Financial Statement Analysis and Security Valuation

Financial Statement Analysis and Security Valuation

Fifth Edition

Stephen H. Penman
Columbia University

FINANCIAL STATEMENT ANALYSIS AND SECURITY VALUATION, FIFTH EDITION
International Edition 2013

Exclusive rights by McGraw-Hill Education (Asia), for manufacture and export. This book cannot be re-exported from the country to which it is sold by McGraw-Hill. This International Edition is not to be sold or purchased in North America and contains content that is different from its North American version.

10 09 08 07 06 05 04 03 02 01
20 15 14 13 12
CTP MPM

When ordering this title, use ISBN 978-007-132640-7 or MHID 007-132640-5

Printed in Singapore

www.mhhe.com

About the Author

Stephen H. Penman is the George O. May Professor in the Graduate School of Business, Columbia University. He also serves as codirector of Columbia's Center for Excellence in Accounting and Security Analysis. Prior to his appointment at Columbia in 1999, Penman was the L. H. Penney Professor in the Walter A. Haas School of Business at the University of California at Berkeley. From 1990 to 1995 he served as Chairman of the Professional Accounting Program and Chairman of the Accounting Faculty at Berkeley. He has served as a Visiting Professor at the London Business School, as the Jan Wallander Visiting Professor at the Stockholm School of Economics, and in the Cheng Tsang Mun Chair Visiting Professorship at Singapore Management University.

Professor Penman received a first-class honors degree in Commerce from the University of Queensland, Australia, and M.B.A. and Ph.D. degrees from the University of Chicago. His research deals with the valuation of equity and the role of accounting information in security analysis. Professor Penman has published widely in finance and accounting journals and has conducted seminars on fundamental analysis and equity valuation for academic and professional audiences. In 1991 he was awarded the Notable Contribution to Accounting Literature Award by the American Accounting Association and the American Institute of Certified Public Accountants, and in 2002 he was awarded the American Accounting Association and Deloitte & Touche Wildman Medal for the first edition of *Financial Statement Analysis and Security Valuation,* published by McGraw-Hill/Irwin. In 2011 Penman received the Rodger F. Murray Prize from the Institute for Quantitative Research in Finance. His book, *Accounting for Value,* was published by Columbia University Press in 2011. He is an editor of the *Review of Accounting Studies* and is on the editorial board of the *Schmalenbach Business Review.*

Preface

Financial statements are the lens on a business. Financial statement analysis calibrates the lens to bring the business into focus. Imperfections in the financial statements can dirty the lens and distort the picture. Financial statement analysis deals with the imperfections in financial statements to improve the focus.

Financial statements have many uses, but the predominant one is to provide information for investing in businesses. Every day millions of shares and corporate bonds are traded in the world's capital markets, and prices are set to value these securities. Investors wish to know what firms are worth so they can ascertain at what price to trade. They turn to financial statement analysis to get an indication of the underlying value of firms. This book focuses on these investors.

Underlying value is sometimes referred to as *fundamental value,* and the analysis of information about fundamental value is referred to as *fundamental analysis.* This book is about fundamental analysis. Financial statement analysis is central to fundamental analysis. Indeed, in this book, fundamental analysis is developed as a matter of appropriate financial statement analysis. As the lens on a business, financial statements, focused with the techniques of financial statement analysis, provide a way of interpreting the business that enables investors to understand the value it generates for shareholders.

The experience in stock markets in the late 1990s and the 2000s suggests that such understanding is sorely needed. During the 1990s, share prices rose considerably above the value that was indicated by earnings, book values, sales, and other fundamental information, only to collapse as the bubble burst. Spurred on by suspect analysis from those representing themselves as analysts, suspect financial reporting from some companies, the hyping of shares by corporate managements, and the speculative discussions of "talking heads" in the media, investors ignored sound analysis in a wave of "irrational exuberance." With a subsequent decline in share prices, compounded by a financial crisis, investors saw risk in action. That risk, in part, is the risk of paying too much for a share. The time has come to return to fundamentals, for fundamental analysis protects from the risk of paying too much. This book lays out the techniques of sound fundamental analysis.

THE APPROACH

Conceptual Framework

Good analysis comes from good understanding. And good understanding is provided by a conceptual framework that helps you—the student analyst—organize your thinking. In this information age, large amounts of information about firms are readily available to be processed. A conceptual framework guides you in using this information intelligently and economically—to turn the information into knowledge.

This book works from a conceptual framework that helps you understand how businesses work, how they generate value, and how the value they generate is captured (or not captured) in financial statements. The framework helps you translate your knowledge of a business into a valuation. The framework helps you interpret what you see in financial statements. It gives you answers to the many important questions facing analysts. What "fundamentals" should the analyst focus on—dividends, cash flows, or earnings? How is an analyst's earnings forecast converted into a valuation? How can an investor rely on earnings when earnings are sometimes measured with doubtful accounting methods? What role does the balance sheet play? What is a growth company and how is growth valued? What does a firm's price-earnings (P/E) ratio tell you? What does its price-to-book ratio tell you? How does one determine what the P/E or price-to-book should be?

Most important, the framework gives you the security that your analysis is a sound one. The framework is built block by block from "first principles" so that you see clearly where the analysis comes from and, by the end of the book, have a firm understanding of the principles of fundamental analysis. You will also be able to distinguish good analysis from poor analysis.

Practical Tools

This book is about understanding, but it is primarily about doing. Concepts and frameworks are important only if they lead to analysis tools. Each chapter of the book ends with a list of **Key Concepts,** but also with the **Analyst's Toolkit** that summarizes the key analysis tools in the chapter. By the end of the book, you will have a complete set of tools for practical analysis. The Toolkit is efficiently organized so that the analyst proceeds in a disciplined way with the assurance that his or her analysis is coherent and does not overlook any aspect of the value generation in a firm. The book identifies too-simple methods of analysis and shuns ad hoc methods. However, it also strives to develop simple schemes, with a sense of trade-off between the benefit of more complicated analysis over the cost. At all points in the book, methods are illustrated with applications to firms such as Google, Cisco Systems, Nike, Microsoft, Coca-Cola, and many more.

Most of the analysis and valuation material in the book can be built into a spreadsheet. So, as the book develops, you are given directions for building and embellishing a spreadsheet program, with further instructions on the book's Web site. By the end of the book, you will have a comprehensive analysis and valuation product that you can apply to almost any firm and use for active investing. A comprehensive guide to building spreadsheets—Build Your Own Analysis Product (BYOAP)—is on the book's Web site. Off-the-shelf spreadsheet products are available (many with faults), but you will find it much more satisfying to build your own, and certainly you will learn more this way.

Valuation and Strategy

The tools in the book are those that a security analyst outside the firm uses to advise clients about investing in the firm. These analysts present their recommendations in an equity research report. After studying this text, you will have the ability to write a persuasive, state-of-the-art equity research report. But the tools are also those that a manager within a firm uses to evaluate investments. The analyst outside the firm values the firm on the basis of what he or she understands the firm's strategy to be, while the manager within the firm uses the same tools to evaluate investments and choose the strategy. The techniques that are used to assess the value of a firm's strategy are also the techniques used to choose among strategies, so this book integrates valuation analysis and strategy analysis.

Accounting-Based Approach to Valuation

Valuation texts typically use discounted cash flow analysis to value businesses. However, analysts typically forecast earnings to indicate business value, and equity research reports primarily discuss firms' earnings, not their cash flows, to get a sense of whether the firm is making money for investors. "Buy earnings" is indeed the mantra of investing. The stock market focuses on earnings; analysts' and managements' earnings forecasts drive share prices, and when a firm announces earnings that are different from analysts' earnings estimates, the stock price responds accordingly. Revelations of overstated earnings result in large drops in stock prices—as with the Xerox, Enron, Qwest, WorldCom, Krispy Kreme, and other accounting scandals that broke as the stock market bubble burst. Investment houses are increasingly moving from cash flow valuation models to earnings-based valuation models.

This book focuses on earnings forecasting and the methods for converting earnings forecasts to a valuation. The reason will become clear as you proceed through the book: Earnings, appropriately measured, give a better indication of the value generation in a business, so the analysis of earnings prospects leads to a firmer understanding of fundamental value. Graham and Dodd and the fundamental analysts of earlier generations emphasized "earnings power." This book maintains that focus, but in a way that is consistent with the principles of modern finance. One must be careful, for there is a danger in paying too much for earnings.

The Quality of the Accounting

With an understanding of how accounting should work, you will develop an appreciation in this book of what is good accounting and what is poor accounting. By the end of the book you will recognize the defects in financial statements that are issued by firms and will have developed a critique of the "generally accepted accounting principles" and disclosure rules that determine what is in the statements. You will also understand how the accounting in reports can be distorted, as well as discover tools that detect the distortion and give you an indication of the quality of the accounting that a firm uses.

Integrating Finance and Accounting

Financial statements are prepared according to the dictates of accounting principles, and you take accounting courses to learn these accounting principles. Your appreciation of financial statements from these courses is often in terms of the accounting used to prepare them, not in terms of what the financial statements say about investing in businesses. Principles of finance guide investment analysis and you typically take finance courses to learn these principles. However, the investment analysis in these courses often does not employ financial statements or accounting concepts in any systematic way. Often you see finance and accounting as distinct or, if you see them as related, the relationship is vague in your mind. Finance courses are sometimes dismissive of accounting, while accounting courses sometimes propose analysis that violates the principles of finance. This book integrates your learning from finance and accounting courses. By integrating financial statement analysis and fundamental analysis, the book combines accounting concepts with finance concepts. Accounting is viewed as a matter of accounting for value and the accounting for value is appropriated for investment analysis. The organized structure of the financial statements helps organize fundamental analysis. Accounting principles for measuring balance sheets and income statements are incorporated as principles for measuring value. All analysis is performed in a way that is consistent with the principles of modern finance and with an appreciation of what is good accounting and what is poor accounting.

Activist Approach

Investment texts often take the view that capital markets are "efficient," such that market prices always reflect the underlying value of the securities traded. These texts are primarily concerned with measuring risk, not with valuation. The investor is viewed as relatively passive, accepting prices as fair value, concerned primarily with managing risk through asset allocation. This text takes an activist's perspective. Active investors do not "assume that the market is efficient." Rather, active investors challenge the market price with sound analysis, checking whether that price is a fair price. Indeed, they exploit what is perceived to be mispricing in the market to earn superior returns. Active investors adopt the creed of fundamental analysts: Price is what you pay, value is what you get. They believe that an important risk in equity investing is the risk of paying too much for a share, so active investors seek to gain an appreciation of value independently of price. Whether or not the market is efficient, you will find this perspective engaging.

Negotiating with Mr. Market

Benjamin Graham saw equity investing as a matter of "negotiating with Mr. Market" over the price to pay. The book shows how to carry out these negotiations. In the spirit of comparing price with value, analysts typically think of calculating a "true" intrinsic value for a stock and comparing that to Mr. Market's price quote. This is not bad thinking but, with so many uncertainties involved, establishing one true number for the intrinsic value with confidence is difficult. The book takes a different approach: Understand how earnings forecasts relate to value, reverse engineer the market price to understand the forecast that Mr. Market is making, and then challenge that forecast. This recognizes that valuation is not a game against nature, but rather a game against other investors; one does not have to find the true value but rather what other investors are thinking. Financial statement analysis that challenges this thinking is then the focus in the dialogue with Mr. Market.

New to This Edition

This edition of the book emphasizes this theme of challenging market prices. A new chapter, Chapter 7, applies the valuation models of Chapters 5 and 6 as tools for active investing. The process is refined in Part Three of the book after the financial statement analysis of Part Two, for it is this financial statement analysis that elicits the information to evaluate whether market prices are reasonable. Many of the active investing themes and tools of my recent book, *Accounting for Value* (Columbia University Press, 2011), are elaborated upon in this edition.

Here are the significant changes for the fifth edition, now running to 20 chapters rather than 19:

- The new Chapter 7—"Valuation and Active Investing"—has been added to Part One of the book.
- Chapters 5 and 6 on valuation have been written more succinctly with some of the material moved to the new Chapter 7.
- Material in all chapters has been updated to incorporate new accounting standards.
- Comparisons between U.S. GAAP accounting and international (IFRS) accounting are made where relevant.
- Examples, illustrations, and graphical material have been updated, now current as of 2010.
- New cases have been added to a number of chapters and the cases in earlier editions have been updated to 2010.
- New end-of-chapter exercises have been added.
- Chapter 15 (previously Chapter 14) on simple forecasting and valuation has been extensively revised and simplified.
- Chapter 19 on risk and return in equity investing returns to the theme of active investing.

When I wrote the first edition of this book (in 1999), world equity markets were experiencing what, in retrospect, is seen as a market bubble. The book was couched in terms of challenging the high price-earnings and price-to-book ratios at that time with fundamental analysis. The episode is an important historical lesson in overvaluation, so that perspective continues in this edition, beginning in Chapter 1. But since then we have experienced not only the bursting of that bubble, but also a credit crisis and a plunge in stock prices, with price multiples now lower than historical benchmarks. This edition thus emphasizes that the analysis techniques it offers are just as applicable to challenging underpricing as well as overpricing. It also warns of the risk of investing in uncertain times and points out that, just as bubbles can perpetuate for some time, so can depressed prices.

The Overview

Chapter 1 introduces you to financial statement analysis and fundamental analysis, and sets the stage for the rest of the book. Chapter 2 introduces you to the financial statements. The remainder of the book is in five parts:

- **Part One** (Chapters 3–7) develops the thinking that is necessary to perform fundamental analysis. It integrates finance concepts with accounting concepts and shows you how the structure of accounting can be exploited for valuation analysis. Good thinking about valuation is captured in a valuation model, so this part of the book introduces accrual-accounting valuation models that provide the framework for the practical analysis that follows in the rest of the book. Alternative models are discussed as competing technologies, so you develop an appreciation of the strength and weaknesses of alternative approaches. Part One ends with an application of these models to active investing.

- **Part Two** (Chapters 8–13) lays out the financial statement analysis that identifies value generation in a business and provides information for forecasting. In this part of the book you will see the lens being focused on the business.

- **Part Three** (Chapters 14–16) deals with forecasting. The value of a firm and its shares is based on the payoffs it is expected to yield investors; thus, using the information from the financial statement analysis, this part of the book shows you how to forecast payoffs. The forecasting is developed within a financial statement framework so that forecasting is an exercise in pro forma financial statement analysis. The analysis then shows how to convert forecasts into valuations of firms and their strategies.

- **Part Four** (Chapters 17 and 18) deals with accounting issues that arise with the use of accounting-based valuation. It shows how to accommodate different accounting methods for measuring earnings and how to analyze the quality of the accounting used in financial statements.

- **Part Five** (Chapters 19 and 20) lays out the fundamental analysis of risk, both equity risk and credit risk, and provides a pro forma analysis that integrates equity analysis and credit analysis. Here, again, the emphasis is on active investing: How does the investor handle risk in investing, particularly the risk of paying too much?

PUTTING IT ALL TOGETHER: A TOOLKIT FOR ANALYSTS AND MANAGERS

The best way to tackle this book is to see yourself as putting together a Toolkit for analyzing financial statements and valuing businesses and business strategies. As a professional analyst or business planner, you want to be using the best technologies available, to get an edge on the competition. So approach the book in the spirit of sorting out what are good methods and what are poor ones. You require methods that are practical as well as conceptually sound.

As you read the text, you find answers to the following questions:

- How are fundamental values (or "intrinsic values") estimated?
- How does one pull apart the financial statements to get at the relevant information to value equities?
- What is the relevance of cash flows? Of dividends? Of book values? How are these measures treated in a valuation?
- What is growth? How does one analyze growth? How does one value a growth firm?
- What are the pitfalls in buying growth?
- How does one challenge the growth expectations implicit in stock prices?
- How does ratio analysis help in valuation?
- How does profitability tie into valuation?
- How does one analyze the quality of financial reports?
- How does one deal with the accounting methods used in financial statements?
- How is financial analysis developed for strategy and planning?
- What determines a firm's P/E ratio? How does one calculate what the P/E should be?
- What determines a firm's market-to-book (P/B) ratio? How does one calculate what the P/B should be?
- How does one evaluate risk? For equity? For debt?
- How does one evaluate an equity research report? What does a good one look like?
- How does one trade on fundamental information?

USING THE BOOK

Background Requirements

To comprehend the text material, you should have a basic course in financial accounting and a basic course in finance. A second course in financial accounting and a course in investments or corporate finance will be helpful but not necessary. Indeed, you may find yourself motivated to take those courses after reading this book.

Chapter Features

The text is written with features designed to enhance your efforts in learning the material. Each chapter of the book begins with a **flow chart** that lays out the material covered in the chapter and connects that material to the preceding and upcoming chapters. This chart will help you see clearly where you've been and where you are going, and how it all ties together. Each chapter also opens with **The Analyst's Checklist,** which has two lists: one covering the conceptual points in the chapter and the other a set of tasks that you should be able to perform after working the chapter. This outlines the goals of the chapter, setting you up for mastery of the material at hand. Each chapter concludes with **The Analyst's Toolkit,** a convenient resource complete with page references, that summarizes the analysis tools in the chapter—ideal for studying and review.

End-of-Chapter Material

Each chapter ends with a set of concept questions, exercises, and minicases. Working through this material will enhance your understanding considerably. These problems are designed, not so much to test you, but to further your learning with practical analysis. Each problem makes a point. **Concept questions** reinforce the thinking in the chapter. **Exercises** apply methods covered in the chapter. **Drill Exercises** lead you gently into the analysis. **Applications** focus on issues involving specific companies. **Minicases,** designed for classroom discussion, are more contextual and involve a broader set of issues, some involving ambiguity. They are written more concisely than full cases so that you do not have to handle a large amount of detail, and classroom time is used more efficiently to make the point. However, the minicases involve considerable analysis and insight, providing stimulus for group discussion.

As with the chapter material, the Exercises and Minicases often use the same real world companies to make different points in different parts of the book. To help you refer back to earlier material on the same company, the Exercises and Minicases are marked with an easy-to-identify **Real World Connection** tagline.

The Continuing Case

A continuing case for one company—Kimberly-Clark Corporation—weaves its way through the book. At the end of each chapter (through Chapter 16), you receive a new installment of the case which shows how the principles and methods in that chapter are applied to Kimberly-Clark and build on the analysis of previous chapters. By the end, you have a demonstration of the application of the book, in total, to one company as a model for other companies. Work the case, then check your solution against that on the book's Web site.

Web Site Reinforcement

The material in the text is supplemented with further analysis on the book's Web site at **www.mhhe.com/penman5e**. The **Student Center** on the Web site contains the following:

- **Chapter supplements** for each chapter in the book. The flow chart at the beginning of each chapter of the text refers you to the Web site, and **The Web Connection** at the end of each chapter summarizes what you will find in the supplements.

- **Solutions to the Continuing Case.**

- **Additional exercises** for each chapter, along with solutions. Work these exercises and correct yourself with the solutions to reinforce your learning.

- **Accounting Clinics I–VII** review accounting issues that are particularly relevant to equity and credit analysis. Among the topics covered are accrual accounting, fair value and historical cost accounting, accounting for debt and equity investments, accounting for stock compensation, pension accounting, and the accounting for taxes.

- **Build Your Own Analysis Product (BYOAP)** on the Web site shows you how to build your own financial statement analysis and valuation spreadsheet product using the principles and methods in the book. It is not a final product that you can immediately appropriate; rather it is a guidebook for constructing your own. As such, it is a learning device; rather than mechanically applying a black-box product, you learn by doing. With the completed product you can analyze financial statements; forecast earnings, residual earnings, abnormal earnings growth, cash flows, and dividends; and then value firms and strategies with a variety of techniques. Add your own bells and whistles. In short, the product is the basis for preparing an equity research report and for carrying out due diligence as a professional. You will find the building process will give you a feeling of accomplishment, and the final product—of your own construction—will be a valuable tool to carry into your professional life or to use for your own investing. Spreadsheet engines for specific tasks are available in the chapter supplements on the Web page for each chapter. Off-the-shelf products are also available. **eVal 2000,** authored by Russell Lundholm and Richard Sloan, is available through McGraw-Hill/Irwin. Also check out the spreadsheet tool of Dan Gode and James Ohlson, at **www.godeohlson.com**, that more closely follows the scheme in this book.

- **Links** to firms' financial statements and to many other sources of financial information. You will also find engines to screen and analyze stocks and to help you build your own analysis tools.
- **Market Insight** (Educational Version) from Standard & Poor's contains financial information on 370 companies. Access codes are available from your instructor.

Resources for Instructors

The book is accompanied by ancillaries that support the teaching and learning. The **Instructor Center** on the book's Web site contains the following:

- **Solutions Manual** with detailed solutions to the end-of-chapter material.
- **Teaching Notes** with advice for teaching from the book, alternative course outlines, a number of teaching tools, and a commentary on each chapter of the book.
- **PowerPoint** slides for each chapter.
- **Test Bank** containing further problems and exercises.
- **Accounting Clinics** to cover the accounting issues in the book in more detail.
- **Chapter Notes** for each chapter.

Acknowledgments

This book capsulates what I have learned as a student of the subject. I am indebted to many writers and professors for that learning. The book has the investment philosophy of Graham, Dodd, and Cottle's *Security Analysis,* the book assigned for my first finance course as an undergraduate. It also incorporates the accounting concepts from my study of accounting theory at the University of Queensland and from reading the classics of Paton and Littleton, Sprouse and Moonitz, and Edwards and Bell, to name a few. It reflects my training in the principles of "modern finance," first as a graduate student at the University of Chicago and subsequently from colleagues at Berkeley.

I have learned much from carrying out research on accounting and valuation. In seminars, workshops, and informal discussions, I have been stimulated by the insights of many colleagues at universities around the world. I have a particular debt to Jim Ohlson, whose theoretical work on accounting valuation models has inspired me, as have our many conversations on research and teaching. I am also indebted to my students at Berkeley, the London Business School, and Columbia University, who have worked with draft versions of this book and given me valuable feedback. Peter Easton and his students at The Ohio State University, the University of Melbourne, and the University of Chicago also used drafts of the first edition and were generous with their comments.

My appreciation also goes to Lorraine Seiji at Berkeley, whose dedication to preparing the manuscript for the first edition was outstanding. Terrence Gabriel and Clarissa Peña at Columbia provided similar support for this edition. Luis Palencia, Doron Nissim, Nir Yehuda, Paul Tylkin, and Mingcherng Deng have helped in preparing the graphical material for the various editions, and Feng Chen, Mingcherng Deng, Guohua Jiang, Siyi Li, and Nir Yehuda provided valuable accuracy checking and help with supporting materials. To them all I am grateful. Nancy Banks, as always, gave strong support. The administrations at Berkeley, the London Business School, and the Columbia Business School, and my colleagues at these schools, lent support at various stages of the book's preparation. The entire team at McGraw-Hill/Irwin have been outstanding. Stewart Mattson has overseen the development of the book with an expert hand. Instructors, too many to mention, gave feedback on their experience with earlier editions.

Anonymous reviewers of the various editions went out of their way to help improve the manuscript. I am very thankful to them. Now identified, they are listed below. Bruce Johnson requires special mention. He went through the manuscript for the first edition word by word, challenged it, and persuaded me to make numerous improvements.

Pervaiz Alam
Kent State University

Holly Ashbaugh
University of Wisconsin, Madison

Scott Boylan
Washington and Lee University

Shelly Canterbury
George Mason University

Agnes Cheng
University of Houston

Michael Clement
University of Texas at Austin

Richard Dumont
Post University

Peter Easton
The Ohio State University

Jocelyn Evans
College of Charleston

Patricia Fairfield
Georgetown University

John Giles
North Carolina State University, Raleigh

Richard Gore
Boise State University

Bruce Johnson
University of Iowa

Sok-Hyon Kang
George Washington University

Sungsoo Kim
Rutgers University, Camden

Charles Lee
Cornell University

Yong Lee
University of Houston at Victoria

Gerald Lobo
Syracuse University

G. Brandon Lockhart
University of Nebraska, Lincoln

Ronald King
Washington University

Arijit Mukherji
University of Minnesota

David Ng
Cornell University, Ithaca

Jane Ou
Santa Clara University

Richard Sloan
University of Michigan

Lenny Soffer
Northwestern University

Greg Sommers
Southern Methodist University

Theodore Sougiannis
University of Illinois

Carolyn Spencer
Dowling College

Thomas Stober
University of Notre Dame

K. R. Subramanyan
University of Southern California

Gary Taylor
University of Alabama

Mark Trombley
University of Arizona

James Wahlen
Indiana University

Clark Wheatley
Florida International University, Miami

Scott Whisenant
University of Houston

Lin Zheng
Mercer University, Atlanta

Stephen H. Penman
Columbia University

Brief Contents

Contents

Chapter 4   3.5

Cash Accounting, Accrual Accounting, and Discounted Cash Flow Valuation   110

Chapter 5   4

Accrual Accounting and Valuation: Pricing Book Values   140

Chapter 6   4

Accrual Accounting and Valuation: Pricing Earnings   178

Week 5: - 3.5

W. 7

List of Cases

List of Accounting Clinics

Financial Statement Analysis and Security Valuation

Chapter **One**

Introduction to Investing and Valuation

LINKS

This chapter

This chapter introduces investing and the role of fundamental analysis in investing.

Link to next chapter

Chapter 2 introduces the financial statements that are the focus of fundamental analysis.

Link to Web page

Go to the book's Web site for this chapter at **www.mhhe.com/ penman5e**. It explains how to find your way around the site and gives you more of the flavor of using financial statement analysis in investing.

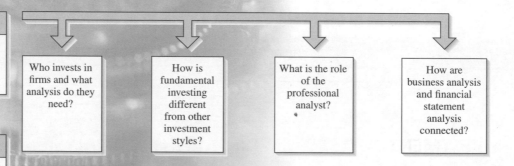

Who invests in firms and what analysis do they need?

How is fundamental investing different from other investment styles?

What is the role of the professional analyst?

How are business analysis and financial statement analysis connected?

Financial statements are the primary information that firms publish about themselves, and investors are the primary users of financial statements. Firms seek capital from investors and prepare financial statements to help investors decide whether to invest. Investors expect the firm to add value to their investment—to return more than was invested—and read financial statements to evaluate the firm's ability to do so. Financial statements are also used for other purposes. Governments use them in social and economic policy-making. Regulators such as the antitrust authorities, financial market regulators, and bank inspectors use them to control business activity. Employees use them in wage negotiations. Senior managers use them to evaluate subordinates. Courts, and the expert witnesses who testify in court, use financial statements to assess damages in litigation.

Each type of user needs to understand financial statements. Each needs to know the statements' deficiencies, what they reveal, and what they don't reveal. **Financial statement analysis** is the method by which users extract information to answer their questions about the firm.

This book presents the principles of financial statement analysis, with a focus on the investor. Many types of investment are entertained. Buying a firm's equity—its common shares—is one, and the book has a particular focus on the shareholder and prospective shareholder. Buying a firm's debt—its bonds—is another. The shareholder is concerned with profitability, the bondholder with default, and financial statement analysis aids in evaluating both. Banks making loans to firms are investors, and they are concerned with default. Firms themselves are also investors when they consider strategies to acquire other firms, go into a new line of business, spin off a division or restructure, or indeed acquire or disinvest in an asset of any form. In all cases financial statements must be analyzed to make a sound decision.

In market economies, most firms are organized to make money (or "create value") for their owners. So financial statements are prepared primarily with shareholders in mind: The statements are formally presented to shareholders at annual meetings and the main "bottom-line" numbers they report are earnings (for the owners) in the income statement and the book value of owners' equity in the balance sheet. But much of the financial statement analysis for investors is relevant to other parties. The shareholder is concerned with profitability. But governmental regulators, suppliers, the firms' competitors, and employees are concerned with profitability also. Shareholders and bondholders are concerned with the riskiness of the business, but so are suppliers and employees. And securities litigation, which involves expert witnesses, usually deals with compensation for loss of profits—or loss of value—to investors. Thus much of the financial statement analysis in this book is relevant to these users as well.

Investors typically invest in a firm by buying equity shares or the firm's debt. Their primary concern is the amount to pay—the value of the shares or the debt. The analysis of information that focuses on valuation is called **valuation analysis, fundamental analysis,** or, when securities like stocks and bonds are involved, **security analysis.** This book develops the principles of fundamental analysis. And it shows how financial statement analysis is used in fundamental analysis.

In this chapter we set the stage.

INVESTMENT STYLES AND FUNDAMENTAL ANALYSIS

Millions of shares of business firms are traded every day on the world's stock markets. The investors who buy and sell these shares ask themselves: Am I trading at the right price? What are the shares really worth? They attempt to answer these questions while a discordant background chorus—the printed press, "talking heads" on television financial networks, and Internet chatrooms—voices opinions about what the price should be. They turn to investment advisers who provide an almost endless stream of information and recommendations to sort out. They hear claims that some shares are overpriced, some underpriced, and they hear theories that stock markets can be caught up in the fads and fashions—even mania—that are said to drive share prices away from their appropriate values.

In the absence of any clear indication of what stocks are worth, investors cope in different ways. Some—**intuitive investors**—rely on their own instincts. They go on hunches. Some—called **passive investors**—throw up their hands and trust in "market efficiency." They assume that the market price is a fair price for the risk taken, that market forces have driven the price to the appropriate point.

These investment styles are simple and don't require much effort. But both types of investors run risks beyond those inherent in the firms they buy: Paying too much or selling for too little damages investment returns. The intuitive investor has the problem of the intuitive bridge builder: One may be pleased with one's intuition but, before building gets under way, it might pay to check that intuition against the calculations prescribed by modern engineering. Not doing so might lead to disaster. The passive investor is in danger if stocks are mispriced. It is tempting to trust, as a matter of faith, that the market is efficient, and much economic theory says it should be. But it is good practice to check. Both types of investors run the risk of trading with someone who has "done his homework," someone who has analyzed the information thoroughly.

Consider the following:

Dell, Inc., the leading manufacturer of personal computers, reported earnings for fiscal year 2000 of $1.7 billion on sales of $25.3 billion. At the time, the total market value of Dell's shares was $146.4 billion, over three times the combined market value for General Motors Corporation and Ford Motor Company, the large U.S. automobile manufacturers with combined sales of $313.5 billion and combined earnings of $13.144 billion. Dell's shares traded at an earnings multiple of 87.9—its price-earnings (P/E) ratio—compared with a P/E of 8.5 for General Motors and 5.0 for Ford.

General Motors and Ford have had their problems. Dell has been a very successful operation with innovative production, "direct marketing," and a made-to-order inventory system. The intuitive investor might identify Dell as a good company and feel confident about buying it. But at 88 times earnings? The P/E ratio for the Standard & Poor's Index (S&P 500) stocks at the time was 33 (very high compared to the historical average of 16), and microcomputer stocks as a whole traded at 40 times earnings. To pay 88 times earnings seems expensive. The intuitive investor should recognize that good companies might be overpriced, good companies but bad buys. He might be advised to check the price with some analysis. The passive investor believes that both companies are appropriately priced and ignores the P/E ratios. But with such an extraordinary P/E, she might be advised to check her beliefs. She is at risk of paying too much. As it turned out, Dell's per-share stock price declined from $58 in 2000 to $29 in 2003, a loss of 50 percent. By 2011, Dell was trading at $14 per share.

The risk of incurring such a loss can be reduced by thoroughly examining information about firms and reaching conclusions about the underlying value that the information implies. This is fundamental analysis and the investor who relies on fundamental analysis is a **fundamental investor.** Fundamental investors ask: Is a P/E of 88 for Dell too expensive? To answer, they make a calculation of what P/E is reasonable given the available information about Dell. They ask: What multiple of earnings is Dell really worth? They also ask whether the P/E ratios for General Motors and Ford are too low. Should they sell Dell and buy Ford? Fundamental investors distinguish price from value. The creed they follow is "price is what you pay, but value is what you get." They "inspect the goods" as a buyer does with any purchase. You could well be cynical and accept price as value, but price is the cost of the investment, not its value. Oscar Wilde's observation is to the point: "Cynics know the cost of everything, and the value of nothing."

"What you get" from the investment is future payoffs, so the fundamental investor evaluates likely payoffs to ascertain whether the asking price is a reasonable one. The **defensive investor** does this as a matter of prudence, to avoid trading at the wrong price. The **active investor** uses fundamental analysis to discover mispriced stocks that might earn exceptional rates of return. Box 1.1 contrasts passive and active investors in more technical terms used by investment advisers.

Fundamental investors speak of discovering intrinsic values, warranted values, or fundamental values. **Intrinsic value** is the worth of an investment that is justified by the information about its payoffs. But this term should not be taken to imply precision. Unlike bridge engineering, fundamental analysis does not take away all uncertainty. It offers principles which, followed faithfully, reduce uncertainty. The analysis in this book develops these principles in a deliberate, systematic way so investors have the security that their investment decisions are sound, intelligent ones. The analysis highlights how errors can be made by following simplistic approaches, and how value can be lost by ignoring basic principles.

Investors buy gambles. They buy a chance to earn a high return against the chance of losing their investment. Passive and active investors differ in their approaches to handling this risk.

Passive investors see risk in business operations delivering less value than expected. They understand that there is a chance that firms' sales will be less than anticipated, that profits from sales will not materialize. But passive investors trust that this **fundamental risk** is efficiently priced in the market. The passive investor realizes, however, that risk can be reduced by diversification and that the market will not reward risk that can be eliminated through diversification. So she holds a diversified portfolio of investments to deal with risk. But, once diversified, the passive investor believes that she is price-protected, with higher risk investments efficiently priced to yield higher expected returns. All she desires from an analyst is information about the level of risk she is taking on, sometimes referred to as *beta risk*. She buys **betas,** and quantitative analysts supply these risk measures using models like the capital asset pricing model (CAPM) and variants—so-called *beta technologies.* No doubt you have been exposed to these models in finance courses.

Fundamental investors see another source of risk, the risk of paying too much (or selling for too little). That is, they are concerned that securities are not efficiently priced. They see **price risk** in addition to the inherent fundamental risk in business operations. So they carry out an analysis to challenge the market price. Like those who supply betas, they design technologies to do this, sometimes referred to as *alpha technologies* to differentiate them from beta technologies. It is these technologies with which this book is concerned. Active fundamental investors see a reward in this endeavor, for they see the possibility of identifying stocks that can earn abnormal returns—higher expected returns than those implied by beta risk. Indeed, the trade term for these abnormal returns is **alphas** (in contrast to betas), and *alpha technologies* are brought to bear to predict alphas.

Index investing is an extreme form of passive investing. The index investor buys the market portfolio of stocks or a portfolio like the S&P 500 Index, which closely resembles the market. The market portfolio provides the ultimate diversification, so the investor does not even have to know the beta. The investor does not have to think about anything, and transaction costs are low. However, the index investor is in danger of paying too much. Consider the returns (including dividends) for the S&P 500 for the years 2000–2010 here, along with the P/E ratios for the index at the end of each year. The index investor did very well in the bull market of the late 1990s, with the returns of 33.0 percent, 28.6 percent, and 21.0 percent for

the three years, 1997–1999. Her subsequent experience was a little painful, for the return on the S&P 500 over the years 2000–2005 was −6.6 percent (an average annual return of −1 percent). The total return over the 11 years 2000–2010 was just 4.7 percent (an average of 0.4 percent per year). Compare this with the annual return on intermediate-term government bonds of 6 percent. Indeed, the S&P 500 stocks underperformed long-term Treasury bonds for the last 5-year, 10-year, and 25-year periods prior to 2010. However, the index investor rides out the market, in the belief that stocks are "for the long run"; the historical average annual return to stocks has been 12.1 percent, compared with 6 percent for corporate bonds, and 3.5 percent for Treasury bills.

	S&P 500 Returns	S&P 500 P/E Ratio
2000	−9.1	26.4
2001	−11.9	46.5
2002	−22.1	31.9
2003	28.7	22.8
2004	10.9	20.7
2005	4.9	17.9
2006	15.8	17.4
2007	5.5	22.2
2008	−37.0	25.4
2009	26.5	21.9
2010	15.1	16.3

The fundamental investor recognizes these statistical averages but appreciates that these returns are not guaranteed. He also notes another statistic: The historical average P/E ratio for the S&P 500 is 16. P/E ratios over 30 suggest that stocks are too expensive. However, the fundamental investor then begins an investigation as to whether times have changed, whether higher P/E ratios are now justified. Further, rather than holding all of the stocks in the index, he differentiates between those stocks he feels are undervalued in the market, those he thinks are efficiently priced, and those he thinks are overvalued. The indexer's action is HOLD; the active investor expands his action alternatives to BUY, HOLD, or SELL.

It is easy, with hindsight, to say that selling stocks at the end of 1999 would have been a good idea. The appropriate question is whether an analysis in 1999 would have indicated so in advance. The passive investor is skeptical. She points to the fact that active investment funds typically do not perform much better than the S&P 500 Index, net of costs of running the funds. The fundamentalist replies: If no one does fundamental research, how can the market become efficient?

Information is gold to the investor; so much of the book explains how the analyst identifies the appropriate information and organizes it in a way to indicate intrinsic value. Organizing the accounting information—financial statement analysis—is of particular importance. The analyst does not want to be overwhelmed by the huge amount of information available on firms and so looks for efficient ways of organizing the information, of reducing it to manageable proportions. He desires simple, straightforward schemes but is wary of ad hoc schemes that are too simple. A simple (and popular) scheme says "buy firms with low P/E ratios and sell firms with high P/E ratios" for price relative to earnings is supposed to tell us how cheap or expensive those earnings are. Selling Dell, with a high P/E in 2000, would have worked. But buying General Motors or Ford, with low P/E ratios of 8.5 and 5.0, respectively, would not; General Motors' stock declined from $80 per share in 2000 to $4 in 2008 (and then went bankrupt), and Ford's declined from $29 to $3 over the same period. The thorough analyst understands that using just one piece of information—earnings here—runs the danger of paying too much; other important information is involved in determining whether a low P/E ratio is justified or, indeed, represents an overpricing rather than an underpricing. Rather than comparing price to earnings, he compares price to value implied by the complete set of information.

Traders in securities are not alone in valuing investments. Within firms, managers daily make investment decisions. They too must ask whether the value of the investment is greater than its cost. And they too, as we will see, must forecast payoffs to ascertain this value.

BUBBLE, BUBBLE, TOIL, AND TROUBLE

History serves up lessons, and the last two decades has provided many. Trillions of dollars were invested in stock markets around the world in the 1990s. By the end of that decade, nearly 50 percent of adults in the United States held equity shares, either directly or through retirement accounts. In the United Kingdom, this figure was 25 percent, in Germany, 15 percent, and in France, 13 percent. These numbers were up considerably from 10 years earlier. Stock markets in Asia and the Pacific also became very active. Firms in Europe and Asia that once went to banks for capital began raising funds through public stock markets. An equity culture was emerging where firms traded more and more with individual equity investors or their intermediaries. Unfortunately, the growing equity culture was not matched with a growing understanding of how to value stocks. Trillions of dollars were lost as a stock market bubble burst in 2000 and investors found their savings shrunk significantly.

The experience repeated that of a decade earlier in Japan. On December 29, 1989, the Nikkei 225 Index of Japanese stocks soared to a high of 38,957, a 238 percent gain over a five-year period. Twelve years later in 2001, the Nikkei 225 fell below 10,000 for a loss of over 75 percent from the 1989 high. By 2005, the index had recovered to only 11,800, and stood at 9,800 in 2011. The stock prices of the 1980s were a bubble, and the bubble burst. The repercussions in Japan were long-term. Some claim that equity investing is rewarded in the long run, but the long run has been a long time coming. On March 10, 2000, the NASDAQ Composite Index in the United States peaked at 5,060, up 574 percent from the beginning of 1995. By mid-2002, the index was below 1,400, down 75 percent from the high, and was still only at 2,750 in 2011. The S&P 500 Index was down 45 percent and the London FTSE 100 and the Eurotop 300 had lost more than 40 percent. Again, a bubble had burst, leaving investors to wonder how long the long run would be. We are reminded that the Dow Index did not recover its 1929 euphoric level until 1954. During the 1970s, after the bull market of the late 1960s, the Dow stocks returned only 4.8 percent over 10 years and ended the decade down 13.5 percent from their 1960s high. As we saw in Box 1.1, the S&P 500 returned only 4.7 percent from 2000 to 2010.

In January 2000, prior to the bursting of the bubble, Alan Greenspan, chairman of the U.S. Federal Reserve Bank, expressed concern. He asked whether the boom would be remembered as "one of the many euphoric speculative bubbles that have dotted human history." In 1999 he said, "History tells us that sharp reversals in confidence happen abruptly, most often with little advance notice. . . What is so intriguing is that this type of behavior has characterized human interaction with little appreciable difference over the generations. Whether Dutch tulip bulbs or Russian equities, the market price patterns remain much the same."

Indeed, while the usual reference to bubbles is to Dutch tulip bulbs in the seventeenth century or to the South Seas Bubble in the eighteenth century, there had been more recent experience. In 1972, the pricing of the technology stocks of the day—Burroughs, Digital Equipment, Polaroid, IBM, Xerox, Eastman Kodak—looked like a bubble waiting to burst. These stocks were part of the "Nifty Fifty" stocks, deemed a "must buy," that included Coca-Cola, Johnson & Johnson, and McDonald's Corporation. The average P/E ratio for the Nifty Fifty was 37 in 1972, nothing like the P/E of over 300 for the NASDAQ 100 stocks in 2000, but considerably above the historical average to that point of 13. The bubble did burst. The S&P 500 P/E ratio declined from 18.3 in 1972 to 7.7 by 1974. The FT 30-share index in London (prior to the days of the FTSE 100) dropped from 543 in May 1972 to 146 in January 1975.

Stock market bubbles damage economies. People form unreasonable expectations of likely returns and so make misguided consumption and investment decisions. Mispriced stocks attract capital to the wrong businesses. Entrepreneurs with poor business models raise cash too easily, deflecting it from firms that can add value for society. Investors borrow to buy paper rather than real productive assets. Debt burdens become intolerable. Banks that feed the borrowing run into trouble. Retirement savings are lost and a pension crisis develops. And, while we have learned something of macroeconomic management since then, the euphoria of the late 1920s and the subsequent depression of the 1930s teach us that systematic failure is possible. Indeed, that was the fear in the market crash of 2008. Bubble, bubble, toil and trouble.

How Bubbles Work

Bubbles work like a chain letter. You may have joined a chain letter as a teenager for fun (and not much consequence), or as an adult trying to get enough signatures to lobby for a good cause (hopefully with consequence). One letter writer writes to a number of people, instructing each to send the letter on to a number of other people with the same instruction. Letters proliferate, but ultimately the scheme collapses. If the letter involves money—each person in the chain is paid by those joining the chain—the scheme is sometimes referred to as a *Ponzi scheme* or a *pyramid scheme*. A few that are early in the chain make considerable money, but most participants are left with nothing.

In a bubble, investors behave as if they are joining a chain letter. They adopt speculative beliefs that are then fed on to other people, facilitated in recent years by talking heads in the media, bloggers, and indeed by analysts and poor financial reporting. Each person believes that he will benefit from more people joining the chain, by their buying the stock and pushing the price up. A bubble forms, only to burst as the speculative beliefs are not fulfilled.

The popular investing style called **momentum investing** has features of a chain letter. Advocates of momentum investing advise buying stocks that have gone up, the idea being that those stocks have momentum to continue going up more. What goes up must keep on going up. Indeed, this happens when speculation feeds on itself as the chain letter is passed along.

Analysts During the Bubble

As the renowned fundamental investor Warren Buffett observed, the boom in technology and Internet stocks of the late 1990s was a chain letter, and investment bankers were the "eager postmen." He might well have added sell-side analysts (who recommend stocks to retail investors), some of whom worked with their investment banking colleagues to push stocks at high prices to investors. During the bubble, analysts were recommending buy, buy, buy. In the year 2000, only 2 percent of sell-side analysts' stock recommendations in the United States were sells. Only after the NASDAQ index dropped 50 percent did analysts begin to issue sell recommendations. This is not very helpful. One would think that, with such a drop in price, recommendations would tend to change from sell to buy rather than the other way around.

To be fair to analysts, it is difficult to go against the tide of speculation. An analyst might understand that a stock is overvalued, but overvalued stocks can go higher, fed along by the speculation of the moment. The nature of a bubble is for prices to keep rising. So, making a sell call may be foolish in the short run. Analysts are afraid to buck the trend. If they turn out to be wrong when the herd is right, they look bad. If they and the herd are wrong together, they are not penalized as much. But there are big benefits for the star analyst who makes the correct call when the herd is wrong.

The issue calls into question what analysts do. Do they write equity research reports that develop a valuation for a company, or do they speculate on where the stock price will go based on crowd behavior? They might do either or both. However, they should always justify their position with good thinking based on fundamentals. Unfortunately, during the 1990s bubble, many analysts promoted poor thinking. They fed the speculation. See Box 1.2.

More Toil and Trouble

The years 2005–2007 saw a bubble of another sort, largely in financial stocks. A real-estate boom in the United States fed housing prices, poor lending practices, and excessive risk taking by banks. The bubble burst. The sorry aftermath, a financial crisis, reduced the market value of stocks by 37 percent in 2008 and resulted in wide unemployment. Premium Wall Street banks such as Bear Stearns, Merrill Lynch, and Lehman Brothers failed. The U.S. government bailed out the AIG insurance firm, Citigroup, and many others, including the mortgage companies Fannie Mae and Freddie Mac. Goldman Sachs and Morgan Stanley required government assistance. A credit crisis extended to sovereign countries, with Iceland, Ireland, Greece, Portugal, and Spain in the headlines but doubts also arising as to the creditworthiness of the United States. Stock prices were depressed, with the S&P 500 index falling below 700 in March 2009 from 1500 in mid-2007. P/E ratios fell below 10.

It is hard to see how a fundamental investor could have foreseen such a devastating macro event. But there are lessons here. Bubbles can work in reverse: Rather than prices becoming inflated, they become depressed. During the mid-1970s, in a period of general pessimism amid oil price shocks, the S&P 500 P/E ratio fell below 7 and its price-to-book ratio below 1. This was a time for the fundamental investor to ask: Are stocks cheap? Investors who bought then did very well. Buying stocks (selectively) in early 2009 also paid off handsomely. By 2011, P/E ratios stood at 12, with Dell, Microsoft, Cisco Systems, and other highly priced firms in 2000 now selling at P/E ratios of 10 and less. Was this the time to buy again? A careful analysis of the fundamentals engages the question.

When speculative fever is high, analysts are tempted to abandon good thinking and promote speculative thinking. They may be compromised because their firms make money from brokerage commissions, so they want analysts to promote stock buying. Their investment banking arm may reward analysts for recommending stocks of their corporate clients. Analysts may be reluctant to make sell recommendations on the firms they cover, in fear of being cut off from further information from those firms. Or, more likely, they may simply get caught up in the speculative fever of the moment.

There was no shortage of speculative analysis during the 1990's bubble, particularly in the coverage of technology, Internet, and telecommunication stocks. Here are some examples. Understand the fallacy in each point.

- Profits were dismissed as unimportant. Most Internet stocks reported losses, but analysts insisted at the time that this did not matter. What was important, they said, was the business model. Well, both are important. A firm has to make profits and, even though it may have losses currently, there must be reasonable scenarios for earning profits. See Box 1.3. As it turned out, the losses reported for dot.com firms during the bubble were a good indicator of outcomes. Many of these firms did not survive.
- Commentators insisted that traditional financial analysis was no longer relevant. The "new economy" demands new ways of thinking, they said. They offered no persuasive new thinking, but discarded the old.
- Analysts appealed to vague terms like "new technology," "Web real estate," "customer share of mind," "network effects," and indeed, "new economy" to recommend stocks. Pseudoscience labels; sound science produces good analysis, not just labels.
- Analysts claimed that the firms' value was in "intangible assets" (and so claimed that the firm must be worth a lot!), but they didn't indicate how one tests for the value of the intangible assets. One even saw analysts calculating the value of intangible assets as the difference between bubble prices and tangible assets on the balance sheet. Beware of analysts recommending firms because they have "knowledge capital." Knowledge is value in this information age, but knowledge must produce goods and services, the goods and services must produce sales, and the sales must produce profits. And knowledge assets must be paid for. Inventors and engineers must be paid. Will there be good profits after paying for knowledge?

- Analysts relied heavily on nonfinancial metrics like page views, usage metrics, customer reach, and capacity utilization. These metrics may give some indication of profitability but they don't guarantee it. The onus is on the analyst to show how these indicators translate into future profits.
- Analysts moved from focusing on P/E ratios and earnings growth to focusing on price-to-sales (P/S) ratios and sales growth. Sales growth is important, but sales ultimately must produce profits. With analysts' focus on price-to-sales ratios, firms began to manufacture sales through accounting practices like grossing up commissions and barter transactions in advertising.
- Analysts' forecasts of growth rates were high compared to past history. Analysts consistently maintained that companies could maintain exceptional revenue and earnings growth rates for a long time. Analysts' "long-term growth rates" (for 3–5 years in the future) are typically too optimistic in boom times. History says that high growth rates usually decline toward average rates quite quickly.
- Rough indicators of mispricing were ignored without justification. A P/E of 33 for the S&P 500 at the height of the bubble is a waving red flag. A P/E of 87.9 for Dell, Inc., flashes a warning. One should have good reasons for buying at these multiples.
- Historical perspective was ignored. Cisco Systems, with a market value of half a trillion dollars, traded at a P/E of 135 in 1999. There has never been a company with a large market value that has traded with a P/E over 100.
- Simple calculations didn't add up. At one point in 1999, an online discount airline ticket seller traded at a market value greater than the total for all U.S. airlines. Internet companies traded at a market value, in total, of over $1 trillion, but had total revenues of only $30 billion, giving them an average price-to-sales ratio of 33. This looks high against the historical average P/S ratio of just 1. All the more so when one recognizes that these firms were reporting losses totaling $9 billion. For $1 trillion, an investor could have purchased quite a number of established firms with significant profits.
- Analysts did not examine the quality of earnings that firms were reporting. The emphasis was on firms reporting earnings that bettered analysts' forecasts, not on the quality of the accounting that went into those earnings.

Fundamental Analysis Anchors Investors

Fundamental analysis anchors the investor against the winds of speculation, fad, and fashion. With a sense of value, fundamental analysis challenges prices fed by speculation, whether it be optimism that drives prices above fundamental value or pessimism that depresses prices downward. Fundamental analysis cuts through poor thinking, like that in Box 1.2. Fundamental

From 1996 to 2000, the prices of Internet stocks soared to such a degree that commentators referred to the phenomenon as speculative mania. The stock price of Amazon.com, Inc. the leading Internet book retailer, rose from $20 in June 1998 to $200 by January 1999 (adjusted for stock splits), at the same time it was reporting losses. Yahoo!'s stock rose from $25 to $225 over the same period, giving it a P/E ratio of 1,406 and a price-sales ratio of 199. Shares in America Online (AOL), another Internet portal, rose from $20 in June 1998 to $150 by April 1999 (before its acquisition of Time Warner), giving it a P/E ratio of 649, a price-sales ratio of 46, and a market capitalization of $2\frac{1}{2}$ times that of General Motors.

To investigate whether these prices represent value or speculative mania, the fundamental investor asks what are reasonable expectations for these firms. AOL was reporting annual sales revenue of $3.1 billion at the time, 80 percent from the subscriptions of 18 million members, and the remainder from online advertising and Internet commerce. The fundamental investor might ask: What anticipated sales growth over the next 10 years is required to justify a price of 46 times sales? Well, if AOL were to maintain its 1998 profit margin of $8\frac{1}{2}$ percent of sales, he might calculate that AOL needs $291 billion in sales in 10 years, or a 9,387 percent increase over current sales, about 57 percent per year. (You will see how to make these calculations later.)

Perspective might tell him this forecast is a high number. Among the largest U.S. firms in stock market value, General Motors had 1998 sales of $154 billion, General Electric's 1998 sales were $100 billion, and Microsoft's were $16 billion. Walmart, the largest U.S. retailer, had 1998 sales of $138 billion and experienced sales growth of 17 percent per year in the 1990s. He might then take a defensive position and not hold AOL stock. Or he might take an active position and sell it short. Or he might come to the conclusion that AOL's future prospects justify the current price of its shares.

The thorough fundamental investor would not be satisfied by assuming that AOL would maintain its profit margin at the 1998 level. He would forecast future profit margins as well. He would investigate alternative strategic scenarios and anticipate the payoffs from the scenarios. And he would ask whether a reasonable scenario could be developed that would justify the current market price.

investors see that prices tend to converge to fundamentals over time, so the investor anchored to the fundamentals has the best prospect for the long run. See Box 1.3.

THE SETTING: INVESTORS, FIRMS, SECURITIES, AND CAPITAL MARKETS

To value business investments we need to have a good understanding of how a business works, how it adds value, and how it returns value to investors. We begin here to build a picture of the firm and its investors—sketchy at first—to be filled out as the book proceeds.

When individuals or institutions invest in firms, they give up cash in hope of a higher return of cash in the future. The investment gives them a **claim** on the firm for a return. This claim is formalized in a *contract,* which may not be tradable (like most partnership interests and bank loan agreements), or in a *security,* which can be traded in security markets (like stocks and bonds).

Corporate claims vary from simple "plain vanilla" types such as equity and debt to more complicated contingent claims. *Contingent claims* such as convertible bonds, options, and warrants are derivative claims whose payoffs are based on the price of firms' stocks or bonds, usually stocks. Despite their contractual complexity, contingent claims are relatively easy to value: Once the value of the stocks or bonds is determined, standard option-pricing techniques can be used to get the derivative price. The techniques follow the principles of financial engineering (which will not concern us in this book). Equity and debt claims are more basic: Their value is "fundamental" to valuing the contingent claims. Their pricing is guided by principles of fundamental analysis (on which we very much focus in this book).

The *equity* is the most important corporate claim, and the **value of the equity** is a particular focus for financial analysis. It is the primary claim, so much so that common stock is sometimes referred to as the fundamental security. The equity is the owners' claim on the

FIGURE 1.1 The Firm, Its Claimants, and the Capital Market

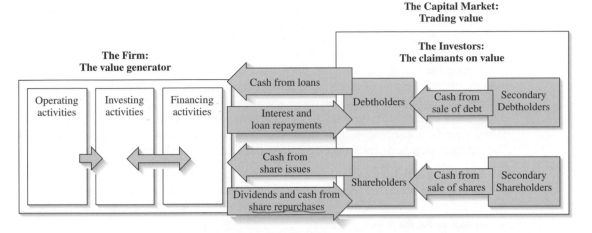

business, often referred to as *owners' equity* or *shareholders' equity*. This claim is the residual claim on the value of the firm after other claimants have been satisfied. It is, by far, the most difficult claim to value and it is the valuation of this claim, *equity valuation,* with which we will be preoccupied. But we also will be concerned with debt claims. Debt claims are relatively simple claims for return of interest and principal. So they are relatively simple to value.

Figure 1.1 depicts the *debtholders* and *shareholders* and the cash flows between them and the firm. We ignore the holders of contingent claims here to keep it simple. Debtholders (bondholders, banks, and other creditors) make loans to the firm in exchange for a claim for a **payoff** in the form of interest payments and loan repayments, as shown. Shareholders contribute cash in exchange for equity shares that entitle them to a payoff in the form of dividends or cash from share repurchases. The amount of the payoff, less the amount paid for the claim, is called the **return.**

When a firm sells debt or equity claims it trades in the *capital market*. The capital market can be a formal, organized stock exchange where public, "listed" firms trade; an informal market involving intermediaries such as venture capitalists, private equity firms, banks, and investment brokers; or a simple process of raising capital from family and friends.

Holders of claims also may sell claims in the capital market if they wish to liquidate their investment. They sell to secondary investors and receive cash, as indicated by the arrows in the diagram, in exchange for surrendering their claims to the new investors. So you see from the diagram that the payoffs to claimants (indicated by the arrows flowing to them) come both from the firm and from sales of their claims in the capital market. For shareholders, the payoffs are in the form of dividends from the firm and proceeds from the sale of shares, either to the firm in a share repurchase (where the firm buys back shares) or to other investors in the stock market. Debtholders receive interest and a settlement payment, either by the firm redeeming the debt before or at maturity or by selling the debt in the bond market.

The value of a claim traded in the capital market is based on the anticipated payoffs that the firm will ultimately pay on the claim. So the diagram describes the firm as the *value generator*. Debtholders want enough value generated to recover interest and principal. Shareholders get the residual value after the return to the bondholders. To the extent their goals are financial ones, shareholders want to maximize the value generated by the firm. Indeed, as owners they have the authority, in most cases, to hire and fire management to ensure that management strives to increase firm value and the value of their residual claim.

It is always the case that the value of the claims on a firm must add up to the **value of the firm:**

$$\text{Value of the firm} = \text{Value of debt} + \text{Value of equity} \qquad \textbf{(1.1)}$$

This just states that the total value that a firm generates must be divided among the various claims to that value (just the two basic claims are given here). So, in valuation, we can think of valuing the firm and dividing the firm's value among claimants, or we can think of valuing the claims, the sum of which is the value of the firm. The value of the firm is sometimes referred to as the value of the enterprise or **enterprise value.**

We will have much more to say about value generation in a business. To start, the diagram shows the firm involved in three activities: financing activities, investing activities, and operating activities. Specifics vary, but these three activities are generic to all businesses.

- **Financing activities** are the transactions with claimants that we have just talked about: raising cash for the business in exchange for equity and debt claims and returning cash to claimants. These activities are investing activities for the claimants but financing activities for the firm.

- **Investing activities** use the cash raised from financing activities and generated in operations to acquire assets to be employed in operations. These assets may be physical assets, like inventories, plant, and equipment, or knowledge and intellectual assets, like technology and know-how.

- **Operating activities** utilize the assets in which the firm has invested to produce and sell products. Operating activities combine assets with labor and materials to produce products and services, sell them to customers, and collect cash from customers. If successful, the operations generate enough cash to reinvest in assets or return to claimants.

Understanding these activities is fundamental to understanding the value generation in a business. The picture is very much incomplete here, so these activities are drawn as opaque windows in the diagram. As the book proceeds, we will open these windows to learn more about how the firm generates value for its investors.

THE BUSINESS OF ANALYSIS: THE PROFESSIONAL ANALYST

Many investors find that choosing and managing investments is not their forte, so they turn to professional **financial analysts.** In any field, the professional is someone who has the specialized technology to get a task done. Indeed professionals present themselves as arbiters of good technology, and a profession is judged by its ability to successfully solve the problem at hand. The professional continually asks: What are good techniques, what are poor ones? The professional, like any other producer, sells products to his customers, the investors. As a competitor with others, the professional asks: How can I enhance the technology to get an edge over my competition? What does a good valuation product look like? What's the best way to go about analyzing information on firms? How can I do financial statement analysis most efficiently? What methods add value for my client? Understanding what a good fundamental analysis technology looks like is at the heart of this book.

As types of investments vary, so do the types of professionals who serve investors. Each needs to tailor analysis to the client's need.

Investing in Firms: The Outside Analyst

Many professionals are outside the business, looking in, and we refer to them as outside analysts. Security analysts, investment consultants, money managers, and stockbrokers advise clients on buying and selling corporate securities. Investment bankers and business brokers advise clients on acquiring and selling businesses. Accountants and assessors value firms for tax and estate purposes. And any one of these might serve as an expert witness in litigation involving valuation issues.

Just as there are two main types of business claims, there are two main types of outside analysts. *Credit analysts,* such as those at bond rating agencies (Standard & Poor's, Moody's Investors Service, and Fitch Ratings for example) or bank loan officers, evaluate the riskiness—and thus the value—of business debt. But prime among business analysts is the *equity analyst. Buy-side analysts* perform equity research as money managers, within mutual funds, hedge funds, and other investment vehicles. *Sell-side analysts* provide the research to support retail investors through their brokers (and also "sell" research to the buy side). The equity analyst typically prepares an equity research report. The analyst's main concern: How do I produce an equity research report that is credible and persuasive and gives my client confidence in investing? Many research reports fail this test. They typically close with a prominent buy, hold, or sell recommendation. They present graphs, numbers, and verbiage about the business but it is not always clear how the recommendation follows from the analysis, or indeed whether it is justified. View the material in this book as a guide to preparing an accomplished equity research report.

Investing Within Firms: The Inside Analyst

Inside the firm, business managers invest moneys contributed to the firm in business assets. Business investment begins with an idea, a "strategy." These strategies may involve developing new products, exploring new markets, adopting a new production technology, or beginning an entirely new line of business. Strategy may call for acquiring another firm, spinning off a division, or entering into alliances. To evaluate their ideas, business managers, like outside investors, need to analyze the value that their ideas might generate. Such an evaluation is called **strategy analysis.**

Business managers may have good intuition and may feel confident that their ideas are good ones. But they can be overconfident, too persuaded by their own ideas. They, like the outside intuitive investor, need to submit their intuition to analysis. And their fiduciary relationship to claimants requires that they focus on shareholder value. They must value their ideas: Is the strategy likely to add value? The insider's view on analysis should be no different from that of the outsider. The outside investor must be persuaded to buy shares at the market price and, to decide, looks to analysis. What value is likely to be added over the price? The inside investor must be persuaded to buy an idea or a strategy at what it will cost to implement and, to decide, looks to analysis. What value is likely to be added over the cost?

Business strategists develop appealing ideas and each year new strategy paradigms are offered in business schools and in the financial press. Recent examples are the "centerless corporation" and the "knowledge corporation," both of which require investment in reorganization and intellectual capital. The ideas must be tested. Building conglomerates was popular in the 1960s and 1970s, but most were not successful. Downsizing was a popular idea of the 1990s, but downsizing may reduce revenues as well as costs. Outsourcing and off-shoring followed. Like all strategies, these ideas must be subjected to analysis.

Valuation analysis not only helps with the go/no-go decision on whether to commit to an investment, but it also helps in the planning and execution of the investment. Strategic ideas sometimes can be vague; submitting the ideas to formal analysis forces the planner to think concretely about ideas and to develop the specifics; it turns ideas into concrete, dollar numbers. And it forces the planner to examine alternative ways of doing things. Strategies are revised in response to the numbers until a final, best plan emerges. A good strategy is the result of both good ideas and good analysis. Investing and managing with valuation analysis is called **value-based management.**

The chief financial officer (CFO) typically coordinates analysis for management, and it is her responsibility to institutionalize the best analysis. She and her corporate analysts evaluate broad strategies and specific proposals to acquire firms, spin off businesses, restructure operations, launch new products, and the like. Managers sometimes complain about "bean counters" being too narrowly focused on the numbers, stifling innovation. Yet "manage by the numbers" they must. The onus is on the CFO to adopt an analysis that not only avoids the criticism but actively promotes innovation and the testing of innovative ideas, with the assurance that good ideas that add value will be recognized.

Inside and outside analysts differ in one respect: Inside analysts have far more information to work with. Outside analysts receive the published financial statements along with much supplementary information, but they are typically not privy to "inside information." Because you, as students, are not privy to inside information either, the financial statement analysis in this book is more oriented to the outside analyst. The focus is on financial statements but not on detailed accounting practices. Rather it is on how accounting information can best be handled in valuation analysis. When accounting principles need to be understood for valuation, they will be covered. And impediments to good analysis due to accounting principles will be identified. So we develop a critique of financial statements as they are currently prepared.

THE ANALYSIS OF BUSINESS

The techniques to be developed in this book are for both inside and outside investors. Both invest in business operations. The outside investor talks of buying a stock, but buying a stock is not buying a piece of paper; it is buying a piece of a business. An old adage says, "One does not buy a stock, one buys a business." And it goes on: "If you are going to buy a business, know the business."

An accomplished analyst must know the business she is covering. An analyst seeking to value a telecommunications firm must understand that industry and the firm's position in it. She must know the firm's strategy to build networks, to adapt to technological change, and to meet the challenges of its competitors. She must know the products. She must anticipate consumer demand. She must know whether there is excess capacity in the industry. She must understand the evolving technology path, how voice, data, and multimedia might be delivered in the future. She must understand government regulations. The business context gives meaning to information. The significance of high labor costs of, say, 70 percent of sales is much greater for a firm with low labor input and high capital input than for a consulting firm with a large labor input. To understand whether a P/E ratio of 87.9 for Dell, Inc., is too high, the analyst must understand the computer business, the prospects for sales growth, and the profit margins on different computer products. Some types of firms work on low profit margins (profits relative to sales), while others work on high profit margins, and it might be ridiculous to expect a low-margin firm to improve its profit margin substantially. Normal inventory levels differ between retailers and wholesalers, and between manufacturers and retailers. Depreciation charges should be high if a firm is in an industry with rapidly changing technology or excess capacity.

Analysts specialize by industry sector simply because knowing the nature of the business is a necessary condition for analyzing a business. For example, equity research reports are usually prefaced by a discussion of the industry and financial statement analysis usually compares measures like profit margins and inventory ratios to normal benchmarks for the industry.

Understanding business is of course the subject of a whole business school curriculum, to be filled out by years of experience. The more thorough that knowledge, the more confident one is in business valuation. One treads cautiously when investing in firms about

Managers of firms use valuation analysis to evaluate whether their strategies create value for shareholders. But shareholders and other potential investors also must familiarize themselves with firms' strategies. And they should ask what alternative strategies firms might pursue, for the value of firms is different under different strategies.

Consider America Online discussed in Box 1.3. In early 1999, AOL was an Internet portal whose revenues came from subscriptions, advertising, and e-commerce. Then, in early 2000, AOL announced its merger with Time Warner, the large media company that owned CNN, Turner Broadcasting Systems, publications like *Time* magazine, Warner Brothers film and recording studios, cable systems, and many other assets with valuable brand names. This acquisition was the first big merger of a new Internet company with an old-style media company, bringing distribution and content together.

Clearly AOL was a company in rapid evolution, changing from a portal firm to a content firm in a short space of time. AOL's management would need to understand the value of Time Warner to ensure that they were not overpaying for its shares. They would need to understand the value of AOL's own shares to ensure that, in offering shares to make acquisitions,

they were not issuing shares that were undervalued in the market. And they would need to understand any value-added synergies that would come from combining the firms.

But outside analysts also benefit from understanding how AOL is likely to evolve. An analyst valuing AOL as a stand-alone portal firm in early 1999 would have arrived at a different valuation from one who had anticipated AOL's acquisition strategy. And an analyst surprised by the Time Warner acquisition would revise his valuation after recognizing the implications of the strategy it revealed.

Strategies are adaptive to changing conditions, so valuations must be revised as strategies change. In mid-2002, AOL Time Warner's stock price was down 65 percent from its level at the time of the merger, and $54 billion of goodwill from the acquisition had to be written off the balance sheet (the largest write-off ever). Commentators insisted that the expected benefits from the merger had not been realized. The CEO position at AOL Time Warner passed from Gerald Levin, who engineered the AOL merger, to Richard Parsons, with the challenge to modify the strategy. Would AOL be spun off from Time Warner? Anticipating that strategy was the first step in valuing AOL Time Warner at that point in time.

which one knows little. Do too many investors (and indeed money managers) buy stocks instead of businesses?

Strategy and Valuation

There are many details of a business with which the analyst must be familiar. To focus his thinking he first identifies the **business model**—sometimes also referred to as the *business concept* or the *business strategy*. What is the firm aiming to do? How does it see itself to be generating value? And what are the consequences of the strategy? These questions are often answered in terms of how the firm represents itself to its customers. Home Depot, the warehouse retailer of home-improvement products, follows the concept of providing high-quality materials for do-it-yourselfers at discount prices, but with training and advice. As a consequence, the combination of discount prices with added customer servicing costs implies that the firm must be very efficient in its purchasing, warehousing, and inventory control. The Gap, Inc., aims to present dress-down clothing as fashion items at reasonable prices in attractive stores, a different concept from warehouse retailing. As a consequence, it must manage image through advertising and be creative in fashion design while at the same time keeping production costs low. With considerable retail space, both firms require high turnover in that space. Both have run into declining fortunes, forcing a reevaluation of their strategies.

For the inside investor, the business strategy is the outcome of valuation analysis: A strategy is chosen after determining whether it will add value. For the outside investor, the business strategy is the starting point for analysis, for firms can be valued only under a specified strategy. But the outside investor also should be aware of alternative strategies that have the potential for enhancing value. Some takeovers occur because outside investors believe that more value can be created with new ideas and with new management. Strategies are ever evolving, so the analyst must be attuned to the way firms adapt to change. Indeed, a smart analyst anticipates changes in strategy and the value they might create or destroy. See Box 1.4.

Mastering the Details

Once the business is clearly in mind, the analyst turns to master the details. There are many details of the business to discover, but you can think of them under six categories.

1. Know the firm's products.
   a. Types of products.
   b. Consumer demand for the products.
   c. Price elasticity of demand for the products. Does the firm have pricing power?
   d. Substitutes for each product. Is the product differentiated? On price? On quality?
   e. Brand name association with products.
   f. Patent protection for products.

2. Know the technology required to bring products to market.
   a. Production process.
   b. Marketing process.
   c. Distribution channels.
   d. Supplier network and how the supply chain operates.
   e. Cost structure.
   f. Economies of scale.

3. Know the firm's knowledge base.
   a. Direction and pace of technological change and the firm's grasp of it.
   b. Research and development program.
   c. Tie-in to information networks.
   d. Ability to innovate in product development.
   e. Ability to innovate in production technology.
   f. Economies from learning.

4. Know the competitiveness of the industry.
   a. Concentration in the industry, the number of firms, and their sizes.
   b. Barriers to entry in the industry and the likelihood of new entrants and substitute products. Is there brand protection? Are customer switching costs large?
   c. The firm's position in the industry. Is it a first mover or a follower in the industry? Does it have a cost advantage?
   d. Competitiveness of suppliers. Do suppliers have market power? Do labor unions have power?
   e. Capacity in the industry. Is there excess capacity or undercapacity?
   f. Relationships and alliances with other firms.

5. Know the management.
   a. What is management's track record?
   b. Is management entrepreneurial?
   c. Does management focus on shareholders? Do members of management have a record of serving their own interests? Are they empire builders?
   d. Do stock compensation plans serve shareholders' interests or managements' interests?
   e. What are the details of the ethical charter under which the firm operates, and do managers have a propensity to violate it?
   f. How strong are the corporate governance mechanisms?

6. Know the political, legal, regulatory, and ethical environment.
   a. The firm's political influence.

  b. Legal constraints on the firm, including antitrust law, consumer law, labor law, and environmental law.

  c. Regulatory constraints on the firm, including product and price regulations.

  d. Taxation of the business.

These features are sometimes referred to as the *economic factors* that drive the business. You have studied many of these factors, and more, in courses on business economics, strategy, marketing, and production.

The Key Question: Sustainability of Competitive Advantage

Armed with an understanding of a firm's strategy and a mastery of the details, the analyst focuses on the key question: *How durable is the firm's competitive advantage?*

Microeconomics tells us that competition drives away abnormal returns. With few exceptions, the **forces of competition** are at play, and the critical question is how long those forces take to play out. The key to adding value is to design a business where abnormal returns endure for as long as possible. Firms attempt to counter the forces of competition to gain **competitive advantage.** The more enduring the competitive advantage, the more the firms generate value.

The business strategy and all of the economic factors listed ultimately bear upon competitive advantage. Innovative strategies are adopted to "get ahead of the competition." Products are designed to allure customers from the competition. Brands are built to maintain enduring customer loyalty. Patent protection is sought. Innovative production technologies are adopted for cost advantage. And, yes, politicians are lobbied to protect firms from competition. The inside analyst designs strategies to maintain competitive advantage. The outside analyst understands those strategies and strives to answer the question as to the durability of the firm's competitive advantage.

Financial Statements: The Lens on the Business

Understanding economic factors is a prerequisite to valuation. But we need a way of translating these factors into measures that lead to a valuation. We must recognize the firm's product, the competition in the industry, the firm's ability to develop product innovations, and so on, but we also must interpret this knowledge in a way that leads to a valuation. Economic factors are often expressed in qualitative terms that are suggestive but do not immediately translate into concrete dollar numbers. We might recognize that a firm has "market power," but what numbers would support this attribution? We might recognize that a firm is "under the threat of competition," but how would this show up in the numbers?

Financial statements report the numbers. Financial statements translate economic factors into accounting numbers like assets, sales, margins, cash flows, and earnings, and therefore we analyze the business by analyzing financial statements. We understand the effects of market power from accounting numbers. We evaluate the durability of competitive advantage from sequences of accounting numbers. Financial statement analysis organizes the financial statements in a way that highlights these features of a business.

Financial statements are the lens on the business. However, financial statements often present a blurred picture. Financial statement analysis focuses the lens to produce a clearer picture. Where accounting measurement is defective, analysis corrects. And where the picture in financial statements is incomplete, the analyst supplements the financial statements with other information. To do so, the analyst must know what the financial statements say and what they do not say. He must have a sense of good accounting and bad accounting. This book develops that facility, beginning in the next chapter, where financial statements are introduced. With this facility and a good knowledge of the business, the analyst proceeds to value the business through the lens of the financial statements.

The following valuation methods are covered in this book. All involve financial statement numbers in some way. Each method must be evaluated on its costs and benefits.

METHODS THAT DO NOT INVOLVE FORECASTING

The Method of Comparables (Chapter 3)

This method values stocks on the basis of price multiples (stock price divided by earnings, book value, sales, and other financial statement numbers) that are observed for similar firms.

Multiple Screening (Chapter 3)

This method identifies underpriced and overpriced stocks on the basis of their relative multiples. A stock screener buys firms with relative low price-earnings (P/E) ratios, for example, and sells stocks with high P/E ratios. Or he may screen stocks into buys and sells by screening on price-to-book, price-to-sales, and other multiples.

Asset-Based Valuation (Chapter 3)

Asset-based valuation values equities by adding up the estimated fair values of the assets of a firm and subtracting the value of the liabilities.

METHODS THAT INVOLVE FORECASTING

Dividend Discounting: Forecasting Dividends (Chapter 4)

Value is calculated as the present value of expected dividends.

Discounted Cash Flow Analysis: Forecasting Free Cash Flows (Chapter 4)

Value is calculated as the present value of expected free cash flows.

Residual Earnings Analysis: Forecasting Earnings and Book Values (Chapter 5)

Value is calculated as book value plus the present value of expected residual earnings.

Earnings Growth Analysis: Forecasting Earnings and Earnings Growth (Chapter 6)

Value is calculated as capitalized earnings plus the present value of expected abnormal earnings growth.

CHOOSING A VALUATION TECHNOLOGY

The analyst must have a good understanding of the business. He must understand the firm's competitive advantage. He must understand how the financial statements measure the success of the business. But, with all this understanding, he must then have a way of converting that understanding into a valuation. A valuation technology makes that conversion. The analyst must choose an appropriate technology.

Box 1.5 lists valuation technologies that are commonly used in practice. Some have the advantage of being simple, and simplicity is a virtue. But techniques can be too simple, ignoring important elements. Some techniques are dangerous, containing pitfalls for the unwary. The analyst chooses a technology with costs and benefits in mind, weighing simplicity against the costs of ignoring complexities.

This book covers the techniques in Box 1.5, highlighting their advantages and disadvantages. However, by far the most attention will be given to those techniques that attempt to calculate fundamental value from forecasts, for value is based on the expected payoffs to investing. For these methods, the analyst must identify what is to be forecasted. Does the analyst forecast dividends (and thus use dividend discount methods)? Does the analyst forecast cash flows (and thus use discounted cash flow methods)? Earnings? Book value and earnings? To make the choice the analyst must understand the advantages and disadvantages of each and then adopt a technology that provides the most security to the investor.

Guiding Principles

Years of investing experience have produced a set of principles that fundamental analysts cling to. Box 1.6 lists a number of tenets that will be adhered to as we develop valuation

As we proceed through the book, we will appeal to a number of guiding principles. Here is some of the wisdom, distilled from practice of fundamental analysis over the years:

1. One does not buy a stock, one buys a business.
2. When buying a business, know the business.
3. Value depends on the business model, the strategy.
4. Good firms can be bad buys.
5. Price is what you pay, value is what you get.
6. Part of the risk in investing is the risk of paying too much for a stock.
7. Ignore information at your peril.
8. Don't mix what you know with speculation.
9. Anchor a valuation on what you know rather than speculation.
10. Beware of paying too much for growth.
11. When calculating value to challenge price, beware of using price in the calculation.
12. Stick to your beliefs and be patient; prices gravitate to fundamentals, but that can take some time.

We have referenced the first six points already in this chapter. Points 7, 8, and 9 are discussed in the adjoining text and will be invoked as we organize information in later chapters. Points 10 and 11 are illustrated below. Point 12 warns against the "quick buck." Fundamental investing is not for day traders.

Beware of Paying Too Much for Growth

A P/E ratio indicates the market's expectation of future earnings growth (as we will see explicitly in later chapters). A P/E of 88 for Dell is high by any standard, so the fundamentalist questions whether the market is forecasting too much earnings growth. Point 10 warns us against getting too excited—too speculative—about future growth. Fundamentalists see speculation about growth as one of the prime reasons for the overpricing of stocks. A valuation method needs to build in protection against paying too much for growth. A sound valuation method challenges the market's speculation about growth.

When Calculating Value to Challenge Price, Beware of Using Price in the Calculation

Price is what you pay and value is what you get. So Point 11 warns against referring to the market price when you are calculating value. If you do so, you are clearly being circular and have ruined the ability of your analysis to challenge prices. Yet analysts allow prices to enter in subtle ways. An analyst who increases her earnings forecast because stock prices have increased—and then applies a valuation multiple to those earnings—commits that error. That is so easy to do when there is excitement about a stock, for there is a temptation to justify the price. But the analyst may be joining a chain letter.

After the launch of iPad, when the shares of Apple Inc. traded at $380, an analyst forecast earnings per share for the firm of $28.82 for fiscal year 2011, considerably higher than the average for other analysts. This is fair enough, if the analyst can justify the number. But the analyst also published a price target of $548 per share and, accordingly, issued a buy recommendation. To get this price, the analyst multiplied his 2011 earnings estimate by Apple's average P/E over the last three years of 19. You see the problem. The analyst is pricing earnings on the basis of the market's pricing of earnings, but if that pricing is incorrect he is building mispricing into the calculation. He used price to challenge price rather than value to challenge price. And he compounded the speculation in a high forecast with speculation in the market price. If a P/E of 19 represents a mispricing, he contributed to the perpetuation of the mispricing. No wonder bubbles form. The fundamentalist takes care to apply methods that establish the intrinsic P/E ratio without reference to market prices.

technologies throughout the book. The first six have been invoked already in this chapter. Those numbered 7, 8, and 9 bear on the all-important task of handling the information from which we infer value.

Too-simple techniques ignore information, and point 7 in Box 1.6 warns that the investor ignores information at her peril; she puts herself in danger of trading with someone who knows more than she. Multiple screening methods, for example, use only one or two bits of information, so they can get you into trouble, as we observed with the temptingly low multiples for General Motors and Ford. Rarely can an analyst avoid forecasting the future, and forecasting requires more information. So Box 1.5 divides techniques into those that require forecasting and those that do not. Forecasting uses the full range of information available, but it also requires the appropriate organization of information into a form that facilitates forecasting.

The trouble with forecasting is that it deals with the future, and the future is inherently speculative. The fundamental analyst is wary of speculation so, to exercise due care, he invokes points 8 and 9 in Box 1.6. In organizing the information, the analyst follows the maxim: *Don't mix what you know with speculation.* To cut across speculation, he distinguishes information that is concrete from information that is more speculative. He takes care not to contaminate relatively hard information with soft information that leads to speculation. He views notions like *intangible assets, knowledge capital, new technology,* and *Web real estate* as speculative. He sees current sales as relatively hard information, for customers have been won, but he sees information indicating that the firm might win more customers in the future as more speculative. He does not ignore the more speculative information, but he treats it differently. Current sales are weighed differently than forecasts of long-run growth rates in sales. He treats forecasts for one or two years ahead in a different light than forecasts for the distant future. And he is considerably more uncomfortable with stock valuations that are dependent on forecasting the long run; he sees such a stock as a speculative stock.

Anchoring Value on the Financial Statements

Tenet 9 in Box 1.6 embellishes Tenet 8: *Anchor a valuation on what you know rather than speculation.* Much of what we know about firms is found in the financial statements, so the maxim might read: *Anchor a valuation on the financial statements.* Financial statements contain information of varying quality and the accounting is sometimes suspect, but the information they contain is relatively hard information. Financial statements are based on accounting principles that largely exclude speculative information. They are audited. So, while the analyst always tests the quality of the information in the financial statements and organizes that information based on its perceived quality, financial statements are a good place to start when valuating firms.

Financial statements report two summary numbers, book value of equity and earnings. The book value of equity is the "bottom-line" number in the balance sheet; earnings is the bottom-line number in the income statement. The last two methods in Box 1.5 anchor value on these summary numbers. The form of the valuation is as follows:

$$\text{Value} = \text{Anchor} + \text{Extra value}$$

That is, the analyst takes a particular measure in the financial statements as a concrete starting point and then goes about calculating "extra value" not captured by this measure. The anchor might be the book value of shareholders' equity, so that

$$\text{Value} = \text{Book value} + \text{Extra value}$$

Here book value is the starting point, but the analyst realizes that book value is an incomplete measure of value, so he calculates extra value. In doing so, he calculates the intrinsic price-to-book ratio, the multiple of book value that the equity is worth. Valuation then comes down to the method of calculating value that is not in book value.

Alternatively, the anchor might be earnings, so that

$$\text{Value} = \text{Earnings} + \text{Extra value}$$

In this case, earnings is the starting point and the extra value yields the intrinsic price-earnings ratio, the multiple of earnings that the equity is worth. In both cases, the analyst starts with a hard number (in the financial statements) and adds an analysis of more speculative information.

To discipline that speculation, he carries out a financial statement analysis that distinguishes relatively hard information about the extra value from that which is relatively soft. That being so, he is secure in his valuation and is protected against the winds of speculation. The subsequent chapters in this book develop these themes.

HOW TO USE THIS BOOK

The best way to tackle this book is to see it as an exercise in building a valuation technology. Think of yourself as an investor who wants to have the best methods to protect and enhance your investments. Or think of yourself as one of the professionals we have talked about, an investment analyst or CFO. This will give you focus. If you think in terms of an outside analyst, ask yourself: How would I build the best valuation product for my clients? How would I prepare a credible equity research report? If you think in terms of an inside analyst, ask yourself: How would I write a strategy document or an investment appraisal? You want an analysis that will be practical, but you want one that is also conceptually sound. And you want an analysis that is understandable and easy to use.

This focus will make you demand a lot of the book, and of yourself. It will help you develop your critique of investment products that are being offered by vendors. It will help you develop your critique of the accounting in published financial statements. And, yes, it will also help you critique the book!

There are three ingredients to a good technology: good thinking, good application, and good balance between cost and benefit. Use the book to develop good thinking about businesses and their valuation: The book takes pains to lay out the concepts clearly. Use the book to translate concepts into methods that work in practice: The book builds a practical technique, block-by-block, from the concepts. Much of the analysis can be built into a spreadsheet program, and you might build this spreadsheet as you go, a product to carry over to your professional life. The book gives directions as we proceed, and you will find the BYOAP (Build Your Own Analysis Product) feature on the Web page to be indispensable for this task. Use the book to get a sense of cost-benefit tradeoffs. When is more detail worth it? What do I lose by cutting corners? What "bells and whistles" are worth adding?

The text is self-contained. But you will also find the book's Web page to be a worthwhile companion. It goes into more "real-life" situations, gives you more data to work with, and opens up the broader literature. Please visit the Web site at **www.mhhe.com/penman5e**.

Learning comes from reinforcing concepts by application. Exercises are given at the end of each chapter along with larger cases at the end of each section. They are written with learning in mind, to make a point, not solely as tests. More applications are on the Web page. Work through as many of these as you can. You will see how the analysis comes to life as you go "hands on."

An Outline of the Book

This chapter has introduced you to fundamental investing and has provided a flavor of the fundamental analysis that supports the investing. Financial statements feature prominently in analysis, so the introduction is completed in Chapter 2, where the financial statements are introduced. There you will understand why an analyst might anchor a valuation in the financial statements. The remainder of the book is then presented in five parts.

Good practice is built on good thinking. Part One (Chapters 3–7) lays out that thinking. Part One evaluates each of the methods presented in Box 1.5 and lays out how financial statement information is incorporated in each. By the end of Part One you will have a good sense of what good analysis is and what poor analysis is, and you will have selected a valuation technology with some confidence. Part One closes in Chapter 7 with the application of the valuation approach to active investing that challenges market prices.

Part Two (Chapters 8–13) deals with the analysis of information. It shows how to understand the business through the lens of the financial statements. It also shows how to carry out financial statement analysis with a view to forecasting payoffs.

Part Three (Chapters 14–16) involves forecasting. It lays out the practical steps for developing forecasts from the information analyzed in Part Two. And it demonstrates how to convert those forecasts into a valuation and to apply them to challenge market prices.

Part Four (Chapters 17–18) deals with accounting issues. A discussion of accounting is intertwined with the development of fundamental analysis throughout the book, beginning in Chapter 2. Part Four pulls the accounting analysis together so that you have a sound understanding of how accounting works in valuation. And, to the financial statement analysis of the earlier parts, it adds an accounting quality analysis.

Part Five (Chapters 19 and 20) discusses how to bring fundamental analysis to the evaluation of risk, both the risk of equities and the risk of corporate debt.

The Web Connection

Find the following on the Web page supplement for this chapter:

- A guide to the book's Web site.
- More on investment styles and the styles that equity funds commit to in their marketing.
- More on the history of investing and the returns to different investments.

- More on stock market bubbles.
- More on analysts during the bubble.
- A further introduction to valuation methods.
- The Readers' Corner provides a guide to further reading.
- Web Exercises has additional exercises for you to work, along with solutions.

Key Concepts

active investors buy or sell investments after an examination of whether they are mispriced, in order to earn exceptional rates of return. Compare with **passive investors** and **defensive investors.** *4*

alpha is an abnormal return over the expected return for the investment risk taken. *5*

beta is a measure of risk as prescribed by the capital asset pricing model (CAPM). *5*

business model is the concept or strategy under which a firm operates to add value from selling products or services to customers. *15*

claim is an enforceable contract for returns from an investment. *10*

competitive advantage is the ability to earn abnormal returns by resisting the **forces of competition.**   *17*

defensive investors buy or sell investments after an examination of whether they are mispriced, in order to avoid trading at the wrong price.   *4*

enterprise value is the value of the business (the firm), in contrast to the value of the various claims on the firm.   *12*

financial analyst is a professional who evaluates aspects of investing; particular types are equity analysts, credit analysts, strategy analysts, risk analysts, and bank loan officers.   *12*

financial statement analysis is a set of methods for extracting information from financial statements.   *2*

financing activities of a firm are the transactions between a firm and its claimants that involve cash investments in the firm by claimants and cash returns to claimants by the firm.   *12*

forces of competition are the challenges of others, in the pursuit of profit, to erode a firm's **competitive advantage.** The forces of competition tend to drive away abnormal returns.   *17*

fundamental analysis (or **valuation analysis**) is a set of methods for determining the value of an investment.   *3*

fundamental investors buy investments only after thoroughly examining information about firms and reaching conclusions about the underlying value that the information implies.   *4*

fundamental risk is the chance of losing value because of the outcome of business activities. Compare with **price risk.**   *5*

index investing involves buying and (passively) holding a market index of stocks.   *5*

intrinsic value is what an investment is worth based on forecasted payoffs from the investment. Payoffs are forecasted with information so intrinsic value is sometimes said to be the value justified by the information.   *4*

intuitive investors trade stocks based on their intuition, without submitting that intuition to analysis.   *3*

investing activities of a firm involve the acquisition and disposal of assets used in operations.   *12*

momentum investing follows the rule: Stocks whose price has gone up will go up further.   *7*

operating activities of the firm involve using assets (acquired in **investing activities**) to produce and sell products in markets.   *12*

passive investors buy investments without an examination of whether they are mispriced. Compare with **active investors.**   *3*

payoff is value received from an investment.   *11*

price risk is the chance of losing value from buying or selling investments at prices that differ from intrinsic value.   *5*

return to an investment is the **payoff** to the investment less the amount paid for the investment.   *11*

security analysis is a set of methods for determining the value of an investment when securities like stocks and bonds are involved.   *3*

strategy analysis involves articulating business ideas and discovering the value that might be generated by the ideas.   *13*

valuation analysis is analysis to determine the value of an investment.

value-based management involves making business plans by maximizing the likely value to be generated by the business, and monitoring and rewarding business performance with measures of value added.   *13*

value of the equity is the value of the payoffs a firm is expected to yield for its shareholders (its owners).   *10*

value of the firm (or **enterprise value**) is the value of the payoffs a firm is expected to yield for all its claimants.   *12*

A Continuing Case: *Kimberly-Clark Corporation*

A Self-Study Exercise

At the end of Chapters 1–16, the principles and techniques of the chapter will be applied to Kimberly-Clark Corporation, the consumer products company that manufactures and markets a wide range of health and hygiene products. By following one company throughout the book, you will observe how a comprehensive financial statement analysis and valuation is developed and applied to challenge the market price. By engaging in the case—by carrying out the tasks it asks you to—you will take on the role of an active analyst and, by the end of the book, will have the complete ingredients for an equity research report on the company. Every detail of the analysis cannot be applied to one company, of course, but you will see many of the principles in the text come to life with Kimberly-Clark.

As you follow Kimberly-Clark, you will be guided to sources for the inputs into your analysis. You will be asked, with guidance, to perform certain tasks. The solution to the case for each chapter is on the book's Web site. After completing the tasks, you can check the solution to see how well you have done.

Chapter 1 is merely an introduction to the book. But a number of principles have been laid down. First and foremost is the requirement that, before you engage in valuing a company, you must understand the business the company is in. So your first engagement with Kimberly-Clark here leads you to sources that explain Kimberly-Clark's business model.

KNOWING THE BUSINESS: KIMBERLY-CLARK CORPORATION (TICKER KMB)

You have possibly sniffled into a Kleenex tissue. At a much younger age you may have used a Huggies diaper (or nappy). Add to these brands the familiar names of Scott (paper towels), Scottex, Cottonelle, Viva, Kotex, and WypAll, you get a good idea of what KMB does. Here is a summary statement:

> Kimberly-Clark Corporation manufactures and markets a range of health and hygiene products. The Company is organized into four global business segments. The Personal Care segment manufactures and markets disposable diapers, training and youth pants and swim pants, baby wipes, and feminine and incontinence care products. The Consumer Tissue segment manufactures and markets facial and bathroom tissue, paper towels, wet wipes, and napkins for household use. The K-C Professional segment manufactures and markets facial and bathroom tissue, paper towels, and a range of safety products for the away-from-home market. The Health Care segment sells health care products such as surgical gowns, drapes, infection control products, sterilization wraps, disposable face masks and exam gloves, and other disposable medical products.

This, of course, is a cursory statement. The dedicated analyst tries to find out much more about the details. Where does he look?

Sources of Business Information

First and foremost is the firm's statement of its business. For this, go to its Web page, at **www.kimberly-clark.com**, paying particular attention to its most recent annual report to shareholders. Go to the firm's Facebook page and its RSS News Feed at **investor.kimberly-clark.com/rss.cfm** to see news releases. Finally (and most importantly), go to the firm's most recent annual 10-K filing with the Securities and Exchange Commission, at **www.sec.gov/edgar.shtml**. Read the Business Analysis, Risk Factors, and Management Discussion and Analysis sections of the 10-K. The 10-K is also on the Web page for Chapter 2 of this book.

Of course, you can also Google. Go to **www.google.com** or similar search engine and enter the company's name. Look not only for information on the company but also on the consumer paper products industry and competitors. You will get to various financial information portals—like Google Finance and Yahoo! Finance—and to news reports on the company. Look for company reports, particularly from financial analysts. Look for consumer and marketing analysis. Now is a good time to explore the links to research resources on the book's Web site. Much information on the Internet is behind passwords, for subscribers only. Time to head to your library and its electronic resources. Does your library have company research and industry research available? Look for consumer paper products. Does your library link you to articles in the business and financial press? Can you link to trade publications?

Knowing What Analysts Are Saying

Before beginning your own analysis, understand what "the Street" (in the U.S.) or "the City" (in the UK) is saying. Start with a finance Web site. These Web sites often have a summary of analysts' opinions and their earnings and revenue forecasts, like the one in Exhibit 1.1 from Yahoo! Finance (at **finance.yahoo.com/**). Google's finance Web site is at **www.google.com/finance**. Does your library subscribe to services that provide recent analysts' research reports like Thomson One, Multex, or S&P Market Insight? A number of brokerages allow you to sign up for free trials for their services.

A warning goes along with peeking at analysts' reports before you start your own research: Beware of joining the speculative crowd. Analysts sometimes herd together, and there is considerable reward to an independent analysis that uncovers something the herd does not see.

Here are some questions you should consider as you go through the various sources.

A. What is Kimberly-Clark's core business?
B. What is Kimberly-Clark's strategy for the future?
C. How does Kimberly-Clark intend to grow? Does it grow through acquisitions?
D. What is Kimberly-Clark's competitive environment? Who are its main competitors?
E. What are the main risks facing the firm? Would you describe this as a risky firm?
F. Go to the Yahoo! Finance or Google finance Web sites, enter the ticker (KMB), and observe the information there. Compare the current information with that on March 31, 2011 in Exhibit 1.1. Look at the price plots and observe how KMB has performed in the market. KMB paid a dividend of $2.64 per share in 2010. Can you calculate the return that shareholders earned over the most recent calendar year? Can you spot the P/E ratio and the price-to-book (P/B) ratio?
G. Summarize and discuss the main features of the analysts' reports in Exhibit 1.1.
H. Overall, do analysts (covered in Exhibit 1.1) think KMB shares are reasonably priced, cheap, or expensive?
I. In a press report in *Barron's* on March 31, 2011, Kimberly-Clark's CFO, Mark Buthman pointed to an increase in stock repurchases, to be financed by borrowing. "Our after-tax cost of debt is actually less than our dividend yield," he said. "For every dollar of shares I buy back, I actually save money." What do you think of his statement?
J. How has KMB's stock price fared since March 31, 2011, the date of the report in Exhibit 1.1? Did the analysts' earnings and revenue forecasts in Exhibit 1.1 turn out to be accurate?

EXHIBIT 1.1

Analysts'
Recommendations
and Estimates for
Kimberly-Clark
Corporation from
Yahoo! Finance Web
Page on March 31,
2011.

The header gives the stock price
at close of trading on March 31,
the stock price movements during the day, and basic summary
information. The Analyst Opinion summarizes analysts' buy,
hold, or sell recommendations.
The Analyst Estimates summarize analysts' consensus forecasts for earnings, revenues,
and earnings growth rates, with
comparisons to the industry,
sector, and the S&P 500 firms.

Kimberly-Clark Corporation Comm (NYSE:KMB)

Last Trade:	65.24	Day's Range:	65.16–65.95
Trade Time:	Mar 31, 3:59pm	52wk Range:	59.57–67.24
Change:	↓0.53 (0.81%)	Volume:	1,788,084
Prev Close:	65.77	Avg Vol (3m):	2,719,410
Open:	65.77	Market Cap:	26.38
Bid:	65.25 × 800	P/E (ttm):	14.67
Ask:	65.26 × 100	EPS (ttm):	4.45
1y Target Est:	68.79	Div & Yield:	2.80 (4.30%)

Analyst Opinion

Recommendation Summary*

Mean Recommendation (this week):	2.6
Mean Recommendation (last week):	2.6
Change:	0.0

*(Strong Buy) 1.0–5.0 (Strong Sell)

Price Target Summary

Mean Target:	68.79
Median Target:	69.00
High Target:	82.00
Low Target:	60.00
No. of Brokers:	14

Recommendation Trends

	Current Month	Last Month	Two Months Ago	Three Months Ago
Strong Buy	3	3	3	3
Buy	2	2	2	2
Hold	10	10	10	10
Sell	2	2	2	2
Strong Sell	0	0	0	0

Analyst Estimates

Earnings Est	Current Qtr Mar-11	Next Qtr Jun-11	Current Year Dec-11	Next Year Dec-12
Avg. Estimate	1.18	1.23	4.98	5.35
No. of Analysts	15	15	16	15
Low Estimate	1.10	1.15	4.94	5.24
High Estimate	1.22	1.27	5.04	5.41
Year Ago EPS	1.14	1.20	4.68	4.98

Next Earnings Date: 25-Apr-11

Revenue Est	Current Qtr Mar-11	Next Qtr Jun-11	Current Year Dec-11	Next Year Dec-12
Avg. Estimate	4.99B	5.10B	20.51B	21.19B
No. of Analysts	12	12	13	11
Low Estimate	4.84B	4.95B	20.26B	20.77B
High Estimate	5.09B	5.22B	20.87B	21.65B
Year Ago Sales	4.84B	4.86B	19.75	20.51B
Sales Growth (year/est)	3.10%	4.90%	3.90%	3.30%

Earnings History	Mar-10	Jun-10	Sep-10	Dec-10
EPS Est	1.16	1.13	1.28	1.15
EPS Actual	1.14	1.20	1.14	1.20
Difference	–0.02	0.07	–0.14	0.05
Surprise %	–1.70%	6.20%	–10.90%	4.30%

Growth Est	KMB	Industry	Sector	S&P 500
Current Qtr.	3.5%	–7.7%	16.8%	22.7%
Next Qtr.	2.5%	22.1%	32.5%	31.1%
This Year	6.4%	4.9%	13.5%	18.0%
Next Year	7.4%	12.9%	19.0%	12.9%
Past 5 Years (per annum)	4.53%	N/A	N/A	N/A
Next 5 Years (per annum)	9.10%	13.07%	13.83	10.18%
Price/Earnings (avg. for comparison categories)	13.13	14.18	16.56	13.37
PEG Ratio (avg. for comparison categories)	1.44	1.31	1.33	1.20

Concept Questions

C1.1. What is the difference between fundamental risk and price risk?

C1.2. What is the difference between an alpha technology and a beta technology?

C1.3. Critique the following statement: Hold stocks for the long run, for in the long run, the return to stocks is always higher than bond returns.

C1.4. What is the difference between a passive investor and an active investor?

C1.5. In the late 1990s, P/E ratios were high by historical standards. The P/E ratio for the S&P 500 stocks was as high as 33 in 1999. In the 1970s it was 8. What do you think would be a "normal" P/E ratio—that is, where multiples higher than normal could be called "high" and multiples less than normal could be called "low"? *Hint:* The P/E ratio is the inverse of the E/P ratio, sometimes called the earnings yield. Compare this yield with normal return for stocks of about 10 percent.

C1.6. Should a shareholder be indifferent between selling her shares on the open market and selling them to the firm in a stock repurchase?

C1.7. Some commentators argue that stock prices "follow a random walk." By this they mean that changes in stock prices in the future are not predictable, so no one can earn an abnormal return. Would stock prices follow a random walk if *all* investors were fundamental investors who use all available information to price stocks and agreed on the implications of that information?

C1.8. Consider the case where *all* investors are passive investors: They buy index funds. What is your prediction about how stock prices will behave over time? Will they follow a random walk? *Hint:* Prices would not incorporate any information.

C1.9. Figure 1.2 plots a price-to-value ratio (P/V) for the Dow Jones Industrial Average (DJIA) from 1979 to 1999. A P/V ratio is a metric that compares the market price (P) to an estimate of intrinsic value (V). The intrinsic value in the figure is based on techniques that will be discussed in this book, but how it is calculated is not important for the following questions:

a. Up to 1996, the P/V ratio fluctuated around 1.0. What do you make of this pattern?

b. If you had purchased the Dow 30 stocks each time the P/V ratio fell below 0.8 and had sold them each time the P/V ratio rose above 1.2, would your investment strategy have performed well?

FIGURE 1.2
Price-to-Value Ratio (P/V) for the DJIA at Monthly Intervals. V Is an Estimate of the Intrinsic Value of the Dow.

Source: From the Web page of the Parker Center, Cornell University. The graph is an update of one reported in C. Lee, J. Myers, and B. Swaminathan, "What Is the Intrinsic Value of the Dow?" *Journal of Finance,* October 1999, pp. 1693–1741. The Parker Center Web site is at **www2.johnson.cornell .edu/parkercenter/about.html**.

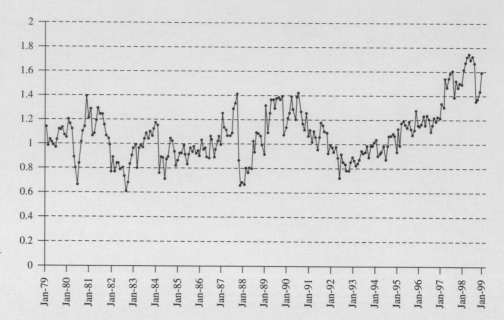

c. What interpretation do you put on the continuing upward movement of the P/V ratio after 1995?

d. Which direction so you think this graph headed after 1999?

Exercises

The exercises at the end of each chapter are divided into *Drill Exercises* and *Applications.* Drill exercises test you on the basics, with simple numerical examples. Application exercises apply the principles and techniques of the chapter to real companies. Drill exercises are important in making sure you have the understanding to proceed to more realistic settings. The degree of difficulty—easy, medium, or hard—is indicated for all exercises.

Drill Exercises

E1.1. Calculating Enterprise Value (Easy)

The shares of a firm trade on the stock market at a total of $1.2 billion, and its debt trades at $600 million. What is the market value of the firm (its enterprise market value)?

E1.2. Calculating Value per Share (Easy)

An analyst estimates that the enterprise value of a firm is $2.7 billion. The firm has $900 million of debt outstanding. If there are 900 million shares outstanding, what is the analyst's estimated value per share?

E1.3. Buy or Sell? (Easy)

A firm reports book value of shareholders' equity of $850 million with 25 million shares outstanding. Those shares trade at $45 each in the stock market. An analyst values the equity by following the scheme: Value = Book value + Extra value. She calculates extra value of $675 million. Should she issue a buy or a sell recommendation to her clients?

Applications

E1.4. Finding Information on the Internet: Dell, Inc. General Motors, and Ford (Easy)

This chapter compared Dell, Inc., General Motors Corp., and Ford Motor Co. Go to the Internet and find sources that will help research these firms. One site to start with is Yahoo!

Finance: **finance.yahoo.com**. Another is Google Finance: **www.google.com/finance**.   Look at the book's Web page for links to further sources.

E1.5.   Enterprise Market Value: General Mills and Hewlett-Packard (Medium)

a. General Mills, Inc., the large manufacturer of packaged foods, reported the following in its annual report for the year ending May 29, 2011 (in millions):

Short-term borrowing	$1,342.6
Long-term debt	5,542.5
Stockholders' equity	6,616.2

The short-term borrowing and long-term debt are carried on the balance sheet at approximately their market value. The firm's 644.8 million shares traded at $36.50 per share when the annual report was released. From these numbers, calculate General Mills's enterprise market value (the market value of the firm).

b. Hewlett-Packard, the computer equipment manufacturer and systems consultant, had 2,126 million shares outstanding in May 2011, trading at $41 per share. Its most recent quarterly report listed the following (in millions):

Investments in interest-bearing debt	
securities and deposits	$12,700
Short-term borrowings	8.406
Long-term debt	14,512
Stockholders' equity	41,795

Calculate the enterprise market value of Hewlett-Packard. The question requires you to consider the treatment of the interest-bearing debt investments. Are they part of the enterprise?

E1.6.   Identifying Operating, Investing, and Financing Transactions: Microsoft (Easy)

Microsoft Corp. reported the following in its annual report to the Securities and Exchange Commission for fiscal year ending June 30, 2011. Classify each item as involving an operating, investing, or financing activity. Amounts are in millions.

a.	Common stock dividends	$ 5,394
b.	General and administrative expenses	4,222
c.	Sales and marketing expenses	13,940
d.	Common stock issues	2,422
e.	Common stock repurchases	11,555
f.	Sales revenue	69,943
g.	Research and development expenditures	9,043
h.	Income taxes	4,921
i.	Additions to property and equipment	2,355
j.	Accounts receivable	14,987

Real World Connection

Exercises E4.14, E6.12, E8.9, E9.9, E11.11, and E18.10 also deal with Microsoft, as do Minicases M9.1 and M13.2.

Minicase **M1.1**

Critique of an Equity Analysis: America Online Inc.

The so-called Internet Bubble gripped stock markets in 1998, 1999, and 2000, as discussed in the chapter. Internet stocks traded at multiples of earnings and sales rarely seen in stock markets. Start-ups, some with not much more than an idea, launched initial public offerings (IPOs) that sold for very high prices (and made their founders and employees with stock options very rich). Established firms, like Disney, considered launching spinoffs with "dot.com" in their names, just to receive the higher multiple that the market was giving to similar firms.

Commentators argued over whether the high valuations were justified. Many concluded the phenomenon was just speculative mania. They maintained that the potential profits that others were forecasting would be competed away by the low barriers to entry. But others maintained that the ability to establish and protect recognized brand names—like AOL, Netscape, Amazon, Yahoo!, and eBay—would support high profits. And, they argued, consumers would migrate to these sites from more conventional forms of commerce.

America Online (AOL) was a particular focus in the discussion. One of the most well-established Internet portals, AOL was actually reporting profits, in contrast to many Internet firms that were reporting losses. AOL operated two worldwide Internet services, America Online and CompuServe. It sold advertising and e-commerce services on the Web and, with its acquisition of Netscape, had enhanced its Internet technology services. See Box 1.3.

For the fiscal year ending June 30, 1999, America Online reported total revenue of $4.78 billion, of which $3.32 billion was from the subscriptions of 19.6 million AOL and CompuServe subscribers, $1.00 billion from advertising and e-commerce, and the remainder from network services through its Netscape Enterprises Group. It also reported net income of $762 million, or $0.73 per share.

AOL traded at $105 per share on this report and, with 1.10 billion shares outstanding, a market capitalization of its equity of $115.50 billion. The multiple of revenues of 24.2 was similar to the multiple of earnings for more seasoned firms at the time, so relatively, it was very high. AOL's P/E ratio was 144.

In an article on the op-ed page of *The Wall Street Journal* on April 26, 1999, David D. Alger of Fred Alger Management, a New York–based investment firm, argued that AOL's stock price was justified. He made the following revenue forecasts for 2004, five years later (in billions):

Subscriptions from 39 million subscribers	$12.500
Advertising and other revenues	3.500
Total revenue	16.000
Profits margin on sales, after tax	26%

To answer parts (*A*) and (*B*), forecast earnings for 2004.

A. If AOL's forecasted price-earnings (P/E) ratio for 2004 was at the current level of that for a seasoned firm, 24, what would AOL's shares be worth in 1999? AOL is not expected to pay dividends. *Hint:* The current price should be the present value of the price expected in the future.

B. Alger made his case by insisting that AOL could maintain a high P/E ratio of about 50 in 2004. What P/E ratio would be necessary in 2004 to justify a per-share price of $105 in 1999? If the P/E were to be 50 in 2004, would AOL be a good buy?

C. What is missing from these evaluations? Do you see a problem with Alger's analysis?

Chapter Two

LINKS

Links to previous chapter

The first chapter introduced active investing based on fundamental analysis and explained how financial statements provide a lens on the business to help carry out the analysis.

This chapter

This chapter gives you a basic understanding of the financial statements with a view to using them as an analysis tool.

Link to Part I

The five chapters in Part One of the book show how financial statements are utilized in valuing business firms.

Link to Web page

The Web page supplement for this chapter shows you how to find financial statements and goes into more detail about the statements.

Introduction to the Financial Statements

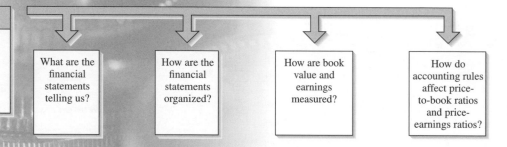

What are the financial statements telling us?

How are the financial statements organized?

How are book value and earnings measured?

How do accounting rules affect price-to-book ratios and price-earnings ratios?

Financial statements contain information that helps the analyst infer fundamental value. The analyst must appreciate what these statements are saying and what they are not saying. She must know where to go in the financial statements to find relevant information. She must understand the deficiencies of the statements, where they fail to provide the necessary information. This chapter introduces the financial statements.

You probably have some familiarity with financial statements, perhaps at the technical level of how they are prepared. This knowledge will help you here. However, our focus is not on the detailed accounting rules, but on the broad principles behind the statements that determine how they are used in analysis. The coverage is skeletal, to be filled out as the book proceeds (and we will come back to a more detailed accounting analysis in Part Four).

Financial statements are the lens on a business. They draw a picture of the business that is brought into focus with financial statement analysis. The analyst must understand how the picture is drawn and how she might then sharpen it with analysis. Two features of the statements need to be appreciated: form and content. *Form* describes how the financial statements are organized. Financial statement analysis is an organized way of extracting information from financial statements, but to organize financial statement analysis, one must first understand how the financial statements themselves are organized. The form of the financial statements sketches the picture. *Content* fills out the form, it colors the sketch. Content describes how line items such as earnings, assets, and liabilities are measured, thus quantifying the message. This chapter lays out the form of the financial statements and then explains the accounting principles that dictate the measurement.

The Analyst's Checklist

After reading this chapter you should understand:

- The broad picture of the firm that is painted by the financial statements.
- The component parts of each financial statement.
- How components of the financial statements fit together (or "articulate").
- The accounting relations that govern the financial statements.
- The stocks and flows equation that dictates how shareholders' equity is updated.
- The concept of comprehensive income.
- The concept of dirty surplus accounting.
- The accounting principles that dictate how the balance sheet is measured.
- How price-to-book ratios are affected by accounting principles.
- The accounting principles that dictate how earnings are measured.
- How price-earnings ratios are affected by accounting principles.
- The difference between market value added and earnings.
- Why fundamental analysts want accountants to enforce the reliability criterion.
- How financial statements anchor investors.

After reading this chapter you should be able to:

- Explain shareholders' equity in terms of assets and liabilities.
- Explain the change in shareholders' equity using the equity statement.
- Explain the change in shareholders' equity using the income statement.
- Explain the change in cash using the cash flow statement.
- Calculate comprehensive income.
- Calculate net payout to shareholders.
- Describe, for a particular firm, the picture that is painted by the financial statements.
- Calculate a premium over book value.
- Identify items in the balance sheet that are measured at fair value.
- Calculate market value added (the stock return).
- Recount the history of price-to-book ratios and price-earnings ratios over the past 50 years.

Financial statements are reported to shareholders. All firms listed for public trading in the United States must also file an annual 10-K report and a quarterly 10-Q report with the Securities and Exchange Commission (SEC). These reports are available online through the SEC's EDGAR database at **www.sec.gov/edgar.shtml**. You should familiarize yourself with this source.

Accounting standards in the United States are issued by the Financial Accounting Standards Board (FASB), subject to oversight by the Securities and Exchange Commission and ultimately the U.S. Congress. Separately, the International Accounting Standards Board (IASB), based in London, has promulgated a set of standards known as International Financial Reporting Standards (IFRS). Partly because of conscious harmonization of activities between the FASB and IASB, these standards are quite similar to those in the United States, though details vary. In 2005, the European Union required listed companies in Europe to conform to IFRS, and many countries are adopting these international standards or are likely to do so. By 2013, about 150 countries are expected to adopt IFRS.

THE FORM OF THE FINANCIAL STATEMENTS

The form of the financial statements is the way in which the statements, and their component parts, relate to each other. Form is given by a set of **accounting relations** that express the various components of financial statements in terms of other components. Understanding these relations is important because, as you will see in later chapters, they structure the way in which we do fundamental analysis. Indeed, many of these relations specify how you develop a spreadsheet program to value firms and their equity.

Firms are required to publish three primary financial statements in the United States, the *balance sheet,* the *income statement,* and the *cash flow statement.* In addition they must report a statement reconciling beginning and ending shareholders' equity for the reporting period. This is usually done in a fourth statement, the *statement of shareholders' equity,* but the information is occasionally given in footnotes. Other countries have similar requirements. The International Accounting Standards Board requires the four statements. The Web page gives examples of financial statements for a number of countries.

Introducing Nike, Inc.

Nike is no doubt familiar to you: The firm's logo is visible on the clothes and shoes that many of us wear, from the greatest sports stars to the smallest of kid pretenders. We will spend considerable time with Nike in this book, analyzing its financial statements and ultimately grappling with a valuation. The **Build Your Own Analysis Product (BYOAP)** on the book's Web site tracks Nike for a number of years up to 2010 and uses the firm as an example of how you develop spreadsheet tools to analyze and value a firm. The four financial statements for fiscal year ending May 31, 2010, are in Exhibit 2.1. Browse the entire 10-K on the SEC EDGAR Web site.

As we emphasized in Chapter 1, one should have a firm knowledge of a firm's business before reading and interpreting its financial statements, more so when it comes to valuation. Box 2.1 provides a summary. You will get a more thorough understanding from reading the Business and Risk Factors sections of its annual 10-K report, along with the Management's Discussion and Analysis there.

In the 1990s, Nike was a hot stock, trading at a price-earnings (P/E) ratio of 35 and a price-to-book (P/B) ratio of 5.1. Its stock price dropped 55 percent from its high on the bursting of the bubble in early 2000, but increased steadily thereafter, from $14.15 in early 2000 to $74 at the time of its 2010 annual report. The stock lost 36 percent of its value during the financial crisis of 2008, but recovered quickly. In 2010 it traded at a P/E of 18.8 and a P/B of 3.67, two numbers that will be the focus of our analysis and valuation.

The Balance Sheet

The balance sheet—sometimes called the Statement of Financial Position—lists assets, liabilities, and stockholders' (shareholders') equity. **Assets** are investments that are expected to generate payoffs. **Liabilities** are claims to the payoffs by claimants other than owners. **Stockholders' equity** is the claim by the owners. So the balance sheet is a statement of the firm's investments (from its investing activities) and the claims to the payoffs from those investments. Both assets and liabilities are divided into current and long-term categories, where "current" means that the assets will generate cash within a year, or that cash will be needed to settle liability claims within a year. Redeemable preferred stock are placed on a "mezzanine" between liabilities and shareholders' equity, as with Nike, but really are a liability from the common shareholders' point of view.

EXHIBIT 2.1
The Financial Statements for Nike, Inc., for Fiscal Year Ending May 31, 2010.
Four statements are published: the balance sheet, the income statement, the cash flow statement, and the statement of shareholders' equity. The notes in the financial statements refer to footnotes in the annual 10-K report.

NIKE, INC.
Consolidated Balance Sheets

	May 31, 2010	May 31, 2009
	(In millions)	
ASSETS		
Current assets:		
Cash and equivalents	$ 3,079.1	$ 2,291.1
Short-term investments (Note 6)	2,066.8	1,164.0
Accounts receivable, net (Note 1)	2,649.8	2,883.9
Inventories (Notes 1 and 2)	2,040.8	2,357.0
Deferred income taxes (Note 9)	248.8	272.4
Prepaid expenses and other current assets	873.9	765.6
Total current assets	10,959.2	9,734.0
Property, plant and equipment, net (Note 3)	1,931.9	1,957.7
Identifiable intangible assets, net (Note 4)	467.0	467.4
Goodwill (Note 4)	187.6	193.5
Deferred income taxes and other assets (Notes 9 and 18)	873.6	897.0
Total assets	$ 14,419.3	$ 13,249.6
LIABILITIES AND SHAREHOLDERS' EQUITY		
Current liabilities:		
Current portion of long-term debt (Note 8)	$ 7.4	$ 32.0
Notes payable (Note 7)	138.6	342.9
Accounts payable (Note 7)	1,254.5	1,031.9
Accrued liabilities (Notes 5 and 18)	1,904.4	1,783.9
Income taxes payable (Note 9)	59.3	86.3
Total current liabilities	3,364.2	3,277.0
Long-term debt (Note 8)	445.8	437.2
Deferred income taxes and other liabilities (Notes 9 and 18)	855.3	842.0
Commitments and contingencies (Note 15)	—	—
Redeemable Preferred Stock (Note 10)	0.3	0.3
Shareholders' equity:		
Common stock at stated value (Note 11):		
Class A convertible—90.0 and 95.3 shares outstanding	0.1	0.1
Class B—394.0 and 390.2 shares outstanding	2.7	2.7
Capital in excess of stated value	3,440.6	2,871.4
Accumulated other comprehensive income (Note 14)	214.8	367.5
Retained earnings	6,095.5	5,451.4
Total shareholders' equity	9,753.7	8,693.1
Total liabilities and shareholders' equity	$ 14,419.3	$ 13,249.6

(*continued*)

EXHIBIT 2.1 **Financial Statements for Nike (*continued*)**

<table>
<tr><td colspan="4" align="center">**Consolidated Statements of Income**</td></tr>
<tr><td></td><td colspan="3" align="center">Year Ended May 31</td></tr>
<tr><td></td><td align="center">2010</td><td align="center">2009</td><td align="center">2008</td></tr>
<tr><td></td><td colspan="3" align="center">(In millions, except per share data)</td></tr>
<tr><td>**Revenues**</td><td>$19,014.0</td><td>$19,176.1</td><td>$18,627.0</td></tr>
<tr><td>Cost of sales</td><td>10,213.6</td><td>10,571.7</td><td>10,239.6</td></tr>
<tr><td>**Gross margin**</td><td>8,800.4</td><td>8,604.4</td><td>8,387.4</td></tr>
<tr><td>Selling and administrative expense</td><td>6,326.4</td><td>6,149.6</td><td>5,953.7</td></tr>
<tr><td>Restructuring charges (Note 16)</td><td>—</td><td>195.0</td><td>—</td></tr>
<tr><td>Goodwill impairment (Note 4)</td><td>—</td><td>199.3</td><td>—</td></tr>
<tr><td>Intangible and other asset impairment (Note 4)</td><td>—</td><td>202.0</td><td>—</td></tr>
<tr><td>Interest expense (income), net (Notes 6, 7 and 8)</td><td>6.3</td><td>(9.5)</td><td>(77.1)</td></tr>
<tr><td>Other (income) expense, net (Notes 17 and 18)</td><td>(49.2)</td><td>(88.5)</td><td>7.9</td></tr>
<tr><td>**Income before income taxes**</td><td>2,516.9</td><td>1,956.5</td><td>2,502.9</td></tr>
<tr><td>Income taxes (Note 9)</td><td>610.2</td><td>469.8</td><td>619.5</td></tr>
<tr><td>**Net income**</td><td>$ 1,906.7</td><td>$ 1,486.7</td><td>$ 1,883.4</td></tr>
<tr><td>Basic earning per common share (Notes 1 and 12)</td><td>$ 3.93</td><td>$ 3.07</td><td>$ 3.80</td></tr>
<tr><td>Diluted earnings per common share (Notes 1 and 12)</td><td>$ 3.86</td><td>$ 3.03</td><td>$ 3.74</td></tr>
<tr><td>Dividends declared per common share</td><td>$ 1.06</td><td>$ 0.98</td><td>$ 0.875</td></tr>
</table>

(continued)

The three parts of the balance sheet are tied together in the following accounting relation:

$$\text{Shareholders' equity} = \text{Assets} - \text{Liabilities} \qquad \textbf{(2.1)}$$

This equation (sometimes referred to as the *accounting equation* or *balance sheet equation*) says that shareholders' equity is always equal to the difference between the assets and liabilities (referred to as *net assets*). That is, shareholders' equity is the residual claim on the assets after subtracting liability claims. From an equity valuation point of view, the shareholders' equity is the main summary number on the balance sheet. It's the accountants' attempt to measure the equity claim. In Nike's case, the shareholders' equity of $9,753.7 million in 2010 is represented by 19 line items, 10 assets totaling to $14,419.3 million and nine liabilities totaling $4,665.6 million, including the redeemable preferred stock. This total of $9,753.7 million is also explained in the shareholders' equity by common stock issued of $3,443.4 million, accumulated other comprehensive income of $214.8 million, and retained earnings of $6,095.5 million. Common stock is the amount of stock issued less any stock repurchased and retired. Stock that is repurchased but not retired is placed on a separate line as **treasury stock**, so **common stock outstanding** is always shares issued (in common stock) less shares in treasury. Nike has no treasury stock. Retained earnings are the accumulated earnings (or profits) less amounts paid out to shareholders. Other comprehensive income is income that is recognized in the balance sheet but which bypasses the income statement. We will discuss it later in this chapter.

The Income Statement

The income statement—Nike's Consolidated Statement of Income in the exhibit—reports how shareholders' equity increased or decreased as a result of business activities. The "bottom line" measure of value added to shareholders' equity is *net income,* also referred to

EXHIBIT 2.1   **Financial Statements for Nike** (*continued*)

Consolidated Statements of Cash Flows

| | Year Ended May 31 | | |
	2010	2009	2008
		(In millions)	
Cash provided by operations:			
Net income	$1,906.7	$1,486.7	$ 1,883.4
Income charges (credits) not affecting cash:			
Depreciation	323.7	335.0	303.6
Deferred income taxes	8.3	(294.1)	(300.6)
Stock-based compensation (Note 11)	159.0	170.6	141.0
Impairment of goodwill, intangibles and other assets (Note 4)	—	401.3	—
Gain on divestitures (Note 17)	—	—	(60.6)
Amortization and other	71.8	48.3	17.9
Changes in certain working capital components and other assets and liabilities excluding the impact of acquisition and divestitures:			
Decrease (increase) in accounts receivable	181.7	(238.0)	(118.3)
Decrease (increase) in inventories	284.6	32.2	(249.8)
(Increase) decrease in prepaid expenses and other current assets	(69.6)	14.1	(11.2)
Increase (decrease) in accounts payable, accrued liabilities and income taxes payable	298.0	(220.0)	330.9
Cash provided by operations	3,164.2	1,736.1	1,936.3
Cash used by investing activities:			
Purchases of short-term investments	(3,724.4)	(2,908.7)	(1,865.6)
Maturities and sales of short-term investments	2,787.6	2,390.0	2,246.0
Additions to property, plant and equipment	(335.1)	(455.7)	(449.2)
Disposals of property, plant and equipment	10.1	32.0	1.9
Increase in other assets, net of other liabilities	(11.2)	(47.0)	(21.8)
Settlement of net investment hedges	5.5	191.3	(76.0)
Acquisition of subsidiary, net of cash acquired (Note 4)	—	—	(571.1)
Proceeds from divestitures (Note 17)	—	—	246.0
Cash used in investing activities	(1,267.5)	(798.1)	(489.8)
Cash used by financing activities:			
Reductions in long-term debt, including current portion	(32.2)	(6.8)	(35.2)
(Decrease) increase in notes payable	(205.4)	177.1	63.7
Proceeds from exercise of stock options and other stock issuances	364.5	186.6	343.3
Excess tax benefits from share-based payment arrangements	58.5	25.1	63.0
Repurchase of common stock	(741.2)	(649.2)	(1,248.0)
Dividends—common and preferred	(505.4)	(466.7)	(412.9)
Cash used by financing activities	(1,061.2)	(733.9)	(1,226.1)
Effect of exchange rate changes	(47.5)	(46.9)	56.8
Net increase in cash and equivalents	788.0	157.2	277.2
Cash and equivalents, beginning of year	2,291.1	2,133.9	1,856.7
Cash and equivalents, end of year	$ 3,079.1	$ 2,291.1	$ 2,133.9
Supplemental disclosure of cash flow information:			
Cash paid during the year for:			
Interest, net of capitalized interest	$ 48.4	$ 46.7	$ 44.1
Income taxes	537.2	765.2	717.5
Dividends declared and not paid	130.7	121.4	112.9

(*continued*)

EXHIBIT 2.1 **Financial Statements for Nike** (*concluded*)

Consolidated Statements of Shareholders' Equity

	Common Stock				Capital in Excess of Stated Value	Accumulated Other Comprehensive Income	Retained Earnings	Total
	Class A		Class B					
	Shares	Amount	Shares	Amount				
					(In millions, except per share data)			
Balance at May 31, 2009	95.3	$ 0.1	390.2	$ 2.7	$ 2,871.4	$ 367.5	$5,451.4	$ 8,693.1
Stock options exercised			8.6		379.6			379.6
Conversion to Class B Common Stock	(5.3)		5.3					—
Repurchase of Class B Common Stock			(11.3)		(6.8)		(747.5)	(754.3)
Dividends on Common stock ($1.06 per share)							(514.8)	(514.8)
Issuance of shares to employees			1.3		40.0			40.0
Stock-based compensation (Note 11):					159.0			159.0
Forfeiture of shares from employees			(0.1)		(2.6)		(0.3)	(2.9)
Comprehensive income (Note 14):								
Net income							1,906.7	1,906.7
Other comprehensive income:								
Foreign currency translation and other (net of tax benefit of $71.8)						(159.2)		(159.2)
Net gain on cash flow hedges (net of tax expense of $27.8)						87.1		87.1
Net gain on net investment hedges (net of tax expense of $21.2)						44.8		44.8
Reclassification to net income of previously deferred net gains related to hedge derivatives (net of tax expense of $41.7)						(121.6)		(121.6)
Reclassification of ineffective hedge gains to net income (net of tax expense of $1.4)						(3.8)		(3.8)
Total comprehensive income						(152.7)	1,906.7	1,754.0
Balance at May 31, 2010	90.0	$0.1	394.0	$ 2.7	$3,440.6	$214.8	$6,095.5	$9,753.7

The accompanying notes to consolidated financial statements are an integral part of this statement.

as *earnings* or *net profit*. The income statement displays the sources of net income, broadly classified as **revenue** (value coming in from selling products) and **expenses** (value going out in earning revenue). The accounting relation that determines net income is

$$\text{Net income} = \text{Revenues} - \text{Expenses} \qquad \textbf{(2.2)}$$

Nike's revenue for 2010 was from sales of its products of $19,014 million. Revenue is sales after deducting estimates for sales returns (sometimes referred to as net revenue). From this net revenue, Nike subtracts operating expenses incurred in earning the revenue along with

Incorporated in 1968, Nike (**www.nike.com**) is a leading manufacturer and marketer of sport and fashion footwear. The firm is headquartered in Beaverton, Oregon.

STRATEGY

Nike aims to dominate the worldwide market for athletic footwear and athletic footwear used for casual and leisure dress. It attempts to accomplish this through extensive promotion, often using high-profile sports figures and endorsements of sporting events.

OPERATIONS

Nike's top-selling footwear are basketball, training, running, and children's shoes, but it also sells tennis, soccer, golf, baseball, football, and other footwear, as well as apparel, brand-name sports equipment, and accessories. It sells its products through retail outlets in the United States and around the world and through independent distributors and licensees. About 42 percent of Nike's sales in 2010 were in the United States.

The firm maintains an active research and development effort to improve its products. Most of its manufacturing facilities are outside the United States, in Asia and South America. It has approximately 34,400 employees, but much of the manufacturing is through independent contractors.

The market for footwear is highly competitive, with Puma and Adidas being major competitors. Changes in consumer preferences, changes in technology, and competition are seen as the main risk factors.

EQUITY FINANCING

Two classes of common shares have equal shares in profits. A total of 484.0 million shares were outstanding at the end of fiscal 2010. Nike has a continuing stock repurchase program and pays dividends. A small number of redeemable preferred shares are held by an Asian supplier.

The company has an active stock compensation plan for employees. In fiscal 2010, options on 6.4 million shares were granted and options on 8.6 million shares were exercised at a weighted-average exercise price of $37.64 per share. There were 36.0 million options outstanding at fiscal year end.

SUMMARY DATA

	2010	2009	2008
Basic earnings per share	$ 3.93	$ 3.07	$ 3.80
Diluted earnings per share	3.86	3.03	3.74
Dividends per share	1.06	0.98	0.88
Book value per share	20.15	17.90	15.93
Price per share, end of year	72.38	57.05	68.37

net interest expense on debt and income from "other" activities, to yield income before income taxes. Finally, taxes are subtracted to yield net income of $1,906.7 million.

The income statement often groups like expenses in categories to report a number of components of net income. Typical groupings in U.S. statements yield the following sequential components:

$$\text{Net revenue} - \text{Cost of goods sold} = \text{Gross margin} \qquad \textbf{(2.2a)}$$

$$\text{Gross margin} - \text{Operating expenses} = \text{Operating income}$$

$$\text{Operating income} - \text{Interest expense} + \text{Interest income} = \text{Income before taxes}$$

$$\text{Income before taxes} - \text{Income taxes} = \text{Income after taxes (and before extraordinary items)}$$

$$\text{Income before extraordinary items} + \text{Extraordinary items} = \text{Net income}$$

$$\text{Net income} - \text{Preferred dividends} = \text{Net income available to common}$$

Only a few of these subtotals appear on Nike's income statement. (Nike reported no extraordinary items.) If a firm has minority interests (or "noncontrolling interests") in its subsidiaries, net income attributable to the minority interests are subtracted to yield income for the common shareholders. You will see examples of this and other variations of the income statement on the Web page for this chapter. Names of line items can differ among companies. *Gross margin* is also referred to as gross profit. Operating income is sometimes referred to as *earnings before interest and taxes (ebit)* by analysts. Interest income is sometimes given as a separate line from interest expense, and sometimes the two are netted as net interest, as with Nike. Although necessary to calculate net income available to common shareholders, preferred dividends are in the statement of shareholders' equity.

Net income is given on a dollar basis and on a per-share basis. *Earnings per share (EPS)* is always earnings (after preferred dividends) for the common shareholder (called ordinary shareholders in the United Kingdom and other countries), so the numerator is net income available to common shareholders. *Basic earnings per share* ($3.93 for Nike in 2010) is net income available to common shareholders divided by the weighted-average of common shares outstanding during the year; a weighted average is used to accommodate changes in shares outstanding from share issues and repurchases. *Diluted earnings per share* ($3.86 for Nike) is based on total common shares that would be outstanding if holders of contingent claims on shares (like convertible bonds and stock options) were to exercise their options and hold common shares.

The Cash Flow Statement

The cash flow statement—Nike's Consolidated Statement of Cash Flows in the exhibit—describes how the firm generated and used cash during the period. Cash flows are divided into three types in the statement: *cash flows from operating activities, cash flows from investing activities,* and *cash flows from financing activities.* Thus the statement reports the cash generated from the three activities of the firm depicted in Figure 1.1 in Chapter 1. Cash from operations is cash generated from selling products, net of cash used up in doing so. Investing cash flows are cash spent on purchasing assets to be employed in the operating activities less cash received from selling assets. Financing cash flows are the cash transactions to raise cash from and disburse cash to the debt and equity claimants that are also depicted in Figure 1.1. The sum of the cash flows from the three activities explains the increase or decrease in the firm's cash (at the bottom of the statement):

$$\text{Cash from operations} + \text{Cash from investment} \qquad \text{(2.3)}$$
$$+ \text{Cash from financing} = \text{Change in cash}$$

Nike reported $3,164.2 million in cash from operations in fiscal 2010, spent a net $1,267.5 million on investments, and disbursed a net $1,061.2 million to claimants, leaving a net decrease in cash of $835.5 million. The line items in Nike's statement give the specific sources of cash in each category. Some, of course, involve cash outflows rather than cash inflows, and outflows are in parentheses. Nike trades around the world and so holds cash in different currencies. Thus the change in cash in U.S. dollar equivalents is also explained by a change in exchange rates over the year: The U.S. dollar equivalent of cash in other currencies decreased by $47.5 million over the year, so the overall increase in cash (in U.S. dollars) was $788 million.

The Statement of Shareholders' Equity

The statement of shareholders' equity—Nike's Consolidated Statement of Shareholders' Equity in the exhibit—starts with beginning-of-period equity in the balance sheet and ends with end-of-period equity, thus explaining how the equity changed over the period. For purposes of analysis, the change in equity is best explained as follows:

$$\text{Ending equity} = \text{Beginning equity} + \text{Comprehensive income} \qquad \text{(2.4)}$$
$$- \text{Net payout to shareholders}$$

This is referred to as the *stocks and flows equation* for equity because it explains how stocks of equity (at the beginning and end of the period) changed with flows of equity during the period. Owners' equity increases from earnings in business activities (comprehensive income) and decreases if there is a net payout to owners. Nike's reported comprehensive income for 2010 was $1,754 million. **Net payout** is amounts paid to shareholders less amounts received from share issues. As cash can be paid out in dividends or share repurchases, net payout is stock repurchases plus dividends minus proceeds from share issues. These items net to a net payout for Nike of $693.4 million, made up of a dividend of $514.8 million plus share repurchase of $754.3 million less share issues (net of forfeitures) of $575.7 million. Note that some shares were issued for the exercise of stock options by employees. With this number, you can see that ending equity of $9,753.7 million is explained by beginning equity of $8,693.1 million plus $1,754.0 million of comprehensive income less $693.4 in net payout. (Sometimes this reconciliation does not quite work due to other small items in the equity statement.)

You'll notice that comprehensive income includes net income of $1,906.7 million reported in the income statement plus some additional income reported in the equity statement. The practice of reporting income in the equity statement is known as **dirty surplus accounting,** for it does not give a clean income number in the income statement. The total of dirty surplus income items (a negative $152.7 million for Nike) is called *other comprehensive income* and the total of net income (in the income statement) and other comprehensive income (in the equity statement) is **comprehensive income:**

$$\text{Comprehensive income} = \text{Net income} + \text{Other comprehensive income} \qquad \textbf{(2.5)}$$

A few firms report other comprehensive income below net income in the income statement and some report it in a separate "Other Comprehensive Income Statement." See the Kimberly-Clark statement in Exhibit 2.2 for an example.[1]

The Footnotes and Supplementary Information to Financial Statements

Nike is a reasonably simple operation in one line of business and its financial statements are also quite simple. However, much more information embellishes these statements in the footnotes. The notes are an integral part of the statements, and the statements can be interpreted only with a thorough reading of the notes.

If you go to Nike's 10-K on the SEC's Web site, you will find the footnotes immediately following the financial statements. The footnotes explain the firm's accounting policies—the accounting methods it used to measure particular line items. The notes provide more information on property, plant and equipment, and intangible assets such as patents, trademarks, and goodwill, and more detail on line items such as accrued expenses in the balance sheet, and selling and administrative expense in the income statement. The income statement in the United States and under international accounting standards is rather a disgrace in the way it aggregates so much into a few line items, with the selling, general, and administrative expense line item in particular covering a multitude of sins. Marketing is so critical for Nike, as is research to give it a technological edge, so it is important to find the amounts spent on these activities in the footnotes. Some information in the footnotes looks a little like boilerplate, but most is important. Look at the debt footnote to understand the firm's borrowing. Look at the compensation footnote, particularly noting how the firm pays its employees with stock options. If a firm has a pension plan for its employees, press on the details, for obligations under these plans can be significant and a big

---

[1]At the date of writing, the FASB issued a new standard that requires the reporting of a separate comprehensive income statement (like that for Kimberly-Clark) or a combined income statement and comprehensive income statement. (Firms could choose between the two formats.) This new requirement converges with IFRS reporting.

concern if they are not fully funded. Watch for off-balance-sheet obligations and structured vehicles. Watch for derivative exposures. Understand the calculation of income taxes. Finally, if the firm has different operating segments, absorb the information on the profitability of these various operations and where risks might lie. We will come back to many of these issues as the book proceeds.

The Articulation of the Financial Statements: How the Statements Tell a Story

The balance sheet is sometimes referred to as a "stock" statement because the balances it reports are **stocks** of value at a point in time. (The word *stock* here should not be confused with stocks as in "stocks and shares" or "stocks" used in the United Kingdom and elsewhere to mean inventory.) The income statement and the cash flow statement are "flow" statements because they measure **flows**—or changes—in stocks between two points in time. The income statement reports part of the change in owners' equity and the cash flow statement reports the change in cash.

The so-called **articulation** of the income statement, cash flow statement, and balance sheet—or the articulation of stocks and flows—is depicted in Figure 2.1. Articulation is the way in which the statements fit together, their relationship to each other. The articulation of the income statement and balance sheet is through the statement of shareholders' equity and is described by the stocks and flows relation (equation 2.4). Balance sheets give the stock of owners' equity at a point in time. The statement of shareholders' equity explains the changes in owners' equity (the flows) between two balance sheet dates, and the income

FIGURE 2.1
The Articulation of the Financial Statements.
The stock of cash in the balance sheet increases from cash flows that are detailed in the cash flow statement. The stock of equity value in the balance sheet increases from net income that is detailed in the income statement and from other comprehensive income, and from net investments by owners that are detailed in the statement of shareholders' equity.

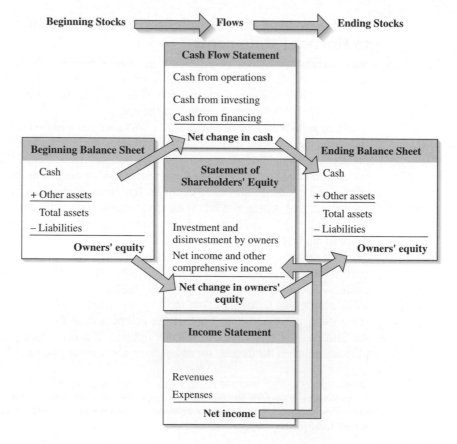

The Balance Sheet
  Assets
  – <u>Liabilities</u>
  = <u>Shareholders' equity</u>

The Income Statement
  Net revenue
  – <u>Cost of goods sold</u>
  = Gross margin
  – <u>Operating expenses</u>
  = Operating income before taxes (ebit)
  – <u>Interest expense</u>
  = Income before taxes
  – <u>Income taxes</u>
  = Income after tax and before extraordinary items
  + <u>Extraordinary items</u>
  = Net income
  – <u>Preferred dividends</u>
  = <u>Net income available to common</u>

Cash Flow Statement (and the Articulation of the Balance Sheet and Cash Flow Statement)
  Cash flow from operations
  + Cash flow from investing
  + <u>Cash flow from financing</u>
  = <u>Change in cash</u>

**Statement of Shareholders' Equity
(and the Articulation of the Balance Sheet and Income Statement)**

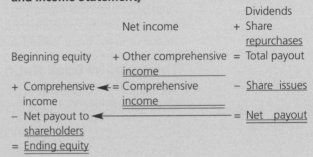

statement, corrected for other comprehensive income in the equity statement, explains the change in owners' equity that comes from adding value by running the business. The balance sheet also gives the stock of cash at a point in time, and the cash flow statement explains how that stock changed over a period.

Much detail buried in the financial statements will be revealed by the financial statement analysis later in the book. But by recognizing the articulation of the financial statements, the reader of the statements understands the overall story that they tell. That story is in terms of stocks and flows: The statements track changes in stocks of cash and owners' equity (net assets). Nike began its 2010 fiscal year with $2,291.1 million in cash on its balance sheet and ended the year with $3,079.1 million in cash. The cash flow statement reveals that the $788 million increase came from a cash inflow of $3,164.2 million in operations, less cash spent in investing of $1,267.5 million, net cash paid out to claimants of $1,061.2 million, and a decrease in the U.S. dollar equivalent of cash held abroad of $47.5 million. But the main focus of the statements is on the change in the owners' equity during the year. Nike's owners' equity decreased from $8,693.1 million to $9,753.7 million over the year by earning $1,754 million in its business activities and paying out a net $693.4 million to its owners. The income statement indicates that the net income portion of the increase in equity from business activities ($1,906.7 million) came from revenue from selling products of $19,014 million, less expenses incurred in generating the revenue of $16,540 million, plus other income of $49.2 million, less net interest of $6.3 million and taxes of $610.2 million.

And so Nike began its fiscal 2010 year with the stocks in place in the 2009 balance sheet to accumulate more cash and wealth for shareholders. Fundamental analysis involves forecasting that accumulation in the future. As we proceed with the analysis in subsequent chapters we will see how the accounting relations we have laid out are important in developing forecasting tools. See Box 2.2 for a summary. Be sure you have Figure 2.1 firmly in mind. Understand how the statements fit together. Understand how financial reporting tracks the evolution of shareholders' equity, updating stocks of equity value in the balance sheet with value added in earnings from business activities. And understand the accounting equations that govern each statement.

MEASUREMENT IN THE FINANCIAL STATEMENTS

To recap, the balance sheet reports the stock of shareholder value in the firm and the income statement reports the flow, or change, in shareholder value over a period. Using the language of valuation, the balance sheet gives the shareholders' net worth and the income statement gives the value added to their net worth from running the business. However, we must be careful with words, for, while financial reporting conveys these ideas conceptually, the reality can be quite different. Value and value added have to be measured, and measurement in the balance sheet and income statement is less than perfect.

The Price-to-Book Ratio

The balance sheet equation (2.1) corresponds to the value equation (1.1) that we introduced in the last chapter. The value equation can be written as

$$\text{Value of equity} = \text{Value of the firm} - \text{Value of debt} \qquad \textbf{(2.6)}$$

The value of the firm is the value of the firm's assets and its investments—sometimes called *enterprise value*—and the value of the debt is the value of the nonowners' claims. So you see that the value equation and the balance sheet equation are of the same form but differ in how the assets, liabilities, and equity are measured. The measure of stockholders' equity on the balance sheet, the *book value of equity,* typically does not tell us the *intrinsic value* of what the equity is really worth. Correspondingly, the net assets are not measured at their values. If they were, there would be no analysis to do! It is because the accountant does not, or cannot, calculate the intrinsic value that fundamental analysis is required.

The difference between the intrinsic value of equity and its book value is called the *intrinsic premium:*

$$\text{Intrinsic premium} = \text{Intrinsic value of equity} - \text{Book value of equity}$$

and the difference between the market price of equity and its book value is called the *market premium:*

$$\text{Market premium} = \text{Market price of equity} - \text{Book value of equity}$$

If these premiums are negative, they are called *discounts* (from book value). Premiums sometimes are referred to as *unrecorded goodwill* because someone purchasing the firm at a price greater than book value could record the premium paid as an asset, purchased goodwill, on the balance sheet; without a purchase of the firm, the premium is unrecorded.

Premiums are calculated for the total equity or on a per-share basis. When Nike published its fiscal 2010 report, the market value for its 484 million outstanding shares (sometimes referred to as market capitalization) was $35,816 million, or $74 per share. With a book value of $9,753.7 million, the market premium was $26,062.3 million: The market saw $26,062.3 million of shareholder value that was not on the balance sheet. With 484 million shares outstanding, the *book value per share (BPS)* was $20.15 and the market premium was $53.85 per share.

The ratio of market price to book value is the *price-to-book ratio* or the *market-to-book ratio,* and the ratio of intrinsic value to book value is the *intrinsic price-to-book ratio*. Nike's price-to-book ratio (P/B) in 2010 was 3.67. Investors talk of buying a firm for a number-of-times book

FIGURE 2.2
Percentiles of Price-to-Book Ratios for All U.S. Traded Firms with Market Capitalization Greater than $200 Million, 1963–2010.
P/B ratios were relatively low in the 1970s and high in the 1960s and 1990s. The median is typically above 1.0.

Source: Standard & Poor's Compustat® data.

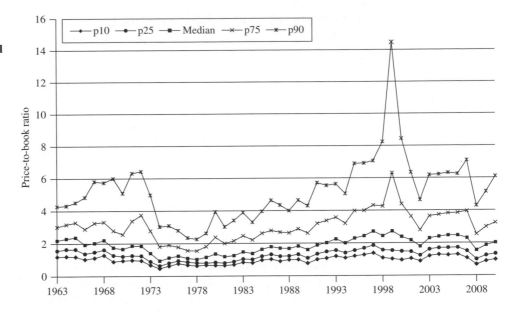

value, referring to the P/B ratio. We will spend considerable time estimating intrinsic price-to-book ratios in this book, and we will be asking if those intrinsic ratios indicate that the market P/B is mispriced.

In asking such questions, it is important to have a sense of history so that any calculation can be judged against what was normal in the past. The history provides a benchmark for our analysis. It was said, for example, that P/B ratios in the 1990s were high relative to historical averages, indicating that the stock market was overvalued. Figure 2.2 tracks selected percentiles of the price-to-book ratio for all U.S. listed firms from 1963 to 2010. Median P/B ratios (the 50th percentile) for these firms were indeed high in the 1990s—over 2.0—relative to the 1970s.[2] But they were around 2.0 in the 1960s. The 1970s experienced exceptionally low P/B ratios, with medians below 1.0 in some years.

What causes the variation in ratios? Is it due to mispricing in the stock market or is it due to the way accountants calculate book values? The low P/B ratios in the 1970s certainly preceded a long bull market. Could this bull market have been forecast in 1974 by fundamental analysis? Were market P/B ratios in 1974 too low? Would an analysis of intrinsic P/B ratios in the 1990s find that they were too high? Nike's P/B of 3.67 in 2010 looks high relative to historical averages. Was it too high? The fundamental analyst sees herself as providing answers to these questions. She estimates the value of equity that is not recorded on the balance sheet.

You can view P/B ratios for other firms through the links on the Web page. You also can find firms with particular levels of P/B ratios using a stock screener from links on the Web site.

---

[2] The median P/B for all firms during the 1990s was considerably lower than that for the Dow Jones Industrial Average stocks (consisting of 30 large firms) and the S&P 500 stocks. The P/B for the S&P 500 index increased from 1.8 in 1990 to over 5.0 by 2000, then decreased to 2.0 by 2010. The P/B ratio was under 1.0 in the 1970s. The average P/B ratio for the S&P 500 index over the 30 years to 2010 was 2.5. The stocks in these indexes tend to be larger than the median stocks but, because they contain a significant portion of the total value of the market, they are representative of the broad market. The Web page for this chapter has S&P 500 P/B ratios.

Measurement in the Balance Sheet

To evaluate the price-to-book ratio, the analyst must understand how book values are measured, for that measurement determines the price-to-book ratio.

The value of some assets and liabilities are easy to measure, and the accountant does so. He applies **mark-to-market accounting,** thus recording these items on the balance sheets, at **fair value** (in accounting terms). These items do not contribute to the premium over book value. But, for many items, the accountant does not, or cannot, mark to market price. He applies **historical cost accounting.** Box 2.3 gives the U.S. GAAP measurement rules for items commonly found on balance sheets, with those carried at fair value and historical cost indicated. International accounting standards broadly follow similar rules.

After reviewing Box 2.3, consider Nike's balance sheet. It lists investments of $3,079.1 million in cash and cash equivalents measured at their fair value. Nike's short-term investments ($2,066.8 million) are mainly in interest-bearing debt securities. These investments are *marked to market*. Nike's accounts payable ($1,254.5 million) is close to market value and, while the long-term debt ($445.8 million) is not marked to market, its book value approximates market value unless interest rates change significantly. So, these items do not contribute to the price premium over book value. Net accounts receivable ($2,649.8 million), accrued liabilities ($1,904.4 million), and taxes payable and "other liabilities" ($914.6 million) involve estimates, but if these are made in an unbiased way, these items, too, are at fair value.

Thus Nike's large market premium of $26,062 million over the book value of its equity arises largely from tangible assets, recorded at (depreciated) historical cost, and unrecorded assets. The latter are likely to be quite significant. Nike's value, it is claimed, comes not so much from tangible assets, but from its innovative design process, its supply chain, and foremost its brand name. None of these assets is on its balance sheet. Nor might we want them to be. Identifying them and measuring their value is a very difficult task, and we would probably end up with very doubtful, speculative numbers. Fundamental analysis deals with the problem of this missing value.

Measurement in the Income Statement

Shareholder value added is the change in shareholders' wealth during a period. This comes from two sources: (1) the increase in the value of their equity and (2) any dividends they receive:

$$\text{Value added} = \text{Ending value} - \text{Beginning value} + \text{Dividend} \qquad \textbf{(2.7)}$$

In terms of market prices,

$$\text{Market value added} = \text{Ending price} - \text{Beginning price} + \text{Dividend} \qquad \textbf{(2.8)}$$

If the market is pricing the intrinsic value correctly, **market value added** is, of course, (intrinsic) value added. The change in value in the market is the **stock return.** The stock return for a period, t, is

$$\text{Stock return}_t = P_t - P_{t-1} + d_t \qquad \textbf{(2.8a)}$$

where $P_t - P_{t-1}$ is the change in price (the **capital gain** portion of the return) and d_t is the dividend part of the return.

The accounting measure that adds to book value—earnings—does not usually equal value added in the stock market. The reason, again, involves the rules for recognizing earnings. Those rules are summarized in Box 2.4. The two driving principles are the **revenue recognition principle** and the **matching principle.** Accounting recognizes that firms add

Generally Accepted Accounting Principles (GAAP) in the United States prescribe the following rules for measuring assets and liabilities in the balance sheet. Items whose carrying values are typically close to fair value are indicated, but note any exceptions mentioned. Accounting Clinics, introduced later in this chapter, take you into the detail for some items.

ASSETS

Cash and Cash Equivalents (*Fair Value*)
Cash and cash equivalents (deposits of less than 90-day maturity) are recorded as the amount of cash held which equals their fair value.

Short-Term Investments and Marketable Securities (*Fair Value*)
Short-term investments—in interest-bearing deposits, short-term paper, and shares held for trading in the short-term—are carried at "fair" market value. An exception is a long-term security held to maturity that is reclassified to short-term because it is due to mature. See long-term securities below.

Also see Accounting Clinic III.

Receivables (*Quasi Fair Value*)
Receivables are recorded at the expected amount of cash to be collected (that is, the nominal claim less a discount for amounts not expected to be received because of bad debts or sales returns). If the estimate of this discount is unbiased, receivables are carried at their fair value. If biased, the carrying amount may not be fair value.

Inventories (*Lower of Cost or Market Value*)
Inventories are recorded at the historical cost of acquiring them. However, the carrying value of inventories is written down to market value if market value is less than historical cost, under the "lower of cost or market" rule. Historical cost is determined under an assumption about the flow of inventory. Under first-in-first-out (FIFO), the cost of more recent inventory goes to the inventory number in the balance sheet, and the cost of older inventory goes to cost of goods sold in the income statement. Under last-in-first-out (LIFO), the balance sheet includes the older costs and cost of goods sold includes the more recent costs. Accordingly, in times of rising inventory prices, the carrying value of inventory in the balance sheet is lower under LIFO than FIFO, but cost of goods sold is higher (and income lower). All else being equal, price-to-book ratios are thus higher for LIFO firms than for FIFO firms. Note that international accounting standards do not permit the use of LIFO.

Long-Term Tangible Assets (*Depreciated Historical Cost*)
Property and plant and equipment are recorded at historical cost (the amount that the firm paid for the assets), less accumulated depreciation. If fair market value is less than amortized historical cost, these assets are impaired (written down to fair value), with the impairment loss as a charge to earnings. In the U.S., assets are never revalued upward to market value.

Recorded Intangible Assets (*Amortized Historical Cost*)
Intangible assets that are recorded on the balance sheet—purchased copyrights, patents, and other legal rights—are recorded at historical cost and then either amortized over the life of the right or impaired if fair value falls below carrying value.

Goodwill (*Historical Cost*)
Goodwill is the difference between the purchase price of an acquired firm and the fair value of net assets acquired. Since FASB Statement No. 142 in 2001, goodwill is carried at cost and not amortized, but is impaired by a write-off if its fair value is deemed to have declined below cost.

Other Intangible Assets (*Not Recorded*)
Assets such as brand assets, knowledge assets developed from research and development, and assets arising from marketing and supplier relationships are not recorded at all, unless acquired in an acquisition as "identifiable intangible assets."

Long-Term Debt Securities (*Some at Fair Value*)
Some investments in bonds and other debt instruments are marked to market, as prescribed by FASB Statement No. 115. For marking to market, these investments are classified into three types:

1. *Investments held for active trading*. These investments are recorded at fair market value and the unrealized gains and losses from marking them to market are recorded in the income statement, along with interest.

2. *Investments available for sale* (investments not held for active trading but which may be sold before maturity). These investments are also recorded at fair market value, but the unrealized gains and losses are reported outside the income statement as part of other comprehensive income (usually in the equity statement), while interest is reported in the income statement.

3. *Investments held to maturity* (investments where the intent is to hold them until maturity). These investments are recorded at historical cost, with no unrealized gains or losses recognized, but with interest reported in the income statement. Fair market values for these investments are given in the footnotes.

Accounting Clinic III gives the details.

Equity Investments (*Some at Fair Value*)
Equity investments are classified into three types:

1. Investments involving less than 20 percent ownership of another corporation. These equity investments are classified as either "held for active trading," "available for

(continued)

sale," or "held to maturity," with the same accounting for debt investments in these categories.

2. Investments involving *20 percent to 50 percent ownership* of another corporation. The equities are recorded using the "equity method." Under the equity method, the investment is recorded at cost, but the balance sheet carrying value is subsequently increased by the share of earnings reported by the subsidiary corporation and reduced by dividends paid by the subsidiary and write-offs of goodwill acquired on purchase. The share of subsidiaries' earnings (less any write-off of goodwill) is reported in the income statement.

3. Investments involving *greater than 50 percent ownership* of another corporation. The financial statements of the parent and subsidiary corporation are consolidated, after elimination of intercompany transactions, with a deduction for noncontrolling (minority) interests in the net assets (in the balance sheet) and net income (in the income statement).

Accounting Clinics III and V give the details.

LIABILITIES

Short-Term Payables (*Fair Value*)
Payables—such as accounts payable, interest payable, and taxes payable—are measured at the contractual amount of cash to satisfy the obligations. Because these obligations are short-term, the contractual amount is close to its discounted present value, so the amount of these liabilities on the balance sheet approximates market value.

Borrowings (*Approximate Fair Value*)
Obligations arising from borrowing—short-term debt, long-term bonds, lease obligations, and bank loans—are recorded at the present value of the contractual amount, so they are at market value when initially recorded. The value of these liabilities changes as interest rates change, but the liabilities are typically not marked to market. However, in periods when interest rates or credit spreads change little, the carrying value of liabilities is typically close to market value. FASB Statement No. 107 requires that the fair market value of liabilities be reported in footnotes, and the debt footnote typically compares market values with carrying values. Some financial institutions mark their debt to fair value.

Accrued and Estimated Liabilities (*Quasi Fair Value*)
Some liabilities arising in operations—including pension liabilities, accrued liabilities, warranty liabilities, unearned (deferred) revenue, and estimated restructuring liabilities—have to be estimated. If the estimates are unbiased present values of expected cash to be paid out on the obligation, these liabilities reflect their value. If biased, these liabilities contribute to a premium over book value. They are sometimes called *quasi-marked-to-market* liabilities, emphasizing that estimation is involved (and can be suspect).

Commitments and Contingencies (*Many Not Recorded*)
If a liability is contingent upon some event, it is recorded on the balance sheet only if two criteria (from FASB Statement No. 5) are satisfied: (1) the contingent event is "probable," and (2) the amount of likely loss can be "reasonably" estimated. Examples include potential losses from lawsuits, product warranties, debt guarantees, and recourse on assignment of receivables or debt. When a liability does not satisfy the two criteria, it must be disclosed in footnotes if it is "reasonably possible." Firms (like Nike) often indicate such a possibility by an entry in the balance sheet with a zero amount and then cover the matter in the footnotes. Understatement of contingent liabilities in the balance sheet reduces the premium over book value.

value by selling products and services to customers. Unless a firm wins customers, it does not "make money." So accounting value is added only when a firm makes a sale to a customer: Revenue is booked. The accountant then turns to the task of calculating the net value added, matching the expenses incurred in gaining revenue against the revenue. Accordingly, the difference between revenue and matched expenses is the measure of value added from trading with customers.

The matching principle, however, is violated in practice, introducing accounting quality problems and, as we will see, difficulties for valuation. See Box 2.4.

Value added in the stock market is speculative value. The market not only prices the earnings from current operations, but it also anticipates sales and earnings to be made in future operations. A firm may announce a new product line. In response, investors revalue the firm in the market based on speculation about future sales and earnings from the product. A firm may announce new strategies, new investment plans, and management changes, and the market prices the anticipated profits from these changes. But none of them affects current earnings. The accountant says: Let's wait and see if these actions win customers;

The accounting measure of value added, earnings, is determined by rules for measuring revenues and expenses.

REVENUES: THE REVENUE RECOGNITION PRINCIPLE

Value is added by businesses from a process—a value creation chain—that begins with strategy and product ideas, and then continues with the research and development of those ideas, the building of factories and distribution channels to deliver the product, the persuading of customers to buy the finished product, and finally the collection of cash from customers. Potentially, value could be recognized gradually, as the process proceeds. However, accounting typically recognizes value added at one point in the process. The two broad principles for *revenue recognition* are:

1. The earnings process is substantially accomplished.
2. Receipt of cash is reasonably certain.

In most cases, these two criteria are deemed to be satisfied when the product or service has been delivered to the customer and a receivable has been established as a legal claim against the customer. The revenue recognized at that point is the amount of the sale.

In a few cases, revenue is recognized during production, but before final sale—in long-term construction projects, for example—and sometimes revenue is not recognized until cash is collected—as in some retail installment sales where there is considerable doubt that the customer will pay. Gains from securities are sometimes recognized prior to sale—in the form of "unrealized" gains and losses—if the securities are trading securities or are available for sale. (See Box 2.3.)

Issues arise when a contract has multiple elements, for example, when a sale of hardware is combined with an agreement to service the hardware and update software. How much of the total revenue should be allocated to the hardware sale and how much to the subsequent services and software updates? At the time of writing, the FASB and IASB were proposing to allocate according to two new criteria for revenue recognition: a "performance obligation" has to be recognized for each component and then that performance obligation has to be "satisfied." These are rather vague criteria, so there is an open question about how they will work in practice.

EXPENSES: THE MATCHING PRINCIPLE

Expenses are recognized in the income statement by their association with the revenues for which they have been incurred. This matching of revenues and expenses yields an earnings number that is net value added from revenues.

Matching is done by direct association of expenses with revenues or by association with periods in which revenue is recognized. Cost of goods sold, for example, is recognized by directly matching the cost of items sold with the revenue from the sale of those items, to yield gross margin. Interest expenses, in contrast, are matched to the period in which the debt provides the financing of the operations that produce revenue.

Revenue recognition and expense matching are violated in practice, reducing the quality of earnings as a measure of value added from customers. Firms themselves may violate the revenue recognition and matching principles, but violations also are admitted (indeed, required) under GAAP. In these cases, there is a difference between value added and accounting value added. Here are some examples of good and poor matching.

Examples of Sound Matching Prescribed by GAAP

- Recording cost of goods sold as the cost of producing goods for which sales have been made and, correspondingly, placing the cost of goods produced, but not sold, in inventory on the balance sheet, to be matched against future revenues when they are sold.

- Recording expenditure on plant as an asset and then allocating the cost of the asset to the income statement (as depreciation expense) over the life of the asset. In this way, income is not affected when the investment is made, but only as revenues from the plant are recognized. Accordingly, income is revenue matched with the plant costs incurred to earn the revenue.

- Recording the cost of employee pensions as expenses in the period in which the employees provide service to produce revenues, rather than in the future when pensions are paid (and employees are not producing, but retired).

Examples of Poor Matching Prescribed by GAAP

- Expensing research and development (R&D) expenditures in the income statement when incurred, rather than recording them as an asset (an investment) in the balance sheet. If the expenditures were recorded as an asset, their cost would be matched (through amortization) against the future revenues that the R&D generates.

- Expensing film production costs as incurred, rather than matching them against revenues earned after the film is released.

Examples of Poor Matching by Firms

- Underestimating bad debts from sales so that income from sales is overstated.

- Estimating long useful lives for plant so that depreciation is understated.

- Overestimating a restructuring charge. The overestimate has the consequence of recording current period's income as

(*continued*)

less than it would be with an unbiased estimate. Further, future income is higher than it would otherwise be because expenses (like depreciation) have already been written off.

THE WORLDCOM CON

In June 2002, WorldCom, the second largest U.S. long-distance telephone carrier through its MCI unit, confessed to overstating income by $3.8 billion over 2001–2002, one of the largest accounting frauds ever. The overstatement was due to a mismatch of revenues with access fees paid to local telephone companies. These fees are necessary to connect long-distance calls through local networks to customers; thus they are a cost of earning current revenue. The WorldCom CFO, however, capitalized these costs as assets in the balance sheet, with the idea of amortizing them against future revenue. This treatment served to inflate income by $3.8 billion and allowed WorldCom to avoid reporting losses. WorldCom shares had traded at a high of $64 per share during the telecom bubble, but they fell below $1 in June 2002, and the firm subsequently filed for bankruptcy with the culprits in jail.

PRO FORMA EARNINGS OFTEN INVOLVE MISMATCHING

During the stock market bubble, corporations often encouraged investors to evaluate them on "pro forma" earnings numbers that differed from GAAP earnings (they still do). Analysts and investment bankers also promoted these numbers. Most pro forma numbers involve mismatching, usually omitting expenses. Indeed they are sometimes referred to as "ebs" (in contrast to eps): Everything but the Bad Stuff. Amazon.com, Inc. for example, referred to earnings before amortization and interest (yes, interest!) in press releases; its GAAP numbers (after amortization and interest) were actually losses.

The most prevalent pro forma number is ebitda, *earnings before interest, taxes, depreciation, and amortization*. This number omits taxes and interest and also depreciation and amortization. Analysts argue that it is a better number because depreciation and amortization are not cash costs, so ebitda is emphasized in telecom and media companies whose large capital investments result in large depreciation charges. However, while the analyst might be wary of mismeasurement of depreciation, depreciation is a real cost, just like wages expense. Plants rust. Telecom networks become obsolescent. Telecoms can overinvest in networks, producing overcapacity. Depreciation expense recognizes these costs.

Reliance on ebitda encourages firms to substitute capital for labor and, indeed, to invest in overcapacity because the cost of overcapacity does not affect ebitda. Ebitda can be used to deceive. The WorldCom con was a scam to inflate ebitda. Expensing access charges as operating costs reduces ebitda. However, by capitalizing the charges, WorldCom not only increased current ebitda, but also increased future ebitda as the amortization of capitalized operating costs is classified as depreciation or amortization; thus the charges are not reflected in ebitda in any period. Growing ebitda would impress the unwary investor and perpetuate the telecom bubble.

let's not book revenues until we have a sale. Investors say: Let's price the anticipated value that will be booked in future revenues.

Thus accounting recognition of value typically lags intrinsic value. Accordingly, fundamental analysis involves anticipation, that is, forecasting value added that has not been recognized in the financial statements but will be recognized in future financial statements as sales are made. In so doing, fundamental analysis estimates value added that is missing from the financial statements. This leads us to the price-earnings ratio.

The Price-Earnings Ratio

The *price-earnings ratio* (P/E) compares current price with earnings. Interpret the P/E ratio as follows. Price, the numerator, is the market's anticipation of value to be added from sales in the future, that is, future earnings. The denominator is current earnings, value added from current sales. So the P/E ratio compares forecasted future earnings to current earnings. If one expects considerably more future earnings than current earnings, the P/E ratio should be high, and if one expects lower future earnings than current earnings, the P/E ratio should be low. To be more concise, the P/E ratio reflects anticipated earnings growth. Accordingly, fundamental analysis evaluates expected earnings growth to estimate *intrinsic P/E ratios*. Intrinsic P/E ratios are then compared to *market P/E ratios* to challenge the market's anticipations.

FIGURE 2.3
Percentiles of Price-Earnings Ratios for All U.S. Traded Firms with Market Capitalization over $200 Million, 1963–2010.
P/E ratios were relatively low in the 1970s and high in the 1960s and 1990s. The median is typically above 10.0. (The figure covers firms with positive earnings only.)

Source: Standard & Poor's Compustat® data.

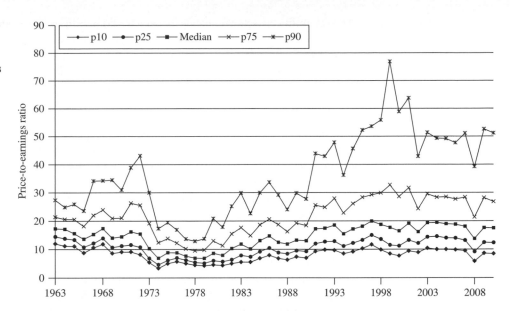

With Nike trading at $74 per share in 2010, its P/E ratio on 2010 earnings per share of $3.93 was 18.8. The analyst's task is to assess whether forecasts of future earnings justify this multiple. Is the P/E ratio now too high? Too Low? As with the P/B ratio, she has the history of P/E ratios in mind and uses these as benchmarks. Figure 2.3 tracks selected percentiles of P/E ratios for U.S. firms. Like P/B ratios, P/E ratios were low in the 1970s, with medians less than 10. But the 1990s saw considerably higher P/E ratios, with medians reaching 20.[3]

Accounting as an Anchor: Don't Mix What You Know with Speculation

As discussed in Chapter 1, Benjamin Graham viewed the value of an investment as "minimum true value" plus "speculative value":

$$\text{Value} = \text{Minimum true value} + \text{Speculative value}$$

Minimum true value is "value justified by the facts" in contrast to value that comes from speculating about future unknowns. The division of course is driven by the fundamental tenets of Chapter 1: *Separate what you know from speculation* and *anchor a valuation on what you know rather than speculation*. Accounting is the primary source of what we know today (or should be), so the fundamental investor looks to accounting reports to supply the first component. It is that component he or she anchors on to assess value:

$$\text{Value} = \text{Anchoring accounting value} + \text{Speculative value}$$

Much of this book is involved in establishing the accounting value on which to anchor, and then using this anchor to challenge the speculation in the market price. But, for the anchor to hold, accounting must be nonspeculative. The fundamental investor says to the accountant: Tell me what you know and leave the speculation to me. Accountants have largely followed this dictum by applying their own dictum, the **reliability criterion.**

---

[3] P/E ratios for the S&P 500 and the Dow index were on the order of 7 to 10 in the mid-1970s and well over 20 in the 1990s. By 2000, the P/E for the S&P 500 reached 33. It stood at 16.3 in 2010. The average P/E ratio for the S&P 500 over the last 50 years has been 16.2. The Web page for the chapter gives P/E ratios for the S&P 500 over the years.

The reliability criterion demands that assets and liabilities be recognized only if they can be measured with reasonable precision and supported by objective evidence, free of opinion and bias. So the reliability criterion rules out recognizing the value of Nike's innovative design, its brand name, or its supply chain on its balance sheet. Estimates of these assets are deemed too subjective, too open to fantasy, even manipulation. Indeed, most intangible assets are omitted from the balance sheet. Knowledge assets developed from research and development (R&D) are usually omitted. Only assets that the firm has purchased—such as inventories, plant, R&D acquired by purchasing a patent, and acquired goodwill—are recorded, for then there is an objective market transaction to justify the measurement. Contingent liabilities, for which the outcome is not probable or which cannot be reasonably estimated, also are not recorded.

The reliability criterion also governs the income statement. Indeed, the revenue recognition principle (see Box 2.4) invokes the reliability criterion: Revenues are recorded only when there is reliable evidence of a customer buying the product. So accountants do not book revenue based on speculation that the firm may get customers in the future—only when they actually do.

The reliability criterion suits the fundamental analyst well. Stock prices are based on speculation about firms' ability to make sales in the future and to generate earnings from those sales. The role of fundamental analysis is to challenge that speculation in order to test whether stocks are appropriately priced. Sales in the current period, and the earnings derived from them after matching expenses, are something that we know with some reliability (unless the accounting is suspect). Don't contaminate that knowledge by mixing it with speculation in the income statement, for the analyst wants to use that knowledge to test speculation. Further, don't mix hard assets in the balance sheet with speculative estimates about the value of unobserved intangible assets. Leave speculation to the analyst. See Box 2.5.

The practice of omitting or understating assets on the balance sheet is called **conservative accounting.** Conservative accounting says: Let's be conservative in valuing assets; let's not speculate about the value of assets. So, if there is uncertainty about the value of an asset, don't book the asset at all. In practicing conservative accounting, accountants write down assets, but they will not write up assets. You understand, then, why price-to-book ratios are typically greater than 1.

Accounting Clinic   I

BASIC ACCOUNTING PRINCIPLES
This chapter has provided an overview of the principles of accounting. Much detail lurks behind the broad principles. Not all will be required of a competent analyst but, as we proceed with the fundamental analysis that is anchored in the financial statements, accounting issues will arise. Those issues will be addressed in the text but, in many cases, the detail is too much to cover. So, on issues important to the equity analyst, you will be introduced to an **Accounting Clinic** on the book's Web site. The purpose of these clinics is to help remedy your scant knowledge of accounting, or to provide a review of material you have covered in accounting courses. You might also want to refer to the texts you have used in previous accounting courses, to refresh your memory.

Accounting Clinic I expands on the basic principles of accounting measurement that are laid out in this chapter.

The book's Web site can be found at **www.mhhe.com/penman5e.**

THE TECHNOLOGY BUBBLE OF 1997–2000

During the stock market bubble of 1997–2000, financial reporting came into question. Commentators claimed that the traditional financial reporting model, developed during the Industrial Age, was no longer relevant for the Information Age. Claims were made that "earnings no longer matter." Balance sheets were said to be useless because, in the "new economy," value comes from knowledge assets and other intangibles that are omitted from balance sheets. To justify lofty price-earnings ratios, technology analysts referred to metrics such as clicks and page views rather than earnings. "Value reporting" that relies on soft information outside the financial statements became the vogue. Was this bubble froth or are these claims justified?

Speculative beliefs feed price bubbles. Speculation overlooks hard information and overemphasizes soft information. The role of financial statements is to anchor the investor on the rising tide of speculation with hard information. As we proceed through the book, we will learn how to anchor analysis in the financial statements. Consider the following:

- Losses reported by new economy firms during the bubble turned out to be a good predictor: Most of these firms failed. Earnings did matter.
- For firms that did survive, the earnings they reported during the bubble were a much better predictor of subsequent earnings than the speculative forecasts of analysts pushing the stocks.
- Most of the intangible assets imagined by speculative analysts vaporized.
- The much-criticized balance sheets also provided good forecasts. The ratio of debt assumed in pursuit of intangible assets (by telecoms, for example) was large relative to tangible assets on the balance sheet, and that ratio predicted demise.

For the main part, accounting authorities resisted the pressure to book intangible assets to the balance sheet. However, financial reporting was rightly criticized after the bubble burst, exposing the poor financial reporting practices of Enron and Arthur Andersen, Xerox, Qwest, and WorldCom,

to mention a few. The problem was largely one of compromised management, directors, and auditors failing to apply accounting principles faithfully rather than an issue with the principles themselves.

THE FINANCING BUBBLE OF 2006–2007

The mention of Enron reminds us of one big accounting failure. If you saw the movie *Enron: The Smartest Guys in the Room*, read the book of the same title by Bethany McLean and Peter Elkind, or saw the musical *ENRON*, you would have observed the celebration at Enron after receiving the news that the SEC had permitted them to use fair-value accounting for the business. They proceeded to build a fair-value-accounting house of cards. In the "mark-to-market" version of fair-value accounting, the firm writes its assets up or down to their market price. That violates the fundamentalist tenet: *When calculating price to challenge price, beware of using price in the calculation* (you are being circular). In another version, the firm "fair-values" assets use managements' expectations (or guesses). In both versions, fair-value accounting allows firms to estimate the present value of future profits, thus bringing speculation into the financial statements. This is not something on which to anchor. For Enron, those expectations were not realized, and the house of cards collapsed.

Despite this experience, the accounting authorities have persisted in promoting fair-value accounting, and the issue again came to a head in the financial crisis. Prior to the global financial crisis of 2008, low interest rates set by the U.S. Federal Reserve Bank fed a financing boom, which, in turn, fed rising real estate prices. Banks originating mortgage loans were able to place them in "available for sale" portfolios and fair value them. As real estate prices rose, so did the prices of mortgages and the securitized mortgage packages traded on Wall Street. Under mark-to-market accounting, banks wrote up their mortgage assets, increasing their capital, enabling them to lend more against bubble real estate prices. Again, prices came into the financial statements until the fictitious values vaporized. We know the sorry aftermath. The fundamental analyst is wary of fair-value accounting. It is not something on which to anchor. It can come back and hit you.

Tension in Accounting

To measure value added from sales to customers, accountants match expenses with revenues. The reliability criterion demands that revenues not be recognized until a customer is won. But the reliability criterion also comes into play in matching expenses, and this creates tension.

In August 2008, the SEC proposed that the United States move to international accounting standards and invited public comment on the proposal. The SEC also outlined a road map for doing so. The road map targets mandatory adopting of IFRS by 2014 but allows certain qualifying U.S. firms (up to 110 of the larger firms) to use IFRS as early as 2009. The SEC laid down certain milestones that would have to be reached for the 2014 objective to be met: (1) continued improvements in IFRS accounting standards, (2) independent funding set up for the IASB, (3) the ability for XBRL (Extensible Business Reporting Language) to accept IFRS data, and (4) sufficient progress in IFRS education and training in the United States. The adoption of IFRS in the United States is taking longer than this road map envisioned. Stay tuned.

The desire for uniform standards across the world is understandable. Some, however, fear that giving a monopoly to one standard setting agency is dangerous. Better, they say, to have competing standards that the market can select from, so that better standards rise to the top. Those advocating convergence say that might lead to a race to the bottom.

As said, IFRS and U.S. GAAP are quite similar. Throughout this book, we will highlight differences between the two when they are important for the analysis at hand. Note the following:

- IFRS requires only two years of comparative income statements while U.S. GAAP requires three.
- IFRS permits expenses in the income statement to be shown by nature (for example, raw material costs, personnel costs) or by function (selling costs, R&D costs) while GAAP requires display by function.
- IFRS requires all deferred tax assets and liabilities to be classified as noncurrent (long term) whereas GAAP requires their classification into current and noncurrent.
- IFRS allows some revaluation of assets in certain circumstances.

According to the reliability criterion, investment in assets with uncertain value cannot be booked on the balance sheet. So GAAP requires that investments in R&D assets and brand assets (developed through advertising) be expensed immediately in the income statement rather then booked to the balance sheet. The result is a mismatch: Current revenues are charged with the investments to produce future revenues, and future revenues are not charged with the (amortized) cost of earning those revenues. There is a tension between the matching principle and the reliability criterion.

The accountant wants to match revenues to expenses but also recognizes that assets of doubtful value should not be placed on the balance sheet. In the case of R&D and advertising, GAAP and IFRS come down on the side of mismatching.

This state of affairs is acceptable to the fundamental investor, for she wants a balance sheet on which to anchor: *Tell me what you know, and leave the speculation to me.* Knowing that there is no "water in the balance sheet," the investor can then go ahead and speculate about the value to be added to the balance sheet, the omitted value from R&D and the brands built by advertising. The valuation procedures in this text supply the tools.

Accounting Quality

Good accounting serves as a check on speculation. Good accounting challenges stock price bubbles. Bad accounting perpetuates bubbles. Bad accounting creates false earnings momentum that feeds price momentum. Look again at Box 2.5. GAAP and IFRS unfortunately do have some undesirable features. Clearly, one cannot anchor on financial statements of doubtful quality. So, as this text proceeds, we will highlight the main accounting quality problems of which you should be aware and show how to handle them. Each chapter in Part Two of the book—dealing with financial statement analysis—ends with an Accounting

Quality Watch covering the main accounting issues in that chapter. Chapter 18 brings this material together for a comprehensive analysis of accounting quality.

Financial statements in the United States are currently prepared according to U.S. Generally Accepted Accounting Principles. But changes are in the wind. Go to Box 2.6 before closing this chapter.

Summary

Financial statements articulate in a way that tells a story. From the shareholder's point of view, the book value of equity in the balance sheet is the "bottom line" to the financial statements. The accounting system tracks shareholders' equity over time. Each period, equity is updated by measuring (accounting) value added from business activities—comprehensive income—and value paid out in net dividends. The statement of shareholders' equity summarizes the tracking. The income statement (along with "other comprehensive income" in the equity statement) gives the details of value added to the business by matching revenues (value received from customers) with expenses (value given up in servicing customers). As well as tracking owners' equity, the financial statements also track changes in a firm's cash position through the cash flow statement, where the change in cash is explained by cash generated in operations, cash spent on investments, and cash paid out in financing activities.

The Web Connection

Find the following on the Web page supplement for this chapter:

- Directions on how to find your way around the SEC's EDGAR database.
- Summary of the filings that firms must make with the SEC.
- Directions to online services for recovering financial statement information.
- XBRL (e**X**tensible **B**usiness **R**eporting **L**anguage) is coming to SEC filings. The Web page takes a look.

- An introduction to IFRS.
- Links to FASB and IASB documents.
- Elaboration on how accounting relations help in building analysis tools.
- More on historical P/B and P/E ratios.
- The Readers' Corner provides a guide to further reading.
- Web Exercises have additional exercises, along with solutions, for you to work.

These features of the financial statements are expressed in a set of accounting relations that define the structure of the statements. Commit these to memory, for they will come into play as we organize the financial statements into spreadsheets for analysis. Indeed, they will become rules that have to be obeyed as we develop forecasted financial statements for valuation.

Accountants calculate the (book) value of equity, but the analyst is interested in the (intrinsic) value of the equity. This chapter outlined the rules that determine the book value of equity in the balance sheet. The chapter also outlined the rules that determine value added—earnings—in the income statement. These rules lead to differences in prices and book values, so understanding them gives you an understanding of price-to-book ratios. The rules also explain why value added in the stock price is not recognized immediately in earnings, so you also have an understanding of the P/E ratio. That understanding will be enhanced as we establish the technology for determining intrinsic P/B and P/E ratios.

Key Concepts

accounting relation is an equation that expresses components of financial statements in terms of other components. *34*

articulation of the financial statements is the way they relate to each other. *42*

asset is an investment that is expected to produce future payoffs. *34*

capital gain is the amount by which the price of an investment changes. *46*

common stock outstanding is the stock (shares) held by common shareholders and is equal to common shares issued less shares in treasury stock. *36*

comprehensive income is total income reported (in the income statement and elsewhere in the financial statements). *41*

conservative accounting is the practice of recording relatively low values for net assets on the balance sheets, or omitting assets altogether. *52*

dirty surplus accounting books income in the equity statement rather than the income statement. *41*

expense is value given up in earning revenue that is recognized in the financial statements. *38*

fair value is the term that accountants use for the value of an asset or liability. Fair value is market value, or an estimate of market value when a liquid market does not exist. *46*

flows in financial statements are changes in stocks between two points in time. Compare with **stocks.** *42*

historical cost accounting records assets and liabilities at their historical cost, then (in most cases) amortizes the cost over periods to the income statement. *46*

intangible asset is an asset without physical form. *47*

liability is a claim on payoffs from the firm other than by the owners. *34*

mark-to-market accounting records assets and liabilities at their market value. *46*

market value added is the amount by which shareholder wealth increases in the market, plus any dividend received. It is equal to the **stock return.** *46*

matching principle is the accounting principle by which **expenses** are matched with the **revenues** for which they are incurred. *46*

net payout is cash distributed to shareholders. *41*

reliability criterion is the accounting principle that requires assets, liabilities, revenues, and expenses to be booked only if they can be measured with reasonable precision based on objective evidence. *51*

revenue is value received from customers that is recognized in the financial statements. *38*

revenue recognition principle is the accounting principle by which revenues are recognized in the income statement. *46*

shareholder value added is the (intrinsic) value added to shareholders' wealth during a period. *46*

stock return is the return to holding a share, and it is equal to the **capital gain** plus dividend. *46*

stockholders' equity is the claim on payoffs by the owners (the stockholders) of the firm. *34*

stocks in the financial statements are balances at a point in time. Compare with **flows.** *42*

treasury stock is stock (shares) that has been repurchased but not retired. *36*

The Analyst's Toolkit

Analysis Tools	Page	Key Measures	Page	Acronyms to Remember	
Financial statements		Assets	34	BPS	book value per share
Balance sheet	34	Basic earnings per share (eps)	40	ebit	earnings before interest
Income statement	36	Book value of equity	44		and taxes
Cash flow statement	40	Book value per share (bps)	44	ebitda	earnings before interest,
Statement of shareholders'		Capital gain	46		taxes, depreciation, and
equity	40	Cash flow			amortization
Financial statement		From operations	40	EPS	earnings per share
footnotes	41	From investing activities	40	FASB	Financial Accounting
Management's discussion		From financing activities	40		Standards Board
and analysis	41	Comprehensive income	41	GAAP	Generally Accepted
Accounting relations		Diluted earnings per share	40		Accounting Principles
Balance sheet equation (2.1)	34	Earnings	38	IASB	International Accounting
Income statement		Earnings before interest and			Standards Board
equation (2.2)	38	taxes (ebit)	39	IFRS	International Reporting
Income statement component		Earnings before interest, taxes,			Standards
equations (2.2a)	39	depreciation, and		P/B	price-to-book ratio
Cash flow statement		amortization (ebitda)	50	P/E	price-earnings ratio
equation (2.3)	40	Expense	38	R&D	research and development
Stocks and flows		Fair value	46	SEC	Securities and Exchange
equation (2.4)	40	Gross margin	39		Commission
Comprehensive income		Liabilities	34		
calculation (2.5)	41	Market value added	46		
Value equation (2.6)	44	Net assets	36		
Value added equation (2.7)	46	Net income (or net profit)	38		
Market value added equation		Net payout	41		
(2.8)	46	Operating income	39		
Stock return equation (2.8a)	46	Premium (or discount) over			
		book value	44		
		Price/earnings ratio (P/E)	50		
		Price-to-book ratio (P/B)	44		
		Revenue	38		
		Shareholder value added	46		
		Stock return	46		

A Continuing Case: *Kimberly-Clark Corporation*

A Self-Study Exercise

In the Continuing Case for Chapter 1, you gained some appreciation of Kimberly-Clark's business, examined its recent stock price history, and discovered what analysts were saying about the stock. It's now time to turn to the financial statements, for it is on those statements that a valuation is anchored. We will go into KMB's financial statements in considerable depth as the book proceeds. For now you need to familiarize yourself with the layout of the statements and appreciate their main features. Exhibit 2.2 presents the firm's 2010 annual financial statements, along with comparative numbers from prior years. Note that Kimberly-Clark has a statement of comprehensive income separate from its statement of stockholders' equity. As we proceed with the firm through the book, we will be referring to

EXHIBIT 2.2
Financial Statements
for Kimberly-Clark
Corporation for Year
Ending December 31,
2010.

KIMBERLY-CLARK CORPORATION AND SUBSIDIARIES
Consolidated Balance Sheet

	December 31	
	2010	**2009**
	(Millions of dollars)	
Assets		
Current assets		
Cash and cash equivalents	$ 876	$ 798
Accounts receivable, net	2,472	2,566
Note receivable	218	—
Inventories	2,373	2,033
Deferred income taxes	187	136
Other current assets	202	331
Total current assets	6,328	5,864
Property, plant and equipment, net	8,356	8,033
Investments in equity companies	374	355
Goodwill	3,403	3,275
Other intangible assets	287	310
Long-term note receivable	393	607
Other assets	723	765
	$19,864	$19,209
Liabilities and Stockholders' Equity		
Current liabilities		
Debt payable within one year	$ 344	$ 610
Redeemable preferred securities of subsidiary	506	—
Trade accounts payable	2,206	1,920
Accrued expenses	1,909	2,064
Accrued income taxes	104	79
Dividends payable	269	250
Total current liabilities	5,338	4,923
Long-term debt	5,120	4,792
Noncurrent employee benefits	1,810	1,989
Long-term income taxes payable	260	168
Deferred income taxes	369	377
Other Liabilities	224	218
Redeemable preferred and common securities of subsidiaries	541	1,052
Stockholders' equity		
Kimberly-Clark Corporation Stockholders' Equity:		
Preferred stock—no par value—authorized 20.0 million shares, none issued	—	—
Common stock—$1.25 par value—authorized 1.2 billion shares; issued 478.6 million shares at December 31, 2010 and 2009	598	598
Additional paid-in capital	425	399
Common stock held in treasury, at cost—71.7 million and 61.6 million shares at December 31, 2010 and 2009	(4,726)	(4,087)
Accumulated other comprehensive income (loss)	(1,466)	(1,833)
Retained earnings	11,086	10,329
Total Kimberly-Clark Corporation Stockholders' Equity	5,917	5,406
Noncontrolling interests	285	284
Total stockholders' equity	6,202	5,690
	$19,864	$19,209

(*continued*)

EXHIBIT 2.2
(*continued*)

Consolidated Income Statement

	Year Ended December 31		
	2010	**2009**	**2008**
	(Millions of dollars, except per share amounts)		
Net sales	$19,746	$19,115	$19,415
Cost of products sold	13,196	12,695	13,557
Gross profit	6,550	6,420	5,858
Marketing, research and general expenses	3,673	3,498	3,291
Other (income) and expense, net	104	97	20
Operating profit	2,773	2,825	2,547
Interest income	20	26	46
Interest expense	(243)	(275)	(304)
Income before income taxes, equity interests and extraordinary loss	2,550	2,576	2,289
Provision for income taxes	(788)	(746)	(618)
Income before equity interests and extraordinary loss	1,762	1,830	1,671
Share of net income of equity companies	181	164	166
Income before extraordinary loss	1,943	1,994	1,837
Extraordinary loss, net of income taxes, attributable to Kimberly-Clark Corporation	—	—	(8)
Net income	1,943	1,994	1,829
Net income attributable to noncontrolling interests	(100)	(110)	(139)
Net income attributable to Kimberly-Clark Corporation	$ 1,843	$ 1,884	$ 1,690
Per share basis			
Basic			
Before extraordinary loss	$ 4.47	$ 4.53	$ 4.06
Extraordinary loss	—	—	(0.2)
Net income attributable to Kimberly-Clark Corporation	$ 4.47	$ 4.53	$ 4.04
Diluted			
Before extraordinary loss	$ 4.45	$ 4.52	$ 4.05
Extraordinary loss	—	—	(.02)
Net income attributable to Kimberly-Clark Corporation	$ 4.45	$ 4.52	$ 4.03

(*continued*)

EXHIBIT 2.2
(*continued*)

Consolidated Cash Flow Statement

| | Year Ended December 31 | | |
	2010	2009	2008
	(Millions of dollars)		
Operating activities			
Net income	$1,943	$1,994	$1,829
Extraordinary loss, net of income taxes, attributable to Kimberly-Clark Corporation	—	—	8
Depreciation and amortization	813	783	775
Stock-based compensation	52	86	47
Deferred income taxes	(12)	141	151
Net losses on asset dispositions	26	36	51
Equity companies' earnings in excess of dividends paid	(48)	(53)	(34)
Decrease (increase) in operating working capital	24	1,105	(335)
Postretirement benefits	(125)	(609)	(38)
Other	71	(2)	(62)
Cash provided by operations	2,744	3,481	2,516
Investing activities			
Capital spending	(964)	(848)	(906)
Acquisitions of businesses, net of cash acquired	—	(458)	(98)
Investments in marketable securities	1	—	(9)
Proceeds from sales of investments	47	40	48
Investments in time deposits	(131)	(270)	(238)
Maturities of time deposits	248	223	314
Proceeds from dispositions of property	9	25	28
Other	9	—	14
Cash used for investing	(781)	(1,288)	(847)
Financing activities			
Cash dividends paid	(1,066)	(986)	(950)
Net decrease in short-term debt	(28)	(312)	(436)
Proceeds from issuance of long-term debt	515	2	551
Repayments of long-term debt	(506)	(278)	(274)
Cash paid on redeemable preferred securities of subsidiary	(54)	(53)	(47)
Proceeds from exercise of stock options	131	165	113
Acquisitions of common stock for the treasury	(803)	(7)	(653)
Shares purchased from noncontrolling interests	—	(293)	—
Other	(48)	(26)	(51)
Cash used for financing	(1,859)	(1,788)	(1,747)
Effect of exchange rate changes on cash and cash equivalents	(26)	29	(31)
Increase (decrease) in cash and cash equivalents	78	434	(109)
Cash and cash equivalents, beginning of year	798	364	473
Cash and cash equivalents, end of year	$ 876	$ 798	$ 364

(*continued*)

EXHIBIT 2.2
(continued)

Consolidated Statement of Stockholders' Equity

(Dollars in millions, shares in thousands)

	Common Stock Issued		Additional Paid-in Capital	Treasury Stock		Retained Earnings	Accumulated Other Comprehensive Income (Loss)	Noncontrolling Interests
	Shares	Amount		Shares	Amount			
Balance at December 31, 2007	478,597	$598	$483	57,676	$(3,814)	$8,748	$(791)	$463
Net income in stockholders' equity	—	—	—	—	—	1,690	—	82
Other comprehensive income:								
Unrealized translation	—	—	—	—	—	—	(900)	(81)
Employee postretirement benefits, net of tax	—	—	—	—	—	—	(687)	(2)
Other	—	—	—	—	—	—	(8)	—
Stock-based awards exercised or vested	—	—	(59)	(2,870)	170	(7)	—	—
Income tax benefits on stock-based compensation	—	—	10	—	—	—	—	—
Shares repurchased	—	—	—	10,232	(641)	—	—	—
Recognition of stock-based compensation	—	—	47	—	—	—	—	—
Dividends declared	—	—	—	—	—	(966)	—	(51)
Additional investment in subsidiary and other	—	—	5	—	—	—	—	(28)
Balance at December 31, 2008	478,597	598	486	65,038	(4,285)	9,465	(2,386)	383
Net income in stockholders' equity	—	—	—	—	—	1,884	—	54
Other comprehensive income:								
Unrealized translation	—	—	—	—	—	—	619	6
Employee postretirement benefits, net of tax	—	—	—	—	—	—	(32)	(2)
Other	—	—	—	—	—	—	3	—
Stock-based awards exercised or vested	—	—	(47)	(3,519)	204	(7)	—	—
Income tax benefits on stock-based compensation	—	—	7	—	—	—	—	—
Shares repurchased	—	—	—	130	(7)	—	—	—
Recognition of stock-based compensation	—	—	86	—	—	—	—	—
Dividends declared	—	—	—	—	—	(996)	—	(45)
Additional investment in subsidiary and other	—	—	(133)	—	1	(17)	(37)	(112)
Balance at December 31, 2009	478,597	598	399	61,649	(4,087)	10,329	(1,833)	284
Net income in stockholders' equity	—	—	—	—	—	1,843	—	44
Other comprehensive income:								
Unrealized translation	—	—	—	—	—	—	326	7
Employee postretirement benefits, net of tax	—	—	—	—	—	—	57	(2)
Other	—	—	—	—	—	—	(16)	—
Stock-based awards exercised or vested	—	—	(37)	(2,862)	170	—	—	—
Income tax benefits on stock-based compensation	—	—	2	—	—	—	—	—
Shares repurchased	—	—	—	12,954	(809)	—	—	—
Recognition of stock-based compensation	—	—	52	—	—	—	—	—
Dividends declared	—	—	—	—	—	(1,085)	—	(47)
Other	—	—	9	—	—	(1)	—	(1)
Balance at December 31, 2010	478,597	$598	$425	71,741	$(4,726)	$11,086	$(1,466)	$285

(continued)

EXHIBIT 2.2
(*concluded*)

Consolidated Statement of Comprehensive Income

	Year Ended December 31		
	2010	**2009**	**2008**
	(Millions of dollars)		
Net income	$1,943	$1,994	$1,829
Other comprehensive income, net of tax:			
Unrealized currency translation adjustments	334	625	(982)
Employee postretirement benefits	55	(34)	(689)
Other	(16)	3	(8)
Total other comprehensive income, net of tax:	373	594	(1,679)
Comprehensive income	2,316	2,588	150
comprehensive income attributable to noncontrolling interests	(106)	(114)	(55)
Comprehensive income attributable to Kimberly-Clark Corporation	$2,210	$2,474	$ 95

more detail in the financial reports, so you might download the full 2010 10-K from the SEC EDGAR Web site or from the firm's Web page at **www.kimberly-clark.com**. If, for some reason, you have difficulty downloading the 10-K, it is on the Web page for Chapter 2 on the book's Web site at **www.mhhe.com/penman5e**.

THE FORM AND CONTENT OF KIMBERLY-CLARK'S FINANCIAL STATEMENTS

Go through the firm's four statements and show that each of the accounting relations in this chapter—2.1 to 2.5—are obeyed in 2010. Be sure to identify comprehensive income and net payout to shareholders. Satisfy yourself that the cash flow statement reconciles to the opening and closing cash balances, as in Figure 2.1, and that the income statement reconciles to the shareholders' equity statement, as also shown in Figure 2.1. Can you "tell the story" of what the financial statements, as a whole, are depicting?

Now dig into the financial statement footnotes in the 10-K. Look at the accounting policies and mark those you don't quite understand. We will discuss many of these later in the text, sometimes with Accounting Clinics available on the book's Web site. Some of the items in the financial statements are highly aggregated. You'll find more detail in the footnotes; add this detail to the financial statements here.

Look at Kimberley-Clark's balance sheet and tick off those assets and liabilities that you think are reported close to their fair value. On what basis are the remaining items measured? From your investigation of the firm in the Chapter 1 case, what assets do you conjecture are missing from the balance sheet? What items in the income statement involve the most mismatching of revenues to expenses?

MARKET VALUES AND MARKET MULTIPLES

You saw in the Chapter 1 case that KMB traded at $65.24 at the end of March 2011, just after its 2010 annual report was published. Using this number and others from the statements, calculate the total market value of the equity. For this you will need to identify shares outstanding; remember that shares outstanding are not the same as shares issued.

Calculate the premium or discount at which KMB trades relative to book value. Also calculate the price-to-book ratio (P/B) and the price-earnings ratio (P/E). Can you provide some explanation for the size of these ratios?

Using the value equation (2.6) and information in the financial statements, make the best calculation you can for the value of the firm (enterprise value).

You may now want to go to Minicase 2.1, which has more questions on the KMB financial statements.

Concept Questions	
	C2.1. Changes in shareholders' equity are determined by total earnings minus net payout to shareholders, but the change in shareholders' equity is not equal to net income (in the income statement) minus net payout to shareholders. Why?

Concept Questions

C2.1. Changes in shareholders' equity are determined by total earnings minus net payout to shareholders, but the change in shareholders' equity is not equal to net income (in the income statement) minus net payout to shareholders. Why?

C2.2. Dividends are the only way to pay cash out to shareholders. True or False?

C2.3. Explain the difference between net income and net income available to common. Which definition of income is used in earnings-per-share calculations?

C2.4. Why might a firm trade at a price-to-book ratio (P/B) greater than 1.0?

C2.5. Explain why some firms have high price-earnings (P/E) ratios.

C2.6. Give some examples in which there is poor matching of revenues and expenses.

C2.7. Price-to-book ratios are determined by how accountants measure book values. Can you think of accounting reasons for why price-to-book ratios were high in the 1990s? What other factors might explain the high P/B ratios?

C2.8. Why are dividends not an expense in the income statement?

C2.9. Why is depreciation of plant and equipment an expense in the income statement?

C2.10. Is amortization of a patent right an appropriate expense in measuring value added in operations?

C2.11. Why is the matching principle important?

C2.12. Why do fundamental analysts want accountants to follow the reliability criterion when preparing financial reports?

Exercises

Drill Exercises

E2.1. Applying Accounting Relations: Balance Sheet, Income Statement, and Equity Statement (Easy)

The following questions pertain to the same firm.

a. The balance sheet reports $400 million in total assets and $250 million in shareholders' equity at the end of a fiscal period. What are the firm's liabilities?

b. The income statement reports $30 million in net income and $175 million in total expenses for the period. What are the firm's revenues?

c. The shareholders' equity statement has a beginning balance for the period of $230 million and the firm had a net payout to shareholders of $12 million. What is the firm's comprehensive income for the year? How much income is reported in the equity statement rather than the income statement?

d. There were no share issues or stock repurchases during the year. How much did the firm pay in dividends?

E2.2. Applying Accounting Relations: Cash Flow Statement (Easy)

A firm reported $130 million increase in cash over a year. It also reported $400 million in cash flow from operations, and a net $75 million paid out to claimants in financing activities. How much did the firm invest in operations?

E2.3. **The Financial Statements for a Bank Savings Account (Medium)**

You received the following statement for 2012 for your savings account at a bank. Cash balances in the account earn interest at a 5 percent rate per annum.

Balance, January 1, 2012	$100
Earnings at an interest rate of 5% p.a.	5
Withdrawals	(5)
Balance, December 31, 2012	100

This statement is effectively a statement of owner's equity for the account. It shows your starting balance, adds your earnings for the year, and subtracts your dividend (the withdrawal), to yield a closing balance.

a. Prepare an income statement, balance sheet, and cash flow statement for this account for 2012.

b. Rather than withdrawing $5 from the account, suppose you left it in the account. What would your financial statements for 2012 then look like?

c. If, before the end of the year, you instructed your bank to invest the earnings of $5 in a mutual fund (and there were no withdrawals), what would the final financial statement from the bank look like?

E2.4. **Preparing an Income Statement and Statement of Shareholders' Equity (Medium)**

From the following information for the year 2012, prepare an income statement and a statement of shareholders' equity, under GAAP rules, for a company with shareholders' equity at the beginning of 2012 of $3,270 million. Amounts are in millions.

Sales	$4,458
Common dividends paid	140
Selling expenses	1,230
Research and development costs	450
Cost of goods sold	3,348
Share issues	680
Unrealized gain on securities available for sale	76
Income taxes	(200)

Also calculate comprehensive income and net payout. Income taxes are negative. How can this be?

E2.5. **Classifying Accounting Items (Easy)**

Indicate where in the financial statements the following appear under GAAP:

a. Investment in a certificate of deposit maturing in 120 days.
b. Expenses for bad debts.
c. Allowances for bad debts.
d. Research and development expenditures.
e. A restructuring charge.
f. A lease of an asset for its entire productive life.
g. Unrealized gain on shares held for trading purposes.
h. Unrealized gain on shares available for sale.
i. Unearned revenue.
j. Preferred stock issued.
k. Preferred dividends paid.
l. Stock option compensation expense.

E2.6. Violations of the Matching Principle (Easy)

Generally accepted accounting principles (GAAP) notionally follow the matching principle. However, there are exceptions. Explain why the following accounting rules, required under GAAP, violate the matching principle.

a. Expenditures on research and development into new drugs are expensed in the income statement as they are incurred.

b. Advertising and promotion costs for a new product are expensed as incurred.

c. Film production costs are expensed prior to the release of films to theaters.

E2.7. Using Accounting Relations to Check Errors (Hard)

A chief executive reported the following numbers for fiscal year 2012 to an annual meeting of shareholders (in millions):

Revenues	$ 2,300
Total expenses, including taxes	1,750
Other comprehensive income	(90)
Total assets, end of year	4,340
Total liabilities, end of year	1,380
Dividends to shareholders	400
Share issues	900
Share repurchases	150
Shareholders' equity, beginning of year	19,140

Show that at least one of these numbers must be wrong because it does not obey accounting relations.

Applications

E2.8. Finding Financial Statement Information on the Internet (Easy)

The Securities and Exchange Commission (SEC) maintains the EDGAR database of company filings with the commission. Explore the SEC's EDGAR site:

www.sec.gov/edgar.shtml.

Look at the "Descriptions of SEC Forms" page to familiarize yourself with the types of filings that firms make. Then click on "Search for Company Filings" for the filings of firms you are interested in. Forms 10-K (annual reports) and 10-Q (quarterly reports) will be of primary interest.

Most firms provide their financial statements on their Web sites, usually under the investor relations tag. The reports are often in a form that can be downloaded into a spreadsheet.

E2.9. Using Accounting Relations: General Mills, Inc. (Medium)

The following numbers appeared in the annual report of General Mills, Inc., the consumer foods manufacturer, for the fiscal year ending May 2010 (in millions of dollars):

	Fiscal 2010	Fiscal 2009
Total assets	17,679	17,875
Total stockholders' equity	5,648	5,417
Total revenues	14,797	14,692
Common share issues	603	521
Common dividends	648	590
Common stock repurchases	692	1,296

The firm has no preferred stock.

For fiscal 2010, calculate

a. Total liabilities at year end.
b. Comprehensive income for the year.

Real World Connection

See Exercises E1.5, E2.9, E3.8, E4.10, E6.8, E11.9, E13.9, E14.15, E15.6, and E16.10 for the material on General Mills.

E2.10.   Using Accounting Relations: Genentech Inc. (Medium)

Consider the following excerpts from Genentech's 2004 income statement and cash flow statement. From the 2004 income statement (in millions):

Revenues	?
Costs and expenses	
Cost of sales	$ 672.5
Research and development	947.5
Marketing, general, and administrative	1,088.1
Collaboration profit sharing	593.6
Special charges	182.7
Other expense—net interest income	(82.6)
Income before tax	1,219.4
Income tax	434.6
Net income	784.8

From the 2004 cash flow statement (in thousands):

Cash flows from operating activities	
Net income	$ 784,816
Adjustments to reconcile net income to net cash provided by operating activities:	
Depreciation and amortization	353,221
Deferred income taxes	(73,585)
Deferred revenue	(14,927)
Litigation-related and other long-term liabilities	34,722
Tax benefit from employee stock options	329,470
Gain on sales of securities available for sale and other	(13,577)
Loss on sales of securities available for sale	1,839
Write-down of securities available for sale	12,340
Loss on fixed asset dispositions	5,115
Changes in assets and liabilities:	
Receivables and other current assets	(362,740)
Inventories	(120,703)
Investments in trading securities	(75,695)
Accounts payable and other current liabilities	335,542
Net cash provided by operating activities	$1,195,838

For 2004, calculate

  a. Revenues.
  b. ebit (earnings before interest and taxes).
  c. ebitda (earnings before interest, taxes, depreciation, and amortization).

The following were reported in Genentech's 2004 balance sheet (in millions):

Current assets	$3,422.8
Total assets	9,403.4
Long-term liabilities	1,377.9
Stockholders' equity	6,782.2

  d. Calculate the long-term assets and short-term liabilities that were reported.

The following were also reported in the 2004 statements (in millions):

	2004	2003
Cash used in investing activities (in the cash flow statement)	$451.6	$1,398.4
Cash and cash equivalents (in the balance sheet)	270.1	372.2

  e. Calculate cash flows from financing activities reported for 2004.

E2.11. Find the Missing Numbers in the Equity Statement: Cisco Systems, Inc. (Easy)
At the end of its 2007 fiscal year, Cisco Systems, Inc., the producer of routers and other hardware and software for the telecommunications industry, reported shareholders' equity of $31,931 million. At the end of the first nine months of fiscal 2008, the firm reported $32,304 million in equity along with $6,526 million of comprehensive income for the period.

  a. What was the net payout to shareholders in the first nine months of 2008?
  b. Cisco paid no dividends and share issues amounted to $2,869 million. What was the amount of shares repurchased during the first nine months of 2008?

Real World Connection
Minicases 7.1 and 15.2 deal with Cisco Systems, as do exercises E2.11 and E19.6.

E2.12. Find the Missing Numbers in Financial Statements: General Motors Corporation (Medium)
General Motors ended its 2007 year (prior to its bankruptcy) with shareholders' equity of −$37,094 million (yes, negative equity!). Six months later, at June 30, 2008, it reported −$56,990 million in equity after paying a dividend of $283 million to shareholders. There were no other transactions with shareholders.

  a. What was comprehensive income for the six months?
  b. The income statement reported a loss of $18,722 million for the six months. What was "other comprehensive income"?
  c. Total expense and other losses in the income statement, including taxes, were $60,895 million. What was revenue for the six months?
  d. The firm reported $148,883 million of total assets at the end of 2007 and $136,046 at June 30, 2008. What were total liabilities at these two dates?
  e. How can a firm have negative equity?

Real World Connection
Exercises E1.4, E2.12, E4.11, and E5.12 also cover General Motors.

E2.13. **Mismatching at WorldCom (Hard)**

During the four fiscal quarters of 2001 and the first quarter of 2002, WorldCom incorrectly capitalized access charges to local networks as assets (as explained in Box 2.4). The amount of costs capitalized were as follows:

First quarter, 2001	$780 million
Second quarter, 2001	$605 million
Third quarter, 2001	$760 million
Fourth quarter, 2001	$920 million
First quarter, 2002	$790 million

Suppose WorldCom amortized these capitalized costs straight-line over five years (20 quarters). Calculate the amount of the overstatement of income before tax for each of the five quarters.

E2.14. **Calculating Stock Returns: Nike, Inc. (Easy)**

The shares of Nike, Inc., traded at $57.83 per share at the beginning of fiscal year 2010 and closed at $73.38 per share at the end of the year. Nike paid a dividend of $1.06 cents per share during the year. What was the return to holding Nike's shares during 2010?

Real World Connection

Nike is covered extensively in this book, both in text material and exercises. See exercises E2.14, E5.13, E6.7, E7.9, E9.12, E14.17, E16.11, E16.13, and E19.5.

Minicase

M2.1

Reviewing the Financial Statements of Kimberly-Clark Corporation

Kimberly-Clark Corporation manufactures and markets a variety of personal care and health products under brand names that include Kleenex, Huggies, Scott, Scottex, Cottonelle, Viva, Kotex, and WypAll. These products are sold worldwide. Founded in 1928, the firm is head-quartered in Dallas, Texas, and has approximately 57,000 employees worldwide.

The firm is organized into four operating segments based on product groupings:

- *Personal Care,* which manufactures and markets disposable diapers, training and youth pants, swimpants, baby wipes, feminine and incontinence care products, and related products. Products in this segment are primarily for household use and are sold under a variety of brand names, including Huggies, Pull-Ups, Little Swimmers, GoodNites, Kotex, Lightdays, Depend, Poise, and other brand names.

- *Consumer Tissue,* which manufactures and markets facial and bathroom tissue, paper towels, napkins, and related products for households use. Products in this segment are sold under the Kleenex, Scott, Cottonelle, Viva, Andrex, Scottex, Hakle, Page, and other brand names.

- *K-C Professional & Other,* which manufactures and markets facial and bathroom tissue, paper towels, napkins, wipers, and a range of safety products for the away-from-home marketplace. Products in this segment are sold under the Kimberly-Clark, Kleenex, Scott, WypAll, Kimtech, KleenGuard, Kimcare, and Jackson brand names.

- *Health Care,* which manufactures and markets health care products such as surgical drapes and gowns, infection control products, face maks, exam gloves, respiratory prod-ucts, pain management products, and other disposable medical products. Products in this segment are sold under the Kimberly-Clark, Ballard, ON-Q, and other brand names.

KMB closed the first quarter of 2011 trading at $65.24 per share. You will find informa-tion of analysts' forecasts and opinions at the time in the first Continuing Case installment in Chapter 1. Prices in earlier years and dividends paid over the prior 12 months are below:

Year	Price per Share, March 31	Annual Dividend per Share
2011	$65.24	$2.64
2010	62.88	2.40
2009	46.11	2.32
2008	64.55	2.12
2007	68.49	1.96

Examine Kimberly-Clark's financial statements for fiscal year ending December 31, 2010, in Exhibit 2.2 with a view to testing your understanding of accounting: What do you not understand? The following questions will help you focus on the pertinent features:

A. Using the numbers in the financial statements, show that the following accounting rela-tions hold in Kimberly-Clark's 2010 statements:

> Shareholders' equity = Assets – Liabilities
> Net income = Revenue – Expenses
> Cash from operations + Cash from investment + Cash from financing + Effect
> of exchange rates = Change in cash and cash equivalents

B. What are the components of other comprehensive income for 2010? Show that the following accounting relation holds (approximately):

Comprehensive income = Net income + Other comprehensive income

C. Calculate the net payout to shareholders in 2010 from the Statement of Stockholders' Equity.

D. Explain how revenue is recognized.

E. Calculate the following for 2010: gross margin, effective tax rate, ebit, ebitda. Calculate the sales growth rate for 2010 and 2009.

F. Explain the difference between basic earnings per share and diluted earnings per share.

G. Explain why some inventory costs are in cost of goods sold and some are in inventory on the balance sheet.

H. Kimberly-Clark spent $698 million on advertising and promotion during 2010. Where is this cost included in the financial statements? Does this treatment satisfy the matching principle?

I. Kimberly-Clark spent $317 million on research and development in 2010. Where is this in the financial statements? Does this treatment satisfy the matching principle?

J. Accounts receivable for 2010 of $2,472 million is net of $80 million (reported in footnotes). How is this calculation made?

K. Why are deferred income taxes both an asset and a liability?

L. What is "goodwill" and how is it accounted for? Why did it change in 2010?

M. Explain why there is a difference between net income and cash provided by operations.

N. What items in Kimberly-Clark's balance sheet would you say were close to fair market value?

O. Based on the stock price at March 31, 2011, calculate the market capitalization of the equity. Calculate the P/E ratio and the P/B ratio at this price. How do these ratios compare with historical P/E and P/B ratios in Figures 2.2 and 2.3?

P. From the price and dividend information above, calculate the stock rate-of-return for each year ending March 31, 2008–2011.

Real World Connection

Follow Kimberly-Clark through the continuing case at the end of each chapter of the text. The solution to this continuing case is on the book's Web site. Exercises E4.9, E7.16, E8.10, E11.10, and E12.6 also cover Kimberly-Clark.

Part One

Financial Statements and Valuation

Chapter 3
Lays out the alternative ways in which financial statements are used for valuation, and shows how valuation models direct how to account for value.

Chapter 4
Introduces cash accounting and accrual accounting for valuation, and lays out discounted cash flow valuation methods that employ cash accounting.

Chapter 5
Introduces valuation methods that anchor equity values on book values and lead to an evaluation of the intrinsic price-to-book ratio.

Chapter 6
Introduces valuation methods that anchor equity values on earnings and lead to an evaluation of the intrinsic price-earnings ratio.

Chapter 7
Applies the valuation methods to challenge the market price.

With the foundations established in Part One, proceed to **The Analysis of Financial Statements (Part Two) Forecasting and Valuation Analysis (Part Three)**

The analyst must choose a technology with which to work. This part of the book lays out alternative techniques that can be employed in equity analysis. The diligent analyst wants the best technology, so the material goes to lengths to contrast the advantages and disadvantages of each technique. By the end of Part One, you will have chosen a technology with which you feel comfortable, one that gives you the security that is necessary for equity investing. Indeed, this part of the book closes with a chapter on how to apply the technology in active investing, and there you will see the methods come to life.

In order to make the appropriate choice, you must have an understanding of the basic principles of fundamental analysis and investing. This part of the book develops that understanding. Crucial to this understanding is an appreciation of the role of a valuation model, for a valuation model directs how analysis is to be done and how valuations are to be carried out. You will understand that valuation models—though often expressed in seemingly cryptic formulas—are really a way of thinking about the analysis and valuation task. You will also understand that a valuation model is actually a statement about how to account for value, thereby tying valuation to the financial statements. You will then see how we accomplish our objective (in Chapter 1) of anchoring value on the financial statements.

Chapter 3 introduces valuation models based on the financial statements, but not before laying out alternative ways of carrying out equity analysis. The chapter describes the method of comparables, multiple screening analysis, and asset-based valuation. These simple schemes are shown to be lacking, and their use comes with the warning that ignoring the principles of sound fundamental analysis is done at one's peril. With the introduction to valuation models in this chapter you will develop an appreciation for how financial statements are utilized in fundamental analysis.

Chapter 4 introduces dividend discounting and discounted cash flow analysis and shows that these valuation techniques embrace cash accounting for value. It identifies the deficiencies of cash accounting (and discounted cash flow analysis) as a method of accounting for value, leading you to an appreciation of how accrual accounting corrects the deficiencies of cash accounting. The discussion of accrual accounting in this chapter builds on the discussion of accounting in Chapter 2, further enhancing your understanding of how accounting works for valuation.

The two "bottom-line" numbers in accrual accounting financial statements are the book value of equity—the bottom-line number in the balance sheet—and earnings (income)—the bottom-line number in the income statement. It is on these two numbers that accrual accounting valuation is anchored. Chapter 5 shows how to value a firm by anchoring value on book value. Chapter 2 showed that book values are typically an imperfect measure of value, but they provide a starting point for valuation. Using book value as a starting point, Chapter 5 goes on to show how the analyst adds value to complete the valuation, determining the intrinsic price-to-book (P/B) ratio. In a complementary way, Chapter 6 shows how to anchor a valuation on earnings, thus determining the intrinsic price-earnings (P/E) ratio.

The purpose of this part of the book is to give you perspective on the issues and to emphasize some important concepts. Above all, it gets you thinking about design issues in developing valuation tools. Some of the concepts will be familiar to you from finance courses. Some will be familiar from accounting courses. The accounting and finance concepts come together here. In finance, people talk of valuation. In accounting, people talk of measurement. But valuation is a matter of measurement (of value generated in the firm). So, in discussing valuation principles, we also introduce the principles of accounting measurement. The point is to show you how accounting works—or maybe doesn't work—to reveal the value in a firm. And we will see how accounting is integrated into valuation analysis so that fundamental analysis and financial statement analysis are much the same thing.

Part Two and subsequent parts of the book are about technique. They are about doing financial statement analysis and fundamental analysis. Part One of the book is less about doing and more about thinking about doing. "Look before you leap" applies to investing but it also applies to the analysis of investing. Sometimes the word "sage" is applied to certain investors, and with good cause. Good techniques must be applied with good judgment, with wisdom. And wisdom helps in the selection of techniques. If you read *The Intelligent Investor* by Benjamin Graham, the acclaimed father of fundamental analysis, you will see that the book is more about attitude and approach to investing than it is about technique.[1] Use this part of the book to understand the basics and use it to cultivate wisdom in investing. We purposefully develop the material slowly, so you can read it in a considered way.

[1] B. Graham, *The Intelligent Investor,* 4th rev. ed. (New York: Harper & Row, 1973).

Chapter Three

How Financial Statements Are Used in Valuation

LINKS

Link to previous chapters

Chapter 1 introduced fundamental analysis and Chapter 2 introduced the financial statements.

This chapter

This chapter shows how fundamental analysis and valuation are carried out and how the financial statements are utilized in the process. It lays out a five-step approach to fundamental analysis that involves the analysis and forecasting of financial statements. Simpler schemes involving financial statements are also presented.

Link to next chapter

Chapter 4 deals with valuation based on forecasting cash flows.

Link to Web page

The Web page supplement offers further treatment of comparables analysis and screening analysis, as well as an extended discussion of valuation techniques and asset pricing.

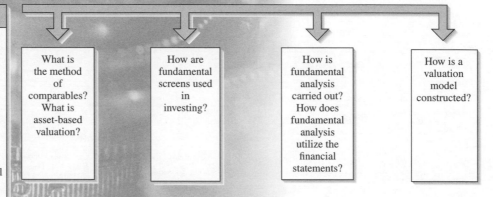

| What is the method of comparables? What is asset-based valuation? | How are fundamental screens used in investing? | How is fundamental analysis carried out? How does fundamental analysis utilize the financial statements? | How is a valuation model constructed? |

This chapter explains how financial statements are used in valuing firms. It is an important chapter, for it sets the stage for developing practical valuation analysis in Chapters 4, 5, and 6. Indeed, the material in the second half of the chapter provides a road map for much of what follows in the rest of the book. As you proceed through the book, you will find yourself looking back to this material to maintain your bearings.

In introducing valuation in Chapter 1, we said that the analyst's first order of business is to choose a technology to work with. You will not be able to commit to a technology until the end of Chapter 6, but this chapter raises the issues involved in making that choice. It lays out the architecture of a competent valuation technology. Here you will develop an appreciation of what a good technology looks like, and you will begin to understand the pitfalls that await those using misguided methods. You also will understand what features of firms are relevant to their valuation, how these features are identified by a competent valuation method, and how they are recognized in financial statements.

In valuation, as with most technologies, there is always a tradeoff between simple approaches that ignore some pertinent features and more elaborate techniques that accommodate complexities. In this book we will always be pushing for the simple approaches, but simple approaches that do not substantially sacrifice the quality of the product. Simple approaches are cheap—they avoid some analysis work—but they can be too cheap, leading to errors. In adopting a simple approach, we want to be sure we know what we are missing relative to a full-fledged analysis. So this chapter begins with simple schemes that use financial statements and progresses to more formal valuation methods. At all points, the tradeoffs are indicated.

The Analyst's Checklist

After reading this chapter you should understand:

- What a valuation technology looks like.
- What a valuation model is and how it differs from an asset pricing model.
- How a valuation model provides the architecture for fundamental analysis.
- The practical steps involved in fundamental analysis.
- How the financial statements are involved in fundamental analysis.
- How one converts a forecast to a valuation.
- The difference between valuing terminal investments and going concern investments (like business firms).
- The dividend irrelevance concept.
- Why financing transactions do not generate value, except in particular circumstances.
- Why the focus of value creation is on the investing and operating activities of a firm.
- How the method of comparables works (or does not work).
- How asset-based valuation works (or does not work).
- How multiple screening strategies work (or do not work).

After reading this chapter you should be able to:

- Carry out a multiple comparison analysis.
- Develop a simple or multiple screen using a stock screener.
- Calculate an array of price multiples for a firm.
- Calculate unlevered price multiples.
- Calculate trailing and forward P/E ratios.
- Calculate a dividend-adjusted P/E ratio.
- Apply asset-based valuation techniques.
- Calculate the breakup value of a firm.
- Value a bond.
- Value a project.
- Calculate the value added from project selection.
- Show that a bond purchased at a price to yield its required return generates no value.
- Calculate the loss to existing shareholders from issuing shares at less than market value.
- Generate "homemade dividends."

Simple valuations use a limited amount of information. The chapter begins with multiple analysis that uses just a few numbers in the financial statements—sales, earnings, or book values, for example—and applies pricing multiples to these numbers. Asset-based valuation techniques are then introduced. These techniques attempt to value equities by summing the market value of the firms' assets, net of liabilities. We will see that asset-based valuation, though seemingly simple, is a doubtful exercise for most firms.

Simple methods run the risk of ignoring relevant information. A full-fledged fundamental analysis identifies all the relevant information and extracts the implications of that information for valuing the firm. The chapter concludes with a broad outline of fundamental analysis technologies that accomplish this. It leads you through the five steps involved and shows how financial statements are incorporated in the process. It stresses the importance of adopting a valuation model that captures value created in the firm and shows how that valuation model provides the architecture for fundamental analysis.

The Analyst's Checklist for Chapter 3 indicates that there is much you will be able to do after reading this chapter, but the primary goal is to provoke your thinking as to what a good valuation technology looks like. With that thinking, you will be prepared to adopt such a technology in the next few chapters.

MULTIPLE ANALYSIS

An acceptable valuation technique must have benefits that outweigh the cost of using it, and its cost-benefit tradeoff must compare favorably with alternative techniques. A full-fledged fundamental analysis comes at some cost because it requires the analyst to consider a large amount of information, which involves considerable effort. We will develop ways of doing this as efficiently as possible but, before proceeding, we should consider shortcuts that avoid those costs. What is lost by taking an easier route? What is gained by taking the more difficult path? Multiple analysis is cheap because it uses minimal information.

A multiple is simply the ratio of the stock price to a particular number in the financial statements. The most common ratios multiply the important summary numbers in the statements—earnings, book values, sales, and cash flows—hence the price-earnings ratio (P/E), the price-to-book ratio (P/B), the price-to-sales ratio (P/S), and the ratio of price-to-cash flow from operations (P/CFO). By using one piece of information in the statements, these multiples are surely parsimonious in using financial statement information. One does not have to know much accounting to calculate these ratios.

Two techniques employ these multiples and variants on them; they are the method of comparables and multiple screening.

The Method of Comparables

The *method of comparables* or *multiple comparison analysis*—sometimes referred to as "comps"—works as follows:

1. Identify comparable firms that have operations similar to those of the target firm whose value is in question.
2. Identify measures for the comparable firms in their financial statements—earnings, book value, sales, cash flow—and calculate multiples of those measures at which the firms trade.
3. Apply an average or median of these multiples to the corresponding measures for the target firm to get that firm's value.

We will attempt to value Dell, Inc., in April 2011 using the method of comparables. Table 3.1 lists the most recent annual sales, earnings, and the book value of equity for Dell and two firms that produce similar personal computer products, Hewlett-Packard Company, which absorbed Compaq Computer, and Lenovo Group, the Hong Kong–listed firm that manufactures ThinkPad and IdeaPad laptops along with desktop computers and workstations. The price-to-sales (P/S), price-to-earnings (P/E), and price-to-book (P/B) ratios for HP and Lenovo are based on their market values in April 2011. Dell is valued by applying the average of multiples for the comparison firms to Dell sales, earnings, and

TABLE 3.1
Pricing Multiples for Comparable Firms to Dell, Inc.

	Sales	Earnings	Book Value	Market Value	P/S	P/E	P/B
Hewlett-Packard Co.	$84,799	$8,761	$40,449	$89,835	1.06	10.3	2.2
Lenovo Group Ltd.	21,540	242	1,763	5,730	0.27	23.7	3.3
Dell, Inc.	50,002	2,635	7,766	?	?	?	?

Dollar numbers are in millions.

TABLE 3.2
Applying Comparable Firms' Multiples to Dell, Inc.

	Average Multiple for Comparables		Dell's Number		Dell's Valuation
Sales	0.67	×	$50,002	=	$33,501
Earnings	17.0	×	2,635	=	44,795
Book value	2.8	×	7,766	=	21,745
Average valuation					33,347

Dollar numbers are in millions.
Dell's actual valuation on April 5, 2011, was $28,041 million.

book values, as seen in Table 3.2. The three multiples give three different valuations for Dell, a bit awkward. So the valuations are averaged to give a value of $33,347 million on 1,918 million shares, or $17.39 per share. The earnings multiple gives the highest valuation of $23.36 per share while the book value multiple yields the lowest valuation of 11.34 per share. Dell was trading at $14.62 per share at the time. On the basis of the average valuation, our analysis says that the stock is cheap.[1]

These calculations are certainly minimal. But the valuation has probably left you a little uneasy, particularly with the different values with different multiples. This is not a valuation that makes one feel secure.

Multiple comparison analysis is easy, but it's cheap in more than one sense of the word. Indeed, there's a real fallacy here. If we have the prices of the comps, we can calculate a value for Dell. But if we want to get a value for Hewlett-Packard (say), would we use the calculated value of $17.39 per share for Dell? This would be circular because Dell's price is based on Hewlett-Packard's price. The analysis is not anchored in something fundamental that tells us about value independently of market prices. It assumes that the market is efficient in setting prices for the comparables. But if this is the case, why doubt that the $14.62 market price for Dell is also efficient and go through the exercise? If the comps are mispriced, then the exercise is also doubtful. In short, the method fails the fundamentalist's tenet in Chapter 1: When calculating value to challenge price, beware of using price in the calculation. Indeed, the method can be dangerous. See Box 3.1.

This method is used extensively and there are situations in which it is justified. If the target firm is a private or thinly traded firm with no reliable traded price, we might get a quick feel for the value of its equity from the comparables, but only if their stocks are efficiently priced. We might also be interested in the price at which a stock should trade, whether that price is efficient or not. Investment bankers floating initial public offerings (IPOs) use the method of comparables to estimate the price at which the market might value the issue. (They might use prices in past comparable IPO transactions rather than comparable prices at the moment.) If the market is mispricing the comps, they estimate it will misprice the IPO also. In litigation for loss of value (in shareholder class action or minority interest suits, for example), the question often asked is what price the stock would have been had certain events occurred, not what it's really worth.

---

[1] In a variation of the calculations (to use more up-to-date information), multiple analysis sometimes uses last-twelve-months (LTM) accounting numbers:

LTM = Number for prior fiscal year + Current year-to-date number − Year-to-date number for prior year

The year-to-date numbers are the sum of quarterly numbers reported to date.

Periodically, initial public offerings for particular types of firms become "hot." The 1990s bull market saw hot issues for theme restaurants, technology and computer stocks, brand fashion houses, business services, and Internet stocks. In a hot IPO market, firms sell for high multiples, encouraging comparable firms to go public also. Investment bankers justify the price of an offering on the basis of multiples received in an earlier offering. If they raise the multiples a little, to get the IPO business, a pyramid scheme can develop, with offering prices based on increasing comparable prices without reference to fundamental value.

In 1995 and 1996, teleservicing firms—firms supplying telemarketing and customer service—were offered to the market. In anticipation of other firms outsourcing these functions to the new firms, investors paid high prices in the IPOs. The pyramiding occurred. Lehman Brothers (later a casualty of the 2008 financial crisis) co-managed one of the initial offers but lost out to other investment banks in handling later IPOs. Quoted in *The Wall Street Journal* on September 15, 1998, Jeffrey Kessler of Lehman Brothers said, "every time we came out with what we thought was a reasonable valuation for a new IPO in this area, the winning bidder had valuations that were way higher. We were outbid [by other investment banks] by, in some cases, over five multiple points, and we scratched our heads and said this was crazy."

Indeed, the stock prices of teleservicing firms dropped dramatically after the IPO boom. A pyramiding IPO market is another stock price bubble. Pricing IPOs on the basis of the speculative price multiples of comparable firms perpetuates the bubble. Beware of prices estimated from comparables, for you may join a chain letter (a pyramid scheme) that leads you to pay too much for a stock.

Conceptual problems aside, the method of comparables also has problems in implementation:

- Identifying comps with the same operating characteristics is difficult. Firms are typically matched by industry, product, size, growth, and some measure of risk, but no two firms are exactly alike. One might argue that Hewlett-Packard, with its printer business, is not the same type of firm as Dell. Lenovo is a Chinese company, traded on a different exchange. Comps are usually competitors in the same industry that might dominate (or be dominated by) the target firm and thus not comparable. Increasing the number of comps might average out errors, but the more comps there are, the less homogeneous they are likely to be.

- Different multiples give different valuations. Applying a comp's P/B ratio to the target's book value yields a different price from applying the comp's P/E ratio to the target's earnings, as we just saw with Dell. Which price should we use? In the example, we simply took an arithmetic average, but it is not clear that this is correct.

- Negative denominators can occur. When the comp has a loss, the P/E has little meaning.

The method of comparables leaves too much room for "playing with mirrors." There is too much freedom for the analyst to obtain a valuation that he, or his client, desires. This is not good if our aim is to challenge speculation.

Other multiples are used in comparison analysis. Some adjust for differences in leverage between firms and some adjust for differences in accounting principle. See Box 3.2.

In carrying out multiple analysis the analyst should have a feel for what typical multiples look like, as a benchmark. Table 3.3 lists percentiles for a number of ratios for all U.S. listed firms for the years 1963–2003. You can see from the table that the median P/B (at the 50th percentile) is 1.7, the median trailing P/E is 15.2, and the median unlevered price-to-sales (P/S) ratio is 0.9. Further back in time (in the 1970s), multiples were lower. On the other hand, multiples in the 1990s were considerably higher than historical ratios. You will find more detail on historical multiples on the book's Web page.

LEVERAGE ADJUSTMENTS

Some multiples are affected by leverage—the amount of debt financing a firm has relative to equity financing. So, to control for differences in leverage between the target firm and comparison firms, these multiples are "unlevered." Typical **unlevered measures** are

$$\text{Unlevered price/sales ratio} = \frac{\text{Market value of equity} + \text{Net debt}}{\text{Sales}}$$

$$\text{Unlevered price/ebit} = \frac{\text{Market value of equity} + \text{Net debt}}{\text{ebit}}$$

where ebit = earnings before interest and taxes (earnings plus net interest and tax expenses). Net debt is total debt obligations less any interest-bearing securities (negative debt) that the firm may hold as assets. Typically the book value of net debt is an approximation of its market value. The numerator in these ratios is the market value of the firm, sometimes referred to as the *unlevered value* or *enterprise value*. Unlevered ratios are sometimes referred to as *enterprise multiples*. Price-to-sales and price-to-ebit ratios should be calculated as unleveled ratios because leverage does not produce sales or earnings before interest and taxes.

The primary enterprise balance sheet multiple is the enterprise price-to-book ratio:

$$\text{Enterprise P/B} = \frac{\text{Market value of equity} + \text{Net debt}}{\text{Book value of equity} + \text{Net debt}}$$

The denominator here is the book value of the enterprise, that is, the net assets employed by the enterprise.

ACCOUNTING ADJUSTMENTS

As their denominators are accounting numbers, multiples are often adjusted for aspects of the accounting that may differ between firms. Depreciation and amortization methods can differ and some analysts feel that depreciation and amortization are not well measured in income statements. A ratio that adjusts for both leverage and the accounting for these expenses is

$$\text{Unlevered price/ebitda} = \frac{\text{Market value of equity} + \text{Net debt}}{\text{ebitda}}$$

where ebitda = earnings before interest, taxes, depreciation, and amortization (ebit plus depreciation and amortization expense). Sometimes, ebitda is referred to as "cash flow" (from operations) but it is only an approximation of cash flow.

Earnings can be affected by one-time events that are particular to one firm. So multiples are adjusted to remove the effects of these events on earnings:

$$\frac{\text{Price/earnings}}{\text{before unusual items}} = \frac{\text{Market value of equity}}{\text{Earnings before unusual items}}$$

VARIATIONS OF THE P/E RATIO

The P/E ratio compares the stock price to annual earnings. Variations are

$$\text{Trailing P/E} = \frac{\text{Price per share}}{\text{Most recent annual EPS}}$$

$$\text{Rolling P/E} = \frac{\text{Price per share}}{\text{Sum of EPS for most recent four quarters}}$$

$$\text{Forward or leading P/E} = \frac{\text{Price per share}}{\text{Forecast of next year's EPS}}$$

The rolling P/E is sometimes indicated as P/E(ttm), where ttm is "total twelve months" to date.

The forward P/E, usually calculated with analysts' forecasts, modifies the trailing P/E for anticipated earnings growth in the coming year.

Price in the numerator of the trailing P/E is affected by dividends: Dividends reduce share prices because value is taken out of the firm. But earnings in the denominator are not affected by dividends. So P/E ratios can differ because of differing dividend payouts. To correct for this difference, trailing P/E ratios are calculated as

$$\text{Dividend-adjusted P/E} = \frac{\text{Price per share} + \text{Annual DPS}}{\text{EPS}}$$

where DPS is dividends per share. The numerator is the **cum-dividend price,** the price before the dividend is paid; the price after the dividend is paid is the **ex-dividend price.** As dividends reduce subsequent earnings, the adjustment is not made with the forward P/E.

The Web page gives some examples of multiple calculations.

Screening on Multiples

The method of comparables takes the view that similar firms should have similar multiples. One would expect this to be the case if market prices were efficient. Investors who doubt that the market prices fundamentals correctly, however, construe multiples a little differently: If firms trade at different multiples, they may be relatively mispriced. Thus stocks are screened for buying and selling on the basis of their relative multiples.

TABLE 3.3 **Percentiles of Common Price Multiples, 1963–2003, for U.S. Listed Firms.**

					Multiple				
Percentile	P/B	Enterprise P/B	Trailing P/E	Forward P/E	P/S	Unlevered P/S	P/CFO	Unlevered P/ebitda	Unlevered P/ebit
95	7.9	12.7	Negative earnings	49.2	8.9	8.1	Negative cash flow	30.1	Negative ebit
75	2.9	2.7	23.5	19.1	1.7	2.0	18.8	10.6	15.3
50	1.7	1.5	15.2	13.1	0.8	0.9	9.9	7.0	9.9
25	1.0	1.0	10.3	9.2	0.3	0.5	5.6	4.8	6.6
5	0.5	0.6	5.9	5.6	0.1	0.2	2.3	2.5	3.3

Notes: CFO is cash flow from operations. Firms with negative denominators are treated as high multiple firms. Thus firms in the upper percentiles of P/E, P/CFO, and P/ebit are those with negative earnings (losses), cash flows, or ebit, as indicated.

Source: Calculated from Standard & Poor's COMPUSTAT data. Forward P/E ratios are based on consensus analysts' one-year-ahead earnings forecasts, on Thomson Financial I/B/E/S database.

Here is how *screening* works in its simplest form:

1. Identify a multiple on which to screen stocks.
2. Rank stocks on that multiple, from highest to lowest.
3. Buy stocks with the lowest multiples and (short) sell stocks with the highest multiples.

Buying low multiples and selling high multiples is seen as buying stocks that are cheap and selling those that are expensive. Screening on multiples is referred to as *fundamental screening* because multiples price fundamental features of the firm. Box 3.3 contrasts fundamental screening with *technical screening*.

Screening on multiples presumes that stocks whose prices are high relative to a particular fundamental are overpriced, and stocks whose prices are low relative to a fundamental are underpriced. Stocks with high multiples are sometimes referred to as **glamour stocks** for, it is claimed, investors view them as glamorous or fashionable and, too enthusiastically, drive up their prices relative to fundamentals. High multiples are also called **growth stocks** because investors see them as having a lot of growth potential. In contrast, stocks with low multiples are sometimes called **contrarian stocks** for they are stocks that have been ignored by the fashion herd. Contrarian investors run against the herd, so they buy unglamorous low multiple stocks and sell glamour stocks. Low multiple stocks are also called **value stocks** because their value is deemed to be high relative to their price.

Fundamental screening is cheap fundamental analysis. You accept the denominator of the screen as an indicator of intrinsic value and accept the spread between price and this number as an indicator of mispricing. It uses little information, which is an advantage. It's quick-stop shopping for bargains. It may be cost effective if a full-blown fundamental analysis is too expensive, but it can lead you astray if that one number is not a good indicator of intrinsic value. For this reason, some screeners combine strategies to exploit more information: Buy firms with both low P/E and low P/B (two-stop shopping), or buy small firms with low P/B and prior price declines (three-stop shopping), for example.

Table 3.4 reports annual returns from investing in five portfolios of stocks selected by screening on P/E and P/B ratios. The investment strategy conjectures that the market overprices firms with high P/E and P/B multiples (glamour stocks or growth stocks) and underprices firms with low multiples (value stocks or contrarian stocks). This is a strategy trolled many times by value-glamour investors and contrarian investors. Clearly, both P/E and P/B rank returns and the differences in returns between portfolio 1 (high multiples) and portfolio 5 (low multiples) indicate that one-stop shopping from screening solely on P/E or P/B would have paid off. Two-stop shopping using both the P/E screen and the P/B screen would have improved the returns: For a given P/E, ranking on P/B adds further returns.

TECHNICAL SCREENS

Technical screens identify investment strategies from indicators that relate to trading. Some common ones are:

Price screens: Buy stocks whose prices have dropped a lot relative to the market (sometimes called "losers") and sell stocks whose prices have increased a lot (sometimes called "winners"). The rationale: Large price movements can be deviations from fundamentals that will reverse.

Small-stocks screens: Buy stocks with a low market value (price per share times shares outstanding). The rationale: History has shown that small stocks typically earn higher returns.

Neglected-stock screens: Buy stocks that are not followed by many analysts. The rationale: These stocks are underpriced because the investor "herd" that follows fashions has deemed them uninteresting.

Seasonal screens: Buy stocks at a certain time of year, for example, in early January. The rationale: History shows that stock returns tend to be higher at these times.

Momentum screens: Buy stocks that have had increases in stock prices. The rationale: The price increase has momentum and will continue.

Insider-trading screens: Mimic the trading of insiders (who must file details of their trades with the Securities and Exchange Commission). The rationale: Insiders have inside information that they use in trading.

FUNDAMENTAL SCREENS

Fundamental screens compare price to a particular number in firms' financial statements. Typical fundamental screens are:

Price-to-earnings (P/E) screens: Buy firms with low P/E ratios and sell firms with high P/E ratios. See Box 3.2 for alternative P/E measures.

Price-to-book value (P/B) screens: Buy firms with low P/B and sell firms with high P/B.

Price-to-cash flow (P/CFO) screens: Buy low price relative to cash flow from operations, sell high P/CFO.

Price-to-dividend (P/d) screens: Buy low P/d, sell high P/d.

The Web page for this chapter discusses these screens in more detail and directs you to screening engines.

TABLE 3.4 Returns to Screening on Price-to-Earnings (P/E) and Priced-to-Book (P/B), 1963–2006.

Annual returns from screening on trailing P/E alone, P/B alone, and trailing P/E and P/B together. The screening strategy ranks firms on the screen each year and assigns firms to five portfolios based on the ranking. For the screen using both P/E and P/B, firms are assigned to five portfolios each year from a ranking on P/E and then, within each P/E portfolio, assigned to five portfolios based on a ranking on P/B. Reported returns are averages from implementing the screening strategies each year from 1963 to 2006.

		Screening on P/E and P/B Alone			
P/E Portfolio	Average P/E	Annual Return	P/B Portfolio	Average P/B	Annual Return
5 (low P/E)	7.1	23.2%	5 (low P/B)	0.61	24.3%
4	10.8	18.1	4	1.08	18.4
3	14.7	14.9	3	1.47	15.4
2	31.3	12.1	2	2.17	12.6
1 (high P/E)	Losses*	13.5	1 (high P/B)	4.55	9.3

		Screening on Both P/E and P/B			
		P/E Portfolio				
		1 (High)	2	3	4	5 (Low)
	1 (High)	4.3%	10.9%	14.2%	17.1%	19.7%
P/B	2	8.8	9.1	13.0	6.0	22.1
portfolio	3	14.4	8.5	12.1	17.0	21.6
	4	15.5	13.4	14.7	18.0	24.3
	5 (Low)	26.4	20.1	20.2	22.6	30.0

*Firms in this loss portfolio have an average E/P of −18.4 percent. Earnings are before extraordinary and special items.

Source: S. H. Penman and F. Reggiani, "Returns to Buying Earnings and Book Value: Accounting for Risk and Growth," forthcoming, *Review of Accounting Studies,* 2013. Earnings and book value are from Standard & Poor's COMPUSTAT data. Annual stock returns are calculated from the monthly returns file of the Center for Research in Security Prices (CRSP) at the University of Chicago Booth School of Business.

But danger lurks! There is no guarantee that these returns, documented after the fact from history, will replicate in the future; we are not sure whether investors would have expected these returns in advance or whether the strategy just "got lucky" in this period. By buying firms with low multiples you could also be taking on risk: The returns in Table 3.4 could reward for risk, with low multiple firms being very risky and high multiple firms having low risk. Indeed, the strategy in the table, though successful on average, has been known to turn against the investor at times, with high P/E rather than low P/E yielding higher returns. That could be uncomfortable, particularly if one had a short position in high P/E stocks. The P/E ratio is the inverse of the E/P ratio, referred to as the *earnings yield*. Just as bonds with higher risk have higher yields, so might it be with stocks. We will see later in the book that leverage (from borrowing) increases E/P (and decreases P/E), so buying a low P/E stock may expose one to leverage risk.

There is an additional caveat in running these investment strategies: They use very little information—only two pieces of financial statement information in the two-stop shopping case—and ignoring information has costs. The fundamentalist's tenet in Chapter 1 is violated: Ignore information at your peril. The price-to-sales ratio is particularly dangerous. See Box 3.4. By relying on little information, the trader is in danger of trading with someone who knows more than he, someone who's done her homework on the payoffs a stock is likely to yield. A low P/E could be low for very good reasons. Indeed, a low P/E stock could be overpriced and a high P/E stock could be underpriced. In such cases, the trader might get caught in the wrong position. Selling Dell with a high P/E of 87.9 in 2000 would have been a good idea, but buying GM or Ford with low P/E ratios of 8.5 and 5.0 at the time would not: GM's and Ford's stock prices declined dramatically in subsequent years. By 2008, GM's per share price had dropped from $80 to just $4, then it went bankrupt. Ford dropped from $29 to $4.50.

The solution to the information problem is to build in a model of anticipations that incorporates all the information about payoffs. This is the subject of formal fundamental analysis that produces the intrinsic value. It is the subject that we begin to develop later in this chapter. But first we look at asset-based valuation.

ASSET-BASED VALUATION

Asset-based valuation estimates a firm's value by identifying and summing the value of its assets. The value of the equity is then calculated by deducting the value of debt: Value of the equity = Value of the firm − Value of the debt. It looks alluringly simple: Identify the assets, get a valuation for each, add them up, and deduct the value of debt.

A firm's balance sheet adds up assets and liabilities, and stockholders' equity equals total assets minus total liabilities, as we saw in Chapter 2. That chapter explained that some assets and liabilities are marked to market. Debt and equity investments are carried at "fair" market value (if part of a trading portfolio or if they are "available for sale"). Liabilities are typically carried close to market value on balance sheets and, in any case, market values of many liabilities can be discovered in financial statement footnotes. Cash and receivables are close to their value (though net receivables involve estimates that may be suspect). However, the bulk of assets that generate value are recorded at amortized historical cost, which usually does not reflect the value of the payoffs expected from them. (Refer back to Box 2.3.)

Further, there may be so-called intangible assets—such as brand assets, knowledge assets, and managerial assets—missing from the balance sheet because accountants find their values too hard to measure under the GAAP "reliability" criterion. Accountants give these assets a value of zero. In Dell's case, this is probably the major source of the difference between market value and book value. The firm has a brand name that may be worth more than its tangible assets combined. It has what is hailed as a unique built-to-order, just-in-time production technology. It has marketing networks and "direct-to-customer" distribution channels that generate value. But none of these assets are on the balance sheet.

PRICE-TO-SALES

During the Internet bubble, the price-to-sales ratio (P/S) was a common metric on which to evaluate stocks. Table 3.3 reports that the median historical P/S ratio is 0.9, but in the period 1997–2000, it was not unusual for new technology firms to trade at over 20 times sales. Why did Internet analysts focus on the price-to-sales ratio? Why were IPOs priced on the basis of comparable P/S ratios? Well, most of these firms were re- porting losses, so the P/E ratio did not work for comparable analysis. But shifting to a P/S ratio brings danger.

What determines the price-to-sales ratio?

Buying a stock on the basis of its P/E ratio makes sense, because a firm is worth more the more it is likely to grow earnings. Buy- ing on the basis of its price-to-book ratio (P/B) also makes sense because book value is net assets, and one can think of buying the assets of a business. But with sales we have to be careful. Sales are necessary to add value, but not sufficient. Sales can generate losses (that lose value), so a consideration of the P/S ratio must be made with some anticipation of the earnings that sales might generate. If current sales are earning losses, beware.

To appreciate a P/S ratio, understand that

$$\frac{P}{S} = \frac{P}{E} \times \frac{E}{S}$$

Here E/S is the profit margin ratio, that is, the fraction of each dollar of sales that ends up in earnings. This "profitability of sales" must be understood in evaluating the P/S ratio, other- wise you are ignoring information at your peril. But, with an appreciation of the profit margin, you are really getting back to the P/E ratio, the first component of the P/S calculation here; the formula says that the P/S ratio is really an undoing of the P/E ratio by ignoring E/S. Analysts sometimes interpret the P/S ratio as indicating expected growth in sales. But growth in earnings (from sales) is what is important, and thus the focus should be earnings growth and the P/E ratio.

PRICE-TO-EBITDA

Price/ebitda is a popular multiple for both multiple compar- isons and screening. Ebitda is earnings before interest, taxes, depreciation, and amortization. Some analysts remove depre- ciation (of plant and equipment) and amortization (of intangi- ble assets like copyrights and patents) from earnings because they are not "cash costs." However, while the analyst must be concerned about how depreciation is measured, depreciation is a real economic cost. Plants must be paid for, and they wear out and become obsolescent. They must be replaced, ulti- mately with cash expenditures. Pricing a firm without consid- ering plant, copyright, and patent expenses pretends one can run a business without these expenses. Just as price/sales omits consideration of expenses, so does price/ebitda. Look back at the discussion of WorldCom in Box 2.4 to see how the ratio can lead us astray.

Asset-based valuation attempts to redo the balance sheet by (1) getting current market values for assets and liabilities listed on the balance sheet and (2) identifying omitted assets and assigning a market value to them. Is this a cheap way out of the valuation problem? The accounting profession has essentially given up on this idea and placed it in the "too difficult" basket. Accountants point out that asset valuation presents some very difficult problems:

- Assets listed on the balance sheet may not be traded often, so market values may not be readily available.
- Market values, if available, might not be efficient measures of intrinsic value if markets for the assets are imperfect.
- Market values, if available, may not represent the value in the particular use to which the asset is put in the firm. One might establish either the current replacement price for an asset or its current selling price (its liquidation value), but neither of these may be indicative of its value in a particular going concern. A building used in computer man- ufacturing may not have the same value when used for warehousing groceries.
- The omitted assets must be identified for their market value to be determined. What is the brand-name asset? The knowledge asset? What are the omitted assets on Dell's balance sheet? The very term "intangible asset" indicates a difficulty in measuring value. Those who estimate the value of brand assets and knowledge assets have a difficult task. Ac- countants list intangible assets on the balance sheet only when they have been purchased in the market, because only then is an objective market valuation available.

Asset-based valuation is used to determine the **breakup value** of a firm. While understanding the value of the firm as a going concern, the investor must always ask whether the assets are worth more as a going concern or broken up. If their breakup value is greater, the firm should be liquidated. Some of the large takeover and restructuring activity of the late 1980s came about when takeover specialists saw that a takeover target's assets were worth more broken up than as a whole. This assessment requires a discovery of the liquidation value (selling prices) of assets.

Fundamental analysis estimates value from utilizing assets in a going-concern business. A comparison of this value with breakup value recognizes the maxim that "Value depends on the business strategy." Proceeding as a going concern is just one strategy for using assets, selling them is another, and the value of the two strategies must be compared.

- Even if individual assets can be valued, the sum of the market values of all identified assets may not (and probably will not) be equal to the value of the assets in total. Assets are used jointly. Indeed, entrepreneurs create firms to combine assets in a unique way to generate value. The value of the "synergy" asset is elusive. Determining the intrinsic value of the firm—the value of the assets combined—is the valuation issue.

Asset-based valuations are feasible in a few instances. For example, we might value an investment fund that invests only in traded stocks by adding up the market values of those stocks. But even in this case, the firm may be worth more than this balance sheet value if one of its assets is the fund's ability to earn superior investment returns. And the market values of the fund's stocks may not be efficient ones—which will be the case if the fund managers can pick mispriced stocks. Asset-based analysis is sometimes applied when a firm's main asset is a natural resource—an oil field, a mineral deposit, or timberlands, for example. Indeed these firms are sometimes called *asset-based companies.* Proven reserves (of oil or minerals) or board feet (of timber) are estimated and priced out at the current market price for the resource, with a discount for estimated extraction costs. See Box 3.5 for an application of asset-based valuation.

Asset-based valuation is not a cheap way to value firms. In fact, it's typically so difficult that it becomes very expensive. This is why accountants dodge it. The difficulty highlights the need for fundamental analysis. The problem of valuing firms is really a problem of the imperfect balance sheet. Fundamental analysis involves forecasting payoffs to get an intrinsic value that corrects for the missing value in the balance sheet. Coca-Cola has a large brand asset that is not on the balance sheet. Therefore, it trades at a high premium over book value. But we will see in this book that the premium can be estimated with fundamental analysis.

FUNDAMENTAL ANALYSIS

The method of comparables, screening analysis, and asset-based valuation have one feature in common: They do not involve forecasting. But the value of a share in a firm is based on the future payoffs that it is expected to deliver, so one cannot avoid forecasting payoffs if one is to do a thorough job in valuing shares. Payoffs are forecasted from information, so one cannot avoid analyzing information. **Fundamental analysis** is the method of analyzing information, forecasting payoffs from that information, and arriving at a valuation based on those forecasts. Because they avoid forecasting, the method of comparables, screening analysis, and asset-based valuation use little information. That makes these methods simple, but this simplicity comes at the cost of ignoring information. Rather than a P/E, P/B, or P/S ratio, the

FIGURE 3.1
The Process of Fundamental Analysis

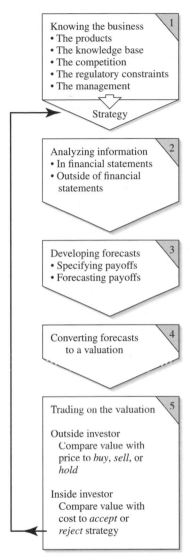

thorough investor screens stocks on a P/V (price-to-value) ratio. Accordingly, she requires a technology to estimate V. Screening on P/E, P/B, or P/S poses the right question: Are earnings, book values, or sales cheap or expensive? But one buys value, not just one aspect of that value.

The Process of Fundamental Analysis

Figure 3.1 outlines the process of fundamental analysis that produces an estimate of the value. In the last step in the diagram, Step 5, this value is compared with the price of investing. This step is the *investment decision.* For the investor outside of the firm, the price of investing is the market price of the stock to be traded. If the valuation is greater than the market price, the analysis says *buy;* if less, *sell.* If the warranted value equals the market price, the analyst concludes that the market in the particular investment is efficient. In the analysts' jargon this is a *hold.* For the investor inside the firm, the price of investing is the cost of the investment. If the calculated value of a strategy or investment proposal is greater than the cost, value is added. The analyst says (in the parlance of project evaluation) *accept* the strategy or the proposal if it is greater than the cost, if less, *reject.*

Steps 1–4 in the diagram show how to get the valuation for this investment decision. The value of an investment is based on the payoffs it is likely to yield, so forecasting payoffs (in Step 3) is at the heart of fundamental analysis. Forecasts cannot be made without identifying and analyzing the information that indicates those payoffs, so information analysis (in Step 2) precedes forecasting. And information cannot be interpreted unless one knows the business and the strategy the firm has adopted to produce payoffs (Step 1).

1. *Knowing the business.* Chapter 1 stressed that understanding the business is a prerequisite to valuing the business. An important element is the firm's strategy to add value. The analyst outside the firm values a given strategy, following the steps in the diagram, and adjusts the valuation as the firm modifies its strategy. The analyst inside the firm is, of course, involved in the formulation of strategy, so she proceeds through the steps to test for the value that alternative strategies might add. So you see a feedback loop in Figure 3.1: Once a strategy has been selected, that strategy becomes the one under which the business is valued as a going concern.

2. *Analyzing information.* With a background knowledge of the business, the valuation of a particular strategy begins with an analysis of information about the business. The information comes in many forms and from many sources. Typically, a vast amount of information must be dealt with, from "hard" dollar numbers in the financial statements like sales, cash flows, and earnings, to "soft" qualitative information on consumer tastes, technological change, and the quality of management. Efficiency is needed in organizing this information for forecasting. Relevant information needs to be distinguished from the irrelevant, and financial statements need to be dissected to extract information for forecasting.

3. *Developing forecasts.* Developing forecasts thus has two steps, as indicated in Step 3 in Figure 3.1. First, specify how payoffs are measured. Then, forecast the specified payoffs. The first step is a nontrivial one, as the validity of a valuation will always depend on how payoffs are measured. Does one forecast cash flows, earnings, book values, dividends, ebit, or return-on-equity? One sees all of these numbers in analysts' research reports. This is a critical design issue that has to be settled before we can proceed.

4. *Converting the forecast to a valuation.* Operations pay off over many years, so typically forecasts are made for a stream of future payoffs. To complete the analysis, the stream of expected payoffs has to be reduced to one number, the valuation. Since payoffs are in the future and investors prefer value now rather than in the future, expected payoffs must be discounted for the time value of money. Payoffs are uncertain so expected payoffs also must be discounted for risk. These two features determine the investor's **discount rate,** otherwise known as the **required return** or **cost of capital.** Therefore, the final step involves combining a stream of expected payoffs into one number in a way that adjusts them for the investor's discount rate.

5. *The investment decision: Trading on the valuation.* The outside investor decides to trade securities by comparing their estimated value to their price. The inside investor compares the estimated value of an investment to its cost. In both cases, the comparison yields the **value added** by the investment. So, rather than comparing price to one piece of information, as in a simple multiple, price is compared to a value number that incorporates all the information used in forecasting. That is, the fundamental analyst screens stocks on their P/V ratios—price-to-value ratios—rather than on a P/E or P/B ratio.

An analyst can specialize in any one of these steps or a combination of them. The analyst needs to get a sense of where in the process his comparative advantage lies, where he can get an edge on his competition. When buying advice from an analyst, the investor needs to know just what the analyst's particular skill is. Is it in knowing a great deal about the business (Step 1)? Is it in discovering and analyzing information (Step 2)? Is it in developing good forecasts from the information (Step 3)? Is it in inferring value from the forecasts (Step 4)? Or is it in the function of developing trading strategies from the analysis while minimizing trading costs (Step 5)? An analyst might be a very good earnings forecaster, for example, but might not be good at indicating the value implied by the forecast.

Financial Statement Analysis, Pro Forma Analysis, and Fundamental Analysis

Financial statements are usually thought of as a place to find information about firms, and indeed we have seen them as such in the "analyzing information" step above. But financial statements play another important role in fundamental analysis.

We have recognized that forecasting payoffs to investments is at the heart of fundamental analysis. Future earnings are the payoffs that analysts forecast, and future earnings will be reported in future income statements. Cash flows might also be forecasted, and cash flows will be reported in future cash flow statements. So financial statements are not only information to help in forecasting; they are also what is to be forecast. Figure 3.2 gives a picture of how financial statements are used in valuation.

Along with earnings and cash flows, the financial statements report many line items that explain how firms produce earnings and cash flows. The income statement reports sales, the costs of production, and other expenses necessary to make the sales. The cash flow statement gives the sources of the cash flows. The balance sheet lists the assets employed to generate earnings and cash. Financial statements, in the jargon of valuation analysis, give the "drivers" of earnings and cash flows. So they provide a way of thinking about how to build up a forecast, a framework for forecasting. If we think of the line items in the financial statements—sales, expenses, assets employed—we will understand the value generation. And if we forecast the complete, detailed statements, we will forecast the factors that drive earnings and cash flows, and so construct forecasts.

Forecasting future financial statements is called **pro forma analysis** because it involves preparing pro forma financial statements for the future. A pro forma statement is one that

FIGURE 3.2
How Financial Statements Are Used in Valuation.
The analyst forecasts future financial statements and converts forecasts in the future financial statements to a valuation. Current financial statements are used as information for forecasting.

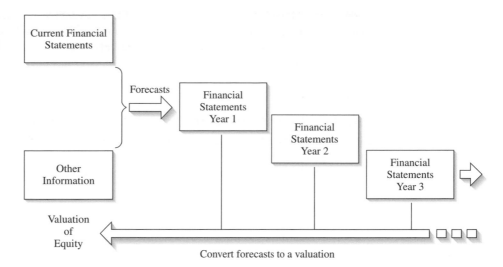

will be reported if expectations are met. Forecasting is at the heart of fundamental analysis and pro forma analysis is at the heart of forecasting. Accordingly, fundamental analysis is a matter of developing pro forma (future) financial statements and converting these pro formas into a valuation. This perspective also directs the analysis of current financial statements. Current financial statements are information for forecasting, so they are analyzed with the purpose of forecasting future financial statements.

THE ARCHITECTURE OF FUNDAMENTAL ANALYSIS: THE VALUATION MODEL

As Figure 3.1 illustrates, fundamental analysis is a process that transforms your knowledge of the business (Step 1) into a valuation and trading strategy (Step 5). Steps 2, 3, and 4 accomplish the transformation. These three steps are guided by the **valuation model** adopted by the analyst. Forecasting in Step 3 is at the heart of analysis, and the analyst cannot begin the analysis without specifying what's to be forecast. The valuation model specifies the payoffs and, accordingly, directs Step 3—the forecasting step—of fundamental analysis. But it also directs Step 2—information analysis—because the relevant information for forecasting can be identified only after defining what is to be forecast. And, it tells the analyst how to do Step 4—converting forecasts to a valuation. So the valuation model provides the architecture for valuation, and a good or poor valuation technology rides on the particular valuation model adopted.

Good practice comes from good thinking. Valuation models embed the concepts regarding how firms generate value. Firms are complex organizations and inferring the value they generate from their many activities requires some orderly thinking. Valuation models supply that thinking. A valuation model is a tool for understanding the business and its strategy. With that understanding, the model is used to translate knowledge of the business into a valuation of the business.

Investment bankers and equity research groups typically have a common discipline, an in-house approach to valuation, that articulates their valuation model. An investment consultant's valuation model is often at the center of its marketing. Many models are being promoted. At one time discounted cash flow (DCF) models were the rage. But now many models focus on "economic profit" and refer to particular economic factors—"value drivers," "fade rates," "franchise factors," and "competitive advantage periods," for example. Are these marketing gimmicks? To what extent, and how, do these factors actually create value? How does one choose between the different models? These are questions that a potential client must ask. And the vendor of the valuation model must have a satisfying answer. The valuation model is at the heart of equity research, and the analyst must have a valuation model that survives scrutiny.

Terminal Investments and Going-Concern Investments

To start you thinking about an appropriate valuation model, refer to Figure 3.3. Suppose you make an investment now with the intention of selling it at some time in the future. Your payoff from the investment will come from the total cash it yields, and this arises from two

FIGURE 3.3

Periodic Payoffs to Investing.

The first investment is for a terminal investment; the second is for a going-concern investment in a stock. The investments are made at time zero and held for T periods when they terminate or are liquidated.

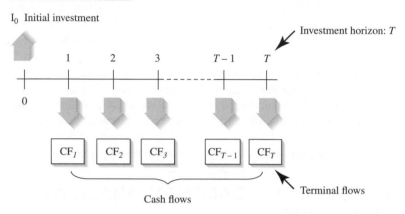

For a terminal investment:

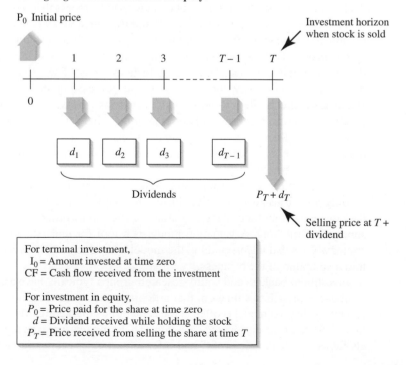

For a going-concern investment in equity:

For terminal investment,
I_0 = Amount invested at time zero
CF = Cash flow received from the investment

For investment in equity,
P_0 = Price paid for the share at time zero
d = Dividend received while holding the stock
P_T = Price received from selling the share at time T

sources: the cash that the investment pays while you are holding it and the cash you get from selling it. These payoffs are depicted for two types of investments on the time line in Figure 3.3. This line starts at the time the investment is made (time zero) and covers T periods, where T is referred to as the **investment horizon.** Investors typically think in terms of annual returns, so think of the periods in the figure as years.

The first investment in the figure is an investment for a fixed term, a **terminal investment.** A bond is an example. It pays a cash flow (CF) in the form of coupon interest each year and a terminal cash flow at maturity. Investment in a single asset—a rental building, for example—is another. It pays off periodic cash flows (in rents) and a final cash flow when the asset is scrapped. The second investment in the figure differs from a bond or a single asset in that it doesn't terminate. This is a feature of investment in an equity share of a firm. Firms are usually considered to be **going concerns,** that is, to go on indefinitely. There is no terminal date and no liquidating payoff that can be forecast. However, an investor may terminate her investment at some time T in the future by selling the share. This leaves her with the problem of forecasting her *terminal payoff.* For an investment in equity, P_0 is the price paid for the share and $d_1, d_2, d_3, \ldots, d_T$ are the dividends paid each year by the firm. The dividends are the periodic cash flow payoffs like the coupon on a bond. P_T is the terminal payoff, the price from selling the share.

Following Figure 3.1, the payoffs for the two types of investments must be converted to a valuation by discounting with the required return. In this book, we will represent 1 + the required return (used in discounting) by the symbol ρ. So, if the required return is 10 percent, $\rho = 1 + 0.10 = 1.10$. When we talk of the required return, we will denote it as $\rho - 1$, so the required return is $1.10 - 1.0 = 0.10$. You may be used to using a symbol (r, say) for the required return and using $1 + r$ as a discount rate. So ρ is equivalent to $1 + r$ and $\rho - 1$ to r. You will see that our convention makes for simpler formulas.

A percentage rate is frequently referred to as the *required return*. Strictly speaking, one means the *required rate of return*.

Valuation Models for Terminal Investments

The standard *bond valuation formula* is an example of a valuation model. The top of Figure 3.4 depicts the cash payoffs for a five-year, $1,000 bond with an annual coupon rate

FIGURE 3.4

Cash Flows for a $1,000, Five-Year, 10 Percent p.a. Coupon Bond and a Five-Year Investment Project.

In both cases a cash investment is made at time 0 and cash flows are received over five subsequent years. The investments terminate at the end of Year 5.

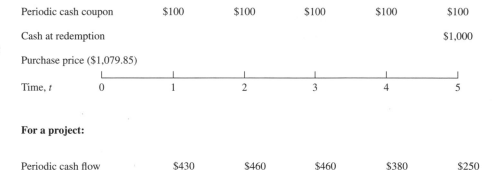

For a bond:

Periodic cash coupon	$100	$100	$100	$100	$100
Cash at redemption					$1,000
Purchase price ($1,079.85)					
Time, t	0	1	2	3	4	5

For a project:

Periodic cash flow	$430	$460	$460	$380	$250
Salvage value					$120
Initial investment ($1,200)					
Time, t	0	1	2	3	4	5

of 10 percent. The layout follows the time line in Figure 3.3. The bond valuation formula expresses the intrinsic value of the bond at investment date zero, as

$$\text{Value of a bond} = \text{Present value of expected cash flows} \qquad \textbf{(3.1)}$$

$$V_0^D = \frac{\text{CF}_1}{\rho_D} + \frac{\text{CF}_2}{\rho_D^2} + \frac{\text{CF}_3}{\rho_D^3} + \frac{\text{CF}_4}{\rho_D^4} + \frac{\text{CF}_5}{\rho_D^5}$$

The ρ_D here is the required return on the bond plus 1. The D indicates the valuation is for debt (as a bond is commonly identified). This model states that future cash flows (CF) from the bond are to be forecasted and discounted at the required payoff rate on the debt, ρ_D. Specifying what's to be forecasted in Step 3 is not difficult here—just refer to the cash flow payoffs as specified in the bond agreement. The formula dictates how these are combined with the required return (Step 4): Cash flows for each period t are weighted by the inverse of the discount rate, $1/\rho_D^t$, to discount them to a "present value."

The only real issue in getting a bond value is calculating the discount rate. This is the rate of return that the lender requires, sometimes called the *cost of capital for debt*. Fixed-income analysts who value debt usually specify different rates for different future periods, that is, they give the discount rate a term structure. We will use a constant rate here to keep it simple. Say this is 8 percent per annum. Then

$$V_0^D = \frac{\$100}{1.08} + \frac{\$100}{(1.08)^2} + \frac{\$100}{(1.08)^3} + \frac{\$100}{(1.08)^4} + \frac{\$1,100}{(1.08)^5} = \$1,079.85$$

This is the amount you would pay for the bond if it were correctly priced, as indicated by the cash outflow at time 0 in the figure.

This of course is the standard *present value formula*. It is often applied for project evaluation inside the firm, that is, for making decisions about whether to invest in projects such as new factories or new equipment. Figure 3.4 also depicts expected cash flow payoffs for a project that requires an outlay of $1,200 at time 0 and runs for five years. The present value formula can again be applied:

$$\text{Value of a project} = \text{Present value of expected cash flows} \qquad \textbf{(3.2)}$$

$$V_0^P = \frac{\text{CF}_1}{\rho_P} + \frac{\text{CF}_2}{\rho_P^2} + \frac{\text{CF}_3}{\rho_P^3} + \frac{\text{CF}_4}{\rho_P^4} + \frac{\text{CF}_5}{\rho_P^5}$$

where P indicates this is for a project and ρ_P is the required payoff per dollar invested in the project, which reflects its risk. The required rate of return for a project is sometimes called a *hurdle rate*. If this is 12 percent ($\rho_P = 1.12$), the value of the investment is $1,530. (Make sure you can calculate this.) This formula is a *project valuation model*. It directs that we should forecast cash flows from the project in Step 3 and combine the forecasts with the required payoff according to the present value formula in Step 4. As with bonds, determining the cost of capital for the project is an issue. But a project's future cash flows are not as transparent as those for bonds, so we must also analyze information to forecast them. So Step 2, information analysis, comes into play. The valuation model directs what to do in the information analysis: Discover information that forecasts future cash flows.

A firm aims to create value for shareholders. The forecasted payoffs in Figure 3.4 are illustrations of two investments that a firm could make with shareholders' money. Consider the bond. If the market is pricing the bond correctly, it will set the price of this bond to yield 8 percent. Thus, if the firm buys the bond, it will pay $1,079.85. What is the anticipated value created by that investment? It's the present value of the payoff minus the cost. This is the *net present value of the investment*, the *NPV*, discovered in Step 5. For the bond priced at $1,079.85, this is zero, so the investment is referred to as a *zero-NPV investment.* Equivalently, it is said that the bond investment does not *create value,* or there is no *value added.* You get what you pay for because it generates payoffs that have the same (present) value as the cost. Of course, if the manager thinks that the market is mispricing the bond—because it has calculated the discount rate incorrectly—then he may buy or sell the bond and create value. This is what bond traders do: They exploit arbitrage opportunities from what they perceive as mispricing of bonds.

Most businesses invest in assets and projects like the one at the bottom of Figure 3.4. This is an example of a *positive-NPV investment,* one that adds value because the value exceeds the cost. In appraising the investment, the manager would conclude that the anticipated net present value was $1,530 − $1,200 = $330, so adopting the project creates value.

Valuation Models for Going-Concern Investments

The valuation of terminal investments like a bond or a project is a relatively easy task. But firms are going concerns, and so are the strategies their managers embark upon. Firms invest in projects but they perpetually roll projects over into new projects. Equity valuation and strategy analysis that involve ongoing operations present two additional complications. First, as going concerns continue (forever?), payoffs have to be forecast for a very long (infinite?) time horizon. This raises practical issues. Second, the attribute to be forecasted to capture value added is not as apparent as that for a single terminal investment. Identifying that attribute requires a good understanding of where value is generated in the business. We deal with these two issues in turn.

Criteria for a Practical Valuation Model

We want a valuation model to capture value generated within the firm, to be sure. But we also want it to be practical. We don't want a fancy valuation model that is cumbersome to apply in practice. The following are some considerations.

1. *Finite forecast horizons.* Going concerns are expected to go on forever but the idea that we have to forecast "to infinity" for going concerns is not a practical one. The further into the future we have to forecast, the more uncertain we will be about our forecast. Indeed, in practice analysts issue forecasts for just a few years ahead, or they summarize the long term with long-term growth rates. We prefer a valuation method for which a **finite-horizon forecast** (for a set number of years, for 1, 5, or 10 years, say) does the job. This dictates the specification of the forecast target in Step 3; it must be such that forecasting the payoff over relatively short horizons is equivalent to forecasting perpetual payoffs for going concerns. And the shorter the horizon, the better.

2. *Validation.* Whatever we forecast must be observable after the fact. That is, when the feature that's been forecasted actually occurs, we can see it. We don't want to forecast vague notions such as "economic profit," "technological advantage," "competitive advantage," or "growth opportunities." These may be important to building a forecast but, as a practical matter, we want to forecast something that can be audited and reported in firms' future financial statements. The ability to validate a forecast requires us to be concrete. So, if "competitive advantage" or "growth opportunities" create value, we want to identify them in terms of a feature that will show up in financial statements. The insistence on validation makes the method credible: An analyst's earnings forecast can be validated in financial reports after the fact to confirm that the forecast was a good (or poor) one. From the investor's point of view, the ability to ascertain product quality is important. He's wary of stock tips that use vague criteria. He demands concreteness.

3. *Parsimony.* We want to forecast something for which the information-gathering and analysis task in Step 2 is relatively straightforward. The fewer pieces of information required, the more parsimonious is the valuation. We want **parsimony.** If we could identify one or two pieces of information as being particularly important—because they summarize a lot of information about the payoff—that would be ideal. And if that information is in the financial statements that are ready at hand, all the better.

What Generates Value?

Firms are engaged in the three activities we outlined in Chapter 1: financing activities, investing activities, and operating activities. Look at Figure 1.1 in Chapter 1 again. Which of these activities adds value?

The economist's answer states that it is the investing and operating activities that add value. Financing activities, the transactions that raise moneys from investors and return cash to them, are of course necessary to run a business. But the standard position among financial economists is that financing activities do not generate value. However, there are some exceptions. We consider transactions with shareholders and debtholders in turn.

Equity Financing Activities

Share Issues in Efficient Markets. A firm with 120 million shares outstanding issues 10 million additional shares at the market price of $42 per share. What happens to the price per share? Well, nothing. The firm's market value prior to the offering was 120 million × $42 = $5,040 million. The offering increases its market value by 10 million × $42 = $420 million, that is, to $5,460 million. With now 130 million shares outstanding, the price per share is still $42. The value of a shareholder's claim is unchanged. The total investment in the firm increases but no value is added to investment. This observation tells us that we should always consider shareholder value on a per-share basis. Value creation is a matter of increasing the per-share value of the equity, not the total value. And managers should not aim at increasing the size of the firm if it not add to per-share value.

Suppose the same firm were to issue 10 million shares but at $32 a share rather than the market price of $42. This issue increases the market value of the firm by 10 million × $32 = $320 million, that is, to $5,360 million. But the per-share price on the 130 million shares after the issue is $41.23. Has this transaction affected shareholder value? Well, yes. Shareholders have lost 77 cents per share. Their equity has been diluted: The per-share value has declined.

These two scenarios illustrate a standard principle: Issuing shares at market value does not affect shareholders' wealth but issuing them at less than market value erodes their wealth. In valuation we might ignore share issues at market value but we cannot ignore issues at less than market value. The latter occurs, for example, when shares are issued to executives and employees under stock compensation plans. If we ignore these transactions we will miss some value that is lost.

The effect of issuing shares at market value is different from the effect of announcing that a share issue will be made. Sometimes the announcement, in advance of the issue, carries information about the value of the firm, about its investment prospects, for example—and so the market price changes. But this effect—sometimes referred to as a *signaling effect*—is generated by new information, not by the issue itself.

Share Issues in Inefficient Markets. The standard view of the effects of financing assumes that the market price of shares reflects their value, that is, the share market is efficient. If so, value received is value surrendered, on both sides of the transaction. But if shares are mispriced, one party can lose at the expense of the other. If management knows

In takeovers, acquiring firms often offer shares of their firm in exchange for shares of the firm they are buying. Questions always arise as to whether particular mergers or acquisitions are value-adding transactions: If the shares in the transactions are efficiently priced, the acquirer pays fair value and expects to earn just a normal rate of return on the acquisition.

An acquirer adds value in an acquisition in three ways:

1. Identifying targets whose shares are undervalued in the market relative to their fundamental value.
2. Identifying targets whose operations, combined with those of the acquirer, will add value.
3. Identifying that the acquirer's own shares are overvalued in the market.

Under the first strategy, the acquirer behaves like any active investor and looks for undervalued assets.

The second strategy looks for so-called synergies from the two combined companies. Cost savings—economies of scale—were said to be the motivation for many bank mergers in the 1990s. Economies from marketing a broad range of financial services under one roof was said to be one of the motivations for the merger of banks, brokerages, and insurance firms, like the merger of Travelers Life, Salomon Smith Barney, and Citibank into Citigroup in 1999. And the announcement of the merger of America Online and Time Warner combined the content of a media company with an Internet portal to that content.

Under the third strategy, the acquirer recognizes that he has "currency" in the form of overvalued stock and so can buy assets cheaply. In the AOL and Time Warner merger, AOL's shares were trading at 190 times earnings and 35 times sales, very high multiples by historical standards. Was AOL using overvalued currency to acquire Time Warner? Indeed, in the agreement to acquire Time Warner, AOL offered its shares at an (unusual) discount of 25 percent of market value, in admission that its shares might have been overvalued. Even at this price, AOL shareholders did well. Although the merger was a failure operationally, AOL shareholders benefitted enormously by using their overpriced shares; they bought Time Warner assets cheaply.

Before going into a transaction, both the acquirer and the target need to understand the value from combining operations. But they also need to understand the value of both the acquirer's shares and the target's shares and how they compare to market values. They then understand value given up and value received.

---

that the shares of their firm are overvalued in the market, they might choose to issue shares. The new shareholder pays the market price but receives less in value. The existing shareholders receive more value than the value surrendered, so they gain. For this reason announcements of share offerings are sometimes greeted as bad news information, and the share price drops. This wealth transfer can only happen in an inefficient market or a market where the manager knows more about the firm's prospects than the market. Buyer beware! Understand the value of the shares before participating in a share issue. See Box 3.6.

Share Repurchases.   Share repurchases are share issues in reverse. So share repurchases at market price do not affect per-share value and share repurchases at more than market value (should they occur) do. But, like share issues, management can make share repurchases when they see that the share price is below intrinsic value. In this case, shareholders who offer their shares lose; those that don't, gain. For this reason, announcements of share repurchases are sometimes seen as signals that the stock is underpriced, increasing share price. In this case, seller beware.

Dividends.   Dividends are part of the return to equity investment so it is tempting to think that they are value for shareholders. Indeed, fundamental analysts once believed that higher payout meant higher value. But modern finance theory sees it differently. Dividends are not what they appear to be.

If a firm pays a dollar of dividends, the shareholders get a dollar. But there is a dollar less in the firm, so the value of the firm drops by a dollar. Shareholders receive the dollar of dividends, but they can sell the share for a dollar less. The dividend payment makes them no better off; it does not create value. In other words, the investor's cum-dividend payoff is not affected. The return to the shareholder is made up of a dividend and a capital gain. A dividend adds to the return but the capital gain is reduced by the amount of the dividend, leaving the return unaffected.

You might have heard these arguments referred to as the **dividend irrelevance concept,** or as the M&M dividend proposition after the two professors who advanced the arguments, Merton Miller and Franco Modigliani. Some investors might prefer dividends to capital gains because they need the cash. But they can sell some of their shares to convert capital gains into dividends. Other investors might prefer no dividends; they can achieve this by buying the stock with the cash from dividends. This ability to make what are called **homemade dividends** means that investors do not care if their return comes from dividends or capital gains. And if its shareholders want dividends, the firm also can create dividends without affecting the firm's investments, by borrowing against the security in the investments and using the proceeds to pay dividends. Of course, if a firm forgoes value-creating projects to pay dividends, it will destroy value. But, given a ready availability of financing, sensible management will borrow or issue shares to pay the dividends rather than affecting good investments.

Homemade dividends and borrowing do involve some transaction costs, but these are usually considered small enough to ignore, given the imprecision we typically have in calculating value. If making homemade dividends is difficult because of illiquidity in the market for the shares (of a nontraded firm, for example), lack of dividends might reduce the value of an investment to a shareholder who desires dividends. The value effect is referred to as the **liquidity discount** (to the value of an equivalent liquid investment). That same shareholder will not demand a liquidity discount, however, if he can generate cash by borrowing against the security of his shares. Just as a firm can borrow to pay dividends (and not affect the value of investments), so shareholders can borrow to generate dividends (and not affect the value of shares).

Like share issues and share repurchases, dividend announcements might convey information that affects stock prices. Dividend increases are often greeted as good news, an indicator that the firm will earn more in the future, and cuts in dividends are often greeted as bad news. These information effects—called *dividend signaling* effects—occur when dividends are announced. The dividend irrelevance notion says that the dividends themselves will not affect (cum-dividend) shareholder value (when the stock goes ex-dividend).

Some argue that dividends might lose value for shareholders if they are taxed at a higher rate than capital gains. This is of no consequence to tax-exempt investors, but the taxable investor might incur more taxes with dividends, and so would prefer to get returns in the form of capital gains.[2] Accordingly, the taxable investor would pay less for a share that pays dividends to yield the same return for a similar share that returns only capital gains. Others argue, however, that investors can shield dividends from taxes with careful tax planning. And some also argue that market prices cannot be lower for dividend-paying stocks because tax-exempt investors (such as the large retirement funds and not-for-profit endowments) dominate the market. A lower price that yields the same after-tax return to a taxable investor as the return without dividends would provide an arbitrage opportunity to the tax-exempt investor, and exploitation of this opportunity would drive the price to yield the same return as a stock with no dividends. Thus dividends have no effect on prices or values. Go to a corporate finance text for the subtleties of this reasoning. Empirical research on the issue has produced conflicting findings.

---

[2] At the time of publication, dividend tax rates and (long-term) capital gains tax rates in the United States were the same (15 percent).

In this book we accept the presumption that "dividends don't matter" and calculate values accordingly. The investor who expects to pay more taxes on dividends than capital gains might reduce the before-tax values that we calculate in this book by the present value of any forecasts of taxes on dividends. (She also might consider buying a stock with similar features that does not pay dividends.) The adjusted valuation involves tax planning because this investor must consider how taxes on dividends can be avoided or deferred by holding high dividend yield stocks in retirement funds and employee savings plans (for example). Similarly, the valuations here might be adjusted for liquidity discounts.

Debt Financing Activities

The bond in Figure 3.4 that yields 8 percent per annum has a market value of $1,079.85. We saw that at this price the bond is a zero-NPV investment; it doesn't add value. Most firms accept debt markets as being efficient and issue and buy bonds and other debt instruments at their market price, so do not add value (over the required return for their risk). The exceptions are financial firms like banks, which can buy debt (lend) at a higher rate than they can sell it (borrow). They add value as financial intermediaries in the capital market. And, as we saw, firms in the business of bond arbitrage might add value if they detect mispricing of bonds.

In debt financing activities, firms sell debt to raise money. They are not in the business of bond arbitrage, so they accept the market price as fair value and sell at that price. The transaction thus does not add value. The firm gets what it pays for. If it issues bonds, it gets cash at exactly the present value of what it expects to pay back. If it borrows from a bank, it gets the amount of cash equal to the present value, at the interest rate, of the principal plus interest it has to pay back in the future. In the jargon of modern finance, **debt financing is irrelevant** to the value of the firm. It is simply a transaction at fair value to bring moneys into the firm for operations.

Some argue that because interest on debt is deductible against income in assessing corporate taxes, issuing debt gains a tax advantage that shareholders cannot get in paying personal taxes. Thus it generates value for the shareholder. This is controversial and you should go to corporate finance texts for a discussion. If one accepts this tax argument, one can add the value of the tax benefit in valuing the firm.

Investing and Operating Activities

Value generation in a business is ascribed to many factors—know-how, proprietary technology, good management, brand recognition, brilliant marketing strategy, and so on. At the root of these factors is good ideas. Good entrepreneurs build good businesses and a good entrepreneur is someone with good ideas. But ideas are vague, as are the factors just mentioned, and it is difficult to see the value of ideas without being more concrete. The value of ideas is ascertained from what firms do, and what firms do is engage in investing and operating activities.

Investing activities use the moneys contributed to the firm in financing transactions to invest in the assets necessary to conduct the business envisioned by ideas. The project in Figure 3.4 is a simple example. It adds value. Value is anticipatory; it is based on expected future payoffs from investing. But there has to be follow-through, and operating activities are the follow-through. Operating activities utilize the investments to produce goods or services for sale, and it is these sales that realize the value anticipated in investing. Simply, a firm cannot generate value without finding customers for its products, and the amount of value received is the amount of value those customers are willing to surrender. Net value added in operations is the value received from customers less the value surrendered by the firm in getting products to customers. So investments generate value, but the anticipated value is determined by forecasting the success of the investment in generating value in operations.

Valuation models are developed with the understanding that it is the operations, and the investment in those operations, that generate value. So valuation models value operations, ignoring value that might be created from share issues and share repurchases. Accordingly, the valuation indicates whether the stock market is mispricing the equity, so that the investor understands whether share transactions are at fair value—or whether the firm has the opportunity to create value for shareholders with share issues or repurchases (by issuing shares in an acquisition, for example).

Valuation Models, the Required Return, and Asset Pricing Models

Step 4 of the valuation process in Figure 3.1 converts forecasts to valuation by discounting with a required return, and the bond valuation model and the project valuation model do just that. This step requires a specification of the required return. The required return has two components:

$$\text{Required return} = \text{Risk-free rate} + \text{risk premium}$$

The risk-free rate, usually measured by the 10-year U.S. Treasury rate, is the return one would require if the investment were risk free. But for a risky investment, one requires additional return for taking on risk, the **risk premium.** If the yield on the U.S. 10-year note is 4.5 percent and you require 5 percent extra return for investing in a stock, your required return is 9.5 percent; this compensates you for the time value of money (with no risk) and for the risk.

The problem is the determination of the risk premium. How much should investors charge for risk (and how much should they discount expected payoffs for risk)? The answer to this question is supposedly supplied by an *asset pricing model*. The *capital asset pricing model (CAPM)* is the most common. It describes the risk premium as determined by the stock's beta and a market risk premium:

$$\text{Required return} = \text{Risk-free rate} + [\text{Beta} \times \text{Market risk premium}]$$

The beta is a measure of how a stock's return moves as the market moves: How sensitive is the stock to the overall market? The market risk premium is the expected return on the market over the risk-free rate. The market risk premium is the amount the market is expected to yield for marketwide risk, so the risk premium for a given stock depends on its beta risk relative to the overall market.

The name "asset pricing model" suggests that the model will give you the price or value of an asset. But it is a misnomer. Asset pricing models yield the required return (the cost of capital), not the value of an asset. An asset pricing model is a so-called beta technology. Valuation models, on the other hand, do yield the value of an asset. As this value can be compared with price, a valuation model is a so-called alpha technology. Asset pricing models are pertinent to valuing an asset, of course, for we have seen that Step 4 in valuation applies the required return. Valuation models show how, giving a required return from an asset pricing model, the asset pricing is completed.

In this text, we do not spend much time on the technology involved in measuring the required return. You should be familiar with the techniques—students sometimes refer to them as "beta bashing"—from your corporate finance courses. Indeed, we will be cautious about using asset pricing models and the required return numbers they yield. They require doubtful estimates—the market risk premium in the capital asset pricing model is particularly difficult to calculate. Estimates involve speculation that the fundamental investor is apprehensive about: plugging in a required return into a valuation model amounts to adding speculation to a valuation. We will be seeking ways to finesse the problem while still recognizing that risk (and discount for risk) is an important aspect of valuation. The appendix to this chapter gives a brief overview of asset pricing models and provides some caveats to using these models for measuring the required return.

Summary

This chapter has given you a road map for carrying out fundamental analysis. Indeed, Figure 3.1 lays out a road map for the rest of the book. It lays out the five steps of fundamental analysis, steps that convert your knowledge of a business and its strategy to a valuation of that business. At the core of the process is the analysis of information (Step 2), making forecasts from that information (Step 3), and converting those forecasts to a valuation (Step 4).

A valuation model provides the architecture for fundamental analysis. A valuation model is a tool for thinking about value creation in a business and translating that thinking into a value. The chapter introduced you to valuation models for bonds and projects and showed that valuation of going concerns is inherently more difficult than valuation of these terminal investments. We concluded that a valuation model must focus on the aspects of the firm that generate value, the investing and operating activities, so setting the stage for the development of appropriate valuation models in the following chapters.

Having gained an understanding of fundamental analysis—at least in outline—you can appreciate the limitations of "cheap" methods that use limited information. The chapter outlined three such methods: the method of comparables, screening analysis, and asset-based valuation. You should understand the mechanics of these methods but also be aware of the pitfalls in applying them.

How are financial statements used in valuation? You don't have a complete answer to this question yet, for that is the subject of the whole book. But you do have an outline.

The Web Connection

Find the following on the Web page supplement for this chapter:

- More on the calculation of multiples.
- More on the method of comparables and price bubbles.
- A discussion of arbitrage.
- Links to screening engines.

- A formal analysis of required returns, abnormal returns, alphas, and betas.
- Surveys of the market risk premium estimates used by a variety of professionals.
- Buying firms with market values less than book value.
- The Readers' Corner guides you to further reading.

Key Concepts

breakup value is the amount a firm is worth if its assets (net of liabilities) are sold off. *84*

contrarian stock is a stock that is out-of-favor and trades at low multiples (viewed by **contrarian investors** as undervalued). *80*

cost of capital is the opportunity cost of having money tied up in an investment. Also referred to as the **normal return,** the **required return,** or, when calculating values, as the **discount rate.** *86*

cum-dividend price is the price inclusive of the dividend received while holding the investment. Compare with **ex-dividend price,** which is price without the dividend. *79*

debt financing irrelevance means that the value of a firm is not affected by debt financing activities, that is, by issuing debt. *95*

discount rate see **cost of capital** *86*

dividend irrelevance means that paying dividends does not generate value for shareholders. *94*

finite-horizon forecasting refers to forecasting for a fixed (finite) number of years. *91*

forecast horizon is a point in the future up to which forecasts are made. *91*

fundamental analysis is the method of analyzing information, forecasting payoffs from that information, and arriving at a valuation based on those forecasts. *84*

glamour stock is a stock that is fashionable and trades at high multiples (viewed by **contrarian investors** as overvalued). Sometimes referred to as a **growth stock.** *80*

going-concern investment is one which is expected to continue indefinitely. Compare with **terminal investment.** *89*

growth stock is a term with many meanings but, in the context of

multiple screening, it is a stock with a high multiple that is contrasted with a **value stock** with a low multiple. *80*

homemade dividends are dividends a shareholder creates for himself by selling some of his shares, thus substituting dividends for capital gains. *94*

investment horizon is the period for which an investment is likely to be held. *89*

liquidity discount is a reduction in the value of an investment due to difficulty in converting value in the investment into cash. *94*

parsimony (in valuation) is the ability to value a firm from a reduced amount of information. *92*

pro forma analysis is the preparation of forecasted financial statements for future years. *86*

required return see **cost of capital** *86*

risk premium is the expected return on an investment over the risk-free return. *96*

terminal investment is an investment that terminates at a point of time in the future. Compare with **going-concern investment.** *89*

unlevered measures are measures that are not affected by how a firm is financed. *79*

valuation model is the architecture for fundamental analysis that directs what is to be forecast as a payoff, what information is relevant for forecasting, and how forecasts are converted to a valuation. *87*

value added (or **value created** or **value generated**) is the value from anticipated payoffs to an investment (**fundamental value**) in excess of value given up in making the investment (the cost of the investment). *86*

value stock is a stock that trades at low multiples (viewed by **value investors** as undervalued). Compare with **growth stock.** *80*

The Analyst's Toolkit

A Continuing Case: *Kimberly-Clark Corporation*

A Self-Study Exercise

In the Continuing Case for Kimberly-Clark in Chapter 2, you gained some familiarity with the financial statements for 2010 and calculated the two basic ratios, the price-to-book (P/B) and price-earnings (P/E). After this chapter you can calculate many more ratios at the March 2011 price of $65.24. Go ahead. You'll now modify your calculation of the trailing P/E in the Chapter 2 case to accommodate the 2010 dividend of $2.64 per share. Calculate the enterprise price-to-book ratio and other unlevered ratios. With analysts' consensus forecasts in the Yahoo! report for the firm in Chapter 1, you will also be able to calculate the forward P/E.

COMPARABLES

Here are three firms that finance Web sites list as comparable consumer product and health firms, with their stock prices at the end of March 2011.

The Procter & Gamble Company (PG)	$62
Energizer Holdings (ENR)	71
Johnson & Johnson (JNJ)	59

You can get descriptions of these firms from their 10-K filings, the Yahoo! finance Web page, or similar financial Web sites. Look at these descriptions and ask whether these firms would serve well as comparables. Can you get better matches? With the firms' stock prices and accounting information in their SEC filings, you can calculate comparison multiples. What do these multiples imply KMB's price should be? How confident are you in your conclusion?

Using the multiples as screens, do you think that KMB's multiples are typically higher or lower than the comps? If so would you recommend taking a buy or sell position on the basis of the difference?

ASSET-BASED VALUATION

Do you think that asset-based valuation will work for KMB?

SOME QUESTIONS TO CONSIDER

Looking back to the firm's financial statements in Exhibit 2.2 in Chapter 2, identify the amount of shares repurchased during 2010. What effect do you think these repurchases had on the stock price?

Identify the amount of dividends paid during 2010. Would these dividends have resulted in an increase in the stock price, or a decrease?

Kimberly-Clark had an equity beta of 0.8 in March 2011. The long-term U.S. government bond rate was 4 percent. If the market risk premium is 5%, what is the required equity return indicated by the capital asset pricing model (CAPM)? What would be the required return if the market risk premium is 6 percent? In Chapter 2, you calculated the prior 12-month stock return for KMB. Would you say that investors covered their cost of capital during that year?

Concept Questions

C3.1. What explains differences between firms' price-to-sales ratios?

C3.2. It is common to compare firms on their price-to-ebit ratios. What are the merits of using this measure? What are the problems with it? *Hint:* ebit leaves something out.

C3.3. It is also common to compare firms on their price-to-ebitda ratios. What are the merits of using this measure? What are the dangers? *Hint:* ebitda leaves something out.

C3.4. Why do trailing P/E ratios vary with dividend payout?

C3.5. If a firm has a P/E ratio of 12 and a profit margin on sales of 6 percent, what is its price-to-sales (P/S) ratio likely to be?

C3.6. If a firm is expected to have a profit margin of 8 percent but trades at a price-to-sales ratio of 25, what inferences would you make?

C3.7. What do traders mean when they refer to stocks as "glamour stocks" and "value stocks?"

C3.8. Why would you expect asset-based valuation to be more difficult to apply to a technology firm, like Microsoft than to a forest products company, like Weyerhaeuser?

C3.9. The yield on a bond is independent of the coupon rate. Is this true?

C3.10. It is sometimes said that firms prefer to make stock repurchases rather than pay dividends because stock repurchases yield a higher EPS. Do they?

C3.11. Your answer to concept question C3.10 should have been: Yes. If share repurchases increase EPS more than dividends, do share repurchases also create more value than dividends?

C3.12. Should a firm that pays higher dividends have a higher share value?

Exercises

Drill Exercises

E3.1. Calculating a Price from Comparables (Easy)

A firm trading with a total equity market value of $100 million reported earnings of $5 million and book value of $50 million. This firm is used as a comparable to price an IPO firm with earnings per share of $2.50 and book value per share of $30 per share. Neither firm pays dividends. What per-share IPO price does the comparable firm imply?

E3.2. Stock Prices and Share Repurchases (Easy)

A firm with 100 million shares outstanding repurchased 10 million shares at the market price of $20 per share. What is the total market value of the equity after the repurchase? What is the per-share value after the repurchase?

E3.3. Unlevered (Enterprise) Multiples (Easy)

A firm reported $250 million in total assets and $140 in debt. It had no interest-bearing securities among its assets. In the income statement it reported $560 million in sales. The firm's 80 million shares traded at $7 each. Calculate

a. The price-to-book ratio (P/B)
b. The unlevered price-to-sales ratio (P/S)
c. The enterprise price-to-book ratio

E3.4. Identifying Firms with Similar Multiples (Easy)

Find a screening engine on the Web, enter a multiple you are interested in, and get a list of firms that have that multiple of a particular size. Choose a particular industry and see how the various multiples—P/E, price-to-book, price-to-sales—differ among firms in the industry.
Screening engines can be found at the following site (among others):

screener.finance.yahoo.com/newscreener.html

E3.5. Valuing Bonds (Easy)

a. A firm issues a zero-coupon bond with a face value of $1,000, maturing in five years. Bonds with similar risk are currently yielding 5 percent per year. What is the value of the bond?
b. A firm issues a bond with a face value of $1,000 and a coupon rate of 5 percent per year, maturing in five years. Bonds with similar risk are currently yielding 5 percent per year. What is the value of the bond?
c. A firm issues the same bond as in part (b) but with an annual coupon rate of 4 percent per year. What is the value of the bond?

E3.6. Applying Present Value Calculations to Value a Building (Easy)

In the year 2012, a real estate analyst forecasts that a rental apartment building will generate $5.3 million each year in rent over the five years 2013–2017. Cash expenses are expected to be $4.2 million a year. At the end of five years, the building is expected to sell for $12 million. Real estate investors require a 12 percent return on their investments. Apply present value discounting techniques to value the building.

Applications

E3.7. The Method of Comparables: Dell, Inc. (Easy)

Here are some accounting numbers and market values (in millions) for Hewlett-Packard and Lenovo Group for 2008. These two computer manufacturers are considered to be comparables for Dell, Inc.

	Sales	Earnings	Book Value	Market Value
Hewlett-Packard Co.	$84,229	$7,264	$38,526	$115,700
Lenovo Group Ltd.	14,590	161	1,134	6,381

a. Calculate price-to-sales, price-earnings (P/E), and price-to-book (P/B) ratios for Hewlett-Packard and Lenovo.

b. Dell reported the following numbers for fiscal year 2008:

Sales	$61,133 million
Earnings	$ 2,947 million
Book value	$ 3,735 million

Apply multiples for Hewlett-Packard and Lenovo to price Dell's 2,060 million outstanding shares. What difficulties did you encounter?

Real World Connection
See Exercises E3.7, E3.12, E5.10, E9.11, and E14.16, and Minicase M16.2.

E3.8. Pricing Multiples: General Mills, Inc. (Medium)

General Mills, the consumer foods company, traded at 1.6 times sales in 2011. It was reporting a net profit margin on its sales of 10.4 percent. What was its P/E ratio?

E3.9. Measuring Value Added (Medium)

a. *Buying a stock.* A firm is expected to pay an annual dividend of $2 per share forever. Investors require a return of 12 percent per year to compensate for the risk of not receiving the expected dividends. The firm's shares trade for $19 each. What is the value added by buying a share at $19?

b. *An investment within a firm.* The general manager of a soccer club is considering paying $2.5 million per year for five years for a "star" player, along with a $2 million upfront signing bonus. He expects the player to enhance gate receipts and television advertising revenues by $3.5 million per year with no added costs. The club requires a 9 percent return on its investments. What would be the value added from the acquisition of the player?

E3.10. Valuation of Bonds and the Accounting for Bonds, Borrowing Costs, and Bond Revaluations (Hard)

On January 1, 2008, Debtor Corporation issued 10,000 five-year bonds with a face value of $1,000 and an annual coupon of 4 percent. Bonds of similar risk were yielding 8 percent p.a. in the market at the time.

a. What did the firm receive for each bond issued?

b. At the end of 2008, the market was still yielding 8 percent on the bonds.
   1. What was the firm's borrowing cost before tax for 2008?
   2. How much interest expense was reported in the income statement for 2008?

    c. At the end of 2009, the yield on the bonds had dropped to 6 percent.

        1. What was the firm's borrowing cost before tax for 2009?

        2. How much interest expense was reported in the income statement for 2009?

    d. Creditor Corporation purchased 2,000 of the bonds in the issue. FASB Statement No. 115 requires firms to mark these financial investments to market.

        1. What were the bonds carried at on the balance sheet at the end of 2009?

        2. What was interest income in the income statement for 2009?

E3.11. Share Issues and Market Prices: Is Value Generated or Lost by Share Issues? (Medium)

    a. XYZ Corporation had 158 million shares outstanding on January 1, 2012. On February 2, 2012, it issued an additional 30 million shares to the market at the market price of $55 per share. What was the effect of this share issue on the price per share?

    b. On February 28, 2012, directors of the same XYZ Corporation exercised stock options to acquire 12 million shares at an exercise price of $30 per share. Prior to this transaction the stock traded at $62 per share. What was the effect of the share issue to the directors on the per-share value of the firm?

E3.12. Stock Repurchases and Value: Dell, Inc. (Easy)

During fiscal year 2011, Dell repurchased 57 million shares on the market for $800 million. There were 1,957 million shares outstanding prior to the repurchase. What was the effect of the repurchases on the per-share price of Dell's stock?

E3.13. Betas, the Market Risk Premium, and the Equity Cost of Capital: Oracle Corporation (Medium)

A risk analyst gives Oracle Corporation, the enterprise software and database management firm, a CAPM equity beta of 1.20. The risk-free rate is 4.0 percent.

    a. Prepare a table with the cost of capital that you would calculate for the equity with the following estimates of the market risk premium:

        4.5%

        6.0%

        7.5%

        9.0%

    b. Other analysts disagree on the beta, with estimates ranging from 0.90 to 1.40. Prepare a table that gives the cost of capital for each estimate of the market risk premium and beta estimates of 0.90 and 1.40.

    c. At the end of May 2011, analysts were forecasting earnings of $2.17 per share for the fiscal year ending May 31, 2012. They were also forecasting that the P/E ratio would be 20 on May 31, 2012. The company is expected to pay $0.24 in dividends per share for the fiscal year. Calculate the current value of the stock in May 2011 for this P/E forecast using the lowest and highest cost of capital estimates from part b.

E3.14. Implying the Market Risk Premium: Procter & Gamble (Easy)

Analysts give Procter & Gamble, the consumer products firm, an equity beta of 0.65. The risk-free rate is 4.0 percent. An analyst calculates an equity cost of capital for the firm of 7.9 percent using the capital asset pricing model (CAPM). What market risk premium is she assuming?

Real World Connection

See Minicases M10.1, M11.1, M12.1, M13.1, M15.1, and M16.1.

Minicases

M3.1

An Arbitrage Opportunity? Cordant Technologies and Howmet International

Cordant Technologies, based in Salt Lake City, manufactures rocket motors, "fasteners" (bolts), and turbine engine components for the aerospace industry. For the first half of 1999, its sales were $1.28 billion, up 7 percent on the same period for the previous year. Net income was $85.7 million, or $2.34 per share, up 16 percent. Cordant's gas turbine business was growing, but production cuts and inventory buildup at Boeing forecast a slowdown in the firm's revenues from other aerospace products. Other data on the firm are as follows:

Rolling 12-month eps to June 30, 1999	$4.11
Book value per share, June 30, 1999	$7.76
Rolling 12-month sales per share to June 30, 1999	$67.20
Profit margin	7.4%
Price per share, September 30, 1999	$32
Market capitalization of equity	$1.17 billion

Analysts were forecasting earnings of $4.00 per share for the full 1999 year and $4.28 for 2000.

Cordant's financial statements consolidate an 85 percent interest in Howmet International, another manufacturer of turbine engine components. Howmet reported net income of $65.3 million for the first half of 1999, up 33 percent, on sales of $742.4 million. Other data on Howmet are:

Rolling 12-month eps to June 30, 1999	$1.21
Book value per share, June 30, 1999	$4.25
Rolling 12-month sales per share to June 30, 1999	$14.28
Profit margin	8.7%
Price per share, September 30, 1999	$14
Market capitalization of equity	$1.40 billion

Analysts were forecasting earnings of $1.24 for 1999 and $1.36 for 2000.

Both firms were categorized by some analysts at the time as "neglected" or "ignored" stocks. Their claim was that the market was irrational not only in overpricing the new technology stocks, but also in underpricing the old, "blue-collar" industrial stocks. For reference, firms like Micosoft, Dell, Yahoo!, and AOL traded at multiples of over 50 times earnings at the time, whereas aerospace firms traded at 11 times earnings.

Calculate price multiples for Cordant and Howmet. Do you see an arbitrage opportunity? What trading strategy do you recommend to exploit the opportunity? Would you call it a riskless arbitrage opportunity?

M3.2

Nifty Stocks? Returns to Stock Screening

In the early 1970s a widely publicized list of the "Nifty Fifty" stocks was drawn up. This list, which included Avon Products, Polaroid, Coca-Cola, McDonald's, Walt Disney, American Express, and Xerox, was touted as a set of "good buys." Most of the firms traded at high multiples. Their P/E ratios were as high as 70 to 90, with an average of 42, while the S&P 500 traded at a multiple of 19 times earnings. Burton Crane, a *New York Times* reporter, wrote the famous words at the time: "Xerox's multiple not only discounts the future but the hereafter as well."

Unfortunately, many of those Nifty Fifty stocks lost considerable value in the subsequent 1970s bear market. Avon's stock fell 80 percent, as did Polaroid's. Coca-Cola, IBM, and Xerox fell dramatically.

The multiples of the Nifty Fifty in 1972 bear a strong resemblance to those of the "nifty" technology stocks of the late 1990s, and indeed to those of mature "quality" firms such as Coca-Cola, General Electric, Pfizer, Merck, and Walt Disney (all of which were in the original Nifty Fifty of 1972). Morgan Stanley published a new set of Nifty Fifty stocks in 1995 that included these stocks. Here are some of the firms with high earnings multiples in September 1999, with their per-share prices at that date:

	P/E	Price per Share ($)
Microsoft (MSFT)	64	90
Dell Computer (DELL)	70	44
Lucent Technologies (LU)	75	64
America Online (AOL)	168	104
Analog Devices (ADI)	65	56
Mattel (MAT)	72	21
CBS Corp. (CBS)	72	46
Cisco Systems (CSCO)	110	68
Home Depot (HD)	51	69
Motorola (MOT)	95	87
Charles Schwab (SCH)	56	34
Time Warner (TWX)	185	61

Track the return to these stocks from October 1999. You might use a price chart that tracks stock splits (for example, Big Charts at **www.bigcharts.com**).

How have these nifty stocks fared?

Here are some less nifty stocks at the time, all of which were in the S&P 500. They have low P/E ratios.

	P/E	Price per Share ($)
Centex (CTX)	7	28
ITT Industries (ITT)	2	32
Seagate Technology (SEG)	7	30
U.S. Airways (U)	3	26
Conseco (CNC)	6	20
Hilton Hotels (HTL)	8	10

How have these stocks fared?

(Note: This case was written in October 1999, without any idea of the outcome.)

The Required Return and Asset Pricing Models

The chapter has introduced the *required return* for an investment, otherwise known as the *normal return* or the *cost of capital* and, in the context of project selection, the *hurdle rate*. The required return is the amount that an investor requires to compensate her for the time value of money tied up in the investment and for taking on risk in the investment. These are her costs of taking on the investment, thus the name, cost of capital. In effect, the cost of capital is the opportunity cost of forgoing an alternative investment with the same risk. To add value, an investment must earn more than the cost of capital, so the required return features in valuation: In converting forecasted payoffs to a valuation, the payoffs must be discounted for the cost of capital.

Considerable time is spent in corporate finance courses estimating the cost of capital. The techniques are called *beta technologies*. This appendix gives an overview. Chapter 19 comes back to the topic with a discussion of how fundamental analysis helps in the assessment of the required return.

MEASURING THE REQUIRED RETURN: BETA TECHNOLOGIES

When you invest, you buy a gamble. Different investments will yield different expected payoffs, but the expected payoff is only one feature of the gamble. You are buying a range of possible outcomes with different probabilities for each, and you must be concerned about the chance of getting payoffs different from those expected. Most people are risk averse (that is, particularly concerned about the downside), so they want to be rewarded with a higher return for taking on risk. They want to earn at least the risk-free return that one would get on a U.S. government bond, say, but they also want a premium for any risk that they take on.

An *asset-pricing model* supplies the technology to calculate required returns. These models have one insight in common: The market will not price an investment to compensate for risk that can be diversified away in a portfolio. They also have a common form. They characterize required returns as determined by the *risk-free return* plus a *risk premium:*

$$\text{Required return} = \text{Risk-free return} + \text{Risk premium}$$

The risk premium is given by (1) expected returns (over the risk-free return) on risk exposures (or "factors") that can't be diversified away, and (2) sensitivities of the returns on a particular investment to these factors, known as *betas*. Multiplying components (1) and (2) together gives the effect of an exposure to a particular risk factor on the risk premium, and the total risk premium is the sum of the effects of all risk factors.

The well-known *capital asset pricing model (CAPM)* identifies the market return (the return on all investment assets) as the (only) risk factor. Box 3.7 outlines the CAPM. The risk premium is the expected return on the whole market over the risk-free rate multiplied by the sensitivity of the investment's return to the market return, its *beta*. The risk-free rate is readily measured by the yield on a U.S. government bond that covers the duration of

Asset Pricing Models: A Quick Review   3.7

THE CAPITAL ASSET PRICING MODEL

The CAPM states that the required return for an investment *i* for a period is determined by

Required return (*i*) = Risk-free return
+ [Beta (*i*) × Market risk premium]

The market risk premium is the expected return from holding all risky assets over that from a risk-free asset. The portfolio of all risky assets (stocks, bonds, real estate, human capital, and many more) is sometimes called "the market portfolio" or "the market." So

Market risk premium = Expected return on the market
− Risk-free return

The beta for an investment measures the expected sensitivity of its return to the return on the market. That is, it measures how the price of the investment will move as the price of the market moves. It is defined as

$$\text{Beta}(i) = \frac{\text{Covariance (return on } i\text{, return on the market)}}{\text{Variance (return on the market)}}$$

The covariance measures the sensitivity but, as it is standardized by the variance of the market, it is scaled so that the market as a whole has a beta of 1.0. A beta greater than 1 means the price of the investment is expected to move up more than the market when the market goes up and drop more when the market declines.

The risk premium for the investment is its beta multiplied by the market risk premium. In early 2011, the risk-free rate (on 10-year U.S. Treasury notes) was 3.5 percent. Commercial services that publish beta estimates were giving Nike a beta of about 0.9. So, if the market risk premium was 5 percent, then the required return for Nike given by the CAPM was 8 percent:

8.0% = 3.5% + (0.9 × 5.0%)

The risk premium for Nike was 4.5 percent, made up of 5.0 percent for the risk in the market as a whole less 0.5 percent for risk that is lower than that for the market.

The CAPM is based on the idea that one can diversify away a considerable amount of risk by holding the market portfolio of all investment assets. So the only risk that an investor needs to take on—and the only risk that will be rewarded in the market—is the risk that one cannot avoid, the risk in the market as a whole. The normal return for an investment is thus determined by the risk premium for the market and the investment's sensitivity to market risk.

The required return given by the CAPM is based on two expectations, expected sensitivities to the market and the expected market risk premium. Expectations are difficult to estimate. This is the challenge for a beta technology.

MULTIFACTOR PRICING MODELS

The market is said to be a risk factor. A risk factor is something that affects the returns on all investments in common, so it produces risk that cannot be diversified away. The market is the only risk factor in the CAPM because the model says that risk produced by other factors can be diversified away. Beta analysts suggest, however, that there are other risks, in addition to market risk, that cannot be negated. So they build multifactor models to capture the risk from additional factors:

Required return (*i*) = Risk-free return + [Beta1 (*i*) × Risk premium for factor 1] + [Beta2 (*i*) × Risk premium for factor 2] + · · · · + [Beta*k*(*i*) × Risk premium for factor *k*]

The risk premium for each of the *k* factors is the expected return identified with the factor over the risk-free return. The market is usually considered to be risk factor 1, so the beta analyst needs to deal with the measurement problems in the CAPM. But the analyst must also identify the additional factors, calculate their expected risk premiums, and calculate the factor betas that measure the sensitivities of a given investment to the factors. Such a task, if indeed possible, is highly conjectural. We will take a fairly skeptical approach to standard beta technologies in this book—which of course requires us to come up with an alternative way of handling risk and the required return.

the investment, so the CAPM leaves the analyst with the task of measuring the market risk premium and a stock's beta.

Alternatively, *multifactor pricing models* insist that additional factors are involved in determining the risk premium. The box reviews these models. These models expand the task to identifying the relevant risk factors and estimating betas for each factor. The *arbitrage pricing theory (APT)* is behind these multifactor models. It characterizes investment returns as being sensitive to a number of economy-wide influences that cannot be diversified away, but is silent as to what these might be and indeed as to the numbers of factors.

One might be the CAPM market factor, and the enhancement in practice comes from identifying the other factors. Some that have been suggested are shocks resulting from changes in industrial activity, the inflation rate, the spread between short and long-term interest rates, and the spread between low- and high-risk corporate bonds.[1] Firm size and book-to-market ratio are among other characteristics that have been nominated as indicating firms' exposures to risk factors.[2] But these are conjectures.

Playing with Mirrors?

Clearly, this is a tricky business. Not only must the elusive risk factors be identified, but the unobservable risk premiums associated with them also must be measured, along with the beta sensitivities. With these problems it's tempting to play with mirrors, but coming up with a solid product is a challenge. Even the one-factor CAPM is demanding. Betas have to be estimated and there are many commercial services that sell betas, each claiming its betas are better than those of the competition. No one knows the true beta and inevitably betas are measured with error. But even if we get a good measure of beta, there is the more difficult problem of determining the market risk premium. We used 5 percent for the market risk premium in calculating Nike's equity cost of capital in Box 3.7. But estimates range from 3 percent to 9.2 percent in texts and research papers. With this degree of uncertainty, estimates of required returns are likely to be highly unreliable. An 8 percent market risk premium would yield a required return for Nike of 10.7 percent. A 3 percent market risk premium would yield a required return of 6.2 percent. We might well be cynical about the ability to get precise measures of required returns with these methods. There are a number of surveys of academics and professionals that ask what number they use for the market risk premium. At the time of writing (early 2011), the average was 5.5 percent. Go to the Web page for this chapter for sources and updates.

Indeed, there is a case to be made that using these beta technologies is just playing with mirrors. If Nike's cost of capital can range from 6.2 percent to 10.7 percent depending on the choice of a number for the market risk premium, we cannot be very secure in our estimate. Disappointingly, despite a huge effort to build an empirically valid asset pricing model, research in finance has not delivered a reliable technology. In short, we really don't know what the cost of capital for most firms is.

If you have confidence in the beta technologies you have acquired in finance courses, you may wish to apply them in valuation. In this book, we will be sensitive to the imprecision that is introduced because of uncertainty about the cost of capital. Analysis is about reducing uncertainty. Forecasting payoffs is the first order of business in reducing our uncertainty about the worth of an investment, so our energies in this book are devoted to that aspect of fundamental analysis rather than the measurement of the cost of capital. We will, however, find ways to deal with our uncertainty about the cost of capital. Indeed, we will bring fundamental analysis to the task of estimating the cost of capital and develop strategies for finessing the problem of measuring the cost of capital. You may wish to jump to Chapters 7 and 19, to get a flavor of the approach and how it relates to standard beta technologies.

---

[1] See, for example, N-F. Chen, R. Roll, and S. A. Ross, "Economic Forces and the Stock Market," *Journal of Business,* July 1986, pp. 383–403.
[2] See E. F. Fama and K. R. French, "The Cross-Section of Expected Stock Returns," *Journal of Finance,* June 1992, pp. 427–465.

Chapter **Four**

Cash Accounting, Accrual Accounting, and Discounted Cash Flow Valuation

LINKS

Link to previous chapter

Chapter 3 outlined the process of fundamental analysis and depicted valuation as a matter of forecasting future financial statements.

This chapter

This chapter introduces dividend discounting and discounted cash flow valuation, methods that involve forecasting future cash flow statements. The chapter also shows how cash flows reported in the cash flow statement differ from accrual earnings in the income statement and how ignoring accruals in discounted cash flow valuation can cause problems.

Link to next chapter

Chapters 5 and 6 lay out valuation methods that forecast income statements and balance sheets.

Link to Web page

The Web page supplement provides further explanation and additional examples of discounted cash flow analysis, cash accounting, and accrual accounting.

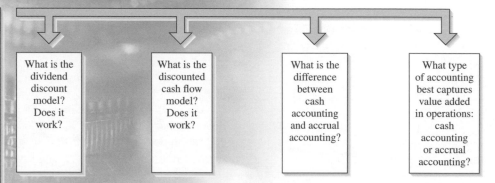

| What is the dividend discount model? Does it work? | What is the discounted cash flow model? Does it work? | What is the difference between cash accounting and accrual accounting? | What type of accounting best captures value added in operations: cash accounting or accrual accounting? |

The previous chapter described fundamental analysis as a matter of forecasting future financial statements, with a focus on those features in the statements that have to do with investing and operating activities. Which of the four financial statements should be forecasted and what features of these statements involve the investing and operating activities?

This chapter examines valuation technologies based on forecasting cash flows in the cash flow statement. First we deal with valuations based on forecasting cash flows to shareholders—dividends—known as *dividend discount analysis*. Second, we deal with valuations based on forecasting cash flow from operations and cash investment. Forecasting cash flow from operations and cash investment and discounting them to a present value is called *discounted cash flow analysis*. Both techniques prove to be unsatisfactory, for the simple reason that cash flows do not capture value added in a business.

As a student in an introductory financial accounting course, you were no doubt introduced to the difference between cash accounting and accrual accounting. The cash flow statement tracks operating and investment activities with cash accounting. Accordingly, discounted cash flow analysis is a cash accounting approach to valuation. Income statements and balance sheets, on the other hand, are prepared according to the principles of accrual accounting. This chapter explains the difference between cash accounting and

The Analyst's Checklist

After reading this chapter you should understand:

- How the dividend discount model works (or does not work).
- How a constant growth model works.
- What is meant by cash flow from operations.
- What is meant by cash used in investing activities.
- What is meant by free cash flow.
- How discounted cash flow valuation works.
- Problems that arise in applying cash flow valuation.
- Why free cash flow is not a measure of value added.
- Why free cash flow is a liquidation concept.
- How discounted cash flow valuation involves cash accounting for operating activities.
- Why "cash flow from operations" reported in U.S. and IFRS financial statements does not measure operating cash flows correctly.
- Why "cash flow in investing activities" reported in U.S. and IFRS financial statements does not measure cash investment in operations correctly.
- How accrual accounting for operations differs from cash accounting.
- The difference between earnings and cash flow from operations.
- How accruals affect the balance sheet and the income statement.
- Why analysts forecast earnings rather than cash flows.

After reading this chapter you should be able to:

- Calculate the value of a perpetuity.
- Calculate the value of a perpetuity with growth.
- Apply the discounted cash flow model.
- Make a simple valuation from free cash flows.
- Calculate cash flow from operations from a cash flow statement.
- Calculate cash used in investing from a cash flow statement.
- Calculate free cash flow.
- Calculate after-tax net interest payments.
- Calculate levered and unlevered cash flow from operations.
- Calculate total accruals from a cash flow statement.
- Calculate revenue from cash receipts and revenue accruals.
- Calculate expenses from cash payments and expense accruals.
- Explain the difference between earnings and cash from operations.
- Explain the difference between earnings and free cash flow.

accrual accounting and so sets the stage for valuation techniques in the next two chapters that involve forecasting accrual accounting income statements and balance sheets rather than the cash flow statement. After explaining how accrual accounting works and how it differs from cash accounting, the chapter asks why those differences are relevant in valuation. In the spirit of choosing the best technology, we ask two questions. What problems arise when we forecast cash flows? Can accrual accounting help in remedying those problems?

THE DIVIDEND DISCOUNT MODEL

Many investment texts focus on the dividend discount model in their valuation chapter. At first sight, the model is very appealing. Dividends are the cash flows that shareholders get from the firm, so value should be based on expected dividends. In valuing bonds we forecast the cash flows from the bond, so, in valuing stocks, why not forecast the cash flows from stocks?

The dividend discount model is stated as follows:

$$\text{Value of equity} = \text{Present value of expected dividends} \qquad \textbf{(4.1)}$$

$$V_0^E = \frac{d_1}{\rho_E} + \frac{d_2}{\rho_E^2} + \frac{d_3}{\rho_E^3} + \frac{d_4}{\rho_E^4} + \cdots$$

(The ellipsis in the formula indicates that dividends must be forecast indefinitely into the future, for years 5, 6, and so on.) The model instructs us to forecast dividends and to convert the forecasts to a value by discounting them at one plus the equity cost of capital, ρ_E. One might forecast varying discount rates for future periods but for the moment we will treat the discount rate as a constant. The dividend discount model is a straight application of the bond valuation model in the last chapter to valuing equity. That model works for a terminal investment. Will it work for a going-concern investment under the practical criteria we laid down at the end of the last chapter?

Well, going concerns are expected to pay out dividends for many (infinite?) periods in the future. Clearly, forecasting for infinite periods is a problem. How would we proceed by forecasting (realistically) for a finite period, say 10 years? Look again at the payoffs for an equity investment in Figure 3.3 in the last chapter. For a finite horizon forecast of T years, we might be able to predict the dividends to Year T but we are left with a problem: The payoff for T years includes the terminal price, P_T, as well as the dividends, so we also need to forecast P_T, the price at which we might sell at the forecast horizon. Forecasting just the dividends would be like forecasting the coupon payments on a bond and forgetting the bond repayment. This last component, the terminal payoff, is also called the **terminal value.** So we have the problem of calculating a terminal value such that

$$\text{Value of equity} = \text{Present value of expected dividends to time } T \qquad \textbf{(4.2)}$$
$$+ \text{ Present value of expected terminal value at } T$$

$$V_0^E = \frac{d_1}{\rho_E} + \frac{d_2}{\rho_E^2} + \frac{d_3}{\rho_E^3} + \cdots + \frac{d_T}{\rho_E^T} + \frac{P_T}{\rho_E^T}$$

You can see that this model is technically correct, for it is simply the present value of all the payoffs from the investment that are laid out in Figure 3.3. The problem is that one of those payoffs is the price that the share will be worth T years ahead, P_T. This is awkward, to say the least: The value of the share at time zero is determined by its expected value in the future, but it is the value we are trying to assess. To break the circularity, we must investigate fundamentals that determine value.

A method often suggested is to assume that the dividend at the forecast horizon will be the same forever afterward. Thus

$$V_0^E = \frac{d_1}{\rho_E} + \frac{d_2}{\rho_E^2} + \frac{d_3}{\rho_E^3} + \cdots + \frac{d_T}{\rho_E^T} + \left(\frac{d_{T+1}}{\rho_E - 1} \right) \Big/ \rho_E^T \qquad \textbf{(4.3)}$$

The terminal value here (in the bracketed term) is the *value of a perpetuity,* calculated by capitalizing the forecasted dividend at $T + 1$ at the cost of capital. This terminal value is then discounted to present value.

If an amount is forecasted to evolve in a predictable way in the future, its present value can be captured in a simple calculation. Two examples are a perpetuity and perpetual growth at a constant rate.

THE VALUE OF A PERPETUITY

A **perpetuity** is a constant stream that continues without end. The amount each period is sometimes referred to as an **annuity,** so a perpetuity is an annuity that continues forever. To value that stream, one just capitalizes the constant amount expected. If the dividend expected next year, d_1 is expected to be a perpetuity, the value of the dividend stream is

$$V_0^E = \frac{d_1}{\rho_E - 1}$$

So, if a dividend of $1 is expected each year forever and the required return is 10 percent per year, then the value of the perpetuity is $10.

THE VALUE OF A PERPETUITY WITH GROWTH

If an amount is forecasted to grow at a constant rate, its value can be calculated by capitalizing the amount at the required return adjusted for the growth rate:

$$V_0^E = \frac{d_1}{\rho_E - g}$$

Here g is one plus the growth rate (and ρ_E is one plus the required return). So, if a $1 dividend expected next year is expected to grow at 5 percent per year in perpetuity, the value of the stream, with a required return of 10 percent, is $20. Note that, in both the case of a perpetuity and a perpetuity with growth, the value is established at the beginning of the year when the perpetuity begins. So for a perpetuity beginning in year 1, the value is at time 0. For a perpetuity beginning at time $T + 1$ in models 4.3 and 4.4, the value of the perpetuity is at time T (and so that value is discounted at ρ_E^T, not ρ_E^{T+1}).

CONSTANT GROWTH MODELS

The calculation for the perpetuity with growth is sometimes referred to as a *constant growth valuation model*. So the model with growth above is referred to as the *constant growth dividend model* (and sometimes as the *Gordon growth model* after its author). It is a simple model, but applicable only if constant growth is expected.

This perpetuity assumption is a bold one. We are guessing. How do we know the firm will maintain a constant payout? If there is less than full payout of earnings, one would expect dividends to grow as the retained funds earn more in the firm. This idea can be accommodated in a terminal value calculation that incorporates growth:

$$V_0^E = \frac{d_1}{\rho_E} + \frac{d_2}{\rho_E^2} + \frac{d_3}{\rho_E^3} + \cdots + \frac{d_T}{\rho_E^T} + \left(\frac{d_{T+1}}{\rho_E - g}\right) / \rho_E^T \qquad \textbf{(4.4)}$$

where g is 1 plus a forecasted growth rate.[1] The terminal value here is the *value of a perpetuity with growth*. If the constant growth starts in the first period, the entire series collapses to $V_0^E = d_1/(\rho_E - g)$, which is sometimes referred to as the *constant growth model*. See Box 4.1.

What would we do, however, for a firm that might be expected to have zero payout for a very long time in the future? For a firm that has exceptionally high payout that can't be maintained? What if payout comes in stock repurchases (that typically don't affect shareholder value) rather than dividends?

---

[1] Setting the growth feature as 1 plus the growth rate corresponds to setting ρ_E equal to 1 plus the required return. The capitalization rate in the denominator of the terminal value is thus equal to $(\rho_E - 1) - (g - 1)$, that is, the required return minus the growth rate, (which is the same as $\rho_E - g$). Setting g = 1 + growth rate allows for negative growth rates (in spreadsheet calculations, for example) so that a negative growth rate of 5 percent (say) is given by $1.0 - 0.05 = 0.95$.

The truth of the matter is that dividend payout over the foreseeable future doesn't mean much. Some firms pay a lot of dividends, others none. A firm that is very profitable and worth a lot can have zero payout and a firm that is marginally profitable can have high payout, at least in the short run. Dividends usually are not necessarily tied to value creation. Indeed, firms can borrow to pay dividends, and this has nothing to do with their investing and operating activities where value is created. Dividends are distributions of value, not the creation of value.

These observations just restate what we covered in the last chapter: Dividends are not relevant to value. To be practical we have to forecast over finite horizons. To do so, the dividend discount model (equation 4.2) requires us to forecast dividends up to a forecast horizon plus the terminal price. But payoffs (dividends plus the terminal price) are insensitive to the dividend component: If you expect a stock to pay you more dividends, it will pay off a lower terminal price; if the firm pays out cash, the price will drop by this amount to reflect that value has left the firm. Any change in dividends will be exactly offset by a price change such that, in present value terms, the net effect is zero. In other words, paying dividends is a zero-NPV activity. That's dividend irrelevance! Dividends do not create value. If dividends are irrelevant, we are left with the task of forecasting the terminal price, but it is price that we are after. Box 4.2 summarizes the advantages and disadvantages of the dividend discount model.

This leaves us with the so-called **dividend conundrum:** Equity value is based on future dividends, but forecasting dividends over a finite horizon does not give an indication of value. The dividend discount model fails the first criterion for a practical analysis established in the last chapter. We have to forecast something else that is tied to the value creation. The model fails the second criterion—validation—also. Dividends can be observed after the fact, so a dividend forecast can be validated for its accuracy. But a change in a dividend from a forecast may not be related to value at all, just a change in payout policy, so ex-post dividends cannot validate a valuation.

The failure of the dividend discount model is remedied by looking inside the firm to the features that do create value—the investing and operating activities. Discounted cash flow analysis does just that.

THE DISCOUNTED CASH FLOW MODEL

We saw in Chapter 1 that the value of the firm (enterprise value) is equal to the value of the debt plus the value of the equity: $V_0^F = V_0^D + V_0^E$. The *value of the firm* is the value of its investing and operating activities, and this value is divided among the claimants—the debtholders and shareholders. One can calculate the value of the equity directly by forecasting

FIGURE 4.1

Cash Flows from All Projects for a Going Concern.

Free cash flow is cash flow from operations that results from investments minus cash used to make investments.

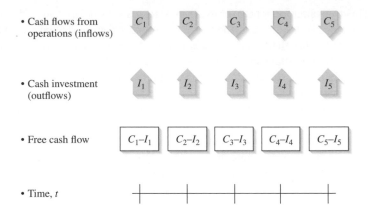

cash flowing to equity holders, as with the dividend discount model. But one can also value the equity by forecasting the cash flowing from the firm's investing and operating activities (the value of the firm), and then deduct the value of the debt claim on those cash flows. Discounted cash flow analysis does that.

Investing and operating activities are generally referred to simply as *operating activities,* with investing in operations implicit. Accordingly, the *value of the operations* is used to mean the value of the investing and operating activities of the firm, and the terms, *value of the operations, value of the firm,* and *enterprise value* are the same thing.

We saw in Chapter 3 that we can value a project by forecasting its cash flows. This is a standard approach in project evaluation. The firm is just a lot of projects combined; to discover the value of the firm, we can calculate the present value of expected cash flows from all the projects in the firm's operations. The total cash flow from all projects is referred to as the *cash flow from operations.* Going concerns invest in new projects as old ones terminate. Investments require cash outlays, called *capital expenditures* or *cash investment* (in operations).

Figure 4.1 depicts the cash flow from operations, C_t, and the cash outflows for investments, I_t, for five years for a going concern. After a cash investment is made in a particular year (Year 2, say), cash flow from operations in subsequent years (Year 3 and beyond) will include the cash inflow from that project until it terminates. In any particular year, operations yield a net cash flow, the difference between the cash flow from operations (from previous investments) and cash outlays for new investment, $C_t - I_t$. This is called *free cash flow* because it is the part of the cash from operations that is "free" after the firm reinvests in new assets.[2]

If we forecast free cash flows, we can value the firm's operations by applying the present value formula:

$$\text{Value of the firm} = \text{Present value of expected free cash flows} \qquad \textbf{(4.5)}$$

$$V_0^F = \frac{C_1 - I_1}{\rho_F} + \frac{C_2 - I_2}{\rho_F^2} + \frac{C_3 - I_3}{\rho_F^3} + \frac{C_4 - I_4}{\rho_F^4} + \frac{C_5 - I_5}{\rho_F^5} + \cdots$$

[2] Be warned that you will encounter a multitude of "cash flow" definitions in practice: operating cash flow, free cash flow, financing cash flow, and even ebitda (used to approximate "cash flow" from operations). You need to understand what is meant when the words *cash flow* are being used.

This is a valuation model for the firm, referred to as the *discounted cash flow (DCF) model*. The discount rate here is one that is appropriate for the riskiness of the cash flows from all projects. It is called the *cost of capital for the firm* or the *cost of capital for operations*.[3]

The equity claimants have to share the cash flows from the firm's operations with the debt claimants, so the value for the common equity is the value of the firm minus the value of the net debt: $V_0^E = V_0^F - V_0^D$. *Net debt* is the debt the firm holds as liabilities less any debt investments that the firm holds as assets. As we saw in Chapter 2, debt is typically reported on the balance sheet at close to market value so one can usually subtract the book value of the net debt. In any case, the market value of the debt is reported, in most cases, in the footnotes to the financial statements. When valuing the common equity, both the debt and the preferred equity are subtracted from the value of the firm; from the common shareholder's point of view, preferred equity is really debt.

You should have noticed something: This model, like the dividend discount model, requires forecasting over an infinite horizon. If we are to forecast (realistically) for a finite horizon, we will have to add value at the horizon for the value of free cash flows after the horizon. This value is called the **continuing value.** For a forecast of cash flows for T periods, the value of equity will be

$$V_0^E = \frac{C_1 - I_1}{\rho_F} + \frac{C_2 - I_2}{\rho_F^2} + \frac{C_3 - I_3}{\rho_F^3} + \cdots + \frac{C_T - I_T}{\rho_F^T} + \frac{CV_T}{\rho_F^T} - V_0^D \qquad \textbf{(4.6)}$$

The continuing value is not the same as the terminal value. The terminal value is the value we expect the firm to be worth at T, the terminal payoff to selling the firm at T. The continuing value is the value omitted by the calculation when we forecast only up to T rather than "to infinity." The continuing value is the device by which we reduce an infinite-horizon forecasting problem to a finite-horizon one, so our first criterion for practical analysis is really a question of whether a continuing value can be calculated within a reasonable forecast period. How do we calculate the continuing value so that it captures all the cash flows expected after T? Well, we can proceed in the same way as with the dividend discount model if we forecast that the free cash flows after T will be a constant perpetuity. In this case we capitalize the perpetuity:

$$CV_T = \frac{C_{T+1} - I_{T+1}}{\rho_F - 1} \qquad \textbf{(4.7)}$$

Or, if we forecast free cash flow growing at a constant rate after the horizon, then

$$CV_T = \frac{C_{T+1} - I_{T+1}}{\rho_F - g} \qquad \textbf{(4.8)}$$

where g is 1 plus the forecasted rate of growth in free cash flow. Look again at Box 4.1.

Exhibit 4.1 reports actual cash flows generated by The Coca-Cola Company from 2000 to 2004. Suppose that these actual cash flows were those you had forecasted—with perfect foresight—at the end of 1999 when Coke's shares traded at $57. The exhibit demonstrates how you might have converted these cash flows to a valuation. Following model 4.6, free cash flows to 2004 are discounted to present value at the required return of 9 percent. Then the present value of a continuing value is added to complete the valuation of the firm

---

[3] Chapter 14 covers the cost of capital for operations and how it relates to the cost of capital for equity. In corporate finance courses, the cost of capital for the firm is often called the weighted-average cost of capital (WACC).

EXHIBIT 4.1
Discounted Cash Flow Valuation for The Coca-Cola Company.
(In millions of dollars except share and per-share numbers.)
Required return for the firm is 9 percent.

	1999	2000	2001	2002	2003	2004
Cash from operations		3,657	4,097	4,736	5,457	5,929
Cash investments		947	1,187	1,167	906	618
Free cash flow		2,710	2,910	3,569	4,551	5,311
Discount rate $(1.09)^t$		1.09	1.1881	1.2950	1.4116	1.5386
Present value of free cash flows		2,486	2,449	2,756	3,224	3,452
Total present value to 2004	14,367					
Continuing value (CV)*						139,414
Present value of CV	90,611					
Enterprise value	104,978					
Book value of net debt	4,435					
Value of equity (V^E_{1999})	100,543					
Shares outstanding	2,472					
Value per share	$40.67					

$$^*CV = \frac{5,311 \times 1.05}{1.09 - 1.05} = 139,414$$

$$\text{Present value of CV} = \frac{139,414}{1.5386} = 90,611$$

(enterprise value). The continuing value is that for a perpetuity with growth at 5 percent, as in calculation 4.8: Free cash flows are expected to grow at 5 percent per year after 2004 indefinitely. The book value of net debt is subtracted from enterprise value to yield equity value of $100,543 million, or $40.67 per share. Exercise E4.8 and Minicase M4.1 at the end of this chapter look at Coca Cola's free cash flows from 2005–2010.

Here are the steps to follow for a DCF valuation:

1. Forecast free cash flows to a horizon.
2. Discount the free cash flows to present value.
3. Calculate a continuing value at the horizon with an estimated growth rate.
4. Discount the continuing value to the present.
5. Add 2 and 4.
6. Subtract net debt.

Free Cash Flow and Value Added

One can conclude that Coke is worth $40.67 per share because it can generate considerable cash flows. But now look at Exhibit 4.2 where cash flows are given for General Electric for the same five years. GE earned one of the highest stock returns of all U.S. companies from 1993–2004, yet its free cash flows are negative for all years except 2003.

Suppose you were thinking of buying GE in 1999. Suppose also that, again with perfect foresight, you knew then what GE's cash flows were going to be and had sought to apply a DCF valuation. Well, the free cash flows are negative in all but one year and their present value is negative! The last cash flow in 2004 is also negative, so it can't be capitalized to yield a continuing value. And if, in 2004, you had looked back on the free cash flows GE had produced, you surely would not have concluded that they indicate the value added to the stock price.

Exhibit 4.2 also gives the cash flows for Starbucks, the ubiquitous coffee chain, for 1996–2000. Starbucks has been quite successful, with coffee shops in so many countries that

EXHIBIT 4.2
Firms with Negative
Free Cash Flows:
General Electric
Company and
Starbucks
Corporation.

General Electric (in millions of dollars, except EPS and DPS)

	2000	2001	2002	2003	2004
Cash from operations	30,009	39,398	34,848	36,102	36,484
Cash investments	37,699	40,308	61,227	21,843	38,414
Free cash flow	(7,690)	(910)	(26,379)	14,259	(1,930)
Earnings	12,735	13,684	14,118	15,002	16,593
Earnings per share (EPS)	1.29	1.38	1.42	1.50	1.60
Dividends per share (DPS)	0.57	0.66	0.73	0.77	0.82

Starbucks Corporation (in thousands of dollars, except EPS)

	1996	1997	1998	1999	2000
Cash from operations	135,236	97,075	147,717	224,987	314,080
Cash investments	148,436	206,591	214,707	302,179	363,719
Free cash flow	(13,200)	(109,516)	(66,990)	(77,192)	(49,639)
Earnings	42,127	57,412	68,372	101,693	94,564
Earnings per share (EPS)	0.55	0.70	0.78	1.12	1.02

it has become a worldwide name. During the years 1996–2000, the firm's stock price more than doubled. Yet the free cash flows are consistently negative. Again, if you were standing at the beginning of 1996 and were given these (future) cash flows and asked to value the firm, you would have a great deal of trouble. As the free cash flows are negative up to 2000, your continuing value would have to be more than 100 percent of the value, yet you have no idea how to calculate it. Any calculation would be highly speculative. See Box 4.3.

Why does DCF valuation not work for these firms? The short answer is that free cash flow does not measure value added from operations. Cash flow from operations is value flowing into the firm from selling products but it is reduced by cash investment. If a firm invests more cash in operations than it takes in from operations, its free cash flow is negative. And even if investment is positive NPV (it adds value), free cash flow is reduced. Investment is treated as a "bad" rather than a "good." Of course, the return to investments will come later in cash flow from operations, but the more investing the firm does for a longer period in the future, the longer the forecasting horizon has to be to capture these cash inflows. GE has continually found new investment opportunities so its investment has been greater than its cash inflow. Starbucks, a growing firm, is continually opening more stores and that investment gives it negative free cash flow even though the investments are made to add value. Many growth firms—that generate a lot of value—have negative free cash flows. Exercise E4.12 at the end of the chapter gives an example of another very successful firm—Walmart—with negative free cash flows.

How can a firm double its stock price while generating negative cash flows? Well, free cash flow is not really a measure about adding value in operations. It confuses investments (and the value they create) with the payoffs from investments, so it is partly an investment or a liquidation concept. A firm decreases its free cash flow by investing and increases it by liquidating or reducing its investments. But a firm is worth more if it invests profitably, not less. If an analyst forecasts low or negative free cash flow for the next few years, would we take this as a lack of success in operations? GE's positive free cash flow in 2003 might have been seen as bad news because it resulted mostly from a decrease in investment. Indeed, Coke's increasing cash flows in 2003 and 2004 in Exhibit 4.1 result partly from a decrease in investment. Decreasing investment means lower future cash flows, calling into question the 5 percent growth rate used in Coke's continuing value calculation. Exercise 4.8 rolls Coke forward to 2006–2007 where you see similar difficulties emerging.

Valuation is a matter of disciplining speculation about the future. In choosing a valuation technology, two of the fundamentalist's tenets come into play: *Don't mix what you know with speculation* and *Anchor a valuation on what you know rather than on speculation*. A method that puts less weight on speculation is to be preferred, and methods that admit speculation are to be shunned. We know more about the present and the near future than about the long run, so methods that give weight to what we observe at present and what we forecast for the near future are preferred to those that rely on speculation about the long run. To slightly misapply Keynes's famous saying, in the long run we are all dead. This consideration is behind the criterion that a good valuation technology is one that yields a valuation with finite-horizon forecasts, and the shorter the horizon the better. Going concerns continue into the long run, of course, so some speculation about the long run is inevitable. But, if a valuation rides on speculation about the long run—about which we know little—we have a speculative, uncertain valuation indeed.

Discounted cash flow valuation lends itself to speculation. The General Electric and Starbucks cases in Exhibit 4.2 are good examples. An analyst trying to value GE in 1999 may have a reasonably good feel for likely free cash flows in the near future, 2000 and 2001, but that would do her little good. Indeed, if she forecast the cash flows over the five years, 2000–2004 with some confidence, that would do little good. These cash flows are negative, so she is forced to forecast (speculate!) about free cash flows that may turn positive many years in the future. In 2010, 2015, 2020? These cash flows are hard to predict; they are very uncertain. In the long run we are all dead. The same can be said for Starbucks. A banker or analyst trying to justify a valuation might like the method, of course, for it is tolerant to plugging in any numbers, but a serious investor does not want to rely on such speculation.

Speculation about the long run is contained in the continuing value calculation. So another way of invoking our principles is to say that a valuation is less satisfactory the more weight it places on the continuing value calculation. You can see with GE and Starbucks that, because cash flows up to the forecast horizon are negative, a continuing value calculation drawn at the forecast horizon would be more than 100 percent of the valuation. A valuation weighted toward forecasts for the near term is preferable, for we are more certain about the near term than the long run. But GE's and Starbucks's near term cash flows do not lend themselves to a valuation.

Free cash flow would be a measure of value from operations if cash receipts were matched in the same period with the cash investments that generated them. Then we would have value received less value surrendered to gain it. But in DCF analysis, cash receipts from investments are recognized in periods after the investment is made, and this can force us to forecast over long horizons to capture value. DCF analysis violates the matching principle (see Box 2.4 in Chapter 2).

A solution to the GE and Starbucks valuation problem is to have a very long forecast horizon. But this offends the first criterion of practical analysis that we established in Chapter 3. It requires too much speculation about the long run. It is the long run that we are very uncertain about. See Box 4.3.

Box 4.4 summarizes the advantages and disadvantages of DCF analysis.

THE STATEMENT OF CASH FLOWS

Cash flows are reported in the statement of cash flows, so forecasting cash flows amounts to preparing pro forma cash flow statements for the future. But the cash flows in a U.S. statement and cash flow statements prepared under international accounting standards are not quite what we want. Exhibit 4.3 gives "cash provided by operations" and "cash used in investing activities" from the statement of cash flows for Nike, Inc., for fiscal year 2010. The extract is from Nike's full cash flow statement in Exhibit 2.1 in Chapter 2. Nike reported 2010 cash flow from operations of $3,164.2 million and cash used in investing of $1,267.5 million, so its free cash flow appears to be the difference, $1,896.7 million.

ADVANTAGES

Easy concept: Cash flows are "real" and easy to think about; they are not affected by accounting rules.

Familiarity: Cash flow valuation is a straightforward application of familiar present value techniques.

DISADVANTAGES

Suspect concept: Free cash flow does not measure value added in the short run; value gained is not matched with value given up.

Investment is treated as a loss of value.

Free cash flow is partly a liquidation concept; firms increase free cash flow by cutting back on investments.

Forecast horizons: Typically, long forecast horizons are required to recognize cash inflows from investments, particularly when investments are growing.Continuing values have a high weight in the valuation.

Not aligned with what people forecast: Analysts forecast earnings, not free cash flow.

WHEN IT WORKS BEST

When the investment pattern produces positive constant free cash flow or free cash flow growing at a constant rate; a "cash cow" business.

DCF is useful when equity investments are terminal or the investor needs to "cash out," as in leverage buyout situations and private equity investment where debt must be paid down or investors must be paid out within a certain time frame, so the ability to generate cash is important.

Cash flow from operations is calculated in the statement as net income less items in income that do not involve cash flows. (These noncash items are the accruals, to be discussed later in the chapter.) But net income includes interest payments, which are not part of operations but rather cash flows to debtholders out of the cash generated by operations. They are financing cash flows. Firms are required to report the amount of interest paid as supplementary information to the cash flow statement; Nike reported $48.4 million in 2010 (see Exhibit 4.3). Net income also includes interest income earned on cash that is temporarily invested in interest-bearing deposits and marketable securities like bonds. These investments are not investments in operations. Rather, they are investments to store excess cash until it can be invested in operations later, or to pay off debt or pay dividends later. They also are financing flows. The supplementary information in Exhibit 4.3 reports $42.1 million of interest income on these securities for 2010.

The difference between interest payments and interest receipts is called *net interest payments*. In the United States, net interest payments are included in cash flow from operations, so they must be added back to the reported free cash flows from operations to get the actual cash that operations generated. However, interest receipts are taxable and interest payments are deductions for assessing taxable income, so net interest payments must be adjusted for the tax payments they attract or save. The net effect of interest and taxes is *after-tax net interest payments,* calculated as net interest payments $\times$ (1 − tax rate). Cash flow from operations is

$$\text{Cash flow from operations} = \text{Reported cash flow from operations} \qquad \textbf{(4.9)}$$
$$+ \text{After-tax net interest payments}$$

The first part of Box 4.5 calculates Nike's cash flow from operations for 2010 from its reported number. For many firms, interest payments are greater than interest receipts so cash flow from operations is usually larger than the reported number.

EXHIBIT 4.3
Operating and Investing Portion of the 2010 Cash Flow Statement for Nike, Inc.

Source: Annual 10-K report for 2010.

NIKE, Inc.
Partial Consolidated Statement of Cash Flows
(in millions of dollars)

	Year Ended May 31		
	2010	**2009**	**2008**
Cash provided by operations			
Net income	$ 1,906.7	$1,486.7	$1,883.4
Income charges (credits) not affecting cash:			
Depreciation	323.7	335.0	303.6
Deferred income taxes	8.3	(294.1)	(300.6)
Stock-based compensation	159.0	170.6	141.0
Impairment of goodwill, intangibles and other assets	—	401.3	—
Gain on divestitures	—	—	(60.6)
Amortization and other	71.8	48.3	17.9
Changes in certain working capital components and other assets and liabilities excluding the impact of acquisition and divestitures:			
Decrease (increase) in accounts receivable	181.7	(238.0)	(118.3)
Decrease (increase) in inventories	284.6	32.2	(249.8)
(Increase) decrease in prepaid expenses and other current assets	(69.6)	14.1	(11.2)
Increase (decrease) in accounts payable, accrued liabilities and income taxes payable	298.0	(220.0)	330.9
Cash provided by operations	3,164.2	1,736.1	1,936.3
Cash used by investing activities			
Purchases of short-term investments	(3,724.4)	(2,908.7)	(1,865.6)
Maturities and sales of short-term investments	2,787.6	2,390.0	2,246.0
Additions to property, plant and equipment	(335.1)	(455.7)	(449.2)
Disposals of property, plant and equipment	10.1	32.0	1.9
Increase in other assets, net of other liabilities	(11.2)	(47.0)	(21.8)
Settlement of net investment hedges	5.5	191.3	(76.0)
Acquisition of subsidiary, net of cash acquired	—	—	(571.1)
Proceeds from divestitures	—	—	246.0
Cash used by investing activities	(1,267.5)	(798.1)	(489.8)
Supplemental information			
Interest paid	$ 48.4	$ 46.7	$ 44.1
Interest income	42.1	56.2	121.2

The U.S. and IFRS statement of cash flows has a section headed "cash flow from investing activities." But the investments there include the "investments" of excess cash in interest-bearing securities. These are not investments in operations, so

Cash investment in operations = Reported cash flow used in investing **(4.10)**
   − Net investment in interest-bearing securities

Net investment is investments minus liquidations (purchases minus sales) of investments. Nike's revised cash investment in operations is calculated in Box 4.5, to complete the calculation of its free cash flow. The adjustments to investment are the first two items in the

NIKE, Inc., 2010 (in millions of dollars)			
Reported cash flow from operations			3,164.2
Interest payments		48.4	
Interest income*		(42.1)	
Net interest payments		6.3	
Taxes (36.3%)†		2.3	
Net interest payments after tax (63.7%)			4.0
Cash flow from operations			3,168.2
Reported cash used in investing activities		1,267.5	
Purchases of interest-bearing securities	3,724.4		
Sales of interest-bearing securities	(2,787.6)	936.8	
Cash investment in operations			330.7
Free cash flow			2,837.5

*Interest payments are given as supplemental data to the statement of cash flows, but interest receipts usually are not. Interest income (from the income statement) is used instead; this includes accruals but is usually close to the cash interest received.
†Nike's statutory tax rate (for federal and state taxes) is 36.3 percent, as indicated in the tax footnotes to the financial statements.

investing section of the cash flow statement in Exhibit 4.3. The adjusted investment in operations is now equal to the sum of net capital expenditures on property, plant, and equipment, and costs of acquisitions, along with the other remaining investment items in Exhibit 4.3. You see that the adjustment makes quite a difference to Nike's free cash flow number.

Cash flow from operations is sometimes referred to as the *unlevered cash flow from operations* but the "unlevered" is redundant. The reported cash flow from operations is sometimes called the *levered cash flow from operations* because it includes the interest from leverage through debt financing. But levered cash flow is not a useful measure. Dividends are the cash flows to shareholders and these are calculated after servicing not just interest but the repayment of principal to debtholders also.

The Cash Flow Statement under IFRS

The cash flow statement under IFRS is similar to the U.S. statement, with a few exceptions:

1. Under IFRS, firms can classify dividends paid and received as either operating or financing activity. If a firm chooses to classify dividends paid as an operating activity, the analyst must transfer it to the financing section: Dividends paid are a distribution of cash from operations to shareholders, not cash used up in operations. But dividends received are appropriately operating items if they are dividends from investing in other businesses as part of the business plan.

2. Firms can classify interest paid and received as either operating or financing activity. If classified as an operating activity, the analyst must adjust cash from operations for the net interest (after tax), as in the United States (equation 4.9 and Box 4.5).

3. Taxes paid are in cash from operations (as in the United States), unless they can be specifically identifiable with a financing or investing activity.

NIKE, INC., 2010

FROM THE CASH FLOW STATEMENT			A COMMON APPROXIMATION		
(in million of dollars)			**(in millions of dollars)**		
Earnings		1,906.7	Earnings before interest and taxes (ebit)		2,523.2
Accrual adjustment		1,257.5	Taxes on ebit (at 36.3%)		915.9
Levered cash flows from operations		3,164.2			1,607.3
Interest payments	48.4		+ Depreciation and amortization	395.5	
Interest receipts	(42.1)		+ Change in operating working capital	694.7	1,090.2
Net interest payments	6.3		Cash flow from operations		2,697.5
Tax at 36.3%	2.3	4.0	– Cash investments:		
Cash flow from operations		3,168.2	Capital expenditures	325.0	
Cash investment in operations		330.7	Acquisitions	—	325.0
Free cash flow		2,837.5	Free cash flow		2,372.5

Change in operating working capital is the change in current assets minus current liabilities after eliminating cash and cash equivalents, short-term investments and short-term borrowings, and deferred taxes. The number on the cash flow statement is used here. Depreciation and amortization are also from the cash flow statement.

As the second method is only an approximation, the two methods differ. Accrual items in Nike's cash flow statement other than depreciation and amortization and change in operating working capital have been ignored in the approximation. Note that is it common to deduct only capital expenditures (Cap-Ex) as investments, but one must ensure that the number includes all investment expenditures such as acquisitions.

Purchases and sales of interest-bearing securities are classified as cash investing activities, as in the United States, so the same adjustment to cash investment must be made (equation 4.10 and Box 4.5).

Forecasting Free Cash Flows

For DCF analysis we need forecasts of free cash flow that will be reported in the cash flow statement in the future. However, developing such forecasts without first forecasting sales and earnings is difficult. These are accrual numbers, so forecasts of free cash flow are made by converting earnings forecasts into forecasts of cash flows from operations, then deducting anticipated investment in operations. The difference between earnings (net income) and cash from operations is due to income statement **accruals,** the noncash items in net income, and these accruals are indicated by the difference between net income and cash from operations in the cash flow statement. The accruals in Nike's 2010 statement total $1,257.5 million. Deducting these accruals from net income—and making the adjustment for after-tax interest—produces cash flow from operations. Box 4.6 shows you how to convert Nike's earnings to cash flow from operations and, with a deduction for new investments in operations, to free cash flow.

Forecasting future accruals is not all that easy. People resort to shortcuts by forecasting earnings before interest and taxes (ebit), deducting taxes that apply to ebit, then making the accrual adjustment by adding back depreciation and amortization (in the cash flow statement) plus the change in working capital items involved in operations. This is only an approximation, and somewhat cumbersome. We will show a much more direct and quicker way to do this in Chapter 11. The common method that starts with ebit is demonstrated for Nike in Box 4.6.

We must ask whether the exercise of converting earnings forecasts to cash flows is a useful one, particularly if we end up with the negative free cash flows we saw for General Electric and Starbucks in Exhibit 4.2. Can we value a firm from earnings forecasts rather than cash flow forecasts and save ourselves the work in making the conversion? The answer is yes. Indeed we will now (in the next chapter) show that taking the accruals out of earnings can actually introduce more complications to the valuation task and produce a more speculative valuation.

CASH FLOW, EARNINGS, AND ACCRUAL ACCOUNTING

Analysts forecast earnings rather than cash flows. And the stock market appears to value firms on the basis of expected earnings: A firm's failure to meet analysts' earnings forecasts typically results in a drop in share price, while beating earnings expectations usually results in an increased share price. In short, earnings drive stock prices.

There are good reasons to forecast earnings rather than free cash flows if we have valuation in mind. The difference between earnings and cash flow from operations is the accruals. We now show how accruals in principle capture value added in operations that cash flows do not. And we also show how accrual accounting treats investment differently from cash accounting to remedy the problems we have just seen in forecasting free cash flows.

Earnings and Cash Flows

Exhibit 4.4 gives the statement of income for Nike, Inc., for fiscal 2010 along with prior years' comparative statements. The income statement recognizes value inflows from selling products in revenues, and reduces revenues by the value outflows in expenses to yield a net number, net income, as we saw in Chapter 2.

There are three things you should notice about income statements:

1. Dividends do not appear in the statement. Dividends are a distribution of value, not a part of the value generation. So they do not determine the measure of value added, earnings. Dividends do reduce shareholders' value in the firm, however; appropriately, they reduce the book value of equity in the balance sheet. Accountants get this right.

2. Investment is not subtracted in the income statement, so the value-added earnings number is not affected by investment, unlike free cash flow. (An exception is investment in research and development, so the value-added measure may be distorted in this case.)

3. There is a matching of value inflows (revenues) to value outflows (expenses). Accountants follow the **matching principle,** which says that expenses should be recorded in the same period that the revenues they generate are recognized, as we saw in Chapter 2. Value surrendered is matched with value gained to get net value added from selling goods or services. Thus, for example, only those inventory costs that apply to goods sold during a period are recognized as value given up in cost of sales (and the remaining costs— value not yet given up—are recorded as inventories in the balance sheet); and a cost to pay pensions to employees arising from their service during the current period is reported as an expense in generating revenue for the period even though the cash flow (during the employees' retirement) may be many years later.

EXHIBIT 4.4
Income Statements for Nike, Inc.

Source: Annual 10-K report.

NIKE, Inc.
Consolidated Statements of Income

	Year Ended May 31		
	2010	2009	2008
	(In millions)		
Revenues	$19,014.0	$19,176.1	$18,627.0
Cost of sales	10,213.6	10,571.7	10,239.6
Gross margin	8,800.4	8,604.4	8,387.4
Selling and administrative expense	6,326.4	6,149.6	5,953.7
Restructuring charges	—	195.0	—
Goodwill impairment	—	199.3	—
Intangible and other asset impairment	—	202.0	—
Interest expense (income), net	6.3	(9.5)	(77.1)
Other (income) expense, net	(49.2)	(88.5)	7.9
Income before income taxes	2,516.9	1,956.5	2,502.9
Income taxes	610.2	469.8	619.5
Net income	$ 1,906.7	$ 1,486.7	$ 1,883.4

Cash flow from operations adds value and is incorporated in revenue and expenses. But to effect the matching of revenues and expenses, the accountant modifies cash flows from operations with the accruals. Accruals are measures of noncash value flows.

Accruals

These are of two types, *revenue accruals* and *expense accruals*.

Revenues are recorded when value is received from sales of products. To measure this value inflow, revenue accruals recognize value increases that are not cash flows and subtract cash inflows that are not value increases. The most common revenue accruals are receivables: A sale on credit is considered an increase in value even though cash has not been received. Correspondingly, cash received in advance of a sale is not included in revenue because value is not deemed to have been added: The recognition of value is deferred (as deferred or unearned revenue) until such time as the goods are shipped and the sale is completed.

Expense accruals recognize value given up in generating revenue that is not a cash flow. Cash payments are modified by accruals by recognizing amounts incurred in generating revenues but not yet paid and amounts paid in the past for generating revenues in the current period. Pension expense is an example of an expense incurred in generating revenue that will not be paid until later. Wages payable is another example. A prepaid wage for work in the future is an example of cash paid for expenses in advance. Depreciation arises from cash flows in the past for investments in plant. Plants wear out. Depreciation is that part of the cost of the investment that is deemed to be used up in producing the revenue of the current period. Income tax expense, includes taxes due for the period but not paid and cost of goods sold excludes cash paid for production of merchandise that has not yet been sold.

Accruals for a period are reported as the difference between net income and cash flow from operations in the statement of cash flows. We saw in Box 4.6 that Nike had $1,257.5 million in accruals in 2010.

Accruals change the timing for recognizing value in the financial statements from when cash flows occur. Recognizing a receivable as revenue or recognizing an increase in a pension obligation as expense recognizes value ahead of the future cash flow; recognizing deferred

	Nike, 2010
Cash flow from operations	3,168.2
− Net interest payments (after tax)	(4.0)
+ Accruals	(1,257.5)
= Earnings	1,906.7
Free cash flow	2,837.5
− Net interest payments (after tax)	(4.0)
+ Accruals	(1,257.5)
+ Investments	330.7
= Earnings	1,906.7

revenue or depreciation recognizes value later than cash flow. In all cases, the concept is to match value inflows and outflows to get a measure of value added in selling products in the market. Timing is important to our first criterion for practical valuation analysis, a reasonably short forecast horizon. You readily see how recognizing a pension expense 30 years before the cash flow at retirement is going to shorten the forecast horizon. We will now see how deferring recognition until after a cash flow also will shorten the forecast horizon.

Investments

The performance measure in DCF analysis is free cash flow, not cash flow from operations. Free cash flow is cash generated from operations after cash investments, $C - I$, and we saw that investments are troublesome in the DCF calculation because they are treated as decreases in value. But investments are made to generate value; they lose value only later as the assets are used up in operations (as depreciation). The value lost in operations occurs after the cash flow. The earnings calculation recognizes this. Effectively, earnings adds investment back to the free cash flow to correct the error in free cash flow as a measure of value added:

$$\text{Earnings} = \text{Free cash flow} - \text{Net cash interest} + \text{Investments} + \text{Accruals} \quad \textbf{(4.11)}$$

Because accrual accounting places investment in the balance sheet as assets, it does not affect income. Accrual accounting then recognizes decreases in those assets in subsequent periods in the form of depreciation accruals (and other amortizations) as assets lose value in generating revenue. Box 4.7 explains the differences between cash flow and earnings, with a demonstration for Nike. Note that investments are really accruals also, so accruals plus investment is sometimes referred to as total accruals.

To appreciate the full details of how accrual accounting works, you must grasp a good deal of detail. Here we have seen only a broad outline of how the accounting works to measure value flows. This will be embellished later—particularly in Part Four of the book—but now would be a good time to review a financial accounting text and go to Accounting Clinic II.

The outline of earnings measurement here nominally describes how the accounting works, and our expression for earnings above looks like a good way to measure value added. But there is no guarantee that a particular set of accounting rules—U.S. GAAP or international accounting standards, for example—achieves the ideal. Yes, depreciation nominally matches value lost to value gained, but whether this is achieved depends on how the depreciation is actually measured. This is true for all accruals. Cash flows are objective, but the accruals depend on accounting rules, and these rules may not be good ones. Indeed, in the case of depreciation, firms can choose from different methods. Many accruals

Accounting Clinic

II

HOW ACCRUAL ACCOUNTING WORKS

Accounting Clinic II, on the book's Web site, lays out in more detail how accrual accounting works and contrasts accrual accounting with cash accounting. After going through this clinic you will understand how and when revenues are recorded and why cash received from customers is not the same as revenues recorded under accrual accounting. You also will understand how accrual accounting records expenses. You will see how the matching principle—to measure value added—that was introduced in Chapter 2 is applied through the rules of accrual accounting. You also will recognize those cases where GAAP violates the principle of good matching. And you will appreciate how accrual accounting affects not only the income statement but also the balance sheet.

involve estimates, which offer a potential for error. Accruals can be manipulated to some degree. R&D expenditures are expensed in the income statement even though they are investments. These observations suggest that the value-added measure, net income, may be mismeasured, so a valuation technique based on forecasting earnings must accommodate this mismeasurement. Indeed, one rationale for DCF analysis is that the accounting is so suspect that one must subtract or "back out" the accruals from income statements to get to the "real cash flows." We have seen in this chapter that this induces problems, however. We will see in the next two chapters how accrual accounting valuation models accommodate accounting measurement issues.

Accruals, Investments, and the Balance Sheet

If you return to Exhibit 2.1 in Chapter 2 you will see Nike's 2010 comparative balance sheet. The investments (which are not placed in the income statement) are there—inventories, land, buildings, equipment, and intangible assets. But the statement also has accruals. Shareholders' equity is assets minus liabilities, so one cannot affect the shareholders' equity through earnings without affecting assets and liabilities also. Thus, as earnings add to shareholders' equity, they also add to assets minus liabilities. Credit sales, recognized as a revenue accrual on Nike's income statement, produce receivables on the balance sheet and estimates of bad debts and sales returns reduce net receivables. Inventories are costs incurred ahead of matching against revenue in the future. Nike's property, plant, and equipment are investments whose costs will later be matched against revenues as the assets are used up in producing those revenues. On the liability side, Nike's accrued liabilities and accounts payable are accruals. Accrued marketing and promotion costs, for example, are costs incurred in generating revenue but not yet paid for.

Indeed all balance sheet items, apart from cash, securities that absorb excess cash, and debt and equity financing items, result from either investment or accruals. To modify free cash flow according to the accounting relation (equation 4.11), investments and accruals are put in the balance sheet.

Box 4.8 gives some examples of specific accruals and how they affect both the income statement and the balance sheet.

The investments and accruals in the balance sheet take on a meaning of their own, either as assets or liabilities. An asset is something that will generate future benefits. Accounts receivable are assets because they are cash to be received from customers in the future. Inventories are assets because they can generate sales and ultimately cash in the future. A liability is an obligation to give up value in the future. Accrued compensation, for example,

Here are some examples of accrual accounting and the way it affects the income statement and the balance sheet:

Accrual Item	Effect on Income Statement	Effect on Balance Sheet
Booking a sale before cash is received	Increase in revenue	Increase in accounts receivable
Booking rent expense before paying cash	Increase in rent expense	Increase in rent payable
Paying rent in advance	No effect	Increase in prepaid expenses
Booking wages expense before paying cash	Increase in wages expense	Increase in wages payable
Booking the cost of pensions	Increase in pension wages expense	Increase in pension liability
Paying wages in advance	No effect	Increase in prepaid expenses
Purchasing inventories	No effect	Increase in inventories
Selling inventories	Increase in cost of goods sold	Decrease in inventories
Purchasing plant and equipment	No effect	Increase in property, plant, and equipment (PPE)
Recognizing depreciation of plant	Increase in depreciation expense	Decrease in PPE
Recognizing interest due but not paid	Increase in interest expense	Increase in interest payable
Recognizing taxes due to the government	Increase in tax expense	Increase in taxes payable
Recognizing taxes that ultimately will be paid on reported income but which are not yet due to the government	Increase in tax expense	Increase in deferred taxes

is a liability to pay wages; a pension liability, an obligation to pay pension benefits. Property, plant, and equipment are assets from investment but subtracting accumulated depreciation recognizes that some of the ability to generate future cash has been given up in earning revenues to date. So net assets (assets minus liabilities) are anticipated value that comes from investment but also anticipated value that is recognized by accruals.

To close, go back to the cash flows for General Electric and Starbucks in Exhibit 4.2. We saw there that valuating these firms on the basis of their negative free cash flows was hopeless. The exhibit also gives the earnings for these firms. We understand now that these earnings differ from the free cash flows because of the accruals and investments recognized by accrual accounting. In contrast to the free cash flows, the earnings are positive and indeed growing at a fairly regular rate. Earnings look like a better basis for valuing a firm than cash flows. The next two chapters show how this is done.

Some versions of DCF valuation handle the free cash flow problem by dividing investment into "maintenance capital expenditure" and "growth investment." Maintenance capital expenditure is investment to maintain operations at their current level—replacing existing assets, for example—whereas growth investment is investment to enlarge operations. This is really a form of accrual accounting where maintenance capital expenditure is a measure of depreciation, expensed immediately in the income statement, with growth investment placed on the balance sheet. So it is a question of whether this is good accrual accounting. Distinguishing the two types of investment is quite difficult in practice where firms are dynamically changing their business, dropping products and adding new ones, investing in new locations, outsourcing, and so on, never really having the same business. Maintenance capital expenditure is an elusive notion requiring too much judgment for the fundamental investor. Note further, that practitioners of this type of (modified) DCF valuation make the mistake of not depreciating the growth investment that is implicitly placed on the balance sheet, so it is never charged against cash flows.

Summary

A valuation model is a tool for thinking about the value creation in a business and translating that thinking into a valuation. This chapter introduced the dividend discount model and the discounted cash flow model. These models forecast cash flows. The dividend discount model focuses on the cash flow distributions to shareholders (dividends); the discounted cash flow model focuses on the investing and operating activities of the firm, where value is generated.

The chapter demonstrated, however, that dividends and cash flows from investing and operating activities, summarized in free cash flow, are doubtful measures of value added. Indeed, as a value-added measure, free cash flow is perverse. Firms reduce free cash flows by investing, whereas investment is made to generate value. Thus very profitable firms with investment opportunities, like General Electric and Starbucks, generate negative free cash flow. Firms increase free cash flow by liquidating investments. So we preferred to call free cash flow a liquidation concept rather than a value-added concept and, in doing so, called into question the idea of forecasting free cash flows to value firms. We recognized, of course, that forecasting free cash flows for the long run captures value. But that goes against our criterion of working with relatively short forecast horizons and avoiding speculative valuations with large continuing values. Forecasting where a firm will be in 2030 is not an easy task. But the problem is primarily a conceptual one as well as a practical one: Free cash flow is not a measure of value added.

How might we deal with the problems of cash flow valuation? The chapter outlined the principles of accrual accounting that determine earnings (in the income statement) and book values (in the balance sheet). It showed that accrual accounting measures earnings in a way that, in principle at least, corrects for deficiencies in free cash flow as a measure of value added. Under accrual accounting, investments are not deducted from revenues (as they are with free cash flow), but rather they are put in the balance sheet as an asset, to be matched as expenses against revenues at the appropriate time. Additionally, accrual accounting recognizes accruals—noncash value—as part of value added. Accordingly, accrual accounting produces a number, earnings, that measures the value received from customers less the value given up in winning the revenues, that is, value added in operations.

The Web Connection

Find the following on the Web page supplement for this chapter:

- Further examples of discounted cash flow valuation.
- Further discussion of the problems with DCF valuation.
- Further demonstration of the difference between cash and accrual accounting.

- A discussion of the question: Is cash king?
- A discussion of the statement: Cash valuation models and accrual valuation models must yield the same valuation.
- The cash flow statement under IFRS.

Analysts forecast earnings rather than cash flows, and—as we now see—for very good reasons. The next two chapters develop valuation methods based on forecasts of earnings and book values. That is, they are based on forecasted income statements and balance sheets rather than forecasted cash flow statements. We will see that these methods typically yield valuations with less reliance on long-term continuing values. The investor is thus more assured, for he or she is putting more weight on "what we know" rather than speculation.

There is one further subtle point to be gleaned from this chapter. A valuation model specifies what aspect of the firm's activities is to be forecasted, and we have concluded that it is the investing and operating activities. But a valuation model also specifies how those activities are to be measured. This chapter investigated cash accounting for investing and operating activities, but it also raised the possibility of using accrual accounting (which we will do in the next two chapters). Here is the subtle point: A valuation model tells you how to *account* for the value generation. *A valuation model is really a model of pro forma accounting for the future.* Should you account for the future in terms of dividends? Should you account for the future in terms of cash flows? Or should you use accrual accounting for the future? You see, then, that accounting and valuation are very much alike. Valuation is a matter of accounting for value.

Accordingly one can think of good accounting and bad accounting for valuation. This chapter has suggested that accrual accounting might be better than cash accounting. But is accrual accounting as specified by U.S. GAAP or international accounting standards good accounting for valuation? We must proceed with a critical eye toward accounting prescribed by regulators.

Key Concepts

accrual is a noncash value flow recorded in the financial statements.   *123*

annuity the annual amount in a constant stream of payoffs.   *113*

continuing value is the value calculated at a forecast horizon that captures value added after the horizon.   *116*

dividend conundrum refers to the following puzzle: The value of a share is based on expected dividends but forecasting dividends (over finite horizons) does not yield the value of the share.   *114*

matching principle is the accounting principle that recognizes expenses when the revenue for which they are incurred is recognized.   *124*

perpetuity is a periodic payoff that continues without end.   *113*

terminal value is what an investment is expected to be worth in the future when it terminates or when it may be liquidated.   *112*

The Analyst's Toolkit

A Continuing Case: *Kimberly-Clark Corporation*

A Self-Study Exercise

THE CASH FLOW STATEMENT

You examined Kimberly-Clark's cash flow statement in the continuing case for Chapter 2. Now go back to that statement (in Exhibit 2.2) and recalculate "cash provided by operations" for 2008–2010 with the adjustments in this chapter (equation 4.9). The firm's combined federal and state tax rate is 36.8 percent. Also recalculate cash used for investing appropriately to identify actual investment in operations (equation 4.10). Finally, calculate free cash flow for each year. The following, supplied in footnote 21 (Supplemental Data) in the 10-K, will help you with these calculations:

	Year Ended December 31		
Other Cash Flow Data	**2010**	**2009**	**2008**
Interest paid	$248	$290	$319
Income taxes paid	582	764	538
Interest Expense:			
Gross interest cost	$255	$288	$318
Capitalized interest on major construction projects	(12)	(13)	(14)
Interest expense	$243	$275	$304

Cash Flows and Accruals

Identify the amount of accruals that are reported in the cash flow statement. Then reconcile your calculations of free cash flow for 2008–2010 to net income, following the accounting relation 4.11. Look at the accrual items in the cash flow statement for 2010 and identify which assets or liabilities these affect on the balance sheet. Which items on the balance sheet are affected by the items listed in the investment section of the cash flow statement?

Discounted Cash Flow Valuation

Suppose you were valuing KMB at the end of 2007 and that you received the free cash flows that you just calculated as forecasts for 2008–2010. Attempt to value the equity with a DCF valuation. Identify aspects of the valuation about which you are particularly uncertain. Kimberly-Clark had 406.9 million shares outstanding at the end of 2010 and had net debt of $5,294 million. You should verify these numbers on the 2010 balance sheet.

For these calculations, use a required return for the firm of 8 percent.

Concept Questions

C4.1. Investors receive dividends as payoffs for investing in equity shares. Thus the value of a share should be calculated by discounting expected dividends. True or false?

C4.2. Some analysts trumpet the saying "Cash is King." They mean that cash is the primary fundamental that the equity analyst should focus on. Is cash king?

C4.3. Should a firm that has higher free cash flows have a higher value?

C4.4. After years of negative free cash flow, General Electric reported a positive free cash flow of $14,259 million in 2003. Look back at GE's cash flows displayed in Exhibit 4.2. Would you interpret the 2003 free cash flow as good news?

C4.5. Which of the following two measures gives a better indication of the value added from selling inventory: (a) cash received from customers minus cash paid for inventory, or (b) accrual revenue minus cost of goods sold? Why?

C4.6. What explains the difference between cash flow from operations and earnings?

C4.7. What explains the difference between free cash flow and earnings?

C4.8. Interest payments should not be part of cash flow from operations. Why?

C4.9. Company X has negative free cash flows but strong earnings that yield a return on equity of 27 percent. Which of the following statements is more likely to be true?

    a. The company is wasting cash on unproductive activities.

    b. The company is investing heavily.

C4.10. In 2010, a newspaper interviewed a money manager who claimed the mantle of a fundamental investor. He laid out his investment philosophy: He "seeks companies that are likely to generate strong cash flows yet are priced very cheaply." "Cash is king," he says so he is investing in Intel, Microsoft, Macy's, DuPont, Xerox, and Radio Shack, firms with significant amounts of cash. Critique his approach.

Exercises

Drill Exercises

E4.1. A Discounted Cash Flow Valuation (Easy)

At the end of 2012, you forecast the following cash flows (in millions) for a firm with net debt of $759 million:

	2013	2014	2015
Cash flow from operations	$1,450	$1,576	$1,718
Cash investment	1,020	1,124	1,200

You forecast that free cash flow will grow at a rate of 4 percent per year after 2015. Use a required return of 10 percent in answering the following questions.

    a. Calculate the firm's enterprise value at the end of 2012.

    b. Calculate the value of the equity at the end of 2012.

E4.2. A Simple DCF Valuation (Easy)

At the end of 2012, you forecast that a firm's free cash flow for 2013 will be $430 million. If you forecast that free cash flow will grow at 5% per year thereafter, what is the enterprise value? Use a required return of 10 percent.

E4.3. Valuation with Negative Free Cash Flows (Medium)

At the end of 2012, you forecast the following cash flows for a firm for 2013–2016 (in millions of dollars):

	2013	2014	2015	2016
Cash flow from operations	730	932	1,234	1,592
Cash investments	673	1,023	1,352	1,745

What difficulties would you have in valuing this firm based on the forecasted cash flows? What would explain the decreasing free cash flow over the four years?

E4.4. Calculate Free Cash Flow from a Cash Flow Statement (Easy)

The following summarizes the parts of a firm's cash flow statement that have to do with operating and investing activities (in millions):

Net income		$2,198
Accruals in net income		3,072
Cash flow from operations		5,270
Cash in investing activities:		
Purchase of property and plant	$2,203	
Purchase of short-term investments	4,761	
Sale of short-term investments	(547)	6,417

The firm made interest payments of $1,342 million and received $876 in interest receipts from T-bills that it held. The tax rate is 35 percent.

Calculate free cash flow.

E4.5. Reconciling Accrual and Cash Flow Numbers (Medium)

a. A firm reports earnings of $735 million and cash flow from operations of $1,623 million. What was the dollar amount of accruals listed in the cash flow statement?

b. A firm with no net debt reports cash flow from operations of $4,219 million in its cash flow statement after adding $1,389 million in accruals to earnings. It reported cash investments in operations of $2,612 million. What was the firm's free cash flow and earnings for the period?

c. A firm reported revenues of $623 million on its income statement. Accounts receivable at the beginning of the year were $281 million and $312 million at the end of the year. How much cash was received from customers?

d. A firm paid $128 million in income taxes during a year. Income taxes payable at the beginning of the year were $67 million and $23 million at the end of the year. There were no deferred taxes. What was the income tax expense on its income statement for the year?

E4.6. Accrual Accounting and Cash (Medium)

a. A firm reported $405 million in revenue and an increase in receivables of $32 million. What was the cash generated by the revenues?

b. A firm reported wages expense of $335 million and cash paid for wages of $290 million. What was the change in wages payable for the period?

c. A firm reported net property, plant, and equipment (PPE) of $873 million at the beginning of the year and $923 million at the end of the year. Depreciation on the PPE was $131 million for the year. There were no disposals of PPE. How much new investment in PPE was there during the year?

Applications

E4.7. Calculating Cash Flow from Operations and Cash Investment for Coca-Cola (Easy)

The Coca-Cola Company reported "Net cash provided by operating activities" of $7,150 million in its 2007 cash flow statement. It also reported interest paid of $405 million and interest income of $236 million. Coke has a 36 percent tax rate. What was the company's cash flow from operations for 2007?

Coca-Cola Company also reported "Net cash used in investing activities" of $6,719 million in its 2007 cash flow statement. As part of this number, it reported "Purchases of investments" (in interest-bearing securities) of $99 million and "Proceeds from disposal of investments" of $448 million. What cash did it spend on investments in operations? What was Coca-Cola's free cash flow for 2007?

E4.8.   Converting Forecasts of Free Cash Flow to a Valuation: Coca-Cola Company (Medium)

After reviewing the discounted cash flow valuation of Coca-Cola in Exhibit 4.1, consider the free cash flows below that were reported by Coke for 2004–2007. They are based on the actual reported cash flows but are adjusted for interest and investments in interest-bearing securities (in millions of dollars).

	2004	2005	2006	2007
Cash flow from operations	$5,929	$6,421	$5,969	$7,258
Cash investments	618	1,496	2,258	7,068
Free cash flow	5,311	4,925	3,711	190

Pretend that you are sitting at the beginning of 2004, trying to value Coke, given these numbers as forecasts. What difficulties would you encounter in trying to value the firm at the beginning of 2004? What do you make of the declining free cash flows over the four years?

Real World Connection

Other material on Coca-Cola can be found in Exhibit 4.1 and Minicase M4.1 in this chapter, Minicase M5.2 in Chapter 5, Minicase M6.1 in Chapter 6, and Exercises E12.7, E15.7, E16.12, E17.7, and E20.4.

E4.9.   Cash Flow and Earnings: Kimberly-Clark Corporation (Easy)

Kimberly-Clark Corporation (KMB) manufactures and markets consumer paper products under brand names that include Kleenex, Scott, Cottonnelle, Viva, Kotex, and WypAll. For fiscal year 2004, the firm reported the following numbers (in millions):

Net income (in income statement)	$1,800.2
Cash flow from operations (in cash flow statement)	2,969.6
Interest paid (in footnote to cash flow statement)	175.3
Interest income (from income statement)	17.9

The cash investment section of the 2004 cash statement was reported as follows (in millions):

Investing Activities:

Capital spending	$(535.0)
Investments in marketable debt securities	(11.5)
Proceeds from sales of investments in marketable debt securities	38.0
Net increase in time deposits	(22.9)
Proceeds from disposition of property	30.7
Other operating investments	5.3
Cash used for investing activities	$(495.4)

The firm has a combined federal and state tax rate of 35.6 percent. Calculate:

a. Free cash flow generated in 2004.

b. The accrual component of 2004 net income.

Real World Connection

Follow the Continuing Case for Kimberly-Clark. See also Exercises E7.16, E8.10, 11.10, and 12.6, and Minicase M5.3.

E4.10. **A Discounted Cash Flow Valuation: General Mills, Inc. (Medium)**

At the beginning of its fiscal year 2006, an analyst made the following forecast for General Mills, Inc., the consumer foods company, for 2006–2009 (in millions of dollars):

	2006	2007	2008	2009
Cash flow from operations	$2,014	$2,057	$2,095	$2,107
Cash investment in operations	300	380	442	470

General Mills reported $6,192 million in short-term and long-term debt at the end of 2005 but very little in interest-bearing debt assets. Use a required return of 9 percent to calculate both the enterprise value and equity value for General Mills at the beginning of 2006 under two forecasts for long-run cash flows:

a. Free cash flow will remain at 2009 levels after 2009.
b. Free cash flow will grow at 3 percent per year after 2009.

General Mills had 369 million shares outstanding at the end of 2005, trading at $47 per share. Calculate value per share and a value-to-price ratio under both scenarios.

Real World Connection

See Exercises E1.5, E2.9, E3.8, E6.8, E11.9, E13.9, E14.15, E15.6, and E16.10.

E4.11. **Free Cash Flow for General Motors (Medium)**

For the first nine months of 2005, General Motors Corporation reported the following in its cash flow statement. GM runs an automobile operation supported by a financing arm, and both activities are reflected in these statements.

Condensed Consolidated Statements of Cash Flows (unaudited)	Nine Months Ended September 30	
	2005	2004
	(dollars in millions)	
Net cash provided by operating activities	$ 3,676	$ 12,108
Cash flows from investing activities:		
Expenditures for property	(5,048)	(4,762)
Investments in marketable securities—acquisitions	(14,473)	(9,503)
Investments in marketable securities—liquidations	16,091	10,095
Net originations and purchases of mortgage servicing rights	(1,089)	(1,151)
Increase in finance receivables	(15,843)	(31,731)
Proceeds from sales of finance receivables	27,802	16,811
Operating leases—acquisitions	(12,372)	(10,522)
Operating leases—liquidations	5,029	5,831
Investments in companies, net of cash acquired	1,367	(85)
Other	(1,643)	808
Net cash (used in) investing activities	$ (179)	$(24,209)

Net interest paid during the 2005 period was $4,059 million, compared with $3,010 million in the corresponding 2004 period. General Motors' tax rate is 36 percent.

An analyst made a calculation of free cash flow from these numbers as follows (in millions):

	2005	2004
Cash flow from operations	$3,676	$ 12,108
Cash flow in investing activities	(179)	(24,209)
Free cash flow	$3,497	$(12,101)

She opened her report to her clients, written the day after GM's third quarter report was published, with the words, "GM has dramatically increased its free cash flow. As a result, we are edging towards upgrading our recommendation from SELL to HOLD."

Calculate the appropriate free cash flow number for the two nine-month periods. What mistakes is the analyst making in suggesting that the increase in free cash flow is good news?

Real World Connection

See Exercises E1.4, E2.12, and E5.12.

E4.12. Cash Flows for Walmart Stores (Easy)

Walmart has been the most successful retailer in history. The panel below reports cash flows and earnings for the firm from 1988 to 1996 (in millions of dollars, except per-share numbers):

	1988	1989	1990	1991	1992	1993	1994	1995	1996
Cash from operations	536	828	968	1,422	1,553	1,540	2,573	3,410	2,993
Cash investments	627	541	894	1,526	2,150	3,506	4,486	3,792	3,332
Free cash flow	(91)	287	74	(104)	(597)	(1,966)	(1,913)	(382)	(339)
Net income	628	837	1,076	1,291	1,608	1,995	2,333	2,681	2,740
EPS	0.28	0.37	0.48	0.57	0.70	0.87	1.02	1.17	1.19

The cash flows are unlevered cash flows.

a. Why would such a profitable firm have such negative free cash flows?
b. What explains the difference between Walmart's cash flows and earnings?
c. Is this a good firm to apply discounted cash flow analysis to?

E4.13. Accruals and Investments for PepsiCo (Easy)

PepsiCo, the beverage and food conglomerate, reported net income of $6,338 million for 2010 and $8,448 million in cash flow from operations. How much of the net income reported was accruals?

PepsiCo reported the following in the investment section of its cash flow statement for 2010 (in millions of dollars):

Capital spending	(3,270)
Sales of property, plant, and equipment	81
Acquisitions and investments in affiliates	(4,279)
Divestitures	12
Short-term investments, by maturity:	
More than three months purchases	(12)
More than three months maturities	29
Three months or less, net	(229)
Net cash used for investing activities	(7,668)

How much did PepsiCo invest in operations during 2010?

Real World Connection

See Minicase M5.2 in Chapter 5, Minicase 6.1 in Chapter 6, and Exercise E10.9 in Chapter 10 for more on PepsiCo.

E4.14. An Examination of Revenues: Microsoft Corp. (Medium)

Microsoft Corp. reported $62.484 billion in revenues for fiscal year 2010. Accounts receivable, net of allowances, increased from $11.192 billion in 2009 to $13.014 billion.

Microsoft has been criticized for underreporting revenue. Revenue from software licensed to computer manufacturers is not recognized in the income statement until the manufacturer sells the computers. Other revenues are recognized over contract periods with customers. As a result, Microsoft reported a liability, unearned revenue, of $14.830 billion in 2010, up from $14.284 billion in 2009.

What was the cash generated from revenues in 2010?

Real World Connection

See Exercises E1.6, E6.12, E8.9, E9.9, E11.11, E18.10, and E20.4, and Minicases M9.1 and M13.2 for related material on Microsoft.

Minicase

M4.1

Discounted Cash Flow Valuation: Coca-Cola Company

The Coca-Cola Company has been a very profitable company, typically trading at high multiples of earnings, book values, and sales. This case asks you to value the company using discounted cash flow analysis, and to appreciate the difficulties involved. Exhibit 4.1 in the text provides a guide. But also keep in mind the lesson from Exhibit 4.2.

Coca-Cola, established in the nineteenth century, is a manufacturer and distributor of non-alcoholic beverages, syrups, and juices under recognized brand names. It operates in nearly 200 countries around the world. At the beginning of 2008, Coke traded at $62 per share, with a P/E of 23.9, a price-to-book ratio of 6.6, and a price-to-sales ratio of 5.0 on annual sales of $28.9 billion. With 2,318 million shares outstanding, the market capitalization of the equity was $143.7 billion, putting it among the top 20 U.S. firms in market capitalization.

Exhibit 4.5 provides a partial statement of cash flow for Coca-Cola for three years, 2008–2010, along with some additional information.

Suppose that you were observing the stock price at the beginning of 2008 and were trying to evaluate whether to buy the shares. Suppose, further, that you had the actual cash flow statements for the next three years (as given in the exhibit), so you knew for sure what the cash flows were going to be.

A. Calculate free cash flows for the firm for the three years using the information given Exhibit 4.5.

B. Attempt to value the shares of Coca-Cola at the beginning of 2008. Use a cost of capital of 9 percent for the firm.

List the problems you run into and discuss the uncertainties you have about the valuation.

Below are the free cash flows reported by Coke for 2004–2007 (in millions of dollars). They are based on the actual reported cash flows but are adjusted for interest and investments in interest-bearing securities.

	2004	2005	2006	2007
Cash flow from operations	$5,929	$6,421	$5,969	$7,258
Cash investments	618	1,496	2,258	7,068
Free cash flow	$5,311	$4,925	$3,711	$ 190

If you used these cash flows for your forecasts, what difficulties would you encounter in trying to value the Coca-Cola Company at the beginning of 2004? What do you make of the declining free cash flows over the four years?

Real Connection

See Minicases M5.2 and M6.1 on Coca-Cola. Exercises E4.7, E4.8, E12.7, E15.7, E16.12, E17.7, and E20.4 deal with Coca-Cola.

EXHIBIT 4.5
Operating and
Investing Cash Flows
as Reported for the
Coca-Cola Company,
2008–2010.

THE COCA-COLA COMPANY AND SUBSIDIARIES
Consolidated Statements of Cash Flows

	Year Ended December 31		
	2010	2009	2008
	(In millions)		
Operating Activities			
Consolidated net income	$11,859	$6,906	$5,874
Depreciation and amortization	1,443	1,236	1,228
Stock-based compensation expense	380	241	266
Deferred income taxes	617	353	(360)
Equity (income) loss—net of dividends	(671)	(359)	1,128
Foreign currency adjustments	151	61	(42)
Significant (gains) losses on sales of assets—net	(645)	(43)	(130)
Other significant (gains) losses—net	(4,713)	—	—
Other operating charges	264	134	209
Other items	477	221	153
Net change in operating assets and liabilities	370	(564)	(755)
Net cash provided by operating activities	9,532	8,186	7,571
Investing Activities			
Purchases of short-term investments	(4,579)	(2,130)	—
Proceeds from disposals of short-term investments	4,032	—	—
Acquisitions and investments for operations	(2,511)	(300)	(759)
Purchases of other investments for operations	(132)	(22)	(240)
Proceeds from disposals of bottling companies and other investments	972	240	479
Purchases of property, plant and equipment	(2,215)	(1,993)	(1,968)
Proceeds from disposals of property, plant and equipment	134	104	129
Other investing activities	(106)	(48)	(4)
Net cash provided by (used in) investing activities	(4,405)	(4,149)	(2,363)
Other information:			
Interest paid	733	355	438
Interest income	317	249	333
Borrowings at the end of 2010:	$23,417 million		
Investment in debt securities at the end of 2010:	$11,182 million		
Statutory tax rate:	35.6%		

Source: 10-K filing for Coca-Cola Company for 2010.

Chapter **Five**

Accrual Accounting and Valuation: Pricing Book Values

LINKS

Link to previous chapters

Chapter 4 showed how accrual accounting modifies cash accounting to produce a balance sheet that reports shareholders' equity. However, Chapter 2 explained that book value is not the value of shareholders' equity, so firms typically trade at price-to-book ratios different from 1.0.

This chapter

This chapter shows how to estimate the value omitted from the balance sheet and thus how to estimate intrinsic price-to-book ratios.

Link to next chapter

Chapter 6 complements this chapter. While Chapter 5 shows how to price the book value of equity, the "bottom line" of the balance sheet, Chapter 6 shows how to price earnings, the "bottom line" of the income statement.

Link to Web page

Go to the Web page supplement for more applications of the techniques in this chapter.

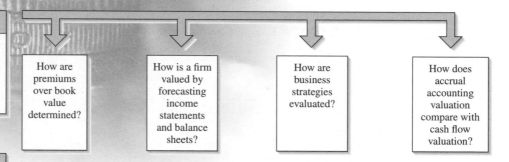

| How are premiums over book value determined? | How is a firm valued by forecasting income statements and balance sheets? | How are business strategies evaluated? | How does accrual accounting valuation compare with cash flow valuation? |

Firms typically trade at a price that differs from book value. Chapter 2 explained why: While some assets and liabilities are marked to market in the balance sheet, others are recorded at historical cost, and yet others are excluded from the balance sheet. Consequently, the analyst is left with the task of estimating the value that is omitted from the balance sheet. The analyst asks: What is the premium over book value at which a share should trade?

This chapter lays out a valuation model for calculating the premium and intrinsic value. It also models strategy analysis, and provides directions for analyzing firms to discover the sources of value creation.

The Analyst's Checklist

After reading this chapter you should understand:

- What "residual earnings" is.
- How forecasting residual earnings gives the premium over book value and the P/B ratio.
- How residual earnings are driven by return on common equity (ROCE) and growth in book value.
- The difference between a Case 1, 2, and 3 valuation.
- How the residual earnings model captures value added in a strategy.
- The advantages and disadvantages of using the residual earnings model and how it contrasts to dividend discounting and discounted cash flow analysis.
- How residual earnings valuation protects the investor from paying too much for earnings added by investment.
- How residual earnings valuation protects the investor from paying for earnings that are created by accounting methods.

After reading this chapter you should be able to:

- Calculate residual earnings.
- Calculate the value of equities and strategies from forecasts of earnings and book value.
- Calculate an intrinsic price-to-book ratio.
- Calculate value added in a strategy.
- Convert an analyst's earnings forecast into a valuation.

THE CONCEPT BEHIND THE PRICE-TO-BOOK RATIO

Book value represents shareholders' investment in the firm. Book value is also assets minus liabilities, that is, net assets. But, as Chapter 2 explained, book value typically does not measure the value of the shareholders' investment. The value of the shareholders' investment—and the value of the net assets—is based on how much the investment (net assets) is expected to earn in the future. Therein lies the concept of the P/B ratio: Book value is worth more or less, depending upon the future earnings that the net assets are likely to generate. Accordingly, the intrinsic P/B ratio is determined by the expected return on book value.

This concept fits with our idea that shareholders buy earnings. Price, in the numerator of the P/B ratio, is based on the expected future earnings that investors are buying. So, the higher the expected earnings relative to book value, the higher the P/B ratio. The *rate of return on book value*—sometimes referred to as the *profitability*—is thus a measure that features strongly in the determination of P/B ratios.

This chapter supplies the formal valuation model to implement this concept of the P/B ratio, as well as the mechanics to apply the model faithfully. The formality is important, for formality forces one to be careful. In evaluating P/B ratios, one must proceed formally because one can pay too much for earnings if one is not careful.

Beware of Paying Too Much for Earnings

A basic precept of investing is that investments add value only if they earn above their required return. Firms may invest heavily—in an acquisition spree, for example—but that investment, while producing more earnings, adds value only if it delivers earnings above the required return on the investment. This maxim refines the P/B concept: The P/B ratio prices expected return on book value, but it does not price a return that just yields the required return on book value.

The analysis in this chapter is designed to prevent you from making the mistake of paying for earnings that do not add value. As you apply the model and methods in this chapter, you will see that P/B ratios should increase only if earnings from investments yield a return that is greater than the required return on book value. Indeed, with the tools in this chapter, you can assess whether the market is overpaying (or underpaying) for earnings and so detect cases where the P/B ratio is too high or too low.

PROTOTYPE VALUATIONS

Fundamental analysis anchors valuation in the financial statements. Book value provides an anchor. The investor anchors his valuation with the value that is recognized in the balance sheet—the book value—and then proceeds to assess value that is not recognized—the premium over book value:

$$Value = Book\ value + Premium$$

Two prototypes introduce you to the methods.

Valuing a Project

Suppose a firm invested $400 in a project that is expected to generate revenue of $440 a year later. Think of it as buying inventory and selling it a year later. After subtracting the $400 cost of the inventory from the revenue, earnings are expected to be $40, yielding a rate of return of 10 percent on the investment. The required rate of return for the project is 10 percent. Following historical cost accounting, the asset (inventory) would be recorded on the balance sheet at $400. How much value does this project add to the book value? The answer, of course, is zero because the asset is expected to earn a rate of return equal to its cost of capital. And the project would be worth its book value.

A measure that captures the value added to book value is **residual earnings** or **residual income.** For the one period for this project (where the investment is at time 0),

$$Residual\ earnings_1 = Earnings_1 - (Required\ return \times Investment_0)$$

For earnings of $40, residual earnings is calculated as

$$Residual\ earnings = \$40 - (0.10 \times \$400) = \$0$$

If the project were to generate revenues of $448 and so earn $48, a rate of return of 12 percent on the investment of $400, residual earnings would be calculated as

$$Residual\ earnings = \$48 - (0.10 \times \$400) = \$8$$

The required dollar earnings for this project is $0.10 \times \$400 = \$40$. Residual earnings is the earnings in excess of these required dollar earnings. If the project earns $40, residual earnings is zero; if the project earns $48, residual earnings is $8. Residual earnings is sometimes referred to as **abnormal earnings** or **excess profit.**

A model that measures value added from forecasts of residual earnings is called the **residual earnings model:**

Value = Book value + Present value of expected residual earnings

The one-period project with an expected rate of return of 10 percent earns a residual earnings of zero. So the value of the project is

$$\text{Value} = \$400 + \frac{\$0}{1.10} = \$400$$

This project is worth its historical cost recorded on the balance sheet; there is no value added. If the project were expected to earn at a 12 percent rate, that is, earn residual earnings of $8,

$$\text{Value} = \$400 + \frac{\$8}{1.10} = \$407.27$$

In this case the project is worth more than its historical-cost book value because it is anticipated to generate positive residual earnings; there is value added, a premium over book value.

The residual earnings value for a terminal project is always the same as that calculated with discounted cash flow methods. For the project yielding $448 in sales, the DCF valuation is:

$$\text{Value (DCF)} = \frac{\$448}{1.10} = \$407.27$$

Valuing a Savings Account

How much is a simple savings account worth? Well, surely it is worth its book value—the balance on the bank statement—because that is the amount you would get out of the account if you cashed it in. The book value is the liquidation value. But it is also the going-concern value of the account.

Exhibit 5.1 lays out forecasts of book values, earnings, dividends (withdrawals), and free cash flows for 2013–2017 for a $100 investment in a savings account at the end of

EXHIBIT 5.1

Forecasts for a Savings Account with $100 Invested at the End of 2012, Earning 5 percent per Year.

		Forecast Year				
	2012	2013	2014	2015	2016	2017
Scenario 1: *Earnings withdrawn each year (full payout)*						
Earnings		$ 5	$ 5	$ 5	$ 5	$ 5
Dividends		5	5	5	5	5
Book value	$100	100	100	100	100	100
Residual earnings		0	0	0	0	0
Free cash flows		5	5	5	5	5
Scenario 2: *No withdrawals (zero payout)*						
Earnings		$ 5	$ 5.25	$ 5.51	$ 5.79	$ 6.08
Dividends		0	0	0	0	0
Book value	$100	105	110.25	115.76	121.55	127.63
Residual earnings		0	0	0	0	0
Free cash flows		0	0	0	0	0

2012, under two scenarios. In the first scenario, earnings are paid out each year so that book value does not change. The required return for this savings account is 5 percent—that is, the opportunity cost of the rate available at another bank across the street in an account with the same risk. So, forecasted residual earnings for each year is $5 − (0.05 × $100) = $0. As this asset is expected to yield no residual earnings, its value is equal to its book value, $100.

In the second scenario in Exhibit 5.1, no withdrawals are taken from the account. As a result, both earnings and book values grow as earnings are reinvested in the book values to earn within the account (numbers are rounded to two decimal places). But residual earnings is still zero for each year. For 2013, residual earnings is $5 − (0.05 × $100) = $0; for 2014, residual earnings is $5.25 − (0.05 × $105) = $0; for 2015, residual earnings is $5.5125 − (0.05 × $110.25) = $0, and so on. In all years, the rate of return on book value is equal to the required return. As expected residual earnings are zero, the value of this asset at the end of 2012 is its book value, $100.

Note that in Scenario 1, forecasted dividends are $5 and, with no investment back into the account, free cash flows are also $5 each year. In Scenario 2, cash generated is reinvested in the account, so forecasted dividends are zero, and free cash flows (cash flows minus investment back into the account) are zero. Yet the two scenarios have the same value.

These examples from the savings account bring out some important principles that also apply to the valuation of equities:

1. An asset is worth a premium or discount to its book value only if the book value is expected to earn nonzero residual earnings.
2. Residual earnings techniques recognize that earnings growth does not add value if that growth comes from investments earning the required return. In the second scenario, there is more earnings growth than in the first scenario, but that growth comes from reinvesting earnings in book values to earn at the required return of 5 percent. After charging earnings for the required return on the investment, there is no addition to residual earnings, even though there is growth in earnings. Accordingly, the value of the asset is the same for the case with no earnings growth.
3. Even though an asset does not pay dividends, it can be valued from its book value and earnings forecasts. Forecasting zero dividends in the second scenario will not work, but we have been able to value it from earnings and book values.
4. The valuation of the savings account does not depend on dividend payout. The two scenarios have different expected dividends, but the same value: The valuation based on book values and earnings is insensitive to payout. This is desirable if, indeed, dividends are irrelevant to value, as discussed in Chapter 3.
5. The valuation of the savings account is unrelated to free cash flows. The two scenarios have different free cash flows but the same value. Even though the account for Scenario 2 cannot be valued by forecasting free cash flows over five years—they are zero—it can be valued from its book value.

The Normal Price-to-Book Ratio

The value of the savings account is equal to its book value. That is, the price-to-book ratio is equal to 1.0. A P/B ratio of 1.0 is an important benchmark case, for it is the case where the balance sheet provides the complete valuation. It is also the case where the forecasted return on book value is equal to the required rate of return, and forecasted residual earnings is zero—as with both the savings account and the project earning a 10 percent return.

The required return is sometimes referred to as the normal return for the level of risk in the investment. Accordingly, as an investment with a P/B of 1.0 earns a normal return, a P/B of 1.0 is sometimes referred to as a **normal P/B ratio.**

A MODEL FOR ANCHORING VALUE ON BOOK VALUE

The prototypes show us how to value assets by anchoring on their book value and then adding extra value by forecasting future residual earnings. The anchoring principle is clear:

> *Anchoring principle:* If one forecasts that an asset will earn a return on its book value equal to its required return, it must be worth its book value.

Correspondingly, if one forecasts that an asset will earn a return on book value greater than its required return—positive residual earnings—it must be worth more than book value; there is extra value to be added. The valuation model that captures the extra value for the equity of a going-concern is

$$\text{Value of common equity } (V_0^E) = B_0 + \frac{\text{RE}_1}{\rho_E} + \frac{\text{RE}_2}{\rho_E^2} + \frac{\text{RE}_3}{\rho_E^3} + \cdots \qquad \textbf{(5.1)}$$

where RE is residual earnings for equity:

$$\text{Residual earnings} = \text{Comprehensive earnings} - (\text{Required return for equity} \times \text{Beginning-of-period book value})$$

$$\text{RE}_t = \text{Earn}_t - (\rho_E - 1)B_{t-1}$$

B_0 is the current book value of equity on the balance sheet, and the residual earnings for each period in the future is the comprehensive earnings available to common equity for the period less a charge against the earnings for the book value of common equity at the beginning of the period, B_{t-1}, earning at the required return, $\rho_E - 1$. This required return for equity is also called the equity cost of capital. We will deal with the issue of the required return in Chapter 7. For the moment, see it as the return supplied by a beta technology like the capital asset pricing model (CAPM) (discussed in the appendix to Chapter 3), or just as your own hurdle rate for investing in equities.

We saw in Chapter 2 that Nike, Inc., reported $1,754 million of comprehensive income in 2010 on book value (assets minus liabilities) of $8,693 million. If Nike's shareholders require a 9 percent return, then its 2010 residual earnings was $1,754 - (0.09 \times 8,693) = $971.6 million. Nike added $971.6 million in earnings over a 9 percent return on the shareholders' investment in book value.

We calculate the value of equity by adding the present value of forecasted residual earnings to the current book value in the balance sheet. The forecasted residual earnings are discounted to present value at 1 plus the equity cost of capital, ρ_E. We calculate the intrinsic premium over book value, $V_0^E - B_0$, as the present value of forecasted residual income. This premium is the missing value in the balance sheet. The intrinsic price-to-book ratio is V_0^E/B_0. This makes sense: If we expect a firm to earn income for shareholders over that required on the book value of equity (a positive RE), its equity will be worth more than its book value and should trade at a premium. And the higher the earnings relative to book value, the higher will be the premium.

TABLE 5.1

Price-to-Book Ratios and Subsequent Residual Earnings, 1965–1995.

High-P/B firms yield high residual earnings, on average, and low-P/B firms yield low residual earnings. Residual earnings for P/B ratios close to 1.0 (in Levels 14 and 15) are close to zero.

Source: Company: Standard & Poor's Compustat® data.

P/B Level	P/B	Residual Earnings Each Year after P/B Groups Are Formed (Year 0)					
		0	1	2	3	4	5
1 (high)	6.68	0.181	0.230	0.223	0.221	0.226	0.236
2	3.98	0.134	0.155	0.144	0.154	0.154	0.139
3	3.10	0.109	0.113	0.106	0.101	0.120	0.096
4	2.59	0.090	0.089	0.077	0.093	0.100	0.099
5	2.26	0.076	0.077	0.069	0.068	0.079	0.071
6	2.01	0.066	0.067	0.059	0.057	0.076	0.073
7	1.81	0.057	0.048	0.043	0.052	0.052	0.057
8	1.65	0.042	0.039	0.029	0.039	0.050	0.044
9	1.51	0.043	0.034	0.031	0.038	0.046	0.031
10	1.39	0.031	0.031	0.028	0.036	0.047	0.028
11	1.30	0.024	0.026	0.023	0.035	0.036	0.030
12	1.21	0.026	0.028	0.023	0.036	0.039	0.038
13	1.12	0.016	0.021	0.012	0.031	0.039	0.026
14	1.05	0.009	0.008	0.009	0.026	0.034	0.032
15	0.97	0.006	0.005	0.011	0.018	0.031	0.017
16	0.89	−0.007	−0.011	−0.004	0.008	0.029	0.015
17	0.80	−0.017	−0.018	−0.004	0.006	0.023	0.008
18	0.70	−0.031	0.030	−0.030	−0.010	0.015	−0.001
19	0.58	−0.052	−0.054	−0.039	−0.015	−0.003	−0.008
20 (low)	0.42	−0.090	−0.075	−0.066	−0.037	−0.020	−0.039

Table 5.1 shows that P/B ratios forecast subsequent residual earnings. This table groups all NYSE and AMEX firms into one of 20 groups based on their P/B ratio. The first group (Level 1) includes the firms with the highest 5 percent of P/B ratios, while the bottom group (Level 20) includes those with the lowest 5 percent. The median P/B for Level 1 is 6.68, while that for Level 20 is 0.42, as indicated in the P/B column of the table. The table gives the median RE for each level for the year that firms are grouped (Year 0) and for the subsequent five years. The RE is standardized by book value in Year 0. You can see that the RE entries in Years 1 to 5 are related to the P/B ratios in Year 0: High-P/B firms pay high RE, on average, while low-P/B firms pay low RE. Levels 14 and 15 have P/B close to 1.0 in Year 0 (a zero premium) and, correspondingly, their RE payoffs are close to zero. Price-to-book ratios higher than 1.0 yield positive RE and low P/B ratios yield negative RE. In short, the data for actual firms behave just as the model says.[1]

The residual earnings model always yields the same value that we would get from forecasting dividends over an infinite forecasting horizon. This is important to appreciate, so that you can feel secure about the valuation, because share value is based on the dividends that the share is ultimately expected to pay. The residual earnings model substitutes earnings and book values for dividends. That substitution means that we are really forecasting dividends; however, we get an appreciation of the ultimate dividends that a firm will pay using forecasts of earnings and book values over forecast horizons that are typically shorter than those required for dividend discounting methods. This is what we want for a practical valuation method. The savings account example makes this abundantly clear. In a zero-payout case where dividends might not be paid out for 50 years (say), we would have to forecast dividends very far into the future. But using a residual earnings method, the valuation is immediate—it is given by the current book value.

[1] The same required return for equity of 10 percent is used for all firms in the table. But using a CAPM cost of capital (and thus adjusting firms' required returns for their betas) gives similar patterns.

Return on common equity, ROCE, is comprehensive earnings to common earned during a period relative to the book value of net assets put in place at the beginning of the period. For period 1,

$$ROCE_1 = \frac{\text{Comprehensive earnings to common}_1}{\text{Book value}_0}$$

Comprehensive earnings to common are after preferred dividends and the book value is (of course) the book value of common shareholders' equity. Sometimes this measure is referred to as return on equity (ROE), but we will use ROCE to be clear that it is the return to common shareholders whose shares we are pricing. The ROCE is also referred to as a *book rate of return* or an *accounting rate of return* to distinguish it from the rate of return earned in the market from holding the shares.

Comprehensive income for Nike, Inc., for 2010 was $1,754 million, and the book value of common shareholders' equity at the beginning of the year was $8,693 million. So Nike's ROCE for 2010 was $1,754/$8,693 = 20.18%. This is quite high. But of course, most of Nike's assets—customer relationships, brand, supply chain—are not on its balance sheet, but the earnings from those assets are coming through comprehensive income. The high ROCE explains why Nike traded at a relatively high P/B of 3.67.

Earnings are earned throughout the period and will change with changes in book values through share issues, stock repurchases, or dividends. But book value is measured at a point in time. For short periods, like a fiscal quarter, this does not matter much. But for longer periods, like a full fiscal year, it might. So ROCE for a year is often calculated as

$$ROCE_1 \equiv \frac{\text{Comprehensive earnings}_1}{\frac{1}{2}(B_1 + B_0)}$$

The denominator is the average of beginning and ending book value for the year. This calculation is approximate. More strictly, the denominator should be a weighted average of book values during the year. Significant errors will occur only if there are large share issues or stock repurchases near the beginning or end of a year.

The calculation can be done on a per-share basis:

$$ROCE_1 \equiv \frac{EPS_1}{BPS_0}$$

(with EPS based on comprehensive income). BPS is book value of common equity divided by shares outstanding (and shares outstanding is issued shares minus shares in treasury). The EPS are weighted down for share issues and repurchases during the year by the weighted-average calculation. So this calculation keeps the numerator and denominator on the same per-share basis.

The three calculations typically give different answers but the difference is usually small. It is, however, dangerous to compare ROCE over time with calculations based on per-share amounts because share issues and repurchases affect EPS and BPS differently.

Residual Earnings Drivers and Value Creation

Residual earnings is the return on common equity, expressed as a dollar excess return rather than a ratio. For every earnings period t, we can restate residual earnings as

$$\text{Residual earnings} = (\text{ROCE} - \text{Required return on equity}) \times \text{Book value of common equity} \qquad \textbf{(5.2)}$$

$$\underset{(1)}{\text{Earn}_t - (\rho_E - 1)B_{t-1}} = \underset{(2)}{[\text{ROCE}_t - (\rho_E - 1)]B_{t-1}}$$

where $\text{ROCE}_t = \text{Earn}_t/B_{t-1}$ is the **rate of return on common equity.** Box 5.1 takes you through the calculation of ROCE. Thus residual earnings compares ROCE to the required return, $\rho_E - 1$, and expresses the difference as a dollar amount by multiplying it by the beginning-of-period book value. Nike's (comprehensive) ROCE for 2010 was 20.18 percent (from Box 5.1). If its required return on equity (the equity cost of capital) was 9 percent, then its residual earnings was $(0.2018 - 0.09) \times $8,693 = 971.6 million, which is the same number as we got before (adjusted for rounding error). If ROCE equals the required return, RE will be zero. If we forecast that the firm will earn an ROCE equal to its cost of capital indefinitely in the future, intrinsic price will be equal to book value. If we forecast that ROCE will be greater than the cost of capital, the equity should sell at a premium. If we forecast that ROCE will be less than the cost of capital, the equity should sell at a discount.

RE is determined by two components, **(1)** and **(2)** in expression 5.2. The first is ROCE and the second is the amount of the book value of the equity investment (assets minus liabilities, or net assets) that are put in place in each period. These two components are called **residual earnings drivers.** Firms increase their value over book value by increasing their ROCE above the cost of capital. But they further increase their value by **growth in book value (net assets)** that will earn at this ROCE. For a given ROCE (greater than the cost of capital), a firm will add more value with more investments earning at that ROCE. Indeed these two drivers are sometimes referred to as *value drivers.* Determining the premium or discount at which a share should sell involves forecasting these two drivers. Figure 5.1 depicts how forecasts of the two drivers, along with the current book value, yield current value. You can see how this model can be a strategy analysis tool: Increase value by adopting strategies that increase ROCE above the required return and grow book values (net assets) that can earn at an ROCE above the required return. That, of course, is what business is all about! And that will drive the financial statement analysis in Part Two of the book to discover the value in a business.

On the next page selected firms ranked by their P/B ratios in 2010, along with the ROCE they earned in 2010 and their book value growth rates for the year.

FIGURE 5.1 **The Drivers of Residual Earnings and the Calculation of the Value of Equity**
Residual earnings is driven by return on common equity (ROCE) and the book value of investments put in place. Valuation involves forecasting future ROCE and the growth in the book values of net assets, discounting the residual earnings that they produce to present value, and adding the current book value.

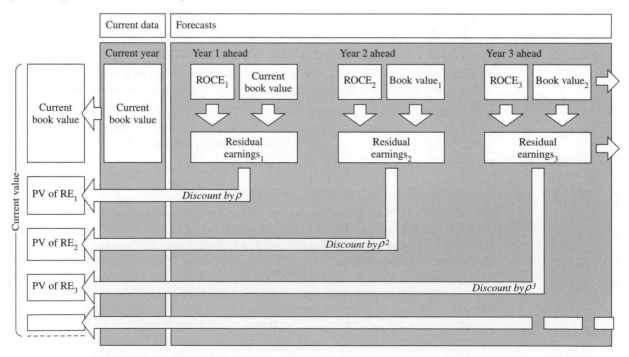

A number of large insurance companies, including John Hancock Mutual Life Insurance and Metropolitan Life Insurance, have converted from mutual companies owned by policyholders to companies owned by shareholders. The process of "demutualization" involves issuing shares to policyholders and new investors in an initial public offering.

When these two firms demutualized, analysts conjectured that they would be priced at book value. They were earning 9 percent–12 percent return on equity and analysts did not expect this rate of return to improve. Why might they trade at book value? Well, if the return that investors require to buy the initial share issue is also 9 percent–12 percent, the firms would be expected to generate zero residual earnings from their book values, and so should be priced at book value.

John Hancock's initial public offering was on January 27, 2000, when it became John Hancock Financial Services, Inc. The firm's ROCE was 12 percent. It issued 331.7 million shares, 229.7 million to policyholders. These shares traded at $17¼ per share, a little above book value of $15 per share.

	P/B	ROCE	Book Value Growth Rate
H. J. Heinz Co.	6.1	42.3%	55%
Coca-Cola Company	5.1	41.9%	25%
Kimberly-Clark Corp.	4.5	32.7%	10%
Dell, Inc.	3.8	39.3%	38%
Nike, Inc.	3.7	20.2%	12%
Exxon Mobil Corp.	2.9	23.4%	33%
Cisco Systems, Inc.	2.1	17.4%	15%
Macy's, Inc.	1.9	16.6%	19%
General Electric Co.	1.8	10.6%	1%
Kraft Foods, Inc.	1.6	8.1%	38%
J. P. Morgan Chase & Co.	1.1	10.2%	7%
Banco Santander, S.A.	1.0	11.8%	10%
Sony Corp.	0.9	3.6%	6%
Panasonic Corp.	0.8	−0.9%	6%
Bank of America Corp.	0.6	−1.0%	−1%

You can see that P/B is related to ROCE and growth in book value. Banco Santander, S.A. and J. P. Morgan Chase have a P/B close to 1.0 and correspondingly earned an ROCE of 11.8 and 10.2 percent, roughly equal to what is considered to be the typical required return on equity. Thus residual earnings for these firms were roughly zero, appropriate for a normal P/B ratio of 1.0. Other firms have considerably higher P/B and, correspondingly, higher ROCE and growth rate in book value. Sony, Panasonic, and Bank of America have P/B less than 1.0 and also have low ROCE and book value growth rates. Now look at Box 5.2.

A few firms do not give the full story, of course, so look at Figure 5.2. This figure plots 2010 ROCE for the S&P 500 firms on their P/B. The regression line through the plots shows that higher P/B is associated with higher ROCE on average. The plot is typical of most years. Of course, many firms do not fall on the regression line and it is the task of financial analysis to explain why. Is it growth in book value, the second driver? Or is it because ROCE in the future will be different from the present?

For a historical picture of ROCE and book value growth, Figure 5.3 plots percentiles of ROCE over the years 1963–2010 for U.S. firms. The median ROCE over all years is

FIGURE 5.2
Price-to-Book Ratios for S&P 500 Firms and Subsequent Return on Common Equity (ROCE).
The figure plots ROCE in 2010 on price-to-book ratios (P/B) at the end of 2010. The line through the dots is the regression line for the relationship between ROCE and P/B: ROCE is positively related to P/B.

Source: Standard & Poor's COMPUSTAT® data.

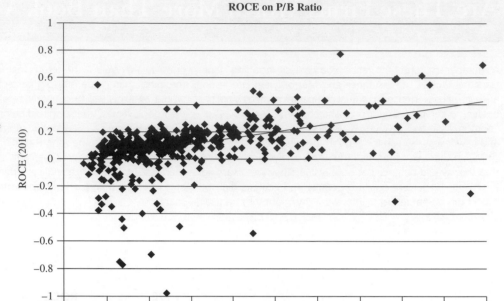

FIGURE 5.3
Percentiles of ROCE for all U.S. Traded Firms with Market Capitalization over $200 million, 1963–2010.
The median ROCE over all years is 13.7 percent.

Source: Standard & Poor's COMPUSTAT® data.

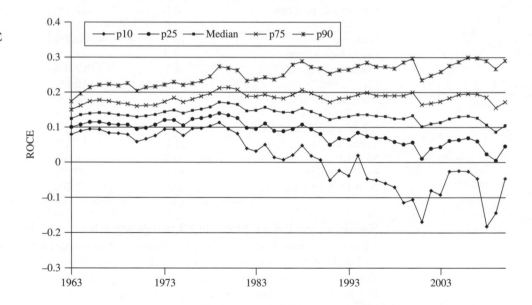

13.7 percent, but there is considerable variation. Accordingly, there has been considerable variation in P/B ratios, as indicated in Figure 2.2 in Chapter 2. The average ROCE for the S&P 500 over the 30 years to 2010 (based on a market-value weighting of stocks in the index) has been 18 percent (and the average S&P 500 P/B ratio has been 2.5).

A Simple Demonstration and a Simple Valuation Model

Exhibit 5.2 presents forecasts of comprehensive earnings and dividends over five years for a firm with $100 million in book value at the end of the current year, Year 0. The required equity return is 10 percent and we must value the equity at time 0.

EXHIBIT 5.2
Forecasts for a
Simple Firm
In millions of dollars.
Required return is
10 percent.

		Forecast Year				
	0	**1**	**2**	**3**	**4**	**5**
Earnings	12.00	12.36	12.73	13.11	13.51	13.91
Dividends	9.09	9.36	9.64	9.93	10.23	10.53
Book value	100.00	103.00	106.09	109.27	112.55	115.93
RE (10% charge)		2.36	2.43	2.50	2.58	2.66
RE growth rate			3%	3%	3%	3%

Future book values are forecasted using the stocks and flows equation of Chapter 2:

Ending book value = Beginning book value + Comprehensive income − Net dividend

The expected book value at the end of Year 1, in millions, is $103 = $100 + 12.36 − 9.36. Residual earnings for Year 1 is $12.36 − (0.10 × 100) = $2.36 million, and similarly for subsequent years. You can see that forecasted residual earnings is growing at a 3 percent rate per year after Year 1, so a simple valuation capitalizes the residual earnings forecasted for Year 1 as a perpetuity with growth:

$$V_0^E = B_0 + \frac{RE_1}{\rho_E - g}$$

With $g = 1.03$ and $\rho_E = 1.10$, the valuation is

$$V_0^E = \$100 + \frac{\$2.36}{1.10 - 1.03} = \$133.71 \text{ million}$$

The intrinsic price-to-book ratio (P/B) is $133.71/$100 = 1.34. This is a *simple valuation model:* A constant growth rate is applied to the forecast for the forward year. The forecast horizon is very short, just one year ahead.

This simple example demonstrates that the RE model gives the same valuation that would result from forecasting dividends indefinitely into the future. Dividends are expected to grow at 3 percent per year in this example, so

$$V_0^E = \frac{d_1}{\rho_E - g} = \frac{9.36}{1.10 - 1.03} = 133.71 \text{ million}$$

This is a stylized case in which the dividend discount model works because the payout is tied directly to earnings with a fixed payout ratio, and growth in dividends is the same as growth in residual earnings. As we saw in Chapter 4, this is not usually the case, as the savings account with zero payout makes abundantly clear. However, the accrual accounting model supplies the desired valuation.

APPLYING THE MODEL TO EQUITIES

The forecasting long-run (to infinity) that is required for the going-concern model (5.1) is a challenge. The criteria for a practical valuation technique in Chapter 3 require finite forecast horizons, the shorter the better. For a forecast over a T-period horizon,

$$V_0^E = B_0 + \frac{RE_1}{\rho_E} + \frac{RE_2}{\rho_E^2} + \frac{RE_3}{\rho_E^3} + \cdots + \frac{RE_T}{\rho_E^T} + \frac{V_T^E - B_T}{\rho_E^T} \qquad \textbf{(5.3)}$$

where $V_T^E - B_T$ is the forecast of the intrinsic premium at the forecast horizon.

Current book value is of course in the current balance sheet, leaving us with the task of forecasting residual earnings and the horizon premium. We also need to choose a forecast horizon. The **horizon premium**—the stock's expected value relative to book value T periods from now—appears to be a particular challenge. Indeed, the model appears circular: To determine the current premium, we need to calculate a premium expected in the future. The calculation of this premium is the problem of determining a continuing value at the horizon. This section focuses on the problem.

Here are the steps to follow for a residual earnings valuation:

1. Identify the book value in the most recent balance sheet.
2. Forecast earnings and dividends up to a forecast horizon.
3. Forecast future book values from current book values and your forecasts of earnings and dividends.

$$\text{Book value} = \text{Beginning Book value} + \text{Earnings} - \text{Dividends}$$

4. Calculate future residual earnings from the forecasts of earnings and book values.
5. Discount the residual earnings to present value.
6. Calculate a continuing value at the forecast horizon.
7. Discount the continuing value to present value.
8. Add 1, 5, and 7.

Case 1 applies these steps to Flanigan's Enterprises, Inc., a firm operating chain restaurants and beverage stores. The first two lines give the firm's basic earnings per share (EPS) and dividends per share (DPS) for 2000 through 2003. Let's play the same game as in Chapter 4 and pretend that we are forecasting at the end of 1999 but know for sure what the subsequent earnings and dividends are going to be. From forecasts of EPS and DPS we can compute successive book values per share (BPS) by adding EPS to beginning-of-period BPS and subtracting DPS. So the forecast of BPS for the end of 2001, for example, is 4.76, as shown below the valuation.

With a forecast of EPS and BPS we can forecast RE. The cost of capital is 9 percent, so RE for 2001 is $0.80 - (0.09 \times 4.20) = 0.422$ or, calculating it from the forecasts of ROCE and book value, RE is $(0.1905 - 0.09) \times 4.20 = 0.422$, as also shown below the valuation.

Now suppose we wished to value this firm at the end of 1999. We would take the present value of the RE forecasts (the discount factors are 1.09^t), sum them, and add the sum to the 1999 book value of $3.58 per share. This gives us a valuation of $4.53 per share, as shown. The calculated premium over book value is $4.53 - 3.58 = 0.95$. Is our valuation correct? Well, it would be if we forecasted RE after 2003 to be zero. You see the RE are declining over the years toward zero. Although the book value driver of RE is increasing, the ROCE driver is declining, and in 2003 it is 9.0 percent, equal to the cost of capital. It looks as if RE from 2003 and onward might be zero. If so, we have completed the valuation. We can write it as

$$V_0^E = B_0 + \frac{RE_1}{\rho_E} + \frac{RE_2}{\rho_E^2} + \frac{RE_3}{\rho_E^3} \quad \textbf{Case 1} \tag{5.4}$$

where, in this case, Year 0 is 1999 and Year T (three years ahead) is 2002.

Compare this calculation with model 5.3. The horizon premium is missing in the calculation here and this makes sense: If RE after the forecast horizon is forecasted to be zero, then the forecast of the premium at that point must be zero. We have forecasted $V_T^E - B_T = 0$.

The Forecast Horizon and the Continuing Value Calculation

How typical is a Case 1 valuation? Well, let's return to General Electric (GE), the firm for which discounted cash flow analysis failed in Chapter 4. Case 2 displays the same five years

CASE 1

Flanigan's Enterprises, Inc.

Required rate of return is 9 percent. In this case, residual earnings is expected to be zero after 2003.

		Forecast Year			
	1999	**2000**	**2001**	**2002**	**2003**
EPS		0.73	0.80	0.71	0.47
DPS		0.11	0.24	0.25	0.27
BPS	3.58	4.20	4.76	5.22	5.42
ROCE		20.4%	19.0%	14.9%	9.0%
RE (9% charge)		0.408	0.422	0.282	0.000
Discount rate (1.09^t)		1.09	1.188	1.295	1.412
Present value of RE		0.374	0.355	0.217	0.000
Total present value of RE to 2003	0.95				
Value per share	4.53				

How the forecasts are developed (for 2001):

Forecasting Book Value per Share (BPS)		**Forecasting Residual Earnings**	
Beginning BPS (a)	4.20	Forecasted ROCE (b/a)	19.05%
Forecasted EPS (b)	0.80	Cost of equity capital	−9.00
Forecasted DPS	(0.24)	Excess ROCE (c)	10.05%
Ending BPS	4.76	RE $(a \times c)$	0.422
		Alternatively,	
		RE $= 0.80 - (0.09 \times 4.20)$	0.422

CASE 2

General Electric Co.

Required rate of return is 10 percent. In this case, residual earnings is expected to be constant, but nonzero, after 2004.

		Forecast Year				
	1999	**2000**	**2001**	**2002**	**2003**	**2004**
EPS		1.29	1.38	1.42	1.50	1.60
DPS		0.57	0.66	0.73	0.77	0.82
BPS	4.32	5.04	5.76	6.45	7.18	7.96
ROCE		29.9%	27.4%	24.7%	23.3%	22.3%
RE (10% charge)		0.858	0.876	0.844	0.855	0.882
Discount rate (1.10^t)		1.100	1.210	1.331	1.464	1.611
Present value of RE		0.780	0.724	0.634	0.584	0.548
Total present value of RE to 2004	3.27					
Continuing value (CV)						8.82
Present value of CV	5.48					
Value per share	13.07					

The continuing value:

$$CV = \frac{0.882}{0.10} = 8.82$$

Present value of continuing value $= \dfrac{8.82}{1.6105} = 5.48$

Note: Allow for rounding errors.

as earlier, but now the EPS, DPS, and BPS are given. Again pretending these actual numbers are numbers forecasted in 1999, forecasted RE and ROCE have been calculated. We charge GE a 10 percent cost for using equity capital. The sum of the present values of the RE up to 2004 (3.27 per share), added to the 1999 book value of 4.32 per share, yield a valuation of 7.59 per share. But this is not correct because GE is earning a positive RE in 2004 and will probably continue with positive RE in subsequent years. GE has a declining ROCE driver, but its growth in book value more than offsets this to maintain its RE. The valuation of 7.59 per share is missing the continuing value, the continuing premium in model 5.3.

The continuing value is the value of residual earnings beyond the horizon. Look at the series of RE forecasts for GE up to the 2004 horizon. You can see that RE is fairly constant. Suppose we forecast that RE beyond 2004 is going to be the same as the 0.882 in 2004: The subsequent RE will be a perpetuity. The value of the perpetuity is the capitalized amount of the perpetuity: $0.882/0.10 = 8.82$, as shown below the valuation. And as this is the value of expected REs after 2004, it is also the value of the expected premium at the end of 2004. So we can replace model 5.3 with

$$V_0^E = B_0 + \frac{RE_1}{\rho_E} + \frac{RE_2}{\rho_E^2} + \cdots + \frac{RE_T}{\rho_E^T} + \left(\frac{RE_{T+1}}{\rho_E - 1}\right) / \rho_E^T \quad \textbf{Case 2} \qquad (5.5)$$

where, in GE's case, T is five years ahead. So the 1999 valuation is $13.07 = 4.32 + 3.27 + 8.82/1.6105$. The calculated premium is $13.07 - 4.32 = 8.75$. The RE forecasts for 2005 and beyond supply the continuing value (CV) at the end of 2004 and this is the expected premium in 2004: $V_5^E - B_5 = 8.82$.

We refer to the case of constant RE after the forecast horizon as Case 2. You might expect Case 1 to be typical: A firm might earn a positive RE for a while (ROCE greater than the cost of capital), but eventually competition will drive its profitability down so its ROCE will equal the cost of capital. High ROCE do decline, as illustrated by both Flanigan's Enterprises and GE, but it is more common for ROCE and RE to level off at a positive amount. If so, Case 2 applies.

Note that we are able to value General Electric, even though its free cash flows are negative. By applying accrual accounting, we have dealt with the problem that haunted us in Chapter 4. Exercise E5.11 looks at GE in 2004.

As there is no expected growth in RE after the forecast horizon, we can refer to Case 2 as the no-growth valuation. Case 3 is a growth valuation, demonstrated with Nike, for the fiscal years 2006 to 2011. With the exception of the recession year, 2009, Nike's residual earnings are growing, with declining ROCE but growing book values. It is probably unreasonable to expect RE to be constant or zero after 2011. If the growth is forecast to continue, the continuing value calculation can be modified by adding a growth rate:

$$V_0^E = B_0 + \frac{RE_1}{\rho_E} + \frac{RE_2}{\rho_E^2} + \frac{RE_3}{\rho_E^3} + \cdots + \frac{RE_T}{\rho_E^T} + \left(\frac{RE_{T+1}}{\rho_E - g}\right) / \rho_E^T \quad \textbf{Case 3} \qquad (5.6)$$

where g is 1 plus the rate of growth.[2] Nike's RE growth rate in 2011 is 2.108/2.017, that is about 4.5 percent ($g = 1.045$). If this rate were expected to continue after 2011, the forecasted RE for 2012 would be $2.108 \times 1.045 = 2.203$. So the continuing value is 48.95, and

---

[2] The growth rate has to be less than the cost of capital or the terminal value calculation "blows up." It is unreasonable to expect a firm's RE to grow at a rate greater than the cost of capital indefinitely (and so have an infinite price). Growth could be negative at a horizon (g < 1). This is typically a case of a positive RE declining toward zero.

CASE 3

Nike, Inc.
Required rate of return is 9 percent. In this case, residual earnings is expected to grow at a 4.5 percent rate after 2011.

			Forecast Year			
	2006	**2007**	**2008**	**2009**	**2010**	**2011**
EPS		2.96	3.80	3.07	3.93	4.28
DPS		0.71	0.88	0.98	1.06	1.20
BPS	14.00	16.25	19.17	21.26	24.13	27.21
ROCE		21.1%	23.4%	16.0%	18.5%	17.7%
RE (9% charge)		1.700	2.338	1.345	2.017	2.108
Discount rate (1.09^t)		1.090	1.188	1.295	1.412	1.539
Present value of RE		1.560	1.968	1.039	1.429	1.370
Total present value of RE to 2011	7.37					
Continuing value (CV)						48.95
Present value of CV	31.81					
Value per share	53.18					

The continuing value:

$$CV = \frac{2.108 \times 1.045}{1.09 - 1.045} = 48.95$$

$$\text{Present value of continuing value} = \frac{48.95}{1.539} = 31.81$$

Note: Allow for rounding errors.

its present value at the end of 2006 is 31.81, as indicated at the bottom of the case study. The value at the end of 2006 is $V_0^E = 14.00 + 7.37 + 31.81 = 53.18$.

Case 3, along with Cases 1 and 2, completes the set of cases we are likely to meet in practice. The long-term level of RE and its growth rate are sometimes referred to as the **steady-state condition** for the firm. The growth rate distinguishes the growth of Case 3 from the no-growth of Case 2. (For Case 2, g = 1.0.) Look at Box 5.3 for some technical issues when calculating continuing values.

Beware of Paying Too Much for Growth

You probably get the feeling that determining a long-term growth rate is the most uncertain part of a valuation. In our examples, we extrapolated growth rates from what we saw up to the forecast horizon—no-growth for GE based on the constant residual earnings and positive growth for Nike based on the growth rate in the horizon year. Growth up to the forecast horizon gives some information about long-term growth, but it is unwise to extrapolate—even worse to assume a rate. Rather we should investigate the information that informs about the growth rate. Accordingly, analyzing and forecasting growth will be a focus of our financial statement analysis in Part Two of the text.

At this point, we might well remind ourselves of the fundamentalist dictum in Chapter 1: *Beware of paying too much for growth.* Fundamental investors see growth as risky; unless the firm has "barriers to entry"—maybe due to a protected brand, like Nike—growth can easily be competed away. The stock market tends to get overexcited about growth prospects, with most bubbles forming around exaggerated growth expectations. Fundamental investors are thus careful about buying growth. *The risk in investing is the risk of paying too much* and that often comes down to paying too much for growth. It is easy to plug in a growth rate to a formula but that can be dangerous.

Once we have our valuation framework in place in this and the next chapter, we proceed in Chapter 7 to the task of applying the framework in a way that protects us from paying too much

A continuing value is always calculated at the end of a period on the basis of a forecast for the following period. So a continuing value at the end of Year T is based on a forecast of residual earnings for T + 1:

$$CV_T = \frac{RE_{T+1}}{\rho_E - g}$$

This continuing value is discounted to present value at the discount rate for Year T, ρ_E^T.
   The following calculations give the same value:

$$V_0^E = B_0 + \frac{RE_1}{\rho_E} + \frac{RE_2}{\rho_E \times (\rho_E - g)} \quad (1)$$

$$V_0^E = B_0 + \frac{RE_1}{\rho_E} + \frac{RE_2}{\rho_E^2} + \frac{RE_2 \times g}{\rho_E^2 \times (\rho_E - g)} \quad (2)$$

Calculation (1) draws the continuing value at the end of Year 1 based on residual earnings for Year 2 growing at the rate, g. Calculation (2) draws the continuing value at the end of Year 2 based on residual earnings for Year 3, but also has residual earnings in Year 2 growing at the rate, g into Year 3
   The following valuations for Home Depot illustrate (with a required return of 10 percent and a 4 percent growth rate). Home Depot, the warehouse retailer, has a book value of $12.67 per share, with residual earnings of $1.713 and $1.755 forecasted for Year 1 and Year 2 ahead respectively.

$$V_0^E = \$12.67 + \frac{1.713}{1.10} + \frac{1.755}{1.10 \times (1.10 - 1.04)} = \$40.82 \quad (1)$$

$$V_0^E = \$12.67 + \frac{1.713}{1.10} + \frac{1.755}{1.21} + \frac{1.755 \times 1.04}{1.21 \times (1.10 - 1.04)} \quad (2)$$

$$= \$40.82$$

for growth. At this stage you should have some assurance that the methods here are helpful. We saw in Chapter 4 that discounted cash flow valuation often leaves us with a high proportion of the calculated value in the speculative continuing value. Indeed, for General Electric we saw that over 100 percent of the value was in the continuing value. In contrast, our Case 2 valuation for GE here captured a considerable part of the value in the book value and short-term forecasts about which we are more confident. That is the result of using accrual accounting—income statements and balance sheets rather than cash flows—which typically brings the future forward in time. Nevertheless, there remains a continuing value calculation to take care of.

Converting Analysts' Forecasts to a Valuation

Analysts typically forecast earnings for one or two years ahead and then forecast intermediate-term growth rates for subsequent years, usually three to five years. These forecasts are available on Yahoo! and Google Finance Web sites. The forecasts for one and two years ahead are somewhat reliable (but buyer beware!); however, analysts' growth rate forecasts are often not much more than a guess. In any case, given the forecasts, the investor asks: How can the forecasts be converted to a valuation?

   Table 5.2 gives consensus analysts' forecasts for Nike, Inc., made after fiscal 2010 financial statements were published. A consensus forecast is an average of forecasts made by sell-side analysts covering the stock. The forecasts for 2011–2012 are point estimates, and those for 2013–2015 are the forecasts implied by the analysts' five-year intermediate-term EPS growth rate of 11 percent per year. Analysts typically do not forecast dividends, so one usually assumes that the current payout ratio—DPS/EPS—will be maintained in the future. Nike paid $1.06 per share in dividends during 2010 on EPS of $3.93, so its payout ratio was 27 percent. You can see from the table that Nike's residual earnings, calculated from the analysts' forecasts, are growing. Analysts do not forecast earnings for the very long run, but if we were to forecast that RE after 2015 were to grow at a rate equal to the typical rate of growth in Gross Domestic Product (GDP) of 4 percent, we would establish a continuing value of $70.62, as indicated in the table. The value implied by the analysts' forecasts is $77.24 per share. At the time, Nike's shares traded at $74 each. So, on these calculations, Nike is reasonably priced.

TABLE 5.2   Converting Analysts' Forecasts to a Valuation: Nike, Inc. (NKE)

Analysts forecast EPS two years ahead ($4.29 for 2011 and $4.78 for 2012) and also forecast a five-year EPS growth rate of 11 percent. Forecasts for 2013–2015 apply this consensus EPS growth rate to the 2012 estimate. Dividends per share (DPS) are set at the 2010 payout rate of 27 percent of earnings. Required rate of return is 10 percent. Years labeled A are actual numbers, years labeled E are expected numbers.

	2010 A	2011 E	2012 E	2013 E	2014 E	2015 E
EPS	3.93	4.29	4.78	5.31	5.89	6.54
DPS	1.06	1.16	1.29	1.43	1.59	1.77
BPS	20.15	23.28	26.77	30.65	34.95	39.72
ROCE		21.3%	20.5%	19.8%	19.2%	18.7%
RE (9% charge)		2.477	2.685	2.901	3.132	3.395
Discount rate $(1.09)^t$		1.090	1.188	1.295	1.412	1.539
Present value of RE		2.272	2.260	2.240	2.218	2.206
Total PV to 2015	11.20					
Continuing value (CV)						70.62
Present value of CV	45.89					
Value per share	77.24					

The continuing value based on the GDP growth rate:

$$CV = \frac{3.395 \times 1.04}{1.09 - 1.04} = 70.62$$

Note: Allow for rounding errors.

In this Nike valuation, we used the average historical GDP growth rate of 4 percent as the long-run growth rate. With the calculated value of $77.24 close to the market price of $74, we have learned something else: Given that the analysts' forecasts are reasonable, the market is pricing Nike on the basis of a 4 percent GDP growth rate in the long run. This makes some sense: In the long run, we expect residual earnings for all firms to grow at the GDP growth rate. Box 5.4 provides more justification for using a GDP growth rate, at least as a first guess, and also gives you a feel for how well the valuation model of this chapter works on average.

Although the GDP growth rate may work well on average, it is probably not appropriate for all firms. While we might expect all firms to grow at the GDP rate in the long run, some (including Nike) may be able to sustain a higher growth rate for a considerable period of time. Yet others may never achieve growth at the GDP rate. We have more work to do in investigating growth and Chapter 7 takes up the task.

BUILD YOUR OWN VALUATION ENGINE

The mechanics of the valuations in Cases 1, 2, 3, and Table 5.2 can easily be handled in a spreadsheet. The spreadsheet requires the following inputs: (1) current book value, (2) earnings and dividend forecasts up to a given forecast horizon, (3) a required return, and (4) a long-term growth rate to calculate the continuing value. You then build in the spreadsheet calculations to forecast future book values, residual earnings, a continuing value, and finally the present value of the forecasts. The standard spreadsheet has forecasts for two years ahead (that's what analysts forecast) and applies a growth rate for years thereafter. A more flexible engine allows for different forecast horizons.

Value-to-price ratios compare calculated value to the current market price. If a V/P ratio is more than 1.0, a buy recommendation is implied. If the V/P ratio is less than 1.0, a sell recommendation is implied.

The graph below tracks median V/P ratios for all U.S. listed firms from 1975 to 2001. Value is estimated using analysts' consensus forecasts for two years ahead, converting them into a residual earnings forecast (as in Table 5.2), and then applying a GDP growth rate of 4 percent for growth in residual earnings thereafter. That is,

$$V_0^{\mathcal{E}} = B_0 + \frac{RE_1}{\rho} + \frac{RE_2}{\rho^2} + \frac{RE_2 \times g}{\rho^2(\rho - g)}$$

The required return, ρ, is set at the risk-free rate (on U.S. government 10-year obligations) for each year plus a 5 percent risk premium. This valuation is only approximate as the continuing value and the required return will be different for different firms.

Even though the valuation is approximate, you can see that V/P ratio oscillates around 1.0. When the V/P ratio is above 1.0—indicating prices are too low—it tends to revert to 1.0 as prices adjust to fundamentals. When V/P is below 1.0—indicating prices are too high—it tends to revert back to 1.0. The pattern could be due to discount rates changing as market-wide risk changes, so one does have to be careful. We have used a risk premium of 5 percent at all points in time in calculating V here. But in bad times, like the 1970s, investors might require a higher risk premium, pushing prices down. In good times, like the 1990s, the risk premium declines, so prices rise. This is the "efficient markets" interpretation of the graph.

The graph of the V/P ratio also tells us that the GDP long-term growth rate that we used for Nike in Table 5.2 also works for the average firm. It is a good first guess at the growth rate. But guesses are not sufficient; what works on average may not work for firms that are different from average. The challenge is to identify superior (or inferior) growth. That challenge is taken up in the financial statement analysis of Part Two of this text.

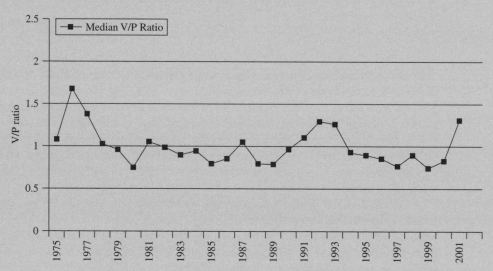

Source: Prices are from Standard & Poor's COMPUSTAT®. Analysts' earnings forecasts are from Thomson Financial I/B/E/S data.

With these inputs, you can calculate a value at the press of a button. Further, to understand your uncertainty about the valuation, the engine can show how the value changes with different inputs. For example, you might be comfortable with inputting your own hurdle rate for the required return—9 percent, say—but you are unsure of the long-term growth rate. The GDP growth rate was applied in Table 5.2, but you might look at the sensitivity of the valuation to a 3 percent or 2 percent rate: What is the stock worth if it delivers only 2 percent growth? If you believe 2 percent is conservative and the stock is trading below the calculated value, you may feel comfortable in buying the stock. If, on the other hand, you see that, by experimenting with alternative growth rates, a 6 percent growth rate is required to justify the market price, then you might see the stock as too expensive.

With such scenario experimentation, you are focusing on the most important aspect of valuation: understanding your uncertainty. We will build on this theme in Chapter 7, with the spreadsheet engine developed further for the purpose. The engine will then be expanded by building in the financial statement analysis of Part Two of the book until you have developed a full analysis and valuation product. The Build Your Own Analysis Product (BYOAP) on the book's Web site will be your guide.

You might be tempted to appropriate an off-the-shelf valuation spreadsheet. You can do this—it's available within BYOAP in fact—but nothing helps your learning more than building the product yourself. You will be proud of the results. You will be more secure in using the product to value firms and to challenge market prices. You will find yourself adding bells and whistles. And you will find yourself taking the product into your professional life and using it for your personal investing.

APPLYING THE MODEL TO PROJECTS AND STRATEGIES

The RE method also can be used to value projects within the firm. At the beginning of the chapter we demonstrated this for a simple one-period project. Multiperiod project evaluation is typically done using NPV analysis (of cash flows), as for the project in Figure 3.4 in Chapter 3 that required an investment of $1,200. Table 5.3 accounts for that project using accrual accounting. The revenue is from the cash inflow but depreciation has been deducted to get the net income from the project. The depreciation is calculated using the straight-line method, that is, by spreading cost less estimated salvage value (the depreciation base) over the five years. The book value of the project each year is its original cost minus accumulated depreciation. And this book value follows the stocks and flows equation, similar to equities:

$$\text{Book value}_t = \text{Book value}_{t-1} + \text{Income}_t - \text{Cash flow}_t$$

So the book value in Year 1 is $1,200 + 214 - 430 = $984, and similiarly for subsequent years. (The cash flow comes from the revenues.) At the end of Year 5, the book value is zero as the assets in the project are sold for estimated salvage value. This is standard accrual accounting.

TABLE 5.3 **Project Evaluation: Residual Earnings Approach.**
Hurdle rate: 12 percent.

		Forecast Year				
	0	**1**	**2**	**3**	**4**	**5**
Revenues		$430	$460	$460	$380	$250
Depreciation		216	216	216	216	216
Project income		214	244	244	164	34
Book value	$1,200	984	768	552	336	0
Book rate of return		17.8%	24.8%	31.8%	29.7%	10.1%
Residual project income (0.12)		70	126	152	98	(6)
Discount rate (1.12^t)		1.120	1.254	1.405	1.574	1.762
PV of RE		62.5	100.5	108.2	62.3	(3.4)
Total PV of RE	330					
Value of project	$1,530		Value added = $330			

TABLE 5.4 Strategy Evaluation.
Hurdle rate: 12 percent.

	0	1	2	3	4	5	6 . . .
				Forecast Year			
Residual Earnings Approach							
Revenues		$430	$890	$1,350	$1,730	$1,980	$1,980 . . .
Depreciation		216	432	648	864	1,080	1,080
Strategy income		214	458	702	866	900	900 . . .
Book value	$1,200	2,184	2,952	3,504	3,840	3,840	3,840 . . .
Book rate of return		17.8%	21.0%	23.8%	24.7%	23.4%	23.4%
Residual strategy income (0.12)		70.0	195.9	347.8	445.5	439.2	439.2 . . .
PV of RE		62.5	156.2	247.5	283.0	249.3	
Total PV of RE	999						
Continuing value[1]						3,660	
PV of CV	2,077						
Value of strategy	$4,276		Value added:	$3,076			
Discounted Cash Flow Approach							
Cash inflow		$430	$890	$1,350	$1,730	$2,100	$2,100 . . .
Investment	$(1,200)	(1,200)	(1,200)	(1,200)	(1,200)	(1,200)	(1,200) . .
Free cash flow	(1,200)	(770)	(310)	150	530	900	900 . . .
PV of FCF		(687.5)	(247.2)	106.8	336.7	510.7	
Total PV of FCF	20						
Continuing value[2]						7,500	
PV of CV	4,256						
Value of strategy	$4,276		Net present value:	$3,076			

[1]CV = 439.2/0.12 = $3,660.
[2]CV = 900/0.12 = $7,500.

The value of the project is its book value plus the present value of expected residual income calculated from the forecasts of net income and book values. This value of $1,530 is the same as the discounted cash flow valuation in Chapter 3. The forecasts of RE have captured the value added over the cost of the investment: The present value of the forecasts of RE of $330 equals the NPV we calculated in Chapter 3.

Strategy involves a series of ongoing investments. Table 5.4 evaluates a strategy which (to keep it simple) requires investing $1,200 in the same project as before but in each year indefinitely. The revenues are those from all overlapping projects in existence in a given year: The revenue in Year 1 is $430 from the project begun in Year 0, the revenue in Year 2 of $890 is the second year's revenue ($460) from the project begun in Year 0 plus the first year's revenue from the project begun in Year 1 ($430), and so on. Depreciation is the same as before ($216 per year for a project), so total depreciation is $216 times the number of projects operating at a time. By the fifth year into the strategy there are five projects operating each year with a steady stream of $1,980 in revenues and $1,080 in depreciation. Book value at all points is accumulated net investment less accumulated depreciation.

You see from the calculations that the strategy adds $3,076 of value to the initial investment of $1,200 if the required return is 12 percent, and this value added is the present value of expected residual income from the project. You also see from the second panel that this value added equals the NPV of the strategy calculated using discounted cash flow analysis.

ADVANTAGES

Focus on value drivers:	Focuses on profitability of investment in net assets and growth in net assets, which drive value; directs strategic thinking to these drivers.
Incorporates the financial statements appropriately:	Incorporates the value already recognized in the balance sheet (the book value); to add value to the balance sheet, it forecasts the income statement, which typically is a better measure of value added than the cash flow statement.
Uses accrual accounting:	Uses the properties of accrual accounting that recognize value added ahead of cash flows, matches value added to value given up, and treats investment as an asset rather than a loss of value.
Forecast horizon:	Forecast horizons can be shorter than for DCF analysis and more value is typically recognized in the immediate future.
Versatility:	Can be used with a wide variety of accounting principles (see text below and Chapter 17).
Aligned with what people forecast:	Analysts forecast earnings (from which forecasts of residual earnings can be calculated).
Protection:	Protects from paying too much for growth.
Reduces reliance on speculation:	The valuation relies less on the uncertain continuing value calculation and speculation about long-run growth.

DISADVANTAGES

Accounting complexity:	Requires an understanding of how accrual accounting works (see Chapters 2 and 3).
Suspect accounting:	Relies on accounting numbers, which can be suspect (must be applied along with an accounting quality analysis; see Chapter 18).

Many of the strategic planning products marketed by consulting firms—with such names as economic profit models, economic value-added models, value driver models, and shareholder value-added models—are variations on the residual earnings model. To guide strategy analysis, they focus on the two drivers of residual income and of value added: return on investment and growth in investment. They direct management to maximize return on investment and to grow investments that can earn a rate of return greater than the required return. These value-added measures are used, in turn, to evaluate and reward management on the success of their strategies.

FEATURES OF THE RESIDUAL EARNINGS VALUATION

Box 5.5 lists the advantages and disadvantages of the residual earnings approach. Compare it to summaries for the dividend discount and discounted cash flow (DCF) models in Chapter 4. Some of the features listed will be discussed in more detail later in the book (as indicated). Some are discussed below.

Book Value Captures Value and Residual Earnings Captures Value Added to Book Value

The residual earnings approach employs the properties of accrual accounting that (typically) bring value recognition forward in time. More value is recognized earlier within a forecasting period, and less value is recognized in a continuing value about which we usually have greater uncertainty.

Residual earnings valuation recognizes the value in the current book value on the balance sheet, for a start; in addition, value is usually recognized in RE forecasts earlier than for free cash flow forecasts. You can see this by comparing the value captured in forecasts for one and two years ahead with the two methods in the strategy example we just went through: Free cash flows forecasts are negative for Years 1 and 2 but RE forecasts are positive. Scenario 2 for the savings account, earlier in the chapter, provides an extreme example: Forecasted free cash flows are zero, yet a savings account can be valued immediately from the current book value, without forecasting at all. The comparison of the General Electric valuation here with the attempt to apply DCF valuation to its negative free cash flows in Chapter 4 drives the point home. In short, RE valuation honors the fundamentalist's dictum to put less weight on speculation, particularly about a continuing value.

Protection from Paying Too Much for Earnings Generated by Investment

The stock market is often excited by earnings growth, and it rewards earnings growth with a higher price. Analysts tend to advocate growth firms. Momentum investors push up stock prices of growth firms, anticipating even more growth. However, growth in earnings does not necessarily imply higher value. Firms can grow earnings simply by investing more. If those investments fail to earn a return above the required return, they will grow earnings but they will not grow value. So, growth comes with a caveat: An investor should not pay for earnings growth that does not add value.

A case in point is a firm that grows earnings dramatically through acquisitions. The market often sees acquisitive firms as growth firms and gives them high P/E multiples. But, if an acquirer pays fair value for an acquisition, it may not add value to the investment: Even though the acquisition adds a lot of earnings, the investment just earns the required return. Or worse, should an acquirer overpay for the acquisition—as is often the case with empire builders—he may actually destroy value while adding earnings growth.

During the 1990s, a number of firms went on acquisition sprees. Some acquisitions were for strategic reasons, while others appeared to be growth for growth's sake. Tyco International, a firm with $8,471 million in assets in 1996, grew to become a conglomerate with $111,287 million in assets by 2001. Its businesses included electronic components, undersea cables, medical supplies, fire suppression equipment, security systems, and flow control products, and it also ran a financing arm. It became a darling of the market, with its stock price increasing from $53 per share in 1996 to $236 (split-adjusted) in 2001. In 2002, much of its market value evaporated, with the price falling to $68, as the value of the acquisitions—and the accounting employed in reporting earnings from the acquisitions— came into question. WorldCom grew from a small Mississippi firm to the number two telecommunications firm in the United States, acquiring (among others) MCI. Its stock price rose to over $60, but by 2002, due to an accounting scandal, it was trading at 25 cents per share and ultimately went bankrupt. Both Tyco and WorldCom were led by aggressive empire builders (who subsequently resigned under doubtful circumstances), both borrowed heavily to make acquisitions, and both ultimately ran into difficulties in servicing that debt. General Electric, on the other hand, made many acquisitions that significantly added value.

The residual earnings model has a built-in safeguard against paying too much for earnings growth: Value is added only if the investment earns over and above its required return. Look at Exhibit 5.3. This is the same simple example as in Exhibit 5.2 except that, in addition to paying a dividend of $9.36 million, the firm issues shares in Year 1 for $50 million, giving it a net dividend in Year 1 of −$40.64 million. Book value at the end of Year 1 is thus $153.00 million. The investment, earning at a 10 percent rate, is expected to contribute $5 million additional earnings in Year 2, and earnings for Years 3 to 5 also increase.

EXHIBIT 5.3   **Forecasts for a Simple Firm with Added Investment**

In millions of dollars. This is the same firm as that in Exhibit 5.2 except the firm is expected to make a share issue of $50 million in Year 1, to be invested in assets earnings 10 percent per year. Required return is 10 percent per year.

	0	1	2	3	4	5
		Forecast Year				
Earnings	12.00	12.36	17.73	18.61	19.56	20.57
Net dividends	9.09	(40.64)	9.64	9.93	10.23	10.53
Book value	100.00	153.00	161.09	169.77	179.10	189.14
RE (10% charge)		2.36	2.43	2.50	2.58	2.66
RE growth rate			3%	3%	3%	3%

Yet forecasted residual earnings are unchanged. And the calculated value is the same as before:

$$V_0^E = \$100 + \frac{\$2.36}{1.10 - 1.03} = \$133.71 \text{ million.}$$

Although the investment produces more earnings, it does not add value.

Protection from Paying Too Much for Earnings Created by the Accounting

Accrual accounting can be used to create earnings. By recognizing lower earnings currently, a firm can shift earnings to the future. An unwary investor, forecasting higher earnings, might think that the firm is worth more. But earnings created by the accounting cannot create value.

Exhibit 5.4 illustrates this, again with the same firm as in Exhibit 5.2. At the end of Year 0, the management writes down inventory—in accordance with the lower of cost or market rule—by $8 million. Accordingly, Year 0 earnings and book values are $8 million lower. Inventory (on the balance sheet) becomes future cost of goods sold. If the inventory written down is to be sold in Year 1, cost of goods sold for Year 1 will be $8 million lower, and (with no change in revenues) earnings are expected to be $8 million higher. You can see, by comparing the $20.36 million forecast for Year 1 with the previous $12.36 million, that future earnings have been created. A perceptive analyst will increase his earnings forecast appropriately. But this is not earnings we should pay for.

EXHIBIT 5.4   **Forecasts for a Simple Firm with an Inventory Write-down**

In millions of dollars. This is the same example as in Exhibit 5.2, except the firm has written down inventory in Year 0 by $8 million, reducing cost of goods sold in Year 1 by $8 million. Required return is 10 percent per year.

	0	1	2	3	4	5
		Forecast Year				
Earnings	4.00	20.36	12.73	13.11	13.51	13.91
Dividends	9.09	9.36	9.64	9.93	10.23	10.53
Book value	92.00	103.00	106.09	109.27	112.55	115.93
RE (10% charge)		11.16	2.43	2.50	2.58	2.66
RE growth rate				3%	3%	3%

Residual earnings for Year 1 is now $20.36 - (0.10 \times 92.00) = \$11.16$ million, while that for subsequent years is unaffected (and growing at a 3 percent rate). The valuation is

$$V_0^E = \$92 + \frac{11.16}{1.10} + \left[\frac{2.43}{1.10 - 1.03} / 1.10 \right] = \$133.71 \text{ million}$$

The valuation is unchanged from before. The accounting has created earnings, but not value, and the residual earnings valuation has protected us from paying too much for the earnings created. How does the built-in safeguard work? Well, one can only generate future earnings by reducing current book values—that is how accounting works. Provided we carry the lower book value ($92 million here instead of $100 million) along in the valuation with the higher future earnings, we are protected: The higher earnings are exactly offset by the lower book value.

Inventory write-downs are just one way of shifting income to the future. Others include write-downs and impairments of plant assets (that reduce future depreciation charges), restructuring charges of whole businesses, and deferral of revenue recognition. We will embellish more as we introduce accounting issues as the text proceeds.

Capturing Value Not on the Balance Sheet— for All Accounting Methods

Residual earnings valuation corrects for the value that accountants do not include on the balance sheet. Chapter 2 showed how accounting rules for measuring assets and liabilities typically yield a book value that differs from value, usually lower. Residual earnings valuation solves the problem of the imperfect balance sheet, adding a premium by forecasting the earnings that the book values will produce.

Accordingly, residual earnings valuation applies for all accounting methods for the balance sheet. Under GAAP, firms are required to expense R&D expenditures rather than book them as investments on the balance sheet as assets (Under IFRS, firms can put "development" on the balance sheet, but not "research.") Investment in brands through advertising and promotion expenditures must also be expensed, so the brand asset is missing from the balance sheet. But we saw that, although Nike has significant amounts of these "intangible assets" missing from the balance sheet (with P/B of 3.7), the shares can be valued with a Case 3 valuation. With no R&D or brand asset, subsequent amortization of the asset cost is zero, so future earnings are higher. Combined with a charge on the lower book values in the residual earnings calculation, residual earnings are higher. These higher residual earnings compensate for the lower book values, to produce a valuation that corrects the low book value. Nike's 2011 residual earnings of 2.477 per share and relatively high ROCE of 21.3 percent in Table 5.2 reflect strong earnings. But these measures also reflect that earnings are coming from low book values because brand and the other intangible assets—which generate the earnings—are not on the balance sheet. This makes sense: If assets are missing from the balance sheet, the P/B ratio should be higher, and a higher P/B means that residual earnings are expected to be higher.

A method based on accounting numbers might be seen as suspect. For this reason, some advocate discounted cash flow analysis, for cash flows are "real" and cannot be affected by accounting methods. However, you can see, both in the discussion here and in the example in Exhibit 5.4, that residual earnings valuation adjusts for the accounting, and so works for all accounting methods. This, too, makes sense, for value is based on the economics of the business, not on the accounting methods it uses. There are some subtleties—the forecast horizon can be affected by the accounting methods used—but these subtleties are left for later chapters.

Residual Earnings Are Not Affected by Dividends, Share Issues, or Share Repurchases

In Chapter 3 we saw that share issues, share repurchases, and dividends typically do not create value if stock markets are efficient. But, as residual earnings is based on book values and these transactions with shareholders affect book values, won't residual earnings (and thus the valuation) be affected by expected dividends, share issues, and share repurchases? The answer is no. These transactions affect both earnings and book values in the residual earnings calculation such that their effect cancels to leave residual earnings unaffected. Go to the Web supplement for this chapter for a demonstration.

What the Residual Earnings Model Misses

The residual earnings model captures the anticipated value to be generated within the business by applying shareholders' investment to earn profits from selling products and services to customers. We have recognized, however, that shareholders can also make money if shares are issued at a price greater than their fair value. This can happen if the market price is inefficient or if management (who acts on shareholders' behalf) has more information about the value of the firm than the buyers of the share issue. Gains also can be made (by some of the shareholders) from stock repurchases: If shares are repurchased at a price that is less than fair value, the shareholders who participate in the repurchase lose value to those who chose not to participate. In short, owners make money from selling or buying the firm at a price that is different from fair value.

The residual earnings model calculates (appropriately) that there is no value added from an anticipated share issue or repurchase at fair value. However, this is not so if the share issue or repurchase is at a price that is different from fair value: The gain or loss to the existing shareholders is not captured by the model. This might be the case when a firm uses overpriced shares to acquire another firm by issuing shares rather than paying cash. We will see how to correct for this deficiency when we apply the model in all its dimensions in Chapter 16.

The Web Connection

Find the following on the Web page for this chapter:

- Further applications of residual earnings valuation.
- A spreadsheet program to help you develop residual earnings pro formas.
- Further discussion of the features of residual earnings valuation.

- A demonstration of how residual earnings are insensitive to dividends, share issues, and share repurchases.
- A demonstration of how residual earnings techniques solve the problems with dividend discounting.
- Directions to finding analysts' forecasts on the Web.
- The Readers' Corner takes you to papers that cover residual earnings valuation.

Summary

This chapter has outlined an accrual accounting valuation model that can be applied to equities, projects, and strategies. The model utilizes information from the balance sheet and calculates the difference between balance sheet value and intrinsic value from forecasts of earnings and book values that will be reported in future forecasted income statements and balance sheets.

The concept of residual earnings is central in the model. Residual earnings measures the earnings in excess of those required if the book value were to earn at the required rate of return. Several properties of residual earnings have been identified in this chapter. Residual earnings treats investment as part of book value, so that an investment that is forecast to earn at the required rate of return generates zero residual earnings and has no effect on a value calculated. Residual earnings is not affected by dividends, or by share issues and share repurchases at fair value, so using the residual income model yields valuations that are not sensitive to these (value-irrelevant) transactions with shareholders. The calculation of residual earnings uses accrual accounting, which captures added value over cash flows. Residual earnings valuation accommodates different ways of doing accrual accounting. And residual earnings valuation protects us from paying too much for earnings growth generated by investment and earnings created by accounting methods.

Above all, the residual earnings model provides a way of thinking about a business and about the value generation in the business. To value a business, it directs us to forecast profitability of investment and growth in investment, for these two factors drive residual earnings. And it directs management to add value to a business by increasing residual earnings, which, in turn, requires increasing ROCE and growing investment. The analyst also understands the business from the model and develops his or her valuation accordingly.

Key Concepts

horizon premium is the difference between value and book value expected at a forecast horizon. *152*

normal price-to-book ratio applies when price is equal to book value, that is, the P/B ratio is 1.0 *145*

residual earnings is comprehensive earnings less a charge against book value for required earnings. Also referred to as **residual income, abnormal earnings,** or **excess profit.** *142*

residual earnings driver is a measure that determines residual earnings; the two primary drivers are **rate of return on common equity (ROCE)** (on p. 147) and **growth in book value.** *148*

residual earnings model is a model that measures value added to book value from forecasts of residual earnings. *143*

steady-state condition is a permanent condition in forecast amounts that determines a continuing value. *155*

The Analyst's Toolkit

Analysis Tools	Page	Key Measures	Page	Acronyms to Remember	
Residual earnings equity		Continuing value (CV)		AMEX	American Stock Exchange
valuation	145	Case 1	152	BPS	book value per share
Case 1 (5.4)	152	Case 2	154	CAPM	capital asset pricing model
Case 2 (5.5)	154	Case 3	154	CV	continuing value
Case 3 (5.6)	154	Growth in book value	148	DPS	dividends per share
Converting an analyst's		Price/book ratio (P/B)	141	EPS	earnings per share
forecast to a valuation	156	Return on common equity	147	GDP	gross domestic product
Residual earnings project		Residual earnings (RE)	142	NYSE	New York Stock Exchange
valuation	159	Value-to-price ratio	158	P/B	price-to-book ratio
Residual earnings strategy				RE	residual earnings
valuation	160			ROCE	return on common equity
Value-to-price ratios	158				

A Continuing Case: *Kimberly-Clark Corporation*

A Self-Study Exercise

CONVERTING ANALYSTS' FORECASTS TO A VALUATION

Exhibit 1.1 in the Chapter 1 introduction to Kimberly-Clark gives consensus analysts' forecasts made in March 2011 when the stock price stood at $65.24 per share. These forecasts are in the form of point estimates for 2011 and 2012 and an estimated five-year growth rate. Find these forecasts in the exhibit. An annual dividend of $2.80 per share was indicated for 2011 at the time. With book value information from the financial statements in Exhibit 2.2 in Chapter 2, calculate the firm's traded P/B ratio in March 2011.

With analysts' forecast of a five-year growth rate, you can forecast analysts' EPS estimates for the years 2013–2015. Do this and, from these forecasts, lay out the corresponding return on common equity (ROCE) and residual earnings. You will need the book value per share at the end of 2010; you can calculate this from the balance sheet given in the Kimberly-Clark case in Chapter 2. For the residual earnings calculations, use a required return for equity of 8 percent.

Now go ahead and value KMB's shares from this pro forma. Assume a long-term growth rate in residual earnings after the five-year forecast period of 4 percent, roughly equal to the average GDP growth rate. What is your intrinsic price-to-book ratio? What is your V/P ratio? What reservations did you develop as you went about this task?

Using Spreadsheet Tools

As you proceed through the book, you will see that most of the analysis can be built into a spreadsheet program. The BYOAP feature on the Web site shows you how to do this, but you might wait until Chapter 8 to get into this. At this point, you might build your own valuation engine, as suggested in this chapter, or experiment with the spreadsheet valuation tool on the Web page supplement for this chapter. Insert your forecasts into the spreadsheet there and specify growth rates and the required return. By changing forecasts, growth rates, and the required returns, you can see how sensitive the valuation is to the uncertainty about these features.

Concept Questions

C5.1. Information indicates that a firm will earn a return on common equity above its cost of equity capital in all years in the future, but its shares trade below book value. Those shares must be mispriced. True or false?

C5.2. Jetform Corporation traded at a price-to-book ratio of 1.01 in May 1999. Its most recently reported ROCE was 10.1 percent, and it is deemed to have a required equity return of 10 percent. What is your best guess as to the ROCE expected for the next fiscal year?

C5.3. Telesoft Corp. traded at a price-to-book ratio of 0.98 in May 1999 after reporting an ROCE of 52.2 percent. Does the market regard this ROCE as normal, unusually high, or unusually low?

C5.4. A share trades at a price-to-book ratio of 0.7. An analyst who forecasts an ROCE of 12 percent each year in the future, and sets the required equity return at 10 percent, recommends a hold position. Does his recommendation agree with his forecast?

C5.5. A firm cannot maintain an ROCE less than the required return and stay in business indefinitely. True or false?

C5.6. Look at the Case 2 valuation of General Electric in the chapter. Why are residual earnings fairly constant for 2000–2004, even though return on common equity (ROCE) is declining?

C5.7. An advocate of discounted cash flow analysis says, "Residual earnings valuation does not work well for companies like Coca-Cola, Cisco Systems, or Nike, which have substantial assets, like brands, R&D assets, and entrepreneurial know-how off the books. A low book value must give you a low valuation." True or false?

C5.8. When an analyst forecasts earnings, it must be comprehensive earnings. Why?

C5.9. Comment on the following: "ABC Company is generating negative free cash flow and is likely to do so for the foreseeable future. Anyone willing to pay more than book value needs their head read."

Exercises

Drill Exercises

E5.1. Forecasting Return on Common Equity and Residual Earnings (Easy)

The following are earnings and dividend forecasts made at the end of 2012 for a firm with $20.00 book value per common share at that time. The firm has a required equity return of 10 percent per year.

	2013	2014	2015
EPS	3.00	3.60	4.10
DPS	0.25	0.25	0.30

a. Forecast return of common equity (ROCE) and residual earnings for each year, 2013–2015.
b. Based on your forecasts, do you think this firm is worth more or less than book value? Why?

E5.2. ROCE and Valuation (Easy)

The following are ROCE forecasts made for a firm at the end of 2010.

	2011	2012	2013
Return of common equity (ROCE)	12.0%	12.0%	12.0%

ROCE is expected to continue at the same level after 2013. The firm reported book value of common equity of $3.2 billion at the end of 2010, with 500 million shares outstanding. If the required equity return is 12 percent, what is the per-share value of these shares?

E5.3. A Residual Earnings Valuation (Easy)

An analyst presents you with the following pro forma (in millions of dollars) that gives her forecast of earnings and dividends for 2013–2017. She asks you to value the 1,380 million shares outstanding at the end of 2012, when common shareholders' equity stood at $4,310 million. Use a required return for equity of 10 percent in your calculations.

	2013E	2014E	2015E	2016E	2017E
Earnings	388.0	570.0	599.0	629.0	660.4
Dividends	115.0	160.0	349.0	367.0	385.4

a. Forecast book value, return on common equity (ROCE), and residual earnings for each of the years 2013–2017.
b. Forecast growth rates for book value and residual earnings for each of the years 2014–2017.
c. Calculate the per-share value of the equity from this pro forma. Would you call this a Case 1, 2, or 3 valuation?
d. What is the premium over book value given by your calculation? What is the P/B ratio?

E5.4. Residual Earnings Valuation and Target Prices (Medium)

The following forecasts of earnings per share (EPS) and dividend per share (DPS) were made at the end of 2012 for a firm with a book value per share of $22.00:

	2013E	2014E	2015E	2016E	2017E
EPS	3.90	3.70	3.31	3.59	3.90
DPS	1.00	1.00	1.00	1.00	1.00

The firm has an equity cost of capital of 12 percent per annum.

a. Calculate the residual earnings that are forecast for each year, 2013 to 2017.
b. What is the per-share value of the equity at the end of 2012 based on the residual income valuation model?
c. What is the forecasted per-share value of the equity at the end of the year 2017?
d. What is the expected premium in 2017?

E5.5. Residual Earnings Valuation and Return on Common Equity (Medium)

A firm with a book value of $15.60 per share and 100 percent dividend payout is expected to have a return on common equity of 15 percent per year indefinitely in the future. Its cost of equity capital is 10 percent.

a. Calculate the intrinsic price-to-book ratio.
b. Suppose this firm announced that it was reducing its payout to 50 percent of earnings in the future. How would this affect your calculation of the price-to-book ratio?

E5.6. Using Accounting-Based Techniques to Measure Value Added for a Project (Medium)

A firm announces that it will invest $150 million in a project that is expected to generate a 15 percent rate of return on its beginning-of-period book value each year for the next five years. The required return for this type of project is 12 percent; the firm depreciates the cost of assets straight-line over the life of the investment.

a. What is the value added to the firm from this investment?
b. Forecast free cash flow for each year of the project. What is the net present value of cash flows for the project?

E5.7. Using Accounting-Based Techniques to Measure Value Added for a Going Concern (Medium)

A new firm announces that it will invest $150 million in projects each year forever. All projects are expected to generate a 15 percent rate of return on its beginning-of-period book value each year for five years. The required return for this type of project is 12 percent; the firm depreciates the cost of assets straight-line over the life of the investment.

a. What is the value of the firm under this investment strategy? Would you refer to this valuation as a Case 1, 2, or 3 valuation?
b. What is the value added to the initial investment of $150 million?
c. Why is the value added greater than 15 percent of the initial $150 million investment?

E5.8. Creating Earnings and Valuing Created Earnings (Medium)

The prototype one-period project at the beginning of the chapter was booked at its historical cost of $400. Suppose, instead, that the accountant wrote down the investment to $360 on the balance sheet at the beginning of the period. See the investment as consisting of $360 of plant (booked to the balance sheet) and $40 advertising (which cannot be booked to the balance sheet under GAAP). Revenues of $440 are expected from the project and the required return is 10 percent.

a. Forecast earnings from this project for the year.
b. Forecast the rate of return on the book value of this investment and also the residual earnings.
c. Value the investment.

Applications

E5.9. Residual Earnings Valuation: Black Hills Corp (Easy)

Black Hills Corporation is a diversified energy corporation and a public utility holding company. The following gives the firm's earnings per share and dividends per share for the years 2000–2004.

	1999	2000	2001	2002	2003	2004
EPS		2.39	3.45	2.28	2.00	1.71
DPS		1.06	1.12	1.16	1.22	1.24
BPS	9.96					

Suppose these numbers were given to you at the end of 1999, as forecasts, when the book value per share was $9.96, as indicated. Use a required return of 11 percent for calculations below.

a. Calculate residual earnings and return of common equity (ROCE) for each year, 2000–2004.
b. Value the firm at the end of 1999 under the assumption that the ROCE in 2004 will continue at the same level subsequently. Would you call this a Case 1, Case 2, or Case 3 valuation?
c. Based on your analysis, give a target price at the end of 2004.

E5.10. Valuing Dell, Inc. (Easy)

In September 2008 the shares of Dell, Inc., the computer maker, traded at $20.50 each. In its last annual report, Dell had reported book value of $3,735 million with 2,060 million shares outstanding. Analysts were forecasting earnings per share of $1.47 for fiscal year 2009 and $1.77 for 2010 Dell pays no dividends. Calculate the per-share value of Dell in 2008 based on the analysts' forecasts, with an additional forecast that residual earnings will grow at the anticipated GDP growth rate of 4 percent per year after 2010. Use a required return of 10 percent.

Real World Connection

Exercises E3.7, E3.12, E7.6, E9.11, and E14.16 deal with Dell, as does Minicase M16.2.

E5.11. Valuating: General Electric Co. (Medium)

General Electric Co. reported a per-share book value of $10.47 in its balance sheet on December 31, 2004. In early 2005, analysts were forecasting consensus earnings per share of $1.71 for 2005 and $1.96 for 2006. The required return for equity is 10 percent. The dividend payout ratio for 2005 is expected to be 50 percent of earnings. Calculate the value per share in early 2005 with a forecast that residual earnings will grow at a long-term growth rate of 4 percent, the average GDP growth rate, after 2006.

Real World Connection

Exercises E6.10, E7.7, and E11.8 also deal with General Electric.

E5.12. Valuing Dividends or Return on Equity: General Motors Corp (Easy)

In April 2005, General Motors traded at $28 per share on book value of $49 per share. Analysts were estimating that GM would earn 69 cents per share for the year ending December 2005. The firm was paying an annual dividend at the time of $2.00 per share.

  a. Calculate the price-to-book ratio (P/B) and the return on common equity (ROCE) that analysts were forecasting for 2005.
  b. Is the P/B ratio justified by the forecasted ROCE?
  c. An analyst trumpeted the high dividend yield as a reason to buy the stock. (Dividend yield is dividend/price.) "A dividend yield of over 7 percent is too juicy to pass up," he claimed. Would you rather focus on the ROCE or on the dividend yield?

Real World Connection

Exercises E1.4, E2.12, and E4.11 also deal with General Motors.

E5.13. Converting Analysts' Forecasts to a Valuation: Nike, Inc. (Medium)

Nike reported book value per share of $15.93 at the end of its 2008 fiscal year. Analysts were forecasting earnings of $3.90 per share for 2009 and $4.45 for 2010, and were also forecasting a five-year growth rate in EPS of 13 percent per year. Prepare a five-year pro forma of earnings based on these forecasts and convert the forecasts to a valuation with the added forecast that residual earnings will grow at the GDP growth rate of 4 percent per year after 2013. Use a required return of 10 percent in your calculations. Table 5.2 in this chapter will help you.

Nike traded at $60 per share at the time. Based on your calculations, do you think Nike is reasonably priced? What does your analysis tell you about the long-run growth rate that the market is forecasting for Nike?

E5.14. Residual Earnings Valuation and Accounting Methods (Hard)

Refer back to the valuation in Exercise 5.3. In that pro forma, an analyst forecast $388 million of earnings for 2013 on a book value at the end of 2012 of $4,310 million, that is, a return on common equity of 9 percent. The forecasts were made at the end of 2012 based on preliminary reports from the firm.

When the final report was published, however, the analyst discovered that the firm had decided to write-down its inventory at the end of 2012 by $114 million (following the lower-of-cost-or-market rule). As this was inventory that the analyst forecasted would be sold in 2013 (and thus the impairment affects cost of goods sold for that year), the analyst revised her earnings forecast for 2013. For questions (a) and (b), ignore any effect of taxes.

  a. What is the revised earnings forecast for 2013 as a result of the inventory impairment assuming no change in the sales forecast? What is the revised forecast of return on common equity (ROCE) for 2013?

    b. Show that the revision in the forecast of 2013 earnings does not change the valuation of the equity.

    c. Recognize, now, that the firm's income tax rate is 35 percent. Do your answers to questions (a) and (b) change?

E5.15. **Impairment of Goodwill (Hard)**

A firm made an acquisition at the end of 2010 and recorded the acquisition cost of $428 million on its balance sheet as tangible assets of $349 million and goodwill of $79 million. The firm used a required return of 10 percent as a hurdle rate when evaluating the acquisition and determined that it was paying fair value.

    a. What is the projected residual income from the acquisition for 2011?

    b. By the end of 2011, the tangible assets from the acquisition had been depreciated to a book value of $301 million. Management ascertained that the acquisition would subsequently earn an annual return of only 9 percent on book value at the end of 2011. What is the amount by which goodwill should be impaired under the FASB and IASB requirements for impairment?

Minicases   **M5.1**

Value-Added Growth? Tyco and Citigroup

Textbooks often talk about adding value from "investment opportunities." The idea is a little vague and indeed can be a little dangerous: Will investments actually add value? Investors often talk of buying earnings growth, but that, too, can be dangerous: Does earnings growth actually add value? This chapter has introduced residual earnings as a measure of value added. Below are some numbers for Tyco International, the international conglomerate, and Citigroup, the large money-center bank, during their growth periods. Analyze these numbers and ask: Did these firms add value?

TYCO INTERNATIONAL LTD.

Tyco International Ltd. is a leading global supplier of security products and services, fire protection products, valves and controls, and other industrial products. The firm grew considerably through serial acquisitions in the 1990s. By increasing book value (net assets) from $3.1 billion in 1996 to $31.7 billion in 2001, largely through acquisition, the firm reported earnings per share growth from $0.08 in 1996 to $7.68 by 2001. The numbers from 1997 onwards are below. The market, apparently impressed, rewarded the growth, with the share price increasing from $53 in 1996 to $236 by the end of 2001. (These prices are adjusted to 2010 shares for subsequent stock splits.)

Earnings, Book Values, and Stock Prices for Tyco International Ltd., 1997–2005

	1997	1998	1999	2000	2001	2002	2003	2004	2005
Earnings (billions)	$ (0.39)	1.17	1.02	2.76*	3.46	(9.18)	0.98	2.88	3.0
EPS	$ (0.96)	2.96	2.48	6.54*	7.68	(18.48)	1.96	5.76	6.04
Book value of equity (billions)	$ 3.43	9.90	12.37	17.03	31.73	24.16	26.48	30.4	32.6
Stock price per share	$ 90	151	156	222	236	68	106	143	115
Price-to-book (P/B)	4.8	6.2	6.1	5.6	3.4	1.4	2.0	2.3	1.8
Trailing P/E	—	53	74	34	31	—	54	24	19
Net debt (billions)	$ 2.7	4.5	8.9	10.3	20.4	18.6	17.4	12.8	9.9

*Excluding gains on asset sales; earnings including those gains were $4.52 billion. Numbers in parentheses are negative. Per share numbers are adjusted to 2010 shares for subsequent stock splits.

Tyco was priced by the market as a growth company. Was this growth to pay for? Use a cost of capital of 10 percent in answering the question.

CITIGROUP, INC.

In 1998, Sanford Weill of Travelers Group developed the idea of a "financial supermarket"; one-stop shopping for banking, investments, and insurance with the merging of Travelers (insurance), Citicorp (banking), and Salomon Smith Barney (brokerage, wealth management, and investment banking) to form Citigroup. A good idea? The panel below reports results for the combined group for selected years from 1996 to 2008. The stock price increased from $15 to almost $56 by 2006, with earnings per share growth from $1.50 to $4.39. Did the super-merger add value? Again use a cost of capital of 10 percent for your analysis.

Earnings, Book Values, and Stock Prices for Citigroup, Inc., for Selected Years, 1996–2008.

	1996	1998	2000	2002	2004	2006	2008
Earnings (billions)	$ 7.6	7.0	13.5	15.3	17.0	21.5	(27.7)
EPS	$ 1.50	1.35	2.69	2.99	3.32	4.39	(5.59)
Book value of equity (billions)	$ 40.5	48.8	64.5	85.3	108.2	119.8	71.0
Stock price per share	$ 15.13	24.85	51.06	35.19	48.18	55.70	6.71
Price-to-book (P/B)	1.3	1.7	4.0	2.1	2.3	2.3	0.5

Growth and Risk

The fundamental investor sees growth as risky and thus is careful in paying too much for growth. Can you see in these numbers that growth is risky? Can you also see in Tyco's numbers that debt is risky?

M5.2

Analysts' Forecasts and Valuation: PepsiCo and Coca-Cola I

PepsiCo, Inc. (PEP) is a global food, snack, and beverage company operating in more than 200 countries with brands that include Quaker Oats, Tropicana, Gatorade, Lay's, and, of course, Pepsi. The products include oat, rice, and grain-based foods as well as carbonated and noncarbonated beverages. The largest operations are in North America, Mexico, Russia, and the United Kingdom.

In April 2011, PepsiCo traded at $67.00 per share on a book value at the end of 2010 of $21,273 million with 1,581 million shares outstanding. Analysts were forecasting per-share earnings of $4.48 for fiscal year ending December 31, 2011, and $4.87 for the 2012 year. The indicated dividend for 2011 was 1.92 per share. The street was using 9 percent as a required rate of return for PepsiCo's equity.

The Coca-Cola Company (KO) also operates in over 200 countries worldwide and competes intensively with PepsiCo in the market for carbonated and noncarbonated beverages. Among its brands are Coke, Diet Coke, Fanta, and Sprite.

In April 2011, Coke also traded at $67.00 per share on a book value of $31,003 million with 2,292 million shares outstanding at the end of 2010. Analysts were forecasting $3.87 in earnings per share for fiscal year ending December 31, 2011, and $4.20 for 2012. The indicated dividend per share was $1.88. The equity is considered to have the same required return as PepsiCo.

A. For both firms, calculate the expected return on common equity (ROCE) for 2011 and the expected growth in residual earnings for 2012 that are implied by the analysts' forecasts.

B. Value both firms with a forecast that the residual earnings growth rate for 2012 will continue into the long run.

C. Now value the firms with a forecast that residual earnings will grow at the GDP growth rate of 4 percent per year after 2012.

D. Why might you expect the long-run growth rate to be less than the residual earnings growth rate in 2012?

E. Given the analysts' forecasts, is the market, at $67 per share, forecasting a long-term growth rate higher or lower than the 4 percent rate?

F. Why do these firms trade at such high price-to-book ratios? Why do these firms have such a high ROCE?

G. Would you feel comfortable buying these firms at $67 a share?

Real World Connection

See Minicase M6.1 in Chapter 6 for a parallel investigation using P/E ratios. See also Minicase M4.1 in Chapter 4 for discounted cash flow analysis applied to Coca-Cola. Exercises E4.7, E12.7, E15.7, E16.12, E17.7, and E20.4 also deal with Coca-Cola, and Exercises E4.13 and 10.9 deal with PepsiCo.

M5.3

Kimberly-Clark: Buy Its Paper?

In an article in *Barron's* on April 21, 2008, a commentator remarked, "As one of the world's largest makers of bathroom tissue and baby diapers, Kimberly-Clark knows a thing or two about bottoms. Lately, however, shares of the venerable household-products company, whose Kleenex brand is virtually synonymous with tissue, look to be near a bottom of another sort."

With Shares trading at $63.20, down to a near low from a 52-week high of $72.79, the trailing P/E of 15 was low by historical standards. "This is as cheap as it gets for this company" claimed a portfolio manager. In 2007, Kimberly-Clark (KMB) grew sales by 9 percent, compared with just over 5 percent the year before. Even though it absorbed increased raw material costs without increasing prices, the firm grew operating profit by 24.5 percent. Analysts expected that the firm would be able to pass those costs on to customers in 2008 and 2009, further accelerating earnings growth. Benefits from the firm's Competitive Improvement Initiative and Strategic Cost Reduction Plan, both begun in 2005 to streamline marketing, manufacturing, and administrative operations, were evident, and its research and development operation was producing new products like GoodNites Sleep Boxers and SleepShorts disposable training pants.

The *Barron's* article concluded, "Kimberly shares are a lot like Kleenex: Every investor should tuck some in a pocket." This case asks whether you agree.

At the time, the consensus analysts' estimate of earnings per share for the year ending December 31, 2008, was $4.54 and $4.96 for 2009, up from the $4.13 earnings per share reported for 2007. At the end of 2007, the firm also reported book value of $5,224 million on 420.9 million outstanding shares. Morningstar, a provider of financial information and mutual fund rankings, was forecasting a dividend of $2.32 per share for 2008.

A. Calculate the forward P/E and price-to-book (P/B) at which Kimberley-Clark was trading.

B. Using the analysts' forecasts, value KMB with an additional forecast that residual earnings will grow at the GDP growth rate of 4 percent per year after 2009. Use a required return of 9 percent.

C. The dividend payout ratio for 2008 is expected to be maintained in 2009. Based on your calculations, what target price would you forecast for the end of 2009?

D. Consumers require tissues, paper towels, and diapers in good times and bad, so Kimberly-Clark has a fairly low equity beta of 0.6. Thus, a 9 percent required return may be a bit high. If the equity risk premium for the market as a whole is 5 percent and the risk-free rate is 5 percent, show that the required return from the capital asset pricing model (CAPM) for a beta of 0.6 is 8 percent. What would your valuation of KMB be if the required return were 8 percent? Also test the sensitivity of your valuations to a required return of 10 percent.

E. At a price of $63.20, what is the market's implied forecast of the residual earnings growth rate after 2009 for a 9 percent required return? What is its forecast of the earnings-per-share growth rate for 2010?

F. Do you agree with the conclusion in the *Barron's* article? What aspect of your calculations are you most uncomfortable with?

Real World Connection

The Continuing Case at the end of each chapter covers Kimberly-Clark. Also see Exercises E4.9, E7.16, E8.10, E11.10, and E12.6. Kimberly-Clark is also the subject of Minicase M2.1.

Chapter **Six**

Accrual Accounting and Valuation: Pricing Earnings

LINKS

Link to previous chapter

Chapter 5 showed how to price book values in the balance sheet and calculate intrinsic price-to-book ratios.

This chapter

This chapter shows how to price earnings in the income statement and calculate intrinsic price-earnings ratio.

Link to next chapter

Chapter 7 goes live, to show how the valuation approaches in Chapters 5 and 6 are applied in active investing.

Link to Web page

The Web page supplement has more applications of the techniques in this chapter.

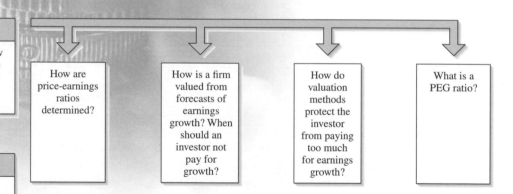

How are price-earnings ratios determined?

How is a firm valued from forecasts of earnings growth? When should an investor not pay for growth?

How do valuation methods protect the investor from paying too much for earnings growth?

What is a PEG ratio?

The last chapter showed how to anchor valuations on the book value, the bottom line of the balance sheet. This chapter shows how to anchor valuations on earnings, the bottom line of the income statement. By anchoring on book value, the analyst develops the price-to-book ratio (P/B). By anchoring on earnings, the analyst develops the price-earnings ratio (P/E). So, while the last chapter asked how much one should pay per dollar of book value, this chapter asks how much one should pay per dollar of earnings.

The Analyst's Checklist

After reading this chapter you should understand:

- What a P/E ratio means.
- What "abnormal earnings growth" is.
- How forecasting abnormal earnings growth yields the intrinsic P/E ratio.
- What is meant by a normal P/E ratio.
- The difference between ex-dividend earnings growth and cum-dividend earnings growth.
- The difference between a Case 1 and Case 2 abnormal earnings growth valuation.
- How both abnormal earnings growth valuation and residual earnings valuation put less weight on a speculative, long-term continuing value.
- The advantages and disadvantages of using an abnormal earnings growth valuation and how the valuation compares with residual earnings valuation.
- How abnormal earnings growth valuation protects the investor from paying too much for earnings growth.

After reading this chapter you should be able to:

- Calculate cum-dividend earnings.
- Calculate abnormal earnings growth.
- Calculate the value of equities from forecasts of earnings and dividends.
- Calculate intrinsic forward P/E and trailing P/E ratios.
- Calculate continuing values for the abnormal earnings growth model.
- Convert an analyst's EPS forecast to a valuation.
- Evaluate a PEG ratio.

THE CONCEPT BEHIND THE PRICE-EARNINGS RATIO

P/B ratios differ from 1.0 because accountants do not measure the full value of the equity in the balance sheet. However, the missing value is ultimately realized in the future earnings that assets produce, and these earnings can be forecasted: A price-to-book ratio is determined by expected earnings that have not yet been booked to book value, and the higher the future earnings relative to book value, the higher the P/B ratio. The last chapter took you through the exercise of estimating the missing value in the balance sheet.

A parallel idea lies behind the P/E ratio. As share prices anticipate future earnings, the P/E ratio compares the value of expected future earnings (in the numerator) to current earnings (in the denominator). Just as the P/B ratio is based on expected earnings that have not yet been booked to book value, the P/E ratio is based on expected earnings that have not yet been booked. So P/E ratios are high when one forecasts considerably higher future earnings than current earnings, and P/E ratios are low when future earnings are forecasted to be lower than current earnings. In short, the P/E ratio prices earnings growth.

This chapter anchors a valuation on earnings rather than book value, though you will see that the methods are quite similar to those of Chapter 5. The chapter supplies the formal valuation model to implement the concept of the P/E ratio rigorously, as well as the mechanics to apply the model faithfully. The formality is warranted, for one can pay too much for earnings growth if one is not careful.

Beware of Paying Too Much for Earnings Growth

History shows that high P/E stocks—so-called growth stocks—have been rewarding investments during bubble periods: Investors, excited about growth, push up prices, and momentum trading takes over to yield yet higher prices and yet higher P/E ratios. But history also shows that, overall, growth expectations are not realized: High P/E stocks have yielded lower returns than low P/E stocks, and lower returns than broad indexes. Chapter 5 came with a warning: Beware of earnings growth; use valuation methods that build in protection from paying too much for earnings growth.

This warning sets the stage for this chapter: A sound P/E valuation prices earnings growth but does not price growth that does not add value. This chapter not only supplies the appropriate valuation but also one that typically puts less weight on speculative, long-run continuing values. Accordingly, like residual earnings valuation, the valuation is adept at challenging the speculation in the market's P/E ratio.

From Price-to-Book Valuation to P/E Valuation

As both the P/B ratio and the P/E ratio are based on the same earnings expectations, valuation methods that anchor on earnings must yield the same valuation as methods that anchor on book values. Indeed, we can quickly show this by returning to the Case 3 valuation of Nike, Inc., in Chapter 5. Nike's pro forma for the residual earnings (RE) valuation at the end of 2006 is reproduced here with one extra line: the change in residual earnings forecasted each year. (The 2012 numbers are based on residual earnings growing at 4.5 percent, as in the P/B valuation.)

| | 2006 | Forecast Year | | | | | |
		2007	2008	2009	2010	2011	2012
EPS		2.96	3.80	3.07	3.93	4.28	4.65
DPS		0.71	0.88	0.98	1.06	1.20	1.12
BPS	14.00	16.25	19.17	21.26	24.13	27.21	30.74
Residual earnings (9% charge)		1.700	2.338	1.345	2.017	2.108	2.203
Change in residual earnings			0.638	−0.993	0.672	0.091	0.095

Rather than anchoring on book value, anchor on the forward earnings of $2.96 per share. Earnings are just the change in book value (before dividends), so correspondingly add to this anchor by forecasting the subsequent change in residual earnings (ΔRE) as follows:

$$V_0^E = \frac{1}{\rho_E - 1}\left[EPS_1 + \frac{\Delta RE_2}{\rho_E} + \frac{\Delta RE_3}{\rho_E^2} + \frac{\Delta RE_4}{\rho_E^3} + \frac{\Delta RE_5}{\rho_E^4} + \frac{\Delta RE_6}{\rho_E^4(\rho_E - g)} \right] \qquad \textbf{(6.1)}$$

With the forecasts above, a required return of 9 percent, and an RE growth rate of 4.5 percent after 2011 (as in Chapter 5), the per-share value for Nike is

$$V_{2006}^E = \frac{1}{0.09}\left[2.96 + \frac{0.638}{1.09} + \frac{-0.993}{1.09^2} + \frac{0.672}{1.09^3} + \frac{0.091}{1.09^4} + \frac{0.095}{1.09^4(1.09 - 1.045)} \right]$$

$$= \$53.18$$

This is the same value we obtained in Chapter 5 (allowing for rounding error). Changes in residual earnings are growth in residual earnings, so we are adding growth to forward earnings. Thus we have the intrinsic forward P/E ratio that incorporates growth expectations: $V_{2006}^{E} = \$53.18/\$2.96 = 17.97$. One aspect may give you pause: Forward earnings is a forecasted number (yours or an analyst's), so we are anchoring on a forecast rather than something in the present. But the forward earnings is earnings for the current fiscal year (not yet ended), and we may well have up to three quarterly earnings already. But we can anchor on the number only if we feel it is something we are fairly confident about (rather than pure speculation). If not, forecast the forward earnings as equal to the trailing actual earnings.

Thinking of growth as residual earnings growth is a bit awkward. We would prefer to think of a P/E in terms of earnings growth rather than residual earnings growth. And indeed we can.

PROTOTYPE VALUATION

In anchoring a valuation on earnings rather than book value, appreciate that earnings is a measure of change in value—a flow rather than a stock. To convert flows to stocks, simply capitalize the flow. The stock of value implied by earnings is

$$\text{Capitalized earnings} = \frac{\text{Earnings}}{\text{Required return}}$$

The way to think about anchoring value on earnings is as follows:

$$\text{Value} = \text{Capitalized earnings} + \text{Extra value for forecasted earnings growth}$$

To value earnings we always start with the anchor of capitalized earnings, and then ask what extra value must be added for anticipated earnings growth.

A savings account is easy to value, so we will begin with this simple asset as a prototype for valuing equities. Exhibit 6.1 presents the same savings account as in Exhibit 5.1 in

EXHIBIT 6.1
Forecasts for a
Savings Account with
$100 Invested at the
End of 2012, Earning
5 Percent per Year

	2012	2013	2014	2015	2016	2017
				Forecast Year		
Earnings withdrawn each year (full payout)						
Earnings		5	5	5	5	5
Dividends		5	5	5	5	5
Book value	100	100	100	100	100	100
Residual earnings		0	0	0	0	0
Earnings growth rate		0	0	0	0	0
Cum-dividend earnings		5	5.25	5.51	5.79	6.08
Cum-dividend earnings growth rate			5%	5%	5%	5%
No withdrawals (zero payout)						
Earnings		5	5.25	5.51	5.79	6.08
Dividends		0	0	0	0	0
Book value	100	105	110.25	115.76	121.55	127.63
Residual earnings		0	0	0	0	0
Earnings growth rate			5%	5%	5%	5%
Cum-dividend earnings		5	5.25	5.51	5.79	6.08
Cum-dividend earnings growth rate			5%	5%	5%	5%

Chapter 5. The account involves $100 invested in 2012 to earn a 5 percent rate each year, from 2013 and thereafter. Two dividend payout scenarios are presented, full payout and no payout.

In both cases, expected residual earnings are zero, so the asset can be valued at its book value of $100 in 2012 using the residual earnings model. However, the asset also can be valued by capitalizing forward 2013 earnings of $5:

$$\text{Value of savings account} = \frac{\text{Forward Earnings}}{\text{Required return}} = \frac{\$5}{0.05} = \$100$$

For the savings account, there is no extra value for anticipated earnings growth. However, you will notice that, while the earnings growth rate in the full-payout scenario is zero, it is 5 percent per year in the no-payout scenario. Yet the value of the account is the same in both cases. According to our calculations, we will not pay for the 5 percent growth. The growth of 5 percent comes from reinvesting earnings, but the reinvested earnings earn only the required return. The equivalent valuations for the two accounts demonstrate the principle that one does not pay for growth that comes from an investment that earns only the required return, for such an investment does not add value.

A little more formalism captures this idea and protects us from paying too much for growth. The earnings growth rates in the two scenarios look different, but in fact they are not. The earnings from the full-payout account are actually understated, for the dividends from the account can be reinvested in an identical account to earn 5 percent. So, for example, the $5 withdrawn in 2013 can be reinvested to earn 5 percent, or $0.25 in 2014, so that the total expected earnings for 2014 are $5.25, the same as the zero-payout account. Earnings from an asset arise from two sources, earnings earned by the asset and earnings earned from reinvesting dividends in another asset. So, by reinvesting dividends for all years, the earnings in the two payout scenarios here are the same; in the no-payout case, earnings are reinvested in the same account—that is, earnings are retained—and in the full-payout case, earnings can be reinvested in a different account, in both cases earning 5 percent.

The total earnings from both sources are referred to as **cum-dividend earnings,** that is, earnings with the dividend reinvested. Earnings without the reinvestment of dividends are called **ex-dividend earnings.** Value is always based on expected cum-dividend earnings and the P/E ratio is always based on cum-dividend earnings growth, for we must keep track of all sources of earnings from the investment. For 2014, the earnings with reinvestment of the dividends from the prior year is

$$\text{Cum-dividend earnings}_{2014} = \text{Earnings}_{2014} + (\rho - 1)\text{dividend}_{2013}$$

where ρ is (as before) 1 plus the required return. So, for the full-payout savings account, cum-dividend earnings for 2014 are $\text{Earnings}_{2014} + (0.05 \times \text{Dividend}_{2013}) = \$5 + (0.05 \times \$5) = \$5.25$.

On a cum-dividend basis, earnings growth in the two scenarios is the same, 5 percent per year, as you can see from the cum-dividend earnings line in Exhibit 6.1. However, in both cases, the earnings growth is not growth that we will pay for. We only pay for earnings growth that is greater than the required return. Earnings that are due to growth at the required return are called **normal earnings.** For any period, t

$$\text{Normal earnings}_t = \rho \text{Earnings}_{t-1}$$

So, for the savings account, normal earnings in 2014 $= 1.05 \times \$5 = \$5.25$, that is, the prior year's earnings growing at 5 percent. The part of cum-dividend earnings for which we will pay is the cum-dividend earnings growth over these normal earnings, that is, the **abnormal earnings growth:**

$$\text{Abnormal earnings growth}_t = \text{Cum-dividend earnings}_t - \text{Normal earnings}_t$$
$$= [\text{Earnings}_t + (\rho - 1)\text{dividend}_{t-1}] - \rho\text{Earnings}_{t-1}$$

As cum-dividend earnings for the savings account in 2014 are $5.25, and as normal earnings also are $5.25, abnormal earnings growth is zero. And so for years 2015 and beyond. We will not pay for growth because, while we forecast growth, we do not forecast abnormal growth.

With these basic concepts in place, we now can move from the simple prototype to the valuation of equities. Here is a summary of the concepts we carry with us:

1. An asset is worth more than its capitalized earnings only if it can grow cum-dividend earnings at a rate greater than the required return. This recognizes that one pays only for growth that adds value.
2. When forecasting earnings growth, one must focus on cum-dividend growth. Ex-dividend growth ignores the value that comes from reinvesting dividends.
3. Dividend payout is irrelevant to valuation, for cum-dividend earnings growth is the same irrespective of dividends.

Box 6.1 solves a riddle about earnings growth for the S&P 500.

The Normal Forward P/E Ratio

The *forward P/E* is price relative to the forecast of next year's earnings. For the savings account, the forward P/E ratio in 2012 is $100/$5 = 20. This is a particularly special P/E, referred to as the **normal forward P/E:**

$$\text{Normal forward P/E} = \frac{1}{\text{Required return}}$$

That is, the normal forward P/E is just $1 capitalized at the required return. For the savings account, the forward P/E is 1/0.05 = 20.

The normal P/E embeds a principle that applies to all assets, including equities. If one forecasts no abnormal earnings growth (as with the savings account), the forward P/E ratio must be 1/required return. Or, put differently, if one expects the growth rate in cum-dividend earnings to be equal to the required return, the forward P/E ratio must be normal. That is, a normal P/E implies that normal earnings growth is expected. For a required (normal) return of 10 percent for an equity investment, say, the normal forward P/E is 1/0.10, or 10. For a required return of 12 percent, the normal forward P/E is $1/0.12 = 8.33$. If one forecasts cum-dividend earnings to grow at a rate greater than the required return, the P/E must be above normal: One pays extra for growth above normal. If one forecasts cum-dividend earnings to grow at a rate lower than the required return, the P/E ratio must be lower than normal: One discounts for low growth.

The Normal Trailing P/E Ratio

Chapter 3 distinguished the *trailing P/E*—the multiple of current earnings—from the *forward P/E*—the multiple of earnings forecasted one year ahead. Having calculated the value of the savings account from forecasts of forward earnings and earnings growth, calculating the trailing P/E is, of course, straightforward: Just divide the calculated value by the earnings reported in the last income statement. But there is an adjustment to make.

For the savings account in Exhibit 6.1, the trailing year is 2012, suppose that $100 were invested in the account at the beginning of 2012 to earn 5 percent. Earnings for 2012 would be $5 and, if these earnings were paid out as dividends, the value of the account at the end of 2012 would still be $100. So it would appear that the trailing P/E is $100/\$5 = 20$, the same as the forward P/E. However, this is incorrect. How could the value of one more year of earnings be the same? Suppose the $5 earnings for 2012 were not paid out, so that the value in the account was $105. The P/E ratio then becomes $105/\$5 = 21$. The latter is the correct trailing P/E.

The amount that $1 of earnings is worth—the P/E multiple—should not depend on dividends. The $5 of earnings for a savings account produces $105 in value for the owner of the account—the $100 at the beginning of the period that produced the earnings, plus the $5 of earnings. If she leaves the earnings in the account, the owner has $105; if she withdraws the earnings, she still has $105, with $100 in the account and $5 in her wallet. The trailing P/E is 21. Thus, the trailing P/E must always be based on cum-dividend prices:

$$\text{Trailing P/E} = \frac{\text{Price} + \text{Dividend}}{\text{Earnings}}$$

This measure is the dividend-adjusted P/E introduced in Chapter 3. The adjustment is necessary because dividends reduce the price (in the numerator) but do not affect earnings (in the denominator). The adjustment is not necessary for the forward P/E because both prices and forward earnings are reduced by the current dividend. P/E ratios published in the financial press do not make the adjustment for the trailing P/E. If the dividend is small, it matters little, but for high-payout firms, published P/E ratios depend on dividends as well as the ability of the firm to grow earnings.

Whereas the normal forward P/E is 1/Required return, the **normal trailing P/E** is

$$\text{Normal trailing P/E} = \frac{(1 + \text{Required return})}{\text{Required return}}$$

For the savings account, the normal trailing P/E is $1.05/0.05 = 21$ (compared with 20 for the forward P/E). For a required return of 10 percent, the normal trailing P/E is $1.10/0.10 = 11$ (compared with 10 for the forward P/E), and for a required return of 12 percent, it is $1.12/0.12 = 9.33$ (compared with 8.33 for the forward P/E). The normal forward P/E and the normal trailing P/E always differ by 1.0, representing one current dollar earning at the required return for an extra year.

A Poor P/E Model

The following model for valuing equities from forward earnings is quite common:

$$\text{Value of equity} = \frac{\text{Earn}_1}{\rho_E - g}$$

where g is (1 plus) the forecasted earnings growth rate. (You perhaps have seen this model with the letter r used to indicate the required return rather than ρ.) The model looks as if it should value earnings growth. The formula modifies the capitalized earnings formula (which worked for a savings account) for growth; indeed, the model is simply the formula for a perpetuity with growth. With this model, the forward P/E ratio is $1/(\rho_E - g)$.

This model is simple, but it is wrong. First, it is applied with forecasts of ex-dividend growth rates rather than cum-dividend growth rates. Ex-dividend growth rates ignore growth from reinvesting dividends. The higher the dividend payout, the higher the omitted value calculated by the formula with ex-dividend growth rates. Second, the formula clearly does not work when the earnings growth rate is greater than the required return, for then the denominator is negative. For the savings account, the required return is 5 percent, but the expected cum-dividend growth rate is also 5 percent, so the denominator of this formula is zero (and the calculated value of the savings account is infinite!). For equities, the cum-dividend growth rate is often higher than the required return, resulting in a negative denominator: This is the case for the S&P 500 in Box 6.1, for example. A growth rate slightly lower than the required return would have you paying a very high price—and overpaying for growth.

This is a poor model; it leads you into errors. The denominator problem is a mathematical problem, but behind this mathematical problem lurks a conceptual problem. We need a valuation model that protects us from paying too much for growth.

A MODEL FOR ANCHORING VALUE ON EARNINGS

The prototype valuation of the savings account gives us an anchor: capitalized forward earnings. It also indicates the anchoring principle:

Anchoring Principle. If one forecasts that cum-dividend earnings will grow at a rate equal to the required rate of return, the asset's value must be equal to its earnings capitalized.

Correspondingly, one adds extra value to the anchor if cum-dividend earnings are forecasted to grow at a rate greater than the required return: The asset must be worth more than its earnings capitalized. Abnormal earnings growth is the metric that captures the extra value, so the value of the equity for a going concern is

$$\text{Value of equity} = \text{Capitalized forward earnings} + \text{Extra value for}$$
$$\text{abnormal cum-dividend earnings growth}$$

$$V_0^E = \frac{\text{Earn}_1}{\rho_E - 1} + \frac{1}{\rho_E - 1}\left[\frac{\text{AEG}_2}{\rho_E} + \frac{\text{AEG}_3}{\rho_E^2} + \frac{\text{AEG}_4}{\rho_E^3} + \cdots\right]$$

$$= \frac{1}{\rho_E - 1}\left[\text{Earn}_1 + \frac{\text{AEG}_2}{\rho_E} + \frac{\text{AEG}_3}{\rho_E^2} + \frac{\text{AEG}_4}{\rho_E^3} + \cdots\right] \quad \textbf{(6.2)}$$

where AEG is abnormal (cum-dividend) earnings growth for years after the forward year, Year 1. (The ellipses indicate that forecasts continue on into the future, for equities are going concerns.) You see from the first version of the formula here that the discounted value of abnormal earnings growth supplies the extra value over that from capitalized forward earnings. The discounting calculates the value at the end of Year 1 of growth from Year 2 onward, and the value from growth is then capitalized (to convert the value of flows to a stock of value). As both the value of growth and forward earnings are capitalized, the second version of the formula simplifies the calculation. So, to value a share, proceed through the following steps:

1. Forecast one-year-ahead earnings (Year 1).
2. Forecast abnormal earnings growth (AEG) after the forward year (Year 2 onwards).
3. Calculate the present value (at the end of Year 1) of expected abnormal earnings growth after the forward year.
4. Capitalize the total of forward earnings and the value of abnormal earnings growth.

Figure 6.1 directs you through these three steps. As with residual earnings valuation, earnings must be comprehensive earnings; otherwise, value is lost in the calculation. Simply stated, the model says that value is based on future earnings, but with earnings from normal growth subtracted.

FIGURE 6.1 **Calculation of Equity Value Using the Abnormal Earnings Growth Model**
Abnormal earnings growth is the difference between cum-dividend earnings and normal earnings. The present value of abnormal earnings growth for Year 2 and beyond is added to forward earnings for Year 1, and the total is then capitalized to calculate equity value.

$$\text{Abnormal earnings growth}_t = \text{Cum-dividend earnings}_t - \text{Normal earnings}_t$$
$$\text{Cum-dividend earnings}_t = \text{Earnings}_t + (\rho_E - 1) \text{ dividend}_{t-1}$$
$$\text{Normal earnings}_t = \rho_E \text{ Earnings}_{t-1}$$

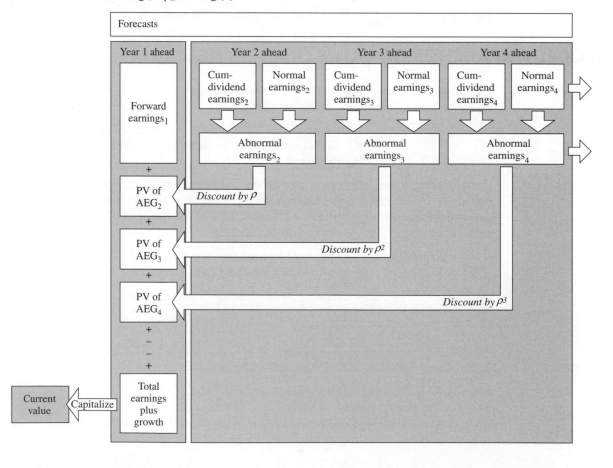

The intrinsic forward P/E is obtained by dividing the value calculated by forward earnings: V_0^E/Earn_1. If no abnormal earnings growth is forecasted,

$$V_0^E = \frac{\text{Earn}_1}{\rho_E - 1}$$

and the P/E is normal:

$$\frac{V_0^E}{\text{Earn}_1} = \frac{1}{\rho_E - 1}$$

This model is referred to as the *abnormal earnings growth model,* or the *Ohlson-Juettner model* after its architects.[1]

Measuring Abnormal Earnings Growth

As for the savings account, abnormal earnings growth (AEG) is earnings (with dividends reinvested) in excess of earnings growing at the required return:

$$\text{Abnormal earnings growth}_t = \text{Cum-dividend earn}_t - \text{Normal earn}_t$$

$$= [\text{Earn}_t + (\rho_E - 1)\text{d}_{t-1}] - \rho_E\text{Earn}_{t-1} \qquad \textbf{(6.3)}$$

Calculations can be made on a per-share basis or on a total dollar basis. When working on a per-share basis, dividends are dividends per share; when working on a total dollar basis, dividends are net dividends (dividends plus share repurchases minus share issues). Here are calculations of abnormal earnings growth for 2010 for two firms, Dell, Inc., and Nike, Inc. The required return in both cases is 9 percent.

	Dell, Inc.	Nike, Inc.
EPS 2010	$0.73	$3.93
DPS 2009	$0.00	$0.98
Earnings on reinvested dividends	0.00	0.088
Cum-dividend earnings 2010	0.73	4.018
Normal earnings from 2009:		
Dell: 1.25 × 1.09; Nike: 3.07 × 1.09	1.363	3.346
Abnormal earnings growth (AEG) 2010	−0.633	0.672

As Dell pays no dividends, cum-dividend EPS is the same as reported EPS ($0.73). Nike paid DPS of $0.98 in 2009, so cum-dividend EPS for 2010 is the reported EPS of $3.93 plus $0.088 from reinvesting the 2009 dividend at 9 percent. In both cases, normal earnings for 2010 is 2009 EPS growing at the "normal" rate of 9 percent. Notice that Dell's AEG is negative because the firm grew earnings at less than the required rate of 9 percent.

Abnormal earnings growth can be expressed in terms of growth rates relative to required return rates:

$$\text{Abnormal earnings growth}_t = [\text{G}_t - \rho_E] \times \text{Earnings}_{t-1} \qquad \textbf{(6.3a)}$$

where G_t is 1 plus the cum-dividend earnings growth rate for the period. That is, AEG is the dollar amount by which a prior year's earnings grow, cum-dividend, relative to the required rate. If G_t is equal to the required rate of return, there is no abnormal earnings growth. With cum-dividend EPS of $4.018 for 2010, Nike's cum-dividend earnings growth rate was

---

[1] See J. A. Ohlson and B. E. Juettner-Nauroth, "Expected EPS and EPS Growth as Determinants of Value," *Review of Accounting Studies,* July–September, 2005, pp. 349–365.

$4.018/3.07 = 30.88$ percent (plus 1). So, with a required return of 9 percent, Nike's AEG for 2010 was $3.07 \times (1.3088 - 1.09) = \$0.672$ per share, as before.

A Simple Demonstration and a Simple Valuation Model

Exhibit 6.2 applies the abnormal earnings growth model to the simple prototype firm used in Chapter 5. This firm has a required return of 10 percent and its earnings are expected to grow at 3 percent a year. A 3 percent growth rate looks low, but looks can be deceiving because the firm has a high payout ratio (76 percent of earnings).

Based on the earnings and dividend forecasts and the future book values they imply, residual earnings for the firm are forecasted to grow at a 3 percent rate, as indicated in the exhibit. So the firm can be valued with a Case 3 residual earnings valuation by capitalizing Year 1 residual earnings at this growth rate, as in Chapter 5:

$$V_0^E = 100 + \frac{2.36}{1.10 - 1.03} = 133.71 \text{ million}$$

EXHIBIT 6.2 Forecasts for a Firm with Expected Earnings Growth of 3 Percent per Year
In millions of dollars. Required return is 10 percent per year.

		Forecast Year				
	0	1	2	3	4	5
Residual earnings forecasts:						
Earnings	12.00	12.36	12.73	13.11	13.51	13.91
Dividends	9.09	9.36	9.64	9.93	10.23	10.54
Book value	100.00	103.00	106.09	109.27	112.55	115.92
Residual earnings (RE)		2.360	2.431	2.504	2.579	2.656
RE growth rate			3%	3%	3%	3%
Abnormal earnings growth forecasts:						
Earnings	12.00	12.36	12.73	13.11	13.51	13.91
Dividends	9.09	9.36	9.64	9.93	10.23	10.53
Earnings on reinvested dividends		0.909	0.936	0.964	0.993	1.023
Cum-dividend earnings		13.269	13.667	14.077	14.499	14.934
Normal earnings		13.200	13.596	14.004	14.424	14.857
Abnormal earnings growth (AEG)		0.069	0.071	0.073	0.075	0.077
Abnormal earnings growth rate			3%	3%	3%	3%
Cum-dividend earnings growth rate		10.57%	10.57%	10.57%	10.57%	10.57%
Normal earnings growth rate		10.0%	10.0%	10.0%	10.0%	10.0%

The Calculations:

Earnings on reinvested dividends refers to the prior year's dividend earning at the required return. So, for Year 2, earnings on reinvested dividends is $0.10 \times 9.36 = 0.936$.

Cum-dividend earnings adds earnings on reinvested dividends to the ex-dividend earnings forecasted. So, cum-dividend earnings for Year 2 is $12.73 + (0.10 \times 9.36) = 13.667$.

Normal earnings is the prior year's earnings growing at the required return. So, for Year 2, normal earnings is $12.36 \times 1.10 = 13.596$.

Abnormal earnings growth is cum-dividend earnings − normal earnings. So, for Year 2, AEG = $13.667 - 13.596 = 0.071$.

Abnormal earnings growth is also the prior year's earnings multiplied by the spread between the cum-dividend growth rate and the required rate. So, for Year 2, AEG is $(1.1057 - 1.10) \times 12.36 = 0.071$.

Allow for rounding errors.

The exhibit also forecasts abnormal earnings growth (AEG), in order to apply the abnormal earnings growth model. Abnormal earnings growth each year is cum-dividend earnings less normal earnings. Calculations are described at the bottom of the exhibit using both the equation 6.3 and 6.3a methods. You see that AEG is growing at 3 percent after Year 1. So, the AEG for Year 2 can be capitalized with this growth rate:

$$V_0^E = \frac{1}{0.10}\left[12.36 + \frac{0.071}{1.10 - 1.03}\right] = 133.71 \text{ million}$$

(Allow for rounding errors.) This is a *simple valuation model* where growth at a constant rate begins after the forward year. The forward P/E ratio is 133.71/12.36 = 10.82, higher than the normal P/E of 10. You will notice at the bottom of the exhibit that the cum-dividend earnings growth rate is 10.57 percent, higher than the required return of 10 percent, and accordingly the P/E ratio is greater than the normal P/E. You also will notice that the cum-dividend earnings growth rate is considerably higher than the 3 percent rate forecasted for (ex-dividend) earnings.[2] And you will notice that the RE model and the AEG model give us the same valuation.

Anchoring Valuation on Current Earnings

The valuation in this example prices forward earnings so, strictly speaking, it anchors on forecasted earnings rather than the current earnings in the financial statements. The value can also be calculated by anchoring on current (trailing) earnings: Capitalize current earnings, and then add the value of forecasted AEG from Year 1 onward. That is, shift the application of the model one period back in time. So, for the example in Exhibit 6.2,

$$V_0^E + d_0 = 133.71 + 9.09 = \frac{1.10}{0.10}\left[12.00 + \frac{0.069}{1.10 - 1.03}\right] = 142.80 \text{ million}$$

The value obtained is the cum-dividend value (price plus dividend) appropriate for valuing current earnings. The trailing P/E is $142.80/$12.00 = 11.90, higher than the normal trailing P/E of 11 (for a required return of 10 percent). The $12.00 here is earnings for Year 0 and the $0.069 is forecasted AEG for Year 1, which is expected to grow at a 3 percent rate. The capitalization rate is 1.10/0.10, the normal trailing P/E, rather than 1/0.10, the normal forward P/E. The formal model for the calculation is

$$V_0^E + d_0 = \frac{\rho_E}{\rho_E - 1}\left[\text{Earn}_0 + \frac{\text{AEG}_1}{\rho_E} + \frac{\text{AEG}_2}{\rho_E^2} + \frac{\text{AEG}_3}{\rho_E^3} + \cdots\right] \quad \textbf{(6.4)}$$

Clearly, with no AEG after the current year, the trailing P/E is normal.

Anchoring valuation on current earnings anchors on actual earnings in the financial statements rather than a forecast of earnings. However, there is a good reason to apply the model to forward earnings rather than current earnings. As we will see when we come to analyze financial statements, current earnings often contain nonsustainable components—unusual events and one-time charges, for example—that do not bear on the future. By focusing on forward earnings and using current earnings as a base for the forecast, we effectively focus on the sustainable portion of current earnings that can grow. Indeed, the

---

[2] Strictly, cum-dividend earnings for any year ahead are earnings for that year plus earnings from all dividends paid and reinvested from Year 1 up to that year (as for the zero-payout savings account in Exhibit 6.1). So, for Year 3 for the simple valuation in Exhibit 6.2, cum-dividend earnings are the $13.11 EPS for that year, plus the Year 2 dividend invested for one year, plus the earnings from the reinvested Year 1 dividend. However, as dividends earn at the required return and earnings at the required return are subtracted in the AEG calculation, it makes no difference to the valuation—and is certainly simpler—if we just include the earnings on the prior year's dividends in cum-dividend earnings.

financial statement analysis of Part Two of the book aims to identify sustainable earnings that are a sound anchor for forecasting forward earnings.

The Web page for this chapter provides a spreadsheet to help you develop abnormal earnings growth pro formas.

APPLYING THE MODEL TO EQUITIES

The example in Exhibit 6.2 is similar to our prototype savings account example, except that this firm has some abnormal earnings growth whereas the savings account had none. The firm is simple because AEG is forecasted to grow at a constant rate immediately after the first year ahead. Model 6.2 requires infinite forecasting horizons, so, to value equities, we need continuing values to truncate the forecast horizon. In the simple example, this occurs just one year ahead.

There are two types of continuing value calculations. Case 1 applies when one expects subsequent abnormal earnings growth at the forecast horizon to be zero. Case 2 applies when one expects more abnormal earnings growth after the forecast horizon.

Case 1 is illustrated using General Electric Company with a required return of 10 percent. The EPS and DPS numbers in Case 1 are GE's actual numbers for 2000–2004, the same numbers used to value GE using residual earnings methods in the last chapter. As in the last chapter, we treat the numbers as forecasts and value GE's shares at the end of 1999. Recall that we attempted to value GE using discounted cash flow techniques in Chapter 4 but ran into difficulties. However, we found we could value it with residual earnings methods. The AEG valuation here produces the same $13.07 per share value as the RE valuation in Chapter 5.

The Case 1 valuation is based on a forecast that AEG will be zero after 2004. While the analyst forecasts positive AEG for 2004, he notes that the average AEG is close to zero over 2001–2004 and so forecasts zero AEG subsequently. Zero AEG implies, of course, that cum-dividend earnings are expected to grow after 2004 at the required rate of return, just like the savings account. The total AEG over 2001–2004, discounted to the end of 2000, is $0.017 per share. Added to forward earnings for 2000 of $1.29 yields $1.307, which when capitalized at the 10 percent rate, yields the valuation of $13.07 per share. Now go to Box 6.2.

CASE 1

General Electric Co. (GE)

In this case, abnormal earnings growth is expected to be zero after 2004. Required rate of return is 10 percent.

			Forecast Year			
	1999	2000	2001	2002	2003	2004
DPS		0.57	0.66	0.73	0.77	0.82
EPS		1.29	1.38	1.42	1.50	1.60
DPS reinvested ($0.10 \times DPS_{t-1}$)			0.057	0.066	0.073	0.077
Cum-dividend earnings (EPS + DPS reinvested)			1.437	1.486	1.573	1.677
Normal earnings ($1.10 \times EPS_{t-1}$)			1.419	1.518	1.562	1.650
Abnormal earnings growth (AEG)			0.018	−0.032	0.011	0.027
Discount rate (1.10^t)			1.100	1.210	1.331	1.464
Present value of AEG at year 2000			0.016	−0.026	0.008	0.018
Total PV of AEG		0.017				
Total earnings to be capitalized		1.307				
Capitalization rate		0.10				
Value per share $\left(\dfrac{1.307}{0.10}\right)$	13.07 ←					

Note: Allow for rounding errors.

Fundamentalist principles (in Chapter 1) emphasize that we should *separate what we know from speculation* and *anchor on what we know*. This is particularly important when valuing growth, for growth is speculative.

In Chapter 4, we pointed out that discounted cash flow (DCF) analysis often puts a lot of the value into the continuing value. This is problematic for the continuing value is the most uncertain part of a valuation, dealing as it does with the long term. For General Electric (GE) in Chapter 4, more than 100 percent of the valuation is in the continuing value. We would much prefer a valuation method where the value comes from the present ("what we know") or the near-term future (what we forecast with some confidence). We suggested that earnings might supply some level of comfort.

Indeed, for General Electric in Case 1, the continuing value at the forecast horizon, 2004, is zero, compared with more than 100 percent in the DCF valuation. We valued GE with five years of forecasts. We may have some uncertainty about these forecasts—and would prefer a valuation based on one or two years of forecasted earnings—but probably feel more comfortable with this valuation than one that speculates about a large continuing value.

The difference between DCF valuation and the valuation here is, of course, the accounting: Cash accounting versus accrual accounting. Accrual accounting brings the future forward in time, leaving less value in a continuing value.

The residual earnings valuation for GE in Chapter 5 also used accrual accounting, but the Case 2 valuation there has a nonzero continuing value (in equation 5.5). Is it then the case that AEG valuation gives us a more secure valuation than an RE valuation? It does look like it, but in fact no. The residual earnings valuation gives the same valuation as the AEG valuation for the same forecast horizon. Forecasting that RE will be a constant at the forecast horizon in a Case 2 residual earnings valuation is the same as forecasting that AEG = 0, for it is always the case that AEG = change in RE. By forecasting that RE will be positive but constant, we are just forecasting that there will be value missing from the balance sheet. But there will be no added value for growth. See Box 6.3.

If expected AEG = 0, then the P/E is normal, as demonstrated with the savings account. So forecasting that GE will have zero AEG in 2005 and beyond is equivalent to forecasting that its P/E will be normal. (By 2008, GE's P/E was approximately normal. See Exercise E6.10.)

Proceed now to the Case 2 valuation of Nike, Inc. You will see that there is now a continuing value containing a growth speculation. In this case, we do not escape some speculation about the long run. But we separate that speculation (in the continuing value) from what we are more confident about (in near-term forecasts).

A Case 2 valuation is demonstrated using Nike, Inc., with a required rate of return of 9 percent. The EPS and DPS up to 2011 are the same as those in Chapter 5 where we valued the firm using residual earnings methods with a continuing value based on a forecast that residual earnings after 2011 would grow at 4.5 percent. The EPS for 2012 here is that which would result from this growth rate.

Case 2 differs from Case 1 because AEG is expected to continue to grow after the forecast horizon, so the valuation adds a continuing value that incorporates this growth. With the forecasted AEG for 2012 of $0.095 expected to grow at a rate of 4.5 percent, the continuing value for Nike at the end of 2011 is $2.111 per share. Adding the present value of this continuing value at the end of 2007 to the total present value of AEG up to the end of 2011 ($0.332) and the forward earnings for 2007 ($2.96) yields $4.787 of earnings to be capitalized, resulting in a value of $53.18 per share.

This is the same value calculated with residual earnings methods in Chapter 5. And it is also the same as the value using forecasted changes in residual earnings in equation 6.1 in this chapter. Indeed, you can see that the AEG for Nike here equals the change in residual earnings in equation 6.1. As both are anchored on forward earnings, the two valuations must be the same. Go to Box 6.3 for a formal demonstration that $\Delta RE = AEG$.

Converting Analysts' Forecasts to a Valuation

In Chapter 5 we converted analysts' forecasts for Nike to a valuation using residual earnings methods. Here we do the same for Google, Inc., the supplier of Web-based software,

CASE 2
Nike, Inc.

In this case, abnormal earnings are expected to grow at a 4.5 percent rate after 2011. Required rate of return is 9 percent.

	2006	Forecast Year					
		2007	2008	2009	2010	2011	2012
DPS		0.71	0.88	0.98	1.06	1.20	1.30
EPS		2.96	3.80	3.07	3.93	4.28	4.65
DPS reinvested ($0.09 \times DPS_{t-1}$)			0.064	0.079	0.088	0.095	0.110
Cum-dividend earnings			3.864	3.149	4.018	4.375	4.760
Normal earnings ($1.09 \times EPS_{t-1}$)			3.226	4.142	3.346	4.284	4.665
Abnormal earnings growth (AEG)			0.638	−0.993	0.672	0.091	0.095
Discount rate (1.09^t)			1.090	1.188	1.295	1.412	
Present value of AEG at end 2007			0.585	−0.836	0.519	0.064	
Total PV of AEG to 2011		0.332					
Continuing value (CV)						2.111	
Present value of CV		1.495					
Total earnings to be capitalized		4.787					
Capitalization rate		0.09					
Value per share $\left(\dfrac{4.787}{0.09}\right)$	53.18						

The continuing value:

$$\text{CV at 2011} = \frac{0.095}{1.09 - 1.045} = 2.111$$

$$\text{Present value of continuing value} = \frac{2.111}{1.412} = 1.495$$

particularly Web search, whose revenues come largely from online advertising. In Table 6.1, analysts' consensus EPS forecasts made in early 2011 for 2011 and 2012 are entered, along with forecasts for 2013–2015 from applying their intermediate-term (five-year) consensus EPS growth rate of 17.4 percent to the 2012 estimate. The table values the firm at the end of 2010 based on these forecasts.

The calculations in the table show that analysts are forecasting abnormal earnings growth after the forward year, 2011. Analysts do not provide forecasts more than five years ahead, so the continuing value here is based on a 4 percent long-term growth rate, the typical GDP growth rate. By doing so, we are refusing to speculate; we are relying on a historical average ("what we know"). The calculated value is $693.09 per share. Google traded at $624 at the time, so this value is in excess of the market's valuation. What could be wrong? Analysts' five-year growth rates are typically optimistic, more so (probably) for this hot stock. Alternatively, the market price is cheap. Could it be the case that the long-term growth rate of 4 percent here is too optimistic? Maybe Google can produce a higher growth rate than the average for the economy—in which case the stock may indeed be cheap. We will return to these issues when we apply the valuations here to active investing in Chapter 7.

BUILD YOUR OWN VALUATION ENGINE

As with residual earnings valuation, the mechanics of the valuations in Cases 1 and 2 and Table 6.1 can be built into a spreadsheet. The spreadsheet requires the following inputs: (1) earnings and dividend forecasts up to a given forecast horizon, (2) a required return, and (3) a long-term growth rate to calculate the continuing value. The standard spreadsheet has

TABLE 6.1
Converting Analysts' Forecasts to a Valuation: Google, Inc., 2010
Analysts forecast EPS two years ahead ($33.83 for 2011 and $39.47 for 2012) and also give a five-year EPS growth rate of 17.4 percent. Forecasts for 2013–2015 apply this consensus growth rate to the 2012 forecast. Google pays no dividends. Required rate of return is 11 percent.

	2010A	2011E	2012E	2013E	2014E	2015E
DPS		0.00	0.00	0.00	0.00	0.00
EPS		33.83	39.47	46.34	54.40	63.87
DPS reinvested ($0.11 \times DPS_{t-1}$)			0.00	0.00	0.00	0.00
Cum-dividend earnings			39.47	46.34	54.40	63.87
Normal earnings ($1.11 \times EPS_{t-1}$)			37.55	43.81	51.44	60.38
Abnormal earnings growth (AEG)			1.92	2.53	2.96	3.49
Discount rate (1.11^t)			1.11	1.232	1.368	1.518
Present value of AEG			1.730	2.054	2.164	2.300
Total PV of AEG to 2015	8.25					
Continuing value (CV)						51.85
Present value of CV	34.16					
Total earnings to be capitalized	76.24					
Capitalization rate	0.11					

Value per share $\left(\dfrac{76.24}{0.11}\right)$ 693.09 ←

The continuing value:

$$CV \text{ at } 2015 = \frac{3.49 \times 1.04}{1.11 - 1.04} = 51.85$$

$$\text{Present value of continuing value} = \frac{51.85}{1.518} = 34.16$$

forecasts for two years ahead (that's what analysts forecast) and applies a growth rate for years thereafter. A more flexible engine allows for different forecast horizons. There are examples on the Web page for this chapter.

The spreadsheet can be set up to calculate abnormal earnings growth for each period after the forward year as in Cases 1 and 2 but, if you have built the residual earnings valuation engine in Chapter 5, simply calculate the AEG as the change in residual earnings. Provided your continuing value has AEG growing at the same rate as the residual earnings, your engine will produce the same valuation as the residual earnings engine.

Use the tool to understand your uncertainty about the valuation by changing the inputs. For example, if you are unsure about the required return, you might test to see how sensitive the valuation is entering a different number. How sensitive is the valuation to the growth rate? Is it the case that the stock looks overpriced or underpriced for any range of reasonable growth rates? The GDP growth rate was applied in Table 6.1, but you might look at the sensitivity of the valuation to a 3 percent or 2 percent rate: What is the stock worth if it delivers only 2 percent growth? If you think 2 percent is conservative and the stock is trading below the calculated value, you may feel comfortable in buying the stock. If, on the other hand, you see that, by experimenting with alternative growth rates, a 6 percent growth rate is required to justify the market price, then you might consider the stock to be too expensive.

The engine is a good tool for converting analysts' forecasts to a valuation. But, in the end, you will want to develop your own forecasts based on the financial statement analysis in the next part of the book. That will allow for much more sensitivity analysis, for it will get to the core of the valuation generation. The Build Your Own Analysis Product (BYOAP) on the book's Web site will be your guide to this full analysis and valuation spreadsheet.

The AEG model and the RE model look different but are really quite similar. Both require forecasts of earnings and dividends, although the RE model adds the extra mechanical step of calculating book value forecasts from these forecasts.

Structurally, the two models are similar. The RE starts with book value as an anchor and then adds value by charging forecasted earnings by the required return applied to book value. The AEG model starts with capitalized earnings as an anchor and then adds value by charging forecasted (cum-dividend) earnings by the required return applied to prior earnings, rather than book value.

This structural difference is just a different arrangement of the inputs. A little algebra underscores the point. Abnormal earnings growth can be written in a different form:

$$AEG_t = [Earn_t + (\rho_E - 1)d_{t-1}] - \rho_E Earn_{t-1}$$
$$= Earn_t - Earn_{t-1} - (\rho_E - 1)(Earn_{t-1} - d_{t-1})$$

Using the stocks and flows equation for accounting for the book value of equity (Chapter 2), $B_{t-1} = B_{t-2} + Earn_{t-1} - d_{t-1}$, so $Earn_{t-1} - d_{t-1} = B_{t-1} - B_{t-2}$. Thus,

$$AEG_t = Earn_t - Earn_{t-1} - (\rho_E - 1)(B_{t-1} - B_{t-2})$$
$$= [Earn_t - (\rho_E - 1)B_{t-1}] - [Earn_{t-1} - (\rho_E - 1)B_{t-2}]$$
$$= RE_t - RE_{t-1}$$

So, abnormal earnings growth is always equal to the change in residual earnings. You can see this by comparing the changes in residual earnings with the AEG for the prototype firm in Exhibit 6.2:

	1	2	3	4	5
Residual earnings	2.360	2.431	2.504	2.579	2.656
Change in residual earnings		0.071	0.073	0.075	0.077
Abnormal earnings growth		0.071	0.073	0.075	0.077

You can also see the equivalence by comparing the AEG for Nike in the Case 2 valuation with the changes in RE in the Nike valuation at the front of this chapter.

So, forecasting that there will be no abnormal earnings growth is the same as forecasting that residual earnings will not change. Or, as abnormal earnings growth of zero means that (cum-dividend) earnings are growing at the required rate of return, forecasting this normal growth rate is the same as forecasting that residual earnings will not change. Correspondingly, forecasting cum-dividend earnings growth above normal is the same as forecasting growth in residual earnings. Accordingly, one set of forecasts gives us both valuations, as the Case 2 valuation for Nike and the equivalent valuation based on changes in residual earnings at the front of this chapter demonstrate.

The rearrangement of the inputs leads to the different anchors and different definitions of adding value to the anchors. Yet the underlying concepts are similar. AEG valuation enforces the point that a firm cannot add value from growing earnings unless it grows earnings at a rate greater than the required rate of return. Only then does it increase its P/E ratio. But that is the same as saying that the firm must grow residual earnings to increase its P/B ratio. That is, added value comes from investing to earn a return greater than the required return, and that added value has its manifestation in both growth in residual earnings and growth in cum-dividend earnings over a normal growth rate.

In one sense, the AEG valuation is more convenient for one does not have to worry about book values. However, the RE model gives us more insight into the value creation (that produces growth) so is more useful when we come to analysis in Part Two of the book.

FEATURES OF THE ABNORMAL EARNINGS GROWTH MODEL

Box 6.4 lists the advantages and disadvantages of the abnormal earnings growth model. Compare it to similar summaries for the dividend discount model (in Chapter 4), the discounted cash flow model (in Chapter 4), and the residual earnings model (in Chapter 5).

We have emphasized that AEG valuation, like the residual earnings valuation, protects us from paying too much for earnings growth. In this section we will discuss some other features of the model.

ADVANTAGES

Easy to understand:	Investors think in terms of future earnings and earnings growth; investors buy earnings. Focuses directly on the most common multiple used, the P/E ratio.
Uses accrual accounting:	Embeds the properties of accrual accounting by which revenues are matched with expenses to measure value added from selling products.
Versatility:	Can be used under a variety of accounting principles (Chapter 17).
Aligned with what people forecast:	Analysts forecast earnings and earnings growth.
Forecast horizon:	Forecast horizons are typically shorter than those for DCF analysis and more value is typically recognized in the immediate future. There is less reliance on continuing values.
Protection:	Protects from paying too much for growth.

DISADVANTAGES

Accounting complexity:	Requires an understanding of how accrual accounting works.
Concept complexity:	Requires an appreciation of the concept of cum-dividend earnings and abnormal earnings growth.
Sensitive to the required return estimate:	As the value derives completely from forecasts that are capitalized at the required return, the valuation is sensitive to the estimate used for the required return. Residual earnings valuations derive partly from book value that does not involve a required return.
Use in analysis:	The residual earnings model provides better insight into the analysis of value creation and the drivers of growth (in Part Two of the book).
Application to strategy:	Does not give an insight into the drivers of earnings growth, particularly balance sheet items; therefore, it is not suited to strategy analysis.
Suspect accounting:	Relies on earnings numbers that can be suspect. Should be implemented along with an earnings quality analysis. (Chapter 18).

Buy Earnings

The abnormal earnings growth model adopts the perspective of "buying earnings." It embodies the idea that the value of a firm is based on what it can earn. As earnings represent value added from selling products and services in markets, the model anticipates the value to be added from trading with customers, by matching revenues from those customers with the value given up in expenses.

The AEG model embraces the language of the analyst community. P/E ratios are more often referred to than P/B ratios. Analysts talk of earnings and earnings growth, not residual earnings and residual earnings growth. So, converting an analyst's forecast to a valuation is more direct with this model than with the residual earnings model. (The language of the (Wall) street does not recognize how dividends affect growth, however; analysts talk of ex-dividend earnings growth rates, not cum-dividend rates.)

Abnormal Earnings Growth Valuation and Residual Earnings Valuation

On the other hand, the AEG model does not give as much insight into the value creation as the residual earnings model. Firms invest in assets and add value by employing these assets in operations. The residual earnings (RE) model explicitly recognizes the investment in assets, then recognizes that value is added only if that return is greater that the required return. The residual earnings model is a better lens on the business of generating value, the cycle of investment and return on investment. Accordingly, we have not proposed the AEG model as a model for strategy analysis (as we did with the RE model), for strategy analysis involves investment. The central question in strategy analysis is whether the investment will add value. When we come to analysis in Part Two of the book, we will focus on the RE model, for it provides more insight into value generation within a business.

Abnormal Earnings Growth Is Not Affected by Dividends, Share Issues, or Share Repurchases

We saw in Chapter 5 that residual earnings valuation is not sensitive to expected dividend payout or share issues and share repurchases. This is also the case with the AEG model.

With respect to dividends, you can prove this to yourself using the simple example in Exhibit 6.2. Rather than paying a dividend, reinvest the dividends in the firm at the 10 percent rate. Subsequent earnings within the firm will increase by the amount of the reinvested dividends. Cum-dividend earnings—the amount of earnings earned in the firm plus that earned by reinvesting the dividends outside the firm—will be exactly the same as if the shareholder reinvested the dividends in a personal account (as in the exhibit). AEG will not change, nor will the valuation. (You also saw this with the savings account.) This simulates the earnings for an investor who receives the dividend but uses the cash to buy the stock, which is priced to yield a 10 percent required return. He effectively undoes the dividend, with no effect on value. The same logic applies if the payouts in Exhibit 6.2 are from stock repurchases rather than dividends. A firm adds value by finding investments that yield abnormal earnings growth, not by keeping cash in the firm or paying it out.

Accounting Methods and Valuation

The residual earnings model accommodates different accounting principles. As we saw in Chapter 5, this is because book values and earnings work together. Firms may create higher future earnings by the accounting they choose, but to do so they must write down book values. When the higher earnings are combined with the lower book values (in a residual earnings valuation), value is unaffected.

The AEG model, at first glance, looks as if it might not have this feature. A manager can create higher future earnings by writing down book values, and the AEG model values future earnings without carrying book values as a correcting mechanism. We do not want to pay for growth that does not add value, and accounting methods can create growth in earnings that we do not want to pay for. As it happens, the AEG model, like the residual earnings model, provides protection against paying for growth that is created by accounting. Box 6.5 explains.

Make sure you read the section titled "A Lesson for the Analyst" in Box 6.5. The trailing P/E indicates expected earnings from sales in the future relative to the earnings recognized from current sales. To measure the value added from sales, accounting methods match expenses with revenues. If that matching underestimates current expenses (by underestimating bad debts, for example), current earnings are higher. However, future earnings are lower—earnings are "borrowed from the future." Because more current earnings are recognized and less future earnings are expected (and value is not affected), the trailing P/E is lower. With lower future earnings, the forward P/E is higher. The converse is true if a firm recognizes more expenses in current earnings.

Exhibit 6.2 presented pro forma earnings and earnings growth for valuing the equity of a prototype firm. Suppose the manager of this firm has decided to create more earnings for Year 1 by writing down inventory by $8 in Year 0. This accounting adjustment changes the accounting numbers, but should not affect the value. Here is the revised pro forma:

Creating Earnings with Accounting: Modifying Exhibit 6.2 for a Write-Down

	Forecast Year					
	0	1	2	3	4	5
Earnings	4.00	20.36	12.73	13.11	13.51	13.91
Dividends	9.09	9.36	9.64	9.93	10.23	10.54
Book value	92.00	103.00	106.09	109.27	112.55	115.92
Earnings on reinvested dividends			0.936	0.964	0.993	1.023
Cum-dividend earnings			13.667	14.077	14.499	14.934
Normal earnings			22.396	14.004	14.424	14.857
Abnormal earnings growth			(8.729)	0.073	0.075	0.077
Abnormal earnings growth rate					3%	3%

EFFECT ON VALUATION

As a result of the $8 write-down, the $12 reported for Year 0 earnings is now $4 (and the book value is $92 instead of $100). Correspondingly, Year 1 forward earnings increase by $8 to $20.36 because cost of goods sold is lower by $8. Cum-dividend earnings for Year 2 are not affected but, because those earnings are now compared to normal earnings of $22.396, on the high base of $20.36 for Year 1, abnormal earnings growth for Year 2 is (a decline of) –$8.729. Subsequent years are unaffected. The AEG valuation at the end of Year 0 is

$$V_0^E = \frac{1}{0.10}\left[20.36 - \frac{8.729}{1.10} + \frac{0.073}{1.10 - 1.03}\bigg/1.10\right] = 133.71$$

This is the same as the value before the accounting change. While forward Year 1 earnings have increased, the higher earnings of $20.36 mean higher normal earnings for Year 2 and consequently lower earnings growth of –$8.729. The net effect is to leave the value unchanged.

EFFECT ON P/E RATIOS

While valuations are not affected by accounting methods, P/E ratios certainly are. The forward P/E for this firm is now $133.71/$20.36 = 6.57, down from 10.82. The trailing (dividend-adjusted) P/E is now ($133.71 + $9.09)/$4.00 = 35.70, up from 11.90. Shifting income from current earnings to forward earnings increases the trailing P/E; there is now more anticipated earnings growth next year and the P/E prices growth. However, shifting income to the future decreases the forward P/E—there is now less anticipated growth after the forward year, and the value of the earnings (in the numerator) does not change.

A LESSON FOR THE ANALYST

There is a lesson here. The diligent analyst distinguishes growth that comes from accounting from growth that comes from real business factors. If growth is induced by the accounting, he changes the P/E ratio, but he does not change the valuation. Applying the AEG model (or indeed the residual earnings model) protects him from making the mistake of pricing earnings that are due to accounting methods.

We opened this chapter with the caveat that we do not want to pay for growth that does not add value. We do not want to pay for earnings growth from added investment that earns only the required return. But we also do not want to pay for growth that is created by accounting methods. Using the residual earnings model or the abnormal earnings growth model protects us from both dangers.

THE FED MODEL

Alan Greenspan, chairman of the Federal Reserve Bank during the 1990s, was known for his statements regarding the "irrational exuberance" of the stock market. According to *Barron's,* he used an earnings yield screen. See Box 6.6.

The "Greenspan model" or the "Fed model" compares the expected *earnings yield* with the 10-year Treasury yield to assess whether stocks are overpriced. The expected earnings yield, measured as forward earnings/price, is just the inverse of the forward P/E ratio, so an earnings yield of 4.75 percent (at the time of the newspaper report) implies a forward P/E

From an article in *Barron's* in 1998:

Fed Chairman Alan Greenspan hasn't said much about the stock market this year, but his favorite valuation model is just about screaming a sell signal. The so-called Greenspan model (or Fed model) was brought to our attention last summer by Edward Yardeni, economist at Deutsche Morgan Grenfell, who found it buried in the back pages of a Fed report. The model's very presence in such a report was noteworthy because the Fed officials normally don't tip their hand about their views on the stock market. The model surfaced at a particularly interesting time: Stocks were near a high point, and the Greenspan model indicated that the market was about 20 percent higher than it should have been.

That turned out to be a pretty good call. By October 1998, stocks had fallen as much as 15 percent from their summer high point. By year-end, of course, the Dow had recovered to around 7900, but it still remained about 5 percent below its peak for the year.

Now that the Dow has climbed above 8600, Greenspan's model is again flashing a warning signal. To be exact, the Greenspan model now indicates that stocks are 18 percent overvalued.

The Fed's model arrives at its conclusions by comparing the yield on the 10-year Treasury note to the price-to-earnings ratio of the S&P 500 based on expected operating earnings in the coming 12 months. To put stocks and bonds on the same footing, the model uses the *earnings yield* on stocks, which is the inverse of the (forward) P/E ratio. So while the yield on the 10-year Treasury is now 5.60 percent, the earnings yield on the S&P 500, based on a (forward) P/E ratio of 21, is 4.75 percent.

In essence, the Fed's model asks, Why would anyone buy stocks with a 4.75 percent earnings return, when they could get a bond with a 5.60 percent yield?

The Fed's model suggests the S&P should be trading around 900, well under its current level of 1070.

Source: "Is Alan Addled? 'Greenspan Model' Indicates Stocks Today Are Overvalued by About 18%," *Barron's,* March 16, 1998, p. 21.

of 21.05. A Treasury yield of 5.60 percent implies a forward P/E of 17.86. The Fed model says that stocks are likely to be overpriced when the forward P/E for stocks rises above the P/E for Treasury notes. Is this a good screen?

Is the Fed model well calibrated? One expects the forward P/E for stocks to be different from that for bonds because stocks and bonds have different risk and thus different required returns. The forward P/E of 17.86 for a bond is the normal P/E for a required return of 5.60 percent. Stocks are more risky; if the required return is 10 percent, the normal P/E is 10, considerably less than the P/E for a riskless government bond. However, P/E ratios also incorporate growth, and the Fed model does not explicitly build in growth after the forward year. A bond has no abnormal earnings growth (it is similar to a savings account), so the normal P/E is the appropriate P/E. But stocks with a normal P/E of 10 could be worth a P/E of 21 if abnormal earnings growth is anticipated after the forward year. Without forecasts of subsequent earnings, the P/E of 21 cannot be challenged effectively. The Fed model asks: Why would anyone buy stocks with a 4.75 percent earnings return, when they could get a bond with a 5.60 percent yield? Well, they would do so if they saw growth that they were willing to pay for. An earnings yield screen is too simplistic.

The two errors in applying the Fed model—ignoring differences in risk and expected growth—work in the opposite direction. Stocks should have a lower P/E because they are more risky, but they should have a higher P/E if they can deliver growth. By demanding that stocks have an earnings yield no less than the yield on Treasury notes, the model is saying that growth can never be high enough to compensate for the error of treating stocks as riskless securities like Treasury notes.

But we must be careful; perhaps more growth means more risk. We understand that growth (in the continuing value calculation) is the most uncertain aspect of a valuation; there is a lot of risk in the growth estimate. One expects that you cannot get more growth without taking on more risk, at least on average. This interplay between risk and growth—and between the required return and growth rate in a valuation—is something we will focus

As P/E ratios involve the capitalization of earnings by the required return, and as the required return varies as interest rates change, P/E ratios should be lower in periods of high interest rates and higher in times of low interest rates. Correspondingly, earnings yields should be higher in times of high interest rates and lower in times of low interest rates. The figure below indicates that P/E ratios and interest rates have moved in the opposite directions in recent history.

When interest rates on government obligations were high in the late 1970s and early 1980s, P/Es were low; when interest rates were relatively low in the 1990s, P/Es were relatively high. But the relationship between P/E and interest rates is not strong. This is because expectations of future earnings growth are more important in determining the P/E than changes in interest rates.

Of course we must be cautious in our interpretations because the market may have been inefficient at times in pricing earnings. Were P/E ratios too low in the 1970s? Too high in the 1990s? Was the market underestimating future earnings growth in the 1970s and overestimating it in the 1990s?

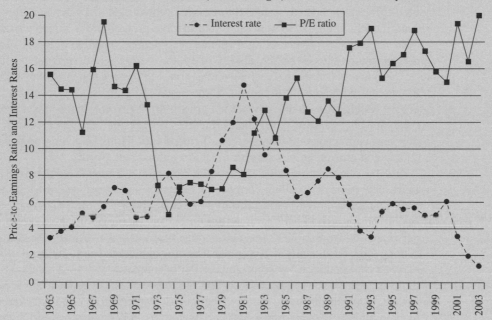

Median P/E Ratios and Interest Rates (in Percentages) on One-Year Treasury Bills

Source: P/E ratios were calculated from Standard & Poor's COMPUSTAT® data. Interest rates are from the Federal Reserve Statistics Release (**www.federalreserve.gov**).

on in the next chapter. But for the moment, heed the warning: Beware of paying too much for growth.

The comparison of earnings yields to Treasury rates does remind us that earnings yields and P/E ratios should change as interest rates change. See Box 6.7.

PEG RATIOS

In recent years, the PEG ratio has come into prominence. The PEG (P/E-to-earnings-growth) ratio compares the P/E ratio to a forecast of percentage earnings growth rate in the following year:

$$\text{PEG ratio} = \frac{\text{P/E}}{\text{1-year-ahead percentage earnings growth}}$$

The P/E in the numerator is usually the forward P/E, but sometimes the trailing P/E is used. If the forward P/E is used, the appropriate measure of growth in the denominator of the PEG ratio is the forecasted one-year growth after the forward year, that is, growth for two years ahead. The ratio compares the traded P/E, the market's assessment of earnings growth after the forward year, with actual growth forecasts. Analysts' growth forecasts are typically used. If the ratio is less than 1.0, the screener concludes that the market is underestimating earnings growth. If it is greater than 1.0, the screener concludes that the market is too optimistic about growth. With a market price of $624 and a forward P/E of $624/$33.83 = 18.4 in early 2011 and a forecasted two-year-ahead growth rate of 17.4 percent (in Table 6.1), Google's PEG ratio was 1.06.

The benchmark PEG ratio of 1.0 is consistent with the ideas in this chapter. If the required return for a stock is 10 percent (and thus the forward P/E is 10), the market is pricing the stock correctly if earnings are expected to grow (cum-dividend) at the required rate of 10 percent. If an analyst indeed forecasts a growth rate of 10 percent after the forward year, the PEG ratio is 10/10 = 1.0. (Note that the growth rate is in percentage terms.) If, however, an analyst forecasts a growth rate of 15 percent, the PEG ratio is 10/15 = 0.67 and the analyst questions whether, at a P/E of 10, the market is underpricing expected growth.

Caution is called for in screening on PEG ratios. First, the benchmark of 1.0 applies only for a required return of 10 percent. If the required return is 12 percent, the normal P/E is 8.33 which, when divided by normal growth of 12 percent, yields a benchmark PEG of 0.69. Second, standard calculations (incorrectly) use the forecasted growth rate in ex-dividend earnings rather than the cum-dividend rate. Third, screening on just one year of anticipated growth ignores information about subsequent growth.

For this reason, some calculations of the PEG ratio use annualized five-year growth rates in the denominator. In 2002, Ford Motor Company's shares traded at $7.20 each on analysts' consensus forecast of forward EPS of $0.43, giving a P/E of 16.7. Analysts were forecasting $0.65 in per-share earnings for two years ahead. As the firm indicated 40 cents per-share dividends in 2002, the cum-dividend forecast for two years ahead was $0.69, assuming a required return of 10 percent. Thus the anticipated cum-dividend growth rate for two years ahead was 60.5 percent, and Ford's PEG ratio was 16.7/60.5 = 0.28. This PEG ratio indicates that Ford was underpriced. But the two-year-ahead growth rate is probably due to the fact that the forward year was a particularly bad year for Ford. Ford would not be able to maintain a 60 percent growth rate into the future (and certainly did not). Indeed, analysts at the time were forecasting only an average 5 percent annual growth rate over the next five years. Using this growth rate in the denominator of the PEG ratio yields a ratio of 3.3.

Summary

The valuation methods in this chapter complement those in Chapter 5. They yield intrinsic P/E ratios rather than P/B ratios. Rather than anchoring valuation on book value, the methods here anchor valuation on earnings. However, the form of the valuation is similar. With P/B valuation, one adds value to book value for earnings in excess of normal earnings (at the required return) on book value; with P/E valuation, one adds value to capitalized earnings for earnings in excess of normal earnings (at the required return) on prior earnings.

Abnormal earnings growth—earnings growth in excess of normal earnings growth—is the central concept for the valuation. This concept, in turn, requires an appreciation that, when the analyst focuses on earnings growth, she must focus on cum-dividend earnings growth because future earnings involve not only earnings earned in the firm but also earnings from reinvesting any dividends to be received.

As with residual earnings valuation, the application of the methods in this chapter protects the investor from paying too much for earnings. These methods also protect the investor from paying for earnings created by accounting methods.

The Web Connection

Find the following on the Web page for this chapter:

- Further applications of abnormal earnings growth valuation.
- A spreadsheet program to help you develop abnormal earnings growth pro formas and valuations.
- Further examples of reverse engineering.

- A further demonstration that AEG valuation and residual earnings valuation yield the same value.
- Some pointers for evaluating the quality of an analyst's stock report and buy-or-sell recommendation.
- The Readers' Corner points you to further reading.

Key Concepts

abnormal earnings growth is earnings growth in excess of growth at a rate equal to the required return. Compare with **normal earnings growth.** *183*

cum-dividend earnings are earnings that include earnings on prior dividends paid. Compare with **ex-dividend earnings.** *182*

ex-dividend earnings are earnings without consideration to the earnings that can be earned on dividends. Compare with **cum-dividend earnings.** *182*

normal earnings growth is earnings growth at a rate equal to the required return. *182*

normal forward P/E is a price-earnings ratio that is appropriate when earnings are expected to grow (cum-dividend) after the forward year at a rate equal to the required return; that is, normal earnings growth is expected. *183*

normal trailing P/E is a price-earnings ratio that is appropriate when earnings are expected to grow (cum-dividend) after the current year at a rate equal to the required return. *184*

The Analyst's Toolkit

Analysis Tools	Page	Key Measures	Page	Acronyms to Remember	
Abnormal earnings growth		Abnormal earnings growth	183	AEG	abnormal earnings growth
model (6.2)	185	Continuing value		EPS	earnings per share
Case 1	190	Case 1	190	DPS	dividends per share
Case 2	192	Case 2	192	GDP	gross domestic product
Normal forward P/E	183	Cum-dividend earnings	182	PEG	price-to-earnings growth
Normal trailing P/E	184	Earnings yield	197	RE	residual earnings
Abnormal earnings		Ex-dividend earnings	182		
growth (6.3), (6.3a)	187	Forward P/E ratio	183		
Trailing P/E model (6.4)	189	Normal earnings	182		
Converting an analyst's		Normal forward P/E ratio	183		
forecast to a valuation	191	Normal trailing P/E ratio	184		
PEG ratio	199	PEG ratio	199		

A Continuing Case: *Kimberly-Clark Corporation*

A Self-Study Exercise

CONVERTING ANALYSTS' FORECASTS TO A VALUATION

In the Kimberly-Clark case for Chapter 5, you were asked to convert analysts' earnings forecasts into a valuation using residual earnings methods. You can now do the same using abnormal earnings growth methods. Exhibit 1.1 in Chapter 1 gives consensus analysts' forecasts made in March 2011 when the stock price stood at $65.24 per share. These earnings forecasts are in the form of point estimates for years 2011 and 2012 and an estimated five-year earnings growth rate. KMB paid an annual dividend per share of $2.64 in 2010 and a dividend of $2.80 per share was indicated for 2011 at the time.

Calculate the forward P/E ratio. Also, using information in the 2010 financial statements in Exhibit 2.2 in Chapter 2, calculate the trailing P/E in March 2011.

With the five-year growth rate, you can forecast analysts' EPS estimates for the years 2013–2015. Do this and, from these forecasts, pro forma the corresponding abnormal earnings growth. Use a required return for equity of 8 percent for the calculations.

Now go ahead and value KMB's shares from this pro forma. You might adapt the spreadsheet engine on the Web page for this chapter to make this valuation. Assume a long-term growth rate after the five-year forecast period of 4 percent, roughly equal to the average GDP growth rate. What is your intrinsic forward P/E ratio? What is your intrinsic trailing P/E ratio? Did you get the same value as in the residual earnings application in the last chapter?

Using Spreadsheet Tools

As in the continuing case for Chapter 5, you can experiment with spreadsheet tools that carry out a valuation. Look at the engine on the Web page supplement for this chapter. Better still, develop your own spreadsheet engine.

Concept Questions	C6.1. Explain why analysts' forecasts of earnings-per-share growth typically underestimate the growth that an investor values if a firm pays dividends.
	C6.2. The historical earnings growth rate for the S&P 500 companies has been about 8.5 percent. Yet the required growth rate for equity investors is considered to be about 10 percent. Can you explain the inconsistency?
	C6.3. The following formula is often used to value shares, where Earn₁ is forward earnings, r is the cost of capital, and g is the expected earnings growth rate.

$$\text{Value of equity} = \frac{\text{Earn}_1}{r - g}$$

Explain why this formula can lead to errors.

C6.4. A firm's earnings are expected to grow at a rate equal to the required rate of return for its equity, 12 percent. What is the trailing P/E ratio? What is the forward P/E ratio?

C6.5. The normal forward P/E and the normal trailing P/E always differ by 1.0. Explain why.

C6.6. Explain why, for purposes of equity valuation, earnings growth forecasts must be for cum-dividend earnings growth, yet neither cum-dividend growth rates nor valuation are affected by expected dividends.

C6.7. Abnormal earnings growth is always equal to growth of (change in) residual earnings. Correct?

C6.8. A P/E ratio for a bond is always less than that for a stock. Correct?

C6.9. In an equity research report, an analyst calculates a forward earnings yield of 12 percent. Noting that this yield is considerably higher than the 7 percent yield on a 10-year Treasury, she heads her report with a buy recommendation. Could she be making a mistake?

C6.10. How do you interpret a PEG ratio?

C6.11. Look at Figure 2.3 in Chapter 2, which tracks median P/E ratios from 1963 to 2010. Explain why P/E ratios were low in the 1970s and high in the 1960s and 1990s.

C6.12. The earnings-to-price ratio for the S&P 500 stocks declined significantly from the late 1970s to the late 1990s. As this ratio is a "return" per dollar of price, some claimed that the decline indicated that the required return for equity investing had declined, and they attributed the increase in stock prices over the period to the decline in the required return. Why is this reasoning suspect?

C6.13. Why might an analyst refer to a leading (forward) P/E ratio rather than a trailing P/E ratio?

C6.14. Can a firm increase its earnings growth yet not affect the value of its equity?

C6.15. P/E ratios were quite low in 2008–2012 (about 11–12 on average), even though interest rates were also very low (with 10-year Treasury yields below 3.5 percent). Explain how this could be.

Exercises

Drill Exercises

E6.1. Forecasting Earnings Growth and Abnormal Earnings Growth (Easy)

The following are earnings and dividend forecasts made at the end of 2010. The firm has a required equity return of 10 percent per year.

	2011	2012	2013
EPS	3.00	3.60	4.10
DPS	0.25	0.25	0.30

a. Forecast the ex-dividend earnings growth rate and the cum-dividend earnings growth rate for 2012 and 2013.

b. Forecast abnormal earnings growth (in dollars) for 2012 and 2013.

c. Calculate the normal forward P/E for this firm.

d. Based on your forecasts, do you think this firm will have a forward P/E greater than its normal P/E? Why?

E6.2. P/E Ratios for a Savings Account (Easy)

Suppose you own a savings account that earned $10 over the past year. Your only transaction in the account has been to withdraw $3 on the last day of this 12-month period. The account bears an interest rate of 4 percent per year.

a. What is the value of the account after the $3 withdrawal?

b. What is the trailing P/E and forward P/E for this account?

E6.3.   **Valuation from Forecasting Abnormal Earnings Growth (Easy)**

An analyst presents you with the following pro forma (in millions of dollars). The pro forma gives her forecasts of earnings and dividends for 2013–2017. She asks you to value the 1,380 million shares outstanding at the end of 2012. Use a required return for equity of 10 percent in your calculations. (This is the same pro forma that was used for a residual earnings valuation in Exercise E5.3.)

	2013	2014	2015	2016	2017
Earnings	388.0	570.0	599.0	629.0	660.45
Dividends	115.0	160.0	349.0	367.0	385.40

a. Forecast growth rates for earnings and cum-dividend earnings for each year, 2014–2017.
b. Forecast abnormal earnings growth (in dollars) for each of the years 2014–2017.
c. Calculate the per-share value of the equity at the end of 2012 from this pro forma. Would you call this a Case 1 or Case 2 abnormal earnings growth valuation?
d. What is the forward P/E ratio for this firm? What is the normal forward P/E?

E6.4.   **Abnormal Earnings Growth Valuation and Target Prices (Medium)**

The following forecasts of earnings per share (EPS) and dividend per share (DPS) were made at the end of 2012:

	2013	2014	2015	2016	2017
EPS	3.90	3.70	3.31	3.59	3.90
DPS	1.00	1.00	1.00	1.00	1.00

The firm has an equity cost of capital of 12 percent per annum. (This is the same pro forma used in the residual earnings valuation in Exercise E5.4.)

a. Calculate the abnormal earnings growth (in dollars) that is forecast for each year, 2014 to 2017.
b. What is the per-share value of the equity at the end of 2012 based on the abnormal earnings growth valuation model?
c. What is the expected trailing P/E at the end of 2017?
d. What is the forecasted per-share value of the equity at the end of 2017?

E6.5.   **Dividend Displacement and Value (Medium)**

Two firms, A and B, which have very similar operations, have the same book value of $100 at the end of 2012 and their cost of capital is 11 percent. Both are forecast to have earnings of $16.60 in 2013. Firm A, which has 60 percent dividend payout, is forecast to have earnings of $17.80 in 2014. Firm B has zero payout.

a. What is your best estimate of firm B's earnings for 2014?
b. Would you pay more, less, or the same for firm B relative to firm A in 2012?

E6.6.   **Normal P/E Ratios (Easy)**

Prepare a schedule that gives the normal trailing and forward P/E ratios for the following levels of the cost of equity capital: 8, 9, 10, 11, 12, 13, 14, 15, and 16 percent.

Applications

E6.7.   **Calculating Cum-Dividend Earnings Growth Rates Nike (Easy)**

In early fiscal year 2009, analysts were forecasting $3.90 for Nike's earnings per share for the fiscal year ending May 2009 and $4.45 for 2010, with a dividend per share of 92 cents expected for 2009. Compare the cum-dividend earnings growth rate forecasted for 2010 with the ex-dividend earnings growth rate, using a required rate of return of 10 percent.

Real World Connection

See Exercises E2.14, E5.13, E7.9, E9.12, E14.17, E16.11, E16.13, and E19.5 on Nike.

E6.8. Calculating Cum-Dividend Earnings: General Mills (Easy)

General Mills reported earnings and paid dividends from 2006 to 2010 as follows:

	2006	2007	2008	2009	2010
Basic EPS	1.53	1.65	1.93	1.96	2.32
DPS	0.67	0.72	0.78	0.86	0.96

Calculate cum-dividend earnings per share for General Mills for each year, 2007–2010. Also calculate abnormal earnings growth (in dollars) for each of these years. Assume a required return of 8 percent for General Mills.

Real World Connection

Exercises E1.5, E2.9, E3.8, E4.10, E11.9, E13.9, E14.15, E15.6, and E16.10 also deal with General Mills.

E6.9. Residual Earnings and Abnormal Earnings Growth: IBM (Medium)

Consider the following pro forma for International Business Machines Corp. (IBM) based on analysts' forecasts in early 2011.

	2011	2012	Next Three Years
Earnings per share	13.22	14.61	Growth at 11%
Dividends per share	3.00	3.30	Growth at 11%

The book value of IBM's common equity at the end of 2010 was $23.0 billion, or $18.77 per share. Use a required return for equity of 10 percent in calculations

a. Forecast residual earnings for each of the years 2011–2015.
b. Forecast abnormal earnings growth (in dollars) for each of the years 2012–2015.
c. Show that abnormal earnings growth is equal to the change in residual earnings for every year.

Real World Connection

Exercises E14.14 and E15.9 deal with IBM, as does Minicase M13.3.

E6.10. A Normal P/E for General Electric? (Easy)

In early 2008, General Electric (GE) shares were trading at $26.75 each. Analysts were forecasting $2.21 in EPS for 2008 and $2.30 for 2009. A dividend of $1.24 was indicated for 2008. Use a required return of 9 percent for the questions below.

a. What is GE's normal forward P/E? What was the P/E at which it traded?
b. The estimated abnormal earnings growth for 2009 indicates that GE's stock should be trading at about a normal P/E. Show this.

E6.11. Challenging the Level of the S&P 500 Index with Analysts' Forecasts (Medium)

The S&P 500 index stood at 1271 in early 2006. Based on analysts' consensus EPS forecasts for calendar year 2006, the forward P/E ratio for the index was 15.0 at the time. Those same analysts were giving the S&P 500 a PEG ratio of 1.47, based on forecasts for 2007. The payout ratio for this portfolio of stocks was 27 percent at the time and investment banks typically published estimates of the equity risk premium of 5 percent over the current 10-year Treasury rate of 5 percent.

  a. Calculate the abnormal earnings growth for 2007 (in dollars) that is implied by the forecasts.
  b. What should be the level of the S&P 500 if (cum-dividend) earnings are forecasted to grow at 10 percent after the forward year? Why is the P/E based on analysts' forecasts different?
  c. Setting the long-term abnormal earnings growth rate equal to 4 percent (the average growth rate for GDP), what do analysts' forecasts say about the level of the S&P 500 index?
  d. What conclusions can your draw from this analysis?

E6.12. **Valuation of Microsoft Corporation (Medium)**

In 2010, some fundamental investors believed that Microsoft, after being overpriced in the stock market for many years, was now a firm to buy. Microsoft's shares traded at $24.30 in September 2010, down from a peak of $60 (split-adjusted) in January 2000.

Analysts' consensus earnings-per-share forecasts for Microsoft's 2011 and 2012 fiscal years (ending in June) were $2.60 and $2.77, respectively. A dividend of $0.40 per share was indicated for fiscal year 2011.

  a. Calculate Microsoft's normal forward P/E and the forward P/E at which it traded in September 2010. Use a required return of 9 percent.
  b. Calculate the intrinsic P/E implied by the analysts' forecasts with the assumption that there will be no abnormal earnings growth after 2012.
  c. If you forecast that there will be significant abnormal earnings growth after 2012, do you think this stock is appropriately priced at $24.30?
  d. Calculate Microsoft's traded PEG ratio based on analysts' forecasts of earnings for fiscal years 2011 and 2012.

Real World Connection

Coverage of Microsoft continues in Exercises E1.6, E4.14, E8.9, E9.9, E11.11, E18.10, and E20.4, and in Minicases M9.1 and M13.2.

E6.13. **Using Earnings Growth Forecasts to Challenge a Stock Price: Toro Company (Medium)**

Toro Company, a lawn products maker based in Minnesota, traded at $55 per share in October 2002. The firm had maintained a 20 percent annual EPS growth rate over the previous five years, and analysts were forecasting $5.30 per share earnings for the fiscal year ending October 2003, with a 12 percent growth rate for the five years thereafter. Use a required return of 10 percent in answering the following questions.

  a. How much is a share of Toro worth based on the forward earnings of $5.30 only (ignoring any subsequent earnings growth)?
  b. Toro maintains a dividend payout of 10 percent of earnings. Based on the forecasted EPS growth rate of 12 percent, forecast cum-dividend earnings for the five years, 2004–2008.
  c. Forecast abnormal earnings growth (in dollars) for the years 2004–2008.
  d. Do your calculations indicate whether or not Toro is appropriately priced?

E6.14. **Abnormal Earnings Growth Valuation and Accounting Methods (Hard)**

Refer back to the valuation in Exercise E6.3. In the pro forma there, an analyst forecasted earnings of $388 million for 2013. The forecast was made at the end of 2012 based on preliminary reports from the firm.

When the final report was published, however, the analyst discovered that the firm had decided to write down its inventory at the end of 2012 by $114 million (following the lower-of-cost-or-market rule). As this was inventory that the analyst had forecasted would be sold in 2013 (and thus the impairment affects cost of goods sold for that year), the analyst revised her earnings forecast for 2013. For questions (a) and (b), ignore any effect of taxes.

a. What is the revised earnings forecast for 2013 as a result of the inventory impairment assuming no change in sales forecasts?

b. Show that the revision in the forecast of 2013 earnings does not change the valuation of the equity.

c. Now assume that the firm's income tax rate is 35 percent. Do your answers to questions (a) and (b) change?

E6.15. **Is a Normal Forward P/E Ratio Appropriate? Maytag Corporation (Easy)**

A share of Maytag Corp., another appliance manufacturer, traded at $28.80 in January 2003. Analysts were forecasting earnings per share of $2.94 for 2003 and $3.03 for 2004, with dividends per share of 72 cents indicated for 2003. Analysts' 3–5 year growth rate for earnings per share after 2004 was 3.1 percent.

a. Calculate the normal forward P/E ratio for Maytag if its equity cost of capital is 10 percent. Compare the normal P/E to the actual traded P/E at the time.

b. Do the forecasts of earnings after 2003 indicate that the traded P/E is the appropriate pricing for the firm's shares?

Real World Connection

Minicase M16.3 deals with the takeover of Maytag by Whirlpool. Exercise E20.6 deals with Maytag also.

Minicase   **M6.1**

Analysts' Forecasts and Valuation: PepsiCo and Coca-Cola II

PepsiCo, Inc. (PEP) is a global food, snack, and beverage company operating in more than 200 countries with brands that include Quaker Oats, Tropicana, Gatorade, Lay's, and of course Pepsi. The products include oat, rice, and grain-based foods as well as carbonated and noncarbonated beverages. The largest operations are in North America, Mexico, Russia, and the United Kingdom.

In April 2011, PepsiCo traded at $67 per share, with a forward P/E of 15.0. Analysts were forecasting per-share earnings of $4.48 for fiscal year ending December 31, 2011, and $4.87 for 2012. The indicated dividend for 2011 was 1.92 per share. The street was using 9 percent as a required rate of return for PepsiCo's equity.

The Coca-Cola Company (KO) also operates in over 200 countries worldwide and competes intensively with PepsiCo in the market for carbonated and noncarbonated beverages. Among its brands are Coke, Diet Coke, Fanta, and Sprite.

In April 2011, Coke also traded at $67 with a forward P/E of 17.3. Analysts were forecasting $3.87 in earnings per share for fiscal year ending December 31, 2011; and $4.20 for 2012. The indicated dividend per share was $1.88. The equity is considered to have the same required return as PepsiCo.

A. Value both firms with a forecast that abnormal earnings growth (AEG) will continue after 2012 at the same level as in 2012.

B. Now value the two firms with a forecast that abnormal earnings growth (AEG) will grow at the GDP growth rate of 4 percent per year after 2012.

C. Given that you accept the analysts' forecasts for 2011 and 2012, is the market, at $67 per share, forecasting a long-term growth rate for AEG that is higher or lower than the 4 percent rate?

D. Calculate the PEG ratio for both of the firms. What do you make of this ratio?

Real World Connection

See Minicase M5.2 in Chapter 5 for a parallel investigation using P/B ratios. Also see Minicase M4.1 in Chapter 4 for an application of discounted cash flow analysis to Coca-Cola. Exercises E4.7, E4.8, E12.7, E15.7, E16.12, E17.7, and E20.4 also deal with Coca-Cola, and Exercises E4.13 and E10.9 deal with PepsiCo.

Chapter **Seven**

Valuation and Active Investing

LINKS

Links to previous chapters

Chapters 5 and 6 laid out two valuation models, one based on pricing book values and one based on pricing earnings.

This chapter

This chapter shows how to apply valuation models in active investing.

Link to next chapter

Chapter 8 begins the financial statement analysis for implementing the active investing of this chapter.

Link to Web page

The Web page for this chapter has more on active investing. Go to **www.mhhe.com/penman5e**

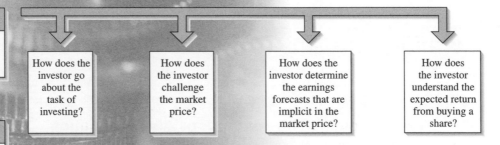

How does the investor go about the task of investing?

How does the investor challenge the market price?

How does the investor determine the earnings forecasts that are implicit in the market price?

How does the investor understand the expected return from buying a share?

Passive investors accept market prices as fair value. Fundamental investors, in contrast, are active investors. They see that *price is what you pay, value is what you get*. They understand that *the primary risk in investing is the risk of paying too much* (or selling for too little). The fundamentalist actively challenges the market price: Is it indeed a fair price? This might be done as a defensive investor concerned with overpaying or as an investor seeking to exploit mispricing.

This chapter leads you into active investing, with the price-to-book (P/B) and price-earnings (P/E) valuation models of Chapters 5 and 6 as the tools. These models are skeletal—more tools will be added as the book proceeds—but they are sufficient to demonstrate the approach. How do we apply these models in active investing? How do we use these models to challenge the market price?

The Analyst's Checklist

After reading this chapter you should understand:

- How the fundamental investor operates.
- Why it is unnecessary to calculate "intrinsic value."
- Why growth rates in a valuation are speculative.
- That we really do not know the cost of capital.
- How the investor applies the principle of "separate what you what you know from speculation" in practice.
- How the investor challenges the market price.
- How the investor ascertains the growth forecast implicit in the market price.
- How the investor understands the expected return from investing at a given price.

After reading this chapter you should be able to:

- Reverse engineer the market price to ascertain the market's earnings forecast.
- Plot the future earnings growth path that is implicit in the market price.
- Calculate the expected return from buying at the current market price.
- Evaluate the current level of a stock market index like the S&P 500.
- Challenge the market price of a stock.
- Take the first steps in engaging in active investing.

HOW THE FUNDAMENTAL INVESTOR OPERATES

To answer these questions, we must put ourselves in the mind-set of the active investor. That means discarding some common misconceptions.

Common Misconceptions About Valuation

Standard valuation methods often proceed with the pretense that we know the inputs to a valuation model. Indeed, valuation models lend themselves to "playing with mirrors." The fundamentalist does not play that game. Fundamental investors strive for honesty, at all points understanding what is known and what is uncertain.

The following points highlight some common misconceptions about valuation and warn of pitfalls to avoid in handling valuation models. For illustration, we will work with the residual earnings valuation model of Chapter 5. For a two-year-ahead forecast,

$$V_0^E = B_0 + \frac{RE_1}{\rho} + \frac{R\dot{E}_2}{\rho(\rho - g)} \tag{7.1}$$

The idea of "intrinsic value" is not useful. Even though valuation models seemingly produce a number for "value" as the output of the valuation process, it is not helpful to think of the notion of true "intrinsic value." Deferring to Graham and Dodd, the fathers of fundamental analysis,

> He [the investor] is concerned with the intrinsic value of the security and more particularly with the discovery of the discrepancies between intrinsic value and price. We must recognize, however, that intrinsic value is an elusive concept. In general terms it is understood to be that value which is justified by the facts, e.g., the assets, earnings, dividends, definite prospects— as distinct, let us say, from market quotations established by artificial manipulation or distorted by psychological excesses. But it is a great mistake to imagine that intrinsic value is as definite and as determinable as is the market price.
>
> —Benjamin Graham and David Dodd, *Security Analysis* (New York: McGraw-Hill Book Company, 1934), p. 17.

With intrinsic value being inherently uncertain, the idea of discovering true intrinsic value is doubtful or even misguided. This may come as a surprise, because the models tell us to plug in numbers on the right-hand side to deliver an intrinsic value (V) on the left-hand side. A valuation model does not deliver a certain intrinsic value because the inputs themselves are uncertain. Forecasts (for two years in the equation 7.1 model above) are estimates. But the two other inputs, the required return, ρ, and the long-term growth rate, g, are also uncertain.

We do not know the required return. Standard valuation practices pretend we know the required return because it is supplied by an asset pricing model such as the capital asset pricing model (CAPM). But, as the appendix to Chapter 3 made clear, estimates of the required return from these models are highly uncertain, particularly the estimate of the "market risk premium," which is anyone's guess. The value from a valuation model is quite sensitive to the required return used, yet we really don't know what the required return is. It is quite disappointing that, after 60 years of dedicated endeavor, modern finance has not come up with a way for determining the required return. You and I may have our own required return for investing—our own hurdle rate—and we can certainly use that in the model. But the idea that the required return can objectively be determined is fiction. Using the CAPM is largely playing with mirrors.

We do not know the long-term growth rate. Benjamin Graham had the following to say about valuation models:

> The concept of future prospects and particularly of continued growth in the future invites the application of formulas out of higher mathematics to establish the present value of the favored issue. But the combination of precise formulas with highly imprecise assumptions can be used to establish, or rather justify, practically any value one wishes, however high, for a really outstanding issue.
>
> —Benjamin Graham, *The Intelligent Investor*, 4th rev. ed. (New York: Harper and Row, 1973), pp. 315–316.

Graham was skeptical about valuation formulas in general but, in this quote, the focus is on long-term growth rates, the g in the continuing value of valuation formulas— "continued growth" as he called it. We do not know the long-term growth rate, or can estimate it only with considerable uncertainty. Graham recognized the scheme of the sell-side investment banker who can choose almost any growth rate (and a required return) to justify the "due diligence" valuation he wants for floating shares. But buy-side fundamental investors acknowledge that the long-term growth rate is highly uncertain, so they do not "assume" long-term growth rates. They do not play that game.

A valuation model is nominally a device for giving us some certainty about the correct value, but you can see from these points that the model can actually serve to compound our uncertainty: Garbage in, garbage out. You might then well ask how useful valuation models are in getting a value, V, to challenge the market price, P. The next point below answers this question and shows how the fundamental investor indeed plays the game and how she plays with valuation models to do so.

Investing is a game against other investors. Equity investing is not a game against nature, but a game against other investors. So it serves little purpose to use a valuation model to discover the "true" intrinsic value, as if it existed somewhere out there. Rather, valuation models should be used to understand how an investor thinks differently from other investors in the market. Thus, the right question to ask of a model is not what the "right" value is but rather whether the model can help the investor understand the perceptions of other investors embedded in the market price—so those perceptions can be challenged. The investor is "negotiating with Mr. Market" (in Benjamin Graham's words) and, in those negotiations, the onus is not on the investor to produce a valuation, but rather to understand Mr. Market's valuation, in order to accept it or reject his asking price. As a valuation is based on forecasts, valuation models are appropriately applied to understand Mr. Market's forecasts: What forecasts are behind Mr. Market's price? Are those forecasts reasonable?

This view of the investing game leads us directly to our application of valuation models to active investing. But first, let's review some fundamentalist principles laid down in Chapter 1.

Applying Fundamental Principles

Chapter 1 gave 12 commonsense principles that guide the investor. We pick up three of them here:

1. Don't mix what you know with speculation.
2. Anchor a valuation on what you know rather than speculation.
3. Beware of paying too much for growth.

The first point is behind the criticism of standard valuation approaches: Don't build speculation about the required return or a growth rate into a valuation. We really don't know these numbers, so don't mix them with what we do know. Use valuation models to challenge the market price with value based on what we do know.

The second point tells us to anchor a valuation on what we know. Identify the value indicated by what we know—"value justified by the facts" in Graham's words—and then go about adding value for speculation:

$$\text{Value} = \text{Value based on what we know} + \text{Speculative value} \qquad \textbf{(7.2)}$$

$$\qquad\qquad\qquad\qquad \textbf{(1)} \qquad\qquad\qquad\qquad\qquad \textbf{(2)}$$

This breaks a valuation down into component (1) that is relatively "hard" and component (2) that is "soft" in the sense that it is far more speculative. As we will see, what we know comes from analysis of information, particularly financial statement information. The fundamental investor asks: What is the value implied by the fundamentals (before I go about adding value for speculative growth)?

The third point says that speculation centers on growth. That is clear from the valuation model in equation 7.1: We know book value—it's on the face on the balance sheet—and we may have relatively firm information about forward earnings or even earnings two years ahead. So we can determine a value implied by these numbers. But it is the growth rate, g, where our uncertainty lies. Indeed, we have stressed in prior chapters that it is the continuing value (containing the growth rate) about which we are most uncertain. It is easy to plug in a speculative growth number into a valuation model like 7.1 and overpay for growth. Chapter 1 gave a history of markets being over-excited about growth in boom times and too pessimistic in depressed times.

The fundamentalist understands that he must challenge the market's speculation and that speculation concerns growth. He does this by anchoring on what he knows. It is here that valuation models come into play and realize their potential. So let's play the game—the game against other investors—using our valuation models.

CHALLENGING SPECULATION IN THE MARKET PRICE

We will find that our financial statement analysis of the next part of this text will typically give us near-term forecasts to which we can anchor along with book value. That leaves us two unknowns in the valuation model, the growth rate and the required return. As the game is against other investors, active investing does not plug in numbers for ρ and g and pretend to get an "intrinsic value," but turns the valuation model around and asks what are the growth rate or expected return that is implicit in the market price. The exercise is called **reverse engineering**: Rather than inserting inputs into a valuation formula to get a V, set V equal to P and ask what inputs explain the current market price, P.

We first illustrate with the simple example that introduced the valuation models in the last two chapters. The simple residual earnings valuation model took the form,

$$V_0^E = B_0 + \frac{RE_1}{\rho - g} = \$100 + \frac{2.36}{1.10 - 1.03} = \$133.71$$

Book value is \$100 and forward residual earnings is forward earnings of \$12.36 minus a charge against book value at 10 percent: $RE_1 = \$12.36 - (0.10 \times 100) = \$2.36$. Following standard valuation procedures, we set a growth rate for residual earnings of 3 percent to yield a \$133.71 value. But now let's apply the model in reverse-engineering mode. Suppose your personal hurdle rate for this investment is 10 percent, and suppose that the equity traded at \$133.71. Then, setting value equal to price in reverse-engineering mode,

$$P_0 = \$133.71 = \$100 + \frac{2.36}{1.10 - g}$$

One can now solve for g. For a price of \$133.71, $g = 1.03$ or a 3 percent growth rate (of course). If the price were \$147.2, $g = 1.05$, or a 5 percent growth rate: Given the current book value and a forecast of earnings one year ahead, the market is forecasting a 5 percent long-term growth rate for residual earnings. This is the market's **implied residual earnings growth rate.**

Rather than guessing at a growth rate, we have reverse engineered to understand Mr. Market's growth rate. To do this we have first "anchored on what we know," as in equation 7.2. We know the book value and we have good information (say) about forward earnings, so we anchor on these two numbers. But rather than adding our own speculation about growth, we turn the problem around and use the anchoring numbers to discover Mr. Market's growth forecast.

Alternatively, we can reverse engineer to discover the market's **implied expected return.** Specifying a growth rate of 3 percent,

$$P_0 = \$133.71 = \$100 + \frac{RE_1}{ER - 1.03}$$

The solution is $ER = 1.10$, a 10 percent return (of course). This is given by a simple formula,

$$ER = \left[\frac{B_0}{P_0} \times ROCE_1 \right] + \left[\left(1 - \frac{B_0}{P_0} \right) \times (g - 1) \right] \tag{7.3}$$

This formula is referred to as the *weighted-average expected return formula* because it is a weighted average of the forward return on common equity (ROCE) and the growth rate, with the book-to-price supplying the weights.[1] (The book-to-price is simply the reciprocal

---

[1] The formula works only for forward ROCE greater than the growth rate (which it typically is).

of the price-to-book, of course.) With a book-to-price of $100/$133.71 = 0.748 and a forward ROCE of $12.36/$100 = 12.36 percent,

$$\text{ER} = [0.748 \times 12.36\%] + [0.252 \times 3\%] = 10.0\%$$

Note, importantly, that ER is not the *required return* but the *expected return* from buying shares at the current market price. If the market price is $147.2, then the expected return from buying at the current market price (with the same 3 percent growth rate) is 9.36 percent. That makes sense: With a higher price for the same expectations, one will get a lower expected return.

You can see that the active investor has two ways to challenge the market price.

First, understand the market's growth forecast and then ask if that growth rate is justified, too high, or too low. You will have to do more analysis to be secure in your answer, and the financial statement analysis of the next part of the text is set up to deal with the question. But appreciate that the onus is not on you, the investor, to come up with a growth rate (or a valuation), but just to accept or reject the market's growth rate as reasonable. After identifying the market's forecast of growth, you might conclude that (with the help of the analysis to come) the implied growth rate is difficult to achieve. So you would conclude that buying the stock runs the risk of paying too much. You don't know the intrinsic value, but you do not have to; all you need to do is assess the risk of overpaying. You might also see an opportunity to earn superior returns when the implied growth rate seems low.

Second, the investor might assess the risk of paying too much (or the opportunity provided by a cheap stock) by calculating the expected return to buying at the market price. If the stock is expensive (the price is high), the expected return will be low; if the stock is cheap, the expected return will be high.

The two methods provide an enhanced screening to the simple screening analysis of Chapter 3 that we judged as too simple: Rather than screen stocks on P/E or P/B, screen them on their implied growth rates or their expected returns. We will get to refinements later in the book, but you see the basic idea.

But there is a problem. To get the implied growth rate, we had to input a required return, and to get an expected return we have to input a growth rate. But we have concluded that both the required return and the growth rate are something we are typically quite unsure about. One can always input one's own hurdle rate or a ceiling growth rate—the GDP growth rate, for example—but this problem needs to be dealt with. We will deal with this later in the book after more tools are on the table. For the moment we proceed with some real-life examples.

Reverse Engineering the S&P 500

In May 2011, the S&P 500 stock index traded at 1357 on a book value of 588 and thus a price-to-book of 2.3. S&P forward earnings for the index (supplied on Standard and Poor's Web site) was 98.76, thus forward ROCE was 98.76/588 = 16.8 percent. What long-term growth rate was the market forecasting for the S&P 500 firms at the 1357 level for the index? The 10-year risk-free Treasury rate at the time was 3.3 percent and the consensus estimate of the market risk premium was 5.7 percent. So set the required return at 3.3% + 5.7% = 9%, then reverse engineer. By pricing at 2.3 times book value, the market was pricing a dollar of book value as follows:

$$2.3 = 1.0 + \frac{(0.168 - 0.09) \times 1.0}{1.09 - g}$$

(The numerator is the residual earnings for a dollar of book value.) The solution for g is 1.03, a 3 percent grow rate. If one expects residual earnings to grow in the long run at the historical GDP growth rate of 4 percent, then one would conclude that the S&P 500 is underpriced.

FIGURE 7.1

Price-to-Book Ratio (P/B) and Implied Residual Earnings Growth Rates for the S&P 500, 1982–2008. The measures are at the end of December of each year. The implied growth rate is indicated on the left axis, and the P/B on the right axis. Implied residual earnings growth rates are calculated by reverse engineering the end-of-year S&P 500 index with a required return of 9 percent and forward earnings measured with analysts' consensus of forward earnings forecasts for the following year.

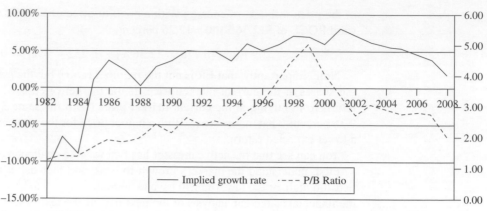

Sources: The S&P 500 index is from Standard and Poor's Web site; book value is from the COMPUSTAT data through WRDS; and analysts' forecasts are from IBES, supplied through WRDS.

One might question the 4 percent GDP rate as an appropriate benchmark. However, the average growth rate for this reverse-engineering exercise on the index typically does approximate the average GDP growth rate, though with some variation. Figure 7.1 plots the price-to-book ratio for the S&P 500 at year-end from 1982–2008, along with implied growth rates. The calculation of implied growth rates is the same as above, but now with forward ROCE based on analysts' consensus earnings forecasts for the index. The implied growth rates range from –11.2 percent in 1982 to 8.0 percent in 2001, but the average is 4.2 percent, much like the typical GDP growth rate. The implied growth rates deviate from the average 4.2 percent—particularly during the bubble of the 1990s—but revert back to the mean. The 4 percent rate seems to be a good measure for central tendency.

Would this analysis detect when the market is underpricing or overpricing growth? If it does, it would predict future returns. Figure 7.2 suggests so. That figure plots the same implied growth rates as in Figure 7.1, but now with an overlay of returns for the S&P 500 over the following year. It appears that the implied growth rates predict returns on the index,

FIGURE 7.2

Implied Growth Rates and Year-ahead Returns for the S&P 500, 1982–2008. Implied growth rates are indicated on the left axis and year-ahead returns on the right axis.

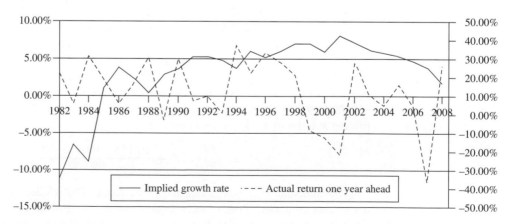

FIGURE 7.3

Expected Year-Ahead Returns and Actual Year-Ahead Returns for the S&P 500, 1982–2008.

Expected returns are inferred from the level of the index at the end of December of each year using book value at that date and analysts' consensus forward earnings forecasts for the following year, along with a GDP growth rate of 4 percent. The actual return is the return for the index for the next calendar year. The expected return is indicated on the left axis, and the actual return on the right axis.

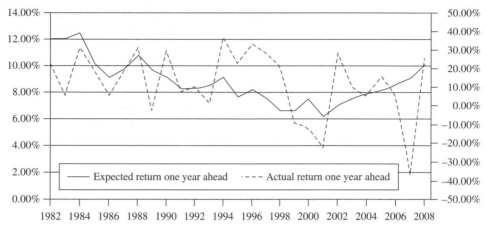

Sources: The S&P 500 index and dividends for the index are from the Standard and Poor's Web site; book value is from the COMPUSTAT data through WRDS; and analysts' forecasts are from IBES, supplied through WRDS.

with higher growth rates predicting lower subsequent returns and vice versa. The correlation is –0.25, and the correlations with returns for two years ahead and three years ahead are –0.26 and –0.33, respectively.[2] It appears that challenging the market's growth forecast would have paid off during this period.

If one accepts the GDP rate as the expected long-term growth rate, the alternative method of reverse engineering to the expected return can be applied. With a price-to-book of 2.3, the book-to-price for the index in May 2011 was 0.435. Applying the weighted-average expected return formula in equation 7.3,

$$ER = [0.435 \times 16.8\%] + [0.565 \times 4\%]$$

$$= 9.57\%$$

If the investor has a hurdle rate of 9 percent for buying equities, then an investment in the S&P 500 would seem reasonable.

Is this measure of expected return a good predictor of actual returns earned? Figure 7.3 suggests so. The figure plots the implied expected return (ER) on the index with a GDP growth rate of 4 percent. The implied expected returns predict the actual year-ahead returns in the figure; the correlation is 0.29. The average expected return over the years, 1982–2008 is 8.8 percent, close to the 9 percent. The period included the 1990s bubble years when, due to high prices, the expected return was low (6.8 percent in 1998 and 6.6 percent 1999, for example). The low expected return in those years was a warning of the actual poor returns that were to follow.

[2] The correlation between the growth rates and year-ahead returns in excess of the 10-year U.S. government bond yield is −0.14. (Excess returns adjust for changing interest rates.)

The pictures do give some encouragement for active investing. They also deliver a warning to passive investors who just buy the market portfolio, perhaps with an index fund or an exchange traded fund (ETF) tied to a market index. Beware: you may be overpaying.

We have to be careful of mechanical schemes, here as always. They are a good first cut but use limited information. Risk can change as economies go into recession or into a financial crisis. At times an investor might require a higher or lower return because of changes in market uncertainty. In these illustrations, with a 9 percent return benchmark at all points, we have not allowed for changing risk. More needs to be flushed out, including a fundamental analysis of risk.

Challenging the Price of a Stock

In May 2011, Google, Inc. was trading at $535 per share, or 3.7 times book value of $143.92 per share at the end of its 2010 fiscal year. Analysts were forecasting a consensus estimate of $33.94 EPS for 2011 and $39.55 for 2012. If we were fairly confident about these near-term forecasts we could break down the valuation into two parts following equation 7.2:

Value = Value based on book value and near-term forecasts + Value of speculative growth

$$\qquad\qquad\qquad\qquad\textbf{(1)}\qquad\qquad\qquad\qquad\qquad\qquad\textbf{(2)}$$

The residual earnings model provides us with the anchoring value (without growth):

$$V_0^E = B_0 + \frac{RE_1}{\rho} + \frac{RE_2}{\rho(\rho-1)} + \textit{Value of Speculative Growth}$$

$$\qquad\qquad\qquad\textbf{(1)}\qquad\qquad\qquad\textbf{(2)}$$

You see that component (1) is simply the valuation in model 7.1 without growth (that is, with g set to 1.0). The value from growth is now in component (2). Accordingly, component (1) is referred to as the **no-growth valuation.** To anchor on two years of forecasts, we must be fairly confident in our predictions; otherwise only one year, the forward year, is used (as in the S&P 500 example). The financial statement analysis in the next part of the book yields these forecasts.

A pro forma that delivers Google's no-growth valuation is laid out in Exhibit 7.1. Your hurdle rate is 10 percent. This is, of course, the Case 2 valuation of Chapter 5 where residual earnings after two years is forecasted to continue at the same level (that is, with no growth).

With no value recognized for speculative growth, we account for $359.54 of the $535 in market value, made up of $143.92 in book value and $17.77 + $197.85 = $215.62 from the short-term forecasts. Thus the amount of the market price unexplained by the accounting is $175.46. That is the value that the market is placing on speculative growth.

Figure 7.4 shows how we have deconstructed the market price into three components: (1) book value, (2) value from short-term earnings, and (3) the speculative value the market places on subsequent growth. These are building blocks that help us understand our uncertainty. The three blocks parse out uncertainty into what we know for sure—book value—what we know with some confidence—value from short-term forecasts—and what we are quite uncertain about—value from long-term growth prospects. It is the latter where our serious uncertainty lies. It is the latter where we risk overpaying for growth. The diagram confronts us: Do we want to pay $175.46 for risky growth?

EXHIBIT 7.1
No-Growth Valuation for Google, Inc.
A 10 percent required return is used for calculating residual earnings.

	2010A	2011E	2012E
EPS		33.94	39.55
DPS		0.00	0.00
BPS	143.92	177.86	217.41
Residual earnings (10% charge)		19.548	21.764
Growth in residual earnings			11.3%
Growth in EPS			16.5%

$$Value\ of\ Equity_0 = B_0 + \frac{Earnings_1 \times r.B_0}{1+r} + \frac{Earnings_2 \times r.B_1}{(1+r) \times r} + Value\ of\ Speculative\ Growth$$

$$= \$143.92 + \frac{19.548}{1.10} + \frac{21.764}{1.10 \times 0.10} \quad + Value\ of\ Speculative\ Growth$$

$$= \$143.92 + 17.77 + 197.85 \quad + Value\ of\ Speculative\ Growth$$

$$= \$359.54 \quad + Value\ of\ Speculative\ Growth$$

We are now in a position to ask Mr. Market for his growth rate. The answer comes quickly by bringing growth back into our valuation, substituting price for value, and reverse engineering:

$$Price\ of\ Equity_0 = \$535 + \$143.92 + \frac{19.548}{1.10} + \frac{21.754}{1.10 \times (0.10 - g)}$$

With value set to Google's market price of $535, we can infer the market's long-term growth rate: The implied growth rate for Google after 2012 is 4.7 percent per year.

This growth rate is the residual earnings growth rate, a little difficult to get our minds around. But we can convert the growth rate to an **implied earnings growth rate** by reverse engineering the residual earnings calculation:

$$Earnings\ forecast_t = (Book\ value_{t-1} \times Required\ return) + Residual\ earnings_t \quad \textbf{(7.4)}$$

FIGURE 7.4
Building Blocks for the Market's Valuation for Google, Inc., May 2011.
The no-growth value is the sum of the first two components, $359.54, and the speculative value for growth is the third component, $175.46.

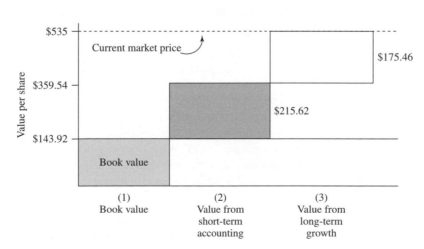

FIGURE 7.5
EPS Growth Path for 2012–2018, Implied by the Market Price of $535 for Google, Inc.

Google's residual earnings two years ahead (2012) is $21.764 per share in Exhibit 7.1, so the residual earnings forecasted for the third year ahead (2013) at a growth rate of 4.7 percent is $22.787. Thus, with a per-share book value of $217.41 forecasted for the end of 2012 (in Exhibit 7.1), the forecast of EPS for 2013 is $44.53 and the forecasted growth rate over 2012 EPS is 12.6 percent. Extrapolating in the same way to subsequent years, one develops the earnings growth path that the market is forecasting, displayed in Figure 7.5. The growth path divides the BUY zone and the SELL zone: If an analyst sees growth at a higher rate than this path, then issue a BUY recommendation; if lower, issue a SELL recommendation.

The 4.7 percent residual earnings growth rate is an average rate for the long term. Modifications permit the more realistic picture of a declining growth rate over time. The 4.7 percent rate looks something like the GDP growth rate, perhaps a little higher. Exhibit 7.1 shows Google growing residual earnings at 11.3 percent in 2012, indicating that the firm might be able to maintain a growth rate above 4.7 percent for some years. On the other hand, one might expect that all firms will look like the average firm in the very long run, with growth at the GDP growth rate. This accepts the view that exceptional growth, like Google's, is ultimately eroded away. With a 2012 growth rate of 11.3 percent, reversion to a long-term GDP growth rate of (say) 4 percent is given by weighting the two with weights that sum to one:

$$\text{Growth rate for 2013} = (0.8 \times 11.3\%) + (0.2 \times 4.0\%) = 9.84\%$$

(and so on, recursively, for years after 2013). The 2013 growth rate is lower than the 11.3 percent for 2012 because it is on a path to decline to 4 percent in the long run. Applying the weights to subsequent years, the forecasted growth rate for 2014 is 8.67 percent, declining to 4 percent eventually. So we establish a **fade pattern** for growth with the growth path depicted in Figure 7.6. This path yields a value of $570.32. The figure compares this fade pattern to a path with weights of (0.9, 0.1) which yields a value of $657.84. The weights are somewhat arbitrary but are a device for experimenting in challenging the market price of $535. What does our information indicate will be the most likely path for Google? You can see that it is a question of how long above-average growth can be sustained. That is the issue of *sustainable competitive advantage,* but now we have some concreteness by bringing numbers to the evaluation of sustained competitive advantage.

FIGURE 7.6
Residual Earnings Growth Paths for Google, Inc., for Alternative Weights Applied to Short-term and Long-term Growth Rates.
The (0.684, 0.316) weights are those implied by the market price of $535.

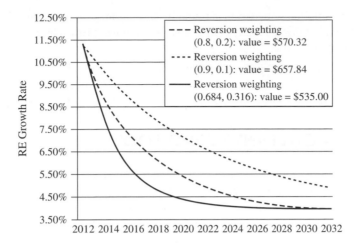

We can make that challenge to the market price directly by "backing out" the weights implicit in the market price. The implicit weights are (0.684, 0.316), and they imply the third growth path in Figure 7.6 that has the growth rate decaying to 4 percent much faster. The path can be converted to an EPS growth path as in Figure 7.2. This is the path that the market sees Google following as it reverts to the GDP growth rate in the long run. Can this path be justified? Or does the analyst see Google maintaining competitive advantage and superior growth for much longer? Is $535 too much or too little to pay for growth?

You can see that we have challenged the market price with this analysis. But we have challenged the price by challenging the market's forecast of the growth path. We have more work to do, to establish the anchoring no-growth value and to get a handle on the question as to whether the market's growth forecast is justified. But we now have a scheme to play the game against other investors, that is, to engage in active investing.

The alternative scheme is to apply the weighted average return formula to estimate the expected return to buying Google at the current market price. Exercise E7.11 asks you to do that.

Reverse Engineering with the Abnormal Earnings Growth Model

The illustration above applies the residual earnings model of Chapter 5. The analysis can be done alternatively with the abnormal earnings growth (AEG) model of Chapter 6. For two years of forecasts,

$$V_0^E = \frac{1}{\rho - 1}\left[\text{EPS}_1 + \frac{\text{AEG}_2}{\rho - g}\right] \qquad (7.5)$$

Parsing out the model into its no-growth and growth components,

$$V_0^E = \underbrace{\frac{1}{\rho - 1}\left[\text{EPS}_1 + \frac{\text{AEG}_2}{\rho - 1}\right]}_{(1)} + \underbrace{\textit{Value of Speculative Growth}}_{(2)} \qquad (7.5a)$$

The implied growth rate is found by solving for g in equation 7.5. That refers to growth in AEG, but that is readily converted to an earnings growth by reverse engineering the AEG calculation:

$$\text{Earnings forecast}_t = \text{Normal earnings forecast}_t + \text{AEG}_t - \text{Forecast}$$
$$\text{of earnings from reinvesting prior year's dividends} \quad \textbf{(7.6)}$$

With these earnings forecasts, one can plot the market's EPS growth path, as in Figure 7.5.

BUILD YOUR OWN ACTIVE INVESTING TOOL

In Chapters 5 and 6 you were encouraged to build a spreadsheet engine that delivers a value from inputs of book values, earnings forecasts, growth rates, and the required return. It is a short step to adapt those spreadsheets for active investing.

This can be done in two ways. First, set up a program to solve directly for implied growth rates, with current price as an input. The weighted average expected return formula 7.3 governs the template for the implied expected return. Or, second, use the spreadsheets you have already developed and just experiment with growth rates or required returns that yield a value equal to the current market price. In both cases you will have to add the feature that converts residual earnings growth rates or AEG growth rates to earnings forecasts, following formulas 7.4 and 7.6. If you can work with graphic functions, you might display plots like those in Figures 7.5 and 7.6.

The Web Connection

Find the following on the Web page for this chapter:

- Further examples of reverse engineering.
- Consensus estimates of the market risk premium from surveys of analysts, academics, and investors.

- More discussion of the difficulties in applying asset pricing models like the CAPM.
- More help in building spreadsheets for active investing.

Summary

A valuation model is a useful tool, but the investors must understand how to operate the tool effectively. Valuation models can be used naively, yielding valuations that are just the product of speculative inputs. Rather than being a tool for challenging speculation, they can build in speculation.

This chapter has shown how to handle valuation models in active investing. A valuation model cannot deliver a reliable intrinsic value. But that does not matter, for active investing does not require us to discover intrinsic value. All that is required is to accept or reject the market valuation. For that, the tools of reverse engineering come into play, with valuation models used to infer the market's growth forecast that then can be challenged. Alternatively, with a forecast of growth, one can apply the valuation model to estimate the expected return to buying a stock at the current market price.

There is more to be done to develop a full toolbox for active investing. Most important, we need to analyze the information that anchors us in challenging the market price and the growth rate implicit in that price. That is the subject of the next part of the book.[3]

---

[3] The active investing of this chapter is treated with more detail in S. Penman, *Accounting for Value* (New York, Columbia University Press, 2011).

Key Concepts

fade pattern is the pattern a characteristic takes in evolving from the present or near future to the very long term. *220*

implied earnings growth rate is the forecast of earnings growth rate that is embedded in the market price. *219*

implied expected return is the expected rate of return from buying at the current market price. *214*

implied residual earnings growth rate is the forecast of the growth rate in residual earnings that is embedded in the market price. *214*

no-growth valuation is a valuation based on current and near-term accounting numbers with no growth expected. *218*

reverse engineering is the process of inferring information from the current market price by running valuation formulas backward. *214*

The Analyst's Toolkit

Analysis Tools	Page	Key Measures	Page	Acronyms to Remember	
Reverse engineering	214	Implied expected return	214	AEG	abnormal earnings growth
— for implied growth rates	214	Implied earnings growth rate	220		
— for expected returns	214	Implied AEG growth rate	221	B/P	book-to-price ratio
Weighted-average		Implied residual earnings		EPS	earnings per share
expected return	214	growth rate	214	ER	expected return
No-growth value	218	Value of speculative growth	218	ETF	exchange traded fund
Valuation building blocks	219			DPS	dividends per share
Implied earnings growth path	220			GDP	gross domestic product
BUY/SELL zones	220			P/E	price/earnings ratio
Fade patterns	220			P/B	price-to-book ratio
				RE	residual earnings
				ROCE	return on common equity

A Continuing Case: *Kimberly-Clark Corporation*

A Self-Study Exercise

In the Kimberly-Clark (KMB) case for Chapters 5 and 6, you were asked to convert analysts' consensus earnings forecasts to a valuation. The issue of the appropriate long-term growth rate arose, and it was suggested that you use the 4 percent GDP growth rate. The continuing case now asks you to go into reverse-engineering mode to understand the market's forecast and to challenge the price. You do not have the full toolkit to do this at this stage, but you will see that you are starting to get a handle on the problem.

ACTIVE INVESTING

In the earlier editions of the case you embraced analysts' five-year earnings growth rate. These growth rates are notoriously imprecise, so discard them. They are not something on which you can anchor. Work now with the EPS earnings estimates for 2011 and 2012, $4.98 and $5.35 respectively. The stock traded at $65.24 when these forecasts were made. Suppose your hurdle rate for investing in KMB is 8 percent and that you are reasonably comfortable with using the two years of forecasts.

Understanding Your Uncertainty

Assemble a building-block diagram for KMB like the one in Figure 7.4. What part are you most uncertain about? What price is the market putting on growth?

Reverse Engineering

Calculate the no-growth value for KMB. Now estimate the growth after 2012 that is forecasted by the market price. Plot the forecasted EPS growth rate, as in Figure 7.5. You probably will work with the residual earnings valuation model, but you might also try your hand at applying the abnormal earnings growth model, as in equations 7.5 and 7.5a. You might also experiment with different fade rates, with the growth rate fading to a (very) long-term rate of 4 percent, as in Figure 7.6.

Now reverse engineer the expected return from buying KMB at $65.24 per share. The weighted-average expected return formula is the tool. Set the growth rate initially at the GDP growth rate, but also look at the expected return for different growth rates. Ask, for example, what the expected return would be if KMB delivered no growth. What would be the expected return with 5 percent growth?

Suppose your hurdle rate is 8 percent and that you refuse to pay for residual earnings growth in excess of 3 percent. Would you buy this stock?

Using Spreadsheet Tools

You can build a spreadsheet program that conducts the reverse-engineering exercise. If you have built spreadsheets for the P/B and P/E valuation models, you might just run with those programs, experimenting with different inputs to discover growth rates and expected returns that yield the market price.

Concept Questions

C7.1. Why is a fundamental investor suspicious about a required return estimated from the capital asset pricing model (CAPM)?

C7.2. Why do valuation models lend themselves to "playing with mirrors"?

C7.3. "Investing is not a game against nature, but a game against other investors." What does this statement mean? What does it imply about how to conduct equity investing?

C7.4. Benjamin Graham was concerned about "the concept of future prospects and particularly of continued growth in the future." Why was he concerned?

C7.5. Growth is risky. Explain.

C7.6. A firm currently has a growth rate for residual earnings of 16 percent. Would you expect that growth rate to be higher, lower, or about the same in five years time?

C7.7. Why would you expect an abnormally high growth to fade toward average growth for the economy in the long run?

C7.8. A firm currently has a growth rate for residual earnings of 16 percent, but investors agree that the very long-term growth rate should be the GDP growth rate of 4 percent. What determines the speed by which the 16 percent rate fades to the 4 percent rate over time?

C7.9. A high P/E stock typically is one with high earnings growth expectations. Would you also expect that stock to be high risk? Are CAPM betas higher for high P/E stocks?

C7.10. A share is trading at $16.34. The no-growth value is $12.92. What do you infer from this comparison?

C7.11. A share trades at a P/B ratio of 0.8. The no-growth value indicates a P/B of 1.2. What do you infer from this comparison?

Exercises

Drill Exercises

E7.1. Reverse Engineering Growth Rates (Easy)

a. A share traded at $26 at the end of 2012 with a price-to-book ratio of 2.0. Analysts were forecasting earnings per share of $2.60 for 2013. Your required return for equity is 10 percent. What is the growth rate for residual earnings that the market expects beyond 2013?

b. A firm with a book value of $27.40 per share at the end of 2012 is expected to earn an EPS of $4.11 in 2013. Your required return for investing in the shares of this firm is 9 percent. What is the expected growth rate for residual earnings after 2013 that is implied by a market price of $54?

(This exercise and Exercise E7.2 can be worked together.)

E7.2. Reverse Engineering Expected Returns (Easy)

a. A share traded at $26 at the end of 2012 with a price-to-book ratio of 2.0. Analysts were forecasting earnings per share of $2.60 for 2013. If you expect no growth in residual earnings after 2013, what is the expected return from buying this stock?

b. A firm with a book value of $27.40 per share at the end of 2012 is expected to earn an EPS of $4.11 in 2013. If you expect subsequent growth in residual earnings to be at a rate of 4 percent per year, what is the expected return from buying this stock at a market price of $54 per share?

E7.3. Reverse Engineering Earnings Forecasts (Easy)

The equity of a firm trades at 2.6 times book value of $239.0 million at the end of 2012 and your required return is 9 percent. The forward earnings forecast for 2013 is $33.46 million and the firm pays no dividends.

a. What is the growth rate for residual earnings after 2013 that is implied by the market price?

b. What is the forecast of earnings for 2014 that is implicit in the market price?

E7.4. Expected Returns for Different Growth Rates (Easy)

A firm whose shares are trading at 2.2 times book value is forecasted to earn a return on book value of 15 percent next year. Calculate the expected return to buying this stock for the following forecasts of residual earnings growth after the forward year: 3 percent, 4 percent, and 6 percent. What is the expected return if no growth is expected?

E7.5. Reverse Engineering with the Abnormal Earnings Growth Model (Medium)

Analysts forecast forward earnings of $2.11 per share and a forecast of $2.67 for two years ahead. The firm pays no dividends. The required return is 9 percent.

a. What is the long-term growth rate in abnormal earnings growth (AEG) implied by a market price of $105.69?

b. What is the market's forecast of EPS for three years ahead?

Applications

E7.6. Reverse Engineering Growth Rates: Dell, Inc. (Easy)

In September 2008, Dell's shares traded at $20.50 each. In its last annual report, Dell had reported book value of $3,735 million with 2,060 million shares outstanding. Analysts were forecasting earnings per share of $1.47 for fiscal year 2009 and $1.77 for 2010. Dell pays no dividends.

Given the analysts' forecasts, what was the market's forecast of the residual earnings growth rate after 2010?

E7.7. Building Blocks for a Valuation: General Electric (Medium)

General Electric Co. (GE) reported a per-share book value of $10.47 in its balance sheet on December 31, 2004. In early 2005, analysts were forecasting consensus earnings per share of $1.71 for 2005 and $1.96 for 2006.

a. Calculate the value per share in early 2005 with a forecast that residual earnings will grow at a long-term GDP growth rate of 4 percent after 2006.
b. GE traded at $36 per share in early 2005. Construct a building-block diagram, like that in Figure 7.4, displaying the components of this $36 price that are attributable to book value, short-term earnings expectations, and speculation about long-term growth.
c. What is the forecast of the residual earnings growth rate after 2006 that is implied by the $36 market price?

Real World Connection

See Exercises E5.11, E6.10, and E11.8 on General Electric.

E7.8. The S&P 500 During Boom and Bust (Easy)

a. At the end of 2008, after the S&P 500 had returned –37.0 percent for the year during the financial crisis, the S&P 500 index stood at 903. Analysts were forecasting forward earnings of 73.0 on book value at the end of 2008 of 451. If the required return for investing in equities is 9 percent, what is the growth forecast that is implicit in the index price of 903? How does this number compare with the average implied growth rates for the index in Figure 7.1?
b. Repeat the exercise at the end on 1999 when the index stood at 1,469 with a book value of 294. Forward earnings' estimates at the time were 50.1.

E7.9. The Market's Forecast of Nike's Growth Rate (Easy)

The shares of Nike, Inc., traded at $74 after its financial statements for fiscal year 2010 were published. The balance sheet reported book value per share of $20.15. Analysts were forecasting EPS of $4.29 for 2011 and $4.78 for 2012. A dividend of $1.16 was indicated for 2011. Your required return is 9 percent.

a. What is the forecast of the residual earnings growth rate after 2012 that is implicit in the market price?
b. What is the market's forecast of EPS for 2013 and 2014?

Real World Connection

Other exercises on Nike are in E2.14, E5.13, E6.7, E9.12, E14.17, E16.11, E16.13, and E19.5.

E7.10. Expected Return from buying Novartis (Easy)

Novartis, the pharmaceutical firm, traded at a price-to-book ratio of 2.1 in May 2011. It is forecasted to have a return on common equity (ROCE) of 19 percent for 2011. What is the expected return from buying a Novartis share if you forecast that residual earnings will grow at 4 percent per year in the future?

E7.11.   The Expected Return to Buying a Google Share (Medium)

Exhibit 7.1 lays out a pro forma for Google, Inc., as of May 2011. Refer to the exhibit to answer the following questions:

a. Working with EPS forecasts for just one year ahead (2011), calculate the expected return to buying Google with a forecast of a 4 percent growth rate for residual earnings after the forward year. What is the expected return for a 5 percent growth rate and a 6 percent growth rate? What is the expected return if no growth is expected?

b. Now repeat the exercise with two years of EPS forecasts (2011 and 2012) with the forecasted growth rates being for the third year (2013) onwards.

Real World Connection

Minicases M7.2 and M19.1 also deal with Google.

E7.12.   Growth for a Hot Stock: Netflix (Easy)

Netflix delivers movies for home entertainment, initially via efficient mail distribution but with prospects of dominating the new technology of electronic delivery. With the failure of Blockbuster and other traditional retail outlets, Netflix was a market favorite in 2011, trading at $157 per share and a forward P/E of 42. Analysts were forecasting EPS of $3.71 for 2011 and $4.84 for 2012 on a book value per share at the end of 2010 of $5.50. The firm pays no dividends. You have a required return of 11 percent for this company: With so much growth built into the price, you see it as risky.

a. How much of the $157 price is value the market places on growth?

b. What is the expected growth rate for residual earnings that is implicit in the market price? Do you consider this growth rate normal?

E7.13.   Sellers Wants to Buy (Medium)

Mark Sellers, a hedge fund manager with Sellers Capital in Chicago, wrote a piece in the *Financial Times* on September 9, 2006, arguing that Home Depot, the warehouse retailer, was worth $50 per share. Home Depot traded at $34 per share at the time. Analysts were forecasting a consensus $2.98 earnings per share for fiscal year 2007 and $3.26 for 2008. A forward dividend of $0.60 per share was indicated for 2007 and $0.70 for 2008, with the dividend payout ratio maintained at the 2008 level in subsequent years. Home Depot reported a book value of $26,909 million for fiscal year ending January 2006, with 2,124 shares outstanding.

Use a required return of 10 percent per year in answering the following questions:

a. Given the analysts' forecasts, what is the growth rate for residual earnings after 2008 that is implied by Mr. Sellers's $50 valuation?

b. What are the earnings-per-share growth rates for 2009 and 2010 that are implied by Mr. Sellers's $50 valuation?

Real World Connection

See Exercises E15.11 and E15.12 on Home Depot.

E7.14.   Reverse Engineering Growth Forecasts for the S&P 500 Index (Medium)

With the S&P price index at 1270 in early 2006, the S&P 500 stocks traded at 2.5 times book value. On most recent (2005) annual earnings, the stocks in the index earned a weighted average return on their common equity of 18 percent. Use a required equity return of 10 percent for this "market portfolio."

a. Calculate the residual earnings growth rate that the market is forecasting for these stocks.

b. Suppose you forecast that a return on common equity of 18 percent will be sustained in the future. What is the growth in the net assets that you would then forecast at the current level of the index?

E7.15.   The Expected Return for the S&P 500 (Medium)

On January 1, 2008, the S&P 500 index stood at 1468 with a price-to-book ratio of 2.6. Expected earnings for the index for calendar year 2008 were 72.56. These earnings estimates, compiled from analysts' consensus earnings forecasts for the 500 stocks in the index, are in the same dollar units as the index.

   a. What is the forecast of return on common equity (ROCE) for the index for 2008?

   b. If you expect residual earnings growth for the corporate sector to equal the GDP growth rate of 4 percent for the economy as a whole, what is the implied expected return to buying the S&P 500 at 1468?

   c. The risk-free rate at the time was 4 percent. If you require a risk premium of 5 percent to buy equities, would you have bought an index fund that tracks the S&P 500 index?

   d. In 1999, the price-to-book ratio for the S&P 500 was much higher, at 5.4. Trailing ROCE was 23 percent. With the same GDP growth rate for growth in residual earnings, calculate the implied expected return to buying the S&P 500 at that point in time. Would you have purchased a market index fund that tracks the S&P 500 index?

E7.16.   Inferring Implied EPS Growth Rates: Kimberly-Clark Corporation (Medium)

In March 2005, analysts were forecasting consensus earnings per share for Kimberly-Clark (KMB) of $3.81 for fiscal year ending December 31, 2005, and $4.14 for 2006, up from $3.64 for 2004. KMB traded at $64.81 per share at the time. The firm paid a dividend of $1.60 in 2004 and a dividend of $1.80 was indicated for 2005, with dividends growing at 9 pecent a year for the five years thereafter. Use a required return of 8.9 percent for the following calculations.

   a. Calculate the trailing and forward P/E ratio at which KMB traded in March 2005. Also calculate the normal trailing and forward P/E ratios for KMB.

   b. Calculate the market's implied growth rate for abnormal earnings growth (AEG) after 2006.

   c. What are the earnings-per-share growth rates that the market was forecasting for the years 2007–2010?

   d. Analysts were forecasting an EPS growth rate of 8.0 percent per year over these years. What do you conclude from the comparison of these growth rates with those you calculated in part (c) of the exercise?

   e. Analyst average buy/hold/sell recommendation, on a scale of 1 to 5 (with 5 being a strong buy), was 2.6. Is this rating supported by their forecasts?

Real World Connection

The continuing case at the end of each chapter follows Kimberly-Clark. See also Exercises E4.9, E8.10, E11.10, E12.6 and Minicases M2.1 and M5.3.

Minicases

M7.1

Challenging the Market Price: Cisco Systems, Inc.

Cisco Systems, Inc. (CSCO), manufactures and sells networking and communications equipment for transporting data, voice, and video and provides services related to that equipment. Its products include routing and switching devices; home and office networking equipment; and Internet protocol, telephony, security, network management, and software services. The firm has grown organically but also through acquisition of other networking and software firms. Cisco's Web site is **www.cisco.com**.

Cisco was a darling of the Internet boom, one of the few firms with concrete products. Indeed its products were important to the development of the infrastructure for the Internet age and the expansion in telecommunications. At one point, in early 2000, the firm traded with a total market capitalization of over half a trillion dollars, exceeding that of Microsoft, and its shares traded at a P/E of over 130. With the bursting of the Internet bubble and the overcapacity in telecommunications resulting from overinvestment by telecommunications firms, Cisco's growth slowed. Faced with a sales slump, CEO John Chambers overhauled the management to streamline the company. By 2004 its revenue had recovered to the $22.0 billion level.

Subsequently, Cisco's sales continued to grow, reaching $39.5 billion by 2008. The company acquired the home networking company Linksys and cable set-top box maker Scientific Atlanta, along with WebEx web-conferencing software and Flip video cameras. However, sales then remained flat, standing at $36.2 billion in 2009. Profit margins declined and EPS in 2009 was $1.05, down from $1.35 in 2008. Rivals Motorola and Juniper Networks were gaining ground. Cisco's diversification, via acquisitions, into cable set-top boxes and videoconferencing equipment had not proved successful, with cable companies cutting back on orders for the cable boxes and customers using Skype or Google Talk to conference for no cost. Mr. Chambers began another shake-up of the company.

At the beginning of 2010, Cisco was trading at $24 per share, or 3.6 times book value of $6.68 at the end of its July 2009 fiscal year. Analysts were forecasting a consensus estimate of $1.42 EPS for fiscal year 2010 and 1.61 for 2011. The forward P/E of 16.9 implies some growth expectations, and indeed the growth rate forecasted for 2011 EPS over 2010 is 13.4 percent. Cisco paid no dividends at the time.

A. Bring all the tools in this chapter to an evaluation of whether Cisco's price is appropriate. You will not be able to resolve the issue without some detailed forecasting of Cisco's future earnings (which you should not attempt at this stage). Rather, using the analysts' forecasts for 2010 and 2011, quantify the earnings forecasts for subsequent years implicit in Cisco's $24 price. Identify the speculative components of Cisco's price using the building block approach. Figures 7.4 and 7.5 should be helpful to you.

B. If, through diligent analysis, you concluded that Cisco's long-run residual earnings growth rate can be no more than 4 percent per year, what is the expected rate of return from buying Cisco at $24?

C. What is the no-growth value for Cisco? What is the expected return from buying Cisco if no growth is expected? Calculate the expected return for different growth rates, including negative growth rates. Does this exercise give you a feeling for the range of possible payoffs from buying Cisco?

D. By August 2011, the stock price had fallen to $15, back to 1997 levels. What lessons do you learn from Cisco's decline in fortunes?

You might repeat the exercise for Cisco at a later date—August 2011, for example. You might also set up a spreadsheet program that can continue the investigation as prices, book value, and forecasts for Cisco change over time. This would also be a ready tool to apply to other firms.

Real World Connection

Minicase M15.2 also covers Cisco, as do Exercises E2.11 and E19.6.

M7.2

Reverse Engineering Google: How Do I Understand the Market's Expectations?

Valuation models can be dangerous if used naively: An analyst can plug in any growth rate or required return estimate to get a desired valuation. Indeed, a valuation model can be a vehicle to build speculation into the valuation: Choose a speculative growth rate—or speculative near-term forecasts—and you will get a speculative valuation. Garbage in, garbage out.

Remember the fundamentalist dictum: *Beware of paying too much for growth*. We would like to apply valuation models in a way that disciplines speculation about growth. Chapters 5 and 6 have shown that residual earnings and abnormal growth models protect us from paying too much for earnings growth from investment that does not add value. They also protect us from paying for earnings growth generated by accounting methods. But they cannot protect us from our own foolish speculation.

Benjamin Graham hit the nail on the head:

> The concept of future prospects and particularly of continued growth in the future invites the application of formulas out of higher mathematics to establish the present value of the favored issue. But the combination of precise formulas with highly imprecise assumptions can be used to establish, or rather justify, practically any value one wishes, however high, for a really outstanding issue.[1]

Reverse engineering gives us a way of handling valuation models differently: Rather than using a model to get a value, use a model to understand the forecasts implicit in the market price. This fits well with active investing. Investing is not a game against nature, but rather a game against other investors. For the active investor, there is no "true" intrinsic value to be discovered. Rather, he or she is playing against others; active investors "win" if they find that others' expectations (embedded in the market price) are not justified by sound analysis. Thus, the right question is not whether a valuation model gives you the "right" value but rather whether the model can help you understand what expectations explain the market price. With this understanding, the investor then compares those expectations to his or her own. Rather than challenging the price with a "true" intrinsic value, the active investor challenges price by challenging others' expectations. Reverse engineering is the vehicle.

At this point, you have not done the analysis to form confident expectations, but you can do the reverse engineering to understand others' expectations. This case asks you to do so with Google, Inc., a firm for which the market has had high expectations.

---

[1] B. Graham, *The Intelligent Investor,* 4th rev. ed. (New York: Harper and Row, 1973), pp. 315–316.

After coming to the market at just under $100 per share in a much heralded IPO in August 2004, Google's shares soared to over $700 by the end of 2007. The firm, with revenues tied mostly to advertising on its Web search engine and Web application products, held out the promise of the technological frontier. It certainly delivered sales and earnings growth, increasing sales from $3.2 billion in 2004 to $16.6 billion in 2007, with earnings per share increasing over the same years from $2.07 to $13.53. One might be concerned about buying such a hot stock. This case asks you to challenge the market price in mid-2008, but to do so by challenging the forecasts implicit in the market price. Tease out those forecasts using the abnormal earnings growth valuation model.

In mid-2008, Google traded at $520. Analysts at the time were forecasting EPS of $19.61 for 2008 and $24.01 for 2009, yielding a forward P/E of 26.5. Analysts' consensus five-year EPS growth rate was 28 percent.

A. Apply abnormal earnings growth (AEG) valuation to value Google based on these forecasts. Beta shops report a typical beta for Google of about 2.0, so use a high required return of 12 percent (against the current risk-free rate of 4 percent).

B. Analysts' intermediate-range forecasts (up to five years ahead) are notoriously optimistic, especially for a "hot stock" like Google. Anchoring on only the 2008 and 2009 forecasts, estimate the growth rate in abnormal earnings growth (AEG) that the market is forecasting for years after 2009. What does your answer tell you about analysts' five-year growth rate?

C. Build a valuation building block diagram, like that in Figure 6.3 in the text, and plot the EPS growth rates for 2010 to 2012 that are forecasted by the market price.

D. How would you now go about challenging the market price of $520? Calculate Google's PEG ratio. Does this help you?

E. Suppose you conclude that the highest (AEG) growth rate that Google can maintain (in perpetuity) is 6 percent. What is the expected return to buying the stock at $520 with this growth rate?

Real World Connection

Minicase 19.1 also deals with the valuation of Google.

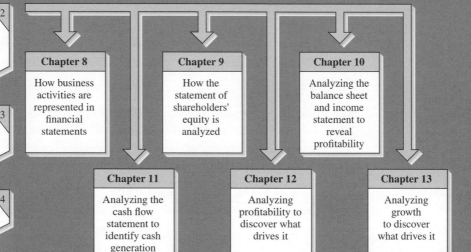

Part Two

The Analysis of Financial Statements

Knowing the business 1
- The products
- The knowledge base
- The competition
- The regulatory constraints
- The management

Strategy

Analyzing information 2
- In financial statements
- Outside of financial statements

Forecasting payoffs 3
- Specifying payoffs
- Forecasting payoffs

Converting forecasts to a valuation 4

Trading on the valuation 5

Outside investor:
Compare value with price to *buy*, *sell*, or *hold*

Inside investor:
Compare value with cost to *accept* or *reject* strategy

Chapter 8

How business activities are represented in financial statements

Chapter 9

How the statement of shareholders' equity is analyzed

Chapter 10

Analyzing the balance sheet and income statement to reveal profitability

Chapter 11

Analyzing the cash flow statement to identify cash generation

Chapter 12

Analyzing profitability to discover what drives it

Chapter 13

Analyzing growth to discover what drives it

Part One of the book was concerned with concepts and with developing good thinking about valuation. Parts Two and Three apply good thinking to develop practical analysis.

The five steps in valuation analysis that were laid out in Chapter 3 are displayed here. Forecasting, in Step 3, is at the heart of the process and Part Three of the book focuses on forecasting. But to forecast, the forecaster must first analyze information in Step 2 of the process. This part of the book develops the financial statement analysis for Step 2 as a platform for forecasting in Step 3.

The valuation models outlined in Chapters 5 and 6 guide the forecasting. To add value to book value (and determine the price-to-book ratio), we must forecast future residual earnings, and to add value to capitalized earnings (and determine the price-earnings ratio), we must forecast abnormal earnings growth. We have seen that residual earnings and abnormal earnings growth amount to the same thing, so the analysis that supports the forecasting is the same.

Accordingly, the culmination of this part of the book is the analysis of the two drivers, ROCE and growth in investment that earns at the ROCE. In analyzing financial statements, we discover the factors that drive current ROCE and growth and use them as a starting point for forecasting future ROCE and growth. Forecasting then becomes a question of how future ROCE and growth will be different from current ROCE and growth.

Step 1 of the valuation process requires that the analyst "know the business" before proceeding to Step 2. To begin financial statement analysis, the analyst must know how financial statements report the business that she has come to understand. Chapter 8 shows how business activities that drive value are represented in financial statements and shows how published financial statements are modified to highlight those activities. The modifications put the statements in a form that readies them for analysis.

Chapters 9, 10, and 11 analyze the financial statements. Chapter 9 deals with the statement of shareholders' equity, with a focus on uncovering comprehensive income and comprehensive ROCE, for correct analysis can proceed only if earnings are comprehensive. Chapter 10 analyzes the income statement and balance sheet. Here the focus is on distinguishing the firm's operating and financing activities and establishing the profitability of the two activities. Chapter 11 analyzes the statement of cash flows to identify the free cash flow from operations and the cash flows involved with financing.

Chapters 12 and 13 are the high point of this part of the book. They dissect the statements to discover the drivers of ROCE and earnings growth and so establish the platform for forecasting.

The financial statement analysis is done with a purpose: to discover what aspects of the financial statements tell us about the features of the business that determine a firm's value. You may have done some "ratio analysis" before—calculating ratios such as the current ratio or the inventory turnover—but after doing the calculations, you may have been left wondering: What now do I do with these ratios? In particular, what do the ratios tell me about the value of the firm? This part of the book outlines how you go about financial statement analysis in a systematic way to get an answer.

Chapter **Eight**

Viewing the Business Through the Financial Statements

LINKS

Link to previous chapters

Chapter 1 introduced the firm's operating, investing, and financing activities. Chapter 2 introduced the financial statements. Chapters 5 and 6 outlined valuation models that anchor on those financial statements, and Chapter 7 utilized those models in active investing.

This chapter

This chapter shows how the three business activities are depicted in the financial statements. It also shows how the statements are redesigned to highlight these activities and to prepare the statements for applying the valuation models in Chapters 5 and 6.

Link to next three chapters

Chapters 9, 10, and 11 reformulate the statements according to the design developed in this chapter.

Link to Web page

Build your own financial statement spreadsheet based on the chapter; for assistance visit the text's Web site at **www.mhhe.com/ penman5e**

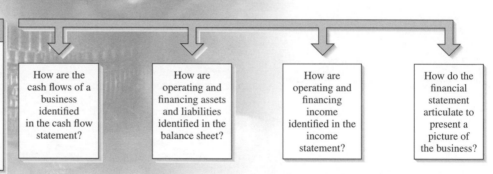

| How are the cash flows of a business identified in the cash flow statement? | How are operating and financing assets and liabilities identified in the balance sheet? | How are operating and financing income identified in the income statement? | How do the financial statement articulate to present a picture of the business? |

Every share purchase is in fact the purchase of a business. And anyone who buys a business should know that business. This maxim, recognized in Chapter 1, requires the analyst to investigate "what makes the business tick." This might be done through factory visits and interviews with management. But we also observe the business through financial statements. Financial statements are the lens on the business, so we need to get a feel for not only how the business operates but also how its operations are represented in financial statements. Then we will understand the story behind the numbers.

This chapter builds on the introduction to businesses in Chapter 1 and the introduction to financial statements in Chapter 2. Chapter 2 showed how financial statements depict "stocks" and "flows" and how these articulating stocks and flows tell a story. This chapter shows how the three business activities introduced in Chapter 1—financing, investing, and operating activities—are depicted through stocks and flows in the statements. The key element is the separation of operating and investment activities from financing activities in the

The Analyst's Checklist

After reading this chapter you should understand:

- How businesses are set up to generate value.
- How the financial statements are organized to reveal value added for shareholders.
- Why reformatting financial statements is necessary for analysis.
- How operating, investing, and financing activities are depicted in reformatted financial statements.
- The four types of cash flows in a business and how they relate to each other.
- How reformulated statements tie together as a set of stocks and flows.
- What operating activities involve.
- What financing activities involve.
- What determines dividends.
- What determines free cash flow.
- How free cash flow is disbursed.
- Why free cash flow is a dividend from operating activities to the financing activities.
- Why free cash flow does not affect the accounting for value added.

After reading this chapter you should be able to:

- Apply the treasurer's rule.
- Lay out the form of reformulated cash flow statements, balance sheets, and income statements.
- Explain how net operating assets change over time.
- Explain how net financial obligations change over time.
- Explain how free cash flow is generated.
- Explain how free cash flow is disposed of.
- Add new accounting relations to your set of analyst's tools.
- Calculate return on net operating assets and net borrowing cost from reformulated statements.
- Build an elementary spreadsheet that sets you up for analyzing the value generation of a business. This spreadsheet can be embellished as you proceed through the rest of the book.

financial statements, for it is the operating and investing activities that typically generate value, not the financing activities.

Chapter 2 introduced the financial statements in the form in which they are presented under GAAP accounting. That form does not quite give the picture we want to draw for valuation purposes. To sharpen our focus, we reformulate the statements in this chapter in a way that aligns the statements with the business activities. This reformulation readies the statements for the analysis in subsequent chapters which uncovers the factors that determine residual earnings and abnormal earnings growth, the primary valuation attributes in Chapters 5 and 6.

The emphasis in the chapter is on design. The redesign of financial statements provides the template for building a spreadsheet program that inputs the financial statements in a way that readies them for analysis. In Chapter 2 the form of the financial statements was given by a set of accounting relations. Here, too, the form of the reformulated financial statements is given by a set of accounting relations. These accounting relations provide the architecture for the spreadsheet program that can, with further embellishments in subsequent chapters, be used to analyze financial statements and value firms. At the end of the chapter you will be given explicit directions for designing the spreadsheet, with Nike, the firm whose financial statements were presented in Chapter 2, as an example.

BUSINESS ACTIVITIES: THE CASH FLOWS

In Figure 1.1 in Chapter 1 we depicted the transactions between the firm and its shareholders and debtholders. The firm, however, was left as a black box, although we recognized that the firm is engaged in financing activities, investing activities, and operating activities. Our aim in this and subsequent chapters is to fill out that box. Figure 8.1 begins to build the picture, to be completed in Figures 8.2 and 8.3. Figure 8.1 is similar to Figure 1.1 in Chapter 1, where cash flows to and from debtholders and shareholders are depicted. The cash flows to and from the debtholders and the firm have been reduced to a net flow, the *net debt financing flow,* labeled *F* in the figure. This involves the net cash flow to bondholders, banks, and other creditors, that is, cash paid to debtholders in interest and principal repayments less cash paid into the firm from borrowing more from these creditors. Similarly, the *net dividend to shareholders* (*d* in the figure) is cash paid in dividends and stock repurchases less cash contributions to the firm from shareholders. The transactions between the two claimants and the firm are the firm's *financing activities*—debt and equity financing—and these take place in capital markets where the firm and these claimants trade.

Debt financing flows involve payments to and from debt issuers as well as debtholders. A firm always begins with cash contributions from shareholders. Cash is a nonproductive asset so, until it is invested in operations, firms invest this cash in bonds or other interest-bearing paper and deposits, referred to as **financial assets** or sometimes as *marketable securities*. These financial assets are purchased in the capital market from debt issuers—governments (T-bills and bonds), banks (interest-bearing deposits), or other firms (corporate

FIGURE 8.1

Cash Flows between the Firm and Claimants in the Capital Market

Cash received from debtholders and shareholders is (temporarily) invested in financial assets. Cash payments to debtholders and shareholders are made by liquidating financial assets. Net financial assets are debt purchased from issuers, net of debt issued to debtholders. Net financial assets can be negative (that is, if debt issued to debtholders is greater than debt purchased).

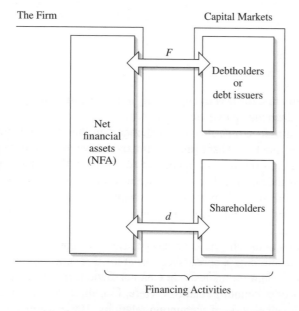

Key: *F* = Net cash flow to debtholders and issuers
         d = Net cash flow to shareholders
       NFA = Net financial assets = Financial assets – Financial liabilities

FIGURE 8.2

Cash Flows to Claimants and Cash Flows Within the Firm
Cash generated from operations is invested in net financial assets (that is, it is used to buy financial assets or to reduce financial liabilities). Cash investment in operations is made by reducing net financial assets (that is, by liquidating financial assets or issuing financial obligations). Cash from operations and cash investment may be negative (such that, for example, cash can be generated by liquidating an operating asset and investing the proceeds in a financial asset).

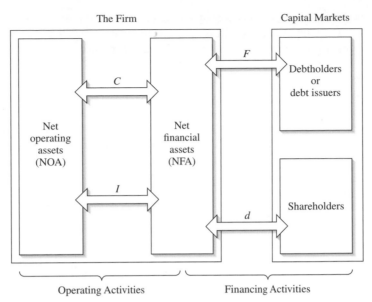

Key: F = Net cash flow to debtholders and issuers
        d = Net cash flow to shareholders
        C = Cash flow from operations
        I = Cash investment
      NFA = Net financial assets
      NOA = Net operating assets = Operating assets – Operating liabilities

bonds or commercial paper). They involve a cash payment out of the firm in exchange for the financial assets. Like the issue of debt, the purchase of debt is also a financing activity. It is lending rather than borrowing, but both amount to buying and selling bonds or other financial claims. A firm can be a buyer of debt (of a debt issuer) if it has excess cash or can be an issuer of debt (to a debtholder) if it needs cash. In the first case it holds financial assets and interest and principal repayments flow into the firm. In the second case it has **financial obligations** or **financial liabilities,** and interest and principal repayments are paid out of the firm. In the first case, the net debt financing flow, F, is cash paid to buy debt assets less cash received in interest and from the sale of the debt. In the second case, the net debt financing flow, F, is cash paid in interest and to redeem debt obligations less cash received in issuing debt. Thus the net financing flow, F, is the net cash flow from borrowing and lending.

Firms often issue debt and hold debt at the same time. Thus they hold both financial assets and financial obligations. The net debtholding is *net financial assets,* financial assets minus financial obligations, as depicted in Figure 8.1, or, if financial obligations are greater than financial assets, *net financial obligations.* Correspondingly, the net debt financing flow is the net cash outflow with respect to both borrowing and lending.

Figure 8.2 completes the cash flow picture. Firms typically are not primarily in the business of buying bonds but hold bonds only temporarily to invest idle cash. They invest in *operating assets*—land, factories, inventories, and so on—that produce products for sale. This is the firm's *investing activities* and the cash flows involved are *cash investment* or *cash flow in investment activities,* labeled I in the figure. To invest in operating assets, firms sell financial assets and buy operating assets with the proceeds. The arrows go both ways in the diagram because firms can also liquidate operating assets (in discontinued operations, for example) and buy financial assets with the proceeds. The operating assets, set to work, produce net cash flows (cash inflows from selling products less cash outflows from paying wages, rent, invoices, and so on) and this cash flow is referred to as *cash flow from operations.* This cash is invested in financial assets by buying debt, or used to reduce the firm's own debt. Cash from operations is never "left lying around" but is invested in financial assets to earn interest until needed. When needed, financial assets are liquidated to make cash investment in operations. Note that the term "investing activities" means investment in operating assets, not financial assets; indeed, investment in operating assets involves a liquidation of net financial assets.

Cash flow from operations and cash flow for investing activities were introduced in Chapter 4. We can now state a very important accounting identity known as the *cash conservation equation* or the *sources and uses of cash equation.* The four cash flows in Figure 8.2 always obey the relationship

Free cash flow = Net dividends to shareholders

$$+ \text{ Net payments to debtholders and issuers} \qquad \textbf{(8.1)}$$

$$C - I = d + F$$

That is, cash flow from operations less cash investment in operations always equals the net cash flows paid to debtholders (or issuers) and shareholders. The left-hand side, $C - I$, is the *free cash flow.* If operations generate more cash than is used in investment, free cash flow is positive. If operations produce less cash than is needed for new investment, free cash flow is negative. A positive free cash flow is used either to pay net interest and buy bonds (F) or to pay net dividends (d). A negative free cash flow requires that a firm either issue bonds (negative F) or issue shares (negative d) to satisfy the cash shortfall. The cash conservation equation is called an identity because it's always true. Cash generated must be disposed of; the sources of cash must be equal to its uses.

You see now how a firm may have financial obligations rather than financial assets (as is often so). Financial obligations are just negative financial assets. If free cash flow is negative, a firm can sell off financial assets to get cash; if these assets are all sold and if the firm chooses not to reduce its net dividend, however, the firm will have to issue debt to get the cash. Thus the firm becomes a net debtor rather than a creditor, a holder of net financial obligations rather than net financial assets. In either case it just trades in the debt market. If free cash flow is positive, the firm buys others' bonds with the cash or buys its own bonds (redeems them), holding net dividends constant. If free cash flow is negative, it sells bonds—either its own bonds or others' bonds which it holds. This is debt financing activity, and although sometimes it's done with banks (where the firm might have a loan or an interest-bearing deposit), you can think of it as trading in bonds. In doing so, the firm will have to cover any net dividend it wants to pay and, of course, net cash interest also generates or uses cash. The *treasurer's rule* summarizes this:

If $C - I - i > d$, then lend or buy down own debt.

If $C - I - i < d$, then borrow or reduce lending.

Here i is the net interest cash outflow (interest paid minus interest received). Net interest is after tax, as calculated in Chapter 4, because net cash paid is after receiving a tax deduction for interest. See Box 8.1.

MICROSOFT CORPORATION: POSITIVE FREE CASH FLOW

In its second quarter for 2004, Microsoft generated $4,064 million in free cash flow and received $338 million in interest, net of tax, from short-term marketable securities it held. It paid a net $2,270 million in cash out to shareholders, leaving $2,132 million with which it purchased short-term interest-bearing securities.

In its second quarter for 2005, Microsoft generated $3,200 million in free cash flow and received $242 million in interest, net of tax, for short-term marketable securities it held. In this quarter, the firm paid out a large special net dividend to shareholders of $33,672 million, leaving a cash shortfall. Accordingly, it sold $30,230 million of marketable securities to provide cash for the dividend.

The calculations for the treasurer's trading in debt are as follows (in millions):

		2nd Quarter 2004		2nd Quarter 2005
Cash flow from operations		$4,236		$3,377
Cash investment in operations		172		177
Free cash flow		4,064		3,200
Cash interest received (after tax)		338		242
Cash available for shareholders		4,402		3,442
Net dividend:				
Cash dividend	$1,729		$33,498	
Share repurchases	730		969	
Share issues	(189)	2,270	(795)	33,672
Purchase (sale) of financial assets		$2,132		$(30,230)

GENERAL ELECTRIC CORPORATION: NEGATIVE FREE CASH FLOW

During 2002, General Electric generated $34.8 billion in cash flow from operations but made $61.2 billion further investment in operations, including $7.7 billion of capital expenditure on property, plant, and equipment, $21.6 billion in acquisitions, and $18.1 billion investment in financing receivables. Accordingly, its free cash flow was negative to the amount of –$26.4 billion. As it paid out $8.1 billion to shareholders, it had to borrow $40.6 billion to cover this payout, the free cash deficit, and $6.1 billion in interest payments on debt.

The calculations for the treasurer's trading in debt are as follows (in millions):

Cash flow from operations		$34,848
Cash investment in operations		61,227
Free cash flow		(26,379)
Interest paid (after tax)		6,082
Cash available to shareholders		(32,461)
Net dividend:		
Cash dividend	$7,157	
Share repurchases	985	8,142
Net issue of debt		$40,603

As the treasurer had $57.8 billion of debt to repay, he issued $98.4 billion of new debt (for a net debt issue of $40.6 billion).

The cash flows in Box 8.1 are summarized in reformulated cash flow statements below (in millions). The reformulated statement distinguishes cash flows associated with operating activities from cash flows associated with financing activities. As free cash flow must be paid out either to shareholders or net debtholders, the statement obeys the cash conservation equation: $C - I = d + F$.

	Microsoft			GE
	1Q, 2004	1Q, 2005		2002
Cash flow from operations (C)	$4,236	$3,377		$34,848
Cash investment (I)	(172)	(177)		(61,227)
Free cash flow (C – I)	4,064	3,200		(26,379)
Equity financing flows (d):				
Dividends and share repurchases	$2,459	$34,467	$8,142	
Share issues	(189) 2,270	(795) 33,672	—	8,142
Debt financing flows (F):				
Net purchase of financial assets	2,132	(30,230)		—
Interest on financial assets (after tax)	(338)	(242)		—
Net issue of debt	—	—		(40,603)
Interest paid on debt (after tax)				6,082
Total financing flows (d + F)	$4,064	$3,200		$(26,379)

The Reformulated Cash Flow Statement

The accountant keeps track of the cash flows in a statement of cash flows. The design of a statement of cash flows that keeps track of the four cash flows in Figure 8.2 is below (items in parentheses are negative amounts):

Reformulated Statement of Cash Flows		
Cash flow from operations		C
Cash investment		(I)
Free cash flow		$C - I$
Equity financing flows:		
Dividends and share repurchases	XX	
Share issues	(XX)	d
Debt financing flows:		
Net purchase of financial assets	XX	
Interest on financial assets (after tax)	(XX)	
Net issue of debt	(XX)	
Interest on debt (after tax)	XX	F
Total financing flows		$d + F$

This reformulated statement is a little different from the GAAP statement of cash flows introduced in Chapter 2. It corresponds to the thought process of the treasurer or chief financial officer who is considering financing needs, and we want financial statements that reflect business activities. See Box 8.2.

The Reformulated Balance Sheet

The cash flows in Figure 8.2 are flows into and out of stocks of net assets depicted by boxes. So a cash investment, for example, is a flow that reduces the stock of net financial assets and increases the stock of operating assets. The balance sheet keeps track of the stock of financial assets and obligations, and so reports the net indebtedness. The balance sheet keeps track of the stock of operating assets as well. Published balance sheets list assets and liabilities, usually classified into current and long-term categories. This division is useful for credit analysis (as we will see in Chapter 20). But for equity analysis, the published statements are better reformulated into operating and financial assets and operating and financial liabilities. Operating assets and liabilities are simply the assets and liabilities used in the business of selling to customers. Financing assets are assets and liabilities used in the financing of the business. The former are involved in trading with customers and suppliers, the latter in trading in capital markets.

A dummy balance sheet that makes the distinction looks like this:

Balance Sheet				
Assets		**Liabilities and Equity**		
Operating assets	OA	Operating liabilities		OL
Financial assets	FA	Financial obligations		FO
		Common stockholders' equity		CSE
Total assets	OA + FA	Total claims		OL + FO + CSE

Financing items can be assets or obligations (liabilities), as we have discussed. But operating items also can be positive or negative. If they are positive, they are called **operating assets** (OA). If they are negative, they are called **operating liabilities** (OL). Accounts receivable is an operating asset because it arises from selling products in operations. Accounts payable is an operating liability because it arises from buying goods and services in operations. So are wages payable, pension liabilities, and other accrued expenses. We will deal with these classifications in more detail when we analyze actual balance sheets in Chapter 10 and reformulate them along the lines of this dummy statement. For now, note that operating liabilities arise as part of operations whereas financial liabilities arise as part of the financing activities to get cash to run the operations.

To distinguish operating and financing activities, it helps to regroup these items in the balance sheet:

Reformulated Balance Sheet				
Operating Assets		**Financial Obligations and Owners' Equity**		
Operating assets	OA	Financial obligations		FO
Operating liabilities	(OL)	Financial assets		(FA)
		Net financial obligations		NFO
		Common shareholders' equity		CSE
Net operating assets	NOA			NFO + CSE

Net operating assets (NOA) = OA − OL

Net financial assets (NFA) = FA − FO

Common shareholders' equity (CSE) = NOA + NFA

Usually NFA is negative, in which case it is net financial obligations (NFO):

$$CSE = NOA - NFO$$

The difference between operating assets and operating liabilities is the *net operating assets* (NOA). The difference between financial assets and financial obligations is the *net financial assets* (NFA). These are the two boxes in Figure 8.2. If NFA is negative, we have *net financial obligations* (NFO), as in this dummy statement. If NFA is positive, it is placed on the left-hand side. The book value of common stockholders' equity, CSE, was previously indicated as *B*. The last two identities under the statement restate the standard balance sheet equation (Assets – Liabilities = Owners' equity) in terms of the two net stocks for operating and financial activities. The owners' equity is seen as an investment in net operating assets and net financial assets, and the investment in net financial assets can be negative.

BUSINESS ACTIVITIES: ALL STOCKS AND FLOWS

The picture in Figure 8.2 is not complete: How does the income statement fit in? Well, firms raise cash from capital markets to invest in financing assets which are then turned into operating assets. But they then use the operating assets in operations. This involves buying inputs from suppliers (of labor, materials, and so on) and applying them with the net operating assets (such as factories, plant, and equipment) to produce goods or services that are sold to customers. Financing activities involve trading in capital markets. *Operating activities* involve trading with these customers and suppliers in *product and input markets*. Figure 8.3 completes the picture.

FIGURE 8.3
All Stocks and Flows for a Firm
Net operating assets employed in operations generate operating revenue (by selling goods and services to customers) and incur operating expenses (by buying inputs from suppliers). Δ indicates changes.

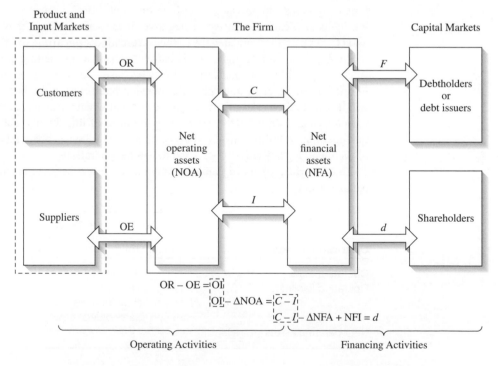

$$OR - OE = OI$$
$$OI - \Delta NOA = C - I$$
$$C - I - \Delta NFA + NFI = d$$

Operating Activities   Financing Activities

Key: F = Net cash flow to debtholders and issuers   NOA = Net operating assets
       d = Net cash flow to shareholders   OR = Operating revenue
       C = Cash flow from operations   OE = Operating expense
       I = Cash investment   OI = Operating income
       NFA = Net financial assets   NFI = Net financial income

Trading with suppliers involves giving up resources, and this loss of value is called **operating expense** (OE in the figure). The goods and services purchased have value in that they can be combined with the operating assets to yield products or services. These products or services are sold to customers to obtain **operating revenue,** or value gained (OR in the figure). The difference between operating revenue and operating expense is called **operating income:** $OI = OR - OE$. If all goes well, operating income is positive: The firm adds value. If not, operating income is negative: The firm loses value.

Figure 8.3 depicts the stocks and flows involved in the three business activities—financing, investing, and operating activities. It is common, however, to refer to the operating and investment activities together as operating activities (as in the figure), because investment is a matter of buying assets for operations. So analysts distinguish operating activities (which include investing activities) from financing activities (as in the figure).

The Reformulated Income Statement

The income statement summarizes the operating activities and reports the operating income or operating loss. The operating income is combined with the income and expense from financing activities to give the total value added to the shareholder, comprehensive income, or earnings:

Reformulated Income Statement		
Operating revenue		OR
Operating expense		(OE)
Operating income		OI
Financial expense	XX	
Financial income	(XX)	(NFE)
Comprehensive income		CI

Both operating income and net **financial expense** are after tax. (Chapter 10 shows how to calculate the after-tax amounts.) Operating revenues and operating expenses are not cash flows. They are measures of value in and value out as determined by the accountant. To capture that value, the accountant adds accruals to the cash flows, as we saw in Chapter 4. Similarly, interest income and interest expense (and other **financing income** and expenses) are not necessarily cash flows. As with operating income, the accountant determines what interest income and expense should be by making an accrual: As cash interest on a discount bond (for example) does not represent the effective borrowing cost, the accountant uses the effective interest method to adjust the cash amount. The net amount of effective interest income (on financial assets) and effective interest expense (on financial obligations) is called **net financial income** (NFI) or, if interest expense is greater than interest income, **net financial expense** (NFE).

ACCOUNTING RELATIONS THAT GOVERN REFORMULATED STATEMENTS

We now have three reformulated statements. Just as published statements are governed by the accounting relations laid out in Chapter 2, so the reformulated statements are also governed by accounting relations. The cash flow and income statements are statements of flows over a period—operating flows and financing flows—and the balance sheet is a statement of the stocks—operating and financing stocks—at the end of a period. The flows during a period flow into and out of the stocks, as in the diagram, so the changes in the stocks are explained by the flows.

The flows and the changes in stocks are linked at the bottom of Figure 8.3. These links between stocks and flows are accounting relations. Accounting relations not only govern the form of the statements—how different components relate to each other—but they also describe what drives, or determines, each component. Financial analysis is a question of what drives financial statements, what drives earnings and book values. So the accounting relations we are about to lay out will become analysis tools in subsequent chapters. The accounting relations below also dictate the structure of a financial statement analysis spreadsheet that will provide those tools. We will end this chapter by giving directions for developing such a spreadsheet. The accounting relations, as stated here, look a bit technical, but they will come to life as you apply them in analysis and valuation. Keep your eye on the prize: We are producing tools for discovering the value generation in a business.

The Sources of Free Cash Flow and the Disposition of Free Cash Flow

Free cash flow is generated by cash from operations net of cash investment. But we can also depict the generation of free cash flow in terms of the accrual accounting income statements and balance sheets. Moving from left to right in Figure 8.3, we see how free cash flow is generated:

$$\text{Free cash flow} = \text{Operating income} - \text{Change in net operating assets} \qquad \textbf{(8.2)}$$
$$C - I = \text{OI} - \Delta\text{NOA}$$

where the Greek delta, Δ, indicates changes. Operations generate operating income, and free cash flow is the part of this income remaining after reinvesting some of it in net operating assets. In a sense, free cash flow is a dividend from the operations, the cash from operating profits after retaining some of the profits as assets.

The right-hand side of the figure explains the disposition of free cash flow:

$$\text{Free cash flow} = \text{Change in net financial assets} \qquad \textbf{(8.3a)}$$
$$- \text{Net financial income} + \text{Net dividends}$$
$$C - I = \Delta\text{NFA} - \text{NFI} + d$$

That is, free cash flow is used to pay net dividends, with the remainder invested in net financial assets, along with net financial income. Box 8.2 provided an example for Microsoft where, in 2004, the firm applied its free cash flow to purchase financial assets (net of interest received) and paid out cash to shareholders. If the firm has net financial obligations,

$$\text{Free cash flow} = \text{Net financial expenses} \qquad \textbf{(8.3b)}$$
$$- \text{Change in net financial obligations} + \text{Net dividends}$$
$$C - I = \text{NFE} - \Delta\text{NFO} + d$$

That is, free cash flow is applied to pay for net financial expenses, reduce net borrowing, and pay net dividends. Box 8.1 provided an example for General Electric, where, in fact, the free cash flow was negative so the firm had to increase its net financial obligations.

The Drivers of Dividends

Running all the way from left to right in Figure 8.3, you see how the value created in product and input markets and recorded in the accounting system flows through to the final dividend to shareholders: Operations yield value (operating income) that is invested in net operating assets; excess (or "free") cash from operations is invested in net financial assets, which yield net interest income; then these financial assets are liquidated to pay dividends. If operations need cash (negative free cash flow), financial assets are liquidated or financial obligations are created through borrowing. Alternatively, cash is raised from shareholders (a negative dividend) and temporarily invested in financial assets until needed to satisfy the negative free cash flow. And so the world turns.

The last point of this dividend generation is stated by the accounting relation to the right in Figure 8.3:

$$\text{Net dividends} = \text{Free cash flow} + \text{Net financial income} \qquad \textbf{(8.4a)}$$
$$- \text{Change in net financial assets}$$

$$d = C - I + \text{NFI} - \Delta\text{NFA}$$

which is a reordering of the free cash flow relation (8.3a). That is, dividends are paid out of free cash flow and interest earned on financial assets and by selling financial assets. If free cash flow is insufficient to pay dividends, financial assets are sold (or financial obligations incurred) to pay the dividend.

If the firm is a net debtor,

$$\text{Net dividends} = \text{Free cash flow} - \text{Net financial expenses} \qquad \textbf{(8.4b)}$$
$$+ \text{Change in net financial obligations}$$

$$d = C - I - \text{NFE} + \Delta\text{NFO}$$

which is a reordering of the free cash flow relation (8.3b). That is, dividends are generated from free cash flow after servicing interest, but also by increasing borrowing. You see why dividends might not be a good indicator of the value generation in a business (at least in the short run): A firm can borrow to generate dividends (at least in the short run).

Dividends in these relations are net dividends, so cash is paid in by shareholders if free cash flow after net interest is less than net borrowing.

The Drivers of Net Operating Assets and Net Indebtedness

By reordering these accounting relations we explain changes in the balance sheet. From equation 8.2,

$$\text{Net operating assets (end)} = \text{Net operating assets (beginning)} \qquad \textbf{(8.5)}$$
$$+ \text{Operating income} - \text{Free cash flow}$$

$$\text{NOA}_t = \text{NOA}_{t-1} + \text{OI}_t - (C_t - I_t)$$

or

$$\text{Change in net operating assets} = \text{Operating income} - \text{Free cash flow}$$

$$\Delta\text{NOA}_t = \text{OI}_t - (C_t - I_t)$$

Operating income is value added from operations, and that value increases the net operating assets. So, for example, a sale on credit increases both operating revenue and operating assets through a receivable; and purchase of materials on credit or a deferral of compensation increases both operating expense and operating liabilities through an accounts payable or wages payable. (This is just the debits and credits of accounting at work.) Free cash flow reduces net operating assets as cash is taken from operations and invested in net financial assets. Or, expressing the change in NOA as $\Delta\text{NOA} = \text{OI} - C + I$, you see that operating income and cash investment increase NOA, and NOA is reduced by the cash flows from operations that are invested in net financial assets.

Correspondingly, the change in net financial assets is determined by the income from net financial assets and free cash flows, along with dividends:

$$\text{Net financial assets (end)} = \text{Net financial assets (begin)} \qquad \textbf{(8.6a)}$$
$$+ \text{Net financial income}$$
$$+ \text{Free cash flow} - \text{Net dividends}$$

$$\text{NFA}_t = \text{NFA}_{t-1} + \text{NFI}_t + (C_t - I_t) - d_t$$

or

Change in net financial assets = Net financial income + Free cash flow − Net dividends

$$\Delta\text{NFA}_t = \text{NFI}_t + (C_t - I_t) - d_t$$

The net financial income earned on net financial assets adds to the assets, free cash flow increases the assets (as the cash from operations is invested in financial assets), and the assets are liquidated to pay net dividends. If the firm holds net financial obligations rather than net financial assets,

Net financial obligations (end) = Net financial obligation (begin)   **(8.6b)**
+ Net financial expense
− Free cash flow + Net dividends

$$\text{NFO}_t = \text{NFO}_{t-1} + \text{NFE}_t - (C_t - I_t) + d_t$$

or

Change in net financial obligations = Net financial expense − Free cash flow
+ Net dividends

$$\Delta\text{NFO}_t = \text{NFE}_t - (C_t - I_t) + d_t$$

That is, interest obligations increase net indebtedness, free cash flow reduces indebtedness, and the firm has to borrow to finance the net dividend.

These accounting relations, remember, tell us what drives the various aspects of the (reformulated) statements. Net operating assets are driven by operating income and reduced by free cash flow, as in equation 8.5. Or, stated differently, NOA is increased by operating revenue, reduced by operating expenses, increased by cash investment, and reduced by cash from operations (which is not "left lying around" but invested in financial assets). The relations for net financial assets and obligations, equations 8.6a and 8.6b, explain what determines the borrowing or lending requirement and so restate the treasurer's rule: The amount of new debt to be purchased (and put on the balance sheet) is determined by the free cash flow after interest and the net dividend.

TYING IT TOGETHER FOR SHAREHOLDERS: WHAT GENERATES VALUE?

Figure 8.4 shows how reformulated statements articulate via accounting relations. It shows the accounting relations governing each statement (within each box) and the stocks and flow relations that explain ending stocks in the balance sheet in terms of beginning balance sheet stocks and the flows over the period. These flows are from the income statement and cash flow statement. Operating income increases net operating assets, and net financial expense increases net financial obligations. The income statement explains where these flows come from. Free cash flow decreases net operating assets and also decreases the net indebtedness. The cash flow statement explains where the free cash flow come from. Dividends are paid out of the net financial obligations—by liquidating financial assets (to get the cash) or by issuing debt. In short, the financial statements track the operating and financing flows of a business and show how they update the stocks of net operating assets, net financial obligations, and (as $\Delta\text{CSE} = \Delta\text{NOA} - \Delta\text{NFO}$) the change in shareholders' equity.

The stocks and flows relations for NOA and NFO (or NFA) are similar in form to the stocks and flows equation for common stockholders' equity introduced in Chapter 2:

$$\text{CSE}_t = \text{CSE}_{t-1} + \text{Comprehensive income} - \text{Net dividends}_t$$

FIGURE 8.4   **The Articulation of Reformulated Financial Statements.**

This figure shows how reformulated income statements, balance sheets, and the cash flow statements report the operating and financing activities of a business, and how the stocks and flows in Figure 8.3 are identified in the financial statements. Operating income increases net operating assets and net financial expense increases net financial obligations. Free cash flow is a "dividend" from the operating activities to the financing activities: Free cash flow reduces net operating assets and also reduces net financial obligations. Net dividends to shareholders are paid out of net financial obligations.

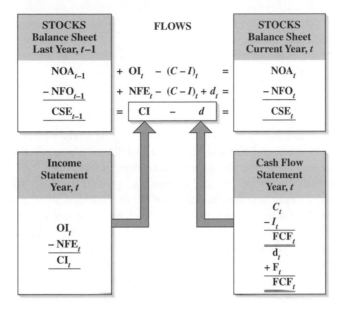

That is, common equity is driven by comprehensive income (earnings) and is reduced by net dividends. The expressions for NOA and NFO (in Figure 8.4 and equations 8.5 and 8.6b) also have a driver and a dividend. NOA is driven by operating income and reduced by a "dividend," free cash flow that is paid to the financing activities. And the net financial obligations are driven by the free cash flow received from the operating activities along with the financial expense they themselves incur, and they pay a dividend to the shareholders.

The aim of the accounting system is to track value created for shareholders. The stocks and flows equation for shareholders indeed says this: Owners' equity is driven by a value-added measure, comprehensive income, and reduced by net distributions to owners. But common equity is also the net total of stocks in the balance sheet, the difference between net operating assets and net financial obligations:

$$CSE_t = NOA_t - NFO_t$$

So changes in common equity are driven by the drivers that change NOA and NFO. Figure 8.5 depicts how common shareholders' equity is generated by NOA and NFO. Line 1 explains the change in net operating assets from the beginning of a period and line 2 explains the change in net financial obligations. Line 3 explains the change in common equity (for the case of net financial obligations). The difference between the flows for NOA and NFO (line 1 minus line 2) explains the flow for common equity. The change in the common equity is explained by comprehensive income minus net dividends, but it is also explained by the flows that explain the net operating assets and net financial obligations.

FIGURE 8.5 **Change in Common Stockholders' Equity Is Explained by Changes (Flows) in Net Operating Assets (NOA) and Net Financial Obligations (NFO).**
Subtract line 2 from line 1 and you see that free cash flow $(C - I)$ does not affect the change in common stockholders' equity.

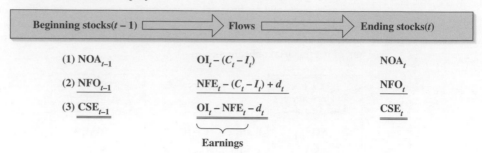

You'll notice in this explanation of the change in shareholders' equity that although the free cash flow affects NOA and NFO, free cash flow drops out in the difference between the two when explaining the change in shareholders' equity: Take line 2 from line 1 to get line 3 and free cash flow drops out. The accounting says that free cash flow does not add value to shareholders. Free cash flow is a driver of the net financial position, not the operating activities, and the amount of free cash flow is irrelevant in determining the value of owners' equity. Rather, the profits from operating activities (OI) and financing activities (NFE), which together give earnings, increase or decrease shareholder wealth. Free cash flow is just a dividend of excess cash from the operating activities to the financing activities, not a measure of the value added from selling products. And free cash flows, just like dividends to shareholders, have little to do with value generated.

This makes eminent sense. Both Microsoft and General Electric in Boxes 8.1 and 8.2 have added tremendous value for shareholders. Microsoft has large positive free cash flow. General Electric has large negative free cash flow. But it does not matter. Earnings matter; accrual accounting gets it right.

BUILD YOUR OWN ANALYSIS ENGINE

As we proceed through this part of the text, you will be able to build most features into a spreadsheet that will perform a complete analysis of a firm. In the next part of the book, on valuation, you will be able to combine the analysis spreadsheet with the valuation engines you produced in Chapters 5–7 to produce a complete analysis and valuation spreadsheet that you can activate to challenge market prices. The Build Your Own Analysis and Valuation Product (BYOAP) guide on the book's Web site gives the full directions for developing the final product, with examples for Nike, Inc. You can, of course, appropriate the spreadsheet for Nike there, but your learning will be considerably enhanced if you build your own spreadsheet progressively as we proceed through the book.

Figure 8.4 gives the summary financial statement numbers that appear in a financial statement analysis and valuation spreadsheet. Of course, we will add more detail as we proceed—the various types of net operating assets, net financial obligations, operating income, and more that make up these totals—but these summary numbers are primary. Figure 8.4 also gives the accounting relations that govern each statement and the articulation between the statements, and these relations govern the spreadsheet. These relations must hold in the spreadsheet, otherwise the analysis and valuation that the spreadsheet sheet delivers will

The 2010 financial statements for Nike, Inc., the athletic footwear manufacturer, are given in Exhibit 2.1 in Chapter 2. Reformulation of financial statements involves rearranging the statements according to the design in this chapter. We will go into the detail of reformulating Nike's statements in Chapter 10. To add some live numbers to the rather cryptic presentation you have just gone through, the main summary numbers from Nike's reformulated balance sheets and income statement are given below in the same form as Figure 8.4, together with the numbers for the accounting relations that explain how the financial statements articulate.

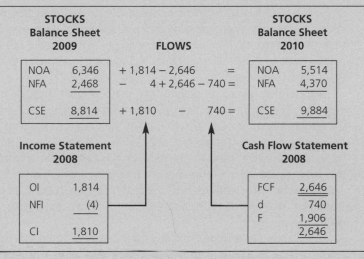

You might ask where the $2,646 million in free cash flow came from. Is it from the cash flow statement? Well, one could extract it from there with the adjustments we made in Chapter 4. However, we have an accounting relation (8.2) that tells us the free cash flow once we have identified operation income (OI) and net operating assets (NOA):

$$C \quad I = OI - \Delta NOA$$
$$- 1,814 - (5,514 - 6,346)$$
$$= 2,646$$

You can see how accounting relations are going to be useful as analysis tools: Some numbers have to be input from financial statements, but others just fall out by applying the relations that connect accounting numbers to each other. A spreadsheet will embed many analysis tools such as this, provided you have set it up to obey the accounting relations.

be in error. Put more positively, if the spreadsheet is built on this template, the analyst is secure, knowing that the spreadsheet has integrity in identifying the value generation in a business.

There is, of course, much to be added before we get to a full analysis and valuation product, and the next few chapters will occupy us in building a complete, functional spreadsheet. We now have only the skeleton, to be fleshed out as we proceed. However, Box 8.3 will get you started. It gives the summary numbers in Figure 8.4 from the financial statements for Nike in Chapter 2. Don't be too concerned about how these are identified at the moment—that is the task of the next three chapters. But put the numbers into a spreadsheet and see how they articulate. In so doing, you will see how the spreadsheet provides tools that give insights. Observe the calculation of free cash flow at the bottom of Box 8.3. We don't have to calculate free cash flow—a problem we found difficult in Chapter 4—for it is supplied by the press of a button using an accounting relation. We shall see many other features pop out as we proceed, provided we have built a spreadsheet with integrity.

Summary

This chapter has laid out the bare bones of how a business works and how business activities are highlighted in reformulated financial statements. The key point for discovering the value generation is the separation of operating (and investing) activities from financing activities. The separation leads to a set of accounting relations that describe the drivers of reformulated statements and connect the statements together. These relations are summarized in the Analyst's Toolkit below, and you should try to commit them to memory. More importantly, you should appreciate what they are saying. Taken as a whole, these relations outline how value is passed from shareholders to the firm in share issues and, with value added, passed back to shareholders. Figures 8.3 and 8.4 summarize this well. Put them firmly in your mind as you continue.

The chapter, indeed, is skeletal and there is much flesh to be added in the following chapters. You have been given the form of the reformulated statements that distinguish the operating and financing activities of the firm, but the form has to be filled out. The distinction between the two types of activities is important for, as we observed in Chapter 3, it is the operating activities that are typically the source of the value generation, so it is these operating activities—and the return on net operating assets (RNOA)—that we will be particularly focused on as we analyze firms. Indeed, as we proceed with financial statement analysis, we will work with reformulated statements, not the published GAAP statements.

The accounting relations that govern the reformulated statements are also tools for the analyst. They explain how to pull the statements apart to get at the drivers. And they explain how to manipulate the statements to express one component in terms of others. The relations are stated in stark, technical terms here, but they, too, will come to life as the analysis develops. As a set, they provide the architecture for a spreadsheet program that can be used to analyze reformulated statements and value firms. You will find yourself referring back to them and, as you do, you will appreciate how the summary of the financial statements in terms of these relations provides a succinct expression of the "story behind the numbers."

The Web Connection

Find the following on the Web page for this chapter:

- More directions for putting the framework in this chapter into a spreadsheet.
- More demonstration of how the framework works to produce analysis tools.
- A discussion of the FASB and IASB financial statement design project, which aims to report financial statements more in line with the reformulations in this chapter.
- Your first introduction to the Build Your Own Analysis Product (BYOAP) spreadsheet tool, a complete spreadsheet for analysis and valuation that you can build as the book proceeds.

Key Concepts

financial asset is an asset held to store cash temporarily and which is liquidated to invest in operations or pay dividends. Also called **marketable securities.** *236*

financial expense is an expense incurred on **financial obligations.** *243*

financial income is earnings on **financial assets.** *243*

financial obligation or **financial liability** is an obligation incurred to raise cash for operations or to pay dividends. *237*

net financial expense is the difference between **financial expense** and **financial income.** If financial income is greater than financial expense, it is referred to as **net financial income.** *243*

operating asset is an asset used in operations (to generate value from selling products and services). *241*

operating expense is a loss of value from selling products (in operations). *243*

operating income is net value added from operations. *243*

operating liability is an obligation incurred as part of operations (to generate value from selling products and services). *241*

operating revenue is value gained from selling products (in operations). *243*

The Analyst's Toolkit

Analysis Tools	Page	Key Measures	Page	Acronyms to Remember	
The treasurer's rule	238	Common stockholders' equity		BYOAP	Build Your Own Analysis Product
If $C - I - i > d$, then lend or buy down debt		(CSE)	242		
		Financial assets (FA)	236	CI	comprehensive income
If $C - I - i < d$, then borrow or reduce lending		Financial obligations (FO)	237	CSE	common shareholders' equity
		Free cash flow	238		
Accounting relations		Net financial assets (NFA)	237	FA	financial asset
Cash conservation equation		Net financial obligations (NFO)	237	FO	financial obligation
$C - I = d + F$ (8.1)	238	Net financial expense (NFE)	243	NFA	net financial assets
Free cash flow sources equation		Net financial income (NFI)	243	NFE	net financial expense
		Net operating assets (NOA)	242	NFI	net financial income
$C - I = OI - \Delta NOA$ (8.2)	244	Operating asset (OA)	241	NFO	net financial obligations
Free cash flow disposition equations		Operating expense (OE)	243	NOA	net operating assets
		Operating income (OI)	243	OA	operating assets
$C - I = \Delta NFA - NFI + d$ (8.3a)	244	Operating liabilities (OL)	241	OE	operating expense
		Operating revenue (OR)	243	OI	operating income
$C - I = NFE - \Delta NFO + d$ (8.3b)	244			OL	operating liabilities
Dividend driver equations				OR	operating revenue
$d = C - I + NFI - \Delta NFA$ (8.4a)	245				
$d = C - I - NFE + \Delta NFO$ (8.4b)	245				
Net operating asset driver equation					
$\Delta NOA = OI - (C - I)$ (8.5)	245				
Net financial asset (or obligation) driver equations					
$\Delta NFA = NFI + (C - I) - d$ (8.6a)	246				
$\Delta NFO = NFE - (C - I) + d$ (8.6b)	246				

A Continuing Case: *Kimberly-Clark Corporation*

A Self-Study Exercise

Kimberly-Clark's financial statements for 2010 are presented in Exhibit 2.2 as part of the the continuing case for Chapter 2. Over the next three chapters, you will be reformulating these statements following the design in this chapter. Then, in Chapters 12 and 13 you will be performing a full analysis of the reformulated statements in preparation for valuing the company in Part Three of the book. This module of the continuing case prepares you for what is to come.

You will be helped by delving into the full 10-K report for 2010. Download it from the SEC's EDGAR Web site and go through the footnotes to the financial statements. You will be referring to these footnotes constantly over the next few chapters, so get a sense of their layout. The detail is not important at this stage, but do familiarize yourself with the broad content. The KMB case for Chapter 2 gives download instructions. If, for some reason, you have difficulty downloading the 10-K, it is on the Web page for chapter 2 on the book's Web site.

THE TREASURER'S RULE

Using the cash flow statement for 2010 in Exhibit 2.2 in Chapter 2 and any other information you glean from the 10-K, lay out the sequence that concludes with the treasurer's trading in debt, as in Box 8.1.

Now take this information and present it in the form of a summary cash flow statement (as in Box 8.2) that obeys the equation: Free cash flow = Distributions to shareholders + Distributions to net debtholders. One question you will have to resolve is the treatment of the increase in cash and cash equivalents of $78 million over the year.

IDENTIFYING OPERATING ACTIVITIES

The rationale for the reformulation of the financial statements sketched out in this chapter is to separate operating activities from financing activities. Typically value is generated in operating activities—trading with customers and suppliers—not in financing activities that merely involve passing cash to and from investors. Reformulation sets us up to examine value added. You will carry out a full reformulation of Kimberly-Clark's balance sheet and income statement in Chapter 10. For now, go through the balance sheet and income statement in Exhibit 2.2 and identify those items you think are involved in operations and those involved in financing activities. If you are ambitious, you can follow through and calculate totals for net operating assets, net financial obligations, operating income, and net financial expenses. You could also set up a stocks and flow diagram like the one for Nike in Box 8.3, but you best wait until Chapter 10.

Concept Questions

C8.1. Why can free cash flow be regarded as a dividend, that is, as a distribution of value rather than the value created?

C8.2. A firm has positive free cash flow and a net dividend to shareholders that is less than free cash flow. What must it do with the excess of the free cash flow over the dividend?

C8.3. How can a firm pay a dividend with zero free cash flow?

C8.4. Distinguish an operating asset from a financial asset.

C8.5. Distinguish an operating liability from a financial liability.

C8.6. If an analyst has reformulated balance sheets and income statements, she does not need a cash flow statement to calculate free cash flow. True or false?

C8.7. What drives free cash flow?

C8.8. What drives dividends?

C8.9. What drives net operating assets?

C8.10. What drives net financial obligations?

C8.11. Free cash flow does not affect common shareholders' equity. True or false?

C8.12. Explain why profitable companies sometimes have negative free cash flows (like General Electric in this chapter).

Exercises

Drill Exercises

E8.1. Applying the Cash Conservation Equation (Easy)

a. A firm generated $143 million in free cash flow and paid a net dividend of $49 million to shareholders. How much was paid to debtholders and debt issuers?

b. A firm paid a dividend to shareholders of $162 million and repurchased stock for $53 million. There were no share issues. The firm received net cash of $86 million from debt financing transactions. What was its free cash flow?

E8.2. A Question for the Treasurer (Easy)

A firm generated $220 million in free cash flow. It paid out $35 million in dividends and there were no share issues or repurchases. It incurred $6 million in net interest expense (after tax). The boss wants to know what happened to the amount left over. Your answer is:

a. Impossible to track it.

b. It must have been spent on paying down debt or invested in interest-bearing debt.

c. It has been invested back into the business operations.

d. Most likely some combination of (b) and (c).

E8.3. What Were the Payments to Shareholders? (Easy)

a. A firm generated $410 million in free cash flow and spent $340 million of this paying net interest and buying down its net debt. What was the net payout to shareholders?

b. The same firm issued shares for $50 million and there were no share repurchases. What was the cash dividend paid to shareholders?

E8.4. Applying the Treasurer's Rule (Medium)

a. A firm generated free cash flow of $2,348 million and paid net interest of $23 million after tax. It paid a dividend of $14 million and issued shares for $54 million. There were no share repurchases. What did the treasurer do with the remaining cash flow and for how much?

b. A firm generated a negative free cash flow of $1,857 million, but the board of directors, understanding that the firm was quite profitable, maintained the dividend of $1.25 per share on the 840 million shares outstanding. The firm also paid $32 million in net interest (after tax). What are the responses open to the treasurer?

E8.5. Balance Sheet and Income Statement Relations (Easy)

a. A firm holding $432 million in interest-bearing financial assets and with financing debt of $1,891 million, reported shareholders' equity of $597 million. What were its net financial assets? What were its net operating assets?

b. The same firm reported $108 million in comprehensive income and net financial expense, after tax, of $47 million. What was its after-tax operating income?

E8.6.   Using Accounting Relations (Medium)

Below are a balance sheet and an income statement that have been reformulated according to the templates laid out in this chapter. Ignore income taxes.

Balance Sheet

Assets			Liabilities and Equity		
	2012	**2011**		**2012**	**2011**
Operating assets	205.3	189.9	Operating liabilities	40.6	34.2
Financial assets	45.7	42.0	Financial liabilities	120.4	120.4
			Shareholders' equity	90.0	77.3
	251.0	231.9		251.0	231.9

Income Statement
2012

Operating revenues	134.5
Operating expenses	(112.8)
Operating income	21.7
Interest revenues	2.5
Interest expenses	(9.6)
Comprehensive income	14.6

a. How much was paid out in net dividends during 2012?
b. What is free cash flow for 2012?

E8.7.   Using Accounting Relations (Medium)

Below are financial statements that have been reformulated using the templates in this chapter. Some items are missing; they are indicated by capital letters.

Income Statement
Six Months to June 30, 2012

Revenues		A
Operating expenses		
Cost of sales	2,453	
Research and development expenses	507	
Selling, administrative, and general expenses	2,423	
Other operating expenses, including taxes	2,929	B
Operating income after tax		850
Net financial expenses after tax		
Interest expense	153	
Interest income	C	59
Comprehensive income		791

Balance Sheet
June 30, 2012

	June 2012	December 2011		June 2012	December 2011
Operating assets	28,631	30,024	Operating liabilities	G	8,747
Financial assets	D	4,238	Financial liabilities	7,424	6,971
			Common equity	18,470	H
	33,088	E		33,088	F

CSE

Cash Flow Statement
Six Months Ending June 30, 2012

Cash flow from operations	584
Cash investment	I
Free cash flow	J
Net dividends (dividends and share repurchases – share issues)	K
Payment to net debtholders	L
Total financing flows	M

a. Supply the missing numbers using the accounting relations laid out in this chapter.

b. What were the total new operating accruals in the first half of 2012?

c. How much new net debt was issued during this period?

E8.8. Inferences Using Accounting Relations (Hard)

A firm with no financial assets or financial obligations generated free cash flow of $8.4 million in 2009. At the end of 2008 it had a market value of $224 million, or 1.6 times book value. At the end of 2009 it had a market value of $238 million, twice book value.

a. What was the rate of return from investing in the stock of this firm for 2009?

b. What were the earnings for this firm for 2009?

Applications

E8.9. Applying the Treasurer's Rule: Microsoft Corporation (Medium)

At the end of its June 30, 2008, fiscal year, Microsoft Corporation reported $23.7 billion in short-term interest-bearing investments and cash equivalents. The firm had no debt obligations. Subsequently, in September of that year, the firm announced a $40 billion stock repurchase and its intention to raise the annual dividend to 52 cents a share, from 44 cents, or to a total of $4.7 billion.

Cash flow from operations for fiscal year 2009 was projected to be $23.4 billion, up from $21.6 billion for 2008; interest receipts were expected to be $702 million; and the firm was expected to maintain cash investment at the 2008 level of $3.2 billion. Cash receipts from the issue of shares to employees were expected to be $2.5 billion. The firm's tax rate is 36 percent.

a. By applying the treasurer's rule, lay out the strategy for Microsoft's treasurer for managing cash flows.

b. Microsoft is actively looking for acquisitions to enhance its presence in the Web search and Web applications area. What would be the effect on the treasurer's plan if Microsoft decided to make a $4.2 billion cash acquisition?

c. For many years, Microsoft has carried no debt (obligations). At the time of the share repurchase announcement, Microsoft also said that it had received authorization from its board of directors for debt financing up to $6 billion. Why would the management seek such authorization at this stage?

Real World Connection

Exercises dealing with Microsoft are E1.6, E4.14, E6.12, E9.9, E11.11, E18.10, and E20.4. Also see Minicases M9.1 and M13.2.

E8.10.   Accounting Relations for Kimberly-Clark Corporation (Medium)

Below are summary numbers from reformulated balance sheets for 2007 and 2006 for Kimberly-Clark Corporation, the paper products company, along with numbers from the reformulated income statement for 2007 (in millions).

	2007	**2006**
Operating assets	$18,057.0	$16,796.2
Operating liabilities	6,011.8	5,927.2
Financial assets	382.7	270.8
Financial obligations	6,496.4	4,395.4
Operating income (after tax)	2,740.1	
Net financial expense (after tax)	147.1	

a. Calculate the following for 2007 and 2006:
   (i)   Net operating assets.
   (ii) Net financial obligations.
   (iii) Shareholders' equity.
b. Calculate free cash flow for 2007.
c. Show that the accounting relation for change in net operating assets (equation 8.5 in the chapter) works for Kimberly-Clark.
d. What was the net payment to shareholders (the net dividend) in 2007?

Real World Connection

Follow Kimberly-Clark through the continuing case at the end of each chapter. Also see Exercises E4.9, E7.16, E11.10, and E12.6, and Minicases M2.1 and M5.3.

Chapter **Nine**

The Analysis of the Statement of Shareholders' Equity

LINKS

Link to previous chapter

Chapter 8 laid out a design for financial statements that prepares them for analysis.

This chapter

This chapter reformulates the statement of owners' equity according to the design in Chapter 8. The reformulation highlights comprehensive income.

Link to next chapter

Chapter 10 continues the reformulation with the balance sheet and the income statement.

Link to Web page

For more applications of Chapter 9 content, visit the text's Web site at **www.mhhe.com/ penman5e**.

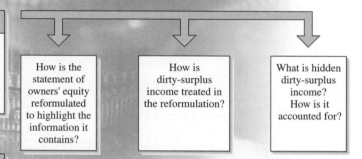

How is the statement of owners' equity reformulated to highlight the information it contains?

How is dirty-surplus income treated in the reformulation?

What is hidden dirty-surplus income? How is it accounted for?

The statement of shareholders' equity is usually not considered the most important part of the financial statements and is often ignored in analysis. However, it is the first statement that the analyst should examine before going on to the other statements. It is a summary statement, tying together all transactions that affect shareholders' equity. By analyzing the statement, the analyst ensures that all aspects of the business that affect shareholders' equity are included in his analysis to value the equity.

We saw in Part One of the book that when accounting income is used in valuation, it must be comprehensive income. Otherwise value is lost in the calculation. The accounting relations in the last chapter hold only if income is comprehensive. We will use these relations as analysis tools in later chapters, but the tools will work only if income is on a comprehensive basis. Unfortunately, earnings reported in most income statements in most countries is not comprehensive, including earnings reported in statements prepared under U.S. GAAP and international accounting standards. The analysis of the statement of shareholders' equity makes the correction.

Value is generated for equity holders through operations, not by equity financing activities. We saw in Chapter 3 that share issues and repurchases at market value do not create value in efficient capital markets. But share issues are sometimes made in exchange for goods and services in operations, mostly for employee compensation. Unfortunately, GAAP

The Analyst's Checklist

After reading this chapter you should understand:

- How statements of shareholders' equity are typically laid out.
- Why reformulation of the statement is necessary.
- What is reported in "other comprehensive income" and where it is reported.
- What "dirty-surplus" items appear in the statement of shareholders' equity.
- How stock options work to compensate employees.
- How stock options and other contingent equity claims result in a hidden expense.
- How management can create value (and losses) for shareholders with share transactions.
- How accounting hides losses from share transactions.

After reading this chapter you should be able to:

- Reformulate a statement of shareholders' equity.
- Distinguish the creation of value from the distribution of value in the equity statement.
- Calculate the net payout to shareholders.
- Calculate comprehensive income and comprehensive ROCE from the equity statement.
- Calculate payout and retention ratios.
- Calculate the expense from exercise of stock options.
- Calculate gains and losses from put options.
- Calculate losses from the conversion of securities into common stock.

and IFRS accounting confuses the financing and operating aspects of these transactions; that is, it confuses the moneys raised for financing with the expenses incurred in operations. The analysis of the statement of shareholders' equity sorts out this accounting.

REFORMULATING THE STATEMENT OF OWNERS' EQUITY

The statement of owners' equity provides the reconciliation of beginning and ending owners' equity according to the stocks and flows equation introduced in Chapter 2: The change in owners' equity is explained by comprehensive income for the period plus capital contributions from share issues, less dividends paid in cash and stock repurchases. The GAAP statement is often—and unnecessarily—more complicated than this, however, so part of the analysis involves simplifying it. The simplified statement for a fiscal period has the following form:

Reformulated Statement of Common Shareholders' Equity

Beginning book value of common equity

\+ Net effect of transactions with common shareholders
    + Capital contributions (share issues)
    − Share repurchases
    − Dividends
    = Net cash contribution (negative net dividends)

\+ Effect of operations and nonequity financing
    + Net income (from income statement)
    + Other comprehensive income
    − Preferred dividends
    = Comprehensive income available to common

Closing book value of common equity

Notice three things about this statement:

1. With a view to valuing the common shareholders' equity, the reformulated statement excludes preferred equity. From the common shareholders' point of view, the preferred equity is an obligation to pay other claimants before themselves, and it is treated as a liability. So the beginning and ending balances refer only to common shareholders' equity.

2. The net addition to common equity from transactions with shareholders—the negative net dividend—is separated from the addition to shareholders' equity that arises from business activities.

3. The total effect of operations and nonequity financing on the common shareholders is isolated in *comprehensive income*. This has three components: net income reported in the income statement, *other comprehensive income* reported outside the income statement, and preferred dividends. As preferred stock is effectively debt from the common shareholders' viewpoint, preferred dividends are an "expense" in calculating comprehensive income, just like interest expense.

Running with Nike

The analysis of financial statements in this and subsequent chapters will be demonstrated with the 2010 statements of Nike, Inc., that were presented in Exhibit 2.1 in Chapter 2. You will see a complete analysis of this firm as we proceed. The Build Your Own Analysis Product (BYOAP) feature on the book's Web site takes the Nike analysis back to earlier years. After covering the material in the book and in that Web module, you will have a complete analysis history for Nike for a 15-year period, 1996–2010. Take the Nike analysis in the book and in BYOAP as a model for the analysis of any firm, and use BYOAP to develop spreadsheets that deliver a concrete analysis and valuation product.

We emphasized in Chapter 1 that the first step in analysis and valuation is "knowing the business." Box 2.1 in Chapter 2 gives some background on the company; however, in practice a much deeper understanding of a firm is required to carry out a capable analysis. For a start, check the Business Section (Item 1) of the firm's 10-K report on EDGAR.

Reformulation Procedures

Exhibit 9.1 presents the GAAP statement of shareholders' equity for Nike, along with reformulated statements in the form of the template on the previous page.

Reformulation follows three steps.

1. Restate beginning and ending balances for the period for items that are not part of common shareholders' equity:
   a. *Preferred Stock.* Preferred stock is included in shareholders' equity in the GAAP statement, but it is a liability for the common shareholders. So reduce the balances by the amount of preferred stock in those balances (and ignore any preferred stock transactions during the period in the reformulation). An exception is mandatory **redeemable preferred stock** which, under GAAP, is not part of equity but rather is reported on the balance sheet in a "mezzanine" between liabilities and equity. Nike's preferred stock is redeemable (in the mezzanine in the balance sheet in Exhibit 2.1), so no adjustment is required.
   b. *Noncontrolling Interests.* Both GAAP and IFRS report noncontrolling interests (also called minority interests) within the equity statement. These minority interests in

EXHIBIT 9.1 **GAAP Statement and Reformulated Statement of Common Shareholders' Equity for Nike, Inc., May 31, 2010**

The reformulated statement separates transactions with shareholders from comprehensive income.

NIKE, INC.
GAAP Statement of Shareholders' Equity
(in millions, except per share data)

| | Common Stock | | | | Capital in Excess of Stated Value | Accumulated Other Comprehensive Income | Retained Earnings | Total |
| | Class A | | Class B | | | | | |
	Shares	Amount	Shares	Amount				
Balance at May 31, 2009	95.3	$0.1	390.2	$2.7	$2,871.4	$367.5	$5,451.4	$8,693.1
Stock options exercised			8.6		379.6			379.6
Conversion to Class B Common Stock	(5.3)		5.3					—
Repurchase of Class B Common Stock			(11.3)		(6.8)		(747.5)	(754.3)
Dividends on Common Stock ($1.06 per share)							(514.8)	(514.8)
Issuance of shares to employees			1.3		40.0			40.0
Stock-based compensation (Note 11):					159.0			159.0
Forfeiture of shares from employees			(0.1)		(2.6)		(0.3)	(2.9)
Comprehensive income (Note 14):								
Net income							1,906.7	1,906.7
Other comprehensive income:								
Foreign currency translation and other (net of tax benefit of $71.8)						(159.2)		(159.2)
Net gain on cash flow hedges (net of tax expense of $27.8)						87.1		87.1
Net gain on net investment hedges (net of tax expense of $21.2)						44.8		44.8
Reclassification to net income of previously deferred net gains related to hedge derivatives (net of tax expense of $41.7)						(121.6)		(121.6)
Reclassification of ineffective hedge gains to net income (net of tax expense of $1.4)						(3.8)		(3.8)
Total Comprehensive income						(152.7)	1,906.7	1,754.0
Balance at May 31, 2010	90.0	$0.1	394.0	$2.7	$3,440.6	$214.8	$6,095.5	$9,753.7

Note: Footnotes to the 10-K indicate Nike had $130.7 million in dividends payable at the end of 2010 and $121.4 million at the end of 2009.

Reformulated Statement of Common Equity		
Balance at May 31, 2009		$8,814.5
Transactions with shareholders		
Stock issued for stock options	379.6	
Stock issued to employees (net)	37.1	
Stock repurchased	(754.3)	
Cash dividends	(505.5)	(843.1)
Comprehensive income		
Net income reported	1,906.7	
Net translation gain (loss)	(159.2)	
Net hedging gains (loss)	6.5	1,754.0
Stock-based compensation		159.0
Balance at May 31, 2010		$9,884.4

Note: The beginning balance in the reformulated statement is calculated as follows:

Reported balance	$8,693.1
Dividends payable	121.4
	$8,814.5

The ending balance is calculated as follows:

Reported balance	$9,753.7
Dividends payable	130.7
	$9884.4

subsidies are clearly not common shareholder interests, so must be deducted from opening and closing balances.

   c. *Dividends Payable.* GAAP requires dividends payable to common shareholders to be reported as a liability. But shareholders cannot owe dividends to themselves. And dividends payable do not provide debt financing. Common dividends payable are part of the equity that the common shareholders have in the firm. So instead of reporting them as liabilities, reclassify them to the balances of shareholders' equity, as calculated in the notes to Nike's reformulated statement in Exhibit 9.1.

2. Calculate *net transactions with shareholders* (the *net dividend*). This calculation nets dividends and stock repurchases against cash from share issues, as in the exhibit. Dividends must be cash dividends (calculated as follows), and not dividends declared as dividends payable:

Cash dividends = Dividends reported – Change in dividends payable

With dividends payable of $121.4 million and $130.7 million at the end of 2009 and 2010, respectively, Nike's cash dividends paid are $514.8 – 130.7 + 121.4 = $505.5 million, which is the number for cash dividends in the cash flow statement.

3. Calculate *comprehensive income.* Comprehensive income combines net income and other income reported in the equity statement. Besides net income, the GAAP statement for Nike reports currency translation gains and losses and gains and losses on hedging instruments. You can see in the GAAP statement that a total is drawn for comprehensive income after these items. The income reported outside net income is referred to as *other comprehensive income,* so comprehensive income is net income plus other comprehensive income. Note that all items in other comprehensive income are after tax. That is, they are reported net of any tax that they draw.[1] Be careful to exclude any income that goes to the noncontrolling interests.

---

[1] Sometimes income is reported in the equity statement on lines outside of comprehensive income. An example is income from restatements of prior years' earnings. This should be included in comprehensive income.

You will notice that there is a line at the bottom of the reformulated statement—$159.0 million for stock-based compensation—that falls outside of both transactions with shareholders and comprehensive income. When firms issue stock options, GAAP and IFRS (correctly) require the value of the options to be booked as compensation, and this goes into the income statement as wages expense. But, oddly, shareholders' equity is credited for the same amount, effectively canceling the expense in the net income that has also been added to shareholders' equity. This is clearly wrong. It implies that incurring wages expense has no effect on shareholders' equity. Stock options are (contingent) liabilities for shareholders, not equity; shareholders will lose equity if the options are exercised with shares issued for less than market price. So increasing equity by $159 million is perverse. The accounting around stock options is a mess that we will clean up later in this chapter. For the moment, leave the $159 million for stock-based compensation stranded in the reformulated statement as a plug.

You will notice in this reformulation that we have not made any use of the distinction between stated value (or par value) of shares and additional (or excess) paid-in capital. This is of no importance for equity analysis; better to know the company's telephone number than the par value of its stock. Retained earnings is a mixture of accumulated earnings, dividends, share repurchases, and stock dividends already identified in the reformation, so does not bear on the analysis. Conversions of one class of common to another with zero effect do not change the book value of equity (as with Nike). Indeed, different classes of common stock can be ignored, provided they share in earnings equally. So can stock splits and stock dividends; splits change the number of shares but do not change a given shareholder's claim.

DIRTY-SURPLUS ACCOUNTING

Reporting income items as part of equity rather than in an income statement is known as *dirty-surplus accounting*. An equity statement that has no income other than net income from the income statement is a **clean-surplus accounting** statement. The terms are pejorative, and appropriately so. Under dirty-surplus accounting, the income in the income statement is not "clean," it is not complete. "Net" income or profit, as used under GAAP and international accounting standards, is really a misnomer.

Table 9.1 lists the **dirty-surplus items** you are likely to see in the United States. Income items are designated as part of operating income or financial income (expense) to categorize them in a reformulated income statement (later). Some of the items you will rarely see. The three most common are unrealized gains and losses on securities, foreign currency translation gains and losses, and unrealized gains and losses on certain derivatives.

1. *Unrealized gains and losses on securities available for sale.* FASB Statement No. 115 distinguishes three types of securities:

   - Trading securities
   - Securities available for sale
   - Securities held to maturity

   Trading securities are those held in a portfolio that is actively traded. These securities are marked to market value in the balance sheet and the unrealized gains and losses from changes in market value are reported in the income statement. Securities that are not actively traded but which might be sold before maturity are available for sale. These also are marked to "fair" market value but the unrealized gains and losses are

TABLE 9.1
Dirty-Surplus Accounting: U.S. GAAP
All dirty-surplus income items are reported net of tax.

Operating Income Items

Changes in accounting for contingencies (FASB Statement No. 11)
Additional minimum pension liability (FASB Statement No. 87)
Tax benefits of loss carryforwards acquired (FASB Statement No. 109)
Tax benefits of dividends paid to ESOPs (FASB Statement No. 109)
Unrealized gains and losses on equity securities available for sale
    (FASB Statement No. 115)
Foreign currency translation gains and losses (FASB Statement No. 52)
Gains and losses on derivative instruments designated as cash-flow hedges
    (FASB Statement No. 133)
Some adjustments of deferred tax valuation allowances (FASB Statement No. 109)
Change in funding status of pension plans (FASB Statement No. 158)
Restatements of prior years' income due to a change in accounting principles
    (FASB Statement No. 154)

Financing Income (or Expense) Items

Preferred dividends
Unrealized gains and losses on debt securities available for sale (FASB Statement No. 115)

---

reported as part of other comprehensive income. Securities that management intends to hold to maturity are recorded at cost on the balance sheet, so no unrealized gains and losses are reported. Realized gains and losses on all types of securities are reported in the income statement as part of net income. The rules apply to both debt securities and equity securities involving less than 20 percent ownership interest. Go to Accounting Clinic III.

2. *Foreign currency translation gains and losses.* The assets and liabilities of majority-owned foreign subsidiaries, measured in the foreign currency, must be consolidated into the statements of a U.S. parent in U.S. dollars. If the exchange rate changes over the reporting period, the value of the assets and liabilities changes in U.S. dollars. The resulting gain or loss is a translation gain or loss, to be distinguished from gains and losses on foreign currency transactions. Most transaction gains and losses are reported as part of net income. Translation gains and losses are part of other comprehensive income.

3. *Gains and losses on derivative instruments.* FASB Statement No. 133 requires most derivatives to be marked to fair value on the balance sheet, either as assets or liabilities. If the instrument hedges an existing asset or liability or a firm commitment by the company—a so-called *fair value hedge*—the gain or loss from marking the instrument to fair value is recorded as part of net income. (Under certain conditions, the gain or loss is offset in the income statement by the gain or loss on the hedged item.) If the instrument hedges the cash flow from an anticipated future transaction—a so-called *cash flow hedge*—the gain or loss is recorded to the equity statement, and then removed from the equity statement to net income on the expiration of the hedge when the hedged transaction affects earnings.[2]

---

[2] See M. A. Trombley, *Accounting for Derivatives and Hedging* (New York: McGraw-Hill/Irwin, 2003) for a primer on the accounting for derivatives. As these hedging gains and losses will be matched against realized gains and losses on the hedged items in subsequent income statements, they are more appropriately classified as deferred income or deferred charges in the liability and asset sections of the balance sheet. We leave them in the equity statement here to maintain the reported number for comprehensive income. But note that they represent income that is likely to be reversed in subsequent periods when the corresponding gains and losses on the hedged items are recognized on termination of the hedge.

Accounting Clinic   III

ACCOUNTING FOR MARKETABLE SECURITIES

Further detail on the accounting for securities is covered in Accounting Clinic III on the book's Web site. The clinic covers debt securities held by firms and equity securities representing less than 20 percent interest in other corporations. The accounting for equity investments with more than 20 percent interest is covered in Accounting Clinic V.

Comprehensive Income Reporting Under U.S. GAAP and IFRS

FASB Statement No. 130 requires comprehensive income to be identified in the financial statements. It distinguishes net income from *other comprehensive income* and permits the sum of the two, *comprehensive income,* to be reported in one of three ways:

1. Report comprehensive income in the statement of shareholders' equity by adding net income to other comprehensive income items reported in the equity statement.
2. Add other comprehensive income to net income in the income statement, and close the total comprehensive income to shareholders' equity.
3. Present a separate statement of other comprehensive income apart from the income statement, and close it to equity along with net income from the income statement.

Most firms follow the first approach, as with Nike. So you now observe dirty-surplus income items added together into a number called "other comprehensive income" and other comprehensive income and net income added to "total comprehensive income"—all within the equity statement. This presentation facilitates the task of identifying comprehensive income. However, it is not, in fact, comprehensive from the common shareholders' point of view. First, it omits preferred dividends, and, second, certain hidden items (which we will identify later in this chapter) are not included.

Other comprehensive income under IFRS consists of items similar to those in the United States, with the addition of actuarial gains and losses on pension assets and asset revaluation gains and losses. Under IAS 1 (Revised 2007) firms choose to report a single statement of comprehensive income or two statements, a statement of operations and a statement of comprehensive income. Comprehensive income cannot be displayed in the statement of changes in shareholders' equity (as is permitted under GAAP).

In June 2011 (at the time of writing of this edition of the book), the FASB decided to conform to the IFRS presentation, effective for U.S. GAAP for fiscal years ending after December 15, 2012. Nike must now choose to present the comprehensive income portion of its equity statement in Exhibit 9.1 as an add-on to its income statement or in a separate statement following the income statement. Under the first option, comprehensive income becomes the bottom line in the income statement, with this total closed to the equity statement. Under the second option, net income is the bottom line of the income statement (as at present) but also the top line of the separate comprehensive income statement which, with other comprehensive income added, totals to comprehensive income (which is then closed to the equity statement). However, our reformulated statement will be exactly the same. Examples of IFRS presentation and the new GAAP presentation are on the Web page for this chapter.

Note that GAAP and IFRS sometimes use different terminology. *Stocks* are *shares* under IFRS, *common stock* is *share capital,* and *additional paid-in capital* is called *share premium* (but the accounting for these items is identical).

RATIO ANALYSIS

What does the reformatted statement of changes in owners' equity reveal? It gives the growth in equity over a period. And it distinguishes clearly between the growth in equity from new investment or disinvestment by the owners and additions to equity from running the business. Accordingly, the reformulated statement distinguishes the creation of value from the distribution of value. Indeed, both return on common equity (ROCE) and growth in equity—the two drivers of residual earnings—can be identified in the statement. A set of ratios analyzes the statement to refine this information.

Payout and Retention Ratios

The disinvestment by shareholders is described by payout and retention ratios. The standard *dividend payout ratio* is the proportion of income paid out in cash dividends:

$$\text{Dividend payout} = \frac{\text{Dividends}}{\text{Comprehensive income}}$$

A calculation that you commonly see compares dividends to net income rather than comprehensive income. The dividend payout ratio involves payout in the form of dividends, but total **payout** is dividends plus share repurchases. Some firms pay no dividends but have regular stock repurchases. The *total payout ratio* is

$$\text{Total payout ratio} = \frac{\text{Dividends} + \text{Stock repurchases}}{\text{Comprehensive income}}$$

calculated with total dollar amounts rather than per-share amounts. The difference between this ratio and the dividend payout ratio gives the percentage of earnings paid out as stock repurchases.

Note that stock dividends and stock splits are not involved. These simply change the share units, with no effect on the claim of each shareholder. Some splits and stock dividends involve a reclassification from retained earnings to additional paid-in capital, but again this has no effect on the value of claims.

Although the dividend payout ratio suggests that dividends are paid out of earnings, they are really paid out of book value, out of assets. So a firm can pay a dividend even if it reports a loss. Payout, as a proportion of book value, is the rate of disinvestment by shareholders:

$$\text{Dividends-to-book value} = \frac{\text{Dividends}}{\text{Book value of CSE} + \text{Dividends}}$$

$$\text{Total payout-to-book value} = \frac{\text{Dividends} + \text{Stock repurchases}}{\text{Book value of CSE} + \text{Dividends} + \text{Stock repurchases}}$$

Usually ending book value of common shareholders' equity (CSE) is used in the denominator in these calculations (although, with dividends paid out over the year, average CSE is also appropriate).

Retention ratios focus on earnings retained rather than earnings paid out. The *standard retention ratio* involves only cash dividends (but can be modified to incorporate stock repurchases):

$$\text{Retention ratio} = \frac{\text{Comprehensive income} - \text{Dividends}}{\text{Comprehensive income}}$$

$$= 1 - \text{Dividend payout ratio}$$

Shareholder Profitability

The reformulated statement yields the comprehensive rate of return on common equity, ROCE, the profitability of the owners' investment for the period. ROCE is also the growth rate in equity from business activities. For Nike, the 2010 ROCE (using average equity for the year) is

$$\text{ROCE}_t = \frac{\text{Comprehensive income}}{\tfrac{1}{2}\,(\text{CSE}_t + \text{CSE}_{t-1})}$$

$$= \frac{1,754.0}{\tfrac{1}{2}\,(8,814.5 + 9,884.4)} = 18.8\%$$

The ROCE calculated on beginning common equity is 19.9 percent.

Note that the income statement and balance sheet are not needed to calculate ROCE; rather, they provide the detail to analyze ROCE.

Growth Ratios

The growth in shareholders' equity is simply the change from beginning to ending balances. *Growth ratios* explain this growth as a rate of growth.

The part of the growth rate resulting from transactions with shareholders is the net investment rate:

$$\text{Net investment rate} = \frac{\text{Net transactions with shareholders}}{\text{Beginning book value of CSE}}$$

Nike's net investment rate was a negative 9.6 percent because net cash was paid out; shareholders disinvested. The part of the growth rate that comes from business activities is given by the ROCE on beginning equity, 19.9 percent for Nike. The rate of growth of owners' equity from both sources—new shareholder financing and business activities—is the growth rate in common stockholders' equity:

$$\text{Growth rate of CSE} = \frac{\text{Change in CSE}}{\text{Beginning CSE}}$$

$$= \frac{\text{Comprehensive income} + \text{Net transactions with shareholders}}{\text{Beginning CSE}}$$

Nike's 2008 growth rate was 10.3 percent.

If ROCE is calculated with beginning CSE in the denominator, then

$$\text{Growth rate of CSE} = \text{ROCE} + \text{Net investment rate}$$

For Nike, the growth rate in common equity is 19.9 percent − 9.6 percent = 10.3 percent.

HIDDEN DIRTY SURPLUS

The distinction between comprehensive income and transactions with shareholders in the reformulated statement of owners' equity separates the creation of value from the raising of funds and the distribution of value to shareholders. The premise is that transactions with shareholders do not create value. This is so when share transactions are at market value, but when shares are issued at less than market value, shareholders lose. We have a problem: these losses do not appear in GAAP or IFRS financial statements.

Issue of Shares in Operations

When firms grant shares to employees at less than market price, the difference between market price and issue price is treated under GAAP and IFRS as (deferred) compensation to employees and ultimately amortized as an expense to the income statement. This is appropriate accounting, for the discount from market value is compensation to employees and a loss of shareholder value. More frequently, though, shares are not granted to employees. Rather, *stock options* are granted and shares are issued later when the options are exercised. Unfortunately, GAAP and IFRS accounting do a poor job of reporting the effects of stock options on shareholder value.

Four events are involved in a stock option award: the grant of the option, the vesting of the option, the exercise of the option, and the lapse of the option. At the grant date, employees are awarded the right to exercise at an exercise price; the vesting date is the first date at which they can exercise the option; the exercise date is the date on which they actually exercise at the exercise price; and the lapse date is the date on which the option lapses should the employee choose not to exercise. Clearly the employee exercises if the stock is "in the money" at exercise date, that is, if the market price is greater than the exercise price.

If the **call option** is granted in the money at grant date (with the exercise price set at less than the market price at grant date), accounting treats the difference between the market price and exercise price as compensation. That compensation is then recognized in the income statement over the vesting period, as in the case of a stock grant at less than market price. However, most options are granted "at the money," with exercise price equal to the market price at grant date. As time elapses and the market price of the stock moves "into the money," no additional compensation expense is recorded. Further, when options are indeed exercised, no compensation expense is recorded. You see on the first line in Nike's statement of equity that the amount received on exercise is recorded as issued shares, but, unlike the stock grants, the expense—the difference between the market price and the issue price—is not recorded.

The appropriate accounting is to record the issue of shares at market price and recognize the difference between the market price and issue price as an expense. In the absence of this accounting there is a **hidden dirty-surplus expense.** The expense is not merely recorded in equity rather than the income statement; it is not recorded at all. But there has been a distribution of wealth to employees and that distribution has come at the expense of the shareholders: The value of their shares must drop to reflect the **dilution** of their equity. GAAP accounting treats this transaction, which is both a financing transaction—raising cash—and an operational transaction—paying employees—as if it is just a financing transaction. This hidden dirty-surplus accounting creates a hidden expense. Box 9.1 calculates Nike's loss from the exercise of stock options during 2010.

Some commentators argue that, because options are granted at the money, there is no expense. Employees—and particularly management, who benefit most—say this adamantly.

Stock option loss is the difference between the exercise price and the market price of the shares at the date of exercise. This is the amount that shareholders lose by not issuing the shares at market price. The amount can be calculated in two ways.

METHOD 1

If options are **nonqualifying options,** the firm receives a tax deduction for the difference between market price and exercise price (and the employee is taxed on that difference). As firms report the **tax benefit** from the exercise of options in the cash flow statement the amount of the tax deduction—the stock option loss—can be imputed using the firm's tax rate. Nike's tax rate, gleaned from the tax footnote to the financial statements, is 36.3 percent. So, from the tax benefit of $58.5 million reported in the cash flow statement (in Exhibit 2.1 in Chapter 2), the loss is $58.5/0.363 = 161.1 million. As the expense is a tax deduction, the after-tax option loss is calculated as follows (in millions):

Stock option loss	$58.5/0.363	$161.1
Tax benefit at 36.3%		(58.5)
Stock option loss, after tax		$102.6

METHOD 2

If there is no reported tax benefit to work from, the calculation must estimate the market price at exercise date. Nike's average stock price during 2010 was $64. With 8.6 million options exercised, the calculation is as follows:

Estimate market value of shares issued 8.6 × $64		$550.4
Exercise (issue) price, from equity statement (less tax benefit of $58.5)		321.1
Stock option loss, before tax		229.3
Tax benefit at 36.3%		83.2
Stock option loss, after tax		$146.1

This calculation is tentative. If employees exercised below the $64 price, the expense would be lower (and some tax allocations are ignored here). Indeed, the Method 2 number is higher than the Method 1 number.

Method 2 must be used for **incentive options,** where the firm does not receive a tax benefit (nor is the employee taxed until the shares are sold).

But there is no expense only if the options fail to move into the money. They also say that, as the exercise of options does not involve a cash payment by the firm, there is no expense. However, paying employees with stock options that are exercised substitutes for paying them with cash, and recording the expense is recording the cash-equivalent compensation: The firm is effectively issuing stock to employees at market price and giving them a cash amount equivalent to the difference between market and exercise prices to help pay for the stock. From a shareholder's point of view, it makes no difference whether employees are paid with cash or with the value of the shares that shareholders have to give up; the shareholders are simply paying employees with their own paper rather than with cash. Recognizing this expense is at the heart of accrual accounting for shareholder value, for accrual accounting looks past cash flows to value flows; it sees an award of valuable stock for wages as no different from cash wages. If you are hesitant in viewing stock compensation as an expense, think of the case where a firm pays for all its operations—its materials, its advertising, its equipment—with stock options. (Indeed some sports stars have asked to be paid with stock options for promotions!) If the hidden expenses were not recognized, the income statement would have only revenues on it and no expenses. Stock options produce revenues and profits for shareholders if they provide an incentive for employees and management. But GAAP accounting does not match the cost of the options against these revenues and profits. Value added must be matched with value lost.

With the large growth in stock compensation in the 1990s, the hidden expense became quite significant, particularly in the high-tech sector. The Financial Accounting Standards Board addressed the issue, but in writing Statement No. 123R came to an unsatisfactory conclusion. This statement requires compensation to be recognized at grant date at an amount equal to the value of the option, priced using option-pricing formulas. The compensation

Accounting Clinic

ACCOUNTING FOR STOCK COMPENSATION

GAAP accounting for stock options in the United States employs *grant-date accounting*. The International Accounting Standards Board (IASB) also requires grant date accounting under IFRS 2. Accounting Clinic IV leads you through grant-date accounting.

Accounting Clinic IV also lays out *exercise date accounting* and takes you through the complete accounting that measures the effects of stock options on shareholders. Unearned compensation costs are recorded at grant date, and then recognized as expense in the income statement over the period when employee services are given. Accordingly, the compensation cost is matched against the revenues that the employees produce. Subsequent to grant date, further losses are recognized as options go into the money. Here are the steps to effect sound accrual accounting for stock options:

1. Recognize the option value at grant date as a contingent liability, along with a deferred (unearned) compensation asset. The two items can be netted on the balance sheet. The option value at grant date is the amount recognized with grant-date accounting under FASB Statement No. 123R. The grant-date value given to employees is compensation, but it is contingent upon the options going into the money, so it is a contingent liability to issue shares. The deferred compensation asset is similar to that which arises from stock issues to employees at less than market value.

2. Amortize the deferred compensation over an employee service period, usually the vesting period.

3. Mark the contingent liability to market as options go into the money to capture the value of the option overhang, and recognize a corresponding unrealized loss from stock options.

4. Extinguish the liability against the share issue (at market value) at exercise date. If options are not exercised, extinguish the liability and recognize a windfall gain from stock options.

For more on appropriate exercise date accounting, go also to the Web page for this chapter.

is then recognized in the income statement over a service period, usually the vesting period.[3] The credit goes to shareholders' equity, incorrectly as we have seen with Nike. The international accounting standard on the issue, IFRS 2, requires similar treatment. This treatment is called *grant date accounting.* But the granting of options yields an expense only in recognition of possible exercise. If the option lapses (because the stock does not go into the money), no expense is incurred, but the accounting maintains the expense. An expense is realized only if the option is exercised. The difference between the market price and exercise price at exercise date is the loss to shareholders. Recognizing this expense, as in Box 9.1, is called *exercise date accounting.* In 2010, Nike reported $159 million in before-tax stock option expense using grant date accounting. Box 9.1 calculates an expense of $161.1 million, before tax, from the exercise of options during 2010. Now go to Accounting Clinic IV.

Significantly, the Internal Revenue Service recognizes that an expense is incurred when options are exercised and gives the firm a tax deduction for it (if certain conditions are met). The firm books this tax benefit to equity, often as an addition to the proceeds from the share issue. So the $379.6 million that Nike received from the exercise of stock options (in Exhibit 9.1) represents $321.1 million received from the share issue plus $58.5 million in tax benefits. So, the accounting recognizes the tax benefit of the expense, increasing equity, but not the associated expense!

Exhibit 9.2 presents a reformulated statement of shareholders' equity for Nike that reports the loss from the exercise of stock options as part of comprehensive income. As GAAP records an expense based on grant date accounting, we have to be careful not to double count. So you see in the reformulated statement that the after-tax loss on exercise of stock options, $102.6 million, has been reduced by the $159 million that has

---

[3] Taxes are allocated for the expense, so income is reduced by the after-tax amount.

EXHIBIT 9.2
Reformulated
Statement of
Common Equity
for Nike, Inc., with
Recognition of Losses
from the Exercise
of Stock Options
(in millions of dollars)

Balance at May 31, 2009			$8,814.5
Transactions with shareholders			
Stock issues for stock options	(321.1 + 161.1)	482.2	
Stock issued to employees (net)		37.1	
Stock repurchased		(754.3)	
Cash dividends		(505.5)	(740.50)
Comprehensive income			
Net income reported		1,906.7	
Net translation gains and losses		(159.2)	
Net hedging gains and losses		6.5	
Loss on the exercise of stock			
options (after-tax)	102.6		
less stock compensation recorded	159.0	56.4	1,810.4
Balance at May 31, 2010			$9,884.4

been recognized under grant-date accounting. That, of course, gets rid of the $159 million embarrassing "plug" in the reformulated statement in Exhibit 9.1. The difference between market price and exercise price, $161.1 million has been added to share issues to report them as if they were issued at market value (and thus add no value). Now the reformulated statement records transactions with shareholders at market value with any loss from issuing shares at less than market value appropriately recognized in comprehensive income. It's all a bit messy to handle, but that's what poor GAAP accounting leaves us with. The difference between the grant date and exercise date expenses can be quite large if options go well into the money after grant date.[4]

The loss from exercise of options in the current period is a legitimate loss that should be reported. But when an investor buys a stock, he is concerned about how he could lose from these instruments in the future. Accordingly, valuation focuses on the expected losses from future exercise of options. This expected loss is referred to as the **option overhang.** It can be estimated as the loss incurred if outstanding options were exercised at the current market price. At the end of 2010, Nike had 36.0 million options outstanding with a weighted-average exercise price of $46.60. The closing market price for its shares at fiscal year end was $72.38. So the option overhang is estimated as follows (in millions):

Market price of shares to be issued for options	36.0 × $72.38 = $2,606
Exercise price	36.0 × $46.60 = 1,678
	928
Tax benefit (at 36.3%)	337
Contingent liability (option overhang)	591

This drag on the value of the shares amounts to $1.22 per share (with 484 million shares outstanding). Note that the liability for the expected loss is reduced by the expected tax benefit on exercise. The measure of the option overhang here is a floor valuation; it should also include option value for the possibility it might increase. We return to the complete treatment in Chapter 14 when we formally build contingent claims into equity valuation.

Firms use options and warrants for other operating expenses beside wages. See Box 9.2.

---

[4] Subtracting the $159 million recognized as "stock-based compensation" in the equity statement is indeed quite a messy solution. That number is really a contingent liability, and should be so classified (see Accounting Clinic IV). But reversing out the GAAP accounting to recognize the liability and its termination at exercise is almost impossible.

In 2001, Reebok, Nike's rival, entered into a 10-year license agreement with the National Football League (NFL) giving the company exclusive rights to design, develop, and sell NFL footwear, apparel, and accessories in exchange for stock **warrants** valued at $13.6 million. These warrants gave the NFL the right to purchase up to 1.6 million shares of Reebok's common stock at various exercise prices, with an expiration date of 2012.

Reebok recorded an intangible asset ("licenses" below) and then amortized this asset over 10 years. So its intangible asset footnote for 2003 reported the following (in thousands):

Amortizable intangible assets:	
Licenses	$13,600
Other intangible assets	4,492
	$18,092
Less accumulated amortization	3,656
	$14,436
Nonamortizable intangible assets:	
Company tradenames and trademarks	27,860
	$42,296

You see that Reebok recognized the license asset and is amortizing the license cost along with other amortizable intangible assets. So the license expense is being matched against revenue from NFL branded products in the income statement over the term of the license. This is appropriate accounting.

However, the issue of the warrants was recorded as a share issue in the equity statement in 2001, as required by GAAP.

But the GAAP accounting is inappropriate. The issue of a warrant—like the issue of a stock option—is not an issue of equity but, rather, an obligation for the shareholders to surrender value in the future should the warrants be exercised. From the shareholders' point of view a warrant is a (contingent) liability, and appropriate accounting for shareholder value requires it to be recognized as such. Further, if and when the warrants are exercised, the difference between the exercise price and the market price of the stock at the time, over and above the $13.6 million already recognized, is a further loss to shareholders.

The diligent equity analyst recognizes that GAAP fails to track the effects of this transaction on shareholder value. Many of the warrants have an exercise price of $27.06 per share. At the end of 2004, Reebok's shares traded at $44.00, so the warrants were well in the money and likely to be exercised. The analyst anticipates that there will be a loss of shareholder value when this happens and builds this into her valuation. This is the warrant overhang. For now, note that a rough calculation of the warrant overhang (at the end of 2004) is the amount of value that the shareholders would have to give up if the warrants were exercised at the end of 2004: The difference between the market price of the share and the exercise price at the end of 2004 is $44.00 − $27.06 = $16.94 per warrant. Chapter 14 modifies this calculation to recognize that the warrants cannot be exercised in 2004, but rather in 2012, so option value must be added to this rough calculation.

Issue of Shares in Financing Activities

Hidden losses occur not only with employee stock options but with the exercise of all **contingent equity claims.** Call and put options on the firm's own stock, warrants, rights, convertible bonds, and convertible preferred shares are all contingent equity claims that, if exercised, require the issue (or repurchase) of shares at a price that is different from market value. Look at Box 9.3.

Box 9.4 covers the accounting for convertible bonds and convertible preferred stock and shows how GAAP and IFRS accounting do not recognize the full cost of financing with these instruments. The accounting is not comprehensive, even though a nominal number, comprehensive income, is reported.

Handling Diluted Earnings per Share

Firms report two earnings-per-share numbers, basic EPS and diluted EPS. Basic EPS is simply earnings available to common (after preferred dividends) divided by the number of outstanding shares. Diluted EPS is an "as if" number that estimates what earnings per share would be if holders of contingent equity claims like stock options, warrants, convertible

In Dell's statement of shareholders' equity for the fiscal year ending February 1, 2002, the following line item appeared (in millions):

	Shares	Amount
Repurchase of common shares	68	$3,000

This line suggests a routine stock repurchase. But further investigation reveals otherwise. Dividing the $3 billion paid out by the 68 million shares purchased, the average per-share purchase price is $44.12. But Dell's shares did not trade above $30 during the year, and the average price was $24. Footnotes reveal that Dell was forced to repurchase shares at the strike price of $44 on **put options** written to investors. In previous years, Dell had gained from these options as the stock price continued to rise during the bubble. But with the share price falling (from a high of $58 in 2000) as the stock market bubble burst, Dell was caught as these options went under water. Using the average price of $24 for 2002 as the market price when the shares were repurchased, the loss from the exercise of put options is as follows:

Market price for shares repurchased $24 × 68 million	$1,632 million
Amount paid for shares repurchased	(3,000)
Loss on exercise of put options	$1,368 million

(The loss is not tax deductible.) This loss should be reported as part of comprehensive income, but it was not. On the 2,670 million shares outstanding before the repurchase, the loss is $0.51 per share, a significant amount compared to Dell's reported EPS of $0.48. Dell effectively ran two types of businesses, a computer business earning $0.48 per share in 2002 and a business of betting on its own stock, earning a loss of $0.51 per share.

The omission of this loss is a concern to the investor, and the investor must be vigilant. Shareholders lose when share prices fall, of course, but when the firm has written put options, the shareholder suffers twice; the loss from the price decline is levered. In 2002, Electronic Data Systems Corporation (EDS) announced that the firm had some accounting problems and that contract revenue would not be as previously expected. The stock price dropped 70 percent on the bad news. Later, the firm indicated that the drop in price would trigger the exercise of put options. The price dropped further.

Put options are sometimes referred to as **put warrants.** Firms make similar commitments to buy back stock through **forward share purchase agreements.** They disclose the existence of put options and share purchase agreements in footnotes. In buying a stock of Dell in 2002, one must be aware of the put option overhang, for it might require further repurchases that lose value for shareholders. At the end of fiscal 2002, Dell had a further put option overhang for 51 million shares to be repurchased at $45 per share. In September 2002, when the shares were trading at $25, the options were in the money by $20 per share, a total of $1.020 billion, projecting a loss of $0.39 per outstanding share. Analysts were forecasting $0.80 EPS for fiscal 2003, but that is GAAP earnings. Expected comprehensive earnings was $0.39 less, or $0.41 per share.

FASB STATEMENT NO. 150

In 2003, the FASB issued Statement 150 to reform the accounting for these put obligations. Firms are now required to recognize a liability, measured at fair value, when the contract is written. Subsequently, as the stock price changes, this liability is measured at the amount of cash that would be required to settle the obligation at the reporting date. This, of course, is the difference between the exercise price and market price at reporting date. The revaluation of the liability is booked to the income statement as interest cost. So, the rule sees a put option contract (appropriately) as a borrowing: The firm borrows the amount that the contract is worth and then repays the "loan" in cash or shares. The amount lost on the contract is the interest cost on the loan. The accounting under Statement 150 effectively puts the liability for the option overhang on the balance sheet and records losses, as interest, as the option moves into the money (and so the shareholders must give up more value). If the option does not go into the money, a gain is recognized.

Accordingly, Statement 150 brings the hidden expense into the income statement and also puts a hidden (off-balance-sheet) liability on the balance sheet. Note, however, that GAAP does not apply the same treatment to call options, (call) warrants, and other convertible securities. See Box 9.2.

debt, and convertible preferred shares were to exercise their option to convert those claims to common shares; rather than shares outstanding, the denominator is shares outstanding plus shares that would be outstanding should conversion take place. (Accounting Clinic IV gives more detail.)

Convertible securities are securities, such as bonds and preferred stock, that can be converted into common shares if conditions are met. Textbooks propose two methods to record the conversion of a convertible bond or a convertible preferred stock into common shares:

1. The *book value method* records the share issue at the book value of the bond or preferred stock. Common equity is increased and debt or preferred stock is reduced by the same amount, so no gain or loss is recorded.

2. The *market value method* records the share issue at the market value of the shares issued in the conversion. The difference between this market value and the book value of the security converted is recorded as a loss on conversion.

The book value method is almost exclusively used in practice. It involves a hidden dirty-surplus loss. The market value method reports the loss. It accords the treatment of convertible securities the same treatment as nonconvertible securities. On redemption of nonconvertible securities before maturity, a loss (or gain) is recognized. The only difference with convertible securities is that shares rather than cash are used to retire them. In both cases there is a loss to the existing shareholders.

Convertible bonds carry a lower interest rate than nonconvertible bonds because of the conversion option. GAAP accounting records only this interest expense as the financing cost, so it looks as if the financing is cheaper. But the full financing cost to shareholders includes any loss on conversion of the bonds into common shares—and this loss is not recorded.

In the 1990s, financing with convertible preferred stock became common. Only the dividends on the preferred stock were recorded as the financing cost, not the loss on conversion. Suppose a convertible preferred stock issue had no dividend rights but, to compensate, set a favorable conversion price to the buyer of the issue. Under GAAP accounting it would appear that this financing had no cost.

In September 2008, in the midst of the credit crisis on Wall Street, Goldman Sachs invited Warren Buffett, the legendary fundamental investor, to contribute much-needed equity capital to the firm. Buffett seemingly got a very good deal. For a $5 billion cash infusion, he received perpetual preferred equity shares carrying a 10 percent dividend (redeemable by Goldman Sachs) plus warrants to buy 43.5 million common shares at $115 per share (for a total of another $5 billion). The $115 conversion price was set at the current share price, a three-year low for Goldman. The stock price rose to $135 within three days, putting Mr. Buffett's warrants well into the money.

It remains to be seen at what price Mr. Buffett exercises. But any difference between the exercise price and the market price at that point will be a loss for shareholders. GAAP accounting will not, however, record that loss. At a stock price of $135 per share, the prospective loss—the warrant overhang—was $20 per share, or a total of $870 million for the 43.5 million shares.

Handle the diluted EPS number with care. While diluted EPS gives an indication of likely dilution to the common shareholders, it is not a number to be used in valuing the common shareholders' equity. It comingles the current shareholders' claim on earnings with those of possible future shareholders. The claims of current and future shareholders are quite different. Both will share in future earnings should options be exercised, but only current shareholders share in current earnings. Further, they share future earnings differently. When claims are converted to common equity, the loss will fall on current shareholders, while the new shareholders will gain as current shareholders effectively sell the firm to new shareholders at less than market price. The two earnings claims must be differentiated and the diluted EPS does not do this. With a focus on valuing the current outstanding shares, one must focus on basic EPS, adjusted of course for the failure of the accounting to record losses (to current shareholders) when claims are converted to common equity.

Share Transactions in Inefficient Markets

The maxim that share issues and repurchases at market value do not create value recognizes that in efficient stock markets, value received equals value surrendered; both sides of the transaction get what they paid for. In a share repurchase, for example, the firm gives up, and the seller receives, cash equal to the value of the stock.

But we recognized in Chapter 3 that if stock markets are inefficient, a firm can buy back shares at less than they are worth and issue shares at more than they are worth. The other side of the transaction—the shareholder who sells the shares or the new shareholder who

Dell, Inc., explains its put option transactions (examined in Box 9.3) as "part of a share-repurchase program to manage the dilution resulting from shares issued under employee stock plans." It is common for firms to explain share repurchases in this way. The exercise of stock options increases shares outstanding and, as we have seen, dilutes existing shareholders' value. Buying back shares reduces shares outstanding. But does it reverse the dilution?

The answer is no. If shares are purchased at fair value, there is no change in the per-share value of the equity; the shareholder does not get extra value to compensate for the loss of value from stock options. Maintaining constant shares outstanding with share repurchases only gives the appearance of reversing the dilution.

During the stock market bubble in the 1990s, employees exercised options against the shareholders as prices soared. Firms then repurchased shares "to manage dilution." But purchasing shares at bubble prices (above intrinsic value) destroys value for shareholders. Shareholders lost twice, once with the employee options, and again with the repurchases. As some firms borrowed to finance the share repurchases, they were left with large debts that led to significant credit problems as the bubble burst.

buys—loses value. But the existing shareholders who do not participate in the transaction gain. These gains (or losses if shareholders lose in the transaction) are not revealed in the accounts.

Even if stock markets are efficient with respect to publicly available information, a firm's management might have private information about the value of their firm's shares and issue or repurchase shares at prices that are different from those that will prevail when the information is subsequently made public. Such transactions also generate value for existing shareholders. (In the United States there are legal constraints on this practice, however.)

The active investor who conjectures that the market may be inefficient at times is wary of share transactions with firms. As with all his trading in the stock market, he tests the market price against an estimate of intrinsic value. But he is particularly careful in this case because the firm's management may have a better feel for intrinsic value than he.

The active investor who understands the intrinsic value of a stock understands when it might be overvalued or undervalued. And he understands that management might use the mispricing to their advantage. The management might, for example, use overvalued shares to make acquisitions, to acquire other firms cheaply. Indeed this is a reason why an investor might buy overvalued shares: He sees that value can be generated by using the shares as currency in an acquisition. But this is a tricky business: If investors force up the prices of shares that are already overpriced, a price bubble can result. The fundamental investor bases his actions on a good understanding of the firm's acquisition possibilities and its acquisition strategy.

As for the management, they can take advantage of share mispricings to create value for shareholders with share transactions. They can choose to finance new operations with debt rather than equity if they feel the stock price is "too low." But they also can choose to exercise their stock options when the price is high—a double whammy for shareholders. They might also have misguided ideas about stock issues and repurchases. See Box 9.5.

THE EYE OF THE SHAREHOLDER

We have characterized the financial statements as a lens on the business. For equity analysis, the lens must be focused to the eye of the shareholder. GAAP and IFRS accounting is inadequate for equity analysis because it does not have its eye on the shareholder. It does not account faithfully for the welfare of the shareholder, and nowhere else is this more apparent than with the accounting in the statement of shareholders' equity.

GAAP and IFRS comingle preferred equity and noncontrolling interests with common equity in the equity statement. GAAP and IFRS fail to see a sale of shares at less than market value as a loss for shareholders. If the shareholders did so on their own account, they surely would make a loss. When the firm forces it on them, they also make a loss. The accounting fails to understand the distinction between cash transactions with shareholders (to raise cash and to pass out unneeded cash as a matter of financing) and value added (or lost) from operations that can be embedded in a share issue. It also fails to see that transactions between claimants—convertible bondholders and common shareholders, for example—can involve losses for the common shareholders.

In short, GAAP and IFRS accounting does not honor the property rights of the common shareholder. This is so despite the fact that financial reports are prepared nominally for the shareholder, company directors (including the audit committee) have a fiduciary duty to the shareholders, and management and auditors formally present the financial reports to shareholders at the annual meeting. The accounting does not honor the shareholders as the owners of the firm. Consequently, the equity analyst must repair the accounting, as we have done in this chapter and will continue to do as we move to valuation in later chapters.

BUILD YOUR OWN ANALYSIS ENGINE

As a first step in building a complete analysis and valuation spreadsheet, download an equity statement for a firm and reformat it in the form of this chapter. You can download the statement from the 10-K report on the SEC EDGAR Web site or from the firm's own Web site. Financial statements are usually under the Investor Relations tag on firms' Web sites and are often available in downloadable form. There is no program that will allow you to automatically reformat the statement; this has to be done manually.

For learning purposes, you might first use the current year for Nike with the examples in this chapter as a guide. You might also work with Kimberly-Clark in the Continuing Case where the solution is given on the book's Web site. Of course, you can also go to the Statement of Shareholders' Equity page for the analysis and valuation product, BYOAP, on the book's Web site that covers Nike. Although you can appropriate the template there, you will learn more by building a product yourself.

You might reformulate the equity statement in the form of Exhibit 9.1. This works as an approximation if the firm has few stock options or other contingent equity claims. Otherwise, apply the form in Exhibit 9.2. Box 9.1 will guide you in calculating the loss from the exercise of stock options, and the stock compensation footnote to the financial statements will provide more information. Check the equity footnote to see if there are other contingent claims involved.

ACCOUNTING QUALITY WATCH

As we proceed with the financial statement analysis in Part Two of the book, we will address accounting issues as they arise. The text will provide an outline of how the relevant accounting works—as we did for marketable securities and employee stock options in this chapter—and refer you to Accounting Clinics on the book's Web site for further elaboration—as we did with Accounting Clinics III and IV on marketable securities and stock compensation in this chapter.

This chapter has identified quality lapses in GAAP and IFRS accounting. With an eye on the shareholder, the analyst needs to maintain a watch on the following. The issues arise both in GAAP and IFRS accounting.

Accounting Item	Quality Problem
Dividends payable	GAAP treats dividends payable as a liability. Rather, it is part of shareholders' equity. Shareholders have a claim to these dividends that have been declared but not paid. They do not owe them to others.
Unrealized gains and losses on securities	Unrealized gains and losses on available-for-sale debt and equity securities are reported as part of other comprehensive income in the equity statement rather than in the income statement. Thus, the full performance of an investment portfolio is not reported in the income statement. Worse, as firms report realized gains and losses in the income statement, they can "cherry pick" gains into the income statement (and earnings per share) by selling securities that have appreciated in value while holding those on which they have experienced losses and reporting those unrealized losses in the equity statement.
Translation gains and losses	A gain or loss results from holding assets and liabilities in foreign currencies when exchange rate change is not recognized in the income statement. (The effect is booked to equity in the equity statement, bypassing the income statement.)
Preferred dividends	Preferred dividends are treated as a distribution of equity rather than a cost to (common) shareholders.
Stock compensation credits to equity	GAAP recognizes deferred compensation from grant of stock options as a credit to equity, as if shareholders' equity increases by compensating employees. This is a liability—to give up value on the exercise of options—not an increase in equity.
Grant-date stock option accounting	GAAP recognizes stock option compensation at option grant date. However, the expense (to the shareholder) is incurred at exercise date as shares are issued for less than market price. If granted options are not exercised, GAAP overstates wages' expense. If options are exercised, GAAP typically understates wages' expense.
Accounting for warrants and options	GAAP does not report the loss to shareholders when warrants and (call and put) options on the firm's stock are exercised and shares are issued or repurchased at prices differing from market price.
Accounting for convertible bonds and preferred stock	GAAP converts these claims to equity at their book value. Thus, no loss is recognized on the conversion.
Omitted borrowing costs	As losses are not recognized on conversion of nonequity financing instruments (like convertible bonds) into equity, borrowing costs are understated.
Omitted (off-balance-sheet) liabilities	Outstanding obligations to issue shares at less then market price are not recognized on the balance sheet. These include the option overhang from outstanding stock options.

One needs to understand how the accounting works, but one also needs to understand when the accounting does not work for the equity analyst. When do accounting quality issues frustrate the analyst? Some of these quality issues arise just because of practical difficulties in accounting measurement. Others arise because the accounting standard setters do not get it right, as we have seen in this chapter. And yet others arise because firms use the license available within GAAP to manipulate the accounting.

Box 9.6 starts our Accounting Quality Watch. It lists the accounting quality issues we have encountered in this chapter. We will add to this list as we proceed so that, when we go specifically into the analysis of accounting quality in Chapter 18, we will have considerable background.

The Web Connection

Find the following on the Web page for this chapter:

- Accounting for the equity statement and comprehensive income under IFRS.
- Display of the new GAAP presentation of comprehensive income that will be required from 2012 onward.
- Further examples of reformulated statements of shareholders' equity.
- Further discussion of hidden expenses.

- More coverage of footnotes that pertain to the equity statement.
- More on GAAP and IFRS accounting for convertible securities.
- More discussion on the appropriate accounting for contingent claims on equity.
- A discussion of accelerated stock repurchase programs (that also involve dirty-surplus accounting).
- The Readers' Corner explores the issues raised in this chapter.

Summary

Misclassifications in the financial statements can lead to erroneous analysis of the financial statements and to erroneous valuations. Reformatting the statements classifies items correctly. The GAAP statement of equity sometimes comingles the results of operations with the financing of the operations. This chapter reformulates the statement to distinguish the creation of value in a firm from the distribution of value to shareholders in net dividends. The reformulation identifies dirty-surplus items in the statement and yields comprehensive income and comprehensive ROCE.

Omission in the financial statements is more pernicious than misclassification, and the chapter sensitizes the analyst to expenses that can arise from exercise of contingent claims but which are hidden by GAAP and IFRS accounting. Failure to recognize these expenses in forecasting can lead to overvaluation of firms.

As always, a sense of perspective must be maintained in analyzing the statement of equity. For some firms with few dirty-surplus items and no stock compensation, there is little to be discovered. For many firms there are just two items—translation gains and losses and unrealized gains and losses on securities—that appear outside the income statement. And for many firms, the amounts of these items are small. In the United States, one can sometimes glance at the statement and dismiss the items as immaterial. In other countries, the practice of dirty-surplus accounting is quite extensive. In the United States, the use of stock options in compensation is widespread.

Key Concepts

call option is a claim that gives the holder the right, but not the obligation, to buy shares at a particular price (the exercise price). *268*

clean-surplus accounting produces a statement of shareholders' equity that contains only net income (closed from the income statement) and transactions with shareholders. *263*

contingent equity claim is a claim that may be converted into common equity if conditions are met. Examples are **call options, put options,** and **convertible securities.** *272*

convertible securities are securities (such as bonds and preferred stock) that can be converted into common shares if conditions are met, but which have additional claims also. *274*

dilution (to existing shareholders) occurs when shares are issued to new shareholders at less than market value. *268*

dirty-surplus item is an accounting item in shareholders' equity other than transactions with shareholders or income closed from the income statement. *263*

forward share purchase agreement is an agreement to buy back shares at a specified price in the future. *273*

hidden dirty-surplus expense is an expense that arises from the issue of shares but is not recognized in the financial statements. *268*

incentive options are employee stock options that are not taxed to the employee on exercise and are not tax deductible for the issuing firm. *269*

nonqualifying options are employee stock options that are taxable to the employee

on exercise and tax deductible to the issuing corporation. *269*

option overhang is the value of stock options unexercised. *271*

payout is amounts paid to shareholders. The term is sometimes used to refer only to dividends, sometimes to dividends and stock repurchases. Compare with **retention.** *266*

put option is a claim that gives the holder the right, but not the obligation, to sell shares at a particular price (the exercise price). *273*

redeemable preferred stock are preferred stock that can be redeemed by the issuer under specified conditions. *260*

retention is paying out less than 100 percent of earnings. Compare with **payout.** *267*

tax benefit is a tax deduction or credit given for specified transactions. *269*

warrant is similar to a **call option** but usually of longer duration. A **put warrant** is similar to a **put option.** *272*

The Analyst's Toolkit

(continued)

The Analyst's Toolkit (concluded)

Analysis Tools	Page	Key Measures	Page
The market value method	274	Gains and losses on put options	273
		Loss on conversion of a convertable security	274
		Ratios	
		Dividend payout	266
		Total payout	266
		Dividends-to-book value	266
		Total payout-to-book value	260
		Retention	267
		New investment rate	267
		Comprehensive ROCE	267
		Growth rate of common shareholders' equity	267
		Tax benefit on issue of shares in exercise of employee stock options	269
		Unrealized gains and losses on securities available for sale	263

A Continuing Case: *Kimberly-Clark Corporation*

A Self-Study Exercise

You are now ready to begin an analysis of Kimberly-Clark's financial statements with a view, ultimately, of using the analysis to value KMB's shares.

As always, start with the equity statement. This is given in Exhibit 2.2 in the Continuing Case for Chapter 2. The layout is similar to the Nike statement in this chapter, although you will note that KMB has non controlling interests. KMB also reports a separate comprehensive income statement outside of the equity statement. Row totals are not given, so first confirm that the beginning and ending balances total to the amount of shareholders' equity in the balance sheet. Kimberly-Clark issues shares when employees exercise stock options. The firm repurchases stock into treasury.

REFORMULATION

Your task is to reformulate this equity statement for 2010 along the lines of the Nike reformulation in this chapter. Go through and mark off the items that are transactions with shareholders and those that are part of comprehensive income. Then ask yourself if there are any hidden dirty-surplus expenses. You should familiarize yourself with the stock compensation footnote in the annual report and also the stockholders' equity footnote. You should note that dividends payable are given in the balance sheet (in the Chapter 2 installment of the Continuing Case). Kimberly-Clark's tax rate is 36.8 percent.

RATIO ANALYSIS

State in one or two sentences what the reformulated statement you have drawn up is saying. Then carry out a ratio analysis that embellishes the story. Why do you think this firm is paying out so much cash to shareholders?

BUILD YOUR OWN ANALYSIS ENGINE FOR KMB

You might enter your reformulated equity statement into a spreadsheet. After you have covered the next chapter, you can add the balance sheet and income statement. Then, in subsequent chapters, you can use spreadsheet operations to analyze the statements and derive valuations from that analysis. The BYOAP feature on the book's Web site will guide you.

Concept Questions

C9.1. Why is income in the equity portion of the balance sheet called "dirty-surplus" income?

C9.2. Why can "value be lost" if an analyst works with reported net income rather than comprehensive income?

C9.3. Are currency translation gains and losses real gains and losses to shareholders? Aren't they just an accounting effect that is necessary to consolidate financial statements prepared in different currencies?

C9.4. In accounting for the conversion of convertible bonds to common stock, most firms record the issue of shares at the amount of the book value of the bonds. The issue of the shares could be recorded at their market value, with the difference between the market value of the shares and the book value of the bonds recorded as a loss on the conversion. Which treatment best reflects the effect of the transaction on the wealth of the existing shareholders?

C9.5. The compensation vice president of General Mills was quoted in *The Wall Street Journal* on January 14, 1997, as saying that option programs are "very attractive for shareholders" because they cut fixed costs and boost profits. So, for General Mills's 1996 year, selling, general, and administrative expenses, which include compensation, dropped by $222 million, or 9 percent, while pretax earnings from continuing operations rose by $194 million, or 34 percent. At the same time, the firm was distributing about 3 percent of its stock to employees annually.

What's wrong with this picture?

C9.6. Before it found the practice to be too expensive, Microsoft (and a number of other firms) was in the habit of repurchasing some of the shares that it issued each year as employees exercised stock options. The rationale, according to commentators, was to avoid the dilution from shares issued to employees.

a. Do share issues from the exercise of employee stock options cause dilution?

b. Do share repurchases reverse dilution?

c. Why would Microsoft feel that repurchasing shares is "too expensive"?

C9.7. Cisco Systems, the networking equipment firm, reported a tax benefit from the exercise of stock options of $537 million in its fiscal 2004 shareholders' equity statement. Over the previous years, the tax benefits had cut more than 25 percent off the firm's tax bills. Commentators saw this tax relief as a major source of value for the shareholders. Is this correct?

C9.8. In February 1999, Boots, the leading retail chemist in the United Kingdom, announced plans to reform its employee option compensation scheme. In the future, it said, the firm will purchase its own shares to provide shares to issue when options are exercised, and it will charge the difference between the market price and the issue price for the options against profits. The charge for the first year was expected to be £63 million ($103 million). What do you think of this scheme?

C9.9. In September 1999, Microsoft agreed to buy Visio Corporation for stock valued at $1.26 billion. Visio sells a popular line of technical drawing software. At the time, Microsoft had $14 billion of cash on its balance sheet. Why might Microsoft pay for the acquisition with its own stock rather than in cash?

Exercises

Drill Exercises

E9.1. Some Basic Calculations (Easy)

a. A firm listed total shareholders' equity on its balance sheet at $237 million. Preferred shareholders' equity was $32 million. What is the common shareholders' equity?

b. From the following information, calculate the net dividend to shareholders and comprehensive income (in millions):

Common shareholders' equity, beginning of period	$1,081
Common share issues	230
Common share repurchases	45
Common dividends	36
Common shareholders' equity, beginning of period	$1,292

c. A firm reported $62 million of comprehensive income in its statement of shareholders' equity but $87 million as net income in its income statement. What explains the difference?

E9.2. Calculating ROCE from the Statement of Shareholders' Equity (Easy)

From the following information, calculate the return on common equity for the year 2012 (amounts in millions of dollars). There were no share repurchases.

Common stockholders' equity, December 31, 2011	174.8
Dividends paid to common stockholders	8.3
Share issue on December 31, 2012	34.4
Common stockholders' equity, December 31, 2012	226.2

E9.3. A Simple Reformulation of the Equity Statement (Easy)

From the following information, prepare a reformulated statement of common shareholders' equity for 2012. Amounts are in millions.

Balance, December 31, 2011	$1,206
Net income	241
Foreign currency translation loss	(11)
Unrealized gain on debt securities held	24
Issue of shares	45
Common dividends	(94)
Preferred dividends	(15)
Balance, December 31, 2012	$1,396

The beginning and end-of-year balances include $200 million of preferred stock.

E9.4. **Using Accounting Relations that Govern the Equity Statement (Medium)**

The following is a statement of common shareholders' equity with some numbers missing (in millions of dollars).

Balance, December 31, 2011	?
Net income	?
Common dividends	(132)
Preferred dividends	(30)
Issue of common stock	155
Unrealized gain on securities held for sale	13
Foreign currency translation loss	(9)
Balance, December 31, 2012	?

a. The market value of the equity was $4,500 million at December 31, 2011, and $5,580 million at December 31, 2012. At both dates, the equity traded at a premium of $2,100 million over the book of the common equity. What was net income for 2012?

b. Fill out the missing numbers in the equity statement and reformulate it to identify comprehensive income for the common shareholders for 2012.

E9.5. **Calculating the Loss to Shareholders from the Exercise of Stock Options (Easy)**

In 2007, an employee was granted 305 options on the stock of a firm with an exercise price of $20 per option. In 2012, after the options had vested and when the stock was trading at $35 per share, she exercised the options. The firm's income tax rate is 36 percent. What was the after-tax cost to shareholders of remunerating this employee with options?

E9.6. **Reformulating an Equity Statement with Employee Stock Options (Medium)**

Reformulate the following statement of shareholder's equity. The firm's tax rate is 35 percent.

Balance, end of fiscal year 2011	$1,430
Share issues from exercised employee stock options	810
Repurchase of 24 million shares	(720)
Cash dividend	(180)
Tax benefit from exercise of employee stock options	12
Unrealized gain on debt investments	50
Net income	468
Balance, end of fiscal year 2012	$1,870

Applications

E9.7. **A Simple Reformulation: J. C. Penney Company (Easy)**

Reformulate the following statement of shareholders' equity statement for J. C. Penney Company. Dividends paid consisted of $24 million in preferred dividends and $225 million in common dividends.

J. C. PENNEY COMPANY, INC., AND SUBSIDIARIES
Consolidated Statements of Stockholders' Equity

($ in millions)	Common Stock	Preferred Stock	Reinvested Earnings	Accumulated Other Comprehensive (Loss)/Income	Total Stockholders' Equity
January 29, 2000	3,266	446	3,590	(74)	7,228
Net loss			(705)		(705)
Net unrealized change in investments				2	2
Currency translation adjustments				(14)	(14)
Other comprehensive income from discontinued operations				16	16
Total comprehensive (loss)/income			(705)	4	(701)
Dividends			(249)		(249)
Common stock issued	28				28
Preferred stock retired		(47)			(47)
January 27, 2001	$3,294	$399	$2,636	$(70)	$6,259

E9.8. Reformulation of an Equity Statement and Accounting for the Exercise of Stock Options: Starbucks Corporation (Hard)

The statement of shareholders' equity below for Starbucks Corporation, the retail coffee vendor, is for fiscal year 2007.

($ in thousands)	Common Stock Shares	Common Stock Amount	Additional Paid-In Capital	Other Additional Paid-In Capital	Retained Earnings	Accumulated Other Comprehensive Income/(Loss)	Total
Balance, October 1, 2006	756,602,071	$756	$	$39,393	$2,151,084	$37,273	$2,228,506
Net earnings					672,638		672,638
Unrealized holding loss, net						(20,380)	(20,380)
Translation adjustment, net of tax						37,727	37,727
Comprehensive income							689,985
Stock-based compensation expense			106,373				106,373
Exercise of stock options, including tax benefit of $95,276	12,744,226	13	225,233				225,246
Sale of common stock, including tax provision of $139	1,908,407	2	46,826				46,828
Repurchase of common stock	(32,969,419)	(33)	(378,432)		(634,356)		(1,012,821)
Balance September 30, 2007	738,285,285	$738	$ 0	$39,393	$2,189,366	$54,620	$2,284,117

a. Reformulate the statement to distinguish comprehensive income from transactions with shareholders
b. Calculate the after-tax loss to shareholders from the exercise of stock options during the year.
c. The following information is provided in the equity footnote in the firm's 10-K for 2007:

	Shares Subject to Options	Weighted Average Exercise Price per Share	Weighted Average Remaining Contractual Life (Years)
Outstanding, October 1, 2006	69,419,871	16.83	6.2
Granted	12,298,465	36.04	
Exercised	(12,744,226)	10.23	
Canceled/forfeited	(3,458,007)	30.92	
Outstanding, September 30, 2007	65,516,103	20.97	6.2
Exercisable, September 30, 2007	40,438,082	14.65	5.0
Vested and expected to vest, September 30, 2007	63,681,867	20.60	6.2

At balance sheet date in 2007, Starbucks' shares traded at $28.57 each. Provide an estimate of the option overhang at that date.

Real World Connection
Material on Starbucks can be found in Exercises E10.10, E12.9, E13.8, and E15.8.

E9.9. Loss on the Conversion of Preferred Stock: Microsoft Corporation (Easy)
In 1996, Microsoft issued 12.5 million convertible preferred shares carrying a dividend of 2.75 percent for $980 million. The shares were converted into common shares in December 1999, with each preferred share receiving 1.1273 common shares. At the time of conversion, Microsoft's common shares traded at $88 each. What was the loss to shareholders from the conversion?

Real World Connection
See Exercises E1.6, E4.14, E6.12, E8.9, E11.11, E18.10, and E20.4. Minicases M9.1 in this chapter and M13.2 also deal with Microsoft.

E9.10. Conversion of Stock Warrants: Warren Buffett and Goldman Sachs (Easy)
In September 2008, in the midst of the credit crisis on Wall Street, Goldman Sachs invited Warren Buffett, the legendary fundamental investor, to contribute much-needed equity capital to the firm. Buffett seemingly got a very good deal. For a $5 billion cash infusion, he received perpetual preferred equity shares carrying a 10 percent dividend (redeemable by Goldman Sachs) plus warrants to buy 43.5 million common shares at $115 per share (for a total of another $5 billion). The $115 conversion price was set at the current share price, a three-year low for Goldman. In June 2011, Goldman's shares traded at $136 each. If Buffet exercised the warrants at that price, what is the loss to Goldman's shareholders?

E9.11. Reformulation of an Equity Statement with Hidden Losses: Dell, Inc. (Hard)

The following is a condensed version of the statement of shareholders' equity for Dell, Inc., for fiscal year ending January 31, 2003 (in millions of dollars):

Balance at February 1, 2002	$4,694
Net income	2,122
Unrealized gain on debt investments	26
Unrealized loss on derivative instruments	(101)
Foreign currency translation gain	4
Comprehensive income	2,051
Shares issued on exercise of options,	
including tax benefits of $260	418
Repurchase of 50 million shares	(2,290)
Balance of January 31, 2003	$4,873

Other information:

1. Dell's tax rate is 35 percent.
2. The share repurchase occurred when the stock traded at $28 per share.

   a. What was the loss to shareholders from the exercise of stock options?

   b. Prepare a reformulated statement of shareholders' equity for 2003 for Dell, Inc. The reformulated statement should identify comprehensive income and include all hidden items.

Real World Connection

Exercises E3.7, E3.12, E5.10, E14.16, and E20.4 also deal with Dell. Minicase M16.2 covers Dell also.

E9.12. Ratio Analysis for the Equity Statement: Nike (Easy)

Using the statement of shareholders' equity in Exhibit 9.2, carry out a ratio analysis that highlights the information about Nike in that statement.

Real World Connection

Further Nike Exercises are in E2.14, E5.13, E6.7, E7.9, E14.17, E16.11, E16.13, E19.5, and E20.4.

E9.13. Losses from Put Options: Household International (Hard)

Household International (acquired by HSBC in 2003 and now known as HSBC Finance Corporation) is one of the largest U.S. lenders to consumers with poor credit histories, carrying receivables for auto loans, Mastercard and Visa credit card debt, and a significant amount of private noncredit card debt. In September 2002, Household issued 18.7 million shares, raising about $400 million. The issue, combined with a decision to sell $7.5 billion of receivables and deposits, was cheered by analysts concerned about the subprime lender's liquidity and credit rating.

However, closer inspection revealed that Household International might have to use the cash raised for purposes other than bolstering its reserves. While the firm issued shares at a price of $21.40 per share, about the same time it also repurchased 2.1 million shares at an average price of $53.88 under forward purchase agreements when the market price of the shares was $27.

a. What was the loss to shareholders from the repurchase of shares under the forward purchase agreements?
b. At the end of its third quarter for 2002, when the stock price stood at $28.31, there were outstanding contracts to repurchase 4.9 million shares at a weighted-average price of $52.99 per share. Make a rough calculation of the option overhang that shareholders were facing?
c. Why does issuing shares at one price and using the proceeds to repurchase shares at a higher price lose value for shareholders?

Minicase

M9.1

Analysis of the Equity Statement, Hidden Losses, and Off-Balance-Sheet Liabilities: Microsoft Corporation

Microsoft has undoubtedly been the most successful software firm ever. Between 1994 and 2000, the firm's revenues increased from $2.8 billion to $23.0 billion, and its earnings from $708 million to $9.4 billion. Over the two year period from 1998 to 2000, its stock price increased from $36 per share to almost $120, giving it a trailing P/E ratio of 66 and a market capitalization at the height of the stock market bubble of over half a trillion dollars. By 2005, Microsoft was trading at $40 per share (on a pre-split basis) with a market capitalization of $275 billion and a trailing P/E ratio of 25.

Microsoft's success has been due to a strong product, market positioning, and innovative research and marketing. In terms of the buzzwords of the time, Microsoft has significant "knowledge capital" combined with dominant market positioning and network externalities. These intangible assets are not on its balance sheet, and accordingly the price-to-book ratio was over 12 in 2000. Yet, to develop and maintain the knowledge base, Microsoft had to attract leading technical experts with attractive stock option packages, with consequent costs to shareholders. Unfortunately, GAAP accounting did not report this cost of acquiring knowledge, nor did it report significant off-balance-sheet liabilities to pay for the knowledge. Knowledge liabilities, as well as knowledge assets, were missing from the balance sheet.

This case asks you to uncover the knowledge costs and the associated liabilities and to deal with other imperfections in the statement of shareholders' equity.

Microsoft's income statement for the first nine months of its June 30, 2000, fiscal year follows, along with its statement of shareholders' equity at the end of the nine months and the shareholders' equity footnote. At the time, Microsoft's shares were trading at $90 each. Reformulate the equity statement and then answer the questions that follow.

MICROSOFT CORPORATION
Income Statements
(in millions, except earnings per share)
(Unaudited)

	Nine Months Ended March 31, 2000
Revenue	$17,152
Operating expenses	
Cost of revenue	2,220
Research and development	2,735
Sales and marketing	2,972
General and administrative	825
Other expenses (income)	(13)
Total operating expenses	8,739
Operating income	8,413
Investment income	2,055
Gains on sales	156

	Nine Months Ended March 31, 2000
Income before income taxes	10,624
Provision for income taxes	3,612
Net income	$ 7,012
Earnings per share:	
Basic	$ 1.35
Diluted	$ 1.27

Stockholders' Equity Statement (in millions) (Unaudited)

	Nine Months Ended March 31, 2000
Common stock and paid-in capital	
Balance, beginning of period	$13,844
Common stock issued	2,843
Common stock repurchased	(186)
Proceeds from sale of put warrants	472
Stock option income tax benefits	4,002
Balance, end of period	20,975
Retained earnings	
Balance, beginning of period	13,614
Net income	7,012
Net unrealized investment gains	2,724
Translation adjustments and other	166
Comprehensive income	9,902
Preferred stock dividends	(13)
Common stock repurchased	(4,686)
Balance, end of period	18,817
Total stockholders' equity	$39,792

Extract from the footnotes to the financial statements:

Stockholders' Equity

During the first three quarters of fiscal 2000, the Company repurchased 54.7 million shares of Microsoft common stock in the open market. In January 2000, the Company announced the termination of its stock buyback program.

To enhance its stock repurchase program, Microsoft sold put warrants to independent third parties. These put warrants entitle the holders to sell shares of Microsoft common stock to the Company on certain dates at specified prices. On March 31, 2000, 163 million warrants were outstanding with strike prices ranging from $69 to $78 per share. The put warrants expire between June 2000 and December 2002. The outstanding put warrants permit a net-share settlement at the Company's option and do not result in a put warrant liability on the balance sheet.

During 1996, Microsoft issued 12.5 million shares of 2.75 percent convertible exchangeable principal-protected preferred stock. Net proceeds of $980 million were used to repurchase common shares. The Company's convertible preferred stock matured on December 15, 1999. Each preferred share was converted into 1.1273 common shares.

A. What was the net cash paid out to shareholders during the nine months?

B. What was Microsoft's comprehensive income for the nine months?

C. Discuss your treatment of the $472 million from "proceeds from sale of put warrants." Why would Microsoft sell put warrants? How does GAAP account for put warrants, put options, and future share purchase agreements?

D. If the put warrants are exercised rather than allowed to lapse, how would GAAP accounting report the transactions? How would you report the effect on shareholder value?

E. The equity statement shows that Microsoft repurchased $4.872 billion in common shares during the nine months. The firm had a policy of repurchasing the amount of shares that were issued in exercise of employee stock options, to "reverse the dilution," as it said. Microsoft discontinued the policy in 2000, as indicated in the shareholders' equity footnote. Does a repurchase reverse the dilution of shareholders' equity? Are repurchases at the share prices that prevailed in 2000 advisable from a shareholder's point of view?

F. Calculate the loss to shareholders from employees exercising stock options during the nine months. Microsoft's combined federal and state statutory tax rate is 37.5 percent.

G. The following is the financing section of Microsoft's cash flow statement for the nine months (in millions):

	Nine months ending March	
Financing	**1999**	**2000**
Common stock issued	$1,102	$1,750
Common stock repurchased	(1,527)	(4,872)
Put warrant proceeds	757	472
Preferred stock dividends	(21)	(13)
Stock option income tax benefits	2,238	4,002
Net cash from financing	$2,549	$1,339

Notice that the tax benefits from the exercise of stock options are included as financing cash flows. Later in 2000, the Emerging Issues Task Force of the Financial Accounting Standards Board required these tax benefits to be reported in the cash from operations section of the statement of cash flows. Which is the correct treatment?

H. The income statement reports income taxes of $3,612 million on $10,624 million of income. Yet press reports claimed that Microsoft paid no taxes at the time. Can you see why? What does the act of paying no taxes on a large income tell you about the quality of Microsoft's reported income?

I. Review the shareholders' equity footnote. What issues arise in the footnote that should be considered in valuing Microsoft's shares?

Microsoft's annual report for the year ending May 31, 2000, reported the following in the stock option footnote:

Stock Option Plans

For various price ranges, weighted-average characteristics of outstanding stock options at June 30, 2000, were as follows:

Range of Exercise Prices	Outstanding Options		
	Shares	Remaining Life (Years)	Weighted-Average Price
$ 0.56–$ 5.97	133	2.1	$ 4.57
5.98– 13.62	104	3.0	10.89
13.63– 29.80	135	3.7	14.99
29.81– 43.62	96	4.5	32.08
43.63– 83.28	198	7.3	63.19
83.29–119.13	166	8.6	89.91

The weighted average Black-Scholes value of options granted under the stock option plans during 1998, 1999, and 2000 was $11.81, $20.90, and $36.67, respectively. Value was estimated using a weighted-average expected life of 5.3 years in 1998, 5.0 years in 1999, and 6.2 years in 2000, no dividends, volatility of 0.32 in 1998 and 1999 and 0.33 in 2000, and risk-free interest rates of 5.7 percent, 4.9 percent, and 6.2 percent in 1998, 1999, and 2000, respectively.

What information does this footnote give you about the off-balance-sheet knowledge for the option overhang? Can you estimate the amount of the liability?

Microsoft has never borrowed, but in September 2010, the firm announced that it planned to borrow $5 billion at a very low interest rate (less than 1 percent) at the time. Microsoft had strong free cash flow and $36.8 billion in cash and short-term investments sitting on its balance sheet. Commentators were speculating that Microsoft planned a stock repurchase, but given its cash position, it clearly had no need to borrow. The stock, trading at $24, shot up 5.3 percent on the announcement. Can you explain why the market would greet such an announcement so positively?

Real World Connection

Minicase M13.2 also deals with Microsoft, as do Exercises E1.6, E4.14, E6.12, E8.9, E9.9, E11.11, E18.10, and E20.4.

Chapter **Ten**

The Analysis of the Balance Sheet and Income Statement

LINKS

Link to previous chapter

Chapter 9 reformulated and analyzed the statement of owners' equity.

This chapter

This chapter continues the reformulation and analysis with the balance sheet and income statement. The reformulation follows the design in Chapter 8.

Link to next chapter

Chapter 11 analyzes the cash flow statement.

Link to Web page

More applications and analysis are on the text's Web site at **www.mhhe.com/ penman5e**.

What assets and liabilities are classified as operating? As financing?	What items in the income statement are classified as operating? As financing?	How are taxes allocated to the operating and financing components of the income statement?	What ratios are calculated from reformulated statements? What do they mean?

The reformulated statement of shareholders' equity of the last chapter yields the overall profitability measure, the comprehensive return on common shareholders' equity, which, along with growth, drives residual earnings and value. The balance sheet and income statement give the detail to discover the sources of profitability and growth. This chapter takes you through the reformulation of the two statements in preparation for the analysis of profitability and growth in Chapters 12 and 13.

Profitability that generates value comes from a firm's business operations. Thus the analysis begins with a reformulation of the statements, following the templates of Chapter 8, to distinguish operating activities from financing activities. This reformulation enforces the rule that one cannot value a firm without knowing the business, for distinguishing operating activities identifies the business the firm is in. And distinguishing operating items from financing items in financial statements requires understanding the role of each item in the business and how it contributes to the profitability of the firm. Reformulation of the financial statements—the lens on the business—brings the business activities into sharper focus. We understand the business, the strategy, and the value it generates, through the lens of reformulated financial statements. Before beginning this chapter, put Figure 8.8 in Chapter 8 in front of you; it will be your guide.

The main aim of reformulating the balance sheet and income statements, however, is to discover the drivers of ROCE (return on common equity) and growth in preparation for forecasting and valuation. This discovery is made through ratio analysis, combined as always with a good knowledge of the business. This chapter introduces ratios calculated from these statements; these ratios become part of the comprehensive analysis of profitability and growth in Chapters 12 and 13.

The Analyst's Checklist

After reading this chapter you should understand:

- Why the analyst reformulates income statements and balance sheets.
- How operating and financing components of the two statements are identified.
- What assets and liabilities typically fall into operating and financing categories.
- Why income taxes are allocated to different parts of the income statement.
- What balance sheet and income statement ratios reveal.
- How one learns about a firm's strategy through the reformatted financial statements.
- How firms manage "cash."

After reading this chapter you should be able to:

- Reformulate income statements and balance sheets.
- Add footnote information to reformulated statements.
- Prepare a reformulated income statement on a comprehensive income basis.
- Allocate income taxes between operating income and financing income (or expense).
- Calculate effective tax rates for operations.
- Prepare and interpret a common-size, comparative analysis.
- Prepare and interpret a trend analysis.
- Calculate income statement ratios—including ratios that reveal the profitability of sales.
- Calculate balance sheet ratios—including financial leverage ratios and operating liability leverage ratios.

REFORMULATION OF THE BALANCE SHEET

The typical balance sheet usually divides assets and liabilities into current and noncurrent (long-term) categories. For assets, this division is based on liquidity, and for liabilities, it is based on maturity, with the aim of giving an indication of the firm's ability to meet creditors' claims on cash. The analysis of credit risk in Chapter 20 will employ this division, but in Chapter 8 we overrode this classification with one that identifies the different sources of profitability, the operations and the financing activities. To discover a firm's ability to generate profits, we need to reformulate the balance sheet into operating and financing assets and liabilities. Following the template of Chapter 8, operating assets and liabilities net to **net operating assets (NOA),** sometimes referred to as **enterprise assets,** and financing assets and liabilities net to **net financial assets (obligations)**, sometimes called net debt.

Exhibit 10.1 lays out a typical balance sheet. It lists the standard line items you see in published statements. Balance sheets for specific firms do not include all these items, of course, and some items are often aggregated or grouped into "other assets" or "other liabilities" categories. In some industries you will see special line items that are not listed here.

From Chapter 8 you'll remember that operating assets and liabilities are those involved in the business, in selling goods and services. Financing assets and liabilities are those that are involved in raising cash for operations and disbursing excess cash from operations. Before reformulating the statement, be sure to have an answer to the question: What business is the firm in? For it is the answer to this question that defines the operating assets and liabilities. Also keep in mind the parallel classification in the income statement (discussed later): Operating assets and liabilities generate operating income and financial

EXHIBIT 10.1
The Typical
Balance Sheet

Assets	Liabilities and Stockholders' Equity
Current assets:	Current liabilities:
Cash	Accounts payable
Cash equivalents	Accrued expenses
Short-term investments (marketable securities)	Deferred (unearned) revenues
Deposits and advances	Advances from customers
Accounts receivable (less allowances)	Warranty liabilities
Short-term notes receivable	Short-term notes payable
Other receivables	Short-term borrowings
Inventories	Deferred taxes (current portion)
Prepaid expenses	Current maturities of long-term debt
Deferred income taxes (current portion)	
Long-term assets:	Long-term liabilities:
Noncurrent receivables	Bank loans
Long-term debt investments	Bonds payable
Long-term equity investments—	Long-term notes payable
less than 20% ownership	Lease obligations
Long-term equity investments—	Commitments and contingencies
equity method	Deferred taxes (noncurrent portion)
Property, plant, and equipment	Pension liabilities
(less accumulated depreciation)	Postemployment liabilities
Land	
Buildings	
Equipment	
Leased assets	Redeemable preferred stock
Leasehold improvements	
Construction in progress	
Intangible assets	
Patents	
Licenses, franchises, and business rights	
Copyrights and trademarks	Equity:
Goodwill	Minority (noncontrolling)
Software development costs	interest
Deferred taxes (noncurrent portion)	Preferred equity
Deferred charges	Common equity

assets and liabilities are those that produce financial income or incur financial expenses. See Box 10.1.

Issues in Reformulating Balance Sheets

The GAAP balance sheet for the typical nonfinancial firm is reformulated into operating and financial items as in Exhibit 10.2. This layout follows the template in Chapter 8. The following issues arise. Footnote information helps sort out the issues.

- *Cash.* Working cash, or **operating cash,** which is needed as a buffer to pay bills as they fall due, is an operating asset. This is non–interest bearing, in the form of cash on hand or in a checking account. Just as the firm needs to invest in plant and equipment to carry out operations, it also has to invest in working cash. However, interest-bearing cash equivalents (investments with less than three months maturity) or cash invested in short-term

Reformulating balance sheets involves distinguishing assets and liabilities that are used in business operations—where the firm makes its money—from assets and liabilities that are used in financing—to raise cash for operations and temporarily store excess cash from operations. A firm "makes its money" by selling goods and services to customers, so identifying operating assets requires knowledge of goods and services the firm is delivering to customers.

Assets and liabilities with similar names on balance sheets may be financing items for one firm but operating items for another. Consider the following.

BANKS

Banks hold mainly (what look like) financial assets and financial liabilities in the form of customer deposits, bonds, and loans. But they make money from the spread between the interest they pay on their financial liabilities and the interest they earn on their financial assets. These apparent financial assets and liabilities are operating assets and liabilities.

CAPTIVE FINANCE SUBSIDIARIES

Automobile manufacturers like General Motors and Chrysler consolidate finance subsidiaries into their financial statements. These finance subsidiaries hold (what look like) financial assets and liabilities. But they are used to support customers' purchases of automobiles, and often generous credit terms are used in promotions as effective price reductions. The finance subsidiaries are an integral part of operations and their assets and liabilities should be classified as such. The interest earned from the financing is operating income.

RETAILERS WITH CREDIT FACILITIES

Retailers make money from selling goods but often also make money from providing credit to customers. Accordingly, their interest income from credit cards they issue and other credit facilities is operating income, and the financing receivables that generate the income are operating assets.

EXHIBIT 10.2
The Classification of Operating and Financing Items in the Balance Sheet for Nonfinancial Firms

The Reformulated Balance Sheet	
Assets	**Liabilities and Stockholders' Equity**
Financial assets:	Financial liabilities:
Cash equivalents	Short-term borrowings
Short-term investments	Current maturities of long-term debt
Short-term notes receivable (?)	Short-term notes payable (?)
Long-term debt investments	Long-term borrowing (bank loans, bonds payable, notes payable)
	Lease obligations
	Preferred stock
Operating assets:	Operating liabilities:
All else	All else
	Minority (noncontrolling) interest
	Common equity

securities are financial assets—they are investments of excess cash over that required to meet liquidity demands. Typically firms lump cash and cash equivalents together, so identifying the working cash is difficult. If the analyst knows the type of business well, she might impute the required working cash (as 0.5 percent of sales, say) but, as many firms have cash swept daily into interest-bearing accounts, she would be safe in classifying all cash as a financial asset.

- *Short-term notes receivable.* Notes can be written by customers for goods received in trade, with or without interest, and, with interest, by borrowers. If the notes are temporary investments of excess cash, treat them as financial assets. If they are trade notes, treat them as operating assets. Trade notes can be treated as financial assets if they bear the market rate of interest: The trade receivable has been converted to a financial claim. But if the firm is using credit to attract customers, treat the notes as operating assets: The firm is effectively offering a lower interest rate instead of a lower price for goods shipped. Correspondingly, the interest income should be classified as operating income, part of the income from selling goods with favorable credit terms. Finance receivables (for financing product sales) fall in the same category. See Box 10.1 again.

- *Debt investments.* For nonfinancial firms, investments in bonds and other interest-bearing investments are financial assets. Under FASB Statement No. 115, both current and noncurrent investments are marked to market (carried at market value on the balance sheet) if they are available for sale. They are recorded at cost if the firm intends to hold them to maturity. (The accounting for securities is covered in Accounting Clinic III in Chapter 9.) The footnotes give a schedule of all securities showing their historical costs and fair values, along with the associated unrealized gains and losses which are income or expense in comprehensive income. Banks make money on the spread between borrowing and lending rates, so in their case, debt investments and debt liabilities are operating items.

- *Long-term equity investments.* Long-term equity investments (in the shares of other firms) are investments in the operations of other companies, and so they are classified as operating assets. If the holding is less than 20 percent of the shares of another corporation, they are recorded on the balance sheet at market value if "available for sale" or at cost if "held to maturity." If the holding is greater than 20 percent and less than 50 percent, they are recorded as equity investments under the *equity method.* The equity method carries these investments at cost plus accumulated share of income of the subsidiary, less dividends paid by the subsidiary and any write-offs of the goodwill on purchase. If the holding is greater than 50 percent, **consolidation accounting** combines the financial statements of the related firms into one set of financial statements, so equity investments do not appear on the consolidated statement. Go to Accounting Clinic V.

   Equity investments in subsidiaries include the parent's share of net financial assets of subsidiaries. Thus they are investments in financial assets and obligations of these subsidiaries as well as their operating assets. Ideally we would like to go back into the subsidiaries' financial statements to sort out the operating and financial activities and divide the equity investments accordingly. This is often difficult to do if the subsidiary is not a public corporation, so as an expediency, treat the entire investment as an investment in an operating subsidiary.

- *Short-term equity investments.* Short-term marketable equity investments can be an exception to classifying equities as operating assets. If they are part of a trading portfolio, they are operating assets. If they are used to temporarily mop up excess cash, they are financial assets. These investments are marked to market.

- *Short-term notes payable.* Short-term notes can be written to generate cash, in which case they are financial obligations. However, notes also can be written because of trade obligations, for the purchase of inventory, for example. If these are non–interest bearing, or carry an interest rate less than the market rate for this type of credit, classify them as operating liabilities; if they are interest bearing at market rates, treat them as financial liabilities. A note written to satisfy a trade obligation results from operating activities but

Accounting Clinic   V

ACCOUNTING FOR EQUITY INVESTMENTS AND ACCOUNTING FOR BUSINESS COMBINATIONS

Accounting Clinic III covers the accounting for debt securities and equity securities that represent less than 20 percent ownership of another corporation. Accounting Clinic V deals with equity investments of 20 percent–50 percent ownership, where the *equity method* applies, and the case of majority control (over 50 percent ownership), where *consolidation accounting* applies.

Firms acquire shares of other firms in mergers and acquisitions. Accounting Clinic V also covers the accounting for these *business combinations,* along with issues related to recognition, amortization, and the impairment of the goodwill acquired in business combinations.

if it is interest bearing at market rate, the operating liability (the accounts payable) has effectively been converted into a financial liability (the note payable).

- *Accrued expenses.* These include liabilities to pay for the whole variety of operating expenses, including rent, insurance, wages, and taxes. Treat them as operating liabilities. But interest payable on financial obligations is a financing item.

- *Deferred revenues (Unearned revenues).* These include receipts from customers that are not yet recognized as revenue (because the firm has not performed on the sale) and obligations to complete performance such as warranties and guarantees. Treat them as operating liabilities.

- *Leases.* Leases that are capitalized are placed on the asset side of the balance sheet as a lease asset at the present value of the expected payouts under the lease agreement. The lease asset is an operating asset. The lease obligation is reported under liabilities and classified as a financial obligation in reformulated statements. Interest expense on the lease obligation is reported with other interest expenses in the income statement. Leases that are capitalized and placed on the balance sheet are called **capital leases.** Capital leases are essentially in-substance purchases granting the firm a right to use the asset for most of its useful life. Accordingly, if an asset satisfies criteria that indicate an in-substance purchase, the lease asset is treated similarly to any other property, plant, or equipment. And the obligation to service the lease is treated as if the firm had purchased the asset and borrowed to finance the purchase: The lease obligation is an effective loan to finance the purchase of the asset. Leases that are deemed not to be effective purchases are called **operating leases.** They do not appear on the balance sheet but the rent payments are included as rent expense in the income statement.

- *Deferred tax assets and liabilities.* Deferred taxes arise almost always from accounting differences in calculating the operating income component of taxable income and reported book income. So treat them as operating assets or liabilities.

- *Dividends payable.* These are classified as shareholders' equity, not a liability, as explained in the last chapter.

- *Preferred stock.* From a common shareholders' focus, preferred stock are financial obligations.

- *"Other" items.* Balance sheets typically have a line for "other assets" and "other liabilities." The detail can be discovered from footnotes and sometimes from the management discussion and analysis (MD&A). If these sources prove fruitless, these items can be assumed to be operating. If any of the other liabilities are material amounts, firms are required to disclose them.

- *Minority (noncontrolling) interest.* It might be tempting to view minority interest in a consolidated subsidiary as a financial obligation from the common shareholders' point of view, an interest that has to be satisfied. But the **minority interest** (now more commonly called **noncontrolling interest**) is not an obligation, like debt, that is satisfied with cash generated from free cash flow. Rather it is an equity sharing in the results of the consolidated operations. In the reformulated statements treat it as a separate line item that shares with the common equity in the operating and financing assets and liabilities. The reformulated statement with minority interest has the following form: NOA − NFO = CSE + Minority interest.

Some people have trouble thinking of operating liabilities as part of operations and not part of the financial indebtedness. Indeed, you may have seen these included in debt and debt ratios in other books. As obligations to creditors, they are debt, and if we were making calculations to evaluate credit risk—or the ability to pay off debt—we would include these in relevant ratios (as in Chapter 20). However, our purpose here is to get a sense of operating profitability relative to the net assets put in place. To the extent that a firm has operating liabilities, it reduces its net investment in operations, its net operating assets. For example, to the extent that a firm can induce suppliers to give credit, this reduces the investment required of shareholders. The following examples illustrate:

- Dell, Inc. is renowned in the computer business for its made-to-order system that keeps its investment in inventories low. Dell's fiscal 2011 balance sheet reports $1,301 million in inventory, only 2.1 percent of sales. However, Dell also reports $11,293 million in accounts payable. Dell has managed to get inventory suppliers to give credit to "finance" the inventory (and other supplies), so, in effect, Dell has negative investment in inventory. This generates value for shareholders as the shareholders do not need to use their funds to purchase inventories; indeed, creditors have supplied funds to finance other operating assets besides inventory. And shareholders need not service interest on financing debt.
- Oracle Corporation, the large software and information management firm, reports deferred revenue of $6,802 million as a liability in its 2011 balance sheet. This is cash that has been given to Oracle by customers in advance of receiving services from the firm. This cash can generate shareholder value because it can be used to purchase operating assets for which shareholders would otherwise have to provide funds. Shareholders can use their money elsewhere.
- Whirlpool Corporation, the appliance manufacturer, included sales warranties of $217 million in its accrued liabilities for 2010. These obligations to service sales effectively net against receivables from the sales; receivables are effectively reduced by the expected amount to be paid on warranty claims.

Exhibit 10.3 reproduces the published comparative balance sheets for Nike, Inc., for 2008–2010, along with reformulated balance sheets. We introduced Nike in Chapter 2 and began an analysis of the firm in the last chapter with a reformulation of its equity statement. Notice several things about the reformulated statement (numbers below correspond to the numbers flagging items to the right in the reformulated statement):

1. The reformulation maintains the balance sheet equation: CSE = NOA − NFO. The balances of common shareholders' equity (CSE) agree with those in the reformulated equity statement (in Chapter 9).

EXHIBIT 10.3
GAAP Consolidated Balance Sheets and Reformulated Balance Sheets for Nike, Inc., 2008–2010.
The reformulated balance sheet reformats the GAAP statement into net operating assets (operating assets minus operating liabilities), net financial assets (financial assets minus financial obligations), and common shareholders' equity (net operating assets plus net financial assets).
Numbers in parentheses to the right of the reformulated statement refer to points on the reformulation made in the text.

NIKE, INC.
Consolidated Balance Sheets
(in millions)

	May 31		
	2010	2009	2008
Assets	(in millions)		
Current assets:			
Cash and equivalents	$ 3,079.1	$ 2,291.1	$ 2,133.9
Short-term investments (Note 6)	2,066.8	1,164.0	642.2
Accounts receivable, net (Note 1)	2,649.8	2,883.9	2,795.3
Inventories (Notes 1 and 2)	2,040.8	2,357.0	2,438.4
Deferred income taxes (Note 9)	248.8	272.4	227.2
Prepaid expenses and other current assets	873.9	765.6	602.3
Total current assets	10,959.2	9,734.0	8,839.3
Property, plant, and equipment, net (Note 3)	1,931.9	1,957.7	1,891.1
Identifiable intangible assets, net (Note 4)	467.0	467.4	743.1
Goodwill (Note 4)	187.6	193.5	448.8
Deferred income taxes and other assets (Notes 9 and 18)	873.6	897.0	520.4
Total assets	$14,419.3	$13,249.6	$ 12,442.7

Liabilities and Shareholders' Equity

	2010	2009	2008
Current liabilities:			
Current portion of long-term debt (Note 8)	$ 7.4	$ 32.0	$ 6.3
Notes payable (Note 7)	138.6	342.9	177.7
Accounts payable (Note 7)	1,254.5	1,031.9	1,287.6
Accrued liabilities (Notes 5 and 18)	1,904.4	1,783.9	1,761.9
Income taxes payable (Note 9)	59.3	86.3	88.0
Total current liabilities	3,364.2	3,277.0	3,321.5
Long-term debt (Note 8)	445.8	437.2	441.1
Deferred income taxes and other liabilities (Notes 9 and 18)	855.3	842.0	854.5
Commitments and contingencies (Note 15)	—	—	—
Redeemable preferred stock (Note 10)	0.3	0.3	0.3
Shareholders' equity:			
Common stock at stated value (Note 11):			
Class A convertible—90.0 and 95.3 shares outstanding	0.1	0.1	0.1
Class B—394.0 and 390.2 shares outstanding	2.7	2.7	2.7
Capital in excess of stated value	3,440.6	2,871.4	2,497.8
Accumulated other comprehensive income (Note 14)	214.8	367.5	251.4
Retained earnings	6,095.5	5,451.4	5,073.3
Total shareholders' equity	9,753.7	8,693.1	7,825.3
Total liabilities and shareholders' equity	$14,419.3	$13,249.3	$12,442.7

Notes refer to footnotes in the published financial statements. Refer to the 2010 10-K report.

(continued)

EXHIBIT 10.3   (*concluded*)

Reformulated Balance Sheets (in millions)

	2010		2009		2008		
Net operating assets							
Operating assets							
Working cash[1]	$ 95.1		$ 95.9		$ 93.1		**(4)**
Accounts receivable, less allowance for doubtful accounts	2,649.8		2,883.9		2,795.3		
Inventories	2,040.8		2,357.0		2,438.4		
Prepaid expenses and other current assets	873.9		765.6		602.3		
Property, plant, and equipment, net	1,931.9		1,957.7		1,891.1		
Goodwill	187.6		193.5		448.8		
Identifiable intangible assets	467.0		467.4		743.1		
Deferred income taxes and other assets	1,122.4		1,169.4		747.6		
Total operating assets	9,368.5		9,890.4		9,759.7		
Operating liabilities							
Accounts payable—non–interest bearing[2]	$ 1,166.3		$ 953.4		$ 1,221.7		**(7)**
Accrued liabilities[3]	1,773.7		1,662.5		1,790.0		**(6)**
Income taxes payable	59.3		86.3		88.0		
Deferred income taxes and other liabilities	855.3	3,854.6	842.0	3,544.2	854.5	3,954.2	
Net operating assets		$ 5,513.9		$ 6,346.2		$ 5,805.5	**(2)**
Net financial assets							
Financial assets							
Cash equivalents[1]	2,984.0		2,195.2		2,040.8		**(4)**
Short-term investments	2,066.8		1,164.0		642.2		
Total financial assets	5,050.8		3,359.2		2,683.0		
Financial liabilities							
Current portion of long-term debt	7.4		32.0		6.3		
Notes payable[4]	138.6		342.9		177.7		
Accounts payable—interest bearing[2]	88.2		78.5		65.9		**(7)**
Long-term debt	445.8		437.2		441.1		
Redeemable preferred stock	0.3		0.3		0.3		**(5)**
Total financial liabilities	680.3	4,370.5	890.9	2,468.3	691.3	1,991.7	**(3)**
Common shareholders' equity[3]		$ 9,884.4		$ 8,814.5		$ 7,797.3	**(1) (6)**

[1]Cash and cash equivalents are split between operating cash and cash investments. Operating cash is estimated at 1/2 percent of sales.
[2]Interest-bearing accounts payable are classified as financing obligations.
[3]Accrued liabilities exclude dividends payable that have been included in shareholders' equity.
[4]Notes payable are interest bearing.

2. Net operating assets (NOA) is the difference between operating assets and operating liabilities.

3. Net financial assets (NFA) is the difference between financial assets and financial obligations.

4. Cash and cash equivalents have been divided up between operating cash and financial assets. Operating cash has been estimated at 1/2 percent of sales.

5. Redeemable preferred stock is a financial obligation.

6. Dividends payable, reported as an accrued liability in the GAAP statement, is included in shareholders' equity (as in the reformulated equity statement in Chapter 9).

7. The diligent analyst reviews the notes to the financial statements and brings further information onto the face of the reformulated statements. Look into "other assets" and "other liabilities" items particularly and also "accrued liabilities." If long-term investments are reported, check footnotes to see if these are equity investments (an operating asset) or debt investments (a financial asset).

Strategic Balance Sheets

A reformulated balance sheet gives insight into how a firm organizes its business. Indeed, we might refer to it as a **strategic balance sheet.**

Nike's reformulated balance sheet tells us that Nike conducts business by investing shareholders' equity in net operating assets with additional investment in net financial assets. It gives the composition of both, along with changes from the previous year. The positive net financial assets reveal the firm's current financing strategy: Rather than financing operations through borrowing, the firm does so through equity and indeed is a net lender rather than borrower. Operating assets list the type of assets that the firm invests in to run the business, while the operating liabilities indicate how much operating credit suppliers provide to finance those assets. These liabilities are not financing debt, for they arise from operations and indeed mean that Nike does not have to issue financing debt to finance the operations. They are also financing that shareholders do not have to provide. Indeed, due partly to supplier credit, Nike has significant financial assets that it can pay out in dividends or stock repurchases to shareholders (which it does).

Exhibits 10.4 and 10.5 present strategic balance sheets for Dell, Inc., and General Mills, Inc. What do these statements say about the strategies of these firms?

Dell, Inc.

Dell has a large amount of financial assets and little debt. So, like Nike, it has net financial assets rather than net financial obligations; the firm generates considerable cash flow and invests that cash flow in interest-bearing securities. But the striking feature of Dell's strategic balance sheet is the negative net operating assets: Shareholders' equity in 2011 is represented by a net investment in financial assets of $9.032 billion and a negative investment in operations of –$1.266 billion. This is rare for a manufacturing firm. How can it be? Well, it reflects Dell's strategy: Keep operating assets low with just-in-time inventory, require a credit card before shipping retail customer sales (thus keeping accounts receivable low), outsource production (reducing investment in plant and equipment), require cash up front for servicing contracts (and thus amass large deferred revenues), and, importantly, require suppliers to carry Dell's payables and thus supply operating credit. Accordingly, shareholders have a negative investment in the firm. That negative investment means that they can take cash out of the firm to invest elsewhere, as they do in the form of stock repurchases. In short, the shareholders of Dell are playing a float. That play adds value, as we will see when we come to value Dell. At this point it is important to appreciate how the reformulated, strategic balance sheet provides insights into the value generation that we wish to evaluate.

An insurance company works on a float to add value. Minicase 10.2 prepares a strategic balance sheet for a property casualty insurer that becomes the starting point for valuation.

General Mills, Inc.

Both Nike and Dell have positive net financial assets (negative net financial obligations). General Mills in Exhibit 10.5 is more typical with more financing debt than debt

EXHIBIT 10.4
Reformulated,
Strategic Balance
Sheet for Dell, Inc.,
for Fiscal Year 2011

DELL, INC.
Strategic Comparative Balance Sheet, 2011
(in millions)

	2011		2010	
Operating assets				
Working cash		$ 40		$ 40
Accounts receivables		6,493		5,837
Financing receivables		4,442		3,038
Inventories		1,301		1,051
Property, plant, and equipment		1,953		2,181
Goodwill		4,365		4,074
Intangible assets		1,495		1,694
Other assets		3,481		3,988
		23,570		21,903
Operating liabilities				
Accounts payable	$11,293		$11,373	
Accrued liabilities	4,181		3,884	
Deferred service revenue	6,676		6,069	
Other liabilities	2,686	24,836	2,605	23,931
Net operating assets		(1,266)		(2,028)
Net financial assets				
Cash Equivalents	13,873		10,595	
Short-term investments	452		373	
Long-term investments	704		781	
	15,029		11,749	
Short-term borrowing	(851)		(663)	
Long-term debt	(5,146)		(3,417)	
		9,032		7,669
Common shareholders' equity		7,766		5,641

assets held. Thus it is a net debtor with $5.648 billion in net financial obligations: The financing strategy involves taking on leverage through borrowing. The firm has $17.066 billion in operating assets to finance, with considerable investment in land, building, and equipment and intangible assets (these are investments in purchasing its many brands such as Pillsbury, Progresso, Green Giant, Old El Paso, Häagen-Dazs, and Uncle Tobys). It also has invested a considerable amount in acquisitions, as indicated by the $6.593 billion goodwill number. With $5.605 billion in operating liabilities, net operating assets stand at $11.461 billion, of which about half is financed by borrowing and half by common shareholders plus small noncontrolling minority equity interests in subsidiaries. Note that minority interest in a subsidiary is not a financing obligation but rather an equity share that shares in the subsidiary with the common shareholders at General Mills.

Net financial assets ("cash") are also strategic assets. Box 10.2 explains.

EXHIBIT 10.5
Reformulated,
Strategic Balance
Sheet for General
Mills, Inc., 2010

GENERAL MILLS, INC.
Strategic Comparative Balance Sheet, 2010
(in millions)

	2010		2009	
Operating assets				
Working cash	$ 60		$ 60	
Receivables	1,042		953	
Inventories	1,344		1,347	
Prepaid expenses	379		469	
Land, building, and equipment	3,128		3,035	
Goodwill	6,593		6,663	
Intangible assets	3,715		3,747	
Deferred tax assets	43		16	
Other assets	762		895	
	17,066		17,185	
Operating liabilities				
Accounts payable	$ 850		$ 803	
Deferred tax liabilities	875		1,165	
Other liabilities	3,880	5,605	3,414	5,382
Net operating assets		11,461		11,803
Net financial obligations				
Current portion of debt	107		509	
Notes payable	1,050		813	
Long-term debt	5,269		5,754	
Cash equivalents	(613)	5,813	(690)	6,386
		5,648		5,417
Noncontrolling interest		245		244
Common shareholders' equity		5,403		5,173

REFORMULATION OF THE INCOME STATEMENT

The income statement reports the profits and losses that the net operating assets and net financial assets have produced. The presentation of the GAAP and IFRS statement varies, but the typical line items found in the income statement are given in Exhibit 10.6.

The reformulated statement groups these items into operating and financing categories. However, the reformulated statement is on a comprehensive basis, so it also includes dirty-surplus items reported within the equity statement. Exhibit 10.7 gives the layout. The two components in the template in Chapter 8—**operating income** and **net financial expense**—are identified, including dirty-surplus income and expense discovered in the reformulation of the equity statement. Operating income is sometimes referred to as **enterprise income** or **net operating profit after tax (NOPAT).** Within operating income, further distinctions are made. We need to understand the profitability of trading with customers, so operating income from sales is distinguished from operating income not coming from sales. For example, equity income in subsidiaries, booked under the equity method, is a net number—sales minus operating expenses in the subsidiary—and is not generated by top-line sales. Nor are merger charges or gains and

Financial assets (in the form of cash and cash equivalents and short-term and long-term debt investments) are sometimes just referred to as "cash." Having identified these financial assets, the analyst asks: What does the firm intend to do with the "cash?" As a basic rule, firms should not hold cash without purpose, but rather pass it out to shareholders: Cash is a zero residual earnings asset (adding no value) that shareholders can just as well hold on their own account. Indeed, they may have investment opportunities to use the cash. Financial assets are held for the following (financing, investment, and operating) purposes:

1. For payout to shareholders (in dividends and stock repurchases) in the near future.
2. For payment of an upcoming debt maturity. (The payment does not affect net financial assets.)
3. For capital expenditures or acquisitions in the near future.
4. As "insurance" against bad times in operations: If cash flow turns negative, the firm has financial assets to alleviate the cash crunch.

The first use, payout to shareholders, is the default. After reporting considerable financial assets in its 2008 balance sheet, Nike announced a stock repurchase program that continued through 2010. Dell, with significant financial assets, has a continuing stock repurchase program. Dell is making some acquisitions, but neither firm has significant debt to retire. If cash were held for investment in operations, the analyst would be keen to discover the investment strategy.

The fourth use of financial assets is often controversial. Firms can borrow in difficult times if firm value is there to back up the loans; if the value is not there, the shareholders may be better off with liquidation of the firm, with the cash from financial assets paid out earlier safely in their pockets. Some complain that financial assets cushion management rather than shareholders. Nevertheless, borrowing in bad times is difficult—particularly when credit generally contracts in the economy as it did in the financial crisis of 2008—so firms may hold cash as protection. General Motors, Ford, and Chrysler, the U.S. automobile firms, traditionally held large amounts of cash, and angry shareholders often demanded payout. The firms always replied that the cash was needed for a "rainy day." Indeed, General Motors held $52.6 billion in cash in 2005, but a "cash burn" subsequently ensued as the firm reported considerable losses in its operations, leaving it with little in cash in 2008 and ending with bankruptcy. If financial assets are used in operations in this way, they must be classified as operating assets and charged with the required (risky) return in a valuation: The cash is being put as risk in operations.

There is another reason that one might see considerable cash on a U.S. balance sheet. Under U.S. tax law, income earned by U.S. firms in overseas subsidiaries is not taxed until cash is repatriated back to the United States. That means that firms hold cash in overseas subsidiaries to avoid the tax. If they have little investment opportunities in the foreign subsidiaries, cash accumulates there but appears on the consolidated U.S. balance sheet. In 2004, the United States declared a one-year "tax holiday" that allowed firms to repatriate cash back to the States at considerably lower tax rates.

FINANCIAL ASSETS AS A MINIMUM VALUATION

Benjamin Graham, in the depths of the 1930s depression, advised buying firms whose market price was lower than their cash value (more common then than now). Having identified net financial assets and net operating assets we can view the valuation of common equity as

Value of common equity = Value of net operating assets
+ Value of net financial assets

If the equity is trading at less than the value of the net financial assets, the market is implicitly saying that the operations (the enterprise) have a negative value. Typically the equity is worth at least the net financial assets, so cash supplies the minimum valuation (before adding the value of the business). Dell traded at $14.25 in February 2011. With $9.032 billion of net financial assets on its strategic balance sheet and 1.918 billion shares outstanding, the minimum per-share value is $4.71. The market was valuing Dell's operations at $9.54.

---

losses on asset sales, for example. Finally, the reformulated statement allocates taxes so that income in each part of the statement is net of taxes it attracts.

Tax Allocation

Income taxes are reported in two ways. The income tax expense reported in the income statement applies to income above the tax line in the income statement. The firm may also pay taxes on items below the tax line, including the income reported in the equity statement. However, extraordinary items and other items below the tax line are reported net of tax, as

EXHIBIT 10.6
The Typical Income Statement

Net sales (sales minus allowances)
+ Other revenue (royalties, rentals, license fees)
− Cost of sales
= Gross margin

− Marketing and advertising expenses
− General expenses
− Administrative expenses
± Special items and nonrecurring items
     Restructuring charges
     Merger expenses
     Gains and losses on asset sales
     Asset impairments
     Litigation settlements
     Environmental remediation
− Research and development expense

+ Interest revenue
− Interest (expense)
± Realized gains and losses on securities
± Unrealized gains and losses on trading securities
+ Equity share in subsidiary income

− Income before tax
= Income taxes

− Income before extraordinary items and discontinued operations
± Discontinued operations
± Extraordinary items
    Abnormal gains and losses
= Net income or loss
− Noncontrolling interest
= Net income or loss to shareholders

are the dirty-surplus items. Thus no tax needs to be allocated to them. These after-tax items have been listed below the items to which the reported tax expense applies, in both operating and financing sections in the template in Exhibit 10.7.

The two components of income, operating and financing, both have tax consequences. Only one income tax number is reported in income statements, so this number must be allocated to the two components to put both on an after-tax basis. Referred to as **tax allocation,** this is done by first calculating the tax benefit of deducting net interest expense on debt for tax purposes and allocating it to operating income. The tax benefit—sometimes referred to as the **tax shield** from debt—is calculated as

$$\text{Tax benefit} = \text{Net interest expense} \times \text{Tax rate}$$

and the after-tax net interest expense is

$$\text{After-tax net interest expense} = \text{Net interest expense} \times (1 - \text{Tax rate})$$

Firms are taxed on a schedule of tax rates, depending on the size of their income. The tax rate used in the calculation is the **marginal tax rate,** the highest rate at which income is taxed, for interest expense reduces taxes at this rate. This marginal rate is not to be confused with the **effective tax rate,** which is tax expense divided by income before tax in the income statement (and incorporates any tax benefits the firm generates). The effective tax rate is reported in footnotes, but it is not to be used for the tax allocation. With little gradation in

EXHIBIT 10.7

The Form of the Reformulated Comprehensive Income Statement
(1) Operating items are separated from financing items.
(2) Operating income from sales is separated from other operating income. (3) Tax is allocated to components of the statement, with no allocation to items reported on an after-tax basis

Reformulated Comprehensive Income Statement
Net sales
– Expenses to generate sales
Operating income from sales (before tax)
– Tax on operating income from sales
+ Tax as reported
+ Tax benefit from net financial expenses
– Tax allocated to other operating income
Operating income from sales (after tax)
± Other operating income (expense) requiring tax allocation
Restructuring charges and asset impairments
Merger expenses
Gains and losses on asset sales
Gains and losses on security transactions
– Tax on other operating income
± After-tax operating items
Equity share in subsidiary income
Operating items in extraordinary income
Dirty-surplus operating items in Table 9.1
Hidden dirty-surplus operating items
Operating income (after tax)
– Net financial expenses after tax
+ Interest expense
– Interest revenue
± Realized gains and losses on financial assets
= Net taxable financial expense before tax
– Tax benefit from net financial expenses
= Net taxable financial expenses after tax
± Gains and losses on debt retirement
± Dirty-surplus financial items in Table 9.1 (including preferred dividends)
± Hidden dirty-surplus financing items
– Minority interest
= **Comprehensive income to common**

tax rates in the United States, the marginal rate is almost always the maximum **statutory tax rate** for federal and state taxes combined. These rates are reported in the tax footnote or can be inferred there.

Without the tax benefit of debt, taxes on operating income would be higher, so the amount of the benefit that reduces the net interest expense is allocated to operating income. Thus the tax on operating income is

Tax on operating income = Tax expense as reported + (Net interest expense × Tax rate)

If there is net interest income (more financial assets than financial obligations), then the financial activities attract tax rather than reduce it, and this tax reduces the tax on operating activities. In both cases, the idea is to calculate after-tax operating income that is insensitive to the financing activities: What would after-tax operating income be if there were no financing activities? This provides a measure of the profitability from operations that takes into account the tax consequences of conducting operations.

The one circumstance where this tax calculation is not done is when the firm cannot get the benefit of tax deduction for interest expense because it has losses for tax purposes. In this case the marginal tax rate is zero. But this is not common in the United States. A net

Accounting Clinic

VI

ACCOUNTING FOR INCOME TAXES

Income taxes are recorded by matching taxes with the income that draws the tax, so the analyst understands the after-tax consequences of earnings income (or losses). As the income may not be taxed (on the firm's tax return) at the same time as it is reported (in the income statement), this matching leads to deferred tax liabilities and deferred tax assets.

Accounting Clinic VI takes you through the details of deferred tax accounting and covers other tax issues such as operating loss carryforwards and valuation allowances against deferred tax assets. It also shows how taxes are allocated over various components of income in reported financial statements.

operating loss (or NOL) for tax purposes can be carried back and deducted from taxable income in the previous two years or carried forward to income for 20 future years. So a firm loses the tax benefit only if the loss cannot be absorbed into taxable income over the carryback and carryforward periods.

Preferred dividends typically are not deductible in calculating taxes, so no benefit arises. An exception is preferred dividends paid to an ESOP for which the tax benefit is recognized as a dirty-surplus item and brought into the income statement. In a recent innovation, firms issue preferred stock through a wholly owned trust from which firms borrow the proceeds of the issue. In the consolidation of the trust into the firm's accounts, the firm gets the tax benefits of interest paid to the trust and recognizes the preferred dividends paid by the trust. This effectively gives the firm a tax benefit for the preferred dividends paid.

Returning to Exhibit 10.7, you see that tax on financing activities has been calculated on items that attract or reduce taxes (interest), but not on items, such as preferred dividends, that do not, or on items that are reported after tax. The tax benefit from financing activities is then added to the reported tax to calculate the tax on operating income. The tax on operating income from sales is then reduced by the amount of tax that other operating income attracts. Accordingly, tax is allocated within the statement to the income it attracts, with components that reduce taxes allocated a negative tax. Box 10.3 gives a simple example and contrasts the top-down approach, outlined above, with a bottom-up approach.

The tax allocation produces a revised effective tax rate that applies to the operations:

$$\text{Effective tax rate for operations} = \frac{\text{Tax on operating income}}{\substack{\text{Operating income before tax, equity income,} \\ \text{and extraordinary and dirty-surplus items}}}$$

The benefits of tax planning (from using investment tax allowances and credits, and locating operations in low-tax jurisdictions for example) arise from operations. The effective tax rate is a measure of those benefits. As income from equity in subsidiaries, extraordinary items, and dirty-surplus items is reported after tax, the denominator excludes these income items. Accounting Clinic VI deals with the accounting for income taxes.

Before proceeding, look at Box 10.4.

The allocation of taxes to calculate operating income after tax is applied to the simple income statement on the left using a top-down approach and a bottom-up approach. The firm has a 35 percent statutory tax rate.

GAAP Income Statement		Top-Down Tax Allocation			Bottom-Up Tax Allocation		
Revenue	$4,000	Revenue		$4,000	Net income		$350
Operating expenses	(3,400)	Operating expenses		(3,400)	Interest expense	$100	
Interest expense	(100)	Operating income before tax		600	Tax benefit	35	65
Income before tax	500	Tax expense:			Operating income after tax		$415
Income tax expense	(150)	Tax reported	$150				
Net income	$ 350	Tax benefit for interest	35	(185)			
		($100 x 0.35)					
		Operating income after tax		$ 415			

The top-down approach adjusts the reported tax for that which applies to financing activities. The bottom-up approach works up from the bottom line, net income, and calculates operating income after-tax as net income adjusted for the after-tax financing component of net income.

The effective tax rate on operating income is $185/$600 = 30.8\%$. Why is this rate less than the statutory tax rate of 35 percent? Well, because operations generate tax benefits. So, if the firm receives research and development tax credits or credits for investment in certain industrial zones, it lowers its tax rate. These credits arise from operations, so the operations are allocated the benefit. Financing activities draw no such benefit, so are taxed at the statutory rate.

Issues in Reformulating Income Statements

Apart from the tax allocation, reformulating the income statement, as with the balance sheet, is a mechanical reclassification exercise. But, as with the balance sheet, the analyst must know the business. Interest income is usually earned on financial assets, but interest income on a finance receivable from financing customer purchases is operating income. The following issues arise in the reformulation:

- Lack of disclosure is often a problem:

    The share of income of a subsidiary may include both financing income and operating income, but the two components are often not identifiable. As the investment in the subsidiary in the balance sheet is identified as an operating item, so should this corresponding income statement item.

    Detailing some expenses is often frustrating. In particular, selling, administrative, and general expenses are usually a large number with little explanation provided in the footnotes.

    Interest income is often lumped together with "other income" from operations. If this is the case, estimate interest income by applying an interest rate to the average balances of financial assets during the period. If financial assets are all current assets, this rate is the short-term interest rate.

- Under GAAP, interest that finances construction is capitalized into the cost of assets on the balance sheet. It is treated as a construction cost just like the labor and materials that

The term *operating income* is used to mean different things in different circumstances:

1. Even though GAAP does not recognize the term, firms sometimes tag a line in their income statement as Operating Income. However, the analyst must be careful. Operating income so reported often includes interest income on financial assets and excludes some expenses associated with operations.

2. Operating Income is used by (Wall) Street analysts to refer to recurring income, that is, income adjusted for one-time charges such as restructuring charges and gains from asset sales.

3. Firms sometimes refer to operating income—or pro forma income—in their press releases as different from GAAP income. Be particularly careful in this case. These pro forma income numbers sometimes exclude significant expenses.

4. Operating income is also used in the way it is defined in the chapter. As such, it also goes under the name of **NOPAT, net operating profit after tax.** Sometimes it is referred to as **enterprise income.**

---

go into the asset. This accounting practice confuses operating and financing activities; labor and material costs are investments in assets, and interest costs are costs of financing assets. The result may be that little interest expense appears in the income statement for debt on the balance sheet. But it is difficult to unscramble this capitalized interest: It is depreciated, along with other construction costs, through to the income statement and so is hard to trace. As the depreciation expense that includes interest is an operating expense, the practice also distorts the operating profitability.

- Reformulated statements can be prepared for segments of the firm—from the detail provided in the footnotes—to reveal more of the operations.

Analysis of the equity statement is a prerequisite for the reformulation of the income statement, for that reformulation identifies dirty-surplus items that have to be brought into the income statement. Exhibit 10.8 gives the reformulated equity statement for Nike, with comprehensive income—to which the reformulated income statement must total—identified.

EXHIBIT 10.8
Reformulated Statement of Shareholders' Equity for Nike, Inc. (in millions).
The statement identifies $1,810.4 million in comprehensive income.

Balance at May 31, 2009			$8,814.5
Transactions with shareholders			
Stock issues for stock options		$ 482.2	
Stock issued to employees (net)		37.1	
Stock repurchased		(754.3)	
Cash dividends		(505.5)	(740.5)
Comprehensive income			
Net income reported		1,906.7	
Net translation gains and losses		(159.2)	
Net hedging gains and losses		6.5	
Loss on the exercise of stock options (after-tax)	102.6		
Less after-tax stock compensations expense in net income	159.0	56.4	1,810.4
Balance at May 31, 2010			$9,884.4

Exhibit 10.9 gives the GAAP comparative income statement for Nike for 2010, along with the reformulated statement. Note the following in the reformulated statement (numbers flag items in the exhibit):

1. Dirty-surplus items have been brought into the statement so the "bottom line" for 2010 is the comprehensive income calculated in Exhibit 10.8 (and so for 2009 and 2008).

2. The reformulation distinguishes operating income that comes from sales from operating income that does not come from sales. This distinction gives a clean measure of the profit margin from sales and also a clean measure of the effective tax rate on operating income. Operating income from items reported net of tax are separately identified.

3. Taxes have been allocated using federal and state statutory rates, 35 percent for the federal rate plus the state 1.3 percent rate. The rates are ascertained from the tax footnote. Nike's effective tax rate on operating income from sales for 2010 is 24.19 percent (612.5/2,532.2 = 24.19%). Note that this is lower than the statutory rate because operations attract tax concessions.

4. Detail on expenses has been discovered in the footnotes. For example, the advertising component of selling and administrative expenses are in the reformulated statement. However, more detail on the large administrative and general expenses is not available. You will often be frustrated by such a lack of disclosure.

The reformulation of Nike's financial statements for prior years is continued on the BYOAP feature on the book's Web site. See Box 10.5.

EXHIBIT 10.9
GAAP Consolidated Statements of Income and Reformulated Income Statements for Nike, Inc., 2008–2010.
The reformulated statement reformats the GAAP statement into operating income (operating revenue minus operating expense) and net financial income (financial income minus financial expense), adds dirty-surplus income items, and makes the appropriate tax allocation. Numbers to the right of the reformulated statement refer to points on the reformulation in the text.

NIKE, INC.
GAAP Income Statements
(in millions, except per-share data)

	Year Ended May 31		
	2010	**2009**	**2008**
Revenues	$19,014.0	$19,176.1	$18,627.0
Cost of sales	10,213.6	10,571.7	10,239.6
Gross margin	8,800.4	8,604.4	8,387.4
Selling and administrative expense	6,326.4	6,149.6	5,953.7
Restructuring charges (Note 16)	—	195.0	—
Goodwill impairment (Note 4)	—	199.3	—
Intangible and other asset impairment (Note 4)	—	202.0	—
Interest expense (income), net (Notes 6,7 and 8)	6.3	(9.5)	(77.1)
Other (income) expense, net (Notes 17 and 18)	(49.2)	(88.5)	(7.9)
Income before income taxes	2,516.9	1,956.5	2,502.9
Income taxes (Note 9)	610.2	469.8	619.5
Net income	$ 1,906.7	$ 1,486.7	$ 1,883.4
Basic earnings per common share (Notes 1 and 12)	$ 3.93	$ 3.07	$ 3.80
Diluted earnings per common share (Notes 1 and 12)	$ 3.86	$ 3.03	$ 3.74
Dividends declared per common share	$ 1.06	$ 0.98	$ 0.875

Notes refer to footnotes in the published statements. Refer to 2010 10-K.

(continued)

EXHIBIT 10.9 (*concluded*)

Reformulated Income Statements
(in millions of dollars)

	2010		2009		2008		
Operating revenues		19,014.0		19,176.1		18,627.0	
Cost of sales		10,213.6		10,571.7		10,239.6	
Gross margin		8,800.4		8,604.4		8,387.4	
Operating expenses							
Administrative expenses		3,970.0		3,798.3		3,645.4	**(4)**
Advertising[1]		2,356.4		2,351.3		2,308.3	**(4)**
Other expense (income)[2]		(49.2)		(88.5)		68.5	**(4)**
Operating income from sales (before tax)		2,523.2		2,543.3		2,365.2	
Taxes							
Taxes as reported	610.2		469.8		619.5		
Tax on financial items and other operating income	2.3	612.5	213.1	682.9	(50.2)	569.3	**(3)**
Operating income from sales (after tax)		1,910.7		1,860.4		1,795.9	**(2)**
Other operating income (before tax items)							
Gains on divestitures[2]					60.6		
Restructuring charges			(195.0)				
Goodwill impairment			(199.3)				
Intangible asset impairment			(202.0)				
			596.3				
Tax on other operating income			216.5	(379.8)	22.1	38.5	**(2)(3)**
Other operating income (after tax items)							
Currency translation gains (losses)[4]		(159.2)		(335.3)		165.6	**(1)(2)**
Hedging gains (losses) and other[4]		6.5		451.4		(117.3)	**(1)(2)**
Effect of stock option exercise		56.4		126.4		30.9	
Operating Income (after tax)		1,814.4		1,723.1		1,913.6	
Financing income (expense)							
Interest income[5]		30.1		49.7		115.8	**(4)**
Interest expense		36.4		40.2		38.7	
Net interest income (expense)		(6.3)		9.5		77.1	
Tax effect (at 36.3%)[3]		2.3		3.4		28.1	**(3)**
Net interest income (expense)		(4.0)		6.1		49.0	
Preferred dividends		0.0		0.0		0.0	
Net financing income (expense)		(4.0)		6.1		49.0	
Comprehensive income		1,810.4		1,729.2		1,962.6	**(1)**

[1]Broken out from selling and administrative expenses.
[2]Other expenses in the GAAP statement in 2008 included gains from divestitures.
[3]Statutory tax rate is 36.3%, including both federal and state taxes. See tax footnote in 10-K.
[4]These items are dirty-surplus income reported in the equity statement.
[5]Interest income is netted against interest expense in the GAAP statements.
[6]Preferred dividends are less than $0.05 million.
Some columns may not add due to rounding error.

The reformulation of Nike's 2008–2010 financial statements in this chapter continues an analysis of the firm on the Build Your Own Analysis Product (BYOAP) feature on the book's Web site. By going to this feature, you can trace Nike over an extended period, giving yourself more information for a valuation in 2010. Below are some summary numbers from the reformulated statements on BYOAP (in millions of dollars).

	2010	2009	2008	2007	2006	2005	2004
Sales	19,014	19,176	18,627	16,326	14,955	13,740	12,253
Operating income (after tax)	1,757	1,661	1,862	1,502	1,323	1,264	1,035
Comprehensive income	1,810	1,667	1,911	1,544	1,346	1,261	1,019
Net operating assets	5,514	6,346	5,806	4,939	4,916	4,782	4,551
Net financial assets	4,370	2,468	1,992	2,179	1,499	939	289
Common shareholders' equity	9,884	8,814	7,797	7,118	6,364	5,721	4,840

Value Added to Strategic Balance Sheets

A reformulated income statement identifies the earnings flowing from the strategic balance sheet; operating income reports the earnings flowing from the net operating assets; and net financing income (expense) reports the earnings flowing from the net financial assets (obligations).

Exhibits 10.10 and 10.11 present the reformulated income statements for Dell, Inc., and General Mills, Inc. Dell reports net financial income flowing from the net financial assets on its strategic balance sheet while General Mills reports net financial expense flowing from its considerable net financial obligations. While Dell has large net financial assets, it reports a net interest expense in its income statement because interest rates on financial assets at the time were very low. For both firms, operating income that pertains to the net operating assets is separated from the financing income, and that operating income is broken down into operating income from sales and other operating income. Dell's other operating income has only after-tax items, but General Mills's statement has tax allocated to before-tax items within other operating income: Restructuring charges are tax deductions, so reduce taxes, and divestiture gains increase taxes.

Residual Income from Operations

Reformulated income statements and balance sheets are designed to identify the value added to the strategic balance sheet. The focus is on the operating activities, for that is where the firm trades with customers and suppliers to add value. We calculated residual earnings for the equity in Chapter 5, but now we can identify residual earnings from the operating component of the shareholders' equity. The value-added measure is referred to as **residual operating income (ReOI).** It is calculated as

$$\text{Residual operating income}_t = \text{Operating income}_t - (\text{Required return} \times \text{Net operating assets}_{t-1})$$

$$\text{ReOI}_t = \text{OI}_t - (\rho - 1)\text{NOA}_{t-1}$$

Here OI is operating income from the reformulated income statement, and NOA is net operating assets at the beginning of the year. If the required return for General Mills is 8 percent, residual operating income for 2010 is $1,177 - (0.08 \times 11,803) = 232.8$ million. That is, General Mills added $232.8 million in operations over the operating income required for a normal return on the book value of operations.

EXHIBIT 10.10
Reformulated Income Statement for Dell, Inc., for Fiscal Year 2011.
Dell's comprehensive income comes from revenues from customers, other operating income, and net financing income from its net financial assets. Each component of the income statement carries the appropriate tax allocation.

DELL, INC.
Reformulated Comparative Income Statement for Fiscal Year 2011
(in millions)

	Year Ending February 1			
		2011		**2010**
Operating revenues		$ 61,494		$ 52,902
Cost of revenue		50,098		43,641
Gross margin		11,396		9,261
Operating expenses				
Administrative and general expenses		6,572		5,846
Advertising expenses		730		619
Research and development		661		624
Operating income from sales (before tax)		3,433		2,172
Taxes				
Taxes as reported	715		591	
Taxes benefit of net financial expense	29	744	52	643
Operating income from sales (after tax)		2,689		1,529
Other operating income (all after tax)				
Foreign currency translation gain (loss)		79		(29)
Unrealized gain (loss) on derivatives		(112)		(323)
Operating income (after tax)		2,656		1,177
Financing income (expense)				
Interest income		116		71
Interest expense		199		219
Net interest expense		83		148
Tax effect (at 35%)		29		52
Net interest expense after tax		54		96
Unrealized gains (losses) on financial assets		(2)		6
Net financing expense after tax		56		90
Comprehensive income		$ 2,600		$ 1,087

Dell provides an illuminating case of how reformatted strategic balance sheets and income statements identify the sources of value creation. When discussing the strategic balance sheet, we pointed out that Dell's negative net operating assets mean that its shareholders have negative investment in the business and that negative investment means they can withdraw cash from the business and invest it elsewhere. Residual 2011 operating income for Dell (with a required return of 9 percent) is

$$\text{ReOI}_{2011} = \$2,656 - (0.09 \times -\$2,028) = \$2,839 \text{ million}$$

Dell's residual operating income from operations is actually greater than its operating income! Why? Well, the negative net operating assets means that Dell effectively runs a float that shareholders can invest elsewhere at 9 percent, and this value-adding feature is picked up in the residual operating income calculation. The reformulated statements identify two drivers of residual operating income: Operating income from trading with customers plus the value of strategically structuring operations to deliver a float. In valuing Dell, we will keep these two drivers in mind: Dell can grow ReOI by increasing sales

EXHIBIT 10.11
Reformulated Income
Statement for
General Mills, Inc.,
for Fiscal Year 2010.
General Mills's
comprehensive income
comes from revenues
from customers and
before-tax and after-
tax other operating
income, less net
interest expense on its
net financial
obligations.

GENERAL MILLS, Inc.
Reformulated Comparative Income Statement for Fiscal Year 2010
(in millions)

		Year Ending May 25		
		2010		**2009**
Operating revenues		$ 14,797		$ 14,691
Cost of sales		8,923		9,458
Gross margin		5,874		5,233
Administrative and general expenses		2,109		2,012
Advertising		909		732
Research and development		219		207
Operating income from sales (before tax)		2,637		2,282
Taxes				
Taxes as reported	771		720	
Tax on other operating income	12		(16)	
Tax benefit of net interest	151	934	144	848
Operating income from sales (after tax)		1,703		1,434
Other operating income (before-tax items)				
Divestive gains (restructuring charges)	(31)		43	
Tax effect (at 37.5%)	12	(19)	16	27
Other operating income (after-tax items)				
Earnings from joint ventures		102		92
Foreign currency translation gain (loss)		(163)		(288)
Gain (loss) on hedge derivatives and securities		14		(3)
Pension charges		(460)		(761)
Operating income (after tax)		1,177		501
Net financing expense				
Interest expense		409		405
Interest income		7		22
Net interest expense		402		383
Tax effect (at 37.5%)		(151)		(144)
Net financing expense after tax		251		239
Noncontrolling interest		5		9
Comprehensive income		$ 921		$ 253

and margins to produce operating income in the income statement and also by expanding the float in its management of assets and its relationships with customers and suppliers. Looking back, the decline in Dell's stock price in recent years can be attributed to a slowing of sales growth, a decline in profit margins, and a contraction of the float.

COMPARATIVE ANALYSIS OF THE BALANCE SHEET AND INCOME STATEMENT

To make judgments about a firm's performance, the analyst needs benchmarks. Benchmarks are established by reference to other firms (usually in the same industry) or to the same firm's past history. Comparison to other firms is called *cross-sectional analysis*. Comparison to a firm's own history is called *time-series analysis*. Financial statements are prepared

EXHIBIT 10.12
Comparative Common-Size Income Statements for Nike, Inc., and General Mills, Inc., for 2010. Dollar amounts in millions. Percentages are per dollar of sales.
Common-size income statements reveal the profitability of sales and the effect of each expense item on the profitability of sales.

	Nike		General Mills	
	$	%	$	%
Revenue	19,014	100.0	14,797	100.0
Cost of sales	10,214	53.7	8,923	60.3
Gross margin	8,800	46.3	5,874	39.7
Operating expenses				
Administrative	3,970	20.9	2,109	14.3
Advertising	2,356	12.4	909	6.1
Other expense (income)	(49)	(0.3)	219	1.5
Operating income from sales (before tax)	2,523	13.3	2,637	17.8
Tax on operating income from sales	612	3.2	934	6.3
Other operating income from sales (after tax)	1,911	10.0	1,703	11.5
Other operating income (expense)	(154)	(0.8)	(526)	(3.6)
Operating income (after tax)	1,757	9.2	1,177	7.9
Net financing income (expense)	(4)	0.0	(256)	(1.7)
Comprehensive income to common	1,753	9.2	921	6.2

for cross-sectional comparisons using the techniques of *common-size analysis*. The statements are compared over time using *trend analysis*.

Common-Size Analysis

Common-size analysis is simply a standardization of line items to eliminate the effect of size. Line items are expressed per dollar of an attribute that reflects the scale of operations. However, if that attribute is chosen carefully, and if reformulated statements are used, the scaling will reveal pertinent features of a firm's operations. And when compared across firms, or across time, common-size statements will identify unusual features that require further investigation.

Common-Size Income Statements

Exhibit 10.12 places Nike's and General Mills's reformulated income statements on a common-size basis. Revenues and expenses, along with net comprehensive income, are expressed as a percentage of the revenue.

The comparative common-size statements reveal two things:

- How firms do business differently and the different structure of revenues and expenses that result. Looking at operating expenses, the firms have similar cost components, but Nike has the lowest cost of sales per dollar of revenue (53.7 percent) and thus a higher percentage gross margin (46.3 percent). General Mills maintains the lowest administrative expenses at 14.3 percent of sales, and has lower advertising expenses (6.1 percent of sales).

- Operating profitability per dollar of sales. As each operating item is divided by sales revenue, the common-size number indicates the proportion of each dollar of sales the item represents. Thus the number for an operating expense is the percentage of sales that is absorbed by the expense, and the number for operating income is the percentage of sales that ends up in profit. The latter is particularly important:

Operating profit margin from sales = Operating income from sales (after tax)/Sales

EXHIBIT 10.13
Comparative
Common-Size
Balance Sheets for
Nike, Inc. and
General Mills Inc.,
for 2010. Dollar
amounts in millions.
Common-size balance
sheets reveal the
percentage makeup of
operating assets and
operating liabilities.

	Nike		General Mills	
	$	%	$	%
Operating assets				
Operating cash	95	1.0	60	0.4
Accounts renewable	2,650	28.3	1,042	6.1
Inventories	2,041	21.8	1,344	7.9
Prepaid expenses	874	9.3	379	2.2
Property, plant, and equipment	1,932	20.6	3,128	18.3
Goodwill	188	2.0	6,593	38.6
Identifiable intangibles	467	5.0	3,715	21.8
Deferred taxes and other assets	1,122	12.0	805	4.7
	9,369	100.0	17,066	100.0
Operating liabilities				
Accounts payable	1,166	30.2	850	15.2
Accrued liabilities	1,774	46.0	3,880	69.2
Income taxes payable	59	1.5	—	—
Deferred taxes and other	855	22.2	875	15.6
	3,855	100.0	5,605	100.0
Net operating assets	5,514		11,461	

Nike's profit margin from sales (after-tax) is 10 percent, compared with an 11.5 percent margin for General Mills. Ratios also can be calculated for operating income before tax and for total operating income, as in the exhibit. Reviewing the expense ratios, we see that Nike, despite a higher percentage gross margin, had a lower profit margin from sales than General Mills primarily because of higher administrative and advertising expenses.

The final comprehensive income number, expressed as a percentage of sales, is the (comprehensive) *net profit margin*. The comparison of this number to the operating profit margin reveals how much the firms increased or decreased their profits through financing activities. Nike earned a net 9.2 cents of comprehensive income for every dollar of sales, compared to 6.2 cents for General Mills.

Common-Size Balance Sheets

Common-size balance sheets often standardize on total assets, but a more informative approach, using reformulated statements, standardizes operating assets and liabilities on their totals. The operating section of the comparative common-size balance sheets for the two firms is shown in Exhibit 10.13. The percentages describe the relative composition of the net assets in the operating activities. You can easily spot the differences when the balance sheets are in this form; compare the relative amounts of investments in accounts receivable, inventory, property, plant, and equipment, and so on, for the two companies.

Trend Analysis

Exhibit 10.14 presents trends for Nike, Inc., from 2006 to 2010. The numbers on which the analysis is based are in the BYOAP tool on the text's Web site. See Box 10.5. **Trend analysis** expresses financial statement items as an index relative to a base year. In Nike's case, the index is 100 for the base year of 2005.

EXHIBIT 10.14 **Trend Analysis of Selected Financial Statement Items for Nike, Inc., 2006–2010. Base = 100 for 2005.**
Trend analysis reveals the growth or decline in financial statement items over time.

Income Statement						
	2010	**2009**	**2008**	**2007**	**2006**	**Base in 2005 ($ in millions)**
Sales	138.4	139.6	135.6	118.8	108.8	13,740
Cost of sales	134.0	138.7	134.3	120.2	109.8	7,625
Gross margin	143.9	140.7	137.2	117.1	107.7	6,115
Operating expenses	147.7	142.6	138.8	118.3	105.5	4,250
Operating income from sales (before tax)	135.3	136.4	126.8	114.4	112.9	1,865
Operating income from sales (after tax)	157.3	153.1	147.8	119.3	112.9	1,215
Operating income	139.0	131.4	147.3	118.8	104.7	1,264
Comprehensive income to common	139.0	132.2	151.5	122.4	106.7	1,261

Balance Sheet						
Operating assets	132.9	140.3	138.5	112.4	108.5	7,049
Operating liabilities	171.0	156.9	168.2	131.6	120.2	2,267
Net operating assets	114.8	132.4	124.4	103.3	102.9	4,782
Net financial assets	467.8	264.2	212.1	232.1	154.3	939
Common shareholders' equity	172.8	154.1	138.8	124.4	111.3	5,721

Trend analysis gives a picture of how financial statement items have changed over time. The index for net operating assets indicates whether the firm is growing investments in operations, and at what rate, or is liquidating. The index for common stockholders' equity tracks the growth or decline in the owners' investment. And the index for net financial obligations tracks the net indebtedness. Similarly, the indexes for the income statement track the income and the factors that affect it. Of particular interest are sales, operating income from sales, and comprehensive income.

The picture drawn for Nike is one of sales growth over the five years, resulting in growth in operating income from sales, after tax, of 57.3 percent and growth in comprehensive income of 39 percent over the five years. The indexes for specific line items indicate where the growth has come from, and year-to-year changes indicate the periods that have contributed most to growth. Cost of sales has grown slower than sales and, correspondingly, gross margins have grown at a higher rate than sales. From the balance sheet trends, we observe that net operating assets have grown slower than sales, indicating that, as time has evolved, more sales have been earned for each dollar invested in these assets.

Year-to-year changes in the index represent year-to-year growth rates. For example, Nike's 2009 sales growth rate was (139.6 − 135.6)/135.6, or 2.9 percent, compared with the 2008 growth rate of (135.6 − 118.8)/118.8, or 14.1 percent. Comparisons of growth rates raise questions for the analyst. In 2009, sales grew by 2.9 percent, but net operating assets grew by a much larger amount, 6.4 percent. Why? Balance sheet detail on the composition of net operating assets supplies the answer. Was it inventory buildup? Was it new investment in plant? Why did net operating assets decline in 2010? Why did operating expenses grow faster than sales revenue in 2010? Such questions provoke the analyst to further investigation.

Common-size and trend analysis can be combined by preparing trend statements on a common-size basis. This facilitates the comparison of one firm's trends with those of comparable firms.

PROFIT MARGIN RATIOS

Profit margins are the percentage of sales that yield profits:

$$\text{Operating profit margin (PM)} = \frac{\text{OI (after tax)}}{\text{Sales}}$$

This profit margin is based on the total operating income on the last line of operating income before financial items. It can be divided into profit margin from income generated by sales and profit margin from income that does not come from sales:

$$\text{Sales PM} = \frac{\text{OI (after tax) from sales}}{\text{Sales}}$$

$$\text{Other items PM} = \frac{\text{OI (after tax) from other items}}{\text{Sales}}$$

These two margins sum to the operating profit margin. A common other operating item is the share of income (or loss) of subsidiaries. This income is from sales reported in the subsidiary, not from the reported sales in the parent's income statement. Including it in the analysis of the profitability of the sales in the parent's income statement results in an incorrect assessment of the profit margin on sales. Nike's sales PM is 10.0 percent in Exhibit 10.12, its other items' PM is –0.8 percent, so its total operating profit margin is 9.2 percent. The bottom-line margin ratio is

$$\frac{\text{Net (comprehensive)}}{\text{income profit margin}} = \frac{\text{Comprehensive income}}{\text{Sales}}$$

Nike's bottom-line margin is 9.2 percent.

EXPENSE RATIOS

Expense ratios calculate the percentage of sales revenue that is absorbed by expenses. They have the form

$$\text{Expense ratio} = \frac{\text{Expense}}{\text{Sales}}$$

This ratio is calculated for each expense item in operating income from sales so

$$1 - \text{Sales PM} = \text{Sum of expense ratios}$$

Expense ratios are given in Exhibit 10.12. Cost of sales for Nike absorb 53.7 percent of sales. The firm's total expense ratios sum to 86.8 percent before tax and 90.0 percent after tax, with the remaining 10.0 percent of sales providing operating income after tax.

RATIO ANALYSIS

From the reformulated statements, we can calculate two ratios that summarize the profitability of the operating activities and the financing activities: return on net operating assets (RNOA), which is operating income after tax relative to net operating assets, and net borrowing cost (NBC), which is net financial expenses after tax relative to net financial obligations. If a firm has net financial assets (rather than net financial obligations), like Nike, the profitability of the financing activities is measured by return on net financial assets (RNFA).

For Nike, Inc., the return on net operating assets for 2010 was

$$\text{RNOA} = \frac{1,814}{\frac{1}{2}\,(5,514 + 6,346)} = 30.6\%$$

Nike's 2008 net return on net financial assets was

$$\text{RNFA} = \frac{49}{\frac{1}{2}\,(1,992 + 2,179)} = 2.3\%$$

The RNOA based on operating income from sales was 32.2 percent. For General Mills, the 2010 RNOA was

$$\text{RNOA} = \frac{1,177}{\frac{1}{2}\,(11,461 + 11,803)} = 10.1\%$$

COMPOSITION RATIOS

The percentages in common-size balance sheets (as in Exhibit 10.13) are composition ratios:

$$\text{Operating asset composition ratio} = \frac{\text{Operating asset}}{\text{Total operating assets}}$$

$$\frac{\text{Operating liability}}{\text{composition ratio}} = \frac{\text{Operating liability}}{\text{Total operating liabilities}}$$

The ratios for individual items sum to 100 percent within their category.

OPERATING LIABILITY LEVERAGE

The composition of net operating assets can be highlighted by comparing operating liabilities to net operating assets:

$$\text{Operating liability leverage (OLLEV)} = \frac{\text{Operating liabilities}}{\text{Net operating assets}}$$

The **operating liability leverage** ratio gives an indication of how the investment in net operating assets has been reduced by operating liabilities. It is called a leverage ratio because it can lever up the return on net operating assets (RNOA) with a lower denominator. For Nike, the operating liability leverage ratio at the end of 2010 is 69.9 percent compared to 48.9 percent for General Mills. The operating liability composition ratios reveal which liabilities have contributed to the operating liability leverage.

FINANCIAL LEVERAGE

A second leverage ratio gives the relative size of net financial assets or obligations. General Mills has net debt in 2010, while Nike holds net financial assets. The differences are captured by ratios that compare totals for net operating assets and net financing obligations to owners' equity. These ratios are

$$\text{Capitalization ratio} = \text{NOA/CSE}$$

and

$$\text{Financial leverage ratio (FLEV)} = \text{NFO/CSE}$$

which is negative if the firm has positive net financial assets. **Financial leverage** is the degree to which net operating assets are financed by common equity. It is always the case that

$$\text{Capitalization ratio} - \text{Financial leverage ratio} = 1.0$$

Thus, either measure can be used as an indication of the degree to which net financial assets are financed by common equity or net financial debt, but it is usual to refer to the financial leverage ratio. It is called a leverage ratio because, as we will see in Chapter 12, borrowing levers the ROCE up or down.

General Mills had a capitalization ratio of 2.03 and a financial leverage ratio of 1.03 at the end of 2010. Nike's financial leverage ratio in 2010 was −0.44 and its capitalization ratio was 0.56. Nike, with net financial assets, is negatively levered.

The RNOA based on operating income from sales was 14.6 percent. General Mill's 2010 net borrowing cost was

$$\text{NBC} = \frac{251}{\frac{1}{2}\,(5{,}813 + 6{,}386)} = 4.1\%$$

These returns are, of course, after tax (and after the tax benefit of debt). The calculations use the average of beginning and ending balances in the denominator; they can be inaccurate if there are large changes in balance sheet items other than halfway through the year. Net borrowing cost is particularly sensitive to the timing of large changes in debt. Always compare the NBC against the cost of debt reported in the debt footnotes, as a check.

These profitability ratios will be analyzed in detail in Chapter 12. The common-size analysis of the statements yield a number of ratios that will be used in that analysis. These ratios are summarized in Boxes 10.6 and 10.7.

Box 10.8 maintains the Accounting Quality Watch begun in the last chapter.

The Accounting Quality Watch, begun in Box 9.6 in the last chapter, continues here with a list of quality issues in the balance sheet. The quality of the accounting in the balance sheet also affects the income statement, as indicated below. The Quality Watch continues in the next chapter with the quality of cash flows. Further earnings quality issues are identified in the Quality Watch in Chapter 13, where sustainable earnings are the focus.

Accounting Item	The Quality Problem
Assets	
Held-to-maturity debt investments	Held-to-maturity debt investments (typically classified as financial assets) are carried at historical cost. This may not indicate their "cash value." Identify market values from footnotes if available. (Historical cost is usually a reasonable approximation of market value.)
Held-to-maturity equity investments	"Held-to-maturity" equity investments (permanent investments) are carried at historical cost when they involve less than 20 percent ownership of another firm (see Accounting Clinic III). So the balance sheet does not give an indication of the value of the investments. Nor does the income statement: Only dividends from the investments are recorded there, and dividends are not an indicator of value. The analyst needs to find a market value for the securities (if traded) or identify the share of income in the investee, as in the equity method.
Marked-to-market equity investments available for sale	Marking equity investments to market solves the problem of the held-to-maturity treatment. However, further issues arise. First, unrealized gains and losses from the marking to market are not reported in the income statement but rather in the equity statement. This not only misreports the performance of the equity portfolio in the income statement, but it also permits firms to "cherry pick" realized gains into the income statement and report unrealized losses in the equity statement. (Reformulating the income statement on a comprehensive-income basis solves the problem.) Second, market prices can be bubble prices, so bubbles are brought into the financial statements. (They can also be depressed prices in an illiquid market.) Third, fair-value accounting allows estimates of the market price when market prices are not available—so-called Level 3 estimates—and these estimates can be suspect.
Receivable allowances	Allowance for bad debts can be biased. Decreases in allowances increase earnings (through lower bad-debt expense) and increases decrease earnings. The same issue arises with allowances on other assets, for example, a bank's allowance against loans for default.
Deferred tax assets	Deferred tax valuation allowances reduce deferred tax assets for the probability that the tax benefit will not materialize. The estimates involved are suspect, and earnings can be increased by changing the allowance. Refer to the deferred tax footnote for details of the valuation allowance.
Goodwill	The price paid for an acquisition is divided between the fair value of identifiable (tangible and intangible) assets acquired and goodwill. As tangible and intangible assets have to be subsequently depreciated or amortized against earnings, firms might allocate more of the purchase price to goodwill (that is not amortized, but rather subject to impairment).
Liabilities	
Deferred (unearned) revenue	Revenue must be recognized as goods are shipped or services performed. With multiyear contracts, firms defer revenue to later years when performance takes place, creating a deferred revenue liability. The amount deferred is subject to judgment: Firms can defer too little (aggressive revenue recognition) or too much (conservative revenue recognition). In either case, current revenues may not be a good indication of future revenues.
Accrued expenses	These are often estimates that can be biased. Watch particularly for estimated warranty liabilities (for servicing warranties and guarantees on products) and estimated restructuring costs.
Lease obligations	Lease obligations, under capitalized leases, are on the balance sheet but those for operating leases are not. Check the footnotes for off-balance-sheet lease obligations.
Pension liabilities	This involves a number of actuarial assumptions and the choice of a discount rate, so is a "soft" number. Pension expense (in the income statement) is affected by changes in the estimated liability from changing these assumptions.
Dividends payable	This should be classified as shareholders' equity, not a liability.
Contingent liabilities	Check the footnotes for any off-balance-sheet, contingent liabilities (for product liability or environmental clean-up lawsuits, for example).
Other liabilities	Dig into footnotes to see what these involve.
Preferred stock	GAAP classifies preferred stock as equity (or, if it is redeemable, between liabilities and equity). This is a liability from the common shareholders' point of view.

BUILD YOUR OWN ANALYSIS ENGINE

If you followed the advice for building an analysis spreadsheet in Chapter 8, you would have entered the summary financial statement numbers for Nike into a spreadsheet and seen how these numbers tie together. Now is the time to get more detail into the spreadsheet. The re-formulated balance sheet and income statement for Nike in this chapter guides you. You might also work with General Mills or with Kimberly-Clark in the Continuing Case at the end of this chapter. (The book's Web site gives the solution for the Continuing Case.)

You should download these firms' financial statements from their annual 10-K reports and read the financial statement footnotes to discover more detail to add to the financial statements. There is no program that will automatically reformulate the statements; you must do this manually after understanding the business and reaching a judgment as to what items pertain to the operating and financing activities. This analysis is your responsibility! The business section of the 10-K will help you, as will the Management Discussion and Analysis section.

With these fully reformulated financial statements, along with the equity statement from the last chapter, you now have the financial statements in a form to begin a full financial statement analysis. If you need more help in setting up these financial statements, the BYOAP guide on the book's Web site will help you.

Summary

We can put what we have done in this chapter in perspective by listing eight steps for financial statement analysis:

1. Reformulate the statement of stockholders' equity on a comprehensive income basis.
2. Calculate the comprehensive rate of return on common equity, ROCE, and the growth in equity from the reformulated statement of common stockholders' equity.
3. Reformulate the balance sheet to distinguish operating and financial assets and obligations.
4. Reformulate the income statement on a comprehensive-income basis to distinguish operating and financing income. Make sure taxes are allocated.
5. Compare reformulated balance sheets and income statements with reformulated statements of comparison firms through a comparative common-size analysis and trend analysis.
6. Reformulate the cash flow statement.
7. Carry out the analysis of ROCE.
8. Carry out an analysis of growth.

Chapter 9 performed the first two steps. This chapter covers steps 3–5, the next chapter covers step 6, and the analysis of ROCE and growth in steps 7 and 8 is done in Chapters 12 and 13.

Reformulation of the income statement and balance sheet is necessary to calculate ratios that correctly measure the results of the firm's activities. If financing items are classified as operating items, we get an incorrect measure of both operating profitability (RNOA) and financing profitability (NBC or RNFA). This chapter has led you through the reformulations. Reformulation looks like a mechanical exercise, but it requires a good knowledge of the business, an understanding of how the firm makes money. Indeed, reformulation prompts the analyst to understand the business better. It requires her to dig into the footnotes and the management discussion and analysis to understand the GAAP statements and to incorporate more detail in the reformulated statements. With a rich set of reformulated statements accompanied by comparative common-size and trend statements, the analyst is prepared to proceed to the analysis of profitability and growth in Chapters 12 and 13.

The Web Connection

Find the following on the Web page for this chapter:

- Further examples of reformulated balance sheets and income statements.
- Further discussion on distinguishing between operating and financing items.
- More discussions on why firms hold cash.
- A discussion of financial disclosure (and lack thereof) and how poor transparency in the financial reports frustrates the analyst.

- Directions to finding tax rates and more directions for tax allocation.
- Differences in balance sheet and income statement accounting under GAAP and IFRS.
- The Readers' Corner.

You will sometimes find that lack of disclosure makes it difficult to classify items into operating and financing categories. The problem can be serious if a significant portion of earnings is in shares of subsidiaries' earnings under the equity method (where the firm holds less than 50 percent of the equity of a subsidiary). Reconstructing consolidated statements, or preparing statements on a segmented basis, helps rectify this problem. But to the extent that disclosure is insufficient, profitability measures will be less precise. At the other extreme, if disclosures—on the profitability of segments, for example—are plentiful, the analysis is improved.

Key Concepts

capital lease is a lease of an asset for substantially all of the asset's useful life and for which a lease asset and a lease obligation are placed on the balance sheet. *297*

common-size analysis compares financial statement items to financial statement totals to standardize for size and to highlight the composition of the financial statement. *315*

consolidation accounting is the accounting process by which financial statements for one or more related firms are combined into one set of financial statements. *296*

effective tax rate is the average tax rate on income. *305*

enterprise assets are the net assets used in operating activities, otherwise called **net operating assets (NOA).** *293*

enterprise income is income from the firm's operations, otherwise called **operating income** or **net operating profit after tax (NOPAT).** *303*

financial leverage is the degree to which net operating assets are financed by net financial obligations. *319*

marginal tax rate is the rate at which the last dollar of income is taxed. *305*

minority interest is the share of shareholders in subsidiaries other than the common shareholders of the parent company. Also called **noncontrolling interest.** *298*

net financial assets (obligations) are net assets used in financing activities. Distinguish from **net operating assets.** *293*

net financial expense is the expense generated by a firm's nonequity financing activities. *303*

net operating assets (NOA) are net assets used in operating a business, otherwise called **enterprise assets.** Distinguish from **net financial assets (obligations).** *293*

net operating profit after tax (NOPAT) is income from a firm's business operations, otherwise referred to as **enterprise income.** *303*

noncontrolling interest is the same as **minority interest.** *298*

operating cash is cash used in operations (compared to cash invested in financial assets). *294*

operating income is income from a firm's business of selling products and services, otherwise called **enterprise income** or **net operating profit after tax (NOPAT).** *303*

operating lease is a lease which does not entitle the lessee to use the lease asset for substantially all of the asset's useful life and for which no asset or obligation is recognized on the balance sheet. *297*

operating liability leverage is the degree to which investment in net operating assets is made by operating creditors. *319*

residual operating income (ReOI) is operating income in excess of the net operating assets earning at the required return. *312*

statutory tax rate is the tax rate applied to corporate income by statute. *306*

strategic balance sheet is a reformulated balance sheet that gives insight into how the business is organized. *301*

tax allocation involves attributing income taxes to the appropriate component of income that attracts the taxes. *305*

tax shield is the effect that interest on debt has of reducing corporate taxes. *305*

trend analysis expresses financial statement items as an index relative to a base year. *316*

The Analyst's Toolkit

Analysis Tools	Page	Key Measures	Page	Acronyms to Remember	
Reformulated balance sheets	293	Effective tax rate for operations	307	CSE	common shareholders' equity
Reformulated income statements	303	Net financial income (or expense) after tax	303	FLEV	financial leverage
Tax allocation	304			NBC	net borrowing cost
—Top-down method	308	Operating income after tax (OI)	303	NFA	net financial assets
—Bottom-up method	308			NFE	net financial expense
Common-size analysis	315	Ratios		NFO	net financial obligations
Trend analysis	316	Income statement ratios	318	NOL	net operating loss
Ratio analysis of the income statement and balance sheet	318	Operating profit margin (PM)		NOA	net operating assets
		Sales PM		NOPAT	Net operating profit after tax
		Other items PM		OI	operating income
		Net (comprehensive) income profit margin		OLLEV	operating liability leverage
		Expense ratio		PM	profit margin
		Balance sheet ratios	319	ReOI	residual operating income
		Operating liability leverage (OLLEV)		RNFA	return on net financial assets
		Financial leverage (FLEV)		RNOA	return on net operating assets
		Capitalization ratio		ROCE	return on common equity
		Residual operating income	312		

A Continuing Case: *Kimberly-Clark Corporation*

A Self-Study Exercise

Having reformulated Kimberly-Clark's 2010 equity statement in Chapter 9, you are now ready to move on to the balance sheet and income statement. These are given in Exhibit 2.2 in the Continuing Case for Chapter 2. You should have the reformulated equity statement beside you (in the solution to the case for Chapter 9 on the book's Web site), for all items in comprehensive income, identified there, must be included in the reformulated (comprehensive) income statement.

At this point it is imperative to have a good read of the full 10-K. The management discussion and analysis (MD&A) and the financial summary have considerable detail that will help you decide which items are operating and which are part of KMB's financing activities. If you have not downloaded the 10-K already, do so now, or retrieve it from the Web page supplement to Chapter 2.

REFORMULATION

Your task is to reformulate the balance sheets for 2008, 2009, and 2010 and the income statement for 2009 and 2010 along the lines of those for Nike, Dell, and General Mills in this chapter. Go to the 2008 10-K for the 2008 balance sheet. Go through and mark off the items you consider to be operating items and those you deem to be involved in financing activities. As you read the 10-K, note any detail that can be brought up to the face of the statements to make them more informative. You will find, for example, that advertising expenses were $512 million, $559 million, and $698 million for the years 2008, 2009, and 2010, respectively, and R&D expenditure was $297 million, $301 million, and $317 million for these years.

To carry out the reformulation of comprehensive income for 2009, you need to examine the equity statement for 2009 to identify other comprehensive income. To save you the trouble, comprehensive income for 2009 is given here, with the inclusion of the effect of the exercise of stock options:

Comprehensive income for 2009 (in millions)	
Net income	$1,884
Currency translation gain	619
Pension liability adjustment	(32)
Loss on cash flow hedge	3
Net effect of exercised stock options (after tax)	67
Comprehensive income	$2,541

For the balance sheet, allocate $50 million to working cash each year (about 1/4 percent of sales). The notes receivable in the balance sheet are receivables in a financing subsidiary. Interest on these receivables of $8 million for 2009 and $14 million for 2010 is included in interest income in the income statement. Be sure you identify all relevant components on the income statement, separating operating income from sales from other operating income, and making the appropriate tax allocation. Kimberly-Clark's statutory tax rate is 36.8 percent.

RATIO ANALYSIS

State in two or three sentences what the reformulated statements you have prepared are saying. Then calculate the return on net operating assets and net borrowing cost for 2010 and 2009. Carry out a common-size analysis of the income statement that reveals information about the profitability of operations. Also calculate financial leverage (FLEV) and operating liability leverage (OLLEV).

BUILDING YOUR OWN ANALYSIS ENGINE FOR KMB

You might add your reformulated statements into the spreadsheet you began building in the last chapter. You will then be set up to analyze these statements within the spreadsheet as you move to Chapters 12 and 13. The BYOAP feature on the book's Web site will guide you.

Concept Questions

C10.1.   Why are reformulated statements necessary to discover operating profitability?

C10.2.   Classify each of the following as a financial asset or an operating asset:

    a. Cash in a checking account used to pay bills.
    b. Accounts receivable.
    c. Finance receivables for an automobile firm.
    d. Cash in 90-day interest-bearing deposits (cash equivalents).
    e. Debt investments held to maturity.
    f. Short-term equity investments.
    g. Long-term equity investments held to maturity.
    h. Goodwill.
    i. Lease assets.
    j. Deferred compensation.

C10.3.   Classify each of the following as a financial liability, an operating liability, or neither:

    a. Accrued compensation.
    b. Deferred revenues.
    c. Preferred stock.
    d. Deferred tax liability.
    e. Lease obligations.
    f. Interest-bearing note payable.

C10.4.   From the point of view of the common shareholders, minority interest is a financial obligation. Correct?

C10.5.   What is meant by saying that debt provides a tax shield?

C10.6.   When can a firm lose the tax benefit of debt?

C10.7.   What does an operating profit margin reveal?

C10.8.   What does it mean to say that a firm is negatively levered?

Exercises

Drill Exercises

E10.1.   Basic Calculations (Easy)

    a. The following numbers were extracted from a balance sheet (in millions):

Operating assets	$547
Financial assets	145
Total Liabilities	322

Of the total liabilities, $190 million were deemed to be financing liabilities. Prepare a reformulated balance sheet that distinguishes items involved in operations from those involved in financing activities.

b. An income statement consists of the following line items (in millions):

Revenue	$4,356
Cost of goods sold	3,487
Operating expenses	428
Interest income	56
Interest expense	132

The firm pays no taxes. Prepare a reformulated income statement that distinguishes items involved in operations from those involved in financing activities.

E10.2. Tax Allocation (Easy)

A firm reported $818 million of net income in its income statement after $140 million of net interest expense and income tax expense of $402 million. Calculate operating income after tax and net financial expense after tax, using a statutory tax rate of 35 percent.

E10.3. Effective Tax Rates (Medium)

Consider the following short income statement (in millions):

Operating income before taxes	$100
Interest expense before taxes	10
Tax expense	25
Net income	$ 65

The statutory tax rate is 35 percent. What is the effective tax rate on net income before tax? What is the effective tax rate on operating income?

E10.4. Tax Allocation: Top-Down and Bottom-Up Methods (Easy)

From the following income statement (in millions), calculate operating income after tax, using both the top-down and bottom-up methods. Use a tax rate of 37 percent.

Revenue	$ 6,450
Cost of goods sold	(3,870)
Operating expenses	(1,843)
Interest expense	(135)
Income taxes	(181)
Net income	$ 421

E10.5. Reformulation of a Balance Sheet and Income Statement (Easy)

Reformulate the following balance sheet and income statement for a manufacturing concern. Amounts are in millions. The firm bears a 36 percent statutory tax rate.

Balance Sheet

Assets		Liabilities and Equity	
Operating cash	$ 23	Accounts payable	$1,245
Cash equivalents	435	Accrued expenses	1,549
Accounts receivable	1,827	Deferred tax liability	712
Inventory	2,876		
Property, plant, and equipment	3,567	Long-term debt	3,678
		Preferred stock	432
		Common equity	1,112
Total assets	$8,728	Liabilities and equity	$8,728

Income Statement	
Revenues	$7,493
Operating expenses	6,321
Interest expense	221
Income before tax	951
Income tax	295
Net income	656
Preferred dividends	26
Net income available to common	$ 630

E10.6. Reformulation of a Balance Sheet, Income Statement, and Statement of Shareholders' Equity (Medium)

The following financial statements were reported for a firm for fiscal year 2012 (in millions of dollars):

Balance Sheet					
	2012	2011		2012	2011
Operating cash	60	50	Accounts payable	1,200	1,040
Short-term investments (at market)	550	500	Accrued liabilities	390	450
Accounts receivable	940	790	Long-term debt	1,840	1,970
Inventory	910	840	Common equity	1,870	1,430
Property and plant	2,840	2,710			
	5,300	4,890		5,300	4,890

Statement of Shareholders' Equity	
Balance, end of fiscal year 2011	1,430
Share issues	822
Repurchase of 24 million shares	(720)
Cash dividend	(180)
Unrealized gain on debt investments	50
Net income	468
Balance, end of fiscal year 2012	1,870

The firm's income tax rate is 35%. The firm reported $15 million in interest income and $98 million in interest expense for 2012. Sales revenue was $3,726 million.

a. Reformulate the balance sheet for 2012 in a way that distinguishes operating and financing activities. Also reformulate the equity statement.
b. Prepare a reformulated statement of comprehensive income.

E10.7. Testing Relationships in Reformulated Income Statements (Medium)

Fill in the missing numbers, indicated by capital letters, in the following reformulated income statement. Amounts are in millions of dollars. The firm's marginal tax rate is 35 percent.

Operating revenues		5,523
Cost of sales	3,121	
Other operating expenses	1,429	
Operating income before tax		A
Tax as reported	B	
Tax benefit of interest expense	C	
Operating income after tax		D
Interest expense before tax	E	
Tax benefit	(F)	
Interest expense after tax		42
Comprehensive income		610

What is the firm's effective tax rate on operating income?

Applications

E10.8.   Price of "Cash" and Price of the Operations: Realnetworks, Inc. (Easy)

In October 2008, the 142,562 thousand outstanding shares of Realnetworks, Inc., traded at $3.96 each. The most recent quarterly balance sheet reported $454 million in net financial assets and $876 million in common shareholders' equity.

a. What is the price-to-book ratio for the firm's equity?
b. What is the book value of the firm's net operating assets?
c. At what price is the market valuing the business operations?

E10.9.   Analysis of an Income Statement: Pepsico, Inc. (Easy)

Pepsico, Inc. reported the following income statement for 1999 (in millions of dollars):

Net sales	20,367
Operating expenses	(17,484)
Restructuring charge	(65)
Operating profit	2,818
Gain on asset sales	1,083
Interest expense	(363)
Interest income	118
	3,656
Provision for income taxes	1,606
Net income	2,050

a. Reformulate this statement to distinguish operating items from financing items and operating income from sales from other operating income. Identify operating income after tax. The firm's statutory tax rate is 36.1 percent.
b. Calculate the effective tax rate on operating income from sales.

Real World Connection

Exercise E4.13 deals with Pepsico, as do Minicases M5.2 and M6.1.

E10.10.   Coffee Time: A Reformulation for Starbucks Corporation (Medium)

(This exercise builds on Exercise E9.8 in Chapter 9, but can be worked independently.)

Below are comparative income statements and balance sheets for Starbucks Corporation, the retail coffee vendor, for fiscal year ending September 30, 2007, along with a statement of shareholders' equity. Read the statements along with the notes under them, then answer the following questions:

a. Prepare a reformulated equity statement for fiscal year 2007 that separates net payout to shareholders from comprehensive income.
b. Prepare a reformulated comprehensive income statement for fiscal year 2007, along with reformulated balance sheets for 2007 and 2006.
c. For fiscal year 2007, calculate the following: return on common equity (ROCE), return on net operating assets (RNOA), and net borrowing cost (NBC). Use beginning-of-year balance sheet amounts in denominators. Also calculate the financial leverage ratio (FLEV) at the beginning of the 2007 fiscal year.

STARBUCKS CORPORATION
Consolidated Statements of Earnings
(in thousands of dollars, except earnings per share)

	Fiscal Year Ended	
	September 30, 2007	**October 1, 2006**
Net revenues:		
Company-operated retail	$7,998,265	$6,583,098
Specialty:		
Licensing	1,026,338	860,676
Food service and other	386,894	343,168
Total specialty	1,413,232	1,203,844
Total net revenues	9,411,497	7,786,942
Cost of sales including occupancy costs	3,999,124	3,178,791
Store operating expenses	3,215,889	2,687,815
Other operating expenses	294,136	253,724
Depreciation and amortization expenses	467,160	387,211
General and administrative expenses	489,249	479,386
Total operating expenses	8,465,558	6,986,927
Income from equity investees	108,006	93,937
Operating income	1,053,945	893,952
Net interest and other income	2,419	12,291
Earnings before income taxes	1,056,364	906,243
Income taxes	383,726	324,770
Earnings before cumulative efffect of change in accounting principle	672,638	581,473
Cumulative effect of accounting change for FIN 47, net of taxes		17,214
Net earnings	$ 672,638	$ 564,259
Per common share:		
Earnings before cumulative efffect of change in accounting principles—basic	$ 0.90	$ 0.76
Cumulative effect of accounting change for FIN 47, net of taxes		0.02
Net earnings—basic	$ 0.90	$ 0.74
Earnings before cumulative efffect of change in accounting principles—diluted	$ 0.87	$ 0.73
Cumulative effect of accounting change for FIN 47, net of taxes		0.02
Net earnings—diluted	$ 0.87	$ 0.71
Weighted average shares outstanding:		
Basic	749,763	766,114
Diluted	770,091	792,556

Consolidated Balance Sheets
(in thousands of dollars, except share data)

	Fiscal Year Ended	
	September 30, 2007	October 1, 2006
Assets		
Current assets:		
Cash and cash equivalents	$ 281,261	$ 312,606
Short-term investments—available-for-sale securities	83,845	87,542
Short-term investments—trading securities	73,588	53,496
Accounts receivable, net	287,925	224,271
Inventories	691,658	636,222
Prepaid expenses and other currrent assets	148,757	126,874
Deferred income taxes, net	129,453	88,777
Total current assets	1,696,487	1,529,788
Long-term investments—available-for-sale securities	21,022	5,811
Equity and other investments	258,846	219,093
Property, plant, and equipment, net	2,890,433	2,287,899
Other assets	219,422	186,917
Other intangible assets	42,043	37,955
Goodwill	215,625	161,478
Total Assets	$5,343,878	$4,428,941

Liabilities and Shareholders' Equity

	September 30, 2007	October 1, 2006
Current liabilities:		
Commercial paper and short-term borrowings	$ 710,248	$ 700,000
Accounts payable	390,836	340,937
Accrued compensation and related costs	332,331	288,963
Accrued occupancy costs	74,591	54,868
Accrued taxes	92,516	94,010
Other accrued expenses	257,369	224,154
Deferred revenue	296,900	231,926
Currrent portion of long-term debt	775	762
Total current liabilities	2,155,566	1,935,620
Long-term debt	550,121	1,958
Other long-term liabilities	354,074	262,857
Total liabilities	3,059,761	2,200,435
Shareholders' equity:		
Common stock ($0.001 par value)—authorized, 1,200,000,000 shares; issued and outstanding, 738,285,285 and 756,602,071 shares, respectively, (includes 3,420,448 common stock units in both periods)	738	756
Other additional paid-in-capital	39,393	39,393
Retained earnings	2,189,366	2,151,084
Accumulated other comprehensive income	54,620	37,273
Total shareholders' equity	2,284,117	2,228,506
Total liabilities and shareholders' equity	$5,343,878	$4,428,941

Consolidated Statements of Shareholders' Equity
(in thousands of dollars, except share data)

	Common Stock		Additional Paid-in Capital	Other Additional Paid-in Capital	Retained Earnings	Accumulated Other Comprehensive Income/(Loss)	Total
	Shares	Amount					
Balance, October 1, 2006	756,602,071	$756	$	$39,393	$2,151,084	$37,273	$2,228,506
Net earnings					672,638		672,638
Unrealized holding loss, net						(20,380)	(20,380)
Translation adjustment, net of tax						37,727	37,727
Comprehensive income							689,985
Stock-based compensation expense			106,373				106,373
Exercise of stock options, including tax benefit of $95,276	12,744,226	13	225,233				225,246
Sale of common stock, including tax provision of $139	1,908,407	2	46,826				46,828
Repurchase of common stock	(32,969,419)	(33)	(378,432)		(634,356)		(1,012,821)
Balance, September 30, 2007	738,285,285	$738	$ 0	$39,393	$2,189,366	$54,620	$2,284,117

Notes:

1. Short-term and long-term investments, available for sale, are debt securities.
2. Short-term investments listed as trading securities are investments in equity mutual funds as part of a defined contribution plan for employees. The corresponding deferred compensation liability ($86,400 thousand in 2007) is included in accrued compensation and related costs.
3. $40,000 thousand of cash and cash equivalents in both 2007 and 2006 is working cash used in operations.
4. Net interest and other income in the 2007 income statement includes the following (in thousands of dollars):

Interest income	$ 19,700
Interest expense	(38,200)
Realized gain on available-for-sale investments	3,800
Gain on assets sales	26,032
Other operating charges	(8,913)
	$ 2,419

5. Income from equity investees is reported after tax.
6. The firm's combined state and federal statutory tax rate is 38.4 percent.
7. Unrealized holding losses in comprehensive income refer to losses on available-for-sale debt securities.

Real World Connection

Starbucks is dealt with also in Exercises E9.8, E12.9, E13.8, and E15.8.

E10.11. A Bite of the Apple: Apple Inc. (Medium)

Apple Inc., under the leadership of Steve Jobs, has been a huge success over the past few years, with new products such as iPhone and iPad received enthusiastically by consumers. The firm's stock price increased from $91 at the beginning of 2009 to $350 by mid-year 2011. The income statement and balance sheet for the first quarter of 2011 are shown below. The firm has a statutory tax rate of 37 percent.

a. Reformulate the statements for the 2011 fiscal quarter in a way that shows how Apple adds value through its business. The long-term marketable securities are debt securities. "Other income and expenses" on the income statement is largely income on financial assets.

b. You will observe that Apple holds a large amount of "cash" on its balance sheet, invested largely in government and corporate bonds and commercial paper. It earned an average of only 0.75 percent (on an annual basis, before tax) on this cash during the quarter. With the free cash flow for the full fiscal year ending September 2011 projected to be $14.6 billion, the figure could become much higher. Apple pays no dividends. What could be Apple's thinking in holding so much cash?

c. Why does Apple have no financing debt?

d. You will notice in your reformulation that Apple has negative net operating assets. What do you infer from this? Calculate residual income from operations for the quarter (using a rough guess of the required return) to provide some insights.

APPLE, INC.
Condensed Consolidated Statements of Operations (Unaudited)
(in millions, except share amounts which are reflected in thousands and per share amounts)

	Three Months Ended		Six Months Ended	
	March 26, 2011	March 27, 2010	March 26, 2011	March 27, 2010
Net sales	$24,667	$13,499	$51,408	$29,182
Cost of sales	14,449	7,874	30,892	17,146
Gross margin	10,218	5,625	20,516	12,036
Operating expenses:				
Research and development	581	426	1,156	824
Selling, general and administrative	1,763	1,220	3,659	2,508
Total operating expenses	2,344	1,646	4,815	3,332
Operating income	7,874	3,979	15,701	8,704
Other income and expense	26	50	162	83
Income before provision for income taxes	7,900	4,029	15,863	8,787
Provision for income taxes	1,913	955	3,872	2,335
Net income	$ 5,987	$ 3,074	$ 11,991	$ 6,452
Earnings per common share:				
Basic	$ 6.49	$ 3.39	$ 13.02	$ 7.12
Diluted	$ 6.40	$ 3.33	$ 12.83	$ 7.00
Shares used in computing earnings per share:				
Basic	923,196	907,548	921,245	905,545
Diluted	935,944	922,878	934,549	921,331

APPLE, INC.
Condensed Consolidated Balance Sheets (Unaudited)
(in millions except share amounts)

	March 26, 2011	September 25, 2010
Current assets: Assets		
Cash and cash equivalents	$15,978	$11,261
Short-term marketable securities	13,256	14,359
Accounts receivable, less allowances of $57 and $55, respectively	5,798	5,510
Inventories	930	1,051
Deferred tax assets	1,683	1,636
Vendor non-trade receivables	5,297	4,414
Other current assets	4,055	3,447
Total current assets	46,997	41,678
Long-term marketable securities	36,533	25,391
Property, plant and equipment, net	6,241	4,768
Goodwill	741	741
Acquired intangible assets, net	507	342
Other assets	3,885	2,263
Total assets	$ 94,904	$ 75,183
Liabilities and Shareholders Equity		
Current liabilities:		
Accounts payable	$ 13,714	$ 12,015
Accrued expenses	7,022	5,723
Deferred revenue	3,591	2,984
Total current liabilities	24,327	20,722
Deferred revenue—noncurrent	1,230	1,139
Other noncurrent liabilities	7,870	5,531
Total liabilities	33,427	27,392
Commitments and contingencies		
Shareholders' equity		
Common stock, no par value; 1,800,000,000 shares authorized; 924,674,079 and 915,970,050 shares issued and outstanding, respectively	12,326	10,668
Retained earnings	49,025	37,169
Accumulated other comprehensive income (loss)	126	(46)
Total shareholders' equity	61,477	47,791
Total liabilities and shareholders' equity	$ 94,904	$ 75,183

Minicases

M10.1

Financial Statement Analysis: Procter & Gamble I

Formed in 1837 by William Procter and James Gamble as a small family-operated soap and candle company, Procter & Gamble Co. is now a leading consumer products company with over $83 billion in revenues. Headquartered in Cincinnati, Ohio, the firm's products are sold in more than 180 countries.

P&G's product range covers laundry detergents, toothpaste, baby diapers, paper towels, beauty and health products, shampoos, snacks, and pet food. The firm is better known by its brands: Charmin, Pampers, Bounty, Tide, Downy, Cascade, Olay, Tampax, Crest, Head and Shoulders, Pringles, and more. The maintenance of these brands, along with innovative packaging and effective distribution through the retail supply chain, is critical to the success of the company's operations. Product innovation and marketing, along with streamlined production and distribution, have contributed to growth, but the firm has also purchased brands through acquisition of other companies. In fiscal 2006, the firm acquired Gillette for $53.4 billion, adding Gillette's shaving and grooming products to its range along with Duracell batteries.

The branded consumer products business is very competitive, and P&G battles the likes of Unilever, Avon, Clorox, Kimberly-Clark, L'Oreal, Energizer, and Colgate. Like these companies, continual innovation is essential to the firm's continuing profitability, so the firm maintains an extensive research and development operation, including marketing research, and spends considerable amounts on advertising and promoting its brands.

Learn more about the firm by going to its Web site at **www.pg.com**. Go to the Investor page, download the firm's annual report, and read the management letter and the Management Discussion and Analysis. Also look at the firm's 10-K in its EDGAR filing with the SEC. Though always having a gloss, management communications are helpful in understanding the strategy and how the management is executing on that strategy. The stress on brand innovation and research is evident in P&G's management letters.

After understanding the company, go to the financial statements, which, along with the footnotes to the statements, are our main focus for financial statement analysis. Survey the management certification on its financial reporting and internal controls. Make sure the auditor's letter does not contain anything unusual. Make a list of the footnote headings so you are reminded of where to go for more detail.

Now you are ready for analysis. We will be engaged with P&G through a series of minicases, beginning with this chapter and continuing through Chapter 16. At each stage we will add another feature to the analysis so that, by the end of Chapter 13, you will have a thorough analysis that prepares you to value the firm. The minicases in Chapters 14 to 16 carry the analysis into a full valuation of P&G.

At this point, you are required to reformulate the income statements and balance sheets to ready them for analysis. Exhibit 10.15 presents the published income statements for 2008 to 2010, along with statement of shareholders' equity for the three years and balance sheets for 2007 to 2010. Additional information provided after the statements will aid you. As advertising and research and development (R&D) are so important to P&G, make sure you include these as line items in the reformulated statements.

If you are adept at spreadsheet analysis, you might put the reformulated statements into a spreadsheet that can then be used to apply the financial statement analysis in later chapters. You could also build annual reports for years after 2010 into the spreadsheet, as they become available, so that you continue to track the firm as it evolves. The BYOAP feature on the Web site will guide you in this task.

After carrying out the reformulations, compare the statements to those for General Mills in Exhibits 10.5 and 10.11. Though devoted primarily to packaged food products, General Mills is a similar brand marketing company. Do the statements reveal the same sort of business organization? How do they differ?

Now compare the statements to those for Nike (in Exhibits 10.3 and 10.9) and Dell (in Exhibits 10.4 and 10.10). What are the differences, and what do they tell you about how the respective firms run their businesses?

A. Calculate the return on common equity (ROCE) for each year 2008 to 2010.

B. Calculate the return on net operating assets (RNOA) for the same years.

C. What was the operating profit margin from sales for each year?

D. Calculate expense ratios (as a percentage of sales) for advertising and R&D for each year. Do you see trends?

E. Calculate sales growth rates for 2009 and 2010 and also growth rates for operating income from sales.

F. Calculate growth rates for net operating assets for 2008 to 2010. Do you see a trend? Is there any one balance sheet item that particularly affects the growth?

G. Calculate P&G's financial leverage ratio at the end of 2010.

H. Comment on any aspect of the financial statements that you see as unusual.

Real World Connection
This case continues with Minicases M11.1, M12.1, M13.1, M15.1, and M16.1.

EXHIBIT 10.15
Comparative
Financial Statements
for Fiscal Year 2010
for Procter &
Gamble Co.
The financial
statements should be
read with the
accompanying
footnotes.

Consolidated Statements of Earnings
(amounts in millions except per share amounts; Years ended June 30)

	2010	2009	2008
Net sales	$ 78,938	$ 76,694	$ 79,257
Cost of products sold	37,919	38,690	39,261
Selling, general and administrative expense	24,998	22,630	24,017
Operating income	16,021	15,374	15,979
Interest expense	946	1,358	1,467
Other non operating income (expense), net	(28)	397	373
Earnings from continuing operations before income taxes	15,047	14,413	14,885
Income taxes on continuing operations	4,101	3,733	3,594
Net earnings from continuing operations	10,946	10,680	11,291
Net earnings from discontinued operations	1,790	2,756	784
Net earnings	$ 12,736	$ 13,436	$ 12,075
Basic net earnings per common share:			
Earnings from continuing operations	$ 3.70	$ 3.55	$ 3.61
Earnings from discontinued operations	0.62	0.94	0.25
Basic net earnings per common share	4.32	4.49	3.86
Diluted net earnings per common share:			
Earnings from continuing operations	3.53	3.39	3.40
Earnings from discontinued operations	0.58	0.87	0.24
Diluted net earnings per common share	4.11	4.26	3.64
Dividends per common share	$ 1.80	$ 1.64	$ 1.45

(continued)

EXHIBIT 10.15
(*continued*)

Consolidated Balance Sheets
(in millions of dollars, June 30)

	2010	2009	2008	2007
Current assets				
Cash and cash equivalents	$ 2,879	$ 4,781	$ 3,313	$ 5,354
Investment securities	—	—	228	202
Accounts receivable	5,335	5,836	6,761	6,629
Inventories				
Materials and supplies	1,692	1,557	2,262	1,590
Work in process	604	672	765	444
Finished goods	4,088	4,651	5,389	4,785
Total inventories	6,384	6,880	8,416	6,819
Deferred income taxes	990	1,209	2,012	1,727
Prepaid expenses and other current assets	3,194	3,199	3,785	3,300
Total current assets	18,782	21,905	24,515	24,031
Property, plant, and equipment				
Buildings	6,868	6,724	7,052	6,380
Machinery and equipment	29,294	29,042	30,145	27,492
Land	850	885	889	849
Total property, plant, and equipment	37,012	36,561	38,086	34,721
Accumulated depreciation	(17,768)	(17,189)	(17,446)	(15,181)
Net property, plant, and equipment	19,244	19,462	20,640	19,540
Goodwill and other intangible assets				
Goodwill	54,012	56,512	59,767	56,552
Trademarks and other intangible assets, net	31,636	32,606	34,233	33,626
Net goodwill and other intangible assets	85,648	89,118	94,000	90,178
Other noncurrent assets	4,498	4,348	4,837	4,265
Total assets	128,172	134,833	$143,992	$138,014
Current liabilities				
Accounts payable	7,251	5,980	$6,775	5,710
Accrued and other liabilities	8,559	8,601	10,154	9,586
Taxes payable	—	—	945	3,382
Debt due within one year	8,472	16,320	13,084	12,039
Total current liabilities	24,282	30,901	30,958	30,717
Long-term debt	21,360	20,652	23,581	23,375
Deferred income taxes	10,902	10,752	11,805	12,015
Other noncurrent liabilities	10,189	9,146	8,154	5,147
Total liabilities	66,733	71,451	74,498	71,254
Shareholders' equity				
Convertible Class A preferred stock, stated value $1 per share (600 shares authorized)	1,277	1,324	1,366	1,406
Nonvoting Class B preferred stock, stated value $1 per share (200 shares authorized)	—	—	—	—
Common stock, stated value $1 per share (10,000 shares authorized; shares issued: 2010—4,007.6, 2009—4,007.3)	4,008	4,007	4,002	3,990
Additional paid-in capital	61,697	61,118	60,307	59,030
Reserve for ESOP debt retirement	(1,350)	(1,340)	(1,325)	(1,308)
Accumulated other comprehensive income	(7,822)	(3,358)	3,746	617
Treasury stock, at cost (shares held: 2010—1,164.1, 2009—1,090.3)	(61,309)	(55,961)	(47,588)	(38,772)
Retained earnings	64,614	57,309	48,986	41,797
Noncontrolling interest	324	283	—	—
Total shareholders' equity	61,439	63,382	69,494	66,760
Total liabilities and shareholders' equity	128,172	134,833	$143,992	138,014

Note: In 2008 and 2007, noncontrolling interest was not identified in the balance sheet.

(*continued*)

EXHIBIT 10.15   (*continued*)

Consolidated Statements of Shareholders' Equity
(dollars in millions/shares in thousands)

Dollars in millions/Shares in thousands	Common Shares Outstanding	Common Stock	Pre-ferred Stock	Additional Paid-In Capital	Reserve for ESOP Debt Retirement	Accumulated Other Comprehensive Income (loss)	Non-controlling Interest	Treasury Stock	Retained Earnings	Total
Balance, June 30, 2007	3,131,946	$3,990	$1,406	$59,030	$(1,308)	$ 617	$ 252	$(38,772)	$41,797	$67,012
Net earnings									12,075	12,075
Other comprehensive income:										
Financial statement translation						6,543				6,543
Hedges and investment securities, net of $1,664 tax						(2,906)				(2,906)
Defined benefit retirement plans, net of $120 tax						(508)				(508)
Total comprehensive income										$ 15,204
Cumulative impact for adoption of new accounting guidance[1]									(232)	(232)
Dividends to shareholders:										
Common									(4,479)	(4,479)
Preferred, net of tax benefits									(176)	(176)
Treasury purchases	(148,121)							(10,047)		(10,047)
Employee plan issuances	43,910	12		1,272				1,196		2,480
Preferred stock conversions	4,982		(40)	5				35		—
ESOP debt impacts					(17)				1	(16)
Noncontrolling interest							38			38
Balance, June 30, 2008	3,032,717	4,002	1,366	60,307	(1,325)	3,746	290	(47,588)	48,986	69,784
Net earnings									13,436	13,436
Other comprehensive income:										
Financial statement translation						(6,151)				(6,151)
Hedges and investment securities, net of $452 tax						748				748
Defined benefit retirement plans, net of $879 tax						(1,701)				(1,701)
Total comprehensive income										$ 6,332
Cumulative impact for adoption of new accounting guidance[1]									(84)	(84)
Dividends to shareholders:										
Common									(4,852)	(4,852)
Preferred, net of tax benefits									(192)	(192)
Treasury purchases	(98,862)							(6,370)		(6,370)
Employee plan issuances	16,841	5		804				428		1,237
Preferred stock conversions	4,992		(42)	7				35		—
Shares tendered for Folgers coffee subsidiary	(38,653)							(2,466)		(2,466)
ESOP debt impacts					(15)				15	—
Noncontrolling interest							(7)			(7)
Balance, June 30, 2009	2,917,035	4,007	1,324	61,118	(1,340)	(3,358)	283	(55,961)	57,309	63,382
Net earnings									12,736	12,736
Other comprehensive income										
Financial statement translation						(4,194)				(4,194)

(*continued*)

EXHIBIT 10.15 (*concluded*)

Consolidated Statements of Shareholders' Equity
(dollars in millions/shares in thousands)

Dollars in millions/Shares in thousands	Common Shares Outstanding	Common Stock	Pre-ferred Stock	Additional Paid-In Capital	Reserve for ESOP Debt Retirement	Accumulated Other Comprehensive Income (loss)	Non-controlling Interest	Treasury Stock	Retained Earnings	Total
Hedges and investment securities, net of $520 tax						867				867
Defined benefit retirement plans, net of $465 tax						(1,137)				(1,137)
Total comprehensive income										$ 8,272
Dividends to shareholders:										
Common									(5,239)	(5,239)
Preferred, net of tax benefits									(219)	(219)
Treasury purchases	(96,759)							(6,004)		(6,004)
Employee plan issuances	17,616	1		574				616		1,191
Preferred stock conversions	5,579		(47)	7				40		—
ESOP debt impacts					(10)				27	17
Noncontrolling interest				(2)			41			39
Balance, June 30, 2010	**2,843,471**	**$ 4,008**	**$ 1,277**	**$ 61,697**	**$ (1,350)**	**$ (7,822)**	**$ 324**	**$ (61,309)**	**$ 64,614**	**$ 61,439**

Notes:

1. Advertising expense and research and development expenses for 2008–2010 are as follows (in millions of dollars):

	2010	2009	2008
Advertising	$8,567	$7,519	$8,520
Research and development	1,950	1,864	1,946

2. "Other nonoperating income" in the income statement consists of the following:

Income for noncontrolling interest	(110)	(86)	(78)
Interest income	12	14	17
Gains (losses) from asset sales	70	469	434
	(28)	397	373

3. "Accrued and other liabilities" and "other noncurrent liabilities" consist largely of pension obligations and other postretirement benefit liabilities.

4. The combined federal, state and local statutory tax rate is 38 percent.

5. Earnings from discontinued operations result from the divestiture of the global pharmaceuticals business in 2009 and the Folgers coffee division in 2008. Gains from these divestitures are included in discontinued operations.

M10.2

Understanding the Business Through Reformulated Financial Statements: Chubb Corporation

Chubb Corporation is a property and casualty insurance holding company providing insurance through its subsidiaries in the United States, Canada, Europe, and parts of Latin America and Asia. Its subsidiaries include Federal, Vigilant, Pacific Indemnity, Great Northern, Chubb National, Chubb Indemnity, and Texas Pacific Indemnity insurance companies.

The insurance operations are divided into three business units. Chubb Commercial Insurance offers a full range of commercial customer insurance products, including coverage for multiple peril, casualty, workers' compensation, and property and marine. Chubb Commercial Insurance writes policies for niche business through agents and brokers. Chubb

Specialty Insurance offers a wide variety of specialized executive protection and professional liability products for privately and publicly owned companies, financial institutions, professional firms, and health care organizations. Chubb Specialty Insurance also includes surety and accident businesses, as well as reinsurance through Chubb Re. Chubb Personal Insurance offers products for individuals with fine homes, automobiles, and possessions who require more coverage choices and higher limits than standard insurance policies.

Chubb's balance sheets for 2009 and 2010 are in Exhibit 10.16. Its 2010 comparative income statement is also given, along with a statement of comprehensive income that Chubb reports outside both the equity statement and the income statement. You are asked to reformulate these statements in a way that captures how Chubb carries out its business operations and that reveals the profitability of those operations. The statutory tax rate is 35 percent, but note that the effective tax rate on investment income is only 19.1 percent because much of it is interest on tax-exempt bonds.

First you should understand how insurers "make money." Insurance companies run underwriting operations where they write insurance policies and processes and pay claims on

EXHIBIT 10.16

Balance Sheet, Income Statement, and Comprehensive Income Statement for Chubb Corporation, 2010

THE CHUBB CORPORATION
Balance Sheet
(in millions of dollars)

	December 31	
	2010	**2009**
Assets		
Invested assets		
Short term investments	$ 1,905	$ 1,918
Fixed maturities		
Tax exempt (cost $19,072 and $18,720)	19,774	19,587
Taxable (cost $15,989 and $ 16,470)	16,745	16,991
Equity securities (cost $1,285 and $1,215)	1,550	1,433
Other invested assets	2,239	2,075
Total invested assets	42,213	42,004
Cash	70	51
Accrued investment income	447	460
Premiums receivable	2,098	2,101
Reinsurance recoverable on unpaid losses and loss expenses	1,817	2,053
Prepaid reinsurance premiums	325	308
Deferred policy acquisition costs	1,562	1,533
Deferred income tax	98	272
Goodwill	467	467
Other assets	1,152	1,200
Total assets	$50,249	$50,449
Liabilities		
Unpaid losses and loss expenses	$22,718	$22,839
Unearned premiums	6,189	6,153
Long term debt	3,975	3,975
Dividend payable to shareholders	112	118
Accrued expenses and other liabilities	1,725	1,730
Total liabilities	34,719	34,815

(continued)

EXHIBIT 10.16
(continued)

THE CHUBB CORPORATION
Balance Sheet
(in millions of dollars)

	December 31	
	2010	**2009**
Commitments and contingent liabilities (Note 6 and 13)	—	—
Shareholders' equity		
Preferred stock—authorized 8,000,000 shares; $1 par value; issued—none	—	—
Common stock—authorized 1,200,000,000 shares; $1 par value; issued 371,980,460 shares	372	372
Paid-in surplus	208	224
Retained earnings	17,943	16,235
Accumulated other comprehensive income	790	720
Treasury stock, at cost—74,707,547 and 39,972,796 shares	(3,783)	(1,917)
Total shareholders' equity	15,530	15,634
Total liabilities and shareholders' equity	$ 50,249	$ 50,449

Consolidated Statements of Income
(in millions of dollars)

	Years Ended December 31		
	2010	**2009**	**2008**
Revenues			
Premiums earned	$11,215	$11,331	$11,828
Investment income	1,665	1,649	1,732
Other revenues	13	13	32
Realized investment gains (losses), net			
Total other-than-temporary impairment losses on investments	(6)	(132)	(446)
Other-than-temporary impairment losses on investments recognized in other comprehensive income	(5)	20	—
Other realized investment gains, net	437	135	75
Total realized investment gains (losses), net	426	23	(371)
Total revenues	13,319	13,016	13,221
Losses and expenses			
Losses and loss expenses	6,499	6,268	6,898
Amortization of deferred policy acquisition costs	3,067	3,021	3,123
Other insurance operating costs and expenses	425	416	441
Investment expenses	35	39	32
Other expenses	15	16	36
Corporate expenses	290	294	284
Total losses and expenses	10,331	10,054	10,814
Income before federal and foreign income tax	2,988	2,962	2,407
Federal and foreign income tax	814	779	603
Net income	$ 2,174	$ 2,183	$ 1,804
Net income per share			
Basic	$ 6.81	$ 6.24	$ 5.00
Diluted	6.76	6.18	4.92

(continued)

EXHIBIT 10.16
(*concluded*)

Consolidated Statements of Comprehensive Income
(in millions of dollars)

	Year Ended December 31		
	2010	**2009**	**2008**
Net income	$2,174	$2,183	$1,804
Other comprehensive income (loss), net of tax			
Change in unrealized appreciation or depreciation of investments	69	1,223	(669)
Change in unrealized other-than-temporary impairment losses on investments	7	(6)	—
Foreign currency translation gains (losses)	(18)	170	(226)
Change in postretirement benefit costs not yet recognized in net income	12	98	(284)
	70	1,485	(1,179)
Comprehensive income	$2,244	$3,668	$625

those policies. They are also involved in investment operations where they manage investments in which the considerable "float" from insurance operations is invested. Accordingly, you see both investment assets and liabilities on the balance sheet as well as assets and liabilities associated with insurance. You also see revenues and expenses associated with both activities in the income statement. Your reformulation should separate the items identified with the two activities.

After you have carried out the reformulations, answer the following questions:

A. Why are some investments listed at market value on the balance sheet while others are listed at cost?

B. Why are net operating assets in the insurance operations negative? What is the business interpretation?

C. Why is it desirable to distinguish the two types of income?

D. Why is it desirable to have income from an insurer reported on a comprehensive basis? Think: cherry picking.

E. What, approximately, is the value of the investment operation?

F. Summarize what the reformulated statements are telling you about Chubb's business.

Real World Connection

Minicase M14.1 on Chubb extends this case to valuation.

Chapter **Eleven**

The Analysis of the Cash Flow Statement

LINKS

Link to previous chapter

Chapter 10 reformulated the balance sheet and income statement to capture the operating and financing activities.

This chapter

This chapter reformulates the cash flow statement to capture the operating and financing activities.

Link to next chapter

Chapter 12 lays out the analysis of the reformulated financial statements.

Link to Web page

Review the statement of cash flows for more companies—visit the book's Web site at **www.mhhe.com/ penman5e**.

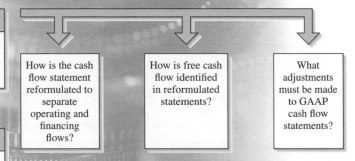

| How is the cash flow statement reformulated to separate operating and financing flows? | How is free cash flow identified in reformulated statements? | What adjustments must be made to GAAP cash flow statements? |

This chapter completes the preparation of the financial statements for analysis by reformulating the cash flow statement. The cash flow statement describes the cash generation in a business, and reformulation highlights the cash flows that are important to analysis.

If the equity analyst chooses to apply discounted cash flow (DCF) analysis (as in Chapter 4), the cash flow statement becomes the primary focus. This analyst has the task of forecasting free cash flows; to do so, he must have a good appreciation of cash flow generation and the statement that reports it.

If the equity analyst is using accrual accounting valuation (as in Chapters 5 and 6), he is concerned with profitability rather than cash flow, so his primary focus is on the balance sheet and income statement. But he cannot ignore the cash flow statement. Equity valuation relies on accrual accounting numbers and accrual accounting numbers can be distorted. A difference between accrual accounting earnings and operating cash flow is a "red flag" that could indicate manipulation, so the analyst must scrutinize the cash flows as well as accrual accounting earnings. Indeed, earnings will be compared to cash flows in the analysis of the quality of earnings in Chapter 18.

Equity valuation issues aside, the analysis of the cash flow statement is necessary for *liquidity analysis* and *financial planning,* which will be covered in Part Five of the book. **Liquidity analysis** is involved in assessing the risk of debt, for liquidity (cash) is required to settle debt. So liquidity analysis is very much the tool of the credit analyst. **Financial planning** is the tool of the treasurer. She must ensure that financing is in place to meet the needs for cash—to make investments and cover dividends, as well as servicing debt.

The Analyst's Checklist

After reading this chapter you should understand:	After reading this chapter you should be able to:
• How free cash flow can be calculated from reformulated income statements and balance sheets without a cash flow statement.	• Calculate free cash flow from reformulated income statements and balance sheets.
• How the cash conservation equation ties the cash flow statement together to equate free cash flow and financing cash flow.	• Calculate free cash flow by adjusting GAAP cash flow statements.
• The difference between the direct and indirect calculations of cash from operations.	• Reformulate GAAP statements of cash flow to identify operating, investing, and financing cash flows distinctly.
• Problems that arise in analyzing cash flows from GAAP statements of cash flow.	• Reconcile the free cash flow from GAAP statements to that calculated from reformulated income statements and balance sheets.
• What reformulated cash flow statements tell you.	
• How to examine the quality of reported cash flow.	

To understand the needs for cash, she must analyze the ability of the firm to generate cash. Like valuation analysis, liquidity analysis and financial planning are prospective: The credit analyst and the treasurer are concerned about the ability of the firm to generate cash in the future, and they use current financial statements to forecast future cash flow statements. The analysis here, like that of the other statements, prepares you for forecasting. Chapter 20 completes the task.

Unfortunately, GAAP and IFRS statements of cash flow are not in the form that identifies the cash flows used in these analyses, and indeed they misclassify some cash flows. Operating cash flows are confused with financing flows. This chapter reformulates the statement to distinguish the cash flows appropriately.

An important lesson emerges from this chapter. Forecasting free cash flow is best done by forecasting reformulated income statements and balance sheets rather than cash flow statements. We can contemplate forecasting cash flow statements, but this is difficult without first forecasting the outcome of operations, understood from reformulated income statements and balance sheets. Once those statements are forecasted, free cash flow forecasts can be calculated immediately, as the first section of the chapter shows.

THE CALCULATION OF FREE CASH FLOW

Free cash flow—the difference between cash flow from operations and cash investment in operations—is the main focus in DCF analysis, liquidity analysis, and financial planning. Free cash flow, the net cash generated by operations (after cash investment), determines the ability of the firm to pay off its debt and return cash to shareholders.

If the analyst has gone through the analysis of the balance sheet and income statement in Chapter 10, he does not need a cash flow statement to get the free cash flow. If those statements are appropriately formatted, then the free cash flow is given by a quick calculation. In Chapter 8 we saw that

Method 1:	$C - I = OI - \Delta NOA$			
	Operating income	2010		$1,814
	Net operating assets	2010	$5,514	
	Net operating assets	2009	6,346	832
	Free cash flow	2010		$2,646
Method 2:	$C - I = \Delta NFA - NFI + d$			
	Net financial income	2010		$4
	Net financial assets	2010	$4,370	
	Net financial assets	2009	2,468	1,902
	Net dividend	2010		740
	Free cash flow	2010		$2,646

$$\text{Free cash flow} = \text{Operating income} - \text{Change in net operating assets} \quad \textbf{(11.1)}$$
$$C - I = OI - \Delta NOA$$

That is, free cash flow is operating income (in a reformulated income statement) less the change in net operating assets in the balance sheet.

For this quick calculation to work, the operating income must, of course, be comprehensive. Just as comprehensive income and changes in the book value of equity explain dividends to shareholders, so comprehensive operating income and the change in the book value of the net operating assets explain the "dividend" from the operating activities to the financing activities, the free cash flow.

The numbers for operating income and net operating assets for Nike, Inc., from Exhibits 10.3 and 10.9 in Chapter 10 are in Box 11.1, and free cash flow is calculated from these numbers under Method 1. Nike generated income from operations of $1,814 million, but the reduction of investment in net operating assets of $832 million resulted in free cash flow of $2,646 million.

There is a second way to calculate free cash flow from reformulated statements. In Chapter 8 we also saw that free cash flow is applied as follows:

$$\text{Free cash flow} = \text{Net financial expense} \quad \textbf{(11.2)}$$
$$- \text{Change in net financial obligations}$$
$$+ \text{Net dividends}$$

$$C - I = NFE - \Delta NFO + d$$

that is, free cash flow is used to pay for net financial expense, reduce debt, and pay net dividends. If minority (noncontrolling) interests are involved, the calculation is

$$C - I = NFE - \Delta NFO + d + \text{Minority interest in income} \quad \textbf{(11.2a)}$$
$$- \Delta \text{Minority interest in the balance sheet}$$

Again, the net financial expense must be comprehensive (of unrealized gains and losses on financial assets, for example, and of the tax benefit from interest expense). This second calculation is given for Nike, Inc., under Method 2 in Box 11.1. The net dividend is from the reformulated statement of common shareholders' equity in Exhibit 9.2 in Chapter 9. As Nike is a holder of net financial assets (rather than net financial obligations), the calculation just changes the signs. Thus, equation 11.2 becomes

$$C - I = \Delta\text{NFA} - \text{NFI} + d \qquad\qquad \textbf{(11.2b)}$$

If the balance sheet and income statement have been reformulated, these calculations are straightforward. You'll agree that these methods are much simpler than the alternative approaches to calculating free cash flow in Chapter 4. But, you may ask, "Can't I simply read the cash flows on the statement of cash flows?" This is not as easy as you would think.

GAAP STATEMENT OF CASH FLOWS AND REFORMULATED CASH FLOW STATEMENTS

For cash flow forecasting, we need to distinguish clearly the net cash generated by operations (the free cash flow) from the flows that involve paying that cash flow out to the firm's claimants. If operations use cash (and thus have negative free cash flow), we need to distinguish that negative free cash flow from the cash flows that involve claimants paying into the firm to cover the free cash flow deficit. An analyst forecasting free cash flow for discounted cash flow analysis must not confuse the free cash flow with the financing flows. And a treasurer forecasting the cash needs of the business must forecast the cash surplus or deficit as distinct from the financing flows that will dispose of the surplus or will be needed to meet the deficit.

As with the income statement and balance sheet, the template in Chapter 8 guides the reformulation of the cash flow statement to identify cash flows appropriately. Review that chapter before beginning this one; focus on Figure 8.3. Four types of cash flow are identified there. Two are cash flows generated by the operating activities within the firm: *cash from operations (C)* and *cash investments in those operations (I)*. Two involve financing activities between the firm and its claimants outside the firm: *net dividends to shareholders (d)* and *net payments to debtholders and issuers (F)*. The reformulated cash flow statement gives the details of these four flows.

The four cash flows are tied together according to the cash conservation equation that was introduced in Chapter 8:

Free cash flow = Net payments to shareholders + Net payments to debtholders and issuers

$$C - I = d + F$$

Free cash flow from operations (on the left) is applied (on the right) to financing payments to shareholders (as net dividends, d) and debtholders and issuers (as interest and principal payments, F). Free cash flow can be negative, in which case at least one of the financing flows to claimants must be negative, in the form of either cash from share issues, debt issues, or the liquidation of financial assets.

The GAAP statement of cash flows has the appearance of giving us the free cash flow and the flows for financing activities, but it somewhat confuses the two. The form of the statement appears below, along with the form of the reformulated statement that follows the cash conservation equation.

GAAP Statement of Cash Flows
Cash flow from operations
− Cash used in investing activities
+ Cash from financing activities
= Change in cash and cash equivalents

Reformulated Statement of Cash Flows
Cash flow from operations
− Cash investments
= Free cash flow from operating activities
Cash paid to shareholders
+ Cash paid to debtholders and issuers
= Cash paid for financing activities

The GAAP statement can come in two forms, one using the direct method and one using the indirect method. Box 11.2 explains the direct and indirect presentations. Cash flow statement presentation under IFRS is similar, though some details differ. Refer to the book's Web site, **www.mhhe.com/penman5e**.

Reclassifying Cash Transactions

Exhibit 11.1 gives Nike's 2010 comparative statement of cash flows. This statement uses the indirect method of presentation. Nike reports cash from operations of $3,164.2 million and cash investment of $1,267.5 million for 2010, so we might conclude that free cash flow equals the difference, $1,896.7 million. This number disagrees with our earlier calculation (in Box 11.1) of $2,646 million. Which is correct?

The GAAP statement suffers from a number of deficiencies for equity analysis purposes, including transparent misclassifications of cash flow. Here are the main problems we encounter in trying to discover free cash flow from the GAAP statement.[1] Examples are in the accompanying boxes with the same numbers as the points below. Some points have already been encountered in Chapter 4.

1. **Change in cash and cash equivalents.** The GAAP statement is set up to explain the change in cash and cash equivalents (flagged 1 in Nike's statement). But cash generated has to be disposed of somewhere. Any change in cash needed for operations (working cash) is an investment in an operating asset that should be included in the cash investment section. The change in cash equivalents that earn interest is an investment of excess cash (over that needed for operations) in financial assets that should be in the debt financing section.

2. **Transactions in financial assets.** Investments in financial assets such as short-term marketable securities and long-term debt securities are included in the investments section rather than in the financing section in the GAAP and IFRS statement. Nike's purchases and sales of financial assets are flagged in Exhibit 11.1. These investments are a disposition of free cash flow, not a reduction of free cash flow. If a firm invests its (surplus) free cash flow from operations in financial assets, the GAAP classification gives the appearance that the firm is reducing its free cash flow further. Similarly, sales of

---

[1] For a more detailed review, see H. Nurnberg, "Perspectives on The Cash Flow Statement under FASB Statement No. 95," Occasional Paper, Center for Excellence in Accounting and Security Analysis, Columbia Business School, September 2006, available at **www.gsb.columbia.edu/ceasa/research/papers/ occasional_papers**.

The direct and indirect cash flow statements differ in their presentation of cash flow from operations.

DIRECT METHOD

The direct method lists the separate sources of cash inflow and cash outflow in operations in the following form:

Cash inflows
Cash from sales
Cash from rents
Cash from royalties
Cash from interest received
Cash outflows
Cash paid to suppliers
Cash paid to employees
Cash paid for other operating activities
Cash paid for interest
Cash paid for income taxes

The difference between cash inflows and cash outflows is cash from operations.

The cash from operations section of the 2010 comparative cash flow statement for Northrop Grumman Corp., the defense contractor, uses the direct method:

	Year Ended December 31 (in millions)	
	2010	**2009**
Operating activities		
Sources of cash		
Cash received from customers		
Progress payments	$ 6,401	$ 8,561
Collections on billings	28,140	25,161
Cash provided by operating activities	34,541	33,722
Uses of cash		
Cash paid to suppliers and employees	29,775	29,250
Interest paid	280	269
Income taxes paid	1,071	774
Other cash payments	962	1,398
Cash used in operating activities	32,088	31,691
Net cash provided by operating activities	$ 2,453	$ 2,031

INDIRECT METHOD

The indirect method calculates cash from operations by subtracting accrual (noncash) components of net income:

$$\begin{array}{l} \text{Net income} \\ -\ \text{Accruals} \\ \hline =\ \text{Cash from operations} \end{array}$$

See Exhibit 11.1 for an example.

The indirect method has the feature of identifying the accruals made in calculating net income, so it reconciles net income to cash flow. But the direct method has the advantage of listing the individual cash flows that generate the net cash, so is more informative about the sources of cash flows. (If the direct method is used, a reconciliation of cash flow from operations to net income must be supplied in footnotes.) Almost all firms use the indirect method.

financial assets to provide cash for operations (or to pay dividends) are classified in GAAP statements as decreases in investment flows rather than financing flows. These sales satisfy a free cash flow shortfall, they do not create it. Consequently, the GAAP statement can give the wrong impression of a firm's liquidity. See the box numbered 2 in this section on Lucent Technologies. Nike's net purchase of financial assets (purchases minus sales) was $936.8 million, so investment in operations is overstated by this amount.

EXHIBIT 11.1
GAAP Consolidated
Statements of Cash
Flows for Nike, Inc.,
2008–2010.
Numbers on the right-
hand side flag the
adjustments numbered
in the text.

NIKE, INC.
GAAP Statements of Cash Flows
(in millions)

	Year Ended May 31		
	2010	**2009**	**2008**
Cash provided by operations:			
Net income	$ 1,906.7	$ 1,486.7	$ 1,883.4
Income charges (credits) not affecting cash:			
Depreciation	323.7	335.0	303.6
Deferred income taxes	8.3	(294.1)	(300.6)
Stock-based compensation (Note 11)	159.0	170.6	141.0
Impairment of goodwill, intangibles and other assets (Note 4)	—	401.3	—
Gain on divestitures (Note 17)	—	—	(60.6)
Amortization and other	71.8	48.3	17.9
Changes in certain working capital components and other assets and liabilities excluding the impact of acquisition and divestitures:			
Decrease (increase) in accounts receivable	181.7	(238.0)	(118.3)
Decrease (increase) in inventories	284.6	32.2	(249.8)
(Increase) decrease in prepaid expenses and other current assets	(69.6)	14.1	(11.2)
Increase (decrease) in accounts payable, accrued liabilities and income taxes payable	298.0	(220.0)	330.9
Cash provided by operations	3,164.2	1,736.1	1,936.3 **(3)(4)**
Cash used by investing activities:			
Purchases of short-term investments	(3,724.4)	(2,908.7)	(1,865.6) **(2)**
Maturities and sales of short-term investments	2,787.6	2,390.0	2,246.0 **(2)**
Additions to property, plant and equipment	(335.1)	(455.7)	(449.2)
Disposals of property, plant and equipment	10.1	32.0	1.9
Increase in other assets, net of other liabilities	(11.2)	(47.0)	(21.8)
Settlement of net investment hedges	5.5	191.3	(76.0)
Acquisition of subsidiary, net of cash acquired (Note 4)	—	—	(571.1)
Proceeds from divestitures (Note 17)	—	—	246.0
Cash used by investing activities	(1,267.5)	(798.1)	(489.8)
Cash used by financing activities:			
Reductions in long-term debt, including current portion	(32.2)	(6.8)	(35.2)
(Decrease) increase in notes payable	(205.4)	177.1	63.7
Proceeds from exercise of stock options and other stock issuances	364.5	186.6	343.3
Excess tax benefits from share-based payment arrangements	58.5	25.1	63.0
Repurchase of common stock	(741.2)	(649.2)	(1,248.0)
Dividends—common and preferred	(505.4)	(466.7)	(412.9)
Cash used by financing activities	(1,061.2)	(733.9)	(1,226.1)
Effect of exchange rate changes	(47.5)	(46.9)	56.8
Net increase in cash and equivalents	788.0	157.2	277.2 **(1)**
Cash and equivalents, beginning of year	2,291.1	2,133.9	1,856.7
Cash and equivalents, end of year	$ 3,079.1	$ 2,291.1	$ 2,133.9
Supplemental disclosure of cash flow information:			
Cash paid during the year for:			
Interest, net of capitalized interest	$ 48.4	$ 46.7	$ 44.1
Income taxes	537.2	765.2	717.5
Dividends declared and not paid	130.7	121.4	112.9

Change in Cash: Nike, Inc. 1

Nike's cash and cash equivalents increased by $788.0 million in 2010. In the reformulated balance sheet in Exhibit 10.3, we attributed this to investment in cash equivalents (financial assets) of $787.2 million and an increase in operating cash of $0.8 million. So reclassify $0.8 million as cash investment in operations and $787.2 million as a debt financing flow for the purchase of financial assets.

Transactions in Financial Assets: Lucent Technologies 2

Lucent Technologies is the telecommunications network supplier that was spun off from AT&T in 1996. The firm includes the research capabilities of the former Bell Laboratories. With the heavy network investment during the telecom boom of the late 1990s, Lucent became a "hot stock," with its share price rising to $60 by late 1999, yielding a P/E of 52. The firm was a darling of technology analysts, but some were concerned about the firm's declining cash flow from operations. Net income and cash from operations are given below for the years 1997–1999, along with the investment section of the firm's cash flow statement (in millions of dollars).

	Fiscal Year Ending September 30		
	1999	**1998**	**1997**
Net income	$ 4,766	$ 1,035	$ 449
Accruals	(5,042)	825	1,680
Cash from operating activities	(276)	1,860	2,129
Cash in investing activities:			
Capital expenditures	(2,215)	(1,791)	(1,744)
Proceeds from the sale or disposal of property, plant, and equipment	97	57	108
Purchases of equity investments	(307)	(212)	(149)
Sales of equity investments	156	71	12
Purchases of investment securities	(450)	(1,082)	(483)
Sales or maturity of investment securities	1,132	686	356
Dispositions of businesses	72	329	181
Acquisitions of businesses—net of cash acquired	(264)	(1,078)	(1,584)
Cash from mergers	61	—	—
Other investing activities—net	(69)	(80)	(68)
Net cash used in investing activities	(1,787)	(3,100)	(3,371)

Despite increasing profits, free cash flow (the difference between cash from operating activities and cash used in investing activities) appears to be negative in each of the three years. This is not unusual if a firm is increasing its investment to generate profits. However, Lucent reported a shortfall of cash from operations, before investment, of $276 million in 1999 (the shortfall after adding back after-tax net interest payments is $191 million). Cash investment also declined in 1999, but the $1,787 million number is misleading. This is the amount after selling interest-bearing investments for $1,132 million, as you see in the investing section of the statement. The net proceeds from these investments, after purchases of $450 million, is $682 million. So the actual investment in operations was $1,787 + $682 = $2,469 million, not $1,787 million, and the deficits between reported cash flow from operations and the actual investment in operations is a $2,745 million.

Free cash flow calculated from GAAP numbers can be quite misleading. A firm like Lucent, faced with a cash shortfall, can sell securities in which it is storing excess cash to satisfy the shortfall. Under GAAP reporting, it looks as if it is increasing free cash flow by doing so, making it look less serious than it is. GAAP reporting mixes the cash flow deficit with the means employed to deal with the deficit.

Postscript: Lucent's negative cash flow in 1999 was an indicator of things to follow. With the bursting of the telecom bubble, Lucent's share price declined to below $2 per share by 2003. The firm's accounting came into question. See Minicase M18.2 in Chapter 18 where these same cash flow statements are investigated to raise accounting issues.

3. **Net cash interest.** Cash interest payments and receipts for financing activities are included in cash flow from operations under GAAP rather than classified as financing flows. See the adjustment for Nike, with an accommodation for related taxes, under point 4 below. Also see the accompanying box numbered 3 for more extreme examples. Note that IFRS allows firms to choose between the operating and financing section to classify net interest payments.

An exception to including net interest in operations is interest capitalized during construction. This is classified by GAAP, inappropriately, as cash investment in constructed assets (see the note on interest payments at the bottom of Nike's cash flow statement in Exhibit 11.1). But interest to finance construction projects is not part of the cost of construction and should be classified as a financing cash flow. Unfortunately, disclosure is usually not sufficient to sort this out.

Interest Payments: Westinghouse and Turner Broadcasting System

3

An extreme case of interest payments distorting cash flow from operations appears in the 1991 cash flow statement for Westinghouse. The reported cash flow was $703 million but that was after $1.006 billion of interest payments. If these interest payments had been classified as financing outflows, the cash flow from operations figure, before tax, would have been $1.709 billion, or 243 percent higher.

The peculiarity of treating interest as an operating flow can be seen in the case of zero coupon or deep discount debt. The repayment of the principal at face value is a financing flow, but GAAP requires the difference between face value and the issue amount (the issue discount) to be treated as an operating cash flow at maturity rather than part of the repayment of principal. So repayment of debt reduces operating cash flow. Accordingly, in 1990 Turner Broadcasting System deducted $206.1 million of issue discounts on zero coupon senior notes repaid in calculating an operating cash flow of $25.8 million. This is correct accounting according to GAAP, but the reported operating cash flow is an 89 percent distortion of the actual $231.9 million number.

4. **Tax on net interest.** Just as cash from interest income and expense is confused with operating cash flows, so are taxes paid on financing and operating income. All tax cash flows are included in cash from operations, even though some apply to financial income or are reduced by financial expenses. We seek to separate after-tax operating cash flows from after-tax financing cash flows, but the GAAP statement blurs this distinction. The accompanying box numbered 4 calculates Nike's after-tax net interest to adjust GAAP cash flow from operations.

Cash interest payments must be disclosed by firms in footnotes: Nike's disclosure of its interest payments is found at the bottom of the cash flow statement in Exhibit 11.1. Convert these interest payments to an after-tax basis at the marginal tax rate. Cash interest receipts are usually not reported. The accrual number in the income statement has to be used for interest receipts; this number will equal the cash number only if the opening and closing interest accruals are the same.

5. **Noncash transactions.** Nike had no noncash transactions in 2010, but it did report noncash transactions in 2000. See the accompanying box numbered 5. In a **noncash transaction,** an asset is acquired or an expense is incurred by the firm by assuming a liability

Taxes on Net Interest Payments: Nike, Inc.   4

Nike's 2010 net interest payments after tax are calculated as follows (in millions of dollars):

Interest receipts	$ 42.1
Interest payments	48.4
Net interest payments before tax	6.3
Taxes (36.3%)	2.3
Net interest payments after tax	4.0

The after-tax net interest payments of $4.0 million are added to cash from operations in the reformulated statement and classified instead as a financing out flow.

Note that interest receipts and payments are not the same as interest income and expense in the income statement (that include accruals). Interest payments (but not interest receipts) are published at the foot of the cash flow statement, or are provided in footnotes.

(by writing a note, for example) or by issuing stock. An acquisition of another firm for stock is a noncash transaction. Capitalized leases are recorded as assets and liabilities, but there is no cash flow for the purchase. A noncash transaction can involve an asset exchange (one asset for another) or a liability exchange, or a conversion of debt to equity or vice versa. With the exception of asset and liability exchanges within operating and financing categories, these noncash transactions affect the Method 1 and Method 2 calculations of free cash flow because they affect NOA or NFO. Implicitly we interpret these as if there were a sale of something for cash and an immediate purchase of something else with that cash. The GAAP statement recognizes these transactions as not involving cash flows. This of course is strictly correct, but it obscures the investing and financing activities, and the "as-if" cash flow accounting uncovers them. Consider the following additional examples.

- Debt that is converted to equity is not indicated as a payment of a loan (in the financing section) in a GAAP statement even though the proceeds from the loan were recorded there in an earlier year when the debt was issued. It looks like the borrowings are never paid off.
- If a firm acquires an asset by writing a note, the payment of the note is recorded in subsequent years but the original amount that is being paid off is not (nor is the investment in the asset).
- For leases, no cash flow is recorded at the inception of the lease, but subsequent lease payments are divided between interest and principal repayments and recorded in the operating and financing sections, respectively, in the GAAP statement. The firm appears to be paying off a phantom loan.
- For an installment purchase of plant assets, only the initial installment is classified as investment. Subsequent payments are classified as financing flows. However, when a firm sells an asset, all installments are investing inflows from the liquidation.

The upshot of all this is that we don't get a complete picture of firms' investment and financing activities in the GAAP statement. Noncash transactions are often reported in supplemental disclosures so that implicit cash flows can be reconstructed.

Tying It Together

Box 11.3 summarizes the adjustments that must be made to the GAAP statement of cash flows and makes the adjustment to Nike's statement. The numbers accompanying selected items flag them as one of the five adjustments in the last section.

Noncash Transactions: Nike, Inc.   5

At the foot of its 2000 statement of cash flows, Nike reported the following (in millions of dollars):

Assumption of long-term debt to acquire property,
   plant, and equipment $108.9

This transaction was not incorporated in the GAAP cash flow statement. To adjust the statement, add $108.9 million to cash investments and $108.9 million to issue of debt in financing activities. The transaction is equivalent to issuing debt for cash, then using the cash to buy property, plant, and equipment.

The free cash flow of $2,836 million in Nike's reformulated statement differs slightly from the $2,646 million calculated under Method 1 and Method 2 in Box 11.1. This often happens (and sometimes the difference is greater). Because of incomplete disclosures, precisely reconciling the cash flow statement to the income statement and balance sheet is usually not possible. The likely reasons for the differences in the calculation are:

- "Other assets" and "other liabilities" can't be classified into operating and financing items appropriately. In particular, interest receivable and payable (financing items) cannot be distinguished from operating items in these "other" categories.
- Cash dividends (in the cash flow statement) differ from dividends in the reformulated statement of equity, implying a dividend payable that cannot be discovered (usually lumped into "other liabilities").
- Cash received in share issues or paid for share repurchases (in the cash flow statement) differs from the amount for those share transactions in the statement of equity, as with Nike. The difference implies a receivable (for shares issued but not paid for) or a payable that has not been discovered.
- The details for adjustments 3, 4, and 5 in the previous section are not available. Watch for noncash transactions, particularly acquisitions with shares rather than cash.
- Differences arise from GAAP's failure to treat the effect of employee stock options correctly, including the ultimate tax effect on exercise (that is recorded as a financing item rather than an operating item in the cash flow statement). See Chapter 9.
- When foreign subsidiaries are involved, balance sheet items are translated into dollar amounts at beginning and end-of-year exchange rates, while cash flow items are translated at average exchange rates. This results in a difference between the changes in balance sheet numbers and the corresponding items in the cash flow statement.

Let's not miss the forest for the trees. Calculations aside, what is the picture drawn here? Following the reformulated statement, Nike had a free cash flow from operations of $2,836 million because cash investments were less than cash from operations. The firm used this cash to pay out a net $823 million to shareholders and $2,013 million in net debt transactions to distribute the cash surplus.

If you are building spreadsheet analysis engines as you proceed through this book, you are probably aware that there is nothing further to be done at this stage. If you built the reformulated equity statement, balance sheet, and income statement of the last two chapters into a spreadsheet, you have an engine to deliver free cash flow by incorporating the accounting relations that underlie the Method 1 and 2 calculations in Box 11.1.

REFORMULATING GAAP CASH FLOW STATEMENTS

GAAP free cash flow	
– Increase in operating cash	1
+ Purchase of financial assets	2
– Sale of financial assets	2
+ Net cash interest outflow (after tax)	3,4
– Noncash investments	5
= Free cash flow	
GAAP financing flow	
+ Increase in cash equivalents	1
+ Purchase of financial assets	2
– Sale of financial assets	2
+ Net cash interest outflow (after tax)	3,4
– Noncash financing	5
= Financing cash flow	

NIKE, INC.
Reformulated Cash Flow Statement, 2010
(in millions)

	Free cash flow		
	Reported cash from operations		$3,164
3,4	Net interest payments (after tax)		4
			3,168
	Cash investments reported	$1,268	
1	Investment in operating cash	1	
2	Net investment in financial assets	(937)	332
	Free cash flow		$2,836
	Financing flows to claimants		
	Debt financing:		
	Decrease in notes payable	205	
	Reductions in long-term debt	32	
2	Net purchases of financial assets	937	
3,4	Net interest payments (after tax)	4	
1	Investments in cash equivalents	835	2,013
	(net of exchange rate effects on cash)		
	Equity financing:		
	Share issues	(423)	
	Share repurchases	741	
	Dividends	505	823
	Total financing flows		$2,836

CASH FLOW FROM OPERATIONS

Our calculations following Methods 1 and 2 yield a number for free cash flow but do not distinguish the two components, cash flow from operations and cash investment, in the free cash flow number. For that we need the cash flow statement. But, again, we run into problems with the reporting. The reason is that some of the cash flows that we might view as investment flows are included in cash from operations in the GAAP statement. Investment in research and development is reported as part of cash from operations rather than part of the investment section. And investments in short-term assets are classified as cash from operations. Consider inventories. Investments in inventory are necessary to carry out operations just like plant and equipment. However, they are not treated as investments. Rather, the cash spent on building up inventory reduces GAAP cash from operations just like cash spent in inventory that is shipped to customers.

Potentially we could make further adjustments to cash flow from operations for these investments. But that should be done only if there is a clear purpose. For many analysis tasks, it is free cash flow that is needed, and a misclassification of an investment as an operating rather than investment flow does not affect this number. Because expenditures on R&D activities, a long-run investment, are classified as a decrease in cash from operations in financial statements, the R&D expenditures are added back to calculate the appropriate cash from operations. But the misclassification does not affect the calculation

The Accounting Quality Watch in Box 9.6 in Chapter 9 and Box 10.8 in Chapter 10 continues here with quality issues that arise with reported cash flows. The three items listed below are covered in the chapter. Further discussion of the quality of the cash flow from operations number, and its use in analysis, then follows.

Accounting Item	The Quality Problem
Cash flow from operations	Reported cash flow from operations reported under GAAP includes interest payments and receipts. These are not cash flows from operations, but rather financing flows. (IFRS allows firms to choose the operating section or the financing section for reporting net interest payments.)
Taxes on net interest	These taxes are included in cash flow from operations, along with the net interest. They should be reclassified to the financing section of the statement.
Transactions in financial assets	Purchases and sales of these "investments" are incorrectly classified as net cash investments in operations (under both GAAP and IFRS). They are financing flows.

THE QUALITY OF CASH FLOW FROM OPERATIONS

Commentators sometimes point to "cash from operations" as a pristine number on which to judge the operating performance of a firm. But the fundamental analyst is cynical.

Cash Flow and Noncash Charges

Cash flow from operations is often promoted as a better number than earnings on which to rely because it dismisses noncash charges like depreciation. Analysts often view those charges as coming from "bookkeeping rules" that do not affect the cash generation. However, one ignores depreciation to one's peril. Depreciation is not a cash flow in the period when it is charged, but it certainly comes from cash outflows, made earlier, for investments. And those investments are necessary to maintain cash from operations. If one refers to cash flows rather than earnings, one should refer to net cash flow—cash flow from operations less the cash invested to deliver cash from operations—which, of course, is free cash flow.

In 2007, Caterpillar, Inc., the manufacturer of construction and mining equipment, reported cash flow from operations of $7,935 million. This was more than the $3,541 million reported in earnings. However, the cash flow number was after adding back $1,797 million from earnings for depreciation of

plant and equipment. Looking at the investment section of the cash flow statement, the analyst would find that the current expenditure in plant and equipment was $3,040 million. These expenditures were necessary to generate cash from operations in the future. Touting cash from operations without considering the cash expenditures (or depreciation) needed to maintain the cash from operations gives a false impression of the ability of the firm to generate cash from operations.

Delaying Payments

Firms can increase cash flow simply by delaying payments on accounts payable and other operating obligations. The delay does not affect earnings. Home Depot, the warehouse retailer, reported cash from operations of $5,942 million for fiscal year 2002, up from $2,977 million from the year earlier. But $1,643 million of the amount reported in 2002 came from an increase in accounts payable and taxes payable.

Advertising and R&D Expenditures

Because advertising and research and development expenditures are treated as cash from operations rather than cash investment under GAAP, cash from operations can be increased by reducing these expenditures (with adverse consequences for the future).

Advancing Payments of Receivables

Firms can increase cash flow by selling or securitizing receivables. This does not, however, represent an ability to generate cash from sales of products. In 2001, TRW, Inc., earnings dropped to $68 million from $438 million in 2000 while operating cash flow increased by $338 million. Most of this increase was due to the firm selling receivables for $327 million. (The firm disclosed this in footnotes.)

Noncash Transactions

Firms can increase cash from operations by paying for services with debt or share issues. Deferring the payment of wages with a payable or pension promise increases cash flow, as does compensation "paid" with stock options rather than cash.

Structured Finance

With the help of a friendly banker, firms might structure borrowing to make the cash flows received from the borrowing look like operating cash flows rather than financing cash flows. Enron was a case in point: Funneled through an off-balance-sheet vehicle, loans were disguised as natural gas trades between Enron and its bank, and the cash receipts from the effective loan were reported as cash from operations.

(continued)

Capitalization Policy Affects Cash from Operations

If a cash outflow is treated as an investment and thus capitalized on the balance sheet, it falls into the investment section of the cash flow statement rather than the cash from operations sections. So, if a firm is aggressively capitalizing what would otherwise be operating costs, it increases its cash flow from operations. Routine maintenance costs may be treated as property, plant, and equipment, for example.

Mismatching

The basic problem with cash flow from operations is that it does not match inflows and outflows well. You see this in the Caterpillar example above. As another example, a firm making acquisitions increases cash flow from operations from new customers acquired. But the cost of acquiring those cash flows is not in the cash flow section of the statement.

of free cash flow from the statement. The treatment of investment in brand name through advertising, which also reduces GAAP cash flow from operations, is similar.

Cash flow from operations is best seen as a diagnostic to challenge the quality of accrual accounting. We will do this in Chapter 18. But the analyst must handle the "cash flow from operations" number carefully. Box 11.4 continues the Accounting Quality Watch with a focus on cash flows.

Summary

The analyst looks to the cash flow statement to assess the ability of the firm to generate cash. Free cash flow is a particular focus, for free cash flow is necessary to anticipate liquidity and financing requirements in the future. And free cash flow forecasts are required if the analyst employs discounted cash flow methods for valuation. Subsequent chapters that involve forecasting cash will rely on the analysis of this chapter.

Unfortunately, the GAAP statement of cash flows is a little messy. But, having reformulated income statements and balance sheets appropriately, free cash flow can be calculated simply by Methods 1 and 2 laid out in this chapter. So we will see in the forecasting part of the book that once forecasted (reformulated) income statements and balance sheets are prepared, forecasting free cash flow involves one simple calculation from these statements. It is hard to think of forecasting free cash flow without thinking of future sales, profitability, and investments that will be reported in the income statement and balance sheet, so forecasting these statements is needed to forecast free cash flow. And if those statements are in reformulated form, the forecasted free cash flow drops out of them immediately. This is a very efficient way of proceeding.

This chapter has presented the adjustments that are necessary to read the free cash flow from the GAAP statement of cash flows. These adjustments reformulate the statement to categorize cash flows correctly, so that free cash flow is identified and shown to be equal to the financing flows.

The Web Connection

Find the following on the Web page for this chapter:

- Further examples of reformulated statements.
- Further discussion of problems raised by the GAAP presentation of the cash flow statement.
- Further examples of cash flow manipulation.
- Presentation of the cash flow statement under international accounting standards.
- The Readers' Corner.

Key Concepts

financial planning is planning to arrange financing to meet the future cash flow needs of the business. *342*

liquidity analysis is the analysis of current and future cash relative to the claims on cash. *342*

noncash transaction involves the acquisition of an asset or the incurring of an expense by assuming a liability or by issuing stock, without any cash involved. *350*

The Analyst's Toolkit

A Continuing Case: *Kimberly-Clark Corporation*

A Self-Study Exercise

With the equity statement, the balance sheet, and the income statement reformulated in the Continuing Case for Chapters 9 and 10, all that remains is to reformulate the cash flow statement.

FREE CASH FLOW FROM BALANCE SHEETS AND INCOME STATEMENT

Before reformulating the cash flow statement, calculate free cash flow for 2009 and 2010 from the balance sheets and comprehensive income statements you reformulated in the last chapter. Apply Method 1 and Method 2.

REFORMULATE THE CASH FLOW STATEMENT

Now reformulate the GAAP cash flow statement for 2010 in Exhibit 2.2. The work you did in Chapter 4 will take you partway. Note the information given there (on page 131) on interest paid during 2010 and the tax rate.

The number for free cash flow that you get from the reformulated cash flow statement will differ from that which you obtained from the balance sheets and income statement. Why might this be? Search the 10-K for likely explanations.

State in a few sentences what the reformulated cash flow statement is saying. What's the basic message?

Concept Questions	C11.1. Is cash flow analysis important for valuing firms?
	C11.2. For what purposes might forecasting cash flows be an analysis tool?
	C11.3. For a pure equity firm (with no net debt), how is free cash flow disposed of?
	C11.4. By investing in short-term securities to absorb excess cash, a firm reduces its cash flow after investing activities in its published cash flow statement. What is wrong with this picture?
	C11.5. Do you consider the direct method to be more informative than the indirect method of presenting cash flow from operations?
	C11.6. GAAP cash flow statements treat interest capitalized during construction as investment in plant. Do you agree with this practice?
	C11.7. Why is free cash flow sometimes referred to as a liquidation concept?
	C11.8. Why might an analyst not put much weight on a firm's current free cash flow as an indication of future free cash flow?
	C11.9. Consider the following quote from the CFO of Lear Corp. (in *The Wall Street Journal*, May 8, 2002, p. C1): "Sales of receivables and operating cash flows are entirely separate events. We see sales of receivables as a low-cost financing method; it shouldn't generate operating cash flow." Do you agree?
	C11.10. Explain why very profitable firms sometimes have negative free cash flows.

Exercises

Drill Exercises

E11.1. Classification of Cash Flows (Easy)

State whether the following transactions affect cash flow from operations, free cash flow, financing flows, or none of them.

a. Payment of a receivable by a customer
b. Sale to a customer on credit
c. Expenditure on plant
d. Expenditure on research and development
e. Payment of interest
f. Purchase of a short-term investment with excess cash
g. Sale of accounts receivable

E11.2. Calculation of Free Cash Flow from the Balance Sheet and Income Statement (Easy)

A firm reported comprehensive income of $376 million for 2012, consisting of $500 million in operating income (after tax) less $124 million of net financial expense (after tax). It also reported the following comparative balance sheet (in millions of dollars):

	Balance Sheet					
	2012	**2011**		**2012**	**2011**
Operating cash	60	50	Accounts payable	1,200	1,040
Short-term investments (at market)	550	500	Accrued liabilities	390	450
Accounts receivable	940	790	Long-term debt	1,840	1,970
Inventory	910	840			
Property and plant	2,840	2,710	Common equity	1,870	1,430
	5,300	4,890		5,300	4,890

Calculate free cash flow using Method 1 and Method 2.

E11.3.   Analyzing Cash Flows (Medium)

Consider the following comparative balance sheets for the Liquidity Company:

	December 31	
	2012	**2011**
Operating cash	$ 435,000	$ 50,000
Accounts receivable	40,000	-0-
Inventories	100,000	-0-
Land (unamortized cost)	400,000	800,000
Plant assets	200,000	200,000
Less: accumulated depreciation	(100,000)	-0-
	1,075,000	1,050,000
Accounts payable	25,000	-0-
Capital stock	1,050,000	1,050,000
	$1,075,000	$1,050,000

The company paid a dividend of $150,000 during 2012 and there were no equity contributions or stock repurchases.

a. Calculate free cash flow generated during 2012.
b. Where did the increase in cash come from?
c. How would your calculation in part (a) change if the firm invested in short-term deposits rather than paying a dividend?

E11.4.   Free Cash Flow for a Pure Equity Firm (Easy)

The following information is from the financial report of a pure equity company (one with no net debt). In millions of dollars.

Common shareholders' equity, December 31, 2011	174.8
Common dividends, paid December 2012	8.3
Issue of common shares on December 31, 2012	34.4
Common shareholders' equity, December 31, 2012	226.2

The firm had no share repurchases during 2012.
   Calculate the firm's free cash flow for 2012.

E11.5.   Free Cash Flow for a Net Debtor (Easy)

The following information is for a firm that has net debt on its balance sheet (in millions of dollars).

Common shareholders' equity, December 31, 2011	174.8
Common dividends, paid December 2012	8.3
Issue of common shares, December 2012	34.4
Common shareholders' equity, December 31, 2012	226.2
Net debt, December 31, 2011	54.3
Net debt, December 31, 2012	37.4

There were no share repurchases during 2012. The firm reported net interest after tax of $4 million on its income statement for 2012, and this interest was paid in cash.
   Calculate the firm's free cash flow for 2012.

E11.6. Applying Cash Flow Relations (Easy)

A firm reported free cash flow of $430 million and operating income of $390 million.

a. By how much did its net operating assets change during the period?

b. The firm invested $29 million cash in new operating assets during the period. What were its operating accruals?

c. The firm incurred net financial expenses of $43 million after tax, paid a dividend of $20 million, and raised $33 million from share issues. What was the change in its net debt position during the period?

E11.7. Applying Cash Flow Relations (Medium)

An analyst prepared reformulated balance sheets for the years 2012 and 2011 as follows (in millions of dollars):

	2012	2011
Operating assets	$640	$590
Financial assets	250	110
	890	700
Financial debt	170	130
Operating liabilities	20	30
Common equity	700	540
	$890	$700

The firm reported $100 million in comprehensive income for 2012 and no net financial income or expense.

a. Calculate the free cash flow for 2012.

b. How was the free cash flow disposed of?

c. How can a firm with financial assets and financial liabilities have zero net financial income or expense?

Applications

E11.8. Free Cash Flow and Financing Activities: General Electric Company (Easy)

The following summarizes free cash flows generated by General Electric from 2000–2004 (in millions of dollars).

	2000	2001	2002	2003	2004
Cash from operations	30,009	39,398	34,848	36,102	36,484
Cash investments	37,699	40,308	61,227	21,843	38,414
Free cash flow	(7,690)	(910)	(26,379)	14,259	(1,930)

a. Explain why such a profitable firm as General Electric can have negative free cash flow.

b. In 2005, the firm announced that the years of building its set of businesses was "largely behind it," so it would be slowing its investment activity. What is the likely effect on free cash flow? How will GE's financing activities likely change? What are the financing alternatives in light of the changed free cash flow?

Real World Connection

Exercises E5.11, E6.10, and E7.7 also deal with General Electric.

E11.9. Method 1 Calculation of Free Cash Flow for General Mills, Inc. (Easy)

Refer to the reformulated balance sheets and income statements for General Mills, Inc., in Exhibits 10.5 and 10.11 in Chapter 10. Calculate free cash flow for 2010 from these statements.

Real World Connection

Coverage of General Mills in Exercises E1.5, E2.9, E3.8, E4.10, E6.8, E13.9, E14.15, E15.6, and E16.10.

E11.10.   Free Cash Flow for Kimberley-Clark Corporation (Medium)

Below are summary numbers from reformulated balance sheets for 2007 and 2006 for Kimberly-Clark Corporation, the paper products company, along with numbers from the reformulated income statement for 2007 (in millions of dollars).

	2007	2006
Operating assets	$18,057.0	$16,796.2
Operating liabilities	6,011.8	5,927.2
Financial assets	382.7	270.8
Financial obligations	6,496.4	4,395.4
Operating income (after tax)	$2,740.1	
Net financial expense (after tax)	147.1	

a. The net payout to shareholders (dividends and share repurchases minus share issues) in 2007 was $3,405.9 million. Calculate free cash flow using Method 1 and Method 2.

b. The firm reported cash flow from operations of $2,429 million in its 2007 cash flow statement and also reported net interest payments of $142.4 million. It reported $898 million in cash spent on investing activities, but this was after including a net $56 million from liquidating short-term interest-bearing securities. The firm's statutory tax rate is 36.6 percent. Calculate free cash flow from these reported numbers.

Real World Connection

Follow Kimberly-Clark through the continuing case at the end of each chapter. Also see Exercises E4.9, E7.16, E8.10, and E12.6 and Minicases M2.1 and M5.3.

E11.11.   Extracting Information from the Cash Flow Statement with a Reformulation: Microsoft Corporation (Medium)

For many years, Microsoft has generated considerable free cash flow. Up to 2004, it paid no dividends and had no debt to pay off, so it invested the cash in interest-bearing securities. Its balance sheet at the end of its second (December) quarter for fiscal year ending June 2005 reported the following among current assets (in millions of dollars):

	June 30, 2004	December 31, 2004
Cash and equivalents	$ 15,982	$ 4,556
Short-term investments	44,610	29,948

You can see a significant reduction in both cash and short-term investments. During the second quarter, Microsoft decided to pay its first dividend in the form of a large special dividend. Exhibit 11.2 gives the cash flow statement for the quarter, along with a note on interest received on the investments listed above. The firm's tax rate is 37.5 percent.

Answer the following questions about the quarter ended December 31, 2004:

a. What were the cash dividends paid to common shareholders?
b. What was the net dividend paid out to shareholders?
c. Calculate (unlevered) cash flow from operations for the quarter.
d. Calculate cash invested in operations.
e. Calculate free cash flow.

f. Why was the "net cash from investing" number reported for 2004 so different from that for 2003? Is the large difference due to a change in Microsoft's investment in its operations?

g. Microsoft maintains $60 million in operating cash. What was its net investment in financial assets during the quarter (before any effect of exchange rates)?

After answering these questions, you have the ingredients to construct a reformulated cash flow statement. Go ahead and do it.

Real World Connection

Exercises on Microsoft are E1.6, E4.14, E6.12, E8.9, E9.9, E18.10, and E20.4. Mini-cases M9.1 and M13.2 also deal with Microsoft.

EXHIBIT 11.2
Cash Flow Statement for Microsoft Corporation for Fiscal Second Quarter, 2005

Cash Flow Statements (In millions of dollars, unaudited)	Three Months Ended December 31	
	2003	**2004**
Operations		
Net income	$ 1,549	$ 3,463
Depreciation and amortization	300	108
Stock-based compensation	3,232	551
Net recognized (gains)/losses on investments	(321)	74
Stock option income tax benefits	148	99
Deferred income taxes	(985)	68
Unearned revenue	2,774	3,354
Recognition of unearned revenue	(3,166)	(3,166)
Accounts receivable	(1,004)	(1,398)
Other current assets	607	373
Other long-term assets	55	7
Other current liabilities	1,256	17
Other long-term liabilities	129	69
Net cash from operations	4,574	3,619
Financing		
Common stock issued	189	795
Common stock repurchased	(730)	(969)
Common dividends	(1,729)	(33,498)
Net cash from financing	(2,270)	(33,672)
Investing		
Additions to property and plant	(172)	(176)
Acquisition of companies net of cash acquired	—	(1)
Purchases of investments	(22,377)	(16,013)
Maturities of investments	825	19,536
Sales of investments	19,775	20,068
Net cash from investing	(1,949)	23,414
Net change in cash and equivalents	355	(6,639)
Effect of exchange rates on cash and equivalents	26	54
Cash and equivalents, beginning of period	5,768	11,141
Cash and equivalents, end of period	$ 6,149	$ 4,556

Note: Interest

Microsoft has no debt, so paid no interest during the three months. Interest received from investments was $378 million.

Minicase   **M11.1**

Analysis of Cash Flows: Procter & Gamble II

Exhibit 11.3 presents the 2010 comparative cash flow statement for Procter & Gamble (P&G). If you worked the Procter & Gamble case in the last chapter (Minicase M10.1), you will have some familiarity with the company. Working that case will set you up to deal with this installment quickly, but in any case you should have the financial statements in the case (in Exhibit 10.15) before you when you work this case. The firm's statutory tax rate is 38 percent.

A. Using Method 1, calculate P&G's free cash flow for 2010. Then calculate the free cash flow from the cash flow statement in Exhibit 11.3, making the necessary adjustments to correct misclassifications. Do the two numbers agree? Why might they differ?

B. Using the Method 2 calculation for free cash flow, can you back out the net payout to shareholders?

C. Calculate the net payout to shareholders from the cash flow statement. Does it agree with your calculation in Part B of the case? Does it agree with the number from the shareholders' equity statement?

D. What is the relevance of the supplemental disclosure at the bottom of Procter & Gamble's cash flow statement?

E. Present a reformulated statement of cash flows for the firm.

F. State in words the message that this reformulated statement is conveying.

EXHIBIT 11.3
Comparative Cash Flow Statement for Procter and Gamble for 2010

	Amounts in millions; Years ended June 30		
	2010	**2009**	**2008**
Cash and cash equivalents, beginning of year	$ 4,781	$ 3,313	$ 5,354
Operating activities			
Net earnings	12,736	13,436	12,075
Depreciation and amortization	3,108	3,082	3,166
Share-based compensation expense	453	516	555
Deferred income taxes	36	596	1,214
Gain on sale of businesses	(2,670)	(2,377)	(284)
Change in accounts receivable	(14)	415	432
Change in inventories	86	721	(1,050)
Change in accounts payable, accrued and other liabilities	2,446	(742)	297
Change in other operating assets and liabilities	(305)	(758)	(1,270)
Other	196	30	(127)
Total operating activities	16,072	14,919	15,008
Investing activities			
Capital expenditures	(3,067)	(3,238)	(3,046)
Proceeds from asset sales	3,068	1,087	928
Acquisitions, net of cash acquired	(425)	(368)	(381)
Change in investments	(173)	166	(50)
Total investing activities	(597)	(2,353)	(2,549)

(*continued*)

EXHIBIT 11.3
(*concluded*)

	Amounts in millions; Years ended June 30		
	2010	**2009**	**2008**
Financing activities			
Dividends to shareholders	(5,458)	(5,044)	(4,655)
Change in short-term debt	(1,798)	(2,420)	2,650
Additions to long-term debt	3,830	4,926	7,088
Reductions of long-term debt	(8,546)	(2,587)	(11,747)
Treasury stock purchases	(6,004)	(6,370)	(10,047)
Impact of stock options and other	721	681	1,867
Total financing activities	(17,255)	(10,814)	(14,844)
Effect of exchange rate change on cash and cash equivalents	(122)	(284)	344
Change in cash and cash equivalents	(1,902)	1,468	(2,041)
Cash and cash equivalents, end of year	$ 2,879	$ 4,781	$ 3,313
Supplemental disclosure			
Cash payments for			
Interest	$ 1,184	$ 1,226	$ 1,373
Income taxes	4,175	3,248	3,499
Assets acquired through noncash capital leases	20	8	13
Divestiture of coffee business in exchange for shares of P&G stock	—	2,466	—

Real World Connection

Minicases M12.1, M13.1, M15.1, and M16.1 continue the analysis and valuation of Procter & Gamble.

Chapter Twelve

The Analysis of Profitability

LINKS

Link to previous chapters

Chapters 9, 10, and 11 reformulated the financial statements to prepare them for analysis.

This chapter

This chapter lays out the analysis of profitability that is necessary for forecasting future profitability and valuation.

Link to next chapter

Chapter 13 lays out the analysis of growth, to complete the analysis of the financial statements.

Link to Web page

The Web site applies the analysis in this chapter to a wider range of firms (**www.mhhe.com/penman5e**).

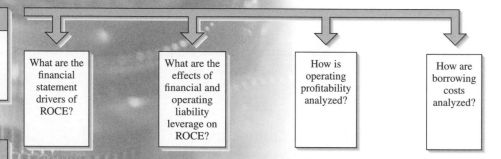

What are the financial statement drivers of ROCE?

What are the effects of financial and operating liability leverage on ROCE?

How is operating profitability analyzed?

How are borrowing costs analyzed?

The price-to-book valuation model of Chapter 5 directs us to forecast future residual earnings to value equities. The price-earnings valuation model of Chapter 6 directs us to forecast abnormal earnings growth, which is the same as residual earnings growth. Residual earnings are determined by the profitability of shareholders' investment, ROCE, and the growth in investment. So forecasting involves forecasting profitability and growth. To forecast, we need to understand what drives profitability and growth. The analysis of the drivers of ROCE is called **profitability analysis** and the analysis of growth is called **growth analysis.** This chapter covers profitability analysis. The next chapter covers growth analysis.

The reformulation of financial statements in the preceding chapters readies the statements for analysis. This and the next chapter complete the financial statement analysis.

Profitability analysis establishes where the firm is now. It discovers what drives current ROCE. With this understanding of the present, the analyst begins to forecast by asking how future ROCE will be different from current ROCE. To do so she forecasts the drivers that we lay out in this chapter. The forecasts, in turn, determine the value, so much so that the profitability drivers of this chapter are sometimes referred to as *value drivers*. Part Three of the book carries the analysis of this chapter over to forecasting and valuation.

Value is generated by economic factors, of course. Accounting measures capture these factors. In identifying the profitability drivers, it is important to understand the aspects of the business that determine them. Profitability analysis has a mechanical aspect, and the analysis here can be transcribed to a spreadsheet program where the reformulated statements are fed in and numerous ratios are spat out. But the purpose is to identify the sources of the value generation. So as you go through the mechanics, continually think of the activities of the firm that produce the ratios. Profitability analysis focuses the lens on the business.

With this thinking, profitability analysis becomes a tool for management planning, strategy analysis, and decision making, as well as valuation. The manager recognizes that generating higher profitability generates value. He then asks: What drives profitability? How will profitability change as a result of a particular decision, and how does the change translate into value created for shareholders? If a retailer decides to reduce advertising and adopt a "frequent buyer" program instead, how does this affect ROCE and the value of the equity? What will be the effect of an expansion of retail floor space? Of an acquisition of another firm?

The purpose of analysis is to get answers to questions like these. So you will find a number of "what-if" questions in this chapter. And you will see how analysis provides the answers to these questions.

THE ANALYSIS OF RETURN ON COMMON EQUITY

As we have seen, the return on common stockholders' equity (CSE) is calculated as

$$\text{Return on common equity (ROCE)} = \frac{\text{Comprehensive income}}{\text{Average CSE}}$$

We have also seen how the reformulated statements of Chapter 10 yield profitability measures for a firm's operations—return on net operating assets (RNOA)—and for its financing activities—net borrowing cost (NBC) or the return on net financial assets (RNFA). These are the drivers of ROCE.

Figure 12.1 shows how ROCE is broken down into its drivers, so follow this figure as we go through the analysis. The analysis proceeds over three levels. First, the effects of operating and financing activities are analyzed. Second, the effects of profit margins and asset turnovers on operating profitability are identified. Third, the drivers of profit margins, asset turnovers, and net borrowing costs at the lowest level of the figure are calculated. Acronyms that will be used as we proceed are given in The Analysts' Toolkit at the end of the chapter.

FIGURE 12.1 The
Analysis of Profitability
The breakdown of return
on common equity
(ROCE) into its drivers.

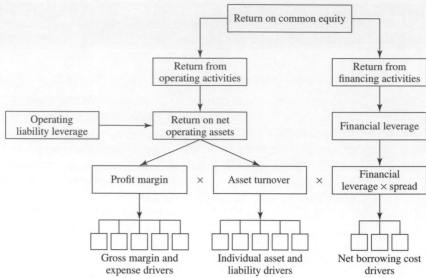

FIRST-LEVEL BREAKDOWN: DISTINGUISHING FINANCING AND OPERATING ACTIVITIES AND THE EFFECT OF LEVERAGE

The first breakdown of ROCE distinguishes the contribution of the operating and financing activities. This involves the effect of leverage, which "levers" the ROCE up or down through liabilities. Leverage is also sometimes referred to as "gearing."

Financial Leverage

Financial leverage is the degree to which net operating assets are financed by borrowing with net financial obligations (NFO). The measure FLEV = NFO/CSE, introduced in Chapter 10, captures financial leverage. To the extent that net operating assets are financed by net financial obligations rather than equity, the return on the equity is affected. The typical FLEV is about 0.4, but there is considerable variation among firms.

Financial leverage affects ROCE as follows (see Box 12.1):

$$
\begin{aligned}
\text{Return on common equity} = {}& \text{Return on net operating assets} \qquad\quad \textbf{(12.1)} \\
& + (\text{Financial leverage} \times \text{Operating spread})
\end{aligned}
$$

$$\text{ROCE} = \text{RNOA} + [\text{FLEV} \times (\text{RNOA} - \text{NBC})]$$

This expression for ROCE says that the ROCE can be broken down into three drivers:

1. Return on net operating assets (RNOA = OI/NOA).
2. Financial leverage (FLEV = NFO/CSE).
3. Operating spread between the return on net operating assets and the net borrowing cost (SPREAD = RNOA − NBC).

$$ROCE = \frac{\text{Comprehensive earnings}}{\text{Average CSE}}$$

Comprehensive earnings in the numerator of ROCE is composed of operating income and net financial expense, as depicted in a reformulated income statement. Common shareholders' equity (CSE) in the denominator is net operating assets minus net financial obligations. Thus

$$ROCE = \frac{OI - NFE}{NOA - NFO}$$

(Balance sheet amounts are averages over the period.) The operating income (OI) is generated by the net operating assets (NOA), and the operating profitability measure, RNOA, gives the percentage return on the net operating assets. The net financial expense (NFE) is generated by the net financial obliga-

tions (NFO), and the rate at which the NFE is incurred is the net borrowing cost (NBC). So the ROCE can be expressed as

$$ROCE = \left(\frac{NOA}{CSE} \times RNOA\right) - \left(\frac{NFO}{CSE} \times NBC\right)$$

where, to remind you, RNOA = OI/NOA and NBC = Net financial expense/NFO. This expression for ROCE is a weighted average of the return from operations and the (negative) return from financing activities.

We get more insights by rearranging this expression:

$$ROCE = RNOA + \left[\frac{NFO}{CSE} \times (RNOA - NBC)\right]$$

$$= RNOA + (\text{Financial leverage} \times \text{Operating spread})$$

$$= RNOA + (FLEV \times SPREAD)$$

Both operating income and net financial expense must be after tax and comprehensive of all components, as in the reformulated income statements of Chapter 10; otherwise, this breakdown will not work.

This formula says that the ROCE is levered up over the return from operations if the firm has financial leverage and the return from operations is greater than the borrowing cost. The firm earns more on its equity if the net operating assets are financed by net debt, provided those assets earn more than the cost of debt.

Figure 12.2 depicts how the difference between ROCE and RNOA changes with financial leverage according to the formula. If a firm has zero financial leverage, equation 12.1 says that ROCE equals RNOA. If the firm has financial leverage, then the difference between ROCE and RNOA is determined by the amount of the leverage and the **operating spread** between RNOA and the net borrowing cost. We will simply refer to the operating spread as the SPREAD. If a firm earns an RNOA greater than its after-tax net borrowing cost, it is said to have **favorable financial leverage** or **favorable gearing:** The RNOA is "levered up" or "geared up" to yield a higher ROCE. If the SPREAD is negative, the leverage effect is unfavorable. Box 12.2 gives a demonstration with General Mills, whose reformulated balance sheet is presented in Exhibit 10.5 in Chapter 10. The example highlights the "good news/bad news" nature of financial leverage: Financial leverage generates a higher return for shareholders if the firm earns more on its operating assets than its borrowing cost, but financial leverage hurts shareholder return if it doesn't. Accordingly, leverage is a component of the risk of equity as well as its profitability, as we will see in Chapter 14. We will also ask the following question in that chapter: Can a firm increase its equity value by increasing its ROCE through financial leverage, or will it reduce its equity value because of the increase in risk?

How does the analysis change when a firm like Nike has net financial assets (NFA) rather than net financial obligations (NFO)? In this case, financial income will be greater than financial expense and the firm will have a positive return on financing activities

FIGURE 12.2
How Financial Leverage Affects the Difference Between ROCE and RNOA for Different Amounts of Operating Spread
FLEV is financial leverage and the SPREAD is the difference between RNOA and the net borrowing cost.

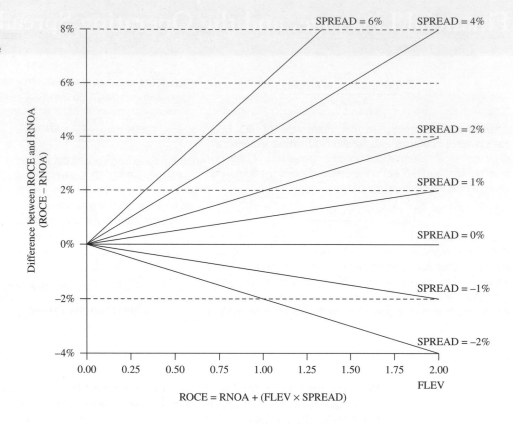

$$ROCE = RNOA + (FLEV \times SPREAD)$$

(RNFA) rather than net borrowing costs. Return on common equity is related to RNOA as follows:

$$ROCE = RNOA - \left[\frac{NFA}{CSE} \times (RNOA - RNFA) \right] \qquad \textbf{(12.2)}$$

where RNFA = Net financial income/NFA, the return on net financial assets. Here a positive spread reduces the ROCE: Some of shareholders' equity is invested in financial assets and if financial assets earn less than operating assets, ROCE is lower than RNOA. Box 12.3 demonstrates this with Nike.

Operating Liability Leverage

Just as financial liabilities can lever up the ROCE, so can operating liabilities lever up the return on net operating assets. Operating liabilities are obligations incurred in the course of operations and are distinct from financial obligations incurred to finance the operations. Chapter 10 gave a measure of the extent to which the net operating assets (NOA) are comprised of operating liabilities (OL), the operating liability leverage:

$$\text{Operating liability leverage (OLLEV)} = \frac{OL}{NOA}$$

The typical OLLEV is about 0.4. Operating liabilities reduce the net operating assets that are employed and so lever the return on net operating assets. To the extent that a firm

General Mills, a large manufacturer of packaged foods, has had considerable stock repurchases over the years, leaving it fairly highly leveraged. In Exhibit 10.5 in Chapter 10 you see that, for fiscal 2010, its average shareholders' equity was $5.533 billion, with average net financial obligations of $6.1 billion. Its average financial leverage was 1.102, based on these average balance sheet amounts.

The firm's ROCE for 2010 was 16.7 percent. Further analysis reveals that this number was driven by the high leverage:

$$ROCE = RNOA + [FLEV \times (RNOA - NBC)]$$
$$16.7\% = 10.1\% + [1.102 \times (10.1\% - 4.1\%)]$$

ROCE can exaggerate underlying operating profitability: RNOA is 10.1 percent but the high financial leverage, combined with a SPREAD over a borrowing cost of 4.1 percent, yields a much higher ROCE. Beware of firms boasting high ROCE: Is it driven by financial leverage rather than business operations?

A What-If Question

What if the RNOA at General Mills fell to 2 percent? What would be the effect on ROCE?

The answer is that the ROCE would turn negative:

$$-0.3\% = 2.0\% + [1.102 \times (2.0\% - 4.1\%)]$$

The unfavorable leverage would produce losses and a negative ROCE on a positive RNOA. That is the "bad news" aspect of leverage.

General Mills has minority interest on its balance sheet. This complicates the ROCE calculation. See Box 12.5.

can get credit in its operations with no explicit interest, it reduces its investment in net operating assets and levers its RNOA. But credit comes with a price. Suppliers who provide credit without interest also charge higher prices for the goods and services they supply than would be the case if the firm paid cash. And so operating liability leverage, like financial leverage, can be unfavorable as well as favorable.

To compute the leverage effect, first estimate the implicit interest that a supplier would charge for credit, using the firm's short-term borrowing rate for financial debt:

$$\text{Implicit interest on operating liabilities} = \text{Short-term borrowing rate (after tax)} \times \text{Operating liabilities}$$

Then calculate a return on operating assets, ROOA, as if there were no operating liabilities:

$$\text{Return on operating assets (ROOA)} = \frac{\text{OI} + \text{Implicit interest (after tax)}}{\text{Operating assets}}$$

RNOA is driven by operating liability leverage as follows:

$$\text{Return on net operating assets} = \text{Return on operating assets} \quad\quad \textbf{(12.3)}$$
$$+ \text{(Operating liability leverage}$$
$$\times \text{Operating liability leverage spread)}$$
$$RNOA = ROOA + (OLLEV \times OLSPREAD)$$

where OLSPREAD is the **operating liability leverage spread**, that is, the spread of the return on operating assets over the after-tax short-term borrowing rate:

$$OLSPREAD = ROOA - \text{Short-term borrowing rate (after tax)}$$

This leverage expression for RNOA is similar in form to the financial leverage equation (12.1) for ROCE: RNOA is driven by the rate of return on operating assets as if there were no operating liability leverage, ROOA, plus a leverage premium that is determined by the amount of operating liability leverage, OLLEV, and the operating liability leverage spread, OLSPREAD. The effect can be **favorable operating liability leverage**—if ROOA

Nike has been very profitable. For fiscal 2008, the firm reported an ROCE of 25.9 percent on average common equity of $7.458 billion. But Nike had considerable (average) financial assets of $2.086 billion from cash generated from its operations, giving it an average financial leverage that was negative: –0.280. The firm's return on average net financial assets was 2.3 percent.

The ROCE masks the profitability of operations of 35.0 percent:

$$ROCE = RNOA - [NFA/CSE \times (RNOA - RNFA)]$$

$$25.9\% = 35.0\% - [0.280 \times (35.0\% - 2.3\%)]$$

The RNOA of 35.0 percent is weighted down by the lower return on financing activities in the overall ROCE.

A What-If Question

What if the company used $1.0 billion of its financial assets to pay a special dividend? What would be the effect on ROCE?

The answer is that with $1.0 billion less in average financial assets and common equity, the average financial leverage would have been –0.168 rather than –0.280, and the ROCE would have been

$$29.5\% = 35.0\% - [0.168 \times (35.0\% - 2.3\%)]$$

Note: Dividends (and stock repurchases) increase ROCE.

---

is greater than the short-term borrowing rate—or unfavorable—if ROOA is less than the short-term borrowing rate. See Box 12.4 for an analysis of General Mills's operating liability leverage.

Operating liability leverage can add value for shareholders, so is important to identify if the analyst is to discover the source of the value generation. A firm that carries $400 million in inventory but has $400 million in accounts payable to the suppliers of the inventory effectively has zero net investment in inventory. The suppliers are carrying the investment in inventory which represents investment in the operations that the shareholders do not have to make (and can, rather, invest elsewhere to generate returns). Dell, Inc., whose reformulated balance sheets and income statements are presented in Exhibits 10.4 and 10.10 in Chapter 10, is a case of a firm using operating liability leverage. Indeed, Dell has so many operating liabilities that its net operating assets are negative. Cast back to the discussion on Dell surrounding those exhibits to see how its extreme operating liability leverage adds value for shareholders: The operating liability leverage produces residual income from operations that is greater than income from operations!

Summing Financial Leverage and Operating Liability Leverage Effects on Shareholder Profitability

Shareholder profitability, ROCE, is affected by both financial leverage and operating liability leverage. Without either type of leverage, ROCE would be equal to ROOA, the rate of return on operating assets. Operating liability leverage levers RNOA over ROOA and financial leverage levers ROCE over RNOA:

$$ROCE = ROOA + (RNOA - ROOA) + (ROCE - RNOA)$$

So, for the General Mills examples in Boxes 12.2 and 12.4, the ROCE of 16.7 percent is determined as follows:

$$ROCE = 7.1\% + (10.1\% - 7.1\%) + (16.7\% - 10.1\%)$$
$$= 7.1\% + 3.0\% + 6.6\%$$
$$= 16.7\%$$

General Mills had average net operating assets of $11.632 billion during fiscal year 2010 of which $5.494 billion was in operating liabilities. Thus its operating liability leverage ratio was 0.472. Its borrowing rate on its short-term notes payable was 1.1 percent, or 0.7 percent after tax. It reported operating income of $1.177 billion, but applying the after-tax short-term borrowing rate to operating liabilities, this operating income includes implicit after-tax interest charges of $38 million. So on average operating assets of $17.126 billion,

$$\text{ROOA} = \frac{1{,}177 + 38}{17{,}126} = 7.09\%$$

The effect of operating liability leverage is favorable:

RNOA = 10.1% = 7.09% + [0.472 × (7.09% − 0.7%)]

A What-If Question

What if suppliers were to charge the short-term borrowing rate of 1.1 percent explicitly for the credit supplied in accounts payable? What would be the effect on General Mills value?

The answer is probably none. The interest would be an additional expense. But to stay competitive, the supplier would have to reduce prices of goods sold to the firm by a corresponding amount so that the total price charged (in implicit plus explicit interest) remains the same. But supplier markets may not work as competitively as this supposes, so firms can exploit operating liability leverage if they have power over their suppliers. Like Dell, Inc., they can add value in their supplier relationship, that is, through operating liability leverage. Refer back to the discussion of Dell in Chapter 10.

A couple of complications can arise when analyzing leverage effects. First, the presence of a minority (noncontrolling) interest calls for a modification. See Box 12.5. Second, if net borrowing is close to zero or borrowing rates are considerably higher than lending rates, it can happen that firms report net interest expense (interest expense greater than interest income) in the income statement but an average net financial asset position in the balance sheet (or vice versa). (This happened to Nike in 2010.) Also, because of small average net financial obligations (in the denominator), you can sometimes calculate a very high net borrowing cost. This problem arises because, strictly, average net borrowing should be an average of daily balances, not just the beginning and ending balances. An analyst typically does not have access to daily numbers, although using amounts from quarterly reports alleviates the problem. One can always refer to the debt footnote for borrowing costs.

Return on Net Operating Assets and Return on Assets

A common measure of the profitability of operations is the *return on assets* (ROA):

$$\text{ROA} = \frac{\text{Net income} + \text{Interest expense (after tax)}}{\text{Average total assets}}$$

(Minority interest in income, if any, is added to the numerator.) The net income in the numerator is usually reported net income rather than comprehensive income. But, this aside, the ROA calculation mixes up financing and operating activities. Interest income, part of financing activities, is in the numerator. Total assets are operating assets plus financial assets, so financial assets are in the base. Thus the measure mixes the return on operations with the (usually lower) return from investing excess cash in financial assets. Operating liabilities are excluded from the base. Thus the measure includes the cost of operating liabilities in the numerator (in the form of higher input prices as the price of credit) but excludes the benefit of operating liability leverage in the base. The RNOA calculation appropriately distinguishes operating and financial items. As interest-bearing financial assets are negative financial obligations, they do not affect the return on

The presence of minority (noncontrolling) interest calls for a slight revision in the calculations of the effect of financial leverage. Minority interest, unlike debtholder interests, does not affect the overall profitability of equity, the leverage, or the SPREAD. It just affects the division of rewards between different equity claimants. The minority, like the majority common, shares the costs and benefits of leverage. So the additional step with minority interest (MI) is to distinguish ROCE for all common claimants from that for the (majority) common owners of the parent corporation in the consolidation:

$$ROCE = ROCE \text{ before MI} \times \text{MI sharing ratio}$$

where ROCE is the return on common equity to the shareholders of the parent company (the majority) and

$$ROCE \text{ before MI} = \frac{\text{Comprehensive income before MI}}{CSE + MI}$$

$$\frac{\text{Minority interest}}{\text{sharing ratio}} = \frac{\text{Comprehensive income}/}{\text{Comprehensive income before MI}}{CSE/(CSE + MI)}$$

The first ratio here gives the return to total common equity, minority and majority. The second ratio gives the sharing of the return. Use ROCE before minority interest when applying the financing leveraging equation 12.1, as we did with General Mills in Box 12.2.

This calculation is cumbersome. Minority interests are typically small in the United States, and one can (as an approximation) usually treat minority interest as a reduction in consolidated operating income and net operating assets.

operations. Operating liabilities reduce the needed investment in operating assets, providing operating liability leverage, so they are subtracted in the base.

Thus ROA typically measures a lower rate of return than RNOA. The median ROA for all U.S. nonfinancial firms from 1963 to 2010 was 7.1 percent. This is below what we would expect for a return to risky business investment: It looks more like a bond rate. The median RNOA was 10.5 percent, more in line with what we expect as a typical return from running businesses. ROA is a poor measure of operating profitability.

Table 12.1 compares ROA and RNOA for selected firms for 2007. You can see that ROA understates operating profitability. Look particularly at Nike and General Mills. The RNOA measures identify Microsoft, Genentech, and Cisco Systems as the exceptional companies they indeed are.

Operating liability leverage (OLLEV) and the amount of financial assets relative to total assets explain the difference between RNOA and ROA, and you can see in the table that firms with the largest differences have high numbers for these ratios. Microsoft had an

TABLE 12.1
Return on Net Operating Assets (RNOA) and Return on Assets (ROA) for Selected Firms for 2007 Fiscal Year
ROA typically understates operating profitability because it fails to incorporate operating liability leverage and includes the profitability of financial assets.

Industry and Firm	RNOA, %	ROA, %	Operating Liability Leverage (OLLEV)	Financial Assets/ Total Assets, %
Biotech				
Genentech, Inc.	40.4%	20.9%	0.44	30.2%
Amgen, Inc.	15.3	9.9	0.25	19.6
High-tech				
Microsoft Corp.	134.3	21.2	2.86	43.4
Oracle Corp.	27.8	14.1	0.59	23.0
Cisco Systems, Inc.	49.1	14.8	1.02	41.4
Retailers				
Walmart Stores, Inc.	14.4	8.9	0.50	4.2
The Gap, Inc.	25.5	11.1	1.12	27.9
Oil producers and refiners				
ExxonMobil Corp.	41.4	17.7	0.95	14.6
Chevron Corp.	26.0	13.4	0.82	6.9
Nike and General Mills				
Nike, Inc.	35.0	16.5	0.65	23.6
General Mills, Inc.	15.1	8.5	0.44	2.5

RNOA of 134.3 percent in 2007, but inclusion of financial assets (43.4 percent of total assets) in the ROA measure and the omission of the operating liability leverage of 2.86 reduces the profitability measure to 21.2 percent.

These observations reinforce two points. To analyze profitability effectively, two procedures must be followed:

1. Income must be calculated on a comprehensive (clean-surplus) basis.
2. There must be a clean distinction between operating and financing items in the income statement and balance sheet.

You will get "clean" measures only if these two elements are in place. So you can see the payoff to your work in this and the preceding chapters.

Financial Leverage and Debt-to-Equity Ratios

A common measure of financial leverage is the *debt-to-equity ratio,* calculated as total debt divided by equity. This measure is useful in credit analysis but, for the analysis of profitability, it confuses operating liabilities (which create operating liability leverage) with financial liabilities (which create financial leverage). And, as usually defined, it does not net out financial liabilities against financial assets.

The difference can be sizable: The median debt-to-equity ratio for U.S. firms from 1963 to 2004 was 1.22 while the median FLEV was 0.43. Microsoft had 43.4 percent of its assets in financial assets at the end 2007 and, with an operating liability leverage of 2.86, had no financial obligations. Its debt-to-equity ratio was 1.02, but all the debt in the debt-to-equity ratio was operating debt. So using the firm's debt-to-equity ratio as an indication of financial leverage would be quite misleading: Microsoft's FLEV (which includes the financial assets as negative debt) was –0.619.

SECOND-LEVEL BREAKDOWN: DRIVERS OF OPERATING PROFITABILITY

In the first-level breakdown, RNOA is isolated as an important driver of the ROCE. Following the scheme in Figure 12.1, RNOA can be broken down further into its drivers so that

$$\text{ROCE} = \text{RNOA} + [\text{FLEV} \times (\text{RNOA} - \text{NBC})] \qquad \textbf{(12.4)}$$

$$= (\text{PM} \times \text{ATO}) + [\text{FLEV} \times (\text{RNOA} - \text{NBC})]$$

The two drivers of RNOA are

1. Operating profit margin (PM):

$$\text{PM} = \text{OI (after tax)/Sales}$$

This we calculated as a common-size ratio in Chapter 10. The profit margin reveals the profitability of each dollar of sales.

2. Asset turnover (ATO):

$$\text{ATO} = \text{Sales/NOA}$$

The asset turnover measures sales revenue per dollar of net operating assets put in place. It measures the ability of the NOA to generate sales. It is sometimes referred to as its inverse, $1/\text{ATO} = \text{NOA/Sales}$, which indicates the amount of net operating assets used to generate a dollar of sales: If the ATO is 2.0, the firm is using 50 cents of net operating assets to generate a dollar of sales.

With $1,814 million of operating income and $5,930 million in average net operating assets, Nike generated an RNOA of 30.6 percent in 2010. With sales revenue of $19,014 million, the operating income amounted to an operating profit margin (PM) of 9.54 percent. The sales yielded an asset turnover (ATO) of 3.21 on the $5,930 million of operating assets. Thus RNOA = PM × ATO = 9.54% × 3.21 = 30.6%.

In 2010, General Mills's sales of $14,797 million earned $1,177 million of operating income on $11,632 million of average net operating assets. Thus its RNOA was 10.1 percent, made up of an operating PM of 7.95 percent and an asset turnover of 1.27. You can see that Nike's higher RNOA came from both a higher PM and a higher ATO: Nike gets more profit per dollar of sales but also generated high sales per dollar of net operating assets. Nike requires 31.2 cents invested in net operating assets for every dollar of sales while General Mills needs 78.7 cents.

This decomposition of operating profitability is known as the *DuPont model*. It says that profitability in operations comes from two sources. First, RNOA is higher the more of each dollar of sales ends up in operating income; second, RNOA is higher the more sales are generated from the net operating assets. The first is a profitability measure; the second is an efficiency measure. A firm generates profitability by increasing margins and can lever the margins up by using operating assets and operating liabilities more efficiently to generate sales.

The average (after-tax) profit margin is about 5.3 percent and the average asset turnover is about 2.0. But it is clear that a firm can produce a given level of RNOA with a relatively high profit margin but low turnover, or with a relatively high turnover but a low margin. Figure 12.3 plots median PM and ATO for various industries from 1963 to 2000. You see from the figure that industries with low asset turnovers tend to have high profit margins, and industries with high asset turnovers tend to have low profit margins. The figure draws a curve—sloping down to the right—that connects dots with the same 14 percent RNOA but different PMs and ATOs. An industry with a 30 percent margin and an ATO of 0.47 (like water supply) has the same 14 percent RNOA as a firm with a 2 percent margin and an ATO of 7.0 (like grocery stores).

Table 12.2 gives median RNOAs, PMs, and ATOs for a number of industries. It ranks industries on their median ROCE and also gives their median financial leverage (FLEV) and

FIGURE 12.3

Profit Margin and Asset Turnover Combinations for Various Industries, 1963–2000

Industries with high profit margins tend to have low asset turnovers, and industries with low profit margins tend to have high asset turnovers.

Source: M. Soliman, "Using Industry-Adjusted DuPont Analysis to Predict Future Profitability," working paper, Stanford University, 2003. With permission.

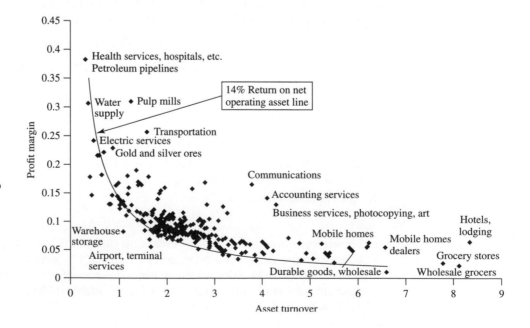

TABLE 12.2
Median Return on Common Equity (ROCE), Financial Leverage (FLEV), Operating Liability Leverage (OLLEV), Return on Net Operating Assets (RNOA), Profit Margins (PM), and Asset Turnovers (ATO) for Selected Industries, 1963–1996

Source:
Company: Standard & Poor's
Compustat® data.

Industry	ROCE, %	FLEV	OLLEV	RNOA, %	PM, %	ATO
Pipelines	17.1%	1.093	0.154	12.0%	27.8%	0.40
Tobacco	15.8	0.307	0.272	14.0	9.3	1.70
Restaurants	15.6	0.313	0.306	14.2	5.0	2.83
Printing and publishing	14.6	0.154	0.374	13.6	6.5	2.20
Business services	14.6	0.056	0.488	13.5	5.2	2.95
Chemicals	14.3	0.198	0.352	13.4	7.1	1.91
Food stores	13.8	0.364	0.559	12.0	1.7	7.39
Trucking	13.8	0.641	0.419	10.1	3.8	2.88
Food products	13.7	0.414	0.350	12.1	4.4	2.74
Telecommunications	13.4	0.743	0.284	9.1	12.5	0.76
General stores	13.2	0.389	0.457	11.3	3.5	3.55
Petroleum refining	12.6	0.359	0.487	11.2	6.0	1.96
Transportation equipment	12.5	0.369	0.422	11.2	4.5	2.47
Airlines	12.4	0.841	0.516	9.0	4.3	1.99
Utilities	12.4	1.434	0.272	8.2	14.5	0.59
Wholesalers, nondurable goods	12.2	0.584	0.461	10.2	2.3	3.72
Paper products	11.8	0.436	0.296	10.2	5.9	1.74
Lumber	11.7	0.312	0.384	10.4	4.0	2.60
Apparel	11.6	0.408	0.317	10.1	4.0	2.55
Hotels	11.5	1.054	0.201	8.5	8.2	1.04
Shipping	11.4	0.793	0.205	9.1	12.6	0.61
Amusements and recreation	11.4	0.598	0.203	10.1	9.5	1.10
Building and construction	11.4	0.439	0.409	10.6	4.5	2.06
Wholesalers, durable goods	11.2	0.448	0.354	9.9	3.4	2.84
Textiles	10.4	0.423	0.266	9.3	4.3	2.09
Primary metals	9.9	0.424	0.338	9.4	5.0	1.80
Oil and gas extraction	9.1	0.395	0.263	8.3	13.0	0.57
Railroads	7.3	0.556	0.362	7.1	9.7	0.78

operating liability leverage (OLLEV). This table gives you a sense of the typical amounts for these measures. The median ROCE over all industries is 12.2 percent, and the median RNOA is 10.3 percent. The difference is due to financial leverage and a positive SPREAD. The median FLEV over all industries is 0.403, but there is considerable variation. You can see that some industries—pipelines, utilities, and hotels—have produced ROCE through highly favorable financial leverage. Others—business services, printing and publishing, and chemicals—use little financial leverage to yield a high ROCE. Some—such as business services—have used operating liability leverage rather than financial leverage to lever ROCE. Others—such as trucking and airlines—have used both forms of leverage.

The PM and ATO tradeoff is apparent from the table. Some industries—printing and publishing and chemicals—produce a higher than average RNOA with both high profit margins and high asset turnovers. But industries with high margins typically have lower turnovers, and vice versa. Compare pipelines with food stores: Similar RNOAs are generated with quite dissimilar margins and turnovers. Capital-intensive industries such as pipelines, shipping, utilities, and communications have low turnovers but high margins. Firms in competitive businesses—food stores, wholesalers, apparel, and general retail—often have low profit margins but generate RNOA through higher turnover.

Margins and turnovers reflect the technology for delivering products. Businesses with large capital investments—like telecommunications—typically have low turnovers and high margins. Firms that generate customers with advertising—like apparel makers—typically have lower margins (after advertising expense) but, as a result of the advertising, high turnovers. Margins and turnovers also reflect competition. An industry where high turnover can be achieved—food stores that can generate a lot of sales per square foot of retail space—will attract competition. That competition erodes margins, if there is little barrier to entry, as sales prices fall to maintain turnover (as with food stores).

THIRD-LEVEL BREAKDOWN

Profit Margin Drivers

We now move to the final step in the scheme in Figure 12.1, breaking down the profit margin and asset turnover into their drivers. The common-size analysis of the income statement in Chapter 10 broke the profit margin into two components:

$$\text{PM} = \text{Sales PM} + \text{Other items PM} \qquad \textbf{(12.5)}$$

Other items in the income statement include shares of subsidiary income, special items, and gains and losses on asset sales. These sources of income are not a result of sales revenue at the top of the income statement. So calculating a PM that includes these items distorts the profitability of sales. The sales PM, based on operating income before other items, includes only expenses incurred to generate sales, thus isolating the profitability of sales.

The two components of the profit margin have further components:

$$\text{Sales PM} = \text{Gross margin ratio} - \text{Expense ratios} \qquad \textbf{(12.6)}$$

$$= \frac{\text{Gross margin}}{\text{Sales}} - \frac{\text{Administrative expense}}{\text{Sales}} - \frac{\text{Selling expense}}{\text{Sales}}$$

$$- \frac{\text{R\&D}}{\text{Sales}} - \frac{\text{Operating taxes}}{\text{Sales}}$$

$$\text{Other operating items PM} = \frac{\text{Subsidiary income}}{\text{Sales}} + \frac{\text{Other equity income}}{\text{Sales}} \qquad \textbf{(12.7)}$$

$$+ \frac{\text{Special items}}{\text{Sales}} + \frac{\text{Other gains and losses}}{\text{Sales}}$$

These component ratios are known as *profit margin drivers*. The drivers can be analyzed further by business segment if segment disclosures are available. Clearly, profit margins are increased by adding to gross margins (reducing cost of sales), by adding other items income, and by reducing expenses per dollar of sales.

Turnover Drivers

The net operating assets are made up of many operating assets and liabilities and so the overall ATO can be broken down into ratios for the individual assets and liabilities:

$$\frac{1}{\text{ATO}} = \frac{\text{Cash}}{\text{Sales}} + \frac{\text{Accounts receivable}}{\text{Sales}} + \frac{\text{Inventory}}{\text{Sales}} + \cdots + \frac{\text{PPE}}{\text{Sales}} \qquad \textbf{(12.8)}$$

$$+ \cdots - \frac{\text{Accounts payable}}{\text{Sales}} - \frac{\text{Pension obligations}}{\text{Sales}} - \cdots$$

Again, the balance sheet amounts are averages over the year. The turnover is expressed here as a reciprocal of the ATO, which is the amount of net operating assets to support a dollar of sales, as are the individual turnovers. Thus the individual turnovers aggregate conveniently (in a spreadsheet, for example) to the overall turnover. However, conventionally, individual turnover ratios are expressed as sales per dollar of investment in the asset. For example,

$$\text{Accounts receivable turnover} = \frac{\text{Sales}}{\text{Accounts receivable (net)}}$$

and

$$\text{PPE turnover} = \frac{\text{Sales}}{\text{Property, plant, and equipment (net)}}$$

(The PPE turnover is sometimes called the *fixed asset turnover.*)

A firm increases its turnover (and thus RNOA) by maintaining operating assets at a minimum while increasing sales. But the ATO is also affected by operating liability turnovers, and this of course reflects operating liability leverage: Operating liability leverage increases ATO and, if operating liability leverage is favorable, RNOA.

Turnover ratios are sometimes referred to as *activity ratios* or *asset utilization ratios.* Some activity ratios are calculated in different ways but with the same concept in mind. So, for example,

$$\text{Days in accounts receivable} = \frac{365}{\text{Accounts receivable turnover}}$$

(sometimes called *days sales outstanding*). This gives the typical number of days it takes to collect cash from sales. It highlights that efficiency is increased by turning sales into cash quickly and is often used as a metric to evaluate collection departments. A typical number is 35 days, but it varies considerably from industry to industry, with department stores and hotels having less than 15 days and pharmaceuticals over 50 days. With an accounts receivable turnover of 6.85, Nike's days in accounts receivable is 53. General Mills, with an accounts receivable turnover of 15.15, has 24 days in accounts receivable.

The inventory turnover ratio is sometimes measured as

$$\text{Inventory turnover} = \frac{\text{Cost of goods sold}}{\text{Inventory}}$$

This differs from the sales/inventory calculation by not being affected by changes in profit margins. Using this definition, the efficiency of inventory management is sometimes expressed in terms of the average number of days that inventory is held, its shelf life:

$$\text{Days in inventory} = \frac{365}{\text{Inventory turnover}}$$

Inventory turnover increases if inventory builds up when sales are slow, so it is often taken as a red flag warning indicating a drop in demand. But the measure will also increase if firms are building up inventories in anticipation of more sales. The ratio is best applied in wholesaling or retailing concerns where there is just one type of inventory, finished goods inventory. In a manufacturing concern, inventories include materials and work in progress, which take different times to complete into finished goods. Footnotes sometimes break down inventory into finished goods and other inventories, in which case ratios for finished goods inventory can be calculated. Advertising and promotion reduce the inventory turnover but, as they incur additional expenses, they also reduce the profit margin. The management issue is the net effect of RNOA.

A metric that assesses the ability to get operating liability leverage by extending credit from suppliers is

$$\text{Days in accounts payable} = \frac{365 \times \text{Accounts payable}}{\text{Purchases}}$$

where

$$\text{Purchases} = \text{Cost of goods sold} + \text{Change in inventory}$$

But note that supplier credit has a cost: The supplier might raise prices to compensate. So the manager has to ask if operating liability leverage is favorable.

The profit margins and asset turnovers for Nike and General Mills are given in Table 12.3, along with their drivers. The profit margin drivers sum to the overall PM, and the inverse of the turnover drivers sum to the inverse of the overall ATO.

TABLE 12.3   Second- and Third-Level Breakdown: Nike and General Mills, 2009–2010

	Nike				General Mills			
	2010		2009		2010		2009	
Second Level								
RNOA	30.6%		28.4%		10.1%		4.1%	
Profit margin	9.54%		8.99%		7.95%		3.41%	
Asset turnover	3.21		3.16		1.27		1.19	
Third Level								
Profit margin drivers (%)								
Gross margin ratio	46.3		44.9		39.7		35.6	
Administrative expense ratio	(20.9)		(19.8)		(14.3)		(13.7)	
Advertising expense ratio	(12.4)		(12.3)		(6.1)		(5.0)	
Other expense ratio	0.3		0.5		(1.5)		(1.4)	
Sales PM before tax	13.3		13.3		17.8		15.5	
Tax expense ratio	(3.2)		(3.6)		(6.3)		(5.8)	
Sales PM	10.0		9.7		11.5		9.8	
Other items PM	(0.5)	9.5	(0.7)	9.0	(3.6)	7.9	(6.4)	3.4
Asset turnover drivers (inverse)								
Cash turnover	0.005		0.005		0.004		0.004	
Accounts receivable turnover	0.146		0.148		0.066		0.069	
Inventory turnover	0.116		0.125		0.090		0.093	
Prepayment turnover	0.043		0.036		0.029		0.033	
PPE turnover	0.102		0.101		0.208		0.209	
Goodwill and intangibles turnover	0.036		0.048		0.700		0.715	
Other asset turnover	0.060		0.050		0.058		0.091	
Operating asset turnover	0.506		0.512		1.157		1.212	
Accounts payable turnover	(0.056)		(0.057)		(0.056)		(0.059)	
Accrued expenses turnover	(0.090)		(0.090)		—		—	
Taxes payable turnover	(0.004)		(0.005)		—		—	
Other liability turnover	(0.045)	0.311	(0.044)	0.316	(0.314)	0.787	(0.314)	0.839

Note: Columns may not add precisely due to rounding error.

What if Nike increased its accounts receivable turnover from 6.85 to General Mills's level of 15.15 while maintaining the current level of sales? How would RNOA change?

Answer: The increase would reduce average accounts receivable by $1,395 million to $1,255 million, increase the overall asset turnover from 3.21 to 4.19, and increase RNOA from 29.6 percent to 40.0 percent. However, this is so only if the reduction in customers' payment terms has no effect on sales and margins. A complete sensitivity analysis traces the effects through to all the determinants of RNOA: How will sales, margins, and asset turnovers be affected?

What if Nike's gross margin ratio of 46.3 percent declines to 44.9 percent in 2009 due to higher production costs?

Answer: A reduction in the gross margin ratio of 1.4 percent is an after-tax reduction of 0.89 percent at Nike's 36.3 percent tax rate. This results in a drop in the (after-tax) overall profit margin from 9.54 percent to 8.65 percent and a drop of RNOA from 30.6 percent to 27.8 percent.

What if General Mills increased its annual advertising expenditures by $200 million to $1,109 million, resulting in $1,200 million in additional sales at the same gross margin percentage?

Answer: The increased advertising would result in an extra $476 million of gross margin at the current gross margin ratio of 39.7 percent. Net of the $200 million in additional advertising expenses, the additional pretax income would be $276 million, or $173 million after tax. Accordingly, the profit margin ratio would increase to 8.4 percent. If receivables, inventory, and other net assets increase proportionally to support the sales, the ATO remains the same, so RNOA increases to 8.4 percent × 1.27 = 10.7 percent. Clearly, if the increased sales that the advertising draws were lower margin sales, the RNOA would be less.

The details in Table 12.3 provide a more granular view of the profitability. Changes over years are particularly informative for the analyst forecasting the future because they indicate how RNOA is evolving and thus its likely path ahead. (One needs more than two years for a good look.) Table 12.3 indicates that Nike's higher profitability in 2010 over General Mills comes from a higher gross margin, though higher advertising and administrative expense ratios to maintain sales cut into the overall profit margin. Gross margin, of course, reflects production costs. General Mills requires lower receivables and inventories to maintain sales, but higher investment in property, plant, and equipment. General Mills's lower ATO also comes from the investments in acquisitions (goodwill) and brands (intangible assets) to grow sales whereas Nike maintains its brand through advertising. Nike's increase in RNOA is due largely from an enhanced gross margin, which bodes well for the future, though sales are flat. All other drivers are fairly stable. General Mills's RNOA increased significantly in 2010 over 2009, also with an increasing gross margin on flat sales and fairly constant asset turnovers. But the increase is also explained by charges for its pension plan and currency losses (in other items) in 2009.

Key Drivers

The big issue for both firms: Can they grow sales while at the same time maintaining the enhanced gross margins? Can they do it without a considerable increase in the advertising expense ratio? Can they do it without large investment that will reduce their asset turnovers? These questions and the analysis here point to the *three key drivers:* sales, operating profit margin, and asset turnover. Simply put, a firm increases value by growing sales, earning high income per dollar of sales (PM), and keeping its net operating assets that generate the sales as low as possible (ATO). Accordingly, these three drivers will appear prominently when we come to valuation in the next part of the book.

Analysis does not end with the calculation of ratios. Indeed the calculations are the tools of analysis. The analyst takes these tools and asks what-if questions—and gets answers. See Box 12.6. The profitability analysis for Nike continues on the BYOAP feature on the book's Web site. See Box 12.7 for a summary for years 2000–2008.

The profitability analysis for Nike is continued on the Build Your Own Analysis Product (BYOAP) feature on the book's Web site, which provides a full analysis of the firm from 2000–2010. Here are some of the salient numbers up to 2008:

	2008	2007	2006	2005	2004	2003	2002	2001	2000
Sales revenue ($ billions)	18.6	16.3	15.0	13.8	12.3	10.7	9.9	9.5	9.0
Profitability:									
Return on common equity (%)	25.9	25.1	24.1	26.1	23.0	10.3	17.0	16.5	16.6
Return on net operating assets (%)	35.0	33.5	29.5	29.4	23.3	9.6	14.4	12.9	13.3
Profit margin (%)	10.1	10.1	9.6	10.0	8.4	4.0	6.5	6.1	6.2
Asset turnover	3.5	3.3	3.1	3.0	2.8	2.4	2.2	2.1	2.1
Leverage:									
Financial leverage	−0.280	−0.269	−0.198	−0.116	−0.160	0.116	0.216	0.342	0.295
Operating liability leverage	0.646	0.579	0.515	0.479	0.462	0.383	0.283	0.258	0.290

You see that Nike's return on common equity (ROCE) increased over the years even though financial leverage declined: In 2000, Nike was positively levered, but by 2004 it had become a holder of net financial assets. The increase in ROCE is explained by operations: RNOA increased from 13.3 percent in 2000 to 35.0 percent by 2008 (but declined to 30.6 in 2010, as we have seen). Not only did profit margins from operations increase, but so did asset turnovers, accompanied by an increase in operating liability leverage. The increased asset turnover was accompanied by significant sales growth but with the firm requiring lower net operating assets to support sales.

These measures are the drivers of growth. They are embellished by a deeper analysis of drivers, as in Table 12.3. We turn to the formal analysis of growth in the next chapter.

Borrowing Cost Drivers

The final component of ROCE is the operating spread, RNOA − NBC. As the RNOA component of this spread has been analyzed, this leaves the analysis of the net borrowing cost or, in the case of net financial assets, the return from net financial assets.

The net borrowing cost is a weighted average of the costs for the different sources of net financing. It can be calculated as

$$\text{NBC} = \left[\frac{\text{FO}}{\text{NFO}} \times \frac{\text{After-tax interest on financial obligations (FO)}}{\text{FO}} \right]$$

$$- \left[\frac{\text{FA}}{\text{NFO}} \times \frac{\text{After-tax interest on financial assets (FA)}}{\text{FA}} \right]$$

$$- \left(\frac{\text{FA}}{\text{NFO}} \times \frac{\text{Unrealized gains on FA}}{\text{FA}} \right) + \left(\frac{\text{Preferred stock}}{\text{NFO}} \times \frac{\text{Preferred dividend}}{\text{Preferred stock}} \right) + \cdots$$

General Mills's 2010 after-tax net borrowing cost of 4.1 percent is made up of after-tax interest expense and interest income components, weighted as follows. Refer again to the reformulated statements in Exhibits 10.5 and 10.11.

$$\text{NBC} = \left[\frac{6{,}752}{6{,}100} \times \frac{256}{6{,}752} \right] - \left[\frac{652}{6{,}100} \times \frac{5}{652} \right]$$

$$= \left[1.11 \times 3.79\% \right] - \left[0.11 \times 0.77\% \right]$$

$$= 4.1\% \text{ (allow for rounding error)}.$$

The weights are calculated from balance sheet averages. This calculation separates the after-tax borrowing cost for the obligations (3.79 percent) from the return on financial assets (0.77 percent).

A lower rate of return on financial assets than the borrowing rate on obligations increases the composite net borrowing cost over that for the obligations. The difference in the rates for the two components is called the **spread between lending and borrowing rates** (−3.02 percent here). Banks make money with higher lending than borrowing rates and thus (if they are successful) their overall net rate is higher than the borrowing rate. General Mills has a negative lending and borrowing rate spread, typical of nonfinancial firms.

As with all calculations, these numbers should be checked for their reasonableness. Footnotes give rates for some borrowings as a benchmark. If your calculated borrowing costs seem "out of line," you may have misclassified operating and financing items (and this means that your RNOA is also incorrect). It may be that disclosures are not sufficient to make a clear distinction. To the extent this is material, it will affect not only the net borrowing cost but also financial and operating leverage calculations. The inability to unravel capitalized interest will introduce errors. And errors will be made if the averaging of balance sheet amounts does not reflect the timing of changes in those amounts during the period.

BUILD YOUR OWN ANALYSIS ENGINE

You are now at the stage where you can build your own financial statement analysis engine along the lines of this chapter. The spreadsheet starts with a reformatting of the equity statement (as in Chapter 9) to isolate comprehensive income, followed by the reformatting of income statements and balance sheets to separate operating and financing activities (Chapter 10). If you also want a statement of cash flow, remember the lesson learned in Chapter 11: Once you have appropriately reformatted income statement and balance sheets, free cash flow falls out by the press on a button. To add the financing section of the cash flow statement, simply take the net payout to shareholders in the equity statement and identify cash flow to net debtholders as the remainder of the free cash flow.

With income statements and balance sheets reformatted into their appropriate cells in the spreadsheet, the decomposition of the ROCE into its drivers follows by the press of a button once you have entered the template for the calculations. If you enter reformatted statements for a number of years you will have a detailed history of the evolution of a firm's profitability and the drivers of the profitability. Keep your eye on the key drivers: sales growth, operating profit margins, and asset turnovers.

Once you have built the spreadsheet, experiment with sensitivity analysis. That involves asking "what-if" questions for different scenarios, such as those in Box 12.6. Observe how RNOA and ROCE can change as particular drivers change. As we proceed, you will see how that exercise will help you get an insight into risk, for the analysis of risk involves understanding outcomes under different scenarios. You will also see how the sensitivity analysis also involves simulating management (albeit as a desk job!). You ask: How can this firm be managed differently and what would be the effect on profitability and its drivers?

Note one important structural point in the scheme in Figure 12.1: The various measures are nested such that any change within the system can be tracked back directly to ROCE. So, for example, the effect of a change in a profit margin driver at the lowest level of ROCE is automatically delivered by the program if the spreadsheet follows the structure of the figure. And ROCE, of course, drives residual earnings and value—that is where we are headed.

With this analysis tool, you are ready for forecasting and valuation. The final stage of the project will be to combine your valuation engines (Chapter 5 and 6) with your analysis

The Web Connection

Find the following on the Web page for this chapter:

- Further exploration of the effects of financial leverage, with consideration of both risk and profitability effects.
- Further exploration of operating liability leverage and how it is particularly pertinent for an insurance company.

- Profitability analysis when firms classify expenses by nature rather than function.
- A spreadsheet engine to carry out profitability analysis.
- The Readers' Corner.

engine here to give you a complete analysis and valuation product. This is Part Three of the book. Again, BYOAP on the Web site will guide you.

Summary

This chapter has laid out the analysis of profitability. The analysis is summarized in Figure 12.1. The methods are orderly, with lower levels of analysis nested in higher levels. And the analysis aggregates up from the bottom to ROCE at the top, so it is amenable to simple programming. Once the reformulated income statement and balance sheet are entered into a spreadsheet program and the template in Figure 12.1 overlaid, the analysis proceeds automatically.

The analysis uncovers the financial statement drivers of the return on common equity, but each of these drivers refers to an aspect of business activity. The analysis here is a way of penetrating the financial statements to observe those activities. But it is also a way of organizing your knowledge of the business and understanding the effects of business activities on value. Understanding how the business affects the financial statement drivers means that the analyst understands how the business affects ROCE and, in turn, how the business affects residual earnings and the value of the business. So, for example, the analyst understands how a change in the profit margin or asset turnover affects residual earnings. And the analyst—or the manager of the business—can ask "what-if" questions of how ROCE and the value might change with a planned or unplanned change in margins or turnovers.

Key Concepts

favorable financial leverage (or **favorable gearing**) is an increase in ROCE over RNOA, induced by borrowing.   *367*

favorable operating liability leverage is an increase in return on net operating assets over return on operating assets, induced by operating liabilities.   *369*

growth analysis is the analysis of the determinants of growth in residual earnings.   *364*

operating liability leverage spread is the difference between the return on operating assets and the implicit borrowing rate for operating liabilities.   *369*

operating spread is the difference between operating profitability and the net borrowing cost.   *367*

profitability analysis is the analysis of the determinants of return on common equity (ROCE).   *364*

spread is a difference between two rates of return. Examples are the **operating spread,** the **operating liability leverage spread,** and the **spread between borrowing and lending rates.**   *367*

spread between borrowing and lending rates is the difference between the return on financial obligations and the return on financial assets.   *381*

The Analyst's Toolkit

Analysis Tools	Page	Key Measures	Page	Acronyms to Remember	
The analysis of financial leverage equations 12.1, 12.2	366	Return on common equity (ROCE)	365	ATO	asset turnover = sales/NOA
The analysis of operating liability leverage equation 12.3	369	Return on net operating assets (RNOA)	366	CSE	common shareholders' equity
		Net borrowing cost (NBC)	366	FLEV	financial leverage = NFO/CSE
DuPont analysis of return on net operating assets equation 12.4	373	Return on net financial assets (RNFA)	368	NBC	net borrowing cost = NFE/NFO
		Financial leverage (FLEV)	366	NFA	net financial assets
Analysis of profit margin equations 12.6, 12.7	376	Operating liability leverage (OLLEV)	368	NFE	net financial expenses
		The operating spread (SPREAD)	366	NFI	net financial income
Analysis of asset turnovers equation 12.8	376	Operating liability leverage spread (OLSPREAD)	369	NOA	net operating assets
				OA	operating assets
Analysis of borrowing costs	380	Return on operating assets (ROOA)	369	OI	operating income
What-if analysis	379			OL	operating liabilities
		Minority interest sharing ratio	372	OLLEV	operating liability leverage = OL/NOA
		Operating profit margin (PM)	373	OLSPREAD	operating liability leverage spread = ROOA – short-term borrowing rate
		Asset turnover (ATO)	373		
		Sales profit margin	376	PM	profit margin = OI/sales
		Other operating items profit margin	376	PPE	property, plant, and equipment
		Gross margin	376		
		Expense ratios	376	RNFA	return on net financial assets = NFI/NFA
		Individual asset turnover ratios	376		
		Days in accounts receivable	377	RNOA	return on net operating assets = OI/RNOA
		Days in inventory	377		
		Days in accounts payable	377		
		Borrowing cost drivers	380	ROA	return on assets = net income + interest expense (after tax)/total assets
		Spread between lending and borrowing rates	381		
				ROOA	return on operating assets = (OI + implicit interest on OL)/OA
				SPREAD	operating spread = RNOA – NBC

A Continuing Case: *Kimberly-Clark Corporation*

A Self-Study Exercise

In the Continuing Case for Chapter 10, you reformulated Kimberly-Clark's balance sheets and income statements. The reformulation prepares the statements for analysis, which you will carry out here.

PROFITABILITY ANALYSIS FOR KMB

Proceed with a comprehensive profitability analysis of Kimberly-Clark for 2009 and 2010. Let Figure 12.1 in this chapter be your guide; proceed through the three levels of analysis. Be sure to distinguish operating profitability from the effects of financing activities, and then analyze the operating activities in detail. Show how the leveraging equations for financial leverage and operating liability leverage work for KMB. For the latter, set the short-term borrowing rate, before tax, at 1.2 percent.

WHAT DOES THE ANALYSIS MEAN?

After making the requisite calculations, state in words what the array of numbers mean. How would you discuss KMB's performance if you were an analyst talking to clients?

SENSITIVITY ANALYSIS: WHAT IF?

After you have completed the analysis, introduce some "what-if" questions and supply the answers. Examine the effects of changes in margins and turnovers on profitability. What if gross margins decline? What if advertising becomes less productive? What if individual asset turnovers change?

BUILDING YOUR OWN ANALYSIS ENGINE FOR KMB

If you entered KMB's reformulated statements into a spreadsheet in Chapter 10, you might add profitability analysis to that spreadsheet. The BYOAP feature on the book's Web page will guide you. Also look at the profitability analysis engine on the Web page for this chapter. Once you have the analysis automated, you can apply it to the sensitivity analysis that supplies answers to the what-if questions you raised above. Just change the inputs (the reformulated statements) and the program will supply the answer at the press of a button.

Concept Questions

C12.1. Under what conditions would a firm's return on common equity (ROCE) be equal to its return on net operating assets (RNOA)?

C12.2. Under what conditions would a firm's return on net operating assets (RNOA) be equal to its return on operating assets (ROOA)?

C12.3. State whether the following measures drive return on common equity (ROCE) positively, negatively, or depending on the circumstances:

   a. Gross margin.

   b. Advertising expense ratio.

   c. Net borrowing cost.

   d. Operating liability leverage.

   e. Operating liability leverage spread.

   f. Financial leverage.

   g. Inventory turnover.

C12.4. Explain why borrowing might lever up the return on common equity.

C12.5. Explain why operating liabilities might lever up the return on net operating assets.

C12.6. A firm should always purchase inventory and supplies on credit rather than paying cash. Correct?

C12.7. A reduction in the advertising expense ratio increases return on common equity and share value. Correct?

C12.8. A firm states that one of its goals is to earn a return on common equity of 17–20 percent. What is wrong with setting a goal in terms of return on common equity?

C12.9. Why might operating losses increase after-tax borrowing cost?

C12.10. Some retail analysts use a measure called "inventory yield," calculated as gross profit-to-inventory. What does this measure tell you?

C12.11. Return on total assets (ROA) is a common measure of profitability. The historical average is about 7.0 percent. The historical yield on corporate bonds is about 6.6 percent. Why is the ROA so low? Would not investors expect more than a 0.4 percent higher return on risky operations?

C12.12. Low profit margins always imply low return on net operating assets. True or false?

C12.13. A firm has financial assets invested in short-term government bonds but has no financial obligations.

   a. Suppose RNOA exceeds ROCE. Explain how this can be due to the financial assets.

   b. Suppose now that ROCE exceeds RNOA. Explain how this can happen to this firm.

   c. Apple Inc. has no financial obligations but had $68.8 billion of financial assets in March 2011. Does it belong in case (a) or (b)?

Exercises

Drill Exercises

E12.1. Leveraging Equations (Easy)

The following information is from reformulated financial statements (in millions):

	2012	2011
Operating assets	$2,700	$2,000
Short-term debt securities	100	400
Operating liabilities	(300)	(100)
Bonds payable	(1,300)	(1,400)
Book value	1,200	$ 900
Sales	2,100	
Operating expenses	(1,677)	
Interest revenue	27	
Interest expense	(137)	
Tax expense (tax rate = 34%)	(106)	
Earnings (net)	$ 207	

a. (1) Calculate the dividends, net of capital contributions, for 2012.
   (2) Calculate ROCE for 2012; use average book value in the denominator.
   (3) Calculate RNOA for 2012; use the average net operating assets in the denominator.
   (4) Supply the numbers for the formula

$$ROCE = PM \times ATO + [\text{Financial leverage} \times (RNOA - \text{Borrowing cost})]$$

b. The firm's short-term borrowing rate is 4.5 percent after tax. Supply the numbers for the formula

$$RNOA = ROOA + (OLLEV \times OLSPREAD)$$

c. Repeat the exercise in part (a) using the following information (in millions):

	2012	2011
Operating assets	$2,700	$2,000
Short-term debt securities	1,000	800
Operating liabilities	(300)	(100)
Book value	3,400	$2,700
Sales	2,100	
Operating expenses	(1,677)	
Interest revenue	90	
Tax expense (tax rate = 34%)	(174)	
Earnings	$ 339	

E12.2.   First-Level Analysis of Financial Statements (Easy)

A firm whose shares traded at three times their book value on December 31, 2012, had the accompanying financial statements. Amounts are in millions of dollars. The firm's marginal tax rate is 33 percent. There are no dirty-surplus income items in the equity statement.

a. The firm paid no dividends and issued no shares during 2012, but it repurchased some stock. Calculate the amount of stock repurchased.

b. Calculate the following measures:
  Return on common equity (ROCE)
  Return on net operating assets (RNOA)
  Financial leverage (FLEV)
  The operating spread (SPREAD)
  Free cash flow

c. Does it make sense that this firm's shares should trade at three times book value?

Balance Sheet, December 31, 2012

Assets	2012	2011	Liabilities and Shareholders' Equity	2012	2011
Operating cash	$ 50	$ 20	Accounts payable	$ 215	$ 205
Short-term investments	150	150	Long-term debt	450	450
Accounts receivable	300	250			
Inventories	420	470	Common equity	1,095	1,025
Property and plant (net)	840	790			
	$1,760	$1,680		$ 1,760	$1,680

Income Statement, Year Ended December 31, 2012

Sales		$3,295
Interest income		9
Operating expenses	$3,048	
Interest expense	36	
Tax expense	61	(3,145)
Net income		$ 159

E12.3. Reformulation and Analysis of Financial Statements (Medium)

This exercise continues Exercise 10.6 in Chapter 10. The following financial statements were reported for a firm for fiscal year 2012 (in millions of dollars):

Balance Sheet						
	2012	**2011**			**2012**	**2011**
Operating cash	60	50	Accounts payable		1,200	1,040
Short-term investments (at market)	550	500	Accrued liabilities		390	450
Accounts receivable	940	790	Long-term debt		1,840	1,970
Inventory	910	840				
Property and plant	2,840	2,710	Common equity		1,870	1,430
	5,300	4,890			5,300	4,890

Statement of Shareholders' Equity	
Balance, end of fiscal year 2011	1,430
Share issues	822
Repurchase of 24 million shares	(720)
Cash dividend	(180)
Unrealized gain on debt investments	50
Net income	468
Balance, end of fiscal year 2012	1,870

The firm's income tax rate is 35%. The firm reported $15 million in interest income and $98 million in interest expense for 2012. Sales revenue was $3,726 million.

a. Prepare a reformulated balance sheet and comprehensive income statement (as required in Exercise 10.6).

b. Calculate free cash flow for 2012.

c. Calculate the operating profit margin, asset turnover, and return on net operating assets for 2012. (For simplicity, use beginning-of-period balance sheet amounts in denominators.)

d. Calculate individual asset turnovers and show that they aggregate to the total asset turnover.

e. Show that the financing leverage equation holds for this firm:

$$ROCE = RNOA + (FLEV \times Operating\ spread)$$

f. Calculate the after-tax net borrowing cost. If this borrowing cost were to be sustained in the future, what would the rate of return of common equity (ROCE) be if operating profitability (RNOA) fell to 6% and financial leverage decreased to 0.8?

g. The implicit cost of credit for accounts payable and accrued liabilities is 3% (after tax). Show that the following leverage equation holds in this example:

$$RNOA = ROOA + [OLLEV \times (ROOA - 3.0\%)]$$

E12.4. Relationship Between Rates of Return and Leverage (Medium)

a. A firm has a return on common equity of 13.4 percent, a net after-tax borrowing cost of 4.5 percent, and a return of 11.2 percent on net operating assets of $405 million. What is the firm's financial leverage?

b. The same firm has a short-term borrowing rate of 4.0 percent after tax and a return on operating assets of 8.5 percent. What is the firm's operating liability leverage?

c. The firm reported total assets of $715 million. Construct a balance sheet for this firm that distinguishes operating and financial assets and liabilities.

E12.5. Profit Margins, Asset Turnovers, and Return on Net Operating Assets: A What-If Question (Medium)

A firm earns a profit margin of 3.8 percent on sales of $435 million and employs net operating assets of $150 million to do so. It considers adding another product line that will earn a 4.8 percent profit margin with an asset turnover of 2.3.

What would be the effect on the firm's return on net operating assets of adding the new product line?

Applications

E12.6. Profitability Measures for Kimberly-Clark Corporation (Easy)

Below are summary numbers from reformulated balance sheets for 2007 and 2006 for Kimberly-Clark Corporation, the paper products company, along with numbers from the reformulated income statement for 2007 (in millions).

	2007	2006
Operating assets	$18,057.0	$16,796.2
Operating liabilities	6,011.8	5,927.2
Financial assets	382.7	270.8
Financial obligations	6,496.4	4,395.4
Operating income (after tax)	$ 2,740.1	
Net financial expense (after tax)	147.1	

a. Calculate the following for 2007 and 2006:
   (1) Net operating assets
   (2) Net financial obligations
   (3) Shareholders' equity
b. Calculate return on common equity (ROCE), return on net operating assets (RNOA), financial leverage (FLEV), and net borrowing cost (NBC) for 2007. Use beginning-of-period balance sheet numbers in denominators.
c. Show that the financing leverage equation works with your calculations.
d. Calculate the operating profit margin (PM) and asset turnover (ATO) for 2007 and show that RNOA = PM × ATO. Sales for 2007 were $18,266 million.

Real World Connection

Exercises E4.9, E7.16, E8.10, and E11.10 also cover Kimberly-Clark, as does Minicases M2.1 and M5.3. The Continuing Case at the end of each chapter is a comprehensive analysis of the firm.

E12.7. Analysis of Profitability: The Coca-Cola Company (Easy)

Here is a reformulated income statement for the Coca-Cola Company for 2007 (in millions):

Sales	$28,857
Cost of sales	10,406
Gross margin	18,451
Advertising expenses	2,800
General and administrative expenses	8,145
Other expenses (net)	81
Operating income from sales (before tax)	7,425
Tax	1,972
Operating income from sales (after tax)	5,453
Equity income from bottling subsidiaries (after tax)	668
Operating income	6,121
Net financial expense (after tax)	140
Earnings	$ 5,981

Summary balance sheets for 2007 and 2006 are as follows (in millions):

	2007	2006
Net operating assets	$26,858	$18,952
Net financial obligations	5,114	2,032
Common shareholders' equity	$21,744	$16,920

For the following questions, use average balance sheet amounts.

a. Calculate return on net operating assets (RNOA) and net borrowing cost (NBC) for 2007.
b. Calculate financial leverage (FLEV).
c. Show that the financing leverage equation that explains the return on common equity (ROCE) holds for this firm.
d. Calculate the profit margin and asset turnover (ATO) for 2007 and show that RNOA = PM × ATO.
e. Calculate the gross margin ratio, the operating profit margin ratio from sales, and the operating profit margin ratio.

Real World Connection
Coca-Cola is covered in Exercises E4.7, E4.8, E15.7, E16.12, E17.7, and E20.4 and also in Minicases M4.1, M5.2, and M6.1.

E12.8. A What-If Question: Grocery Retailers (Medium)
In the late 1990s, many grocery supermarkets shifted from regular storewide sales to issuing membership in discount and points programs, much like frequent flyer programs run by the airlines.

A supermarket chain with $120 million in annual sales and an asset turnover of 6.0 ponders whether to institute a customer membership program. It currently earns a profit margin of 1.6 percent on sales. Its marketing research indicates that a customer membership program would increase sales by $25 million and would require an additional investment in inventories of $2 million but no additional retail floor space. Costs to run the membership program, including the discounts offered to members, would reduce profit margins to 1.5 percent.

What would be the effect on the firm's return on net operating assets of adopting the customer membership program?

E12.9. Financial Statement Reformulation and Profitability Analysis for Starbucks Corporation (Medium)
Refer to the financial statements for Starbucks, the coffee vendor, in Exercise E10.10 in Chapter 10. Be sure to read the notes under the financial statements.

a. Prepare a reformulated income statement for fiscal year 2007 and reformulated balance sheets for 2007 and 2006 in a way that distinguishes operating and financing activities and identifies taxes applicable to various components of income.
b. For fiscal year 2007, calculate the following: return on common equity (ROCE), return on net operating assets (RNOA), and net borrowing cost (NBC). Use beginning-of-year balance sheet amounts in denominators.
c. Calculate the financing leverage ratio (FLEV) at the beginning of the year and show that the following leverage equation for 2007 is satisfied:

$$ROCE = RNOA + [FLEV \times (RNOA - NBC)]$$

    d. Calculate the operating profit margin ratio (PM) and the asset turnover (ATO). Also calculate the operating profit margin ratio from sales.

    e. Calculate the operating liability leverage ratio at the beginning of 2007.

    f. The firm's borrowing cost on its short-term commercial paper is 5.5 percent, or 3.6 percent after tax. Show how operating liability leverage levers up the return of net operating assets.

Real World Connection
See Exercises E9.8, E10.10, E13.8, and E15.8 on Starbucks Corporation.

Minicase	**M12.1**

Financial Statement Analysis: Procter & Gamble III

Financial statements for the Procter & Gamble Co. are presented in Exhibit 10.15 in Chapter 10. If you worked Minicase 10.1, you will have reformulated the statements in preparation for financial statement analysis. If not, do so now.

Proceed to carry out a comprehensive profitability analysis for fiscal years 2008–2010 along the lines of this chapter. Figure 12.1 will guide you. If you have built the reformulated statements into a spreadsheet, you might add this profitability analysis to the spreadsheet. The BYOAP guide on the book's Web site will help. (There is also an analyis spreadsheet on the Web page for this chapter.) You might also extend the analysis to subsequent years, as they become available, to track P&G's profitability and its drivers as the firm evolves. The financial statements for 2005–2008 are available on the Web page for this chapter, both in their original form and in their reformulated form, to provide further history.

Your analysis should have the following features:

A. Operating profitability should be distinguished from return on common equity. Apply the financing leverage equation to highlight the difference. How much leverage does P&G carry? Is the firm favorably leveraged?

B. Distinguish operating income from sales from other operating income. Calculate return on net operating assets (RNOA) with total operating income and then only with operating income from sales

C. Carry out an analysis of operating liability leverage. Footnotes to the firm's financial statements reveal that its short-term borrowing rate averaged 1.8 percent (before tax). The firm's combined federal, state, and local statutory tax rate is 38 percent.

D. Carry out a comprehensive analysis of profit margins and asset turnovers.

After making the various calculations, step back and ask what they all mean. Refer to the background on P&G in Minicase 10.1 before you begin your interpretation. As a benchmark, you might compare the measures you have calculated with those for General Mills in this chapter. As a packaged food products company, General Mills is not quite a comparable company but, like P&G, it is primarily a brand management operation.

Comment on the change in P&G's profitability from 2008 to 2010.

Now conduct some sensitivity analysis. Ask some "what-if" questions. What would be the effect on ROCE if operating profitability fell? What would be the effect on RNOA if profit margins changed? If asset turnovers changed? How might an increase in advertising expenditures affect profitability? If you have built the analysis into a spreadsheet, you will be able to answer these questions with the press of a button.

A final question: After excluding nonsales items from operating income, the return on net operating assets is quite low for a brand company. Why?

Real World Connection

Minicases M10.1, M11.1, M13.1, M15.1, and M16.1 also deal with the analysis and valuation of Procter & Gamble. See also Exercise E3.14.

Chapter **Thirteen**

The Analysis of Growth and Sustainable Earnings

LINKS

Link to previous chapter

Chapter 12 laid out the analysis of profitability.

This chapter

This chapter lays out the analysis of growth that readies the analyst for forecasting future growth.

Link to next chapter

Part Three of the book applies the analysis of profitability and growth to forecasting and valuation.

Link to Web page

Explore the text's Web site for more applications of Chapter 13 content (**www.mhhe.com/penman5e**).

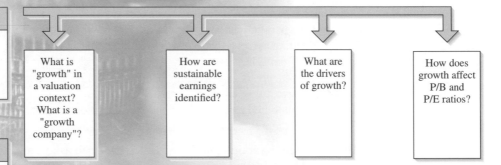

| What is "growth" in a valuation context? What is a "growth company"? | How are sustainable earnings identified? | What are the drivers of growth? | How does growth affect P/B and P/E ratios? |

Forecasting growth is a critical aspect of P/B valuation in Chapter 5 and P/E valuation in Chapter 6. Yet forecasting growth is probably the most uncertain aspect of valuation. Chapter 7 recognized the problem and turned it around: First understand the growth forecast in the market price, then challenge that forecast with your own forecast of growth. This chapter supplies the analysis to develop that forecast.

Analysts often talk of growth in terms of a firm's ability to grow earnings. The chapter begins by reminding you that earnings growth is not a valid growth concept for valuation because, as explained in Chapters 5 and 6, firms can grow earnings without adding value. Rather, residual earnings growth and abnormal earnings growth are the relevant measures. Residual earnings growth is the focus when evaluating P/B ratios, and abnormal earnings growth is the focus when evaluating P/E ratios, but they are both measures for the same purpose: detecting added value from earnings growth.

The ability to grow residual earnings is very much at the heart of the question of whether a firm has durable competitive advantage: Can the firm sustain and grow residual earnings? Accordingly, the evaluation of sustainable earnings features prominently in this chapter.

The Analyst's Checklist

After reading this chapter you should understand:

- Why growth analysis focuses on residual earnings growth and abnormal earnings growth, rather than earnings growth.
- What a growth firm is.
- What constitutes sustainable earnings.
- What is meant by transitory earnings.
- How to analyze sustainable profitability.
- How sustainable earnings and growth analysis help answer the question of whether a firm has durable competitive advantage.
- What drives growth of the common shareholders' investment.
- How P/E and P/B ratios relate to each other.

After reading this chapter you should be able to:

- Complete an analysis of a change in return on net operating assets (RNOA).
- Complete an analysis of growth in investment.
- Complete an analysis of growth in residual earnings.
- Identify core or sustainable earnings in income statements.
- Identify transitory or unusual items in income statements.

WHAT IS GROWTH?

The term *growth* is often used vaguely, or with a variety of meanings. People talk of "growth firms"—and of paying more for a growth firm—but their meaning is not always clear. Sometimes the term is used to mean growth in sales, sometimes growth in earnings, and sometimes growth in assets. Generally growth is seen as a positive attribute, an ability to generate value. But what is growth? What is a **growth firm?**

The valuation models of Chapters 5 and 6 provide the answer to this question.

Chapter 5 showed that one pays a premium over book value based on the ability of a firm to earn residual earnings (RE), where residual earnings is the difference between earnings and the required return on book value. For any year t,

$$\text{Residual earnings}_t \ (\text{RE}_t) = \text{Earnings}_t - [(\rho_E - 1) \times \text{Common shareholders' equity}_{t-1}]$$

where $\rho_E - 1$ is the required return for equity. Shareholders invest in firms, and the book value of their equity—the firm's net assets—measures this investment. Firms apply the net assets in operations to add value for shareholders. Residual earnings measure the value added to book value over that required to cover the cost of capital. So a sensible way of viewing growth that ties into value creation is in terms of growth in residual earnings: A growth firm is one that can grow residual earnings.

Chapter 6 showed that one pays more than a normal P/E based on the ability of a firm to generate abnormal earnings growth (AEG), where abnormal earnings growth is the difference between cum-dividend earnings and a charge for the prior year's earnings growing at the required rate. For any year t,

$$\text{Abnormal earnings growth}_t \ (\text{AEG}_t) = [\text{Earnings}_t + (\rho_E - 1)d_{t-1}] - \rho_E \text{Earnings}_{t-1}$$

where d_{t-1} is the net dividend paid in the prior year. Firms do not add to their P/E ratio if they can only grow earnings at the required rate of growth. They add value only if they can grow earnings at a rate greater than the required rate, that is, if they can deliver abnormal earnings growth. So another way of viewing growth that ties into the value creation is in terms of the ability of a firm to deliver abnormal earnings growth.

In both Chapters 5 and 6, we warned against paying too much for earnings growth. We emphasized that earnings growth alone is not a good measure of growth because earnings growth can be created by investment (that may not add value) and by accounting methods (that do not add value). We showed how residual earnings and abnormal earnings growth measures isolate that part of earnings growth that is to be valued from the part which is not. Charging earnings for required earnings—required earnings on book value in the case of residual earnings and required earnings on prior earnings in the case of abnormal earnings growth—protects the investor from paying too much for earnings growth created by investment and accounting methods. In short, residual earnings growth and abnormal earnings growth are the growth measures we must focus on if we have valuation in mind.

Residual earnings is the relevant growth measure when evaluating the price-to-book (P/B) ratio. Abnormal earnings growth is the relevant growth measure when evaluating the price-earnings (P/E) ratio. However, we showed in Chapter 6 (in Box 6.3) that the two measures are just different ways of looking at the same thing: *Abnormal earnings growth is equal to the change in residual earnings.* If a firm has no growth in residual earnings, its abnormal earnings growth must be zero: The firm is a "no-growth" firm. If a firm has residual earnings growth it must also have abnormal earnings growth: The firm is a "growth company." For most of this chapter, we will analyze growth in residual earnings with the understanding that the factors that grow residual earnings also produce abnormal earnings growth. Residual earnings growth involves both balance sheet and income statement features, so we gain a better appreciation of the determinants of growth from the analysis of growth in residual earnings.

Box 13.1 introduces you to some growth and no-growth cases. In each case, observe that abnormal earnings growth is equal to the change in residual earnings.

Warnings About Growth

The growth histories shown in Box 13.1 are helpful in extrapolating to the future and will be more so once we have uncovered the drivers of growth. But the examples here also provide some lessons:

1. *Growth is difficult to sustain.* General Electric delivered substantial growth up to 2000, continually increasing residual earnings. Indeed, GE was one of the great growth companies of the last half of the twentieth century. But Box 13.1 shows quite a different picture in the first decade of the twenty-first century. The lesson: Growth is difficult to sustain. Unless a firm has a clear, sustainable competitive advantage, market forces will eventually erode growth. That competitive advantage may be a technological advantage, as with Microsoft or Cisco Systems in their early days, a dominant first-mover position as with Google, or a brand, as with Nike. But even these firms are challenged, as is now evident with Microsoft and Cisco Systems. The moat around the castle is ultimately bridged.

2. *Growth is risky.* Buying a firm where the market price has a lot of growth built in is dangerous. Growth can be competed away, but also growth gets hit in bad times. Nike's residual earnings declined during the downturn of 2008 to 2010. Much of General Electric's growth came from its finance arm, but that suffered terribly during the financial crisis, producing the negative residual earnings.

A GROWTH FIRM: GENERAL ELECTRIC, 1993–2000

(in millions of dollars)	2000	1999	1998	1997	1996	1995	1994	1993
Sales	129,853	111,630	100,469	90,840	79,179	70,028	60,109	55,701
Sales growth rate	16.3%	11.1%	10.6%	14.7%	13.1%	16.5%	7.9%	5.0%
Common equity	50,492	42,557	38,880	34,438	31,125	29,609	25,387	25,824
Earnings	12,735	10,717	9,296	8,203	7,280	6,573	4,726	4,315
ROCE	29.9%	27.6%	26.2%	27.2%	22.5%	23.9%	18.5%	17.5%
Residual earnings	7,628	6,065	5,221	4,994	3,190	3,273	1,653	1,358
Abnormal earnings growth	1,563	844	227	1,804	(83)	1,620	295	—

Up to 2000, General Electric maintained a high growth rate in sales and earnings, with increasing ROCE and increasing equity investment. Accordingly, residual earnings (based on a required return of 12 percent) was on a growth path and abnormal earnings growth was (mainly) positive.

A NO-GROWTH FIRM: GENERAL ELECTRIC, 2001–2010

(in millions of dollars)	2010	2009	2008	2007	2006	2005	2004	2003	2002	2001
Sales	150,211	150,278	181,581	172,488	151,586	149,702	152,363	134,187	131,698	125,913
Sales growth rate	0.0%	−17.2%	5.3%	13.8%	1.3%	−1.7%	13.5%	1.9%	4.6%	−3.0%
Common equity	118,936	117,291	104,665	115,559	111,509	108,633	110,181	79,180	63,706	54,824
Earnings	11,644	11,025	17,410	22,208	20,742	16,720	16,593	15,589	14,118	13,684
ROCE	9.9%	9.9%	15.6%	19.6%	18.8%	15.3%	17.5%	21.8%	25.8%	27.1%
Residual earnings	(2,463)	(2,198)	4,160	8,475	7,387	3,636	4,355	6,243	7,539	7,625
Abnormal earnings growth	(265)	(6,358)	(4,315)	1,088	3,751	(719)	(1,888)	(1,296)	(86)	(3)

General Electric failed to maintain the residual earnings growth of the 1990s after 2000. Sales continued to grow, though at a slower rate, and the slower sales growth translated into lower earnings growth rates. Significantly, ROCE declined on slower growing equity investment, leading to lower residual earnings and negative abnormal earnings growth. With its finance arm hurt badly during the financial crisis, residual earnings were in fact negative at the end of the decade. The growth company of the 1990s became a no-growth firm, even one losing value. Its share price declined from $52 in 2000 to $14 in 2010.

A GROWTH FIRM: NIKE, 2001–2010

(in millions of dollars)	2010	2009	2008	2007	2006	2005	2004	2003	2002	2001
Sales	19,014	19,176	18,627	16,326	14,955	13,740	12,253	10,697	9,893	9,489
Sales growth rate	−0.8%	2.9%	14.1%	9.2%	8.8%	12.1%	14.6%	8.1%	4.3%	5.5%
Common equity	9,884	8,815	7,797	7,118	6,365	5,721	4,840	4,028	3,839	3,495
Earnings	1,753	1,667	1,911	1,695	1,452	1,433	1,019	406	599	495
ROCE	18.9%	20.1%	25.6%	25.1%	24.0%	27.1%	23.0%	10.3%	19.1%	18.8%
Residual earnings	739	756	1,089	951	786	850	479	(31)	280	241
Abnormal earnings growth	(17)	(333)	138	165	(64)	371	510	(311)	39	31

Apart from the recession period at the end of the decade, Nike grew sales and earned a high ROCE, increasing investment, increasing residual earnings, and delivering positive abnormal earnings growth. Can Nike maintain growth in the future?

For these reasons, we were careful in Chapter 7 to identify the market's growth expectations and anchor ourselves to a no-growth valuation. We were then in a position to ask: Do I want to pay for growth? To answer that question, we need to understand what drives growth.

CUTTING TO THE CORE: SUSTAINABLE EARNINGS

The analysis of growth starts with an identification of earnings on which growth is possible. Earnings from a one-time special contract cannot grow; earnings depressed by a labor strike are not a basis for continuing growth; earnings from gains on asset sales or restructurings probably will not be repeated in the future. Earnings that can repeat in the future, and grow, are called **sustainable earnings, persistent earnings, core earnings,** or **underlying earnings.** We will mostly use the term, *core earnings*. Earnings based on temporary factors are called **transitory earnings** or **unusual items.**

As core earnings are the base for growth, we begin the analysis of growth with an analysis that distinguishes core earnings purged of transitory components. Earnings are composed of operating income from the business and net financing expenses, so the exercise amounts to an identification of core operating income and core net borrowing cost. Identifying core earnings is sometimes referred to as **normalizing earnings** because it establishes "normal" ongoing earnings unaffected by one-time components.

Identifying these core (sustainable) earnings is a starting point not only for evaluating growth prospects, but also for answering this question: Does the firm have durable competitive advantage?

Core Operating Income

Operating income consists of core (sustainable) operating income and unusual (transitory) items:

$$\text{Operating income} = \text{Core operating income} + \text{Unusual items}$$

Incorporating the distinction between operating income from sales and other operating income (in Chapter 10),

$$\text{Operating income} = \text{Core operating income from sales} + \text{Core other operating income}$$
$$+ \text{Unusual items}$$
$$\text{OI} = \text{Core OI from sales} + \text{Core other OI} + \text{UI}$$

Exhibit 13.1 lays out a template that adds to the reformulation of income statements in Chapter 10 to distinguish core (sustainable) and unusual operating income. Typical unusual items are listed there but the list is not exhaustive. The standard income statement identifies some items as "extraordinary" and these are of course unusual. But unusual items often appear above the extraordinary items section of the income statement also. Read the footnotes and Management Discussion and Analysis for clues. The better you know the business, the better you will be in identifying these items. See Box 13.2.

With forecasting in mind, we are interested in components that have no bearing in the future. Thus the unusual items category should include not only items that won't be repeated in the future but also items that appear each period but can't be forecast. Currency gains and losses and gains and losses from derivatives trading for an industrial firm are good examples. We might expect these as a normal feature of operations each period but presumably we cannot predict them: There will be either gains or losses in the future but we can't predict which, so their expected value is zero. A currency gain or loss is transitory; we don't expect it to persist. And so with all income items that are a result of marking balance sheet items to market value, because changes in market values are typically not predictable. Separate these gains and losses from current core income; otherwise, core income will be affected by an item that is not representative of the future. Accordingly, we establish core operating income, which is a basis for predicting future operating income.

EXHIBIT 13.1
Reformulation of the Operating Income Section of the Income Statement to Identify Core Income and Unusual Items.
Core operating income is core income from sales plus core other operating income. Taxes are allocated to each component.

Reformulated Operating Income

Core operating income
  Core sales revenue
− Core cost of sales
= Core gross margin
− Core operating expenses
= Core operating income from sales before tax
− Tax on core operating income from sales
    + Tax as reported
    + Tax benefit from net financial expenses
    − Tax allocated to core other operating income
    − Tax allocated to unusual items
= Core operating income from sales
+ Core other operating income
    + Equity income in subsidiaries
    + Earnings on pension assets
    + Other continuing income not from sales
    − Tax on core other operating income
= Core operating income
± Unusual items
    − Special charges
    − Special liability accruals
    ± Nonrecurring items
    − Asset write-downs
    ± Changes in estimates
    − Start-up costs expensed
    ± Profits and losses from asset sales
    − Restructuring charges
    ± Profits and losses from discontinued operations
    ± Extraordinary operating items
    ± Accounting changes
    ± Unrealized gains and losses on equity investments
    + Gains from share issues in subsidiaries
    ± Currency gains and losses
    ± Derivative gains and losses (operations)
    − Tax allocated to unusual items
= Comprehensive operating income

Issues in Identifying Core Operating Income

Here are the main issues in identifying sustainable operating income:

1. *Deferred (unearned) revenue.* Firms typically recognize revenue when goods are delivered or services are rendered. In sales contracts that cover a number of years—for example, a contract for the sale of computer hardware with subsequent servicing, consulting, and software upgrades—revenue from the contract is deferred (as unearned) until the rendering of service and booked as a liability, deferred (unearned) revenue. Estimates are involved so firms can be aggressive (booking too much revenue to the current income statement) or conservative (deferring too much to the future). Both have implications for the sustainability of earnings. The latter is actually more common: Defer revenue and bleed it back to the income statement in the future so as to give a picture of growth.

As with all analysis, knowing the firm's business is essential to identifying its core income. A firm's core business is defined by its business strategy, so the analyst must know the firm's business model before classifying items in the income statement.

Start-up costs for beginning new businesses are expensed in the income statement and would appear to be one-time charges. But for a retail chain such as The Gap, the clothes retailer, or Starbucks, the coffee vendor, which are continually opening new stores as a matter of business strategy, these costs are ongoing.

Research and development expenditures on a special project might be considered a one-time expense, but R&D expenditures as part of a continuing R&D program—as is the case for a drug company like Merck & Co.—are persistent.

THE ANALYSIS OF R&D: MERCK & CO.

(in billions of dollars)	2010	2009	2008
Sales	46.0	27.4	23.8
R&D	11.0	5.8	4.8
R&D/Sales	23.9%	21.2%	20.2%

Merck's expenditures for R&D are persistent and growing, and increasing as a percentage of sales. The analyst views R&D expenses as core expenses but sees the increase in R&D as a percentage of sales as a red flag. Will Merck's R&D as a percentage of sales in 2010 revert to pre-2010 levels in the future?

Does the 2010 rate indicate that research is becoming less successful in producing new products?

THE ANALYSIS OF ADVERTISING COSTS: COCA-COLA CO.

Marketing is an essential part of brand firms' core strategy. A firm like Coca-Cola spends heavily on advertising to maintain its brand name. A one-time marketing campaign might be a transitory item but repetitive advertising, like Coke's, is persistent.

(in billions of dollars)	2010	2009	2008
Revenues	35.1	31.0	31.9
Cost of goods sold	12.7	11.1	11.4
Gross profit	22.4	19.9	20.5
Selling, administrative, and general	14.0	11.7	12.1
Operating income (before tax)	8.4	8.2	8.4
Advertising expenses	2.9	2.8	3.0
Advertising expenses/sales	8.3%	9.0%	9.4%

Coke's income statement is very aggregated, with only two operating expense items. Advertising expenses are included in selling, administrative, and general expenses but are detailed in footnotes. As with R&D, the analyst must be sensitive to a change in the advertising-to-sales ratio. Is the decline in 2010 temporary? Is it due to lower advertising expenditures or higher sales growth? Is the firm generating more sales from its advertising?

Microsoft Corporation defers a large amount of revenue. At the end of its 2010 fiscal year, its unearned revenue liability stood at $14,830 million compared with revenue in the income statement of $62,484 million. In the accrual section of the cash flow statement (between net income and cash flow from operations), Microsoft reported the following (in millions):

	2010	2009	2008
Deferral of unearned revenue	$ 29,374	$ 24,409	$ 24,532
Recognition of unearned revenue	(28,813)	(25,426)	(21,944)

The numbers in parentheses are the "bleedback" for previously deferred revenue recognized in the current period. One can see the amount by which current revenue is being reduced by deferrals and increased by bleedback. One would be concerned if more current revenue was coming from bleedback than was being deferred for, if revenue contracts are growing, it should go the other way. If sales growth is reported, but with considerable bleedback, the growth is not likely to be sustainable. Unearned revenue is sometimes referred to as a "cookie jar": Firms can dip into the cookie jar when they need more earnings in the income statement.

When firms decide to restructure, they often write off the expected costs of restructuring against income before the actual restructuring begins, and recognize an associated liability, or "restructuring reserve," that is reduced later as restructuring costs are incurred. If the firm later finds that it has overestimated the charge, it must increase income for the correction. As with deferred revenue, this is known as **bleeding back** to income.

In moving its business away from computer hardware to a focus on information technology in the early 1990s, IBM wrote off considerable income with restructuring charges— $3.7 billion, $11.6 billion, and $8.9 billion, respectively, for 1991–1993, a total of $24.2 billion. Examination of the firm's cash flow statement for subsequent years reveals the following item as an adjustment to net income to calculate cash from operations:

	1994	1995	1996	1997	1998
Effect of restructuring charges (in millions)	(2,772)	(2,119)	(1,491)	(445)	(355)

These amounts are negative; that is, they are deductions from net income to get cash from operations. Accordingly, they have an increasing effect on income: Income would have been lower by these amounts had the charges been recorded as incurred. But a further issue needs to be investigated: If IBM had overestimated the restructuring charges in 1991–1993, the differences between subsequent income and cash from operations could, in part, be due to the reversal of the restructuring charges. Was IBM bleeding back the earlier restructuring charges to increase operating income? See Minicase M13.3.

When new management arrives at a firm, they are tempted to take restructuring charges to show they are innovating. The market often greets the restructuring as good news. If the new managers overestimate the restructuring charge, they get an added benefit: They can bleed it back to future income and report earnings improvement on their watch. This is a scheme to grow earnings. The diligent analyst is attuned to these schemes.

FASB Statement 146, issued in 2002, restricts a firm's ability to manipulate income with restructuring charges. Firms must recognize the restructuring liability when an obligation to pay restructuring costs is incurred, not when the firm merely develops a plan to restructure.

Microsoft is helpful in reporting these two lines, so is transparent about the matter. Many firms do not report this detail. Beware of firms that have multiyear revenue contracts and inspect the revenue recognition footnote carefully.

2. *Restructuring charges, asset impairments, and special charges.* These are mostly unusual, but note that firms can have repetitive restructuring charges. Eastman Kodak, the photographic company, reported restructuring charges every year from 1992 to 2003 as it adapted its technology to the arrival of the digital age, and in 2004 Kodak indicated that $1.5 billion more charges would be made from 2004 to 2006.

   Restructuring charges and asset impairments must be handled with care—their effects may not be just "one-time." If a firm writes down inventory, future cost of goods sold will be lower if the inventory is subsequently sold. If a firm writes down property, plant, and equipment, future depreciation will be lower. Lower expenses mean higher future core income; the perceptive analyst recognizes this and adjusts her forecasts accordingly. Worse, if a firm overestimates a restructuring charge, it must "bleed it back" to future income, creating earnings. See Box 13.3.

   Merger charges taken to cover the costs of mergers and acquisition also require scrutiny. Is the firm lumping operating expenses into these charges? Is the firm overestimating the charge in order to increase future income to make the merger appear more profitable?

3. *Research and development.* A drop in R&D expenditure increases current earnings but may damage future earnings. Investigate whether changes in R&D are temporary. See Box 13.2.

4. *Advertising.* A drop in advertising expenditures increases current earnings but may damage future earnings. Investigate whether changes in advertising are temporary. See Box 13.2.

5. *Pension expense.* Firms report the cost of providing defined benefit pension plans as part of the cost of operating expenses. Pension expense, however, is a composite number, and the analyst must be aware of its makeup. The following summarizes the pension expense footnote for IBM from 2001 to 2004.

INTERNATIONAL BUSINESS MACHINES (IBM)
Components of Pension Expense, 2001–2004
(in millions of dollars)

	2004	2003	2002	2001
Service cost	1,263	1,113	1,155	1,076
Interest cost	4,071	3,995	3,861	3,774
Expected return on plan assets	(5,987)	(5,931)	(6,253)	(6,264)
Amortization of transition asset	(82)	(159)	(156)	(153)
Amortization of prior service cost	66	78	89	80
Actuarial losses (gains)	764	101	105	(24)
Net pension expense	95	(803)	(1,199)	(1,511)

Pension expense has six components, and you see all six components in IBM's summary.

- *Service cost:* The present value of the actuarial cost of providing future pensions for services of employees in the current year. This cost is, in effect, wages for employees to be paid in pension benefits when employees retire.
- *Interest cost:* The interest cost on the obligation to pay benefits, the effect of the time value of money as the date to pay pensions comes closer and the net present value of the obligation increases. This cost recognizes that, as wages will be paid in the future, the firm must pay wages with interest.
- *Expected return on plan assets:* The expected earnings on the assets of the pension fund, which reduce the cost of the plan to the employer. The expected earnings on plan assets is the market value of the assets multiplied by an expected rate of return. To make the pension expense less volatile in the financial statements, the expected return on plan assets is deducted in the calculation of pension expense, not actual gains and losses. If the difference between accumulated actual and expected gains and losses exceeds a limit, the difference is amortized into pension expense (none appears in IBM's pension expense). Differences between expected returns and actual returns are reported in other comprehensive income.
- *Amortization of prior service cost:* The amortization of the cost of pension entitlements for service periods prior to the adoption or amendment of a plan. The amortization is over the estimated remaining service years for employees at the time of the change in the plan.
- *Amortization of transition asset or liability:* The amortization of the initial pension asset or liability established when pension accounting was first adopted.
- *Actuarial gains and losses:* Changes in the pension liability due to changes in actuaries' estimates of employees' longevity and turnover.

Service cost is a part of the core cost of paying employees. Interest cost is also a core cost; it is the cost, effectively paid to employees, to compensate them for the time value of money from receiving wages later, as a pension, rather than in the current year.

Accounting Clinic   VII

ACCOUNTING FOR PENSIONS

Accounting Clinic VII on the book's Web site gives a more thorough coverage of the accounting for pensions. The clinic explains how pension plans work and how defined benefit plans differ from defined contribution plans. The clinic also explains how the pension liability in the balance sheet is calculated as well as providing more detail on the pension expense in the income statement. The Web page for this chapter goes through the pension expense for Boeing company.

Like service cost, interest cost is repetitive. Amortizations of prior service costs and transition assets and liabilities smooth out these items so, while they may eventually disappear, the smoothing is done over such a long period that they should be treated as repetitive rather than unusual. Actuarial gains and losses are also smoothed, but are subject to shocks.

Expected returns on plan assets, however, must be handled with care. You will notice that, from 2001 to 2003, IBM's net pension expenses were negative (that is, gains), primarily because of this item. These earnings on pension plan assets reduce IBM's obligation to support employees in retirement, so they are legitimately part of income. However, they are not earnings from the core business (of selling computers and technology in the case of IBM). The analyst must be careful to disentangle these earnings and attribute them to the profitability of the pension fund rather than the profitability of the business. For this reason they are identified outside of core income from sales in the template in Exhibit 13.1. Other dangers lurk in the pension expense number. See Box 13.4.

Accounting Clinic VII takes you through the accounting for pensions.

6. *Changes in estimates.* Some expenses like bad debts, warranty expenses, depreciation, and accrued expenses are estimates. When estimates for previous years turn out to be incorrect, the correction is made in the current year. Bad debts are usually estimated as a percentage of accounts receivable that is likely to go bad. If the estimate for last year (say) was found to be too high—fewer creditors went bad than expected—the correction is made to the current year's bad debt expense. Thus the reported expense does not reflect the credit costs of the current period's sales. Firms also change estimates of residual values of lease receivables. The effect of these changes in estimates should be classified as unusual, leaving the core expense to reflect current operations. Unfortunately, published reports often do not give the necessary detail, although Schedule II in the 10-K helps. A particularly pernicious change in estimate can follow restructuring charges. See Box 13.3.

7. *Realized gains and losses.* Many realized gains and losses (on asset sales, for example) are not detailed in the income statement. But they can be found in the cash flow statement in the reconciliation of cash flow from operations and net income. Beware of "cherry picking." See Box 13.5.

8. *Unrealized gains and losses on equity investments.* These arise from equity holdings of less than 20 percent. They are due to marking the holdings to market value in the balance sheet. The market value of the holdings indicates their value, but changes in market value do not. Market values follow a "random walk," so changes in market value do not predict future changes in market value. Treat these unrealized gains and losses as transitory.

9. *Unrealized gains and losses from applying fair value accounting.* Firms may exercise a "fair value option" under FASB Statement 159 or IAS 9 to revalue certain assets and

The expected return on plan assets component of pension expense must be handled with care. Below are three warnings.

1. RETURNS ON PENSION FUND ASSETS CAN BE A SIGNIFICANT PORTION OF EARNINGS

Pension expense is reduced by expected earnings on assets of the pension fund, and expected earnings on a fund's assets are of course based on the amount of the fund's assets. Pension plans invest in equities and, during the 1990s bull market, the prices of equities increased significantly, increasing the assets in these plans and the expected earnings on the plans. Such was the increase that for some firms, the expected earnings on fund assets, reported as a reduction in pension expense, was a significant part of the firm's earnings.

General Electric

General Electric sponsors a number of pension plans for its employees. Its 2001 pension footnote reported a service cost of $884 million, but $4,327 million in expected returns on plan assets was also reported, along with $2,065 million in interest on the pension liability. The net pension expense (with all components) was actually a gain of $2,095 million. This pension gain was netted against other expenses in the income statement. The $4,327 million in expected returns on plan assets was 22.0 percent of earnings before tax.

IBM Corporation

IBM reported a pension service cost of $931 million for 1998. But it also reported $4,862 million in expected returns on plan assets, along with $3,474 million in interest on the pension liability. The expected returns on plan assets were 53.1 percent of operating income before tax. IBM's expected return on plan assets for 1999–2001 were 45.9 percent, 51.5 percent, and 57.2 percent of pretax income, respectively.

Earnings on pension plan assets are earnings from the operation of running a pension fund, not earnings from products and services. In all cases, list the expected return on plan assets as a separate component of core income so profit margins can be identified without this component, as in Exhibit 13.1.

General Motors Corporation

For many years prior to its 2009 bankruptcy, General Motors reported that it was seemingly profitable. But most of the earnings came from expected returns on pension plan assets. A penetration of the income statement would have revealed that the firm was not making much from producing automobiles. The pension fund was underfunded by over $70 billion by 2002. How could a firm making nothing from manufacturing hope to cover the shortfall? Yet the income statement, driven by expected returns on pension assets, made the company look as if the profits were there to share.

2. RETURNS ON PENSION ASSETS CAN PERPETUATE A CHAIN LETTER

Consider the following scenario. In an overheated stock market, the assets of pension funds are inflated above their intrinsic values. Accordingly, the earnings of the firms sponsoring the pension funds for their employees are inflated through the reduction of pension expense for earnings of the pension funds. Analysts then justify a higher stock price for these firms based on the inflated earnings. So inflated stock prices feed on themselves. A chain letter is created.

As an extreme, consider the case of a company during the stock market bubble whose pension fund is invested solely in the shares of the company (so employees could share in the success of the company). The earnings of the company would be exaggerated by the returns on the pension fund from the run-up of the firm's share price. Analysts look to earnings to assess the worth of firms' shares relative to their market price, but if the earnings reflect the market price of the shares, the analysis—if not done carefully—is circular. Good analysis penetrates the sources of firms' earnings and understands that stock prices are based on firms' ability to generate earnings from their core business, not the appreciation in stock prices.

Pension funds in the United states are permitted to hold only 10 percent of their assets in the sponsoring firm's shares, but they may well hold shares whose returns are highly correlated with the firm's own shares, inducing a similar effect.

3. BEWARE OF EXPECTED RATES OF RETURN ON PLAN ASSETS

Expected earnings of plan assets are calculated as an expected rate of return multiplied by the market value of the plan assets. The expected rate of return is an estimate that can be biased. Indeed, in the late 1990s, firms were using an expected rate of return of 10 percent and higher, considerably more than the 7 percent rate used in the early 1980s. Exxon used a 7 percent rate in 1975 but a 9.5 percent rate in 2000. General Motors went from 6 percent to 10 percent, GE from 6 percent to 9.5 percent, and IBM from 4.8 percent to 10 percent. Over the same time, the yield on long-term government bonds fell from 8 percent to 5.5 percent. The ambitious expected return in 2000—perhaps influenced by the high bubble returns during the 1990s—led to higher pension gains in earnings when applied to high pension asset values.

The subsequent bursting of the bubble led to much lower returns—indeed, large negative returns—and firms revised their expected rates of return downward. The consequence was much lower pension gains in earnings in 2002, due in part from the drop in asset prices and in part from the lower expected rates of return. Indeed, many firms with defined benefit plans found that their pension obligations were underfunded and, in retrospect, their past earnings that incorporated the pension gains were overstated. An analyst with an understanding of pension accounting would have anticipated this scenario during the bubble.

INTEL

In the rising stock market of the 1990s, firms' holdings of equity securities appreciated. The sale of the shares sometimes provided a significant portion of profits.

In its third quarter report for 1999, Intel reported net income of $1,458 million, with no indication of unusual items. Its cash flow statement, however, reported $556 million in gains on sales of investments, along with a $161 million loss on retirements of plant, as add backs to net income to calculate cash from operations.

DELTA AIR LINES

Delta reported operating income (before tax) of $350 million for its September quarter in 1999. However, notes to the report indicated that these earnings included pretax gains of $252 million from selling its interest in Singapore Airlines and Priceline.com.

IBM

IBM reported before-tax operating income of $4,085 million for its quarter ending June 1999. However, footnotes revealed that this income included a $3,430 million gain from the sale of IBM's Global Network to AT&T. This gain reduced selling, general, and administrative expenses in the income statement!

You see that the disclosure of these gains is often not transparent. The analyst must be careful to look for these gains—in the cash flow statement or in the footnotes—and separate them from core income from core operations. And watch firms with big equity portfolios: Microsoft had $9 billion in equity investments in 2002 and can realize gains into income should operating profitability from other operations decline.

As with gains from pension plan assets, gains from share appreciation can lead to mispricing and even create share price bubbles. Firms may sell shares when they feel that the shares are overvalued in the market. If an analyst mistakenly attributes profits that include these gains to persistent operating profits, he will overprice the firm. But he will overprice it more if the gains themselves are generated by mispricing. So the mispricing feeds on itself.

BEWARE OF CHERRY PICKING

Firms holding available-for-sale equity investments recognize unrealized gains and losses as part of other comprehensive income in the equity statement as market prices of the equity shares change. They recognize realized gains and losses in the income statement when shares are sold. Refer again to Accounting Clinic III. It is tempting—especially in a year when income is down—to sell shares whose prices have appreciated in order to increase income reported in the income statement, while keeping shares whose prices have declined unsold, with the unrealized losses reported in the equity statement. This practice is referred to as *cherry picking.* Beware of firms with large investment portfolios, like Intel and Microsoft. Beware of the practice with insurance companies who hold large investment portfolios.

The lesson is clear: Investment portfolios must be evaluated on a comprehensive income basis so that gains, possibly cherry-picked, are netted against losses for a comprehensive assessment of portfolio performance. Appropriate reformulation of the income statement takes care of the problem.

---

liabilities to fair value. The associated unrealized gains and losses are transitory, except when they offset a component of core income.

10. *Income taxes.* Unusual aspects of income tax expense such as one-time or expiring credits and loss carryforwards can be found in the tax footnote.

11. *Other income.* Review the details of "other income" in footnotes, if provided. Often interest income is included with operating income in "other income."

Most operating items reported in other comprehensive income (in the equity statement) are unusual items rather than core income. Although including these items in a reformulated statement only to take them out again to identify core income seems pointless, there are four reasons for doing so. First, the discipline of identifying all the sources of profitability is important; otherwise, something might be left out. For example, hidden dirty-surplus expense must be identified for a complete evaluation of management's actions; cherry picking (in Box 13.5) is identified only if income is on a comprehensive basis. Second, the accounting relationships that govern the financial statement analysis work only if earnings are on a comprehensive basis. For example, the leveraging equations of Chapter 12 require earnings to be comprehensive; the short-cut calculations of free cash flow in Chapter 11 (Free cash flow = OI − ΔNOA) work only if earnings are on a comprehensive basis. Third, the other comprehensive income items reveal the risk to which the business is subject. Translation gains and losses, for example, show how a firm can be hit by exchange rate changes. Fourth, we will see when we come to forecasting in Part Three of the book that the integrity of the forecasting process relies on financial statements prepared (and reformulated) on a comprehensive income basis. Indeed, an analysis and valuation spreadsheet, like that in BYOAP, will not work otherwise.

For many firms, the separation of operating income into operating income from sales and other operating income (in the Chapter 10 reformulation of the income statement) makes the division between core income and unusual, transitory items. So operating income from sales is core income and other operating income identifies unusual items. That is the case with Nike (in Exhibit 10.9) and Dell (in Exhibit 10.10).

However, this is not the case for General Mills in Exhibit 10.11. General Mills reports a share of earnings from joint ventures. As these earnings are not from top-line sales, they are other operating income. However, they are core earnings, for the ventures continue into the future. General Mills also has a defined benefit pension plan, and expected returns from plan assets are included in operating income from sales but, of course, are not part of the income from sales. Exhibit 13.2 presents a reformulated statement for General Mills that includes income from joint ventures in core income (but not core income from sales) and separates earnings from pension assets from income from sales. Pension returns are continuing (and thus core) but the separation allows the assessment of core profit margins from sales without the contamination of pension returns.[1] One-time pension charges are, on the other hand, unusual items.

To assess the profitability of the component parts of the income statement effectively, income taxes must be allocated to the component income that attracts the taxes, as in Exhibits 13.1 and 13.2. Taxes must thus be allocated not only over operating and financing components, but within the operating components also. See Box 13.6.

Core Operating Profitability

With the identification of core operating income, the analyst can distinguish core return on net operating assets (RNOA) from the transitory effects on RNOA:

Return on net operating assets = Core RNOA + Unusual items to net operating assets

$$RNOA = \frac{Core\ OI}{NOA} + \frac{UI}{NOA}$$

Separating income from sales from other operating income within the core RNOA,

$$RNOA = \frac{Core\ OI\ from\ sales}{NOA} + \frac{Core\ other\ OI}{NOA} + \frac{UI}{NOA}$$

To the extent that RNOA is driven by unusual, transitory items, it is said to be of "low quality." It is not sustainable.

---

[1] Pension gains are subtracted from core income from sales on one line in the reformulated statement. GAAP credits these gains to various line items, depending on where the pension cost is recorded. Unfortunately, firms do not report the allocation of the credit to line items.

EXHIBIT 13.2   **Identification of Core Operating Income and Unusual Items for General Mills, Inc., for Fiscal Years 2010 and 2009**

Core operating income consists of continuing, sustainable income while unusual items are one-time components. Core income from sales is distinguished from core income not from sales. All income components are after tax (in millions of dollars).

		Year Ending May 25		
		2010		**2009**
Core operating revenues		14,797		14,691
Cost of sales		8,923		9,458
Gross margin		5,874		5,233
Administrative and general expenses		2,109		2,012
Advertising		909		732
Research and development		219		207
		2,637		2,282
Expected return on pension assets		(429)		(416)
Core operating income from sales (before tax)		2,208		1,866
Taxes				
Taxes as reported	771		720	
Tax on pension returns	(161)		(156)	
Tax benefit from divestiture gains	12		(16)	
Tax benefit from net interest expense	151	773	144	692
Core operating income from sales (after tax)		1,435		1,174
Core other operating income				
Expected return on pension assets	429		416	
Tax (at 37.5%)	161	268	156	260
Earnings from joint ventures (after tax)		102		92
Core operating income		1,805		1,526
Unusual items				
Divestiture gains (restructuring charges)	(31)		43	
Tax benefit (at 37.5%)	12	(19)	16	27
Foreign currency translation gain (loss)		(163)		(288)
Gain (loss) on hedge derivatives and securities		14		(3)
Pension charges		(460)		(761)
Operating income (after tax)		1,177		501
Net financing expense				
Interest expense		409		405
Interest income		7		22
Net interest expense		402		383
Tax benefit (at 37.5%)		(151)		(144)
Net financing expense after tax		251		239
Noncontrolling interest		5		9
Comprehensive income		921		253

With average net operating assets of $11,632 million, General Mills earned an RNOA of 10.1 percent in 2010. Using income components in Exhibit 13.2, we see that the RNOA was generated by a return of core operating income from sales of 12.3 percent (after tax), plus a return of 3.2 percent from other core income, less a negative return from one-time items of 5.4 percent. Core RNOA (from both sales and other core income) was 15.5 percent. Clearly, the return from the core business is higher than the overall RNOA of 10.1 percent would suggest.

If an income statement is reformulated to identify different sources of income, each type of income must be allocated the income taxes it attracts so the after-tax contribution of each source of income is identified. GAAP income statements are reformulated as follows. The firm has a 35 percent statutory tax rate.

GAAP Income Statement		Reformulated Statement		
Revenue	$ 4,000	Core revenue		$ 4,000
Operating expenses	(3,400)	Core operating expenses		(3,400)
Restructuring charge	(300)	Core operating income before tax		600
Interest expense	(100)	Taxes:		
Income before tax	200	Tax reported	$ 45	
Income tax	45	Tax benefit of interest	35	
Net earnings	$ 155	Tax on benefit unusual items	105	185
		Core operating income after tax		415
		Unusual Items:		
		Restructuring charge	$300	
		Tax deduction	(105)	195
		Operating income		220
		Interest expense	$100	
		Tax on interest	(35)	65
		Net earnings		$ 155

Net earnings are the same before and after the tax allocation, of course. The restructuring charge, like interest expense, draws a tax deduction, so unusual items after tax are $195. The tax savings from the restructuring charge, like that from interest, is an adjustment to reported tax to calculate tax on operating income. Accordingly, the total tax on operating income is $185, that is, the tax that would have been paid had the firm not had a deduction for the restructuring charge and interest. In the same vein, taxes are allocated to pension earnings in General Mills's income statement in Exhibit 13.2.

Having identified core RNOA, break it down into its profit margin and turnover components:

$$\text{RNOA} = (\text{Core sales PM} \times \text{ATO}) + \frac{\text{Core other OI}}{\text{NOA}} + \frac{\text{UI}}{\text{NOA}}$$

where

$$\text{Core sales PM} = \frac{\text{Core OI from sales}}{\text{Sales}}$$

This core sales PM uncovers a profit margin that is unaffected by other income or unusual items, so it really "cuts to the core" of the firm's ability to generate profits from sales. General Mills had a core sales PM of 9.7 percent, which, with an asset turnover of 1.27, explains its core RNOA from sales of 12.3 percent.

Core Borrowing Cost

The net financing expense component of the income statement can also be broken into core expense and one-time effects. The breakdown yields core net borrowing cost, the number to apply in forecasting future borrowing costs:

Net borrowing cost = Core net borrowing cost + Unusual borrowing costs

$$\text{NBC} = \frac{\text{Core net financial expenses}}{\text{NFO}} + \frac{\text{Unusual financial expenses}}{\text{NFO}}$$

As before, unusual financial items are those that are not likely to be repeated in the future or are unpredictable. They include realized and unrealized gains and losses on financial items and unusual interest income or expenses. The before-tax core rates should agree roughly with the borrowing rates reported in the debt footnote. Core borrowing cost will reflect changes in these rates and, as the rates are after tax, this includes changes due to changes in tax rates. The analysis for a net financial asset position proceeds along the same lines.

ANALYSIS OF GROWTH

With sustainable profitability as a base, we are in a position to analyze growth. Residual earnings, the focus for growth, are driven by return on common equity (ROCE) and the amount of common shareholders' equity:

$$\text{Residual earnings}_t = (\text{ROCE}_t - \text{Cost of equity capital}) \times \text{CSE}_{t-1}$$

So, growth in residual earnings is driven by increases in ROCE and growth in common shareholders' equity. We consider each in turn.

Growth Through Profitability

The financing leverage equation in Chapter 12 tells us that ROCE is driven by operating profitability (RNOA), the amount of financial leverage (FLEV), and the spread of operating profitability over the net borrowing cost (NBC):

$$\text{ROCE} = \text{RNOA} + [\text{FLEV} \times (\text{RNOA} - \text{NBC})]$$

Figure 13.1 adds the analysis of sustainable profitability to this breakdown, along with the drivers of profitability. The analyst asks how these drivers might change in the future. Can the firm increase core profitability or is it likely to be competed away? What is the likely change in core profit margins and asset turnovers? These are the questions we ask to query whether a firm has durable competitive advantage.

FIGURE 13.1 **Sustainable Drivers of Return on Common Equity (ROCE)**
Return on common equity is driven by core profitability, financial leverage, and net borrowing-costs. Operating profitability, RNOA, is driven by core (sustainable) operating profitability and one-time, unusual items. Net borrowing costs (NBC) are determined by core borrowing costs and one-time, unusual items.

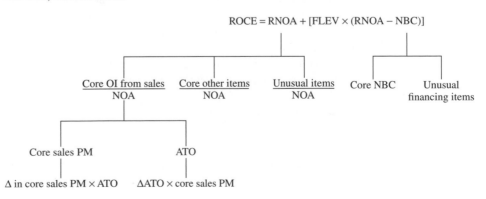

Change in RNOA	= Change in core sales profit margin at previous asset turnover level	+ Change due to change in asset turnover
	+ Change due to change in other core income	+ Change due to change in unusual items

$$\Delta RNOA_{2010} = (\Delta core\ sales\ PM_{2010} \times ATO_{2009})$$
$$+ (\Delta ATO_{2010} \times Core\ sales\ PM_{2010})$$
$$+ \Delta \left(\frac{Core\ other\ OI}{NOA} \right) + \Delta \left(\frac{UI}{NOA} \right)$$

Table 12.3 in Chapter 12 reports RNOA, profit margins, and asset turnovers for 2010 and 2009 for Nike and General Mills. The following analyzes the year-to-year changes. Nike's core operating income is equal to its operating income from sales because it has no other core income. General Mills's core operating income is identified in Exhibit 13.2.

NIKE

Nike's increase in RNOA of 2.2 percent, from 28.4 percent in 2009 to 30.6 percent in 2010, is explained as follows:

$$\Delta RNOA_{2010} = 2.2\%$$
$$= (0.35\% \times 3.16) + (0.05 \times 10.0\%)$$
$$+ 0 + (-1.62\% + 2.26\%)$$

(allow for rounding error). You see that core profit margins increased, by 0.35 percent, producing a 1.1 percent boost to RNOA. Turnover also increased by 0.05, producing a 0.5 percent increase. Accordingly, core profitability increased by 1.6%. Unusual items explained the remaining increase of 0.6 percent.

GENERAL MILLS

General Mills's increase in RNOA from 4.1 percent to 10.1 percent is explained as follows:

$$\Delta RNOA_{2010} = 6.0\%$$
$$= (1.71\% \times 1.19) + (0.07 \times 9.70)$$
$$+ (3.18\% - 2.85\%) + (-5.40\% + 8.30\%)$$

The increase in RNOA of 6.0 percent is due to a 2.9 percent increase from one-time items and a 0.33 percent increase from core income outside of sales. Core income from sales contributed 2.73 percent to the increase in RNOA, and that increase came from an increase in core profit margins of 2.04 percent and 0.68 percent from enhancement in the asset turnover.

To gain insights into these forecasts, the analyst discovers how profitability changed in the current period. By far the most important issue is the explanation for the change in current core profitability. Following the design in Figure 13.1, Box 13.7 carries out such an analysis for Nike, Inc., and General Mills, Inc., the two firms analyzed in Chapter 12. Note the formula at the beginning of the box (that is also indicated in Figure 13.1). The contribution of a change in the core sales profit margin is assessed holding the asset turnover for the previous year constant, while the contribution of the change in asset turnover is assessed holding the current profit margin constant. From Box 13.7 you see that Nike's operating profitability is driven by an increase in core income from sales, with both an increase in core profit margin and an increase in asset turnover contributing. General Mills's increase in profitability also came from core profitability, with increase in core profit margins adding 2 percent and enhancement in asset turnovers adding 0.7 percent. But the big increase in overall RNOA came from unusual items.

Operating Leverage

Changes in core sales PM are determined by how costs change as sales change. Some costs are **fixed costs:** They don't change as sales change. Other costs are **variable costs:** They change as sales change. Depreciation, amortization, and many administrative expenses are fixed costs, while most labor and material costs in cost of sales are variable costs. The difference between sales and variable costs is called the *contribution margin* because it is this amount that contributes to covering fixed costs and providing profits. Thus

$$\text{Sales PM} = \frac{\text{Sales} - \text{Variable costs} - \text{Fixed costs}}{\text{Sales}}$$

$$= \frac{\text{Contribution margin}}{\text{Sales}} - \frac{\text{Fixed costs}}{\text{Sales}}$$

The first component here is called the *contribution margin ratio.* This is sometimes calculated

$$\text{Contribution margin ratio} = 1 - \frac{\text{Variable costs}}{\text{Sales}} = \frac{\text{Contribution margin}}{\text{Sales}}$$

This ratio measures the change in income from a change in one dollar of sales. For a firm with variable costs that are 75 percent of sales, the contribution margin ratio is 25 percent: The firm adds 25 cents to income for each dollar increase in sales (and the fixed costs don't explain changes in profit margins).

The sensitivity of income to changes in sales is called the *operating leverage* (not to be confused with operating liability leverage). Operating leverage is sometimes measured by the ratio of fixed to variable expenses. But it is also measured by

$$\text{OLEV} = \frac{\text{Contribution margin}}{\text{Operating income}} = \frac{\text{Contribution margin ratio}}{\text{Profit margin}}$$

(Again, don't confuse OLEV with OLLEV!) If you are dealing with core income, then this calculation should include only core items. If there are fixed costs, OLEV will be greater than 1. The measure is not an absolute for the firm but changes as sales change. However, at any particular level of sales, it is useful to indicate the effect of a change in sales on operating income. Applying it to core operations,

$$\% \text{ Change in core OI} = \text{OLEV} \times \% \text{ Change in core sales}$$

An analyst inside the firm will have a relatively easy task of distinguishing fixed and variable costs. But the reader of annual financial reports will find it difficult. The depreciation and amortization component of fixed costs must be reported in the 10-K report, and it can be found in the cash flow statement. But other fixed costs—fixed salaries, rent expense, administrative expenses—are aggregated with variable costs in different line items on the income statement.

Analysis of Changes in Financing

Changes in RNOA partially explain changes in ROCE. The explanation is completed by an examination of financing. The leveraging effect on ROCE is given by the leveraging equation at the top of Figure 13.1. Leverage effects on ROCE come from two sources, change in the amount of leverage (FLEV) and the net borrowing cost.

Box 13.8 shows how changes in leverage can affect ROCE. The analysis there comes with a warning: Issuing debt at market value to add financing leverage does not add value but it can have a significant effect on ROCE. Indeed, changes in ROCE due to leverage can mask the contribution of operating profitability to the value creation, and it is the business operations that add value. We pick up on this point in the next chapter.

Analysis of Growth in Shareholders' Equity

Residual earnings are driven not only by the rate of return on common equity but also by the amount of common shareholders' equity that earns at that rate.

In 1996, Reebok had a considerable change in its financing. It borrowed approximately $600 million and applied the proceeds to repurchase its shares. The consecutive reformulated balance sheets below show the large increase in net financial obligations and a corresponding decrease in shareholders' equity. This produced a large increase in financial leverage, from 0.187 to 0.515 (based on average balance sheet amounts).

REEBOK INTERNATIONAL LIMITED
Summary Reformulated Balance Sheets
(in millions of dollars)

	1996	1995
Net operating assets	1,135	1,220
Net financial obligations	720	287
Common shareholders' equity	415	933
ROCE	18.9%	19.2%
RNOA	14.1%	16.9%
Net borrowing cost (NBC)	4.9%	4.8%
Financial leverage (FLEV)	0.515	0.187

Reebok's ROCE dropped by only 0.3 percent in 1996, but this masks a considerably higher drop of 2.8 percent in operating profitability. The ROCE was maintained with borrowing. Had Reebok maintained its 1995 leverage of 0.187, the ROCE on a 14.1 percent RNOA would have been 15.8 percent:

$$ROCE = RNOA + (FLEV \times SPREAD)$$
$$ROCE_{1996} = 14.1 + [0.187 \times (14.1 - 4.9)]$$
$$= 15.8\%$$

Instead, Reebok reported an ROCE of 18.9 percent.

For most firms, issuing debt does not create value: They buy and sell debt at its fair value. The value generation is in the operations. Yet financial leverage can lever the ROCE above RNOA. Accordingly, firms can create ROCE by issuing debt. Beware of increases in ROCE. Analyze the change in profitability to see if it is driven by core operations or by changes in leverage.

Firms often state that their objective is to increase return on common equity. Maximizing ROCE is not entirely satisfactory. Maximizing RNOA is, and to the extent that increases in ROCE come from operations, increasing ROCE is a desirable goal, provided the cost of capital is covered. Tying management bonuses to ROCE would be a mistake: Management could increase managerial compensation by issuing debt.

Growing residual earnings generates value, as noted. But residual earnings are driven by ROCE, and ROCE can be generated by borrowing (which does not create value). There seems to be a contradiction. The riddle is solved in the next chapter.

BEWARE OF LIQUIDATIONS OF FINANCIAL ASSETS

Just as borrowing increases ROCE, so do sales of financial assets. Financial assets are negative debt and their liquidation increases leverage. But sales of T-bills at (fair) market value do not add value. Watch for firms that sell off their financial assets when RNOA is declining; they may be masking a decline in operating profitability. In the GAAP cash flow statement, they also look as if they are increasing free cash flow, because GAAP classifies sales of financial assets as reducing investment in operations. See the Lucent Technologies example in Chapter 11.

The overall effect of a sale of financial assets depends, of course, on what the proceeds are used for. If they are invested in operating assets, they may well enhance profitability—but through operations, not financing activities. If they are used to retire debt, there is no effect on leverage. If they are used to pay dividends, there is an increase in leverage.

The shareholders' investment requirement is driven by the need to invest in net operating assets. But to the extent that debt is used to finance net operating assets, the shareholders' investment is reduced:

$$\Delta CSE = \Delta NOA - \Delta NFO$$

As net operating assets are put in place to generate sales, sales are a driver of net operating assets and, thus, the shareholders' investment. The asset turnover (ATO) indicates the amount of net operating assets required to support sales. As ATO = Sales/NOA,

$$NOA = Sales \times \frac{1}{ATO}$$

So

$$\Delta CSE = \Delta\left(\text{Sales} \times \frac{1}{\text{ATO}}\right) - \Delta NFO$$

Sales require investment in net operating assets and the inverse of the asset turnover, 1/ATO, is the amount of net operating assets in place to generate $1 of sales. Nike's 2010 ATO was 3.21, so 1/3.21, or 31.2 cents of net operating assets, were in place to generate $1 of sales. The change in CSE can be explained by three components:

1. Growth in sales.
2. Change in net operating assets that support each dollar of sales.
3. Change in the amount of net debt that is used to finance the change in net operating assets rather than equity.

Sales growth is the primary driver. But sales growth requires more investment in net operating assets, which is financed by either net debt or equity.

Nike's common equity grew by $1,069.9 million in 2010, from $8,814.5 million in 2009 to $9,884.4 million. That largely came from an increase in net financial assets rather than a result of operations. Net operating assets actually declined by $832.3 million on a slight decline in sales of $162.1 million and a decrease in the net operating assets required to support sales, 31.2 cents per dollar of sales in 2010 versus 31.7 cents in 2009. (Apply the above formula to tie these drivers together.)

GROWTH, SUSTAINABLE EARNINGS, AND THE EVALUATION OF P/B RATIOS AND P/E RATIOS

The analysis of current and past growth is a prelude to forecasting future growth in order to evaluate P/E and P/B ratios; the next part of the book proceeds with forecasting. We have two ratios on which we can base our pricing: the P/B ratio and the P/E ratio. Before proceeding to forecasting and valuation you should understand how these ratios are related to each other, and how each is related to growth. In this section, we look at the relationship between P/B ratios and trailing P/E ratios and draw some lessons from the comparison.

Remember that zero abnormal earnings growth (AEG) implies no growth in residual earnings (RE), and positive AEG means there is positive growth in residual earnings. To reinforce this idea, Box 13.9 gives the benchmark case of a firm, Whirlpool Corporation, with a normal forward P/E and a normal trailing P/E ratio. The normal P/E valuation can be developed either by forecasting zero AEG or by forecasting no growth in residual earnings.

How Price-to-Book Ratios and Trailing P/E Ratios Articulate

The Whirlpool example is a case of normal P/E ratios but a nonnormal P/B ratio. To focus on the question of how P/E and P/B ratios are related, ask the following question: Must a firm with a high P/B ratio also have a high P/E ratio? Can a firm with a high P/B ratio have a low P/E ratio?

In order to appreciate the empirical relationship between the two ratios, Table 13.1 splits U.S. firms at their median (trailing) P/E and P/B each year from 1963 to 2001 and counts the number of times firms had a high P/B (above the median) and a high P/E (above the median), a low P/B (below the median) and a low P/E (below the median), and so on. You see

The table below gives an analyst's forecast of Whirlpool's earnings for 1995, 1996, and 1997 and the forecasted residual earnings calculated from the forecasted earnings. The forecast was made at the end of 1994.

WHIRLPOOL CORP.

Analyst Forecast, December 1994

(amounts in dollars per share)

Required return of 10%

	1993A	1994A	1995E	1996E	1997E
EPS		4.43	4.75	5.08	5.45
DPS		1.22	1.28	1.34	1.41
BPS	22.85	25.83	29.30	33.04	37.07
RE		2.15	2.17	2.15	2.15
Cum-dividend earnings			4.87	5.21	5.58
Normal earnings			4.87	5.23	5.58
ΔRE			0.02	(0.02)	0.00
AEG			0.02	(0.02)	0.00

RESIDUAL EARNINGS VALUATION ON FORWARD RESIDUAL EARNINGS

Because the 1995 RE forecast is similar to subsequent forecasted RE, Whirlpool is valued at $47.53 per share by capitalizing the 1995 RE forecast as a perpetuity at the cost of capital of 10 percent:

$$V_{1994}^E = CSE_{1994} + \frac{RE_{1995}}{\rho_E - 1} = \$25.83 + \frac{\$2.17}{0.10} = \$47.53$$

This value is close to Whirlpool's market price at the time of $47.25.

FORWARD EARNINGS VALUATION

The pro forma forecasts no growth in residual earnings from the forward year, 1995 onward. But no growth in residual earnings means abnormal earnings are zero, as shown (approximately) in the pro forma. With this expectation, the shares can be valued by capitalizing forward earnings, and the forward P/E must be 10, the normal forward P/E for a required return of 10 percent.

$$V_{1994}^E = \frac{\$4.75}{0.10}$$

= $47.50, or 10 times forward earnings of $4.75.

RESIDUAL EARNINGS VALUATION ON CURRENT (TRAILING) RESIDUAL EARNINGS

The actual 1994 RE is $4.43 − (0.10 × $22.85) = $2.15. This is similar to the RE forecasted for the future. So, as no growth in RE is forecasted, we could have valued the firm by capitalizing the current 1994 RE:

$$V_{1994}^E = \$25.83 + \frac{\$2.15}{0.10} = \$47.33$$

TRAILING EARNINGS VALUATION

With no growth in residual earnings from the current year onward, and thus zero abnormal earnings growth, the shares can be valued by capitalizing trailing earnings, and the (cum-dividend) trailing P/E must be 11, the normal P/E for a required return of 10 percent:

$$V_{1994}^E + d_{1994} = 11 \times \$4.43 = \$48.73$$

So, as the dividend is $1.22, the ex-dividend value is $47.51 (allowing for approximation error).

This is a case of a firm with both a normal trailing P/E and a normal forward P/E, but a nonnormal P/B.

that the relationship between P/B and P/E is positive: Firms with high P/B tend to have high P/E, and firms with low P/B tend to have low P/E also. Indeed two-thirds of cases fall on this diagonal. But one-third falls on the other diagonal: Firms can trade at a high P/B and a low P/E or a high P/B and a low P/E. What explains which of these cells a firm will fall into?

To answer this question, let's consider high, low, and normal P/Bs and P/Es in Table 13.2. Remember a normal P/B is equal to 1.0 and a normal trailing P/E is equal to $\rho_E/(\rho_E - 1)$. There are nine cells, labeled **A** to **I**, and we want to enter the conditions under which firms fall into a particular cell. As with tic-tac-toe, start with the central cell, **E**. We know that expected future residual earnings must be zero here because P/B is normal. We also know that expected future RE must be the same as current RE for the P/E to be normal. Expected AEG

TABLE 13.1
Frequency of High
and Low P/B and P/E
Ratios, 1963–2001

P/E Ratio	P/B Ratio	
	High	**Low**
High	23,146	10,848
	34.0%	16.0%
Low	10,849	23,147
	16.0%	34.1%

TABLE 13.2
Cell Analysis of the
P/B–P/E Relationship

P/E Ratio	P/B Ratio		
	High	**Normal**	**Low**
High	A	B	C
Normal	D	E	F
Low	G	H	I

TABLE 13.3
Cell Analysis of the
P/B–P/E
Relationship: Filling
in the Cells

P/E Ratio	P/B Ratio		
	High $(\overline{RE} > 0)$	**Normal** $(\overline{RE} = 0)$	**Low** $(\overline{RE} < 0)$
High	A $\overline{RE} > RE_0$	B $\overline{RE} > RE_0$ $RE_0 < 0$	C $\overline{RE} > RE_0$ $RE_0 < 0$
Normal	D $\overline{RE} = RE_0$ $RE_0 > 0$	E $\overline{RE} = RE_0$ $RE_0 = 0$	F $\overline{RE} = RE_0$ $RE_0 < 0$
Low	G $\overline{RE} < RE_0$ $RE_0 > 0$	H $\overline{RE} < RE_0$ $RE_0 > 0$	I $\overline{RE} < RE_0$

Key: $\overline{RE}$ = Expected future residual earnings.
   RE_0 = Current residual earnings.

must be zero. If we indicate the stream of expected future RE by $\overline{RE}$ (for short) and current
RE by RE_0, it must be that $\overline{RE} = RE_0 = 0$ for firms in this central cell. That is, for both P/B
and P/E to be normal, a firm must have zero expected future RE and current RE that is also
zero (and thus current and future ROCE equal the cost of capital). This condition is entered
in cell **E** in the solution to the problem in Table 13.3.

Now look at the other cells for a normal P/B, cells **B** and **H**. Here forecasted future RE
must be zero. But, for high P/E in cell **B**, future RE must be forecasted as being higher than
current RE (and forecasted AEG is positive). Thus RE_0 must be less than zero (and current
ROCE must be less than the cost of capital). Correspondingly, firms should trade at a normal P/B and a low P/E in cell **H** when current RE is greater than zero (and current ROCE

is greater than the cost of capital). In the other cells for a normal P/E (cells **D** and **F**), expected future RE must be at the same level as current RE but, as these are cases of non-normal P/B, it must be that both current and future RE are greater than zero (cell **D**) or less than zero (cell **F**). Whirlpool falls into cell **D**.

The conditions for the four corner cells follow the same logic. To attribute both a high P/E and a high P/B to a firm (cell **A**), we must forecast future RE to be greater than zero and this RE must be greater than current RE. A firm can also have a high P/B and a low P/E. This is the cell **G** case where we expect residual earnings to be positive in the future but current residual earnings are even higher. And a firm can have a high P/E but a low P/B. This is the cell **C** case where we expect low (and negative) RE in the future but current RE is even lower. Finally cell **I** contains firms that have both forecasts of low and negative RE in the future but currently have a higher RE than the long-run level.

We can summarize all this in one statement: P/B is determined by the future RE a firm is expected to deliver but P/E is determined by the difference between current RE and the forecast of future RE, that is, growth in RE from current levels.

Look at Box 13.10 for examples of firms that fall into the various cells. It looks as if the market is giving these firms the appropriate cell classification. But we could use the analysis to screen for firms that might be mispriced. Certain combinations of P/E, P/B, and current RE and forecasted RE are ruled out, so if these occur, mispricing is indicated. If a firm were reporting a high ROCE and RE, and reliable analysts' forecasts indicated positive RE in the future, we would expect the stock to trade at a P/B above 1.0. And if analysts' forecasts indicated that the current RE was particularly high and would be lower in the future, we would expect the P/E to be below normal and would classify the firm as a cell **G** firm. If the market were giving the firm a high P/B and a high P/E (as a cell **A** firm), it might be mispriced. (Of course, the market could be valuing earnings beyond the analysts' forecast horizon.)

You can summarize equity analysis and take positions based on the analysis in this way: Put a firm in the appropriate cell based on forecasts of RE and then compare your classification with that of the market. In the late 1990s, the market placed many firms in cell **A**. Some claimed that earnings at that time were exceptionally high and could not be sustained. That claim puts firms in cell G. Who was correct? History shows the latter applied to many firms.

Trailing Price-Earnings Ratios and Transitory Earnings

Because the trailing P/E is an indicator of the difference between current and future profitability, it is affected by current profitability. If a firm with strong ROCE forecasts has an exceptionally good year, it will have a low P/E and fall into cell **G**, like US Airways in 1998. A firm with poor prospects can fall into cell **C** with a high P/E because its current year's earnings are temporarily depressed, like Rocky Shoes. Earnings that are abnormally high or temporarily depressed are affected by transitory earnings or unusual earnings.

The effect of transitory earnings on the P/E has historically been referred to as the **Molodovsky effect,** after the analyst Nicholas Molodovsky, who highlighted the phenomenon in the 1950s. Table 13.4 shows the Molodovsky effect at work. The table shows the relationship between trailing P/E and earnings growth for three P/E groups from 1968 through 2004. The "high"-P/E group had an average P/E of 49.8, the "medium" group an average P/E of 13.1, and the "low" group an average P/E of 6.5. The table gives median year-to-year cum-dividend EPS growth rates for each P/E group, for the year when firms were assigned to the P/E group (Year 0) and for four subsequent years. Look at the medium P/E level. These firms had subsequent earnings in the four years following Year 0 at 13 percent to 15 percent per year. Now look at the high- and low-P/E levels. High-P/E firms had

A. High P/B–High P/E

Nike, Inc. The market gave Nike a P/B of 4.1 and a P/E of 21 in 2005, both high relative to normal ratios. Current residual earnings were $642 million and analysts were forecasting earnings that indicated higher residual earnings (and positive abnormal earnings growth) in the future. This is a cell **A** firm.

B. Normal P/B–High P/E

Westcorp. Westcorp, a financial services holding company, reported earnings for 1998 of $0.65 per share and an ROCE of 5.4 percent. Analysts in 1999 forecasted earnings of $1.72 for 1999 and $2.00 for 2000, which translate into an ROCE of 13.6 percent and 14.1 percent, respectively. With a forecasted ROCE at about the (presumed) cost of capital but increasing from the current level, this is a cell **B** firm. The market gave the firm a P/B of 1.10 and a P/E of 24.

C. Low P/B–High P/E

Rocky Shoes & Boots, Inc. Like Nike, a footwear manufacturer, Rocky Shoes reported an ROCE of 1.8 percent for 1998 with earnings of $0.21 per share. Analysts forecast an ROCE of 6.2 percent for 1999 and 7.8 percent for 2000, on earnings of $0.72 and $0.95, respectively. The market gave the firm a P/B of 0.6 and a P/E of 33, appropriate for a firm with forecasted ROCE less than the (presumed) cost of capital but with increasing ROCE.

D. High P/B–Normal P/E

Whirlpool Corp. Whirlpool, with a positive but constant RE, was a cell **D** firm in 1994. Whirlpool was priced at 11 times earnings (cum-dividend), and at 1.8 times book value, as we saw in Box 13.9.

E. Normal P/B–Normal P/E

Horizon Financial Corp. Horizon Financial Corp., a bank holding company, reported an ROCE of 10.3 percent for fiscal 1999. Analysts forecasted that ROCE would be 10.6 percent for 2000 and after, roughly at the same level. If the equity cost of capital is 10 percent, this firm should have a normal P/B and a normal P/E. The stock traded at 11 times earnings and 1.0 times book value.

F. Low P/B–Normal P/E

Rainforest Cafe Inc. In 1999, analysts covering Rainforest Cafe, a theme restaurant ("a wild place to eat"), forecasted earnings of $0.62 per share for 1999 and $0.71 for 2000, or an ROCE of 6.8 percent and 7.2 percent. The stock traded at a P/B of 0.6, reflecting the low anticipated ROCE. The ROCE for 1998 was 6.5 percent. With 1998 profitability similar to forecasted profitability, the stock should sell at a normal P/E ratio. And indeed it did: The P/E at the time of the forecasts was 11.

G. High P/B–Low P/E

US Airways Group. US Airways reported an ROCE of 81 percent in 1998. Analysts deemed 1998 to be a particularly good year and forecast ROCE for 1999 and 2000 down to 29 percent and 33 percent. The stock traded at 12.6 times book value, consistent with high ROCE in the future, but at a P/E of only 4.

H. Normal P/B–Low P/E

America West Holdings. America West Holdings, the holding company for America West Airlines, had an ROCE of 15.0 percent in 1998. Analysts forecasted in 1999 that the ROCE would decline to 11.7 percent by 2000. The market gave the stock a P/B of 1.0 in 1999, in line with the forecasted ROCE equaling the cost of capital. But the P/E was 7, consistent with the expected drop in the ROCE.

I. Low P/B–Low P/E

UAL Corporation. United Airlines's holding company traded at a P/B of 0.7 in mid-1999 and a P/E of 6. It reported an ROCE of 29.2 percent for 1998, but its ROCE was expected by analysts to drop to 10.6 percent (before a special gain) in 1999 and to 9.1 percent in 2000.

---

relatively high earnings growth in the years following Year 0, whereas low-P/E firms had relatively low earnings growth. Thus the data confirm that P/E indicates future growth in earnings.

Now look at the growth rates in Year 0, the current year. Whereas P/E is positively related to future earnings growth, it is negatively related to current earnings growth. High-P/E firms are typically those whose earnings are down now but will rebound in the future. The low-P/E firms in the table have large increases in current earnings but these are not sustained subsequently. In short, the trailing P/E is affected by temporary aspects of current

TABLE 13.4   **Subsequent Earnings Growth for Different Levels of P/E, 1968–2004**

High-P/E firms in the current year (Year 0) have higher cum-dividend earnings growth in
subsequent years than low-P/E firms. However, the relationship between P/E and growth is negative
in the current year.

		Year After Current Year (Year 0)				
P/E Level	**P/E**	**0**	**1**	**2**	**3**	**4**
Cum-dividend EPS growth by P/E level						
High	49.8	−35.8%	54.1%	16.6%	19.1%	17.2%
Medium	13.1	18.4%	14.8%	13.1%	14.8%	15.6%
Low	6.5	23.9%	2.2%	7.1%	11.5%	14.4%

Earnings growth is the year-to-year change in EPS divided by (the absolute value of) prior year's EPS. EPS is adjusted for payout in
the prior period and so is cum-dividend, with dividends reinvested at a 10 percent rate.

Source: Standard & Poor's Compustat® data.

earnings. Indeed, because of this effect a P/E can be high, but without much growth after
the transitory effect has worked its way out.

P/E Ratios and the Analysis of Sustainable Earnings

The analysis of sustainable earnings in this chapter identifies the transitory aspects of
current earnings and so helps to ascertain the Molodovsky effect on the trailing P/E ratio.
If earnings are temporarily high (and cannot be sustained), one should pay less per dollar of earnings—the P/E should be low. If, on the other hand, earnings can be sustained—
or can grow because they are temporarily depressed—one should pay a higher multiple.
Sustainable earnings analysis focuses on the future—for it is future earnings that the investor is buying—and helps the investor discount earnings for that part which is not
sustainable.

As investors buy future earnings, it makes sense that a P/E valuation should focus on
the forward P/E and thus the pricing of next year's earnings and growth after that year.
Forward earnings are considerably less affected by the transitory items that do not contribute to permanent growth. For evaluation of the forward P/E, sustainable earnings
analysis very much comes into play for, to forecast forward earnings after observing
current earnings, we wish to identify the core earnings that can be sustained in the
forward year.

Price-to-Book and Growth

It is common to refer to a high P/B stock as a growth stock. Indeed, Wall Street labeling
refers to a high P/B as "growth" and a low P/B as "value." But this is not necessarily the
case. Table 13.1 indicates that high P/B tends to be associated with high P/E (growth)
and low P/B with low P/E (low growth). But a third of the firms fall on the other diagonal there. We have seen that a high P/B stock can fall into cell G (where declining
residual earnings is forecast) and a low P/B can be in cell C (with growing residual earnings). A drug company that has a high P/B (because R&D assets are not on the balance
sheet) can have negative growth (with declining residual earnings). P/B is not the focus
for growth, rather it is P/E (and, to avoid the transitory earnings effect, specifically the
forward P/E).

Summary

Firms change over time and their financial statements change accordingly. This chapter has laid out the analysis of the changes in financial statements that are particularly relevant for forecasting growth. The focus has been on changes in ROCE and growth in investment which drive residual earnings growth and abnormal earnings growth.

A change in ROCE is analyzed by distinguishing changes that are due to operating profitability (changes in RNOA) and changes in the financing of operations. In both cases, core or sustainable components that are likely to drive profitability in the future are distinguished from transitory or unusual components that are nonrecurring. So the analyst "cuts to the core" of what will drive profitability in the future. Growth in equity investment, which combines with ROCE to produce growth in residual earnings, is determined primarily by sales growth but also by changes in the net operating asset investment needed to support sales growth and by changes in financing of this investment.

The analysis here has given an answer to the question raised at the beginning of the chapter: What is a growth firm? A growth firm is one that can increase its residual earnings. To do so, a growth firm will have the following features:

1. Sustainable, growing sales.
2. High or increasing core profit margins.
3. High or improving asset turnovers.

On the other hand, the chapter warns against growth that comes from financial leverage. The next chapter expands upon this theme.

Durable competitive advantage is an important feature in valuation. The analysis of sustainable earnings and growth in this chapter gives insights into whether a firm has such advantage. Sustaining high core profit margins indicates competitive advantage. Growing residual earnings with sales growth and high core margins points to competitive advantage. And growing sales with both high core margins and high asset turnover yields higher residual earnings because less investment is required.

Valuation involves the residual earnings expected in the future, so see the analysis here as a tool for forecasting. How will the future be different from the present? The analysis of the chapter lays out the features that will drive changes in the future and so is a tool for forecasting, strategy analysis, and in valuation in the next part of the book.

Box 13.11 completes the Accounting Quality Watch, begun in Chapter 9 and continued through the chapters on financial statement analysis.

The Web Connection

Find the following on the Web page for this chapter:

- Additional examples of the analysis of core earnings and the questions it answers, with an application to Boeing Company.
- Further discussion of pension issues with a look at Boeing Company.

- A historical analysis of how past growth forecasts future growth and an introduction to fade diagrams.
- A discussion of "value" versus "growth" investing.
- The Readers' Corner.

This chapter has cautioned the analyst about a number of accounting issues that arise when identifying sustainable earnings. These issues are accounting quality concerns, for they can yield earnings that are "low quality" as an indicator of future earnings. So we add them to the Accounting Quality Watch, begun in Chapter 9 and continued through Chapter 10 and Chapter 11. With the full list of quality issues, you will be prepared to tackle the formal analysis of accounting quality in Chapter 18.

Accounting Item	The Quality Problem
Deferred revenue	Firms can defer too much earnings to the future and thus create too much earnings growth. Conversely, firms can defer too little earnings and so report unsustainable earnings currently.
Restructuring charges	Firms can make excessive restructuring charges in one year and bleed them back to earnings in future years, giving the appearance of growth. FASB Statement 146 now limits the practice.
Selling, general, and administrative expense	SG&A is a large, aggregated number that covers a multitude of sins. Penetrate its composition.
Gains and losses on asset sales	These are often hidden in SG&A expense but are not a part of the core business.
R&D and advertising	Firms can increase earnings by temporarily reducing R&D and advertising expenditures. This not only inflates current earnings, but damages future earnings that the expenditures would otherwise produce.
Pension accounting	Pension accounting brings prices into the income statement with the danger that earnings can reflect price bubbles. Returns on pension plan assets are commingled with core operating income from the business, contaminating profit margins. Expected returns on plan assets can be overestimated.
Cherry picking	Firms can cherry pick realized gains on investments into the income statement and report unrealized losses in the equity statement. Restate the income statement on a comprehensive income basis.
Changes in estimates	Firms can affect earnings by changes in estimates (of bad debts, warranty liabilities, and accrued expenses, for example).

Key Concepts

bleeding back (to income) is the practice of reversing charges in prior years to increase income. *399*

fixed costs are costs that do not change with sales. Compare with **variable costs.** *408*

growth firm is a firm that grows residual earnings (that is, it has abnormal earnings growth). *393*

Molodovsky effect is the effect of transitory earnings on the P/E ratio. *414*

normalizing earnings is the process of purging earnings of transitory, abnormal components. *396*

sustainable earnings (also called **persistent earnings, core earnings,** or **underlying earnings**) are current earnings that are likely to be maintained in the future. Compare with **transitory earnings.** *396*

transitory earnings (or **unusual items**) are current earnings that are not likely to be repeated in the future. Compare with **sustainable earnings.** *396*

variable costs are costs that vary with sales. Compare with **fixed costs.** *408*

The Analyst's Toolkit

A Continuing Case: *Kimberly-Clark Corporation*

A Self-Study Exercise

In the Continuing Case for Chapter 12, you carried out a comprehensive profitability analysis for Kimberly-Clark for both 2010 and 2009 based on the reformulated financial statements you prepared in Chapter 10. Now it's time to compare the profitability for the two years.

ANALYSIS OF THE CHANGE IN PROFITABILITY FOR KMB

Let Figure 13.1 and Exhibit 13.1 in this chapter be your guide to identifying Kimberly-Clark's core income and analyzing what determined the change in its profitability from 2009 to 2010. The template in Exhibit 13.1 simply takes the reformulation you carried out in Chapter 10 a step further, in order to distinguish the core component of operating income. Some components of noncore income will be evident from the prior reformulation. You will discover others from the reconciliation of net income to cash flow from operations in the cash flow statement. Here is some further information that will help you refine the analysis.

Organization Optimization Initiative

Footnote 5 to the financial statements detailed initiatives the firm took in 2009 to reduce the worldwide workforce. The initiative resulted in a $128 million pretax charge to the income statement, $44 million to cost of goods sold, and $84 million to marketing expenses.

Defined Benefit Pension Plan

The following from the pension footnote gives the composition of the net pension expense included in the income statement (dollar amounts in millions). The firm used a 7.9 percent rate for the expected return on pension plan assets.

	2010	2009	2008
Service cost	$ 70	$ 82	$ 88
Interest cost	353	357	373
Expected return on plan assets	(336)	(269)	(370)
Amortization of prior service cost	5	5	8
Recognized net actuarial loss (gain)	100	111	57
Other	3	28	7
Net periodic benefit cost	$ 195	$ 314	$ 163

Concept Questions

C13.1. What is a growth firm?

C13.2. In analyzing growth, should the analyst focus on residual earnings, abnormal earnings growth, or both?

C13.3. What measure tells you that a firm is a no-growth firm?

C13.4. What features in financial statements would you look for to identify a firm as a growth company?

C13.5. Why would an analyst wish to distinguish the part of earnings that is sustainable?

C13.6. What are transitory earnings? Give some examples.

C13.7. Are unrealized gains and losses on financial assets persistent or transitory income?

C13.8. Distinguish operating leverage from operating liability leverage.

C13.9. The higher a firm's contribution margin ratio, the more leverage it gets from increasing sales. Correct?

C13.10. Would you see a high profit margin of, say, 6 percent for a grocery retailer as sustainable?

C13.11. What determines growth in equity investment in a firm?

C13.12. A firm can have a high trailing P/E ratio, yet have a low expected earnings growth rate in the future. Is this so?

C13.13. For a firm with a normal trailing P/E ratio, expected future residual earnings must be the same as current residual earnings. Correct?

C13.14. Can a firm have a high P/E ratio yet a low P/B ratio? How would you characterize the growth expectations for this firm?

C13.15. Firms with high unsustainable earnings should have low trailing P/E ratios. Is this correct?

C13.16. Why would we expect a firm with a large write-off to have a high trailing P/E?

Exercises

Drill Exercises

E13.1. Identifying Transitory Items (Easy)

Classify each of the following items as either part of core income or unusual (transitory) income.

a. Depreciation expense
b. Unrealized gains on equity securities
c. Realized gains on equity securities
d. Gain on the disposal of property
e. Earnings in subsidiaries under the equity method
f. Research and development expenses
g. Expected returns on pension plan assets

E13.2. Forecasting from Core Income (Medium)

A firm reported the following income statement (amounts in millions):

Net sales	$ 496
Cost of goods sold	240
Selling and administrative expense	18
Restructuring charges	12
Loss on asset sale	18
Operating income	178
Interest expense	18
Income before taxes	160
Income taxes	40
Net income	120

The firm's tax rate is 35 percent. You have been asked to forecast the future profit margin based on this information. What is your best estimate?

E13.3. Analyzing a Change in Core Operating Profitability (Easy)

The following numbers were calculated from the financial statements for a firm for 2012 and 2011:

	2012	2011
Core profit margin	4.7%	5.1%
Asset turnover	2.4	2.5

Calculate core return of net operating assets (core RNOA) and show how much of its change from 2011 to 2012 is due to the change in profit margin and the change in asset turnover. Box 13.7 will help you.

Note: Exercises E13.3 to E13.5 are all connected and can be worked as one exercise.

E13.4. Analyzing a Change in Return on Common Equity (Easy)

The following numbers were calculated from the financial statements for a firm for 2012 and 2011:

	2012	2011
Return on common equity (ROCE)	15.2%	13.3%
Return on net operating assets (RNOA)	11.28%	12.75%
Net borrowing cost (NBC)	2.9%	3.2%
Average net financial obligations (millions)	$ 2,225	$ 241
Average common equity (millions)	$ 4,756	$ 4,173

Explain how much of the change in ROCE from 2011 to 2012 is due to operating activities and how much is due to financing activities. Box 13.8 will help you.

E13.5. Analyzing the Growth in Shareholders' Equity (Easy)

The following numbers were calculated from the financial statements for a firm for 2012 and 2011:

	2012	2011
Return on common equity (ROCE)	15.2%	13.3%
Return on net operating assets (RNOA)	11.28%	12.75%
Sales (millions)	$16,754	$11,035
Average net operating assets (millions)	$ 6,981	$ 4,414
Average net financial obligations (millions)	$ 2,225	$ 241
Average common equity (millions)	$ 4,756	$ 4,173

Explain to what extent the change in common equity from 2011 to 2012 is due to sales growth, net assets required to support sales, and borrowing.

E13.6. Calculating Core Profit Margin (Easy)

A firm reports operating income before tax in its income statement of $73.4 million on sales of $667.3 million. After net interest expense of $20.5 million and taxes of $18.3 million, its net income is $34.6 million. The following items are included as part of operating income:

Start-up costs for new venture	$ 4.3 million
Merger-related charge	$13.4 million
Gains on the disposal of plant	$ 3.9 million

The firm also reports a currency translation gain of $8.9 million as part of other comprehensive income.

Calculate the firm's core operating income (after tax) and core percentage profit margin. The firm's marginal tax rate is 39 percent.

E13.7. Explaining a Change in Profitability (Medium)

Consider the following financial information:

Summary Balance Sheets at December 31

	2009	2008	2007
Cash	$ 100	$ 100	$ 120
Short-term investments	300	300	330
Accounts receivable	900	1,000	1,250
Inventory	2,000	1,900	1,850
Property, plant, and equipment (net of accumulated depreciation)	8,200	9,000	10,500
Total assets	11,500	12,300	14,050
Accrued liabilities	600	500	550
Accounts payable	900	1,000	1,100
Bank loan	0	0	3,210
Bonds payable	4,300	4,300	1,000
Deferred taxes	490	500	600
Total liabilities	6,290	6,300	6,460
Preferred stock (8%)	1,000	1,000	1,000
Common stock	1,400	2,000	2,000
Retained earnings	2,810	3,000	4,590
Owners' equity	$ 5,210	$ 6,000	$ 7,590

Summary Income Statements

	2009	2008
Sales	$ 22,000	$ 24,000
Cost of goods sold	(13,000)	(13,100)
Selling and administration	(8,000)	(8,250)
Restructuring charges	(190)	0
Interest income	24	25
Interest expense	(430)	(430)
Earnings before taxes and extraordinary items	404	2,245
Tax expense	(134)	(675)
Earnings before extraordinary items	270	1,570
Gain due to retirement of bonds, net of taxes	0	100
Net income	$ 270	$ 1,670

Prepare a succinct analysis that explains the change in ROCE from 2008 to 2009. The marginal tax rate is 34 percent, and dividends paid on preferred stock cannot be deducted for tax purposes.

Applications

E13.8. Identification of Core Operating Income and Margins for Starbucks Corporation (Medium)

The consolidated statement of earnings for Starbucks Corporation for 2007 is given in Exercise E10.10 in Chapter 10. The firm's statutory tax rate is 38.4 percent. Note 4 on "net interest and other income," under the statements, identifies some components of earnings. For the 2007 fiscal year, identify

a. Core operating income from sales.
b. Other core operating income.
c. Core operating profit margin from sales.
d. Unusual items.

Real World Connection
See Exercises E9.8, E10.10, E12.9, and E15.8 on Starbucks.

E13.9.   **Forecasting from Core Income: General Mills (Medium)**
The following are selected numbers from the income statements reported by General Mills for 2008 and 2007 (dollars in millions):

	2008	2007
Sales	$13,652	$12,441
Operating income	2,228	2,058
Interest, net	422	427
Income before taxes	1,806	1,631
Income taxes	622	560
Earnings from joint ventures	111	73
Net income	1,295	1,144

The firm's statutory tax rate at the time was 38.5 percent. Further investigation revealed that operating income was after restructuring charges of $21 million in 2008 and $39 million in 2007.

a. Calculate core income from sales and total core income for both years.
b. The income for 2008 was earned on a base of $12,572 million of net operating assets. What was core RNOA for 2008?
c. What is your best forecast of the operating profit margin and core RNOA for 2009 based on this information?
d. Why would earnings from joint ventures be reported after the tax line on the income statement?

Real World Connection
Other exercises on General Mills are in E1.5, E2.9, E3.8, E4.10, E6.8, E11.9, E14.15, E15.6, and E16.10.

Minicases

M13.1

Financial Statement Analysis: Procter & Gamble IV

This case continues the financial statement analysis of Procter & Gamble Co. begun in Minicase 10.1 and developed further in Minicases 11.1 and 12.1. This installment covers issues in dealing with core income.

Financial statements for Procter & Gamble are presented in Exhibit 10.15 in Chapter 10. If you worked Minicase 10.1, you will have reformulated the income statements and balance sheets to distinguish operating activities from financing activities. This case refines the reformulation to identify core, sustainable earnings. If you worked Minicase 12.1, you will have carried out an analysis of profitability. This case adds an analysis of growth.

To start, calculate residual earnings for the years 2008 to 2010 and note changes over time. Use a required return of 8 percent. The risk-free rate was about 3.8 percent at the time, so an 8 percent required return implies a 4.2 percent risk premium suitable for a firm with a beta less than 1.0. What is the trend in residual earnings? Does P&G appear to be a growth company? Comment on both the level and the change in residual earnings from 2008 to 2010.

For valuation, we are interested in the residual earnings (growth) that a firm can deliver in the future. These past residual earnings numbers are affected by transitory earnings that do not bear on the future. So cut to the core: Reformulate the income statement further to identify core (sustainable) income. For Procter & Gamble, this is fairly straightforward, but the accounting for its defined benefit pension plans poses problems. The information given to you at the bottom of the case will be helpful.

With sustainable earnings identified, identify core profit margins and carry out an analysis of core profitability (core return on net operating assets). Explain how core profitability changed from year to year. What are the primary drivers of the change in residual earnings from 2008 to 2010?

Finally, forecast operating income and total earnings for 2011 based on your analysis. What is your forecast of return on net operating assets (RNOA) for 2011? What is your forecast of residual earnings?

Information needed to identify core earnings:

1. Look at the information provided with the financial statements in Exhibit 10.15.
2. The following, from the pension footnote, gives details of the net pension cost included in earnings and also the expected rate of return applied to pension assets.

Net periodic benefit cost. Components of the net periodic benefit cost were as follows:

	Years Ended June 30					
	2010	2009	2008	2010	2009	2008
	Pension Benefits			Other Retiree Benefits		
Service cost	$ 218	$ 214	$ 263	$ 103	$ 91	$ 95
Interest cost	579	551	539	253	243	226
Expected return on plan assets	(437)	(473)	(557)	(429)	(444)	(429)
Prior service cost (credit) amortization	15	14	14	(21)	(23)	(21)
Net actuarial loss amortization	91	29	9	20	2	7

Curtailment and settlement gain	3	6	(36)	14	—	(1)
Gross benefit cost (credit)	469	341	232	(60)	(131)	(123)
Dividends on ESOP preferred stock	—	—	—	(83)	(86)	(95)
Net periodic benefit cost (credit)	469	341	232	(143)	(217)	(218)

Assumptions used to determine net periodic benefit cost:

	Years Ended June 30			
	2010	2009	2010	2009
	Pension Benefits (%)		Other Retiree Benefits (%)	
Discount rate	5.0%	6.0%	5.4%	6.4%
Expected return on plan assets	7.1	7.4	9.1	9.3
Rate of compensation increase	3.5	3.7	—	—

The pension footnote has the following narrative:

> Several factors are considered in developing the estimate for the long-term expected rate of re-turn on plan assets. For the defined benefit retirement plans, these include historical rates of return of broad equity and bond indices and projected long-term rates of return obtained from pension investment consultants. The expected long-term rates of return for plan assets are 8%–9% for equities and 5%–6% for bonds. For other retiree benefit plans, the expected long-term rate of return reflects the fact that the assets are comprised primarily of Company stock. The expected rate of return on Company stock is based on the long-term projected return of 9.5% and reflects the historical pattern of favorable returns.

What issues does this raise?

Real World Connection

Minicases M10.1, M11.1, M12.1, M15.1, and M16.1 also cover Procter & Gamble.

M13.2

A Question of Growth: Microsoft Corporation

By 2005, Microsoft Corporation, the premier software firm of the computer age, had matured into an established firm. Maturity, however, often brings slower growth and many observers claimed that Microsoft was beginning to show such symptoms. Outside its core business centered around the Windows operating systems and related applications such as Microsoft Office, the firm had struggled to make an impact with new products and services. In particular, in Internet-based services that generate subscription, advertising, and transaction revenues, it lagged behind rivals such as Google and Yahoo!. Apple's recent launch of its iTunes music service and its success with iPod left Microsoft looking somewhat dated.

At its annual meeting with analysts on July 28, 2005, Chairman Bill Gates acknowledged that Microsoft was "playing catch-up on search" but added that, within three years, it would make significant advances over the current state of the technology. CEO Steve Ballmer announced a new focus on growth through an expansion into Internet services. The software industry, he insisted, was moving from "delivering bits to delivering bits and services. The Internet's transformative impact on the software business has just begun." The shift from software to services was hailed as a new business model for generating growth. New areas would involve communications, Web-based storage, and tools to permit workers to collaborate better. Analysts advised caution. Few details of the new plan were offered at the meeting, and Microsoft had previously emphasized Web-services initiatives with less than stellar results.

Despite the skepticism about Microsoft's ability to deliver growth, the press release accompanying fiscal 2005 results indicated otherwise. "We closed out a record fiscal year with strong revenue growth in the fourth quarter driven by healthy, broad-based demand across all customer segments and channels," said Chris Liddell, chief financial officer at Microsoft. "While continuing to invest in the business, we also returned $44 billion to investors through share repurchases and dividends during the fiscal year. These results provide solid momentum heading into fiscal 2006, which is shaping up to be a strong year for growth and investment. We expect double digit revenue growth next year, kicking off the strongest multiyear product pipeline in the company's history."

Microsoft's income statements for 2002–2005 and balance sheets for 2001–2005 are summarized in Exhibit 13.3. The income statements are supplemented with details of other comprehensive income reported in the equity statement. Reformulate these statements, being sure to distinguish operating activities from financing activities and, within operating activities, income from Microsoft's core software business from income from its investment portfolio. The firm's statutory tax rate is 37 percent.

Discuss the following. Use a required return of 9 percent if needed for calculations.

A. With valuation in mind, what measures would you focus on to evaluate Microsoft's growth from 2002 to 2005? Focus on the core business rather than investment income. Would you say that Microsoft has been a growth company? Is there any indication that growth is slowing?

B. Explain the change in return on common equity (ROCE) for 2005 over that for 2004.

C. Microsoft paid out $44 billion to shareholders during fiscal year 2005, including a large special dividend of $33.5 billion. Explain how such a big payout affects return on common equity (ROCE). What would Microsoft's ROCE for 2004 have been if its financial leverage had been the same as that at the end of 2005? It has been said that firms can increase ROCE simply by selling off their holdings of Treasury bills. Is this true?

D. Microsoft has considerable unearned revenues. Analysts have been concerned that Microsoft might use these deferred revenues to create earnings growth. How could this happen?

E. Examine Microsoft's investment income. Is there any suggestion of cherry picking?

Real World Connection

Microsoft Exercises are E1.6, E4.14, E6.12, E8.9, E9.9, E11.11, E18.10, and E20.4. Minicases M9.1 and M13.2 also cover Microsoft.

EXHIBIT 13.3
Summary Financial Statements for Microsoft Corporation, Fiscal Years Ending June 30, 2001–2005

	Yearly Income Statements (in billions of dollars)			
	2005	**2004**	**2003**	**2002**
Revenue	39.79	36.83	32.19	28.36
Operating expenses:				
Cost of revenue	6.20	6.72	6.06	5.70
Research and development	6.18	7.78	6.60	6.30
Sales and marketing	8.68	8.30	7.55	6.25

(continued)

EXHIBIT 13.3
(*concluded*)

General and administrative	4.17	5.00	2.43	1.84
	25.23	27.80	22.64	20.09
Operating income	14.56	9.03	9.55	8.27
Investment income	2.07	3.17	1.50	(0.40)
Income before taxes	16.63	12.2	11.05	7.87
Income taxes	4.38	4.03	3.52	2.51
Net income	12.25	8.17	7.53	5.36
Investment income is comprised of the following:				
Interest income	1.27	1.67	1.70	1.76
Dividends	0.19	0.20	0.18	0.27
Realized gains (losses) on investments	0.61	1.30	(0.38)	(2.43)
	2.07	3.17	1.50	(0.40)
Other comprehensive income (from equity statement):				
Gains (losses) on derivatives	(0.06)	0.10	(0.10)	(0.09)
Unrealized investment gains (losses)	0.37	(0.87)	1.24	0.01
Translation adjustments	0.0	0.05	0.12	0.08
	0.31	(0.72)	1.26	0.00

Yearly Balance Sheets
(in billions of dollars)

	2005	**2004**	**2003**	**2002**	**2001**
Cash and cash equivalents	4.85	15.98	6.44	3.02	3.92
Short-term investments	32.90	44.61	42.61	35.64	27.68
Accounts receivable	7.18	5.89	5.20	5.13	3.67
Inventories	0.49	0.42	0.64	0.67	0.08
Deferred taxes	1.70	2.10	2.51	2.11	1.52
Other	1.62	1.57	1.57	2.01	2.34
Total current assets	48.74	70.57	58.97	48.58	39.21
Property and equipment	2.35	2.33	2.22	2.27	2.31
Equity investments	10.10	10.73	11.83	12.19	12.70
Debt investments	0.90	1.48	1.86	2.00	1.66
Goodwill	3.31	3.12	3.13	1.43	1.51
Intangible assets	0.50	0.57	0.38	0.24	0.40
Deferred taxes	3.62	1.83	2.16	—	—
Other long-term assets	1.30	1.76	1.18	0.94	1.04
Total assets	70.82	92.39	81.73	67.65	58.83
Accounts payable	2.09	1.72	1.57	1.21	1.19
Accrued compensation	1.66	1.34	1.42	1.15	0.74
Income taxes payable	2.02	3.48	2.04	2.02	1.47
Short-term unearned revenue	7.50	6.51	7.23	5.92	4.40
Other liabilities	3.61	1.92	1.71	2.45	1.45
Total current liabilities	16.88	14.97	13.97	12.75	9.25
Long-term unearned revenue	1.67	1.66	1.79	1.82	1.22
Other long-term liabilities	4.15	0.93	1.06	0.90	1.07
	22.70	17.56	16.82	15.47	11.54
Shareholders' equity	48.12	74.83	64.91	52.18	47.29
	70.82	92.39	81.73	67.65	58.83

Note: For 2001–2002, deferred taxes were a net liability and were included in other liabilities.

M13.3

Analysis of Sustainable Growth: International Business Machines

International Business Machines Corporation (IBM) was once the dominant computer manufacturer in the world and, from 1960 to 1980, the leading growth company. Indeed, in those years IBM became the very personification of a growth company. However, with the advent of decentralized computing and the personal computer in the 1980s, IBM's growth began to slow. Under the leadership of Louis Gerstner Jr., the firm transformed itself in the early 1990s from a mainframe manufacturer to an information technology company, providing technology, system software, services, and financing products to customers. Mr. Gerstner's book, *Who Says Elephants Can't Dance? Inside IBM's Historic Turnaround,* published in 2002, gives the play-by-play. From revenues of $64.8 billion in 1991, IBM grew to a firm with $88.4 billion in revenues in 2000.

In turning around the business, IBM took large restructuring charges against its income in the early 1990s, resulting in net losses of $2.861 billion, $4.965 billion, and $8.101 billion for 1991–1993, respectively. Subsequently the firm delivered the earnings growth of yesteryear. You can see at the bottom of the income statements in Exhibit 13.4 that earnings per share grew from $2.56 in 1996 to $4.58 in 2000.

At a number of points, this chapter has analyzed the components of IBM's earnings in order to understand their sustainability. From the information extracted from IBM's financial statement footnotes below, restate the income statements from 1996 to 2000 in Exhibit 13.4 to identify core operating income that arises from selling products to customers. The footnotes are from the firm's 1999 10-K filing; you may also wish to look at the corresponding footnotes for other years. The extracts from the firm's cash flow statement in Exhibit 13.4 will also help you in your task.

Do you get a different picture of IBM's income growth during the last half of the 1990s than is suggested by growth in earnings per share?

EXHIBIT 13.4	INTERNATIONAL BUSINESS MACHINES CORPORATION AND SUBSIDIARY COMPANIES

EXHIBIT 13.4
Income
Statements and
Selected
Components of
the Cash Flow
Statements for
IBM, 1996–2000

INTERNATIONAL BUSINESS MACHINES CORPORATION AND SUBSIDIARY COMPANIES
Consolidated Statements of Earnings
(dollars in millions except per share amounts)

	For the Year Ended December 31				
	2000	**1999**	**1998**	**1997**	**1996**
Revenue	$88,396	$87,548	$81,667	$78,508	$75,947
Cost of revenue	55,972	55,619	50,795	47,899	45,408
Gross profit	32,424	31,929	30,872	30,609	30,539
Operating expenses					
Selling, general, and administrative	15,639	14,729	16,662	16,634	16,854
Research, development, and engineering	5,151	5,273	5,046	4,877	5,089
Total operating expenses	20,790	20,002	21,708	21,511	21,943
Operating income	11,634	11,927	9,164	9,098	8,596

(continued)

EXHIBIT 13.4
(*concluded*)

Other income, principally interest	617	557	589	657	707
Interest expense	717	727	713	728	716
Income before income taxes	11,534	11,757	9,040	9,027	8,587
Provision for income taxes	3,441	4,045	2,712	2,934	3,158
Net income	8,093	7,712	6,328	6,093	5,429
Preferred stock dividends	20	20	20	20	20
Net income applicable to common stockholders	$ 8,073	$ 7,692	$ 6,308	$ 6,073	$ 5,409
Earnings per share of common stock:					
Assuming dilution	$ 4.44	$ 4.12	$ 3.29	$ 3.00	$ 2.51
Basic	$ 4.58	$ 4.25	$ 3.38	$ 3.09	$ 2.56

Operating and Investing Section of Cash Flow Statements
(dollars in millions)

	At December 31				
	2000	**1999**	**1998**	**1997**	**1996**
Cash flow from operating activities					
Net income	$ 8,093	$ 7,712	$ 6,328	$ 6,093	$ 5,429
Adjustments to reconcile net income to cash provided from operating activities					
Depreciation	4,513	6,159	4,475	4,018	3,676
Amortization of software	482	426	517	983	1,336
Effect of restructuring charges			(355)	(445)	(1,491)
Deferred income taxes	29	(713)	(606)	358	11
Gain on disposition of fixed and other assets	(792)	(4,791)	(261)	(273)	(300)
Other changes that (used) provided cash					
Receivables	(4,720)	(1,677)	(2,736)	(3,727)	(650)
Inventories	(55)	301	73	432	196
Other assets	(643)	(130)	219	(1,087)	(545)
Accounts payable	2,245	(3)	362	699	319
Other liabilities	122	2,817	1,257	1,814	2,294
Net cash provided from operating activities	9,274	10,111	9,273	8,865	10,275
Cash flow from investing activities					
Payments for plant, rental machines, and other property	(5,616)	(5,959)	(6,520)	(6,793)	(6,599)
Proceeds from disposition of plant, rental machines, and other property	1,619	1,207	905	1,130	1,314
Investment in software	(565)	(464)	(250)	(314)	(295)
Purchases of marketable securities and other investments	(1,079)	(3,949)	(4,211)	(1,617)	(1,613)
Proceeds from marketable securities and other investments	1,393	2,616	3,945	1,439	1,470
Proceeds from sale of the Global Network		4,880			
Net cash used in investing activities	$(4,248)	$(1,669)	$(6,131)	$(6,155)	$(5,723)

Extracts from 1999 Footnotes

D. Acquisitions/Divestitures

In December 1998, the company announced that it would sell its Global Network business to AT&T. During 1999, the company completed the sale to AT&T for $4,991 million. More than 5,300 IBM employees joined AT&T as a result of these sales of operations in 71 countries. The company recognized a pretax gain of $4,057 million ($2,495 million after tax, or $1.33 per diluted common share). The net gain reflects dispositions of plant, rental machines, and other property of $410 million, other assets of $182 million, and contractual obligations of $342 million.

M. Other Liabilities

Other liabilities (of $11,928 million in 1999) principally comprises accruals for nonpension postretirement benefits for U.S. employees ($6,392 million) and nonpension postretirement benefits, indemnity, and retirement plan reserves for non-U.S. employees ($1,028 million).

Also included in other liabilities are noncurrent liabilities associated with infrastructure reduction and restructuring actions taken through 1993. Other liabilities include $659 million for postemployment preretirement accruals and $503 million (net of sublease receipts) for accruals for leased space that the company vacated.

P. Taxes

The significant components of activities that gave rise to deferred tax assets and liabilities that are recorded on the balance sheet were as follows:

Deferred Tax Assets (dollars in millions)			
	At December 31		
	1999	**1998**	**1997**
Employee benefits	$ 3,737	$ 3,909	$ 3,707
Alternative minimum tax credits	1,244	1,169	1,092
Bad debt, inventory, and warranty reserves	1,093	1,249	1,027
Infrastructure reduction charges	918	863	1,163
Capitalized research and development	880	913	1,196
Deferred income	870	686	893
General business credits	605	555	492
Foreign tax loss carryforwards	406	304	202
Equity alliances	377	387	378
Depreciation	326	201	132
State and local tax loss carryforwards	227	212	203
Intracompany sales and services	153	182	235
Other	2,763	2,614	2,507
Gross deferred tax assets	13,599	13,244	13,227
Less: Valuation allowance	647	488	2,163
Net deferred tax assets	$12,952	$12,756	$11,064

Deferred Tax Liabilities (dollars in millions)

	At December 31		
	1999	**1998**	**1997**
Retirement benefits	$3,092	$2,775	$2,147
Sales-type leases	2,914	3,433	3,147
Depreciation	1,237	1,505	1,556
Software cost deferred	250	287	420
Other	2,058	1,841	1,413
Gross deferred tax liabilities	$9,551	$9,841	$8,683

The valuation allowance at December 31, 1999, principally applies to certain state and local and foreign tax loss carryforwards that, in the opinion of management, are more likely than not to expire before the company can use them.

As part of implementing its global strategies involving the relocation of certain of its manufacturing operations, the company transferred certain intellectual property rights to several non-U.S. subsidiaries in December 1998. Since these strategies, including this transfer, result in the anticipated utilization of U.S. federal tax credit carryforwards, the company reduced the valuation allowance from that previously required.

A reconciliation of the company's effective tax rate to the statutory U.S. federal tax rate is as follows:

	At December 31		
	1999	**1998**	**1997**
Statutory rate	35%	35%	35%
Foreign tax differential	(2)	(6)	(3)
State and local	1	1	1
Valuation allowance related items		(1)	
Other		1	
Effective rate	34%	30%	33%

For tax return purposes, the company has available tax credit carryforwards of approximately $1,919 million, of which $1,244 million have an indefinite carryforward period, $199 million expire in 2004 and the remainder thereafter. The company also has state and local and foreign tax loss carryforwards, the tax effect of which is $633 million. Most of these carryforwards are available for 10 years or have an indefinite carryforward period.

Q. Selling and Advertising

Selling and advertising expense is charged against income as incurred. Advertising expense, which includes media, agency, and promotional expenses, was $1,758 million, $1,681 million, and $1,708 million in 1999, 1998, and 1997, respectively.

S. Research, Development, and Engineering

Research, development, and engineering expense was $5,273 million in 1999, $5,046 million in 1998, and $4,877 million in 1997. Expenses for product-related engineering included in these amounts were $698 million, $580 million, and $570 million in 1999, 1998, and 1997, respectively.

The company had expenses of $4,575 million in 1999, $4,466 million in 1998, and $4,307 million in 1997 for basic scientific research and the application of scientific advances to the development of new and improved products and their uses. Of these amounts, software-related expenses were $2,036 million, $2,086 million, and $2,016 million in 1999, 1998, and 1997, respectively. Included in the expense each year are charges for acquired in-process research and development.

Extracts from Footnotes for 1996–2000

Retirement Plans

Cost of the Defined Benefit Plans (dollars in millions)					
	2000	**1999**	**1998**	**1997**	**1996**
Service cost	$ 1,008	$ 1,041	$ 931	$ 763	$ 96
Interest cost	3,787	3,686	3,474	3,397	3,427
Expected return on plan assets	(5,944)	(5,400)	(4,862)	(4,364)	(4,186)
Net amortization of unrecognized net actuarial gains, net transition asset, and prior service costs	(117)	(126)	(93)	(173)	(196)
Net periodic pension (benefit) cost	$(1,266)	$ (799)	$ (550)	(377)	$ (159)
Expected return on plan assets	10.0%	9.5%	9.5%	9.5%	9.25%
Discount rate for liability	7.25%	7.75%	6.5%	7.0%	7.75%

Real World Connection

See how leverage also contributed to IBM's earnings-per-share growth in Chapter 14. Exercises E6.9, E14.14, and E15.9 also cover IBM.

Part **Three**

Forecasting and Valuation Analysis

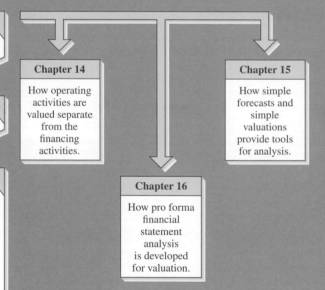

Knowing the business   1
- The products
- The knowledge base
- The competition
- The regulatory constraints
- The management

Strategy

Analyzing information   2
- In financial statements
- Outside of financial
  statements

Forecasting payoffs   3
- Specifying payoffs
- Forecasting payoffs

Converting forecasts   4
to a valuation

Trading on the valuation   5

Outside investor:
  Compare value with
  price to *buy*, *sell*, or
  hold

Inside investor:
  Compare value with
  cost to *accept* or
  reject strategy

Chapter 14

How operating
activities are
valued separate
from the
financing
activities.

Chapter 15

How simple
forecasts and
simple
valuations
provide tools
for analysis.

Chapter 16

How pro forma
financial
statement
analysis
is developed
for valuation.

Part Two of the book analyzed financial statements in preparation for forecasting. This part of the book does the forecasting that leads to a valuation of the firm, its equity, and its strategies. It covers Steps 3 and 4 of fundamental analysis.

The forecasting is developed gradually to enable you to see the building blocks clearly. And it is done with an eye to discovering simple forecasting schemes that make the task easier. Chapter 14 begins by showing that forecasting can be simplified by ignoring the financing activities if net financial obligations are measured on the balance sheet at market value. This has considerable practical advantages besides simplifying the forecasting: If financial leverage can be ignored, the analyst does not have to be concerned with continual changes in the equity cost of capital caused by changes in leverage. He need only focus on the operations and the risk of operations. And that focus leads him to evaluate price-to-book ratios and price-earnings ratios for the operations rather than for the equity.

The analyst looks for good, quick approximations before doing a lot of work. Chapter 15 lays out a scheme for making simple forecasts based only on the analysis of the operating activities in the current financial statements. These simple forecasts lead to simple valuations that usually are only approximate, although they are often a good first cut at the valuation. These simple forecasts and simple valuations are also useful analytical devices for asking "what-if" questions, employing reverse engineering schemes of Chapter 7, and prompting the analyst to find the broader information that leads to a better forecast and a sound valuation.

Chapter 16 develops a comprehensive scheme for forecasting, valuation, and strategy analysis utilizing the analyst's complete knowledge of the business. The knowledge is incorporated in a full set of pro forma financial statements for the future which can be converted to a valuation. The building blocks are laid out in the form of a template that can be incorporated in a standard spreadsheet analysis.

The financial statement analysis in Part Two of the book establishes where the firm is currently. Forecasting involves preparing pro forma financial statements to indicate where the firm will be in the future. The forecasting question is: How will the drivers of residual earnings and earnings growth differ in the future from their current levels?

Chapter **Fourteen**

The Value of Operations and the Evaluation of Enterprise Price-to-Book Ratios and Price-Earnings Ratios

LINKS

Link to previous chapter

Part Two of the book showed how to analyze the operating and financing activities of a firm and the profitability and growth they generate.

This chapter

This chapter develops valuations based on operating profitability and growth and shows how to calculate intrinsic price-to-book ratios and price-earnings ratios for operations.

Link to next chapter

Chapter 15 will develop simple forecasting and valuation methods based on the valuation models for operations in this chapter.

Link to Web page

Apply the methods of this chapter to valuing the operations of firms—visit the text Web site at **www.mhhe.com/ penman5e**.

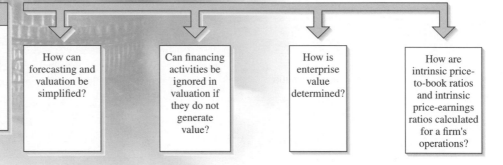

How can forecasting and valuation be simplified?

Can financing activities be ignored in valuation if they do not generate value?

How is enterprise value determined?

How are intrinsic price-to-book ratios and intrinsic price-earnings ratios calculated for a firm's operations?

The residual earnings model of Chapter 5 and the abnormal earnings growth model of Chapter 6 give us two approaches to value equities from the financial statements: price book values or price earnings. The analysis of financial statements in Part Two of the book provides an understanding of what drives residual earnings and abnormal earnings growth. We are now in a position to apply the analysis tools of Part Two to develop valuations using residual earnings and abnormal earnings growth methods.

With valuation in mind we want to forecast the aspects of the business that generate value. In Part Two of the book, we took pains to distinguish operating activities from financing activities with the understanding that it is operations that generate value. This chapter shows how this distinction is incorporated in developing forecasts for valuation. It shows that if net financial obligations are measured in the balance sheet at market value, financing activities can be ignored in forecasting. You will see that this makes forecasting easier. In particular, complications that arise from the effect of financial leverage on residual earnings, abnormal earnings growth, and the cost of capital can be ignored. You will also see that this protects you from paying too much for earnings growth, for leverage

The Analyst's Checklist

After reading this chapter you should understand:

- How, for an asset at fair market value on the balance sheet, expected residual income in the future must be zero.
- How a valuation based on forecasting residual income from operations differs from a residual earnings (RE) valuation based on forecasting full comprehensive income.
- Why forecasted residual income (or expense) on financial assets and liabilities is typically zero.
- How return on net operating assets and growth in net operating assets are the two drivers of residual operating income.
- How a valuation based on forecasting abnormal operating income growth differs from an abnormal earnings growth (AEG) valuation.
- How the required return for operations and the required return for equity are related.
- How financial leverage affects ROCE, earnings growth, and the required return for equity.
- How financial leverage affects a valuation.
- Why earnings growth that is created by leverage should not be valued.
- The effects of stock repurchases on value.
- The difference between enterprise (unlevered) price multiples and levered multiples.

After reading this chapter you should be able to:

- Calculate residual operating income.
- Calculate abnormal operating income growth.
- Value a firm using the residual operating income model and the abnormal operating income growth model.
- Identify the drivers of residual operating income.
- Use reformulated balance sheets to value the financing activities of a business.
- Analyze the effect of a change in financial leverage on the value of a firm.
- Analyze the effect of financial leverage on ROCE, earnings growth, equity cost of capital, and P/B and P/E ratios.
- Calculate a weighted-average cost of capital using market values for debt and equity.
- Calculate the cost of capital for equity from the cost of capital for operations and the cost of debt.
- Explain the difference between a levered and unlevered price-to-book ratio.
- Explain the difference between a levered an unlevered price-earnings ratio.
- Calculate an unlevered price-to-book ratio using the residual operating income model.
- Calculate an unlevered P/E ratio using the abnormal operating income growth model.
- Reconcile levered and unlevered multiples.

creates earnings growth but usually does not add value. The simplification leads to a focus on income from operations rather than bottom-line earnings, and to a focus on net operating assets rather than common equity in the balance sheet.

The focus on operations brings a focus to *enterprise* or *unlevered* price-to-book ratios and price-earnings ratios rather than the more conventional *levered* ratios. If the financial assets and liabilities are measured at market value on the balance sheet, they do not contribute to the premium over book value. Rather it is the net operating assets that determine the premium. So an (enterprise) price-to-book ratio that reflects the pricing of the net operating assets gives a better measure of the omitted value in the balance sheet and of the value that, once calculated and added to book value, gives the value of the firm. Similarly, as value generating growth comes from the operating activities, an (enterprise) price-earnings ratio that prices operating income gives a better indication of the ability of a firm to add value through earnings growth.

A MODIFICATION TO RESIDUAL EARNINGS FORECASTING: RESIDUAL OPERATING INCOME

Let's remind ourselves of the residual earnings model for valuing equity:

$$V_0^E = \text{CSE}_0 + \text{Present value of forecasted residual earnings} \quad \textbf{(14.1)}$$

$$= \text{CSE}_0 + \frac{\text{RE}_1}{\rho_E} + \frac{\text{RE}_2}{\rho_E^2} + \frac{\text{RE}_3}{\rho_E^3} + \cdots$$

where

Residual earnings (RE) = Earnings − Required earnings on book value of equity

$$\text{RE}_t = \text{Earn}_t - (\rho_E - 1)\,\text{CSE}_{t-1}$$

This RE model instructs us to anchor the valuation of equity on the book value of equity, then add value for earnings forecasted in excess of the required earnings on book value. The required rate of return is the cost of capital for equity, $\rho_E - 1$.

We understand from this model that, if an asset is forecasted to earn at its required rate of return, forecasted residual earnings will be zero and the asset will be worth its book value. Correspondingly, if the book value of an asset is equal to its intrinsic value, then the residual earnings that it is expected to yield will be zero. We can make use of these properties in valuing equities. If some assets are measured in the balance sheet at market value and if market value equals intrinsic value, then we know we don't have to forecast the residual earnings that they will produce; their forecasted residual earnings are zero. We only have to forecast residual earnings from assets not at market value. Accordingly, we can calculate the value of equity as

$$V_0^E = \text{CSE}_0 + \text{Present value of forecasted residual earnings from net assets not at fair market value}$$

To carry out this valuation we have to be able to distinguish the earnings from assets or liabilities at market value from those that are not. The income from operating assets is usually earned by using assets jointly, which makes it impossible to identify the income from the separate assets. However, we have seen that we can usually separate operating income (generated by the net operating assets) from net financial expense (generated by the net financial obligations). And, net financial obligations are typically measured on the balance sheet at close to market value.

The two components of earnings identified by the reformulation of financial statements in Part Two of the book are listed in Table 14.1 along with the balance sheet component that

TABLE 14.1
Components of Earnings and Book Value, and Corresponding Residual Earnings Measures

Earnings Component	Book Value Component	Residual Earnings Measure
Operating income (OI)	Net operating assets (NOA)	Residual operating income: $\text{OI}_t - (\rho_F - 1)\,\text{NOA}_{t-1}$
Net financial expense (NFE)	Net financial obligations (NFO)	Residual net financial expense: $\text{NFE}_t - (\rho_D - 1)\,\text{NFO}_{t-1}$
Earnings	Common stockholders' equity (CSE)	Residual earnings: $\text{Earn}_1 - (\rho_E - 1)\,\text{CSE}_{t-1}$

generates them. Beside each component is the corresponding residual earnings measure. To get the residual earnings measure, each income component is matched with the corresponding balance sheet component and charged with the required earnings rate (the cost of capital) for the component. We will discuss the cost of capital in the next section but for now recognize that the required return for the different sources of income depends on the riskiness of that activity. Note that ρ_D is 1 plus the cost of capital for net debt (or, as it may be, the required return on net financial assets), and ρ_F is 1 plus the cost of capital for operating activities. In all cases the residual earnings is earnings in excess of the earnings (or expense) required for the asset (or liability) in the balance sheet to be earning at the relevant cost of capital.

Residual earnings from net operating assets is *residual operating income,* and we will refer to it as ReOI:

$$\text{Residual operating income} = \text{Operating income (after tax)}$$
$$- \text{Required income on net operating assets}$$
$$\text{ReOI}_t = \text{OI}_t - (\rho_F - 1)\text{NOA}_{t-1}$$

Residual operating income charges the operating income with a charge for using the net operating assets. Residual operating income is also referred to as "economic profit" or "economic value added," and some consulting firms have taken these terms as trademarks for their valuation products. For Nike, with after-tax operating income of $1,814 million in 2010 and net operating assets at the beginning of the year of $6,346 million, the residual operating income for 2010 was $\text{ReOI}_{2010} = 1,814 - (0.091 \times 6,346) = \$1,236.5$ million for a required return of 9.1 percent.

Similarly, residual earnings from the net financial obligations is *residual net financial expense* $= \text{NFE}_t - (\rho_D - 1)\text{NFO}_{t-1}$, or, if the firm has net financial assets, *residual net financial income.* Thus residual net financial expense is net financial expense less the required cost of the net debt.

With forecasts of ReOI and residual net financial expense, we can value the NOA and NFO. But if the NFO are measured at market value, it must be that forecasted residual net financial expenses are zero: For $100 million of debt at an interest rate of 5 percent, interest expense is $5 million and residual net financial expense $= \$5 - (0.05 \times 100) = 0$. Thus, the value of the net financial obligations, $V_0^{\text{NFO}} = \text{NFO}$; the book value of the net financial obligations is their value.

The *value of the net operating assets, V_0^{NOA},* is

$$\text{Value of operations} = \text{Net operating assets} + \text{Present value of expected residual}$$
$$\text{operating income}$$

$$V_0^{\text{NOA}} = \text{NOA}_0 + \frac{\text{ReOI}_1}{\rho_F} + \frac{\text{ReOI}_2}{\rho_F^2} + \frac{\text{ReOI}_3}{\rho_F^3} + \cdots \qquad \textbf{(14.2)}$$
$$+ \frac{\text{ReOI}_T}{\rho_F^T} + \frac{\text{CV}_T}{\rho_F^T}$$

That is, the value is the book value of the NOA, plus the present value of expected residual operating income from these assets to a forecast horizon, plus a continuing value that is the value of expected residual operating income after the horizon. This model is the same form as the residual earnings model 14.1 but applies to the net operating assets instead of the common shareholders' equity.

Corresponding to the three cases for the residual earnings model in Chapter 5, the continuing value for the residual operating income model can take three forms:

$$\text{Case 1:} \qquad CV_T = 0$$

$$\text{Case 2:} \qquad CV_T = \frac{\text{ReOI}_{T+1}}{\rho_F - 1}$$

$$\text{Case 3:} \qquad CV_T = \frac{\text{ReOI}_{T+1}}{\rho_F - g}$$

In Case 1 we expect residual operating income (ReOI) to be zero after the forecast horizon because we expect the net operating assets to earn at the cost of capital. In Case 2 we expect ReOI to be at a constant, permanent level, and in Case 3 we expect ReOI to grow perpetually at the rate g. The analyst's task, then, is to forecast the level and growth of residual operating income at the forecast horizon.

The value of the operations is also called the *value of the firm*. It is also sometimes referred to as **enterprise value.** The value of the equity is $V_0^E = V_0^{\text{NOA}} - V_0^{\text{NFO}}$. So if the NFO are measured at market value on the balance sheet—that is, expected residual net financial expenses are zero—then (recognizing that NOA – NFO = CSE) the value of the equity is

Value of common equity = Book value of common equity   **(14.3)**
          + Present value of expected residual
           operating income

$$V_0^E = CSE_0 + \frac{\text{ReOI}_1}{\rho_F} + \frac{\text{ReOI}_2}{\rho_F^2} + \frac{\text{ReOI}_3}{\rho_F^3} + \cdots + \frac{\text{ReOI}_T}{\rho_F^T} + \frac{CV_T}{\rho_F^T}$$

This model is the *residual operating income model.*

Table 14.2 values Nike using the model. The forecasts are for operating income and net operating assets, not total earnings and common shareholders' equity; the financing components of the income statement and the balance sheet are ignored. The forecasts imply the return on net operating assets (RNOA) numbers indicated, with declining profitability up to 2014, as is common. Residual operating income, calculated as described at the bottom of the table, is forecasted to grow after 2014 at the 4 percent average GDP growth rate. With the continuing value implied by this growth rate, the value of the operations at the end of 2010—the enterprise value—is $32,273 million and the value of the equity (that includes Nike's 2010 net financial assets) is $36,644 million, or $75.71 per share. Nike's shares traded at $74 at the time, so one could view the pro forma here as one that is (approximately) consistent with the forecasts implied by the market price. We might then ask whether this pro forma (that justifies the current market price) is a reasonable one. If, through analysis, we forecasted higher residual operating income in the future, we would conclude that Nike is underpriced, given we accepted the 9.1 percent required return as reasonable.

The residual operating income model makes sense. If debt and financial assets are zero residual earnings producers, then they add no value to their recorded value. We are going to get the valuation by forecasting the profitability of the operations that do add value. The model makes the forecasting task easier, too. It requires us to forecast operating income and net operating assets but we can forget about forecasting net financial expenses and net financial obligations. Of course if financial items are not measured at market value,

TABLE 14.2 **Residual Operating Income Valuation for Nike, Inc.**
Required return for operations is 9.1 percent. (Amounts in millions of dollars except per-share numbers)

	2010A	2011E	2012E	2013E	2014E
Operating income (OI)		1,950	2,042	2,102	2,146
Net operating assets (NOA)	5,514	6,287	6,549	6,814	7,089
RNOA (%)		35.4%	32.5%	32.1%	31.5%
Residual operating income (ReOI)		1,448	1,470	1,506	1,526
Discount rate (1.091^t)		1.091	1.190	1.299	1.417
PV of ReOI		1,327	1,235	1,159	1,077
Total PV of ReOI	4,798				
Continuing value (CV)					31,118
PV of CV	21,961				
Enterprise value	32,273				
Book value of net financial assets	4,371				
Value of common equity	36,644				
Value per share (on 484 million shares)	$ 75.71				

The continuing value calculation:

$$CV = \frac{1,526 \times 1.04}{1.091 - 1.04} = 31,118$$

$$PV\,of\,CV = \frac{31,118}{1.417} = 21,961$$

Residual operating income (ReOI) is $OI_t - (\rho_F - 1)NOA_{t-1}$. So, for 2012,
ReOI $= 2,042 - (0.091 \times 6,287) = 1,470$

Allow for rounding errors.

the RE model in equation 14.1 must be used. But if the market value of these items is available, we can substitute the market value for the book value and proceed with ReOI valuation. Fair values of many financial items can be found in statement footnotes. (In any case, book value is usually a reasonable approximation to market value.) If the financial reporting is such that operating and financing activities cannot be separated, the RE model must be used.

Remember that for financial institutions, apparent interest-bearing financial assets and liabilities are really operating assets and liabilities. These firms make profits from financial assets and liabilities. The market value of these assets and liabilities might reflect their value generally, but they might not reflect the value in use to a particular firm. The analyst must explore how the firm makes money from financial items and forecast the residual operating income from them.

A final caveat: The market value of assets and liabilities on the balance sheet can be taken as their fair value only if the market value is an efficient one. See Box 14.1.

The Drivers of Residual Operating Income

We saw in Chapter 5 that residual earnings can be broken down into two components:

Residual earnings = (ROCE − Required return for equity) × Common equity

$$RE_t = [ROCE_t - (\rho_E - 1)]\,CSE_{t-1}$$

$$\quad\quad\quad\quad\quad (1) \quad\quad\quad\quad\quad\quad (2)$$

Equity investments that involve less than 20 percent ownership and are "available for sale" are carried on the balance sheet at market value. Market values are also given in the footnotes for "held-to-maturity" equity investments that are carried at cost on the balance sheet.

Microsoft Corporation held the following equity investments on its 1999 balance sheet:

Equity Securities (in millions of dollars)	Cost	Gains Recognized	Market Value
At market value on the balance sheet			
Comcast Corporation— common stock	$ 500	$1,394	$ 1,894
MCI WorldCom, Inc.— common stock	14	1,088	1,102
Other	849	1,102	1,951
Unrealized hedge loss		(785)	(785)
At cost on the balance sheet	3,845	—	6,100
	$5,208		$10,262

The analyst might accept the market values of these equity investments as their values, considerably simplifying the valuation.

But what if these securities were mispriced in the market? In 1999, the investments were in "hot" technology and telecommunications stocks during a bubble. Might not the shares of technology companies be overpriced? Basing Microsoft's intrinsic value on the market price of these stocks could result in an overvaluation: One would be incorporating bubble prices in the valuation. Indeed, Microsoft recorded subsequent losses on its investment portfolio of $1,743 million as the technology bubble burst, reversing the gains in 1999. Intel Corp., having recognized an unrealized gain of $3.188 billion on marking its technology investments to market value in 1999, followed up by recognizing a loss on those same investments of $3.596 billion in 2000. Cisco Systems booked a gain of $3.240 billion followed by a loss of $3.812 billion.

These considerations require the analyst to investigate the value behind the market values of equities. Just as the analyst queries the market price of Microsoft through fundamental analysis, he also queries the price of Microsoft's equity investments through fundamental analysis of those investments.

Mark-to-market accounting brings prices into the financial statements. The fundamentalist's alarm sounds again: *when doing an analysis to challenge price, beware of putting price into the calculation*. Marking mortgage loans to market during the real estate bubble of 2005–2007 put hot air into the balance sheets of banks, thus booking assets that vaporized in the subsequent financial crisis.

We referred to the two components, ROCE and book value, as residual earnings drivers: RE is driven by the amount of shareholders' investment and the rate of return on this investment relative to the cost of equity capital. Residual operating income can similarly be broken down into two components:

$$\text{Residual operating income} = (\text{RNOA} - \text{Required return for operations}) \times \text{Net operating assets}$$

$$\text{ReOI}_t = [\text{RNOA}_t - (\rho_F - 1)]\, \text{NOA}_{t-1}$$

$$(1) \qquad\qquad (2)$$

The two components of ReOI are RNOA and net operating assets, and we refer to these as *residual operating income drivers:* ReOI is driven by the amount of net operating assets put in place and the profitability of those assets relative to the cost of capital.

Value is added to book value through the operations, and our breakdown tells us that this is done by earning an RNOA that is greater than the cost of capital for operations and by putting investments in place to earn at this rate. The combination produces growth in residual operating income. Accordingly, forecasting and valuation involve forecasting the two drivers, future RNOA and future NOA. We will see how these forecasts are developed in the next two chapters.

A MODIFICATION TO ABNORMAL EARNINGS GROWTH FORECASTING: ABNORMAL GROWTH IN OPERATING INCOME

Let us remind ourselves of the abnormal earnings growth model for valuing equity:

$$V_0^E = \text{Capitalized [Forward earnings + Present value of abnormal earnings growth]}$$

$$= \frac{1}{\rho_E - 1}\left[\text{Earn}_1 + \frac{\text{AEG}_2}{\rho_E} + \frac{\text{AEG}_3}{\rho_E^2} + \frac{\text{AEG}_4}{\rho_E^3} + \cdots\right] \qquad \textbf{(14.4)}$$

where

$$\text{Abnormal earnings growth}_t \text{ (AEG)} = \text{Cum-dividend earnings}_t - \text{Normal earnings}_t$$

$$= [\text{Earnings}_t + (\rho_E - 1)\text{d}_{t-1}] - \rho_E\text{Earnings}_{t-1}$$

$$= [G_t - \rho_E] \times \text{Earnings}_{t-1}$$

where G_t is the cum-dividend earnings growth rate for the period. The AEG model instructs us to forecast forward (one-year ahead) earnings, then add value for subsequent cum-dividend earnings forecasted in excess of earnings growing at the required rate of return for equity. We understand from this model that earnings growth in itself does not add value, only abnormal growth over the required growth. If abnormal earnings growth is expected to be zero, the equity will be worth just the capitalized value of its forward earnings.

Consider now where abnormal growth comes from. It does not come from financing activities. Debt is always expected to earn (or incur expenses) at the required return on the debt so, residual income from the financing activities is expected to be zero. So the change in residual income, period-to-period, is also expected to be zero, and abnormal earnings growth is always equal to the change in residual income.

Abnormal earnings growth is generated by operations. This makes sense for, once again, it is the operations that add value. As the financing activities do not contribute to growth over the required return, we focus on abnormal growth in operating income.

Abnormal Growth in Operating Income and the "Dividend" from Operating Activities

When introducing earnings growth in Chapter 6, we recognized that growth in (ex-dividend) earnings—the growth that analysts typically forecast—is not the growth that we should focus on. Earnings growth rates will be lower the more dividends are paid, but dividends can be reinvested to earn more, adding to growth. So any analysis of growth must focus on cum-dividend earnings growth. In focusing on growth in the operating income component of earnings, we also must not make the mistake of focusing on growth in operating income if cash that otherwise could be reinvested in operations is paid out of the operations. Dividends are net cash payments to shareholders out of earnings (that they can reinvest). What is the cash paid out of operations (that can be reinvested elsewhere)? What are the "dividends" from the operating activities?

Our depiction of business activities in Chapter 8 supplies the answer to this question. Look at Figure 8.3, which summarizes business activities, and Figure 8.4, which summarizes how those activities are represented in reformulated financial statements. Net dividends, *d*, are the dividends from the financing activities to the shareholders. Net payments to bondholders and debt issuers, *F*, are the "dividends" from the financing activities to these claimants. But the "dividend" from the operating activities to the financing activities is the free cash flow. Business works as follows: Operations pay a dividend to the financing activities—in the form of free cash flow—and the financing activities apply this cash to pay dividends to the outside claimants. Indeed, the reformulated cash flow statement is a statement that reports the cash dividend from the operating activities (free cash flow) and how that dividend is divided among cash to debtholders and cash to shareholders in the financing activities: $C - I = d + F$.

Accordingly, *abnormal operating income growth* is calculated as

Abnormal operating income growth$_t$ (AOIG)

$$= \text{Cum-dividend operating income}_t - \text{Normal operating income}_t$$
$$= [\text{Operating income}_t + (\rho_F - 1)\text{FCF}_{t-1}] - \rho_F \text{Operating income}_{t-1}$$

where free cash flow (FCF) is, of course, cash from operations minus cash investment $(C - I)$. Compare this measure to abnormal earnings growth (AEG) above. Operating income is substituted for earnings, and free cash flow is substituted for dividends. And, as the income is from operations, the required return that defines normal growth is the required return for operations. A firm delivers abnormal operating income growth if growth in operating income—cum-dividend, after reinvesting free cash flow—is greater than the normal growth rate required for operations. Note that just as AEG equals the change in residual earnings, so AOIG equals the change in ReOI.

Just as AEG can be expressed in terms of cum-dividend growth rates relative to the required rate, so can abnormal operating income growth:

$$\text{Abnormal operating income growth}_t \text{ (AOIG)} = [G_t - \rho_F] \times \text{Operating income}_{t-1}$$

where G_t is now the cum-dividend operating income growth rate.

Table 14.3 lays out the abnormal earnings growth measures that correspond to the operating and financing components of earnings, in a similar way to the residual earnings breakdown in Table 14.1. A calculation for abnormal growth in net financial expense is included there, for completeness, but (like residual net financing expense) it is not a measure we will make use of because it is expected to be zero. (Note, for completeness, that the "dividend" for debt financing is the cash payment to debtholders, F.)

With an understanding of abnormal growth in operating income, we can lay out an *abnormal operating income growth model* to value the operations and the equity. Forecasting abnormal operating income growth yields the value of the operations, just as forecasting residual operating income yields the value of the operations. So,

TABLE 14.3
Earnings Components and Corresponding Abnormal Earnings Growth Measures

Earnings Component	Abnormal Earnings Growth Measure
Operating income (OI)	Abnormal operating income growth: $[\text{OI}_t + (\rho_F - 1)\text{FCF}_{t-1}] - \rho_F\text{OI}_{t-1}$ $[G_t - \rho_F] \times \text{OI}_{t-1}$
Net financing expense (NFE)	Abnormal net financial expense growth: $[\text{NFE}_t + (\rho_D - 1)F_{t-1}] - \rho_D\text{NFE}_{t-1}$
Earnings	Abnormal earnings growth: $[\text{Earn}_t + (\rho_E - 1)d_{t-1}] - \rho_E\text{Earn}_{t-1}$ $[G_t^E - \rho_E] \times \text{Earn}_{t-1}$

Value of net operating assets = Capitalized [Forward operating income   **(14.5)**
                                + Present value of abnormal operating
                                income growth]

$$V_0^{NOA} = \frac{1}{\rho_F - 1}\left[OI_1 + \frac{AOIG_2}{\rho_F} + \frac{AOIG_3}{\rho_F^2} + \frac{AOIG_4}{\rho_F^3} + \cdots\right]$$

The value of the equity subtracts the net financial obligations. You see that this is the same form as the AEG model (equation 14.4) except that operating income is substituted for earnings, and the cost of capital for the operations is substituted for the equity cost of capital. Like the ReOI model, this AOIG model simplifies the valuation task, for we need only forecast operating income and can ignore the financing aspects of future earnings. As the model values the enterprise or the firm before deducting the net financial obligations, the model (like the ReOI model) is referred to as an *enterprise valuation model* or a *valuation model for the firm*.

Table 14.4 applies the model to valuing Nike, as in Table 14.2. The layout is the same as that for the abnormal earnings growth valuations in Chapter 6. As with the ReOI model, operating income and net operating assets are forecasted, but the net operating asset forecasts are then applied to forecast free cash flows: $C - I = OI - \Delta NOA$, as in the Method 1 calculation in Chapter 11. Free cash flow does not have to be forecasted in addition to the other forecasts—it is calculated directly from those forecasts. Expected abnormal operating income growth is calculated from forecasts of operating income and free cash flow, as described at the bottom of the table, and those forecasts are converted to a valuation as prescribed by the model. Note that AOIG is equal to the change in ReOI in each period (in Table 14.2). The valuation is, of course, the same as that obtained using ReOI methods.

Eye on the Future: Sustainable Income

With valuation in mind, we are interested in residual operating income and abnormal operating income growth in the future. The number that projects into the future is core (sustainable) operating income:

$$\text{Core ReOI}_t = \text{Core OI}_t - (\rho_F - 1)\text{NOA}_{t-1}$$

Core operating income excludes all unusual, transitory items discovered in the reformulated income statement (and, of course, is after tax). Core operating income in Nike's 2010 statement is $1,910.7 million. So Nike's **core residual operating income** for 2010 was $1,910.7 - (0.091 \times 6,346) = $1,333.2 million. Core RNOA, identified in the last chapter, drives core residual operating income. This is the base for forecasting: Can Nike grow core residual operating income?

THE COST OF CAPITAL AND VALUATION

Valuation combines forecasts with the cost of capital to get a present value. The preceding models show how this is done, but now we have encountered three costs of capital: the cost of capital for equity, ρ_E; the cost of capital for debt, ρ_D; and the cost of capital for operations, ρ_F. These need a little explanation. Why do they differ? They are calculated

TABLE 14.4 **Abnormal Operating Income Growth Valuation for Nike, Inc.**
Required return for operations is 9.1 percent. (Amounts in millions of dollars except per-share number)

	2010A	2011E	2012E	2013E	2014E
Operating income (OI)		1,950	2,042	2,102	2,146
Net operating assets (NOA)	5,514	6,287	6,549	6,814	7,089
Free cash flow (C − I = OI − ΔNOA)		1,777	1,780	1,837	1,871
Income from reinvested free cash flow (at 9.1%)			107.1	162.0	167.2
Cum-dividend OI			2,149.1	2,264.0	2,313.2
Normal OI			2,127.5	2,227.8	2,293.3
Abnormal OI growth (AOIG)			21.6	36.2	19.9
Discount rate			1.091	1.190	1.299
PV of AOIG			19.8	30.4	15.3
Total PV of AOIG		65.5			
Continuing value (CV)					1,197
PV of continuing value		921.4			
Forward OI for 2011		1,950.0			
		2,936.9			
Capitalization rate		0.091			
Enterprise value	32,273				
Book value of net financial assets	4,371				
Value of common equity	36,644				
Value per share (on 484 million shares)	$ 75.71				
Cum-dividend growth rate in OI			10.2%	10.9%	10.0%

The continuing value calculation:

$$CV = \frac{61.0}{1.091 - 1.04} = 1,196.9$$

$$PV\,of\,CV = \frac{1,196.9}{1.299} = 921.4$$

The forecast of 2015 AOIG of 61.0 for the continuing value calculation is 2014 residual operating income of $1,526 growing at the 4% GDP growth rate (to be consistent with the ReOI valuation in Table 14.2).

Income from reinvested free cash flow is the prior year's free cash flow earning at the required return of 9.1%. So, for 2012, income from reinvested free cash flow is 0.091 × 1,177 = 107.1.

Cum-dividend OI is operating income plus income from reinvesting free cash flow. So, for 2012, cum-dividend OI is 2,042 + 107.1 = 2,149.1.

Normal OI is the prior year's operating income growing at the required return. So, for 2012, normal OI is 1,950 × 1.091 = 2,127.5.

Abnormal OI growth (AOIG) is cum-dividend OI minus normal OI. So, for 2012, AOIG is 2,149.1 − 2,127.5 = 21.6. AOIG is also given by $OI_{t-1} \times (G_t - \rho_F)$. So, for 2012, AOIG is (1.102 − 1.091) × 1,950 = 21.6.

Allow for rounding errors.

using the beta technologies discussed in the appendix to Chapter 3 (and in corporate finance texts). The issue here is how the fundamental analyst handles them. But first let's make sure we understand the concepts.

The Cost of Capital for Operations

Residual earnings is earnings for the equity holders and so is calculated and discounted using the cost of capital for equity, ρ_E. Residual operating income is earnings for the operations and so is calculated and discounted using a cost of capital for the operations, ρ_F. Payoffs must be discounted at a rate that reflects their risk, and the risk for the operations may be different from the risk for equity. The risk in the operations is referred to as *operational risk, firm risk,* or *enterprise risk.* Operational risk arises from factors that may hurt operating profits. The sensitivity of sales and operating expenses to recessions and other shocks determines the operating risk. Airlines have relatively high operating risk because people fly less during recessions, and fuel costs are subject to shocks in oil prices. The required return that compensates for this risk is called the *cost of capital for operations* or the *cost of capital for the firm.* This is what we have labeled ρ_F (where F is for "firm").

If you have taken a corporate finance class, you are familiar with this concept. The cost of capital for operations is sometimes referred to as the *weighted-average cost of capital,* or *WACC,* because of the following relationship:

$$\text{Cost of capital for operations} = \text{Weighted-average of cost of equity} \qquad \textbf{(14.6)}$$
$$\text{and cost of net debt}$$

$$= \left(\frac{\text{Value of equity}}{\text{Value of operations}} \times \text{Equity cost of capital} \right)$$

$$+ \left(\frac{\text{Value of debt}}{\text{Value of operations}} \times \text{Debt cost of capital} \right)$$

$$\rho_F = \frac{V_0^E}{V_0^{\text{NOA}}} \cdot \rho_E + \frac{V_0^D}{V_0^{\text{NOA}}} \cdot \rho_D$$

That is, the required return to invest in operations is a weighted average of the required return of the shareholders and the cost of net financial debt, and the weights are given by the relative values of the equity and debt in the value of the firm. See Box 14.2 for examples of the calculation.

The Cost of Capital for Debt

The cost of capital for debt is a weighted average of all components of net financial obligations, including preferred stock and financial assets. It is typically referred to as the cost of capital for debt but is better thought of as the cost of capital for all net financial obligations.

In Chapter 10 we allocated income taxes to operating and financing components of the income statement to restate net financial expenses on an after-tax basis. So too must the cost of net debt be calculated on an after-tax basis. The calculation is

$$\text{After-tax cost of net debt } (\rho_D) = \text{Nominal cost of net debt} \times (1 - t)$$

where t is the marginal income tax rate we used in Chapter 10. IBM (in Box 14.2) indicates in its financial statement footnotes that its average borrowing rate for debt in 2010 was about 4.8 percent per year. With a tax rate of 36 percent, this is an after-tax rate of 3.1 percent. The after-tax cost of debt is sometimes referred to as the **effective cost of debt,** just like NFE is the effective financial expense, because what the firm effectively pays in interest is not the

The cost of capital for operations (also referred to as the cost of capital for the firm) is calculated as the weighted average of the cost of capital for equity and the (after-tax) cost of capital for the net debt (the net financial obligations). Accordingly, it is often called the *weighted-average cost of capital (WACC)*. The calculation is done in two steps:

1. Apply an asset pricing model such as the capital asset pricing model (CAPM) to estimate the equity cost of capital. For the CAPM, the inputs are the risk-free rate, the firm's equity beta, and the market risk premium. See the appendix to Chapter 3.

2. Apply the WACC formula 14.6 to convert the equity cost of capital to the cost of capital for the operations. The weights are determined, in principle, by the (intrinsic) value of the operations and the value of the net financial obligations. As the value of the equity is unknown, the market value of the equity is typically used. The book value of the net financial obligations approximates their value.

Here are the calculations for four firms, IBM, Dell, Nike, and General Mills for 2010 when the 10-year Treasury rate was 3.6 percent and the market risk premium was deemed to be 5 percent. Equity beta estimates are those supplied by beta services. The cost of capital for debt is itself a weighted average of the interest rates on the various components of net debt and is ascertained from the debt footnote and the yield on financial assets. The rates for Dell and Nike are yields on their net financial assets. The market value of operations is the market value of equity plus the book value of the net financial obligations. (Market values are in millions of dollars.)

	Nike	General Mills	Dell	IBM
Equity beta	0.9	0.4	1.4	0.7
Equity cost of capital	8.1%	5.6%	10.6%	7.1%
Cost of capital for debt (after tax)	1.2%	3.3%	1.0%	3.1%
Market value of equity	35,816	23,634	30,688	193,600
Net financial obligations	(4,371)	5,813	(9,032)	17,973
Market value of operations	31,445	29,447	21,656	211,573
Cost of capital for operations	9.1%	5.1%	14.6%	6.8%

For General Mills and IBM, with net financial obligations, the cost of capital for operations is less than that for equity, while for Nike and Dell, with net financial assets, the cost of capital for operations is greater than that for equity. For a given level of operating risk, holding (low-risk) financial assets makes the equity cost of capital lower than if the firm borrows.

The WACC calculation for General Mills:

$$\left(\frac{23,634}{29,447} \times 5.6\% \right) + \left(\frac{5,813}{29,447} \times 3.3\% \right) = 5.1\%$$

The WACC calculation for Nike enters the net financial assets as negative debt:

$$\left(\frac{35,816}{31,445} \times 8.1\% \right) + \left(\frac{-4,371}{31,445} \times 1.2\% \right) = 9.1\%$$

The calculation comes with a warning. See Box 14.3.

nominal amount but that amount less the taxes saved. So when we use ρ_D to indicate the cost of debt, always remember that this is the effective cost of capital for net financial obligations.

Operating Risk, Financing Risk, and the Cost of Equity Capital

The calculation of the WACC in equation 14.6 is a bit misleading because it looks as if the cost of capital for operations is determined by the costs of debt and equity. However, the operations have their inherent risk, and this depends on the riskiness of the business, not on how the business is financed. Thus a standard notion in finance—another Modigliani and Miller concept—states that the cost of capital for the firm is unaffected by the amount of debt or equity in the financing of the operational assets. Rather than the required return for operations being determined by the cost of capital for equity and debt, the return that equity and debt investors require is determined by the riskiness of the operations. The operations have their inherent risk, and this is imposed on the equity holders and the debtholders. The way to think about it is to see the cost of equity determined by the following formula. This

A basic tenet of fundamental analysis (introduced in Chapter 1) dictates that the analyst should always be careful to distinguish what she knows from speculation about what she doesn't know. Fundamental analysis is done to challenge speculative stock prices, so it must avoid incorporating speculation in any calculation. Unfortunately, standard cost-of-capital measures are speculative, so they must be handled with care. The appendix to Chapter 3 explained that, despite the elegant asset pricing models at hand, we really do not have a sound method to estimate the cost of capital.

SPECULATION ABOUT THE EQUITY RISK PREMIUM

Cost of capital measures that use the capital asset pricing model—like those in Box 14.2—require an estimate of the market risk premium. We used 5 percent, but estimates range, in texts and academic research, from 3.0 percent to 9.2 percent. With such a range, Dell's equity cost of capital (with a beta of 1.4) would range from 7.8 percent to 16.5 percent.

The truth is that the market risk premium is a guess; it is a speculative number. Add to this the uncertainty as to what the actual beta is, and we have a highly speculative number for the cost of capital. Building this speculative number into a valuation results in a speculative valuation.

USING SPECULATIVE PRICES IN WEIGHTED-AVERAGE COST OF CAPITAL CALCULATIONS

We have warned against incorporating (possibly speculative) stock prices in a valuation. Thus, we warned of speculative pension fund gains in earnings in Chapter 13 and, in this chapter in Box 14.1, we warned about relying on (possibly speculative) equity prices on the balance sheet, and mark-to-market mortgages for banks.

The WACC calculation in equation 14.6 weights equity and debt costs of capital by their respective (intrinsic) values. The standard practice is to use market values instead of intrinsic values in the weighting, as in the calculations in Box 14.2. This is done under the assumption that market prices are efficient. But we carry out fundamental valuations to question whether market prices are indeed efficient. If we build speculative prices into our calculation, we compromise our ability to challenge those prices.

Indeed, you can see that the WACC calculation is circular: We wish to estimate the cost of capital in order to estimate equity value, but the estimate requires that we know the equity value! We need methods to break this circularity—without reference to speculative market prices. We return to this problem in Chapter 19.

is just a rearrangement of the WACC calculation (equation 14.6), putting the equity cost of capital on the left-hand side rather than the cost of capital for operations:

Required return for equity = Required return for operations   **(14.7)**
+ (Market leverage × Required return spread)

$$\rho_E = \rho_F + \frac{V_0^D}{V_0^E}(\rho_F - \rho_D)$$

     (1)   (2)

For IBM (in Box 14.2), the cost of equity capital is 6.8% + [17,973/193,600 × (6.8% − 3.1%)] = 7.1%. Just as the payoff to shareholders has two components, operating and financing, the required return to investing for those payoffs has two components, **operating risk** and **financing risk** components. Component **1** is the risk the operations impose on the shareholder, and the return this requires is the cost of capital for the operations. If the firm has no net debt, the cost of equity capital is equal to the cost of capital for the operations, that is, $\rho_E = \rho_F$. If IBM had no net debt, the shareholders would require a return of 6.8 percent, according to the CAPM calculation. This is sometimes referred to as the case of the **pure equity firm.** But if there are financing activities, component **2** comes into play; this is the additional required return for equity due to financing risk. As you can see, this premium for financing risk depends on the amount of debt relative to equity (the financial leverage) and the spread between the cost of capital for operations and that for debt. This makes sense. Financing risk arises because of leverage and the possibility of that leverage turning unfavorable. Leverage is unfavorable when the return from operations is less than the cost of debt, so the equity is more risky the more debt there is and the riskier the operations are relative to the cost of debt. In Box 14.2, the CAPM required return for operations is lower for IBM than for Dell. But the equity investors require a higher financing premium for IBM than for Dell because of IBM's higher leverage. So the financing risk premium is 0.3 percent for IBM (7.1% − 6.8%) and a negative 4.0 percent for Dell (10.6% − 14.6%) because Dell has negative leverage.

The leverage here is measured with the values of the debt and equity; it is referred to as **market leverage** to distinguish it from the **book leverage** (FLEV) discussed in Chapter 12.

How much are we willing to trust these calculations? Box 14.3 provides a warning about using cost of capital estimates in fundamental analysis. We have to finesse this problem and will do so when we go active again in Chapter 19. But you have the idea from Chapter 7: Focus on the expected return from buying at the current market price rather than a speculative "cost of capital."

FINANCING RISK AND RETURN AND THE VALUATION OF EQUITY

Leverage and Residual Earnings Valuation

You will have noticed that the expression for the required return for equity in equation 14.7 has a similar form to the expression for the drivers of ROCE in Chapter 12. Both formulas are given below, so you can compare them:

$$\text{Return on common equity} = \text{Return on net operating assets} \\ + (\text{Book leverage} \times \text{Operating spread})$$

$$\text{ROCE} = \text{RNOA} + \left[\frac{\text{NFO}}{\text{CSE}} \times (\text{RNOA} - \text{NBC}) \right]$$

$$\text{Required return for equity} = \text{Required return for operations} \\ + (\text{Market leverage} \times \text{Required return spread})$$

$$\rho_E = \rho_F + \frac{V_0^D}{V_0^F} (\rho_F - \rho_D)$$

The equity return in both cases is driven by the return on operating activities plus a premium for financing activities, where the latter is given by the financial leverage and the spread. The only difference is that the second equation refers to required returns rather than accounting returns and the leverage is market leverage rather than book leverage.

The comparison is insightful. Leverage increases the ROCE (and thus residual earnings) if the spread is positive, as we saw in Chapter 12. This is the "good news" aspect of leverage. But at the same time, leverage increases the required return to equity because of the increased risk of getting a lower ROCE if the spread turns negative. This is the "bad news" aspect of leverage. "More risk, more return" is an old adage that you can see at work here. And you can see it at work in the RE valuation model: Equity value is based on forecasted RE and the rate at which RE is discounted to present value. The ROCE drives residual earnings. Given a positive spread between RNOA and the net borrowing cost, leverage will yield a higher ROCE and thus a higher RE. This is the good news effect on the present value. But at the same time the discount rate will increase to reflect the increased financing risk. This is the bad news effect on the present value. What is the net effect on the calculated value?

A standard notion in finance is that the two leverage effects are exactly offsetting, so leverage has no effect on the value of the equity. This is demonstrated in Table 14.5. The first valuation (A) values the equity from an operating income forecast of $135 million for all years in the future on a constant level of net operating assets. The perpetual forecasted ReOI of $18 million is capitalized at the cost of capital for operations of 9 percent to get a valuation (on 600 million shares) of $2.00 per share. The table then gives the valuation (B) for the equity using the RE model. The RE is calculated and capitalized using the equity cost of capital of 10 percent rather than the cost of capital for operations of 9 percent, but the valuation remains the same. Free cash flow after interest payments is paid out in dividends so, to keep it simple, there is no change in leverage forecasted from using free cash flow to buy down debt. But the final valuation (C) does have a leverage change. It is an RE valuation for the same firm recapitalized with a debt-for-equity swap. Two hundred shares were tendered in the swap at their value of $2.00 per share, reducing equity by $400 million and increasing debt by $400 million (leaving the net operating assets unchanged). The resulting leverage change increases the required return that shareholders demand from 10 percent to 12.5 percent, as indicated, to compensate them for the additional financing risk. It also increases ROCE from 12 percent to 16.7 percent, and residual earnings from $20 million to $25 million. But it does not change the per-share valuation of the equity.

In Chapter 13 (Box 13.8) we saw that Reebok's change in residual earnings and ROCE in 1996 was driven largely by a large change in financial leverage. Now look at Box 14.4. It analyzes the effect of Reebok's large stock repurchase on the value of the firm and its equity. You'll notice the large increase in ROCE that resulted from the big change in leverage in this transaction. Firms can increase ROCE with leverage. But the increased ROCE has no effect on the value of the firm.

The equivalence of valuations A, B, and C in Table 14.5 demonstrates that we can use either RE or ReOI forecasting to value equity. But the RE valuation is more complicated. The examples were constructed with just one leverage change. In reality, forecasted leverage will change every period as earnings, dividends, debt issues, and maturities change the equity and debt. So we have to adjust the discount rate every period. This tedious process requires more work, but there will be no effect on the value calculated. If, however, we apply residual operating income valuation, we remove all need to deal with financing activities. The operating income approach is a more efficient way of doing the calculation. It not only recognizes that expected residual earnings from net financing assets are zero but also recognizes that changes in RE and the equity cost of capital that are due to leverage are not a consideration in valuation. Accordingly, the non–value generating financing activities are ignored and we can concentrate on the source of value creation, the operating activities.

Leverage and Abnormal Earnings Growth Valuation

You will notice that, as financial leverage increased with Reebok's stock repurchase, forecasted earnings per share also increased—from $2.30 without the repurchase to $2.56 after the repurchase. Just as financial leverage increases ROCE (provided the spread is positive), financial leverage also increases earnings per share. An increase in leverage along with a stock repurchase increases earnings per share even more. With abnormal earnings growth

TABLE 14.5
Leverage Effects on
the Value of Equity:
Residual Earnings
Valuation

	0	1	2	3
A. ReOI Valuation of a Firm with 9% Cost of Capital for Operations and 5% After-Tax Cost of Debt				
Net operating assets	1,300	1,300	1,300	1,300→
Net financial obligations	300	300	300	300→
Common shareholders' equity	1,000	1,000	1,000	1,000→
Operating income		135	135	135→
Net financial expense (300 × 0.05)		15	15	15→
Earnings		120	120	120→
Residual operating income, ReOI [135 − (0.09 × 1,300)]		18	18	18→
PV of ReOI (18/0.09)	200			
Value of common equity	1,200			
Value per share (on 600 shares)	2.00			

$$P/B = \frac{1,200}{1,000} = 1.2$$

	0	1	2	3
B. RE Valuation of the Same Firm: Cost of Equity Capital = 9.0% + [300/1,200 × (9.0% − 5.0%)] = 10.0%				
Net operating assets	1,300	1,300	1,300	1,300→
Net financial obligations	300	300	300	300
Common shareholders' equity	1,000	1,000	1,000	1,000
Earnings		120	120	120→
ROCE		12%	12%	12%→
Residual earnings, RE [120 − (0.10 × 1,000)]		20	20	20→
PV of RE (20/0.10)	200			
Value of common equity	1,200			
Value per share (on 600 shares)	2.00			

$$P/B = \frac{1,200}{1,000} = 1.2$$

	0	1	2	3
C. RE Valuation for the Same Firm After Debt-for-Equity Swap: Cost of Equity Capital = 9% + [700/800 × (9% − 5%)] = 12.5%				
Net operating assets	1,300	1,300	1,300	1,300→
Net financial obligations	700	700	700	700→
Common shareholders' equity	600	600	600	600→
Operating income		135	135	135→
Net financial expense (700 × 0.05)		35	35	35→
Earnings		100	100	100→
ROCE		16.7%	16.7%	16.7%→
Residual earnings, RE [100 − (0.125 × 600)]		25	25	25→
PV of RE (25/0.125)	200			
Value of common equity	800			
Value per share (on 400 shares)	2.00			

$$P/B = \frac{800}{600} = 1.33$$

Reebok International Ltd.: Effect of Stock Repurchase and Borrowing on the Value of the Firm and the Value of the Equity

14.4

Note 2 to Reebok's 1996 financial statements reads:

2. Dutch Auction Self-Tender Stock Repurchase

On July 28, 1996, the Board of Directors authorized the purchase by the Company of up to 24.0 million shares of the Company's common stock pursuant to a Dutch Auction self-tender offer. The tender offer price range was from $30.00 to $36.00 net per share in cash. The self-tender offer, commenced on July 30, 1996, and expired on August 27, 1996. As a result of the self-tender offer, the Company repurchased approximately 17.0 million common shares at a price of $36.00 per share. Prior to the tender offer, the Company had 72.5 million common shares outstanding. As a result of the tender offer share repurchase, the Company had 55.8 million common shares outstanding at December 31, 1996. In conjunction with this repurchase and as described in Notes 6 and 8, the company entered into a new credit agreement underwritten by a syndicate of major banks.

At a purchase price of $36.00 per share, $601.2 million was paid to repurchase the 16.7 million shares. The company borrowed this amount at current market borrowing rates and so, with a reduction in equity and an increase in debt, leverage increased substantially. Here is the 1996 balance sheet and financial leverage compared with balance sheet and leverage as they would have been if the repurchase and simultaneous borrowing had not taken place (in millions of dollars):

	Actual 1996 Balance Sheet with Stock Repurchase	"As-If" 1996 Balance Sheet Without Stock Repurchase
Net operating assets	1,135	1,135
Net financial obligations	720	119
Total equity	415	1,016
Minority interest	34	34
Common stockholders' equity	381	982
Financial leverage (FLEV)	1.73	0.12

Note: Financial leverage (FLEV) is based on average net financial obligations and average equity over the year, not the year-end amounts.

The following is the forecasted 1997 income statement based on analysts' consensus EPS forecast of $2.56 made in early 1997. It is compared with an "as-if" statement showing how that forecasted statement would have looked without the financing transaction (in millions of dollars):

	Pro Forma 1997 Income Statement with Stock Repurchase	"As-If" Pro Forma 1997 Income Statement Without Stock Repurchase
Operating income	187	187
Net financial expense (4% of NFO)	(29)	(5)
Minority interest in earnings	(15)	(15)
Earnings forecast	143	167
Shares outstanding (millions)	55.840	72.540
Forecasted EPS	2.56	2.30
Forecasts for 1997		
RNOA	16.5%	16.5%
SPREAD	12.5%	12.5%
ROCE	37.5%	17.0%

The forecast of operating income is unchanged by the change in leverage, since no NOA have been affected. Forecasted RNOA and the SPREAD also remain unchanged. But the change in leverage produces a big change in forecasted ROCE.

You see that a firm can earn a higher ROCE simply by increasing leverage (provided the spread is positive). But this has nothing to do with the underlying profitability of the operations. The financing adds no value. Here a $2,542 million valuation of Reebok's equity is compared with an "as-if" valuation of the 72.54 million shares had the leverage not changed:

	Valuation with Stock Repurchase	"As-If" Valuation Without Stock Repurchase
Value of NOA	3,472	3,472
Book value of NFO	720	119
Value of equity	2,752	3,353
Value of minority interest	210	210
Value of common equity	2,542	3,143
Value per share	45.52	43.33

(continued)

The operations were not affected by the financing, so their value is unaffected. It seems, however, that value per share increased. But the $45.52 per-share valuation is based on analysts' forecasts at the end of 1996 and is approximately the market price at that date. The stock was repurchased in August 1996, however, at $36 per share. If the 16.7 million shares had been repurchased at the $43.33 price that reflects the value in the later analysts' forecasts, the valuations before and after the transaction would be as follows:

	Valuation with Repurchase at $43.33 per Share	Valuation Without Repurchase
Value of NOA	3,472	3,472
Book value of NFO	843	119
Value of equity	2,629	3,353
Value of minority interest	210	210
Value of common equity	2,419	3,143
Value per share	43.33	43.33

The valuation without the repurchase is the valuation at the end of 1996 as if there had not been a share repurchase, as before. The valuation with the repurchase just reflects a reduction of equity by the amount of the repurchase of $43.33 × 16.7 million shares = $724 million, and an increase in debt by the same amount. We saw in Chapter 3 that issuing or repurchasing shares at market value does not affect per-share price, and we see it here again. But we further see that issue of debt at market value also does not affect per-share value of $43.33. And we see that a change in leverage does not affect per-share value.

Of course, ex post (after the fact), the shareholders who did not participate in the stock repurchase did benefit from it. The $36.00 may have been a fair price, but the value went up subsequently: Our calculated value is $45.52 per share and that is close to the market value in early 1997. Without the repurchase, the per-share value would have gone from $36.00 to $43.33 based on analysts' forecast revisions. But the per-share value went to $45.52. The difference of $2.19 is the per-share gain to shareholders who did not participate in the repurchase from repurchasing the stock at $36.00 in August rather than at the later higher price. It is the loss to those who did repurchase (from selling at $36.00 rather than $43.33) spread over the remaining shares.

Could Reebok have made the large stock repurchase because its analysis told it that the shares were underpriced? Reebok's share price rose from $36, the repurchase price in August 1996, to $43 in early 1997, so after the fact, shareholders who tendered their shares in the repurchase lost and those who did not gained. Did Reebok's management choose to make the stock repurchase when they thought the price was low? (Reebok's share prices subsequently dropped considerably.) Again, be careful which side of a share repurchase you choose to be on!

valuation, we have said that we should pay more for earnings growth. But should we pay for EPS growth that comes from leverage? Table 14.6 shows that the answer is no.

This table applies abnormal earnings growth methods to the same firm as in Table 14.5. The first valuation (A) applies the AOIG model of this chapter. As net operating assets do not change, free cash flow is the same as operating income, and cum-dividend operating income (after reinvesting free cash flow) is forecasted to equal normal operating income. Thus abnormal operating income growth from Year 2 onward is forecasted to be zero and, accordingly, the value of the operations is equal to forward operating income ($135 million) capitalized at the required return for operations of 9 percent, or $1,500 million. The value of the equity, after subtracting net financial obligations, is $1,200, or $2.00 per share, the same valuation (of course) as that using ReOI methods.

Valuation (B) applies an AEG valuation rather than an AOIG valuation. Thus, earnings and reinvested dividends are the focus rather than operating income and free cash flows. There is full payout, so dividends are the same as earnings. Now, however, the cost of equity capital is 10.0 percent, so abnormal earnings growth after the first year is forecasted to

TABLE 14.6
Leverage Effects on the Value of Equity: Abnormal Earnings Growth Valuation

	0	1	2	3
A. AOIG Valuation of a Firm with 9% Cost of Capital for Operations and 5% After-Tax Cost of Debt				
Operating income		135	135	135→
Net financial expense (300 × 0.05)		15	15	15→
Earnings		120	120	120→
EPS (on 600 million shares)		0.20	0.20	0.20→
Free cash flow (C − I = OI − ΔNOA)		135	135	135→
Reinvested free cash flow (at 9%)			12	12→
Cum-dividend operating income			147	147→
Normal operating income (at 9%)			147	147→
Abnormal operating income growth (AOIG)			0	0→
Value of operations (135/0.09)	1,500			
Net financial obligations	300			
Value of equity	1,200			
Value per share (on 600 million shares)	2.00			
Forward P/E = 2.00/0.20 = 10				
B. AEG Valuation of the Same Firm: Cost of Equity Capital = 9.0% + [300/1,200 × (9% − 5%)] = 10.0%				
Operating income		135	135	135→
Net financial expense (300 × 0.05)		15	15	15→
Earnings		120	120	120→
EPS (on 600 million shares)		0.20	0.20	0.20→
Dividend (*d* = Earn − ΔCSE)		120	120	120→
Reinvested dividends (at 10%)			12	12→
Cum-dividend earnings			132	132→
Normal earnings (at 10%)			132	132→
Abnormal earning growth (AEG)			0	0→
Value of equity (120/0.10)	1,200			
Value per share (on 600 million shares)	2.00			
Forward P/E = 2.00/0.20 = 10				
C. AEG Valuation for the Same Firm After Debt-for-Equity Swap: Cost of Equity Capital = 9% + [700/800 × (9% − 5%)] = 12.5%				
Operating income		135	135	135→
Net financial expense (700 × 0.05)		35	35	35→
Earnings		100	100	100→
EPS (on 400 million shares)		0.25	0.25	0.25→
Dividends (*d* = Earn − ΔCSE)		100	100	100→
Reinvested dividends (at 12.5%)			12.5	12.5→
Cum-dividend earnings			112.5	112.5→
Normal earnings			112.5	112.5→
Abnormal earnings growth (AEG)			0	0→
Value of equity (100/0.125)	800			
Value per share (on 400 million shares)	2.00			
Forward P/E = 2.00/0.25 = 8				

be zero. Therefore, the value of the equity is forward earnings of $120 million capitalized at 10 percent, or $1,200 as before. Value per share is $2.00, which is forward EPS of $0.20 capitalized at 10 percent.

Valuation (C) is after the same debt-for-equity swap as in Table 14.5. The change in leverage decreases earnings (as there is now more interest expense with the same operating income) but increases EPS to $0.25. The valuation shows that this increase in EPS does not change the per-share value of the equity, for the cost of equity capital increases to 12.5 percent as a result of the increase in leverage to offset the increase in EPS. The equity value—forward EPS of $0.25 capitalized at a cost of equity capital of 12.5 percent—is $2.00, unchanged.

This example confirms that we can use either AEG or AOIG valuation methods to price earnings growth. But it also suggests that we are better off using AOIG methods that focus on the growth from operations. In practice, leverage changes each period so, if we were to use AEG valuation, we would have to change the equity cost of capital each period. It is easier to ignore the leverage and focus on the operations. Indeed, financing activities do not generate abnormal earnings growth, so why complicate the valuation (with a changing cost of capital from changing leverage) when leverage does not produce abnormal earnings growth?

Ignoring financing activities makes sense if you understand that a firm can't make money by issuing bonds at fair market value: These transactions are zero-NPV (and zero-residual income). If you forecast that a firm will issue bonds in the future and thus change its leverage—and the bond issue will be zero-NPV—current value cannot be affected. Similarly, an increase in debt to finance a stock repurchase cannot affect value if the stock repurchase is also at fair market value.

Leverage Creates Earnings Growth

The added leverage in Table 14.6 increased EPS from $0.20 to $0.25 but did not change the per-share value. The example provides a warning: Beware of earnings growth that is created by leverage. Leverage produces earnings growth, but not abnormal earnings growth. So the growth created by leverage is not to be valued. The point underscores another point made throughout this book: Growth is risky. See Box 14.5 for a full explanation.

During the 1990s, many firms made considerable stock repurchases while increasing borrowings. The effect was to increase earnings per share. Below are some numbers for IBM.

INTERNATIONAL BUSINESS MACHINES (IBM) Share Repurchases and Financial Leverage, 1995–2000						
	2000	**1999**	**1998**	**1997**	**1996**	**1995**
Share repurchases, net ($ billions)	6.1	6.6	6.3	6.3	5.0	4.7
Increase in net debt ($ billions)	2.4	1.2	4.4	4.6	0.8	2.3
Financial leverage (FLEV)	1.21	1.10	1.22	0.98	0.68	0.62
Earnings per share	4.58	4.25	3.38	3.09	2.56	1.81

IBM delivered considerable per-share earnings growth during the 1990s. We saw in Chapter 13 that a significant portion of that growth came from pension fund gains, asset sales, and bleeding back of restructuring charges. The effect of the significant stock repurchases and the increase in financial leverage on the earnings per share further calls into question the quality of IBM's earnings-per-share growth.

In introducing the P/B and P/E valuation models, Chapters 5 and 6 warned about paying too much for earnings and earnings growth. Beware of paying for earnings created by investment, for investment may grow earnings but not grow value. Do not pay for earnings created by accounting methods, for accounting methods do not add value. We now have another warning: Do not pay for earnings growth created by financing leverage. Here is the complete caveat:

- Beware of earnings growth created by investment.
- Beware of earnings growth created by accounting methods.
- Beware of earnings growth created by financial leverage.

Just as valuation models protect the investor from paying too much for earnings growth from the first two sources, so the models, faithfully applied, protect the investor from paying too much for earnings growth created by leverage.

The examples in Tables 14.5 and 14.6 looked at the effect of a one-time change in leverage. However, leverage changes each period, and if leverage increases each period (and the leverage is favorable), forecasted earnings and EPS will continue to grow. But the growth is not growth to be paid for. The following pro formas compare the earnings growth and value of two firms with the same operations, one levered and the other not. The levered firm has higher expected earnings growth, but the same per-share equity value as the unlevered firm.

EARNINGS GROWTH WITH NO LEVERAGE

The pro forma below gives a forecast of earnings and EPS growth for a pure equity firm (no financial leverage) with 10 million shares outstanding. The forecast is at the end of Year 0. The firm pays no dividends and its required return on operations is 10 percent (and so, with no leverage, the required return for the equity is also 10 percent). Dollar amounts are in millions, except per-share amounts.

	0	1	2	3	4
Net operating assets	100.00	110.00	121.00	133.10	146.41
Common equity	100.00	110.00	121.00	133.10	146.41
Operating income (equals comprehensive income)		10.00	11.00	12.10	13.31
EPS (on 10 million shares)		1.00	1.10	1.21	1.33
Growth in EPS			10%	10%	10%
RNOA		10%	10%	10%	10%
ROCE		10%	10%	10%	10%
Residual operating income		0	0	0	0
Free cash flow (= OI − ΔNOA)		0	0	0	0
Cum-dividend OI			11.00	12.10	13.31
Normal OI			11.00	12.10	13.31
Abnormal OI growth			0	0	0
Value of equity	100.00				
Per-share value of equity (10 million shares)	10.00				
Forward P/E ratio	10.0				
P/B ratio	1.0				

The forecast of RNOA of 10 percent yields residual operating income of zero. As forecasted residual income is zero, the equity is worth its book value of $100 million in Year 0, and the per-share value is $10. The P/B ratio is 1.0, a normal P/B.

The forecasts of operating income and free cash flow yield a forecast of zero abnormal operating income growth. So the firm (and the equity) is worth forward operating income capitalized at the required return of 10 percent, or $100 million, and $10 per share. The forward P/E ratio is 10.0, a normal P/E for a cost of capital of 10 percent.

The earnings and EPS growth rates are both forecasted to be 10 percent and, accordingly, as 10 percent is also the required rate of return, abnormal earnings growth is forecasted to be zero.

(continued)

EARNINGS GROWTH WITH LEVERAGE

The pro forma below is for a firm with the same operations, but with the operating assets in Year 0 financed by $50 million in debt and $50 million in equity (now with 5 million shares outstanding). The after-tax cost of the debt is 5 percent. This change in leverage could be induced by a debt-for-equity swap or a share repurchase.

	0	1	2	3	4
Net operating assets	100.00	110.00	121.00	133.10	146.41
Net financial obligations	50.00	52.50	55.12	57.88	60.77
Common equity	50.00	57.50	65.88	75.22	85.64
Operating income		10.00	11.00	12.10	13.31
Net financial expense		2.50	2.63	2.76	2.89
Comprehensive income		7.50	8.37	9.34	10.42
EPS (on 5 million shares)		1.50	1.68	1.87	2.08
Growth in EPS			11.67%	11.57%	11.48%
RNOA		10%	10%	10%	10%
ROCE		15.0%	14.6%	14.2%	13.9%
Residual operating income		0	0	0	0
Free cash flow (= OI – ΔNOA)		0	0	0	0
Cum-dividend OI			11.00	12.10	13.31
Normal OI			11.00	12.10	13.31
Abnormal OI growth			0	0	0
Value of equity	50.00				
Per-share value of equity (5 million shares)	10.00				
Forward P/E ratio	6.67				
P/B ratio	1.00				

You will notice that, while earnings are lower than in the no-leverage case, EPS is higher and both earnings growth and EPS growth are higher. An analyst forecasting the higher growth rate of over 11 percent might be tempted to give this firm a higher valuation than the pure equity firm where the growth rate is just 10 percent. But that would be a mistake. Both ReOI and AOIG valuations yield the same $10 per-share value as is the case with no leverage. Just as the higher ROCE here is discounted by the appropriate valuation, so is the higher earnings growth. Beware of paying for growth.

While the valuation does not change with leverage, the P/E does. The forward P/E ratio is now 6.67 rather than 10.0, even though abnormal earnings growth is expected to be zero. You will understand the reason in the next section, but here is a hint: P/E ratios are determined not only by growth but also by the cost of capital, and the equity cost of capital increases with financing leverage. Exercise E14.10 explores this example further.

There is a formal accounting relation that ties leverage to growth in earnings:

$$\text{Earnings growth rate}_t = \text{OI growth rate}_t$$

$$+ [\text{Earnings leverage}_{t-1} \times (\text{OI growth rate}_t - \text{NFE growth rate}_t)]$$

$$g_t^{\text{Earn}} = g_t^{\text{OI}} + \text{ELEV}_{t-1}\left[g_t^{\text{OI}} - g_t^{\text{NFE}}\right] \tag{14.8}$$

Here earnings leverage (ELEV_{t-1}) is leverage in the income statement in the prior year, measured by NFE/Earnings, that is, the degree to which net financial expenses affect earnings. Typically, $g_t^{\text{OI}} > g_t^{\text{NFE}}$ so the effect of leverage on earnings growth is "favorable." Demonstrate this formula with the example above.

FIGURE 14.1

Median Financial Leverage for U.S. Firms, 1963–2010

Financial leverage is net financial obligations to common equity (FLEV). The median is for listed firms with a market capitalization over $200 million.

Source:
Standard & Poor's
Compustat® data

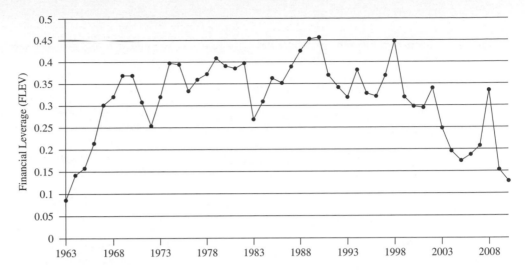

The increase in corporate debt during the 1990s contributed to strong earnings growth that the market rewarded with high earnings multiples. Figure 14.1 tracks financial leverage (FLEV) for U.S. firms from 1963 to 2010. For IBM, the outcome was favorable—it was able to maintain a favorable leverage position. But debt has a downside, and this downside risk increases the required return: If leverage becomes unfavorable, earnings will decline, perhaps precipitously. For some firms, the downside of debt became apparent in the early 2000s as they struggled to cover debt service, with large losses of shareholder value. Vivendi, Quest (and the many telecoms), United Airlines (and the many air carriers) are just a few examples. You can see the deleveraging after 2000 in Figure 14.1. The episode was repeated in the 2008 credit crisis, especially among highly levered financial firms. In many cases, the debt was issued to make doubtful acquisitions that also produced earnings growth. Analysts must be cautious of earnings growth from acquisitions, but especially when the growth is financed with debt. A similar warning attaches to stock repurchases, for stock repurchases always involve an increase in leverage: The stock repurchase must be financed either by borrowing or by liquidating financial assets. See Box 14.6.

Debt and Taxes

Some people argue that, because interest is tax-deductible if paid by a corporation but is not deductible if paid by shareholders, there are tax savings to corporate borrowing. Shareholders can borrow on personal account to lever their equity, but they can also lever their equity by borrowing within the firm. If they borrow within the firm, they add value because they get a tax deduction for the interest cost incurred.

The claim is controversial. First, interest can (in the United States) be deducted on shareholders' own tax returns to the extent that it is matched by investment income. Second, the interest that is deductible by corporations is taxable in the hands of debtholders who receive the interest, and they will require a higher interest rate to compensate them for the taxes, mitigating the tax advantage to the corporate debt. The spread between interest rates on tax-free debt (like municipal debt) and corporate debt suggests this is so. Third, free cash flow must either be used to reduce corporate net debt or to make distributions to shareholders: $C - I = d + F$. Both uses have tax effects. If cash flow is applied to reduce

Firms make stock repurchases for very good reasons: They are a method of paying out cash to shareholders. If a firm has significant holdings of financial assets and no investment opportunities for the cash, it should pay it out to shareholders, who may indeed have those opportunities. The shareholders can be no worse off, for at the very least, they can invest the cash in the same interest-bearing financial assets as the firm.

However, stock repurchases must be evaluated with care. Selling financial assets at fair value and paying the proceeds out with a fair-value repurchase of stock does not create value; nor does issuing debt at fair value to finance a repurchase. But management may have reasons for stock repurchases other than passing out idle cash:

1. In a 2003 management survey,* 76 percent of respondents said that increasing earnings per share was an important factor in share repurchase decisions. Repurchases indeed increase earnings per share, but growth in earnings per share from share repurchases does not create value. If management's bonuses are tied to earnings per share, one can see how they might favor repurchases.

2. In the same survey, 68 percent of respondents said that reversing the dilutive effects of employee stock options is also important. But stock repurchases do not reverse dilution. See the discussion in Box 9.5 in Chapter 9.

3. Share repurchases are sometimes made when a firm is flush with cash as a result of its success. That can coincide with a high stock price. Buying back overpriced stock destroys value for shareholders, even though increasing earnings per share. Indeed, if the stock price is EPS driven, management may be tempted to buy back overpriced stock to perpetuate EPS growth. You see how a price bubble could result.

4. Alternatively, management can create value for shareholders by actively timing the market: "Buy low" applies to firms buying their own stock as well as to investors.

Accordingly, management should be aware of the intrinsic value of the shares when they engage in share purchases (or issues). The 2003 management survey found that 86.4 percent of managers say they repurchase when they consider their stock a good value.

If management is repurchasing stock with shareholders' funds, check their insider trading filings with the SEC: Is management buying or selling on their own account? Be particularly vigilant when you estimate that the stock is overpriced in the market.

During the late 1990s Microsoft made a number of stock repurchases when its stock price was as high as $60 (on a split-adjusted basis). Commentators questioned whether Microsoft was buying its "overpriced stock." See Box 9.5 in Chapter 9 for a commentary. In September 2008, Microsoft announced a $40 billion stock repurchase when its price was down to $25. Could it be that Microsoft thought its shares were underpriced?

Up to September 2010, Microsoft had never borrowed, but in that month the firm announced that it planned to borrow $5 billion at the very low interest rates (less than 1 percent) at the time. Microsoft had strong free cash flow and $36.8 billion in cash and short-term investments sitting on its balance sheet. Commentators were speculating that Microsoft planned a stock repurchase, but given its cash position it clearly had no need to borrow. What could Microsoft be up to? An answer: Microsoft thought the stock price, then $24, was cheap and thus it was a time to repurchase. But they might also have thought that, with interest rates at an historical low, this was the time to borrow. A stock repurchase financed by cheap debt is a pure financing arbitrage play. The stock market seemed to think so: The stock shot up 5.3 percent on the announcement.

*A. Brav, J. Graham, C. Harvey, and R. Michaely, "Payout Policy in the 21st Century," *Journal of Financial Economics,* 2005, pp. 483–527.

debt, shareholders lose the supposed tax advantage of debt; if the firm wishes to maintain the debt, it must distribute cash flow to shareholders who are then taxed on the distributions. Either way, free cash flow is taxed, and shareholders cannot get the tax advantage of debt without incurring taxes at the personal level.

You can delve into these issues in a corporate finance text. Armed with the shareholders' personal tax rates and the corporate tax rate, you can revise the value calculations here by incorporating the present value of tax benefits if you are convinced that debt adds value. But, with an eye on the shareholder, do not fall into the trap of thinking only about the tax benefit of debt without considering taxes on distributions to shareholders and debtholders.

Box 14.7 considers two other ways that firms might generate value for shareholders from debt.

Typically it is argued that firms cannot create value by issuing debt: If the debt is issued at fair market value, the transaction is a zero-net present value transaction—or, equivalently, a zero-residual net financial expense transaction. Banks and other financial institutions make money from the spread between lending rates and borrowing rates and so create value from transacting in debt. And bond traders who discover mispricing of bonds also create value from transacting in debt. But for the firm that uses debt for financing, debt transactions are deemed not to create value.

There are exceptions, however.

1. Consider the following scenario. A firm with a particular risk profile that is given an AA bond rating issues debt with a yield to maturity of 6 percent. Subsequently, it engages in more risky business and the bonds accordingly are downgraded to a BBB rating. The price of the bonds drops to yield a 9 percent return commensurate with the firm's new risk level. The firm then redeems the bonds and books a gain.

   Firms can transfer value from bondholders to shareholders in this way. There is a message for bondholders: Beware and write bond agreements that give protection from this scenario. There is also a message for shareholders: Bondholders can be exploited in this way. There is also a message for the valuation analyst: Firms can create value for shareholders in this scenario. Applying residual earnings techniques will incorporate this value. If the scenario is anticipated, the analyst forecasts a realized gain from the redemption of bonds and, accordingly, a negative residual net financial expense (that is, residual income from bonds).

2. Just as management might time a share issue or repurchase, they can time debt issues and repurchases. If managers think that the firm's bonds are overpriced—because the market underestimates the default probability—they might issue bonds to take advantage of the perceived mispricing. Correspondingly an underpricing of bonds may promote a repurchase of the debt. Debt might also be issued when management deems interest rates to be low and expects them to be higher in the future. Shares of a

firm with low-interest debt are worth more after interest rates rise, for one is then buying debt cheap. In 2010 to 2011, firms issued a huge amount of debt while the Federal Reserve kept interest rates low, anticipating that rates would rise as inflation (from the Fed's permissive monetary policy) set in. See the Microsoft example in Box 14.6.

Corporate finance is usually taught with the view that markets are efficient, so firms buy and sell their debt and equity at fair market prices. If so, financing activities add little value. But if one entertains market mispricing, a different view of corporate finance emerges: Like an activist investor, the firm buys its debt and equity when they are cheap and issues them when they are overpriced. (Of course, issues have to be coordinated with the need for investment funds for operations.) At a minimum, the firm takes the view of the defensive investor and avoids trading at the wrong price. Accordingly, capital structure—the debt versus equity composition of the financing—is not an indifferent or "irrelevant" issue but rather an outcome of the firm's activist approach to the capital market. But to engage, management must have a good understanding of the appropriate value of the firm.

With a good understanding of the value of the operations, an active investor might also employ leverage. An investor who sees a stock is underpriced might borrow to lever up what she sees as a gain to buying low. But, alternatively, she might be attracted to a firm where the operations are deemed to be underpriced but which also has considerable leverage that will lever up earnings when they eventuate. Again, shareholders can lever on their own account, or the firm can lever for them. But the idea of employing leverage in investing is quite dangerous, and most fundamental investors avoid high leverage. Leverage, after all, is risky. One must be very sure of one's belief in the underpricing to add leverage. For the defensive investor, the caution goes the other way: If one has the slightest suspicion that a stock may be overpriced, avoid it most surely if it has leverage; leverage will only increase the pain if suspicions turn out to be justified. One point is fundamental: Understand the value of the firm without leverage so the effect of added leverage can be appropriately assessed. The enterprise valuation techniques of this chapter do so.

MARK-TO-MARKET ACCOUNTING: A TOOL FOR INCORPORATING THE LIABILITY FOR STOCK OPTIONS IN VALUATION

The distinction between operating activities and financing activities shows us that there are two ways to proceed in valuation. We can forecast future earnings from an asset or liability (and add the present value of its expected residual earnings to its book value), or we can mark the asset or liability to market. Marking to market is attractive because it relieves us of the forecasting task. But marking to market can only be done if market values are reliable measures of fair value. Market values of financial assets and liabilities typically measure up to this criterion, so we do not have to forecast the income and expenses arising from financing activities.

Chapter 9 explained that shareholders incur losses when employees exercise the stock options they have received as compensation. Yet GAAP accounting does not recognize this loss. In that chapter, we showed how losses from the exercise on stock options are calculated. But that is not the end of the matter. While recognizing the effect of option exercises on current income, it does not accommodate outstanding options that might be exercised in the future, decreasing future comprehensive income. A valuation based on forecasting GAAP operating income will overestimate the value of the firm, leaving the investor with the risk of paying too much for a stock. The analyst must make adjustments. One might think the solution would involve reducing forecasts of GAAP earnings by forecasts of future losses from the exercise of options. Indeed, this is a solution. But forecasting those losses is not an easy task: As the loss is the difference between the market price and the exercise price at the exercise date, one would have to anticipate not only exercise dates but the market price of the stock at those dates.

Mark-to-market accounting—the alternative to forecasting—provides a solution. Fair values of outstanding options can be estimated, with reasonable precision, using option pricing methods. Nike, Inc., was the focus in Chapter 9. Nike's stock option footnote says there were 36.0 million outstanding options at the end of 2010, with a weighted-average exercise price of $46.60. With Nike's stock trading at $72.38 at fiscal-year end, the weighted-average exercise price indicates that many of the outstanding options are in the money. The value of these options—the option overhang—amounts to a contingent liability for shareholders to surrender value by issuing shares at less than market price, just like an obligation under a product liability or environmental damage suit is a contingent liability. That contingent liability must be subtracted in calculating equity value.

The value of this contingent liability is estimated using option pricing methods applied to the outstanding options. This option value reduces the valuation based on forecasts of GAAP income in Tables 14.2 and 14.4, as follows (in millions):

Value of equity before option overhang (from Tables 14.2 and 14.4)		$36,644
Liability for option overhang:		
Black-Scholes value of outstanding options: 36.0 × $41.50	$1,494	
Tax benefit (at 36.3%)	(542)	
Option liability, after tax		952
Value of equity		$35,692
Value per share on 484 million shares		$ 73.74

The option overhang is based on a weighted-average value of all options outstanding, here estimated at $41.50 per option. As the loss on the exercise of option is tax deductible, the overhang is reduced by the tax benefit. The recognition of the option overhang reduces Nike's value to $73.74 per share from the $75.71 in Tables 14.2 and 14.4.

The adjustment here is only approximate. First, Black-Scholes option valuations are only approximate. Because employee options have features different from standard traded options—they may not vest and may be exercised before expiration, for example—modifications are often made. Second, as GAAP and IFRS recognize some of the option value at grant date (under their "grant-date accounting"), the amount calculated here is overstated. Ideally, one would like to subtract the at-the-money option value already recognized and just recognize the added liability for options in the money. However, unraveling the history is just too difficult. Third, basing the option value on the market price is appropriate only if that price represents value. The analyst wishes to get intrinsic value independent of the market price, and this value depends on outstanding options. However, option value and equity value are jointly determined, so this presents problems. Iterative methods can be applied: Start with option values based on intrinsic equity values before considering options ($75.71), then iteratively change equity and option values until convergence is reached. Warrant pricing methods also deal with this problem.[1] Unlike option pricing models that apply to (nondilutive) traded options, warrant pricing models recognize the dilutive effect of employee options. Given these problems, one must keep perspective: Is the issue material?

Mark-to-market methods essentially restate the book value on the balance sheet for an omitted liability. Mark-to-market accounting can be applied to other contingent liabilities. Apply the procedure above to incorporate outstanding put options on the firm's stock, warrants, and other convertible securities into a valuation. For contingent liabilities from lawsuits, deduct the present value of expected losses to be incurred. The contingent liability footnote provides (sparse) information about these liabilities.

ENTERPRISE MULTIPLES

In the example of leverage effects in Table 14.5 you will have noticed that the P/B ratio increased with the increase in leverage, from 1.2 to 1.33. You also will have noticed that the P/E ratio decreased with the increase in leverage in Table 14.6, from 10 to 8. Yet, in both cases, the value of the equity did not change. This suggests that we might be better served to think of P/B and P/E ratios without the effect of leverage.

Enterprise Price-to-Book Ratios

The value of equity is the value of the operations minus the value of the net financial obligations. So the intrinsic price-to-book (P/B) ratio can be expressed as

$$\frac{V_0^E}{\text{CSE}_0} = \frac{V_0^{\text{NOA}} - V_0^{\text{NFO}}}{\text{NOA} - \text{NFO}}$$

If the net financial obligations are measured at market value, they do not contribute to the premium over book value; the difference between price and book value is due to net operating assets not being measured at market value. Yet the expression here tells us that the P/B ratio will vary as the amount of net financial obligations changes relative to the operating assets. That is, the ratio is sensitive to leverage. So differences in firms' P/B ratios can derive from their financing even though price equals book value for financial items.

To avoid this confusion we should focus on the value of the operations relative to their book value. The ratio of the value of the net operating assets to their book value is the **enterprise P/B ratio** or the **unlevered P/B ratio:**

$$\text{Enterprise P/B ratio} = \frac{\text{Value of net operating assets}}{\text{Net operating assets}}$$

$$= \frac{V_0^{\text{NOA}}}{\text{NOA}_0}$$

---

[1] For an application, see F. Li and M. Wong, "Employee Stock Options, Equity Valuation, and the Valuation of Option Grants Using a Warrant-Pricing Model," *Journal of Accounting Research*, March 2005, pp. 97–131.

The value of the net operating assets is, of course, the value of the equity plus the net financial obligations. So, to calculate a market (traded) enterprise P/B, just add the net financial obligations to the market value of the equity.

The standard price-to-book ratio for the equity is referred to as the **levered P/B ratio.** The two P/B ratios reconcile as follows:

Levered P/B ratio = Enterprise P/B ratio
$$\qquad\qquad + [\text{Financial leverage} \times (\text{Enterprise P/B ratio} - 1)] \qquad\qquad \textbf{(14.9)}$$

$$\frac{V_0^E}{\text{CSE}_0} = \frac{V_0^{\text{NOA}}}{\text{NOA}_0} + \text{FLEV}\left(\frac{V_0^{\text{NOA}}}{\text{NOA}_0} - 1\right)$$

where FLEV is book financial leverage (NFO/CSE), as before. The expression also applies to market P/B ratios, by substituting the market price (P) for V. The difference between the two P/B ratios increases with leverage and the distance that the unlevered P/B is from the normal of 1.0. For an unlevered P/B of 1.0, the levered P/B is also 1.0 regardless of leverage. Figure 14.2 shows how the levered P/B ratio changes with leverage for six different levels of the unlevered P/B ratio.

The levered P/B ratio is the one that is commonly referred to. But it is the enterprise P/B on which we should focus. Reebok's levered P/B before its large stock repurchase and

FIGURE 14.2
Levered P/B Ratios and Leverage
The figure shows how the levered P/B ratio (V^E/CSE) changes with financial leverage for different levels of unlevered P/B (V^{NOA}/NOA).

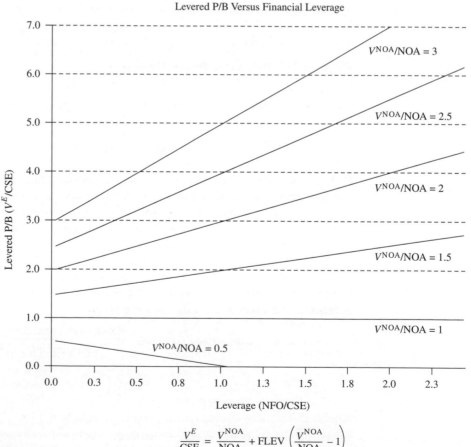

$$\frac{V^E}{\text{CSE}} = \frac{V^{\text{NOA}}}{\text{NOA}} + \text{FLEV}\left(\frac{V^{\text{NOA}}}{\text{NOA}} - 1\right)$$

FIGURE 14.3
Median Levered and Unlevered Price-to-Book Ratios, 1963–2010 for U.S. traded firms with market capitalization over $200 million.

Source:
Standard & Poor's
Compustat® data

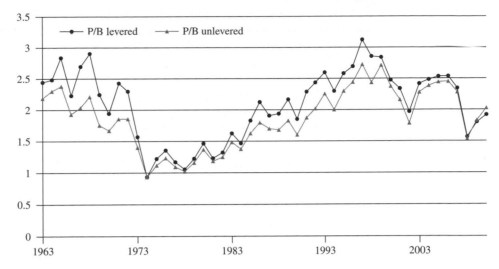

change in leverage (in Box 14.4) was 3.3, but immediately after it was 6.3. This change does not reflect a change in the expected profitability of operations or a change in the premium one would have paid for the operations. It's a leverage-induced change: Reebok's enterprise P/B remained the same at 3.0. And the stock price was unchanged at about $36; this repurchase and financing transaction had no effect on shareholders' per-share value, and this is also indicated by no change in the enterprise P/B ratio.

Figure 14.3 plots the median levered and unlevered price-to-book ratios for U.S. firms from 1963 to 2010. When unlevered P/B ratios were around 1.0 in the mid-1970s, so were the levered ratios. But when unlevered P/B ratios were above 1.0, the levered P/B ratios were higher than the unlevered ratios, the more so the higher the unlevered P/B.

Enterprise Price-Earnings Ratios

The P/E ratio commonly referred to is a multiple of earnings after net interest expense, so it is a **levered P/E.** A levered P/E ratio anticipates earnings growth. However, earnings growth is affected by leverage, and anticipated growth from leverage is not growth to be valued because it creates no abnormal earnings growth. So it makes sense to think of a P/E ratio in terms of growth in earnings from operations. The **enterprise P/E ratio** or **unlevered P/E ratio** prices the operating income on the basis of expected growth in operating income.

The *forward enterprise P/E* is the value of the operations relative to forecasted one-year-ahead operating income:

$$\text{Forward enterprise P/E} = \frac{\text{Value of operations}}{\text{Forward operating income}} = \frac{V_0^{\text{NOA}}}{\text{OI}_1}$$

The value of the operations is the value of the equity plus the net financial obligations. In Table 14.6, the forward enterprise P/E is the value of the operations, $1,500 million relative to Year 1 operating income of $135 million, or 11.11. This enterprise P/E does not change with the increase in leverage in Table 14.6, whereas the levered P/E drops from 10 to 8 despite no change in operating income growth. The drop in the levered P/E reflects an increase in the required return due to leverage. The change in leverage with the Reebok stock repurchase increased forward earnings from 2.30 to 2.56 (in Box 14.4) and reduced the forward levered P/E from 18.8 to 16.9, but with no effect on the value per share. The enterprise P/E did not change.

The *trailing enterprise P/E* compares the value of the operations to current operating income. There is an adjustment, however. Just as the levered trailing P/E must be cum-dividend (with dividends added to the numerator), so must the unlevered P/E. The dividend from operations is the free cash flow, so

$$\text{Trailing enterprise P/E} = \frac{\text{Value of operations} + \text{Free cash flow}}{\text{Current operating income}} = \frac{V_0^{\text{NOA}} + \text{FCF}_0}{\text{OI}_0}$$

The value of the operations is reduced by free cash flow (paid out to the financing activities) so, as the value of the operating income is independent of the cash paid out, free cash flow must be added to the numerator.

The forward levered and unlevered P/E ratios reconcile as follows:

Levered forward P/E = Unlevered P/E + [Earnings leverage **(14.10)**
$\qquad\qquad\qquad\qquad \times$ (Unlevered P/E − 1/Net borrowing cost)]

$$\frac{V_0^E}{\text{Earn}_1} = \frac{V_0^{\text{NOA}}}{\text{OI}_1} + \text{ELEV}_1\left(\frac{V_0^{\text{NOA}}}{\text{OI}_1} - \frac{1}{\text{NBC}_1}\right)$$

Earnings leverage is the extent to which net financial expenses affect earnings: ELEV = NFE/Earnings, and NBC is the net borrowing cost. Think of the terms in parentheses as their reciprocals, operating income yield and the net borrowing cost. If the operating income yield, $\text{OI}_1/V_0^{\text{NOA}}$, is higher than the borrowing cost, the levered P/E is lower than the unlevered P/E, with the amount of the difference depending on the amount of earnings leverage, ELEV. The two ratios are the same when the operating earnings yield is equal to the net borrowing cost. When the unlevered P/E is particularly high (because a lot of operating income growth is expected), the levered P/E is higher than the unlevered P/E.

A similar expression reconciles the levered and unlevered earnings-to-price ratios (which are of course just the reciprocal of the P/E ratios):

$$\frac{\text{Earn}_1}{V_0^E} = \frac{\text{OI}_1}{V_0^{\text{NOA}}} + \frac{\text{NFO}_0}{V_0^E}\left[\frac{\text{OI}_1}{V_0^{\text{NOA}}} - \text{NBC}_1\right] \qquad \textbf{(14.11)}$$

In all these expressions one can substitute market prices (P) for values (V) and so express the relationship between enterprise traded P/E ratios and equity P/E ratios.

The two trailing P/E ratios reconcile in a similar way:

$$\frac{V_0^E + d_0}{\text{Earn}_0} = \frac{V_0^{\text{NOA}} + \text{FCF}_0}{\text{OI}_0} + \text{ELEV}_0\left(\frac{V_0^{\text{NOA}} + \text{FCF}_0}{\text{OI}_0} - \frac{1}{\text{NBC}_0} - 1\right) \qquad \textbf{(14.12)}$$

For a given borrowing cost, you can set up a conversion charts like that for enterprise and levered P/B ratios in Figure 14.2. Figure 14.4 plots median levered and unlevered trailing P/E ratios from 1963 to 2003. Typically, levered P/E ratios are less than unlevered ratios, though the opposite is the case when unlevered P/E ratios are very high (as in the late 1990s).

FIGURE 14.4
Median Levered and Unlevered Trailing Price-to-Earnings Ratios for U.S. Firms, 1963–2003

Source:
Standard & Poor's
Compustat® data

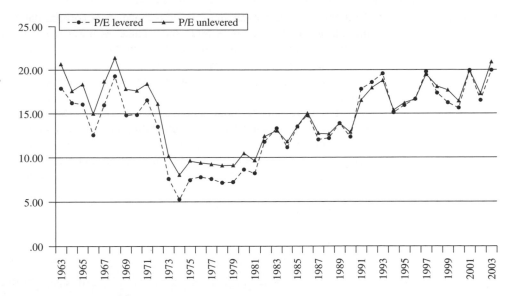

TABLE 14.7 **Relationships between Levered and Unlevered Measures**

Concept	Levered Measure	Unlevered Measure	Relationship
Profitability	ROCE	RNOA	$\text{ROCE} = \text{RNOA} + \text{FLEV}(\text{RNOA} - \text{NBC})$
Cost of capital	ρ_E	ρ_F	$\rho_E = \rho_F + \dfrac{V_0^D}{V_0^E}(\rho_F - \rho_D)$
P/B ratio	V_0^E/CSE_0	$V_0^{\text{NOA}}/\text{NOA}_0$	$\dfrac{V_0^E}{\text{CSE}_0} = \dfrac{V_0^{\text{NOA}}}{\text{NOA}_0} + \dfrac{\text{NFO}_0}{\text{CSE}_0}\left(\dfrac{V_0^{\text{NOA}}}{\text{NOA}_0} - 1\right)$
Forward P/E ratio	V_0^E/Earn_1	$V_0^{\text{NOA}}/\text{OI}_1$	$\dfrac{V_0^E}{\text{Earn}_1} = \dfrac{V_0^{\text{NOA}}}{\text{OI}_1} + \text{ELEV}_1\left(\dfrac{V_0^{\text{NOA}}}{\text{OI}_1} - \dfrac{1}{\text{NBC}_1}\right)$
Trailing P/E ratio	$\dfrac{V_0^E + d_0}{\text{Earn}_0}$	$\dfrac{V_0^{\text{NOA}} + \text{FCF}_0}{\text{OI}_0}$	$\dfrac{V_0^E + d_0}{\text{Earn}_0} = \dfrac{V_0^{\text{NOA}} + \text{FCF}_0}{\text{OI}_0} + \text{ELEV}_0\left(\dfrac{V_0^{\text{NOA}} + \text{FCF}_0}{\text{OI}_0} - \dfrac{1}{\text{NBC}_0} - 1\right)$
Forward earnings yield	$\dfrac{\text{Earn}_1}{V_0^E}$	$\dfrac{\text{OI}_1}{V_0^{\text{NOA}}}$	$\dfrac{\text{Earn}_1}{V_0^E} = \dfrac{\text{OI}_1}{V_0^{\text{NOA}}} + \dfrac{\text{NFO}_0}{V_0^E}\left[\dfrac{\text{OI}_1}{V_0^{\text{NOA}}} - \text{NBC}_1\right]$

The form of the relationship between levered and unlevered P/B ratios and P/E ratios is familiar: The levered amount is the unlevered amount plus a premium that depends on the leverage and a spread. We saw this in the relationship between levered and unlevered accounting returns and required returns. Table 14.7 summarizes the leverage effects we have discussed in this chapter.

Summary

To the extent that accountants get the balance sheet correct, the analyst does not have to make a valuation. If, in the extreme, the balance sheet were perfect—giving the value of the equity—the analyst would have nothing to do; the accountant would have done the valuation. Balance sheets are typically not perfect, so the analyst has to forecast to get the missing value. But to the extent that the balance sheet gives the value, the analyst can avoid forecasting.

This chapter has introduced valuation approaches that recognize the balance sheet values of net financial items as approximating their market values, but recognize that balance sheet amounts for net operating assets are typically not their values. Accordingly, valuation is based on forecasting residual income or abnormal earnings growth from operations. The valuation gives the value of the operations, and the value of the equity is then the value of the operations less the balance sheet value of the net debt (or the fair value of the net debt in the fair-value footnote).

The Web Connection

Find the following on the Web page for this chapter:

- Further explanation of residual operating income methods.
- Further explanation of abnormal operating income growth methods.
- A further demonstration of the equivalence of residual earnings valuation and residual operating income valuation (and the cost of capital adjustments required).
- Demonstrations of how leverage affects ROCE, earnings growth, and valuations.

- More discussion of stock repurchases and their effect on value.
- More discussion of when borrowing can add value.
- More coverage of levered and unlevered P/B and P/E ratios.
- Further examples of the option overhang.
- Demonstration of how residual earnings valuation methods can be applied to the impairment of goodwill.
- Look at the Readers' Corner.

If the net debt on the balance sheet is close to its fair value, the appropriate way of thinking of a book value multiple is in terms of the unlevered or enterprise price-to-book ratio, that is, the pricing of the net operating assets rather than the equity. The chapter has laid out the calculation of the enterprise price-to-book ratio and has shown how it relates, through leverage, to the levered price-to-book ratio.

This chapter also focused on enterprise price-earnings ratios. It recognized that standard P/E ratios—levered P/E ratios—are based on prospective earnings growth that incorporates growth that is created by leverage. Yet, growth from leverage is not valued. Levered P/E ratios change with leverage, even if leverage has no effect on equity value. The analyst therefore prices growth from operations with an enterprise or unlevered P/E ratio. He is thus protected from paying too much for earning growth.

We always want to carry out valuations efficiently. The residual operating income valuation approach and the abnormal operating income growth approach both reduce the forecasting task on which we will embark in the next two chapters. Only the operating components of comprehensive income and the net operating asset component on the balance sheet need to be forecasted. Further, in converting forecasts to a valuation using a required return, one can ignore changes in required returns that are due to changes in financial leverage.

Key Concepts

book leverage is the book value of net financial obligations relative to the book value of common shareholders' equity.   *450*

core residual operating income is residual operating income that excludes one-time, unsustainable income. Also called **sustainable residual operating income.**   *445*

effective cost of debt is the after-tax cost of borrowing.   *447*

enterprise value is the value of the operations.   *440*

financing risk is the risk shareholders have of losing value in borrowing and lending activities.   *449*

levered price-earnings ratio is the price multiple that prices (net) earnings. Compare with **unlevered price-earnings ratio.**   *465*

levered price-to-book ratio is the price multiple of common equity.

Compare with **unlevered price-to-book ratio.**   *464*

market leverage is financial leverage measured by the ratio of the value of net financial obligations to the value of common equity.   *450*

operating risk is the risk shareholders and bondholders have of losing value in operations.   *449*

pure equity firm is a firm with no net debt.   *449*

unlevered price-earnings ratio or **enterprise price-earnings ratio** is the price multiple that prices operating income. Compare with **levered price-earnings ratio.**   *465*

unlevered price-to-book ratio or **enterprise price-to-book ratio** is the price multiple of net operating assets. Compare with **levered price-to-book ratio.**   *463*

The Analyst's Toolkit

A Continuing Case: *Kimberly-Clark Corporation*

A Self-Study Exercise

In the next chapter you will begin to develop a valuation of KMB's shares based on the analysis work you have done to this point. Your task here is to identify residual operating income in the reformulated statements you have prepared. You should do this for total operating income and also for core (sustainable) operating income because it is the sustainable operating income that forecasts the future. With the reformulated statements you have, you will be able to do this only for 2009–2010. If you are ambitious, go back to the 2006–2008 annual reports and do the same for these years. You will then have a five-year history that will provide more insight into the likely path in the future. You will also be able to track the growth in residual operating income over a longer time period.

THE COST OF CAPITAL FOR OPERATIONS

For the residual income calculation, you have to estimate the cost of capital for operations. Follow the procedures in Box 14.2. Strictly the cost of capital should be reestimated each year, but this is a very stable firm, so make the calculation for 2010 and apply it to all years. Calculate the market value of the equity on the basis of the per-share stock price of $65.24 in early 2011. You calculated the equity cost of capital, based on a beta of 0.8, in the Continuing Case for Chapter 3. The firm's debt footnote indicates a weighted-average borrowing rate of 5.2 percent (before tax). Be skeptical of these calculations. See Box 14.3.

TRACK THE DRIVERS OF RESIDUAL OPERATING INCOME

How much of the change in residual operating income over the years is due to profitability (RNOA) and how much to growth in net operating assets? Examine the effect of sales growth. How much of operating income growth comes from core operations? Compare the growth in core operating income with the growth in earnings per share. Why are they different?

THE 2010 STOCK REPURCHASE

The firm repurchased 12,954 thousand shares for $809 million in 2010. What effect will this repurchase have on future operating profitability, return on common equity, and earnings-per-share growth? What effect does the repurchase have on the value per share?

OPTION OVERHANG

The stock option footnote indicates that there are 25,793 thousand employee stock options outstanding at the end of 2010 with a weighted-average exercise price of $61.62. The weighted-average value of these options is estimated at $5.70. Calculate the after-tax option overhang.

ENTERPRISE P/B AND P/E RATIOS

Calculate the levered and enterprise price-to-book ratios in early 2011 when the stock price was $65.24. Also calculate the levered and enterprise trailing P/E ratios. (KMB's 2010 dividend was $2.64 per share.) Show that the levered and unlevered multiples reconcile according to standard formulas.

Concept Questions

C14.1. If assets are measured at their fair (intrinsic) value, the analyst must forecast that residual earnings from those assets will be zero. Is this correct?

C14.2. Why might the market value of the assets of a pure investment fund that holds only equity securities not be an indication of the fund's (intrinsic) value?

C14.3. What drives growth in residual operating income?

C14.4. Explain what is meant by a financing risk premium in the equity cost of capital. When will a financing risk premium be negative?

C14.5. A firm with positive net financial assets will typically have a required return for equity that is greater than the required return for its operations. Is this correct?

C14.6. What is wrong with tying management bonuses to earnings per share? What measure would you propose as a management performance metric?

C14.7. The management of a firm that ties employee bonuses to return on common equity repurchases some of the firm's outstanding shares. What is the effect of this transaction on shareholders' wealth?

C14.8. An increase in financial leverage increases return on common equity (if the operating spread is positive), and thus increases residual earnings. The value of equity is based on forecasted residual earnings, yet it is claimed that the value of equity is not affected by a change in financial leverage. How is this seeming paradox explained?

C14.9. Levered price-to-book ratios are always higher than unlevered price-to-book ratios. Is this correct?

C14.10. During the 1990s and 2000s, many firms repurchased stock and borrowed to do so. What is the typical effect of stock repurchases on earnings-per-share growth and return on common equity? Predict how a firm that excessively engaged in these practices would have fared in the downturn in 2008.

C14.11. Does an increase in financial leverage increase or decrease the (levered) P/E ratio?

C14.12. Noting the large amount of stock repurchases in 2009–2010, an equity strategist at a leading Wall Street firm predicted that earnings per share would increase and "we'll see a jump in P/E ratios." Does he have the correct analysis?

C14.13. Another Wall Street analyst predicted in 2010 that, after the considerable deleveraging during the financial crisis, firms would begin once again to lever up with more borrowing. "They must defend their return on equity," he claimed. As a result, "investors should look for a rise in dividends and share buy-backs and an expansion of P/E multiples, leading to equity market outperformance." Is he correct?

Exercises

Drill Exercises

E14.1. Residual Earnings and Residual Operating Income (Easy)

Here are summary financial statements for a firm (in millions of dollars):

Income Statement, 2012		Balance Sheet, End of 2011	
Operating income	1,400	Net operating assets	10,000
Interest expense	500	Financing debt	5,000
Net income	900	Common equity	5,000

The required return for equity is 12 percent, the required return for operations is 11 percent, and the required return for debt is 10 percent. The firm pays no taxes.

Calculate residual earnings, residual operating income, and residual income from financing activities for 2012.

E14.2. Calculating Residual Operating Income and Its Drivers (Easy)

Here are summary numbers from a firm's financial statements (in millions of dollars):

	2007	2008	2009	2010
Operating income	187.00	200.09	214.10	229.08
Net operating assets	1,214.45	1,299.46	1,390.42	1,487.75

The required return for operations is 10.1 percent. Calculate residual operating income, return on net operating assets (RNOA), and the growth rate for net operating assets for each year 2008–2010.

E14.3. Calculating Abnormal Operating Income Growth (Easy)

Here are summary numbers from a firm's financial statements (in millions of dollars):

	2007	2008	2009	2010
Operating income	187.00	200.09	214.10	229.08
Net operating assets	1,214.45	1,299.46	1,390.42	1,487.75

The required return for operations is 10.1 percent. Calculate abnormal operating income growth (in dollars) for each year 2008–2010.

E14.4. Residual Operating Income and Abnormal Operating Income Growth (Easy)

Here are financial statements for a firm (in millions of dollars):

Income Statement			Balance Sheet, End of Year		
	2012	2011		2011	2010
Operating income	2,700	2,300	Net operating assets	20,000	18,500
Interest expense	800	500	Financing debt	10,000	6,250
Net income	1,900	1,800	Common equity	10,000	12,250

The firm has a required return of 10 percent for operations. Calculate residual operating income for 2012 and 2011 using beginning-of-year balance sheet numbers. Then calculate abnormal operating income growth (in dollars) for 2012.

E14.5. Cost of Capital Calculations (Easy)

From the following data, calculate the cost of capital for operations (WACC). Use the capital asset pricing model to estimate the cost of equity capital.

U.S. Government long-term bond rate	4.3%
Market risk premium	5.0%
Equity beta	1.3
Per-share market price	$40.70
Shares outstanding	58 million
Net financial obligations on balance sheet	$1,750 million
Weighted-average borrowing cost	7.5%
Statutory tax rate	36.0%

Explain why the cost of capital for operations is different from that for equity.

E14.6. Calculating the Required Return for Equity (Medium)

A firm with a required return of 10 percent for operations has a book value of net debt of $2,450 million with a borrowing cost of 8 percent and a tax rate of 37 percent. The firm's equity is worth $8,280 million. What is the required return for its equity?

E14.7. Residual Operating Income Valuation (Easy)

The following forecasts were made at the end of 2012 for a firm with net operating assets of $1,135 million and net financial obligations of $720 million (in millions of dollars):

	2013E	2014E	2015E	2016E
Operating income	187.00	200.09	214.10	229.08
Net operating assets	1,214.45	1,299.46	1,390.42	1,487.75

The required return for operations is 10.1 percent. Forecast residual operating income for these years and, from these forecasts, value the operations and the equity.

E14.8. Abnormal Operating Income Growth Valuation (Easy)

Using the forecasts in Exercise E14.7, forecast abnormal operating income growth and, from these forecasts, value the operations and the equity. The required return for operations is 10.1 percent.

E14.9. Financing Leverage and Earnings Growth (Medium)

At the bottom of Box 14.5 in this chapter there is a formula that shows how leverage affects earnings growth. Apply this formula to explain the increase in the earnings growth rate from 10 percent to 11.67 percent in Year 2 as a result of the increase leverage in the example above it.

E14.10. Growth, the Cost of Capital, and the Normal P/E Ratio (Hard)

Box 14.5 in this chapter demonstrated how increases in leverage can increase earnings-per-share growth. Suppose the leverage change was due to a stock repurchase where the repurchase was financed by the borrowing. Answer the following questions regarding the effect of the stock repurchase.

a. Why does the stock repurchase have no effect on the per-share value of the equity?
b. Why does forecasted earnings for Year 1 decrease from $10.00 million to $7.50 million?
c. Why does forecasted EPS for Year 1 increase while forecasted earnings decrease?

d. The required return prior to the stock repurchase was 10 percent. What is the required return for the equity after the stock repurchase?
e. What is the expected residual earnings (on equity) for Year 1 after the repurchase?
f. Forecast the value of the equity at the end of Year 1 for both the case with no leverage and the case with leverage.
g. Forecast the P/E at the end of Year 1 for both the case with no leverage and the case with leverage. Why are they different?

E14.11. Levered and Unlevered P/B and P/E Ratios (Easy)

A firm has the following summary balance sheet and income statement (in millions):

Net operating assets	$469
Net financial obligations	236
Common equity	$233
Operating income	$ 70
Net financial expense	14
Earnings	$ 56

The firm held the same amount of net financial obligations during the whole year for which the earnings were reported. The equity of this firm trades at a P/B ratio of 2.9. The firm pays no dividends.

a. Calculate the levered trailing P/E ratio for this firm.
b. Calculate the enterprise P/B and P/E ratios.

E14.12. Levered and Unlevered P/E Ratios (Medium)

The following pro forma was prepared for a firm at the end of 2009 (in millions of dollars):

	2009A	2010E	2011E	2012E
Net operating assets	1,300	1,300	1,300	1,300
Net financial obligations	300	300	300	300
Common shareholders' equity	1,000	1,000	1,000	1,000
Operating income		135	135	135
Net financial expense		15	15	15
Earnings		120	120	120

The firm has a required return for its operations of 9 percent and a 5 percent after-tax cost of debt. Pro forma financial statements after 2012 are forecasted to be the same a those in 2012.

a. Forecast the value of the operations and the value of the equity at the end of years 2010 to 2012.
b. Forecast the levered and unlevered P/E ratios at the end of years 2010 to 2012. Make calculations for both the expected trailing P/E and the forward P/E.
c. Can you infer the required return for equity from the levered P/E ratios?

This exercise builds on the examples in Table 14.5 and Table 14.6.

Applications

E14.13. The Quality of Carrying Values for Equity Investments: SunTrust Bank (Easy)

In 1993, SunTrust Bank of Atlanta reported investment securities on its balance sheet of $10,644 million, an increase over the $8,715 million reported for 1992. Footnotes revealed that most of the securities were interest-bearing debt securities. But $1,077 million of the 1993 securities were shares held in the Coca-Cola Company, carried at market value. In 1992, the bank had carried these securities on the balance sheet at their historical cost of $110 million.

Which carrying value for the Coca-Cola shares do you see as the better quality number, the market value or the historical cost?

E14.14. Enterprise Multiples for IBM Corporation (Easy)

IBM's 1,228 million outstanding shares traded at $165 each when its 2010 financial statements were published. Those statements reported common shareholders' equity of $23,046 million and net financial obligations of $17,973 million. Footnotes reveal that the firm's net borrowing cost (after tax) is 3.1 percent.

a. Calculate the levered price-to-book and enterprise price-to-book ratios at the time. What explains the difference between the two multiples?
b. Analysts were forecasting earnings per share of $13.22 for 2011. Calculate the forward levered P/E and forward enterprise P/E ratio.

Real World Connection

Exercises E6.9 and E15.9 deal with IBM, as does Minicase M13.3.

E14.15. Residual Operating Income and Enterprise Multiples: General Mills, Inc. (Easy)

Reformulated balance sheets and income statements for General Mills's 2010 fiscal year are in Exhibits 10.5 and 10.11 in Chapter 10. The firm's 656.5 million outstanding shares traded at $36 each at the time the 2010 statements were published. From these financial statements, calculate the following for fiscal year 2010:

a. Free cash flow.
b. Residual operating income based on beginning-of-year balance sheet numbers. Use a required return for operations of 5.1 percent (the number in Box 14.2).
c. Enterprise price-to-book.

Do you feel comfortable using the 5.1 percent required return from Box 14.2?

Real World Connection

See Exercises E1.5, E2.9, E3.8, E4.10, E6.8, E11.9, E13.9, E15.6, and E16.10.

E14.16. Calculating Residual Operating Income: Dell, Inc. (Medium)

Dell, Inc., reported after-tax operating income of $2,618 million for fiscal year 2008, along with operating assets at the beginning of the year of $13,230 million and operating liabilities of $20,439 million.

Using a cost of capital for operations of 12 percent, calculate Dell's residual operating income for the year. Describe, in words, how Dell generated value during the year.

Real World Connection

Further Dell Exercises are in E3.7, E3.12, E5.10, E7.6, E9.11, and E20.4. Minicase M16.2 covers Dell also.

E14.17. Residual Operating Income Valuation, Nike, Inc., 2004 (Medium)

At the end of its 2004 fiscal year, the 263.1 million outstanding shares of Nike, Inc., traded at $75 each. The following summary numbers are from the 2004 financial report (in millions of dollars).

	Balance Sheet		Income Statement	
	2004	**2003**		**2004**
Net operating assets	4,551	4,330	Operating income	961
Net financial assets	289	(302)	Net financial expense	16

a. Calculate the levered and unlevered (enterprise) price-to-book ratios at which Nike traded at the end of fiscal year 2004.
b. Calculate residual operating income for 2004 using beginning-of-year balance sheet amounts. Use a required return of 8.6 percent for operations.
c. Calculate return on net operating (RNOA) assets for 2004.
d. With this RNOA, forecast operating income and residual operating income for 2005.
e. Calculate the value of a Nike share if the residual operating income you forecasted for 2005 is expected to grow at a 4 percent annual rate after 2005.

Real World Connection
Exercises E2.14, E5.13, E6.7, E7.9, E9.12, E16.11, E16.13, and E19.5 deal with Nike.

E14.18. **Stock Repurchases: Expedia, Inc. (Medium)**

In June 2007, the Web travel firm Expedia, Inc., announced that it would buy back as much as 42 percent of its shares, with the repurchase financed by new borrowings.

a. What is the likely effect on earning per share and earnings per share growth?
b. What is the effect on the risk that the shareholders bear?
c. Will the repurchase add value to shareholders? To answer, consider that the shares traded at a rather high multiple of 26 times analysts' forward earnings estimates at the time.
d. The firm's proxy statement says that executive compensation is tied to (among other things) earnings per share. Is this a desirable way to reward management?

Minicase

M14.1

Valuing the Operations and the Investments of a Property and Casualty Insurer: Chubb Corporation

Chubb Corporation is a property and casualty insurance holding company providing insurance through its subsidiaries in the United States, Canada, Europe, and parts of Latin America and Asia. Its subsidiaries include Federal, Vigilant, Pacific Indemnity, Great Northern, Chubb National, Chubb Indemnity, and Texas Pacific Indemnity insurance companies.

The insurance operations are divided into three business units. Chubb Commercial Insurance offers a full range of commercial customer insurance products, including coverage for multiple peril, casualty, workers compensation, and property and marine. Chubb Commercial Insurance writes policies for niche business through agents and brokers. Chubb Specialty Insurance offers a wide variety of specialized executive protection and professional liability products for privately and publicly owned companies, financial institutions, professional firms, and health care organizations. Chubb Specialty Insurance also includes surety and accident businesses, as well as reinsurance through Chubb Re. Chubb Personal Insurance offers products for individuals with fine homes and possessions who require more coverage choices and higher limits than standard insurance policies.

Before proceeding with this case, you should understand how insurers "make money." Insurance companies run underwriting operations where they write insurance policies and processes and pay claims on those policies. The delay between receipt of premiums and payment of claims produces a "float," so they are also involved in investment operations where they manage investments in which the float is invested. Accordingly, you see both investment assets and liabilities on the balance sheet as well as assets and liabilites associated with insurance. You also see revenues and expenses associated with both activities in the income statement.

A frequently used measure of property and casualty insurance underwriting results is the combined loss and expense ratio. This ratio is the sum of the ratio of incurred losses and related loss adjustment expenses to premiums earned (the loss ratio) and the ratio of underwriting expenses to premiums written (the expense ratio), after reducing both premium amounts by dividends to policyholders. When the combined ratio is under 100 percent, underwriting results are generally considered profitable; when the combined ratio is over 100 percent, underwriting results are generally considered unprofitable.

Chubb's ratios for years 2003–2010 shown on the following page. In their discussion of results for 2010, management noted that underwriting results were "highly profitable" from 2008–2010. The loss ratio for 2005 was attributed to catastrophic losses primarily from Hurricane Katrina. The lower results in 2003 were due to large asbestos and toxic waste claims, but even excluding these, the combined loss and expense ratio would have been 97.5 percent. The combined ratio for 2002 was 106.7 percent and that for 2001 was 113.4 percent, arising from the September 11 attack in New York and surety bond losses relating to the Enron bankruptcy.

	2010	2009	2008	2007	2006	2005	2004	2003
Loss ratio	58.1%	55.4%	58.5%	52.8%	55.2%	64.3%	63.1%	67.6%
Expense ratio	31.2	30.6	30.2	30.1	29.0	28.0%	29.2	30.4
Combined ratio	89.3%	86.0%	88.7%	82.9%	84.2%	92.3%	92.3%	98.0%

These ratios give a good indication of the profitability of the insurance operations, but we need dollar numbers to get to the valuation implications. Further, they do not consider the performance of the investment operations. Chubb's balance sheets for 2010 and 2009 are in Exhibit 10.16 in Chapter 10 as part of the Chubb case M10.2 there. Its 2010 income statement is also given, along with a statement of comprehensive income that Chubb reports outside both the equity statement and the income statement. If you worked Minicase M10.2, you will have reformulated these statements. If not, do so now before you proceed. The reformulation should capture the way that Chubb carries out its business operations, with the analysis of the profitability of the business in mind. In particular, make sure you distinguish the underwriting operations from the investment operations. Chubb has some relatively small real estate operations. Group these with the underwriting operations. The firm's statutory tax rate is 35 percent, but note that the effective tax rate on investment income is only 19.1 percent because much of it is from tax-exempt securities.

Chubb's loss and expense ratios indicate that 2010 was a good year. The stock price, under the ticker CB, rose to $58 on these results. You are required to carry out an analysis that challenges this stock price. You do not have the complete information that you would like for forecasting, but you will be surprised how far you get simply on the basis of the financial statement information before you.

As you proceed, deal with the following:

A. Calculate the residual income from underwriting operations and from the investment operations and decide how you will use these numbers for your valuation. Use a required return of 9 percent for the underwriting operations and 6 percent for investment operations. Why would the two operations have different required returns?

B. Explain how you dealt with the following features in your valuation:

   1. Investment income
   2. Realized investment gains
   3. Unrealized appreciation or depreciation of investments
   4. Book value of investments
   5. Equity investments
   6. Net operating assets
   7. Tax allocation

C. Insurance companies are suspected of cherry picking investments. How did you deal with this?

D. What features of Chubb's accounting—and insurers in general—might give you pause in basing your valuation on the financial statements?

Real World Connection

Minicase M10.2 in Chapter 10 deals with the reformulation on Chubb Corporation's financial statements.

Chapter **Fifteen**

Anchoring on the Financial Statements: Simple Forecasting and Simple Valuation

LINKS

Link to previous chapter

Chapter 14 developed a simplified valuation model based on forecasting operating activities.

This chapter

This chapter develops simple valuation models based on forecasts of operating activities solely from information in the financial statements.

Link to next chapter

Chapter 16 develops valuations based on information both within and outside the financial statements.

Link to Web page

Learn more about simple forecasting and valuation—check out the text's Web site at **www.mhhe.com/penman5e**.

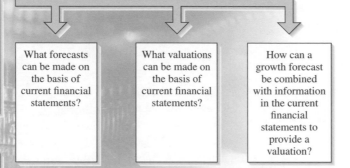

| What forecasts can be made on the basis of current financial statements? | What valuations can be made on the basis of current financial statements? | How can a growth forecast be combined with information in the current financial statements to provide a valuation? |

In valuation, analysts aim for simplicity. They strip away features of the business that are not involved in value generation. And if some features are relatively important and others are of minor importance, analysts concentrate their efforts on those that are important. And they look for useful approximations that give a quick benchmark valuation before proceeding to a more complete, but more complex, valuation. In this spirit, the last chapter stripped away the forecasting of financing activities to simplify valuation.

Simplicity comes not only from fewer factors to forecast, but also from using less information to make forecasts. A potentially large amount of information—from strategic planning, marketing research, the analysis of production costs, and an assessment of the viability of R&D, to name a few—is involved in forecasting. If we can limit ourselves to a small set of information that captures much of the broader information, yet still obtain reasonable value approximations, we are parsimonious in our endeavor.

This chapter develops simple valuations as a prelude to the next chapter, which utilizes the full set of information for forecasting. The focus is on the (limited) information in the financial statements. In many cases—particularly for relatively mature firms—the financial statements aggregate considerable information and can be a reasonable indicator of the future. For example, core profit margins and asset turnovers in current statements are often

The Analyst's Checklist

After reading this chapter you should understand:

- How simple forecasts yield simple but insightful valuations.
- How simple forecasts are developed from the current financial statements.
- How sales forecasts combine with financial statement information to provide simple forecasts.
- When simple forecasts and simple valuations work as reasonable approximations.
- How simple forecasting works as an analysis tool in sensitivity analysis.
- How simple valuation models work in reverse engineering mode to challenge the market price.
- How simple valuation models enhance screening analysis.

After reading this chapter you should be able to:

- Develop simple forecasts from financial statements.
- Integrate sales forecasts into a simple forecast.
- Calculate simple valuations from simple forecasts.
- Calculate enterprise price-to-book ratios and price-earnings ratios from simple forecasts.
- Use simple forecasting in sensitivity analysis.
- Use simple valuation models in reverse engineering to challenge market speculation.
- Use simple valuation models to screen stocks.

good indicators of future margins and turnovers. The chapter asks the question: What forecasts and valuations can be made solely from information in the financial statements? In this chapter you will understand that historical financial statements are not "backward looking" but very much forward looking. (You will also get a sense of the limits of the information provided by financial statements.) With this in mind, the financial statement analysis of Part Two of the book—with its emphasis on core operating income as a basis for forecasting—is set up to elicit the information in the financial statements for forecasting. It is now that you will strike pay dirt from the thorough reformulation and analysis of financial statements.

The focus of financial statement information has particular importance in fundamental analysis. The fundamental analyst, you'll remember, follows the rule of not mixing what he knows with speculation. Forecasting involves considerable speculation—particularly when forecasting the "long term" (for a continuing value calculation, for example). Financial statement information is what we know about the present and the past (subject, of course, to the quality of the accounting). By isolating this more reliable information, we ensure we do not contaminate it with more speculative, softer information.

We saw in Chapter 7 that the separation of hard financial statement information from speculation was the key to challenging the market price. We saw that speculation revolves around growth so we were careful to separate value implied by the financial statements from value based on speculation about long-run growth. By anchoring to the financial statements, we were able to identify the market's speculative growth forecast, which could then be challenged. This chapter simply goes further by developing forecasts from the financial statements and understanding the value they imply in order to strengthen our challenge to the market price.

SIMPLE FORECASTS AND SIMPLE VALUATIONS

Simple forecasts are developed from the financial statement analysis of Part Two of the book. That analysis identified value drivers and established the current state of those drivers; forecasting asks how the future will be different from the present. But the present is an indicator of the future and thus provides a benchmark forecast we can enhance with information outside the financial statements. That information is likely to be more speculative, so the financial statement information also serves to discipline our forecasting: If we forecast that the future will be different from the present, we must have very good reasons. Simple forecasts ground our speculative forecasting on "what we know" from the financial statements.

Simple forecasts are converted to a valuation via the following "simple" version of the residual operating income model of the last chapter:

$$V_0^E = CSE_0 + \frac{ReOI_1}{\rho_F - g}$$

That is, a **simple valuation** is based on forecasting residual operating income for the forward year and applying a growth rate to that forecast. Both the forward-year forecast and the growth rate come from the financial statements. There are variants to this model. One might feel confident in forecasting two years ahead and applying a growth rate at that point (as we did in challenging the market price in Chapter 7). And of course we could also apply the abnormal earnings growth model (applied to the operations), which we will do later in the chapter.

Forward residual operating income is

$$ReOI_1 = OI_1 - (\rho_F - 1)NOA_0$$

Current net operating assets, NOA_0, is available in the reformulated balance sheet, but we also require a forecast of forward operating income, OI_1, and a forecast of the growth rate, g. In a simple valuation, these are elicited from the financial statements. We will show how, but first an introduction.

Introducing PPE, Inc.

We will illustrate the analysis with two firms. One is PPE, Inc., a firm so called because it has just one asset, property, plant, and equipment. This is a dummy firm, so simple that one can see the picture clearly. The other firm is our companion example throughout the book, Nike, Inc. We will work with PPE, Inc., both in this chapter and in the next, where we will add information outside the financial statements to complete a fully fledged valuation.

The reformulated financial statements for PPE, Inc., are shown below. Our interest is in the balance sheet and income statement, but the cash flow statement is also supplied. That statement can be derived from the income statement. Make sure you can do this.[1] The balance sheet reports 7.7 of debt and the income statement shows that this debt incurs interest expense at 4 percent.

---

[1] Free cash flow = $OI - \Delta NOA = 9.8 - 4.5 = 5.3$. Net dividends can be deduced from the change in shareholders' equity using the clean-surplus relation: $d = $ Earnings $- \Delta CSE = 5.3$. Note that, as there is no financing cash flow but an increase in indebtedness in the balance sheet, the debt must be deep discount (zero-coupon) debt (or the interest was not paid).

PPE, INC.
Balance Sheet, December 31, Year 0

Assets	Year 0	Prior Year	Liabilities and Equity	Year 0	Prior Year
Property, plant, and equipment (at cost less accumulated depreciation)	74.4	69.9	Long-term debt (NFO) Common shareholders' equity (CSE)	7.7 66.7	7.4 62.5
Net operating assets (NOA)	74.4	69.9		74.4	69.9

Income Statement, Year 0

Operating income	
Sales of products	124.9
Cost of goods sold (including depreciation of 21.4)	(114.6)
	10.3
Other operating expenses	(0.5)
	9.8
Net financial expense: 0.04×7.4	(0.3)
Earnings	9.5

Statement of Cash Flows, Year 0

Cash flow from operations		
Operating income	9.8	
Depreciation	21.4	31.2
Cash flow in investing activities		
Investment in PPE $(21.4 + 4.5)$		(25.9)
Free cash flow		5.3
Cash flow in financing activities		
Net dividends paid		5.3

These statements supply the numbers for forecasting. Current CSE_0 is 66.7 and current NOA_0 is 74.4. These are the balance sheet numbers to anchor on for a levered and unlevered (enterprise) valuation. Core operating income is identified: With no unusual items, core operating income is 9.8 and core $RNOA = 9.8/69.9 = 14.02$ percent. (We use beginning-of year NOA for simplicity.) PPE, Inc. has a required return for operations of 10 percent, so the current core $ReOI_0 = 9.8 - (0.10 \times 69.9) = 2.81$.

The No-Growth Forecast and Valuation

A no-growth forecast predicts that the forward ReOI will be the same as current core ReOI: $ReOI_1 = ReOI_0 = 2.81$. Thus the no-growth equity valuation (with no growth applied to the forward year forecast) is

$$V_0^E = 66.7 + \frac{2.81}{0.10} = 94.8 \qquad \textbf{(15.1)}$$

The value of the operating activities, enterprise value, is

$$V_0^{NOA} = 74.4 + \frac{2.81}{0.10} = 102.5$$

The difference in the two valuations is, of course, the amount of the debt on the balance sheet, 7.7. The levered P/B is 1.42 and the unlevered (enterprise) P/B is 1.38.

The no-growth forecast implies a particular forecast of forward operating income. You might think that a no-growth forecast would predict year-ahead operating income to be the same as current core operating income, 9.8. But that would be too simple: The firm has added assets over the year and these will earn more income. The no-growth forecast is

$$OI_1 = OI_0 + (\rho_F - 1)\Delta NOA_0$$

That is, forward operating income is forecasted as current operating income plus further income from assets added in the current year (ΔNOA) and earning at the required return. For PPE, $OI_1 = 9.8 + (0.10 \times 4.5) = 10.25$. (It should be clear that, if the added assets earn only at the required return, then forward residual income will be the same as currently.)

The no-growth enterprise value is also forward operating income capitalized:

$$V_0^{NOA} = \frac{OI_1}{\rho_F - 1} = \frac{10.25}{0.10} = 102.5$$

The forward enterprise P/E = 102.5/10.25 = 10, which is the normal P/E for a required return of 10 percent. This is an abnormal operating income growth (AOIG) valuation with no growth. It is equivalent to the residual income valuation above of course: Constant residual income implies no abnormal income growth.

Box 15.1 develops a no-growth forecast and valuation for Nike. The no-growth value is $50.69 per share. Nike traded at $74 at the time, so the market is building in growth. It is the market's growth valuation that we wish to challenge, so let's turn to the growth valuation indicated by the financial statements. But note the no-growth value puts a floor on the valuation: Nike is worth at least $50.19. How much extra do you want to pay for growth?

The Growth Forecast and Valuation

The no-growth forecast sees additions to net assets earning only at the required return: Increased investment adds no value. This is a conservative forecast, and one should always respect a conservative forecast. Indeed, it was the no-growth valuation that we anchored on in challenging the market price in Chapter 7, albeit with two years of forward earnings. But the financial statements may tell us that assets are currently earning an RNOA different from the required return. Indeed, core RNOA for PPE, Inc., is 14.02 percent, higher than the required return. So an alternative forecast predicts that all NOA_0 (including the new additions) will earn at this core profitability:

$$OI_1 = NOA_0 \times Core\ RNOA_0$$

For PPE, $OI_1 = 74.4 \times 14.02\% = 10.43$. Accordingly forward $ReOI_1 = 10.43 - (0.10 \times 74.4) = 2.99$. Relative to current $ReOI_0$ of 2.81, we have growth. The growth rate is 6.44 percent.

Where does this growth come from? ReOI is driven by RNOA and the amount of net operating assets: $ReOI_1 = [RNOA_1 - (\rho_F - 1)] \times NOA_0$. With $RNOA_1$ forecasted to be the same as in the current year, growth comes from the growth in net operating assets. This is easy to see:

$$Growth\ rate\ in\ ReOI_1 = \frac{[RNOA_1 - (\rho_F - 1)]NOA_0}{[RNOA_0 - (\rho_F - 1)]NOA_{-1}}$$

NIKE, INC.

Required return for operations		9.1%
Core operating income	2010	$1,911 million
Net operating assets	2009	$6,346 million
	2010	$5,514 million
Core residual operating income	2010: 1,911 − (0.091 × 6,346)	$1,333 million
No-growth forecast of operating income	2011: 1,911 + (0.091 × −832)	$1,835 million
No-growth forecast of ReOI	2011: 1,835 − (0.091 × 5,514)	$1,333 million
No-growth forecast of AOIG (change in ReOI)	2012	0

Value of Common Equity

$$V_{2010}^E = CSE_{2010} + \frac{ReOI_{2011}}{0.091} = 9,884 + \frac{1,333}{0.091}$$ $24,532 million

Value per share on 484 million shares $50.69

ReOI Valuation of Operations $20,162 million

$$V_{2010}^{NOA} = V_{2010}^E - NFA_{2010} = 24,532 - 4,370$$

$$V_{2010}^{NOA} = NOA_{2010} + \frac{ReOI_{2011}}{0.091} = 5,514 + \frac{1,333}{0.091}$$ $20,162 million

AOIG Valuation of Operations

$$V_{2010}^{NOA} = \frac{OI_{2011}}{0.091} = \frac{1,835}{0.091}$$ $20,162 million

Nike traded at $74 per share when fiscal year 2010 results were reported.

However, if we forecast $RNOA_1 = RNOA_0$, the growth rate becomes

$$\text{Growth rate in } ReOI_1 = \frac{NOA_0}{NOA_{-1}}$$

That is, the forecasted growth in ReOI for the next year is given by the current growth of NOA. The growth forecast is given by growth in the balance sheet, and that is 74.4/69.9 = 1.0644, or 6.44 percent.

Now suppose we apply this forecast to all future periods. That is, we predict that RNOA will be the same as current core RNOA indefinitely but NOA investments will continue to grow at the current rate. In this case, ReOI will also grow indefinitely at this rate. Capitalizing the forecast of ReOI for Year 1 as a perpetuity with growth, we have the simple valuation with growth:

$$V_0^E = CSE_0 + \frac{[\text{Core } RNOA_0 - (\rho_F - 1)]NOA_0}{\rho_F - g} \tag{15.2}$$

The growth rate is the forecasted growth in ReOI from Year 1 on, but in this case it is the forecasted growth in NOA at the current rate, NOA_0/NOA_{-1}. For PPE, Inc., current core RNOA is 14.02 percent, and the current NOA grew at 1.0644 from the previous year.

So, the value of the equity is

$$V_0^E = 66.7 + \frac{(0.1402 - 0.10) \times 74.4}{1.10 - 1.0644} = 150.71$$

The numerator here is $ReOI_1 = 2.99$.

The value of the operations is

$$V_0^{NOA} = NOA_0 + \frac{[Core\ RNOA_0 - (\rho_F - 1)]NOA_0}{\rho_F - g} \qquad \textbf{(15.2a)}$$

With a little rearrangement,

$$V_0^{NOA} = NOA_0 \times \frac{Core\ RNOA_0 - (g - 1)}{\rho_F - g} \qquad \textbf{(15.2b)}$$

For PPE, Inc., the enterprise valuation with the two formulas is

$$V_0^{NOA} = 74.4 + \frac{(0.1402 - 0.10) \times 74.4}{1.10 - 1.0644} = 158.41$$

$$V_0^{NOA} = 74.4 \times \frac{0.1402 - 0.0644}{1.10 - 1.0644} = 74.4 \times 2.13 = 158.41$$

The multiplier in equation 15.2b is the *enterprise price-to-book ratio* (2.13 for PPE, Inc.). The multiplier compares RNOA relative to the growth rate (in the numerator) to the required return relative to the growth rate (in the denominator). You can see the two ReOI drivers, RNOA and NOA, working together here. Remember that g is 1 plus the growth rate, so $g - 1$ is the growth rate. If the RNOA is greater than the required return for operations, then more value is added to book value the higher the RNOA is relative to the growth rate. But growth also contributes: For a given RNOA (higher than the required return), more value is added if growth is higher. If RNOA equals the required return, the enterprise P/B is normal. Note that the multiplier formula only works for RNOA greater than the growth rate (which usually is the case).

Firms can have uneven growth in net operating assets from year to year, so applying the NOA growth rate for the most recent year may not be representative. Better to work with an average growth rate over the last three to five years (provided there has not been an unusual event like an acquisition). That is, normalize the asset growth rate.

Box 15.2 carries out a simple growth valuation for Nike based on an average NOA growth rate of 4.6 percent. The value implied by the financial statement analysis is $73.59, close to the market price at the time of $74. We have learned something about the market price: The market is giving Nike the same value as that indicated by the financial statements, with the same forecast as that uncovered by a financial statement analysis. We also understand from the financial statement benchmark that, if we are to pay more than $74, we must see a growth rate of more than 4.6 percent, and that will involve either an increase in core profitability over the current 30.1 percent or growth in the net operating assets to earn at that rate.

An equivalent abnormal operating income growth (AOIG) valuation applies a growth multiplier to the forecast of forward operating income:

$$V_0^{NOA} = OI_1 \times \frac{1}{\rho_F - 1}\left[1 + \frac{G_2 - \rho_F}{\rho_F - g}\right] \qquad \textbf{(15.3)}$$

where G_2 is 1 + the cum-dividend growth rate in operating income for Year 2 ahead and g is still the growth rate in net operating assets. The multiplier is a *forward enterprise P/E ratio*. The Web page for this chapter provides a demonstration with PPE, Inc. Table 15.1 summarizes the simple no-growth and growth valuations.

NIKE, INC.

Cost of capital for operations		9.1%
Core RNOA	2010	30.1%
Five-year average growth rate for net operating assets	2006–2010	4.6%
Net operating assets	2010	$ 5,514 million
Growth forecast of operating income	2011: 5,514 × 30.1%	$ 1,660 million
Growth forecast of ReOI	2011: (0.301 − 0.091) × 5,514	$ 1,158 million

Value of Common Equity:

$$V_{2010}^{E} = CSE_{2010} + \frac{ReOI_{2011}}{1.091 - 1.046} = 9,884 + \frac{1,158}{0.045}$$

	$35,616 million
Value per share on 484 million shares	
	$73.59

ReOI Valuation of Operations:

$$V_{2010}^{NOA} = V_{2010}^{E} - NFA_{2010} = 35,616 - 4,370$$

	$31,246 million

$$V_{2010}^{NOA} = NOA_{2010} + \frac{(RNOA_{2010} - 0.091) \times NOA_{2010}}{1.091 - 1.046}$$

$$= 5,514 + \frac{(0.301 - 0.091) \times 5,514}{0.045}$$

	$31,246 million

$$V_{2010}^{NOA} = NOA_{2010} \times \frac{RNOA_{2010} - (g-1)}{1.091 - 1.046}$$

$$= 5,514 \times \frac{0.301 - 0.046}{0.045}$$

	$31,246 million

The forward enterprise P/B is 5.67.
Nike traded at $74 when fiscal year 2010 results were reported.

TABLE 15.1 Simple Forecasts and Simple Valuation Models

Simple Forecast	Simple Valuation of the Equity	Simple Valuation of the Operations
No-growth	$$V_0^{E} = CSE_0 + \frac{Core\ ReOI_0}{\rho_F - 1}$$	$$V_0^{NOA} = NOA_0 + \frac{Core\ ReOI_0}{\rho_F - 1}$$ $$= \frac{OI_1}{\rho_F - 1}$$
Growth	$$V_0^{E} = CSE_0 + \frac{[Core\ RNOA_0 - (\rho_F - 1)]NOA_0}{\rho_F - g}$$	$$V_0^{NOA} = NOA_0 + \frac{[Core\ RNOA_0 - (\rho_F - 1)]NOA_0}{\rho_F - g}$$ $$= NOA_0 \times \frac{Core\ RNOA_0 - (g-1)}{\rho_F - g}$$ $$V_0^{NOA} = OI_1 \times \frac{1}{\rho_F - 1}\left[1 + \frac{G_2 - \rho_F}{\rho_F - g}\right]$$

SIMPLE FORECASTING: ADDING INFORMATION TO FINANCIAL STATEMENT INFORMATION

The valuations above are based solely on information in financial statements. This information is (presumably) reliable information—though we will challenge this presumption with the accounting quality analysis in Chapter 18—but it is limited information. One must have perspective. These are simple valuations and for some firms can be simple-minded. They are relevant only for relatively mature firms where the past is a reasonable indication of the future. Simple valuations will not work for a start-up firm with little income (even losses) and most of its prospects based on speculation. Indeed a speculative firm is defined as one where the financial statements provide little valuation to anchor on.

To these benchmark valuations, the analyst may add information about how the future might be different from the present. Here are two examples of adjustments to simple forecasts.

Weighed-Average Forecasts of Growth

If current core RNOA is higher than the required return, the no-growth forecast is a conservative forecast because it predicts that additions to NOA will earn only at the required return rather than at the current RNOA. The growth forecast, on the other hand, can be optimistic: It predicts that NOA will earn at the current RNOA and that current RNOA and growth in NOA will continue indefinitely into the future. History tells us that high profitability tends to decline: Competition erodes profitability, so RNOA fades over time. Can Nike maintain a core RNOA of 30.1 percent in the future? Similarly, high asset growth cannot be maintained indefinitely. The question is one of durable competitive advantage, of course, and Nike has indeed shown that its profitability is durable.

The issue of the duration of competitive advantage comes to the fore when we look at full-information forecasting in the next chapter. But the fact that history tells us that profitability tends to decline over time can be built into our simple forecasts and valuations; after all, it is part of "what we know."

With the expectation that growth in the long run will be at the GDP growth rate, high growth rates in residual operating income might be weighted down to the GDP growth rate of 4 percent:

Weighted-average growth rate for ReOI = (0.7 × Current growth in ReOI)   **(15.4)**
                                   + (0.3 × 4%)

Weighting the 4.6 percent financial statement growth rate we used in the growth valuation of Nike in Box 15.2 with 4 percent GDP growth yields a weighted-average growth rate of 4.42 percent. This produces a valuation of $71.54 per share. For Nike, the adjustment makes little difference because our growth rate is close to the GDP rate. But, for a firm with exceptionally high ReOI growth, the adjustment matters.[2]

Simple Valuations with Short-Term and Long-Term Growth Rates

The idea that growth rates decline over the long term can also be accommodated with the abnormal operating income growth (AOIG) model. Stating the model in multiplier form:

$$V_0^{\text{NOA}} = \text{OI}_1 \times \frac{1}{\rho_F - 1}\left[\frac{G_2 - G_{\text{long}}}{\rho_F - G_{\text{long}}}\right] \qquad \textbf{(15.5)}$$

---

[2] This analysis can be enhanced by forecasting a gradual decay in the growth rate to the GDP growth rate in the long run. See S. Penman, *Accounting for Value* (New York: Columbia University Press, 2011), Chapter 3.

In early fiscal year 2011, analysts following Nike were forecasting EPS of $4.39 for 2011 and $4.64 for 2012, up from $3.93 in 2010. Adjusting for expected net interest income these forecasts translated into operating income forecasts of $2,033 million and $2,140 million. With an expectation of net operating assets in the 2011 balance sheet of $5,768 million, a two-year pro forma is developed as follows:

	2010	2011	2012
Operating income		$ 2,033	$ 2,140
Net operating assets	$5,514	5,768	
Free cash flow (OI − ΔNOA)		1,779	
Reinvested free cash flow (at 9.1%)			162
Cum-dividend operating income			2,302
Cum-dividend operating income growth rate: 2,302/2,033			13.2%

For the valuation: G_2 = 1.132

$\quad\quad\quad\quad\quad\quad G_{long}$ = 1.04 (the GDP growth rate)

$\quad\quad\quad\quad\quad\quad \rho_F$ = 1.091

The value of the operations is:

$$V^{NOA}_{2010} = 2,033 \times \frac{1}{0.091}\left[\frac{1.132 - 1.04}{1.091 - 1.04}\right] = 40,301$$

$$V^{E}_{2010} = V^{NOA}_{2010} + NFA = 40,301 + 4,370 = \$44,671 \text{ million}$$

Value per share on 484 million shares is $92.30.

The market price was $74 at the time. We would conclude that either the market price is too low, analysts' forecasts are too optimistic, or the long-term growth rate is too high. The analysts' forecasts here are considerably higher than the operating income forecasts from the financial statements. Are analysts using information outside the financial statements or are they too optimistic?

OI_1 is a forecast of forward operating income that is multiplied by a multiplier that incorporates two growth rates. G_2 is (1 plus) the growth rate forecasted for cum-dividend operating income two years ahead, and G_{long} is the growth rate for the long term usually set to the GDP growth rate.[3] The model implies a gradual (geometric) decay of the growth rate over time from the short-term to the long-term rate. Note that we are anchoring on short-term forecasts and a GDP growth rate, both of which we might be relatively confident about. For the model to work, the short-term rate must be higher than the long-term rate (which it usually is). Box 15.3 applies this two-stage model to Nike.

Growth in Sales as a Simple Forecast of Growth

The growth models in equations 15.2, 15.2a, and 15.2b forecast growth based on past growth in net operating assets. But another method can be used: A simple forecast of NOA growth can be made from forecasted sales growth. Net operating assets are driven by sales and the asset turnover: NOA = Sales × 1/ATO. Thus if ATO is expected to be constant in the future, forecasting growth in sales is the same as forecasting growth in NOA. A sales forecast, you'll agree, is much easier to think about than an NOA forecast. And ATO typically does not change much. If so, set the growth rate equal to the sales growth rate.

Recognize that RNOA = Profit margin × ATO. So if we forecast a constant ATO, we forecast a constant RNOA if we also forecast constant margins. You see, then, that the simple growth valuation is likely to work best for firms that have fairly constant profit margins and turnovers and steady sales growth. Many retailers have this feature: Their current RNOA along with a sales growth forecast often give a good approximation. Look also at the valuation for the Coca-Cola Company in Box 15.4. On the other hand, firms that are changing their type of business (and thus their sales growth rates, profit margins, and asset turnovers) are not good candidates for a simple growth valuation. More analysis (as in the next chapter) is required.

[3] The two-stage growth model was developed by Ohlson and Juettner-Nauroth. See J. Ohlson and B. Juettner-Nauroth, "Expected EPS and EPS Growth as Determinants of Value," *Review of Accounting Studies,* July–September 2005, pp. 347–364.

Challenging Stock Prices with a Simple Valuation: The Coca-Cola Company 15.4

The 2,318 million outstanding shares of the Coca-Cola Company traded at $60 each when its 2007 financial statements were issued. Analysis of those and earlier financial statements establishes the following history (dollar numbers are in millions):

	2007	2006	2005	2004	2003	2002
Core profit margin	20.7%	20.4%	21.4%	22.4%	21.3%	22.1%
Asset turnover	1.30	1.32	1.36	1.32	1.32	1.35
Core RNOA	26.9%	26.9%	29.1%	29.6%	28.1%	29.8%

Net operating assets	$26,858
Net financial obligations	5,144
Common equity	$21,714

Coke's core profit margin has declined somewhat over the years, but its asset turnover is very stable. That means that net operating assets grow at the same rate as sales. The average annual sales growth rate over the five years up to 2007 was 5.4 percent (ignoring growth from acquisitions in 2007), and this rate is in line with the rate analysts were forecasting for the future. Using this growth rate for the NOA growth rate along with 2007 core RNOA, Coke's value is calculated as follows with a 9 percent required return:

$$V_{2007}^{NOA} = 26,858 + \frac{(0.269 - 0.09) \times 26,858}{1.09 - 1.054}$$

	= $160,402 million
Net debt	5,144
V_{2007}^{E}	$155,258 million
Value per share on 2,318 million shares	$66.98

The $66.98 valuation suggests that the market price is a little low, though this is just a simple valuation. Observe how far we get with just a few ingredients once financial statements have been reformulated and analyzed to highlight the relevant value drivers. And observe that an historical sales growth rate is an input when asset turnovers are fairly stable, as they often are. Given the stability of the ATO, the analysts asks whether profit margins and sales growth in the future will be different from the past.

You see how simple valuations can be used to challenge a stock price. But there is another lesson here. Coke has a big brand-name asset that is not in the balance sheet. Some claim that because accountants do not record brand assets, it is difficult to value such firms. Not so. Valuation involves both the balance sheet and the income statement, and we see here that a valuation with both is indeed plausible. The simple valuation might be too simple, but you can see that modifying it with a more intelligent forecast of future RNOA and growth will give an intelligent valuation even with a deficient balance sheet.

Information in Analysts' Forecasts

Analysts are supposedly industry experts, so the consensus analyst forecast is one point of reference to check on simple forecasts. Any difference could be attributed to the additional information that analysts have relative to the financial statements. But there is one problem: considerable research has shown that forecasts based on financial statement analysis are often better predictors than analysts' forecasts. (The Web page for this chapter provides details.) Analysts tend to be too optimistic in good times—particularly during bubbles—and too pessimistic in bad times. Warren Buffett said that the 1990s stock market bubble was a chain letter and investment bankers were the postmen, but he could also have included analysts who hyped stocks. Analysts' forecasts may contain additional information over the financial statements, but they are also speculative. Two-year ahead forecasts are particularly suspect, as are their intermediate-term EPS growth rates. The Nike valuation in Box 15.3, based on analysts' forecasts, produced a price of $92.30, well above the $74 market price at the time and well above our simple forecasts. One might see the simple forecasts as a check on analysts: Why are their forecasts so different from what we see in the financial statements? Do their research reports, with its firm and industry analysis, point to solid reasons for the difference? Or are the forecasts speculations that feed speculation in the market price? The financial statements are used to challenge the market price, but they can also be used to challenge your analyst.

SIMPLE VALUATION AS AN ANALYSIS TOOL

Simple models provide a rough valuation, but they come to their fore as analysis tools.

Sensitivity Analysis

For the simple growth valuation of Nike, we set core RNOA equal to the 2010 number of 30.1 percent and the growth rate at the historical rate for net operating assets of 4.6 percent. But the simple valuation formulas allow us to enter any values. Accordingly we can entertain what the valuation might be under different scenarios for future profitability and growth.

Setting different values for these features is called **sensitivity analysis.** This tests how a valuation changes as inputs to a model change, how the valuation is sensitive to alternative forecasts of the future. The simple valuation model gives the form in which to conduct sensitivity analysis.

Sensitivity analysis involves varying forecasts of RNOA and growth and observing the effect on the valuation. How does Nike's valuation in Box 15.2 change if we forecast that future RNOA will be 25.0 percent rather than 30.1 percent? Or if we forecast growth to be 3 percent rather than 4.6 percent? Indeed, we can construct a *valuation grid* that gives per-share values for different combined forecasts of the two drivers:

Valuation Grid for Nike, Inc., 2010. Required Return for Operations: 9.1 Percent

RNOA Growth in NOA	25%	30%	33%	36%
0%	40.33	46.59	50.34	54.10
3%	50.12	59.46	65.06	70.66
4%	55.94	67.11	73.82	80.51
5%	64.60	78.50	86.83	95.17
6%	78.85	97.23	108.25	119.28

The valuation grid can be three-dimensional to incorporate different estimates of the required return. The two-dimensional grid here gives price per share, calculated for different combinations of RNOA and growth in NOA. If asset turnovers are forecasted to be constant, growth in NOA is replaced by sales growth.

As well as answering "what-if" questions, the grid expresses our uncertainty. We might be unsure about Nike's profitability in the future, so the grid displays the value of uncertain outcomes: What could the value drop to, or increase to, under reasonable scenarios?

The valuation grid also indicates what combinations of RNOA and growth in NOA justify the current price. A $74 price can be legitimized by forecasting RNOA of 30 percent with a growth rate of about 4.6 percent or, alternatively, an RNOA of 25 percent and a growth rate of 5.5 percent. If we rule out a growth rate of 5.5 percent as too high, we must demand that Nike maintain an RNOA higher than 25 percent to justify its $74 price.

Reverse Engineering to Challenge the Market Price

Chapter 7 applied valuation models to challenge the market price. The technique was that of reverse engineering. One version reverse engineers a valuation model to identify the growth expectations implicit in the market price. Another version calculates the expected return to buying at the market price.

The simple valuation model can be reverse engineered to infer the forecast of growth in the market price. The simple enterprise valuation model is:

$$V_0^{NOA} = NOA_0 + \frac{ReOI_1}{\rho_F - g}$$

Setting the value at Nike's enterprise market value and inserting the NOA and growth forecast for $ReOI_1$, one can calculate g:

Enterprise market price
= Equity market price
    − Net financial assets
= (484 million shares ×
    $74) − $4,370 million
= $31,446 million

Net operating assets (NOA_0)   = $5,514 million
Forward residual income ($ReOI_1$) = $1,158 million
Required return for operations   = 9.1 percent

The reverse engineering model is:

$$\$31,446 = \$5,514 + \frac{1,158}{1.091 - g}$$

The solution for g is 1.046, that is, a 4.6 percent growth rate. The market is forecasting the same growth rate as the simple growth valuation. This residual operating income growth rate can be converted to an operating income growth rate following the procedures in Chapter 7.

It should be clear that one can reverse engineer from a simple valuation model: Given current price, current book value, and simple forecasts for the near term, what is the growth that the market is forecasting? The only difference is that we are now working with unlevered, enterprise valuation models rather than the levered versions in Chapter 7. That makes sense for a growth forecast because it is growth from operations that generates value.

We will return to active, reverse engineering in Chapter 19. For the moment, you can ask the question: What is the growth rate we must see to justify the market price? After reviewing our financial statement analysis, you can then ask: Is that rate reasonable? Box 15.5 does so for Nike.

Summary

This chapter shows how simple forecasts can be developed from current and past financial statements utilizing financial statement analysis of Part Two of the book. With core profitability identified, forecasts can be developed as if that core profitability is sustainable. Add to core profitability a measure of growth, and the analyst has a simple forecast. The simple forecasts yield simple valuations that give the analyst a first, quick-cut feel for the valuation and quick enterprise P/B and P/E ratios.

The analyst who ignores information is at peril. The simple valuations will not work well when information outside the financial statements indicates that future profitability and growth will be different from current profitability and growth. The analyst calculates the simple valuations as starting points but then turns to full-information forecasting (as in the next chapter).

Notwithstanding, the simple valuations are an analysis tool to examine how valuations are sensitive to different scenarios for future profitability and growth—for asking "what-if" questions. And they lend themselves to reverse engineering to uncover the forecasts of profitability and growth that are implicit in the market price. But, most importantly, simple valuations serve as an anchor as the analyst engages in speculation about the future. A valuation that differs from a simple valuation must be justified with sound reasoning as to why the future will be different from the past.

The Web Connection

Find the following on the Web page for this chapter:

- More demonstrations of simple forecasts.
- More applications of two-stage growth forecasting.
- More on anchoring long-term growth on the GDP growth rate.

- More coverage of sensitivity analysis.
- More on weighted-average forecasts and durable competitive advantage.
- More on analysts' forecasts.

Key Concepts

sensitivity analysis tests how value changes with different forecasts of the future or with different measures of the required return. *491*

simple forecasts involve forecasting from information in the current financial statements. *482*

simple valuations are valuations calculated from simple forecasts. *482*

The Analyst's Toolkit

A Continuing Case: *Kimberly-Clark Corporation*

A Self-Study Exercise

You finally have arrived at the point to value Kimberly-Clark's shares. In this chapter, you will carry out a simple valuation, limiting your inputs to those from the financial statements that you have diligently been analyzing. Then, in the next chapter, you will carry out a full pro forma analysis and valuation.

A SIMPLE VALUATION

Proceed to a simple valuation, using the required return for operations you have previously calculated. Limit yourself solely to information you have discovered in current and past financial statements. Calculate enterprise price-to-book and enterprise P/E ratios from the information. What does that information imply the stock price should be at the end of 2010? Remember to deduct the option overhang you calculated in the Continuing Case for Chapter 14. How does your valuation compare with the market price (in March 2011) of $65.24 per share?

REVERSE ENGINEERING AND SENSITIVITY ANALYSIS

The market price embeds expectations of future growth. Assuming Kimberly-Clark can maintain future operating profitability at the level of current core RNOA, what growth rate in residual operating income is the market projecting for the future? Would you say this forecast is reasonable, given the history? What tools might you use to get better insights?

Now start to experiment. What scenarios would justify the market price? Do you see these as reasonable scenarios? Do you see scenarios that would suggest that the stock is underpriced or overpriced? Are these speculations consistent with what you know from the financial statement history?

Concept Questions	
C15.1.	A valuation that simply capitalizes a forecast of operating income for the next year implicitly assumes that residual operating income will continue as a perpetuity. Is this correct?
C15.2.	An analyst forecasts that next year's core operating income for a firm will be the same as the current year's core operating income. Under what conditions is this a good forecast?
C15.3.	When is the forecasted growth rate in residual operating income the same as the forecasted growth rate in sales?
C15.4.	Would you call a firm that is expected to have a high sales growth rate a growth firm?
C15.5.	The higher the anticipated return on net operating assets (RNOA) relative to the anticipated growth in net operating assets, the higher will be the unlevered price-to-book ratio. Is this correct?
C15.6.	What is the effect of increasing the asset turnover (ATO) on enterprise price-to-book, holding all else constant?

Exercises

Drill Exercises

E15.1. A No-growth Forecast and a Simple Valuation (Easy)

An analyst calculates residual operating income of $35.7 million from financial statements for 2012, using a required return for operations of 10 percent. She also forecasts residual operating income at the same level for 2013 and years after on net operating assets of $1,257 million at the end of 2012.

a. What is the analyst's forecast of operating income for 2013?
b. What is the value of the operations based on these forecasts?
c. What is the forward enterprise P/E ratio implied by the forecasts?

E15.2. A Simple Growth Forecast and a Simple Valuation (Easy)

An analyst prepares the following reformulated balance sheet (in millions):

	2012	2011
Net operating assets	$9,682	$9,400
Net financial obligations	1,987	1,876
Common shareholders' equity	$7,695	$7,524

Core operating income (after tax) for 2012 was $990 million. The required return for operations is 9 percent. For ease, use beginning-of-year balance sheet numbers where pertinent in calculations.

a. What was the core return on net operating assets for 2012?
b. Prepare a growth forecast of operating income and residual operating income for 2013 based on this financial statement information.
c. Value the equity based on the information.
d. What is the intrinsic enterprise price-to-book ratio?

E15.3. Two-Stage Growth Valuation (Medium)

An analyst develops the following pro forma at the end of 2012 for a firm that uses a 9 percent hurdle rate for its operations (in millions):

	2012A	2013E	2014E
Operating income		$ 782	$ 868
Net operating assets	$6,400	6,848	7,190
Net financial obligations	756		
Common equity	$5,644		

a. Forecast the cum-dividend operating income growth rate for 2014.
b. Using the two-stage growth model 15.5, value the equity with a long-term growth rate of 4 percent.
c. What is the forward enterprise price/earnings ratio implied by the valuation?

E15.4. Simple Valuation with Sales Growth Rates (Medium)

An analyst forecasts that the current core return on net operating assets of 15.5 percent will continue indefinitely in the future with a 5 percent annual sales growth rate. She also forecasts that the current asset turnover ratio of 2.2 will persist. Calculate the enterprise price-to-book ratio if the required return for operations is 9.5 percent.

E15.5. Simple Forecasting and Valuation (Medium)

An analyst uses the following summary balance sheet to value a firm at the end of 2012 (in millions of dollars):

	2012	2011
Net operating assets	4,572	3,941
Net financial obligations	1,243	1,014
Common shareholders' equity	3,329	2,927

The analyst forecasts that the firm will earn a return on net operating assets (RNOA) of 12 percent in 2013 and a residual operating income of $91.4 million.

a. What is the required rate of return for operations that the analyst is using in his residual operating income forecast?
b. The analyst forecasts that the residual operating income in 2013 will continue as a perpetuity. What value does this imply for the equity?
c. Calculate the forecast of residual earnings (on common equity) for 2013 that is implied by these forecasts. The firm's after-tax cost of debt is 6.0 percent.

Applications

E15.6. Simple Valuation for General Mills, Inc. (Easy)

The following are from the financial statements for General Mills (in millions):

	2008	2007
Net operating assets	$12,847	$12,297
Common equity	6,216	5,319
Core operating income (after tax)	1,560	

There were 337.5 million shares outstanding at the end of fiscal year 2008 and they traded at $60 each. Use a required return for operations of 8 percent in answering the following questions:

a. What is General Mills's no-growth per-share valuation?
b. What is General Mills's per-share valuation based on growth forecasts from these numbers?

Real World Connection

See Exercises E1.5, E2.9, E3.8, E4.10, E6.8, E11.9, E13.9, E14.15, and E16.10.

E15.7. Simple Valuation for the Coca-Cola Company (Medium)

In early 2006, the 2,369 million outstanding shares of the Coca-Cola Company traded at $48.91 each. The price-to-book ratio was 6.3 and the forward P/E was 19.3 based on analysts' consensus EPS forecast for 2007. An analyst extracted the following numbers from Coke's financial statements (in millions of dollars):

	2005	2004	2003	2002
Sales	23,104	21,742	20,857	19,564
Core operating income, after tax	4,944	4,870	4,443	4,324
Net operating assets (average for year)	17,184	16,563	15,735	14,932

a. Calculate the core operating profit margin and asset turnover for each year 2002–2005.
b. Calculate the average sales growth rate over the years 2003–2005.
c. The firm reported common shareholders' equity at the end of 2005 of $16,945 million, along with $1,010 billion in net financial obligations. Using the numbers you calculated, estimate Coke's enterprise value at the end of 2005 and also the value per share. Use a required return for operations of 10 percent. Box 15.4 will help you.

Real World Connection

See Exercises E4.7, E4.8, E12.7, E16.12, E17.7, and E20.4. Also see Minicases M4.1, M5.2, and M6.2 for coverage of Coke.

E15.8. Reverse Engineering for Starbucks Corporation (Medium)

In January 2008, the 738.3 million outstanding shares of Starbucks Corporation traded at $20 each. Analysts' consensus earning-per-share estimates of $1.03 for the fiscal year ending September 30, 2008, gave the firm a forward P/E of 19.4. The firm reported earnings per share for 2007 of $0.90, up from $0.74 a year earlier.

The following information was garnered from the firm's financial statements (in millions):

	2007	2006
Revenues	$9,412	$7,787
Core operating income (after tax)	671	
Net operating assets	3,093	2,565
Net financial obligations	915	337
Common equity	2,178	2,228

OI:
ReOI

a. From these statements, calculate the following for 2007 (with beginning-of-period balance sheet numbers in denominators where applicable):

(1) Core operating profit margin

(2) Core return on net operating assets (core RNOA)

(3) Asset turnover

(4) Growth rate for net operating assets

b. Using these numbers and a required return of 9 percent, forecast residual operating income (ReOI) for fiscal year 2008.

c. What is the stock market's implied rate of growth for residual operating income after 2008?

Real World Connection

Exercises on Starbucks are E9.8, E10.10, E12.9, and E13.8.

E15.9. A Simple Valuation and Reverse Engineering: IBM (Medium)

The following are key numbers from IBM's financial statements for 2004.

Net operating assets, end of year	$42,104 million
Net financial obligations, end of year	12,357 million
Common equity, end of year	29,747 million
Common shares outstanding, end of year	1,645.6 million
Core return on net operating assets	18.8%
Sales growth rate	8.8%

IBM's shares traded at $95 when 2004 results were announced. Use a required return for operations of 12.3 percent to answer the following questions:

a. Forecast operating income and residual operating income for 2005 if IBM maintains the same core RNOA as in 2004.

b. Calculate the per-share value of the equity if IBM were to maintain this profitability in the future and if residual earnings were to grow at the 2004 sales growth rate. Also calculate the implied forward enterprise P/E ratio and the enterprise P/B ratio.

c. What growth rate in residual operating income would justify the current stock price if you were sure that 12.3 percent was a reasonable required return?

Real World Connection

Exercises E6.9 and E14.14 deal with IBM, as does Minicase M13.3.

E15.10. Buffett's Acquisition of Burlington Northern Santa Fe (Medium)

In 2009, Warren Buffett announced that Berkshire Hathaway would acquire all of the 341 million outstanding shares of Burlington Northern Santa Fe (BNSF) railroad for $100 per share, a large premium from the current price. BNSF reported shareholders' equity of $12,798 million in its most recent annual report, with $9,135 million in net financial obligations that Buffett would assume. The corresponding numbers for the prior year were $11,131 million and $9,155 million. The income statement reported $14,016 million in revenue for the year that translated into $2,113 million in after-tax core operating income.

a. On the basis of the current numbers, do you think the $100 per share bid can be justified? What growth rate is implied in the price? (Experiment with "reasonable" estimates of Buffett's required return.)

b. What might Buffett see to justify paying $100 per share? (Think: ATO).

E15.11. Comparing Simple Forecasts with Analysts' Forecasts: Home Depot, Inc. (Medium)

Home Depot, the warehouse retailer, traded at $42 per share when its 2005 financial statements were published. Analysts were forecasting $2.59 earnings per share for 2006 and $2.93 for 2007. There were 2,185 million shares outstanding at the time. Below are income statements for fiscal years 2003–2005, along with information extracted from balance sheets. Home Depot's combined federal and state statutory tax rate is 37.7 percent.

Develop forecasts of earnings for 2006 and 2007 from the financial statements. How close are your forecasts to the analysts' forecasts?

THE HOME DEPOT, INC. AND SUBSIDIARIES
Consolidated Statements of Earnings
(In millions except per-share numbers)

	Fiscal Year Ended		
	January 30, 2005	February 1, 2004	February 2, 2003
Net sales	$73,094	$64,816	$58,247
Cost of merchandise sold	48,664	44,236	40,139
Gross profit	24,430	20,580	18,108
Operating expenses:			
Selling and store operating	15,105	12,588	11,276
General and administrative	1,399	1,146	1,002
Total operating expenses	16,504	13,734	12,278
Operating income	7,926	6,846	5,830
Interest income (expense):			
Interest and investment income	56	59	79
Interest expense	(70)	(62)	(37)
Interest, net	(14)	(3)	42

Earnings before provision for income taxes	7,912	6,843	5,872
Provision for income taxes	2,911	2,539	2,208
Net earnings	$ 5,001	$ 4,304	$ 3,664
Weighted-average common shares	2,207	2,283	2,336
Basic earnings per share	$ 2.27	$ 1.88	$ 1.57
Diluted weighted-average common shares	2,216	2,289	2,344
Diluted earnings per share	$ 2.26	$ 1.88	$ 1.56

From the balance sheet (in millions):

	2005	2004	2003	2002
Net operating assets	$23,833	$20,886	$18,820	$16,753
Net financial assets	325	1,521	982	1,329
Common equity	24,158	22,407	19,802	18,082

E15.12. Valuation Grid and Reverse Engineering for Home Depot, Inc. (Medium)

a. Using the information in Exercise 15.11, calculate the implied growth rate in residual operating income that is implicit in the market price of $42 per share.

b. If you forecast that the growth rate in residual earnings after fiscal year 2006 will be the GDP growth rate of 4 percent, what is the expected return to buying the stock at $42?

c. Prepare a valuation grid showing what the stock is worth for alternative forecasts of return on net operating assets and growth in net operating assets.

Real World Connection

Home Depot is also discussed in E15.11.

Minicases

M15.1

Simple Forecasting and Valuation: Procter & Gamble V

This case continues the financial statement analysis of Procter & Gamble Co. begun in Minicase 10.1 and developed further in Minicases 11.1, 12.1, and 13.1. This fifth installment focuses on forecasting and valuation, with further development in Minicase 16.1 in the next chapter.

Financial statements for Procter & Gamble are presented in Exhibit 10.15 in Chapter 10. If you worked Minicase 10.1, you will have reformulated the income statements and balance sheets to distinguish operating activities from financing activities. If you worked Minicases M12.1 and 13.1, you will have reached an understanding of P&G's core profitability and the factors that drive that profitability. If not, you should do so now.

To start, calculate residual core operating income for the years 2008 to 2010 and note changes over time. Use a required equity return of 8 percent but convert it to an unlevered required return (for operations). In July 2010, just after the fiscal year ended, the 2,844 million outstanding shares of P&G were trading at $62. What is the trend in residual operating income? Does P&G appear to be a growth company? What drives the trend?

A. Develop forecasts of residual operating income for 2011 and growth thereafter based solely on information in the financial statements. Your analysis should include a no-growth forecast, along with a forecast that includes growth. Consider a weighted-average forecast that forecasts GDP growth in the long run. Do you think these forecasts are applicable to P&G? Carry out a sensitivity analysis to changes in inputs by developing a valuation grid.

B. Analysts were forecasting $3.93 in earnings per share for fiscal year 2011. How does the analyst forecast compare with yours?

C. Calculate the (traded) enterprise price-to-book ratio and reconcile it to the levered price-to-book ratio. Now calculate an intrinsic enterprise P/B using equation 15.2b in this chapter. Do you think the $62 price is reasonable?

Real World Connection

Minicases M10.1, M11.1, M12.1, M13.1, and M16.1 also cover Procter & Gamble.

M15.2

Simple Valuation, Reverse Engineering, and Sensitivity Analysis for Cisco Systems, Inc.

Cisco Systems, Inc. (CSCO), manufactures and sells networking and communications equipment for transporting data, voice, and video and provides services related to that equipment. Its products include routing and switching devices; home and office networking equipment; and Internet protocol, telephony, security, network management, and software services. The firm has grown organically but also through acquisition of other networking and software firms. Cisco's Web site is at **www.cisco.com**.

By any stretch of the imagination, Cisco Systems (CSCO) has been a strong growth company. A darling of the Internet boom of the late 1990s, it was one of the few technology companies tied to the Internet and telecommunications that prospered during that era. Its products built the infrastructure of the Internet. While most Internet and telecommunications firms struggled and failed, their supplier, Cisco, capitalized on the new technology. At one point in 2000, its market capitalization was over half a trillion dollars, the largest market capitalization of any firm, ever. Its P/E was over 130. The stock price increased from $10 in 1995 to $77 in 2000, supported by sales growth from $2.0 billion in 1995 to $18.9 billion in 2000.

However, with the subsequent collapse of the technology bubble and the demise of telecommunications firms such as WorldCom, Qwest, and AT&T, growth slowed considerably. Sales that peaked at $22.3 billion in fiscal year 2001 dropped to $18.9 billion by 2003 and recovered to the 2001 level only in 2004. The stock price also tumbled, reaching a low of a little over $8 in late 2002 after the firm reported a net loss for the year. The stock price recovered to $24 by 2004.

Subsequently, Cisco's sales grew, reaching $39.5 billion by 2008. However, from 2008 to 2010, sales remained flat, standing at $40.04 billion in 2010. Profit margins also declined and EPS in 2010 of $1.36 was little changed from the $1.35 in 2008. Rivals Motorola and Juniper Networks were gaining ground. Cisco's diversification, via acquisitions, into cable set-top boxes and videoconferencing equipment was not proving successful, with cable companies cutting back on orders for the cable boxes and customers using Skype or Google Talk to conference for free. Cisco suffered a precipitous decline in government orders during 2010 as state governments cut budgets.

Cisco's 5,655 million shares traded at $20 by the end of 2010 and were down further to $15 by June 2011. On the next page are summary numbers from its financial statements for 2008 to 2010.

Prepare simple valuations based on these statements. Use a required return of 9 percent for Cisco's operations. Then introduce some scenarios for the future—speculation about sales growth and the level of profitability, for example—to see if the current price can be justified or whether reasonable speculation might justify an even higher price. You might also test how your valuations are sensitive to the required return you use. Also use reverse engineering techniques to ask the question: What growth rate is the market forecasting?

A. Would you pay $15 for a share of Cisco Systems?

B. Would you attribute the drop in stock price from 2000 to 2002 to problems in Cisco's operations?

C. Clearly the great Cisco is now challenged. Discuss the lesson here.

D. In 2010, Cisco announced that it would pay a dividend of $0.24 per share for the first time. Why might Cisco be doing this? What effect do you think it had on the share price?

E. In 2010, Cisco borrowed about $5 billion. The firm has a high level of financial assets on its balance sheet; why would it borrow?

F. Goodwill on the 2010 balance sheet stood at $16,674 million, up from $12,121 billion in 2007 because of acquisitions. Given that these acquisitions have not been successful, what do you think might happen to the carrying value of the goodwill in the future?

CISCO SYSTEMS, INC.
Summary Reformulated Income Statements
(in millions of dollars, except per-share amounts)

	2010	2009	2008
Sales	40,040	36,117	39,540
Cost of sales	14,397	13,023	14,194
Gross Margin	25,643	23,094	25,346
Operating expenses	16,479	15,772	15,904
Core operating income before tax	9,164	7,332	9,442
Tax on operating income	1,557	1,424	1,907
Core operating income after tax	7,607	5,898	7,535
Net interest income after tax	160	236	517
Net income	7,767	6,134	8,052
Earnings per share	$ 1.36	$ 1.05	$ 1.35

Summary Reformulated Balance Sheets
(in millions of dollars)

	2010	2009	2008	2007
Net operating assets	18,708	13,971	15,011	15,622
Net financial assets	25,577	24,706	19,342	15,858
Common equity	44,285	38,677	34,353	31,480

Real World Connection

Minicase M7.1 is a reverse engineering study of Cisco, and Exercises E2.1 and E19.6 also deal with the firm.

Chapter **Sixteen**

Full-Information Forecasting, Valuation, and Business Strategy Analysis

LINKS

Link to previous chapter	Link to previous chapters
Chapter 15 developed simple forecasting schemes based on information in financial statements.	Chapters 12 and 13 laid out the analysis of financial statements that uncovers drivers of profitability and growth.

This chapter	
This chapter shows how information outside the financial statements is incorporated to make forecasts that improve upon the simple forecasts in Chapter 15.	This chapter uses the financial statement analysis of Chapters 12 and 13 to develop a framework for full-information forecasting.

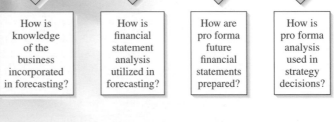

How is knowledge of the business incorporated in forecasting?	How is financial statement analysis utilized in forecasting?	How are pro forma future financial statements prepared?	How is pro forma analysis used in strategy decisions?

Link to next chapter
Chapter 17 begins an investigation of accounting issues that arise in forecasting and valuation.

Link to Web page
Learn how to develop spreadsheet financial models to convert forecasts to valuations—visit the text's Web site at **www.mhhe.com/penman5e**.

The simple forecasting schemes in the last chapter embedded all the concepts needed for valuation. But they did not exploit all of the information that is necessary to make the analyst feel secure about a valuation. The simple schemes focused on profitability and growth in operations, but they were limited to information in the financial statements. Full-information forecasting digs deeper. It forecasts using all information available and, from these forecasts, builds up a forecast of residual earnings and abnormal earnings growth from which a valuation can be made.

Chapters 12 and 13 outlined the factors that drive profitability and growth enabling us to analyze current financial statements. But because those same factors drive future profitability and growth, the driver analysis of those chapters also gives us the framework for forecasting: The analyst forecasts the drivers—future sales, core profit margins, asset turnovers, and so on—to develop forecasts. Financial statement analysis is an analysis of the past, to provide

The Analyst's Checklist

After reading this chapter you should understand:	After reading this chapter you should be able to:
• How forecasting is a matter of financial statement analysis for the future.	• Develop pro forma income statements and balance sheets for the future.
• How financial statement drivers translate economic factors into a valuation.	• Make forecasts of future residual operating income, abnormal operating income growth, and free cash flow from pro forma financial statements.
• How to identify key drivers.	
• How to conduct full-information pro forma analysis.	• Make valuations from pro forma financial statements.
• The 15 steps in pro forma analysis.	• Show how changes in forecasts for specific drivers change pro forma financial statements and valuations.
• The seven steps involved in forecasting residual operating income and abnormal operating income growth.	
• How mergers and acquisitions are evaluated.	• Use pro forma analysis for sensitivity analysis.
• How pro forma analysis is used as a tool in strategy analysis.	• Calculate the effect of a proposed merger or acquisition on per-share value.
	• Use pro forma analysis to evaluate strategy scenarios.

information for forecasts of the future. However, you will see in this chapter that forecasting is a matter of **financial statement analysis of the future.** Much of this chapter takes the analysis of Chapters 12 and 13 and rolls it over to the future.

The drivers of profitability and growth are themselves driven by the "real" economic factors of the business. So knowing the business is an essential first step to discovering the information for full-information forecasting. You will see here how financial statement analysis provides the means of interpreting the many dimensions of business activity in a form that can be used for forecasting. Knowing the firm's strategy is also a prerequisite for forecasting, and you will also see how financial statement analysis interprets strategy. Moreover, you will see how the methods of forecasting are also the methods by which a manager evaluates alternative strategies.

The chapter develops a formal scheme for forecasting. The scheme ensures that all relevant aspects of the business are incorporated and irrelevant aspects are ignored. It is comprehensive and orderly so that no element is lost. By forcing the analyst to forecast in an orderly manner, the scheme disciplines speculative tendencies.

The simple forecasts of the last chapter are a starting point for full-information forecasting. The simple forecasts are based on current profitability and growth in net operating assets. Full-information forecasting asks how future profitability and growth will differ from current levels. If, through analysis of additional information, we forecast that indeed they will, then we will have improved on the simple forecasts and the simple valuations. But we must realize that we are adding speculation, so must be sober in the endeavor.

FINANCIAL STATEMENT ANALYSIS: FOCUSING THE LENS ON THE BUSINESS

We have repetitively said that one cannot value a business without a thorough understanding of the business; knowing the business is a prerequisite to valuation and strategy analysis—Step 1 of fundamental analysis. Before embarking on this chapter, look back to the section titled "The Analysis of Business" in Chapter 1, where the main factors that determine business success are discussed. The analyst must understand the business model and alternative, adaptive strategies available to the firm. She must understand the firm's product, its marketing and production methods, and its knowledge base. She must understand the legal, regulatory, and political constraints on the firm. She must evaluate the management. Most important, she must develop an appreciation of the durability of the firm's competitive advantage, if any.

Understanding these many economic factors is a prerequisite to forecasting. But we need a way of translating these factors into measures that lead to a valuation. We must recognize the firm's product, the competition in the industry, the firm's ability to develop product innovations, and so on, but we must also interpret this knowledge in a way that leads to a valuation. Economic factors are often expressed in qualitative terms that are suggestive but do not immediately translate into concrete dollar numbers. We might recognize that a firm has "market power," but what does this imply for its value? We might recognize that a firm is "under threat of competition," but what does this imply for its value? How are "growth opportunities" valued?

Accounting-based valuation models and our earlier financial statement analysis provide the translation. Market power translates into sales and higher margins; competition reduces them. The technology to produce sales is reflected in the asset turnover. And sales, margins, and turnovers are the drivers of profitability on which valuation is based. The structure of financial statement analysis is the means to interpret what we observe about business. It focuses the lens on the business. There is danger in relying on suggestive notions such as "market power," "competitive advantage," and "breakthrough technology" without a concrete analysis of what they imply for valuation. Investors can get carried away by enthusiasm for such ideas, leading to speculation in stock prices. Forecasting within a financial statement analysis framework disciplines investor exuberance and, indeed, investor pessimism. It brings both the bulls and the bears to a focus on the fundamentals.

There are four points of focus for translating business activities into a valuation.

1. Focus on Residual Operating Income and Its Drivers

The focus for the valuation of operations is on residual operating income (ReOI) for a P/B valuation or abnormal operating income growth (AOIG) for a P/E valuation. But AOIG is just the change in ReOI. So business activities are interpreted by their effect on ReOI. ReOI is driven by return on net operating assets (RNOA) and growth in net operating assets (NOA). RNOA is driven by four drivers:

$$\text{RNOA} = (\text{Core sales PM} \times \text{ATO}) + \frac{\text{Core other OI}}{\text{NOA}} + \frac{\text{Unusual items}}{\text{NOA}}$$

Combining these RNOA drivers with growth in NOA, we can capture the drivers of residual operating income in one expression that contains five drivers:

$$\text{ReOI} = \text{Sales} \times \left[\text{Core sales PM} - \frac{\text{Required return for operations}}{\text{ATO}} \right] \quad \textbf{(16.1)}$$
$$+ \text{Core other OI} + \text{Unusual items}$$

(It is usually the case that unusual items are expected to be zero in the future.) The ATO is sales per dollar of net operating assets, so the ratio of the required return on operations to ATO here is a measure of operational efficiency in using net operating assets to generate sales relative to the required rate of return for those assets. The RNOA drivers—core profit margin, asset turnover, core other income, and unusual items—are in this formula. And growth in NOA is embedded through its drivers: Since NOA is put in place to generate sales, NOA is driven by sales and 1/ATO, that is, by sales and the net operating assets required to generate a dollar of sales.

Forecasting residual operating income involves forecasting these drivers so, with valuation in mind, observations about the business are translated into forecasts of the five drivers:

1. Sales
2. Core sales profit margin
3. Asset turnover
4. Core other operating income
5. Unusual items

Sales is the primary driver because, without customers and sales, no value can be added in operations. Much of our knowledge of the business—its products, its marketing, its R&D, its brand management, to name a few factors—is applied to forecasting sales. And as every basic economics course teaches, dollar sales is sales price multiplied by quantity sold. Both price and quantity involve analysis of consumer tastes, the price elasticity of consumer demand, substitute products, the technology path, competitiveness of the industry, and government regulations, to name a few. But equation 16.1 tells us that sales generate positive ReOI only if they are turned into positive margins. And sales generate positive ReOI only if these margins are greater than the ATO relative to the required return.

As a first step in organizing your business knowledge, attach economic factors to ReOI drivers. What factors drive product prices and product quantities (and thus sales)? Among the answers will be competition, product substitutes, brand association, and patent protection. What factors drive margins? Among the answers will be the production technology, economies of scale and learning, and the competitiveness in labor and supplier markets.

2. Focus on Change

A firm's current drivers are discovered through financial statement analysis. Forecasting involves future drivers, so focus on business activities that may change ReOI drivers from their current levels. The analysis of changes in drivers is a question of earnings sustainability, or more strictly, *ReOI sustainability*. Analyze change in three steps.

Step A. Understand the Typical Driver Pattern for the Industry

Figures 16.1 and 16.2 display historical patterns for the primary drivers. They are based on actual data and show how the drivers change from initial values (in Year 0) over the subsequent five years. All drivers exhibit **mean reversion**: Value drivers tend to become more like the average over time. High levels (of core RNOA, for example) tend to be lower in the future and low levels tend to become higher.

These **driver patterns** have two features:

1. The current level of the driver relative to its typical (median) level for a comparison set of firms.
2. The rate of reversion to a long-run level.

Element 1 is established by the analysis of the current financial statements and element 2 is the subject of forecasting. The rate of reversion to a long-run level is sometimes referred to as the **fade rate** or **persistence rate,** and these displays are often called *fade diagrams*. Some analysts market their equity research as an analysis of fade rates. How long will a nontypical ReOI and nontypical ReOI drivers take to fade to the typical long-run level? How long will a nontypical level persist?

Economic factors affect firms in similar ways within industries, so driver pattern diagrams are best developed by industry. Industry is usually defined by the product brought to market. There are standard classifications, like the Standard Industrial Classification (SIC) system, which classifies firms by nested four-digit industry codes. Within an industry, firms tend to become more like each other over time, or they go out of existence. Thus, analysts talk of ReOI and its drivers fading to levels that are typical for the industry. Firms may have temporary advantages, new ideas, or innovations that distinguish them from others, but the **forces of competition** and the ability of existing and new firms to imitate them drive out the temporary advantage. Correspondingly, if these competitive forces are muted, we expect to see more sustained driver patterns than for a strongly competitive industry. As fade rates are driven by competition, some analysts refer to the period over which a driver fades to a typical level as the **competitive advantage period.**

Figure 16.1 gives historical patterns for the core RNOA driver, along with patterns for core other income and items classified as unusual (both divided by NOA).[1] These figures, track the drivers over five years from a base year (Year 0) for 10 groups of firms that differ in the amount of the drivers in the base year. The top group contains firms with the highest 10 percent in the base year and the bottom group contains firms with the lowest 10 percent. As you would expect, unusual items (in Figure 16.1c) fade out quickly—they are very transitory—but core RNOA (in Figure 16.1a) and other core income (in Figure 16.1b) also fade toward central values, with high profitability (in the upper groups) declining and low profitability (in the lower groups) increasing. The diagrams indicate that the forces of competition are at play to drive core RNOA to common levels. Firms in the top 10 percent of core RNOA in the current year have a median 29 percent RNOA that fades to 18 percent five years later. But there are long-run differences between core RNOA that have to be forecast: Firms with higher core RNOA currently tend to have higher core RNOA later, but differences in core RNOA decrease over time. We will see in Part Four that the accounting partly explains these permanent differences.

When evaluating where RNOA might converge in the future, beware of a common fallacy. Many valuation texts dictate "the rate of return must decline to the required return in the long run." This is incorrect. Box 16.1 explains.

Figure 16.2 gives historical patterns for sales growth rates, changes in core sales profit margins, and changes in asset turnovers. These patterns indicate the sustainability of increases or decreases in the drivers. Sales growth (in Figure 16.2a) is strongly mean reverting: Firms with large increases in sales tend to have lower increases in the future. And large increases or decreases in core sales profit margins (in Figure 16.2b) and asset turnovers (in Figure 16.2c) also tend to be temporary. Average changes in both drivers (represented by the fifth group from the top in Year 0) are close to zero, but all groups converge to this average over time.

The contrarian stock screening strategy (in Chapter 3) shorts stocks with high growth in sales and profits and buys stocks with low growth. The contrarians have these change patterns in mind but believe that the market does not. They believe that the market gets too excited about high sales and profit growth and thinks growth will continue rather than fade; and they believe the market does not understand that drops in sales and profits are often temporary.

---

[1] The patterns in the figures here are averages of patterns from grouping firms on their drivers in 1964, 1969, 1974, 1979, 1984, 1989, and 1994, and tracking their subsequent path.

Valuation texts often claim that the rate of return must equal the required return in the long run and build that principle into forecasts and valuations: If the required return is 10 percent, forecast that RNOA will decline to 10 percent at the forecasting horizon. They have economic theory in mind: Superior profitability will be eroded away as competition sets in, so all firms will just earn the required return for their risk level in the long run. As a statement of economic principle, this is reasonable provided the industry is competitive.

But RNOA (and any measure of rate of return) is an accounting measure and its properties depend on the accounting. GAAP and IFRS accounting have the feature of leaving assets off the balance sheet, so firms may have a rate of return higher than the required return in the future even though they may be earning a competitive "economic rate of return." Even though profits (in the numerator) are competitive profits, the rate of return will be high if the assets that generate the profits are missing in the denominator. A pharmaceutical firm, with the R&D asset missing from its balance sheet, will always have a high RNOA (barring catastrophe). Coca-Cola, with its brand asset missing from the balance sheet, has a high RNOA continually. So does Microsoft, Cisco Systems, and other technology firms. Chapter 17 demonstrates how accounting increases the rate of return.

One might suggest that we should focus on the "economic rate of return." But that is something we cannot see; it's just a concept out of theory. Every measure is, well, just a measure, subject to how one measures, how one does the accounting. Don't get into the business of constructing economic income and return—you will find yourself speculating. And you don't have to. We found in Chapter 5 that residual earnings methods accommodate the accounting: If book value is low (because of missing assets), RNOA is higher to compensate. And, importantly, residual income is correspondingly higher, so adding the higher ReOI to the low book value compensates and yields the appropriate valuation. Don't adjust the RNOA: You will misvalue. And don't necessarily set the RNOA in the long run to a required return of 10 percent (say) if the firm is one that should have a higher RNOA, even if it is in a competitive industry: You will misvalue.

FIGURE 16.1
Driver Patterns for Core RNOA, Core Other Income, and Unusual Operating Items, NYSE and AMEX Firms, 1964–1999

The patterns trace the median drivers over five years for 10 groups formed for different levels of the drivers in Year 0. Firms in the upper groups have high drivers in the current year (Year 0) and firms in the lower groups have low drivers in the current year.

Source: D. Nissim and S. Penman, "Ratio Analysis and Equity Valuation: From Research to Practice," *Review of Accounting Studies,* March 2001, pp. 109–154. Based on Standard & Poor's COMPUSTAT data.

(*a*) Core RNOA. Firms with high core RNOA currently (in the upper groups) tend to have declining profitability in the future; firms with low core RNOA (in the lower groups) tend to have increasing profitability in the future.

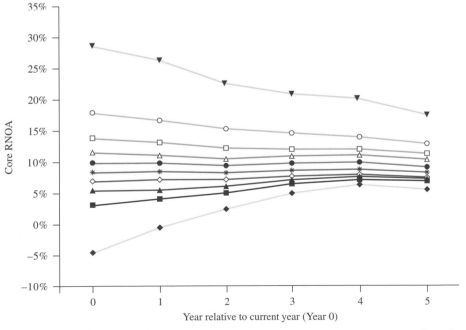

(*continued*)

FIGURE 16.1
(*concluded*)

(*b*) Core other income/NOA. High core other income (for firms in the upper groups) tends to decline subsequently as a percentage of net operating assets; low core other operating income (for firms in the lower groups) tends to increase.

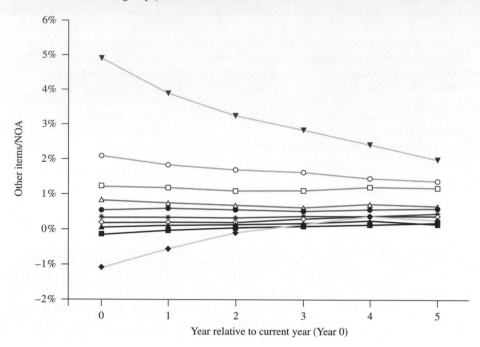

(*c*) Unusual operating items/NOA. Unusual items tend to disappear very quickly—as expected for a transitory item.

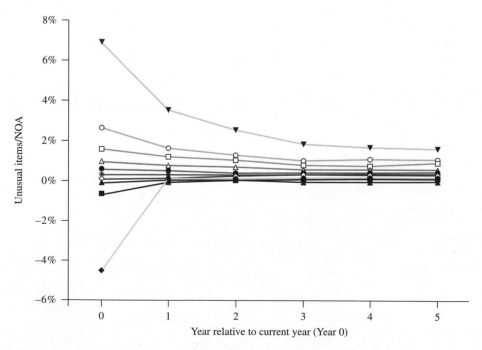

FIGURE 16.2
Driver Patterns for Sales Growth Rates, Changes in Core Sales Profit Margins, and Changes in Asset Turnovers, NYSE and AMEX Firms, 1964–1999

Source: D. Nissim and S. Penman, "Ratio Analysis and Equity Valuation: From Research to Practice," *Review of Accounting Studies,* March 2001, pp. 109–154. Based on Standard & Poor's COMPUSTAT data.

(*a*) Sales growth rates. Sales growth tends to fade quickly: Firms with high sales growth currently (in the upper groups) have lower sales growth subsequently; firms with low current sales growth (in the lower groups) have higher sales growth subsequently.

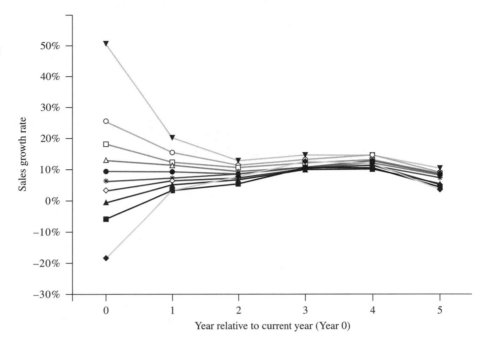

(*b*) Changes in core sales profit margins. Changes in core sales profit margins tend to fade quickly toward common levels close to zero.

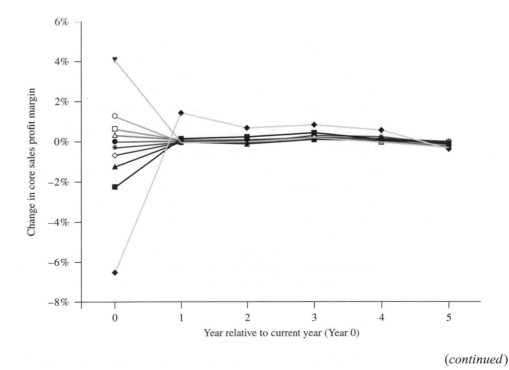

(continued)

FIGURE 16.2
(concluded)

(c) Changes in asset turnovers. Changes in asset turnovers tend to revert toward common levels very quickly; large increases in asset turnovers (in the upper groups) are temporary, as are large decreases in asset turnovers (in the lower groups).

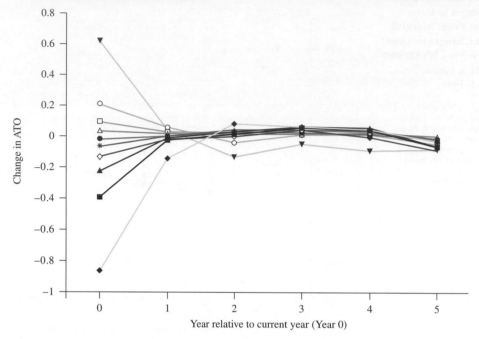

Step B. Modify the Typical Driver Pattern for Forecasts for the Economy and the Industry

Historical industry patterns are a good starting point if the future is likely to be similar to the past. But indications may be to the contrary. Government or trade statistics may forecast a change in the direction for the (global) economy or for the specific industry. Forecasts of recession or a slowdown of GDP growth may signal a change from the past. Shifts in industrywide demand for the product may be indicated by changing demographics or changing consumer tastes. Knowing the business requires a knowledge of industry trends and a knowledge of the susceptibility of the industry to macroeconomic changes.

Step C. Forecast How the Firm's Drivers Will Be Different from the Typical Industry Pattern

Understanding typical drivers for an industry disciplines speculative tendencies. But firms have idiosyncratic features that yield drivers that are predictably different from industry patterns. So full-information forecasting is completed by asking how the firm's future drivers will be different from the typical pattern for the industry.

The main factor in determining fade rates is competition and firms' reactions to it. Competition causes abnormal RNOA to fade, and the ability of the firm to counter the forces of competition sustains RNOA higher than the industry average. Firms both create the forces of competition and counter those forces. Among the ways that they challenge other firms (with examples of specific firms or industries) are:

- Product price reductions (Walmart, Home Depot, and other discount retailers).
- Product innovations (software developers, pharmaceutical companies).
- Product delivery innovations (Dell, Inc., Amazon, and electronic commerce).

- Lower production costs (manufacturers moving production to countries with low labor costs).
- Imitation of successful firms (PC cloners copying IBM; imitating Dell's inventory and distribution system).
- Entering industries where firms are earning abnormal profits (software, biotechnology).

Among ways that firms counter competitive forces (with examples of specific firms or industries) are:

- Brand creation and maintenance; franchising (Coca-Cola, McDonald's).
- Creating proprietary knowledge that receives patent protection (pharmaceutical firms).
- Managing consumer expectations (beer and wine marketing).
- Forming alliances and agreements with competitors, suppliers, and firms with related technology (airline alliances, telecom alliances).
- Exploiting first-mover advantages (Walmart, Google, Internet portal pioneers).
- Mergers (banking, financial services).
- Creating superior production and marketing technologies (Dell, Inc.).
- Staying ahead on technological knowledge and production learning curve (Intel).
- Creating economies of scale that are difficult to replicate (telecom networks, banking networks).
- Creating a proprietary technological standard or a network that consumers and other firms must lock into (Microsoft).
- Government protection and government-allocated privileges (agriculture, media).

Understanding the tension between the forces of competition and the counterforces is crucial to forecasting fade rates. Many actions of firms that challenge and counter competition create temporary advantages, but these advantages often disappear over time. Product innovation draws customers but ultimately is imitated if there is no patent protection. Success draws imitators unless there are natural or government-enforced barriers to entry. These factors yield decreasing returns (to use economists' language). Firms strive to maintain returns or generate increasing returns. A firm that can create a technological standard (like Microsoft with Windows) will enjoy sustained or even growing ReOI as customers are locked in. So will a pharmaceutical firm with patents for products in strong demand (Genentech). So will a firm that has created consumer demand through a strong brand name (Coca-Cola).

Government policy attempts to balance the forces of competition against the forces to counter them. So government policy must be understood. Is the government disposed to free trade and competition? To protection? To political favoritism? What is the antitrust (monopolies) law? What are the trade laws and international trade treaties?

The driver pattern diagrams indicate not only that high profitability tends to decline but also that low profitability tends to increase. Firms on the latter trajectory include those that are entering an industry or establishing new products. These often have low initial profitability that gradually improves. The forecasting challenge is to assess the likely success of new products or innovations. Firms that fade up rather than down also include those whose core income is temporarily depressed because of product transition, competitive challenge, or a labor strike. The forecasting challenge is to assess the extent to which the low profitability is indeed temporary (so will recover) or is permanent. The diagrams here are based on actual data; the patterns therefore are for firms which survived to each future year. Forecasting survival and recovery is important for these low-profitability firms: The forces of

NIKE, INC.

In the face of stiff competition from Adidas, Reebok, and Puma brands, Nike has been able to grow sales and increase core profit margins and core RNOA on growing net operating assets. Accordingly, residual operating income (ReOI) has not only been sustained but has grown:

	2008	2007	2006	2005	2004	2003
Sales (billions)	$18.6	$16.3	$15.0	$13.8	$12.3	$10.7
Sales growth rate	14.1%	9.2%	8.8%	2.1%	14.5%	8.1%
Core profit margin	9.6%	8.9%	9.2%	9.3%	7.9%	7.1%
Asset turnover	3.47	3.31	3.09	2.95	2.76	2.43
Core RNOA	33.4%	29.4%	28.3%	27.4%	21.7%	17.3%
Average NOA (billions)	$ 5.4	$ 4.9	$ 4.8	$ 4.7	$ 4.4	$ 4.4
ReOI (billions)	$ 1.37	$ 1.03	$ 0.95	$ 0.88	$ 0.58	$ 0.38

THE COCA-COLA COMPANY

Coke's management says in its 10-K that "our goal is to use the Company's assets—our brands, financial strength, unrivaled distribution system, global reach and talent, and strong commitment to our management and associates—to become more competitive and accelerate growth in a manner that creates value for our shareholders." Up to 2000, Coke continually grew residual operating income (ReOI) with strong sales growth and sustained core RNOA. From 2000–2007 Coke sustained ReOI but without much growth. While asset turnovers have been sustained, slower sales growth has been accompanied by a decline in core profit margins:

	2007	2006	2005	2004	2003	2002
Sales (billions)	$28.9	$24.1	$23.1	$21.7	$20.9	$19.6
Sales growth rate	19.8%	4.3%	6.3%	4.2%	6.6%	11.5%
Core profit margin	20.7%	20.4%	21.4%	22.4%	21.3%	22.1%
Asset turnover	1.30	1.32	1.36	1.32	1.32	1.35
Core RNOA	26.9%	26.9%	29.1%	29.6%	28.1%	29.8%
Average NOA (billions)	$23.0	$18.4	$17.2	$16.6	$15.7	$14.9
ReOI (billions)	$ 4.1	$ 3.3	$ 3.5	$ 3.4	$ 3.0	$ 3.1

Sales growth in 2007 includes the effect of an acquisition.

competition drive out firms that cannot sustain ReOI in the long run. Chapter 20 deals with bankruptcy prediction.

Fading (up or down) is a typical pattern, but many other driver patterns are possible. A not uncommon pattern is continuing high RNOA, without any fading, along with growth in ReOI because of growth in net operating assets. These are firms that counter competition successfully. Nike is a good example of a firm that has maintained core RNOA and grown ReOI through brand management. Coca-Cola, once a company that continually grew ReOI, just managed to sustain ReOI in the 2000s. See Box 16.2.

3. Focus on Key Drivers

For some firms, particular drivers are more important than others. A number of drivers might change slightly, but one or two drivers might change significantly. Drivers that require particular focus are **key drivers.** For Coca-Cola (in Box 16.2) sales and profit margins are key drivers. A simple forecast might suffice for a non-key driver, but key drivers require thorough investigation of the factors that determine them. In retailing, profit margins are often fairly constant, so forecasting focuses on sales and ATO where there is more uncertainty. Because sales and ATO are driven by sales per square foot, the retail analyst cuts through to this number first.

Box 16.3 identifies key economic factors for selected industries and the ReOI drivers associated with them. It also gives an analysis of key drivers for airlines.

Analysts sometimes identify firms by **value types** according to their key drivers. So Coca-Cola is a *brand management firm* where value is driven by exploiting a brand. A firm where profit margins and asset turnovers quickly revert to typical levels is called a *company of averages*. A firm where value comes from growing sales and net operating assets with sustained RNOA is called a *growth firm*. A firm that has large fixed costs to be covered and where most of sales go to the bottom line after fixed costs are covered—like telecoms—is referred to as being *sales driven*. (This type of firm has increasing ATO as sales increase.) A firm whose product is not yet clearly defined—like a start-up research biotech—is a *speculative* type. These names are helpful to bring focus but are often oversimplifications; be careful not to presume too much by typing a firm.

4. Focus on Choices Versus Conditions

Economic factors and ReOI drivers can change in two ways. They are determined either by a change in the environment the firm is in or by choices made by management. Government regulations and tax rates are determined outside the firm (although the firm might try to influence regulations). Product price is often set by the market. The degree of competition in the industry is often outside management's control. These are **business conditions** under which the firm must operate. But other factors are the result of **strategic choices** made by management. Management chooses the product. Management chooses the location and form of the production process. They choose product quality. They decide on the R&D program. They make alliances with other firms. These choices, taken as a whole, amount to the firm's *strategy*.

Understanding both business conditions and the firm's strategy is a prerequisite for sound forecasting and valuation. When forecasting, the analyst asks how business conditions might change and how management's strategy might change—perhaps in reaction to changes in business conditions. But strategy, as a matter of choice, is itself the subject of valuation analysis.

FULL-INFORMATION FORECASTING AND PRO FORMA ANALYSIS

Full-information forecasting builds up pro forma future financial statements from forecasts of drivers. This is done in an orderly way to ensure that no element is overlooked.

The forecasting scheme follows a straightforward outline. Sales forecasting is the starting point. Then forecasted profit margins are applied to sales to yield forecasts of operating income. And forecasted ATO applied to sales yields the forecast of NOA to complete the ReOI calculation.

We will demonstrate the scheme with PPE, Inc., the merchandising company for which we developed simple forecasts in the last chapter. Here are the relevant numbers in PPE's Year 0 statements (in millions of dollars):

Sales	124.90
Operating income	9.80
Net operating assets	74.42

SELECTED INDUSTRIES

Industry	Key Economic Factors	Key ReOI Drivers
Automobiles	Model design and production efficiency	Sales and margins
Beverages	Brand management and product innovation	Sales
Cellular phones	Population covered (POP) and churn rates	Sales and ATO
Commercial real estate	Square footage, rent per square foot, and occupancy rates	Sales and ATO
Computers	Technology path and competition	Sales and margins
Fashion clothing	Brand management and design	Sales, advertising/sales
Internet commerce	Hits per hour	Sales and ATO
Nonfashion clothing	Production efficiency	Margins
Pharmaceuticals	Research and development	Sales
Retail	Retail space and sales per square foot	Sales and ATO

AIRLINES

Airlines typically operate with a given fleet and a given gate allocation at airports, at least in the short run. Thus with a fixed number of flights their costs are mainly fixed costs, and profitability is driven largely by revenues. Below are statistics for the 10 largest carriers in the United States for 1994 to 1996.

U.S. Industry Statistics	1994	Change	1995	Change	1996	Change
Revenue miles seat (RMS) (thousands)	499,715	4.34%	512,612	2.58%	546,896	6.69%
Available seat miles (ASM) (thousands)	752,841	1.16%	762,550	1.29%	784,502	2.88%
Load factor	66.38%	3.14%	67.22%	1.27%	69.71%	3.70%
Yield (cent per RMS)	12.47	−1.88%	12.84	2.93%	13.08	1.90%
Revenues ($ millions)						
Passenger	62,332	2.38%	65,816	5.59%	71,553	8.72%
Cargo and other	7,572	−0.88%	7,653	1.07%	7,767	1.49%
Total	69,904	2.02%	73,469	5.10%	79,320	7.96%
Costs ($ millions)						
Labor	24,171	2.36%	24,093	−0.32%	25,507	5.87%
Fuel	8,099	−8.35%	8,193	1.16%	10,275	25.41%
Commissions	6,386	−0.05%	6,308	−1.22%	6,307	−0.02%
Rentals and landing fees	7,501	1.54%	7,824	4.31%	7,739	−1.09%
Maintenance	3,210	4.36%	2,989	−6.88%	3,485	16.59%
Depreciation and amortization	3,840	1.61%	3,791	−1.28%	3,825	0.09%
Other	14,741	3.92%	15,061	2.17%	15,767	4.69%
Total costs	67,948	1.01%	68,259	0.46%	72,905	6.81%
Commission rate	10.2%	−2.86%	9.6%	−5.88%	8.8%	−8.33%
Fuel price/gallon ($)	56.7	−8.55%	57.4	1.23%	70	21.95%
Average compensation ($ millions)	58,147	6.47%	59,849	2.93%	61,773	3.21%
Labor productivity[1]	1,811	5.22%	1,894	4.59%	1,900	0.30%
Unit labor cost/ASM	3.21	1.19%	3.16	−1.59%	3.25	2.91%

Note: Industry includes Alaska, America West, American, Continental, Delta, Northwest, Southwest, TWA, United, and US Airways.
[1] Thousands of available seat miles per employee.

(continued)

The size of the fleet and gate allocation defines what the industry calls *available seat miles (ASM)*. A *load factor* determines *revenue miles seat (RMS)* and ticket prices determine the dollar yield per RMS. This yield, along with RMS, drives revenues so, for a given ASM, load factors and yields are the key drivers for airlines. The analyst cuts to these key factors but is also sensitive to any changes in available seat miles with new routes and new gate allocations. Other drivers such as labor productivity, labor costs, commission rates to travel agents, and fuel costs per mile (given in the table above) are also monitored.

HOTELS AND RESORTS

Hotel and resort firms, like Hilton, Marriott, and Starwood, run large fixed-cost facilities with added (fixed and variable) labor costs. Occupancy rates are an important driver but these depend on the price charged for a room. A composite driver—revenue per available room—captures both, so leads the set of factors that drive profitability. These factors are:

- Revenue per available room (REVPAR) at existing properties, calculated as the product of the occupancy rate and the average daily rate charged (ADR).
- Construction of new hotels and disposition of underperforming hotels.
- New contracts to manage or franchise hotels.
- Enhancements in technology to streamline operations and reduce costs.

Starwood Hotels and Resorts (which manages Westin, Sheraton, W, and St. Regis hotels, among others) reported the following REVPAR for the years 2001–2004:

	2004	2003	2002	2001
Worldwide (138 hotels with approximately 49,000 rooms)				
REVPAR	$110.81	$ 98.03	$ 95.46	$101.44
ADR	$161.74	$151.49	$150.42	$155.77
Occupancy	68.5 %	64.7 %	63.5 %	65.1 %
North America (93 hotels with approximately 36,000 rooms)				
REVPAR	$110.13	$ 98.21	$ 94.40	$100.42
ADR	$156.65	$147.15	$145.61	$152.39
Occupancy	70.3 %	66.7 %	64.8 %	65.9 %
International (45 hotels with approximately 13,000 rooms)				
REVPAR	$112.72	$ 97.52	$ 98.65	$104.55
ADR	$177.57	$165.37	$166.35	$166.55
Occupancy	63.5 %	59.0 %	59.3 %	62.8 %
Stock price, end of year	$ 59.50	$ 37.60	$ 26.01	$ 30.59

You see that the stock price tracks REVPAR. Occupancy rates dropped in North America after September 11, 2001, and, in the international operations, after the SARS outbreak in 2003.

These numbers indicate a sales PM of 7.85 percent and an ATO of 1.68. Suppose we forecast from a marketing analysis that sales for PPE, Inc., will increase at a rate of 5 percent per year. Suppose also that we forecast that core profit margins will be the same in the future as they are currently (7.85 percent) and that there will be no other operating income or unusual items. To produce sales, an investment of net operating assets (more property, plant, and equipment) of 56 3/4 cents for each dollar of sales will have to be in place at the beginning of each year. This is just the inverse of the forecasted ATO, so the forecasted ATO is 1.762.

EXHIBIT 16.1

PPE, INC.
Pro Forma Financial Statements, Operating Activities
(in millions of dollars)
(Required return for operations is 10%.)

	Year –1	Year 0	Year 1	Year 2	Year 3	Year 4	Year 5
Income Statement							
Sales		124.90	131.15	137.70	144.59	151.82	159.41
Core operating expenses		115.10	120.86	126.89	133.24	139.90	146.89
Core operating income		9.80	10.29	10.81	11.35	11.92	12.51
Financial income (expense)		(0.30)					
Earnings		9.50					
Balance Sheet							
Net operating assets	69.90	74.42	78.14	82.05	86.15	90.46	94.98
Net financial assets	(7.40)	(7.70)					
Common stockholders' equity (100 million shares outstanding)	62.50	66.72					
Cash Flow Statement							
OI		9.80	10.29	10.81	11.35	11.92	12.51
ΔNOA		4.52	3.72	3.91	4.10	4.31	4.52
Free cash flow $(C - I)$		5.28	6.57	6.90	7.25	7.61	7.99
RNOA (%)		14.02	13.83	13.83	13.83	13.83	13.83
Profit margin (%)		7.85	7.85	7.85	7.85	7.85	7.85
Asset turnover		1.787	1.762	1.762	1.762	1.762	1.762
Growth in NOA (%)		6.5	5.0	5.0	5.0	5.0	5.0
Residual OI (0.10)		1.87	2.853	2.995	3.144	3.301	3.467
Growth in ReOI (%)			5.0	5.0	5.0	5.0	5.0
Abnormal OI Growth (AOIG)				0.142	0.149	0.157	0.165
Growth in AOIG (%)				5.0	5.0	5.0	5.0

Allow for rounding errors.

Based on these forecasts, we can develop the pro forma of Exhibit 16.1. Sales, as you see, are growing at the predicted 5 percent rate. Applying the forecasted PM to forecasted sales each year yields operating income: OI = Sales × PM. Applying the forecasted ATO to sales yields the forecast of net operating assets at the beginning of the year: NOA = Sales/ATO. So we produce the ingredients of residual operating income, OI and NOA. (Allow for some rounding errors when proofing these calculations.) The forecasted ReOI is given at the bottom of Exhibit 16.1. This is growing at a rate of 5 percent per year. So, with PPE's required return for operations of 10 percent, the value of the equity is

$$V_0^E = \text{CSE}_0 + \frac{\text{ReOI}_1}{(\rho_F - g)}$$

$$= 66.72 + \frac{2.853}{1.10 - 1.05}$$

$$= \$123.78 \text{ million}$$

and the intrinsic levered P/B ratio is 1.86. The value of the operations is $131.48 million and the unlevered P/B is 1.77. On 100 million shares outstanding, the per-share value is $1.24.

The drivers of ReOI are given in the pro forma. The RNOA in all years is the same as that forecasted for Year 1 because its drivers, PM and ATO, are forecasted to stay the same: This is a firm with constant profitability but growing investment in NOA.

The pro forma also forecasts abnormal operating income growth (AOIG). By recognizing that AOIG is the change in ReOI, the analysis avoids forecasting cum-dividend operating income and the free cash flow needed to calculate it. As AOIG is forecasted to grow at 5 percent per year, the AOIG equity valuation is

$$V_0^{CSE} = \frac{1}{0.10}\left[10.295 + \frac{0.142}{1.10 - 1.05}\right] - 7.70$$

$$= \$123.78 \text{ million}$$

or \$1.24 per share (allow for rounding error.) That is, the equity value is the value of the operations less the value of the net financial obligations.

The forecasted OI and NOA are also the drivers of free cash flow ($C - I = OI - \Delta NOA$), so the cash flow forecast in the pro forma falls out immediately. These free cash flow forecasts can, in this case, be used to value the firm using discounted cash flow analysis. As the free cash flows are forecasted to grow at 5 percent per year after Year 1, the value of the equity is

$$V_0^E = \frac{\text{Free cash flow}_1}{\rho_F - g} - \text{NFO}_0$$

$$= \frac{6.574}{1.10 - 1.05} - 7.70$$

$$= \$123.78 \text{ million}$$

The pro forma in Exhibit 16.1 is a simple scenario, of course, but it highlights the ingredients in forecasting. The change in asset turnover and growth in net operating assets from current levels might be accompanied by changes in profit margins, but always the three forecasts—sales, PM, and ATO—along with any other operating income and unusual items, will determine the RNOA and growth in NOA, which produce residual operating income and abnormal operating income growth. You might put the PPE example into your spreadsheet program and see how the valuation changes with different predictions of the drivers.

The pro forma financial statements are not complete, but we can fill out the rest of the pro forma with just two further forecasts, one for net dividends and one for borrowing costs. The pro forma has free cash flow forecasts and so, if we forecast dividends and borrowing costs, we can forecast net financial obligations and expenses and fill out the income statement and balance sheet:

$$\text{NFO}_t = \text{NFO}_{t-1} - (C - I)_t + \text{NFE}_t + d_t \quad \text{and} \quad \text{NFE}_t = (\rho_D - 1)\text{NFO}_{t-1}$$

Suppose borrowing costs are 4 percent here. Let's set the future dividend at 40 percent of net income (a 40 percent payout ratio). The pro forma rolls out as in Exhibit 16.2.

Interest expense in the income statement is always 4 percent of net financial obligations in place at the beginning of the period and the change in net financial obligations is always determined by the treasurer's rule: Sell debt to cover the deficiency of free cash flow over interest and net dividends. In this case there is a surplus, as indicated by the debt financing flows in the forecasted cash flow statement. This has been applied to buying bonds, first the firm's own bonds until Year 3 and then others' bonds after Year 3, to yield net financial assets rather than obligations. In Year 2, for example, net financial obligations of 2.97 are determined by Year 1 net financial obligations of 5.43 plus interest of 0.22 for Year 3 minus

EXHIBIT 16.2

PPE, INC.
Pro Forma Financial Statements, All Activities
(in millions of dollars)

	Year –1	Year 0	Year 1	Year 2	Year 3	Year 4	Year 5
Income Statement							
Sales		124.90	131.15	137.70	144.59	151.82	159.41
Core operating expenses		115.10	120.86	126.89	133.24	139.90	146.89
Core operating income		9.80	10.29	10.81	11.35	11.92	12.51
Financial income (expense)		(0.30)	(0.31)	(0.22)	(0.12)	(0.01)	0.10
Earnings		9.50	9.98	10.59	11.23	11.91	12.61
Balance Sheet							
Net operating assets	69.90	74.42	78.14	82.05	86.15	90.46	94.98
Net financial assets	(7.00)	(7.70)	(5.43)	(2.97)	(0.33)	2.51	5.56
Common stockholders' equity							
(100 million shares outstanding)	62.90	66.72	72.71	79.08	85.82	92.97	100.54
Cash Flow Statement							
OI		9.80	10.29	10.81	11.35	11.92	12.51
ΔNOA		4.52	3.72	3.91	4.10	4.31	4.52
Free cash flow (C – I)		5.28	6.57	6.90	7.25	7.61	7.99
Dividends (payout: 40%)		5.28	3.99	4.22	4.49	4.76	5.04
Debt financing		0.00	2.58	2.68	2.76	2.85	2.95
Total financing flows		5.28	6.57	6.90	7.25	7.61	7.99

Allow for rounding errors.

the 2.68 remaining after paying dividends of 4.22 out of the free cash flow of 6.90. With both NOA and NFO forecasted, we have forecasted common stockholders' equity: CSE = NOA − NFO.

The forecasting scheme can get into more detail, and that added detail will add further line items to the pro forma statements. Rather than forecasting profit margins, the detailed forecast predicts gross margins and expense ratios for each component of the margin and so builds up further line items for the forecasted income statement. And rather than forecasting the (total) asset turnover, the detailed forecast predicts individual asset and liability turnovers and so builds up the line items for the forecasted balance sheets. The forecaster decides what level of detail is necessary to improve a forecast, keeping in mind the cost of researching for more information. Box 16.4 builds up a detailed forecast for Nike.

A Forecasting Template

We can pull all this forecasting together as a series of steps:

Step 1. Forecast Sales

The sales forecast is the starting point and usually involves the most investigation. Simple extrapolations with sales growth rates are a way to get going but a complete analysis involves a thorough understanding of the business. The following issues have to be considered:

1. The firm's strategy. What lines of business is the firm likely to be in? Are new products likely? What is the product quality strategy? At what point in the product life cycle is the firm? What is the firm's acquisition and takeover strategy?

After reformulating Nike's financial statements for 2004, an analyst prepares a forecast in order to value Nike's shares. With a thorough knowledge of the business, its customers, and the outlook for athletic and fashion footwear, he first prepares a sales forecast. Then, understanding the production process and the components of cost of goods sold, he forecasts how much gross margin will be earned from sales. Adding forecasts of expense ratios—particularly the all-important driver, the advertising-to-sales ratio—he finalizes his pro forma income statements with a forecast of operating income. His forecasted balance sheet models accounts receivable, inventory, PPE, and other net operating assets based on his assessment of turnover ratios for these items. He arrives at the following forecasts:

Income statement forecasts:

1. Sales for 2005 will be $13,500 million, followed by $14,600 million for 2006. For 2007–2009, sales are expected to grow at a rate of 9 percent per year.

2. The gross margin of 42.9 percent in 2004 is expected to increase to 44.5 percent in 2005 and 2006 as benefits of off-shore manufacturing are reaped, but decline to 42 percent in 2007 and subsequently to 41 percent as labor costs increase and more costly, high-end shoes are brought to market.

3. Advertising, standing at 11.25 percent of sales in 2004, will increase to 11.6 percent of sales to maintain the ambitious sales growth. The recruitment of visible sports stars to promote the brand will also add to advertising costs.

4. Other before-tax expenses are expected to be 19.6 percent of sales, the same level as in 2004.

5. The effective tax rate on operating income will be 34.6 percent.

6. No unusual items are expected or their expected value is zero.

Balance sheet forecasts:

1. To maintain sales, the carrying value of inventory will be 12.38 cents per dollar of sales (an inventory turnover ratio of 8.08).

2. Receivables will be 16.5 cents per dollar of sales (a turnover ratio of 6.06).

3. PPE will fall to 12.8 cents per dollar of sales in 2005 and 2006, from the 13.1 cents in 2004, because of more sales from existing plant. However, with new production facilities coming on line—at higher construction costs—to support sales growth, PPE will increase to 13.9 cents for each dollar of sales (a turnover ratio of 7.19).

4. The holdings of all other net operating assets, dominated by operating liabilities, will be –6.0 percent of sales.

5. A contingent liability for the option overhang of $452 million is recognized.

These forecasts result in the following pro forma and the valuation it implies (in millions of dollars):

	2004A	2005E	2006E	2007E	2008E	2009E
Income Statement						
Sales	12,253	13,500	14,600	15,914	17,346	18,907
Cost of sales	7,001	7,492	8,103	9,230	10,234	11,155
Gross margin	5,252	6,008	6,497	6,684	7,112	7,752
Advertising	1,378	1,566	1,694	1,846	2,012	2,193
Operating expenses	2,400	2,646	2,862	3,119	3,400	3,706
Operating income before tax	1,474	1,796	1,941	1,719	1,700	1,853
Tax at 34.6%	513	621	672	595	588	641
Operating income after tax	961	1,175	1,269	1,124	1,112	1,212
Core profit margin	7.84%	8.69%	8.69%	7.06%	6.41%	6.41%

(continued)

2. The market for the products. How will consumer behavior change? What is the elasticity of demand for products? Are substitute products emerging?

3. The firm's marketing plan. Are new markets opening? What is the pricing plan? What is the promotion and advertising plan? Does the firm have the ability to develop and maintain brand names?

	2004A	2005E	2006E	2007E	2008E	2009E
Balance Sheet						
Accounts receivable	2,120	2,228	2,409	2,626	2,862	3,120
Inventory	1,634	1,671	1,807	1,970	2,147	2,341
PPE	1,587	1,728	1,869	2,212	2,411	2,628
Other NOA	(790)	(810)	(876)	(955)	(1,041)	(1,134)
Net operating assets	4,551	4,817	5,209	5,853	6,379	6,955
Asset turnover (ATO)		2.803	2.803	2.719	2.719	2.719
Operating income		1,175	1,269	1,124	1,112	1,212
Change in NOA		266	392	644	526	576
Free cash Flow		909	877	480	586	636
RNOA (on beginning NOA)		25.82%	26.34%	21.58%	19.00%	19.00%
ReOI (8.6% required return)		783.6	854.7	676.0	608.6	663.4
Present value (PV) of ReOI		721.5	724.7	527.8	437.5	439.2
Total PV to 2009	2,851					
Continuing value*	12,809					19,349
Enterprise value	20,211					
Net financial assets	289					
	20,500					
Option overhang	452					
Value of common equity	20,048					
Value per share on 263.1 million shares: $76.20						

$$*\text{Continuing value} = \frac{663.4 \times 1.05}{1.086 - 1.05} = 19,349$$

   The analyst feels comfortable forecasting five years ahead, but is unsure about the long-term growth rate. Understanding that Nike is an exceptional firm with long-run prospects, he sets the long-term growth rate at 5 percent, above the average GDP growth rate, but has his reservations. With that growth rate, the value comes to $76.20 per share, a little above the market price of $75 per share. With concerns that interest rates are rising—so the required return for operations may well increase from the 8.6 percent applied here—the analyst decides to place a weak sell recommendation on the stock.

   With this Nike model in a spreadsheet program, the analyst is ready to adjust the pro forma and the valuation when new information arrives. When Nike announced actual results for 2005, operating income, after tax, was $1,209 million, considerably above his forecast. He revised his forecast for subsequent years and recalculated the value at $82 per share. The market price, he noted, increased to $87 per share. In this way he rolls over his analysis as time evolves.

   The analyst can also change the numbers to see how sensitive his valuation is to different scenarios about the future. He has a tool for sensitivity analysis. He also has a tool for risk analysis. See Chapter 19. With this example in hand, go to the BYOAP product on the book's Web site where Nike is featured.

Step 2. Forecast Asset Turnover and Calculate Net Operating Assets

The forecasted asset turnover, applied to sales, yields the NOA: NOA = Sales/ATO. Forecasting overall ATO involves forecasting its elements: receivables turnover, inventory turnover, PPE turnover, and so on. Accordingly, the forecaster develops line items on forecasted balance sheets for receivables, inventories, PPE, and so on, that total to NOA.

   The ATO forecast asks what assets need to be put in place to generate the forecasted sales. This of course requires a knowledge of the production technology: What plants need to be built and what level of inventories and receivables need to be carried to maintain the forecasted sales? It also requires a forecast of costs: How much will plants cost to build? In the Americas, in Asia, in Europe?

For PPE, Inc. we forecasted that the amount of assets to be put in place will be proportional to sales. But this is probably unrealistic. Because plants do not always run at the same level of capacity, even without changes in technology the ATO will change if more sales can be generated with existing plants or if a forecasted drop in demand produces idle capacity. The ATO forecast captures the cost (in value lost) of idle capacity and the value gained by producing sales with existing capacity. If full capacity is reached, new plants will have to be built, but they may result in idle capacity to begin with. The Nike forecast in Box 16.4 involves both an increase in PPE turnover as capacity is used and a decrease as new plants come online.

Step 3. Revise Sales Forecasts

Capacity constraints limit sales. Forecasted ATO yields forecasted net operating assets, but if the assets cannot be put in place to produce the sales, the sales forecast must be revised.

Step 4. Forecast Core Sales Profit Margins

Core OI from sales = Sales × Core sales PM, so next forecast core sales PM. This involves forecasting all its components, gross margins, and expense ratios. This also requires a good knowledge of the business. What will be production costs? Is there a learning curve in production? Will technological innovations reduce costs? Will labor costs or material prices change? What will be the advertising budget? How much of each dollar of sales will be spent on R&D?

For firms with operating leverage, profit margins and expense ratios, like ATO, may not be proportional to sales. Variable costs might increase as a constant percentage of sales, but if some costs are fixed over a range of forecasted sales, margins will increase as sales increase over that range. Of course, as sales continue to increase all costs become variable as additional fixed costs are incurred to support the sales, but these fixed costs increase in lumps rather than continuously.

Step 5. Forecast Other Operating Income

The share of income in subsidiaries is the main item here and requires going to the subsidiaries and forecasting their earnings.

Step 6. Forecast Unusual Operating Items

These often can't be forecasted (they are forecasted to be zero). But if you can forecast a restructuring or a special charge, this is subtracted from core operating income to get total operating income.

Step 7. Calculate ReOI and AOIG

With the operating income and net operating asset forecasts and the operating cost of capital, calculate residual operating income: $\text{ReOI}_t = \text{OI}_t - (\rho_F - 1)\text{NOA}_{t-1}$. Remember the shortcut:

$$\text{ReOI} = \text{Sales} \times \left(\text{Core sales PM} - \frac{\text{Required return for operations}}{\text{ATO}} \right) + \text{Core other OI} + \text{UI}$$

Abnormal operating growth is the change in ReOI over the previous period.

The valuation can now be done. In the PPE example, we forecasted that the cost of capital was to remain constant, but we could use different rates in each period if the cost of capital were forecasted to change.

Step 8. Calculate Free Cash Flow

This is simply calculated from other forecasted amounts: $C - I = \text{OI} - \Delta\text{NOA}$.

Step 9. Forecast Net Dividend Payout

What will be the payout policy? Are stock repurchases anticipated? How much of new financing will come from share issues? Remember the net dividend is payout minus net share issues.

Step 10. Forecast Financial Expenses or Financial Income

With a forecast for NFO for the beginning of each year, the forecasted NFE for the next year applies a forecasted borrowing rate: $\text{NFE}_t = (\rho_D - 1)\text{NFO}_{t-1}$, and similarly for financial income with net financial assets. Remember that NFE is after tax and so too is the cost of capital for debt.

Step 11. Calculate Net Financial Obligations or Financial Assets

This, too, is by calculation: $\Delta\text{NFO}_t = \text{NFE}_t - (C_t - I_t) + d_t$. The net dividend is key here as it increases the borrowing requirement. Correspondingly, if funds are raised by share issues, the borrowing requirement is reduced. The amount of net financial obligations might be a matter of firm policy: The firm has a target leverage. If so, net dividend payout is determined by the leverage policy.

Step 12. Calculate Comprehensive Income

$$\text{Earnings} = \text{OI} - \text{NFE}$$

Step 13. Calculate Common Stockholders' Equity

$$\text{CSE}_t = \text{NOA}_t - \text{NFO}_t = \text{CSE}_{t-1} + \text{Earnings}_t - d_t$$

Step 14. Adjust the Valuation for Any Stock Option Overhang

See Chapter 14 for calculation of the option overhang.

Step 15. Adjust for the Value of Any Minority Interest

The value calculated at Step 14 is the value of the equity, to be divided between the common shareholders and the minority interest in subsidiary corporations. Done thoroughly, this involves valuing the subsidiaries in question and subtracting the minority's share. Usually the minority interest is small, so simple approximations work. From the equity value at Step 14, subtract minority interest earnings (in the income statement) multiplied by the intrinsic P/E you have calculated; or subtract minority interest in the balance sheet multiplied by the P/B ratio you have calculated.

Steps 1–6 and 9–10 require forecasting. All other steps up to Step 14 are calculations from forecasted amounts using the accounting relations with which we are familiar from Chapter 8. (Step 7 could also involve a forecast of a change in the cost of capital for operations.) Only Steps 1–7 are necessary for valuation (before the adjustments for stock options and minority interest). Yes, the seven steps.

The analyst can take some additional steps to test the pro forma statements:

1. Ensure that the two calculations of CSE in Step 13 agree. This validates that the pro forma articulates. We then know that we have been tidy and have not lost any element in the valuation.

2. Do a common-size analysis on the pro forma statements and test the numbers against industry norms to see if they are reasonable. Are they consistent with your prediction of how the firm's fade rates will differ from industry fade rates?

With the financial statement analysis of Part Two of the book and the forecasting and valuation analysis of Part Three, you have all the equipment necessary to build a comprehensive analysis and valuation tool. The PPE example in this chapter provides a template for a forecasting spreadsheet. But it is in summary form: To develop a full financial statement pro forma, add the income statement and balance sheet line items that add to the summary numbers here. Adding this pro forma to the analysis spreadsheet that you may have built earlier, you will have a complete analysis and valuation product. The BYOAP feature on the book's Web site leads you through the construction.

You will find developing a product to be very satisfying. The concepts and tools in the book come to life as you apply them; you will understand them better and will appreciate how helpful they are. You will be gratified from working with a tool that has integrity, is consistent with the principles of sound fundamental analysis, and is disciplined by the accounting relations that must be obeyed if we are to avoid mistakes. Accordingly, you will have some added security in equity investing, by protecting yourself from the risk of paying too much for stocks. Take the product into your professional life and use it for your own personal investing. Add bells and whistles as you learn more.

3. Watch for **financial asset buildup.** If operations are forecasted to generate positive free cash flow, financial obligations will be reduced and ultimately financial assets will be generated, as with PPE, Inc. This can't go on indefinitely. You have to ask: What will they do with the financial assets? Will they pay them out as dividends, or does management have a strategy that anticipates new investment that I have overlooked? These questions lead back to the issue that requires an answer before forecasting begins: What is the firm's strategy? Rethinking strategy as a result of forecasted financial asset buildup can induce you to revise the pro forma.

You now have all the tools required for building your own analysis and valuation product. See Box 16.5.

Features of Accounting-Based Valuation

The pro forma analysis highlights a number of desirable features of forecasting ReOI to value equity:

1. The method is efficient. It comes down to forecasting a few drivers: sales, PM, ATO, and their components.
2. The focus is on operations. The method focuses on the part of the business that adds value, the operations.
3. Dividends are irrelevant. The valuation is insensitive to dividend payout, and this is appropriate given our discussion of dividend irrelevance in Chapter 3. We valued PPE, Inc. without a dividend forecast. The dividend forecast comes after Step 7 in the forecasting, and it is at Step 7 that a valuation is made. Indeed, you can change the payout in the example and you will see that the valuation is unaffected. Higher payout just means less cash to buy bonds under the treasurer's rule. Accordingly, only net financial assets are affected, not operating assets or operating income. To state it again, ReOI and AOIG are not affected by payout.
4. Financing is irrelevant. The valuation is not sensitive to financing. Buying and selling debt and the interest incurred on debt do not affect operating income or net operating assets. We could forecast stock issues in the PPE, Inc. pro forma with the proceeds used to reduce debt or purchase financial assets, but this has no effect on the valuation. This complements point 2 above. The focus is on value added and the valuation ignores the zero-residual earnings financing activities.[2]

[2] If you believe that there are tax advantages from corporate debt or tax disadvantages from paying dividends, the valuation can be adjusted by the present value of these tax effects.

5. Investments that add no value do not affect the valuation. To see this, suppose we modify the NOA forecast for PPE, Inc. and predict that at the end of Year 2 PPE will invest another $50 million in operations, financed by an issue of debt. This investment is expected to earn at the same rate as the cost of capital of 10 percent and thus will increase the OI forecast by $5 in Year 3 and after. The ReOI will of course not be affected by the new debt or interest on the debt, but it will not be affected by the investment either. The expected addition to ReOI in Year 3 from the investment will be $5 - (0.10 \times 50) = 0$. The effect on AOIG (the change in ReOI) will also be zero. And so for subsequent years of the investment's life. Accordingly, the firm's value based on the present value of ReOI is unaffected by the new investment. This would be called a zero-NPV investment in DCF analysis, a zero-ReOI investment here. Pro forma ReOI is affected only by investments that add (or decrease) value by earning at a rate different from the cost of capital.

6. Value-generating investments are uncovered and the source of the value generation is identified. By the same reasoning as in point 5, positive and negative ReOI investments that generate or decrease value are discovered by the pro forma analysis. In addition, the pro forma will reveal the reason for the value effect—in the PM or ATO. Suppose we forecast that in Year 1 management will make a new investment that will not produce any increase in sales. The forecasted ATO will decline, RNOA will decline, and so will ReOI. Accordingly, the effect on the valuation will be negative: We have uncovered a negative-value generator. This is an unlikely case, but it could be that frivolous corporate jet. It is sometimes said that management indulges in negative-value projects after free cash flow and financial asset buildup. This scenario is the so-called *free cash flow hypothesis* of management behavior: Management makes poor investments when they have a lot of free cash flow. This has to be monitored and pro forma analysis provides the means of anticipating financial asset buildup.

7. In applying the discount rate, we have to be concerned about only one discount rate, the cost of capital for operations. From the full pro forma statements in Exhibit 16.2, we could calculate RE and AEG from forecasted earnings and CSE and value PPE, Inc. from forecasts of RE and AEG rather than ReOI and AOIG. This would require the calculation of the cost of equity capital. But this varies with financing risk and must be recalculated for each period as financial leverage changes. The cost of capital for operations may also change as operations change but the task of forecasting the discount rate is reduced. Given the difficulty in estimating discount rates, changes in the discount rate for operations are likely to be not only small but also imprecise. So work with constant rates unless the nature of the business changes significantly.

8. The valuation avoids forecasting when mark-to-market accounting suffices, as with the valuation of financing activities and the effect of outstanding stock options.

VALUE GENERATED IN SHARE TRANSACTIONS

In introducing the residual earnings model in Chapter 5, we emphasized that the model does not capture value that may be generated or lost in share transactions. If no share issues or repurchases are anticipated in the future or these transactions are expected to be for cash at fair value, then there is no problem. But if a firm can issue overpriced shares or repurchase underpriced shares, the resulting gain is not reflected in earnings or residual earnings. Nor is it captured by a discounted cash flow valuation. Two types of corporate transactions in particular can involve these gains: mergers (acquisitions) and buyouts.

PPE, Inc. is expected to conclude an acquisition of another firm at the end of Year 1 by issuing 50 million shares to that firm's shareholders. The analyst follows the following steps:

1. Prepare a consolidated balance sheet for the combined firm at the end of Year 1.
2. Forecast the value of the new merged firm at the end of Year 1 from the forecasted balance sheet and the present value of subsequent residual operating income that the balance sheet is anticipated to generate.
3. Calculate the anticipated value per share at the acquisition date (at the end of Year 1) by dividing the merged firm's value by the total shares outstanding for the new firm.
4. Calculate the present value of this per-share value at Year 0.
5. Add the present value of expected per-share dividends from the premerged firm up to the merger date.

Suppose pro forma analysis calculates a value for the merged firm at the end of Year 1 of $280 million. With 150 million shares outstanding (100 million held by the original PPE shareholders and 50 million issued to the shareholders of the acquired firm), the per-share value is $1.87.

This per-share amount will depend on the number of shares issued in the acquisition and this, is turn, depends on the relative price of a PPE share: If PPE shares are overpriced or the acquirees' shares are underpriced, fewer shares will have to be issued. The value of one of PPE's 100 million shares outstanding at Year 0 is calculated as follows:

Present value (at Year 0) of per-share Year 1 value:

$$\frac{1.87}{1.10} \qquad \$1.70$$

Present value of Year 1 dividend per share:

$$\frac{0.04}{1.10} \qquad \underline{0.036}$$

Per-share value of PPE, Inc. $\qquad \underline{\$1.736}$

As a PPE share was valued at $1.24 before the anticipated acquisition, this calculation indicates that the acquisition adds value to the current shareholders.

Real World Connection

See Exercise E16.14 for further calculations.

Mergers and Acquisitions

Mergers and acquisitions often involve the issue of shares. The acquiring firm issues shares to shareholders of the acquired firm (whose shares are retired), or sometimes shareholders of both firms receive shares in a new firm. The acquiring firm adds value in three ways:

1. Buying the acquiree's shares at less than fair value.
2. Using its own overvalued shares (as "overvalued currency") to buy the shares of the acquiree cheaply.
3. Generating value—synergies—by combining the operations of the two firms.

Residual earnings techniques anticipate the value of a business acquired and the synergies generated with pro forma analysis. But they don't capture the division of value between the shareholders of acquired and acquiring firms. Both have shares in the merged firm but their relative share of value depends on the terms of the share transaction. Points 1 and 2 determine those terms and those terms determine how the synergies in point 3 are divided. The acquirer buys the acquiree cheaply—for either reason 1 or 2—if it issues fewer of its shares for the shares of the acquiree, and so its shareholders get a larger share of any synergies from the merger.

The division of value in a merger is resolved in Box 16.6 from the point of view of the acquiring firms' shareholders. The same principles apply if the acquirees' shareholders wish to value an anticipated acquisition of their firm. The focus of the analysis is on the effect of the acquisition on the per-share value of an outstanding share.

A manager evaluates a potential acquisition by going through the same analysis: What is the effect of the transaction on the per-share value of the stock? Points 1, 2, and 3 above determine the answer. If the acquisition is made "cheaply," value is added to each share. If the acquiring firm overpays (either because it pays too much for the acquiree's shares or its own shares are undervalued), per-share value is lost. If there are synergies and, by the terms of the share transaction, the acquiring firms' shareholders share in those synergies, per-share value is added. The analysis in Box 16.6 shows that PPE's acquisition is expected to increase per-share value from the $1.24 calculated from the preacquisition pro formas earlier to $1.736.

As a historical note, empirical studies have shown that much of the value generated in mergers and acquisitions typically goes to the shareholders of the acquiree. Prices of acquirees' shares tend to increase—often by significant amounts—while prices of acquirers' shares tend to be unaffected or even decline. These observations suggest that acquirees can extract most of the value in mergers. The acquirer's share price might decline because the market feels that it is overpaying for the acquisition. But the price might also decline because the market interprets the bid as a signal that the acquirer's shares are overpriced.

Share Repurchases and Buyouts

If members of management feel that their firm's shares are undervalued in the market, they might generate value for shareholders—that is, increase per-share value—by buying back shares. It is for this reason that announcements of share repurchase programs are often seen as a signal of undervaluation, resulting in a share price increase. Research suggests that the market is slow to react, so that buying the shares on the announcement captures subsequent abnormal price appreciation as the market comes to realize that the shares are indeed undervalued.

But the investor must be careful. Share repurchases may just be the firm paying effective dividends. And they may involve distributions of cash not needed for investment—financial asset buildup—to shareholders. Indeed, the announcement of a repurchase may signal that the firm does not have investment opportunities.

The analyst must also be careful in interpreting repurchases in overheated markets: The firm may be paying too much for the shares, and the analyst tests this proposition with an analysis of intrinsic value. Many of the share repurchases in the bull market of the late 1990s did not result in price appreciations. Review Box 14.6 in Chapter 14.

The *buyout* is a stock repurchase on a larger scale, often with borrowing (and is then a *leveraged buyout,* or *LBO*). If management is involved in gaining equity, the buyout is a *management buyout*. These transactions may add per-share value if managements who participate are more motivated to generate value in operations. But they also add value if shareholders interpret the buyout as a recognition that shares are undervalued.

For this reason, firms add the buyout to their set of tools for creating shareholder value. Buyouts were popular after the 1987 stock market crash. They also were proposed as a remedy for increasing the stock prices of "old-economy" firms in the late 1990s. At a time when investors were pricing technology stocks at very high multiples, old-economy firms traded at relatively low multiples. Their managements felt they were undervalued and proposed buyouts. Airlines were trading at multiples of earnings below 10. *The Wall Street Journal* (March 10, 2000, p. 1) reported the chief executive of Continental Airlines as saying, "If the market says this is all we're worth, then we ought to just buy the company."

FINANCIAL STATEMENT INDICATORS AND RED FLAGS

Much of the information needed to determine how future operating income will be different from current core operating income comes from outside the financial statements. But the financial statements themselves provide information that suggests that current income

Each of the following features of financial statements may indicate aspects of the current operational profitability that will not persist into the future. They are flags that cue the analyst to investigate causes and ask whether those causes indeed indicate that current operating income is not indicative of future income.

- Unusually high sales growth rates. High sales growth rates typically do not persist, as fade diagrams suggest.
- Unusually large changes in core RNOA. Large changes in core RNOA often don't persist, as fade diagrams suggest.
- Unusual changes in RNOA components.
  PM components:
      Gross margin ratio
      Advertising-to-sales ratio
      General and administrative expenses-to-sales ratio
      R&D-to-sales ratio
  ATO components:
      Inventories-to-sales ratio
      Accounts receivable-to-sales ratio
      Doubtful debts-to-sales ratio
      Other assets-to-sales ratio
      Operating liabilities-to-sales ratio
- RNOA is different from the industry average.
  Operating profitability typically reverts to the average for the industry.
- Components of RNOA are different from the industry average.
- Changes in RNOA components are different from the industry average.
- Changes in NOA are different from the industry average.
- Low effective tax rates. Low effective tax rates on operating income are usually due to tax concessions that are temporary: Firms' tax rates tend to revert to a common level close to the statutory rate over time.

Footnotes and the management discussion and analysis also provide indicators. Investigate the following:

- Order backlog.
  An accumulated order backlog indicates pending demand for the product. Computer and technology companies use the book-to-bill ratio—the ratio of sales orders outstanding to sales orders filled—as an indicator.
- Management earnings forecasts and sales forecasts.
- Changes in per-unit sales prices.
- Investment plans.
- Operational plans.
- Changes in labor force.
- Contingent liabilities and provisions.
- Expiration of loss carryforwards and loss of tax credits.

Some indicators are referred to as **red-flag indicators** because they indicate deterioration or even distress:

- Slower sales growth.
- Decline in order backlog.
- Increasing sales returns.
  This ratio may indicate growing customer dissatisfaction with the product.
- Increasing accounts receivable-to-sales ratio.
  This ratio may indicate customers are having credit problems or the firm is having difficulties making sales.
- Increasing inventory-to-sales ratio.
  This ratio may indicate inventory is building up due to difficulties in making sales. But it may also indicate a production buildup in anticipation of higher sales in the future.
- Deterioration in gross margin ratio.
  Analysts watch this ratio very closely. A small change in the gross margin ratio has a large effect on operating income.
- Increasing advertising-to-expense ratio.
  Increases in this ratio can indicate a decreasing effectiveness in advertising generating sales. But it can also indicate increased investment in advertising that will generate more future sales.
- Increasing R&D-to-sales ratio.
  If there is a pattern of higher R&D expense relative to sales, the firm may be having less success in generating new sales with product innovations.
- Increasing selling and administrative expenses-to-sales ratio.
  This ratio will increase when sales decline if part of the expenses are fixed costs. Look at increases in the ratio due to variable costs; investigate an increasing ratio on increasing sales because, with fixed costs, the ratio is expected to decline with increases in sales.

may not be indicative of the future. Box 16.7 lists features in financial statements that raise questions. Each suggests that something might be unusual in core income or net operating assets. The analyst investigates to see whether the indicator points to transitory income or whether drivers have shifted to a new permanent level.

BUSINESS STRATEGY ANALYSIS AND PRO FORMA ANALYSIS

We have observed that pro forma analysis and valuation cannot begin without an appreciation of a firm's strategy. But pro forma analysis is also a means of evaluating strategies. Pro forma analysis uncovers the value generation. Thus it is also a means of investigating management strategies that generate value.

Pro forma analysis of residual operating income substitutes for discounted cash flow analysis. Because investments reduce free cash flow, a firm with a great strategy requiring value-added investments can generate negative free cash flows! For a manager who wishes to maximize the value of the firm, the criterion of maximizing the present value of ReOI replaces the criterion of maximizing the net present value of cash flows. Forecasting ReOI cuts to the core of what drives value. It forecasts the drivers of the profitability of operations that connect management choices to value. Much of the framework we have developed in this book for the outside shareholder is, then, the framework for strategy analysis.

Strategy begins with ideas and good strategies begin with innovative ideas. Business strategy books lay out how to think about strategy in a way that leads to innovative ideas. Pro forma analysis converts those ideas into concrete numbers from which the ideas can be valued. But the forecasting framework is not just a method of analysis; it is a way of thinking about the business. And it simplifies that thinking. The manager knows that to generate value, he must focus on the drivers: sales, profit margins, and asset turnovers.

He makes investments that grow sales with high asset turnovers and profit margins. To maximize profit margins, he minimizes expense ratios, and so on down through the drivers of RNOA.

The manager understands the economic factors and how they affect ReOI drivers. She identifies which factors are business conditions and which involve her choices. Her focus is on change. She analyzes the effects of changes in business conditions and the alternatives to deal with those changes with pro forma analysis. She knows the key drivers where the business is most susceptible. And her strategy is always to sustain a high or growing ReOI. She understands the forces of competition that cause ReOI to fade and understands how she can counter the forces of competition to sustain a high ReOI.

Unarticulated Strategy

During the 1990s bubble, it was fashionable to reject financial analysis as the focus for strategic analysis. Some claimed that financial models constrain thinking and lead to mediocre organizations. The new strategists claimed that good thinking cannot be scripted. "Nonlinear thinking" must replace "linear thinking." The "intellectual capital model" must replace the financial model based on balance sheets and income statements, so that firms replace physical assets with knowledge assets as sources of value. Firms must be organized in ways that foster creativity and adaptability to change rather than focusing on the bottom line.

Such ideas are stimulating. They recognize the sources of value in modern economies, the value in human capital, adaptability, and invention. But rejecting financial analysis to embrace these ideas introduces considerable confusion. Ultimately firms must generate sales to add value, whether those sales are generated from investments in physical assets or investments in human capital and knowledge assets. Those sales must generate positive margins. And the RNOA must be high enough to recover investors' required return. We must have an idea of what future income statements and balance sheets will look like. The financial model must be used in conjunction with new ideas, to test those ideas and to discipline over-enthusiasm for and speculation in ideas.

At some level of strategic analysis, however, financial analysis is difficult to apply. Strategic thinking can begin with general ideas that mature to specifics only as the thinking is executed. A firm might adopt a strategy of investing in basic R&D with the chance of discovering valuable products but, without an indication of what that product will be (let alone the sales and margins), financial analysis is very limited. To value a start-up biotech firm, study biochemistry. A firm might invest in reorganizing itself to be more dynamic, to foster creative thinking, and to develop its human capital and knowledge assets, but the form the payoffs will take is not clear.

Such strategies are **unarticulated strategies.** The less articulated the strategy, the less amenable it is to financial analysis. Investments in unarticulated strategies are highly speculative, approaching the form of a pure gamble. Financial information is of minimal use to reduce the uncertainty, although some technical information can be useful. It is for this reason that capital tends to flow to start-ups through venture capitalists (who specialize in technical information) rather than public stock markets where stocks are analyzed by financial analysis.

Nevertheless, the investor understands that ultimately a good strategy must "turn a profit." Strategic thinking, in its initial stages, does not submit to financial analysis well. But ultimately it must. Accordingly, the need for financial analysis of strategy enforces a discipline on strategic thinking, even at its most unarticulated level. The strategic thinker is pressed to develop her ideas further, to refine them to a level of specificity where they can be evaluated with financial analysis. By so doing, unarticulated strategies are articulated. The script is written. And, through the lens of financial analysis, the value generated by the idea becomes more transparent, the investment less speculative.

Scenario Analysis

The pro formas prepared for PPE, Inc. in Exhibits 16.1 and 16.2 and for Nike in Box 16.4 are for one particular scenario. The scenario is a particularly important one for it forecasts expected outcomes from which we wish to derive a valuation. Expected values are averages over a whole range of possible outcomes, however, and the pro forma analysis can be used to model all possible outcomes. What does the pro forma (and the valuation) look like if the sales growth rate is 4 percent rather than 5 percent? What is the effect if the forecasted profit margin drops to 6 percent? The pro forma under each condition is called a scenario, and an analysis that repeats the pro forma analysis under alternative scenarios for the future is called *scenario analysis*. Scenario analysis is the full-forecasting equivalent of the valuation grid applied to simple forecasting in the last chapter.

If you have built the pro forma forecasting framework into a spreadsheet (following the BYOAP road map) you can easily conduct scenario analysis. In doing so, you will understand the full range of possible outcomes and appreciate the upside and downside potential to the investment. Accordingly, scenario analysis is an important tool for assessing fundamental risk—as we will see when we take up the issue of risk and the required return in Chapter 19.

The Web Connection

Find the following on the Web page for this chapter:

- More detailed and "real world" applications of pro forma analysis.

- More on the "one-stop" formula for forecasting residual operating income.
- Demonstration of how alternative valuation models produce the same value, with spreadsheet programs to help.

Summary

This chapter has shown how to convert knowledge of a business into its valuation. Pro forma financial statement analysis is the tool. Pro forma analysis interprets the business in terms of its effect on value. And it provides a framework for developing forecasts and converting those forecasts to a valuation.

The forecasting template in the chapter develops the forecasting and valuation in a series of steps. Be sure you understand these steps and how the structure of the financial statements is used as a tool for forecasting.

As valuation involves forecasting future financial statements, you can see that valuation and accounting are the same thing. Valuation is really a question of accounting for the future. Accounting is often thought of as a method to record the present, but really it is a system to think orderly about the future, a system to guide the development of forecasts of investment payoffs that can be converted to a valuation.

The formal structure of the accounting is of great benefit in valuation. We often have hazy concepts about firms' activities, but getting a handle on their value implications is difficult. We can think a firm is "worth a lot," but measuring the worth is another thing. The accounting forces us to interpret imprecise notions in concrete terms such as margins and turnovers in a way that leads to a value inference. "Competitive advantage" translates into sales growth with higher profit margins. "Strategic position" translates into higher margins and higher turnover. "Technological advantage" translates into lower expense ratios. Saying that an industry will become more competitive translates into lower profit margin forecasts and an explicit calculation of the loss in value. The "cost of idle capacity" is captured in the asset turnover and measured through the value calculation that forecasts this asset turnover. And we can go on. Accounting relations also play an important role, for these relations tie the pro forma together and make its components reconcile so no aspect of the value generation is lost. Most importantly, the analysis disciplines our speculation.

But let's not get carried away. The analysis here relies on getting a good handle on long-term growth. That may be hard to do when our sense of a firm's value comes from the opinion that it is "strategically poised" to benefit from changes in technology or changes in consumer behavior. Measuring these potential benefits in a pro forma analysis might not be easy if the changes are not yet defined. We may feel that a firm has "superior management" that will generate value, but how the management might act to do this might not be clearly articulated. The firm might have R&D that may lead to new products, but what those products will be may be unclear, not to mention the profit margins and turnovers they will deliver. The firm may be positioned to make takeovers, but the firms involved and the timing might be unclear. Pro forma analysis serves to reduce our uncertainty. Pro forma analysis can be used to model our uncertainty (with scenario analysis). But pro forma analysis cannot eliminate our uncertainty. Equity investing is risky.

Key Concepts

business condition is an economic factor that cannot be altered by management. Compare with **strategic choice.** *515*

competitive advantage period is the time that unusually high profitability takes to revert to a normal level. *508*

driver pattern is the behavior of a driver over time. *507*

fade rate is the rate at which a driver reverts to a typical level; also called **persistence rate.** *507*

financial asset buildup is increasing financial assets (from free cash flow net of dividends). *525*

financial statement analysis of the future is the structure of financial statement analysis applied in forecasting. *505*

forces of competition is the tendency of economic factors to force drivers to typical levels. *508*

full-information forecasting is forecasting with complete information about the economic factors affecting the business. Compare with **simple forecasting.** *515*

key driver is a driver that is particularly important to the value generation of a firm. *515*

mean reversion is the tendency of a measure to move toward its average or typical level over time. *507*

red-flag indicator is information that indicates deterioration in a firm's profitability. *529*

strategic choice or **strategic plan** is a decision to determine an economic factor. Compare with **business condition.** *515*

unarticulated strategy is a strategy that is not specific enough to evaluate with pro forma analysis. *531*

value type classifies a firm by its **key driver.** *515*

The Analyst's Toolkit

Analysis Tools	Page	Key Measures	Page	Acronyms to Remember	
Component residual operating income calculation equation 16.1	506	Fade rates	507	AOIG	abnormal operating income growth
		Financial statement indicators	528		
		Red-flag indicators	528	ATO	asset turnover
Fade diagrams	507			CSE	common shareholders' equity
Pro forma analysis	515				
Forecasting template	520			DCF	discounted cash flow
Seven steps to valuation	520			LBO	leveraged buyout
Merger and acquisition valuation	527			NFE	net financial expense
				NFO	net financial obligations
Strategic planning analysis	530			NOA	net operating value
Scenario analysis	531			NPV	net present value
				OI	operating income
				PM	profit margin
				R&D	research and development
				ReOI	residual operating income
				RNOA	return on net operating assets
				UI	unusual items

A Continuing Case: *Kimberly-Clark Corporation*

A Self-Study Exercise

The sensitivity analysis you conducted in the Continuing Case in Chapter 15 gave you a good feel for the pricing of KMB shares. Pro forma analysis enhances sensitivity analysis by allowing for a full range of scenarios that accommodate not only financial statement information but also other information that bears on the firm.

SPREADSHEET ANALYSIS AND INITIALIZATION

If you have not done so already, you should enter KMB data into a spreadsheet like the one outlined in the BYOAP feature on the book's Web site. Calculations will then be so much easier. To incorporate a new scenario, you will simply have to change the inputs, and the rest of the analysis and valuation will be taken care of by the spreadsheet program.

As a benchmark scenario, enter a pro forma implied by the simple forecasting in the Continuing Case for Chapter 15. Remember the key items to be forecasted are operating income and net operating assets. With these two summary numbers, you can calculate the residual operating income (ReOI) for each future period (and abnormal operating income growth) that leads directly to a valuation. After entering the forecasts and calculating ReOI, make sure the ReOI formula 16.1 in this chapter works. A full pro forma analysis contains the line items necessary to get to the two summary numbers, so your spreadsheet should contain all the line items in the firm's reformulated income statement and balance sheet.

Now you are ready to go. Try different scenarios for the future and observe how profitability, growth, cash flows, and per-share value change.

CONTINUING THE CONTINUING CASE

The Continuing Case concludes at this point of the book. However, you will find that, when you come to Chapters 19 and 20, you will want to return to your spreadsheet to model value-at-risk and to gain an appreciation of the firm's prospective liquidity and credit risk. Build the features in those chapters into your spreadsheet and you will have a product of which you can be proud. Also ask: What bells and whistles can I add to enhance the product?

Concept Questions

C16.1. Why is it important to understand the "business concept" before valuing a firm?

C16.2. Explain why a fade diagram is helpful for forecasting.

C16.3. What factors determine the rate at which high operational profitability declines over time?

C16.4. What is meant by the "integrity" of a pro forma?

C16.5. Forecasted dividends affect forecasted shareholders' equity but do not affect the value calculated from forecasted financial statements. Why?

C16.6. What is a red-flag indicator?

C16.7. What is an unarticulated strategy?

C16.8. Why must the effect of a merger or acquisition on shareholder value be calculated on a per-share basis?

C16.9. When might management of a firm consider a leveraged buyout?

C16.10. Why might the shares of the acquiring firm in an acquisition decline on announcement of the acquisition?

Exercises

Drill Exercises

E16.1. A One-Stop Forecast of Residual Operating Income (Easy)

An analyst predicted the following:

1. Sales of $1,276 million.
2. Core profit margin of 5 percent.
3. Asset turnover of 2.2.
4. Core other operating income and unusual items are zero.

The firm's required return for operations is 9 percent.

a. Apply formula 16.1 to calculate the residual operating income (ReOI) implied by these forecasts.
b. How would ReOI change if the analyst dropped her forecast of the core profit margin to 4.5 percent?
c. Given a 5 percent profit margin forecast, what level of asset turnover would yield negative residual operating income?

E16.2. A Revised Valuation: PPE, Inc. (Easy)

Refer to the pro forma for PPE, Inc. in Exhibit 16.1. Modify this pro forma for the following revised forecasts:

1. Sales are expected to grow at 6 percent from their Year 0 level of $124.90 million.
2. Core profit margins are expected to be 7.0 percent.
3. Asset turnovers (on beginning-of-year net operating assets) are expected to be 1.9.

Then answer the following questions:

a. After revising the pro forma, calculate the value of a PPE share. There are 100 million shares outstanding.
b. If dividend payout is expected to be 40 percent of earnings each year, what do you expect the firm's position in net financial obligations to be at the end of Year 3?

E16.3. Forecasting Free Cash Flows and Residual Operating Income, and Valuing a Firm (Medium)

The following forecasts were prepared in 2012 for a firm with a cost of capital for its operations of 12 percent. Amounts are in millions of dollars.

Year	2013E	2014E	2015E	2016E	2017E
Dividends	70	75	75	75	75
Net debt	0	0	0	0	0
Investment expenditures	80	89	94	95	95
Common shareholders' equity	635	665	689	703	712

The common stockholders' equity at the end of 2012 is 596 and there is no net debt.

a. Forecast cash flow from operations and free cash flow for each of the five years.
b. Use residual operating income techniques to value this firm.
c. Attempt to value the firm using discounted cash flow analysis. Do you get the same answer as that for part (b) of the exercise?

E16.4.   Analysis of Value Added (Medium)

A firm has the following summary balance sheet (in millions of dollars):

Net operating assets	441
Net financial obligations	52
Common shareholders' equity	389

The firm is currently earning a return on net operating assets (RNOA) of 14 percent from sales of $857 million and after-tax operating income of $60 million. Its required return on operations is 10 percent. Forecasts indicate that RNOA is likely to continue at the same level in the future with growth in sales of 3 percent per year and growth in net operating assets to support the sales of 3 percent per year.

Management is considering a plan to introduce new products that are expected to increase the sales growth rate to 4 percent a year and maintain the current profit margin of 7 percent. But the plan will require additional investment in net operating assets that will reduce the firm's asset turnover to 1.67.

What effect will this plan have on the value of the firm?

E16.5.   Evaluating a Marketing Plan (Medium)

A firm with a current return on net operating assets of 15 percent anticipates growth in sales of 6 percent per year from its current net operating asset base of $498 million. It also anticipates that sales will deliver 7.5 percent after-tax profit margins and an RNOA of 15 percent on a consistent basis.

a. Value the operations of this firm for a required return on operations of 11 percent.
b. The marketing team believes that if it can structure extended delayed-payment terms with customers, it can increase the sales growth rate to 6.25 percent per year, with no change in profit margins. The effect of the increased receivables would be to reduce the asset turnover ratio to 1.9. Should the marketing plan be adopted?

E16.6.   Forecasting and Valuation (Medium)

The reformulated balance sheet and income statement for a firm's 2012 fiscal year are below (in millions of dollars).

Comprehensive Income Statement		
Sales		3,726
Operating expenses		(3,204)
OI before stock compensation		522
Stock option compensation		(22)
Operating income		500
Interest expense	98	
Interest income	(15)	
	83	
Tax benefit	29	
	54	
Unrealized gain on investments	(50)	
Losses on put options	120	(124)
Comprehensive income		376

Balance Sheet	2012	2011
Net operating assets	3,160	2,900
Net financial obligations	1,290	1,470
Common shareholders' equity	1,870	1,430

At the end of 2012, sales were forecasted to grow at 6 percent per year on a constant asset turnover of 1.25. Operating profit margins of 14 percent (after tax) are expected each year. The firm's tax rate is 35 percent.

a. Forecast return on net operating assets (RNOA) for 2013.
b. Forecast residual operating income for 2013. Use a required return for operations of 9 percent.
c. Value the shareholders' equity at the end of the 2012 fiscal year using residual income methods.
d. Forecast abnormal growth in operating income for 2014.
e. Value the shareholders' equity at the end of 2012 using abnormal earnings growth methods.
f. After reading the stock compensation footnote for this firm, you note that there are employee stock options on 28 million shares outstanding at the end of 2012. A modified Black-Scholes valuation of these options is $15 each. How does this information change your valuation?
g. Forecast (net) comprehensive income for 2013.

E16.7. Valuing a Property-Casualty Insurer (Hard)

The following summarizes the balance sheet and income statement for a property-casualty insurer. Numbers are in millions of dollars.

Balance Sheet		
	2012	**2011**
Operating assets associated with underwriting	$2,450	$2,300
Unpaid claims and unearned premiums	5,300	5,600
Net operating assets in underwriting activities	(2,850)	(3,300)
Investments in debt and equity securities, at market	6,050	5,940
Common equity	3,200	2,640

Net income of $848 million for 2012 comes from the following to which taxes have been allocated.

Loss on underwriting activities, after tax	$ 43
Investment income and realized gains on investments, after tax	891

In addition to net income in the income statement, unrealized losses on available-for-sale investments of $124 million were reported as part of other comprehensive income in the equity statement.

a. Calculate the residual income from underwriting activities for 2012. Use beginning-of-year balance sheet numbers in the calculation and a required return of 9 percent.
b. Value the equity under a forecast that the residual income from underwriting will grow at 2 percent per year in the future.

E16.8. Integrity of Pro Formas (Hard)

An analyst developed the following set of pro forma financial statements as an input into a valuation:

(in millions of dollars)	2012A	2013E	2014E	2015E
Sales		454.0	481.2	510.1
Operating expenses		408.6	433.1	459.1
Operating income		45.4	48.1	51.0
Net financial expenses		6.4	10.5	12.9
Comprehensive income		39.0	37.6	38.1
Net operating assets	227.0	240.6	255.1	270.4
Net financial obligations	130.0	130.0	130.0	130.0
Common equity	97.0	110.6	125.1	140.4
Net dividends		25.0	25.0	25.0
Free cash flow		(19.0)	28.0	29.6

a. Spot the errors in the pro forma.
b. The analyst forecasts from these pro formas that residual operating income will grow at a rate of 8 percent per year. Do the pro formas justify this prediction?

E16.9.   Comprehensive Analysis and Valuation (Hard)

This exercise comes in two parts. Part I involves an analysis of a set of financial statements and Part II involves forecasting and valuation based on those financial statements.

Part I: Analysis

The following is a comparative balance sheet for a firm (in millions of dollars):

	2012	2011		2012	2011
Operating cash	$ 60	$ 50	Accounts payable	$1,200	$1,040
Short-term investments			Accrued liabilities	390	450
(at market)	550	500			
Accounts receivable	940	790	Long-term debt	1,840	1,970
Inventory	910	840			
Property and plant	2,840	2,710	Common equity	1,870	1,430
	$5,300	$4,890		$5,300	$4,890

The following is the statement of common shareholders' equity:

Balance, end of fiscal year 2011	$1,430
Share issues from exercised employee stock options	810
Repurchase of 24 million shares	(720)
Cash dividend	(180)
Tax benefit from exercise of employee stock options	12
Unrealized gain on investments	50
Net income	468
Balance, end of fiscal year 2012	$1,870

The firm's income tax rate is 35 percent. The firm reported $15 million in interest income and $98 million in interest expense for 2012. Sales revenue was $3,726 million.

a. Calculate the loss to shareholders from the exercise of employee stock options.
b. The shares repurchased were in settlement of a forward purchase agreement. The market price of the shares at the time of the repurchase was $25 each. What was the effect of this transaction on the income for the shareholders?

c. Prepare a comprehensive income statement that distinguishes after-tax operating income from financing income and expense. Include gains or losses from the transactions in parts (a) and (b).

d. Prepare a reformulated comparative balance sheet that distinguishes assets and liabilities employed in operations from those employed in financing activities. Calculate the firm's financial leverage and operating liability leverage at the end of 2012.

e. Calculate free cash flow for 2012.

Part II: Forecasting and Valuation

Use a cost of capital for operations of 9 percent. Sales revenue is forecasted to grow at a 6 percent rate per year in the future, on a constant asset turnover of 1.25. Operating profit margins of 14 percent are expected to be earned each year.

a. Forecast return on net operating assets (RNOA) for 2013.

b. Forecast residual operating income for 2013.

c. Value the shareholders' equity at the end of the 2012 fiscal year using residual income methods.

d. Forecast abnormal growth in operating income for 2014.

e. Value the shareholders' equity at the end of 2012 using abnormal earnings growth methods.

f. After reading the stock compensation footnote for this firm, you note that there are employee stock options on 28 million shares outstanding at the end of 2012. These options vest in 2014 and after. A modified Black-Scholes valuation of these options is $15 each. How does this information change your valuation?

g. Forecast (net) comprehensive income for 2013.

Applications

E16.10. Forecasting and Valuation for General Mills, Inc. (Easy)

The following are from the financial statements for General Mills (in millions):

	2010	2009
Net operating assets	$11,461	$11,803
Common equity	5,403	5,173
Sales	14,797	
Core operating income (after tax)	1,805	

At the end of fiscal year 2010, 656.5 million shares were outstanding, and they traded at $60 each. The following forecasts were prepared:

Sales growth rate, 2011–2012	7% per year
Sales growth rate, 2013–2014	6% per year
Sales growth rate after 2014	4% per year

Prepare a pro forma for the years 2011–2014 with a forecast that core profit margins and asset turnovers will be the same as in 2010. Then calculate the per-share value at the end of fiscal year 2010 with the forecast that residual operating income will grow after 2014 at the sales growth rate. Use a required return for operations of 8 percent.

Real World Connection

Exercises on General Mills are E1.5, E2.9, E3.9, E4.10, E6.8, E11.9, E13.9, E14.15, and E15.6.

E16.11. ### Pro Forma Analysis and Valuation: Nike, Inc. (Medium)

At the end of fiscal year 2008, Nike reported $5,806 million in net operating assets and common shareholders' equity of $7,797 million. Develop a pro forma and valuation at the end of fiscal year 2008 with the following forecasts. Then calculate the per-share value of the 491.1 million shares outstanding at the end of fiscal year 2008. Use a required return for operations of 8.6 percent and forecast that residual operating income will grow at an annual rate of 4 percent after 2012. Sales for 2008 were $18,627 million.

Forecast	2009E	2010E	2011E	2012E
Sales growth rate	10.0%	9.0%	8.0%	7.0%
Core profit margin	9.0%	8.5%	8.0%	7.5%
Asset turnover		3.4	3.5	3.6

(After working this exercise, you might go to the BYOAP feature on the Web site and develop alternative forecasts and valuations for Nike using the technology there.)

E16.12. ### One-Stop Residual Operating Income Calculation: Coca-Cola Company (Easy)

The Coca-Cola Company reported an after-tax profit margin of 20.0 percent on its sales of $24,088 million in 2006. It also reported $102 million of other core income, mainly from equity investments in its bottling companies. Further analysis of the financial statements reveals an asset turnover (on net operating assets) of 1.32. Coke uses a hurdle of 9 percent for its investment in operations.

  a. What was Coke's residual operating income for 2006?
  b. What would Coke's residual operating income be if the asset turnover increased to 1.7?

Real World Connection

See exercises E4.7, E4.8, E12.7, E15.7, E17.7, and E20.4, and Minicases M4.1, M5.2, and M6.2.

E16.13. ### A Valuation from Operating Income Growth Forecasts: Nike, Inc. (Medium)

Box 16.4 in this chapter values Nike's shares using residual operating income methods.

  a. Modify the pro forma in Box 16.4 to forecast abnormal operating income growth, and value the shares from these forecasts.
  b. Apply the simple forecast model (equation 15.5 in Chapter 15) that combines short-term and long-term growth rates. Box 15.4 will help you.

Real World Connection

See exercises E2.14, E5.13, E6.7, E7.9, E9.12, E14.17, E16.11, E19.5, and E20.4.

E16.14. ### Evaluating an Acquisition: PPE, Inc. (Hard)

PPE, Inc. is considering an acquisition. The acquisition, to be completed within one year, will bring the acquired firm onto PPE's balance sheet. Management has prepared the following pro forma, which anticipates this acquisition at the end of Year 1. This pro forma modifies the one in the text which yielded a valuation for PPE, Inc. without the anticipated acquisition.

(in millions of dollars)	Year –1	Year 0	Year 1	Year 2	Year 3	Year 4	Year 5	Year 6
Income Statement								
Sales		124.90	131.15	189.00	200.34	212.36	225.10	238.61
Core operating expenses		115.10	120.86	168.87	179.00	189.74	201.13	213.19
Amortization of goodwill				11.00	11.00	11.00	0.00	0.00
Operating income		9.80	10.29	9.13	10.34	11.62	23.97	25.42
Balance Sheet								
Net operating assets other than goodwill	69.90	74.42	94.50	100.17	106.18	112.55	119.30	126.46
Goodwill			33.00	22.00	11.00	0.00	0.00	0.00
Net operating assets	69.90	74.42	127.50	122.17	117.18	112.55	119.30	126.46
Net financial obligations	7.00	7.70	5.71					
Common equity	62.90	66.72	121.79					

The pro forma balance sheet for the combined firm at the end of Year 1 includes the net operating assets of both firms and the goodwill on the purchase. This goodwill is amortized over the three subsequent years. Forecasted sales and operating expenses for the merged firm are given for years after Year 1. The merged firm is expected to have a required return for its operations of 11 percent.

Management anticipates that it will have to issue 120 shares to acquire the firm from its shareholders. PPE, Inc. currently has 100 outstanding shares and, according to the pro forma in the text, is anticipated to pay a dividend of 3.99 cents per share at the end of Year 1.

a. Review the pro forma in Exhibit 16.1 without the acquisition and compare it to the one here. Will the proposed acquisition create value for PPE's shareholders?

b. Prior to FASB Statement No. 142, applicable from 2002 onward, firms amortized goodwill purchased in an acquisition, as in the pro forma here. Statement No. 142 does not require amortization. Rather, goodwill is carried on the balance sheet until it is deemed impaired; then it is written down. Reconstruct the pro forma without any amortization of goodwill.

c. Show that the equity value is the same with the revised pro forma.

Minicases

M16.1

Full Forecasting and Valuation: Procter & Gamble VI

This is the final installment in a series of cases on Procter & Gamble Co. that began in Minicase 10.1 with the reformulation of financial statements and continued with a financial statement analysis in Minicases 11.1, 12.1 and 13.1. Minicase 15.1 carried out a valuation of the firm, using only information from financial statement analysis. This final installment applies full pro forma analysis to forecasting and valuation.

In July 2010, just after 2010 fiscal year-end, the 2,844 million outstanding shares of P&G were trading at $62. Analysts were forecasting $3.93 in earnings per share for fiscal year 2011, giving it a forward P/E of 15.8. The consensus forecast for 2012 was $4.26. Analysts' PEG ratio, based on an estimate of five years of earnings growth, was 1.75.

A. Initializing on the reformulated statements for 2010, develop a pro forma that would justify the market price but which recognizes that profit margins and asset turnovers that P&G has reported in the past. How much would the future have to be different from the past to justify the current market price? To start, use a required equity return of 8 percent but convert it to an unlevered required return (for operations). You may wish to employ a spreadsheet like that in the BYOAP on the book's Web site.

B. Develop a sensitivity analysis that shows how the value per share might change with different forecasts that you consider to be reasonable.

Real World Connection

See Minicases M10.1, M11.1, M12.1, M13.1, and M14.1 on Procter & Gamble.

M16.2

Challenging the Stock Price of Dell, Inc.

Dell's 2008 annual 10-K report begins with the following introduction to the company that explains the main features of it business model.

> Dell listens to customers and delivers innovative technology and services they trust and value. As a leading technology company, we offer a broad range of product categories, including desktop PCs, servers and networking products, storage, mobility products, software and peripherals, and services. According to IDC, we are the number one supplier of personal computer systems in the United States, and the number two supplier worldwide.

> Our company is a Delaware corporation and was founded in 1984 by Michael Dell on a simple concept: By selling computer systems directly to customers, we can best understand their needs and efficiently provide the most effective computing solutions to meet those needs. Our corporate headquarters are located in Round Rock, Texas, and we conduct operations worldwide through subsidiaries. When we refer to our company and its business in this report, we are referring to the business and activities of our consolidated subsidiaries. We operate principally in one industry, and we manage our business in three geographic regions: the Americas; Europe, Middle East and Africa; and Asia Pacific-Japan.

We are committed to managing and operating our business in a responsible and sustainable manner around the globe. This includes our commitment to environmental responsibility in all areas of our business. In June 2007, we announced an ambitious long-term goal to be the "greenest technology company on the planet" and have a number of efforts that take the environment into account at every stage of the product lifecycle. This also includes our focus on maintaining a strong control environment, high ethical standards, and financial reporting integrity.

Business Strategy

Our core business strategy is built around our direct customer model, relevant technologies and solutions, and highly efficient manufacturing and logistics; and we are expanding that core strategy by adding new distribution channels to reach even more commercial customers and individual consumers around the world. Using this strategy, we strive to provide the best possible customer experience by offering superior value; high-quality, relevant technology; customized systems and services; superior service and support; and differentiated products and services that are easy to buy and use. Historically, our growth has been driven organically from our core businesses. Recently, we have begun to pursue a targeted acquisition strategy designed to augment select areas of our business with more products, services, and technology that our customers value. For example, with our recent acquisition of EqualLogic, Inc., a leading provider of high-performance storage area network solutions, and the subsequent expansion of Dell's PartnerDirect channel, we are ready to deliver customers an easier and more affordable solution for storing and processing data.

Our core values include the following:

- *We simplify information technology for customers.*   Making quality personal computers, servers, storage, and services affordable is Dell's legacy. We are focused on making information technology affordable for millions of customers around the world. As a result of our direct relationships with customers, or "customer intimacy," we are best positioned to simplify how customers implement and maintain information technology and deliver hardware, services, and software solutions tailored for their businesses and homes.

- *We offer customers choice.*   Customers can purchase systems and services from Dell via telephone, at a growing number of retail stores, and through our Web site, **www.dell.com,** where they may review, configure, and price systems within our entire product line; order systems online; and track orders from manufacturing through shipping. Customers may offer suggestions for current and future Dell products and services through an interactive portion of our Web site called Dell IdeaStorm. Commercial customers also can interact with dedicated account teams. We plan to continue to expand our recently launched indirect initiative by adding new distribution channels to reach additional consumers and small businesses through retail partners and value-added resellers globally.

- *Customers can purchase custom-built products and custom-tailored services.*   Historically our flexible, build-to-order manufacturing process enabled us to turn over inventory quickly, thereby reducing inventory levels, and rapidly bring the latest technology to our customers. The global IT industry and our competition have evolved, and we are continuing to expand our utilization of original design manufacturers, manufacturing outsourcing relationships, and new distribution strategies to better meet customer needs and reduce product cycle times. Our goal is to introduce the latest relevant technology more quickly and to rapidly pass on component cost savings to a broader set of our customers worldwide.

- *We are committed to being environmentally responsible in all areas of our business.*   We have built environmental consideration into every stage of the Dell product life cycle—from developing and designing energy-efficient products, to reducing the footprint of our manufacturing and operations, to customer use and product recovery.

Product Development

We focus on developing standards-based technologies that incorporate highly desirable features and capabilities at competitive prices. We employ a collaborative approach to product design and development, where our engineers, with direct customer input, design innovative solutions and work with a global network of technology companies to architect new system designs, influence the direction of future development, and integrate new technologies into our products. Through this collaborative, customer-focused approach, we strive to deliver new and relevant products and services to the market quickly and efficiently. Our research, development, and engineering expenses were $693 million for Fiscal 2008, $498 million for Fiscal 2007, and $458 million for Fiscal 2006, including in-process research and development of $83 million related to acquisitions in Fiscal 2008.

Products and Services

We design, develop, manufacture, market, sell, and support a wide range of products that in many cases are customized to individual customer requirements. Our product categories include desktop PCs, servers and networking products, storage, mobility products, and software and peripherals. In addition, we offer a wide range of services.

- *Desktop PCs*—The XPS^{TM} and Alienware lines are targeted at customers seeking the best experiences and designs available, from multimedia capability to the highest gaming performance. The OptiPlex^{TM} line is designed to help business, government, and institutional customers manage their total cost of ownership by offering a portfolio of secure, manageable, and stable lifecycle products. The Inspiron^{TM} line of desktop computers is designed for mainstream PC users requiring the latest features for their productivity and entertainment needs. In July 2007, we introduced the Vostro^{TM} line, which is designed to provide technology and services to suit the specific needs of small businesses.

  Dell Precision^{TM} desktop workstations are intended for professional users who demand exceptional performance from hardware platforms optimized and certified to run sophisticated applications, such as those needed for three-dimensional computer-aided design, digital content creation, geographic information systems, computer animation, software development, computer-aided engineering, game development, and financial analysis.

- *Servers and Networking*—Our standards-based PowerEdge^{TM} line of servers is designed to offer customers affordable performance, reliability, and scalability. Options include high performance rack, blade, and tower servers for enterprise customers and aggressively priced tower servers for small organizations, networks, and remote offices. We also offer customized Dell server solutions for very large data center customers.

  Our PowerConnect^{TM} switches connect computers and servers in small-to-medium-sized networks. PowerConnect^{TM} products offer customers enterprise-class features and reliability at a low cost.

- *Storage*—We offer a comprehensive portfolio of advanced storage solutions, including storage area networks, network-attached storage, direct-attached storage, disk and tape backup systems, and removable disk backup. With our advanced storage solutions for mainstream buyers, we offffer customers functionality and value while reducing complexity in the enterprise. Our storage systems are easy to deploy, manage, and maintain. The flexibility and scalability offered by Dell PowerVault^{TM}, Dell EqualLogic, and Dell | EMC storage systems helps organizations optimize storage for diverse environments with varied requirements.

- *Mobility*—The XPS^{TM} and Alienware lines of laptop computers are targeted at customers seeking the best experiences and designs available from sleek, elegant, thin, and light laptops to the highest performance gaming systems. In Fiscal 2008, we introduced the XPS M1330, an innovative mobile platform featuring a 13.3-inch high definition display and ultra-portable form factor that received awards for its unique design. The Inspiron^{TM} line of laptop computers is designed for users seeking the latest technology and high performance in a stylish and affordable package. The Latitude^{TM} line is designed to help business, government, and institutional customers manage their total cost of ownership through managed product lifecycles and the latest offerings in performance, security, and communications. The Vostro™ line, introduced in July 2007, is designed to customize technology, services, and expertise to suit the specific needs of small businesses. The Precision™ line of mobile workstations is intended for professional users who demand exceptional performance to run sophisticated applications.

- *Software and Peripherals*—We offer Dell-branded printers and displays and a multitude of competitively priced third-party peripheral products, including software titles, printers, televisions, laptop accessories, networking and wireless products, digital cameras, power adapters, scanners, and other products.

  - *Software.* We sell a wide range of third-party software products, including operating systems, business and office applications, anti-virus and related security software, entertainment software, and products in various other categories. We finalized the acquisition of ASAP Software Express Inc., a leading software solutions and licensing services provider, in the fourth quarter of Fiscal 2008. As a result of this acquisition, we now offer products from over 2,000 software publishers.

  - *Printers.* We offer a wide array of Dell-branded printers, ranging from ink-jet all-in-one printers for consumers to large multifunction devices for corporate workgroups. All of our printers feature the Dell Ink and Toner Management System™, which simplifies the purchasing process for supplies by displaying ink or toner levels on the status window during every print job and proactively prompting users to order replacement cartridges directly from Dell.

  - *Displays.* We offer a broad line of branded and non-branded display products, including flat panel monitors and projectors. In Fiscal 2008, we extended our consumer monitor line-up and introduced new innovations such as "True Life" and integrated camera and microphone into some of our monitors. We added the 1201MP projector to our existing projector portfolio. Across our monitors and projector product lines, we continue to win awards for quality, performance, and value.

- *Services*—Our global services business offers a broad range of configurable IT services that help commercial customers and channel partners plan, implement, and manage IT operations and consumers install, protect, and maintain their PCs and accessories. Our service solutions help customers simplify IT, maximizing the performance, reliability, and cost-effectiveness of IT operations. During Fiscal 2008, we acquired a number of service technologies and capabilities through strategic acquisitions of certain companies. These are being used to build-out own service capabilities.

While priding itself on its service to customers, Dell has also done well by its shareholders, regularly topping rankings of firms on value added for shareholders. A $1,000 investment in the company in 1988 had a market value of $351,356 by 1998, an average compound rate of return of 79.7 percent per year. From 1998 to 2000, the stock price increased from $20 to $58 (split-adjusted).

Unfortunately, Dell's stock price has not done as well since 2000 despite significant sales growth and continued profitability. It appears that the $58 price—yielding a P/E of 88—was a bubble price. By the time the 2008 financial statements were published, the stock price stood at $20.

But not all of the stock price decline was due to bursting the bubble. The slide continued as sales growth rates declined and profit margins on consumer computer products became squeezed. By 2011, the stock price stood at $16.00 after reaching a low of $11.50 earlier. Dell was attempting to steady the ship by moving into the corporate market, providing "enterprise solutions" (servers, networking, storage, and IT servicing) for businesses. But competition in this area from IBM, Hewlett Packard, and Oracle (to name a few) is fierce. Dell increased vendor financing. It made several acquisitions in the systems and data management area. It organized itself into a Large Enterprise division, a Public (government) division, a Small and Medium Enterprises division, and a Consumer division. It still maintained its basic customer and supply chain model outlined in its 2008 business strategy statement. By 2011, Dell stood at the cusp of a promised turnaround.

In 2011, analysts were forecasting EPS for fiscal year 2012 of $1.91, up from $1.36 for fiscal year ended January 2011. They were forecasting just two cents more, $1.93, for 2013. Clearly they were not seeing much growth after the forward year. The PEG ratio based on analysts' forecasts for five years ahead was 1.53.

You are asked to evaluate the prospects of a turnaround and the ability of Dell to add to the stock price of $16.00 in 2011. Use a required return of 9 percent in calculations. To help you, the reformulated financial statements for fiscal years 2008 and 2007 and for 2011 and 2010 are below. To get you to an answer, consider the following:

A. How does Dell generate value? What are the main value drivers?

B. How have these drivers changed during the last few years?

C. What are the growth prospects implicit in the market price? Is the market optimistic?

D. Consider some scenarios that would result in a higher stock price. Do you think these scenarios are possible?

DELL, INC.

Reformulated Comparative Income Statement for Fiscal Year 2008
(in millions of dollars)

		Year Ending February 1		
		2008		**2007**
Operating revenues		61,133		57,420
Cost of revenue		49,462		47,904
Gross margin		11,671		9,516
Operating expenses				
Administrative and general expenses		6,595		5,112
Advertising expenses		943		836
Research and development		693		498
Operating income from sales (before tax)		3,440		3,070
Taxes				
Taxes as reported	880		762	
Taxes on net financial income	(135)	745	(96)	666
Operating income from sales (after tax)		2,695		2,404
Other operating income (all after tax)				
Foreign currency translation gain (loss)		17		(11)
Unrealized gain (loss) on derivatives		(38)		30
Other		(56)		23
Operating income (after tax)		2,618		2,446
Financing income (expense)				
Interest income		410		302
Interest expense		23		27
Net interest income		387		275
Tax effect (at 35%)		135		96
Net interest income after tax		252		179
Unrealized gains (losses) on financial assets		56		31
Net financing income after tax		308		210
Comprehensive income		2,926		2,656

DELL, INC.

Strategic Comparative Balance Sheet, 2008
(in millions of dollars)

	2008		2007	
Operating Assets				
Working cash		40		40
Accounts receivables		5,961		4,622
Financing receivables		2,139		1,853
Inventories		1,180		660
Property, Plant and Equipment		2,668		2,409
Goodwill		1,648		110
Intangible assets		780		45
Other assets		3,653		3,491
		18,069		13,230
Operating Liabilities				
Accounts payable	11,492		10,430	
Accrued liabilities	4,323		5,141	
Deferred service revenue	5,260		4,221	
Other liabilities	2,070	23,145	647	20,439
Net Operating Assets		(5,076)		(7,209)
Net Financial Assets				
Cash Equivalents	7,724		9,506	
Short-term investments	208		752	
Long-term investments	1,560		2,147	
	9,492		12,405	
Short-term borrowing	(225)		(188)	
Long-term debt	(362)		(569)	
Redeemable stock	(94)	8,811	(111)	11,537
Common Shareholders' Equity		3,735		4,328

DELL, INC.

Reformulated Comparative Income Statement for Fiscal Year 2011
(in millions of dollars)

	Year Ending February 1			
	2011		**2010**	
Operating revenues		61,494		$52,902
Cost of revenue		$50,098		43,641
Gross margin		11,396		9,261
Operating expenses				
Administrative and general expenses		6,572		5,846
Advertising expenses		730		619
Research and development		661		624
Operating income from sales (before tax)		3,433		2,172
Taxes				
Taxes as reported	715		591	
Taxes on net financial expense	29	744	52	643
Operating income from sales (after tax)		2,689		1,529

DELL, INC.
Reformulated Comparative Income Statement for Fiscal Year 2011
(in millions of dollars)

	Year Ending February 1	
	2011	**2010**
Other operating income (all after tax)		
Foreign currency translation gain (loss)	79	(29)
Unrealized gain (loss) on derivatives	(112)	(323)
Operating income (after tax)	2,656	1,177
Financing income (expense)		
Interest income	116	71
Interest expense	199	219
Net interest expense	83	148
Tax effect (at 35%)	29	52
Net interest expense after tax	54	96
Unrealized gains (losses) on financial assets	(2)	6
Net financing expense after tax	56	90
Comprehensive income	$2,600	$1,087

DELL, INC.
Strategic Comparative Balance Sheet, 2011
(in millions of dollars)

	2011		2010	
Operating assets				
Working cash		40		40
Accounts receivables		6,493		5,837
Financing receivables		4,442		3,038
Inventories		1,301		1,051
Property, plant, and equipment		1,953		2,181
Goodwill		4,365		4,074
Intangible assets		1,495		1,694
Other assets		3,481		3,988
		23,570		21,903
Operating liabilities				
Accounts payable	$11,293		$11,373	
Accrued liabilities	4,181		3,884	
Deferred service revenue	6,676		6,069	
Other liabilities	2,686	24,836	2,605	23,931
Net operating assets		(1,266)		(2,028)
Net financial assets				
Cash Equivalents	13,873		10,595	
Short-term investments	452		373	
Long-term investments	704		781	
	15,029		11,749	
Short-term borrowing	(851)		(663)	
Long-term debt	(5,146)	9,032	(3,417)	7,669
Common shareholders' equity		7,766		5,641

Real World Connection

Exercises E3.7, E3.12, E5.10, E7.6, E9.11, E14.16, and E20.4 cover Dell.

M16.3

The Battle for Maytag: An Analysis of a Takeover

On May 19, 2005, Maytag Corporation (MYG), the home appliance manufacturer, agreed to be acquired by Ripplewood Holdings for $1.13 billion in cash or $14 per share, a 21 percent premium over the closing price of $11.56 the day before.

Maytag is a manufacturer of washing machines, dryers, dishwashers, and other home appliances, including the venerable Hoover vacuum cleaner. Besides Maytag and Hoover, its brands include Jenn-Air and Amana. The company traces its roots back to 1893 when F. L. Maytag started manufacturing farm implements, producing his first wooden-tub washing machine in 1907 from which evolved the appliance now seen as a household necessity. Ripplewood is a private equity firm famous for its investments in depressed Japanese firms in the 1990s.

Maytag prospered for many years but increasingly the market for white goods became very competitive. While rivals such as Whirlpool and General Electric began shifting production to low-cost areas in Asia in the 1990s, Maytag's production remained in North America with a high cost base. In 2004, Maytag announced a restructuring involving a 20 percent cut in its salaried staff. It closed a large refrigerator plant in Galesburg, Illinois, opened a new factory in Mexico, and began discussions with unions on lowering costs at other plants. However, in April 2005, its bonds were downgraded to junk status by all three big rating agencies, and the firm cut its dividends in half. The stock price declined from $30 in April 2004 to $10 a year later.

Timothy Collins, Ripplewood's founder and chief executive, said he aimed "to take action to become a low-cost producer and accelerate growth by introducing new innovative products, expanding in international markets, and pursuing selective acquisitions" (*Financial Times,* May 20, 2005).

In June 2004, the Chinese appliance maker Haier made a bid on behalf of a consortium of investors to acquire Maytag for $16 per share. Then, on July 18, Maytag's competitor Whirlpool entered the fray with a $17 bid. Two days later Haier dropped out, leaving Ripplewood and Whirlpool as the contenders. Maytag's board was concerned that Whirlpool's bid would run into regulatory hurdles as the antitrust authorities considered the possibility of reduced competition in the market. Further, Whirlpool's offer was partly for stock rather than an all-cash offer. Whirlpool, quite persistent, upped its offer to $21 per share, or $1.68 billion.

You are required to establish a price for Maytag based on reasonable scenarios about its future. Maytag is likely to be worth more to Whirlpool, should the antitrust department give its blessing. The strategic options that Ripplwood refers to would seem to be available to Whirlpool. Whirlpool, in addition, might produce more cost efficiencies by merging plants and combining purchasing and marketing systems. Further, its R&D may be of advantage in competing against new Asian entrants such as LG Electronics. You probably cannot estimate these synergies very well, but you can attempt to model the acquisition from Ripplewood's point of view. What scenarios, introduced into a pro forma analysis, would justify its bid of $14 per share? The difference in the $14 per-share offer and the $21

Whirlpool offer might then be seen as the added value from combining the two operations rather than competing against Whirlpool as a stand-alone business. Or was Whirlpool paying too much?

Here are selected financial data that highlight Maytag's problems:

	2004	2003	2002	2001	2000
	In thousands, except per share data				
Net sales	$4,721,538	4,791,866	4,666,031	4,185,051	3,891,500
Gross profit	660,219	859,531	1,004,602	864,842	985,481
Percent of sales	14.0%	17.9%	21.5%	20.7%	25.3%
Operating income	$ 40,348	228,293	359,495	289,152	439,715
Percent of sales	0.9%	4.8%	7.7%	6.9%	11.3%
Income (loss) from continuing operations	$ (9,345)	114,378	191,401	162,367	216,367
Percent of sales	−0.2%	2.4%	4.1%	3.9%	5.6%
Basic earnings (loss) per share—continuing operations	$ (0.12)	1.46	2.46	2.12	2.78
Dividends per share	0.72	0.72	0.72	0.72	0.72
Total assets	$3,020,024	3,024,140	3,104,249	3,131,051	2,647,461
Total notes payable and long-term debt	$ 978,611	970,826	1,112,638	1,213,898	808,436
Cash and cash equivalents	$ 164,276	6,756	8,106	109,370	6,073

However, to get a handle on the issue, you must download the 2004 10-K from the SEC EDGAR Web site and go into the details. The 2004 financial statements are also on the Web site for this chapter. To initialize the pro forma, reformulate the income statement and balance sheet for 2004. Then begin your forecasting, line by line, for a "best guess" scenario. Investigate the sensitivity of your valuation to changes in forecasts and see if you can justify the $14 price—or the $21 price—as falling within the range of feasible scenarios. Use a required return on operations of 10 percent, the minimum that a private equity investor would require.

Postscript: On August 22, 2005, Maytag's board agreed to the Whirlpool offer and paid Ripplewood a $40 million fee for breaking the agreement.

Real World Connection

See Exercises E6.15 and E20.6.

Part Four

Accounting Analysis and Valuation

Knowing the business
- The products
- The knowledge base
- The competition
- The regulatory constraints
- The management

    Strategy   1

Analyzing information
- In financial statements
- Outside of financial statements

2

Forecasting payoffs
- Specifying payoffs
- Forecasting payoffs

3

Converting forecasts to a valuation

4

Trading on the valuation

Outside investor:
  Compare value with price to *buy*, *sell*, or *hold*

Inside investor:
  Compare value with cost to *accept* or *reject* strategy

5

Chapter 17
How do accounting methods, affect measures of profitability, growth, and residual earnings? How do accounting methods affect valuations?

Chapter 18
How can firms use accounting methods to temporarily change their reported profitability? How can such manipulations be detected?

A valuation is as good as the forecasts on which it is based. The valuation analysis in this book is based on forecasting earnings and book values in future financial statements. But earnings and book values are determined in part by accounting methods. So an obvious question arises: If valuation is done on the basis of accounting numbers, won't the valuation be affected by how the accounting is done? Will the valuation depend on whether a firm uses accelerated depreciation methods versus straight-line methods or LIFO versus FIFO accounting for inventories? How does the analyst accommodate the expensing of research and development investments in income statements when these investments are assets that will produce future profits? Does she correct the accounting? This part of the book supplies answers to these questions, lays out the accounting issues that arise in valuation analysis, and shows how the accounting is accommodated.

    Step 3 of the process of fundamental analysis, indicated here, has two aspects. First the analyst must specify what is to be forecasted and how it is measured in such a way as to capture a firm's value. Then, with this specification, he goes about the task of forecasting using the information he has analyzed in Step 2. Accordingly, accounting issues arise in valuation analysis in two ways. First is the issue of the accounting used to measure earnings forecasted for the future: Will forecasted residual earnings and abnormal earnings growth capture value added so that the analyst arrives at a sound valuation? If he forecasts earnings using GAAP, does he capture value? Should he adjust the GAAP accounting? Second is the issue of the accounting in current financial statements that the analyst uses (in Step 2) to forecast future residual earnings. His financial statement analysis has uncovered core profitability as a basis for forecasting future profitability, but the measure of core profitability is based on accounting methods. Is that accounting appropriate? Is it misleading? The first issue is one of the quality of forecasted accounting. The second issue is one of the quality of the current accounting. Chapter 17 deals with the first issue; Chapter 18 examines the second.

In working through this part of the book you will be helped by a good knowledge of accounting. But detailed knowledge of accounting rules is not as important as appreciating how accounting works, particularly for valuation purposes. So the emphasis here will be on explaining the structure of accounting and how it aids—or hinders—valuation analysis. If you are hazy on the details of specific accounting methods, go to one of the many intermediate or advanced financial accounting texts that are available. The Accounting Clinics on the book's Web site will also help you.

Chapter **Seventeen**

Creating Accounting Value and Economic Value

LINKS

Link to previous chapters

Part Three of the book developed the analysis to calculate intrinsic price-to-book (P/B) ratios and price-earnings (P/E) ratios.

This chapter

This chapter shows how accounting policies, applied on a permanent basis, affect forecasts of profitability and growth and the P/B and P/E ratios calculated from these forecasts.

Link to next chapter

Chapter 18 reviews issues that arise when firms use accounting methods to shift income between the present and the future.

Link to Web page

For more examples of how accounting methods are accommodated in valuation, visit the text's Web site at **www.mhhe.com/penman5e**.

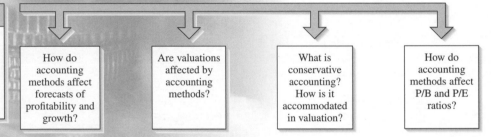

How do accounting methods affect forecasts of profitability and growth?

Are valuations affected by accounting methods?

What is conservative accounting? How is it accommodated in valuation?

How do accounting methods affect P/B and P/E ratios?

In this chapter we resolve a seeming paradox: Value is calculated by forecasting future earnings and earnings are measured using accounting methods, yet a firm's value cannot be affected by the accounting methods it uses.

Generally accepted accounting principles (GAAP) constrain the way that firms can account for their business. However, within GAAP firms have some latitude in choosing accounting methods, and these choices can affect the book values and earnings they report. Further, these choices can affect the future earnings and book values that must be forecasted for valuation purposes. In this chapter we ask how the choice of accounting method—as a matter of permanent accounting policy—affects the forecasts and the valuations made from them. If a firm uses LIFO rather than FIFO for inventory measurement, how will forecasts of residual earnings or abnormal earnings growth differ? Will valuations derived from these forecasts differ? How will price-to-book (P/B) ratios and price-earnings (P/E) ratios be affected? If a firm uses an accelerated depreciation method, capitalizes leases, or expenses costs of intangible assets, what will be the effect on residual earnings, earnings growth, valuations, and P/B and P/E ratios? Discounted cash flow valuations remove the effect of accounting methods (and focus rather on cash flows) under

The Analyst's Checklist

After reading this chapter you should understand:

- How accounting rates of return and residual earnings can be created by accounting methods.
- How growth in earnings, growth in residual earnings, and abnormal earnings growth can be created by accounting methods.
- The difference between economic value added and accounting value added.
- How appropriate valuation techniques produce valuations that are not affected by accounting methods.
- How price-to-book ratios are affected by accounting methods.
- How P/E ratios are affected by accounting methods.
- What "conservative accounting" means and what it implies for analysis of profitability, growth, and valuation.
- How firms create hidden reserves and how they can increase earnings by liquidating hidden reserves.

After reading this chapter you should be able to:

- Value firms in a way that incorporates their accounting methods.
- Forecast profitability and growth for firms with different accounting methods.
- Calculate intrinsic price-to-book ratios that reflect firms' accounting methods.
- Calculate intrinsic P/E ratios that reflect firms' accounting methods.
- Identify when a firm is using conservative accounting.

the suspicion that valuations can be distorted by accounting methods. Do accounting methods indeed distort valuations? Does an analyst have to adjust firms' earnings for accounting methods before proceeding to a valuation?

We will see in this chapter how a firm can use accounting methods that will give it a high rate of return and thus high residual earnings: The firm can make itself look more profitable than it really is. We will also see that a firm's accounting methods can produce high earnings growth. But we will also see that residual earnings and earnings growth created by accounting methods do not affect the valuation of a firm. Residual earnings and earnings growth can be created by real factors and by accounting methods, but it is only the real factors that add economic value. Appropriate use of valuation methods distinguishes real value added from the accounting methods used to measure value added, and so yields valuations that reflect real factors only.

VALUE CREATION AND THE CREATION OF RESIDUAL EARNINGS

Consider a project that involves an investment of $400 at the end of the year 2010 and has a required return of 10 percent per year. The project has a two-year life and is expected to generate sales of $240 in 2011 and $220 in 2012. Depreciation and amortization is the only expense. Table 17.1 uses two different accounting treatments for this project. In Accounting Treatment 1 the initial cost is depreciated straight-line at $200 per year, so project income after depreciation is $40 and $20 for the two years. The book value of the project after

TABLE 17.1
Accounting Treatments for a Project with a Required Return of 10 Percent per Year and a Two-Year Life. Investment in the project is $400.

	2010	2011	2012
Accounting Treatment 1			
Sales		240	220
Depreciation		200	200
Operating income		40	20
Net operating assets	400	200	0
Free cash flow		240	220
RNOA		10%	10%
ReOI (0.10)		0	0
PV of ReOI		0	0
Total PV of ReOI	0		
Value of project	400		
Accounting Treatment 2			
Sales		240	220
Start-up costs and depreciation	(40)	180	180
Operating income	(40)	60	40
Net operating assets	360	180	0
Free cash flow		240	220
RNOA		16.7%	22.2%
ReOI (0.10)		24	22
Present value of ReOI		21.82	18.18
Total PV of ReOI	40		
Value of project	400		

depreciation (the net operating assets [NOA] for the project) declines to $400 at the end of 2011, yielding an expected return on net operating assets (RNOA) of 10 percent for each year, equal to the required return. Accordingly, residual operating income (ReOI) is forecasted to be zero for both years. This project does not add value over its investment cost so its value is its book value in 2010, that is, $400. By discounting the free cash flow numbers (given by operating income minus the change in net operating assets) at the 10 percent rate, you will also see that the project is a zero-NPV project.

The accountant who keeps the books with Accounting Treatment 2 is a conservative accountant. This does not refer to the accountant's clothes, hair style, or political beliefs. The conservative accountant likes to understate assets and overstate liabilities in the balance sheet. So he writes down the project to a book value of $360 in 2010. The reduced book value in 2010 results in reduced charges of $180 in straight-line depreciation in 2011 and 2012. The $40 write-down may be a start-up cost (as in the table) or the part of the $400 investment that involves advertising to launch the project. Both are investments to benefit the future, so might be seen as assets, but GAAP requires both costs to be expensed. The panel gives the ReOI forecasts with this accounting and the valuation from these forecasts.

There are two things to notice from comparing the two accounting treatments, summarized as "accounting effects" and "valuation effects" in Box 17.1. The accounting effects demonstrate the intertemporal feature of accounting. Reducing book values lowers future expenses (in this case depreciation) and thus increases future earnings. Future RNOA is also higher because the higher operating income is divided by a lower book value for net operating assets. And future residual operating income is higher because higher income is compared to lower book values (charged with the cost of capital), to yield higher residual income.

ACCOUNTING EFFECTS

Residual earnings and RNOA can be created by the accounting. Treatment 1 yields forecasted RNOA of 10 percent for both 2011 and 2012 while Treatment 2 yields forecasted RNOA of 16.7 percent and 22.2 percent. Treatment 1 forecasts zero residual operating income for both years while Treatment 2 forecasts $24 and $22.

VALUATION EFFECTS

Residual earnings created by accounting methods does not affect the valuation: The value of the project is the same $400 under the two treatments and both treatments indicate no value added from the investment. Residual income valuation techniques accommodate different accounting methods so that any residual income that is created by the accounting has no effect on the value calculated.

In practice, assets have lower book values when R&D investments are expensed, when promotion and advertising that create brand-name assets are expensed, and when assets are written down excessively. Firms can also maintain low asset values for assets on the balance sheet by using accelerated depreciation for property, plant, and equipment, accelerated amortization of intangibles, and maintaining high bad debt estimates for receivables, for example. Liabilities are overstated with high estimates for deferred revenue, accrued liabilities, and pension liabilities, for example. These practices create higher subsequent rates of return. Thus firms with large successful R&D programs typically generate high RNOA and ROCE in subsequent years when the R&D pays off, as earnings from the R&D are compared to low book values. Drug companies, which have large R&D programs, often report RNOA over 30 percent. Coca-Cola has brand-name assets that are not on the balance sheet and so has an RNOA on the order of 28 percent.

The practice of understating book values is called **conservative accounting.** But just as future RNOA and ROCE can be increased by writing down net assets, so can they be decreased by writing assets up. Writing up assets (or failing to write them down when they are impaired) is referred to as **liberal accounting.** Prior to the adoption of international accounting standards, firms in the United Kingdom and Australia periodically revalued tangible assets upward, yielding lower RNOA and ROCE than comparable U.S. firms.

Liberal accounting is a name sometimes given to less conservative accounting: A firm that capitalizes some software development costs but expenses other R&D is said to use more liberal accounting than a firm that expenses all R&D (Oracle and Microsoft, for example). But both use conservative accounting overall. A benchmark that draws the line between conservative and liberal accounting is **neutral accounting.** This is accounting that yields an expected return on equity equal to the cost of capital, and thus zero residual income, for investments that do not add value. Accounting Treatment 1 is an example of neutral accounting. Conservative and liberal accounting, in contrast, yield profitability that is different from the required return when there in fact is no value added. Conservative accounting produces higher future profitability than the required return; liberal accounting lowers future profitability.

So you see that **economic value added** and **accounting value added** differ. High RNOA and residual earnings are not necessarily indicative of value added. So beware of those who point to accounting measures as indicators of economic value added. Examine products that consultants sell as measures of economic value added. All such measures are accounting measures of some form and the form of the accounting must be considered in accepting the measures as economic value added.

The valuation effect of different accounting methods (described in Box 17.1) is referred to as the **value conservation principle:** Valuations using residual income techniques are not affected by the accounting for current book value. Value is calculated as current book value plus the present value of future residual income forecasted. An accounting method that changes current book value changes future residual income, but it does not change the value calculated because the change in the residual income is exactly offset, in present value terms, by the change in current book value. So expensing R&D creates higher future residual earnings but lower current book value, and the valuation is not affected. Value is affected only by residual income generated by real economic profitability, not accounting-induced profitability.

ACCOUNTING METHODS, PRICE-TO-BOOK RATIOS, PRICE-EARNINGS RATIOS, AND THE VALUATION OF GOING CONCERNS

The example in the last section involves a single project. Similar observations can be made about a going-concern firm which keeps its book values low (or high) continually. Here again the value does not depend on the accounting. But P/B and P/E ratios will. The effects depend on the amount of investment growth, so first we look at the case of no growth in investment and then at the case where a firm grows its investment.

Accounting Methods with a Constant Level of Investment

Going concerns have repetitive investment. Table 17.2, the first in a series of five tables illustrating accounting methods, gives the valuation for a firm that invests $400 in the same zero-value-added project in 2010 (as before) but is also forecasted to invest $400 in each subsequent year, again with zero value added. The table gives forecasted operating income and net operating assets for the firm, and it calculates forecasted RNOA, residual operating income (ReOI), and abnormal operating income growth (AOIG) from these forecasts, along with profit margin, asset turnover, and growth drivers. As before, the project generates $240 in sales in its first year and $220 in its second, and again its cost is depreciated straight-line over two years. The totals for operating income after 2011 are the sum of incomes from the projects put in place over the prior two years, and net operating assets is the sum of the investments just made ($400) and the (partially depreciated) book value of the continuing investment in place.

You see that operating income is $60 once the firm reaches its permanent level of net operating assets of $600. Accordingly, the RNOA is forecasted to be 10 percent in all years, equal to the cost of capital; the ReOI is forecasted to be zero; and the value of the firm is $400, its book value in 2010. The AOIG is also forecasted to be zero after the forward year (2011), so the value of $400 is also equal to capitalized forward operating income. This is neutral accounting: The firm does not add value to its investments (like the project before) and the accounting method confirms this since the rate of return equals the cost of capital, and abnormal income growth equals zero. And for a zero-value-added firm, neutral accounting yields a normal intrinsic P/B ratio of 1.0 and normal trailing and forward P/E ratios, as you see at the bottom of the table. For this reason neutral accounting can be referred to as **normal accounting.**

Look now at Table 17.3. Here the firm's investment and sales are the same as in Table 17.2 in all years, but now conservative accounting is used. The accountant writes off 10 percent (or $40) of investment immediately, charged against income. Consider this as the R&D component of the project or promotion costs that are expensed immediately according to GAAP. Comparing Table 17.3 with Table 17.2, you observe the accounting and valuation effects of conservative accounting relative to normal accounting. Liberal accounting would have the same effect, except in the opposite direction. Box 17.2 lists the

TABLE 17.2
Neutral Accounting: A Firm Investing $400 Each Year with No Value Added (Required return is 10 percent)

	2010	2011	2012	2013	2014
Sales					
From investments in 2010		240	220		
From investments in 2011			240	220	
From investments in 2012				240	220
From investments in 2013					240
		240	460	460	460
Operating expenses (depreciation)					
For investments in 2010		200	200		
For investments in 2011			200	200	
For investments in 2012				200	200
For investments in 2013					200
		200	400	400	400
Operating income		40	60	60	60
Net operating assets (NOA)					
For investments in 2010	400	200			
For investments in 2011		400	200		
For investments in 2012			400	200	
For investments in 2013				400	200
For investments in 2014					400
	400	600	600	600	600
Investment	400	400	400	400	400
Free cash flow	(400)	(160)	60	60	60
RNOA (%)		10.0	10.0	10.0	10.0
Profit margin (%)		16.7	13.0	13.0	13.0
Asset turnover		0.60	0.77	0.77	0.77
Growth in NOA (%)		50	0	0	0
ReOI (0.10)		0	0	0	0
AOIG (0.10)			0	0	0
Value of firm	400	600	600	600	600
Premium over book value	0	0	0	0	0
P/B	1.0	1.0	1.0	1.0	1.0
Trailing P/E		11.0	11.0	11.0	11.0
Forward P/E	10.0	10.0	10.0	10.0	10.0

ReOI value of firm = Book value = 400

AOIG value of firm = Capitalized forward income = $\dfrac{40}{0.10} = 400$

Values in all years in Tables 17.2–17.5 and 17.7 are the value in 2010 growing at the 10 percent cost of capital, less free cash flows paid out. So the forecasted value at the end of 2011 is $(400 \times 1.10) + 160 = 600$ and that at the end of 2012 is $(600 \times 1.10) - 60 = 600$. The P/B ratios are unlevered P/B ratios (or levered P/B if there is no debt financing). As premiums are unaffected by financing they are both the premiums for the firm and premiums for the equity. P/E ratios are also unlevered P/E ratios. For each year they are calculated as (Value + Free cash flow)/OI, as in Chapter 14. The effects on levered P/E ratios are similar; the P/E ratios here are indeed levered P/E ratios if the firm has no net debt, and free cash flows equal dividends.

accounting and valuation effects of conservative accounting for this firm that invests a constant amount each year.

The valuation of $400 in Table 17.3 is the same as that with neutral accounting; again the accounting does not affect the valuation. But note now that intrinsic price-to-book ratios are higher—and permanently so—because of the lower book value. Intrinsic trailing and forward P/E ratios are affected temporarily (because earnings are transitory) but they are unaffected once the permanent level of investment is reached: Earnings are unaffected by the accounting (as, of course, is value). The AOIG is expected to be zero, so the P/E ratio

TABLE 17.3
Conservative Accounting: A Firm Investing $400 Each Year with No Value Added; 10 Percent of Investment Expensed Immediately (Required return is 10 percent)

	2010	2011	2012	2013	2014
Sales					
From investments in 2010		240	220		
From investments in 2011			240	220	
From investments in 2012				240	220
From investments in 2013					240
		240	460	460	460
Operating expenses					
For investments in 2010	40	180	180		
For investments in 2011		40	180	180	
For investments in 2012			40	180	180
For investments in 2013				40	180
For investments in 2014					40
	40	220	400	400	400
Operating income	(40)	20	60	60	60
Net operating assets (NOA)					
For investments in 2010	360	180			
For investments in 2011		360	180		
For investments in 2012			360	180	
For investments in 2013				360	180
For investments in 2014					360
	360	540	540	540	540
Investment	400	400	400	400	400
Free cash flow	(400)	(160)	60	60	60
RNOA (%)		5.6	11.1	11.1	11.1
Profit margin (%)		8.3	13.0	13.0	13.0
Asset turnover		0.67	0.85	0.85	0.85
Growth in NOA (%)		50	0	0	0
ReOI (0.10)		(16)	6	6	6
AOIG (0.10)			22	0	0
Value of firm	400	600	600	600	600
Premium over book value		60	60	60	60
P/B	1.11	1.11	1.11	1.11	1.11
Trailing P/E		22.0	11.0	11.0	11.0
Forward P/E	20	10.0	10.0	10.0	10.0

$$\text{ReOI value of firm} = 360 - \frac{16}{1.10} + \left(\frac{6}{0.10}\right) / 1.10 = 400 \text{ (A Case 2 valuation)}$$

$$\text{AOIG value of firm} = \frac{1}{0.10}\left[20 + \frac{22}{1.10}\right] = 400$$

remains a normal P/E ratio. Research and development and brand-generating firms typically have high RNOA and residual earnings, so they typically have high price-to-book ratios. But that does not mean that they necessarily have high P/E ratios.

The form of the valuation for the firm with conservative accounting differs from that for the firm with neutral accounting. As residual operating income is expected to be greater than zero permanently, the ReOI valuation is a Case 2 valuation (introduced in Chapter 5), as shown at the bottom of Table 17.3: ReOI is a perpetuity, so it is capitalized at the

ACCOUNTING EFFECTS

1. *Operating income* is not affected by conservative accounting once a permanent level of investment is reached. Income is lower with the conservative accounting while the level of investment is being built up (in 2011) but it is the same $60 after 2011. This is always a feature of accounting: Accounting methods don't affect income if there is no change in investment because expenses and revenues are always the same, regardless of whether the accounting is conservative or not.

2. *Net operating assets*, although constant, are lower with conservative accounting and permanently so. As with the project, the accounting affects book value, but it does so permanently.

3. *RNOA* and *residual operating income* (and ROCE and residual earnings) are permanently higher with conservative accounting than with neutral accounting.

4. *Abnormal operating income growth* is not affected by conservative accounting once a permanent level of investment is reached.

VALUATION EFFECTS

1. *Value* is unaffected by the accounting. As with the single project, residual earnings created by the accounting have no effect on the value calculated.

2. *P/B ratios* are nonnormal (greater than 1). Conservative accounting reduces book values and thus induces a premium over book value. Not only is there an effect on current premiums, but there is also a permanent effect on subsequent premiums.

3. *P/E ratios* are not affected by the accounting once the permanent level of investment is reached: Earnings and value are both unaffected by the accounting.

required return. It is sometimes said that continuing values should be calculated at a point in the future where the rate of return is expected to equal the cost of capital. Rates of return decline toward a normal return, it is said, as competition drives excess profits to zero. Excess economic profits may indeed be dissipated through competition, but that does not mean that the accounting measure of profitability, RNOA, will fall to the level of the required return: Conservative accounting will create a permanent level of RNOA above the required return even if there is no real value generated. So a Case 1 valuation (where ReOI is expected to be zero) will typically not apply to an R&D firm, for example.

Accounting Methods with a Changing Level of Investment

In Tables 17.2 and 17.3 the firm reaches a constant level of investment. But the picture changes when the level of investment is forecasted to change. Table 17.4 deals with the same firm as in Table 17.2, except that investment, which again is depreciated straight-line, is forecasted to grow at 5 percent per year. Each dollar of investment is expected to generate the same sales as before but, as investment is growing, so are sales revenue, operating income, and cum-dividend operating income. Because the firm is employing neutral accounting, even though operating income and net operating assets are forecasted to grow, forecasted RNOA is 10 percent and ReOI is zero. The value of the firm is still $400: The expanding investment with growing earnings does not add value.

Look now at Table 17.5. Here the conservative accountant is at work writing off 10 percent of the investment as R&D and promotion expenditures each year. This results in positive residual earnings and a nonnormal P/B ratio, as before, but there are additional effects. Forecasted operating income is increasing through time but is lower in all years than in Table 17.4 because the write-off also increases at a 5 percent rate. But the cum-dividend operating income (after reinvesting the free cash flow "dividend" at the cost of capital) is growing at a rate that is greater than the cost of capital rather than the 10 percent rate in

TABLE 17.4
Neutral Accounting:
A Firm with
Investment Growing
at 5 Percent per Year
with No Value Added
(Required return is
10 percent)

	2010	2011	2012	2013	2014
Sales					
From investments in 2010		240.0	220.0		
From investments in 2011			252.0	231.0	
From investments in 2012				264.6	242.6
From investments in 2013					277.8
		240.0	472.0	495.6	520.4
Operating expenses (depreciation)					
For investments in 2010		200.0	200.0		
For investments in 2011			210.0	210.0	
For investments in 2012				220.5	220.5
For investments in 2013					231.5
For investments in 2014					
		200.0	410.0	430.5	452.0
Operating income (OI)		40.0	62.0	65.1	68.4
Net operating assets (NOA)					
For investments in 2010	400.0	200.0			
For investments in 2011		420.0	210.0		
For investments in 2012			441.0	220.5	
For investments in 2013				463.1	231.5
For investments in 2014					486.2
	400.0	620.0	651.0	683.6	717.7
Investment	400	420	441	463.1	486.2
Free cash flow	(400)	(180)	31	32.5	34.4
RNOA (%)		10.0	10.0	10.0	10.0
Profit margin (%)		16.7	13.1	13.1	13.1
Asset turnover		0.60	0.76	0.76	0.76
Growth in NOA (%)		55	5	5	5
ReOI (0.10)		0	0	0	0
Growth in ReOI (%)		—	0	0	0
Growth in cum-dividend OI (%)		—	10	10	10
AOIG (0.10)			0	0	0
Value of firm	400	620.0	651.0	683.6	717.7
Premium over book value	0	0	0	0	0
P/B	1.0	1.0	1.0	1.0	1.0
Trailing P/E		11.0	11.0	11.0	11.0
Forward P/E	10.0	10.0	10.0	10.0	10.0

ReOI value of firm = 400

AOIG value of firm = $\dfrac{40}{0.10}$ = 400

Growth in cum-dividend OI is growth in operating income adjusted for reinvesting free cash flow at the required return of 10 percent. The free cash flow is the "dividend" from operations.

Table 17.4.[1] Further, ReOI and AOIG are increasing at 5 percent, not constant as before. Nothing has changed here from Table 17.4 except the accounting. The conservative accounting has produced growth in operating income, growth in ReOI, and abnormal income growth: An RNOA above the required return combined with growing net operating assets yields growing ReOI, and growing ReOI implies abnormal income growth.

[1] Reported (ex-dividend) income grows at a slower rate but this does not recognize the earnings from reinvesting dividends. The "dividends" from the operations are the free cash flow and the growth rates in operating income incorporate earnings from this free cash flow invested at 10 percent.

TABLE 17.5
Conservative Accounting: A Firm with Investment Growing at 5 Percent per Year with No Value Added; 10 Percent of Investment Expensed Immediately (Required return is 10 percent)

	2010	2011	2012	2013	2014
Sales					
From investments in 2010		240.0	220.0		
From investments in 2011			252.0	231.0	
From investments in 2012				264.6	242.6
From investments in 2013					277.8
		240.0	472.0	495.6	520.4
Operating expenses					
For investments in 2010	40.0	180.0	180.0		
For investments in 2011		42.0	189.0	189.0	
For investments in 2012			44.1	198.5	198.5
For investments in 2013				46.3	208.4
For investments in 2014					48.6
	40.0	222.0	413.1	433.8	455.5
Operating income	(40.0)	18.0	58.9	61.8	64.9
Net operating assets (NOA)					
For investments in 2010	360.0	180.0			
For investments in 2011		378.0	189.0		
For investments in 2012			396.9	198.5	
For investments in 2013				416.8	208.4
For investments in 2014					437.6
	360.0	558.0	585.9	615.2	646.0
Investment	400	420	441	463.1	486.2
Free cash flow	(400)	(180)	31	32.5	34.2
RNOA (%)		5.0	10.6	10.6	10.6
Profit margin (%)		7.5	12.5	12.5	12.5
Asset turnover		0.67	0.85	0.85	0.85
Growth in NOA (%)		55	5	5	5
ReOI (0.10)		(18.0)	3.10	3.26	3.42
Growth in ReOI (%)		—	—	5	5
Growth in cum-dividend OI (%)		—	127	10.3	10.3
AOIG (0.10)			21.10	0.155	0.163
Growth in AOIG (%)			—	—	5
Value of firm	400.0	620.0	651.0	683.6	717.7
Premium over book value		62.0	65.1	68.4	71.8
P/B	1.11	1.11	1.11	1.11	1.11
Trailing P/E		24.4	11.6	11.6	11.6
Forward P/E	22.2	10.5	10.5	10.5	10.5

$$\text{ReOI value of firm} = 360 - \frac{18}{1.10} + \left(\frac{3.1}{1.10 - 1.05}\right)/1.10 = 400 \text{ (A Case 3 valuation)}$$

$$\text{AOIG value of firm} = \frac{1}{0.10}\left[18 + \frac{21.10}{1.10} + \left(\frac{0.155}{1.10 - 1.05}\right)/1.10\right] = 400$$

Some numbers don't add precisely due to rounding.

As the growing ReOI is just an accounting effect, it does not change the $400 valuation. This is also a zero-value-added firm. But note that the ReOI value calculation (at the bottom of the table) is now a Case 3 valuation that accommodates the growing ReOI: ReOI is capitalized at the 5 percent growth rate. The AOIG valuation also is based on a 5 percent growth rate but the value of $400 is the same as the case with no growth.

ACCOUNTING EFFECTS

1. *Operating income* is lower with conservative accounting if assets are growing.
2. *RNOA* and *residual operating income* are higher with conservative accounting, as before. Although there is an effect on income (in the numerator of RNOA), the effect is proportionally larger on the denominator. But, due to the effect on income in the numerator, rates of return and residual earnings are not as large as with constant investment.
3. *Growth in income* is induced by conservative accounting if assets are growing.
4. *Growth in residual operating income* is induced by conservative accounting if assets are growing.
5. *Abnormal income growth* is induced by conservative accounting if assets are growing.

VALUATION EFFECTS

1. *Value* is unaffected by the accounting, as always.
2. *P/B ratios* are higher with conservative accounting, but no higher than in the no-growth case. But conservative accounting with growth results in increasing premiums over time, reflecting induced residual earnings growth. P/B ratios do not change from the no-growth case because the percentage increase in the numerator is the same as that in the denominator.
3. *P/E ratios* are higher than in the no-growth case: The accounting does not affect firm value but yields lower earnings. The higher P/E ratios reflect the higher forecasted growth in abnormal operating income induced by the accounting.

The accounting and valuation effects of conservative accounting with growing investment for a firm with zero value added are summarized in Box 17.3. The accounting effects for liberal accounting are in the opposite direction.

Table 17.6 summarizes the effects of conservative and liberal accounting that we have observed for operating income, residual operating income, growth in residual operating income, abnormal operating income growth, the P/B ratio, and the P/E ratio. The effects are the same on earnings and residual earnings, but they are compounded by the effects of financial leverage that we examined in Chapter 14. The effects are for the firm that does not add value; the results of neutral accounting are given as a benchmark. The effects are given for declining investment as well as growing investment. Under all conditions (of constant, growing, or declining investment), P/B and P/E ratios are normal for normal accounting. Conservative and liberal accounting produce opposite effects, but the direction of some of the effects depends on whether investment is growing or declining. (Note that declining investment cannot continue indefinitely.) Price-to-book ratios with conservative accounting and growth in investment are higher than normal, but they are unchanged from the no-growth case. But P/E ratios are higher than in the no-growth case (and higher than normal P/E ratios), because conservative accounting yields lower earnings (and value is unaffected). A higher P/E is, of course, appropriate: P/E is higher than normal if positive AOIG is expected, and conservative accounting creates AOIG.

We have observed in earlier chapters that P/E ratios and P/B ratios tend to be above normal. This makes sense in light of our analysis here. Conservative accounting is commonly practiced, so firms tend to have P/B above normal. But firms also have been growing assets, so the conservative accounting produces high P/E ratios as well.

The examples we have been through are for a firm that doesn't add value. The idea is to show you how the accounting can give the appearance of value added when there is none. Economic factors that add value will yield higher forecasted ReOI and AOIG than that

TABLE 17.6 Summary of Accounting Effects for a Firm with Zero Value Added

Accounting Method	Investment Pattern	RNOA	Residual OI		Abnormal OI Growth		P/B	P/E
			Level	Pattern	Level	Pattern		
Neutral	Constant	Normal	Zero	Constant	Zero	Constant	Normal	Normal
Conservative	Constant	Above normal	Positive	Constant	Zero	Constant	Above normal	Normal
Liberal	Constant	Below normal	Negative	Constant	Zero	Constant	Below normal	Normal
Neutral	Growing	Normal	Zero	Constant	Zero	Constant	Normal	Normal
Conservative	Growing	Above normal	Positive	Growing	Positive	Growing	Above normal	Above normal
Liberal	Growing	Below normal	Negative	Declining	Negative	Declining	Below normal	Below normal
Neutral	Declining	Normal	Zero	Constant	Zero	Constant	Normal	Normal
Conservative	Declining	Above normal	Positive	Declining	Negative	Declining	Above normal	Below normal
Liberal	Declining	Below normal	Negative	Growing	Positive	Growing	Below normal	Above normal

A normal RNOA is one that equals the required return for operations; a normal P/B is equal to 1.0; a normal trailing P/E is equal to (1 + Required Return)/Required return; a normal forward P/E is equal to 1/Required return.

generated by the accounting, and thus higher premiums over book value and higher P/E ratios. ReOI and AOIG are always a result of both real and accounting effects.

Because accounting methods don't affect the value, we don't have to worry about distinguishing real profitability from accounting profitability. But there is a proviso. The earnings we forecast must be comprehensive earnings. If any component of earnings is left out of the forecast, we will lose value in the calculation.

An Exception: LIFO Accounting

There is one exception to the principle that accounting methods do not create value. If firms are required to use the same accounting methods in their financial reports as they use for filing tax returns, the choice of accounting will affect their values. If, for example, firms choose methods that reduce or postpone taxes, they will have higher values. In some countries there is a link between tax and financial reporting rules. In the United States the link applies only to LIFO (last in, first out) accounting for inventories; if a firm uses LIFO for tax, it must also use it in its financial reports.

LIFO is a conservative accounting method when inventory quantities and costs are rising. Inventory on the balance sheet is measured at the low prices of older inventory purchases while cost of goods sold is measured at recent, higher purchase prices. The low book values yield higher inventory turnovers, asset turnovers, rates of return, and P/B ratios. It is sometimes said that LIFO results in lower earnings also. But this is not necessarily so. Cost of goods sold equals purchases minus change in inventory; thus if inventories on the balance sheet remain level, cost of goods sold (and earnings) are the same under LIFO and FIFO (first in, first out) accounting, equal to the cost of current purchases. This is another example of what we saw in Table 17.3: The accounting does not affect income when there is no change in net operating assets (in inventories here). But if inventories are growing (and inventory costs are rising), the effects observed in Table 17.5 surface: LIFO yields higher cost of goods sold along with lower gross margins, profit margins, and earnings, and it yields higher P/B and P/E ratios.

If inventories and their costs are expected to grow, the higher LIFO cost of goods sold will result in lower taxes. Firms therefore adopt LIFO for tax and book purposes and so generate value. What adjustments are required to incorporate this added value from using the LIFO method? None: The higher value is incorporated in forecasts of residual income. The lower forecasted taxes increase forecasted after-tax profit margins and RNOA. Accordingly, forecasted residual earnings are higher and so are their present values.

HIDDEN RESERVES AND THE CREATION OF EARNINGS

We have just seen that when investments are growing, conservative accounting depresses earnings and profit margins but raises residual earnings and abnormal income growth. But it is also the case that if the rate of investment subsequently slows, conservative accounting generates higher earnings and profit margins and even higher residual earnings and abnormal income growth.

Look at Table 17.7. This involves the same investment as Table 17.5 up to the year 2014. Then, in 2015, investment is forecasted to level off at the amount in 2014 instead of growing at 5 percent. Sales and expenses from 2016 on are thus forecasted for this level of investment, producing a permanent level of operating income of $72.9. But the ratio of depreciation to revenue declines, yielding higher profit margins. So RNOA increases from 10.6 percent to 11.1 percent by 2016, the same RNOA as that with no growth in investment in Table 17.3. Residual operating income also increases, driven by the higher RNOA, and, as in Table 17.3, is forecasted to be constant. The decline in the rate of growth has generated profit margins, turnovers, RNOA, residual operating income, and (temporarily) abnormal operating income growth.

This example illustrates the phenomenon of **hidden reserves** and their liquidation. Hidden reserves are profits that might have been booked with less conservative accounting. Conservative accounting, with growth, reduces earnings because of higher expenses. But the charging of higher expenses builds up hidden profit reserves that can be realized with a slowing of investment. They are "hidden" because they are book value that is missing from the balance sheet due to conservative accounting: Reporting lower earnings means that net assets (and equity) must be lower by exactly the same amount.[2] If the accounting were not conservative, the net operating assets would be carried at a higher amount. If the growth of investment slows or levels off, or if investment declines, more profits can be generated; this is referred to as **liquidating hidden reserves.** Yes, this is strange! Firms can generate profits by reducing investment. Table 17.5 shows the effect of the creation of hidden reserves (reducing income); Table 17.7 shows the effects of their liquidation (increasing income).

The use of LIFO is a case in point. If physical inventories and inventory costs are increasing, LIFO produces higher cost of goods sold and lower earnings, creating hidden reserves. These hidden reserves are reflected in a lower balance sheet number for inventories over what it would have been under FIFO. In the United States GAAP requires the amount of the hidden reserve, referred to as the *LIFO reserve,* to be reported. It is typically given in footnotes. The LIFO reserve is the cumulative amount of additional earnings that would have been recognized in the past if the firm had used FIFO. It is always the case that

$$\text{LIFO inventory} = \text{FIFO inventory} - \text{LIFO reserve}$$

so you can always calculate what the inventory number would have been if the firm used FIFO. And it is always the case that, for any fiscal period,

$$\text{LIFO cost of goods sold} = \text{FIFO cost of goods sold} + \text{Change in LIFO reserve}$$

---

[2]The term "hidden reserves" is sometimes used to refer to allowances and liabilities that have been overestimated, so excessive bad debt allowances and unearned revenue estimates create hidden reserves. These are just particular cases of conservative accounting. The understatement or omission of any asset, or overstatement of any liability, creates a hidden reserve.

TABLE 17.7   Creation and Liquidation of Hidden Reserves with Conservative Accounting: A Firm with Investment Initially Growing at 5 Percent and Then Leveling Off, with No Value Added; 10 Percent of Investment Expensed Immediately (Required return is 10 percent)

	2010	2011	2012	2013	2014	2015	2016	2017
Sales								
From investments in 2010		240.0	220.0					
From investments in 2011			252.0	231.0				
From investments in 2012				264.6	242.6			
From investments in 2013					277.8	254.7		
From investments in 2014						291.7	267.4	
From investments in 2015							291.7	267.4
From investments in 2016								291.7
		240.0	472.0	495.6	520.4	546.4	559.1	559.1
Operating expenses								
For investments in 2010	40.0	180.0	180.0					
For investments in 2011		42.0	189.0	189.0				
For investments in 2012			44.1	198.5	198.5			
For investments in 2013				46.3	208.4	208.4		
For investments in 2014					48.6	218.8	218.8	
For investments in 2015						48.6	218.8	218.8
For investments in 2016							48.6	218.8
For investments in 2017								48.6
	40.0	222.0	413.1	433.8	455.5	475.8	486.2	486.2
Operating income (OI)	(40.0)	18.0	58.9	61.8	64.9	70.6	72.9	72.9
Net operating assets (NOA)								
For investments in 2010	360.0	180.0						
For investments in 2011		378.0	189.0					
For investments in 2012			396.9	198.5				
For investments in 2013				416.8	208.4			
For investments in 2014					437.6	218.8		
For investments in 2015						437.6	218.8	
For investments in 2016							437.6	218.8
For investments in 2017								437.6
	360.0	558.0	585.9	615.2	646.0	656.4	656.4	656.4
Investment	400	420	441	463.1	486.2	486.2	486.2	486.2
Free cash flow	(400)	(180)	31	32.5	34.2	60.2	72.9	72.9
RNOA (%)		5.0	10.6	10.6	10.6	10.9	11.1	11.1
Profit margin (%)		7.5	12.5	12.5	12.5	12.9	13.0	13.0
Asset turnover		0.67	0.85	0.85	0.85	0.85	0.85	0.85
Growth in NOA (%)		55	5	5	5	1.6	0.0	0.0
ReOI (0.10)		(18.0)	3.10	3.26	3.42	6.02	7.29	7.29
Growth in ReOI (%)		—	—	5	5	76	21	0
Growth in cum-dividend OI (%)		—	127	10.3	10.3	14.0	11.8	10.0
AOIG (0.10)			21.10	0.155	0.163	2.602	1.270	0.0
ReOI value of firm	400.0	620.0	651.0	683.6	717.7	729.3	729.3	729.3
Premium over book value		62.0	65.1	68.4	71.7	72.9	72.9	72.9
P/B	1.11	1.11	1.11	1.11	1.11	1.11	1.11	1.11
Trailing P/E		24.4	11.6	11.6	11.6	11.2	11.0	11.0
Forward P/E	22.2	10.5	10.5	10.5	10.2	10.0	10.0	10.0

$$\text{ReOI value of firm} = 360 - \frac{18}{1.10} + \frac{3.1}{1.21} + \frac{3.25}{1.331} + \frac{3.42}{1.464} + \frac{6.02}{1.611} + \frac{7.29}{0.10} / 1.611 = 400$$

Some numbers don't add exactly due to rounding.

TABLE 17.8 LIFO Reserves and Changes in LIFO Reserves for NYSE and AMEX Firms, 1976–2004

Year	% Change in CPI	LIFO Reserve/Shareholders' Equity, %			Change in LIFO Reserve/ Revenue, %		
		75th Percentile	Median	25th Percentile	75th Percentile	Median	25th Percentile
1976	4.86	14.96	10.07	5.13	0.88	0.39	0.12
1977	6.70	15.48	10.20	4.98	0.93	0.49	0.16
1978	9.02	16.72	10.70	5.36	1.04	0.55	0.23
1979	13.29	20.93	12.85	6.52	1.84	1.06	0.51
1980	12.52	22.63	13.49	6.65	1.50	0.75	0.29
1981	8.92	21.46	12.72	6.35	1.10	0.53	0.12
1982	3.83	20.10	11.57	5.24	0.28	−0.03	−0.50
1983	3.79	18.14	10.40	4.72	0.19	−0.04	−0.43
1984	3.95	16.48	9.48	4.12	0.25	0.02	−0.24
1985	3.80	14.89	7.98	3.23	0.08	−0.10	−0.47
1986	1.10	12.65	6.18	2.27	0.08	−0.10	−0.51
1987	4.43	12.60	6.16	2.35	0.35	0.11	−0.09
1988	4.42	13.37	6.31	2.33	0.56	0.25	0.05
1989	4.65	12.98	6.04	2.32	0.38	0.13	−0.05
1990	6.11	13.30	6.08	2.05	0.32	0.08	−0.09
1991	3.06	12.01	5.42	1.86	0.12	−0.03	−0.27
1992	2.90	12.15	5.28	1.73	0.09	−0.03	−0.21
1993	2.75	10.71	4.52	1.41	0.06	−0.05	−0.30
1994	2.67	10.15	4.41	1.65	0.26	0.07	−0.05
1995	2.54	9.80	4.50	1.94	0.32	0.10	−0.02
1996	3.32	8.49	3.96	1.53	0.11	−0.02	−0.22
1997	1.70	7.61	3.31	1.29	0.06	−0.03	−0.19
1998	1.61	6.37	2.85	1.09	0.01	−0.08	−0.27
1999	2.68	6.42	2.64	0.93	0.07	−0.03	−0.16
2000	3.39	6.56	2.90	1.09	0.16	0.03	−0.07
2001	1.55	6.37	2.52	0.83	0.06	−0.05	−0.22
2002	2.38	7.42	2.99	0.88	0.12	0.00	−0.10
2003	1.88	6.70	2.90	0.79	0.15	0.01	−0.06
2004	3.26	8.75	3.00	0.96	0.48	0.11	0.00
Total		14.05	6.50	2.45	0.40	0.06	−0.13

The table gives the amount of LIFO reserve (as a percentage of shareholders' equity) and the change in the LIFO reserve (as a percentage of revenue). The LIFO reserve is the difference between LIFO inventories and the FIFO carrying amount. The change in the LIFO reserve is the difference between LIFO and FIFO cost of goods sold.

Source: Accounting data is from Standard of Poor's COMPUSTAT files. Consumer price index (CPI) data is from the U.S. Department of Labor Bureau of Labor Statistics.

The difference in after-tax operating income under FIFO and LIFO is the change in the LIFO reserve multiplied by the tax rate. If you want to compare profit margins, turnovers, and RNOA of a LIFO and FIFO firm, you can put them on the same basis by using these relationships.

Table 17.8 gives the median LIFO reserve as a percentage of shareholders' equity for NYSE and AMEX firms using LIFO for the years 1976 to 2004, along with the 75th and 25th percentiles. You see that the median reserve ranged from a high of 13.5 percent of shareholders' equity in 1980 to 3.0 percent by 2004. So, at the median, firms would have had 13.5 percent higher equity in 1980 if they had used FIFO, and 3.0 percent more equity in 2004. LIFO reserves increase when inventory costs rise and the change in the Consumer Price Index (CPI) reported in the table indicates that 1980 was a high inflation year, with inflation, and LIFO reserves, declining through to 2004. The table also gives numbers for changes in the LIFO reserve as a percentage of revenue. Changes in LIFO reserves are the difference between LIFO and FIFO cost of goods sold, so, as the changes are divided by revenue in the table, the numbers are the LIFO effect on before-tax gross margins and profit margins relative to FIFO. At the median, they ranged from 1.06 percent in 1979 to −0.1 percent in 1985 and 1986 as a percentage of revenues.

Just as growing LIFO inventories reduce earnings and increase (hidden) LIFO reserves, declining LIFO inventories create earnings by liquidating LIFO reserves: Lower, older costs are brought into cost of goods sold, yielding higher earnings than under FIFO. The additional earnings are called *LIFO liquidation profits*. (Taxes, deferred by using LIFO when inventories were growing, will also be realized against the liquidation profits.) Table 17.8 indicates there were 12 years when median changes in LIFO reserves were negative, and in each year from 1982 to 2003, except 1988, LIFO reserves declined at the 25th percentile: Over 25 percent of LIFO firms reported higher profits than they would have under FIFO.

A decline in physical inventories reduces the LIFO reserve if inventory costs are rising. But the LIFO reserve will also decline if inventory costs fall, because LIFO costs of goods sold (based on recent, lower prices) are then lower than under FIFO (based on older, higher prices). Often quantities and prices both fall as a result of lower demand for the product. Some companies separate LIFO reserve declines due to inventory liquidation from those due to price declines in their footnotes.

Hidden reserves can arise from any application of conservative accounting. Reducing investment in plant and equipment that has been depreciated rapidly will generate profits. Constant or declining sales after a period of sales growth will yield profits if there has been a policy of overestimating warranty liabilities on bad debts provisions.

Some analysts take special care to recognize hidden reserves and add value to the firm for them. Some maintain that LIFO reserves, which must be reported under U.S. GAAP (usually in footnotes), are an asset whose value must be added to correct the book value. But we have to be careful. Hidden reserves are an accounting phenomenon, and accounting can't generate value. Look at the valuation at the bottom of Table 17.7. This is the same firm as in the previous tables; it does not generate value. And applying residual earnings techniques—now with the forecast horizon at the steady-state year beginning 2006—we get the same valuation as before, $400. (You might do the AOIG valuation also.) The presence of unrealized hidden reserves in Table 17.5 did not give us an incorrect valuation. Provided we forecast ReOI to a steady-state level that recognizes the investment path, hidden reserves are not a concern. Perpetual growth (in the Table 17.5 valuation) means we anticipate hidden reserves will never be realized. But expected realization of hidden reserves (in Table 17.7) does not change the valuation. A forecast of higher ReOI (in Table 17.7) is exactly offset by a forecast of a lower growth rate for ReOI.

By now you should be aware of a number of fallacies with respect to interpreting accounting data. These fallacies often lead to misstatements—in the press and even by analysts—so it is useful to flag them. Box 17.4 lists statements that are sometimes erroneously made about the relationship between accounting numbers and value. Each statement can be true if the accounting captures real phenomena, and often that is the case. But each attribute can also result from accounting methods. Most of the fallacies arise from naively focusing on earnings growth or rates of return. Earnings growth and rates of return can be affected by the accounting, so they must be interpreted by combining forecasted residual earnings with current book value in a residual earnings valuation, or by charging earnings growth for required earnings growth in an AOIG valuation. Don't be too quickly impressed with growing earnings, growing residual earnings, and high rates of return. Reserve judgment until you have tested to see if these attributes are real or induced.

These statements are not necessarily true:

- Firms with higher anticipated earnings growth are worth more.
  Rejoinder: Earnings growth can be created by accounting methods (and by financial leverage) rather than economic factors.
- Firms with high anticipated return on equity are worth more.
  Rejoinder: High return on equity means a higher premium over book value but not a higher value; ROCE can be created by the accounting (and by financial leverage).
- Increasing residual earnings indicate a firm that is adding more and more value.
  Rejoinder: Probably, but growth in residual earnings can be induced with conservative accounting.
- If a firm is earning an RNOA that is higher than the cost of capital, it will add value by investing more.
  Rejoinder: A firm can create a high RNOA through accounting methods but may not be able to add value through investment.

- If RNOA is higher than the cost of capital, a reduction in investment (or slowing of its growth rate) reduces residual earnings.
  Rejoinder: A reduction of investment can create residual earnings if conservative accounting has created hidden reserves.
- Low profit margins mean a firm cannot generate much value from sales.
  Rejoinder: Low profit margins may be induced by conservative accounting depressing earnings, if net assets are growing.
- High asset turnovers mean a firm is efficient in generating sales.
  Rejoinder: High turnovers can be produced by keeping asset values low with conservative accounting.
- Conservative accounting reduces profits and results in higher P/E ratios.
  Rejoinder: Not always; only if investment is growing.

With respect to earnings growth, you now have three warnings about interpreting earnings growth. In Chapters 5 and 6 we saw that investment can generate earnings growth but may not add value. In Chapter 14 we saw that financial leverage can generate earnings growth but does not add value. And here we see that conservative accounting can generate earnings growth but does not add value. In all cases, the use of appropriate valuation techniques determines whether growth adds value. The techniques protect you from paying too much for earnings growth.

CONSERVATIVE AND LIBERAL ACCOUNTING IN PRACTICE

While the focus of some accounting methods is on measuring earnings, all methods have an effect on both earnings and book value. This is just the debits and credits of accounting: One can't affect earnings without also affecting the balance sheet. So all methods can be thought of in terms of their effect on book value and thus on accounting rates of return, residual income, and the P/B ratio. They can be thought of in terms of their effects on earnings, profit margins, and the P/E ratio, but only with changing investment. So think first in terms of the effect on book values. For example, "accelerated depreciation" results in lower book values for property, plant, and equipment; high bad debt estimates result in lower net receivables; and LIFO measurement of cost of goods sold results in lower inventories (when inventory prices are rising). These conservative methods yield higher P/B ratios. They yield lower earnings and higher P/E ratios only with increasing property, plant, and equipment, receivables, and inventories.

The accounting profession in most countries typically takes a conservative approach. It is sometimes claimed that this conservative accounting leads to lower income and lower

CONSERVATIVE ACCOUNTING

Practices that decrease book values:

- Accelerated depreciation of tangible assets.
- Accelerated amortization of intangible assets such as patents and copyrights.
- LIFO inventory methods.
- Underestimates of:
  Net accounts receivable (high bad debt estimates).
  Lease receivables (low residual value estimates).
  Impairment values (high impairment write-offs).
- Overestimates of:
  Pension and postemployment benefit liabilities.
  Warranty liabilities.
  Provisions for restructurings and other future events.
  Deferred revenue.
  Accrued expense liabilities.

Practices that record no book values at all:

- Expensing R&D expenditures.
- Expensing advertising expenditures.
- Expensing investment in intellectual and human capital.

LIBERAL ACCOUNTING

Practices that increase book values:

- Revaluing tangible assets upward.
- Booking brand-name assets.
- Charging no depreciation (some firms in U.K.).
- Overstating deferred tax assets through low valuation allowances (U.S.).

Practices that record no book values at all:

- Omitting contingent liabilities for environmental damage, lawsuits, and stock compensation, for example.

---

rates of return, giving a "conservative" picture of the firm. Don't be confused. Conservative accounting policies will yield lower profits if investments are growing. But they will always result in higher rates of return and thus higher apparent profitability. And if investments are growing, they will result in growing residual income and higher earnings growth. Conservative accounting—supposedly designed to yield a conservative balance sheet—actually produces higher profitability, which is not a conservative view.

Box 17.5 lists common accounting practices that affect book values and accounting rates of return. They are classified as conservative or liberal but many of the conservative methods can be liberal (and some liberal methods conservative) if applied in the opposite direction. For example, accelerated depreciation and amortization methods yield lower book values and higher rates of return and so are conservative. But methods that depreciate or amortize assets very slowly are liberal methods, just like asset revaluations.

The rest of this chapter illustrates the effects of accounting methods.

LIFO Versus FIFO

In 1997 Nike had higher RNOA than Reebok, 25.7 percent compared to Reebok's 16.0 percent. But Nike used LIFO for its U.S. inventories while Reebok used FIFO. Table 17.9 lists some measures for 1996 and 1997 that reflect inventory accounting for the two firms.

Nike's inventory turnover ratios are higher than Reebok's, due in part to lower LIFO inventories. This contributes to a higher RNOA. Nike's large growth in inventory has the effect of lower profit margins because of higher cost of goods sold, but the effect of lower margins on the RNOA is not as great as that of the asset turnover, so RNOA is larger than it would be under FIFO. With the amounts for the LIFO reserve (taken for Table 17.9 from the inventory footnote), we can calculate Nike's RNOA for 1997 as if it were using FIFO. Inventories would be higher by the amount of the LIFO reserve and so then would net operating assets in the denominator of RNOA. Operating income in the numerator would

TABLE 17.9

Nike Versus Reebok: LIFO vs. FIFO

	1997		1996	
	Nike	**Reebok**	**Nike**	**Reebok**
RNOA (%)	25.7	16.0	22.6	14.1
Asset turnover	3.0	3.2	2.7	2.9
Inventory turnover	8.1	6.6	8.3	5.8
Gross margin (%)	40.1	37.0	36.9	38.4
Profit margin (%)	8.7	4.9	8.5	4.8
Inventory ($ thousand)	1,338,640	563,735	931,151	544,522
Growth in inventory (%)	43.8	3.5	47.8	−14.2
LIFO reserve ($ thousand)	20,716	—	16,023	—

TABLE 17.10 Ratios from a Simulated Research and Development Program Using Different Accounting Methods

Year from Beginning of R&D Program	ROCE, %			P/B Ratios			E/P Ratios		
	Expense Method	**Full Costing**	**Successful Efforts**	**Expense Method**	**Full Costing**	**Successful Efforts**	**Expense Method**	**Full Costing**	**Successful Efforts**
14	−92.3	−3.4	−15.2	17.9	2.7	4.5	−0.043	−0.012	−0.035
20	8.1	10.7	11.0	11.4	2.9	5.2	0.016	0.029	0.018
26	54.8	27.8	39.6	7.3	2.7	4.5	0.098	0.101	0.098
32	54.0	26.4	39.3	7.4	2.6	4.5	0.096	0.097	0.096

The table shows how ROCE, P/B ratios, and E/P ratios change as R&D programs mature, for three different accounting methods that differ in the degree of conservative accounting. Expensing R&D is the most conservative accounting, full costing the least conservative. The R&D program generates losses up to Year 14 (for all three methods) because R&D expenses exceed revenues. Positive profitability is reported after Year 14, but the profitability is higher the more conservative the accounting method.

Source: P. Healy, S. Myers, and C. Howe, "R&D Accounting and the Relevance–Objectivity Tradeoff: A Simulation Using Data from the Pharmaceutical Industry," Sloan School of Management, MIT, 1998. See also "R&D Accounting and the Tradeoff between Relevance and Objectivity," *Journal of Accounting Research,* June 2002, pp. 677–710, by the same authors.

be higher by the amount of the change in the LIFO reserve from 1996 to 1997, that is, $4,693 thousand before tax and $2,886 thousand after tax at Nike's 38.5 percent tax rate. The adjusted RNOA (based on average net operating assets in the denominator) is 25.6 percent, immaterially different from the LIFO RNOA. We see that Nike had large increases in inventory but conclude that with the small increase in the LIFO reserve relative to its inventory, it does not have significant cost increase in manufacturing inventories.

These adjustments help in the comparison of firms' ratios. But for valuation purposes they are unnecessary: We can value both Nike and Reebok by forecasting their RNOA as measured, without adjustment for differences in the accounting. However, other considerations aside, Nike, with lower net operating assets under LIFO, has a (slightly) higher intrinsic P/B ratio than Reebok and, with its growth in inventories depressing earnings, a slightly higher intrinsic P/E.

Research and Development in the Pharmaceuticals Industry

Table 17.10 gives ROCE, P/B, and E/P ratios (the reciprocal of the P/E ratios) generated by a simulation of a firm's R&D program. In the simulation a firm spends a set amount each year for basic R&D on a number of drugs with a set probability of success. If the research on a drug is successful, the firm moves to preclinical testing and clinical trials, again with a set probability of a successful outcome. Successful drugs are launched commercially with estimated revenues, production costs, and marketing costs. All estimates, including the probability of R&D success, are based on experience in the drug industry, lending them a certain realism.

The numbers in Table 17.10 are averages over many trials in the simulation. This representative firm starts an R&D program in Year 1, and in early years there are no revenues as drug development moves through to commercial launch. The development period is quite long, and Year 14 is the first year that revenues are generated. The table gives ROCE, P/B, and E/P for that year, as well as Years 20, 26, and 32. The firm is not leveraged, so the ROCE is equal to the RNOA. The three ratios are given for three different accounting methods. The expensing method expenses all drug development costs when incurred, as required under GAAP. The full costing method capitalizes development costs and amortizes them straight-line over 10 years from commercial launch. The successful efforts costing method capitalizes all development costs, writes off unsuccessful projects when they fail to move to the next stage of development, and amortizes successful projects over 10 years from commercial launch. Prices in the E/P and P/B ratios are intrinsic prices calculated from forecasting cash flows in the stimulation.

Expensing R&D is the most conservative accounting, full costing the least. Steady state is reached in Year 26 and you can see that at that point expensing yields the highest ROCE, full costing the lowest. Accordingly, P/B ratios are highest under the expensing method, lowest under full costing. Because the firm commits a set amount of expenditure to R&D each year, once steady state is reached there is no growth in investment. Correspondingly, there is little change in earnings and ROCE (from Year 26 to Year 32), as in the Table 17.3 example earlier. There is also little change in E/P ratios and P/B ratios regardless of accounting method, again as in Table 17.3. And E/P ratios look normal: As there is no growth in ROCE or growth in expenditures (and no growth in earnings or book values), residual earnings are constant, so P/Es are normal.

The steady-state ratios are typical of a mature R&D firm with no growth in its R&D program. With growth, steady-state ROCE would be lower but P/E higher: The steady state would be a Table 17.5 rather than a Table 17.3 example. The ratios for the expensing method prior to steady state are typical of an R&D start-up. Expenditures for R&D are expensed but revenues are not yet forthcoming, so the firm reports very low profitability.

Expensing Goodwill and Research and Development Expenditures

The first line of Table 17.11 gives the reported operating profitability for Glaxo Wellcome, the large U.K. pharmaceutical firm, from 1991 to 1996. Glaxo bought Wellcome in 1995, so earlier figures are preacquisition (the firm is now part of GlaxoSmithKline PLC). Glaxo Wellcome expenses R&D expenditures. The second line gives the profitability recalculated by capitalizing R&D and amortizing it at a rate of 25 percent of declining balance each year. The period was one of growing investment in R&D which, when expensed, reduces operating income in the numerator. But the overall impact of the conservative accounting is to increase the return on operating assets over that from capitalizing and amortizing.

TABLE 17.11
Glaxo Wellcome PLC: Effects of Expensing R&D

Return on Operations, %	1991	1992	1993	1994	1995	1996
As reported	50.6	54.2	51.5	55.5	75.5	96.4
With R&D capitalized	39.8	41.2	39.4	39.4	50.5	55.0

Source: C. Higson, "Value Metrics in Equity Analysis," Institute of Finance and Accounting, London Business School, 1998.

TABLE 17.12
Forte Versus Hilton:
Liberal vs.
Conservative
Accounting

	1991	1992	1993	1994	1995
Forte PLC					
ROCE (%)	1.2	1.2	4.1	2.4	3.8
Depreciation/sales (%)	3.0	3.3	3.6	4.6	4.9
Revaluation reserve/equity (%)	69.8	71.0	67.5	73.9	70.9
P/B	0.58	0.61	0.58	1.03	0.94
Hilton Hotels Corp.					
ROCE (%)	9.0	10.6	10.3	11.1	14.5
Depreciation/sales (%)	9.1	8.9	8.5	8.9	8.6
P/B	2.01	2.06	2.75	2.90	2.37

Prior to 1998, firms in the United Kingdom expensed all goodwill in the year that it was purchased as a dirty-surplus charge to equity. (They now capitalize it and subject it to impairment rules.) This was very conservative accounting. You can see that the write-off from the acquisition of Wellcome in 1995 produced a large reported rate of return of 96.4 percent in 1996. When goodwill is capitalized, the 1996 return falls to 38.6 percent; it falls to 31.5 percent when both R&D and goodwill are capitalized.

Liberal Accounting: Breweries and Hotels

Many breweries, hotels, and leisure companies in the United Kingdom regularly revalue assets upward and also charge little in depreciation. Their argument is that asset values increase rather than decline and regular maintenance slows economic depreciation. Such firms accordingly have low accounting rates of return and low P/B ratios. Table 17.12 compares numbers for Forte PLC, a U.K. hotel and restaurant chain (before it was taken over by Granada in 1996), and Hilton Hotels, the U.S. hotel chain. These firms have large investments in depreciable assets (hotels), yet Forte's depreciation-to-sales ratio is much lower than Hilton's. And a high percentage of Forte's book value comes from revaluations (which are not permitted in the United States). Accordingly, its liberal accounting produced low ROCE and low P/B ratios. Forte's P/B ratios of less than 1.0 forecast negative residual earnings for the future. Hilton's P/B ratios forecast positive residual earnings.

Profitability in the 1990s

In the middle to late 1990s many firms reported strong profitability. In the early 1990s many of those same firms reported low profitability. The low profitability was due partly to recession and also to major restructurings and to the recognition of employee benefit liabilities. Some claim that the subsequent high profitability and earnings growth, though no doubt deriving from cost efficiencies introduced by the restructurings, was partly created by the lower book values from asset write-offs and the recognition of the new liabilities. Correspondingly, the high P/B ratios of the middle to late 1990s were due partly to the accounting having become more conservative.

In the late 1980s, General Motors Corporation traded below book value with correspondingly low book rates of return, as you can see in Table 17.13. After a period of very low profitability in the early 1990s, due significantly to restructuring and recognition of postemployment liabilities, profitability recovered to higher levels in 1994 and 1995, and the firm traded at a premium. Core profit margins recovered, but the higher RNOA relative to 1988 and 1989 was driven by a higher ATO. The higher ATO probably reflects real efficiencies in using assets but also is a result of the accounting in 1990 to 1992. And the higher P/B ratios reflect the lower book values of net operating assets.

TABLE 17.13
General Motors
Corporation: Effects
of Lower Book Values

	1988	1989	1990	1991	1992	1993	1994	1995	1996
Unlevered P/B	0.7	0.8	0.7	0.7	1.2	1.5	1.3	1.2	1.2
RNOA (%)	9.7	7.2	2.5	0.0	−20.8	6.3	11.1	11.0	7.5
Core PM (%)	6.7	6.9	4.1	1.5	1.8	4.2	5.0	5.5	3.8
ATO	1.5	1.0	1.0	1.0	1.3	1.9	2.2	1.9	1.7
NOA ($ billion)	118.3	125.1	124.1	118.4	81.8	63.3	76.7	96.2	95.3

Economic-Value-Added Measures

Consultants in recent years have developed residual earnings measures that adjust GAAP accounting to measure "economic value added" or "economic profit." These products may be good as value-based management tools—as performance incentives to maximize shareholder value—but users should be careful about demanding the adjustments for valuation. These measures redo the accounting, but the accounting may not matter. The measures typically undo accounting conservatism—by capitalizing and amortizing R&D and advertising, for example—but we have seen that this is not necessary. Indeed capitalizing and amortizing introduces the problem of estimating amortization rates to measure the decline in economic value of intangibles. This is a nontrivial exercise.

ACCOUNTING METHODS AND THE FORECAST HORIZON

The analysis in this chapter has shown that, for valuation purposes, we do not have to distinguish real economic profitability from accounting profitability: Accounting methods do not affect the valuation. That is just as well, for—despite consultants' claims that their products measure "economic profit" and "economic value added"—we really cannot observe true economic profitability. While accountants and consultants strive to improve measurement, we are ultimately forced to work with imperfect measurements. There are, however, two provisos to our conclusion:

1. The earnings forecasted must be comprehensive earnings. If any component of earnings is left out of the forecast, value is lost in the calculation.

2. The valuation is insensitive to the accounting only if steady state is predicted. Different accounting methods result in different (Case 1, 2, or 3) steady-state profitability, but once this difference in permanent profitability is recognized, the valuations are the same. If we value firms with forecasts up to a point before steady state is reached, however, we will not get the same valuation.

The first point has been emphasized consistently throughout the book. The second point is clear from comparing the valuations in Tables 17.4 and 17.5. With neutral accounting (in Table 17.4), the forecast horizon is very short; steady state is reached one year ahead. With conservative accounting (Table 17.5), the forecast horizon is longer; steady state is reached two years ahead. In the case of the pharmaceuticals industry in Table 17.10, the accounting takes a considerable amount of time to uncover the profitability of bringing drugs to the market, the more so for (very conservative) GAAP accounting that expenses investment in R&D immediately.

These observations give you a sense of another feature of the accounting that bears upon the valuation. Valuations are uncertain, but more so the further into the future we have to forecast. All else being equal, we prefer to value a firm from forecasts over a short forecasting horizon. Accounting methods that recognize value added earlier are to be preferred to accounting methods that require us to forecast well into the future. The simple valuations of Chapter 15 use very short forecast horizons. Indeed, the forecast horizon is immediate because those valuations rely only on the current financial statements. But those valuations only work if the accounting for the present is good enough to give us an indication of the long run.

The neutral accounting outlined in this chapter appears to be ideal, for it uncovers economic profitability and results in short forecast horizons. However, accounting that purports to be closer to the ideal is a good forecast of the long run only if it is reliable. If the accountant builds in a lot of speculation in short-term measures, we have lost our anchor; we have contaminated what we know with what we don't know. Consultants who measure "economic value added" typically capitalize R&D expenditures as assets on the balance sheet and then amortize this cost to earnings. If the outcome of the R&D program is highly speculative, the book value is also highly speculative. If, in addition, the amortization rates are highly uncertain, earnings also are contaminated by the speculation about the future, and we lose information about what we do know about the current profitability that might help us forecast future profitability. Conservative accounting (that expenses R&D immediately, for example) excludes such speculation and forces us to speculate over longer forecast horizons. Conservative accounting that is justified by uncertainty satisfies the fundamental analyst's desire to leave speculation to the analyst and exclude it from the accounting.

The Quality of Cash Accounting and Discounted Cash Flow Analysis

This discussion brings us back to the point where we embraced accrual accounting valuation models (in Chapter 4). We did so because cash accounting—and discounted cash flow analysis—can lead to long forecasting horizons to uncover the underlying value, especially if free cash flows in the short term are negative. Is free cash flow good accounting for valuation?

Discounted cash flow analysis forecasts cash flows, and its seeming appeal is that it uses reliable numbers. Cash flows are said to be "real" and not affected by accrual accounting rules and estimates. "Cash is king" is the cry, so forecast cash. The implication is that cash flow forecasts are better quality than earnings forecasts for capturing value. But we saw earlier in the book that free cash flow is doubtful as a value-added measure. It is the "dividend" from the operations, not the value created by the operations. For forecasting the long-term, free cash flow is perverse: investment reduces free cash flow but produces higher future cash flows, so the lower the free cash flow, the higher are future free cash flows.

To remind ourselves, Table 17.14 gives the free cash flows for Starbucks during its growth period from 1994 to 1997. As $C - I = OI - \Delta NOA$, the first two lines give operating income and net operating assets. The free cash flows here are negative. Was Starbucks losing value over this period? If we were valuing the firm in 1993 and had been given these cash flows as short-term forecasts for 1994 to 1997, would we accept them as good quality indicators of profitability in the future? As measures of cash flows, they are of course "real." But they are not good quality for valuing the firm.

In contrast, the accrual accounting numbers for Starbucks in Table 17.14—profit margins, asset turnover, RNOA, and growth in net operating assets—give some indication of profitability. They do not necessarily indicate long-run profitability, but they are a starting

TABLE 17.14
**Starbucks
Corporation: Free
Cash Flows and
Accrual Accounting
Measures, 1994–1997
(in thousands of
dollars)**

	1993	1994	1995	1996	1997
Operating income		15,051	24,406	31,081	53,252
Net operating assets	93,589	191,416	342,648	412,958	578,237
Free cash flow (C – I)	—	(82,776)	(126,826)	(39,229)	(112,027)
Core profit margin (%)		5.3	5.2	4.5	5.6
Asset turnover		2.00	1.74	1.84	1.95
Core RNOA (%)		10.6	9.0	8.3	10.9
Growth in NOA (%)		104.5	80.5	20.6	40.0

point to project how this firm can add value from profitability and growth in the future. We begin by recognizing the current profitability and growth and then, with other information about the firm's business plan, product demand, and so on, we forecast into the future. But looking at the free cash flows does not help. Starbucks's new investment each year is large relative to cash flow from operations, so forecasted free cash flows are negative. If investment continues apace as the firm expands into Europe and the Asia/Pacific region, forecasted free cash flows might be negative for a long time after 1997. The forecast horizon might have to be very long indeed to capture the value the firm can generate.

In practice, DCF analysts often adjust forecasted cash flows to get a better quality forecast. They recognize liabilities for pension costs and deferred taxes. They adjust for investments they consider to be unnecessary for sustaining the cash flows. This effectively yields a normal depreciation charge. But any adjustment to a cash flow is an accrual that serves the role of producing higher quality measures of value added. The adjustments are effectively redoing the accounting with particular accrual methods. In the end, the quality of the forecast will depend on the quality of the added accruals, which raises the question of what is good accrual accounting and what is poor accrual accounting.

The alternative approach is to start with GAAP earnings forecasts which already have many of the desired accruals. An analyst might be so distrustful of the estimates in accrual accounting as to back them out altogether. But he would have to then consider whether the resulting number—free cash flow—is really a higher quality number. Better to work with the accrual accounting, subject to the quality analysis of the next chapter.

Discounted cash flow analysis always gives the same valuation as residual earnings techniques if the forecast horizon is long enough. If one forecasts free cash flow to steady state, one recovers the valuation. Again, the issue is a question of working with reasonable horizons. But there are also circumstances where the DCF valuation is the same as the residual earnings valuation with the same forecast horizon. The Web page for this chapter lays out these circumstances and also contrasts other features of DCF and residual earnings valuation.

Growth, Risk, and *Valuation*

We have seen in this chapter that conservative accounting induces future growth when there is growing investment. Effectively, the accounting defers the recognition of income into the future. For example, as R&D accounting expenses investment immediately, it reduces current income but increases expected income in the future, and higher future income on lower current income is earnings growth.

The name, conservative accounting, implies caution. Indeed, conservative accounting is typically applied when investments are risky. Conservative accounting is a reaction to risk;

the conservative accountant defers the recognition of earnings to the future when the outcome to investing is uncertain. R&D accounting is a good example as R&D investing is indeed risky. So is investment to generate future sales by advertising (that is expensed immediately); the investment make not pay off. Accelerated depreciation or accelerated expensing of any kind can be a reaction to risky investing: Be conservative about recognizing earnings. And being conservative results in earnings growth, as we have shown. Historical cost accounting is actually a form of conservative accounting (relative to fair value accounting): Don't recognize earnings until there is a firm contract with a customer, that is, until the uncertainty about selling products in resolved. That pushes the earnings into the future as earnings growth. Fair value accounting, on the other hand, recognizes the (present) value from future sales immediately, putting a lot of risk on the balance sheet (as those holding mortgage-back securities at "fair" value during the financial crises found out to their sorrow).

Now consider the fundamentalist's doctrine: Beware of paying too much for growth, for growth is risky. You can see that the conservative accountant is acting is just the way the fundamentalist wishes, deferring the recognition of earnings to the future to produce growth that is deemed to be risky. That growth becomes the long-term growth part of a valuation, the part of the valuation that is deemed to be speculative, deemed to be risky. Correspondingly, the earnings in the short-term are conservative, earnings to anchor on with some assurance. In contrast to a risky balance sheet under fair value accounting, the balance sheet is solid, also something to anchor on.

We have recognized that adherence to our valuation models accommodates conservative accounting such that the accounting has no effect on the valuation. But the notion that conservative accounting and the growth it produces coincides with risk adds another dimension: If a valuation incorporates a lots of growth, require a higher return, for growth is risky. A higher growth rate requires a higher return, and specifying a higher required return in a valuation protects you from paying too much for growth. We made this point in Chapter 7 and will return to it when we return to active investing in Chapter 19: But, for now recognize that accounting works to indicate growth and risk. Conservative accounting protects us from paying too much for growth, provided we see growth as risky.

Summary

Residual earnings and abnormal earning growth are accounting measures. So are measures marketed by consultants as "economic profit," "economic value added," and the like. These measures are not necessarily measures of (real) value added. They are measures that are determined by real economic factors, but also by the accounting used in their calculation.

In a series of examples, this chapter has shown how accounting can create earnings, profitability, and residual earnings. And it has shown how accounting can create growth in earnings and growth in residual earnings, with the resultant effect on P/B ratios and P/E ratios. A benchmark case of a firm that adds no value with its investment was used to demonstrate the accounting effects. In general, profitability and growth result from both accounting effects and real economic factors that create value.

The chapter has shown that the way to view accounting methods is in terms of their effect on book value, for it is the accounting for book value that generates higher profitability and growth. So accounting methods were categorized as "conservative," "liberal," or "neutral" depending on their effect on book value. Indeed, while people often think of accounting methods in terms of their effect on earnings, the chapter has shown that the accounting does not affect earnings or P/E ratios if investment is constant. But the accounting does, in this case, affect profitability, residual earnings measures, and P/B ratios. Only if investment is increasing does the accounting affect earnings and P/E ratios, and in this case it creates growth in earnings and residual earnings even though no value is added by the growing investment.

The Web Connection

Find the following on the Web page for this chapter:

- Metrics that measure the amount of hidden reserves and the release of hidden reserves.
- A spreadsheet program for analyzing the effect of conservative accounting on profitability and growth.

- A look at cases in which discounted cash flow methods give the same valuation as accrual accounting methods with the same forecast horizon.
- An examination of the accounting issues involved in making valuations from short-term forecasts, with an application to Starbucks Corporation.

Despite the fact that book value and earnings are determined by both economic and accounting factors, the chapter comes with the assurance that firms can be valued if valuations are performed using our accrual accounting valuation models. The proviso is that growth induced by conservative accounting requires a higher discount rate, for growth is risky. The chapter also reconsidered the case where the analyst removes the accruals completely and uses discounted cash flow analysis, reiterating that this cash accounting is poor quality for value.

Key Concepts

accounting value added is (accounting) earnings in excess of that required for book value to earn at the required return. Compare with **economic value added.** *557*

conservative accounting is accounting that understates assets on the balance sheet or overstates liabilities. Compare with **liberal accounting.** *557*

economic value added is value generated from investment in excess of that to compensate for the required return on the investment. Compare with **accounting value added.** *557*

hidden reserve is income that has not been recognized in the past because conservative accounting has been practiced. Equivalently, hidden reserves are amounts of net assets that have not been recognized on the balance sheet because of conservative accounting. An example is the LIFO reserve. *566*

liberal accounting is accounting that overstates (or gives relatively higher) assets on the balance sheet or understates liabilities. Compare with **conservative accounting.** *557*

liquidation of hidden reserve is an increase in income that arises from slowing investments in assets that have been measured with conservative accounting. *566*

neutral accounting or **normal accounting** is accounting that yields an accounting rate of return equal to the required return for investments that add no (economic) value. *557*

value conservation principle is the principle by which value is insensitive to the accounting for book values: Accounting methods affect forecasts of residual earnings but, because of the offsetting effect on book value, do not affect value. *557*

The Analyst's Toolkit

Analysis Tools	Page	Key Measures	Page	Acronyms to Remember	
Analysis of profitability and accounting methods	558	LIFO liquidation profits	569	AOIG	abnormal operating income growth
Analysis of growth and accounting methods	561	LIFO reserve	566	ATO	asset turnover
Analysis of effects of conservative and liberal accounting	570			CV	continuing value
				E/P	reciprocal of P/E ratio
				FIFO	first in, first out
LIFO–FIFO relations	566			LIFO	last in, first out
Analysis of the effect of LIFO on profitability	571			NOA	net operating assets
				OI	operating income
				P/B	price-to-book ratio
Analysis of R&D and profitability	572			P/E	price-earnings ratio
				PM	profit margin
				PV	present value
				R&D	research and development
				RE	residual earnings
				ReOI	residual operating income
				RNOA	return on net operating assets
				ROCE	return on common equity

Concept Questions

C17.1. Firms with a return on net operating assets (RNOA) that is higher than the required return on operations are adding value with their investments and so should trade at a premium over their book value. Is this statement correct?

C17.2. Why are LIFO accounting and the expensing of R&D expenditures referred to as conservative accounting policies?

C17.3. Explain how intrinsic price-to-book (P/B) ratios are affected by conservative accounting (such as expensing R&D expenditures).

C17.4. Does conservative accounting result in higher or lower accounting rates of return?

C17.5. Explain how intrinsic P/E ratios are affected by conservative accounting (such as expensing R&D expenditures).

C17.6. Consultants talk of "economic profit," or "economic value added." What is it? Can it be observed?

C17.7. How is it that accounting policies affect the measurement of residual income but the value calculated using residual income methods may not be affected by accounting policies?

C17.8. A firm that uses LIFO accounting for inventory in times of rising inventory costs will always report lower profit margins than if it used FIFO. Is this correct?

C17.9. A firm using LIFO accounting for inventory is likely to have a lower inventory turnover ratio than one using FIFO. Is this correct?

C17.10. Firms with anticipated earnings-per-share growth are worth more. Is this statement always correct?

C17.11. What is a "hidden reserve"? What does it mean to "release hidden reserves"?

C17.12. What is meant by "steady state"?

C17.13. In the United Kingdom, firms revalue tangible assets upward and recognize the value of brands on the balance sheet. In the United States, this accounting is not permitted. In which country would you expect the average return on common equity for firms to be higher?

C17.14. On January 29, 1999, *The Wall Street Journal* reported: "Sears, Roebuck & Co. is moving toward more conservative accounting methods used by competing credit-card issuers, which will boost its loan losses by about $200 million during the next 5 quarters." What effect should this new policy have had on future return on net operating assets?

C17.15. Expensing research and development costs raises accounting quality issues similar to those raised in cash accounting. Explain.

Exercises

Drill Exercises

E17.1. A Simple Demonstration of the Effect of Accounting Methods on Value (Easy)

You invest $100 (at time 0) and expect to receive $115 in cash in one year. Your required return is 9 percent.

a. Calculate the value of your investment at time 0 using discounted cash flow techniques.
b. Calculate the value of your investment using residual earnings techniques.
c. Suppose that your accountant demanded that you expense $20 of your investment immediately such that the book value of the investment was $80 at time 0. Calculate the value of your investment under this accounting.

E17.2. Valuation of a Project Under Different Accounting Methods (Easy)

Here are some details of an investment in a project with a two-year life and a required return of 9 percent per year. Dollar amounts are in millions.

Initial investment in equipment	$1,500
Initial investment in advertising	700
Total investment	$2,200
Expected revenue, Year 1	$1,540
Expected revenue, Year 2	$1,540

All revenue is received in cash. Investments are depreciated using the straight-line method.

a. Value the project and its value added using discounted cash flow techniques.
b. Value the project using residual earnings techniques with the total initial investment capitalized on the balance sheet. Also calculate expected return on net operating assets (RNOA) for each period.
c. Repeat part b of the question, but with depreciation of $1,300 million in Year 1. Explain why numbers differ. How does the value of the investment change?
d. Repeat the valuation using straight-line depreciation but with the initial investment in advertising expensed immediately, as required by GAAP.
e. Compare the price-to-book ratio and the forward P/E ratio under the alternative accounting treatments for investments in advertising.

E17.3. **Valuation of a Going Concern Under Different Accounting Methods (Medium)**

An entrepreneur develops a business plan that requires an initial investment of $2,200 million with a further investment of $2,200 million each year on an ongoing basis. Investment is expected to yield sales revenue equal to 70 percent of the investment in each of the two years following the investment. Accounting rules require the investment to be depreciated straight-line over those two years. She asks you whether you would like to invest in this business. You have a hurdle rate for investment of this sort of 9 percent per year.

a. Develop a pro forma to assist you in your valuation and calculate the value implied by that pro forma. What are the price-to-book ratio and the forward P/E ratio?

b. After running the analysis by your accountant, you find that GAAP rules require 20 percent of the projected investment each year to be expensed immediately. Revise your pro forma and find our how your valuation will change.

c. Repeat the evaluations in parts a and b for a scenario where investment is expected to grow by 5 percent each year.

Applications

E17.4. **Inventory Accounting, P/B, and P/E Ratios: Ford Motor Company (Medium)**

Ford Motor Company uses the last in, first out (LIFO) method for most of its inventories in its Automotive Division. The amounts of the LIFO reserve reported in footnotes for 1999 were

	1999	1998
LIFO reserve	$1.1 billion	$1.2 billion

Ford reported total shareholders' equity of $27.537 billion at the end of 1999 and $23.409 billion at the end of 1998, and it reported earnings for 1999 of $7.237 billion. The firm's 1.21 billion outstanding shares traded at $53 at the end of 1999. Ford faces a statutory tax rate of 36 percent.

a. What would have been Ford's shareholders' equity at the end of 1999 and 1998 if it had used the first in, first out (FIFO) method to record its inventories?

b. What return on common equity would Ford have reported in 1999 if it had used FIFO?

c. Compare Ford's price-to-book ratios at the end of 1999 under LIFO and FIFO, and explain the difference.

d. Compare the firm's P/E ratio under LIFO and FIFO, and explain the difference.

E17.5. **The Accounting for Research and Development and Economic Profit Measures (Medium)**

Many consultants recognize that expensing R&D investments gives a poor indication of the performance of a firm or its managers because investing in R&D results in lower income. So they adjust GAAP accounting by capitalizing R&D expenditures and amortizing the capitalized amount over the estimated life of the revenues that flow from the expenditures.

a. Below is a series of R&D expenditures that are expected for the years 2009 to 2014 under a firm's R&D program (in millions of dollars). The R&D program began in 2008 with a $100 million investment. Expected net operating assets for the firm are also given for net assets other than those created by the R&D expenditures. Expenditures for R&D are expected to generate $1.60 of revenue over each of the subsequent five years for each dollar spent. Expenses other than R&D expenses are expected to be 80 percent of sales.

	2008A	2009E	2010E	2011E	2012E	2013E	2014E
R&D expenditure	100	100	100	100	100	100	100
Net operating assets	80	80	80	80	80	80	80

Calculate expected operating income, return on net operating assets (RNOA), and residual operating income for each year, 2009 to 2014, under GAAP accounting (where R&D expenditures are expensed against income). Use a required return for operations of 10 percent.

b. Now calculate the RNOA and residual operating income for each year under an accounting that capitalizes R&D expenditures and amortizes them over five years.

c. Compare the RNOA and residual operating income calculated under the two accounting treatments for each year. Why are they different?

d. Forecast RNOA and residual operating income for 2015 under the two accounting treatments. Why do these forecasts differ?

e. Value the firm at the end of 2008 using the two different accounting treatments. Do the valuations differ? Why?

f. If you tried to value this firm by forecasting only to 2011, what difficulties would you face under the two methods?

E17.6. Depreciation Methods, Profitability, and Valuation (Hard)

A start-up firm embarks on an investment program in 2009 to manufacture and market a new switching device to be used in communications. The program requires an initial investment of $600 million in plant and equipment, increasing by $100 million each year for four years up to 2013, and then continuing at $1,000 million per year thereafter.

The founders of the firm are keen to look profitable when they expect to take the firm public in an initial public offering (IPO) in early 2014. After awarding him stock options, they ask the newly hired chief financial officer (CFO) to prepare pro forma statements of earnings and return on investment. The marketing manager supplies the CFO with the following sales forecasts (in millions of dollars), and he and the production manager estimate that operational expenses before depreciation will be 70 percent of sales.

	2010E	2011E	2012E	2013E	2014E	2015E	2016E
Sales	250	1,530	3,540	4,295	4,305	4,410	4,500

Sales after 2016 are expected to be at the level of those in 2016.

The CFO understands that with the rapid technological change that is expected, estimated useful lives of assets are quite uncertain and thinks he can justify either a three-year estimated life or a five-year estimated life for the plant and equipment. So he prepares two sets of pro formas, one depreciating the investments in plant and equipment straight-line over three years, and one depreciating them straight-line over five years.

a. Prepare the operating section of the pro forma income statements and balance sheets under both depreciation methods. Ignore tax effects.

b. Which set of pro formas shows the firm to be more profitable in 2013, just prior to the anticipated public offering? Why?

c. The CFO wishes to show the management that the depreciation method does not affect the intrinsic value of the firm at the time of the IPO. Prepare the calculations to give this demonstration, using the hurdle rate of 10 percent that the founders have set for investments.

d. Despite your calculation, the founders insist that the market will give a higher value if higher earnings are reported at the time of the IPO. What would be your reply to them?

e. The CFO points out that his and the founders' stock options vest in 2018, not at the time of the IPO in 2014. He therefore suggests that the focus should be on profits expected to be reported in 2018. What arguments might be made to justify using one depreciation method over the other?

E17.7. The Quality of Free Cash Flow and Residual Operating Income: Coca-Cola Company (Easy)

At one time, the Coca-Cola Company reported a number called "economic profit" that is very similar to residual operating income. It also reported free cash flow in its annual summary of selected financial data. The respective numbers for 1992–1999 are given below (in millions of dollars), along with what Coke calls total capital (similar to net operating assets) and return on total capital (similar to return on net operating assets):

	1992	1993	1994	1995	1996	1997	1998	1999
Economic profit	1,300	1,549	1,896	2,291	2,718	3,325	2,480	1,128
Free cash flow	873	1,623	2,146	2,102	2,413	3,533	1,876	2,332
Total capital	7,095	7,684	8,744	9,456	10,669	11,186	13,552	15,740
Return on capital	29.4%	31.2%	32.7%	34.9%	36.7%	39.4%	30.2%	18.2%

a. Economic profit and free cash flow are similar, in most years, and their growth patterns are similar. Why?

b. Based on this past history, would you be indifferent in valuing Coke using discounted cash flow methods or residual operating income methods?

Real World Connection

See Exercises E4.7, E4.8, E12.7, E15.7, E16.12, and E20.4 and Minicases M4.1, M5.2, and M6.1.

E17.8. Research and Development Expenditures and Valuation (Medium)

A new pharmaceutical firm has patented a technology and has committed to spending $350 million annually for the next five years to develop further products from the technology. The program is currently spending $350 million on R&D, yielding $1,000 million in sales and a loss of $150 million after R&D, production and advertising costs, and taxes. However, revenues from the R&D are expected to grow by $500 million per year over the next five years, reaching $3,500 million. After that, revenues are expected to grow at 5 percent per year, with growth in R&D expenditures also of 5 percent per year to support the additional sales. Production and advertising costs are expected to be at the same percentage of sales as currently. The firm requires an investment in net operating assets such as to maintain an asset turnover of 1.4. Currently net operating assets stand at $714 million.

a. Value the firm using a hurdle rate for operations of 10 percent.

b. Comment on the quality of the earnings forecasts for the next three years as a basis for valuation.

c. Calculate the forecasted R&D-to-sales ratio for each of the next five years. Why is this ratio an indicator of the quality of the earnings forecasted?

E17.9. **The Quality of Forecasted Residual Operating Income and Free Cash Flow (Medium)**

A start-up begins operations in 2012 by investing $400 million in plant and equipment. It expects to increase investment by $40 million each year, indefinitely, depreciating it straight-line over two years. The investment program is expected to generate sales for the next five years, as follows (in millions of dollars):

	2012A	2013E	2014E	2015E	2016E	2017E
Sales		240	484	530	576	622
Investment	400	440	480	520	560	600

a. Prepare a schedule of pro forma operating income, return on net operating assets (RNOA), residual operating income, and net operating assets for the years 2013 to 2017. Depreciation of the investment is the only operating expense. The firm has a 10 percent hurdle rate for its operations. Calculate the value of this firm using residual operating income methods.

b. Forecast free cash flow for 2013 to 2017. Do you think that forecasted free cash flow is a good quality number on which to base a valuation? What features in the pro forma explain why the pattern of free cash flows is different from that for residual operating income?

Minicase **M17.1**

Advertising, Low Quality Accounting, and Valuation: E∗Trade

New businesses take time to get established, and the new Internet firms of the late 1990s were no exception. Internet portal firms and e-commerce firms traded at high multiples of sales on the promise of large profits, but most of them were generating losses from their sales.

In statements to the press, these firms maintained that their "business model" required them to incur substantial losses in order to generate future profits. Investments were required in infrastructure. Considerable expenditure was required for advertising and promotion to establish a customer base and to create brand recognition. So these firms appealed to investors to ignore the bottom line and focus rather on their ability to generate revenues. Accordingly, the price-to-sales ratio became the typical multiplier that investors referred to. And analysts referred to other indicators like "hit rates" and "page views" (on Web sites) to assess the price-to-sales ratio.

In arguing that the losses they were reporting were not indicative of the value in their business model, Internet entrepreneurs argued that the GAAP accounting they were required to use was of low quality. But clearly investors were left with the question of whether these firms would actually become profitable in the end and whether the size of the profits would justify the high stock prices at which these firms traded. Rather than the crude indicators like hit rates, they looked for more substantial financial analysis.

ONLINE TRADING FIRMS

During 1999 there was a dramatic shift by investors to online stock trading on the Internet. E∗Trade, TD Waterhouse, National Discount Brokers, and others battled with Charles Schwab, the traditional discount broker, and with each other for market share. Morgan Stanley Dean Witter, a more traditional broker, offered online trading through its Discover brokerage. Merrill Lynch, after initially indicating that it might shun the online business, entered the fray in late 1999 with a $29.95 per-trade fee.

Figures as of September 1999 for some of the firms selling online trading services follow. Earnings and sales are rolling 12-month numbers to June 30, 1999 (M = millions; B = billions):

	Sales	EPS	Market Value	P/E Ratio	Price-to-Book Ratio	Price-to-Sales Ratio
E∗Trade	$464M	−0.23	$ 5.75B	—	5.5	12.4
TD Waterhouse	896M	0.25	5.13B	47	2.6	5.7
National Discount Brokers	250M	1.28	458.6M	20	2.6	1.8
Ameritrade	274M	0.15	3.28B	119	9.2	12.0
Charles Schwab	3.361B	4.11	27.6B	56	14.4	8.2

In the fall of 1999, these firms began an advertising war. In the industry, market share is referred to as "share of voice." Customers are sticky, it is said: They tend to stay with the same brokerage, so attracting them—and building a brand name to attract them—is seen as the driver of ultimate success.

Schwab, with a large discount brokerage business prior to the advent of online trading, led with a 25 percent share of voice on the Internet. But in early 1999, E∗Trade increased its share to 14 percent with what was judged a very successful advertising campaign on prime-time TV shows such as *Ally McBeal* and *E.R.* and on the Super Bowl, the most expensive advertising time of all. Others imitated, so that by the end of 1999 it was said that these firms had committed to a total of $1.5 billion in advertising over the subsequent 18 months.[3] To give a sense of perspective, this amount is roughly equal to the annual advertising budget of Coca-Cola.

Estimates varied, but industry analysts maintained that in a market saturated with competitors, it takes $400 to $500 in advertising and inducements to sign up each new customer, with repeat advertising of $100 per customer to retain them and maintain the brand.

E∗TRADE

E∗Trade was one of the first online trading firms to challenge Schwab and the traditional brokers. It spent $322 million on sales marketing for its fiscal year ended September 30, 1999, increasing the number of trading accounts by 1 million to 1.55 million and producing revenues of $657 million. Based on its marketing expenses for the first quarter of fiscal 2000, its annual advertising budget was running at $450 million.

Exhibit 17.1 presents summary financial statements for E Trade Group, the firm that runs E∗Trade, for the September 1999 fiscal year.

A. Why are the earnings reported by start-up firms considered to be a "low quality" number?

B. Why should investors be wary of price-to-sales ratios? Why should they be skeptical about hit rates and page views on Web sites?

C. Develop an analysis that tests E∗Trade's business model with the marketing information in the case.

D. E Trade Group traded at $25 per share at the end of September 1999, giving it a price-to-sales ratio of 10.5. Given your analysis in part (C), was the firm appropriately priced at the time?

E. What other strategies might E∗Trade pursue to add value?

F. By early 2000, the number of online brokerage firms had exploded to about 140 and competition was fierce. The industry needed consolidation, it was said, to deal with the glut in capacity. Should E∗Trade consider acquisitions to consolidate the dominant position it holds and compete more effectively with Charles Schwab? Stock market values for the larger online firms in the preceding table were such as to value each customer account at about $3,000 each.

---

[3] As reported in Joseph Kahn's articles "The Media Business: Advertising: The On-Line Brokerage Battle," *The New York Times,* October 4, 1999, p. C1. Copyright © 1999 by The New York Times Co. Reprinted with permission. Text not being quoted, but is cited in publication.

EXHIBIT 17.1
Summary Financial
Statements for
E Trade Group, Inc.
for 1999

E TRADE GROUP, INC.
Consolidated Balance Sheets
(in thousands, except per-share amounts)

	September 30	
	1999	**1998**
Assets		
Cash and equivalents	$ 124,801	$ 71,317
Cash and investments required to be segregated		
under federal or other regulations	104,500	7,400
Brokerage receivables—net	2,912,581	1,365,247
Mortgage-backed securities	1,426,053	1,012,163
Loans receivable—net	2,154,509	904,854
Investments	830,329	812,093
Property and equipment—net	178,854	54,805
Goodwill and other intangibles	17,211	19,672
Other assets	159,386	101,372
Total assets	$7,908,224	$4,348,923
Liabilities and Shareowners' Equity		
Liabilities		
Brokerage payables	$2,824,212	$1,244,513
Banking deposits	2,162,682	1,209,470
Borrowings by bank subsidiary	1,267,474	876,935
Subordinated notes	0	29,855
Accounts payable, accrued and other liabilities	203,971	101,920
Total liabilities	6,458,339	3,462,693
Company-obligated mandatorily redeemable		
preferred securities	30,584	38,385
Shareowners' equity		
(275 million shares outstanding in 1999)	1,419,301	847,845
Total liabilities and shareowners' equity	$7,908,224	$4,348,923

(*continued*)

EXHIBIT 17.1
(*concluded*)

Consolidated Statements of Operations
(in thousands, except per-share amounts)

	Years Ended September 30	
	1999	**1998**
Revenues		
Transaction revenues	$ 355,830	$162,097
Interest income	368,053	185,804
Global and institutional	110,959	95,829
Other	40,543	28,163
Gross revenues	875,385	471,893
Interest expense	(215,452)	(120,334)
Provision for loan losses	(2,783)	(905)
Net revenues	657,150	350,654
Cost of services	292,910	145,018
Operating Expenses		
Selling and marketing	321,620	124,408
Technology development	76,878	33,926
General and administrative	102,138	50,067
Merger-related expenses	7,174	1,167
Total operating expenses	507,810	209,568
Total cost of services and operating expenses	800,720	354,586
Operating income (loss)	$(143,570)	$ (3,932)
Nonoperating Income (Expense)		
Corporate interest income—net	$ 19,639	$ 11,036
Gain on sale of investments	54,093	0
Equity in income (losses) of investments	(8,838)	531
Other	(71)	(1,098)
Total nonoperating income	64,823	10,469
Pretax income (loss)	(78,747)	6,537
Income tax expenses (benefit)	(31,300)	1,873
Minority interest in subsidiary	2,197	1,362
Income (loss) before cumulative effect of accounting change and extraordinary loss	(49,638)	3,302
Cumulative effect of accounting change, net of tax	(469)	0
Extraordinary loss on early extinguishment of subordinated debt, net of tax	(1,985)	0
Net income (loss)	(52,092)	3,302
Preferred stock dividends	222	2,352
Income (loss) applicable to common stock	($52,314)	$ 950
Income (loss) per share before cumulative effect of accounting change and extraordinary loss		
Basic	($0.19)	$ 0.00
Diluted	($0.19)	$ 0.00
Income (loss) per share		
Basic	($0.20)	$ 0.00
Diluted	($0.20)	$ 0.00

Chapter **Eighteen**

Analysis of the Quality of Financial Statements

LINKS

Link to previous chapter

Chapter 17 showed how accounting methods, consistently applied, affect profitability and earnings growth on a permanent basis.

This chapter

This chapter shows how accounting methods can affect earnings temporarily, making current earnings a poor indicator of future earnings. It also develops diagnostics to detect when reported earnings are of poor quality.

Link to next chapter

Part Five of the book analyzes the fundamental determinants of risk and the cost of capital.

Link to Web page

Explore further examples of accounting quality analysis by visiting the text's Web site at **www.mhhe.com/penman5e**.

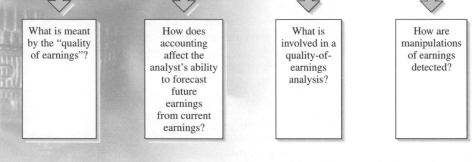

| What is meant by the "quality of earnings"? | How does accounting affect the analyst's ability to forecast future earnings from current earnings? | What is involved in a quality-of-earnings analysis? | How are manipulations of earnings detected? |

Fundamentalists anchor on the financial statements. They do so to challenge the market price. They do so to uncover value drivers for forecasting. They initialize on the current financial statements for full-information pro forma analysis. So they must be assured that the financial statements are of good quality. Otherwise the anchor drifts.

Some analysts specialize in examining the quality of the accounting in financial reports. Quality analysts advise clients—some of whom are other analysts—on the integrity of the accounting in representing the underlying performance of the firm. Accounting methods can be used to "package" the firm, to make it look better than it is. Quality analysts unwrap the packaging, and if the accounting is being used to obscure, they issue warnings. This chapter leads you through a quality analysis.

Analysts' quality warnings and announcements of SEC investigations hit the news headlines, causing sudden drops in share prices. The equity analyst tries to avoid being caught by surprise; the analyst who first gets a sense that there is something wrong with the accounting is very much at an advantage.

With the bursting of the stock market bubble in 2001, accounting quality problems surfaced for many firms. The pressure to produce earnings was too much for some firms, leading them to apply a variety of accounting "tricks" to deliver earnings growth. But such methods can only maintain growth in the short run. As the bubble burst, firms like Xerox,

The Analyst's Checklist

After reading this chapter you should understand:

- How accounting methods and estimates affect the sustainability of earnings.
- What "quality of earnings" means.
- The accounting devices that management can use to manipulate earnings.
- How firms can time transactions to determine their earnings.
- What *disclosure quality* means.
- Situations where accounting manipulation is more likely.
- Why change in net operating assets is the focus of a quality analysis.
- How diagnostics are developed to detect manipulation in financial statements.
- How quality scoring works.

After reading this chapter you should be able to:

- Carry out a complete accounting quality analysis on a set of financial statements.
- Identify sensitive situations where manipulation of the financial statements is more likely.
- Apply a set of diagnostics that raises questions about the quality of the accounting in financial statements.
- Combine accounting quality analysis with the financial statement analysis and red-flag analysis discussed earlier in the book to assess the sustainability of earnings.
- Engage in quality scoring.

Enron, Tyco, Lucent Technologies, WorldCom, Bristol-Myers Squibb, Qwest, Krispy Kreme, and Royal Ahold found their accounting called into question, in most cases with disastrous effects on their stock prices. More recently, the quality of banks' balance sheets, with their inflated "fair values" of mortgage assets during the housing bubble, came into question.

WHAT IS ACCOUNTING QUALITY?

With valuation in mind, we are interested in future earnings; indeed, "buy future earnings" is the investors' creed that we have followed, with all due care, in this book. We use current earnings, and entire financial statements, to help us forecast future earnings. The current financial statements are of poor quality if they mislead us in forecasting. So, if current earnings are not a good indicator of future earnings, the investor would say that the **earnings quality** is poor. Thus, for example, if those earnings contain one-time, unusual items, the analyst recognizes that the earnings quality is poor, so works with a better quality number, core earnings. We did so in Chapter 13. But if, in addition, the firm uses accounting methods that degrade core earnings as an indicator of future earnings, core earnings can be poor quality. So, for example, if a firm underestimates bad debts, warranties, deferred revenue, or depreciation, it reports a higher earnings number that is likely to be lower in the future. So, to a core-earnings analysis, we add an analysis of the accounting quality that produces the earnings.

An accounting quality analysis is imperative because of the **reversal property of accounting:** Earnings induced by accounting methods always reverse in the future. So, if current bad debt estimates are too low (and earnings too high), bad debt expense must be higher in the future (and income lower); if the current depreciation charge is too low, then depreciation must be higher in the future or the firm must impair assets or report a loss on the sale of the asset. If, as we saw in Chapter 13, a restructuring charge is too high, it must be bled back as a gain to income in the future. Indeed, this feature of accounting defines earnings quality: Earnings are of good quality if they do not reverse.

If the low-quality earnings are detected, forecasts can be adjusted to anticipate the reversals. If left undetected, however, low-quality accounting leads to low-quality forecasts and low-quality valuations. Undetected low-quality accounting exposes the investor to a "torpedo," a drop in stock price—not only when accounting malfeasance is exposed by an analyst or an enforcement agency but, more likely, through earnings surprises when subsequent earnings containing the reversals are reported.

Manipulation is often referred to (politely) as **earnings management.** Manipulation that inflates current income is referred to as **borrowing income from the future.** It always involves either an increase in sales or a decrease in expenses, with the reverse in the future. Manipulation can also be done in the other direction. Manipulation that reduces current operating income is called **saving** or **banking income for the future.** It always involves either a decrease in sales or an increase in expenses, again with the reverse in the future. The motivation for borrowing from the future is fairly clear: Management wants to make profitability look better than it really is. Saving income for the future might arise when managers' bonuses are tied to future earnings. An extreme version is called "taking a big bath": A new management writes off a lot of expenses, attributes the lower income (or loss) to the old management it has replaced, and generates more future income on which it will be rewarded.

This intertemporal shifting of income, the hallmark of manipulation, means that earnings quality is not only doubtful in the year of the manipulation but also in subsequent years when the borrowing or saving of income "comes home to roost." Some claim that the large amount of restructuring in the early 1990s produced excessive restructuring charges, which created higher profits in the late 1990s. The market was very excited about earnings in the late 1990s, resulting in high multiples. But these earnings were partly created by the bleed back from the earlier excessive restructuring charges.

Do not confuse the accounting issues in this chapter with those in the last. The last chapter dealt with accounting methods that are applied on a consistent, permanent basis—always expensing research and development (R&D) and advertising expenses, always maintaining accelerated depreciation methods, or always using LIFO for inventory, for instance. Those conservative accounting methods, consistently applied, consistently produce higher accounting rates of return and earnings growth, and liberal accounting does the opposite. This chapter deals with the effects of accounting that are temporary, thus making current earnings a poor indicator of future earnings. If a firm always overestimates bad debts (so always to be "conservative"), it will consistently report a higher return on net operating assets. But if it temporarily increases or lowers its bad debt estimate to change current earnings, it will produce a return on net operating assets that is a poor indicator of future profitability. Accordingly, the term **aggressive accounting** (not liberal accounting) is best used to indicate manipulation that temporarily increases income. And the term **big-bath accounting** might be used to indicate manipulation that temporarily reduces income (not conservative accounting), although the term is typically used when income is reduced by large amounts.

Accounting Quality Watch

It should be clear that much of the apparatus that we have laid out in this book involves a quality-of-earnings analysis. The identification of hidden expenses (in Chapter 9) yielded higher quality earnings. The separation of operating from financing items (in Chapter 10) identifies a component of net income—operating income—that is pertinent for forecasting what's important for value. The financial statement analysis in Chapter 13 drove harder to purge operating income of unusual, transitory items, to cut to sustainable core operating income and core profit margins that are "higher quality" numbers to forecast the future. And the analysis in Chapter 16 hoisted some red flags.

In carrying out this analysis, we have maintained an Accounting Quality Watch that identified quality issues as they arose and which accumulated as you worked through the book. Look back at Box 9.6 in Chapter 9, Box 10.8 in Chapter 10, Box 11.4 in Chapter 11, and Box 13.11 in Chapter 13, so you are well attuned to the issue of accounting quality.

One further element is needed to complete an earnings-quality analysis. Core operating income and its components may be affected by accounting methods. So we have to analyze the quality of the accounting for core operating income. We have to cut through the accounting to get to the core. This is the issue of accounting quality.

Five Questions About Accounting Quality

In analyzing the quality of the accounting, the analyst seeks answers to five questions:

1. **GAAP quality:** Are generally accepted accounting principles deficient? If forecasts are based on GAAP statements but GAAP does not capture all the value-relevant aspects of the firm, valuations will be deficient. We saw in Chapter 9 that GAAP fails to capture the expense of stock compensation comprehensively. In Chapter 13 we saw that GAAP earnings can include stock market bubble gains.

2. **Audit quality:** Is the firm violating GAAP or committing outright fraud? GAAP accounting might be appropriate, but a firm might not be applying GAAP according to the rules. Is it booking receivables without having firm commitments from customers? Is it failing to recognize expenses or recognize liabilities as required? Is it using methods not approved by GAAP? To answer these questions the observer usually has to be close to the business, so audit quality is the province of the auditor and the audit committee of the board of directors. Agencies such as the Securities and Exchange Commission (SEC) and the Public Company Accounting Oversight Board (PCAOB) in the United States play an enforcement role. The analyst typically relies on the audit. But she needs to be sensitive to the possibility of audit failure or to situations where an auditor with a conflict of interest might be generous to management in drawing a line through a gray area. And there is a problem with auditing in the United States: Auditors obey GAAP which can be used to develop form over substance schemes (as we will see) rather than expressing a "true and fair" view of the economics of a firm.

3. **GAAP application quality:** Is the firm using GAAP accounting to manipulate reports? Generally accepted accounting principles restrict the accounting methods that a firm can use but permit some choice among methods. That choice can be taken as a license to manipulate the numbers to achieve a desired effect, and with approval of auditors. The issue is particularly sensitive when estimates are involved—estimates of bad debts, useful lives of assets, warranty expenses, pension costs, and restructuring charges, for example. Managers manage firms but they can also manage earnings.

4. **Transaction quality:** Is the firm manipulating its business to accommodate the accounting? A firm may employ GAAP faithfully but then arrange transactions around the accounting to achieve desired results. This is manipulation of the business, not the accounting, but it exploits features of the accounting. It takes two forms:

    a. **Transaction timing** controls the timing of transactions to affect income. Both **revenue timing** and **expenditure timing** can be involved. Revenue timing—sometimes known as **channel stuffing**—times transactions around revenue recognition rules. Typically GAAP requires revenue to be recognized when goods and services are delivered to customers. Firms might ship a lot of goods prior to the end of the period to increase profits for the period or delay shipping when they wish to defer profits. Expenditure timing times expenditures that go straight to the bottom line in order to manipulate income. Deferring R&D and advertising outlays to the next period increases income, for example, whereas advancing them to the current period decreases income.

b. **Transaction structuring** creates form over substance: Business arrangements are structured to take a form that receives the desired accounting treatment, but investigation of the substance of the transaction reveals a sham.

5. **Disclosure quality:** Are disclosures adequate to analyze the business? Disclosures are made within the financial statements, in the footnotes, and in the management discussion and analysis. Management also gives additional commentary in meetings with analysts. Much of the financial analysis that we have been through relies on good disclosures, to understand the business and how it is represented in the financial statements. For valuation, four types of disclosures are particularly important:

a. Disclosures that distinguish operating items from financial items in the statements.

b. Disclosures that distinguish core operating profitability from unusual items.

c. Disclosures that reveal the drivers of core profitability.

d. Disclosures that explain the accounting used so the analyst can investigate the quality of the application of GAAP.

Without adequate disclosures it is difficult to forecast from a good measure of current core operating income, so low-quality disclosures lead to low-quality valuations.

All five quality questions must be answered to discover the quality of the accounting. GAAP quality (question 1) has arisen at several points in this book, particularly in Chapters 2, 9, and 13. Audit quality (question 2) is a matter of auditing principles and is left to auditing books. In this chapter, we deal with the problem of earnings manipulated by the application of GAAP accounting (question 3) or by transaction timing and structuring (question 4). But disclosure quality (question 5) arises at many points because we can't carry out any analysis with confidence if disclosures are poor.

CUTTING THROUGH THE ACCOUNTING: DETECTING INCOME SHIFTING

Manipulation of earnings with accounting methods or estimates always leaves a trail: By the debits and credits of accounting, one cannot affect the income statement without affecting the balance sheet. Higher revenues mean higher receivables (an asset) or lower deferred revenues (a liability), for example, and lower expenses mean higher prepaid expenses (an asset) or lower accrued expenses (a liability). So, investigation of balance sheet changes provides the clues. For valuation, the focus is on operating income and, correspondingly, net operating assets, so changes in net operating assets are the focus.

Figure 18.1 depicts the effects of earnings manipulation of the accounting numbers. It gives free cash flows, net operating assets (NOA), operating income, and return of net operating assets (RNOA) for scenarios with and without growth in net operating assets. Then, within each scenario, the figure depicts the accounting numbers with and without earnings manipulation. In the no-growth case, without income shifting, Scenario A, free cash flow and operating income are 12 each year on NOA of 100 and, with no growth in NOA, RNOA is a constant 12 percent. In Scenario B, the manager decides to increase operating income in the current year, Year 0, by 10, up to 22. But he cannot do this without affecting the balance sheet: He must also increase net operating assets by the extra 10, up to 110. His manipulation results in an RNOA of 22 percent for Year 0 which, if she were not careful,

FIGURE 18.1
How Accounting Manipulation Leaves a Trail in the Balance Sheet: Four Scenarios

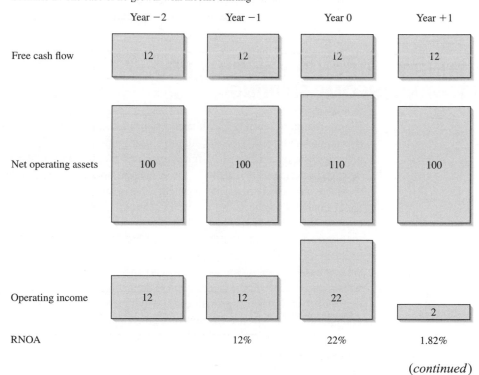

Scenario A: The case of no growth with no income shifting

Scenario B: The case of no growth with income shifting

(*continued*)

FIGURE 18.1
(*concluded*)

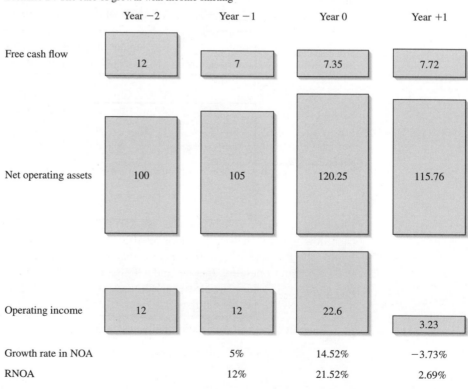

Scenario C: The case of growth with no income shifting

	Year −2	Year −1	Year 0	Year +1
Free cash flow	12	7	7.35	7.72
Net operating assets	100	105	110.25	115.76
Operating income	12	12	12.6	13.23
Growth rate in NOA		5%	5%	5%
RNOA		12%	12%	12%

Scenario D: The case of growth with income shifting

	Year −2	Year −1	Year 0	Year +1
Free cash flow	12	7	7.35	7.72
Net operating assets	100	105	120.25	115.76
Operating income	12	12	22.6	3.23
Growth rate in NOA		5%	14.52%	−3.73%
RNOA		12%	21.52%	2.69%

an analyst might take as indicative of future RNOA. However, the operating income must fall to 2 in Year 1 and the RNOA to 1.82 percent.

You have just observed income shifting and the reversal it always involves: Booking 10 more in income in Year 0 means 10 less in income in Year 1. Accounting cannot change total income over a number of years for a firm; it just moves it between periods. But you have also seen that the income shifting has left a trail in the form of higher net operating assets in Year 0.

The analyst has a problem, however, for NOA can increase with normal business growth. The growth case in Figure 18.1 without income shifting, Scenario C, shows NOA growing at 5 percent per year, along with free cash flow and operating income. However, RNOA is still 12 percent. Introduce income shifting in Scenario D—with an extra 10 recognized in operating income in Year 0—and the RNOA increases to 21.52 percent. The reversal is still evident, however, with operating income falling to 3.23 and RNOA to 2.69 percent in Year 1. The only difference is that growth has muted the reversal; indeed, income shifting managers often engage in the practice in the hope that subsequent growth will bail them out so that the reversal will not look as damaging.

Figure 18.1 teaches us two things. First, change in net operating assets—the trail left by income shifting—is the focus of quality analysis. Second, normal business growth complicates the analysis, so any diagnostic for abnormal changes in NOA must accommodate normal business growth.

Separating What We Know from Speculation

Beginning in Chapter 1, we have abided by the fundamentalist's maxim to distinguish what we know from speculation. We designated the financial statements as concrete information—what we know—that is relatively free from speculation. Yet financial statements contain estimates and estimates involve some speculation. The reliability principle of accounting says that estimates must be based on firm evidence, but estimates they are. There is a tension in accounting: To remedy the defects of cash accounting, accrual accounting adds estimates, but these estimates inevitably add some speculation. Unbiased management and unbiased auditors constrain the speculation, but unfortunately, these agents are not always to be relied on.

In dealing with the resulting quality problem, we maintain the rule to distinguish what we know from that which is more speculative. As a starting point, what do we know? Well, Figure 18.1 simply demonstrates the effect of an accounting relation with which we have been familiar since Chapter 8:

$$\text{Operating income} = \text{Free cash flow} + \text{Change in net operating assets}$$

$$OI = C - I + \Delta NOA \tag{18.1}$$

Make the calculations and you will see that this relation is honored in Figure 18.1. Free cash flow is hard; that is, it cannot be affected by the accounting, as you also see in the figure. The soft part of operating income that has to be challenged is ΔNOA. A big increase in NOA creates operating income and a higher current $RNOA_0$, but results in a high NOA_0 that becomes the base for next year's RNOA: $RNOA_1 = OI_1/NOA_0$. Accordingly $RNOA_1$ declines if NOA_0 has been inflated.

Yet another accounting relation helps us further:

$$\text{Change in net operating assets} = \text{Cash investment} + \text{Operating accruals}$$

$$\Delta NOA = I + \text{Operating accruals} \tag{18.2}$$

Accordingly, in challenging the ΔNOA, the analyst follows two avenues of investigation:

1. Are investments appropriately booked to the balance sheet? Booking investments to the balance sheet is sometimes referred to as *capitalization*. Appropriate accounting capitalizes costs that are incurred to generate revenue in future periods but expenses costs that pertain to revenue in the current period. In this way revenues and expenses are appropriately matched. GAAP demands some mismatching—by expensing R&D and investments in advertising, for example—as we saw in Chapter 2. However, firms have discretion with other items. Investments in property, plant, and equipment are put on the balance sheet (appropriately), but if a firm capitalizes periodic repairs and maintenance in PPE, it increases current earnings and reduces future earnings through higher depreciation charges. This same result occurs by recognizing too much prepaid expense, allocating too much cost to inventories, capitalizing promotion costs, and capitalizing the costs of acquiring customers.

2. Are the accruals appropriate? The list of accruals is long: allowances for bad debts, allowances for sales returns, deferred revenues, warranty accruals, accrued expenses, and pensions liabilities, to name a few (which we will come back to). The accruals are particularly soft numbers; they embed the estimates that are necessary to apply accrual accounting, but estimates can be biased.

With a focus on ΔNOA, Table 18.1 lists typical balance sheet items that lend themselves to manipulation. It also gives the income statement effect of the manipulation. The table is, of course, a road map for the manager who wants to engage in earnings management (reluctantly offered). However, it is also a road map for the analyst who wishes to investigate earnings management. The last column points the analyst to situations where earnings management is more likely to occur. The earnings management in the table is in the direction of increasing earnings; earnings management to decrease earnings is applied in the other direction. So, for example, lower cost of goods sold is reported if a firm fails to write down obsolete inventory, but higher cost of goods sold results from excessive inventory write-downs (leading to lower future cost of goods sold).

Prelude to a Quality Analysis

Before beginning a quality investigation, the analyst should understand four things well:

1. The business.
2. The accounting policy.
3. The business areas where accounting quality is most doubtful.
4. Situations in which management is particularly tempted to manipulate.

On the first point, knowing the business is necessary to get a feel for what the appropriate accounting is for the type of business. What are normal bad debt rates for the business and does the firm's allowance for bad debts seem out of line? What is the standard useful life of depreciable assets in this line of business?

On the second point, the accounting policy for the firm establishes a benchmark for detecting deviations from the policy. A firm's accounting policy is determined from its accounting footnote (usually the first footnote). The policy may be conservative, liberal, or neutral. It determines the level of current and future RNOA. This permanent effect does not frustrate the valuation, as we saw in the last chapter. But deviations from the policy may be manipulations. Beware of firms whose accounting policy is different from the standard for the industry. Watch for firms whose accounting estimates have been incorrect in the past. If a firm regularly recognizes large gains from asset sales, its depreciation charges might be

TABLE 18.1 How Specific Balance Sheet Items Are Managed to Increase Income

Balance Sheet Item	Earnings Management	Effect on Income	Flash Points
Assets			
Gross receivables	Book revenue in advance of its being earned	Higher revenues	Contracts with multiple deliverables; long-term contracting; sales with related parties
Net receivables	Decrease allowances for bad debts and sales returns	Higher revenues or lower selling expenses	Receivables with low credit quality; banks' loan loss reserves
Lease receivables	Increase estimated residual values on lease termination	Higher lease revenues	Aircraft leases; computer leases; equipment leases
Inventories	Book noninventory costs to inventory; fail to write down obsolete inventories	Lower cost of goods sold or SG&A expense	Technological change causing inventory obsolescence; falling inventory prices
Prepaid expenses	Overestimate amount of expenses prepaid	Lower SG&A expense	Considerable expenses paid in advance
Property, plant, and equipment	Book repairs and maintenance to PPE; increase estimated lives or estimated salvage values; excessive impairment charges	Lower depreciation charges that appear all through the income statement, from cost of goods sold down	Capital-intensive manufacturing
Intangible assets	Charge inappropriate expenses to intangible assets; lower amortization rates	Lower amortization expense in SG&A	Knowledge-based companies; capitalized software costs
Deferred charges	Classify too much current expense as deferred expense	Lower SG&A expense	Valuation allowances on deferred tax assets; capitalized costs of acquiring customers
Liabilities			
Deferred revenue	Reduce deferred revenues	Higher revenues	Firms that defer revenues with multiple deliverables
Warranty liabilities	Reduce warranty reserve	Lower selling expenses	Firms with guaranties and warranties on their products
Accrued expenses	Reduce amount of expenses accrued	Lower expenses—applying to all expense lines	All firms
Pension liabilities	Reduce pension liabilities by changing actual assumptions and discount rate	Lower pension expense	Defined benefit pension plans
Unpaid claim reserves	Reduce the reserve	Lower claims expense	Insurance companies

Note: To decrease income, change the direction of the manipulation.

Industry	Flash Point
Banking	Credit losses: Quality of loan loss provisions
Computer hardware	Revenue recognition: Quality of deferred revenue and warranty liabilities
Computer software	Marketability of products: Quality of capitalized research and development
	Revenue recognition of servicing contracts: Quality of receivables and deferred revenue
Retailing	Credit losses: Quality of net accounts receivable
	Rebate programs: Quantity of supplier rebates recognized
Manufacturing	Warranties: Quality of warranty liabilities
	Product liability: Quality of estimated liabilities
Automobiles	Overcapacity: Quality of depreciation allowances
Telecommunications	Technological change: Quality of depreciation allowances and carrying value for inventories
Equipment leasing	Lease values: Quality of carrying values for leases, particularly estimated residual values
Tobacco	Liabilities for health effects of smoking: Quality of estimated liabilities
Pharmaceuticals	R&D: Quality of R&D expenditures
	Product liability: Quality of estimated liabilities
Real estate	Property values: Quality of carrying values for real property
Aircraft and ship manufacturing	Revenue recognition: Quality of estimates under percentage of completion method and "program accounting"
Subscriber services	Development of customer base: Quality of capitalized promotion costs
	Subscriptions paid in advance: Quality of deferred revenue

too high. If it regularly reports losses from asset sales, or restructuring charges, its depreciation might be too low.

On the third point, some businesses have particular flash points where manipulation is more likely. In equipment leasing, it is the estimate of leases' residual values and allowances for defaults. For computer manufacturers, it is sales returns. They could book sales on shipment to retailers but allow returns. They could guarantee distributors' inventories off balance sheet. Product obsolescence is a factor in this industry, so the quality of sales is also in doubt. Box 18.1 gives the typical flash points for a number of industries.

On the fourth point, a number of conditions coincide to make manipulation more attractive to managers. Box 18.2 lists them. The quality analyst needs to be aware of these flash points in order to direct her efforts to cases where manipulation is more likely.

Quality Diagnostics

Following the trail to changes in net operating assets is not as straightforward as one would like. With adequate disclosure and diligence on the part of the analyst, the trail can be uncovered. Unfortunately, disclosures are often inadequate. In response, the analyst develops **quality diagnostics** to help with the detection.

Quality diagnostics are only red flags; they raise questions about accounting quality but do not resolve the question. Each diagnostic can arise for legitimate reasons, and it is up to the quality analyst to dig further to discover whether real operations or the application of accounting methods is the cause. It is at this point that disclosure quality is important, particularly disclosures about the accounting. If disclosures are inadequate, the quality analyst can only flag the possible problem but cannot sort it out. As it happens, red flags are explained by legitimate operational factors in many cases.

Figure 18.2 summarizes a quality analysis that employs these diagnostics. Many of the diagnostics are accounting ratios. Like all financial statement ratios, they should be evaluated relative to the past (in time series) and relative to those for comparison firms (in cross

Institutional conditions:

- The firm is in the process of raising capital or renegotiating borrowing. Watch public offerings.
- Debt covenants are likely to be violated.
- Management changes.
- Auditor changes.
- Management rewards (like bonuses) are tied to earnings.
- Inside trading is strongly in one direction.
- Management is repricing executive stock options.
- Governance structure is weak: Inside management dominates the board; there is a weak audit committee or none at all.
- Regulatory requirements (like capital ratios for banks and insurance companies) are likely to be violated.
- Transactions are conducted with related parties rather than at arm's length.
- Special events such as union negotiations and proxy fights.
- The firm is "in play" as a takeover target.
- Earnings meet analysts' expectations, but just barely.
- The firm engages in exotic arrangements like off-balance-sheet special-purpose entities and stylized derivative contracts.

Accounting and financial statement conditions:

- A change in accounting principles or estimates.
- An earnings surprise.
- A drop in profitability after a period of good profitability.
- Constant sales or falling sales.
- Earnings growing faster than sales.
- Very low positive earnings (that might be a loss without manipulation).
- Small or zero increases in profit margins (that might be a decrease without manipulation).
- Differences in expenses for tax reporting and financial reporting.

- Financial reports are used for other purposes, like tax reporting and union negotiations.
- Accounting adjustments in the last quarter of the year.

CAVEAT EMPTOR: BEWARE WHEN BUYING SHARES FROM THE FIRM

Beware when buying shares, but be particularly careful when buying shares from the firm itself. It is well known that returns to buying stock in an initial public offering (IPO) are not particularly good; indeed, after an initial period when an IPO might be "hot," risk-adjusted stock returns subsequent to an IPO are negative on average. Look at the diagnostics in the table below. They are medians from 1,682 IPOs between 1980 and 1990. The net income-to-sales ratio was high for these firms in the year they went public but declined thereafter. Was management manipulating the accounting to give a better profitability picture for the IPO? Well, look at the abnormal accounting accruals in the table. These are accruals in excess of those you would expect from the increase in sales and capital investments for the year (expressed relative to book value in the table). They were high in the IPO year, increasing income, but considerably lower later. Indeed they were negative later; they reversed. And allowances for bad debts were low in the IPO year, increasing later. As always, the analyst asks whether these patterns are due to legitimate business or to manipulation.

Does the apparent manipulation explain the poor returns from buying IPOs? The market might indeed have been deceived by the good earnings reported with the IPO, thus valuing the firms too high. And then, when prices dropped as lower earnings were reported, the market realized that the earlier earnings were "low quality." Indeed, there is evidence that the amount of implied manipulation predicts post-IPO returns.[*] If so, a quality analyst who diagnosed the accounting would have been able to earn superior returns.

[*]See S. Teoh, I. Welch, and T. Wong, "Earnings Management and the Long-Run Market Performance of Initial Public Offerings," *Journal of Finance*, December 1998, pp. 1935–1974.

Accounting Numbers Around Initial Public Offerings

Diagnostic, %	Year of IPO	Year after IPO					
		1	2	3	4	5	6
Net income/sales	4.6	2.8	2.1	1.6	1.3	1.3	1.8
Abnormal accruals/book value	5.5	1.6	−0.4	−0.8	−2.0	−1.4	−2.7
Allowance for uncollectibles/gross accounts receivable	2.91	3.32	3.46	3.62	3.81	3.77	3.85

Source: S. Teoh, T. Wong, and G. Rao, "Are Accruals During Initial Public Offerings Opportunistic?" *Review of Accounting Studies,* 1998, pp. 175–208.

FIGURE 18.2
**Diagnostics to Detect
Manipulation in
Operating Income**
First investigate the
quality of sales
revenues. Then
investigate the quality
of core expenses.
Finally investigate
unusual items.

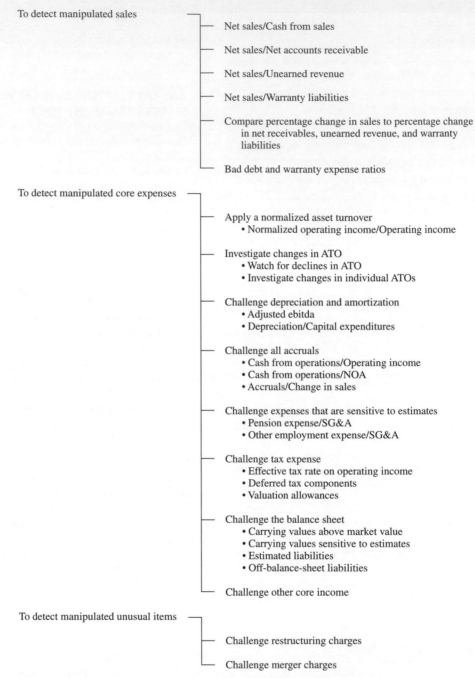

To detect manipulated sales

Net sales/Cash from sales

Net sales/Net accounts receivable

Net sales/Unearned revenue

Net sales/Warranty liabilities

Compare percentage change in sales to percentage change
    in net receivables, unearned revenue, and warranty
    liabilities

Bad debt and warranty expense ratios

To detect manipulated core expenses

Apply a normalized asset turnover
    • Normalized operating income/Operating income

Investigate changes in ATO
    • Watch for declines in ATO
    • Investigate changes in individual ATOs

Challenge depreciation and amortization
    • Adjusted ebitda
    • Depreciation/Capital expenditures

Challenge all accruals
    • Cash from operations/Operating income
    • Cash from operations/NOA
    • Accruals/Change in sales

Challenge expenses that are sensitive to estimates
    • Pension expense/SG&A
    • Other employment expense/SG&A

Challenge tax expense
    • Effective tax rate on operating income
    • Deferred tax components
    • Valuation allowances

Challenge the balance sheet
    • Carrying values above market value
    • Carrying values sensitive to estimates
    • Estimated liabilities
    • Off-balance-sheet liabilities

Challenge other core income

To detect manipulated unusual items

Challenge restructuring charges

Challenge merger charges

section). Look for differences from the past and differences from other firms, and compare
changes from the past with changes from the past for comparison firms.

Equation 18.2 instructs that examining ΔNOA involves examining cash investments and
examining the accruals. So, before beginning, spread the cash flow statement before you.
Cash investments are reported in the investment section and the accruals are reported as the
difference between net income and cash from operations in the cash flow from operations
section. See Box 18.3.

The focus in an accounting quality analysis is on distinguishing "hard" numbers, which result from cash flows, and "soft" numbers in the accruals, which are subject to estimates. The cash flow statement separates "hard" cash flows (from operations and investment) from the accruals.

Accruals are reported between net income and cash from operations in an indirect-method statement of cash flows. These accruals are used in quality diagnostics as follows:

- Compare changes in net accounts receivable with changes in sales for sales quality diagnostics.

- Compare changes in unearned revenue and warranty liabilities with changes in sales for sales quality diagnostics.
- Use the depreciation and amortization number for the adjusted ebitda and depreciation diagnostics.
- Compare changes in prepaid expenses with changes in sales.
- Compare changes in accrued expenses with changes in sales.
- Use the deferred tax number for deferred tax diagnostics.
- Track restructuring charges and their reversals.

Diagnostics to Detect Manipulated Sales

Sales are of good quality if they are unbiased estimates of the cash that the sales will generate. A sale might be booked but there is a chance that goods may be returned or a receivable may not be paid. It might also be that too many or too few sales are booked currently rather than in the future (as unearned revenue). Focus, then, is on net sales after allowances for sales returns, credit losses, and unearned revenue:

$$\text{Net sales} = \text{Cash from sales} + \Delta\text{Net accounts receivable} - \Delta\text{Allowance for sales returns and discounts} - \Delta\text{Unearned revenue}$$

Cash from sales cannot be manipulated by the accounting, so any quality question arises from accruals that affect changes in net receivables (that are net of estimated bad debts), allowances for sales returns and discounts, and unearned revenue. Manipulation diagnostics look for changes in sales relative to cash generated by sales and changes in sales relative to changes in the net operating assets that relate to sales:

Diagnostic: Net sales/Cash from sales

Diagnostic: Net sales/Net accounts receivable

Diagnostic: Net sales/Allowance for sales returns and discounts

Diagnostic: Net sales/Unearned revenue

Schedule II in the 10-K reports allowances for sales returns, discounts, and bad debts. The deferred tax footnote also gives details of allowances not permitted for tax purposes. But lack of disclosure may frustrate some of these calculations. If net sales cannot be calculated as above, use net sales as reported under GAAP, that is, sales less estimated sales returns and discounts.

If firms are aggressively recognizing revenue or underestimating returns and credit losses (and thus do not have legitimate receivables that are being paid off in cash), the first ratio will increase and the second will decrease. If net sales are increasing because of reduced estimates of unearned (deferred) revenue, the last ratio will increase. Changes in these ratios should be investigated over time. Comparisons of percentage changes in net sales to percentage changes in net receivables and unearned revenue are also revealing. Watch increases in sales that are accompanied by decreases in unearned revenue.

Of course these ratios can change for legitimate reasons, like unusual credit sales growth and customers taking longer to pay receivables. Receivables will decline if they are securitized or sold. The ratios can also be red flags about the business, to signal lower customer interest in products or price discounting to attract customers. These are issues pertaining to the overall quality of earnings but not accounting quality.

Challenge bad debt expense with three diagnostics:

Diagnostic: Bad debt expense/Actual credit losses
Diagnostic: Bad debt reserves/Accounts receivable (gross)
Diagnostic: Bad debt expense/Sales

Red *Flag*

In 2000, Gateway, the personal computer manufacturer decided to finance computer sales to high-risk customers that outside financing companies were shunning. Its consumer finance receivables, net of allowances for bad debts, increased from 3.3 percent of sales to 7.3 percent of sales over the year. In the first quarter of 2001, the firm wrote off $100 million of these receivables.

Red *Flag*

At the end of 1999, Bank of America's allowance for credit losses on its bank loans stood at 1.84 percent of outstanding loans of $370.7 billion, and in the prior three years this ratio had not fallen below 1.98 percent. However, at the end of 2000, the ratio was down to 1.75 percent, even though actual charge-offs for bad loans increased to 0.61 percent of loans from 0.55 percent.

Red *Flag*

Xerox Corporation sells copiers to customers under sales-type leases. It books the present value of lease payments plus an estimated residual value of the equipment at the end of the lease. This present value is recognized as revenue and as a lease receivable. In 1999, gross receivables declined from $16,139 million to $14,666 million as customers moved away to digital technology that Xerox was slow to embrace. However, estimated residual values on the leases increased from 4.33 percent of gross lease value to 5.13 percent (even though the equipment was more likely to become obsolete). The stock price subsequently declined dramatically and the firm came under SEC investigation.

Torpedo

In March 2000, the shares of MicroStrategy, a software firm, fell from $227 to $87 (a loss of market value of $6 billion) on revelations that it had practiced aggressive revenue recognition on its software contracts. The firm had booked revenue from multiyear contracts in the first year of the contract rather than as unearned (deferred) revenue.

Diagnostics to Detect Manipulation of Core Expenses

Manipulations are also perpetrated through the recording of expenses. Here is a way to investigate.

1. Investigate Changes in Net Operating Assets with Normalized Asset Turnover

As we have shown, manipulation of operating income leaves a trail: Net operating assets must also change as operating income changes. We have also seen, however, that one expects changes in NOA because of normal business growth. The first metric controls for that growth.

We saw in Chapter 13 that net operating assets are driven by sales and the asset turnover: NOA = Sales/ATO. The amount of NOA that is required for a given level of sales is determined by the normal or usual ATO, and the ΔNOA that should be recorded for the current change in sales is determined by the normal or usual ATO. If the ΔNOA is higher than that expected from the change in sales, suspect manipulation of the expenses.

If you are satisfied with the integrity of sales (from the diagnostics above), calculate

$$\text{Normalized OI} = \text{Free cash flow} + \Delta\text{Normalized NOA}$$
$$= \text{Free cash flow} + \Delta\text{Sales/Normal ATO}$$

This, obviously, is a normalized version of equation 18.1. The normalized ATO is calculated from average asset turnovers over past years or from comparison firms with similar operations and accounting policies. The following diagnostic flags the possible manipulation:

Diagnostic: (Normalized OI)/OI

If this ratio differs from 1.0, a flag is hoisted.

Red *Flag*

Gateway, the computer manufacturer, had always operated on a high asset turnover. In 1999, its ATO was 13.2 on sales of $8,965 million, and even higher in earlier years. In 2000, sales increased by $636 million to $9,601 million, resulting in operating income, after tax, of $231 million. Net operating assets, however, grew by $1,086, more than sales, resulting in a negative free cash flow of $855 million. The firm was investing rapidly in new stores and inventory, providing consumer credit, and increasing accruals, yet sales growth was modest. Normalized operating income was −$855 + (636/13.2) = −$807 million, considerably less than reported operating income. In 2001, Gateway wrote off $876 million of net operating assets and reported an after-tax operating loss of $983 million.

2. Investigate Changes in Asset Turnover

Manipulation of operating expenses always changes both profit margin (PM) and ATO, but in opposite directions: Lower expenses mean higher income to sales but, as net operating assets increase, lower expenses also mean lower sales to net operating assets. So a change in ATO may indicate manipulation. And if firms are using manipulation to increase or maintain profit margins, the corresponding decrease in ATO will signal a subsequent decrease in future profit margins as the accounting reverses.

Table 18.2 pertains to firms grouped on their core RNOA before taxes (Year 0) for the years 1978 to 1996. Group 1 has the highest RNOA, group 10 the lowest. The average core RNOA for each group is given under the group number in the column headings. The table then gives median changes in RNOA and profit margins for each group in the next year (Year 1). These are given for firms with the top third of changes in asset turnover in Year 0 in each group (high-ΔATO firms) and for firms with the lowest third of ΔATO (low-ΔATO firms). For all groups, next year's change in RNOA is lower if the current change in ATO is low, and for all except one group, next year's change in profit margin is lower if the current change in ATO is low. And the differences are higher for firms that have high current RNOA: A high current RNOA is likely to be followed by a decrease in RNOA, but the decrease is likely to be greater if the firm has a small change in ATO.

These relationships may not arise from accounting quality but certainly bear on the overall question of earnings quality. So analyze changes in ATO. Compare changes in sales

TABLE 18.2 **Changes in Return on Net Operating Assets (RNOA) and Profit Margins (PM) for Different Changes in Asset Turnover (ATO)**

Group, Year 0:	1 (High)	2	3	4	5	6	7	8	9	10 (Low)
Core RNOA (%)	57.4	35.5	28.3	23.8	20.2	17.3	14.2	11.3	8.2	3.9
Change in RNOA Next Year, Year 1 (%)										
High ΔATO	−6.72	−0.77	−0.18	−0.61	0.12	0.35	0.74	0.69	0.97	1.49
Low ΔATO	−12.57	−4.90	−2.92	−2.54	−1.41	−0.13	−0.63	−0.45	0.12	0.59
Change in PM Next Year, Year 1 (%)										
High ΔATO	−1.14	−0.32	−0.04	−0.13	−0.15	−0.08	−0.31	0.06	0.32	0.88
Low ΔATO	−2.74	−1.68	−0.94	−1.07	−0.54	−0.51	−0.32	−0.14	0.04	0.29

Source: P. Fairfield and T. Yohn, "Using Asset Turnover and Profit Margin to Forecast Changes in Profitability," unpublished paper, School of Business Administration, Georgetown University, 1999. A published version of this paper (but without this table) is in *Review of Accounting Studies,* 2001, pp. 371–385.

to changes in ATO. Be sensitive to cases where profit margins increase or are constant but the asset turnover declines. This may be the case of a firm that is otherwise experiencing falling margins but wants to maintain profit margins and RNOA at previous levels. And watch for cases where there has been a large increase in NOA but a small or negative change in ATO.

Changes in individual turnovers should be investigated to isolate the possible manipulation. Pay attention to turnovers involving estimates: accounts receivable turnover, PPE turnover, deferred asset turnover, pension liability turnover, and other estimated liability turnovers. Watch for declines in turnovers (or changes in individual items relative to sales). Is there an explanation?

Red *Flag*

Cisco Systems supplies the infrastructure for the Internet economy. Up to 2001, it saw rapid revenue growth on low inventories. For the four quarters of its 2000 fiscal year, the ratios of inventory-to-sales, in percent, were 16.9, 16.0, 17.8, and 21.3, respectively. By the second quarter of 2001, the ratio had increased to 37.5 percent. In the third quarter of 2001, the firm took a charge for an inventory write-down of over $2.2 billion dollars and sales and earnings subsequently slowed dramatically. The inventory buildup represented inventory whose sale prices had declined as the Internet bubble burst.

Torpedo

Sunbeam Corporation, the household appliance manufacturer, hired new management in 1996 to turn its ailing business around. After a major restructuring, its stock rose 50 percent during 1997 with earnings improving to $109 million from a loss of $228 million in 1996. Sales increased by 18.7 percent. However, accounts receivable grew 38.5 percent, from 21.7 percent of sales to 25.3 percent, and inventory grew 57.9 percent, from 16.5 percent of sales to 21.9 percent. The SEC subsequently investigated Sunbeam, leading to a restatement and, ultimately, the bankruptcy of the firm.

3. Investigate Line Items Directly

a. Challenge Depreciation and Amortization Expense. Low depreciation or amortization usually means there will be future write-downs of assets, usually through restructuring charges or losses on disposals of assets. Too high depreciation or amortization results in later gains from asset disposals.

In 1988, General Motors reported $4.9 billion in profits. Analysts claimed that $790 million of this came from extending the useful lives of assets from 35 to 45 years, thereby reducing depreciation, and $270 million came from changing assumptions for estimated residual values on car leases. This accounting continued for a few years, but then came the large restructuring charges of the early 1990s. These charges, it was claimed, were partly corrections for underdepreciation in the past. Indeed, GM had so many restructurings in the 1990s that analysts claimed they could not at any time work out what profits GM was really making.

To investigate, adjust operating income before depreciation and amortization (ebitda) with a normal capital charge:

$$\text{Adjusted ebitda} = \text{OI (before tax)} + \text{Depreciation and amortization} - \text{Normal capital expense}$$

The diagnostic compares this adjusted ebitda to operating income before tax (ebit), which is based on the reported depreciation and amortization:

Diagnostic: (Adjusted ebitda)/ebit

Normal capital expense is approximated by the average capital expenditure over past years or, to accommodate growth, normal depreciation and amortization for the level of sales, calculated from past (Depreciation + Amortization)-to-sales ratios. Also calculate, for the past few years,

Diagnostic: Depreciation/Capital expenditures

If this ratio is less than 1.0, future depreciation is likely to increase.

Electronic Data Systems (EDS) has had many restructurings over the years. Restructurings are a response, in part, to depreciation charges being too low. In the third quarter of 2001, the firm reported (in the cash flow statement) depreciation and amortization expense that was 6.6 percent of revenues, down from 7.2 percent of sales a year earlier, accounting for nearly half of the growth in operating income. Analysts asked: Was the lower charge due to better asset utilization or did it forecast further restructuring charges?

AMR, the parent of American Airlines, reported that operating income, before tax, increased in 2000 to $1,381 million from the $1,156 million in 1999. Notes to the financial statements reveal that the firm increased estimated lives on some of its aircraft from 20 to 25 years and also increased estimated salvage values from 5 percent to 10 percent of cost. The effect was to reduce depreciation for the year by $158 million, with an after-tax effect on income of $99 million, accounting for 80 percent of the increase in income before discontinued operations. Was management correct to claim that the change "more accurately reflects the expected life of its aircraft"?

Some analysts employ models of required depreciation that are more forward looking. These models identify under- or overdepreciation by forecasting write-downs and disposal gains and losses, and they set the appropriate depreciation charge as that which will produce no write-downs, gains, or losses. For example, if there is overcapacity in an industry—as with automobile manufacturing and telecoms in the 1990s—these models forecast that firms will have to write off the excess plant unless current depreciation is adjusted to reflect the cost of the investment in overcapacity. Or if technological change

In June 1998 AT&T, the largest U.S. telecommunications group, made a bid of $45.5 billion to acquire Telecommunications Inc. (TCI), the country's biggest cable television company. AT&T's strategy was to build systems for delivery of voice, television, and Internet service to homes, circumventing the Baby Bells (the local telephone companies).

The press at the time claimed that the purchase price of 14 times 1997 earnings before interest, tax, depreciation, and amortization (ebitda) was "a bit stiff," and indeed AT&T's shares dropped 15 percent in the two weeks after the bid. High or not, quoting prices as multiples of ebitda is appropriate if,

with rapid technological change, there is a question of whether reported depreciation is too low. Indeed the many restructuring charges in the industry at the time were in part adjustments for low depreciation charged in the past. It was also recognized that AT&T would have to spend heavily to upgrade TCI's network to maintain the business under competition.

Quoting a bid price as a multiple of earnings before depreciation and amortization allows the analyst to plug in a normalized depreciation calculated to accommodate technological change and to anticipate expenditures necessary to sustain the business.

will render the current plant obsolete, depreciation is adjusted. These models may also attempt to calculate the depreciation that is necessary to sustain sales, usually approximated by annualizing capital expenditures necessary to replace facilities. This is desirable when there are anticipated increases in the cost of new plants that will replace current plants but will generate the same sales, or where technological change will require the updating of the production facilities to deliver sales. Current depreciation, so adjusted, becomes a better predictor of future depreciation, a higher quality number. Technological change has been rapid in telecommunications and so these methods are desirable there. See Box 18.4.

Other analysts, wary of depreciation and amortization charges, add back depreciation to operating income and work with ebitda as a measure of income from operations for profitability analysis. This is bad analysis. Depreciation is a cost of generating sales, just like wages. Plants rust, wear out, and become obsolete, so value is lost. Depreciation captures value loss; ebitda is a low-quality measure of value added. If the analyst has questions about the quality of depreciation and amortization, she can work with adjusted ebitda, which uses a normal capital charge.

b. Challenge Total Accruals. We have seen that cash flow from operations = OI − New operating accruals. Thus calculate

Diagnostic: CFO/OI

As the accounting does not affect cash flow from operations (CFO), manipulation of operating income (OI) with unjustified accruals will affect this ratio. Also calculate

Diagnostic: CFO/NOA

Any increase in NOA due to manipulation will affect the average NOA in the denominator. Be careful of cash flow metrics, however. Cash flow from operations can itself be manipulated. See Box 11.4 in Chapter 11. Nevertheless, the CFO for firms like Enron and World Com fell dramatically, relative to operating income, prior to their demise.

Torpedo

With new management on board, Sunbeam Corporation reported earnings of $109 million in 1997, up from a loss of $228 million. However, cash flow from operations for 1997 was (a negative) –$8.2 million compared with $14.2 million in 1998. The earlier torpedo box gives some reasons. See also Exhibit 18.2 in Exercise 18.14. Sunbeam was manufacturing sales with a "bill and hold" scheme whereby the firm billed customers who did not need products immediately, with deep discounts and easy credit terms, and storing the merchandise in its own warehouse. The SEC subsequently made the firm reduce 1997 earnings by $71 million.

c. Challenge Individual Accruals   Inspect each accrual listed in the reconciliation of net income to CFO in the cash flow statement, such as changes in prepaid expenses, deferred revenues, and accrued expenses. For each accrual other than depreciation and amortization, look at

Diagnostic: Accrual/ΔSales

For example, a drop in the change in accrued expenses (an accrual in the cash flow statement) may indicate that too few expenses have been recognized. Be particularly aware of accruals that increase income, especially when the change in sales is close to zero, lower than in the past, or negative. (If the change in sales is zero or negative, the ratio form of the diagnostic will not work but accruals and change in sales can still be compared.)

Red *Flag*

Shared Medical Systems, a supplier of information systems to hospitals and physicians, reported earnings of $18.3 million in its first quarter of 1999, almost unchanged from the previous quarter. However, revenues declined from $339.3 million to $287.1 million. Level or increasing earnings on declining sales always waves a red flag. The cash flow statement revealed further ones: Accrued expenses declined from $86.5 million to $61.5 million and the amount of computer software capitalized in the balance sheet increased from $75.7 million to 81.1 million. Manipulation or legitimate business? Well, earnings significantly increased throughout the next year, on rising revenues, so a reversal was not apparent.

Green *Flag*

Microsoft Corporation writes software contracts with multiple deliverables and defers a significant portion of the revenue on these contracts. At the end of its 2005 fiscal year, deferred revenues stood at $9.17 billion or 23.0 percent of sales. The prospect of the firm bleeding this deferred revenue back into income is real, so the analyst has Microsoft on a watch. In 2005, the cash flow statement reveals that Microsoft added $12.5 billion to deferred revenue and transferred $11.3 of deferred revenue to revenue to the income statement. There is no sign of an excessive bleed back.

Red *Flag*

As it promises upgrades and add-ons, Microsoft historically followed the practice of recognizing up to 25 percent of revenue from its Windows software over three or four years. With the launch of Vista in 2008, it changed the policy to record most of the revenue in the period in which the software was sold. In the third quarter for fiscal year 2008, Microsoft reported an increase in earnings of 65 percent. The increase came from sales of the new Vista program and also from the acceleration in revenue recognition.

Red *Flag*

Cisco Systems reported revenue of $4,816 million for its second quarter of 2002 up from the $4,448 million in the preceding quarter and exceeding projections. It looked like the revenue decline, from the $6,000 million per quarter in 2001, was over. However, the firm pointed out that, for the first time, deferred revenue had reversed: The firm had recognized an unusually large amount of revenue on conditional shipments from prior periods.

d. Challenge Other Expense Components that Depend on Estimates.

Diagnostic: Pension expense/Total operating expense

Diagnostic: Other postemployment expenses/Total operating expense

Pensions and other employment expenses can be manipulated by changing actuarial estimates of projected payouts and discount rates for the liabilities, and by changing the expected return on plan assets. Go to the pension footnote and investigate the components of pension expense (as in Chapter 13). To the extent disclosure allows, investigate other components of SG&A expenses; this item tends to be a large one on the income statement.

e. Challenge Tax Expense.   Effective tax rates usually converge to the statutory rate over time. So investigate

Diagnostic: Operating tax expense/OI before taxes

If this rate is below the statutory rate, find out when tax credits are likely to expire. But also investigate the portion of the tax expense that is subject to estimates: deferred taxes. Go to the tax footnote and investigate reasons for changes in deferred tax assets and liabilities. If these are changing at a rate different from sales, a flag is raised.

Deferred taxes are taxes on the difference between income reported in the financial statements (using GAAP) and income reported on the tax return (using tax rules for measuring income). If the firm is using estimates to generate higher GAAP income, it must recognize more deferred taxes. So investigate the extent to which tax expense is composed of deferred taxes. Investigate the components of deferred taxes (in the tax footnote). Watch, particularly, deferred taxes arising from depreciation: If the deferred tax from depreciation relative to depreciation expense is high (compared to similar firms) or increasing relative to investment growth, the firm may be reporting low GAAP depreciation expense by estimating long useful lives for assets. Investigate deferred taxes arising from bad debt estimates, unearned revenue, and warranty expenses. If a firm increases GAAP income by lowering its bad debt estimate, for example, it will also recognize more deferred taxes because bad debts are accounted for on a cash basis on tax returns. Watch deferred taxes arising from sales-type leases that require estimates of residual values for GAAP income measurement.

If a firm has deferred tax assets, one feature requires particular monitoring: the valuation allowance. Deferred tax assets arise from features that yield lower GAAP income to taxable income. If the income tax benefits in these assets are deemed "more likely than not" *not* to be realized in the future, deferred tax assets are reduced by the allowance. But, to say the least, the allowance is a subjective number.

4. Investigate Balance Sheet Line Items Directly

If carrying values of operating assets are too high in the balance sheet, they will have to be written off in the future, reducing RNOA. Particular suspects are:

- Assets whose carrying values are above their market values: These are likely impairment candidates. (Market values may be difficult to ascertain, however.)
- Assets susceptible to nontypical capitalization of expenses, such as start-up costs, advertising and promotion, customer acquisition and product development costs, and software development costs. Look at trends in these assets relative to total operating assets. See Box 18.5.
- Intangible assets whose carrying values and amortization rates are subject to estimate, like software costs and intangible assets acquired in acquisitions.
- Assets recorded at fair value. "Fair values" are often estimates, uncertain at least and biased in the worst case. If fair values are from marking-to-market, they can bring bubble

Prior to 1996, America Online (AOL) capitalized marketing costs in developing a subscriber base on its balance sheet and amortized them over a two-year period. It had been a "hot stock," increasing its share price from $10 in early 1995 to over $35 in April 1996. But concerns about the quality of its capitalized marketing costs set in during 1996 and its price dropped back almost to $10 by September 1996. Analysts queried whether subscribers would renew. To meet the concerns, AOL wrote off the $385 million capitalization in its first fiscal 1997 quarter ending September 1996, producing a loss of $3.80 per share for the quarter. Earnings per share for 1997 were −$2.61 compared to 14 cents in 1996. One might say that 1996 earnings were low quality (they did not reflect appropriate marketing expenses) and that the low quality resulted in lower future earnings. In evaluating the quality of the asset, one would have to consider the retention rate in holding on to new subscribers, and that was the point on which quality analysts were focusing.

prices into the financial statements, as with the marking-to-market of available-for-sale mortgages in the balance sheets of banks during the real estate and financing bubble of 2005 to 2007. See Box 18.6. Read the fair value footnote to the financial statements. Watch firms exercising the "fair value option" under which firms elect to fair value certain assets and liabilities. Banks may elect to fair value their debt such that when their credit rating declines, they recognize gains (on the lower value of their debt), as they did during the financial crisis. As conditions improve, they recognize losses:

Red *Flag*

Enron, the energy company whose demise also brought down its Big 5 auditor, Arthur Andersen, employed fair value accounting extensively for its energy contracts and other investments. These energy contracts were traded in very thin markets, some of them organized by Enron, so fair values were very much an estimate. In 2000, prior to the firm's demise, unrealized gains on marking these contracts to fair value accounted for more than half on the firm's pretax income of $1.41 billion and about a third in 1999. The profits subsequently evaporated as the "fair" values proved to be fictitious. Enron was found to have no value.

The carrying value of operating liabilities should be investigated. Focus on:

- Estimated liabilities such as pension liabilities, other employment liabilities, and deferred revenue. Look at trends in these liabilities relative to total operating liabilities. Investigate warranty liability estimates. Firms are required to reconcile warranty liability estimates to their actual experience with warranty claims.

  Diagnostic: Warranty expense/Actual warranty claims

  Diagnostic: Warranty expense/Sales

  Also monitor estimated liabilities for rebate programs such as frequent-flier programs and incentives on retail credit cards.

- Off-balance-sheet liabilities such as loan guarantees, recourse for assigned receivables or debt, purchase commitments, contingent liabilities for lawsuits and regulatory penalties, and contingent obligations from off-balance-sheet special-purpose entities. These liabilities are usually mentioned in footnotes. The footnote should be studied thoroughly to avoid a surprise in the outcome of the contingency. Environmental liabilities (for cleanup of pollution) can be considerable.

  While focusing on the balance sheet, this analysis is a quality-of-earnings analysis also: If distorted carrying values were recorded at an appropriate amount or the contingent

Many financial institutions report assets and liabilities at "fair value." At the time of writing, the FASB was proposing to require all financial instruments to be reported at fair value. But firms also have an option to elect to use fair values for a wider set of assets and liabilities under GAAP and IFRS, including their own debt. Fair value is defined as "exit value," the amount that an asset can be sold for or someone else would pay to relieve the firm of liability. Other than for financial assets and cases where the value of an asset comes from exposure to market prices (like liquid trading securities), fair value accounting does not make much sense to the fundamental investor. The value of an asset is in its employment in the business, not what it can be sold for. Exit value is liquidation value.

FASB Statement 157 sets three levels for determining "fair value":

Level 1: Prices are available in a liquid market.
Level 2: Prices are not available, but some "market inputs" (like the prices of comparables) are available.
Level 3: No market prices are available.

Level 1 fair values bring prices into the financial statements. Putting prices in the financial statements defies a fundamentalist principle: *when calculating value to challenge price, beware of putting price in the calculation.* The practice induces circularity where the accounting that is supposed to challenge prices incorporates the prices to be challenged. The anchor drifts.

Mark-to-market accounting can even promote bubbles: investors infer higher prices from higher reported book value, but the higher book value is due to higher prices. Prices thus feed on themselves, with accounting as the instrument. In the real estate bubble of the mid-2000s, the market value of mortgages and the securities that packaged them increased to speculative levels. Banks applying mark-to-market accounting for their mortgage assets brought these speculative prices into their balance sheet, increasing capital ratios, encouraging more dubious lending to record even more fair value gains. This is not a balance sheet on which to anchor. Such a bubble must burst, with prices now cascading downward, as the sorry aftermath of the financial crisis tells. Rather than providing accounting to cut across bubble prices, fair value accounting becomes an instrument in promoting bubbles and associated momentum investing. The fundamentalist is always wary: *Price is what you pay, value is what you get.*

Level 2 and Level 3 fair value accounting requires estimates. Level 3 is a particular concern. It involves "marking to model," and we have seen in this book how uncertain the numbers from valuation models can be. Management has much freedom in choosing a required return and a growth rate to get the desired valuation. Add the tendency of management to use accounting to paint the picture they want, and the fundamentalist is increasingly nervous. Fundamentalists think that accounting should not only be independent of prices, but also independent of managers.

---

liabilities were recognized on the balance sheet, income would be lower (through a charge). Omission of this charge yields low quality earnings and results in subsequent earnings surprises.

Diagnostics to Detect Manipulation of Unusual Items

Unusual items are isolated to identify core income in order to improve earnings quality. From an earnings quality point of view they are low quality and thus are discarded for forecasting. But the analyst does have to be careful that unusual items identified indeed have no implications for the future.

A quality issue arises if unusual items involve estimates. A notorious example is estimated restructuring charges and impairments. Firms may decide to restructure in the future but will include an estimate of the cost in current income, along with an estimated liability in the balance sheet. And they may overestimate the liability, take a bath, and bleed back income to income statements in the future as actual expenses are less than anticipated.

Box 18.7 is a case in point. The Borden restructuring there raises another point about estimated charges. Borden included (what the SEC concluded was) $145.5 million of 1992 core operating expense in the 1992 restructuring charge, thus inflating core income. Investigate the components of the charge to see whether this is going on.

Borden, Inc.: Reversal and Reclassification of Restructuring Charge 18.7

In 1992 Borden, the food and chemicals company, took a $642 million special restructuring charge against income and reported a loss of $439.6 million. In 1993, under pressure from the SEC, Borden reversed $119.3 million of the charge retrospectively, increasing 1992 income and reducing 1993 income. In addition, Borden was required to reclassify $145.5 million of the charges that were for "packaging modernization" and marketing as ordinary operating expense.

In the fourth quarter of 1993, Borden took another restructuring charge of $637.4 million for estimated losses on disposal of businesses, unrelated to the earlier charge. Its 1994 third quarter results included a $50 million credit from having overestimated these losses in 1993.

Estimated merger costs also warrant investigation. Firms can overestimate these costs and then bleed back the overestimates to increase profits in the future. This makes the merger look more profitable than it is.

Special charges can of course be underestimated as well as overestimated. The analyst watches for charges that should be taken and are not. AT&T took four major charges between 1986 and 1993. The firm reported an average of nearly 10 percent annual profit growth over the period before the charges were subtracted, from $1.21 per share in 1996 to $3.13 per share in 1995. But the total of the restructuring charges of $14.2 billion exceeded the total reported net income of $10.3 billion over the period. AT&T maintained that the write-offs were caused by rapid technological change that hadn't been anticipated. But quality analysts raised a question: Were the profits before restructuring low quality, overstated profits that would have to be written off later? What was AT&T really making in profits during the period? Would an insightful analyst have adjusted the low quality earnings with "normalized depreciation"? Monitor normalized core operating income relative to reported core operating income. Watch particularly for cases where this ratio is low but other costs to sales are high; these conditions may signal a restructuring.

In view of the AT&T case, one must be skeptical about classifying restructuring charges as unusual. They may be repetitive, particularly during times of technological and organizational change. Citicorp took restructuring charges six years in a row, from 1988 to 1993, when changes shook the banking industry. Eastman Kodak did the same for five out of six years from 1989 to 1994. And Cadbury-Schweppes maintained in its 1996 report that "major restructuring costs are now widely recognized as a recurring item in major food manufacturers, estimated by some analysts as 0.5 percent of sales over the long term," and thus felt it no longer appropriate to exclude these costs from underlying (core) earnings.

Red *Flag*

In the second quarter of its 2002 fiscal year, Cisco Systems reported an increase in revenue after a period of decline. Gross margins were also up, to $2,970 million from $2,692 million in the preceding quarter. The gross margin ratio was 62 percent, much the same as the ratio achieved during Cisco's peak revenue period during the telecom bubble. However, Cisco had written down its inventory in the third quarter of 2001 by over $2.2 billion. The analyst would have raised a red flag in 2001 (p. 606) and would have predicted that the lower inventory would reverse into lower future cost of goods sold, leading to maintained or higher gross margins. Move on to 2002 and a red flag continues to wave over the margins: Can Cisco maintain these margins once the impaired inventory has been sold? (Cisco was quite forthcoming in tracking its utilization of the impaired inventory.)

DETECTING TRANSACTION MANIPULATION

The diagnostics to this point raise concerns about a firm using accounting methods and estimates to alter income, and so address the (third) question of GAAP application quality in the five quality questions we began with. The fourth question, concerning transaction quality, deals with firms' timing or structuring transactions to manipulate income. Short of being fraudulent, firms can choose accounting methods and estimates only as GAAP permits. Where GAAP is inflexible, they can sometimes arrange their business to accommodate GAAP to achieve a desired result.

Core Revenue Timing

Recognizing sales by shipping products in one fiscal year rather than another shifts income. Unfortunately this "channel stuffing" is hard to pick up unless one has details of monthly shipments. Watch for unexpected shipments and sales increases or decreases in the final quarter.

Core Revenue Structuring

A variety of techniques have been employed to manufacture revenue. Unfortunately, they too are difficult to uncover; the investor trusts very much in the auditor.

- Related-party and other-than-at-arm's-length transactions; for example, shipping equipment to an affiliate that does not need the equipment and books it as plant, while the shipper books it as revenue; booking revenues for goods shipped "on consignment" or with an implicit right of return. Look for related-party transactions in the 10-K.
- Structuring lease transactions to quality as sales-type leases.
- Grossing up commission revenue to the top line.
- Swapping inventory in barter transactions.

Red *Flag*

Krispy Kreme rose from a regional doughnut maker to a national taste sensation and a "hot stock" IPO in 2000. As sales faltered, however, the firm shipped high-margin doughnut-making equipment to franchisees, long before they needed it. The company booked the revenue while the equipment sat in trailers controlled by Krispy Kreme. The firm also sold equipment to a franchisee and booked it as revenue immediately before it bought the franchisee for a price that was inflated for the equipment. In 2005, the firm was forced to restate results as far back as 2000, reducing pretax income by over $25 million. Once at a high of $49.37, its shares traded at $7.30 in 2005 after a report from the company on its accounting.

Red *Flag*

Global Crossing sold capacity on its extensive telecom network to telecoms under long-term contracts. In a deal known as a *capacity swap*, the firm exchanged capacity with these firms such that Global Crossing booked revenue for the capacity it "sold" but booked the capacity that it received in exchange as an asset. In a 2001 transaction with Qwest Communications, it signed a $100 million contract to supply capacity, only to "round-trip" the cash by purchasing a similar amount of capacity from Qwest, but booking revenue. Both companies ran into regulatory problems and Global Crossing subsequently filed for bankruptcy.

Core Expense Timing

Firms can time expenditures, and these will affect income if they are expensed immediately. So look at R&D and advertising expenses. Investigate

Diagnostic: R&D expense/Sales

Diagnostic: Advertising expense/Sales

If these ratios are low, a firm might be deferring expenditures to the future to increase current income.

Advertising and R&D expenses may have more the quality of an asset because they may produce future profits. Increasing expenditures will reduce current income but may increase future income. Understand the technology and the markets for products to evaluate whether the expenditures will in fact produce future profits. Look at trends in the ratios over time. Look particularly for earnings that are generated by declining R&D or advertising. These may be low quality earnings because future earnings may suffer from the reduced expenditures.

Releasing Hidden Reserves

If a firm uses conservative accounting (as a matter of policy), we saw in the last chapter (in Table 17.7) that hidden reserves are created. If the growth in investment slows, hidden reserves are liquidated and profits increase. So a firm can slow investments temporarily to increase profits temporarily. This practice is sometimes referred to as *cookie-jar accounting*, dipping into the cookie jar (of hidden reserves) to generate profits. You see this in the case of R&D (which is an extreme case of conservative accounting). But it applies also to assets that are put on the balance sheet but are measured conservatively. So watch firms you have identified as having conservative accounting policies and inspect their changes in inventory, plant, and intangibles.

A particular case is a firm using LIFO for inventories. If inventories are reduced, LIFO liquidation profits are realized as hidden reserves are released. We saw in Table 17.8 in Chapter 17 that over 25 percent of NYSE and AMEX firms on LIFO increased earnings with LIFO liquidations from 1982 to 2003. This is referred to as **LIFO dipping.** The footnotes are helpful here because the inventory note must give the amount of the LIFO reserve and the SEC requires that firms report the impact of LIFO dipping on income. Is it temporary? Firms can dip into LIFO inventories to boost profits temporarily, but a LIFO liquidation can also be the precursor to a long-run decline in the demand for the firm's products. And a drop in the LIFO reserve can follow a drop in prices, not inventory liquidation, and this is more likely to be permanent.

FIFO accounting is less open to manipulation. But because cost of goods sold is based on older costs (and inventory on more recent costs), FIFO cost of goods sold and FIFO earnings are sometimes said to be low quality if inventory costs are rising: Cost of goods sold does not indicate what firms are currently paying for inventory or will have to pay in the future. This is not of great concern, however, in the typical situation of rapid inventory turnover.

Red *Flag*

In 2003, General Motors reported an unusually good year with $3.6 billion in pretax income from continuing operations. Footnotes revealed that cost of goods sold was $200 million lower because of liquidation of LIFO inventories. Without the benefit of this LIFO dipping, future cost of goods sold are likely to increase. The increase will be greater if the firm needs also to replace the inventories at higher prices: Under LIFO, last in (at higher prices) is first out to cost of goods sold.

Other Core Income Timing

Look at the results reported by Coca-Cola Co. from 2001 to 2004 (in millions of dollars):

	2004	2003	2002	2001
Operating income	5,698	5,221	5,458	5,352
Equity income in subsidiaries	621	406	384	152
Other income (loss)	(82)	(138)	(353)	39
Gain on issuances of stock by equity investees	24	8	—	91

Coke, as we have seen, has been very profitable. But a significant share of income from subsidiaries has come from gains that are recognized on a parent's equity investment when a subsidiary issues shares. Some issues were of one subsidiary's shares to another. Coke presumably has "significant influence" in issuing these shares and so might be able to arrange share issues to time the recognition of gains in its own accounts. Coke might maintain that this is a device to represent the real profitability of subsidiaries. But it can also be used for manipulation. And since the gains are from share issues, not operations, they are low quality.

Unusual Income Timing

Firms time asset sales to increase or decrease net income by recognizing gains or losses on the sales. Classifying these gains and losses as unusual deals with the quality issue, but beware of sales that are made of good quality business just to affect income. A firm may sell an asset with low book value relative to its market value to record a gain that increases current income, but future income is impaired by the loss of earnings from the asset.

Organizational Manipulation: Off-Balance-Sheet Operations

Firms can sometimes arrange their affairs to get some aspect of operations off the books. These off-balance-sheet operations are called **shells** and setting them up is called the *shell game.*

R&D Partnerships

Expenditures for R&D reduce income. Firms therefore sometimes set up a shell company—perhaps with other partners—to carry out the R&D. The original company may actually do the research but then charge the R&D partnership, creating revenue for itself to offset its R&D expenditure. If the R&D is unsuccessful, the investment in the shell has to be written off, and past revenues from the R&D would be fictitious.

Pension Funds

Pension funds can become overfunded, as happened in the 1990s with the long bull market in stocks (held by pension funds). This overfunding is technically the property of the employees, but firms find ways to use the overfunding to pay for operational expenses. They apply it to early retirement plans, retiree health benefits, and merger financing, the cost of which would otherwise be borne in the income statement.

Special-Purpose Entities

These entities are designed to hold assets that might otherwise be on a firm's balance sheet, like leased assets and assets that have been securitized. Although the firm may not have control of these entities (and thus the entities are not consolidated), it may have some recourse liability for the obligations of the entity.

JUSTIFIABLE MANIPULATION?

It is claimed that Coca-Cola realizes gains from stock issues to report the underlying profitability in subsidiaries that investors might not otherwise see. General Electric is alleged to "smooth" earnings to give a picture of regular, predictable profit growth (which the company denies).

Managements smooth earnings by borrowing income from the future or by shifting income to the future. They borrow earnings in bad years and bank earnings in good years. All's well and good if they can be sure that a bad year will be followed by good years from which they borrow. Indeed, such practices will help with forecasting as the current year's earnings will be a better indicator of future earnings. One might argue the quality of earnings is better (for forecasting) if they are smoothed!

But what if bad years are followed by bad years? Then the quality of current earnings, increased to make them look better, is doubtful. Thus analyzing this practice is a tricky business and the analyst has to be very sure of a firm's long-run earnings prospects before accepting the manipulated earnings as high quality. Accept a high, manipulated RNOA only if the firm has the real profitability to maintain the RNOA in the future. In Coke's case, what if profitability declined but profits could no longer be propped up with the gains from shares in subsidiaries?

DISCLOSURE QUALITY

News Corporation (of which Rupert Murdoch is chairman) is engaged in publishing, entertainment, television, and sports franchises. Prior to 1998 it ran these businesses through hundreds of companies in scores of countries. Its consolidated statements were hard to sort out, to say the least, and analysts often requested greater transparency. They had difficulty discovering where profits were coming from. And, while a large proportion of revenues and profits came from film, television, and sports in the United States, News Corporation was priced more like a publishing concern than an entertainment company: It traded in 1998 at 8.5 times estimated 1998 earnings as compared to 16 and higher for competitors like Disney, Viacom, and Time Warner. In June 1998 Murdoch announced that the U.S. entertainment assets, including 20th Century Fox, the Fox television network, the Los Angeles Dodgers, and part interest in the New York Knicks and Rangers, would be bundled into a separate company—Fox Group—and a public offering made of 20 percent of its stock. News Corporation's stock price rose 12 percent on the news of the spinoff. Was this the reward for disclosure? Other factors may have contributed but analysts hailed the added transparency that would result as a reason for valuing the earnings higher. "Tracking" or "letter" stocks for a division of a company—like the Hughes Electronics unit of General Motors—have the same effect (and also separate out an earnings stream, which some investors might want), but the shareholder usually doesn't have voting rights.

The News Corporation spinoff indicates that poor disclosure leads to lower valuations: Investors discount the price for the risk from not having information. The price effect of poor disclosure is sometimes couched in terms of the cost of capital: Low-quality disclosure raises the required return to compensate for additional risk.

Disclosure issues permeate all aspects of financial analysis and by now you will have accumulated a list of problems you have had with disclosures in getting to this point. The following (and many more!) should be on your list:

- Consolidation accounting often makes the source of profitability hard to discover.
- Line of business and geographical segment reporting is often not detailed enough.

- Earnings in unconsolidated subsidiaries are hard to analyze. (Think of a firm that has all its earnings in subsidiaries in which it has less than 50 percent ownership: Core profit margins are not transparent.)
- Disclosure is insufficient to reconcile free cash flow in the cash flow statement to free cash flow calculated (as $OI - \Delta NOA$) from the income statement and balance sheet. Some of the problems arise from uncertainty about items to be included in operating income and net operating assets.
- Disclosures to calculate stock compensation overhang are thin.
- Details on selling, general, and administrative expenses are often scarce.

QUALITY SCORING

The array of diagnostics is overwhelming. Would it not be nice to have one overall measure of accounting quality? Such a measure is referred to as a *composite quality score*. A composite score weights a number of diagnostics into one metric, as follows:

$$\text{Composite score} = w_1 D_1 + w_2 D_2 + w_3 D_3 + \cdots + w_n D_n$$

where D is a score and w is the weight given to each of the n scores included in the composite.

To build this score we would need to know what aspect of accounting quality we are trying to capture, which diagnostics are to be included, and the weights to be applied to them. For earnings quality, the answer to the first question is clear: We wish to predict earnings reversals, and the set of diagnostics is that which best does this. One might develop ad hoc scoring, developing a score on a scale of 1 to 10, say, based on a set of diagnostics that are judged important for forecasting earnings reversals. Or one might develop expert systems based on the long experience of quality analysts. But typically the diagnostics and weights are chosen by reference to the data: What set of diagnostics forecast earnings reversals in the history and what weights give the best forecast? Standard statistical methods—of which ordinary-least-squares regression fitting is just one (and probably not the best one)—are applied to develop estimates from the data.

Estimating quality scores from the data has the advantage of reducing the large set of diagnostics to manageable proportions. The data will tell us that a number of diagnostics are correlated—they convey similar information—so they are not all needed. But there is another feature of quality analysis that is also accommodated. As we have noted, diagnostics are only red flags, and there is a very good probability that a measure that indicates quality problems may be justified for sound business reasons. Thus we are open to error. Earnings quality analysis is a probabilistic exercise and the data can tell us how likely we are to make an error with a set of diagnostics. That error can be a so-called Type I error—identifying a firm as having no quality problems when in fact it does—or a Type II error—identifying a firm as having quality problems when in fact it does not. The data give us the probability of making each of these types of errors.

A number of quality scores have been developed over the past several years. Here are just five of them (the Web page for this chapter has more coverage):

- M-scores: Detect manipulation that is likely to result in an SEC investigation: M. Beneish, "The Detection of Earnings Manipulation," *Financial Analysts Journal,* 1999, pp. 24–36.
- F-scores: Discriminate on financial health among low price-to-book firms: J. Piotroski, "Value Investing: The Use of Historical Financial Statement Information to Separate Winners from Losers," *Journal of Accounting Research,* Supplement 2000, pp. 1–41.

- Q-scores: Score how earnings are affected by the release of hidden reserves when conservative accounting is being used: S. Penman and X. Zhang, "Accounting Conservatism, the Quality of Earnings, and Stock Returns," *The Accounting Review,* April 2002, pp. 237–264.

- S-scores: The composite score indicates whether operating income is sustainable or will reverse: S. Penman and X. Zhang, Modeling Sustainable Earnings and P/E Ratios Using Financial Statement Information, 2005. Available at **papers.ssrn.com/sol3/papers.cfm?abstract_id=318967**

- Abnormal accrual scores: Models have been developed that estimate the amount of accruals that are deemed to be abnormal. For example: J. Jones, "Earnings Management During Import Relief Investigations," *Journal of Accounting Research,* Autumn 1991, pp. 193–223 and P. Dechow, R. Sloan, and A. Sweeney, "Detecting Earnings Management," *The Accounting Review,* April 1995, pp. 193–225.

Figure 18.3 shows how discriminating these scores can be. It is based on a calculation of a sustainable earnings score, the S-score, which uses quality diagnostics, calculated from the financial statements, to forecast whether current RNOA will be sustained, increase, or decrease in the future. (Refer back to Figure 18.1 to remind yourself how earnings management plays out through the RNOA.) All U.S.-listed firms from 1979 to 2002 with available data are included in the analysis. The firms in the top third of S-scores have significantly higher RNOA than those in the bottom third in the years after the year when scores were estimated, Year 0, even though both groups have the same RNOA in the S-scoring year. The difference is not trivial—12.8 percent versus 8.8 percent one year ahead.

FIGURE 18.3
Return of Net Operating Assets (RNOA) for Firms with High S-Scores and Low S-Scores, 1979–2002

The S-score ranges from 0 to 1, with a score of 0.5 indicating that current RNOA will be sustained in the future. A score greater than 0.5 indicates that future RNOA will be above current RNOA, and a score less than 0.5 indicates that future RNOA will be below current RNOA. The graph plots average RNOA for the top third of S-scores (High S) and for the bottom third (Low S). Both groups have the same RNOA in the base year, Year 0, when the S-score is estimated, but significantly different RNOA in subsequent years.

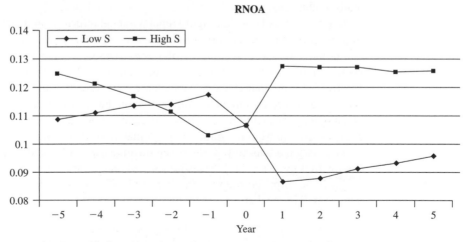

RNOA

Source: S. Penman and X. Zhang. 2005. Modeling Sustainable Earnings and P/E Ratios Using Financial Statement Information. Available at **papers.ssrn.com/sol3/papers.cfm?abstract_id=318967**

FIGURE 18.4
Annual Returns by Calendar Year to a Hedge Portfolio That Takes a Long Position in the Stocks with the Highest 10 Percent of S-Scores and a Short Position in Stocks with the Lowest 10 Percent of S-Scores, 1979–2002

The returns are size-adjusted to subtract the part of the return that is related to risk associated with firm size; that is, each firm's return is reduced by the average return for its size. The long–short position requires zero investment. The combined return to zero investment is positive in all but four years.

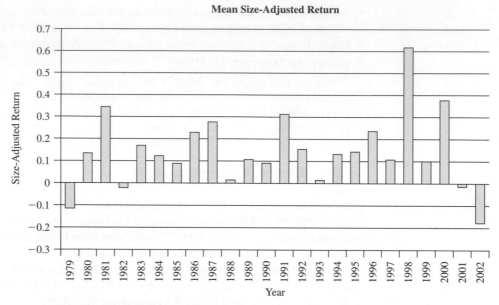

Mean Size-Adjusted Return

Source: S. Penman and X. Zhang. 2005. Modeling Sustainable Earnings and P/E Ratios Using Financial Statement Information. Available at **papers.ssrn.com/sol3/papers.cfm?abstract_id=318967**

ABNORMAL RETURNS TO QUALITY ANALYSIS

Many analysts claim that the market is "fixated" on reported earnings. The market takes earnings at face value, so managers are tempted to manipulate earnings to affect stock prices. A person who believes in efficient markets would maintain that the market sees through any accounting tricks to the real profitability. But a quality analyst who believed otherwise might find that piercing through the accounting will discover mispricing that leads to abnormal returns.

Look at Figure 18.4. That figure reports annual returns from investing long in firms with high S-scores and short in firms with low S-scores, every year from 1979 to 2002. The canceling long and short positions involve zero investment (apart from transactions costs), so should yield zero returns if the long and short sides have similar risk. But the returns are positive in all but four years and quite large—10 percent or higher—in many years. Similar returns have been documented from trading on the amount of accruals relative to cash flows and a variety of quality diagnostics.[1] Of course, traders are increasingly exploiting quality analysis, so returns in the future may not match these historical returns.

Why might a trading strategy based on an analysis of sustainable earnings work? Well, Figure 18.4 gives a clue. If investors as a whole are not perceptive about earnings quality, they will be surprised when the subsequent RNOA are reported. But the competent quality analyst will have taken a position in stocks to benefit from that surprise.

[1] See, for example, R. Sloan, "Do Stock Prices Fully Reflect Information in Accruals and Cash Flows about Future Earnings?" *The Accounting Review,* July 1996, pp. 289–315. Also see the book's Web page for this chapter.

Summary

When forecasting from the current financial statements, the analyst must be concerned with the quality of the accounting used in those statements. If accounting methods and estimates temporarily increase or decrease reported profitability, the analyst knows that the effect will reverse in the future.

This chapter has developed a set of diagnostics to use in an accounting quality analysis. These diagnostics are merely suggestive, flags to raise suspicions about the accounting numbers. They lead to further investigation and to questions to management, to resolve the suspicions that they raise. To reach an overall judgment of accounting quality, the analyst is aware of situations when manipulation is more likely and is aware of the sensitive issues in particular industries. The chapter has outlined situations where the analyst must have particular concerns about the quality of the accounting.

Accounting quality analysis is part of the wider analysis of sustainable earnings. So marry the material in this chapter with that on sustainable earnings in Chapter 13. And use the red-flag analysis of Chapter 16 to raise further questions about the ability of the firm to maintain current profitability in the future.

The Web Connection

Find the following on the Web page for this chapter:

- More on the quality of GAAP accounting.
- A discussion of accounting quality problems that surfaced during the stock market bubble.
- More on fair value accounting and its dangers.

- More examples of doubtful accounting.
- More on composite quality scoring and earnings forecasting.
- More on the abnormal returns that have been reported from using financial statement analysis.
- Look at the Readers' Corner.

Key Concepts

aggressive accounting is accounting that recognizes more current income than alternative accounting methods. Compare with **big-bath accounting.** *592*

audit quality refers to the integrity of the audit in ensuring that generally accepted accounting principles have been adhered to. *593*

banking (or **saving**) **income for the future** refers to the practice of reducing current income and deferring it to the future. Compare with **borrowing income from the future.** *592*

big-bath accounting is accounting that reduces current income (usually by large amounts). Compare with **aggressive accounting.** *592*

borrowing income from the future refers to the (aggressive accounting) practice of recognizing income currently that would

otherwise be recognized in the future. Compare with **banking income for the future.** *592*

channel stuffing is the practice of advancing sales to the current period to recognize more revenue. *593*

disclosure quality is the degree to which financial statements and their footnotes give the detail necessary to analyze them. *594*

earnings management is the practice of shifting earnings between periods. *592*

earnings quality refers to the ability of current earnings to forecast future earnings. Earnings are of good quality if no earnings reversals are forecasted. *591*

expenditure timing is the practice of timing expenditures to selected accounting periods. *593*

GAAP application quality is the degree to which a firm uses GAAP accounting to give a "true and fair" view of the firm's activities: A firm can use accounting methods available within GAAP to give a distorting view of the firm's activities.   *593*

GAAP quality is the degree to which generally accepted accounting principles (GAAP) capture the transactions that are relevant to the valuation of a firm.   *593*

LIFO dipping is the practice of reducing LIFO inventories to increase current income by the liquidation of LIFO reserves.   *615*

quality diagnostics is a measure that raises questions as to the quality of accounting in financial statements.   *600*

revenue timing is the practice of assigning revenue to selected accounting periods.   *593*

reversal property of accounting refers to a feature whereby higher (lower) current earnings will result in lower (higher) earnings in the future.   *591*

shell is an operation that is part of a firm's business but is organized in such a way as to keep the operation off the firm's balance sheet.   *616*

transaction quality refers to the amount of **transaction timing** involved in determining reported earnings.   *593*

transaction structuring involves arranging transactions to achieve a desired accounting effect.   *594*

transaction timing refers to the practice of arranging a firm's business around the accounting rules so as to recognize transactions in particular accounting periods.   *593*

The Analyst's Toolkit

Analysis Tools	Page	Key Measures	Page	Acronyms to Remember	
Five questions about quality	593	Diagnostics		ATO	asset turnover
Prelude to quality analysis	598	Net sales/Cash from sales	603	CFO	cash flow from operations
Diagnostics to detect		Net sales/Net accounts		ebit	earnings before interest
manipulated accounting:		receivable	603		and taxes
Sales	603	Net sales/Unearned		ebitda	earnings before interest,
Core expenses	604	revenue	603		taxes, depreciation, and
Unusual items	612	Bad-debt ratios	604		amortization
Diagnostics to detect		Warranty expense ratios	611	FIFO	first in, first out
transaction timing:		Normalized OI/OI	605	IPO	initial public offering
Core revenue timing	614	Change in asset turnover	605	LIFO	last in, first out
Core expense timing	615	Adjusted ebitda/ebit	607	NOA	net operating assets
Other core income timing	616	Depreciation/Capital		OI	operating income
Unusual income timing	616	expenditures	607	PM	profit margin
Organizational		Cash flow from		R&D	research and development
manipulation	616	operations/OI	608	RNOA	return on net operating
		Cash flow from			assets
		operations/Average NOA	608	SEC	U.S. Securities and
		Expense accrual diagnostics	610		Exchange Commission
		Effective tax rate on		SG&A	selling, general, and
		operations	610		administrative (expenses)
		R&D expense/Sales	615		
		Advertising expense/Sales	615		
		Composite quality score	618		

Concept Questions

C18.1. A firm can create future income by temporarily increasing its bad debt allowance. Is this correct?

C18.2. Low depreciation charges forecast losses in future income statements. Is this correct?

C18.3. A decrease in warranty liabilities increases net sales. Is this correct?

C18.4. Increasing profit margins by underestimating expenses creates net operating assets. Is this correct?

C18.5. Why is a change in the asset turnover an indicator of future profitability?

C18.6. Why do analysts compare cash flow from operations with earnings to assess the quality of the earnings?

C18.7. Why should an analyst view a large merger charge suspiciously?

C18.8. Why should an analyst view an increase in deferred taxes from bad debt allowances suspiciously?

C18.9. IBM reported a 3 percent increase in income for its first quarter of 2000, beating analysts' estimates. But it also reported a decline in revenue. Its stock price dropped in response to the report.

What explanations would you give for the drop in stock price on an earnings increase?

What is your prediction for the change in IBM's asset turnover over the quarter?

C18.10. Excite signed a pact with Netscape in 1999 under which it paid $86.1 million to share revenues from co-branded search-and-directory services. It wrote off two-thirds of the cost—or $56.8 million—against income immediately.

Analysts objected. Why should they?

C18.11. Shares of Pitney Bowes dropped 10 percent after it announced earnings per share from continuing operations of $0.70 for its September quarter of 1999, up from $0.49 in the same quarter in the year before. Revenues also increased 8 percent.

Analysts raised concerns about the quality of the earnings, citing a decrease in the firm's effective tax rate. Why might the effective tax rate be of concern to analysts?

C18.12. If you saw a deferred tax liability from depreciation increase significantly over a year, what might you conclude?

C18.13. A firm has a capital expenditure-to-depreciation ratio of 1.6 over three years. What might you infer from this ratio?

C18.14. Some firms suggest that investors focus on "pro forma" earnings rather than reported earnings. Their pro forma earnings usually exclude amortization of intangibles and shares of losses in subsidiaries. Is this good advice?

C18.15. In July 1999, Federal Reserve Chairman Alan Greenspan stated that corporate profits in the United States were understated, particularly in the technology sector. To what do you think he was referring?

C18.16. The realization principle, which recognizes revenues at point of sale, is said to be an accounting principle that improves the quality of reporting. Companies cannot estimate their future revenues; rather they must have a firm customer before they can recognize revenue. Do you see the realization principle as a desirable accounting principle?

C18.17. Matching costs to revenue—the matching principle—is seen as producing "good quality" earnings numbers. Why?

Exercises

Drill Exercises

E18.1.   Following the Trail: Identifying Hard and Soft Components of Income (Easy)

A firm reported after-tax operating income of $1,298 million. Free cash flow of $234 million was calculated from the cash flow statement.

a. Identify the "hard" and "soft" components of the income.
b. The free cash flow is after $687 million in cash investments. What were the operating accruals for the year?

E18.2.   Income Shifting and Net Operating Assets (Easy)

The chief financial officer of a firm presented the CEO with a set of financial statements showing $2,234 million in after-tax operating income. This number yielded a return on beginning-of-period net operating assets of 9 percent. The CEO complained that this number was below the 12 percent RNOA target they had promised and asked if any "accounting tricks" were available to meet the target.

a. How much must the CFO add to net operating assets to manipulate the income?
b. What is the likely effect of the earnings management on RNOA in the following year?

E18.3.   Following the Trail to the Balance Sheet (Medium)

Indicate which items in the balance sheet can be altered to implement the following earnings management:

a. Increase gross revenues (before allowances).
b. Reduce bad debt expense.
c. Reduce depreciation.
d. Lower selling expenses.
e. Reduce software expenses.

E18.4.   Interpretation of Diagnostics (Easy)

The following lists a number of ratios against the average for the ratio over the prior three years. For each, indicate whether the ratio suggests that return on net operating assets will be higher or lower in the following year.

Ratio	Current Level	Average, Prior Three Years
Bad debt expense/Sales	2.34%	4.12%
Warranty expense/Sales	3.59%	2.30%
Net sales/Accounts receivable	7.34	5.88
Inventory/Sales	0.23	0.12
Depreciation/Capital expenditure	1.3	1.5
Deferred revenue/Sales	0.9	0.25

E18.5.   Normalized Asset Turnover (Medium)

A firm reported after-tax operating income of $136 million, up from $120 million the year before, on a sales increase from $5,106 million to $5,751 million. Net operating assets increased from $2,321 million to $2,614 million. The firm's average asset turnover during the prior three years had been 2.2.

Calculate free cash flow for the year and normalized operating income for the year. What do your calculations indicate about the quality of the $136 million in operating income?

E18.6.   Change in Asset Turnover and Earnings Quality (Medium)

An analyst finds that, for a firm reporting a return on net operating assets of 19 percent, the asset turnover had declined from 2.2 to 1.9.

a. Calculate the profit margin for the year.
b. What does the decrease in the asset turnover tell you about the likelihood of the 19 percent RNOA being maintained in the future?

E18.7.   Red Flags in the Cash Flow Statement (Medium)

Identify the quality red flags in the following portion of a cash flow statement. Revenues for 2012 declined from $456 million in 2011 to $401 million.

In Millions	2012	2011
Net income	$36.5	$28.3
Depreciation	46.0	63.0
Change in accounts receivable, net	(33.3)	12.2
Change in accrued expenses	12.4	(5.2)
Change in deferred revenue	(22.5)	12.3
Change in estimate of restructuring charge	(22.0)	—
Cash flow from operating activities	17.1	110.6
Cash in investing activities:		
Capital expenditure	$61.0	$58.0

Applications

E18.8.   The Quality of Revenues: Bausch & Lomb (Easy)

Bausch and Lomb, Inc., the optical products company, reported the following sales and receivables from 1990 to 1993 (in millions of dollars):

	1990	1991	1992	1993
Net sales	1,368.6	1,520.1	1,709.1	1,872.2
Trade receivables, less allowances	203.0	205.3	277.3	385.0

Subsequently it was discovered that the firm had booked revenues incorrectly, and the SEC investigated. Do the numbers here raise concerns about the quality of the reported revenues?

E18.9.   The Quality of Gross Margins: Vitesse Semiconductor Corp. (Easy)

Vitesse Semiconductor reported the following revenues and cost of goods sold for 2001–2003 (in thousands):

	2003	2002	2001
Revenues	$156,371	$151,738	$383,905
Cost of revenues	73,163	110,155	201,536

Calculate the gross margin ratio (gross margin/sales) for each year. In 2001 the firm took a charge for obsolete inventory of $46.5 million and, in 2002, another $30.5 million. Explain how these charges affect the gross margin ratio in each of the three years.

E18.10.   The SEC and Microsoft (Easy)

a. In 1999, Microsoft Corporation announced that the Securities and Exchange Commission (SEC) was investigating some of its accounting practices. Exhibit 18.1 presents the current liability section of Microsoft's comparative balance sheet at the end of the first quarter of its 2000 fiscal year. Can you see a reason for the SEC's concern?

EXHIBIT 18.1

MICROSOFT CORPORATION
Partial Balance Sheets
(dollars in millions)

	Sept. 30, 1999	June 30, 1999
Current liabilities		
Accounts payable	$ 997	$ 874
Accrued compensation	313	396
Income taxes payable	1,136	1,607
Unearned revenue	4,129	4,239
Other	1,757	1,602
Total current liabilities	$8,332	$8,718

Partial Cash Flow Statements
(dollars in millions)

	Three Months Ended September 30	
	1999	1998
Operations		
Net income	$2,191	$1,683
Depreciation	440	179
Gains in sales	(156)	(160)
Unearned revenue	1,253	1,010
Recognition of unearned revenue from prior periods	(1,363)	(765)
Other current liabilities	(345)	360
Accounts receivable	64	341
Other current assets	(94)	(64)
Net cash from operations	$1,990	$2,584

b. Exhibit 18.1 also gives the cash from operations section of Microsoft's cash flow statement for the same quarter. Microsoft reported revenues of $5.384 billion in the quarter to September 30, 1999, and $4.193 billion for the corresponding quarter for 1998.

Does it appear that the SEC's concerns were justified in the 1999 period?

Real World Connection
See Exercises E1.6, E4.14, E6.12, E8.9, E9.9, E11.11, and E20.4 and Minicases M9.1 and M13.2

E18.11. **Spot the Red Flags in a Cash Flow Statement:**
EDS and Cerner Corporation (Medium)
On the next page are portions of the cash flow statements for Electronic Data Systems (EDS) and Cerner Corporation. Spot the red flags.

ELECTRONIC DATA SYSTEMS AND SUBSIDIARIES

(dollars in millions)

	Years Ended December 31,		
	2001	**2000**	**1999**
Cash flows from operating activities			
Net income	$1,363	$1,143	$ 421
Adjustments to reconcile net income to net cash provided by operating activities:			
Depreciation and amortization	1,482	1,431	1,436
Deferred compensation	98	101	113
Asset write-downs, including acquired in-process R&D	91	43	129
Other	(340)	(187)	(229)
Changes in operating assets and liabilities, net of effects of acquired companies:			
Accounts receivable and unbilled revenue	(882)	(386)	(185)
Prepaids and other	202	(87)	90
Accounts payable and accrued liabilities	(481)	(305)	368
Deferred revenue	(138)	(156)	162
Income taxes	327	(38)	(369)
Total adjustments	359	416	1,515
Net cash provided by operating activities	1,722	1,559	1,936

CERNER CORPORATION

(dollars in thousands)

	Six Months Ended	
	June 29, 2002	**June 30, 2001**
Cash flows from operating activities:		
Net earnings (loss)	$ 24,310	$ (62,655)
Adjustments to reconcile net earnings (loss) to net cash provided by operating activities:		
Depreciation and amortization	27,168	23,580
Common stock received as consideration for sale of license software	—	(750)
Write-off of goodwill impairment	1,272	—
Gain on sale of investment	(4,308)	—
Realized loss on sale of stock	—	385
Write-down of investment	—	127,616
Gain on software license settlement	—	(7,580)
Nonemployee stock option compensation expense	34	56
Equity in losses of affiliates	—	1,093
Provision for deferred income taxes	(29,627)	(44,801)
Changes in assets and liabilities (net of business acquired):		
Receivables, net	(28,817)	(4,582)
Inventory	(1,406)	1,166
Prepaid expenses and other	(4,400)	(5,601)
Accounts payable	4,895	6,644
Accrued income taxes	35,413	5,958
Deferred revenue	(12,641)	(8,304)
Other accrued liabilities	(3,443)	1,160
Total adjustments	(15,860)	96,040
Net cash provided by operating activities	8,450	33,385

(continued)

(concluded)

CERNER CORPORATION		
(dollars in thousands)		
	Six Months Ended	
	June 29, 2002	**June 30, 2001**
Cash flows from investing activities:		
Purchase of capital equipment	(21,493)	(8,150)
Purchase of land, buildings, and improvements	(5,484)	(4,356)
Acquisition of business	(13,429)	—
Investment in investee companies	—	(1,292)
Proceeds from sale of available-for-sale securities	90,119	1,572
Issuance of notes receivable	—	(100)
Repayment of notes receivable	—	89
Capitalized software development costs	(22,915)	(18,179)
Net cash provided by (used in) investing activities	26,798	(30,416)

E18.12. **Tracking Changes in Net Operating Assets and the Asset Turnover: Regina Company (Medium)**

(Based on an analysis by Patricia Fairfield, Georgetown University.)

The Regina Company once marketed a successful line of vacuum cleaners, but then ran into trouble and failed. As you can see from the income statements below, the firm had dramatic sales growth during the 1980s.

Using the income statements and balance sheets below, track operating income (after tax), free cash flow, changes in net operating assets, and asset turnovers over the period. Use a tax rate of 39 percent.

a. For 1988, calculate normalized operating income. What does this number tell you about the earnings quality in 1988?

b. What do the changes in asset turnover tell you about earnings quality in each of the years?

c. What detail in the statements raises further red flags?

REGINA COMPANY				
Comparative Statement of Income				
1985–1988				
(dollars in thousands)				
	Year Ended June 30			
	1985	**1986**	**1987**	**1988**
Net sales	$67,654	$76,144	$128,234	$181,123
Operating costs and expenses				
Cost of goods sold	43,988	46,213	70,756	94,934
Selling, distribution, and administration	9,121	10,366	14,621	21,870
Advertising	9,416	8,557	26,449	39,992
Research and development	673	1,182	1,530	2,423
Total operating costs	63,198	66,318	113,356	159,219
Operating income	$ 4,456	$ 9,826	$ 14,878	$ 21,904
Interest expense	2,930	1,930	1,584	3,189
Income before income taxes	$ 1,526	$ 7,896	$ 13,294	$ 18,715
Income tax expense	405	3,807	6,189	7,761
Net income	$ 1,121	$ 4,089	$ 7,105	$ 10,954

Comparative Balance Sheet
1984–1988
(dollars in thousands)

	Year Ended June 30				
	1984	**1985**	**1986**	**1987**	**1988**
Assets					
Current assets:					
Cash	$ 328	$ 36	$ 63	$ 514	$ 885
Accounts receivable, net	8,551	11,719	14,402	27,801	51,076
Inventory	11,109	6,325	9,762	19,577	39,135
Other	6	475	708	1,449	3,015
Total current assets	$19,994	$18,555	$24,935	$49,341	$ 94,111
Property, plant, and equipment cost	17,219	18,486	19,523	19,736	27,884
Less accumulated depreciation	0	(1,304)	(3,140)	(4,948)	(6,336)
Other assets	1,118	1,775	1,884	1,112	2,481
Total assets	$38,331	$37,513	$43,202	$65,241	$118,140
Liabilities and Stockholders' Equity					
Current liabilities:					
Short-term borrowings	$ 7,500	$ 3,732	$ 2,707	$ 0	$ 0
Current portion of term loan	1,400	1,400	0	900	1,250
Accounts payable	3,082	4,724	7,344	15,072	13,288
Accrued liabilities	3,800	3,091	3,127	5,468	4,710
Income taxes payable	2,349	1,145	1,554	2,619	3,782
Total current liabilities	$18,131	$14,092	$14,732	$24,059	$ 23,030
Long-term debt:					
Term loan	12,600	0	0	0	0
Industrial revenue bonds	0	14,800	14,800	13,900	12,650
Subordinated note	5,000	5,000	0	0	0
Bank debt	0	0	0	5,941	47,432
Mississippi state debt	0	0	0	0	1,975
Total long-term debt	$17,600	$19,800	$14,800	$19,841	$ 62,057
Deferred income taxes	0	118	685	1,254	1,881
Stockholders' equity					
Common stock, $.0001 par value	1	1	1	1	1
Common stock purchase warrant	1,100	1,100	0	0	0
Additional paid-in capital	1,499	1,473	8,010	8,018	8,149
Retained earnings	0	1,121	5,210	12,315	23,269
Less: treasury stock, cost	0	(192)	(236)	(247)	(247)
Total stockholders' equity	$ 2,600	$ 3,503	$12,985	$20,087	$ 31,172
Total liabilities and shareholders' equity	$38,331	$37,513	$43,202	$65,241	$118,140

E18.13.   Quality Diagnostics: Gateway, Inc. (Medium)

Gateway, the computer manufacturer, was a fast-growing company during the 1990s, with continual revenue and earnings growth, bringing admiration from analysts. However, in 2000 revenue growth slowed, from $8,965 million in 1999 to only $9,601 million, despite the opening of over 800 new retail outlets. Operating income was down, at $231 million (after tax) compared with $403 million in 1999. The firm trumpeted its retail expansion, which pleased analysts, and the stock remained around $60. However, in 2001, a torpedo struck: The firm took a restructuring charge of $876 million and reported an after-tax operating loss of $983 million. The stock dropped to $20.

Below are some numbers reported in Gateway's 2000 10-K filing. Go through these numbers and develop diagnostics that point to a quality of earnings issue that might forecast that earnings in 2001 would be degraded.

	2000	1999
	(dollars in thousands)	
Accounts receivable, net:		
Accounts receivable	$ 557,479	$ 662,811
Allowance for uncollectible accounts	(12,724)	(16,472)
	$ 544,755	$ 646,339
Inventory:		
Components and subassemblies	$ 252,085	$ 183,321
Finished goods	62,984	8,849
	$ 315,069	$ 191,870
Property, plant, and equipment	1,308,696	1,092,004
Accumulated depreciation and amortization	(411,282)	(346,344)
	$ 897,414	$ 745,660
Other assets:		
Financing receivables, net of allowance for losses	$ 701,659	$ 295,812
Long-term investments	339,143	212,865
Deferred income taxes	290,596	211,921
Other	283,924	261,548
	$1,615,322	$ 982,146
Accrued liabilities:		
Warranty	$ 127,770	$ 142,729
Other	428,553	466,403
	$ 556,323	$ 609,132
Other current liabilities:		
Deferred revenue	$ 116,089	$ 108,603
Other	34,831	39,699
	$ 150,920	$ 148,302
Other long-term liabilities		
Deferred revenue	$ 62,673	$ 61,200
Warranty	54,910	47,246
Other	23,588	19,414
	$ 141,171	$ 127,860
Total net operating assets	$1,767,000	$ 681,000

E18.14. A Financial Statement Restatement: Sunbeam (Hard)

By the mid-1990s, Sunbeam Corporation, the once celebrated household appliance manufacturer, was reporting lackluster sales and losses. New management, engaged in 1996 to turn the company around, implemented a major restructuring and trumpeted higher sales and profitability. The firm's stock price rose 50 percent over 1997 as results confirmed the predictions.

In 1998, the firm restated its annual reports for 1996 and 1997 with the following introduction:

> Subsequent to the issuance of the Company's Consolidated Financial Statements for the fiscal years ended December 28, 1997, and December 29, 1996, it was determined that the reported results generally inflated 1997 results at the expense of 1996 results.

The firm's stock price dropped from $50 to $10 after the announcement of the restatement.

Part of the restatement had to do with improperly recognized sales. Net sales for 1997 were restated from $1.168 billion down to $1.073 billion but those for 1996 were unchanged. Expenses in both years were affected, however. Exhibits 18.2 and 18.3 are the original and restated cash flow from operations. What were the aspects of the original reports that had to be restated?

EXHIBIT 18.2
From Original Cash
Flow Statement
(in millions of
dollars)

SUNBEAM CORPORATION		
	1997	**1996**
Operating activities		
Net earnings (loss)	$109,415	$(228,262)
Adjustments to reconcile net earnings (loss) to net cash provided by (used in) operating activities		
Depreciation and amortization	38,577	47,429
Restructuring, impairment, and other costs	—	154,869
Other noncash special charges	—	128,800
Loss on sale of discontinued operations, net of taxes	13,713	32,430
Deferred income taxes	57,783	(77,828)
Increase (decrease) in cash from changes in working capital		
Receivables, net	(84,576)	(13,829)
Inventories	(100,810)	(11,651)
Accounts payable	(1,585)	14,735
Restructuring accrual	(43,378)	—
Prepaid expenses and other current assets and liabilities	(9,004)	2,737
Income taxes payable	52,844	(21,942)
Payment of other long-term and nonoperating liabilities	(14,682)	(27,089)
Other, net	(26,546)	13,764
Net cash provided by (used in) operating activities	$ (8,249)	$ 14,163

EXHIBIT 18.3
From Restated Cash
Flow Statement
(in millions of
dollars)

SUNBEAM CORPORATION		
	Restated 1997	**Restated 1996**
Operating activities		
Net earnings (loss)	$ 38,301	$(208,481)
Adjustments to reconcile net earnings (loss) to net cash (used in) provided by operating activities		
Depreciation and amortization	39,757	47,429
Restructuring and asset impairment (benefits) charges	(14,582)	110,122
Other noncash special charges	—	70,847
Loss on sale of discontinued operations, net of taxes	14,017	39,140
Deferred income taxes	38,824	(69,206)
Increase (decrease) in cash from changes in operating assets and liabilities from continuing operations		
Receivables, net	(57,843)	(845)
Proceeds from accounts receivable securitization	58,887	—
Inventories	(140,555)	11,289
Accounts payable	4,261	11,029
Restructuring accrual	(31,957)	—
Prepaid expenses and other current assets and liabilities	(16,092)	39,657
Income taxes payable	52,052	(21,942)
Payment of other long-term and nonoperating liabilities	(1,401)	(27,089)
Other, net	10,288	12,213
Net cash (used in) provided by operating activities	$ (6,043)	$ 14,163

E18.15.   **Stock Market Reactions to Earnings Announcements: Eastman Kodak and Intel (Medium)**

For its September quarter of 1998, Eastman Kodak, the imaging products manufacturer, reported a net profit of $398 million, up 72 percent from one year earlier and in line with analysts' expectations. However, when it was also revealed that its sales had fallen 10 percent to $3.4 billion, its stock price dropped 13 percent.

For the same quarter, Intel, the world's biggest computer chip manufacturer, reported that its net income of $1.6 billion was much the same as a year earlier, but sales rose 9 percent to $6.7 billion. Its stock price increased by 8 percent after the announcement.

a. Calculate the changes in the net profit margins in the September 1999 quarter over the quarter for the year earlier for both firms. Why would the price reaction be so different to the two earnings announcements?

b. Below is the cash flow from the operations section of Eastman Kodak's cash flow statements for the first three quarters of 1998 and 1997. Sales were $9.843 billion for the first three quarters of 1998 and $10.759 billion for the corresponding period for 1997. Do these statements provide any information about earnings quality?

EASTMAN KODAK
Partial Cash Flow Statements
(in millions of dollars)

	Three Quarters	
	1998	**1997**
Cash flows from operating activities		
Net earnings	1,118	749
Adjustments to reconcile above earnings to net cash provided by operating activities, excluding the effect of initial consolidation of acquired companies		
Depreciation and amortization	619	600
Purchased research and development	—	186
Deferred taxes	(63)	(76)
(Gain) loss on sale or retirement of businesses, investments, and properties	(107)	1
Increase in receivables	(216)	(57)
Increase in inventories	(334)	(156)
Decrease in liabilities excluding borrowings	(553)	(285)
Other items, net	(26)	(97)
Total adjustments	(680)	116
Net cash provided by operating activities	438	865

Minicases

M18.1

A Quality Analysis: Xerox Corporation

Xerox Corporation is a long-established company whose very name has been lent to the process of copying documents. The firm develops copying technology through an extensive research program and manufactures and markets a large range of document processing products. Many of its sales are made with lease financing arrangements through its Xerox Credit Corporation in the United States and through other subsidiaries worldwide. The firm's traditional black and white lens copiers (which provided 40 percent of revenues in 1999) were under challenge in the late 1990s from new digital technology, and Xerox developed digital copiers, printers, and production publishers in response.

Xerox initiated a major restructuring of its operations in 1998, and the implementation of the restructuring caused some difficulties in the field. In 1999, total revenues of $19.2 billion were down 1 percent from $19.4 billion in 1998. An announcement that revenues would not meet expectations in October 1999 resulted in a 24 percent share price drop. During 1999 Xerox's share price dropped from $59 to $24. However, income from continuing operations for the full 1999 year, ending December 31, was $1.43 billion, up from $585 million in 1998.

Xerox's income statements for 1997, 1998, and 1999 are reproduced in Exhibit 18.4, along with sections of its cash flow statements. Also given are extracts from the 1999 footnotes.

EXHIBIT 18.4

XEROX CORP.
Income Statements
(dollars in millions, except per-share data)

	Year Ended December 31		
	1999	**1998**	**1997**
Revenues			
Sales	$10,346	$10,696	$ 9,881
Service and rentals	7,856	7,678	7,257
Finance income	1,026	1,073	1,006
Total revenues	19,228	19,447	18,144
Costs and expenses			
Cost of sales	5,744	5,662	5,330
Cost of service and rentals	4,481	4,205	3,778
Inventory charges	0	113	0
Equipment financing interest	547	570	520
Research and development expenses	979	1,040	1,065
Selling, administrative, and general expenses	5,144	5,321	5,212
Restructuring charge and asset impairments	0	1,531	0
Other, net	297	242	98
Total costs and expenses	17,192	18,684	16,003
Income before income taxes, equity income, and minority interests	2,036	763	2,141
Income taxes	631	207	728
Equity in net income of unconsolidated affiliates	68	74	127
Minority interests in earnings of subsidiaries	49	45	88
Income from continuing operations	1,424	585	1,452
Discontinued operations	0	(190)	0
Net income	$ 1,424	$ 395	$ 1,452

(continued)

EXHIBIT 18.4
(concluded)

Partial Cash Flow Statements
(dollars in millions)

	Year Ended December 31		
	1999	**1998**	**1997**
Cash flows from operating activities			
Income from continuing operations	$ 1,424	$ 585	$ 1,452
Adjustments required to reconcile income to cash flows from operating activities			
Depreciation and amortization	935	821	739
Provision for doubtful accounts	359	301	265
Restructuring charge and other charges	0	1,644	0
Provision for postretirement medical benefits, net of payments	41	33	29
Cash charges against 1998 restructuring reserve	(437)	(332)	0
Minorities' interests in earnings of subsidiaries	49	45	88
Undistributed equity in income of affiliated companies	(68)	(27)	(84)
Decrease (increase) in inventories	68	(558)	(170)
Increase in on-lease equipment	(401)	(473)	(347)
Increase in finance receivables	(1,788)	(2,169)	(1,629)
Proceeds from securization of finance receivables	1,495	0	0
Increase in accounts receivable	(94)	(540)	(188)
(Decrease) increase in accounts payable and accrued compensation and benefit costs	(94)	127	250
Net change in other current and noncurrent liabilities	277	(192)	361
Change in current and deferred income taxes	(78)	67	83
Other, net	(464)	(497)	(377)
Total	1,224	(1,165)	472
Cash flows from investing activities			
Cost of additions to land, buildings, and equipment	(594)	(566)	(520)
Proceeds from sales of land, buildings, and equipment	99	74	36
Acquisitions, net of cash acquired	(107)	(380)	(812)
Other, net	(25)	5	45
Total	$ (627)	$ (867)	$(1,251)

Peruse the statements and footnotes. What questions arise about the quality of the earnings reported in 1998 and 1999?

Extracts from Footnotes

The following footnote extracts refer to 1999. Dollar amounts are in millions.

2 Restructuring

In 1998, we announced a worldwide restructuring program intended to enhance our competitive position and lower our overall cost structure. In connection with this program, we recorded a pretax provision of $1,644. The program includes the elimination of approximately 9,000 jobs, net, worldwide, the closing and consolidation of facilities, and the write-down of certain assets. The charges associated with this restructuring program include $113 of inventory charges recorded as cost of revenues and $316 of asset impairments. Included in the asset impairment charge is facility fixed asset write-downs of $156 and other asset write-downs of $160. Key initiatives of the restructuring include:

1. Consolidating 56 European customer support centers into one facility and implementing a shared services organization for back-office operations.
2. Streamlining manufacturing, logistics, distribution, and service operations. This will include centralizing U.S. parts depots and outsourcing storage and distribution.
3. Overhauling our internal processes and associated resources, including closing one of four geographically organized U.S. customer administrative centers.

The reductions are occurring primarily in administrative functions, but also impact service, research, and manufacturing.

The following table summarizes the status of the restructuring reserve (in millions of dollars):

	Total Reserve	Charges Against Reserve	12/31/99 Balance
Severance and related costs	$1,017	$ 717	$300
Asset impairment	316	316	0
Lease cancellation and other costs	198	104	94
Inventory charges	113	113	0
Total	$1,644	$1,250	$394

5 Finance Receivables, Net

Finance receivables result from installment sales and sales-type leases arising from the marketing of our business equipment products. These receivables generally mature over two to five years and are typically collateralized by a security interest in the underlying assets. The components of finance receivables, net at December 31, 1999, 1998, and 1997 follow:

	1999	1998	1997
Gross receivables	$14,666	$16,139	$14,094
Unearned income	(1,677)	(2,084)	(1,909)
Unguaranteed residual values	752	699	557
Allowance for doubtful accounts	(423)	(441)	(389)
Finance receivables, net	13,318	14,313	12,353
Less current portion	5,115	5,220	4,599
Amounts due after one year, net	$ 8,203	$ 9,093	$ 7,754

6 Inventories

The components of inventories at December 31, 1999, 1998, and 1997 follow:

	1999	1998	1997
Finished goods	$1,800	$1,923	$1,549
Work in process	122	111	97
Raw materials	363	464	406
Equipment on operating leases, net	676	771	740
Inventories	$2,961	$3,269	$2,792

7 Investments in Affiliates, at Equity

Investments in corporate joint ventures and other companies in which we generally have a 20 to 50 percent ownership interest at December 31, 1999, 1998, and 1997 follow:

	1999	1998	1997
Fuji Xerox	$1,513	$1,354	$1,231
Other investments	102	102	101
Investments in affiliates, at equity	$1,615	$1,456	$1,332

Xerox Limited owns 50 percent of the outstanding stock of Fuji Xerox, a corporate joint venture with Fuji Photo Film Co. Ltd. (Fuji Photo). Fuji Xerox is headquartered in Tokyo and operates in Japan and other areas of the Pacific Rim, Australia, and New Zealand, except for China. Condensed financial data of Fuji Xerox for its last three fiscal years follow:

	1999	1998	1997
Summary of operations			
Revenues	$7,751	$6,809	$7,415
Costs and expenses	7,440	6,506	6,882
Income before income taxes	311	303	533
Income taxes	201	195	295
Net income	$ 110	$ 108	$ 238
Balance sheet data			
Assets			
Current assets	$3,521	$2,760	$2,461
Noncurrent assets	3,521	3,519	2,942
Total assets	$7,042	$6,279	$5,403
Liabilities and shareholders' equity			
Current liabilities	$2,951	$2,628	$2,218
Long-term debt	169	101	286
Other noncurrent liabilities	1,079	1,028	679
Shareholders' equity	2,843	2,522	2,220
Total liabilities and shareholders' equity	$7,042	$6,279	$5,403

8 Segment Reporting

Our reportable segments are as follows: Core Business, Fuji Xerox, Paper and Media, and Other.

	Document Processing Segments			
	Core Business	Fuji Xerox	Paper and Media	Other
1999				
Information about profit or loss				
Revenues from external customers	$15,224	$ 0	$1,148	$1,830
Finance income	1,016	0	0	10
Intercompany revenues	(206)	0	0	206
Total segment revenues	16,034	0	1,148	2,046
Depreciation and amortization	930	0	0	5
Interest expense	803	0	0	0
Segment profit (loss)	2,014	0	62	(40)
Earnings of nonconsolidated affiliates	13	$ 55	0	0
Information about assets				
Investments in nonconsolidated affiliates	102	1,513	0	0
Total assets	25,319	1,513	86	1,896
Capital expenditures	580	0	0	14

M18.2

A Quality Analysis: Lucent Technologies

Lucent Technologies, Inc., was formed from AT&T's Bell Laboratories research organization after the breakup of AT&T into the Baby Bells. Lucent designs, develops, and manufactures communication systems, supplying these systems to most of the world's telecom operators for both wired and wireless services for voice, data, and video delivery. In 1999 Lucent reported $38.301 billion in revenues, against $31.806 billion in 1998 and $27.611 billion in 1997.

Analysts have complained about the quality of Lucent's reported earnings over the years.

A. What questions arise regarding the quality of Lucent's earnings for 1997, 1998, and 1999 from the partial cash flow statements in Exhibit 18.5?

EXHIBIT 18.5

Partial Consolidated Statements of Cash Flows
(dollars in millions)

	Year Ended September 30		
	1999	1998	1997
Operating activities			
Net income	$4,766	$1,035	$ 449
Adjustments to reconcile net income to net			
cash (used in) provided by operating activities,			
net of effects from acquisitions of businesses			
Cumulative effect of accounting change	(1,308)	0	0
Business restructuring reversal	(141)	(100)	(201)
Asset impairment and other charges	236	0	81
Depreciation and amortization	1,806	1,411	1,499
Provision for uncollectibles	75	149	136
Tax benefit from stock options	367	271	88
Deferred income taxes	1,026	56	(21)
Purchased in-process research and development	15	1,683	1,255
Adjustment to conform Ascend and Kenan's fiscal years	169	0	0
Increase in receivables—net	(3,183)	(2,161)	(484)
Increase in inventories and contracts in process	(1,612)	(403)	(316)
Increase (decrease) in accounts payable	668	231	(18)
Changes in other operating assets and liabilities	(2,320)	155	(397)
Other adjustments for noncash items—net	(840)	(467)	58
Net cash (used in) provided by operating activities	$ (276)	$1,860	$2,129

B. How do deferred tax footnotes help in ascertaining the quality of the accounting? Does the following note (from the 1999 report) raise any quality questions?

The components of deferred tax assets and liabilities at September 30, 1999, and 1998 are as follows:

	September 30		
Deferred Income Tax Assets	**1999**	**1998**	**1997**
Employee pensions and other benefits—net	$ 442	$1,520	$1,777
Business restructuring	6	165	112
Reserves and allowances	1,009	1,137	887
Net operating loss/credit carryforwards	226	239	107
Valuation allowance	(179)	(261)	(234)
Other	344	526	664
Total deferred tax assets	$1,848	$3,326	$3,313
Deferred income tax liabilities			
Property, plant, and equipment	$ 628	$ 399	$ 478
Other	511	391	240
Total deferred tax liabilities	$1,139	$ 790	$ 718

C. Lucent reported effective tax rates of 33.9 percent in 1999, 35.3 percent in 1998, and 36.8 percent 1997. Do these rates raise quality questions?

D. Look at the footnote for the pension cost that follows. Does this note revise your assessment as to the quality of earnings reported from 1997 to 1999?

Components of Net Periodic Benefit Cost

	Year Ended September 30		
	1999	**1998**	**1997**
Pension cost			
Service cost	$ 509	$ 331	$ 312
Interest cost on projected benefit obligation	1,671	1,631	1,604
Expected return on plan assets	(2,957)	(2,384)	(2,150)
Amortization of unrecognized prior service cost	461	164	149
Amortization of transition asset	(300)	(300)	(300)
Amortization of net loss	2	0	0
Charges for plan curtailments	0	0	56
Net pension credit	$ (614)	$ (558)	$ (329)
Postretirement cost			
Service cost	$ 80	$ 63	
Interest cost on accumulated benefit obligation	537	540	
Expected return on plan assets	(308)	(263)	
Amortization of unrecognized prior service cost	53	53	
Amortization of net loss (gain)	6	3	
Charges for plan curtailments	0	0	
Net postretirement benefit cost	$ 368	$ 396	
Pension and postretirement benefits			
Weighted-average assumptions as of September 30			
Discount rate	7.25%	6.0%	
Expected return on plan assets	9.0%	9.0%	
Rate of compensation increase	4.5%	4.5%	

Effective October 1, 1998, Lucent changed its method for calculating the market-related value of plan assets used in determining the expected return-on-asset component of annual net pension and postretirement benefit cost. Under the previous accounting method, the calculation of the market-related value of plan assets included only interest and dividends immediately, while all other realized and unrealized gains and losses were amortized on a straight-line basis over a five-year period. The new method used to calculate market-related value includes immediately an amount based on Lucent's historical asset returns and amortizes the difference between that amount and the actual return on a straight-line basis over a five-year period. The new method is preferable under Statement of Financial Accounting Standards No. 87 because it results in calculated plan asset values that are closer to current fair value, thereby lessening the accumulation of unrecognized gains and losses while still mitigating the effects of annual market value fluctuations.

The cumulative effect of this accounting change related to periods prior to fiscal year 1999 of $2,150 ($1,308 after-tax, or $0.43 and $0.42 per basic and diluted share, respectively) is a one-time, noncash credit to fiscal 1999 earnings. This accounting change also resulted in a reduction in benefit costs in the year ended September 30, 1999, that increased income by $427 ($260 after-tax, or $0.09 and $0.08 per basic and diluted share, respectively) as compared with the previous accounting method. A comparison of pro forma amounts below shows the effects if the accounting change were applied retroactively:

	Year Ended September 30	
	1998	**1997**
Pro forma net income	$1,276.00	$657.00
Earnings per share—basic	$ 0.43	$ 0.23
Earnings per share—diluted	$ 0.42	$ 0.22

The Analysis of Risk and Return

Knowing the business	1
• The products	
• The knowledge base	
• The competition	
• The regulatory constraints	
• The management	

Strategy

Analyzing information	2
• In financial statements	
• Outside of financial statements	

Forecasting payoffs	3
• Specifying payoffs	
• Forecasting payoffs	

Converting forecasts to a valuation	4

Chapter 19
How is fundamental risk analyzed? How is risk handled in active investing?

Chapter 20
How does fundamental analysis aid in the evaluation of default risk on business debt?

Trading on the valuation	5
Outside investor: Compare value with price to *buy*, *sell*, or *hold*	
Inside investor: Compare value with cost to *accept* or *reject* strategy	

Investing involves both risk and return. For much of this book we have been concerned with forecasting payoffs to investing. But forecasts are expected amounts and expected amounts are averages of possible outcomes, so investors must consider the possibility of getting an outcome different from that expected. The chance of getting an outcome different from that expected is the risk of the investment. Of particular concern is getting a "bad outcome," an outcome worse than expected.

This part of the book analyzes business risk. The two chapters here give you an understanding of what determines risk. With that understanding, the investor sets his required return for investing. So these chapters deal with the issue of setting the investor's hurdle rate. It also lays out methods for handling the problem that we really don't know the required return. These methods add to the reverse engineering solutions of Chapter 7 and bring us back to active investing.

Chapter 19 analyzes the risk of equity investment. The risk in equity investing is the risk of not getting the stock return expected. Standard beta models, like the capital asset pricing model, attempt to measure this return risk. These models were outlined in the appendix to Chapter 3 and are covered in detail in corporate finance and investments texts. But the risk in returns is determined by the risk of the underlying business. So Chapter 19 focuses on the fundamental determinants of risk and on how fundamental analysis can help to gain insight into the risk of equity investing. With that understanding the chapter discusses how to handle risk in active investing.

Chapter 20 analyzes the risk of investing in business debt, such as corporate bonds and bank loans. The risk involved is that which a debt ranking agency or a bank loan officer has to evaluate: the risk that a firm might default on its debt. Default risk determines the effective interest rate on the debt—the cost of debt to the firm—and the value of the debt. The emphasis in Chapter 20 is on applying fundamental analysis to determine default risk.

The required return is the final ingredient needed to calculate a value—as indicated in Step 4 in the diagram depicting fundamental analysis here. The required return for equity converts forecasts of the payoffs from business activity to a valuation, typically by discounting or capitalizing those payoffs to present value. Unfortunately, the determination of the required return is elusive. This part of the book attempts to finesse the problem.

Chapter **Nineteen**

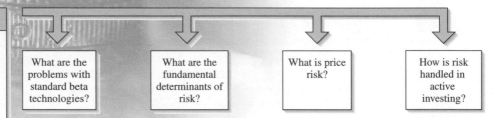

The Analysis of Equity Risk and Return for Active Investing

LINKS

Link to previous chapters

Chapter 3 (and its appendix) reviewed standard beta technologies to measure the cost of capital. Chapter 14 distinguished operating risk and financing risk.

This chapter

This chapter analyzes the fundamental determinants of operating and financing risk in equity investing. It also outlines ways to incorporate risk when valuing firms and trading in their shares.

What are the problems with standard beta technologies?	What are the fundamental determinants of risk?	What is price risk?	How is risk handled in active investing?

Link to next chapter

Chapter 20 analyzes the risk of firms' debt.

Link to Web page

Go to the text's Web site at **www.mhhe.com/penman5e** for further discussion of risk.

Valuation involves both risk and expected return, so we have referred to risk at many points in this text. Risk determines an investor's required return, and expected payoffs must cover the required return before an investment can be said to add value. As the book has proceeded, we have seen that, to value investments and to measure value added, expected payoffs must be discounted for the required return. Indeed, Step 4 of fundamental analysis requires expected payoffs to be discounted using the required return to arrive at a valuation.

But we also have seen that valuations can be quite sensitive to estimates of the required return. In many applications in the book, we have estimated the required return using the standard capital asset pricing model (CAPM). But we have done so with considerable discomfort because of problems in measuring the inputs into the model. Alternative multifactor models have been proposed (as discussed in the appendix to Chapter 3), but these beta technologies only compound the measurement problems. These models are speculative.

So-called asset pricing models seemingly do not refer to fundamentals. They are composed of betas and risk premiums. Betas are defined by expected correlations between

The Analyst's Checklist

After reading this chapter you should understand:

- The difference between the required return and the expected return.
- That precise measures of the cost of capital are difficult to calculate.
- How business investment can yield extreme (high and low) returns.
- How diversification reduces risk.
- Problems with using the standard capital asset pricing model and other beta technologies.
- The fundamental determinants of risk.
- The difference between fundamental risk and price risk.
- How pro forma analysis can be adapted to prepare value-at-risk profiles.
- How the investor finesses the problem of not knowing the required return.
- How to be sensitive to the risk associated with growth.

After reading this chapter you should be able to:

- Identify a firm's risk drivers.
- Generate a value-at-risk profile.
- Incorporate value-at-risk analysis in strategy formulation.
- Deal with the uncertainty about the required return.
- Apply value-at-risk profiles to evaluate implied expected returns estimated with reverse engineering.
- Assign firms to a risk class.
- Carry out pairs trading.
- Estimate the expected return from buying a stock at the current market price.
- Generate growth-return profiles.
- Engage in relative value investing and pairs trading.
- Invest with a margin of safety.

investment returns and market returns, and risk premiums are defined in terms of expected returns. Typically betas and risk premiums are measured from past stock returns. However, risk, like return, is driven by the fundamentals of the firm, the type of business it is engaged in, and its leverage; in short, a firm's operating and financing activities determine its risk. This chapter analyzes the fundamentals that determine risk, so that you can understand why one firm would have a higher required return than another.

THE REQUIRED RETURN AND THE EXPECTED RETURN

The **required return**, also referred to as the **cost of capital**, is the return that an investor demands to compensate him for the risk he bears in making an investment. Both asset pricing models like the CAPM and the fundamental analysis of risk aim to determine what this required return should be. If markets are efficient, the market price will reflect this fundamental risk: The price will be set such that the expected return to buying the shares will equal the required return for risk.

This book, however, has entertained the notion that prices may not be efficient. That is, prices might be set to yield a return different from the required return that compensates for risk. If the price is lower than that indicated by the fundamentals, the investor expects to earn a return higher than the required return; if the price is set higher than that indicated by fundamentals, the investor expects a lower return than the required return. Active investors attempt to identify such mispricing; in other words, they attempt to identify when the expected return is different from the required return. Hence, we distinguish the **expected return** from the required return. The expected return is the return from buying a share at the current market price. The expected return is equal to the required return only if the market price in efficient.

This chapter analyzes fundamental risk with the aim of determining the required return that compensates for that risk. But it also rejoins the earlier active investing analysis of Chapter 7 that determines the expected return. That analysis involves reverse engineering: Given forecasts of profitability and growth, what is the expected return to buying at the current market price? The comparison of this implied expected return with the required return indicates a buy, sell, or hold position.

Despite an enormous amount of research on the issue, measures of the required return (the cost of capital) remain elusive. To be blunt, you will not find a way to estimate the required return with assured precision in this chapter. You will find the material here to be more qualitative than quantitative; the chapter will give you a feel for the risk you face but will not transform that into a percentage return number. It is just too much to think that risk can be reduced to one number like a beta. But the expected return is the focus of the active investor, so the chapter concludes with ways to finesse the difficulties of estimating the required return.

THE NATURE OF RISK

Every year, up to 2007, *The Wall Street Journal* published a "Shareholder Scorecard," which ranked the 1,000 largest U.S. companies by market capitalization on their stock return performance. The year 2007 was a below-average year for stocks, with the S&P 500 stocks earning a return of 5.5 percent. But there was considerable variation around this average. Table 19.1 gives the top and bottom 2½ percent of performers among the 1,000 stocks that year.

The historical average return to investing in U.S. equities has been about 12.5 percent per year. Table 19.1 gives you some idea of how actual returns vary from average returns. There is a chance of doing better than 12.5 percent—very much better as the best performers in the table indicate—and a chance of "losing one's shirt"—as the negative returns in the table indicate. This variation in possible outcomes is the risk of investing.

The investor's perception of this variation determines the return she requires for an investment—how much she will charge in terms of required return to invest—and the return required by investors is the firm's cost of capital. If no variation in returns is expected, the investment is said to be risk free. So the required return for a risky investment is determined as

Required return = Risk-free return + Premium for risk

United States government securities are seen as risk free, and the yields on these securities are readily available. The difficult part of determining a required return is calculating the premium for risk.

The Distribution of Returns

The set of possible outcomes and the probability of outcomes that an investor faces is referred to as the **distribution of returns.** Risk models typically characterize return distributions in terms of probability distributions that are familiar in statistical analysis. A probability distribution assigns to each possible outcome a probability, the chance of getting that outcome. The average of all outcomes, weighted by their probabilities, is the mean of the distribution, or the expected outcome. The investor is seen as having an expected return but also is aware of the probabilities of getting outcomes different from the expected return. And the risk premium she requires depends on her perception of the form of the distribution around the mean.

TABLE 19.1 Best and Worst 2007 Stock Return Performance for the 1,000 Firms in *The Wall Street Journal*'s Shareholder Scorecard

The Best Performers		The Worst Performers	
Company	One-Year Return, %	Company	One-Year Return, %
First Solar	795.2	Countrywide Financial	−78.4
Onyx Pharmaceuticals	425.7	MBIA	−74.1
Mosaic	341.7	Ambac Financial Group	−70.6
CF Industries Holdings	330.0	Washington Mutual	−68.2
Terra Industries	298.7	Pulte Homes	−68.0
SunPower	250.8	Lennar	−65.2
Intuitive Surgical	236.8	MGIC Investment	−63.6
Foster Wheeler	181.1	Office Depot	−63.6
AK Steel Holding	173.6	Advanced Micro Devices	−63.1
Owens-Illinois	168.3	SLM	−58.5
Bally Technologies	166.2	Sepracor	−57.4
Priceline.com	163.4	KB Home	−56.7
GrafTech International	156.5	CIT Group	−55.9
National Oilwell Varco	140.1	Centex	−54.9
Chipotle Mexican Grill	136.6	First Horizon National	−54.9
Amazon.com	134.8	Sovereign Bancorp	−54.4
Jacobs Engineering Group	134.5	AMR	−53.6
Apple	133.5	Liz Claiborne	−53.0
McDermott International	132.1	National City	−52.7
Alpha Natural Resources	128.3	Lexmark International	−52.4
MEMC Electronic Materials	126.1	Rite Aid	−48.7
GameStop	125.4	D.R. Horton	−48.6
Consol Energy	124.2	Freddie Mac	−48.6
FTI Consulting	121.0	Moody's	−48.1
MGI Pharma	120.2	Micron Technology	−48.1

Note: The best performers listed are 2½ percent of the total, as are the worst performers. Stock return includes changes in share prices, reinvestment of dividends, rights and warrant offerings, and cash equivalents (such as stock received in spinoffs).

Source: *The Wall Street Journal*, February 25, 2008. Analysis performed by L.E.K. Consulting LLC. Copyright 2008 by Dow Jones & Co. Inc. Reproduced with permission of Dow Jones & Co. Inc. in the format textbook via Copyright Clearance Center.

Figure 19.1*a* plots the familiar bell-shaped curve of the **normal distribution.** If returns were distributed according to the normal distribution, approximately 68 percent of outcomes would fall within 1 standard deviation of the expected return (the mean) and 95 percent within 2 standard deviations, as depicted. The typical *standard deviation* of annual returns among stocks is about 30 percent. So, with a mean of 12.5 percent, we expect returns to fall between −47.5 percent and +72.5 percent exactly 95 percent of the time if returns follow a normal distribution.

But look at Table 19.1. The stocks listed there are 5 percent of the Shareholder Scorecard's 1,000, that is, 2½ percent with the best performance and 2½ percent with the worst, so their returns are those outside 95 percent of outcomes. The top performers have returns considerably greater than 72.5 percent. Most of the worst performers have 2007 returns below −47.5 percent. Far worse returns are not uncommon; in 2002, for example, all the bottom 2½ percent of stocks had returns worse than −69 percent, in 2001 they all had returns of less than −66 percent, and in the year of the bursting of the bubble, 2000, the 2½ percent worst performers all returned less than −74 percent. Even in a good year,

FIGURE 19.1

(*a*) **The Normal Distribution and** (*b*) **the Typical Distribution of Actual Stock Returns.** (*c*) **The Hypothetical Normal Distribution of S&P 500 Returns and** (*d*) **the Empirical Distribution of S&P 500 returns**

The actual distribution of returns indicates that the chance of getting very low returns or very high returns is higher than indicated by the normal distribution. Even for a large portfolio, like the S&P 500, there are more extreme negative and positive returns than are likely under the normal distribution.

Source for Figure 19.1(*d*): © CRSP. *Center for Research in Security Prices*. The University of Chicago, Booth School of Business. Used with permission. All rights reserved.

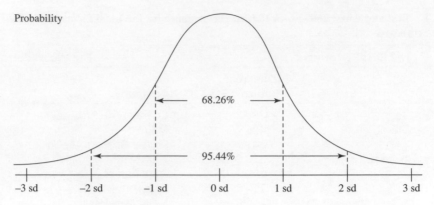

(*a*) The normal distribution. With a normal distribution, there is a 68.26% probability that a return will be within 1 standard deviation (sd) of the mean and a 95.44% probability that a return will be within 2 standard deviations of the mean.

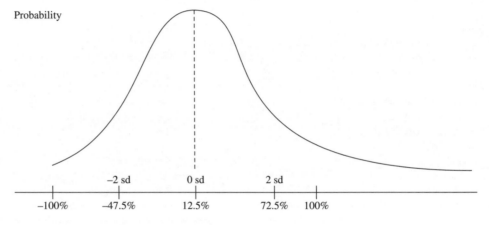

(*b*) The empirical distribution of annual stock returns.

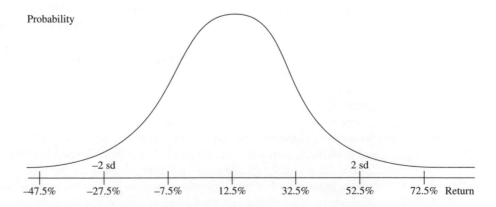

(*c*) The normal distribution of annual returns on the S&P 500 stock portfolio with a mean of 12.5% and a standard deviation of 20%.

FIGURE 19.1
(*concluded*)

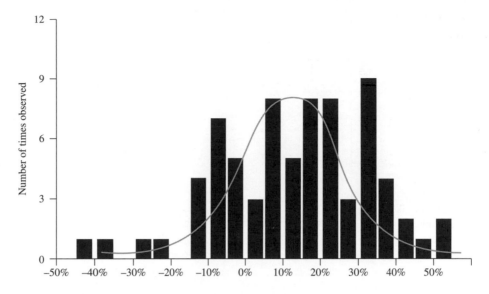

(*d*) The empirical distribution of annual returns on the S&P 500 stock portfolio 1926–1998, superimposed on the normal distribution.

large negative returns are not uncommon: In 1998, when the average return was 24.2 percent, the bottom 2½ percent all returned less than −55 percent.

Figure 19.1*b* compares the actual distribution of annual stock returns to the normal distribution in Figure 19.1*a*. You notice two things. First, stock returns can't be less than −100 percent, but there is significant potential for returns greater than +100 percent, as Table 19.1 also indicates.[1] Second, the probability of getting very high or low returns is greater than if returns were normally distributed. In statistical terms, the first observation says that returns are **skewed** to the right. The second observation says that the distribution of returns is **fat-tailed** relative to the normal; that is, there is a higher probability of falling into the tails (the extremes to the left and right of the 2 sd points) of the distribution, as the comparison of Figures 19.1*a* and *b* indicates.

This all says that in evaluating risk we should be apprehensive of models that rely on the normal distribution. There is a chance of being badly damaged in equity investing: The probability of getting very bad returns (greater than 2 standard deviations from the mean, say) cannot be taken lightly. This is sometimes referred to as **downside risk.** Correspondingly, equity investing has the potential of yielding very large rewards—on the order of 100 percent and greater. This is sometimes referred to as **upside potential.** Indeed, we might view equity investing as buying a significant chance of losing a considerable amount but with the compensation of upside potential. Amazon, in the best performers of the Shareholder Scorecard with a 134.8 percent return in 2007, experienced a large negative return of −80.2 percent in 2000.

The mean and standard deviation do not capture this feature of investing entirely. In assessing risk premiums, the investor might require a higher premium for downside risk and a lower premium for upside potential. His required return for a start-up biotech firm

---

[1] With limited liability, returns cannot be less than −100 percent because losses are limited to the amount invested. That is, stock prices cannot drop below zero. But investing in ventures not protected by limited liability can yield returns less than −100 percent because creditors can make claims against assets outside the business.

FIGURE 19.2

The Effect on the Standard Deviation of Return from Adding More Securities to a Portfolio

The standard deviation declines as the number of securities in the portfolio increases, but the amount of the decline from adding yet more securities is less as the number of securities in the portfolio grows.

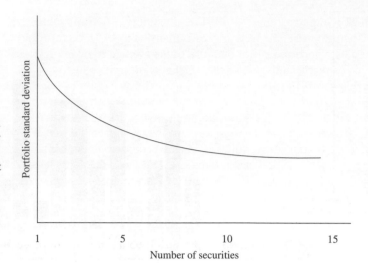

that has a significant probability of losing 100 percent of value but also a significant probability of generating 200 percent returns may be different from his required return for a mature firm like the consumer products firm Procter & Gamble, which has a small chance of either.

Diversification and Risk

A major tenet of modern finance states that the investor reduces risk by holding stocks (or any other investment) in a portfolio with other stocks (or investments). Positive returns cancel negative returns in a portfolio, just like the positive returns in Table 19.1 compensate for the negative returns for anyone holding the 1,000 stocks covered by the Shareholder Scorecard. And if returns on the different investments in the portfolio are not perfectly correlated, the standard deviation of the portfolio return is less than the average standard deviation of return for stocks in the portfolio.

This reduction in the variation of returns in a portfolio is the reduction of risk through **diversification.** Figure 19.2 shows how the standard deviation of return on a portfolio declines as the number of securities in an investment portfolio increases. An investor holding one or two investment assets (stocks, for example) exposes himself to considerable standard deviation of return, but by adding more assets he reduces this variation. At some point, however, adding more investments reduces the standard deviation of return only slightly; there is little further gain to diversification. If the investor holds all available investment assets, he is said to hold the market portfolio and the variation of return for this portfolio is variation that cannot be further reduced. The variation that remains after being fully diversified is **nondiversifiable risk,** or **systematic risk;** it is risk that affects all investments in common. Risk that can be diversified away is called **diversifiable risk** or **unsystematic risk.**

The S&P 500 stocks are typically seen as approximating the market portfolio. The historical standard deviation of returns for the S&P 500 has been about 20 percent per year, around a mean of 12.5 percent. Figure 19.1*c* depicts a normal distribution with a mean of 12.5 percent and a standard deviation of 20 percent. With a standard deviation of 20 percent, we expect returns to fall between –27.5 percent and 52.5 percent (within 2 standard deviations of the mean) 95 percent of the time if they are distributed normally, as Figure 19.1*c* shows. Compare this normal distribution with the distribution of individual stock returns in Figure 19.1*b*. The probability of returns falling between –27 percent and 53 percent in Figure 19.1*c* is greater than that in 19.1*b* because the standard deviation of return on a portfolio is less than that of the average standard deviation for individual stocks. This comparison illustrates the benefits of diversification.

Figure 19.1*d* gives the actual empirical distribution of annual returns for the S&P 500 from 1926 to 1998. You'll notice that the actual distribution of returns in the history does not follow the normal distribution in Figure 19.1*c* exactly. As in the case of individual stocks, some returns are more extreme than would be the case if returns were normally distributed. So portfolios, while giving the benefit of diversification, do not entirely eliminate the chance of getting extreme returns. And that chance is greater than would be predicted by the normal distribution. In 1930 the stock market dropped by 25 percent, followed by a 43 percent drop in 1931 and a 35 percent drop in 1937. In 1974 it dropped by 26 percent, and on "Black Monday" in October 1987 it dropped by 29 percent in one day. On the other hand, 1933 yielded a return of 54 percent, 1935 a return of 48 percent, 1954 a return of 53 percent, 1958 a return of 43 percent, 1995 a return of 38 percent, and 1997 a return of 34 percent. For 2008, the S&P 500 index was down 37.0 percent for the year, another left-tail outcome. Look at Box 1.1 in Chapter 1 for stock market returns since 1999.

What do we learn from these observations? The investor can reduce risk through diversification, and if this can be done without much transaction cost, the market will not reward the investor for bearing diversifiable risk. The investor will be rewarded only for the risk that has to be borne in a well-diversified portfolio. So we must think of risk in terms of factors whose effect on returns cannot be diversified away. But we should also realize that diversification does not entirely eliminate the possibility of getting large (positive and negative) returns.

Asset Pricing Models

An asset pricing model translates the features of the return distribution into a risk premium, and so calculates a required return. Review the material on asset pricing models and beta technologies in the appendix to Chapter 3; for more detail, go to a corporate finance or investments text.[2]

The capital asset pricing model (CAPM), which is widely used, recognizes the diversification property. It says that the only nondiversifiable risk that has to be borne is the risk in the market as a whole. Accordingly, the risk premium for an investment is determined by a premium for the (systematic) risk of the market portfolio and by an investment's sensitivity to that risk, the investment's beta. But the CAPM assumes that returns follow a normal distribution,[3] like that in Figure 19.1*a*. That is, it assumes that if you think about the standard deviation of return, you will have captured all aspects of an investment's risk. But we have seen that the standard deviation underweights the probability of extreme returns (and it is the extreme downside returns that really hurt!).

Even if we accept the CAPM assumptions, we run into severe problems applying it. Warren Buffett, the renowned fundamental investor, claims that the CAPM is "seductively

---

[2] See, for example, R. A. Brealey and S. C. Myers, and F. Allen, *Principles of Corporate Finance*, 10th ed. (New York: McGraw-Hill, 2011); and S. A. Ross, R. W. Westerfield, and J. Jaffe, *Corporate Finance*, 9th ed. (New York: McGraw-Hill, 2010).

[3] On a technical point, the CAPM is also valid if investors have quadratic utility for any form of the return distribution. But we don't know enough about people's utility functions to test if they are quadratic (and they probably are not), whereas we know something about the actual distribution of returns.

precise." It uses fancy machinery and looks as if it gives you a good estimate of the required return. But there are significant measurement problems:

- The CAPM requires estimates of firms' betas, but these estimates typically have errors. A beta estimated as 1.3 may, with significant probability, be somewhere between 1.0 and 1.6. With a market risk premium of 5.0 percent, an error in beta of 0.1 produces an error of 0.5 percent in the required return.
- The market risk premium is a big guess. Research papers and textbooks estimate it in the range of 3.0 percent to 9.2 percent. Pundits keen to rationalize the "high" stock market at the end of the 1990s were brave enough to state that it had declined to 2 percent. With a beta of 1.3, the difference between a required return for a market risk premium of 3.0 percent and one for a market risk premium of 9.2 percent is 8.06 percent.

Compound the error in beta and the error in the risk premium and you have a considerable problem. The CAPM, even if true, is quite imprecise when applied. Let's be honest with ourselves: No one knows what the market risk premium is. And adopting multifactor pricing models adds more risk premiums and betas to estimate. These models contain a strong element of smoke and mirrors.

Warren Buffett made another observation on asset pricing models.[4] The CAPM says that if the price of a stock drops more than the market, it has a high beta: It's high risk. But if the price goes down because the market is mispricing the stock relative to other stocks, then the stock is not necessarily high risk: The chance of making an abnormal return has increased, and paying attention to fundamentals makes the investor more secure, not less secure. The more a stock has "deviated from fundamentals," the more likely is the "return to fundamentals" and the less risky is the investment in the stock.

Buffett's point is that risk cannot be appreciated without understanding fundamentals. Risk is generated by the firm, and in assessing risk, it might be more useful to refer to those fundamentals rather than estimating risk with betas based on (possibly inefficient) market prices.

To see the difficulty in relying on market prices to estimate the required return, consider the weighted-average cost of capital (WACC) calculation for operations (or the cost of capital for the firm), ρ_F, that we outlined in Chapter 14:

$$
\begin{aligned}
\text{Cost of capital for operations} &= \left(\frac{\text{Value of equity}}{\text{Value of operations}} \times \text{Equity cost of capital} \right) \\
&+ \left(\frac{\text{Value of debt}}{\text{Value of operations}} \times \text{Cost of debt capital} \right)
\end{aligned}
\tag{19.1}
$$

$$
\rho_F = \frac{V_0^E}{V_0^{\text{NOA}}} \cdot \rho_E + \frac{V_0^D}{V_0^{\text{NOA}}} \cdot \rho_D
$$

This weighted-average cost of capital requires a measure of the equity cost of capital, ρ_E, as an input. This is often estimated from market prices using the CAPM without reference to fundamentals, producing the reservations that Buffett expresses. But, further, the cost of

---

[4] Buffett's commentary on asset pricing models, along with other aspects of corporate finance, can be found in L. A. Cunningham, ed., *The Essays of Warren Buffett: Lessons for Corporate America* (New York: Cardozo Law Review, 1997).

capital for equity and the after-tax cost of capital for debt, ρ_D, are usually weighted not with intrinsic values as in equation 19.1 but with the market prices of equity and debt. This is odd. We want to estimate the cost of capital for operations in order to get the value of the firm and the value of the equity. We do this to see if the market price is correct. But if we use the market price as an input to the calculation—and assume it is correct—we are defeating our purpose. In valuation we must always try to estimate fundamental value independently of prices to assess whether the market price is a reasonable one. To break the circularity in the WACC calculation, we must assess risk by reference to fundamentals, not market prices.

FUNDAMENTAL RISK

Fundamental risk is the risk that an investor bears as a result of the way a firm conducts its activities. The firm conducts its activities through financing, investment, and operations, as we have seen. The risk from investing and operating activities, combined, is called *operating risk* or *business risk*. If a firm invests and operates in countries with political uncertainty, it has high operating risk. It has high operating risk if it chooses to produce products for which demand drops considerably in recessions. Financing activities that determine financial leverage produce additional risk for shareholders, called *financial risk* or *leverage risk*.

We introduced these two risk components in Chapter 14. We saw that the required return for an equity investor is made up as follows:

Required return for equity = Required return for operations $\hspace{2cm}$ **(19.2)**
$\hspace{4cm}$ + (Market leverage × Required return spread)

$$\rho_E = \rho_F + \frac{V_0^D}{V_0^E}(\rho_F - \rho_D)$$
$$\hspace{1.5cm}\underbrace{\hspace{1cm}}_{(1)}\hspace{1cm}\underbrace{\hspace{2cm}}_{(2)}$$

The two components, operating risk **(1)** and financial risk **(2)**, are the basic *fundamental determinants* of equity risk. But just as payoffs are determined by drivers, so these risks are also driven by further fundamental determinants. Indeed, you see in the expression that financing risk is decomposed into two drivers, market financial leverage and the spread of the required return for operations over the after-tax cost of debt.

To understand the determinants of operating and financing risk, appreciate first what is at risk. Well, shareholder value is at risk, and shareholder value is driven by expectations of future residual earnings:

$$V_0^E = CSE_0 + \frac{RE_1}{\rho_E} + \frac{RE_2}{\rho_E^2} + \frac{RE_3}{\rho_E^3} + \cdots$$

This valuation is based on expected residual earnings (RE). So value is at risk because expected residual earnings are at risk: The firm might not earn the earnings relative to book value that are expected, so anticipated value might not be delivered. Indeed, instead of earnings adding to current book values, the book values might be used up with losses in operations. Accordingly, expected RE are "discounted" for this possibility with a required return, ρ_E, that incorporates the risk. As a consequence, the calculated value reflects risk as well as expected return.

The same drivers that yield RE also can drive RE away from its expected level. Thus, the analysis of risk determinants closely follows the analysis of RE drivers in Chapters 12 and 13.

FIGURE 19.3

The Determinants of Fundamental Risk

Risk of not earning an expected ROCE is determined by the risk of not earning the expected return on operations (operating risk 1), compounded by the risk of financial leverage turning unfavorable (financing risk). The risk of not earning expected residual earnings is the ROCE risk compounded by growth risk (operating risk 2).

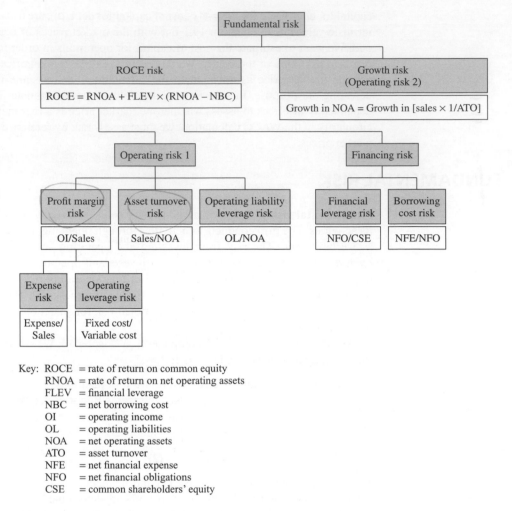

Key: ROCE = rate of return on common equity
RNOA = rate of return on net operating assets
FLEV = financial leverage
NBC = net borrowing cost
OI = operating income
OL = operating liabilities
NOA = net operating assets
ATO = asset turnover
NFE = net financial expense
NFO = net financial obligations
CSE = common shareholders' equity

Residual earnings are generated by return on common equity (ROCE) and growth in investment. So risk is determined by the chance that a firm will not earn the forecasted ROCE or will not grow investments to earn at the ROCE. We deal with these determinants in turn.[5]

Figure 19.3 depicts how the drivers of return on common equity and growth determine fundamental risk. Follow this diagram as we proceed. The risk determinants are expressed in terms of financial statement drivers, but just as economic factors drive residual income, so risk determinants are driven by economic risk factors. Analyzing risk amounts to identifying these economic factors and attaching them to observable features in the financial statements. And identifying economic risk factors amounts to "knowing the business."

---

[5] If value is calculated as discounted free cash flows, the same drivers of risk apply: Free cash flow is just an accounting transformation of residual earnings, as we have seen, so the factors that drive residual earnings also drive free cash flow over the long term. But one would not want to view the variation of free cash flow in the short term as indicative of risk: A negative free cash flow may be caused by large, low-risk investments rather than a bad outcome.

Risk to the Return on Common Equity

We have seen that return on common equity is driven by return on operations and a premium for financing in the same way as the required return in equation 19.2:

$$\text{Return on common equity} = \text{Return on net operating assets} \qquad \textbf{(19.3)}$$
$$+ (\text{Financial leverage} \times \text{Operating spread})$$

$$\text{ROCE} = \text{RNOA} + \frac{\text{NFO}}{\text{CSE}}(\text{RNOA} - \text{NBC})$$

Just as the drivers here determine the expected ROCE, so they determine the risk that the expected ROCE will not be earned. We analyze each in turn.

Operating Risk

The potential variation in return on net operating assets (RNOA) generates operating risk. And variation in RNOA is driven by variation in profit margins and asset turnovers. We refer to the risks that profit margins and asset turnovers will not be at their expected levels as *profit margin (PM) risk* and *asset turnover (ATO) risk*. The RNOA is also determined by operating liability leverage, and we refer to possible variation in operating liability leverage as *operating liability leverage (OLLEV) risk.*

Asset turnover risk recognizes the chance that sales will fall, by a fall either in prices or in volumes, if demand from customers changes or competitors erode market share. If net operating assets are inflexible—they cannot be reduced immediately—ATO falls with a drop in sales, reducing RNOA. The decrease in ATO is, in turn, driven by lower inventory turnover (a buildup of inventory relative to sales and thus excess investment in inventory), lower property, plant, and equipment turnover (and thus value lost in idle capacity), and other individual net asset turnovers. Firms with fixed capital equipment in place, such as investments in large communications networks, are particularly susceptible to ATO risk. Firms with large inventories for which consumer demand can shift to substitute products, such as a new generation of computers or new models of cars, are susceptible to ATO risk.

Profit margin risk is the risk of profit margins changing for a given level of sales. It is driven by *expense risk:* the risk of labor and material costs increasing, per dollar of sales, selling expenses increasing, and so on. Profit margins will also be affected by the fixed and variable cost structure of expenses, which we referred to as *operating leverage (OLEV)* in Chapter 13. If sales fall, profit margins fall by a larger amount if costs are fixed rather than variable (and adaptable to the change in sales). So fixed salary commitments and a tradition that frowns on dismissing employees generate higher profit margin risk. Long-term rental agreements increase profit margin risk.

Operating liability leverage risk is the chance that operating liabilities will fall as a percentage of net operating assets. If the firm gets into difficulties that cause margins and turnovers to fall, suppliers may not grant credit, reducing payables and OLLEV. The ability to collect cash ahead of sales may fall, reducing deferred revenues and OLLEV. These scenarios reduce RNOA and ROCE.

Financing Risk

Financing risk is driven by the amount of financial leverage and the variation in the spread, that is, the RNOA relative to the net borrowing cost. The operating spread varies, of course, as RNOA varies, but the financing component of the spread is the net borrowing cost. So we talk of *financial leverage (FLEV) risk* and *net borrowing cost (NBC) risk* as the determinants of financing risk.

A fall in RNOA reduces the operating spread and the effect on ROCE is magnified, or levered, by the FLEV. As long as the operating spread is positive, financial leverage is favorable (for firms with positive leverage). Should the operating spread turn negative, however, the leverage turns unfavorable, reducing ROCE below RNOA.

Borrowing cost risk increases the chance that operating spreads will decline. Firms with variable-interest-rate debt have higher borrowing cost risk than firms with fixed-rate debt; if interest rates increase with variable-rate debt, ROCE declines, but if interest rates decrease, ROCE increases. Firms that hedge interest rates reduce borrowing cost risk. Net borrowing costs are after-tax, so if firms incur operating losses and cannot get the tax benefit from losses carried forward or back, their after-tax borrowing costs will increase.

Growth Risk

Residual earnings are driven by both ROCE and growth in investment, so ROCE risk is compounded by the risk that common equity will not increase as expected. For a given financial leverage, growth in common equity is driven by growth in net operating assets. So uncertainty about whether the firm can grow investment in net operating assets is an additional aspect of operating risk. That is, uncertainty about a firm's investment opportunities adds to risk.

Growth in net operating assets is driven by sales. For a given asset turnover, the amount of net operating assets to be put in place is determined by sales, so growth risk is driven by the risk of sales not growing as expected. Indeed sales risk is viewed as the foremost business risk, affecting both the growth in net operating assets and the RNOA. A reduction of sales may not reduce net operating assets because net operating assets are inflexible, but if so, it will reduce RNOA and residual earnings as asset turnovers decrease. If net operating assets are flexible, a sales decline will reduce residual earnings through the reduction in net operating assets. This growth risk is labeled operating risk 2 in Figure 19.3 to distinguish it from RNOA risk, which is labeled operating risk 1.

You see how risk components interact, compounding sales risk through the system depicted in Figure 19.3. A fall in sales reduces net operating assets growth and asset turnovers. The fall in asset turnover reduces RNOA, which reduces the operating spread. Operating creditors may reduce credit, reducing operating liability leverage, and borrowing costs may increase because of lower profitability. These effects compound to reduce residual earnings and the compounding effect can cause considerable distress, or even failure. These compounding effects increase the probability of extreme returns.

In valuing the operations by forecasting residual operating income (ReOI), only operating risk needs to be considered, both operating risk 1 and operating risk 2 in Figure 19.3.

VALUE-AT-RISK PROFILING

In Figure 19.1, risk was depicted as a distribution of possible return outcomes. Each possible outcome implies a valuation—how much the investor would be willing to pay for that outcome—so risk can also be depicted as a distribution of values. Plotting that distribution of values—depicting how value might differ from expected value—prepares a *value-at-risk profile*.

Cast back to the full-information, pro forma financial statement forecasting in Chapter 16. Following the template laid out there, we forecasted operating income and net operating assets for the simple firm PPE, Inc., and, from the forecasts, calculated forecasted residual operating income. We then converted these forecasts to a valuation. The pro forma financial statements that we prepared were based on expected sales, profit margins, and turnovers. But a whole range of possible outcomes is possible: The pro forma we prepared is at risk. Value-at-risk profiles are developed by preparing pro forma financial statements for each possible outcome and then calculating the values for each outcome.[6]

To develop value-at-risk profiles, follow the five steps outlined next.

1. *Identify economic factors that will affect the risk drivers in Figure 19.3.* Like valuation more generally, identifying these factors requires "knowing the business." Consider airlines. What factors affect airlines' profits? General economic conditions affect asset turnover risk since airlines sell fewer tickets at lower prices on fixed capacity in recessions than in boom times. Airlines are subject to shocks in oil prices, affecting expense risk. Airlines are subject to changes in government regulation, affecting growth risk. Airlines are subject to price challenges from competitors and new entrants to the industry, affecting RNOA and growth risk.

2. *Identify risk protection mechanisms in place within the firm.* An airline may hedge oil prices to reduce the effects of oil price shocks. Currency risk may be hedged. Incorporation is a risk-protection device to limit liability. The investigation of risk exposures is part of knowing the business. Indeed, the aspects of business that are exposed to risk really define the business. If a gold company hedges its gold reserves against changes in the price of gold, it creates a gold mining business (with risk in production costs) rather than a gold mining and trading business (with risk in production costs and sale prices). If a downstream oil company hedges oil prices, an investor should realize that she is buying a firm that is more like a marketing company than an oil company. A firm hedging currency risk has decided that it is not in the business of trading currencies. If a firm hedges all risks, the investor is buying an investment that is more like the risk-free asset than an equity.

   Disclosure is important to the discovery of risk exposure. Look at the derivatives and financial instrument disclosures. Examine the management discussion and analysis. Just as poor disclosure frustrates the identification of operating assets (what business the firm really is in), so poor disclosure frustrates discovery of risk exposures. A manager seeking to maximize the market value of the firm indicates clearly what type of business the firm is in and so attracts investors who seek the risk and returns to that type of business. If she fails to disclose exposures, she imposes disclosure risk on the investor.[7]

3. *Identify the effect of economic factors on the fundamental risk elements in Figure 19.3.* If valuations are made by forecasting operations, only operating risk drivers need be considered. If valuations are made on the basis of full residual income, both operating and financing drivers need to be considered.

4. *Prepare pro forma financial statements under alternative scenarios for the future fundamental risk drivers.*

5. *Calculate projected residual operating income for each scenario and, from these projections, calculate the set of values that each scenario implies.* Use the risk-free rate (the rate on secure government obligations) to calculate residual incomes and to discount them. (The reason for this will become clear shortly.)

A value-at-risk profile is developed by considering all risk factors to which the firm and its shareholders are exposed. With the profile—and an understanding of the risk factors that generate it—the investor considers his strategy to deal with risk. He chooses his exposures.

---

[6] The value-at-risk analysis here is not to be confused with VaR (value at risk), a measure used to indicate the risk of a trading portfolio.

[7] Some argue that managers should not be concerned with protecting shareholders from risk. With the availability of risk protection instruments on the market and with the ability to diversify, shareholders can protect themselves if they wish, and so arrange their own risk exposures. But to the extent that firms do manage risk, the investor must be aware.

He avoids firms with particular risk features. He uses financial and commodity hedging instruments to protect himself against particular exposures. For example, if he wants exposure to oil price risk, he might buy an oil company, but because he does not want exposure to interest rate risk, he might hedge against interest rate effects on a highly leveraged oil company. Further, the investor understands that risk can be diversified by holding a large portfolio of stocks. Value-at-risk profiles for individual firms are then an input to determining the risk profile of a portfolio of stocks. And the investor understands that portfolios can be engineered to give exposure to one type of risk while minimizing exposure, through diversification, to other types of risk. Value-at-risk profiles help him in weighting his portfolio toward particular types of risk. In implementing his risk-exposure strategy, the investor appreciates the risk protection mechanisms in place within the firm (discussed in Step 2) and mixes his own strategy with that of the firm to engineer his desired exposure to risk.

The identification of economic risk factors in Step 1—and the attachment to financial statement drivers in Step 3—follows closely the identification of the economic determinants of residual earnings in Chapter 16. The preparation of pro forma financial statements in Step 4 completes the full-information forecasting of Chapter 16 by considering not only information about expected residual income but information about the possible variation in residual income also.

The values calculated in Step 5 use the risk-free rate. So for each outcome scenario, using residual operating income valuation,

$$V_0^{\text{NOA}} = \text{NOA}_0 + \frac{\text{OI}_1 - (R-1)\text{NOA}_0}{R} + \frac{\text{OI}_2 - (R-1)\text{NOA}_1}{R^2} \qquad \textbf{(19.4)}$$
$$+ \frac{\text{OI}_3 - (R-1)\text{NOA}_2}{R^3} + \cdots$$

where R is 1 + risk-free rate. Forecasts are made up to a steady-state year.

Most spreadsheet programs have sensitivity analysis features that facilitate this analysis. The example in Table 19.2 keeps it simple by considering only one risk factor (albeit an important one), the variation in the performance of the economy as a whole as measured by the growth in gross domestic product (GDP). This factor is like the "market factor" in the capital asset pricing model. This factor affects only three drivers in the example: sales, profit margins, and asset turnovers. Table 19.2 gives sales for two firms, A and B, for seven growth rates in GDP indicated at the top of the table. Both firms, you notice, have the same sales for a given GDP growth scenario and so have the same sales risk from the GDP factor. But the two firms differ on PM risk and ATO risk. Profit margin risk is driven by operating leverage, the ratio of fixed costs to variable costs. Firm A has a higher fixed-cost component to expenses than B, $20 million compared to $4 million (as indicated at the bottom of the table) and accordingly, with variable costs of 72 percent of sales rather than 88 percent, Firm A has higher operating leverage risk and profit margin risk. Firm A also has less adaptable net operating assets, with $30.7 million invested in inflexible assets compared to $18.7 million for Firm B (as indicated at the bottom of the table). Accordingly, Firm A has higher ATO risk. View the inflexible portion of net operating assets as plant and the variable portion (36 percent of sales for A and 48 percent of sales for B) as inventory and receivables.

These differing sensitivities to the performance of the economy produce different ReOI under the seven scenarios. If GDP grows at 2 percent, both firms will deliver $100 million of sales, a PM of 8 percent, an ATO of 1.50, and an RNOA of 12 percent. And they will deliver $4 million in ReOI over that required with NOA earning at the risk-free rate (assumed to be 6 percent). But Firm A delivers lower RNOA and ReOI than B if GDP growth falls below 2 percent. On the other hand, Firm A delivers considerably

TABLE 19.2 Value-at-Risk Profiles for Two Firms

	Firm A							Firm B						
Scenario:	1	2	3	4	5	6	7	1	2	3	4	5	6	7
Factor: GDP growth	−1%	0%	1%	2%	3%	4%	5%	−1%	0%	1%	2%	3%	4%	5%
Probability of scenario	0.1	0.1	0.2	0.2	0.2	0.1	0.1	0.1	0.1	0.2	0.2	0.2	0.1	0.1
Fundamentals affected														
Sales ($ million)	25	50	75	100	125	150	175	25	50	75	100	125	150	175
Operating expenses ($ million)														
Fixed costs	20	20	20	20	20	20	20	4	4	4	4	4	4	4
Variable costs	18	36	54	72	90	108	126	22	44	66	88	110	132	154
Total expenses	38	56	74	92	110	128	146	26	48	70	92	114	136	158
Operating income ($ million)	−13	−6	1	8	15	22	29	−1	2	5	8	11	14	17
Profit margin	−52%	−12%	1.3%	8.0%	12%	14.7%	16.6%	−4%	4%	6.7%	8.0%	8.8%	9.3%	9.7%
Asset turnover	0.63	1.03	1.30	1.50	1.65	1.77	1.87	0.81	1.17	1.37	1.50	1.59	1.65	1.70
RNOA	−32.7%	−12.3%	1.7%	12.0%	19.8%	26.0%	30.9%	−3.3%	4.7%	9.1%	12.0%	14.0%	15.4%	16.6%
Beginning NOA ($ million)	39.7	48.7	57.7	66.7	75.7	84.7	93.7	30.7	42.7	54.7	66.7	78.7	90.7	102.7
ReOI (R = 1.06)	−15.4	−8.9	−2.5	4.0	10.5	16.9	23.4	−2.8	−0.6	1.7	4.0	6.3	8.6	10.8
Value with limited liability	−40	−49	−16	133	251	366	484	−31	33	83	133	184	234	283

PM risk driver: Firm A: Operating expense = 20 + 72% of sales   Firm B: Operating expense = 4 + 88% of sales

ATO risk driver: Firm A: Net operating assets = 30.7 + 36% of sales   Firm B: Net operating assets = 18.7 + 48% of sales

FIGURE 19.4

Value-at-Risk Profiles for Firm A and Firm B

The profiles are generated for seven scenarios for GDP growth in Table 19.2. Firm A has higher profit margin risk and higher asset turnover risk. These risk factors give Firm A a higher probability of low-value outcomes but also a higher probability of high-value outcomes.

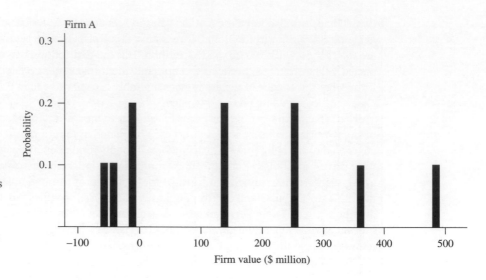

Firm A

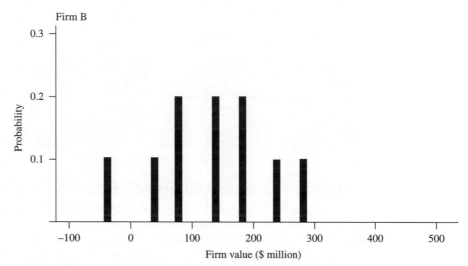

Firm B

more RNOA and ReOI if GDP growth is over 2 percent: Operating leverage and ATO flexibility determine downside risk, but they also work to reward downside risk with upside potential.

The value of each outcome is given at the bottom of Table 19.2. The valuation (again, to keep it simple) is based on each outcome being a perpetuity: $V_0^{NOA} = NOA_0 +$ Forecasted ReOI/0.06. For scenarios 1 and 2 for Firm A and scenario 1 for Firm B, the negative value is the amount of NOA put in place: A perpetual negative RNOA implies all value is lost and, with limited liability, the loss is limited to 100 percent of investment. So the set of possible values reflects not only sales risk, PM risk, and ATO risk but also protection from risk through limited liability. Value-at-risk profiles are completed by attaching the probability of outcomes to the value of outcomes. Profiles for firms A and B are depicted in Figure 19.4

The comparison of the two profiles illustrates the tradeoff between upside potential and downside risk. The expected value of a set of outcomes is the sum of each outcome multiplied by the probability of the outcome. So for both firms, expected sales are $100 million (which happens also to be the median sales in scenario 4). At this level of sales, both firms generate \$4 million in ReOI and, forecasting this ReOI as a perpetuity, both firms' values are $V_0^{\text{NOA}} = 66.7 + 4.0/0.06 = \$133$ million. But the distribution of values around this expected value differ, so the firms are not equivalent investments. Their risk profiles differ. Firm A has the chance of generating considerably higher value than B but takes on a higher chance of losing value on the downside.

The value-at-risk profile for Firm A is similar to the fat-tailed, right-skewed distribution of stock returns that is typically observed, as depicted in Figure 19.1*b*. But now we have uncovered the drivers of those distributions through fundamental analysis. We understand what drives firms' risk. Rather than assuming a return distribution, like the normal distribution, we have determined the form of the distribution through analysis. We understand return distributions—and corresponding value-at-risk profiles—may not be normally distributed. And we understand why the standard deviation of return may not capture all aspects of risk: Operating leverage and ATO risk can combine to give the chance of large returns but also the chance of very poor returns.

The examples here are very stylized. They ignore other aspects of operating risk such as expense risk and operating liability leverage risk. They ignore factors beside GDP growth that might affect sales. They are based on a distribution of sales for just one period. Nevertheless, the examples illustrate the form of the analysis. Other risk factors can be accommodated. Political risk from a change in government or a change in regulations might lead the analyst to specify sales outcomes for both GDP and political outcome scenarios.

The analysis can be performed for longer forecast horizons. Where is the firm likely to be in 3 or 5 years under different scenarios? Extreme "tail" events are rarely observed, but one can model their effect with this apparatus. One can ask questions and get answers: What would have to happen for the stock price to drop, say, 20 percent? How likely is that? Where does the analysis indicate the critical risks lie?

Adaptation Options and Growth Options

The examples for firms A and B specify the response of net operating assets to sales in a simple way: The ATO risk driver has just two components, a fixed component and a component that is proportional to sales. This asset structure does not recognize the variety of ways that a firm can adapt to changes in sales. It is unlikely that a firm would stay in a scenario 1 situation. If it found that, for any reason, the demand for its products faced a scenario 1 outcome, it would adapt. It might liquidate, returning some value to claimants rather than losing all value as in the examples. Or it might adapt into other related or unrelated products.

The ability to liquidate or adapt and avoid worst-case outcomes is called the **adaptation option.** A firm's adaptation option depends on how it is structured, how easily its technology can be liquidated or adapted to alternative use. A farmer can adapt to falling demand for his crop by growing alternative crops or grazing animals. A maker of gasoline-powered automobiles presumably can adapt to solar-powered vehicles should demand shift to them. But a highly specialized producer—the manufacturer of a drug that is replaced by a superior drug—may have few options and may choose to adapt by liquidating. The adaptation option is the ability of firms to "reinvent themselves."

Analysts talk of valuing the adaptation option. The value is captured within the analysis here by specifying more sales outcomes (which will result if the adaptation option is taken) and more complicated ATO drivers for these outcomes, and assigning probabilities that the adaptation will occur. The value in liquidation can also be considered within the analysis.

Analysts also talk of **growth options** and the need to attach a value to them. Like adaptation options, a growth option is an option to adapt, but in particularly good scenarios rather than bad scenarios. The growth option amounts to being able to put assets in place—to expand net operating assets—to exploit new opportunities. Adaptation options limit downside risk; growth options generate upside potential. We characterized growth risk in Figure 19.3 as the risk that sales may not grow. But as with all risks, growth risk has an upside, and firms may have differential ability to capitalize on unexpected growth in sales.

A retailer who signs a lease with an option to rent additional floor space has created an explicit growth option. But most growth operations are not as explicit. Firms create growth options by building excess capacity—in factories, telephone networks, distribution systems, airline routes, and satellite networks. Growth options also come from a firm placing itself "in the right place at the right time." Its knowledge base may give it the ability to capitalize on technological change as it occurs. Its market position, brand name, and customer loyalty may give it the ability to capitalize on product innovations and adapt to changes in consumer tastes. Identifying these options adds to the upside potential in the value-at-risk profile. Indeed we saw Firm A had a built-in growth option (relative to Firm B) by having fixed-cost plant that could be utilized if sales materialized above their expected amount.

These growth options, and the profits and value they may generate, are captured by a value-at-risk analysis. As with Firm A, lay out the sales, profit margin, and asset turnover scenarios if growth options are exercised and assign a probability to these scenarios.

Strategy and Risk

Value-at-risk profiles are a tool for analyzing strategies. The business strategist must not only appreciate the expected value of a strategy but also understand the upside potential and downside risk it generates. And he needs to trade off upside potential for downside risk. So he prepares a value-at-risk profile for each proposed strategy.

Firm A and Firm B in the example above represent different strategies for structuring a business with the same sales outcomes, and these strategies generate different value-at-risk profiles. Strategies with different sales outcomes can be evaluated in the same way. More generally, each component of fundamental risk is explicitly considered in each strategy and its effect on the value-at-risk profile is documented. Should the firm build in growth options? Should it build in adaptation options? What is the cost of these options?

With an understanding of risk, the manager manages risk with *scenario planning*. He lays out the possible scenarios, but he also plans how to run the business in each possible scenario. He plans the adaptation to avoid bad outcomes should pessimistic scenarios be realized. He plans how to handle growth, should it come. This contingent planning, in turn, yields more detailed scenarios and more insights into generating value and reducing risk. Accordingly, value-at-risk analysis is an aid to formulating plans as well as analyzing them for the risk that they involve.

Discounting for Risk

For both firms A and B we calculated a value of $133 million based on expected sales. But this valuation assumed the investments were risk free: The discount rate used in the calculations was the risk-free rate. Given the risk profiles indicated possible variation around the value of $133 million, the risk-averse investor would pay something less than $133 million for the gambles.

The difference between the risk-free valuation and a risk-adjusted valuation is the discount for risk. Buying at the lower risk-adjusted price creates an expected return above the risk-free return; therefore, the discount for risk also can be viewed as an increase in the expected (required) return over the risk-free rate, or as a risk premium in the required return. The valuation question is how to measure this premium (or discount, if that's how you view it).

The standard deviation in the values for Firm A is $198.8 million, compared to $103.3 million for Firm B. One approach might be to determine the risk premium on the basis of this standard deviation. This approach requires a model of how the risk premium is related to standard deviation. Asset pricing models do, but they do not yield a reliable measure of the risk premium. Further, the standard deviation and asset pricing models do not capture the risk in extreme returns that is indicated by the analysis of fundamental risk and observed in stock returns.

The technology to measure the risk premium has not yet been developed in a satisfactory way. The CAPM, the model that is most frequently used, is unsatisfactory for the reasons stated earlier. The analysis here does not give you an alternative. It does describe how business fundamentals determine risk and how outcomes affect value. But it does not tell you how the value-at-risk profile translates into a premium for risk, nor does it yield a number for the required return. Risk is complicated and reducing it to one number is beyond our capabilities at present. This does not, of course, stop you as an investor from setting your hurdle rate on the basis of the analysis base.

PRICE RISK

Fundamental risk arises from the uncertainty of outcomes to business investment, and fundamental risk contributes to uncertainty about stock returns. But there is another aspect of risk with which the investor must be concerned. If prices deviate from fundamental value, the investor can be at risk—and be rewarded—by trading at prices that are not at fundamental value. This risk, which has nothing to do with fundamentals, is called **price risk.** Price risk comes in two forms, market inefficiency risk and liquidity risk.

Market Inefficiency Risk

The passive investor who trusts that the market for shares is efficient recognizes that he is subject to fundamental risk: Efficient market prices will change in response to changes in fundamentals. The active investor maintains that prices can be inefficient. He tries to exploit the inefficiencies, but he also recognizes that the market can be inefficient in an uncertain way. Prices can move against him. **Market inefficiency risk** is the risk of prices moving in a way that is not justified by fundamentals.

Consider two scenarios for exploiting market inefficiency. You might predict that the price at which you will liquidate the investment at some future time, P_T, will be appropriately priced but recognize that the current price, P_0, is mispriced. That is, you predict that you will get a fair price when you sell at time T, and you make an abnormal return by buying the stock at the current price that you judge is incorrect. Alternatively, you might conclude that the stock is appropriately priced at present in P_0 but will be mispriced in the future in P_T. Using V to indicate an intrinsic value, the two scenarios are depicted in the two panels of Figure 19.5. Each panel gives current and expected future market prices for the investment, P_0 and P_T^C. P_T^C (the expected future price with a C attached to it) indicates that the expected price at time T is cum-dividend for dividends paid from 0 to T, for dividends are always part of the return. P_0 and P_T^C are compared to intrinsic values at time 0 and T, V_0 and V_T^C. The intrinsic value at time T is also cum-dividend.

In Scenario A, the fundamental analyst perceives the stock to be currently mispriced and invests to capture an abnormal return as the price returns to fundamental value. An investor

FIGURE 19.5

In These Scenarios for Earning Abnormal Returns, P_0 Is Market Price at Time 0 and V_0 Is Intrinsic Value at Time 0. P_T^C Is Expected Cum-dividend Price at Time T and V_T^C Is Expected Cum-dividend Intrinsic Value at T

In Scenario A the investor expects the cum-dividend price in the future to be at fundamental value but sees the current price as different from fundamental value. Thus she makes abnormal returns as prices move toward fundamental value. In Scenario B the investor sees the current price as equal to fundamental value but expects the price to move away from fundamental value in the future. Thus she makes abnormal returns as prices deviate from fundamental value.

Scenario A: Price gravitates to fundamental value

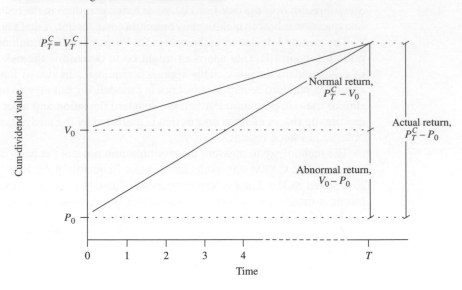

Scenario B: Price deviates from fundamental value

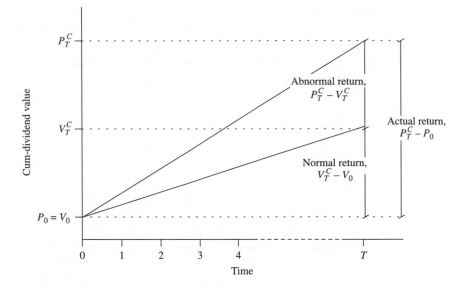

who fails to detect overpricing might buy a stock that is overvalued and then lose value as the price falls in its return to fundamental value. An investor who fails to detect an underpricing (as in the figure) might sell (short) and lose the value as the price rises toward fundamental value. In either case, there is a risk of trading at the wrong price. The risk is referred to as *Scenario A risk*. Scenario A can bring rewards but it also involves risk.

In Scenario B, the investor buys a stock at its fundamental value and sees the stock deviating from fundamental value in the future. So he invests to capture the abnormal return that he predicts. However, a fundamental investor who thinks he is buying at fundamental value but does not anticipate Scenario B may actually lose value should a Scenario B outcome materialize and the stock deviate down from fundamental value. We refer to this risk as *Scenario B risk*. Like all investing, Scenario B can be exploited for reward but also brings risks.

The two scenarios differ in the expectation of how future prices will behave. Scenario A predicts that the market will ultimately recognize the mispricing and correct itself (as future earnings reports become available, for example). Scenario B predicts the market will be "carried away" from fundamental value. In a Scenario B one might, for example, forecast that acquirers, in the process of "empire building," will bid up the price of takeover targets above fundamental value. The investor might buy likely takeover targets in anticipation of this. Or one might forecast inflated prices of takeover targets during "merger booms" as acquirers compete for the acquisitions. One might anticipate supply and demand for stocks and forecast that strong demand for stocks (or lack of demand) will drive them away from their intrinsic values. A number of investors explained the perceived overvaluation of stocks in the 1990s as the effect of baby boomers getting too enthusiastic about stocks and investing their wealth indiscriminately, pushing the price up. These are so-called liquidity theories of stock prices. One might forecast that stock prices will be carried away from fundamentals by fashions, fads, or a herd mentality that introduces misconceived popular beliefs of a stock's worth. Fear might drive stock prices down, as was conjectured about the large drop in stock prices during the credit crisis of 2008. These are so-called psychological theories of the stock market. These theories try to explain how investors can be seemingly irrational. The study of the forces that drive stocks away from their values is called **behavioral finance.**

Scenario A risk and Scenario B risk can be operating at the same time. An investor may think that a stock is undervalued and so buy in anticipation of a Scenario A return, but Scenario B forces can drive the price even lower. In the mid-1990s, many fundamental investors saw stocks as overvalued, so they moved out of stocks, only to find that over the late 1990s stocks became more overvalued (in their view)—and they missed out on a good deal of the bull market. And those who sold short in the mid-1990s had considerable losses. Assured of their insights into fundamentals (and fundamental risk), they were still exposed to price risk.

The risk in both scenarios arises from buying or selling at the wrong price, a price that is not consistent with information about fundamentals. Fundamental analysis is a protection against price risk. This was the appeal to fundamental analysis that we made in the very first chapter of this book: Analysis reduces the uncertainty in investing.

But fundamental analysis alone may not be enough to protect against Scenario B risk. Scenario B arises from factors that drive prices away from fundamentals and understanding those "irrational" market forces helps to predict Scenario B. Indeed, that understanding also helps predict Scenario A because if you think, based on fundamental analysis, that a stock is mispriced and, as well, you have an explanation of why the prices are not at fundamental value, you are doubly assured.

Fundamental analysis does not explain stock prices fully. Stock price theory, based on behavioral theories of price movements, completes the explanation. Understanding price formation protects against price risk. But just as fundamental analysis protects against price risk while it exploits (Scenario A) mispricing, so stock price theory helps in exploiting (Scenario B) mispricing. Unfortunately, the behavioral theory of stock prices is not well developed; it is rather at the level of (interesting) conjecture. Absent such a theory, the fundamental investor might well take the advice of the fundamental analysts of old: Invest for the long term with considerable patience (for prices to ultimately reflect fundamental value). This view asserts the mispricing is a temporary phenomenon that will (ultimately) correct itself.

The manager investing in projects within the firm is not concerned with price risk. The risk in projects and business strategies is fundamental risk. However, that manager must be careful in using hurdle rates for investment that are estimated from market prices, like those based on historical CAPM betas. Such hurdle rates might reflect price risk, not fundamental risk.

Liquidity Risk

Selling at a price less than fundamental value can harm returns. But an investor can get a poor price by simply not finding other investors to sell to. Desiring to sell, the investor may find she has to take a low price to attract a buyer.

The risk of having to trade at a price that is different from intrinsic value because of a scarcity of traders is called **liquidity risk.** Sellers face liquidity risk, but so do buyers who do their fundamental analysis but can't find sellers. Short sellers run considerable risk if they can't find buyers when they wish to buy the stock to cover positions. And the more leveraged the trading position, the worse is the effect of liquidity risk.

Liquidity risk can be a permanent feature of some markets. Shares in privately held firms that rarely trade have considerable liquidity risk. Shares in large publicly traded firms have low liquidity risk. But liquidity risk can change unpredictably also. Investors may lose interest in particular stocks. And if the firm fares poorly, the investor may find it difficult to dispose of shares, to find willing buyers. Entire markets face liquidity risk should investors flee the market in a "crash," and regulators and central bankers are concerned with this "systematic" liquidity risk.

The discount that a seller takes for illiquidity is the *liquidity discount*. Market mechanisms develop to reduce this discount. The stockbroker performs the function of finding buyers or sellers on the other side of a trade and so reduces liquidity risk (for which he charges a fee). The market maker matches buy and sell orders on stock exchanges and so reduces liquidity risk (for which traders pay an implicit fee in the bid–ask spread). Investment banks find buyers for large issues of securities, and specialized brokers arrange for sales of private firms (for which they charge fees). Indeed, transaction costs in trading are the cost of minimizing liquidity risk. Expected returns to investing are reduced by liquidity risk and expected returns to investing are reduced by transaction costs (which reduce liquidity risk).

INFERRING EXPECTED RETURNS FOR ACTIVE INVESTING

A measure of the required return is elusive. You, of course, can specify your own hurdle rate for the risk you perceive, but to pretend that the required return exists out there to be discovered is a false hope. This is a vexing problem for someone wishing to plug a required return into a valuation spreadsheet in the hope of estimating value. However, an active investor is not really concerned with a valuation, but rather in understanding whether the market's valuation is appropriate. As emphasized in Chapter 7, the task is one of challenging the market price to see if it looks cheap or expensive. If it looks cheap, the active investor expects to earn a high return; if it is expensive, returns are expected to be low. The investor thus focuses, not on the required return, but on the *expected return* to buying the stock at the current market price. After all, we understand that there is fundamental risk, but there is also price risk: *Part of the risk in investing is the risk of paying too much* for a stock.

The technique for estimating the expected return is that of reverse engineering. We employed reverse engineering in Chapter 7 to infer the growth forecast implicit in the market price. Understanding the market's forecast, we could then go about asking whether the forecast was reasonable. The considerable financial statement analysis that followed enabled us to meet the challenge. Indeed, we returned to the reverse engineering, now on an enterprise basis, in Chapter 15 where we brought simple valuations based on financial statement analysis to challenge the market price. The simple enterprise valuation model took the form:

$$V_0^{NOA} = NOA_0 + \frac{ReOI_1}{\rho_F - g}$$

(This model can be adapted for longer forecast horizons—we used two years of forecasts in Chapter 7.) For Nike, Inc. (see Box 15.5), we set up the reverse engineering exercise with the value set at the current market enterprise price of $31,446 million and the forecast for forward residual operating income, $ReOI_1$, from the financial statement analysis:

$$\$31,446 = \$5,514 + \frac{1,158}{1.091 - g}$$

Setting the required return at 9.1 percent in the formula, the reversed-engineered value for the growth rate, g, is 4.6 percent. That residual income growth rate can be converted into an easier-to-understand operating income growth rate, as in Chapter 7.

Rather than reverse engineering the growth rate, one can reverse engineer to the expected return for a specified growth rate. For Nike with a growth rate of 4.6 percent,

$$\$31,446 = \$5,514 + \frac{1,158}{ER - 1.046}$$

The solution for the expected return, ER, is of course, 1.091 or a 9.1 percent return. Note that this is not the required return but rather the expected return from buying at the current market price. If enterprise price were $25,000 million, the program would be

$$\$25,000 = \$5,514 + \frac{1,158}{ER - 1.046}$$

The expected return is now 10.54 percent.

A simple formula provides the solution:

$$\text{Expected return for operations} - \left[\frac{NOA_0}{P_0^{NOA}} \times RNOA_1 \right] + \left[\left(1 - \frac{NOA_0}{P_0^{NOA}} \right) \times (g - 1) \right] \quad \textbf{(19.5)}$$

Where NOA_0/P_0^{NOA} is the enterprise book-to-price ratio.[8] You can proof this for Nike where the enterprise book-to-price is $5,514/$31,446 = 0.175 and the forward $RNOA_1$ from the financial statement analysis is 30.1 percent:

$$\begin{aligned} ER &= [0.175 \times 30.1\%] + [(1 - 0.175) \times 4.6\%] \\ &= 5.3\% + 3.8\% = 9.1\% \quad\quad\quad \textbf{(19.5a)} \\ &\quad\; \textbf{(1)} \quad\quad \textbf{(2)} \end{aligned}$$

This is the *weighed-average return formula*: The expected return is a weighted average of the forward RNOA and the growth rate, with the enterprise book-to-price supplying the weights (that sum to one). Note that this is the expected return from buying the firm (the enterprise). The corresponding levered return calculation (applied in Chapter 7) is

$$\text{Expected equity return} = \left[\frac{B_0}{P_0} \times ROCE_1 \right] + \left[\left(1 - \frac{B_0}{P_0} \right) \times (g - 1) \right] \quad \textbf{(19.6)}$$

[8]The formula works only if $RNOA_1$ is greater than the growth rate (which is mostly the case).

The reverse engineering can be adapted for longer forecast horizons (beyond one year here).

Wait a minute! To get the expected return, we need a forecasted growth rate, and this is another unknown. Indeed, we reversed engineered to discover the growth rate for Nike, and for that we set a required return. We can't have it both ways! This, of course, is a problem of one formula with two unknowns.

Growth-Return Profiles

But there is some degree of freedom. We may not know the growth rate but can use the framework to test what the expected return might be for different growth scenarios. The calculation of the expected return for Nike in equation 19.5a is broken down into the two parts indicated. Component (1) is the expected return if there is no growth. So, if one were to forecast that Nike would have no growth, one would expect a 5.28 percent return per year. One might see this as very conservative (involving no speculation about growth) yet also understand that the conservative scenario yields a return of 5.28 percent. But there is also an upside, given by component (2). If growth at the 4 percent GDP growth rate were expected, then the required return is $(1 - 0.175) \times 4\% = 3.3\%$ over the 5.28%, a total of 8.58%. If Nike can deliver 4.6 percent growth, we have seen that the expected return is 9.1 percent.

Alternative scenarios yield a growth-return profile. The growth-return profile for Nike for a price of $74 per share is below and is also plotted in Figure 19.6. It shows how the expected return for buying at the current market price changes with different growth expectations.

Growth–Return Profile for Nike, Inc.	
Price = $74 per share in July 2010	
Growth (%)	**Return (%)**
−3	2.80
−2	3.63
−1	4.45
0	5.28
1	6.10
2	6.93
3	7.75
4	8.58
5	9.40
6	10.23
7	11.05

If the investor is determined never to buy risky growth in excess of the 4 percent GDP growth rate, she understands that will yield an 8.58 percent return. She might feel quite comfortable with that. But the growth-return profile also indicates her upside potential: There is the possibility of higher returns should the higher growth rates eventuate. And there is a downside, and the returns to negative growth are also supplied by the growth-return profile: For negative growth of −3 percent, one expects a return of only 2.8 percent for Nike.

The growth-return profile is a means of understanding alternative possible returns and questioning whether they are sufficient reward for risk: Are the returns adequate given the chances of getting the growth rates that correspond to the returns? If an investor seeks

FIGURE 19.6
Growth-Return
Profile for Nike, Inc.,
for a Market Price
of $74 per Share,
July 2010
The growth-return
profile yields the
expected return from
buying at the market
price for different
growth expectations.
The intercept of the
line is the expected
return with no growth.

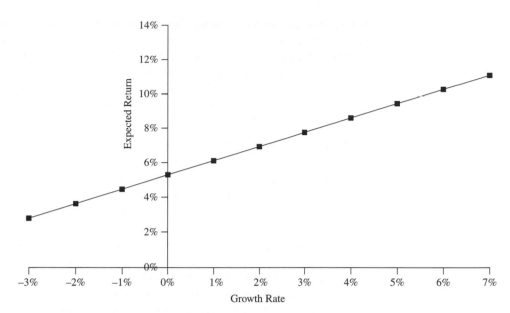

a 9.5 percent return for equity risk and assesses that the 5 percent growth rate needed for a 9.4 percent return from Nike is unlikely, she might look for another investment. If, on the other hand, she deems Nike as able to meet that expectation, she might feel that a 9.4 percent return is quite adequate. If, as a margin of safety, an investor will never pay for more than 2 percent growth, he sees that Nike yields 6.93 percent under this scenario. He may look for another investment, but he should also recognize that growth-return profile points to an upside: There is a chance the investor will do better.

Margin of safety is a concept that is of central importance to fundamental investors. Because they are concerned with the risk of paying too much, they are conservative. They must see that there is a big enough difference between price and value to invest. But identifying "true" value is difficult. Thinking in terms of expected returns helps: Will the stock give me an expected return that contains a margin of safety? Working with growth-return profiles helps: Does a conservative growth estimate yield an expected return that is high enough but also has a margin of safety? What is the upside should the conservative estimate prove to be too conservative?

Finessing the Required Return Problem

The foregoing analysis deals with the problem of not knowing the required return. It is frank and honest: It recognizes that a required return is not available as a prop to tell the investor all about risk. It is just too much to expect to have one number as a sufficient statistic for all the complexities of business risk. The analysis displays payoffs for different uncertain outcomes, but the onus is on the investor to evaluate the risk-return tradeoff. You have to take responsibility for taking on risk; you cannot expect a capital asset pricing model to bail you out. Benchmarks are available, of course. One might demand a return from an equity investment to be higher than the firm's bond yield. One can always set one's own hurdle rate. But there is further help.

Evaluating Implied Expected Returns with Value-at-Risk Profiles

When is an expected return extracted with reverse engineering too high or too low? That question is answered only by reference to the fundamentals, so the investor refers to his value-at-risk profile for the stock. If the expected return from his reverse engineering is low but that profile indicates considerable downside risk, without compensating upside potential, he confirms his opinion that the risk of paying too much is high. If, on the other hand, the implied return is high but the profile indicates low risk, he is more assured that he is not paying too much for the stock. If the growth-return profile indicates that an 8 percent return (say) requires a 6 percent growth rate, but the value-at-risk profile indicates that is unlikely, the investor may avoid the stock.

Investing Within Risk Classes

A value-at-risk profile serves to indicate the risk in an investment. So firms can be assigned to a *risk class* based on their risk profiles, with firms in a given risk class having similar value-at-risk profiles.

Investment analysis can then be conducted for firms within risk classes: Which firms in the risk class have the most favorable prospects? Growth-return profiles can be compared within these risk classes: For firms within a given risk class, which yield the more favorable growth-return profiles? Which has the superior no-growth return? Which yield more favorable returns on the upside and downside?

A refinement involves **pairs trading,** sometimes called *relative value investing.* Pairs trading requires canceling long and short positions in stocks with similar characteristics. If that characteristic is risk (as determined by a value-at-risk profile), the trader is essentially canceling her exposure to the risk: If the risk hits the long position, she is protected by a compensating return to the short position. Place firms in their same risk class, then go long on those with a high implied expected return or superior growth-return profiles and short on those with a low expected return or inferior growth-return profiles. If the risk is indeed the same, the long and short firms should have the same required return, so one is investing on the basis of the relative assessed mispricing. But one is also hedging against the common risk to both. The investor does not have to measure the required return; the measurement problem is finessed.

Analysts concentrate on specific industries and their knowledge of the industry should enable them to generate value-at-risk profiles. Table 19.3 gives "perceived risk" measures from a survey of analysts published in 1985. Analysts were asked to rank the risk of stocks on a scale of 1 to 9, assuming that the stocks were to be added to a well-diversified portfolio. Thus, the risk they were asked to assess is systematic risk. The average responses for each firm are given along with three fundamental attributes that are commonly accepted as indicators of risk. The average perceived risks are in ascending order and seem to be correlated with the fundamentals. Indeed, the correlations between perceived risk and asset size, financial leverage, and earnings variability are −0.46, 0.52, and 0.48, respectively. This analysis is quite primitive but gives promise that analysts can combine their knowledge of business with fundamental analysis to assign firms to risk classes.

Beware of Paying for Risky Growth

This book has emphasized that growth is risky and has developed safeguards against paying too much for growth. If growth is risky, a stock with high expected growth requires a higher return. This makes sense: Expected growth is just more expected earnings, and basic economics tells us that one typically cannot get more earnings without taking on more risk. Again, we do not know how to measure the required return for risk, but the recognition that growth is risky brings a warning: Do not think of growth and the required return as independent inputs to a valuation. Rather, when high growth is forecasted, think in terms of a higher required return.

TABLE 19.3
Analysts' Perceived Risk and Fundamental Attributes for 25 Stocks in 1985

Source: G. E. Farrelly, K. R. Ferris, and W. R. Reichenstein, "Perceived Risk, Market Risk, and Accounting Determined Risk Measures," *Accounting Review,* April 1985, pp. 278–288.

Name of Stock	Perceived Risk Mean	Perceived Risk Variance	Asset Size	Financial Leverage	Variability in Earnings
AT&T	1.89	1.22	11.83	0.165	1.09
Procter & Gamble	2.36	1.74	8.85	0.318	2.79
IBM	2.39	1.52	10.30	0.338	1.95
General Electric	2.69	1.64	9.95	0.468	1.29
Exxon	2.70	1.97	11.33	0.277	2.25
Commonwealth Edison	3.20	2.40	9.32	0.620	1.76
Dow Jones & Co.	3.57	2.38	6.28	0.477	2.96
McDonald's	3.87	2.36	7.97	0.413	2.32
Sears, Roebuck	3.91	1.69	10.24	0.573	1.42
DuPont	4.11	1.91	10.08	0.508	1.64
Safeway	4.28	3.27	8.21	0.691	2.01
Citicorp	4.30	2.37	11.69		1.52
Dr. Pepper	4.32	2.03	5.11	0.215	2.26
General Motors	4.59	2.43	10.57	0.422	
Xerox	4.69	2.45	8.95	0.397	1.04
American Broadcasting Company	4.86	1.83	7.37	0.370	0.47
Holiday Inn Worldwide	5.13	1.86	7.43	0.536	1.34
Tandy	5.54	2.00	6.84	0.225	3.27
Litton Industries	5.66	1.78	8.21	0.552	2.52
RCA	5.67	2.02	8.97	0.855	
Georgia-Pacific	5.88	2.51	8.53	0.450	3.13
Emery Air Freight	5.92	2.58	5.62	0.697	2.28
E.F. Hutton	6.37	2.75	8.64		1.80
U.S. Homes	7.23	2.60	6.63		20.18
International Harvester	8.78	0.41	8.58	0.704	

Note: A blank indicates that data were not available. Perceived risk is a ranking of risk as perceived by analysts, on a scale from 1 to 9; asset size is the natural logarithm of total assets; financial leverage is senior debt divided by total assets; and variability in earnings is the past standard deviation of the price-earnings ratio.

Consider the short-form enterprise valuation model:

$$V_0^{NOA} = NOA_0 + \frac{[\text{RNOA}_1 - (\rho_F - 1)] \times NOA_0}{\rho_F - g}$$

In implementing this model, one might forecast considerable growth. A high growth rate, g (for a given required return), yields a lower denominator and thus a higher valuation. But if growth is risky, the required return, ρ_F, should also be higher. To add higher growth without also adding to the required return would be a mistake.

One can imagine a situation where more growth adds to the required return, one-for-one, such that the denominator is unaffected. If the addition of 1 percent to the growth rate (from a 4 percent growth rate to a 5 percent growth rate, say) adds 1 percent to the required return (from 9 percent to 10 percent, say), the denominator and the value are unaffected. We would not pay for that growth because it does not add value, it's just risky growth.

We do not know how much to add to the required return for growth, and firms can indeed deliver growth that adds to value. But the insight points to a conservative valuation: For every 1 percent added to g, add 1 percent to the required return. As this leaves the calculated value unchanged, it is probably too conservative. It pays nothing for growth so probably builds in too much margin of safety from paying too much for growth. But it is a good starting point for asking how much growth is worth. Note that the weighted average return equations (19.5 and 19.6) still work when the growth they incorporate is risky but a high expected return identified by the reverse engineering should be conservatively appraised: It might be due to higher growth risk rather than mispricing. Set your hurdle rate high if you are buying growth.

Expected Returns in Uncertain Times

Risk requires a higher return, so when there is considerable uncertainty in the economy as a whole, the investor requires a higher return. When a recession is anticipated, the investor takes a conservative approach and thinks in terms of a higher required return. He does so for investing in the market as a whole and more so for firms where the value-at-risk profile indicates susceptibility to economic downturns. This builds in a margin of safety against bad times. Market prices drop in anticipation of recessions and thus expected returns from reverse engineering might increase. However, the conservative investor evaluates these expected returns against a higher benchmark for her required return. As the appropriate required return is indefinite, this exercise is vague, but thinking in a conservative direction is good practice.

As an active investor, understand your tolerance for risk, because it may be quite different from others. In the depths of the financial crisis in the autumn of 2008 when asset prices dropped precipitously—the S&P 500 index dropped below 700—it was said that the crash was partly due to a large revision in the risk premium as investors faced an uncertain world. But individuals' feelings about risk, and the risk premium they require, might differ significantly. If I am heavily leveraged, my house price is falling, and I am in danger of losing my job in the crisis, my risk premium goes up. I dump risky stocks which, coordinated with others in a similar predicament, forces prices down. Indeed, the drop of stock prices at the time was attributed to people deleveraging and running to the safety of cash. You, on the other hand, have no debt, have sold your house, already have a lot of your investments in cash—as a fundamentalist, you saw it coming—and have security of employment. Your risk premium is low relative to others, so you see stocks as a bargain. This is your time to buy.

Summary

This chapter has not given you a precise cost of capital, so we cannot list the cost of capital as one of the key measures at the end of the chapter. We must be realistic and not pretend that a precise measure can be calculated. Fake precision is of no help in practical investing. Rather, take an honest approach, admit that imprecision is inescapable, and think of ways of finessing the problem. The last section of the chapter offered some ways of doing this. The active investor's concern is not with the required return, but with the risk of paying too much for a firm. The focus is thus on the expected return to buying a share at the current market price.

The centerpiece of this chapter is the material in the section on the determinants of fundamental risk. Understand the drivers of fundamental risk; they are summarized in Figure 19.3. And understand how value-at-risk profiles, like those in Figure 19.4, are developed from an analysis of these drivers. With this understanding of risk, refer to a growth-return profile like that in Figure 19.6: What is my expected return for buying risky growth?

An understanding of the fundamental determinants yields a qualitative assessment of risk. Wise and prudent investors understand risk even if they cannot measure it precisely. And they understand that price risk as well as fundamental risk is involved, and how fundamental analysis helps to reduce price risk. Active investors focus on the expected return rather than the required return, and the chapter has provided tools to do so.

The Web Connection

Find the following on the Web page for this chapter:

- More discussion on extreme returns, "tail risk," and how downside risk is rewarded with upside potential.
- More detail from the Shareholder Scorecard for 2007 and other years.
- More on reverse engineering.

- More on Scenario A and Scenario B investing and behavioral factors underlying Scenario B investing.
- Attempts by researchers to estimate the equity risk premium.
- The Readers' Corner.

Key Concepts

adaptation option is the ability to alter the business after a bad outcome. *659*

behavioral finance is the study of why stock prices seemingly behave irrationally. *663*

distribution of returns is the set of possible outcomes that an investor faces with probabilities assigned to those outcomes. *644*

diversification of risk involves reducing risk by holding many investments in a portfolio. *648*

downside risk is the probability of receiving extremely low returns. *647*

expected return is the return that an investor anticipates earning from buying at the current market price. Compare with **required return.** *643*

fat-tailed distribution of outcomes has a probability of extreme (high and low) outcomes that is higher than that for the **normal distribution.** *647*

fundamental risk is the risk that is generated by business activities. Compare with **price risk.** *651*

growth option is the ability to grow assets (and profits) if an opportunity arises. *660*

liquidity risk is the risk of not finding a buyer or seller at the intrinsic value. *664*

market inefficiency risk is the risk of prices changing in a way that is not justified by fundamentals. *661*

normal distribution is a set of outcomes characterized solely by its mean and standard deviation. *645*

pairs trading involves canceling long and short positions in firms with similar characteristics (for example, the same risk). *668*

price risk is the risk of trading at a price that is different from the fundamental value, either because of **market inefficiency risk** or **liquidity risk.** Compare with **fundamental risk.** *661*

required return or **cost of capital** is the return that an investor demands to compensate for risk. Compare with **expected return.** *643*

skewed distribution of outcomes is one that has higher probability in one extreme than the other. *647*

systematic risk or **nondiversifiable risk** is risk that cannot be diversified away in a portfolio. Compare with **unsystematic risk.** *648*

unsystematic risk or **diversifiable risk** is the risk that can be diversified away in a portfolio. Compare with **systematic risk.** *648*

upside potential is the probability of yielding extremely high returns. Compare with **downside risk.** *647*

The Analyst's Toolkit

Concept Questions

C19.1. Why might the normal distribution of returns not characterize the risk of investing in a business?

C19.2. Comment on the following statement. The challenge in measuring the required return for investing is to measure the size of the risk premium over the risk-free rate, but the capital asset pricing model largely leaves this measurement as a guessing game.

C19.3. Can you explain why diversification lowers risk?

C19.4. Why does operating liability leverage increase operating risk?

C19.5. Why are growth stocks often seen as high risk?

C19.6. Explain asset turnover risk.

C19.7. Airlines are said to have high operating risk. Why?

C19.8. Why might stock returns have greater risk than is justified by the fundamentals of the firm's business activities?

C19.9. Should firms manage risk on behalf of their shareholders?

C19.10. Explain the difference between Scenario A and Scenario B investing and the risks involved in each.

Exercises

Drill Exercises

E19.1. Balance Sheets and Risk (Easy)

Below are balance sheets for two firms with similar revenues. Amounts are in millions of dollars. Which firm looks more risky for shareholders? Why?

FIRM A

Assets		Liabilities and Equity	
Cash	17	Accounts payable	14
Accounts receivable	43	Long-term debt	200
Inventory	102		
Property, plant, and equipment	194		
Long-term debt investments	104	Common equity	246
	460		460

FIRM B

Assets		Liabilities and Equity	
Cash	15	Accounts payable	37
Accounts receivable	72	Long-term debt	200
Inventory	107		
Property, plant, and equipment	289	Common equity	246
	483		483

E19.2. Income Statements and Risk (Medium)

The statements below are for two firms in the same line of business (in millions of dollars).

FIRM A

Sales		1,073
Expenses		
Labor and materials	536	
Administration	121	
Depreciation	214	
Selling expenses	84	955
		118
Interest expense		25
Income before taxes		93
Income taxes		34
Income after taxes		59

FIRM B

Sales		1,129
Expenses		
Labor and materials	793	
Administration	42	
Depreciation	79	
Selling expenses	91	1,005
		124
Interest expense		4
Income before taxes		120
Income taxes		43
Income after taxes		77

a. Analyze the risk drivers in these income statements. Which firm looks more risky for stockholders? Why?
b. On the basis of the relationships in these income statements, develop pro forma income statements under the following scenarios:
   (1) Sales drop to $532 million for both firms.
   (2) Sales increase to $2,140 million for both firms. What does this analysis tell you?

E19.3 **Ranking Firms on Risk (Medium)**

Below are income statements and balance sheets for three firms. Rank these firms on what you perceive to be the relative riskiness of their equity from these statements. What features in the statements determined your ranking? All numbers are in millions of dollars. All three firms face a statutory tax rate of 36 percent.

FIRM A Income Statement		
Sales		542
Cost of sales		
Labor and materials	345	
Depreciation	89	434
		108
Selling expenses	9	
Administrative expenses	26	
Research and development expenses	24	59
		49
Net interest expense		7
Income before taxes		42
Income taxes		15
Income after taxes		27

FIRM A Balance Sheet				
Assets			**Liabilities and Equity**	
Cash	7		Accounts payable	42
Short-term investments	4		Long-term debt	104
Accounts receivable	27			
Inventory	64			
Property, plant, and equipment	215		Common equity	171
	317			317

FIRM B
Income Statement

Sales		796
Cost of sales		
Labor and materials	590	
Depreciation	47	637
		159
Selling expenses	53	
Administrative expenses	19	
Research and development expenses	15	87
		72
Net interest expense		4
Income before taxes		68
Income taxes		24
Income after taxes		44

FIRM B
Balance Sheet

Assets		Liabilities and Equity	
Cash	5	Accounts payable	36
Short-term investments	47	Long-term debt	104
Accounts receivable	78		
Inventory	192		
Property, plant, and equipment	159	Common equity	341
	401		481

FIRM C
Income Statement

Sales		649
Cost of sales		
Labor and materials	454	
Depreciation	65	519
		130
Selling expenses	36	
Administrative expenses	28	
Research and development	8	72
		58
Net interest expense		14
Income before taxes		44
Income taxes		16
Income after taxes		28

FIRM C
Balance Sheet

Assets		Liabilities and Equity	
Cash	6	Accounts payable	39
Short-term investments	10	Long-term debt	210
Accounts receivable	66		
Inventory	97		
Property, plant, and equipment	195	Common equity	125
	374		374

E19.4. Analyzing Risk (Hard)

Two firms, Firm A and Firm B, have $1,000 million invested in net operating assets in the same line of business. Firm A has $25 million in net financial obligations while Firm B has $600 million in net financial obligations. Both firms face a statutory tax rate of 36 percent.

Below are forecasted pro forma income statements for the two firms for the upcoming year (in millions of dollars).

FIRM A
Forecasted Income Statement

Sales		2,140
Fixed costs	643	
Variable costs	1,240	1,883
		257
Interest expense		2
Income before taxes		255
Income taxes		91
Income after taxes		164

FIRM B
Forecasted Income Statement

Sales		2,140
Fixed costs	1,240	
Variable costs	643	1,883
		257
Interest expense		48
Income before taxes		209
Income taxes		75
Income after taxes		134

a. Calculate the forecasted return on common equity for the two firms. Would you attribute the difference between the two measures to differences in risk? If so, why is the risk of the equity different for the two firms?

b. Calculate the value of the operations of these two firms, assuming that the residual operating income indicated by the pro forma income statements will continue indefinitely in the future. Use a risk-free rate of 5 percent in your calculations to derive a value that is not risk adjusted.

c. Would you pay more or less for the operations of Firm A than for Firm B? Why?

d. As an equity investor, would your required return be higher for Firm A than Firm B? Why?

e. What would residual operating income for the two firms be if sales fell to $1,500 million? Does this calculation justify your answer to part (c)?

Applications

E19.5. Constructing a Value-at-Risk Profile: Nike Inc. (Medium)

For fiscal year 2004, Nike reported after-tax core profit margins of 7.84 percent on an asset turnover of 2.759. An analyst forecasts that this margin and turnover will persist in the future on a sales growth rate of 5.1 percent per year. Nike reported $4,840 million of common equity and $4,551 million in net operating assets on it 2004 balance sheet. The risk-free rate is 4.5 percent and the required return for operations is 8.6 percent.

a. From this information, calculate the value per share at the end of 2004 on 263.1 million shares outstanding.

b. Generate a value-at-risk profile from scenarios 1–7 below:

Scenario	Sales Growth (%)	Profit Margin (%)	Asset Turnover
1	1.0	4.0	1.5
2	2.0	4.5	1.9
3	3.0	6.0	2.3
4	4.0	6.9	2.5
5	5.1	7.84	2.759
6	6.0	8.0	2.9
7	6.5	8.9	3.1

Real World Connection

Exercises E2.14, E5.13, E6.7, E7.9, E9.12, E14.17, E16.11, E16.13, and E20.4 deal with Nike.

E19.6. A Growth-Return Profile for Cisco Systems, Inc. (Medium)

In November 2009, Cisco Systems' shares traded at $24 each, with a total market equity capitalization of $138.8 billion. The most recent balance sheet reported net operating assets of $13.9 billion, along with $24.7 billion in net financial assets. A financial statement analysis produced a forecast of 57.1 percent for return on net operating assets (RNOA) for the next fiscal year.

a. Calculate the expected return from buying the enterprise at the current market price if no growth is expected after the forward year.

b. Calculate the expected return from buying the enterprise if you expect a growth rate equal to the GDP growth rate of 4 percent after the forward year.

c. Develop a full growth-return profile for Cisco, like that in Figure 19.6.

d. How does this profile help you in your investment decision?

Real World Connection

Cisco is also investigated in Exercise E2.11 and Minicases M7.1 and M15.2.

Minicase

M19.1

Growth, Risk, and Expected Return for Google, Inc.

In May 2011, Google was trading at $535 per share, or 3.7 times book value of $143.92 per share. Analysts were forecasting a consensus estimate of $33.94 EPS for 2011. The forward P/E of 15.8 implies some growth expectation.

Do you wish to pay for this growth? Construct a growth-return profile like that in Figure 19.6 to help answer this question. Be sure to identify the no-growth case and the case with a 4 percent GDP growth rate. Discuss how this profile helps you in your investment decision.

One likes to make investment decisions against benchmarks. In May 2011, the S&P 500 index stood at 1,357, with forward earnings forecasted by analysts at 98.79. Construct a similar profile for the S&P 500. How is the market pricing Google differently from the market as a whole? Which of the two is the more favorable investment for you—buy Google or an index fund that tracks the S&P 500?

Real World Connection

Minicase M7.2 and Exercise 7.11 also deal with Google Inc.

Chapter **Twenty**

The Analysis of Credit Risk and Return

LINKS

Link to previous chapter

Chapter 19 showed how the analysis of fundamentals helps in the evaluation of equity risk. Value-at-risk profiles were developed to aid active investing.

This chapter

This chapter shows how fundamental analysis helps in the evaluation of the risk of a firm defaulting on its debt. Value-at-risk profiles are developed to assess default risk.

Link to Web page

To learn more about risk, visit the text's Web site at **www.mhhe.com/penman5e**.

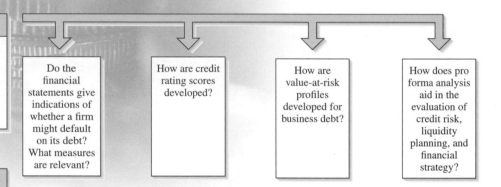

Do the financial statements give indications of whether a firm might default on its debt? What measures are relevant?

How are credit rating scores developed?

How are value-at-risk profiles developed for business debt?

How does pro forma analysis aid in the evaluation of credit risk, liquidity planning, and financial strategy?

Most of the analysis in the book to this point has been concerned with the valuation of the firm and the valuation of the equity claim on the firm. This chapter deals with the other major claim on the firm, the debt. Thus far we have accepted the market value of debt as its value. But buyers and sellers of debt need to know how to establish the market value of debt.

In most debt contracts, the payoffs to debt are specified in the contract. So Step 3 of fundamental analysis—forecasting payoffs—is trivial. But forecasted payoffs have to be discounted (in Step 4) to get a valuation. Discounting requires a measure of the required return for debt, and this required return, like that for equity, depends on the riskiness of the debt: The required return for debt is the risk-free rate for the term of the debt plus a **default premium** that varies with default risk. **Default risk,** or **credit risk,** is the risk of

The Analyst's Checklist

After reading this chapter you should understand:

- How default risk determines the price of credit and the cost of debt capital for the firm.
- What determines default risk.
- How default risk is analyzed.
- What bond rating agencies do.
- How credit scoring models work.
- The difference between Type I and Type II errors in predicting default.
- How pro forma analysis identifies default scenarios.
- How value-at-risk analysis is incorporated into default analysis.
- How financial strategy works.

After reading this chapter you should be able to:

- Reformulate and annotate financial statements in preparation for credit analysis.
- Calculate liquidity, solvency, and operational ratios that are pertinent to credit analysis.
- Calculate credit scores using financial ratios.
- Calculate a probability of bankruptcy using financial ratios.
- Trade off Type I and Type II default forecasting errors.
- Prepare pro formas for default scenarios.
- Prepare value-at-risk profiles for debt.
- Forecast default points.
- Prepare a default strategy.

default; that is, the risk of not receiving timely interest and return of principal as specified in the debt agreement. This chapter brings fundamental analysis to the task of evaluating default risk.

Analysts talk of the required return for debt. But debt taken on by the firm is also credit supplied by those who purchase the debt. Accordingly, we can talk of the required return for debt as also being the **price of credit.** Whatever the terminology, the amount charged by suppliers of credit is the *cost of debt* for the firm.

THE SUPPLIERS OF CREDIT

Suppliers of credit to the firm include the following:

- *Public debt market investors,* who include (long-term) bondholders and (short-term) commercial paper holders. Sometimes public debt is packaged by banks into bundles of *securitized debt obligations* or *collateralized debt obligations,* which are then traded as a package at a price that reflects the underlying credit risk. In turn, *credit default swaps,* which insure the debtholder against default, are also priced on the perceived credit risk. At all points in this chain, keeping track of the underlying risk is important (a point that was not always understood in the securitizations prior to the global financial crisis). Often, publicly traded debt is unsecured, that is, not collateralized by specific assets. Bondholders are protected by bond covenants, which restrict the firm from specified actions that might increase default risk, and violation of a bond covenant is technically a default. To evaluate default risk, investors in this type of debt rely on those corporate disclosures about the overall health of the firm that are required by the Securities and Exchange Commission (SEC) in the United States for all publicly traded securities. They also rely on *bond ratings,* which are published by rating agencies to indicate default risk. Accordingly, it is the rating agencies that are particularly concerned with the analysis of risk, and they develop rating models that involve the analysis of fundamentals.

- *Commercial banks,* which make loans to firms. They are usually closer to a firm's business than a bondholder, so they have access to more information regarding default risk. The loan officer serves as the credit analyst, and loan officers, like bond rating agencies, have models that aid in *credit scoring*. Their credit scoring methods are tied into their bank's internal risk management, to protect the bank and to satisfy regulatory constraints on its exposure to risk. Banks originate loans on the basis of credit scores. They then use credit scoring to measure the quality of loans that they sell to other institutions and to monitor the default risk of loans they retain.
- *Other financial institutions,* such as insurance companies, finance houses, and leasing firms, make loans, much like banks, but usually with specific assets serving as **collateral.** They also arrange specialty financing such as leases of long-term assets.
- *Suppliers* to the firm, who grant (usually short-term) credit upon delivery of goods and services. The credit can be granted with or without explicit interest.

Each supplier of credit has a price for granting credit—the required return—and each needs to analyze the risk of default and charge accordingly. Bondholders charge a yield to maturity based on their risk assessment and set bond prices accordingly. Banks charge an interest rate over a base rate (the prime rate for their safest customers) that depends on default risk. And suppliers charge a higher price for goods and services if the default risk is high. If risk is deemed to be unacceptable, no price is acceptable to the lender, so credit is denied.

The explicit price is only one dimension of the price. Just as a supplier might charge no explicit interest for credit but charge a higher price for goods supplied to compensate, a bondholder will charge a lower yield if bond covenants have more protection, a finance firm will charge less with collateral, and a bank will charge less for loans with personal or parent company guarantees. Such restrictions increase the (implicit) cost of capital to the borrowing firm.

FINANCIAL STATEMENT ANALYSIS FOR CREDIT EVALUATION

Equity analysis calls for a particular ratio analysis (of profitability and growth), which was laid out in Chapters 12 and 13. **Credit analysis** calls for a different analysis, and many of the ratios involved are different from those for equity analysis. As with equity analysis, the emphasis is on forecasting. Rather than identifying those ratios that forecast profitability and growth, credit analysis identifies ratios that indicate the likelihood of default. Therefore, it is also referred to as **default analysis.** As with equity analysis, the credit analyst identifies ratios from financial statements that have first been reformulated for the purpose.

Reformulated Financial Statements

For the equity analysis financial statements were reformulated to uncover what is most important to equity investors, core operating profitability. For credit analysis, the statements must be in a form to uncover what is most important to creditors, the ability to repay the debt.

Reformulation, as before, involves reclassifying items in the financial statements and bringing more dollar detail into the financial statements from the footnotes. In addition, the discovery process leads to some annotation of the statements. *Annotation* involves summarizing features of the financing that cannot be expressed as dollar amounts on the balance sheet but which are pertinent to the risk of default.

Balance Sheet Reformulation and Annotation

The ability to repay amounts to having cash at maturity. Maturities differ, but it is standard practice to distinguish debt as short-term (usually thought of as maturing within one year) and long-term (maturing in more than one year). Published balance sheets are usually prepared with a division into current and noncurrent (long-term) assets and liabilities, so the balance sheet needs little reformulation. Indeed, it is because balance sheets are structured with the creditor in mind that we had to reformulate them for equity analysis. For credit analysis, there is no need to distinguish operating debt from financing debt. Both are claims that have to be paid.

Some reformulation and annotation is called for, however. Here are points to consider:

- Details on different classes of debt and their varying maturities are available in the debt footnotes; these details can be inserted in the body of reformulated statements.
- Debt of unconsolidated subsidiaries (where the parent owns less than 50 percent but has effective control) should be recognized. For example, oil companies sometimes raise cash through joint ventures in which they hold less than 50 percent interest, and they cover the debt of the joint venture if revenues in the venture are insufficient to service its debt. The Coca-Cola Company owns less than 50 percent of some of its bottling companies but effectively borrows through these subsidiaries. The debt of these subsidiaries or joint ventures should be included in a consolidated reformulated statement, on a proportional basis, if the parent company is ultimately responsible for it.
- Long-term marketable securities are sometimes available for sale in the short term if a need for cash arises. For analyzing short-term liquidity, therefore, reclassify them as a short-term asset.
- Remove deferred tax liabilities that are unlikely to revert from liabilities to shareholders' equity. Such deferred taxes, created by a reduction of earnings and equity, are liabilities that are unlikely to be paid. So classify them back to equity.
- Add the LIFO reserve to inventory and to shareholders' equity to convert LIFO inventory to a FIFO basis. FIFO inventory is closer to current cost, so it is a better indicator of cash that can be generated from inventory.
- Off-balance-sheet debt can be recognized on the face of the statement. See Box 20.1.
- Contingent liabilities that can be estimated should be included in the reformulated statements. Contingent liabilities that cannot be estimated should be noted as part of the annotation. Contingent liabilities include liabilities under product, labor, and environmental litigation. In the United States, GAAP requires these liabilities to be put on the balance sheet if the liability is "probable" and the amount of the loss can be "reasonably estimated." Footnote disclosure is otherwise required, unless the possibility of loss is "remote." Inspect the contingent liabilities footnote.
- The risk in derivatives and other financial instruments should be noted. Inspect the financial instruments footnote.

Reformulated Income Statements

The analyst reviews the income statement to assess the ability of the firm to generate operating income to cover net interest payments. Thus the reformulated income statement that distinguishes after-tax operating income from after-tax net financial expense serves debt analysis well. So does the distinction in reformulated statements between core and unusual items for, with a view to future default, the issue is whether future core income will cover future core financial expense.

Reformulated Cash Flow Statements

The reformulated cash flow statement prepared for equity analysis also serves debt analysis. In particular, the reformulation of GAAP cash flow from operations to exclude after-tax net interest identifies (unlevered) cash flow from operations that is available to pay after-tax interest. And the reclassification of investments in financial assets (which GAAP places in the investing section) as financing flows rather than investment flows yields a number for investing cash flows that has integrity, and captures net amounts of bond issuing activity.

Off-balance-sheet financing transactions are arrangements to finance assets and create obligations that do not appear on the balance sheet. Some types of off-balance-sheet financing are:

- Operating leases. Leases that are in substance purchases, called *capital leases*, appear on the balance sheet, with the leased asset as part of property, plant, and equipment and the lease obligation as part of liabilities. Leases that are not in substance a purchase, called *operating leases*, do not appear on the balance sheet; they are summarized in footnotes. However, lessees and lessors have been creative in writing lease agreements to get around the letter of the rules for capitalizing leases. Examine operating leases in the footnotes and assess whether these are effectively an obligation to use an asset for most of its useful life. If so, bring them onto the balance sheet as a capital lease. The lease amount is the present value of the payments under the lease.

- Agreements and commitments can create obligations that should be recognized:

  Third-party agreements: A third party purchases an asset for the firm and the firm agrees to service the third party's debt on the purchase.

  Throughput agreements: A firm agrees to pay for the use of the facilities of another firm.

  Take-or-pay agreements: A firm agrees to pay for goods in the future, regardless of whether it takes delivery.

  Repurchase agreements: A firm sells inventory but agrees to repurchase the inventory at selling price or guarantees a resale price to the customer. Agreements to sell and repurchase debt ("repos") are similar. Prior to its bankruptcy, Lehman Brothers was accused of moving debt off its balance sheet via repos.

- Sales of receivables with recourse. A firm sells its receivables for cash, removing them from the balance sheet, but has an obligation to indemnify the holder of the receivables.

- Unfunded pension liabilities. In some countries (but not the United States) significant pension liabilities may not be on the balance sheet.

- Guarantees of third-party or related-party debt. Watch for guarantees of the debt of nonconsolidated subsidiaries by a parent company.

- **Special-purpose entities,** *off-balance-sheet partnerships*, and *structured finance vehicles*. Firms can create entities in which others have control (so they are not consolidated), to accomplished specific purposes—like the securitization of assets or acquiring assets with off-balance-sheet leases ("synthetic leases"). Although the firm does not have control, it might retain residual risk if these entities run into financial difficulties. The obligations may be in the form of recourse liabilities or put options on the firm's own stock. The Enron affair highlighted the danger of these special-purpose entities, as did banks' holdings of securitized debt and mortgages in *special investment vehicles* (SIVs) during the credit crisis of 2008.

With reformulated financial statements in hand, the ratio analysis can begin. With the two types of maturities in mind—short-term and long-term—ratio analysis groups ratios into two types, short-term *liquidity ratios* and long-term *solvency ratios*. Both sets of ratios are indicators of the ability to repay, but at different maturity dates. The ratio analysis is completed with some of the *operational ratios* that we have already covered.

All three sets of ratios are benchmarked with comparisons to similar firms and with trend analysis over time. The credit analyst looks for deteriorations in the ratios over time and relative to comparison firms.

Short-Term Liquidity Ratios

Short-term creditors—suppliers, short-term paper holders, and long-term lenders of debt that is shortly to mature, for example—are concerned with the firm's ability to have enough cash to repay in the near future. The long-term lender is also interested in short-term liquidity because if the firm cannot survive the short term, there is no long term.

Working capital is current assets minus current liabilities. As *current assets* are those expected to generate cash within one year and *current liabilities* are obligations due to mature within one year, working capital and its components are the focus of liquidity analysis.

The typical balance sheet has five types of current assets:

1. Cash and cash equivalents
2. Short-term investments

3. Receivables

4. Prepaid expenses

5. Inventories

Each item has an expected date for realization into cash. Inventories typically have the longest time to cash as they first have to be sold and converted into a receivable, and then the receivable has to be turned into cash. Short-term investments (to which readily marketable long-term securities can be added in the balance sheet reformulation) may be closer to cash than receivables or prepaid expenses, depending on the maturity of the investments. Under historical cost accounting, the carrying amount for inventories usually understates their cash value, although the lower-of-cost-or-market rule for inventories can give them a market valuation when the firm is in distress.

Three types of current liabilities appear on the typical balance sheet:

1. Trade payables

2. Short-term debt

3. Accrued liabilities

All three are typically close to their cash value.

The balance sheet is a statement of stocks, so it gives the stocks (amounts) of net liquid assets at a point in time. Liquidity flows are in the cash flow statement. Liquidity ratios involve both the balance sheet stocks of cash and near-cash items and flows of cash in the cash flow statement.

Liquidity Stock Measures

$$\text{Current ratio} = \frac{\text{Current assets}}{\text{Current liabilities}}$$

$$\text{Quick (or acid test) ratio} = \frac{\text{Cash} + \text{Short-term investments} + \text{Receivables}}{\text{Current liabilities}}$$

$$\text{Cash ratio} = \frac{\text{Cash} + \text{Short-term investments}}{\text{Current liabilities}}$$

These measures indicate the ability of near-cash assets to pay off the current liabilities. The numerators of these ratios indicate different cash maturities. So, for example, the quick ratio includes only *quick assets* in the numerator by excluding inventories that may take some time to turn into cash (and whose carrying values are not usually their cash values). The cash ratio involves only assets with almost immediate liquidity.

Liquidity Flow Measures

$$\text{Cash flow ratio} = \frac{\text{Cash flow from operations}}{\text{Current liabilities}}$$

$$\text{Defensive interval} = \frac{\text{Cash} + \text{Short-term investments} + \text{Receivables}}{\text{Capital expenditures}} \times 365$$

$$\frac{\text{Cash flow to}}{\text{capital expenditures}} = \frac{\text{Cash flow from operations}}{\text{Capital expenditures}}$$

The first measure indicates how well the cash flow from operations covers the cash needed to settle liabilities in the short term. The second ratio measures the liquidity available to meet capital expenditures without further borrowing. Multiplying by 365 yields the number of days expenditures can be maintained out of near-cash resources. The third measure is free cash flow in ratio form and indicates to what extent capital expenditures can be financed out of cash from operations. Sometimes forecasted expenditures are used in the denominators of the second and third measures.

Long-Term Solvency Ratios

Long-term debtholders watch the firm's immediate liquidity, but they are primarily concerned with its ability to meet its obligations in the more distant future. Focus therefore moves to incorporate the noncurrent sections of the balance sheet in ratios.

Solvency Stock Measures

$$\text{Debt to total assets} = \frac{\text{Total debt (Current + Long-term)}}{\text{Total assets (Liabilities + Total equity)}}$$

$$\text{Debt to equity} = \frac{\text{Total debt}}{\text{Total equity}}$$

$$\text{Long-term debt ratio} = \frac{\text{Long-term debt}}{\text{Long-term debt + Total equity}}$$

The first two ratios capture all debt, the third just long-term debt. The first two differ in the denominator but capture similar characteristics. Net debt can be used in the numerator when financial assets are available to pay off the debt (in this case the denominators of the first and third ratios are reduced by financial assets).

Solvency Flow Measures

$$\frac{\text{Interest coverage}}{\text{(times interest earned)}} = \frac{\text{Operating income}}{\text{Net interest expense}}$$

$$\text{Interest coverage (cash basis)} = \frac{\text{Unlevered cash flow from operations}}{\text{Net cash interest}}$$

$$\text{Fixed-charge coverage} = \frac{\text{Operating income + Fixed charges}}{\text{Fixed charges}}$$

$$\frac{\text{Fixed-charge coverage}}{\text{(cash basis)}} = \frac{\text{Unlevered cash flow from operations + Fixed charges}}{\text{Fixed charges}}$$

$$\text{CFO to debt} = \frac{\text{Unlevered cash flow from operations}}{\text{Total debt}}$$

These ratios are improved (as indicators of the future) by measuring operating income and net interest as core income and expense. The two interest coverage ratios give the number of times operating earnings and cash flow from operations, respectively, cover the interest requirement. The numerators and denominators are from the reformulated income and cash flow statements. Some definitions consider only interest expense, in which case the numerator includes interest income and the denominator excludes it. *Fixed charges* are interest and principal repayments (including those on leases) and preferred dividends, so fixed-charge coverage measures the number of times total debt service is covered. The last ratio measures cash flow relative to total debt repayments to be made, not just the current repayment.

These ratios give not only an indication of solvency but also an indication of a firm's **debt capacity.** Low coverage ratios suggest that a firm has capacity to assume more debt (all else being equal).

Operating Ratios

The ratios just listed pertain directly to liquidity and solvency. But liquidity and solvency are driven in large part by the outcome of operations, so operating ratios are also indicators of debt risk. It is sometimes the case that a firm can be quite profitable in operations and still have short-term liquidity difficulties, but both short-term liquidity and long-term solvency problems are far more likely to be induced by poor operating profitability.

Interest coverage, for example, is just a restatement of the FLEV × SPREAD, and so is driven by financial leverage (FLEV) and the operating spread (SPREAD), that is, the return on net operating assets relative to net borrowing costs. And these measures, in turn, are driven by lower-order drivers. Thus to complete the ratio analysis, analyze profitability and changes in profitability along the lines of earlier parts of the book. And watch for the "red flag" indicators (in Chapter 16) that indicate deterioration. If receivables or inventory turnover increases, for example, liquidity problems could result.

FORECASTING AND CREDIT ANALYSIS

Liquidity, solvency, and operational ratios reveal the current state of the firm. But the credit analyst is concerned with default in the future. Do the ratios predict default? Some of them might be symptoms of financial distress rather than predictors. Discovering that interest coverage is low is important to the analyst. But anticipation of a low interest coverage ahead of time is also important. And so for all ratios. Indeed, once liquidity and coverages have deteriorated, it might be too late.

The analyst thus turns to forecasting. His aim is to produce a credit score that indicates the probability of default.

Prelude to Forecasting: The Interpretive Background

Before forecasting, the analyst must have a good understanding of the conditions under which credit is given to the firm. Such an understanding provides the information necessary for forecasting. It enables the analyst to bring her judgment to supplement quantitative techniques. And it provides perspective to interpret ratios and other financial data. A particular ratio—a current ratio of less than 1.0, for example—might be seen as inadequate for a firm with large inventories and receivables but quite adequate for a firm with no inventories or receivables.

The analyst needs to understand the following points and include salient ones in the annotations to the reformulated statements:

- Know the business. Just as the equity analyst must know the business before attempting to value the equity, so must the credit analyst. Understand the business strategy and understand the drivers of value in the strategy. And understand the risks that the strategy exposes the firm to.
- Appreciate the "moral hazard" problem of debt. The interest of debtholders is not the prime consideration for management. Members of management serve the shareholders (and themselves), not the debtholders. So they can take actions that benefit the shareholders at the expense of debtholders. They can borrow to pay a large dividend to shareholders. They can pursue highly risky strategies with high upside potential and use debt to leverage the upside payoff. If the strategy is successful, shareholders benefit

enormously, but debtholders just get their fixed return. If they fail, debtholders (and shareholders) can lose all.

- Understand the financing strategy. Does the firm have a target leverage ratio? What is the firm's target payout ratio? What sources of financing will the firm rely on? Does the firm hedge interest rate risk? If borrowing across borders, does it hedge currency risk?
- Understand the current financing arrangements. What are the firm's banking relationships? Does it have open lines of credit? When might they expire? What is the current composition of the firm's debt? What debt is secured? What debt has seniority? What are the maturity dates for the debt? What are the restrictions on the firm in its debt agreements?
- Understand the quality of the firm's accounting.
- Understand the auditor's opinion, particularly any qualifications to the opinion.

With this background, the analyst develops forecasts. We cover two forecasting tools here. The first develops credit scores based on predictions from financial ratios. The second brings the pro forma profitability analysis and value-at-risk analysis of earlier chapters to the task of credit analysis.

Ratio Analysis and Credit-Scoring

Figure 20.1 depicts the deterioration of a number of ratios over five years prior to bankruptcy (failure). The graphs are from one of the original studies on bankruptcy prediction by William Beaver in the 1960s, but they apply much the same today. Average ratios for bankrupt firms are compared with those of comparable firms that did not go bankrupt. The ratios for firms going bankrupt are of lower quality than those for nonbankrupt firms, even five years before bankruptcy. And they become significantly worse as bankruptcy approaches. So, benchmarking ratios against those for comparable firms, combined with a trend analysis, does give an indication of future bankruptcy.

Two issues arise in getting default predictions from accounting ratios:

1. Many ratios must be considered, and the analyst needs to summarize the information they provide as a whole. A low interest coverage but a high current ratio may have different implications than a low interest coverage and a low current ratio. A composite credit score needs to be developed.

   A *bond rating* of the sort published by Standard & Poor's and Moody's is a composite score. Standard & Poor's ratings range from AAA (for firms with highest capacity to repay interest and principal) through AA, A, BBB, BB, B, CCC, CC, C to D (for firms actually in default). The ability to repay debt rated BB and below is deemed to have significant uncertainty. Moody's rankings are similar: Aaa, Aa, and A for high-grade debt, then Baa, Ba, B, Caa, Ca, C, and D. These debt ratings are published as an indicator of the required bond yield, and indeed the ratings are highly correlated with yields.

   A bank typically summarizes information about the creditworthiness of a firm in a credit score. This score can be in the form of a number ranging from one to seven or one to nine, or qualitative categories such as "normal acceptable risk," "doubtful," and "nonperforming."

2. Errors in predicting default and the cost of prediction errors have to be considered. The financial ratios of failing and nonfailing firms are different on average but some failing firms can have ratios that are similar to those of healthy firms. A firm going bankrupt could have the same current ratio and interest coverage ratio as one that will survive.

FIGURE 20.1   The Behavior of Selected Financial Statement Ratios over Five Years Prior to Bankruptcy, for Firms That Failed and Comparable Firms That Did not Fail.
Ratios for failed firms (on the dotted line) are of lower quality than those for nonfailed firms (on the solid line), and they deteriorate as bankruptcy approaches.

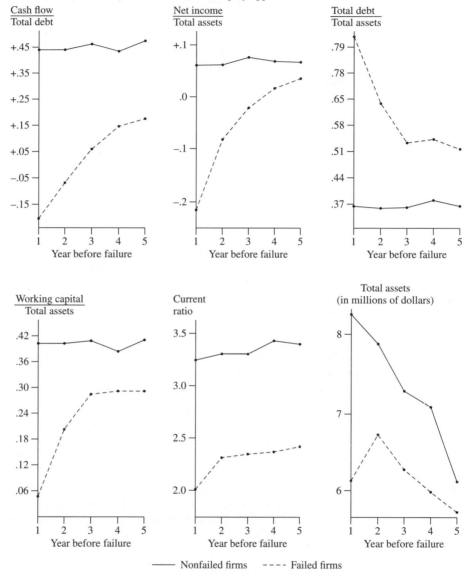

Source: W. H. Beaver, "Financial Ratios as Predictors of Failure," *Journal of Accounting Research,* Supplement, 1966, p. 82.

A bank loan officer might then classify both firms as low default risk, approve loans to both, and generate loan losses for the bank (from the bankrupt firm). Alternatively she might classify them both as having high default risk and deny credit, losing good business for the bank (from the nonbankrupt firm).

The first issue calls for a method of combining ratios into one composite score that indicates the overall creditworthiness of the firm. The second issue calls for a method of trading off the two types of errors that can be made. We deal with each in turn.

Credit Scoring Models

Credit scoring models combine a set of ratios that pertain to default into a credit score. A credit scoring model has the form

$$\text{Credit score} = (w_1 \times \text{Ratio}_1) + (w_2 \times \text{Ratio}_2) + (w_3 \times \text{Ratio}_3) + \cdots + (w_N \times \text{Ratio}_N)$$

That is, the model sums ratios that are weighted by weights w. A variety of statistical techniques can be used to determine the weights, but two common ones are multiple discriminant analysis and logit analysis.

Multiple Discriminant Analysis.   Z-score analysis, pioneered by Edward Altman,[1] utilizes discriminant analysis techniques. The model has been refined over time but the original model, developed in the 1960s, took the form

$$Z\text{-score} = 1.2\left(\frac{\text{Working capital}}{\text{Total assets}}\right) + 1.4\left(\frac{\text{Retained earnings}}{\text{Total assets}}\right)$$

$$+ 3.3\left(\frac{\text{Earnings before interest and taxes}}{\text{Total assets}}\right)$$

$$+ 0.6\left(\frac{\text{Market value of equity}}{\text{Book value of liabilities}}\right) + 1.0\left(\frac{\text{Sales}}{\text{Total assets}}\right)$$

To identify predictors in a model like this, select a sample of firms that went bankrupt in the past and a random sample of firms that did not. Calculate a full set of liquidity, solvency, and operational ratios for these firms. Discriminant analysis, applied to the historical data, then selects those ratios that jointly best discriminate between firms that subsequently went bankrupt and those that did not, and then calculates coefficients on the selected ratios that weight them into a Z-score. The weights are calculated to minimize the differences in Z-scores within bankrupt or nonbankrupt groups but to maximize the differences in scores between the two groups. The Z-score indicates the relative likelihood of a firm not going bankrupt, so a firm with a high score is less likely, a firm with a low score is more likely, and those with intermediate level scores are in a gray area.

The Z-score model is based on firms going bankrupt, but models also can be estimated with default on debt or other conditions of financial distress as the defining event. And the model can be adapted to situations having more than two outcomes. So a model of bond ratings (with several classes) also can be built. Other ratios, such as asset size, interest coverage, the current ratio, and the variability of earnings, have appeared in similar published models.

Logit Analysis.   Logit analysis is based on different statistical assumptions from discriminant analysis and delivers a score between zero and 1 that indicates the probability of default.

[1] E. Altman, "Financial Ratios, Discriminant Analysis, and the Prediction of Corporate Bankruptcy," *Journal of Finance,* September 1968, pp. 589–609.

An early application of logit analysis to bankruptcy prediction by James Ohlson[2] produced the following model:

$$y = -1.32 - 0.407(\text{size}) + 6.03\left(\frac{\text{Total liabilities}}{\text{Total assets}}\right)$$

$$- 1.43\left(\frac{\text{Working capital}}{\text{Total assets}}\right) + 0.0757\left(\frac{\text{Current liabilities}}{\text{Current assets}}\right)$$

$$- 2.37\left(\frac{\text{Net income}}{\text{Total assets}}\right) - 1.83\left(\frac{\text{Working capital flow from operations}}{\text{Total liabilities}}\right)$$

$$+ 0.285\left(\begin{matrix}1 \text{ if net income was negative for the last two years} \\ 0 \text{ if net income was not negative for the last two years}\end{matrix}\right)$$

$$- 1.72\left(\begin{matrix}1 \text{ if total liabilities exceed total assets} \\ 0 \text{ if total liabilities do not exceed total assets}\end{matrix}\right)$$

$$- 0.521\left(\frac{\text{Change in net income}}{\text{Sum of absolute values of current and prior years' net incomes}}\right)$$

Size is measured here as the natural logarithm of total assets divided by the GNP implicit price deflator (with a base of 100 in 1978). Working capital flow is cash flow from operations plus changes in other working capital items. The score from this model is transformed into a probability:

$$\text{Probability of bankrutcy} = \frac{1}{1 + e^{-y}}$$

where e is approximately 2.718282 and y is the score estimated from the ratios above.

The models here serve to indicate the form of credit scoring. The estimates were made quite a while ago, so the analyst should reestimate the models from more recent data. Coefficients will be different and other ratios may be found to be relevant. Nonaccounting information might be included. The models here are unconditional models. Conditional models might be estimated for different conditions, such as industry, country, or macro conditions. Predictors and their coefficients may be different in recessions than in boom times, for example.

It is unrealistic to expect financial ratios to capture all the information that indicates the probability of default. The interpretive background and the annotations to reformulated statements yield other insights, as does the pro forma analysis of the next subsection. So credit analysts use the scores from these types of models to supplement their broader judgment (and as a check on their judgment). The credit scores that combine financial statement scores with other information are typically a ranking from one to seven or one to nine rather than the Z-scores and probabilities estimated here.

Prediction Error Analysis

A bank loan officer who assigns credit scores on a scale of one to nine (say) has to decide at what score he will reject a loan application. Is it three, or is it four or five? A bond rater has to decide what Z-score or probability score indicates significant probability of default

[2] J. A. Ohlson, "Financial Ratios and the Probabilistic Prediction of Bankruptcy," *Journal of Accounting Research*, Spring 1980, pp. 109–131.

in order to assign the firm to a BB or lower rating. Set the cutoff point too high and too many firms are deemed to be high credit risk. Set the cutoff too low and too many firms will be considered safe investments.

Classifying a firm as not likely to default when it actually does default is called a **Type I error.** Classifying a firm as likely to default when it does not default is called a **Type II error.** Both errors have costs. In a Type I error, the bank or bondholder loses in the default. In a Type II error, the bank or bond investor misses out on a good investment. For a bank, the cost of a Type II error may be considerable: It may lose good loans and good customers and business might migrate to banks with better credit models and better error analysis.

Errors are reduced by developing better scoring models. But inevitably these will be gray areas. In his original study, Altman found that firms with Z-scores of less than 1.81 went bankrupt within one year while scores higher than 2.99 always indicated nonbankruptcy. Scores from 1.81 to 2.99 were the gray areas.

Error analysis aims to determine the optimal cutoff for classifying firms. One simple way is to choose a cutoff point that minimizes the total of Type I and Type II errors. This cutoff can be discovered from historical data analysis (preferably on a set of firms that were not used to estimate the credit scoring model), and this historical analysis can be updated through experience. Altman's original analysis found that a Z-score of 2.675 minimized the number of total errors. For Ohlson's logit analysis, a probability of 0.038 gave the optimal cutoff.

This simple method assumes that Type I and Type II errors are equally costly. If this is not so, the bank or the investor must analyze the cost of each type and weight the errors accordingly in setting a cutoff. Many consider a Type I error more costly than a Type II.

Full-Information Forecasting

Credit scoring from ratios uses the limited information in current financial statements. The full information about firms is captured by the pro forma analysis of Chapter 16. This analysis, along with the value-at-risk analysis of the last chapter, can readily be adapted to assess the likelihood of default.

Pro Forma Analysis and Default Prediction

Rather than using current liquidity, solvency, and operational ratios to forecast default, pro forma analysis uses the full information available to the analyst to forecast future liquidity, solvency, and operational ratios that result in default. And pro forma analysis explicitly forecasts the firm's ability to generate cash to meet debt payments.

Scenario 1 in Table 20.1 calculates ratios from the pro formas for PPE, Inc., the firm used in the pro forma analysis of Chapter 16. More ratios could be calculated with more detailed financial statements. The forecasts underlying these pro formas were a sales growth of 5 percent per year, a profit margin (PM) of 7.85 percent, an asset turnover (ATO) of 1.762, and a dividend payout of 40 percent of net income. Under this scenario, the firm is projected to pay down debt from positive free cash flow after dividends by Year 4 and become a holder of net financial assets. Debt to total assets and the debt to equity ratio are thus decreasing and interest and fixed-charge coverages are increasing. The debt is expected to mature at the end of Year 4. But the debt is retired by that date without need of further financing. Default is not anticipated: Scenario 1 is a nondefault scenario. Indeed, the firm is projected to increase its debt capacity.

Scenario 2 gives a different picture. Here sales are expected to decline by 5 percent each year and the profit margins are expected to be only 1 percent. Net operating assets decline with sales but they are not perfectly flexible, so asset turnover decreases. The firm is expected to drop its dividend in Year 1 in anticipation of liquidity problems, but the poor cash flow still leaves a reduced capacity to service the debt. When the debt matures in Year 4, the firm is expected to default. Scenario 2 is a **default scenario.**

TABLE 20.1 **PPE, Inc.: Pro Forma Financial Statements and Default Prediction Under Two Scenarios**

	Year 0	Year 1	Year 2	Year 3	Year 4	Year 5
Scenario 1						
Sales (growth = 5% per year)	124.90	131.15	137.70	144.59	151.82	159.41
Core operating income (PM = 7.85%)	9.80	10.29	10.81	11.35	11.92	12.51
Financial income (expense)	(0.70)	(0.77)	(0.57)	(0.35)	(0.10)	0.18
Net income	9.10	9.52	10.24	11.00	11.82	12.69
Net operating assets (ATO = 1.762)	74.42	78.15	82.05	86.16	90.46	94.99
Net financial assets	(7.70)	(5.71)	(3.47)	(0.97)	1.81	4.91
Common equity	66.72	72.44	78.58	85.19	92.27	99.90
Free cash flow	5.28	6.57	6.90	7.25	7.61	7.99
Dividend	5.28	3.81	4.10	4.40	4.73	5.08
Cash available for debt service	0.0	2.76	2.80	2.85	2.88	2.91
Debt to total assets (%)	10.3	7.3	4.3	1.1	−2.0	−5.2
Debt to equity (%)	11.5	7.9	4.4	1.1	−2.0	−4.9
Interest coverage[*]	14.0	13.4	19.0	32.4	19.2	—
Fixed-charge coverage[†]	—	4.7	4.9	5.0	5.1	—
RNOA (%)	14.0	13.8	13.8	13.8	13.8	13.8
ROCE (%)	14.5	14.3	14.1	14.0	13.9	13.8
Debt service requirement[‡]	0.0	0.0	0.0	0.0	0.0	0.0
Scenario 2						
Sales (decline = 5% per year)	124.90	118.66	112.72	107.09	101.73	96.65
Core operating income (PM = 1%)	9.80	1.19	1.13	1.07	1.02	0.97
Financial income (expense)	(0.70)	(0.77)	(0.69)	(0.60)	(0.52)	(0.42)
Net income	9.10	0.42	0.44	0.47	0.50	0.55
Net operating assets	74.42	74.00	73.60	73.20	72.80	72.40
Net financial assets	(7.70)	(6.86)	(6.02)	(5.15)	(4.25)	Default
Common equity	66.72	67.14	67.58	68.05	68.55	Default
Free cash flow	5.28	1.61	1.53	1.47	1.42	1.37
Dividend	5.28	0.0	0.0	0.0	0.0	0.0
Cash available for debt service	0.0	1.61	1.53	1.47	1.42	1.37
Debt to total assets (%)	10.3	9.3	8.2	7.0	5.8	
Debt to equity (%)	11.5	10.2	8.9	7.6	6.2	
Interest coverage[*]	14.0	1.5	1.6	1.8	2.0	
Fixed-charge coverage[†]	—	1.7	1.7	1.7	1.7	
RNOA (%)	14.0	1.6	1.5	1.5	1.4	1.3
ROCE (%)	14.5	0.6	0.7	0.9		
Debt service requirement[‡]	0.0	0.0	0.0	0.0	4.25	Default

[*]Interest coverage = Operating income/Financial expense.
[†]Fixed-charge coverage = (Operating income + Debt service)/Debt service.
[‡]The debt is zero-coupon, thus there are no interest payments.

Default occurs when *cash available for debt service* is less than the *debt service requirement*:

$$\text{Cash available for debt service} = \text{Free cash flow} - \text{Net dividends}$$

$$= \text{OI} - \Delta\text{NOA} - \text{Net dividends}$$

$$\text{Debt service requirement} = \text{Required interest and preferred dividend payments}$$
$$+ \text{Required net principal payments} + \text{Lease payments}$$

In scenario 2, PPE, Inc., is forecasted to have $1.42 million available for debt service in Year 4 when the debt matures. The debt service requirement is $4.25 million. Thus it is anticipated to default. Note that cash available for debt service is after net dividends, that is, dividends net of new equity financing. So default can be avoided if cash can be raised from equity issues. Similarly, the debt service requirement is for net principal repayments (debt repayments minus new debt issued). So default can be avoided if cash can be raised from issuing new debt (which debt restructuring effectively involves).

Pro forma analysis for equity valuation focuses on forecasting operating income and net operating assets for the residual income calculation. Pro forma analysis for credit evaluation focuses on forecasting cash available for debt service. Accordingly, the "bottom line" in the pro formas in Table 20.1 is the cash available for debt service line. In terms of the forecasting template in Chapter 16, the pro forma analysis for equities is completed at Step 6, where residual income can be calculated. The pro forma analysis for debt is completed at Step 9, where cash available for debt service can be calculated.

Value-at-Risk Profiles and the Probability of Default

Scenario 2 is a default scenario, but it is just one default scenario: It forecasts a particular sales growth, profit margin, and so on. It also forecasts that the dividend would be dropped (to increase cash available for debt service) and that no cash would be raised from new debt to reduce the debt service requirement. Other operating and financing scenarios are possible and the analyst is interested in the full set of default scenarios.

The value-at-risk analysis of the last chapter is a method for examining the full set of likely scenarios. The analysis was applied to equities but is also applicable to debt: Under what set of scenarios is the value of debt at risk?

The equity analysis profiles the possible variation in residual income. The debt analysis profiles the possible variation in cash available for debt service. Follow these steps:

1. Generate profiles of cash available for debt service for a full set of scenarios from pro forma analysis.
2. Establish the debt service requirement.
3. Identify the *default point* where cash available for debt service is below the debt service requirement, and so identify the default scenarios.
4. Assess the probability of the set of default scenarios occurring.

As debt has to be serviced each year, a profile should be generated for each year ahead, with particular attention to years where large amounts of debt are to mature.

A profile of cash available for debt service from Step 1 is depicted in Figure 20.2. The default scenarios are to the left of the point where cash available for debt service is less than the required debt service. To the left of this default point, value is lost to the debtholder; to the right of the default point, debt value is preserved.

The probability of default is the sum of the probabilities of the defaulting scenarios (about 3.5 percent in the figure). Stated formally, the default probability is

Probability of default = Pr {Cash available for debt service < Debt service requirement}

where Pr is probability. This probability is a measure of "distance from default." It is the basis for setting the price of credit (and the cost of debt capital for the firm).

FIGURE 20.2   Value-at-Risk Profile for Debt and the Identification of Default Scenarios.
The profile plots cash available for debt service under alternative scenarios and the probability of
each outcome. The default point—where cash available for debt service is less than the debt service
requirement—distinguishes defaulting scenarios from nondefaulting scenarios. The probability of
default is the total probability of defaulting scenarios.

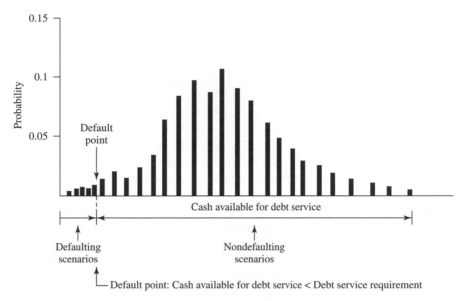

This metric is similar to the value-at-risk (VaR) metric that is commonly used to assess
the market (price) risk of a portfolio of financial assets.[3] The formal definition of VaR is
given by

$$\text{Prespecified probability} = \Pr\{\Delta P_t \le \text{VaR}\}$$

Here ΔP_t is the change in market value of a financial asset over a period t. So VaR is an
amount such that, for a prespecified probability, losses equal to or larger than the VaR
occur. A hedge fund, for example, might assess that it will lose 50 percent of the value of its
fund in one month with a probability of 0.02 percent. It might discover this from historical
simulation of price changes for its portfolio.

Similarly, a bank might assess, for a stated probability, how much of its loan portfolio it
will lose over a year. To do this it might refer to its historical experience in lending, just like
the hedge fund does. Or it might produce the value-at-risk profiles for its current portfolio
which employ fundamental analysis. And a banking syndicate that wishes to sell its loans
to a pension fund might use the profiles to price the sale.

Required Return, Expected Return, and Active Debt Investing

Credit scoring, pro forma default prediction, and value-at-risk profiling are methods the analyst uses to assess default probabilities and thus the required return for investing in debt.
If bond prices set in the market are efficient, they will be based on the required return for
the risk taken. If so, the **yield-to-maturity**—the rate that discounts the expected (coupon
and maturity) cash flows to the market price—will be equal to the required return.

The credit analyst may have another goal in mind, however: She determines default risk
with the view to challenging the market price. She does so by challenging the yield-to-maturity

---

[3] VaR metrics were developed and popularized by J.P. Morgan in 1994, though there were also
antecedents. See J. P. Morgan/Reuters, "Risk Metrics—Technical Document," 4th ed., 1996.

implicit in the market price. The yield-to-maturity is the expected return to buying a bond at the market price. If that expected return is different from the return required for the risk, she deems the bond to be mispriced. She has become an active, fundamental investor. She is engaging in **bond arbitrage.**

ACTIVE BOND INVESTING

With the large amount of sovereign, corporate, and personal debt in the world, a large sector of professional investors is involved with debt investments or **fixed-income investing.** Much of this is passive investing for money-market funds and the like. Some involves **securitization** of different types of debt into packages, which are then sold and traded. But some involves active debt management, sometimes called **debt arbitrage.**

Debt arbitrage is of two types. The most common is technical arbitrage where traders detect relative mispricing between debt instruments that should be priced efficiently in relation to each other according to a pricing formula. So a bond arbitrageur might detect that a 30-year government bond price is out of line with the 10-year bond price according to a model of the yield curve. Or the spread between a BBB-rated corporate bond and an A-rated bond deviates from normal. Or the price of a credit default swap differs too much from the price of the underlying debt. These differences in prices are usually short-lived, so this is the domain of day traders.

Fundamental arbitrage, in contrast, digs deeper into the fundamental information for bond pricing and carries out the type of analysis in this chapter. Fundamental bond arbitrage asks: Is the bond price justified by the fundamentals?

The answer to the question is supplied in much the same way as active investing for equities. First, understand the expected return implicit in the market price. This is so much easier than for equities, for it is simply the internal rate of return that discounts the cash flows from the bond to the current market price; that is, it is the current market yield on the bond. Then the fundamentalist asks: Is this yield sufficient to compensate me for the credit risk I see from my credit analysis? Like equities, he might engage in relative investing or pairs trading by investigating the relative bond prices of firms that are deemed to have the same default risk. Are they out of line?

LIQUIDITY PLANNING AND FINANCIAL STRATEGY

Just as the pro forma analysis of operating profitability can be used to formulate business strategy, so can the pro forma analysis here be used to formulate financial strategy.

Financial planning is the task of the corporate treasurer. Her task is to ensure that the debt and equity financing is in place to support the firm's operational strategy. With targets for the debt-to-equity mix and dividends that are set by management, she plans the financing under the most likely scenario. And she plans, contingently, for scenarios that vary from the likely scenario. How will a surplus of cash under an optimistic operational scenario be applied? To a stock repurchase? To a purchase of bonds? And how will a cash deficiency be handled under a pessimistic scenario?

Planning for pessimistic scenarios sets a **default strategy.** Default planning is part of scenario planning that we introduced in the last chapter. Scenario 2 in the PPE, Inc. example embeds a default strategy: Drop the dividend to generate more cash for debt service. Other strategies (that generate other scenarios to deal with default) are

- Modify operations to reduce operational risk that generates default risk.
- Issue equity.

- Issue or roll over debt; renegotiate borrowing terms.
- Establish an open line of credit.
- Sell off assets.
- Sell off the whole firm (in an acquisition).
- Hedge risks.

Some strategies, such as issuing new debt or equity or rolling over a line of credit, might not be feasible in some scenarios.

Each strategy has a different set of default scenarios and a different value-at-risk profile. And each profile yields a different probability of default and thus a different borrowing cost. The benefit of lowering the cost of capital by reducing the probability of default is traded off against the cost of lowering the probability. Open lines of credit require fees. Hedging is costly. Do the benefits outweigh the costs?

Two principles guide this tradeoff:

1. Strategy indifference. In well-functioning capital markets the arrangements to avoid default might be priced to equal the benefits from avoidance. So the treasurer is indifferent. She might hedge default risk with a financial instrument, but the cost of that hedge will reflect the probability of default and the cost of the firm's debt.
2. Shareholder indifference. Shareholders might be able to hedge themselves against the consequences of default in financial markets and so are indifferent to the firm doing it for them.

The Web Connection

Find the following on the Web page for this chapter:

- Additional methods for bankruptcy prediction that use option pricing techniques and exploit information in equity prices.
- A review of value-at-risk metrics.
- More discussion of hidden off-balance sheet debt.

- A pointer to special-purpose entities and the dangers they pose.
- References that give updated coefficients for *Z*-score and logit bankruptcy scoring models.
- Look at the Readers' Corner.

Summary

This chapter has shown how the analysis of financial statements and the development of pro forma financial statements aid in determining the creditworthiness of a firm.

The risk of default is the primary concern in the analysis of debt. To gain an appreciation of this risk, the credit analyst, like the equity analyst, is familiar with the business and its operations. Like the equity analyst, she understands the risk in the operations. She understands the contracts between the debtholders and the firm. And she understands how financial statements and pro forma analysis of financial statements can help her in evaluating credit risk.

This chapter has laid out an analysis of financial statements for credit evaluation. It has identified a number of liquidity and solvency ratios and has shown how these ratios can be combined to yield credit ratings and to indicate the probability of default.

The pro forma analysis for equities has been adapted to credit analysis, this time with the objective of forecasting cash available for debt service. That analysis generates a value-at-risk profile for debt that depicts cash available for debt service under alternative scenarios and identifies default scenarios. The chapter also shows how these profiles are used in financial strategy analysis and default planning. As the pro forma analysis tools are the same as those for equity analysis, the chapter unifies equity and credit analysis.

Key Concepts

bond arbitrage is active investing that attempts to discover mispriced bonds. *696*

collateral refers to assets that can be repossessed if a debtor defaults. *682*

credit analysis or **default analysis** analyzes information to determine the likelihood of a borrower defaulting on debt. *682*

debt arbitrage is the attempt to find abnormal returns by investing (long and short) in debt. *696*

debt capacity is a firm's ability to borrow. *687*

default is a failure to make timely payments on debt or other violation of a debt agreement. *681*

default premium is the price of debt in excess of the risk-free rate to compensate for **default risk.** *680*

default risk or **credit risk** is the risk that a debtor will **default.** *680*

default scenario is a forecast under which a firm defaults. *692*

default strategy or **default planning** is a strategy to deal with default. *696*

fixed-income investing is investing in debt. *696*

off-balance-sheet financing is financing that creates an obligation that is not shown on a balance sheet. *684*

price of credit is the lending rate charged by a creditor, the creditor's required return (and the borrower's borrowing rate). *681*

securitization is the process whereby debt is put into packages which are then sold and traded. *696*

special-purpose entity is an entity (often a partnership) set up off-balance-sheet to accomplish a specific task, but not controlled by the firm. *684*

Type I default prediction error is classifying as not likely to default a firm which does default. *692*

Type II default prediction error is classifying as likely to default a firm which does not default. *692*

yield-to-maturity is the rate that discounts the expected (coupon and maturity) cash flows of a bond to its market price. *695*

The Analyst's Toolkit

Analysis Tools	Page	Key Measures	Page	Acronyms to Remember	
Reformulation of financial statements for credit analysis	682	Bond ratings	688	ATO	asset turnover
		Debt service requirement	693	CFO	cash from operations
		Credit score	688	FLEV	financial leverage
Z-score (discriminant analysis) credit scoring model	690	Cash available for debt service	693	GAAP	generally accepted accounting principles
Logit default probability scoring model	690	Default point	693		
		Default probability scores	690	NOA	net operating assets
Error analysis for default predictions	691	Ratios	684	OI	operating income
		Liquidity ratios	684	PM	profit margin
Pro forma analysis of default scenarios	692	Current ratio	685	Pr	probability
		Quick ratio	685	RNOA	return on net operating assets
Value-at-risk analysis for debt	694	Cash ratio	685		
Active bond investing	696	Cash flow ratio	685	ROCE	return on common equity
Financial strategy analysis	696	Defensive interval	685	SEC	Securities and Exchange Commission
Default planning	696	Cash flow to capital expenditures	685	SPREAD	operating spread
		Solvency ratios	686		

(continued)

The Analyst's Toolkit (*concluded*)

Analysis Tools	Page	Key Measures	Page	Acronyms to Remember
		Debt to total assets	686	
		Debt to equity	686	
		Long-term debt ratio	686	
		Interest coverage	686	
		Interest coverage (cash basis)	686	
		Fixed-charge coverage	686	
		Fixed-charge coverage (cash basis)	686	
		CFO to debt	686	
		Z-score	690	

Concept Questions

C20.1. Explain what a default premium is.

C20.2. What is the objective in reformulating financial statements for credit analysis? How does the reformulation for credit analysis differ from that for equity analysis?

C20.3. Describe off-balance-sheet financing.

C20.4. What is the "moral-hazard" problem with business debt?

C20.5. Distinguish a Type I error in predicting default from a Type II error.

C20.6. What is a default point?

C20.7. How does pro forma analysis of financial statements help in credit analysis?

C20.8. Why might a deferred tax liability be considered not a liability for credit scoring?

C20.9. What is a default strategy?

C20.10. Explain the danger posed by special-purpose entities.

Exercises

Drill Exercises

E20.1. Credit Scoring: A Decline in Credit Quality? (Medium)

The following numbers are extracted from the financial statements for a firm for 2011 and 2012. Amounts are in millions of dollars.

	2011	2012
Sales	4,238	3,276
Earnings before interest and taxes	154	(423)
Current assets	1,387	976
Current liabilities	1,292	1,390
Total assets	3,245	3,098
Book value of shareholders' equity	1,765	1,388
Retained earnings	865	488

At the end of 2011, the firm's 80 million shares traded at $25 each, but by the end of 2012 they traded at $15. Commentators blamed the drop on an increase in the risk of bankruptcy. Conduct a credit scoring analysis that indicates how much the likelihood of bankruptcy increased over the year.

E20.2. Pro Forma Analysis and Default Points (Medium)

A firm has the following balance sheet and income statement (in millions of dollars):

Balance Sheet	
Operating cash	4
Receivables	29
Inventories	138
Plant and equipment	942
	1,113
Operating liabilities	288
Long-term debt (8%)	695
	983
Stockholders' equity	130
	1,113

Income Statement	
Revenues	908
Operating expenses	817
Operating income	91
Interest expense	55
Income before tax	36
Income taxes	13
Income after tax	23

The long-term debt is 8 percent coupon debt maturing in five years. The statutory tax rate is 38 percent. Prepare pro forma financial statements for the next five years under the two following scenarios. Also forecast cash available for debt service and the debt service requirement under both scenarios. The firm pays no dividends.

a. Sales are expected to grow at 4 percent per year, with the current operating profit margin being maintained and with an asset turnover of 1.14.

b. Sales are expected to decline by 4 percent per year and operating profit margins are expected to decline to 2 percent. With some assets inflexible, asset turnovers are expected to decline to 0.98.

Does either of these two scenarios forecast default on the debt?

E20.3. **Yield-to-Maturity and Required Bond Returns (Easy)**

After analyzing the default risk for a five-year bond with a maturity value of $1,000 and an 8 percent annual coupon, an analyst estimates the required return for the bond at 7 percent per year. The bond has just been issued at a price of $1,000.

  a. What is the value of the bond at a 7 percent required return?
  b. What is the yield-to-maturity with a market price of $1,000?
  c. What is the expected return of buying the bond at a price of $1,000?
  d. Does the analyst think that the bond is appropriately priced by the bond market?

Applications

E20.4. ***Z*-Scoring (Easy)**

Below are ratios for some of the firms that have appeared in this book, for their 1998 fiscal year.

Firm	Working Capital / Total Assets	Retained Earnings / Total Assets	Earnings Before Interest and Taxes / Total Assets	Market Value of Equity / Book Value of Liabilities	Sales / Total Assets
Coca-Cola	−0.12	1.05	0.29	15.4	0.98
Nike	0.34	0.58	0.15	9.0	1.67
Reebok	0.43	0.66	0.06	0.7	1.85
Hewlett-Packard	0.24	0.50	0.13	3.6	1.40
Dell, Inc.	0.38	0.09	0.31	27.9	2.65
Gateway Computer	0.27	0.34	0.19	5.2	2.59
Microsoft	0.45	0.34	0.32	46.7	0.65

  a. Calculate *Z*-scores from these ratios.
  b. Explain why Nike has a different *Z*-score from Reebok.
  c. What reservations do you have about the *Z*-score as an indicator of creditworthiness?

E20.5. **Tracking Credit Risk Measures: Toys "R" Us (Hard)**

Toys "R" Us, Inc., is the world's largest toy retailer, with sales of nearly $12 billion in 1999. It has been challenged in recent years, particularly in e-commerce, losing market share from 20.2 percent in 1993 to 16.8 percent in 1999. The firm's stock price was down to $11 in early 2000 from a high of $36 in 1998. Management had begun, however, to take strategic initiatives to return the firm to the leading position it once enjoyed.

The firm's balance sheets and income statements for fiscal years ending January of 1997 to 2000 are given in Exhibit 20.1, along with share price and shares outstanding information. Track the profitability of the firm over the years and also its creditworthiness, as indicated by relevent ratios and *Z*-scores.

EXHIBIT 20.1
Toys "R" Us, Inc.

Balance Sheets
(in millions of dollars)

	1997	1998	1999	2000
Assets				
Cash	$ 761	$ 214	$ 410	$ 584
Accounts and other receivables	142	175	204	182
Merchandise inventories	2,215	2,464	1,902	2,027
Prepaid expenses and other current assets	42	51	81	80
Total current assets	3,160	2,904	2,597	2,873
Net property, plant, and equipment	4,047	4,212	4,226	4,455
Goodwill	365	356	347	374
Deposits and other assets	451	491	729	651
Total assets	8,023	7,963	7,899	8,353
Liabilities				
Short-term borrowings	304	134	156	278
Accounts payable	1,346	1,280	1,415	1,617
Accrued expenses and other current liabilities	720	680	696	836
Income taxes payable	171	231	224	107
Total current liabilities	2,541	2,325	2,491	2,838
Deferred income taxes	222	219	333	362
Long-term debt	909	851	1,222	1,230
Other liabilities	160	140	229	243
Total liabilities	3,832	3,535	4,275	4,673
Shareholders' Equity				
Common stock	30	30	30	30
Additional paid-in capital	489	467	459	453
Retained earnings	4,120	4,610	4,478	4,757
Foreign currency translation adjustments	(60)	(122)	(100)	(137)
Treasury	(388)	(557)	(1,243)	(1,423)
Shareholders' equity	4,191	4,428	3,624	3,680
Total liabilities and equity	$8,023	$ 7,963	$ 7,899	$ 8,353
Share price	$ 22	$ 27	$ 17	$ 11
Shares outstanding (millions)	288	282	251	240

Income Statements
(in millions of dollars)

	1997	1998	1999	2000
Net sales	$9,932	$11,038	$11,170	$11,862
Cost of sales	6,892	7,710	8,191	8,321
Gross profit	3,040	3,328	2,979	3,541
Selling, advertising, general, and administrative expenses	2,020	2,231	2,443	2,743
Depreciation, amortization, and asset write-offs	206	253	255	278
Restructuring and other charges	60	0	294	0
Total operating expenses	2,286	2,484	2,992	3,021
Operating (loss) income	754	844	(13)	520
Interest expense	98	85	102	91
Interest and other income	(17)	(13)	(9)	(11)
Earnings before income taxes	673	772	(106)	440
Income taxes	246	282	26	161
Net earnings (loss)	$ 427	$ 490	$ (132)	$ 279

E20.6. **Credit Scoring for a Firm with a Ratings Downgrade:
Maytag Corporation (Medium)**

Maytag Corporation is the established manufacturer of washing machines, dryers, dishwashers, and other home appliances—including the venerable Hoover vacuum cleaner. But in 2004 and 2005, the firm faced deteriorating profitability. Competitors had moved manufacturing to low-cost countries while Maytag persisted with its high labor cost manufacturing in the United States.

The following shows how Maytag's sales stalled over the period 2000–2004, with a negative effect on income.

	2004	2003	2002	2001	2000
	(in thousands, except per share data)				
Net sales	$4,721,538	$4,791,866	$4,666,031	$4,185,051	$3,891,500
Gross profit	660,219	859,531	1,004,602	864,842	985,481
Percent of sales	14.0%	17.9%	21.5%	20.7%	25.3%
Operating income	$ 40,348	$228,293	$359,495	$289,152	$439,715
Percent of sales	0.9%	4.8%	7.7%	6.9%	11.3%
Income (loss) from continuing operations	$ (9,345)	$114,378	$191,401	$162,367	$216,367
Percent of sales	−0.2%	2.4%	4.1%	3.9%	5.6%

In April 2005, the firm's bonds were downgraded to junk status by all three major bond rating agencies. Maytag's financial statements for 2004 are on the Web page for Chapter 16. If you worked Minicase M16.3, you will have reformulated these statements.

a. What aspects of the financial statements tell you about the declining credit quality from 2003 to 2004?

b. What scores might you develop from these statements that would indicate the declining credit quality?

Real World Connection

Exercise E6.15 and Minicase M16.3 also deal with Maytag.

Minicase

M20.1

Analysis of Default Risk: Fruit of the Loom

Fruit of the Loom Ltd. fared poorly from 1997 to 1999. Between April 1997 and October 1999, its stock price dropped from $38 to $3, a 92 percent loss in market value.

Fruit of the Loom manufactures men's and boys' underwear. It had an estimated 32 percent share of the U.S. market in 1999, second only to the Sara Lee Corporation's Hanes brand, which holds a 37 percent share. The firm has had a checkered history. It was controlled by a financier, William Farley, who took the firm through a leveraged transaction in the mid-1980s and began considerable cost cutting. It was one of those "small-town America" companies where conflicts between management and labor arose with the cost cutting associated with leveraging and reorganization and with the shipping of production overseas to countries with cheaper labor. Remember the movie *Other People's Money?*

With the cost cutting and dispersion of production came quality control problems and difficulty managing inventories. Financial difficulties in other apparel holdings forced Farley to reduce his stake in Fruit of the Loom and, analysts claimed, distracted him from the business. In late summer 1999, Farley gave up control to Dennis Bookshester, an outside director and a veteran of the retail trade, who found the firm's computer and control systems were in a mess. Some numbers on the firm are shown in Table 20.2.

The problems, most analysts claimed, were fixable. Product market share had declined slightly but was still at a respectable 32 percent. The market was pricing these sales at a low multiple of 0.11. The infrastructure from the cost-cutting program was still in place. Many of the production and inventory coordination problems could be fixed with better computer systems, and computer consultants were working to do so.

In the fall of 1999, some analysts were forecasting that the firm would break even for the rest of 1999 and were forecasting an EPS of $0.79 for the year ending December 31, 2000. Subject to qualifications about the firm's ability to get its systems under control, these analysts were also forecasting continuing profitability in the years after 2000. But other analysts warned that the firm might be heading for bankruptcy.

For the nine months ending October 2, 1999, the firm reported a loss of $253.2 million against a profit of $146.9 million for the same period of the previous year. Exhibit 20.2 presents the firm's financial statements covering the first nine months of 1999.

TABLE 20.2
Fruit of the Loom Ltd.

	1995	1996	1997	1998	1999
Revenues	2,403	2,447	2,140	2,170	2,045
Ebit	50.4	325.3	−283.1	234.9	102.3
Net income	−227.3	151.2	−487.6	135.9	28.1
Dividends	0	0	0	0	0
EPS	−300	1.98	−6.55	1.88	0.39
Net profit margin (%)	−9.5	6.2	−22.8	6.3	1.4
Book value per share	11.78	13.90	5.87	7.61	6.82
P/E ratio	—	19.1	—	73	7.7
P/B ratio	2.11	2.70	4.41	1.86	0.44
Price-to-sales ratio	0.77	1.19	0.86	0.46	0.11

1999 numbers are based on 12 months to June 30, 1999.
Shares outstanding: 66.923 million.

Figures in millions of dollars, except as per-share numbers and ratios.

EXHIBIT 20.2

FRUIT OF THE LOOM LTD.
Condensed Consolidated Balance Sheet
(in thousands of dollars)

	October 2, 1999	January 2, 1999
Assets		
Current assets		
Cash and cash equivalents (including restricted cash)	$ 37,000	$ 1,400
Notes and accounts receivable (less allowance for possible losses of $10,800 and $12,000, respectively)	80,200	109,700
Inventories		
Finished goods	645,200	500,700
Work in progress	135,800	183,100
Materials and supplies	52,500	58,200
Total inventories	833,500	742,000
Due from receivable financing subsidiary	26,800	—
Other	45,400	41,100
Total current assets	1,022,900	894,200
Property, plant, and equipment	1,157,200	1,192,100
Less accumulated depreciation	745,900	758,200
Net property, plant, and equipment	411,300	433,900
Other assets		
Goodwill (less accumulated amortization of $356,200 and $336,200, respectively)	666,300	686,300
Deferred income taxes	36,700	36,700
Other	146,500	238,700
Total other assets	849,500	961,700
	$2,283,700	$2,289,800
Liabilities and Stockholders' Equity		
Current liabilities		
Current maturities of long-term debt	$ 650,200	$ 270,500
Trade accounts payable	87,300	119,700
Other accounts payable and accrued expenses	299,200	226,700
Total current liabilities	1,036,700	616,900
Noncurrent liabilities		
Long-term debt	682,200	856,600
Notes and accounts payable—affiliates	438,600	—
Other	266,000	267,400
Total noncurrent liabilities	1,386,000	1,124,000
Preferred stock	71,70	—
Common stockholders' equity (deficiency)[1]	(211,500)	548,900
	$2,283,700	$2,289,800

[1]Common stockholders' equity at October 2, 1999, includes retained earnings of $20,700 thousand compared to retained earnings of $276,600 thousand at January 2, 1999.

(continued)

EXHIBIT 20.2
(*continued*)

Condensed Consolidated Statement of Operations (Unaudited)
(in thousands of dollars)

	Nine Months Ended	
	Oct. 2, 1999	**Sept. 26, 1999**
Net sales		
Unrelated parties	$1,508,400	$1,678,900
Affiliates	275,000	—
	1,783,400	1,678,900
Cost of sales		
Unrelated parties	1,253,900	1,145,500
Affiliates	355,400	—
	1,609,300	1,145,500
Gross earnings (loss)	174,100	533,400
Selling, general, and administrative expenses	315,400	281,100
Goodwill amortization	19,900	19,900
Operating earnings (loss)	(161,200)	232,400
Interest expense	(72,700)	(74,600)
Other expense—net	(18,100)	(3,100)
Earnings (loss) before income tax provision	(252,000)	154,700
Income tax provision	1,200	7,800
Net earnings (loss)	$ (253,200)	$ 146,900

(*continued*)

A. Stock screeners would say that this stock has all the features of a buy: low P/E, low P/B, and low price-to-sales ratio. How comfortable would you be with issuing a buy recommendation on this stock at a price of $3 per share? What other information would you like to see to make you more secure in your recommendation?

B. Carry out an analysis of financial statement ratios that indicate the likelihood of bankruptcy in October 1999.

C. Calculate a Z-score using the Z-score model in this chapter. Annualize ratios based on nine months for the calculation. How did the firm's Z-score change between January and October 1999?

Note: Fruit of the Loom filed for Chapter 11 bankruptcy protection in December 1999. Warren Buffett subsequently bought the firm out of bankruptcy.

EXHIBIT 20.2
(*concluded*)

Condensed Consolidated Statement of Cash Flows (Unaudited)
(in thousands of dollars)

	Nine Months Ended	
	Oct. 2, 1999	Sept. 26, 1999
Cash flows from operating activities		
Net earnings (loss)	$(253,200)	$ 146,900
Adjustments to reconcile to net cash provided by (used for) operating activities:		
Depreciation and amortization	90,200	84,900
Deferred income tax provision	—	(4,900)
Increase in working capital	(117,000)	(189,100)
Other—net	(24,700)	(13,600)
Net cash provided by (used for) operating activities	(304,700)	24,200
Cash flows from investing activities		
Capital expenditures	(28,000)	(25,000)
Proceeds from asset sales	20,500	68,200
Payment on Acme Boot debt guarantee	—	(60,800)
Other—net	(19,600)	(4,100)
Net cash used for investing activities	(27,100)	(21,700)
Cash flows from financing activities		
Proceeds from issuance of long-term debt	240,200	—
Proceeds under line-of-credit agreements	676,800	754,300
Payments under line-of-credit agreements	(486,800)	(643,400)
Principal payments on long-term debt and capital leases	(236,400)	(122,200)
Increase in affiliate notes and accounts payable	174,700	—
Preferred stock dividends	(1,100)	—
Common stock issued	—	6,800
Common stock repurchased	—	(3,000)
Net cash provided by (used for) financing activities	367,400	(7,500)
Net increase (decrease) in cash and cash equivalents (including restricted cash)	35,600	(5,000)
Cash and cash equivalents (including restricted cash) at beginning of period	1,400	16,100
Cash and cash equivalents (including restricted cash) at end of period	$ 37,000	$ 11,100

Appendix

A Summary of Formulas

CHAPTER 1

CHAPTER 2

CHAPTER 3

$$\text{Unlevered price/sales} = \frac{\text{Market value of equity} + \text{Net debt}}{\text{Sales}}$$

Page 79

$$\text{Unlevered price/ebit} = \frac{\text{Market value of equity} + \text{Net debt}}{\text{ebit}}$$

Page 79

$$\text{Unlevered price/ebitda} = \frac{\text{Market value of equity} + \text{Net debt}}{\text{ebitda}}$$

Page 79

$$\text{Enterprise P/B} = \frac{\text{Market value of equity} + \text{Net debt}}{\text{Book value of equity} + \text{Net debt}}$$

Page 79

$$\text{Trailing P/E} = \frac{\text{Price per share}}{\text{Most recent annual EPS}}$$

Page 79

$$\text{Rolling P/E} = \frac{\text{Price per share}}{\text{Sum of EPS for most recent four quarters}}$$

Page 79

$$\text{Forward or leading P/E} = \frac{\text{Price per share}}{\text{Forecast of next year's EPS}}$$

Page 79

$$\text{Dividend-adjusted P/E} = \frac{\text{Price per share} + \text{Annual DPS}}{\text{EPS}}$$

Page 79

Value of a bond = Present value of expected cash flows

$$V_0^D = \frac{CF_1}{\rho_D} + \frac{CF_2}{\rho_D^2} + \frac{CF_3}{\rho_D^3} + \frac{CF_4}{\rho_D^4} + \cdots + \frac{CF_T}{\rho_D^T}$$

Page 90

(ρ_D is 1 + Required return for the bond)

Value of a project = Present value of expected cash flows

$$V_0^P = \frac{CF_1}{\rho_P} + \frac{CF_2}{\rho_P^2} + \frac{CF_3}{\rho_P^3} + \frac{CF_4}{\rho_P^4} + \cdots + \frac{CF_T}{\rho_P^T}$$

Page 90

(ρ_P is 1 + Hurdle rate for the project)

CHAPTER 4

Value of equity = Present value of expected dividends

$$V_0^E = \frac{d_1}{\rho_E} + \frac{d_2}{\rho_E^2} + \frac{d_3}{\rho_E^3} + \frac{d_4}{\rho_E^4} + \cdots$$

Page 112

(ρ_E is 1 + Required return for the equity)

Value of equity = Present value of expected dividends + Present value of expected terminal price

$$V_0^E = \frac{d_1}{\rho_E} + \frac{d_2}{\rho_E^2} + \frac{d_3}{\rho_E^3} + \cdots + \frac{d_T}{\rho_E^T} + \frac{P_T}{\rho_E^T}$$

Page 112

Perpetuity dividend model:

$$V_0^E = \frac{d_1}{\rho_E} + \frac{d_2}{\rho_E^2} + \frac{d_3}{\rho_E^3} + \cdots + \frac{d_T}{\rho_E^T} + \left(\frac{d_{T+1}}{\rho_E - 1} \right) \Big/ \rho_E^T \qquad \text{Page 112}$$

Dividend growth model:

$$V_0^E = \frac{d_1}{\rho_E} + \frac{d_2}{\rho_E^2} + \frac{d_3}{\rho_E^3} + \cdots + \frac{d_T}{\rho_E^T} + \left(\frac{d_{T+1}}{\rho_E - g} \right) \Big/ \rho_E^T \qquad \text{Page 113}$$

Value of a perpetual dividend stream $= V_0^E = \dfrac{d_1}{\rho_E - 1}$ Page 113

Value of a dividend growing at a constant rate $= V_0^E = \dfrac{d_1}{\rho_E - g}$ Page 113

Value of the firm = Present value of expected free cash flows

$$V_0^F = \frac{C_1 - I_1}{\rho_F} + \frac{C_2 - I_2}{\rho_F^2} + \frac{C_3 - I_3}{\rho_F^3} + \frac{C_4 - I_4}{\rho_F^4} + \frac{C_5 - I_5}{\rho_F^5} + \cdots \qquad \text{Page 115}$$

(ρ_F is 1 + Required return for the firm)

Value of the equity = Present value of expected free cash flows minus value of net debt

$$V_0^E = \frac{C_1 - I_1}{\rho_F} + \frac{C_2 - I_2}{\rho_F^2} + \frac{C_3 - I_3}{\rho_F^3} + \cdots + \frac{C_T - I_T}{\rho_F^T} + \frac{\text{CV}_T}{\rho_F^T} - V_0^D \qquad \text{Page 116}$$

If free cash flows after T are forecasted to be a (constant) perpetuity,

$$\text{CV}_T = \frac{C_{T+1} - I_{T+1}}{\rho_F - 1} \qquad \text{Page 116}$$

If free cash flows are forecasted to grow at a constant rate after the horizon,

$$\text{CV}_T = \left(\frac{C_{T+1} - I_{T+1}}{\rho_F - g} \right) \qquad \text{Page 116}$$

Cash flow from operations = Reported cash flow from operations
+ After-tax net interest payments   Page 120

Cash investment in operations = Reported cash flow from investing
− Net investment in interest-bearing
instruments   Page 121

Earnings = Free cash flow − Net cash interest + Investment + Accruals

$$\text{Earnings} = (C - I) - i + I + \text{Accruals} \qquad \text{Page 126}$$

CHAPTER 5

The value of common equity $(V_0^E) = B_0 + \dfrac{\text{RE}_1}{\rho_E} + \dfrac{\text{RE}_2}{\rho_E^2} + \dfrac{\text{RE}_3}{\rho_E^3} + \cdots$ Page 145

Residual earnings = Comprehensive earnings − (Required return for equity
× Beginning-of-period book value of equity)   Page 145

$$RE_t = Earn_t - (\rho_E - 1)B_{t-1}$$

Residual earnings = (ROCE − Required return on equity)
× Beginning-of-period book value of common equity

$$Earn_t - (\rho_E - 1)B_{t-1} = [ROCE_t - (\rho_E - 1)]B_{t-1}$$ Page 147

Simple valuation model:

$$V_0^E = B_0 + \frac{RE_1}{\rho_E - g}$$ Page 151

Case 1 valuation. RE is forecasted to be zero after some point:

$$V_0^E = B_0 + \frac{RE_1}{\rho_E} + \frac{RE_2}{\rho_E^2} + \frac{RE_3}{\rho_E^3} + \cdots + \frac{RE_T}{\rho_E^T}$$ Page 152

Case 2 valuation. No growth:

$$V_0^E = B_0 + \frac{RE_1}{\rho_E} + \frac{RE_2}{\rho_E^2} + \cdots + \frac{RE_T}{\rho_E^T} + \left(\frac{RE_{T+1}}{\rho_E - 1}\right)\Big/ \rho_E^T$$ Page 154

Case 3 valuation. Growth is forecasted to continue at a constant rate:

$$V_0^E = B_0 + \frac{RE_1}{\rho_E} + \frac{RE_2}{\rho_E^2} + \frac{RE_3}{\rho_E^3} + \cdots + \frac{RE_T}{\rho_E^T} + \left(\frac{RE_{T+1}}{\rho_E - g}\right)\Big/ \rho_E^T$$ Page 154

CHAPTER 6

Value of equity $= V_0^E = \dfrac{1}{\rho_E - 1}\left[Earn_1 + \dfrac{\Delta RE_2}{\rho_E} + \dfrac{\Delta RE_3}{\rho_E^2} + \dfrac{\Delta RE_4}{\rho_E^3} + \cdots \right]$ Page 180

Normal forward P/E $= \dfrac{1}{\text{Required return}}$ Page 183

Normal trailing P/E $= \dfrac{(1 + \text{Required return})}{\text{Required return}}$ Page 184

Value of equity = Capitalized forward earnings
+ Extra value for abnormal cum-dividend earnings growth

$$V_0^E = \frac{Earn_1}{\rho_E - 1} + \frac{1}{\rho_E - 1}\left[\frac{AEG_2}{\rho_E} + \frac{AEG_3}{\rho_E^2} + \frac{AEG_4}{\rho_E^3} + \cdots \right]$$

$$= \frac{1}{\rho_E - 1}\left[Earn_1 + \frac{AEG_2}{\rho_E} + \frac{AEG_3}{\rho_E^2} + \frac{AEG_4}{\rho_E^3} + \cdots \right]$$ Page 185

Abnormal earnings growth$_t$ (AEG$_t$) = Cum-dividend earn$_t$ − Normal earn$_t$ Page 187

$$= [Earn_t + (\rho_E - 1)d_{t-1}] - \rho_E Earn_{t-1}$$

Abnormal earnings growth$_t$ (AEG$_t$) = [G$_t$ − ρ$_E$] × Earnings$_{t-1}$ Page 187

Value of equity (cum-dividend) = Capitalized current earnings
    + Extra value for abnormal cum-dividend abnormal
    earnings growth

$$V_0^E + d_0 = \frac{\rho_E}{\rho_E - 1}\left[\text{Earn}_0 + \frac{\text{AEG}_1}{\rho_E} + \frac{\text{AEG}_2}{\rho_E^2} + \frac{\text{AEG}_3}{\rho_E^3} + \cdots\right]$$ Page 189

$$\text{PEG ratio} = \frac{\text{P/E}}{1\text{-year-ahead percentage earnings growth}}$$ Page 199

CHAPTER 7

Value = Value based on what we know + Speculative value Page 213

Weighted-average expected return formula:

$$\text{ER} = \left[\frac{B_0}{P_0} \times \text{ROCE}_1\right] + \left[\left(1 - \frac{B_0}{P_0}\right) \times (g - 1)\right]$$ Page 214

Value = Value based on book value and near-term forecasts Page 218
    + Value of speculative growth

$$V_0^E = B_0 + \frac{\text{PE}_1}{\rho} + \frac{\text{PE}_2}{\rho(\rho - 1)} + \text{Value of speculative growth}$$ Page 218

Earnings forecast$_t$ = (Book value$_{t-1}$ × Required return) + Residual earnings$_t$ Page 219

$$V_0^E = \frac{1}{\rho - 1}\left[\text{EPS}_1 + \frac{\text{AEG}_2}{\rho - 1}\right] + \text{Value of speculative growth}$$ Page 221

Earnings forecast$_t$ = Normal earnings forecast$_t$ + AEG$_t$
    − Forecast of earnings from prior year's dividends Page 222

CHAPTER 8

Free cash flow = Net dividends to shareholders + Net payments to debtholders and
    issuers

$$C - I = d + F$$ Page 238

Treasurer's rule:

If $C - I - i > d$: Lend or buy down own debt Page 238
If $C - I - i < d$: Borrow or reduce lending

Free cash flow = Operating income − Change in net operating assets

$$C - I = \text{OI} - \Delta\text{NOA}$$ Page 238

Free cash flow = Change in net financial assets − Net financial income
    + Net dividends

$$C - I = \Delta\text{NFA} - \text{NFI} + d$$ Page 244

Free cash flow = Net financial expenses – Change in net financial obligations
+ Net dividends

$$C - I = \text{NFE} - \Delta\text{NFO} + d$$ Page 244

Net dividends = Free cash flow + Net financial income
– Change in net financial assets

$$d = C - I + \text{NFI} - \Delta\text{NFA}$$ Page 245

Net dividends = Free cash flow – Net financial expenses
+ Change in net financial obligations

$$d = C - I - \text{NFE} + \Delta\text{NFO}$$ Page 245

Net operating assets (end) = Net operating assets (beginning)
+ Operating income – Free cash flow

$$\text{NOA}_t = \text{NOA}_{t-1} + \text{OI}_t - (C_t - I_t)$$ Page 245

Change in net operating assets = Operating income – Free cash flow

$$\Delta\text{NOA}_t = \text{OI}_t - (C_t - I_t)$$ Page 245

Net financial assets (end) = Net financial assets (begin)
+ Net financial income + Free cash flow
– Net dividends

$$\text{NFA}_t = \text{NFA}_{t-1} + \text{NFI}_t + (C_t - I_t) - d_t$$ Page 245

Change in net financial assets = Net financial income + Free cash flow
– Net dividends

$$\Delta\text{NFA}_t = \text{NFI}_t + (C_t - I_t) - d_t$$ Page 246

Net financial obligations (end) = Net financial obligations (begin)
+ Net financial expense – Free cash flow
+ Net dividends

$$\text{NFO}_t = \text{NFO}_{t-1} + \text{NFE}_t - (C_t - I_t) + d_t$$ Page 246

Change in net financial obligations = Net financial expense – Free cash flow
+ Net dividends

$$\Delta\text{NFO}_t = \text{NFE}_t - (C_t - I_t) + d_t$$ Page 246

Stocks and flows equation for common stockholders' equity:

$$\text{CSE}_t = \text{CSE}_{t-1} + \text{Comprehensive earnings}_t - \text{Net dividends}_t$$ Page 246

$$\text{CSE}_t = \text{NOA}_t - \text{NFO}_t$$ Page 247

CHAPTER 9

$$\text{Dividend payout} = \frac{\text{Dividends}}{\text{Comprehensive income}}$$ Page 266

$$\text{Total payout ratio} = \frac{\text{Dividends} + \text{Stock repurchases}}{\text{Comprehensive income}}$$

Page 266

$$\text{Dividends-to-book value} = \frac{\text{Dividends}}{\text{Book value of CSE} + \text{Dividends}}$$

Page 266

$$\text{Total payout-to-book value} = \frac{\text{Dividends} + \text{Stock repurchases}}{\text{Book value of CSE} + \text{Dividends} + \text{Stock repurchases}}$$

Page 266

$$\text{Retention ratio} = \frac{\text{Comprehensive income} - \text{Dividends}}{\text{Comprehensive income}}$$

$$= 1 - \text{Dividend payout ratio}$$

Page 267

$$\text{Net investment rate} = \frac{\text{Net transactions with shareholders}}{\text{Beginning book value of CSE}}$$

Page 267

$$\text{Growth rate of CSE} = \frac{\text{Change in CSE}}{\text{Beginning CSE}}$$

Page 267

$$= \frac{\text{Comprehensive income} + \text{Net transactions with shareholders}}{\text{Beginning CSE}}$$

$$\text{Growth rate of CSE} = \text{ROCE} + \text{Net investment rate}$$

Page 267

CHAPTER 10

$$\text{Tax benefit of net debt} = \text{Net interest expense} \times \text{Tax rate}$$

Page 305

$$\text{After-tax net interest expense} = \text{Net interest expense} \times (1 - \text{Tax rate})$$

Page 305

$$\text{Tax on operating income} = \text{Tax expense as reported} + (\text{Net interest expense} \times \text{Tax rate})$$

Page 306

Effective tax rate for operations =

Page 307

$$\frac{\text{Tax on operating income}}{\text{Operating income before tax, equity income, and extraordinary and dirty-surplus items}}$$

$$\text{Residual operating income} = \text{ReOI}_t = \text{OI}_t - (\rho - 1)\text{NOA}_{t-1}$$

Page 312

$$\text{Operating profit margin (PM)} = \frac{\text{OI (after tax)}}{\text{Sales}}$$

Page 318

$$\text{Sales PM} = \frac{\text{OI (after tax) from sales}}{\text{Sales}}$$

Page 318

$$\text{Other items PM} = \frac{\text{OI (after tax) from other items}}{\text{Sales}}$$

Page 318

$$\text{Net (comprehensive) income profit margin} = \frac{\text{Comprehensive income}}{\text{Sales}}$$

Page 318

$$\text{Expense ratio} = \frac{\text{Expense}}{\text{Sales}}$$

Page 318

$1 - \text{Sales PM} = \text{Sum of expense ratios}$ — Page 318

$\text{Operating asset composition ratio} = \dfrac{\text{Operating asset}}{\text{Total operating assets}}$ — Page 319

$\text{Operating liability composition ratio} = \dfrac{\text{Operating liability}}{\text{Total operating liabilities}}$ — Page 319

$\text{Operating liability leverage (OLLEV)} = \dfrac{\text{Operating liabilities}}{\text{Net operating assets}}$ — Page 319

$\text{Capitalization ratio} = \dfrac{\text{Net operating assets}}{\text{Common stockholders' equity}} = \text{NOA/CSE}$ — Page 319

$\text{Financial leverage ratio (FLEV)} = \dfrac{\text{Net financial obligations}}{\text{Common stockholders' equity}} = \text{NFO/CSE}$ — Page 319

$\text{Capitalization ratio} - \text{Financial leverage ratio} = 1.0$ — Page 319

$\text{Return on net operating assets (RNOA}_t) = \dfrac{\text{OI}_t}{\frac{1}{2}\,(\text{NOA}_t + \text{NOA}_{t-1})}$ — Page 318

$\text{Return on net financial assets (RNFA}_t) = \dfrac{\text{NFI}_t}{\frac{1}{2}\,(\text{NFA}_t + \text{NFA}_{t-1})}$ — Page 318

$\text{Net borrowing cost (NBC}_t) = \dfrac{\text{NFE}_t}{\frac{1}{2}\,(\text{NFO}_t + \text{NFO}_{t-1})}$ — Page 319

CHAPTER 11

Free cash flow = Operating income − Change in net operating assets

$$C - I = \text{OI} - \Delta\text{NOA}$$ — Page 344

Free cash flow = Net financial expense − Change in net financial obligations + Net dividends

$$C - I = \text{NFE} - \Delta\text{NFO} + d$$ — Page 344

CHAPTER 12

$$\text{ROCE} = \left(\frac{\text{NOA}}{\text{CSE}} \times \text{RNOA}\right) - \left(\frac{\text{NFO}}{\text{CSE}} \times \text{NBC}\right)$$ — Page 367

$$\text{ROCE} = \text{RNOA} + \left[\frac{\text{NFO}}{\text{CSE}} \times (\text{RNOA} - \text{NBC})\right]$$

$$= \text{RNOA} + (\text{Financial leverage} \times \text{Operating spread})$$

$$= \text{RNOA} + (\text{FLEV} \times \text{SPREAD})$$ — Page 366

$$\text{ROCE} = \text{RNOA} - \left[\frac{\text{NFA}}{\text{CSE}} \times (\text{RNOA} - \text{RNFA})\right]$$ — Page 368

Implicit interest on operating liabilities = Short-term borrowing rate (after tax) × Operating liabilities   Page 369

$$\text{Return on operating assets (ROOA)} = \frac{\text{OI} + \text{Implicit interest (after tax)}}{\text{Operating assets}}$$ Page 369

Return on net operating assets = Return on operating assets + (Operating liability leverage × Operating liability leverage spread)

RNOA = ROOA + (OLLEV × OLSPREAD)   Page 369

OLSPREAD = ROOA − Short-term borrowing rate (after tax)   Page 369

ROCE = ROCE before MI × MI sharing ratio   Page 372

$$\text{ROCE before minority interest (MI)} = \frac{\text{Comprehensive income before MI}}{\text{CSE} + \text{MI}}$$ Page 372

$$\frac{\text{Minority interest}}{\text{sharing ratio}} = \frac{\text{Comprehensive income/Comprehensive income before MI}}{\text{CSE/(CSE} + \text{MI)}}$$ Page 372

ROCE = (PM × ATO) + [FLEV × (RNOA − NBC)]   Page 373

PM = OI (after tax)/Sales   Page 373

ATO = Sales/NOA   Page 373

PM = Sales PM + Other items PM   Page 376

Sales PM = Gross margin ratio − Expense ratios   Page 376

$$\frac{1}{\text{ATO}} = \frac{\text{Cash}}{\text{Sales}} + \frac{\text{Accounts receivable}}{\text{Sales}} + \frac{\text{Inventory}}{\text{Sales}} + \cdots + \frac{\text{PPE}}{\text{Sales}}$$
$$+ \cdots - \frac{\text{Accounts payable}}{\text{Sales}} - \frac{\text{Pension obligations}}{\text{Sales}} - \cdots$$ Page 377

$$\text{Accounts receivable turnover} = \frac{\text{Sales}}{\text{Accounts receivable (net)}}$$ Page 377

$$\text{PPE turnover} = \frac{\text{Sales}}{\text{Property, plant, and equipment (net)}}$$ Page 377

$$\text{Days in accounts receivable} = \frac{365}{\text{Accounts receivable turnover}}$$

(sometimes called days sales outstanding)   Page 377

The inventory turnover ratio is sometimes measured as:

$$\text{Inventory turnover} = \frac{\text{Cost of goods sold}}{\text{Inventory}}$$ Page 377

$$\text{Days in inventory} = \frac{365}{\text{Inventory turnover}}$$ Page 377

$$\text{Days in accounts payable} = \frac{365 \times \text{Accounts payable}}{\text{Purchases}}$$ Page 378

The net borrowing cost is a weighted average of the costs for the different sources of net financing:

$$\text{NBC} = \left(\frac{\text{FO}}{\text{NFO}} \times \frac{\text{After-tax interest on financial obligations (FO)}}{\text{FO}} \right)$$

$$- \left(\frac{\text{FA}}{\text{NFO}} \times \frac{\text{After-tax interest on financial assets (FA)}}{\text{FA}} \right)$$

$$- \left(\frac{\text{FA}}{\text{NFO}} \times \frac{\text{Unrealized gains on FA}}{\text{FA}} \right)$$

$$+ \left(\frac{\text{Preferred stock}}{\text{NFO}} \times \frac{\text{Preferred dividends}}{\text{Preferred stock}} \right) + \cdots \qquad \text{Page 380}$$

CHAPTER 13

$$\text{OI} = \text{Core OI from sales} + \text{Core other OI} + \text{UI} \qquad \text{Page 396}$$

Return on net operating assets = Core RNOA
+ Unusual items to net operating assets   Page 404

$$\text{RNOA} = \frac{\text{Core OI}}{\text{NOA}} + \frac{\text{UI}}{\text{NOA}} \qquad \text{Page 404}$$

$$\text{RNOA} = \frac{\text{Core OI from sales}}{\text{NOA}} + \frac{\text{Core other OI}}{\text{NOA}} + \frac{\text{UI}}{\text{NOA}} \qquad \text{Page 404}$$

$$\text{RNOA} = \left(\text{Core sales PM} \times \text{ATO} \right) + \frac{\text{Core other OI}}{\text{NOA}} + \frac{\text{UI}}{\text{NOA}}$$

where $\text{Core sales PM} = \dfrac{\text{Core OI from sales}}{\text{Sales}}$ Page 406

Net borrowing cost = Core net borrowing cost + Unusual borrowing costs

$$\text{NBC} = \frac{\text{Core net financial expenses}}{\text{NFO}} + \frac{\text{Unusual financial expenses}}{\text{NFO}} \qquad \text{Page 406}$$

| Change in RNOA = | Change in core sales profit margin at previous asset turnover level | + | Change due to change in asset turnover | + | Change due to change in other core income | + | Change due to change in unusual items |

$$\Delta\text{RNOA}_1 = \left(\Delta\text{Core sales PM}_1 \times \text{ATO}_0 \right) + \left(\Delta\text{ATO}_1 \times \text{Core sales PM}_1 \right)$$

$$+ \Delta\left(\frac{\text{Core other OI}}{\text{NOA}} \right) + \Delta\left(\frac{\text{UI}}{\text{NOA}} \right) \qquad \text{Page 408}$$

$$\text{Sales PM} = \frac{\text{Sales} - \text{Variable cost} - \text{Fixed costs}}{\text{Sales}}$$

$$= \frac{\text{Contribution margin}}{\text{Sales}} - \frac{\text{Fixed costs}}{\text{Sales}} \qquad \text{Page 409}$$

$$\text{Contribution margin ratio} = 1 - \frac{\text{Variable costs}}{\text{Sales}} = \frac{\text{Contribution margin}}{\text{Sales}} \qquad \text{Page 409}$$

$$\text{OLEV} = \frac{\text{Contribution margin}}{\text{Operating income}} = \frac{\text{Contribution margin ratio}}{\text{Profit margin}}$$

(Don't confuse OLEV with OLLEV!) — Page 409

% Change in core OI = OLEV × % Change in core sales — Page 409

$$\text{NOA} = \text{Sales} \times \frac{1}{\text{ATO}} \qquad \text{Page 410}$$

$$\Delta\text{CSE} = \Delta\left(\text{Sales} \times \frac{1}{\text{ATO}}\right) - \Delta\text{NFO} \qquad \text{Page 411}$$

CHAPTER 14

Residual operating income = Operating income − (Required return for operations
$\qquad\qquad\qquad$ × Beginning net operating assets)

$$\text{ReOI}_t = \text{OI}_t - (\rho_F - 1)\text{NOA}_{t-1} \qquad \text{Page 439}$$

Value of operations = Net operating assets
$\qquad\qquad\qquad$ + Present value of expected residual operating income

$$V_0^{\text{NOA}} = \text{NOA}_0 + \frac{\text{ReOI}_1}{\rho_F} + \frac{\text{ReOI}_2}{\rho_F^2} + \frac{\text{ReOI}_3}{\rho_F^3} + \cdots + \frac{\text{ReOI}_T}{\rho_F^T} + \frac{\text{CV}_T}{\rho_F^T} \qquad \text{Page 439}$$

Value of common equity = Book value of common equity
$\qquad\qquad\qquad$ + Present value of expected residual operating income

$$V_0^E = \text{CSE}_0 + \frac{\text{ReOI}_1}{\rho_F} + \frac{\text{ReOI}_2}{\rho_F^2} + \frac{\text{ReOI}_3}{\rho_F^3} + \cdots + \frac{\text{ReOI}_T}{\rho_F^T} + \frac{\text{CV}_T}{\rho_F^T} \qquad \text{Page 440}$$

Residual operating income = (RNOA − Required return for operations)
$\qquad\qquad\qquad$ × Net operating assets

$$\text{ReOI}_t = [\text{RNOA}_t - (\rho_F - 1)]\text{NOA}_{t-1} \qquad \text{Page 442}$$

Abnormal operating income growth$_t$ (AOIG)

$\quad$ = Cum-dividend operating income$_t$ − Normal operating income$_t$

$\quad$ = [Operating income$_t$ + $(\rho_F - 1)\text{FCF}_{t-1}$] − ρ_F operating income$_{t-1}$

$\quad$ = [OI_t + $(\rho_F - 1)\text{FCF}_{t-1}$] − $\rho_F \text{OI}_{t-1}$

$\quad$ = [$G_t - \rho_F$] × OI_{t-1} $\qquad\qquad$ Page 443

Value of common equity = Capitalized (Forward operating income + Present value of abnormal operating income growth) − Net financial obligations

$$V_0^E = \frac{1}{\rho_F - 1}\left[OI_1 + \frac{AOIG_2}{\rho_F} + \frac{AOIG_3}{\rho_F^2} + \frac{AOIG_4}{\rho_F^3} + \cdots\right] - NFO_0 \qquad \text{Page 445}$$

Core $ReOI_t$ = Core $OI_t - (\rho_F - 1)\, NOA_{t-1}$ Page 445

Cost of capital for operations = Weighted-average cost of equity and cost of net debt

$$= \left(\frac{\text{Value of equity}}{\text{Value of operations}} \times \text{Equity cost of capital}\right)$$

$$+ \left(\frac{\text{Value of debt}}{\text{Value of operations}} \times \text{Cost of debt capital}\right)$$

$$\rho_F = \frac{V_0^E}{V_0^{NOA}} \cdot \rho_E + \frac{V_0^D}{V_0^{NOA}} \cdot \rho_D \qquad \text{Page 447}$$

After-tax cost of net debt (ρ_D) = Nominal cost of net debt × (1 − Tax rate)   Page 447

Required return on equity = Required return for operations + (Market leverage × Required return spread)

$$\rho_E = \rho_F + \frac{V_0^D}{V_0^E}(\rho_F - \rho_D) \qquad \text{Page 449}$$

Earnings growth rate$_t$ = OI growth rate$_t$ + [Earnings leverage$_{t-1}$ × (OI growth rate$_t$ − NFE growth rate$_t$)]

$$g_t^{Earn} = g_t^{OI} + ELEV_{t-1}\left[g_t^{OI} - g_t^{NFE}\right] \qquad \text{Page 458}$$

$$ELEV = \frac{NFE}{Earnings} \qquad \text{Page 458}$$

Unlevered P/B ratio $= \dfrac{\text{Value of net operating assets}}{\text{Net operating assets}}$

$$= \frac{V_0^{NOA}}{NOA_0} \qquad \text{Page 463}$$

Levered P/B ratio = Unlevered P/B ratio + [Financial leverage × (Unlevered P/B ratio − 1)]

$$\frac{V_0^E}{CSE_0} = \frac{V_0^{NOA}}{NOA_0} + FLEV\left(\frac{V_0^{NOA}}{NOA_0} - 1\right) \qquad \text{Page 464}$$

Forward enterprise P/E ratio $= \dfrac{\text{Value of operations}}{\text{Forward operating income}} = \dfrac{V_0^{NOA}}{OI_1}$ Page 465

$$\text{Trailing enterprise P/E ratio} = \frac{\text{Value of operations} + \text{Free cash flow}}{\text{Current operating income}}$$

$$= \frac{V_0^{\text{NOA}} + \text{FCF}_0}{\text{OI}_0} \qquad \text{Page 466}$$

$$\text{Forward levered P/E ratio} = \frac{V_0^E}{\text{Earn}_1} = \frac{V_0^{\text{NOA}}}{\text{OI}_1} + \text{ELEV}_1\left(\frac{V_0^{\text{NOA}}}{\text{OI}_1} - \frac{1}{\text{NBC}_1}\right) \qquad \text{Page 466}$$

$$\text{Forward levered E/P ratio} = \frac{\text{Earn}_1}{V_0^E} = \frac{\text{OI}_1}{V_0^{\text{NOA}}} + \frac{\text{NFO}_0}{V_0^E}\left[\frac{\text{OI}_1}{V_0^{\text{NOA}}} - \text{NBC}_1\right] \qquad \text{Page 466}$$

$$\text{Trailing levered P/E ratio} = \frac{V_0^E + d_0}{\text{Earn}_0} \qquad \text{Page 466}$$

$$= \frac{V_0^{\text{NOA}} + \text{FCF}_0}{\text{OI}_0} + \text{ELEV}_0\left(\frac{V_0^{\text{NOA}} + \text{FCF}_0}{\text{OI}_0} - \frac{1}{\text{NBC}_0} - 1\right)$$

CHAPTER 15

The no-growth forecast of operating income:

$$\text{OI}_1 = \text{OI}_0 + (\rho_F - 1)\Delta\text{NOA}_0 \qquad \text{Page 484}$$

The no-growth valuation of operations:

$$V_0^{\text{NOA}} = \frac{\text{OI}_1}{\rho_F - 1} \qquad \text{Page 484}$$

The growth forecast of operating income:

$$\text{OI}_1 = \text{NOA}_0 \times \text{Core RNOA}_0 \qquad \text{Page 484}$$

Growth valuation:
    Value of common equity:

$$V_0^E = \text{CSE}_0 + \frac{[\text{Core RNOA}_0 - (\rho_F - 1)]\text{NOA}_0}{\rho_F - g} \qquad \text{Page 485}$$

Value of operations:

$$V_0^{\text{NOA}} = \text{NOA}_0 + \frac{[\text{Core RNOA}_0 - (\rho_F - 1)]\text{NOA}_0}{\rho_F - g}$$

$$= \text{NOA}_0 \times \frac{\text{Core RNOA}_0 - (g - 1)}{\rho_F - g} \qquad \text{Page 486}$$

Unlevered price-to-book ratio:

$$\frac{V^{\text{NOA}}}{\text{NOA}_0} = \frac{\text{Core RNOA}_0 - (g - 1)}{\rho_F - g} \qquad \text{Page 486}$$

Unlevered forward P/E ratio:

$$\frac{V_0^{\text{NOA}}}{\text{OI}_1} = \frac{1}{\rho_F - 1}\left[1 + \frac{G_2 - \rho_F}{\rho_F - g}\right]$$

Page 486

Weighted-average growth rate for ReOI = $(0.7 \times$ Current growth in ReOI)
$+ (0.3 \times 4\%)$

Page 488

A simple valuation with short-term and long-term growth rates:

$$V_0^{\text{NOA}} = \text{OI}_1 \times \frac{1}{\rho_F - 1}\left[\frac{G_2 - G_{\text{long}}}{\rho_F - G_{\text{long}}}\right]$$

Page 488

CHAPTER 16

$$\text{ReOI} = \text{Sales} \times \left(\text{Core sales PM} - \frac{\text{Required return for operations}}{\text{ATO}}\right)$$
$$+ \text{Core other OI} + \text{Unusual items}$$

Page 506

CHAPTER 18

Quality diagnostics:
    Net sales/Cash from sales
    Net sales/Net accounts receivable
    Net sales/Allowance for sales returns and discounts
    Net sales/Unearned revenue

Page 603

    Bad debt expense/Actual credit losses
    Bad debt reserves/Accounts receivable (gross)
    Bad debt expense/Sales

Page 604

$$\frac{\text{Normalized OI}}{\text{OI}}$$

where

Normalized OI = Free cash flow + ΔNormalized NOA
      = Free cash flow + ΔSales/Normal ATO

Page 605

$$\frac{\text{Adjusted ebitda}}{\text{ebit}}$$

Page 607

$$\frac{\text{Depreciation}}{\text{Capital expenditures}}$$

Page 607

$$\frac{\text{Cash flow from operations (CFO)}}{\text{Operating income}}$$

Page 608

$$\frac{\text{CFO}}{\text{Average NOA}}$$

Page 608

$$\frac{\text{Pension expense}}{\text{Total operating expense}}$$

Page 610

$$\frac{\text{Other postemployment expenses}}{\text{Total operating expense}}$$

Page 610

$$\frac{\text{Operating tax expense}}{\text{OI before taxes}}$$

Page 610

Warranty expense/Actual warranty claims
Warranty expense/Sales

Page 611

$$\frac{\text{R\&D expense}}{\text{Sales}}$$

Page 615

$$\frac{\text{Advertising expense}}{\text{Sales}}$$

Page 615

CHAPTER 19

Reverse engineering the expected return:

$$\text{Expected equity return} = \left[\frac{B_0}{P_0} \times \text{ROCE}_1\right] + \left[\left(1 - \frac{B_0}{P_0}\right) \times (g - 1)\right]$$

Page 665

$$\text{Expected return for operations} = \left[\frac{\text{NOA}_0}{P_0^{\text{NOA}}} \times \text{RNOA}_1\right] + \left[\left(1 - \frac{\text{NOA}_0}{P_0^{\text{NOA}}}\right) \times (g - 1)\right]$$

Page 665

CHAPTER 20

$$\text{Current ratio} = \frac{\text{Current assets}}{\text{Current liabilities}}$$

Page 685

$$\text{Quick (or acid test) ratio} = \frac{\text{Cash} + \text{Short-term investments} + \text{Receivables}}{\text{Current liabilities}}$$

Page 685

$$\text{Cash ratio} = \frac{\text{Cash} + \text{Short-term investments}}{\text{Current liabilities}}$$

Page 685

$$\text{Defensive interval} = \frac{\text{Cash} + \text{Short-term investments} + \text{Receivables}}{\text{Capital expenditures}} \times 365$$

Page 685

$$\frac{\text{Cash flow to}}{\text{capital expenditures}} = \frac{\text{(Unlevered) cash flow from operations}}{\text{Capital expenditures}}$$

Page 685

$$\text{Debt to total assets} = \frac{\text{Total debt (current} + \text{long-term)}}{\text{Total assets (liabilities} + \text{total equity)}}$$

Page 686

$$\text{Debt to equity} = \frac{\text{Total debt}}{\text{Total equity}}$$

Page 686

$$\text{Long-term debt ratio} = \frac{\text{Long-term debt}}{\text{Long-term debt} + \text{Total equity}}$$ Page 686

$$\text{Interest coverage} = \frac{\text{Operating income}}{\text{Net interest expense}} \quad \text{(times interest earned)}$$ Page 686

$$\text{Interest coverage} = \frac{\text{Unlevered cash flow from operations}}{\text{Net cash interest}} \quad \text{(cash basis)}$$ Page 686

$$\text{CFO to debt} = \frac{\text{Unlevered cash flow from operations}}{\text{Total debt}}$$ Page 686

$$\text{Cash available for debt service} = \text{Free cash flow} - \text{Net dividends}$$
$$= \text{OI} - \Delta\text{NOA} - \text{Net dividends}$$ Page 693

$$\text{Debt service requirement} = \text{Required interest and preferred dividend payments}$$
$$+ \text{Required net principal payments}$$
$$+ \text{Lease payments}$$ Page 693

Index